LET'S GO:
FRANCE

is the best book for anyone traveling on a budget. Here's why:

No other guidebook has as many budget listings.

In Paris, we list over fifty places to stay for less than $8 per night; in the countryside, hundreds more for much less. We tell you how to get there the cheapest way, whether by bus, plane, or thumb, and where to get an inexpensive and satisfying meal once you've arrived. There are hundreds of money-saving tips for everyone plus lots of information on special student discounts.

LET'S GO researchers have to make it on their own.

No expense accounts, no free hotel rooms. Our Harvard-Radcliffe student researchers travel on budgets as limited as your own.

LET'S GO is completely revised every year.

We don't just update the prices, we go back to the places. If a charming café has become an overpriced tourist trap, we'll replace the listing with a new and better one.

No other budget guidebook includes all this:

Coverage of both the cities and the countryside; in-depth information on culture, history, and the people; distinctive features such as rail, city, and regional maps; tips on work, study, hiking and biking, nightlife and special splurges; and much, much more.

LET'S GO is for anyone who wants to see France on a budget.

LET'S GO:

The Budget Guide to

FRANCE

1989

Sharon Lim-Hing
Editor

M. Zita J. Ezpeleta
Assistant Editor

Written by Harvard Student Agencies, Inc.

PAN BOOKS
London, Sydney and Auckland

Helping Let's Go

If you have suggestions or corrections, or just want to share your discoveries, drop us a line. We read every piece of correspondence, whether a 10-page letter, a postcard, or, as in one case, a collage. All suggestions are passed along to our researcher/writers. Please note that mail received after June 1, 1989 will probably be too late for the 1990 book, but will be retained for the following edition. Address mail to: Let's Go: France, Harvard Student Agencies, Inc.; Thayer Hall-B; Harvard University; Cambridge, MA 02138; USA.

In addition to the invaluable travel advice our readers share with us, many are kind enough to offer their services as researchers. Unfortunately, the charter of Harvard Student Agencies, Inc. enables us to employ only currently enrolled Harvard students both as researchers and editorial staff.

Published in Great Britain by Pan Books Ltd
Cavaye Place, London SW10 9PG
9 8 7 6 5 4 3 2 1

Published in the United States of America
by St. Martin's Press, Inc.

Maps by David Lindroth, copyright © 1989, 1986 by St. Martin's Press, Inc.

ISBN: 0 330 30545 X

Let's Go: France is written by Harvard Student Agencies, Inc., Harvard University, Thayer Hall-B, Cambridge, Mass. 02138, USA.

Let's Go ® is registered trademark of Harvard Student Agencies, Inc.

Printed and bound in the United States of America.

Editor	Sharon Lim-Hing
Assistant Editor	M. Zita J. Ezpeleta
Publishing Manager	Mark D. Selwyn
Managing Editors	Alice K. Ma
	Andrea Piperakis
Production/Communications	
Coordinator	Nathanael Joe Hayashi

Researcher/Writers:

*Brittany, Périgord-Quercy, Basque
   Country, Gascony* — Lisa Ayako Estreich

*Channel Islands, Normandy,
   Alsace-Lorraine* — Shelley Glick

Champagne, the North, Paris — Deborah Levi

*Côte d'Azur, Burgundy, Loire Valley,
   Central France, Auvergne,
   Franche-Comté* — Elizabeth Stuyvesant Potter

*Corsica, Rhône Valley,
   Languedoc-Roussillon* — Christopher S. Russ

*Poitou-Charentes, Auvergne, the Alps,
   Franche-Comté, Central France,
   Burgundy* — Eric Verhoogen

Advertising Manager	Kimberley Harris
Advertising Representatives	Kelly Ann McEnaney
	Charles Emmit Ryan
Legal Counsel	Harold Rosenwald

ACKNOWLEDGMENTS

I would like to thank readers who took the time during or after their voyages to give us feedback. Postcards, notes, and typewritten essays conveyed everything from praise and complaints to *Let's Go* anecdotes and a tip on that wonderful little restaurant hidden away in Mettray.

Next I wish to credit the lifeblood of this organization, the researcher/writers who backpacked, scribbled, and *débrouillé*-ed through the tourist traps, hinterlands, and vintage wines of ye ole Hexagon. Elizabeth Potter tackled snobby tourist offices and accepted genuine kindness in two of the most visited regions, the Côte d'Azur and the Loire Valley. Writing from Burgundy and Central France, Liz also brightened the dark basement office with her ebullient prose and outrageous marginalia. Oblivious to local furor over his lack of socks, Eric Verhoogen ploughed his way around France with the determination of Charles Martel while diligently collecting masses of detail with the precision of Louis Pasteur. Franche-Comté, Auvergne, Poitou-Charentes, and Central France—all nebulous areas were sculpted into form by Eric. With her trusty, rusty 10-speed companion, Lisa Estreich rolled into town after town, seeing marvelous things and meeting strange people in Brittany, Périgord-Quercy, the Basque Country, and Gascony. I am compelled to laud Lisa's careful research and delicate style; for her next birthday I'd like to give her a pen that doesn't blot. Despite a start encumbered by French men falling over their feet and in her way, Deborah Levi headed out to the north and Champagne with an experienced, sympathetic eye. In Paris, Debbie devoted much overtime to updating the Entertainment and Food sections, and turned in the most detailed Paris chapter ever. Shelley Glick braved rich Guernsey dairy products, camped out in stormy Norman weather, and astounded Alsace and Lorraine with her polyglot talents. Shelley also did additional research on camping and dietary concerns. Christopher Russ thumbed, ferried, and sailed through much of the Midi, promptly submitting concise copy.

Back in the depths of the basement, I would like to extend my warmest thanks to Zita ("Tiny Tim") Ezpeleta, who sank her summer into production, leaving the VDT's glow seven times per week to see the moon and returning shortly before sunrise. Zita is now legally blind, but boy—what a trooper! I wish the big Z. success at Harvard Law School; Let's Go has prepared her for the intricacies of contracts and the grind of 1L. Thanks for some of that Brookline, Massachusetts competence go to Mark the Man Selwyn. Thanks also to Jay Dickson the Prince of Pop and Broadway, Joe-Eel Abrams (nephew of Jor-El), Etienne Grauvére, Alice Ma, Isabella Fu, Jenn Brumage, Ellen Rubin, and Jim Sheeny.

Since these are my acknowledgments, I'd like to thank friends who have nothing to do with *Let's Go*. Deepest thanks go to Jacquelyn Black. Hi, Mom! Thanks for everything! Thank you, D. Elizabeth Miller, Brigitte Goutal, the Voullet family of Avignon, Sheema Xanadu Khan, Dr. Melissa Lim, Elizabeth Scarlett, and Yamina Habibi.

—SLH

CONTENTS

x   **Contents**

About Let's Go

In 1960, Harvard Student Agencies, a three-year-old nonprofit corporation established to provide employment opportunities to Harvard and Radcliffe students, was doing a booming business selling charter flights to Europe. One of the extras HSA offered passengers on these flights was a 20-page mimeographed pamphlet entitled *1960 European Guide,* a collection of tips on continental travel compiled by the staff at HSA. The following year, Harvard and Radcliffe students traveling to Europe made notes and researched the first full-fledged edition of *Let's Go: Europe,* a pocket-sized book with a smattering of tips on budget accommodations, irreverent write-ups of sights, and a decidedly youthful slant. The first editions proclaimed themselves to be helpmates to the "adventurous and often pecunious student." Throughout the sixties, the series reflected its era: A section of the 1968 *Let's Go: Europe* was entitled "Street Singing in Europe on No Dollars a Day"; the 1969 guide to America led off with a feature on drug-ridden Haight Ashbury.

During the seventies, *Let's Go* gradually became a large-scale operation, adding regional guides to parts of Europe and slowly expanding into North Africa and nearby Asia. In 1981, *Let's Go: USA* returned after an eight-year hiatus, and in the next year HSA joined forces with its current publisher, St. Martin's Press. Since then, the series has continually blossomed; the additions of *Let's Go: Pacific Northwest, Western Canada, and Alaska* and *Let's Go: California and Hawaii* in 1988 brought the the total numbers of titles to eleven.

Each spring, over 150 Harvard students compete for some 70 positions as *Let's Go* researcher/writers. An editorial staff of 14 carefully reads stacks of 10-page applications and conducts thorough interviews. Those hired possess a rare combination of budget travel sense, writing ability, stamina, and courage. Each researcher/writer travels on a shoestring budget for seven weeks, researching and writing seven days per week, and mailing back their copy to Cambridge—about 500 pages in six installments. Train strikes, grumpy proprietors, noisy hostels, irate tourist officials are all in a day's work, but sometimes things become more serious. The afflictions of the summer of 1988 included one tear gassing, two totaled cars, one concussion, one near-drowning, and, in the most bizarre tale to date, one researcher/writer was chased up a tree by a pack of reindeer.

Back in a cluttered basement in Harvard Yard, an editorial staff of 25 and countless typists and proofreaders spend four months poring over more than 50,000 pages of manuscript as they push the copy through 12 comprehensive stages of intensive editing. In September the collected efforts of the summer are converted from computer diskette to nine-track tapes and delivered to Com Com in Allentown, Pennsylvania, where their computerized typesetting equipment turns them into books in record time. And even before the books hit the stands, the next year's editions are well underway.

LET'S GO: FRANCE

General Introduction

US$1 = 6.41F	1F = US$0.16
CDN$1 = 5.32F	1F = CDN$0.19
UK£1 = 10.83F	1F = UK£0.09
AUS$1 = 5.14F	1F = AUS$0.19
NZ$1 = 4.24F	1F = NZ$0.24

From the snow-capped mountains of the Alps to the rolling, Burgundian vineyards, France offers a landscape as spectacular as it is varied. The country's attraction, however, lies not only in the contrasts between its prehistoric caves and ornate châteaux, its manicured gardens and craggy coasts, but also in the diversity of its people. From Celtic traditions in Brittany, Flemish traces in the north, Spanish influence in the Basque region, and German ties in Alsace and Lorraine, France's heritage has yielded a culture whose richness is reflected in the country's celebrated architecture, language, and cuisine.

Let's Go introduces the budget traveler to the many faces of France. Our researcher/writers travel on a shoestring allowance, so their concerns are the same as yours: how to travel, eat, sightsee, and sleep as economically as possible. We suggest ways to cut costs at every corner.

Let's Go guides you through the maze of preparations for your trip. For instance, this introduction gives you details on how to apply for passports and visas, secure inexpensive flights, and send mail and money overseas. We help you decide what kind of trip to take and whether to invest in a railpass or hostel card.

We divide the country into 21 geographical regions covered in separate chapters. These chapters are organized in a counterclockwise spiral around Paris. Each section begins with an **Introduction** that captures the flavor of the region. The **Orientation and Practical Information** sections which follow prepare you for the reality of your destination. They detail a town's accessibility from other areas, and how to get to the town center from the train or bus station. We list the addresses and phone numbers of the local tourist office, currency exchange, telephone office, post office, train and bus stations, and emergency lines.

Let's Go also provides you with street maps and basic information about airports, student travel offices, and hospitals for larger cities. Regional maps display several provinces together and include the larger cities, most of the smaller towns, sights, and essential geography. We list schedules and fares (one-way) for various forms of transportation.

The **Accommodations** section for each city keeps economy in mind and lists the best values first. The **Food** section follows a similar format. Places to eat or stay remain open year-round unless otherwise indicated. Finally, most town coverage concludes with a **Sights and Entertainment** section, and suggestions for daytrips in the countryside nearby.

A Note on Prices and Currency

We quote prices in effect during the summer of 1988. Given the current inflation rate, 1989 travelers should expect increases of 5-15% over our prices. Note also that the exchange rates listed at the head of this chapter are those of August 10, 1988.

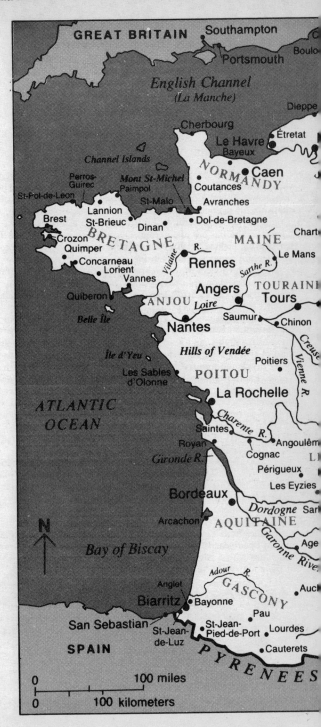

GREAT BRITAIN Southampton
Boulo-
Portsmouth
English Channel
(La Manche)
Dieppe
Cherbourg
Étretat
Le Havre
Bayeux
Channel Islands
NORMANDY Caen
Perros-
Guirec Mont St-Michel
Paimpol Coutances
St-Pol-de-Leon St-Malo
Lannion Avranches
Brest St-Brieuc Dol-de-Bretagne
Crozon Dinan
Quimper BRETAGNE MAINE Chart
Concarneau R. Le Mans
Lorient Vilaine Rennes
Vannes Sarthe R.
Angers TOURAINE
Quiberon ANJOU Loire Tours
Belle Île Saumur Chinon
Nantes Creuse
Île d'Yeu Hills of Vendée Poitiers Vienne R.
Les Sables POITOU
d'Olonne La Rochelle
ATLANTIC
OCEAN Charente R.
Saintes Angoulêm
Royan Cognac L
Gironde R. Périgueux
Les Eyzies
Bordeaux
Dordogne Sarl
N Arcachon AQUITAINE
Garonne River
Bay of Biscay Age
Adour R.
Anglet GASCONY Auc
Biarritz Bayonne
San Sebastian Pau
St-Jean- St-Jean- Lourdes
de-Luz Pied-de-Port
SPAIN Cauterets
PYRENEES

0   100 miles
0   100 kilometers

Planning Your Trip

Though a detailed itinerary may not be necessary for a successful trip, plan ahead. Research the places you'd like to go, ways to get there, and what to do along the way. Travel has become a large industry in France; you will be surprised by how much information is available. Write to the organizations listed in the general and regional introductions of *Let's Go,* and request specific information about hiking, eating, entertainment, or anything that interests you.

No matter which way you choose to travel, remember that traveling isn't a chore. When every city seems to have 1001 points of historical interest, and none of your trains connects with one another, it's easy to forget that a trip is supposed to be an escape, an adventure. Avoid letting cathedrals and museums blur into boredom—take a break from the routine of traveling. Go running on the backroads, or have a picnic in the park. Watch street artists, or sip a *citron pressé.*

When to Go

Traveling during the off-season cuts costs. Fall wine harvests, the Alps in winter, and Paris in spring are some of the enticements of non-summer travel. Air fares are cheaper, and flying standby, except around major holidays, is simple. Getting around proves easy too: You don't have to compete with hordes of summer tourists crowding establishments and driving prices up. Off-season travel, however, does have its drawbacks. Winters in France are usually mild, but the frequent rain and overcast skies can dampen your ramblings. Many hostels and some hotels close down, and museums and tourist offices keep shorter hours.

If you plan to travel during peak season, you should know that all of France seems to go on vacation in July and August. Getting anywhere during these two months, especially August, is difficult. You should reserve seats on trains and try to book accommodations in advance.

Useful Organizations and Publications

To ensure a relaxed, trouble-free voyage, research your trip early. The government and private agencies listed below may provide useful information.

Travel CUTS (Canadian Universities Travel Service), 187 College St., Toronto, Ont. M5T 1P7 (tel. (416) 979-2406). Branch offices in Victoria, Vancouver, Edmonton, Saskatoon, Winnipeg, Toronto, Ottawa, Montreal, Halifax, Burnaby, Calgary, Sudbury, Waterloo, and London. Offers discounted transatlantic flights from Canadian cities, sells the ISIC, FIYTO, and IYHF cards and discount travel passes (e.g., Transalpino and Eurotrain). Sells the Eurailpass/Youthpass. Administers the Student Work Abroad Programme for ages 18-25. Their excellent newspaper, *The Canadian Student Traveler,* is free at all offices and on campuses across Canada.

Council on International Educational Exchange (CIEE)/Council Travel Services, 205 E. 42nd St., New York, NY 10017 (tel. (212) 661-1414; for charter flights (800) 223-7402, or (212) 661-1450 from NY). CIEE is one of the broadest-ranging student travel and educational services. Write, call, or visit for information on low cost travel, educational, and work opportunities. Sells the Eurailpass/Youthpass and hostel cards. Discount fares on major airlines. Issues ISIC. Send US$1 for the annual *CIEE Student Travel Catalog,* or pick one up free at any CIEE office and many campus travel offices. They publish *It Pays To Go Abroad,* a brochure detailing work programs in many countries, including France (free); *Work, Study, Travel Abroad: The Whole World Handbook* (US$8.95, postage US$1); and *Volunteer! The Comprehensive Guide to Voluntary Service in the U.S. and Abroad* (US$4.95, postage US$1). For in-person inquiries, visit the New York Student Center, 356 W. 34th St., New York, NY or any of the branch offices in Amherst, Atlanta, Austin, Berkeley, Boston, Cambridge, Chicago, Dallas, Encino, Long Beach, Los Angeles, Minneapolis, Portland, Providence, San Diego, La Jolla, San Francisco, and Seattle.

Educational Travel Centre (ETC), 438 N. Frances St., Madison, WI 53703 (tel. (608) 256-5551). Flight information, IYHF (AYH) membership cards, Eurail and BritRail passes. Mention *Let's Go* and ETC will send you a free copy of their travel newspaper *Taking Off,* providing information on tours and flights.

THE EUROPE SPECIALIST!

Forsyth Travel Library, 9154 W. 57th St., P.O. Box 2975, Shawnee Mission, KS 66201 (tel. (913) 384-3440 or (800) FORSYTH, that's (800) 367-7984). A mail-order service that stocks a wide range of city, area, and country maps, as well as guides for rail and ferry travel in Europe. Sole North American distributor of the *Thomas Cook Continental Timetables* for trains, covering all of Europe and Britain (US$19.95, including 1st-class postage). Recommended by Eurailpass. Write for catalog and newsletter.

French Consulate. Supplies visas and passport information. In the **U.S.,** 3 Commonwealth Ave., Boston, MA 02116 (tel. (617) 266-1680); Visa Section, 20 Park Plaza, #620, Boston, MA 02116 (tel. (617) 451-6755), or 540 Bush St., San Francisco, CA 94108 (tel. (415) 397-4330), or 934 Fifth Ave., New York, NY 10021 (tel. (212) 606-3688, (212) 983-5660 for U.S. citizens tourist visa). In **Canada,** 2, Elysée Pl., Bonaventura, Montreal B.P. 202, Que. H5A 1B1 (tel. (514) 878-4381). In the **U.K.,** 24 Rutland Gates, London SW7 (tel. 581-5292 in London). In **Australia,** 291 George St., Sydney NSW 2000 (tel. 294-778 or 294-779 in Sydney).

Cultural Services of the French Embassy, 972 Fifth Ave., New York, NY 10021 (tel. (212) 439-1400). General information about France: culture, employment, educational possibilities, and housing.

Press and Information Division of the French Embassy, 4101 Reservoir Rd. NW, Washington, DC 20007-2182 (tel. (202) 944-6000). Write for information about employment and political, social, and economic life.

French Government Tourist Office: In the **U.S.,** 610 Fifth Ave., New York, NY 10020-2452 (tel. (212) 757-1125) or 1 Hallidie Plaza, #250, San Francisco, CA 94102 (tel. (415) 986-4161) or 645 N. Michigan Ave., 6th floor, Chicago, IL 60611 (tel. (312) 337-6301). In **Canada:** 1981, av. McGill College, #490, Montreal, Que. H3A 2W9 (tel. (514) 288-4264) or 1 Dundas St. W., #2405 Box 8, Toronto, Ont. M5G 1Z3 (tel. (416) 593-4717). In **Australia:** Kindersley House, 33 Bligh St., Sydney NSW 2000 (tel. (612) 231-5244). In the **U.K.:** 178 Picadilly, London WIV OAL (tel. (44) 493-65-94). Write for information on any region of France, festival dates, and tips for handicapped travelers.

Interexchange Program, William Sloane House, 2nd floor, 356 W. 34th St., New York, NY 10001 (tel. (212) 947-9533). A service of the United States Student Travel Service. Write for their catalogs on work abroad for U.S. students.

John Muir Publications, P.O. Box 613, Sante Fe, NM 87504 (tel. (505) 982-4078). Publishes 3 books by veteran traveler Rick Steves. *Europe through the Back Door* (revised spring 1987; US$12.95) offers good advice, especially on traveling light, not being the ugly American, and avoiding tourist traps. *Europe in 22 Days* (US$6.95) is an itinerary for those who want to "do" Europe. *Europe 101: History, Art and Culture for the Traveler* (US$11.95) is somewhat simplistic.

Let's Go Travel Services, Harvard Student Agencies, Inc., Thayer Hall-B, Harvard University, Cambridge, MA 02138 (tel. (617) 495-9649). Sells student ID cards; AYH memberships (valid at all IYHF hostels); FIYTO cards for non-students; Eurail, BritRail, and France Vacances passes; transatlantic charter flights; travel guides (including the entire *Let's Go* series); and a line of travel gear—all available on the spot. ISIC, AYH, FIYTO card also available by mail.

Société Nationale de Chemins de Fer (SNCF), 610 Fifth Ave., New York, NY 10020 (tel. (212) 582-2110). French national railway. Schedules and maps of train routes throughout France and Europe. They also operate offices in Beverly Hills, Chicago, Miami, and San Francisco. In Canada, contact their offices in Montreal and Vancouver.

SSA/STA, 220 Faraday St., Carlton, Melbourne, Victory 3053, Australia. Provides standard travel services for Australians. Offers the ISIC.

Wide World Books & Maps, 401 NE 45th St., Seattle, WA 98105 (tel. (206) 634-3453). Useful, free catalog listing the most recent guidebooks to every part of the world. Good if you're planning to extend the boundaries of your European trip.

All large cities in France have an **Office de Tourisme.** Smaller French towns that attract a significant number of visitors have a tax-supported office called the **Syndicat d'Initiative** to provide information on the town and the surrounding area. The address of a town's *syndicat* is listed in its Practical Information section. Each office stocks color brochures and lists of local hotels and restaurants. For a regional view, though, the *syndicats* are a bit nearsighted; write to the French Government Tourist Office (see Useful Organizations above) for information on tourism, culture, lodging, and activities particular to a whole province.

Documents and Formalities

Parts of this section, such as the instructions on how to obtain a passport, apply to every traveler; other parts may not relate to your particular vacation plans. Be sure to look through the entire section and decide which documents you'll need. File all applications early, several weeks or even months before your planned departure date: A backlog at any agency could spoil even the best-laid plans.

Passports

You need a valid passport to enter France and to re-enter your own country. **U.S. citizens** aged 18 and over may apply for a 10-year U.S. passport at one of the several thousand Federal courts or U.S. post offices that accept passport applications, or at any one of the 13 Passport Agencies—in Boston, Chicago, Honolulu, Houston, Los Angeles, Miami, New Orleans, New York, Philadelphia, San Francisco, Seattle, Stamford, or Washington, DC. Those under 18 can obtain a five-year passport. Parents may apply for children under 13. If this is your first U.S. passport, if you are between the ages of 13 and 18, or if your current passport is more than 12 years old or was issued before your 16th birthday, you must apply in person; otherwise, you can renew by mail for US$35. You must submit the following: (1) a completed application form; (2) proof of U.S. citizenship (either a certified copy of your birth certificate, under the seal of the official registrar, naturalization papers, or a previous passport issued no more than 12 years ago); (3) identification bearing your signature and either your photo or personal description, e.g., a driver's license or passport—Social Security cards and credit cards are not valid forms of identification; and (4) two identical, recent, passport-sized photographs. If you are renewing by mail, your old passport will serve as both (2) and (3); do not forget to enclose it with your application. To obtain or renew a passport when ineligible for application by mail, you should bring (1-4) and US$42 (ages 18 or over) or US$27 (ages under 18) in the form of personal check or money order. The Passport Service also requests you write your birth date on your check.

LETS·GO·EUROPE·WITH·USIT

Athens
USIT, Filellinon 1, 105 57 Athens. Tel. (01) 322-5165, (01) 323-0483.

Brussels
Connections Eurotrain, 13 Rue Marche au Charbon/Kolenmarktstraat 13, 1000 Brussels. Tel. 5125060.

Dublin
USIT, 7 Anglesea Street, Dublin 2. Tel: (01) 778117.

London
London Student Travel, 52 Grosvenor Gardens (opposite Victoria Station) London, SWIW OAG. Tel: (01) 730 3402

Paris
USIT Voyages, 6 rue de Vaugirard, 75006 Paris. Tel: 4329 8500 or USIT Voyages, 12 Rue Vivienne, 75002 Paris. Tel: 4296 1588.

Processing usually takes two to three weeks (longer through a clerk of court or post office), but it's wise to apply several months before your departure date. If you are leaving within five working days, the passport office can provide express service while you wait, but you must have valid proof of your departure date (e.g., an airline ticket) and arrive at the office before 1pm. For more details, check with the closest Passport Agency; call U.S. Passport Information (tel. (202) 783-8200-5, a recording that gives a number to call in Washington, DC if you need a passport in an emergency after hours); or write to the Washington Passport Agency, 1425 K St. NW, Washington, DC 20524-0002 (tel. (202) 523-1355).

Canadian citizens may obtain passports by presenting their application in person to one of 20 regional offices (addresses are in the telephone directory), or by mailing their application to the Passport Office, Department of External Affairs, Ottawa, Ont. K1A 0G3. Passport applications are available from passport offices, post offices, and travel agencies. Passport requirements are (1) a completed application, (2) original documentary evidence of Canadian citizenship; and (3) two identical photographs, both signed by the holder, and one certified by a "guarantor," someone who has known you for at least two years and falls into one of a number of categories (e.g., lawyer, mayor, medical doctor, police officer, or notary public). The fee is CDN$25 and may be paid in cash, money order, certified check, or bank draft. The Passport Office recommends that you apply during the winter off-season. A passport may normally be obtained within three to five working days at a regional office; mailed applications normally require two weeks from the day the application is received. A Canadian passport is valid for five years. For more information, consult the *Canadian Passport* brochure and the *Bon Voyage, But . . .* booklet, available free from the Passport Office and at Canadian airports. For public inquiries, consult the Blue Pages of your local directory. Canadian citizens residing in the U.S. should apply at a Canadian consulate.

British Citizens must apply at any one of the passport offices in London, Liverpool, Newport, Peterborough, Glasgow, and Belfast, and must present originals of their birth certificate and marriage certificate as well as two identical copies of recent photos. The fee is £15, which covers a 10-year passport for adults and a five-year passport for ages under 16 (extendable to 10 years upon expiration). The application process averages four weeks.

Australian citizens must apply in person at a local post office or a passport office (usually located in the provincial capital). The fee for those 18 and over is AUS$66, and your passport is valid for 10 years. Those under 18 can get a five-year passport for AUS$27. All children must have passports. For more information, consult your local post office.

New Zealanders must contact their local passport office or consulate for an application which may be filed in person or by mail. Documented evidence of New Zealand citizenship must accompany your application. The fee for a 10-year passport (5 years if you are under age 10, though children may be included on parents' passports up to age 16) is NZ$50. The application process normally requires two weeks, but the office will speed up processing in an emergency.

Record your passport number in a separate, safe place, and photocopy the page with your photograph in case your passport is lost or stolen. These precautions will help prove your citizenship and facilitate the issuing of a new passport. If you lose your passport abroad, notify the nearest embassy or consulate and the local police immediately. It helps if you have registered with the nearest embassy or consulate, a wise precaution if you intend to stay in France for some time. The U.S. consulate can usually issue Americans new passports, given proof of citizenship, within two hours. In an emergency ask for an immediate temporary passport.

Second proof of citizenship can be anything from your birth certificate to driver's license; you should also bring two extra pieces of identification when traveling abroad. Keep these separate from your passport. A few extra passport-type photos also come in handy in case you lose your passport or decide to apply for a visa. For a complete list of all U.S. embassies, consulates, consulates general, and missions abroad, write for *Key Officers of Foreign Serving Posts* (updated 3 times per year), Superintendent of Documents, U.S. Government Printing Office, Washington, DC 20402.

Visas

Visas are required of all visitors to France, except those from Switzerland and the European Common Market countries. A visa is an endorsement or stamp placed in your passport by a foreign government allowing you to visit that country for a specified period of time. Three types of French visas are available.

Transit visas (US$3) are for travelers crossing France for a single, limited period of time (such as train passengers between Belgium and Spain). Their validity period differs with different nationalities (it's 72 hours for U.S. and Canadian citizens). The **court séjour** (90-day, multiple entry) visa costs US$9, but because it becomes valid on its issue date, you can't apply for it much in advance of your trip. The hassle of having to wait until the last minute to apply for this visa has markedly decreased its popularity. Unless you are really just passing through, the best deal is the **visa de circulation,** the "tourist" visa (US$15). It allows unlimited entries for 90 days or less during its five-year validity, although you cannot stay a total of more than six months in any one-year period. Apply for a visa through the nearest French Consulate. If the political situation remains essentially unchanged, visas will be required until at least 1990.

The requirements for any of these visas are a valid passport, a completed application (available from French Consulates and some travel agencies), and the fee in cash, check, or money order. Visas are usually issued within one day (longer through a travel agency). Obtaining a visa by mail takes three weeks, or three to four days by express mail. If you're already in Europe and decide to visit France, apply to the nearest consulate of your own country to help secure a visa. For details, check with a French Embassy or Consulate (see Useful Organizations above for addresses), or write for a free copy of *Visa Requirements of Foreign Governments* from Passport Services (see Passports above).

> **Pending Visa Changes**
> At press time, the French government was modifying long-stay visa requirements. Please contact a French consulate for up-to-date information. Below are the 1988 procedures.

Requirements for a long-stay visa vary with the nature of the stay: work, study, or *au pair*. Anyone staying in France longer than 90 days at one time must have a **carte de séjour** (residency permit). You must present a valid passport, six application forms completed in French, six passport photos, a letter of financial guarantee, and, if you're under 18, proof of parental authorization. If you plan to study in France, you must obtain the permit before arriving. *Au pairs* and others wishing to work in France may obtain residency permits before arrival or as soon as possible after arrival from the local *préfecture* (district office).

Before applying to the nearest French Consulate for a **student visa,** those wishing to study in France must have the residency permit, a medical exam, and a letter of admission to a school or university in France. To obtain a **work visa,** you must first obtain a work permit. After getting a job and a work contract from your French employer, your employer will obtain this permit for you and will forward it with a copy of your work contract to the Consulate nearest you. After a medical checkup and completion of the application, the visa will be issued on your valid passport. Note, however, that is illegal for foreign students to work during the school year, although they can receive permission from their local *Direction départementale du travail et de la main-d'oeuvre étrangère* to work in summer. *Au pairs* are subject to nearly the same requirements as others wishing to work. An **au pair's visa** can be obtained within two weeks with submission of two passport photos, a fee of US$10 to US$14, a medical exam, the original copy of the *au pair's* work contract signed by the *au pair,* and proof of admission to a language school or university program.

Student Identification

The **International Student Identity Card (ISIC)** is the only internationally recognized proof of student status. Although not always the only form of student identification accepted in France, it qualifies you for discounts on admission to museums, historical sites, and festivals and on theater tickets. Essential if you plan to use student charter flights or clubs, the ISIC will also get you lower fares on many forms of transportation, local and international. If you purchase the card in the U.S., it also provides you with US$2000 of medical insurance, plus US$100 per day for up to 60 days in case of in-hospital illness (see Insurance below). The ISIC is well-worth the US$10 cost—see Useful Organizations above for those that sell the card.

No application form is necessary, but you must supply all of the following: (1) current, dated proof of student status (a photocopy of your school ID showing this year's date, a letter on school stationery signed and sealed by the registrar, or a photocopied grade report); (2) a 1½ × 2 inch photo with your name printed in pencil on the back; (3) proof of your birthdate and nationality. The card is valid for 16 months from September 1 of one year through December of the following year. Unfortunately for those taking a year off from school, you cannot purchase a new card in January unless you were in school during the fall semester. If you are about to graduate, be sure to get your card before you leave school, as it will be valid until the end of the year. If you're not a student but are under age 26, inquire about youth discounts anyway—your passport will be your best proof of age.

If you are will be studying at a French university, you will be given a **carte d'étudiant** (student card) by the enrollment office at your school upon presentation of a receipt for your university fees and your residency permit (see Visas above).

The **Federation of International Youth Travel Organizations (FIYTO)** issues a **Youth International Education Exchange Card (YIEE)** to anyone under age 26.

The YIEE, or FIYTO, card is internationally recognized and gives you access to over 8000 discounts, primarily on international and inter-European transport, accommodations, cultural activities, and tours all over Europe. For further information and an application, write to FIYTO, 81 Islands Brugge, DK-2300 Copenhagen S., Denmark. CIEE offices, Travel CUTS, and agencies all over Europe issue the FIYTO card. An **IYHF card** entitles you to discounts on hostels (see Hostels below).

International Driver's License

An International Driving Permit is not necessary but is recommended if you don't speak French (it's basically a translation of your driver's license into 9 languages). Most rental agencies will not ask to see the permit, but will want to see your valid home driver's license. It is available at any branch of the **American Automobile Association** or at the main office, AAA Travel Agency Services, 8111 Gatehouse Rd., Falls Church, VA 22047. It is also available from the **Canadian Automobile Association (CAA),** 2 Carlton St., Toronto, Ont. M5B 1K4 (tel. (416) 964-3170). You will need a completed application, two recent passport-sized photos, a valid U.S. (or Canadian) driver's license (which must always accompany the International Driving Permit), and US$5 (CND$7). You must be over 18 to apply.

If you are going to drive, buy, or borrow a car that is not insured, you will need a "green card," or International Insurance Certificate, to prove you have liability insurance. If you are renting or leasing, you must get the green card (and the coverage too, if your own insurance does not apply abroad) from the rental agency or dealer. If you will be buying a car, you can get a green card by taking out a Europe Tourist Insurance Policy from CAA or AAA Travel Services.

Customs

Customs often evoke more alarm than they should. Just remember a few basic principles: You will not be charged duty on things you brought with you, and you have an allowance of what you can bring into the country—anything exceeding that allowance is charged a duty.

If you are bringing more than 200 cigarettes, 2 liters of wine (1 liter of alcohol over 28.8 proof), or ¼ liter of perfume into France, you must declare such items. Upon re-entering your own country, you must declare all articles acquired abroad. Keep all receipts. **U.S. citizens** may bring in US$400 worth of goods duty-free; they pay 10% on the next US$1000 worth. The duty-free goods must be for personal or household use and cannot include more than 100 cigars or 200 cigarettes (1 carton) and one liter of wine or liquor (you must be 21 or older to bring liquor into the U.S.). All items included must accompany you; you cannot have them shipped separately. Exemptions of persons traveling together may be combined.

While in Europe, you can mail unsolicited gifts back to the U.S. duty-free if they're worth less than US$50; mark the package "unsolicited gift" and indicate the nature of the gift and its retail value. However, you may not mail liquor, tobacco, or perfume into the U.S. If you send back a parcel worth over US$50, the Postal Service will collect the duty plus a handling charge when it is delivered. If you mail home personal goods of U.S. origin, mark the package "American goods returned."

Before departure, **Canadian citizens** should identify or list serial numbers of all valuables on form Y-38 at the Customs Office or point of departure; these goods can then be reimported duty-free. Once every year after seven days' absence, you can bring in goods up to a value of CDN$300, and in addition, goods to a value of CDN$100 any number of times per year after two days' absence. However, these two allowances can't both be claimed on the same trip. Duty-free goods can include no more than 50 cigars, 200 cigarettes, 0.91kg of tobacco, or one liter of alcohol (if you're 16 and over). Anything above the duty-free allowance is taxed. Shipped items will be taxed at a higher rate and may not include alcohol or tobacco products. You can send gifts up to a value of CDN$40 duty-free, but again, you cannot mail alcohol or tobacco. For more information, see the pamphlet *I Declare,* available from the Revenue Canada Customs and Excise Department, Communications Branch, Mackenzie Ave., Ottawa, Ont. K1A OL5.

American or Canadian, you must declare any items that you bought at duty-free shops abroad with your other purchases, and you will have to pay duty on them if they exceed your allowance. Remember, "duty-free" means only that you didn't pay taxes in the country of purchase. When you return from abroad, you may also run into trouble with clothing or jewelry of foreign make that you originally purchased in North America. You must be able to prove their origin with purchase receipts or identifying marks.

According to the U.S. Customs Service's official brochure, *Know Before You Go,* available free by writing the U.S. Customs Service, P.O. Box 7407, Washington, DC 20044, non-prescription drugs and narcotics, obscene publications, lottery tickets, liquor-filled candies, and most plants are all considered "injurious to the well-being of our nation." Write the Animal and Plant Health Inspection Service, U.S. Department of Agriculture, 700 Federal Bldg., 6505 Belcrest Rd., Hyattsville, MD 20782 for *Travelers' Tips on Bringing Food, Plant, and Animal Products into the United States.* They also provide information on restrictions in the wildlife trade. To avoid problems when carrying prescription drugs, make sure the bottles are clearly marked, and have the prescription ready to show the customs officer. Canadians traveling to or from Europe via the U.S. should also note that pain-killers containing codeine—available over-the-counter in Canada—are illegal in the U.S.

If you are an **Australian citizen,** your allowance upon returning home is 250g of tobacco (equivalent to 250 cigarettes) and one liter of alcohol. Before leaving Australia, you must buy an AUS$20 Departure Tax Stamp at a post office or airport (children under 12 exempt). Filling out Customs Form B263 will allow you to reimport your own valuables duty- and trouble-free. You are allowed to bring in up to AUS$400 worth of goods duty-free; if you are under 18 your allowance is AUS$200. Any goods above these limits will be taxed. These goods may not include tobacco, alcohol, or furs and must be carried into the country with you. You may not export more than AUS$5000 in cash. You may mail back personal property; mark it "Australian goods returned" to avoid duty. You may not mail unsolicited gifts duty-free. For additional information, write to the Australian Customs Service, Customs House, 5-11 Constitution Ave., Canberra, ACT 2600 Australia, for their brochure *Australian Customs Information.*

New Zealand citizens can list goods they're taking with them on a Certificate of Export and have a NZ$500 duty-free allowance upon returning home (children included). Those over 16 may bring in 200 cigarettes or 250g of tobacco or 50 cigars (or a combination of the three not weighing more than 250g) and 4.5 liters of wine or beer and 1.125 liters of spirits or liqueur. There are no restrictions on the amount of New Zealand currency that may be brought into or taken out of New Zealand. For more information, contact your nearest Customs Department for the *New Zealand Customs Guide for Travelers.*

Money

Currency and Exchange

The basic unit of currency in France is the franc, which may be divided into 100 centimes and issued in both coins and paper notes. The smallest unit of French currency is the five-centimes piece. The new franc, equal to 100 old francs, was issued in 1960. Old habits die hard, though, especially in the provinces: If an elderly waiter or waitress demands "mille (1000) francs" for two cups of coffee, relax—10F should cover it.

We list the exchange rates valid on August 10, 1988 (when our researchers were in the field); however, rates fluctuate considerably, so check them by scanning the financial pages of a national newspaper or by calling a large local bank. Before leaving home, buy US$50 or so in French bills; this will save you time at the airport.

When changing money, it pays to compare rates. Banks often offer the best rates, but usually charge a commission which can be as much as US$3. Large, local banks or national ones, such as Crédit Agricole or Crédit Lyonnais, have competitive rates and charge the smallest commission. Avoid exchanging money at "tourist" locations such as hotels, airports, train stations, or restaurants; their convenient hours and locations allow them to offer less favorable exchange rates. To minimize losses, exchange fairly large sums at one time, though never more than is safe to carry around. Be sure to procure enough cash to carry you through weekends, holidays, and side trips in isolated areas.

Traveler's Checks

Nothing is likely to cause you more headaches than money: Toting large amounts of cash, even in a moneybelt, is risky. Traveler's checks are the safest and least troublesome means of carrying funds; they can prevent money nightmares from becoming realities.

Traveler's checks are sold by several agencies and many banks, usually for face value plus a commission of 1-2%. American Express checks are perhaps the most widely recognized and the easiest to replace if lost or stolen, though other major checks are sold, exchanged, cashed, and refunded with almost equal ease.

Consult your bank or phone book for the nearest vendor. Several companies provide toll-free numbers which provide assistance with check purchases as well as refund information.

American Express: Call (800) 221-7282 from the U.S. and Canada; call collect (801) 968-8300 from abroad. Checks available in U.S. and Canadian dollars, in British pounds, and in 5 other currencies. The 1% commission is waived for cardholders. Local American Express Travel Service offices will cash personal checks up to US$200, assist in replacing missing travel documents, arrange temporary IDs, and help change airline, hotel, and car rental reservations.

Bank of America: Call (800) 227-3460 from the U.S.; call collect (415) 624-5400 from Canada and abroad. Checks available in U.S. dollars. Free in California, 1% commission elsewhere. A free booklet lists over 40,000 refund offices worldwide. Checkholders get access to a Travel Information hotline and are eligible to join the WorldMoney SafeTravel Network, a comprehensive travel assistance and insurance plan. 45-day individual membership US$8.50; family membership US$16.

Barclays Bank: Call (800) 221-2426 from the U.S. and Canada; (415) 574-7111 from abroad; call collect (01) 937-8091 from London. Checks available in U.S. and Canadian dollars and British pounds in New York and at other regional branches, including those at the British Airways terminals at Kennedy and Heathrow Airports. For other locations write to Barclays, 54 Lombard St., London EC3P 3AH, U.K., or Barclays, 420 Lexington Ave., New York, NY 10163.

Citicorp: Call (800) 645-6556 or (800) 523-1199 from the U.S.; call collect (813) 623-1709 from abroad. Checks available in U.S. dollars, British pounds, Deutschmarks, and Japanese yen at banks throughout the U.S. Checkholders are automatically enrolled in a program called Travel Assist Hotline (a slightly abridged version of Europ Assistance Worldwide's Travel Assist program; see Insurance below), for 45 days from the date of the checks' purchase.

Mastercard International: Call (212) 649-5379. Traveler's checks are available in 11 currencies at many banks and are refundable at over 170,000 locations worldwide.

Thomas Cook: Call (800) 223-7373 from the U.S.; call collect (212) 974-5696 from Canada and abroad. Checks available in U.S. and Canadian dollars, British pounds, and eight other currencies at Thomas Cook offices, local AAA offices, and at some banks. 1% commission.

Visa: Call (800) 227-6811 from the U.S. and Canada; call collect (415) 547-7111 (San Francisco) or (01) 937-8091 (London) from abroad. Checks available in U.S. and Canadian dollars and 12 other currencies. Commission varies with the bank.

Each agency provides refunds if your checks are lost or stolen, and many provide additional services. Inquire about refund hotlines, emergency message relay services, and stolen credit card assistance when you purchase your checks.

You should expect a fair amount of red tape and delay in the event of theft or loss. To expedite the refund process, separate your check receipts and keep them

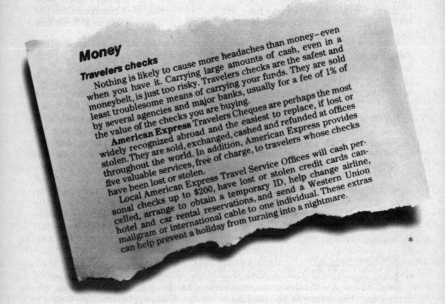

Money

Travelers checks

Nothing is likely to cause more headaches than money–even when you have it. Carrying large amounts of cash, even in a moneybelt, is just too risky. Travelers checks are the safest and least troublesome means of carrying your funds. They are sold by several agencies and major banks, usually for a fee of 1% of the value of the checks you are buying.

American Express Travelers Cheques are perhaps the most widely recognized abroad and the easiest to replace, if lost or stolen. They are sold, exchanged, cashed and refunded at offices throughout the world. In addition, American Express provides five valuable services, free of charge, to travelers whose checks have been lost or stolen.

Local American Express Travel Service Offices will cash personal checks up to $200, have lost or stolen credit cards cancelled, arrange to obtain a temporary ID, help change airline, hotel and car rental reservations, and send a Western Union mailgram or international cable to one individual. These extras can help prevent a holiday from turning into a nightmare.

*

Thanks a lot "Let's Go."
We couldn't have said it better ourselves.

AMERICAN EXPRESS **Travelers Cheques**

*Excerpt from "Let's Go, Europe." © 1984 by Harvard Student Agencies, Inc.

in a safe place. Record check numbers when you cash them (to help you identify which checks are missing), and leave a list of check numbers with someone at home. When you buy your checks, ask for a list of refund centers. American Express and Bank of America have over 40,000 centers worldwide; others provide phone numbers you can call collect (listed above). Most importantly, keep a separate supply of cash or traveler's checks for emergencies.

Buy most of your checks in large denominations (US$50 or US$100) to avoid spending too much time in line at banks, but buy some checks in small denominations (US$10 or US$20) to minimize losses when you must settle for unfavorable exchange rates.

Finally, weigh the costs and benefits of purchasing traveler's checks in your local currency. While U.S. citizens can easily exchange dollars for francs in France, New Zealanders and Australians may have difficulty exchanging their currencies. On the other hand, dealing with double exchange rates (such as Canadian to U.S. dollars and then U.S. dollars to francs) can be expensive.

Credit Cards

Although credit cards are of limited value to the budget traveler since low-cost establishments usually don't honor them, they can be invaluable in an emergency. With major credit cards such as **Visa** or **MasterCard,** you can obtain an instant cash advance in local currency as large as your remaining credit line from banks honoring the card. Such a transfusion of cash can tide you over if your traveler's checks or cash are lost or stolen; indeed, it may be your only source of cash, as many traveler's check vendors will not cash personal checks, and transatlantic money cables take at least 48 hours. Visa has increased the number of its foreign offices and offers the *International Travel Guide* free. Write to Chase Visa, P.O. Box 5111, 1400 Union Turnpike, New Hyde Park, NY 11042. Visa cards are also accepted at over 6000 automated teller machines throughout Europe; you can withdraw up to US$200 per day in the local currency until you reach your credit limit.

American Express Travel Service (tel. (800) 528-4800) staffs over 1400 full-service travel offices that will cash personal checks up to US$1000 in any seven-day period (US$200 in cash and the rest in traveler's checks). In addition, American Express operates over 8000 **automated teller machines** throughout the U.S. and Europe, where cardholders can get up to US$1000 (US$500 in cash and US$500 in traveler's checks). Call (800) CASH-NOW, that's (800) 227-4669, for more information. The card also allows you to use American Express offices as mailing addresses for free; otherwise you may have to pay (or show your AmEx traveler's checks) to pick up your mail. They will also wire to replace cards that have been lost or stolen. The *Traveler's Companion,* a list of full-service offices worldwide, is available from American Express, 65 Broadway, New York, NY 10006.

If your income level is low, you may have difficulty acquiring an internationally recognized credit card. If a family member already has a card, however, it's easy to get joint-account cards. American Express will issue an extra green card for US$25 per year or an extra gold card for US$30 (bills go to your loved ones). Fees for Visa and MasterCard joint-account cards vary from bank to bank.

When looking for places in France that will accept your card, remember that Mastercard is often called Eurocard, and Visa the Carte Bleue. Look for the familiar logos rather than the names.

Sending Money

Sending money overseas is costly and often frustrating. Do your best to avoid it. Carry a credit card or a separate stash of traveler's checks for emergencies.

The quickest and cheapest way to have money sent is to notify your home bank, by mail or telegram, of the amount you need, whether in francs or your home currency, and the name and address of the bank to which it should be **cabled** (preferably the office of a large French bank with many regional branches). This service takes about 24 hours—a bit longer in small cities—and costs anywhere between US$25 and US$80. Before you leave, you can arrange to have your local bank send you money at specified periods, but the procedure is cumbersome and confusing, and most banks are reluctant to do it.

Sending money through a company such as **American Express** costs about as much as sending it through a bank. Normally, the sender must have an American Express card, but certain offices will waive this requirement for a commission. The money is guaranteed to arrive within 72 hours at the designated overseas office, where it will be held for 14 days, and, if unclaimed, returned to the sender. It costs US$15 to send US$500 and US$30 to send US$1000, which is the limit. The first US$200 of any amount will be disbursed in francs, the rest in traveler's checks. This service operates only between American Express offices proper, not their representatives.

Western Union offers a convenient service for cabling money abroad. They operate 24 hours a day, seven days a week. In the U.S., a sender with a **Visa** or **Master-Card** can call Western Union's toll-free number (tel. (800) 325-6000 or (800) 325-4176) and have them cable up to US$2000. If the sender doesn't have a card, she or he must appear at a Western Union office with either cash, American Express travelers checks, or a cashier's check; no money orders are accepted. Transactions of this type are not limited to US$2000. The money will arrive at the central telegram office of the city the sender designates and can be picked up upon presentation of suitable identification. The company covers about 50 cities in France. The money it sends is handled by Citibank in France, and should arrive within two business days, in francs. Money is generally held 14 days; if no one picks it up, it will be returned to the sender minus the original cost of having it sent. It costs about US$34 to send US$300-500.

Finally, U.S. citizens in emergencies can have money sent via the **Citizen's Emergency Center,** Department of State, Room 4811, 2201 C St. NW, Washington, DC 20520 (tel. (202) 647-5225). The center serves only Americans in life or death situations abroad. For a fee of US$15, the center will send the money within 24 hours to the nearest consular office, which will then disburse the cash according to instructions. The center requires the sender's name and address, the name of the recipient, and the reason for sending money. The department prefers not to send sums greater than US$500. The quickest way to have the money sent is to cable the State Department through Western Union or to leave cash, a certified check, a bank draft, or a money order at the department itself.

T.V.A. (Value Added Tax)

In France, you will be charged a national sales tax, the T.V.A., on most goods. The French rate is 18.60% on all goods except books, food, and medicine. There is a 33% luxury tax on such items as video cassettes, watches, jewelry, and cameras.

Shoppers who are not from France can participate in a complex over-the-counter export scheme that exempts them from paying T.V.A. This is only worthwhile if you are buying expensive items. Ask the store for a duplicate pink sales invoice (*bordereau*) and a stamped envelope. At the border, show the invoices and your purchases to the French customs officials, who will stamp the invoices and send a copy back to the vendor, who can then prove that he or she was entitled to deduct T.V.A. and will refund the agreed amount. The refunds are usually sent to your bank account and not your address. You must take the goods out of the country with you within three months of their purchase.

Safety and Security

Insurance

When buying insurance, beware of unnecessary coverage. Your current **medical insurance** policy may cover costs incurred abroad. University term-time medical plans often include insurance for summer travel. Medicare, on the other hand, does not cover foreign travel—except for limited coverage in Canada and Mexico. Canadians are protected by their home province's health insurance plan, but the details vary from province to province. Check with your provincial Ministry of Health or Health Plan Headquarters. Your **homeowners' insurance** (or your family's coverage) often provides against theft during travel. Homeowners are generally covered against loss of travel documents (passport, plane ticket, rail pass, etc.) up to US$500.

Remember that claims can only be filed to your home medical or homeowner's insurance upon return to the U.S. or Canada and must be accompanied by the proper documents, i.e., police reports in cases of theft, doctor's statements (written in English if possible), and all other receipts for which you're requesting reimbursement. Note that some of the plans listed below offer cash advances or guaranteed transferrals, so it is not always necessary to use your own vacation cash to pay doctor bills. Full payment *in cash* before check-out (and sometimes even before treatment) is virtually the rule at most European hospitals. If your coverage doesn't include on-the-spot payments or cash transferrals, budget in emergency money supplies.

When purchased in the U.S., the **ISIC card** will provide you with US$2000 worth of accident insurance plus US$100 per day up to 60 days of in-hospital sickness coverage as long as the card is valid. In addition, **CIEE** offers an inexpensive Trip Safe plan that can extend coverage of medical treatment and hospitalization, accidents, and even charter flights missed due to illness (see Useful Organizations and Publications above).

The following agencies offer insurance against theft, loss of luggage, trip cancellation/interruption, and medical emergencies. You can buy a policy directly from them or, in some cases, from a travel agent operating on their behalf.

Access America, Inc., 600 3rd Ave., P.O. Box 807, New York, NY 10163 (tel. (800) 851-2800). Travel insurance that covers everything from luggage, trip cancellation/interruption, stolen passports, and bail money, to emergency medical evacuation and on-the-spot hospital and doctor payments in cash. US$5 per US$100 of trip cancellation/interruption coverage. Policyholders can call a 24-hour toll-free international number for access to a network of multilingual coordinators.

ARM Coverage, Inc., P.O. Box 310, 120 Mineola Blvd., Mineola, NY 11501 (tel. (800) 645-2424). Their Carefree Travel Insurance offers comprehensive travel insurance, including coverage of luggage loss. US$5.50 per US$100 of trip cancellation/interruption coverage. 24-hour hotline. Underwritten by Hartford.

Edmund A. Cocco Agency, 220 Broadway, #201, P.O. Box 780, Lynnfield, MA 01940 (tel. (800) 821-2488; in MA (617) 595-0262). Trip cancellation/interruption and travel accident and sickness coverage. Coverage for payment of medical expenses "on-the-spot" anywhere in the world and medical evacuation insurance. Group rates available. Protection against bankruptcy or default of airlines, cruise lines, or charter companies. US$5.50 per US$100 of trip cancellation/interruption coverage. 24-hour hotline.

Europ Assistance Worldwide Services, Inc., 1133 15th St. NW, #400, Washington, DC 20005 (tel. (800) 821-2828). Services for members of their Travel Assist program include a 24-hour assistance program in the event of financial, personal, or medical emergencies; comprehensive medical coverage; emergency medical evacuation and repatriation home when necessary; as well as interpretation, legal and medical referrals, transmission of messages, and cash advances.

WorldCare Travel Assistance Association, Inc., 2000 Pennsylvania Ave. NW, #7600, Washington, DC 20006 (tel. (800) 521-4822). 24-hour emergency medical hotline with extensive international network. Membership fee can be annual or per trip. Also offers a Scholarcare program tailored to students and faculty spending a semester or year abroad.

Preventing Theft

A few precautions will see you safely through your travels more effectively than constant mistrust. Steer clear of empty train compartments, and avoid bus and train stations and public parks after dark. When on foot, stick to busy, well-lit streets. Ask the managers of your hotel, hostel, or campground for advice on specific areas, and consider staying in places with a curfew or night attendant. Keep all valuables with you whenever you leave your room, even if it has a lock; others may have a passkey. At night, sleep with valuables on your person; laying your pack alongside the bed isn't necessarily enough to deter thieves.

While traveling, avoid checking luggage on trains, especially if you are transferring en route. Checked belongings may be lost or stolen. Keep your money, passport, and other important documents with you in a pouch or **money-belt** at all times. **Necklace pouches** worn under the shirt prove the most theft-resistant. Look for packs that have zippers designed to accept combination locks; remember, though, that these will not stop a determined thief. If you plan to sleep outside, or simply can't carry everything with you, try to store your gear in sturdy lockers or at the baggage check of a bus or train station. Bomb scares and terrorism, however, have decreased the availability of these lockers. Furthermore, since these lockers are sometimes broken into, always carry essential documents with you.

Pickpockets are fast, practiced, and professional. Pros can unzip a bag in just a few seconds, so wear yours with the opening against your body. They often work in pairs, one providing a distraction and the other grabbing your wallet or purse. Some street children will do anything to distract you; they will even pretend that they are being molested. Be on your guard against the following currently popular scams: someone who blocks your view with a piece of cardboard or a map (pretending to ask directions), groups of youths who feign scuffles and fights, pairs of people who pretend to solicit money or sell posters to support political causes, and people who tell you they have just been robbed themselves and need to "borrow" money. In Metro stations move quickly into the waiting car; thieves may try to grab your bag as you board, just before the doors close.

It's a good idea to make photocopies of all important documents, your passport, identification, credit cards, and the numbers of your traveler's checks. Keep one set of copies in a separate, secure place in your luggage, and leave another set at home. Although copies can seldom substitute for originals, you'll at least have a means of retrieving the information on anything you lose without having to rely on memory.

If you are pickpocketed, check your surroundings carefully. Thieves may throw away your wallet after taking the money, and you might be able to retrieve non-cash objects such as cards. Report the theft to the police station in the area where it occurred.

Drugs

If you're caught with any quantity of drugs in France, you'll be kicked out of the country immediately. Never bring anything across the borders, since drug laws and the severity with which they are enforced vary considerably among different countries (e.g., between Holland and France). In France police may legally stop and search anyone on the street. It is not uncommon for a pusher to increase his profit by first selling drugs to a tourist and then turning that person into the authorities for a reward. If you are arrested, your home country's consulate can visit you, provide a list of attorneys, and inform family and friends; they cannot get you out of jail. You're virtually "on your own" if you become involved, however innocently, in illegal drug trafficking. For more information, write the Bureau of Consular Affairs, CP/PA #5807, Department of State, Washington, DC 20520 (tel. (202) 647-1488) for the pamphlet *Travel Warning on Drugs Abroad.*

Health

The simplest prescription for health while traveling is to keep your body and anything you put into it clean: Eat well, and don't overextend yourself. You'll need plenty of protein (for sustained energy) and fluids (dehydration and constipation are common travel problems). All food, including seafood, dairy products, and fresh produce, is safe in France. The water is chlorinated and also safe, but in parts of the country, the bacteria differ from those found in North American water, and may cause diarrhea. Relying on bottled mineral water your first couple of weeks is a sensible precaution. Write IAMAT (see below) for their useful pamphlets, *How to Avoid Traveler's Diarrhea, How to Adjust to the Heat,* and *How to Adapt to Altitude.*

Although no special immunizations are necessary for travel to France, be sure that your **inoculations** are up-to-date. Typhoid shots remain good for three years, tetanus for 10. *Health Information for International Travel* (US$4.75) provides U.S. Public Health recommendations and other hints. Write the U.S. Government Printing Office, Superintendent of Documents, Washington, DC 20402-9325.

Depending on your plans, you may wish to bring a few of the following: mild antiseptic soap, aspirin, a decongestant, an antihistamine, something for diarrhea, something for motion sickness, earplugs, a thermometer, bandages, contraceptives (remember time zone changes when taking the Pill), mosquito repellent, and a Swiss army knife with tweezers.

Travelers with contact lenses should bring an extra pair, a pair of glasses, or at least a copy of their prescription. Since the pressurized atmosphere of an airplane can dehydrate soft lenses, you should clean them just before leaving; don't drink coffee or alcohol, and don't read for long periods of time. Make sure to bring along adequate supplies of your cleaning solutions. Foreign brands with familiar names may have different formulations from those to which you're accustomed. For heat disinfection you'll need low-wattage voltage and outlet adapters.

Travelers with a chronic medical condition requiring regular treatment should consult their doctors before leaving. Diabetics, for example, may need advice on adapting insulin levels for flights across multiple time zones. Carry an ample supply of all medicines, since matching your prescription with a foreign equivalent may be difficult. Always carry up-to-date prescriptions (in legible, preferably typewritten form, including the medication's trade name, manufacturer, chemical name, and dosage) and/or a statement from your doctor, especially if you take insulin, syringes, or any narcotic drugs. Keep all medicines and syringes in your carry-on luggage.

Travelers with a medical condition that cannot be easily recognized (e.g., diabetes, allergies to antibiotics, epilepsy, heart conditions) should obtain a **Medic Alert identification tag.** This internationally recognized tag indicates the nature of the condition, and provides the number of Medic Alert's 24-hour hotline, through which medical personnel can obtain information about the member's medical history. Lifetime membership costs US$20; contact Medic Alert Foundation International, P.O. Box 1009, Turlock, CA 95381-1009 (tel. (800) ID-ALERT, that's (800) 432-5378). The emergency number is (209) 634-4917.

• At night and on Sundays, the local *commissariat de police* will supply the address of the nearest open *pharmacie* (drugstore) and that of a doctor on duty. For an ambulance to the *hôpital,* look in the phone book under *ambulances municipales.*

Few areas of France are so isolated that you will have to worry about finding competent medical attention. Before you go, write for a directory of English-speaking physicians worldwide from the **International Association for Medical Assistance to Travelers (IAMAT),** 417 Center St., Lewiston, NY 14092 (tel. (716) 754-4883); in Canada, 40 Regal Rd., Guelph, Ont. N1K 1B5 (tel. (519) 836-0102). Membership is free (donation requested), and doctors are on call 24 hours for members. American, Canadian, and British embassies and consulates, and American Express offices can also help you find English-speaking doctors. You may also be able to find a good doctor in the emergency room of a university hospital. As a last resort, go to the largest city nearby and hope that someone at the hospital speaks English. *Let's Go* lists hospitals in most cities; we try to note where English-speaking doctors are available.

For additional information, you might want to write for *The Pocket Medical Encyclopedia and First-Aid Guide* (US$4.95) from Simon & Schuster, 200 Old Tappan Rd., Old Tappan, NJ 07675, Attn: Mail Order Department.

Packing

Pack light. Lay out everything you think you'll need, pack only half of it, and take more money. Remember that you can buy almost anything you'll need in Europe, and that the more luggage you carry, the more you'll look and feel like a tourist.

First decide what kind of luggage is best suited to your trip. A **backpack** is ideal if you plan to cover a lot of ground and want to hike or camp often (see Camping Equipment below). If you intend to stay mainly in cities and towns, consider a **light suitcase.** For unobtrusive travel, choose a large **shoulder bag** that zips or closes securely. This may also be the best choice if you intend to hitch most of the time—it's less intimidating to drivers than a large backpack. Whenever you can, store your luggage in secure lockers while you see the sights; bring a small **daypack** to carry your *Let's Go,* lunch, map, rain poncho, and camera.

Pack solid, dark-colored clothes that won't show the wear they'll eventually receive. If they're loose and layerable, they will be more versatile. Dress neatly and conservatively—you'll fare better when hitching and dealing with elderly hotel owners. Sturdy cotton-blend pants or a wide skirt are cooler for summer and look more polished than jeans. Since French women do not wear them publicly, shorts above the knee will instantly brand a woman as a foreigner and are inappropriate in cities and towns. Remember too that you should dress neatly when visiting any house of worship, whether or not services are being held. Taking clothes that you can wash in a sink and that dry quickly wrinkle-free will save you visits to laundromats.

France is generally fair and warm in summer with temperatures in the 70s (around 25°C), the 80s (30°C) in Paris, and the 90s (35°C) in the south. Winters are mild, averaging about 40°F (5°C) during the day. (See Climate below for details.) Lightweight cottons or blends are a must in summer, with a sweater for cool evenings. Light wool clothing is good for autumn, and will carry you through winter as well except in the north and in the mountains. You'll need **rainwear** in all seasons, and if you plan to camp, it's worth paying a little more for a lightweight poncho that unbuttons to form a groundcloth.

Avoid taking electrical appliances, but if you must, remember that electricity in most European countries is 220 volts AC, twice as much as in North America and enough to fry any of your appliances. If you can use batteries, you'll save money; if you can't, you'll need an **adapter.** In France, as in most of Europe, sockets accommodate mainly two-pin round plugs, but some places may have three-pin plugs. If the appliance is not dual voltage, you'll also need a **converter** (US$15-18). But remember that you can use these converters only in areas with AC current. You can buy adapters and converters when you get to Europe, or order them in advance from the **Franzus Company,** 53 W. 23rd St., New York, NY 10010 (tel. (212) 463-9393). They also offer a line of dual-voltage travel appliances.

The following is a checklist of items you might consider taking: a first-aid kit, needle and thread, string, a small flashlight, a cold-water soap (Dr. Bronner's Castile Soap, available in camping stores, claims to work as everything from clothes detergent to toothpaste), ziplock bags (for damp clothing, soap, or messy foods), waterproof matches, a notebook, English-language maps, a pocket French-English dictionary or phrasebook, and a travel alarm clock. If you take expensive **cameras** or equipment abroad, it's best to register everything with customs at the airport before departure. Since color film is more expensive in France, consider buying a supply before you leave.

Camping Equipment

If you decide on a camping vacation, purchase your equipment before you leave—American packs, for instance, are generally more durable and comfortable than European ones, and often less expensive. As a rule, prices go down in the fall as old merchandise is cleaned out. **Backpacks** come with either an external frame or an internal X- or A-shaped frame. If your load is not extraordinarily heavy and you plan to use the pack mainly as a suitcase, choose an internal-frame model. Less cumbersome, it's more manageable when hitching or on crowded trains, and it's less likely to be mangled by rough handling. A good pack costs US$100-150.

Your **sleeping bag** need not be down; a good synthetic fiber is almost as warm and dries much more quickly. For camping in spring, summer, or fall, a 2½-pound down bag (US$85-150) or a 3½-pound synthetic bag (US$20-50) should be more than adequate. At about US$10, an **ensolite pad** (much warmer than foam rubber) is a real bargain, providing crucial protection from cold, damp, and often rocky ground. Thermarest (US$50) is a hybrid ensolite pad and air mattress which virtually inflates itself—comfy. Good **tents** are expensive (US$70-120 for a 2-person nylon tent with a rain fly and bug netting), but are a sound investment. A **tarpaulin** rigged between two trees will keep you from getting completely soaked in a downpour, but only experienced campers should rough it with just a tarp. A long favorite of climbers, the **bivouac sac** (US$30) is merely an envelope of rip-stop nylon, polymer-coated on one side. Place your sleeping bag inside, and it will keep you much drier and warmer than you might expect. The following organizations provide camping information or supplies.

Ariel Publications, 14417 SE 19th Pl., Bellevue, WA 98007 (tel. (206) 641-0158). Publishes *How to Camp Europe by Train* (US$13).

L.L. Bean, Freeport, ME 04033 (tel. (800) 221-4221 for orders, (800) 341-4341 for customer service). A well-established firm that sells camping equipment and outdoor clothes, its own and other national brands. Publishes a catalog 4 times per year. Open year-round 24 hours.

Mountain Equipment Inc. (MEI), 4776 E. Jensen Ave., Fresno, CA 93725 (tel. (209) 486-8211). Good quality, reasonably priced packs. Send for their catalog and the names of retailers near you who sell MEI products.

National Campers and Hikers Association, Inc., 4804 Transit Rd., Bldg. 2, Depew, NY 14043 (tel. (716) 668-6242). Issues the **International Camping Carnet,** required by some European campgrounds. The US$23 fee includes membership in the association. Short bibliography of travel guides for campers and a list of camping stores in major European cities.

Recreational Equipment, Inc., Commercial Sales, P.O. Box C-88126, Seattle, WA 98188 (tel. (206) 431-5809 or 431-5805). Outdoor equipment cooperative. Lifetime membership (not required) US$10. You must make a purchase every 2-3 years to receive the catalog each season. Sells *Europa Camping and Caravanning,* an encyclopedic catalog of campsites in Europe.

Special Concerns

Traveling Alone

Some cheap accommodations may entail more risks for the lone traveler than savings. Forgo dives and city outskirts in favor of university accommodations, youth hostels, and *foyers,* and remember that centrally located accommodations are usually safest.

Although women traveling alone are at the highest risk, women traveling together are safe virtually anywhere. Remember that hitching is not safe for women alone. Also, consider staying in *foyers* or religious organizations that offer rooms for women only. Foreign women in France, especially Germans and Americans, are frequently beset by unwanted and tenacious followers. Try to exercise reasonable caution without falling prey to the notion that all French men are best avoided.

Cultural sensitivity can often short-circuit threatening situations. French women almost never wear shorts (especially cut-offs), tube tops, or camisoles. Doing so might invite unwanted attention. Follow the example of local women. In the more provincial provinces, the more skin you cover, the less harassment you'll receive. If you're traveling alone, don't say so. Try to look as if you know where you're going, and ask women or couples for directions if you're lost or you feel uncomfortable. Your best answer to verbal harassment is no answer at all. In crowds, you may be pinched, squeezed, or otherwise molested. Wearing a walkman or a conspicuous wedding band may help prevent such incidents. If you are propositioned directly, a loud "*Non!*" or "*Laissez-moi tranquille!*" (lay-say-mwah-tran-keel; leave me alone) is best, with no further explanation. Seek out a policeman or a female passer-by before a crisis erupts, and don't hesitate to scream for help. Always carry change for the phone (emergency numbers aren't free) and enough extra money for a bus or taxi in case you feel threatened. The Practical Information section for every large city lists emergency, police, and consulate phone numbers, and women's centers. Women may also want to consult *The Handbook for Women Travellers,* published by Judy Piatkus Ltd., 5 Windmill St., London W1.

Senior Travelers

Senior citizens enjoy an assortment of discounts on transportation, tours, admission to museums, and more. The following organizations offer information, assistance, and/or discounts to seniors.

American Association of Retired Persons, Special Services Department, 1909 K St. NW, Washington, DC 20049 (tel. (800) 227-7737). Persons aged 50 and older receive benefits from AARP Travel Services and get discounts on hotels, motels, car rental, and sightseeing companies. For a brochure write P.O. Box 38997, Los Angeles, CA 90230. Annual membership US$5.

Elderhostel, 80 Boylston St., #400, Boston, MA 02116 (tel. (617) 426-7788). Weeklong programs in over 30 countries in the Americas and Europe cover a variety of subjects; a fee of US$195-225 includes room, board, tuition, and extracurricular activities. You or your spouse must be 60 or over to enroll.

Mature Outlook, P.O. Box 1205, Glenview, IL 60025. Special domestic and international packages, reduced travel insurance, and other travel discounts. You must be 50 or over. Annual membership costs US$7.50 per couple.

National Council of Senior Citizens, 925 15th St., Washington, DC 20005 (tel. (202) 347-8800). Information on discounts and travel abroad.

Pilot Industries, Inc., 103 Cooper St., Babylon, NY 11702 (tel. (516) 422-2225). Publishes *The Senior Citizen's Guide to Budget Travel* (US$3.95, postage US$1).

Superintendent of Documents, U.S. Government Printing Office, Washington, DC 20402. Write for a free copy of *Travel Tips for Senior Citizens,* which provides information on passports, visas, health, and currency.

Gay and Lesbian Travelers

In general, the French public is not overtly hostile to gay people living openly, especially in the capital. Gay life continues to be rather discreet outside Paris, with more openness in Nice, Lyon, Marseille, Toulouse, and Nantes.

Wherever possible, *Let's Go* lists gay and lesbian information lines, community centers, and bookstores. Paris has a weekly journal *Gai Pied Hebdo,* which is distributed nationally. The best of the gay and lesbian monthly magazines are *Gay International, Gay Men,* and *Lesbia. Illico* is available free in bars and other gay meeting places. Les Mots à la Bouche, 6, rue Ste-Croix de la Bretonnerie, 75004 Paris (tel. 42-78-88-30); Librairie Des Femmes, 74, rue de Seine, 6ème (tel. 43-29-50-75); and Librairie Pluriel, 3, rue Keller, 11ème (tel. 48-06-30-53), are well-regarded Parisian bookstores. There is an information center at La Maison des Femmes, 8, Cité Prost, 11ème (tel. 43-48-24-91). The **Centre du Christ Liberateur, Sexual Minorities,** at 3bis, rue Clairaut, 75017 Paris (tel. 46-27-49-36; Mo. La Fourche), provides legal, medical, pastoral, and psychological help to various sexual minorities. They also operate the gay switchboard, **SOS Homosexualité** (tel. 46-27-49-36). The multilingual staff can also help locate inexpensive housing.

Gaia's Guide, an excellent "international guide for traveling women," lists local lesbian, feminist, and gay information numbers; publications; women's and cultural centers and resources; bookstores; restaurants; hotels; and meeting places. The book, revised annually, should be available at a local bookstore or by mail (US$12.50, postage included). In the U.S. and Canada, write to Giovanni's Room, 345 S. 12th St. NE, Philadelphia, PA 19107; in Britain or Ireland, contact Gaia's Guide, 9-11 Kensington High St., London W8; in Australia or New Zealand, contact Open Leaves, 71 Cardigan St., Carlton, Victoria 3053, Australia.

The *Spartacus Guide for Gay Men* provides similar information (US$24.95, £12.50). Write c/o Bruno Gmunder, Lützowstr. 105, P.O. Box 30 13 45, D-1000 Berlin 30, West Germany. Also consult the *Gayellow Pages,* printed in English, French, German, and Spanish.

The legal minimum age in France for consensual homosexual activity is 15, but since the age of majority is 18, the liberalized law does not always apply to sexual activity between a minor under 18 and an adult.

Disabled Travelers

The French Tourist Board can supply disabled travelers with free handbooks and access guides (see Useful Organizations above), but these directories can be misleading since they are not compiled by disabled travelers. Accurate information about ramps, the width of doors, the dimensions of elevators, and washroom facilities remains difficult to secure. Ask questions directly of restaurants, hotels, railways, and airlines.

All TGV high-speed trains can accommodate wheelchairs, and guide dogs are transported free. Other trains have a special compartment and an escalator for boarding. It is worth writing to the train station at your destination to alert the conductor to your needs. In Paris, travel by Metro is facilitated by wider seats reserved for the disabled, although many stations have stairs rather than escalators or elevators. The new RER network operates a number of stations with lift access and others with flat/ramped access. For car travel, get the *Guide des transports à l'usage des personnes à mobilité réduite* (available free from many tourist offices), which includes a list of gas stations located on *autoroutes* equipped to serve disabled customers.

If you bring a seeing-eye dog into France, you must produce a vaccination certificate for rabies issued in your home country, or a certificate showing there have been no cases of rabies in your country for over three years.

The American Foundation for the Blind, 15 W. 16th St., New York, NY 10011 (tel. (800) 232-5463, in NY (tel. (212) 620-2147). Recommends travel books and issues ID cards to the blind.

L'Association des Paralysés de France, Délégation de Paris, 156, rue d'Aubervilliers, 19*ème* (tel. 40-38-28-96). Publishes *Où ferons-nous étape?* (70F, postage included), which lists hotels and motels all over France accessible to the disabled.

Le Comité National Français de Liaison pour la Réadaption des Handicapés (CNFLRH), 38, bd. Raspail, 75007 Paris (tel. 45-48-90-13). Offers *Touristes quand même! promenades en France pour voyageurs handicapés,* updated in 1986.

Disability Press, Ltd., Applemarket House, 17 Union St., Kingston-upon-Thames, Surrey KT1 1RP. Publishes the *Disabled Traveler's International Phrasebook* (£1.50, outside the U.K. £2.35), listing useful phrases in 8 languages, including French.

The Guided Tour, 555 Ashbourne Rd., Elkins Park, PA 19117 (tel. (215) 782-1370). Year-round full-time travel program for developmentally- and learning-disabled adults as well as separate trips for those with physical disabilities.

Federation of the Handicapped, 211 W. 14th St., New York, NY 10011 (tel. (212) 242-9050). Leads tours for its members. Also plans an annual trip each summer. Annual membership US$4.

Mobility International, USA (MIUSA), P.O. Box 3551, Eugene, OR 97403 (tel. (503) 343-1284, voice and TDD). MIUSA has contacts in 25 countries, and information on travel programs, workcamps, accommodations, access guides, organized study, cultural tours, and opportunities for disabled people to participate in international education programs. In Canada, contact Carolyn Masleck, Canadian Bureau for International Education, 141 Laurier Ave. W., Ottowa, Ont. K1P 5J3. In the U.K., contact Isobelle Mcgrath, DIVE, Central Bureau for Educational Visits and Exchanges, Seymour Mews House, Seymour Mew, London W1H 9PE.

Travel Information Service, Moss Rehabilitation Hospital, 12th St. and Tabor Rd., Philadelphia, PA 19141 (tel. (215) 329-5715). Distributes information on travel for the physically disabled. Nominal postage and handling fee for mailing information; send US$5 for brochures.

Pauline Hephaistos Survey Projects Group, 39 Bradley Gardens, West Ealing, London W13 8HE, England. Will send you *Access Guides* to Paris, Brittany, Jersey, the Loire Valley, and the Channel Ports, detailing hotels, hostels, and points of interest (£3 each).

Wings on Wheels, c/o Evergreen Travel Service, 19505L 44th Ave. W., Lynnwood, WA 98036 (tel. (800) 435-2288). Provides services for disabled travelers.

Dietary Concerns

While you should have little trouble finding tastefully prepared vegetables in France, they are often cooked with salt, butter, or sugar. Vegetarians of all persuasions will have trouble eating cheaply in restaurants, since *menus à prix fixe* almost always feature meat or fish. Ordering a salad may prove cheaper. *Viande* refers only to red meat; if you don't eat pork, chicken, fish, eggs, or dairy products, you should clearly state this to the server. Although the natural foods movement began in Europe, American-style health food merchandizing has not caught on in France, and you may have to search long for a tofu and tahini fix. Health food stores are called *diététiques* or *maisons de régime;* occasionally health food products are referred to as *produits à santé. Let's Go* tries to list inexpensive vegetarian restaurants; also inquire at local *syndicats.* The following organizations, including one for kosher eaters and one for diabetics, may help.

American Diabetes Association, 1660 Duke St., Alexandria, VA 22314 (tel. (800) 232-3472). Write for a reprint of the article "Your Turn to Fly," which provides travel tips (about 75¢).

The Vegetarian Society of the U.K., Parkdale, Dunham Rd., Altrincham, Cheshire WA 14 4QG (tel. (061) 928-07-93). Publishes *The International Vegetarian Handbook,* listing vegetarian and health-conscious restaurants, guesthouses, societies, and health-food stores in Europe. Useful general information, with a small section on France (strongest on Paris).The book is distributed by Thorsons Publishing Group, Ltd., Wellingborough, Northamptonshire (£2.50).

North American Vegetarian Society, P.O. Box 72, Dolgeville, NY 13329 (tel. (518) 568-7970). Sells *The International Vegetarian Handbook* (US$8.95, postage included).

Sephor-Herman Press, 1265 46th St., Brooklyn, NY 11219 (tel. (718) 972-9010). Sells *The Jewish Travel Guide,* which lists kosher restaurants, synagogues, and other Jewish institutions in over 80 countries.

Travelers with Children

A shoestring budget doesn't have to become a boot-lace for family travel. A **car** is almost indispensable when traveling with children, and is easily cheaper than a fistful of rail passes. As for food, if your kids don't take to the subtleties of *haute cuisine,* don't fight the siren song of *le hot dog* or *le croque monsieur* (a grilled ham-and-cheese sandwich). France also offers great ice cream, and older children may enjoy a *demi-panaché* (shandy) made half-and-half with beer and an otherwise odious carbonated lemonade (while you sip true lemonade, the gorgeous *citron pressé*). Not all restaurants have highchairs, but French servers are generally less put out by children than their North American counterparts. Young diners are especially welcome in informal cafeterias, *café-restaurants* and *brasseries.* The French habit of family roadside picnics is another convenience you'll enjoy.

While Paris is less oriented to children's entertainment than London or Copenhagen, it is blessed with many delights, and traveling with your kids gives you a chance to enjoy them. **The Jardins du Luxembourg** have a *guignol* (Punch-and-Judy show), pony rides, go-carts, a carousel, boats to rent and sail on the ornamental ponds, and swings with attendants who, for a tip, will push the swings while you vanish to a cafe. The gardens also maintain some of the few lawns in Paris that children may play on. *Les Invalides* will fascinate older kids with its full-scale dioramas of Napoleon's battles. The **Jardin des Plantes** and the Paris **Zoo** are also fun, and even the most frequented sights, such as the Eiffel Tower and the *bateaux mouches* (tour boats on the Seine), are made new when you see them with children.

Outside Paris, watch for village *fêtes,* which usually have a few rides. Finally, the medieval walled towns of **Avignon, Villeneuve-les-Avignon,** and **Carcassonne** are a child's fairytale dreams realized in stone.

For bedtime stories before or during your trip, follow the twelve little girls around the sights of Paris in Hugo Bemelmans's *Madeline* picture books. *Crin blanc* and

Le ballon rouge, both by Albert LaMorisse, are two poignant stories that exemplify a peculiarly French sentimentality regarding early childhood; Antoine de St-Exupéry's books, especially *Le petit prince,* are in the same vein. The well-known *Tintin* and *Astérix* series appeal to a wide range of ages, and the hardbound copies are both travel- and child-proof (or almost).

If you plan to camp with very young children, you may want to consult *Backpacking with Children* (US$8.95) and *Sharing Nature with Children* (US$6.95), both published by Wilderness Press, 2440 Bancroft Way, Berkeley, CA 94704 (tel. (415) 843-8080).

Nudists

You'll find that most of the coastline offers at least a few nudist beaches, particularly in the south. France was the second country to establish organized naturism in the '30s and '40s. The cult of the sun, as familial as it is hedonistic, has grown steadily: A 1982 survey showed that 86% of the French favor public nude beaches. For more information consult the following:

Fédération Française de Naturisme, 53, rue de la Chausée-d'Antin, 75009 Paris (tel. 42-80-05-21). Free guide book, *France, terre du naturisme,* available in French and English. They also publish a catalog of addresses of nudist beaches, campsites, and pools, as well as an international naturist catalog (150F).

Harmony Books, Crown Publishers, Inc., 34 Englehard Ave., Arenel, NJ 07001. Publishes the *World Guide to Nude Beaches and Recreations* (US$14.95).

Keeping in Touch

Mail

Between major cities in France and the east coast of the U.S., air mail takes five to ten days and is fairly dependable. Send mail from the largest postal office in the area. Surface (*par eau, par terre*) mail is considerably cheaper, but takes one to three months to arrive. It's adequate for getting rid of books or clothing you no longer need in your travels. (See Customs above for details about sending packages duty-free.) If you send a parcel air mail (*par avion, poste aérienne*), you must complete a green customs form for any package over 1kg (2kg for letter-post rate).

Air-mailing a 25g (about an ounce) letter costs 9.60F to the U.S. (9.60F to Canada). *Aérogrammes* are 4.20F, and post cards (*cartes postales*) 3F when mailed to the U.S. Special delivery is called *avec recommandation,* and express mail *exprès postaux.*

If you have no fixed address in France, you can receive mail through **American Express.** American Express will receive and hold mail for up to 30 days (after which they return it to sender). Most big-city American Express offices will hold mail for you free of charge if you have their traveler's checks, but some require that you be an AmEx cardholder. A free pamphlet, *Directory of Travel Service Offices,* contains the addresses of American Express offices worldwide, and can be obtained from any branch or from American Express International Headquarters, American Express Tower, World Financial Center, New York, NY 10285-3130.

Alternatively, make use of the **Poste Restante** system in any locale with a post office. In major cities the central post office handling Poste Restante is open long hours and on weekends. Almost all post offices function as Postes Restantes: To specify a particular post office, you must know its postal code—*Let's Go* lists postal codes for the central post office in the Practical Information section of every city. To ensure the safe arrival of your letter, address it: LAST NAME (in capitals), first name; Poste Restante; city name, R. P. (*Recette Principale*); Postal code, FRANCE. You will have to show your passport as an identification and pay a few francs for every letter received. You can also forward mail from most post offices to Postes Restantes anywhere else in France.

The post office is also the place to send or receive money orders, and to change *postcheques.* In more than 150 post offices in major towns, you can also exchange foreign currency: Look for the *CHANGE* sticker. If you have a Visa or AmEx card, or a Eurocheque guarantee card issued by your bank, you can withdraw money at one of the 780 post offices indicated by a *CB/VISA ou EC* sticker.

Post offices are often open until 7pm (they stop changing money at 6pm) and on Saturday mornings, when banks are closed. Avoid long lines by purchasing stamps at local *tabacs,* or from the yellow coin-operated vending machines outside major post offices.

Telephones and Telegrams

Almost all pay phones in France's cities accept only **Télécartes** (in outlying districts more phones are still coin-operated). You may purchase the card in two different denominations: 40F for 50 *unités,* and 96F for 120 *unités.* One *unité* buys 0.80F of conversation (anywhere from 6 to 18 min. depending on the rate schedule). The *Télécarte* is available at post offices, railway ticket counters, and some *tabacs.*

The best places to call from are phone booths and post offices. If you phone from a cafe, hotel, or restaurant, you risk paying up to 30% more than the usual tariff.

You can make **intercontinental calls** from any pay phone or from a post office. The clerk will assign you to a phone from which you can usually dial direct, and will collect your money when you complete your call. In many towns, you can dial directly overseas from a corner phone booth.

A brief directory:

Operator (*Téléphoniste*): Tel. 10.

International Operator: Tel. 19-33-11.

Directory information (*Renseignements téléphoniques*): Tel. 12.

Direct long-distance calls within France: Tel. 16 + the number.

Direct international calls: Tel. 19 + country code (Australia 61; Canada and the U.S. 1; Ireland 353; and U.K. 44) + the number.

A brief glossary: To dial is *composer;* a collect call is made *en PCV* (pay-say-vay); a person-to-person call, *avec préavis.*

Rates are reduced Monday through Friday 9:30pm-8am and Saturday 2pm-8am for calls to the Common Market and Switzerland; 10pm-10am for Canada and the U.S.; 8pm-8am for Israel; and all day Sunday and bank holidays. Keep in mind any time differences (in general 6 hr. ahead of Eastern Standard Time).

Telegrams can be sent from any post office and can sometimes be called in if you have a local address. International telegrams cost 5F per word (6F to Australia). The address counts as text.

If your itinerary is unplanned and you don't want to be constrained by mailstops or the expense of phone calls, you might also consider **Overseas Access,** a telephone checkpoint service offered by EurAide. EurAide maintains a toll-free number in the U.S. so that family and friends can leave messages which are then relayed to their Munich office for you. As a member, you can then call the Munich office for news from home (US$49 for the first month, US$35 each additional month). In the U.S., contact EurAide, Inc., P.O. Box 2375, Naperville, IL 60565 (tel (312) 983-8880 or (312) 420-2343). In Germany, contact Bahnhofplatz 2, 8000 München 2 (tel. (089) 59-38-89).

Alternatives to Tourism

Work

Finding work in France is extremely difficult. As a result of high unemployment, the French government has become wary of hiring foreigners; before you can obtain a work permit through normal channels, your employer must convince the Ministry of Labor that there is no native capable of filling your position. Even when a foreigner is considered, Common Market country members have priority.

With the exception of *au pair* jobs, it is illegal for foreign students to hold full-time jobs during the school year. Students registered at French universities may get work permits for the summer with a valid visa, a student card from a French university, and proof of a job. If you are not a student in a French university, you can check the fact sheet *Employment in France,* put out by **Cultural Services of the French Embassy,** 972 Fifth Ave., New York, NY 10021 (tel. (212) 439-1400), which provides basic information about work in France and also lists the government-approved organizations through which foreign students must secure their jobs. **CIEE** (see Useful Organizations above), which operates a reciprocal work program with France, is the only U.S. organization so approved. If you are a permanent degree-seeking college or university student, a resident U.S. citizen, and have a good working knowledge of French (at least 2 years of college French), CIEE will issue you a three-month work permit valid at any time of the year for US$82. Under this system, you do not need a job prior to obtaining a work permit. Once you have the permit, you are virtually on your own, since CIEE's Work Abroad Program does not place people. It does, however, provide information on accommodations and job-hunting, as well as assistance from its office in Paris. Jobs available are mostly short-term, unskilled work in hotels, shops, restaurants, farms, and factories. Wages should cover food, lodging, and basic living expenses. Complete information and application are enclosed in the *Student Travel Catalog* (US$1 for postage).

CIEE's *Work, Study, Travel Abroad: The Whole World Handbook* (US$8.95, book rate postage US$1, 1st-class postage US$2.50), available in bookstores or from any CIEE office, is a comprehensive guide to overseas opportunities, containing a work abroad section and country-by-country listings. The handbook also includes a section on long-term employment. For more detail, consult *Emplois d'Eté en France* (US$11, postage US$1), also available from CIEE. *The 1989 Directory of Overseas Summer Jobs* (US$9.95, postage US$2), available from Writer's Digest Books, 1507 Dana Ave., Cincinnati, OH 45207 (tel. (800) 543-4644, in OH (800) 551-0884), lists 50,000 openings worldwide, volunteer and paid.

A good place to start your job search is the **American Chamber of Commerce,** 21, av. Georges V, 75008 Paris (tel. 47-23-80-26 or 47-23-70-28). A *Membership Directory of the French-American Chamber of Commerce* is available from its office at 509 Madison Ave., #1900, New York, NY 10022 (tel. (212) 371-4466). The **Agence Nationale Pour l'Emploi,** 53, av. du Général Leclerc, 92136 Issy-Les-Moulineaux (tel. 46-45-21-26), can give you specific information on job opportunities. When writing to a French employer, send two International Reply Coupons to guarantee a rapid reply by airmail.

Once in France, check help-wanted columns in newspapers, especially *Le Monde, Le Figaro,* and the English-language *International Herald Tribune.* In Paris, check the posted job listings at the Alliance Française, 101, bd. Raspail, 75270 Paris, and at the American Cathedral, 23, av. Georges V, 75008 Paris (tel. 47-20-17-92).

A number of programs offer practical experience to people with technical and business skills. The **Association for International Practical Training (AIPT)** is an umbrella organization for the **IAESTE** program (International Association for the Exchange of Students for Technical Experience), an on-the-job training program for agriculture, math, engineering, computer science, and natural/physical science students who have completed two years at an accredited four-year institution. There is a non-refundable US$75 fee. Apply to the IAESTE Program, c/o AIPT, Park View Bldg., #320, 10480 Little Patuxent Parkway, Columbia, MD 21044 (tel. (301) 997-2200).

Summer positions as tour group leaders are available with **American Youth Hostels (AYH),** P.O. Box 37613, Washington, DC 20013-7613 (tel. (202) 783-6161). You must be at least 21 and are required to take a week-long leadership course (US$250, room and board included). You must also lead a group in the U.S. before taking one to Europe. The **Experiment in International Living (EIL),** Kipling Rd.,

Brattleboro, VT 05301 (tel. (802) 257-7751), requires leadership ability and extensive overseas experience (minimum age 24). Applications are due by late November.

Long-term employment is difficult to secure unless you have skills in high-demand areas (e.g., medicine, computer programming, teaching). One useful booklet, *Employment Abroad: Facts and Fallacies,* covers the major considerations involved in seeking overseas employment and includes many sources of further information. It's available free from Publications Fulfillment, Chamber of Commerce of the United States, 1615 H St. NW, Washington, DC 20062 (tel. (301) 468-5128).

Volunteering

Volunteering is a great way to meet locals, and you may even get room and board in exchange for your work. *Volunteer! The Comprehensive Guide to Voluntary Service in the U.S. and Abroad* is co-published by CIEE (see Useful Organizations above) and the Commission on Voluntary Service and Action. It offers advice on choosing a voluntary service program and lists over 170 organizations in fields ranging from health care and social work to construction. Write to CIEE (US$4.95, book-rate postage US$1, 1st-class postage US$2.50).

CIEE also offers placement in international **workcamps** in the U.S. and Europe each summer. Volunteers from throughout the world live and work together on a two- to four-week project that benefits a local community. A working knowledge of French is required for projects in France, and participants must be at least 18 years old. The camp provides room and board; the application fee is US$100. Write to CIEE International Voluntary Projects, 356 W. 34th St., New York, NY 10001.

Many non-government organizations hire U.S. citizens for work abroad, including the YMCA, Red Cross, CARE, and the United Nations. Refer to *U.S. Non-Profit Organizations in Development Assistance Abroad,* available from Unipub Co., 4611-F Assembly Dr., Lanham, MD 20706 (tel. (800) 274-4888), US$24.50, postage US$2.50). For **YMCA** positions, write to Overseas Personnel Programs, YMCA of the USA, 101 N. Wacker Dr., Chicago, IL 60606 (tel. (800) USA-YMCA, that's (800) 872-9622, (312) 977-0031 for general information).

Volunteers for Peace, a workcamp organization, publishes an annual *Directory* to workcamps in 36 countries, primarily in Europe (US$7, postage included). They also publish a free newsletter. Write to VFP, 43 Tiffany Rd., Belmont, VT 05730 (tel. (800) 259-2759). Placement is quick: Volunteer's reservations are generally confirmed within a week. **Service Civil International** runs workcamps throughout France that aim to advance international peace. Contact them at 129, rue du Faubourg Poissonière, F-75009 Paris (tel. 48-74-60-15). In the U.S., contact S.C.I. c/o Innisfree, Rte. 2, Box 506, Crozet, VA 22932. Apply well in advance. For work in the great outdoors, try a *vacance en chantier,* a workcamp for environmentalists and historic preservationists. Write to **Etudes et Chantiers,** 18, rue de Châtillon, 14ème (tel. 43-45-99-60), for more information about their year-round programs. You might also try **Club du Vieux Manoir,** 10, rue de la Cossonnerie, 75001 Paris (tel. 45-08-80-40), which works to restore churches, castles, fortresses, and other historical monuments throughout France. The club offers summer- and year-long programs. Anyone over age 13 or 15 may apply, depending on the project (application fee US$8). **Compagnons Bâtisseurs,** 5, rue des Immeubles Industriels, 75011 Paris (tel. 43-73-70-63), an international volunteers' association, helps to renovate and convert local buildings into facilities for the mentally, economically, and physically underprivileged. Work includes heavy physical labor, but extensive experience is not necessary. Terms run for two to three weeks, June to October. Volunteers prepare their own food (cooking facilities provided) and sleep in tent or barrack accommodations (also provided), but they must bring their own sleeping bag, make their own travel arrangements, pay a registration fee of 500F, and apply two months in advance.

If working on an archeological dig interests you, the **Archaeological Institute of America** publishes a *Fieldwork Opportunities Bulletin* that lists fieldwork projects (US$8). Contact the AIA at 675 Commonwealth Ave., Boston, MA 02215 (tel. (617) 353-9361). Positions in France as **camp counselors** are also sometimes available: Contact the **Service Pédagogique** of the French Embassy, 972 Fifth Ave., New York, NY 10021 (tel. (212) 439-1400 between 2-5pm EDT).

Au Pair Positions

Lastly, there is the old standby—*au pair* work. Positions are reserved primarily for single women ages 18 to 30 with a minimal knowledge of French (though some men are employed). The *au pair* cares for the children in her or his French family and does light housework five or six hours each day (1 day off per week), while taking courses at a school for foreign students or a French university. *Au pair* positions usually last six to 18 months (in summer the contract can be as short as 3 months). You'll receive room, board, and a small monthly stipend (around 1400F). Be sure to acquire a visa *long séjour* before arriving in France.

The **Cultural Services of the French Embassy** (see Useful Organizations above) offers a detailed information sheet on *au pair* jobs. Organizations offering placement include:

L'Accueil Familial des Jeunes Etrangers, 23, rue du Cherche-Midi, 75006 Paris (tel. 42-22-50-34).

L'A.R.C.H.E, 7, rue Bargue, 75015 Paris (tel. 42-73-34-39).

Study

Study in France allows you to participate in an educational system radically different from your own—your experiences with it can tell you much about French culture and values, and a lot about your own culture as well. French education prepares students for a consecutive series of standard examinations that must be passed in order to proceed from one level of instruction to the next.

A good place to begin investigating study abroad programs is *Work, Study, Travel Abroad: The Whole World Handbook* (see the CIEE listing in Useful Organizations above). *Basic Facts on Foreign Study,* put out by the **Institute of International Education (IIE)** and **CIEE,** is a free brochure that covers the nitty-gritty—from visas to tax returns. IIE's *Vacation Study Abroad* (US$20) lists summer programs, and *Academic Year Abroad* (US$20) provides a thorough guide to both undergraduate and graduate study in Europe run by U.S. colleges and universities; it includes information on scholarships and work opportunities. **UNESCO** publishes *Study Abroad* (US$14.50), available from Unipub (see Volunteering above for address). In addition, IIE's New York office will answer written or telephone inquiries, and maintains a reference library that is open by appointment. Contact them at 809 United Nations Plaza, New York, NY 10017 (tel. (212) 883-8200). For free pamphlets on various fields of study in France and much useful advice, contact the **Cultural Services of the French Embassy** (see Useful Organizations above). The **Franco-American Committee for Educational Travel and Study (FACETS),** 989 Sixth Ave. S., New York, NY 10018 (tel. (212) 475-4343), also provides information on language-study opportunities in France. The **American Center for Students and Artists** is a student advisory service that provides information on both housing and education. Contact the Student Advisory Service, American Cathedral, 23, av. Georges V, 75008 Paris. (Closed in July and Aug.)

Perhaps the most intellectually challenging and culturally rewarding way to study in France is to enroll as a regular student in a French university. Tuition is low (at least by U.S. standards). For details on application procedures, contact the cultural services office at the nearest French consulate or embassy. Apply between February and May of the year in which you wish to attend.

As a student registered in a French university, you will be given a student card (*carte d'étudiant*) by your school upon presentation of your residency permit (see Visas above) and a receipt for your university fees. In addition to the student benefits to which the *carte d'étudiant* entitles you, many benefits are administered by the **Centres Régionaux des Oeuvres Universitaires et Scolaires (CROUS).** Founded in 1955 to improve the living and working conditions of its members, this division of the Oeuvres Universitaires welcomes foreign students. A student card entitles you to subsidized rates at restaurants, accommodations, and various social and cultural services. In Paris, the regional center is at 39, av. Georges-Bernanos, 75231 (tel. 43-29-12-43, poste 345). The CROUS welcome center for foreign students is also at this address. Pick up the helpful guidebook *Je vais en France* (30F) from any French embassy or consulate. The Paris office of CROUS also publishes an annual brochure, *Infos-Etudiants,* listing valuable addresses and information on practically every aspect of student life.

Another way to study in France is to enroll in a year-abroad program run by an American school. If you want to meet French students and experience French culture, however, be wary of programs that cater mainly to Americans; you may find them little different from studying in the U.S.

If your main object is to learn the language, you should investigate an institute for foreigners run by a French university or special language courses offered by various institutions. The **Alliance Française,** Ecole Internationale de Langue et de Civilisation Française, 101, bd. Raspail, 75270 Paris Cédex 06 (tel. 45-44-38-28; Mo. Notre-Dame-des Champs or Mo. Rennes), is the best-knownand least intimidating language school in Paris (150F to enroll and 900-1800F for lessons). It is open year-round, gives classes at all levels, and offers 12 18- to 20-day sessions during the year and 12 to 20 week-long sessions. Most classes progress very slowly, however, since about 15 different nationalities are represented in any given class of 20 students.

The **Institut Catholique de Paris,** 21, rue d'Assas, 75270 Paris Cédex 06 (tel. 42-22-41-80; Mo. St-Placide), offers classes at all levels, though their schedule is less flexible than the Alliance's: Students must register for 15 weeks during the school year. There is also a course given in July. The **Office de Tourisme de Paris** can also give you a list of member language schools.

The **Sorbonne** has been giving its French civilization course since 1919. As well as an academic year course (which can be taken by the semester), the Sorbonne

INSTITUTE FOR AMERICAN UNIVERSITIES

(Chartered by the Regents of the University of the State of New York)

STUDY IN SOUTHERN FRANCE

Semester & Year Programs:

AIX-EN-PROVENCE
French at all levels; European studies:
government, history, literature, art, etc.
AVIGNON
French Language & Civilization
(all in French)
TOULON
Management, economics, law, etc.
(all in French)
ACCELERATED FRENCH - AVIGNON
7-week courses, 6 credit hrs.

Summer Programs:

FRENCH LANGUAGE & LITERATURE
in Avignon
ART IN PROVENCE
in Avignon and Aix
*EUROPEAN STUDIES & FRENCH
LANGUAGE*
in Aix

For details write:
27, place de l'Université
13625 Aix-en-Provence
France

offers four-, six-, and eight-week programs in summer, with both civilization and
language classes at various levels and a special course in commercial French during
the academic year. Write Cours de Civilisation Française, 47, rue des Ecoles, 75005
Paris (tel. 40-46-22-11). It is also possible to take the Cours de Civilisation through
the American Institute for Foreign Study, which will arrange accommodations and
meals for students. Contact **AIFS** at 102 Greenwich Ave., Greenwich, CT 06830
(tel. (203) 863-6096).

Getting There

From North America

It's difficult to generalize about flights to Europe or to offer exact fares. Prices
and market conditions can fluctuate significantly from one week to the next. The
best advice we can offer is to have patience and begin looking for a flight as soon
as possible.

Flexibility is the best strategy. Prices for direct, regularly scheduled flights are
ordinarily beyond the resources of any budget traveler. Consider leaving from a
travel hub; flights from certain cities—e.g., New York, Chicago, Los Angeles, San
Francisco, Seattle, Vancouver, Toronto, and Montreal—are generally cheaper than
flights from smaller cities. The savings on international flights from these cities may
more than pay for the connecting flight or the gasoline you'll spend getting to the
travel hub.

It pays to be flexible in terms of destination as well. Fares to cities only 100km
apart may differ by that many dollars. London and Brussels have remained consistently cheap travel targets. Once in Europe, you should be able to arrange inexpensive ground transportation to your ultimate destination. Cities such as Paris, Amsterdam, and especially London are popular on intra-European budget flights. The
short flight from London to Paris usually costs about US$100 (although train, ferry,
or bus are usually much cheaper).

Sometimes cheaper return flights are available in Europe, so you may want to be daring and wait until you're over there to buy your ticket home. (See Getting Back below.) Be warned, however, that this plan could backfire and leave you temporarily stranded. European metropolises with consistently inexpensive transatlantic fares include London, Paris, Amsterdam, and Athens. If at all possible, consider traveling in the off-season; most major airlines maintain a fare structure that reaches its peak between mid-June and early September.

Finally, shop around. Have a knowledgeable travel agent guide you through the morass of travel options. It's best to inquire at several places. In addition, check the Sunday travel sections of major newspapers, perhaps from several travel centers near you, for bargain fares. Student travel organizations such as CIEE in the U.S. or Travel CUTS in Canada are excellent sources of information; they specialize in budget travel and offer special deals which regular travel agents are unaware of.

A **charter** flight is the most consistently economical option. You can book charters up until the last minute, but most summer flights fill up several months in advance. Charter flights allow you to stay abroad up to one or two years, and often allow you to "mix-and-match" arrivals and departures from different cities. Once you have made your plans, however, the flexibility stops. You must choose your return dates when you book your flight, and if you cancel your ticket within 14 or 21 days of your departure, you will lose some or all of your money. Few travel insurance policies will cover your cancellation unless it's earned by serious unforeseen illness, death, or natural disaster.

Although charter flights are less expensive, they can also be less reliable. Charter companies reserve the right to cancel flights up to 48 hours before departure; they will do their best to find you another flight, but your delay could be days, not just hours. To avoid eleventh-hour problems, pick up your ticket in advance of the departure date.

CIEE (see Useful Organizations above) was among the first on the charter scene and offers flights to destinations worldwide. Their subsidiary, **Council Charters,** offers extremely popular flights, so reserve early. Call (800) 223-7402 ((212) 661-1450 in NY), or write them at the address listed above. Other charter companies include **Travac** (tel. (800) TRAV-800, that's (800) 872-8800, in NY (212) 563-3303); **Uni-Travel** (tel. (800) 325-2222, in MO (314) 727-8888); **DER Tours** (tel. (800) 421-4343, in CA (800) 252-0606); and **Wardair** (tel. (800) 237-0314). In Canada, try **Travel CUTS** (see Useful Organizations above); **European Tourist Information** (tel. (800) 621-1974) specializes in flights from the West Coast to Europe; charter flights to Paris are US$450-550 round-trip.

If you decide to make your transatlantic crossing with a commercial airline, you'll be purchasing greater flexibility, reliability, and comfort. The major airlines offer two options for the budget traveler: standby flights and APEX fares. The advantage of a **standby** fare is flexibility; you can come and go as you please. The disadvantage is that flying standby during peak season can be uncertain. Call individual carriers for the availability and price of standby fares. Tickets are sold in advance or at the airport on the day of departure, but the number of seats available is not known until the few moment before departure. Most travel agents can issue standby tickets, but it's usually necessary to do your own research first, since many travel agents either don't know or are reluctant to tell you about standby options. Major international carriers, however, restrict the number of cities to which one can fly standby; Paris is an extremely rare standby destination, but London is popular, and cheap train or bus connections to France make the flight economical. In 1988, the cheapest standby fare to London on Pan Am, TWA, and British Airways was US$279. TWA offers a discount card (US$50 per year) to full-time students ages 16-26; it entitles them to an additional 10% discount on all fares.

Advanced Purchase Excursion Fares (APEX) provide you with confirmed reservations and allow you to arrive and depart from different cities. Reservations must be made 21 days in advance with 7- to 14-day minimum and 60- to 180-day maximum stay limitations. To change an APEX reservation, you must pay a US$50-100 penalty, and to change a return flight you must pay a US$100 penalty or upgrade

your ticket, which will cost you well over US$100. For summer travel, book APEX fares early—by June you may have difficulty getting the departure date you want.

A few airlines undercut the major carriers by offering bargain fares on regularly scheduled flights. In 1988 **Virgin Atlantic** (tel. (800) 862-8621) flew from Newark to London for US$289 one-way. Remember that competition for seats on these smaller carriers during peak season is fierce, so book early.

In recent years last-minute discount clubs have sprung up, making available unsold seats on scheduled flights, cruises, and tours. They offer their members savings on European travel, including charter flights and tour packages. (Annual dues US$30-50.) Check with some of the following companies: **Unitravel Corp.** (tel. (800) 325-2222); **Access International,** 250 W. 57th St., #511, New York, NY 10107 (tel. (212) 333-7280); **Last Minute Travel Club,** 132 Brookline Ave., Boston, MA 02215 (tel. (800) 527-8646, in Boston 267-9800); **Worldwide Discount Travel Club,** 1674 Meridian Ave., Miami Beach, FL 33139 (tel. (305) 534-2082); **Discount Travel International,** Ives Bldg., #205, Narberth, PA 19072 (tel. (800) 824-4000, in PA (215) 668-2182); and **Stand-Buys Ltd.,** 311 W. Superior, 4th floor, Chicago, IL 60610 (tel. (800) 255-0200, in Chicago (312) 943-5737). When buying a charter ticket, you should be sure to ask about any restrictions that might affect your travel plans.

Enterprising travelers who can travel light might consider flying to Europe as a **courier.** A company hiring you as a courier will use your checked-luggage space for freight; you're left with the carry-on allowance. You must make one to three-month advance reservations and also turn your luggage receipts over to a company representative upon arrival. In return, the company pays the lion's share of your fare. You can fly from New York to Paris and back as a courier for **NOW Voyager** (tel. (212) 431-1616). NOW Voyager also arranges flights from New York to London, Milan, Madrid, and Amsterdam; you can easily get to France from any of these cities. Their one-year membership fee is US$45. Check the phone book for other courier companies who might be willing to "hire" you.

From Within Europe

By Air

If charters to your ultimate destination are booked and commercial flights expensive, you can always fly to London and connect with an intra-European flight to places more remote. Some travel agents can give you specific information on intra-European flights in your home country. If your home currency is strong, though, you'll save more money by taking a chance and making travel arrangements once you arrive overseas. Do in London as you did at home: Check newspapers, travel agents, and student travel organizations for bargain charter flights. The **Airline Advisory Board,** Morley House, Regent St., London (tel. 636-50-00) puts travelers in touch with the cheapest carriers for free. Contact **STA Travel,** 74 Old Brompton Rd., London SW7 3LQ, for information on inexpensive flights throughout Europe. **Magic Bus** offers cheap charter flights within Europe (see By Bus below). A number of **bucket shops** also operate in London; some regular travel agencies allow travelers to buy unsold tickets on commercial flights at unofficially discounted prices. Bucket shops can save you more than 50%—ask around in London.

You may also want to consider special student fares offered within Europe by airlines such as **Olympic Airways**—see a student travel organization such as CIEE about this option. Write CIEE in France at 51, rue Dauphine, 6*ème,* 75006 Paris. Finally, you may wish to check on special deals offered by national airlines for free or reduced-fare travel within the country you're heading for if you fly with them across the Atlantic. For continental travel, some of the lowest fares can be found on Eastern European airlines.

By Train

You can get to France from Britain or anywhere on the continent by train. **Eurotrain,** a group of nine student organizations in Europe, offers 15-30% reductions on point-to-point rail tickets. Eurotrain tickets are valid for two months (6 in Turkey and Morocco). Those under 26 are eligible for these tickets, available at local travel offices in Britain or at Eurotrain, 52 Grosvenor Gardens, London SW1W OAG (tel. (01) 730-81-11). In the U.S., CIEE offices can provide more information (see Useful Organizations above).

Transalpino offers reduced second-class rail fares in Europe, including Greece and Turkey, to anyone under 26. Tickets are valid for two months. Transalpino offices are distributed throughout Europe: The head office is at 71-75 Buckingham Palace Rd., London SW1W 0QL (tel. (01) 834-96-56); in Paris contact them at 14, rue Lafayette, 75009 (tel. 48-24-29-29). **Travel CUTS** (see Useful Organizations above) sells vouchers for both Transalpino and Eurotrain passes.

BIJ tickets remain one of the cheapest options for travelers under 26. They cut up to 50% off regular second-class rail fares on international routes and are valid on the vast majority of trains. They are sold by both Transalpino and Eurotrain. When you buy a BIJ ticket, you specify both your destination and route, and have the option of stopping anywhere along that route for up to two months. The fare between London and Paris is US$32 one-way (ferry crossing included), US$64 round-trip.

By Bus

Magic Bus, after several closings and openings in the last few years, has re-emerged to offer cheap, direct bus service between major cities in Europe. Magic Bus offices are located at Freeway Voyages, 16, rue de Rivoli, 75004 Paris (tel. 42-71-23-23 or 42-71-23-33); 67-68 New Bond St., London; Rokin 38, Amsterdam (tel. (02) 026-44-34). Information on Magic Bus is available from cooperating offices in many other cities. **Miracle Bus** and **Grey-Green Coaches** are two other reasonable coach services running between major cities. For information on Miracle Bus routes, contact their office at 408 Strand, London WC2 (tel. (01) 379-60-55). Contact Grey-Green Coaches at 53 Stamford Hill, London N16 5DT (tel. (01) 800-80-

EUROPE BY YOURSELF

WITH THE YOUTH TRAVEL SPECIALIST

FROM PARIS TO

	✈	🚆
AMSTERDAM	$ 55	35
ATHENS	$ 143	123
BERLIN	$ 94	81
MADRID	$ 150	70
LONDON	$ 48	46
MILAN	$ 94	53
MUNICH	$ 78	65
ROME	$ 112	73
VENICE	$ 130	64

FROM LONDON TO

	✈	🚆
ATHENS	$ 122	178
ROME	$ 102	114
VENICE	$ 92	102

FROM ROME TO

	✈	🚆
AMSTERDAM	$ 127	99
ATHENS	$ 139	79
BERLIN	$ 155	100

ACCOMMODATION

	🛏
PARIS	$ 14
AMSTERDAM	$ 19
ATHENS	$ 11
FLORENCE	$ 16
LONDON	$ 15
MUNICH	$ 19
ROME	$ 19
VENICE	$ 19

 YOUTH & STUDENT TRAVEL CENTER

PARIS V°   20, Rue des Carmes ☎ 43250076
Metro Maubert Mutualité

LONDON   W1P 1HH • 33, Windmill street ☎ 5804554 • 6365915-6
Metro Tottenham Court Rd

ROME   16, Via Genova ☎ 46791 • 297, Corso Vittorio Emanuele ☎ 6872672-3-4

FLORENCE   11-R, Via dei Ginori ☎ 292150

MILAN   2, Via S. Antonio ☎ 72001121

NAPLES   35, Via A. De Gasperi ☎ 5520074

VENICE   3252, Dorso Duro Cà Foscari ☎ 5205660

10) or Rokin 10, Amsterdam. **Euroways Eurolines Ltd.,** 52 Grosvenor Gardens, London SW1W 0AU (tel. (01) 730-82-35), offers express service from London to Paris as well as other points throughout Europe.

By Ferry

Many ferries link France with England and Ireland. **Sealink** and **Townsend Thoresen** offer extensive service across the English Channel. Sealink ferries leave from Victoria Station, London, and are the most frequent (1½-1¾-hr. crossings cost US$46 to Calais and US$53 to Dieppe). Summer crossings are usually very crowded by day. Alternate routes between England and France (4-8 hr.) include Weymouth/Portsmouth or Southampton to Cherbourg; Newhaven to Dieppe; and Portsmouth to Le Havre (about US$30 each). **Brittany Ferries** runs between Plymouth/Cork and Roscoff, and Portsmouth and St-Malo/Caen. There are other convenient Channel crossings from Dover to Oostende or Zeebrugge in Belgium (3¾-4¼ hr.). **Irish Continental Lines** offers ferry service to Cherbourg or Le Havre from Rosslare in Ireland, and to Le Havre from Cork. Irish Continental is rather expensive, but covered by Eurail and Interail passes.

Traveling by hovercraft is quicker (35 min.), but you must book in advance. **Hoverspeed** hovercrafts depart for Calais or Boulogne from Dover (US$46). Service is suspended in rough weather, so you may find yourself waiting for a ferry instead. Hoverspeed also offers combination rail/bus and hovercraft service to and from London, Paris, Brussels, Amsterdam, and points in southwestern France. This service operates from late March to October only; students under 26 travel at youth rates. **Transalpino** offers reduced rates on hovercraft services between Dover and Boulogne. For information, try **Travelloyd,** 8 Berkeley Sq., London W1, or the British Travel Centre, 4-12 Lower Regent St., London SW1. Only agents who hold a Continental Rail Licence may book Dover-Oostende jetfoil service.

For detailed information on ferry and hovercraft service, look in the Practical Information sections of the French ports in question.

Getting Back

British Airways and **Air France** offer youth and student fares from Paris to most large cities in Europe. For charter flights home, contact **Student Travel Association (STA)** (see By Air above); **Euro budget** and **APEX** return tickets from Paris may now be purchased in the U.S. at the time you make your reservation. They are completely non-refundable.

Standby from Paris to New York is 1600F one way. You make a 300F deposit and go to the airport on the day of your flight. Standby passengers board in the order in which their deposits were received; if you're among the lucky, you pay the remaining 1300F on the plane.

Try small, national airlines for cheap flights. **Accueil de Jeunes en France (AJF)** (see Student Accomodations below) flies to London and New York. **Paris International** offices are at 43, bd. Haussmann, 9ème (tel. 47-42-15-80; Mo. Chaussée-d'Antin); 22, rue Sommerand, 5ème (tel. 43-29-64-60; Mo. Maubert-Mutualité); and 49, bd. Montparnasse, 6ème (tel. 45-48-96-35; Mo. Montparnasse). Several charter airlines fly to a wide range of destinations, including Africa and Asia. **Council Charter,** the charter service of CIEE, is located at 31, rue St-Augustin, 75002 Paris, 2ème (tel. 42-66-34-73; Mo. Opéra). This service offers charters to everywhere and an English-speaking staff. **Travel CUTS,** 295-A Regent St., W1R 7YA London (tel. (01) 637-3161), may also be helpful.

Getting Around

By Air

Three main airlines serve major French cities and resorts: **Air France, Air Inter,** and **U.T.A.** (Union des Transports Aériens). Air Inter and U.T.A. offer a wide range of discounts. Generally speaking, though, domestic air travel in Europe is hardly ever an inexpensive option.

By Train

Most European trains are fast, punctual, and convenient. France has a vast rail network, and its national rail company, the **Société Nationale de Chemins de Fer (SNCF),** runs a very tight ship. (See Useful Organizations above for SNCF address.) Trains go almost everywhere, even to rural areas. Off the main lines between cities and large towns, however, service is both less frequent and less convenient: Be prepared for long waits and obscure timetables. Buses fill in shorter gaps in the system, and recently a few unprofitable SNCF train routes have been replaced with SNCF buses, on which rail passes are valid.

Overnight trains will save you money on accommodations, but are a prime target for thieves. You might spend a few extra dollars for a berth in a *couchette* (bunkbed) car. Bring your own food and drink—it's expensive in the restaurant cars. If you'll be traveling during a peak ("red") period and don't want to risk standing for hours, you should reserve a seat in advance. Train discounts apply during the off-peak "blue" and "white" periods.

Every major railroad station in France carries **schedules,** and you can purchase the complete SNCF timetable at newsstands in the stations. SNCF representatives in the U.S. will provide material on France Railpasses and Eurailpass, as well as a booklet of French and European fares. Thomas Cook publishes the *European Timetable,* available from Forsyth Travel Library (see Useful Organizations above). Every major train station provides train information at computer tellers, via various representatives at the station, or, most commonly, on poster timetables.

If you purchase your ticket in France, always remember to validate it (*compostez votre billet*) in the orange ticket punch at the entrance to the platforms. If the ticket is purchased in the U.S. or Canada, these requirements are waived. However, Eurailpass, Eurail Youthpass, or France Vacances holders *must* validate their passes before boarding their first train—otherwise, they may be fined over and above the price of a regular ticket. Any railroad ticket counter (not a regular ticket window) can validate your pass. If you break your journey, you must validate your ticket again after the stopover. Always keep your ticket with you, as you may have to present it during your trip and when you leave the train at your final destination.

Reservations are recommended for longer trips on all international trains, though you can usually find a seat on shorter journeys. To travel between Paris and the southeast of France, take a TGV (*train à grande vitesse*) train, which always requires a reservation fee even if you have a railpass, but will save you hours.

With a **France Railpass** (formerly the France Vacances Special pass), travelers can travel for four days within a 15-day period (US$110 1st class, US$85 2nd class); nine days within a 30-day period (US$190 1st class, US$140 2nd class); or 16 days within a 30-day period (US$250 1st class, US$180 2nd class); the days of use need not be consecutive. The pass includes a *métropass* for the Paris Métro, covering the city's buses, subways, and RER trains for one day with the four-day pass, two days with the nine- and 16-day pass. You also get free transfer from Orly or Roissy Airports to Paris and back, and you are exempted from the surcharge on TGV trains. Other bonuses include a discount on car rentals at over 200 rail stations. (Bought alone, the *métropass* costs US$11 for 2 days.) You can buy the railpasses in North America at offices of the French National Railroad or from travel agents.

The **Carte Vermeille** entitles travelers over 60 to 50% off first- or second-class tickets for trips in the "blue" period. It can be obtained at the larger rail stations (valid for 1 yr., 100F). SNCF offers the **Carte Jeune** to anyone under 26. For 150F, you get a card valid all over France from June 1 to September 30, good for reductions of up to 50% on all "blue" period train routes except those in Paris and its suburbs. The card can also give you a 50% discount on one round-trip ferry ride and bargains at campgrounds, hotels, restaurants, theaters, museums, and discos. The card is available at most youth hostels and *syndicats* in all major cities. Bring a passport-type photo and ID. The **Carré Jeune,** like the Carte Jeune, can get the bearer discounts of up to 50% on "blue" period trips. Unlike the Carte Jeune, it is valid only for four train rides, so make sure the combined savings are more than the Carré Jeune itself. It is valid between October 1 and May 31. SNCF also offers family discounts of up to 50% during "blue" periods, but you must provide proof of marriage and bring ID photos.

Those under 26 may also purchase **BIJ tickets,** which cut up to 50% off regular second-class rail fares on international runs (see From Within Europe By Train above).

If you wish to travel a great deal during your trip, consider purchasing a railpass. The **Eurailpass** is valid for unlimited rail travel in all Western European countries, including the Republic of Ireland, but not Great Britain or Northern Ireland. You can travel first class for periods of 15 days (US$298), one month (US$470), two months (US$650), or three months (US$798). If you're under age 26, you can buy the **Eurail Youthpass,** good for one month of second-class travel (US$320), or two months (US$420). You must buy your Eurailpass or Eurail Youthpass in North America; you may purchase them from a travel agent, CIEE, the Educational Travel Center, or Let's Go Travel Services. Travel CUTS includes a free copy of *Let's Go: Europe* with every Eurailpass they sell. With the **Eurail Saverpass,** three or more people may travel together for 15 consecutive days for US$210 per person. From October to March, two people traveling together may take advantage of this Saverpass.

The **InterRail** pass is an alternative for travelers under 26 who plan to travel in countries not covered by the Eurailpass. The pass allows for one month of unlimited second-class travel in all countries covered by Eurail, plus Great Britain, Morocco, Yugoslavia, Romania, and Hungary. You may purchase the pass only if you can prove you have been a European resident for six months. The pass gives you only a 50% reduction in the country where you buy it, so you should try to purchase it outside France; major rail stations throughout Europe sell the pass (US$240).

Transalpino has no representative in the U.S., so you'll have to purchase tickets from them once you're in Europe. (See From Within Europe By Train above.) You may also purchase the tickets at Eurotrain offices abroad. In Paris, these are located at 3, bd. des Capucines, 75002 (tel. 42-66-00-90), and at the Student Travel Center (STC), 20, rue des Carmes, 75005 (tel. 43-25-00-76). Cannes, Lyon, Nice, Marseille, Lille, and St-Etienne also have Eurotrain offices; check at STC's Travel Services Desk or at any Eurotrain office in Europe for addresses and information.

By Bus

In France, buses usually serve tour groups or fill in gaps in train service. When buses and trains do cover the same routes, the bus is usually less expensive and slower. For routes and fares, check at the local Syndicat d'Initiative or *gare routière* (bus station—usually next to the railway station).

Europabus, run by European Railways, serves major European cities and offers a wide variety of tour packages. For information, contact Europabus, c/o German Rail, 747 Third Ave., 33rd floor, New York, NY 10017 (tel. (800) 223-6063; in NY (212) 308-6447). In France, call the Europabus office at 7, rue Pablo Neruda, 92530 Levallois-Perret (tel. (1) 47-30-82-24), or in Nice, Autocars VFD-Traffort, Gare Routière, Promenade du Paillon (tel. 93-85-24-56).

Magic Bus and **Miracle Bus** offer inexpensive transport to major cities in Europe and beyond (see From Within Europe By Bus).

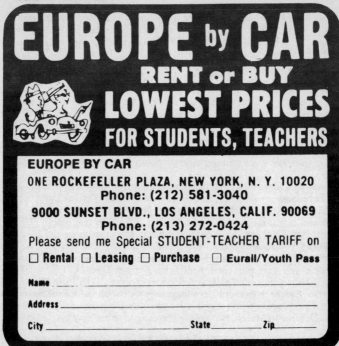
By Car

If you are traveling with a companion or in a group, renting or leasing a car may be the most enjoyable way to see France. It can also prove expensive. Renting costs at least US$200 per week for a four-seater, excluding taxes (33.3%) or deposit. Parking in congested cities is expensive. Nevertheless, the cost falls dramatically when three or more people share the expense.

If you want a car for longer than three weeks, leasing becomes more economical than renting. Most firms lease to 18-year-olds, while rental agencies have an age minimum of 21. Beware, though, that along with the economy of leasing come several potential pitfalls, such as hidden servicing expenses. Some tourists, especially families or small groups of friends, have found a purchase/resale deal plan cheaper than renting for long vacations. You must arrange the deal before you go; contact the AAA or the CAA for advice (see International Driver's License above for addresses).

Most companies require that you have a major credit card. Several U.S. firms offer rental and leasing plans in France. Send for their catalogs, and if you are a student or faculty member, ask about discounts. Compare prices carefully; they vary substantially between firms. Also, make sure that rental prices include the TVA tax. Some companies are **Auto-Europe,** P.O. Box 1097, Camden, ME 04843 (tel. (800) 223-5555; in Canada (800) 237-2465); **France Auto Vacances,** 420 Lexington Ave., New York, NY 10170 (tel. (212) 867-2625); **Europe by Car,** 1 Rockefeller Plaza, New York, NY 10020 (tel. (800) 223-1516); and **Kemwel Group, Inc.,** 106 Calvert St., Harrison, NY.10528-3199 (tel. (800) 678-0678). CIEE and France Auto Vacances offer discounted rental and leasing plans to students and faculty members.

You can also wait till you get to France to make arrangements. **Avis, Hertz, Solvet, Budget,** and **Europcar** operate agencies all over the world, the last two generally being the least expensive. **Europcar** has an office in Paris: 145 av. Malekoff, 75016 Paris (tel. 45-00-08-06). The **French National Railroad (SNCF)** offers a train-plus-car rental package available in about 200 cities. Many firms in the U.S. and France rent campers (sometimes called "motor caravans"), which can also be practical when the cost is split among several people.

Buying a used car in Europe is another option. *How to Buy and Sell a Used Car in Europe* contains useful tips; write for it c/o Gil Friedman, P.O. Box 1295, Mendocino, CA 95460 (tel. (707) 937-0866). If you can afford a new car, contact **Nemet Auto International,** 153-03 Hillside Ave., Jamaica, NY 11432 (tel. (800) 221-0177), a major firm dealing with European car purchase plans and overseas delivery. Send for their catalog of prices and shipping rates. The **Kemwel Group** also has a European car purchase plan. The **National Highway Traffic Safety Administration,** U.S. Department of Transportation, Office of Vehicle Safety Compliance, Washington, DC 20590 (tel. (202) 366-2830), will provide you with information on safety requirements for imported cars.

Once you have a car, you'll have to adjust to the French road system. The speed limit on the *autoroutes* is 130kph, which means that traffic moves at almost 80mph. Somewhat slower are the *Routes Nationales* that run through towns. For a synopsis of French driving regulations, write to the French Government Tourist Office (see Useful Organizations above) for the pamphlet *Motoring in France.* Be aware especially of the *priorité à droite:* Cars approaching from the right have the right of way. Although you do not need an international driving permit to drive in France, it can aid in smoothing over difficulties with police officers, and provides you with an additional piece of identification (see Documents and Formalities above).

Michelins, available in book stores and kiosks, make good road maps. The large map #989 is especially useful. The suggested roads, drawn in yellow, supposedly bypass congested areas.

By Thumb

Hitching in France takes patience: The country ranks among the worst in Europe for hitchhikers. You'll have better luck in regions such as Brittany, with lots of French vacationers and relatively few foreign tourists. Getting out of big cities such as Lyon or traveling along the Riviera can be almost impossible.

The system of primary roads consists of *Autoroutes* (designated by A) and the *Routes Nationales* (the N roads). To get long-distance rides, the *autoroutes* are best, but you must stand on an entrance ramp to get a ride—it is illegal to stand on the *autoroute* itself. If you are more interested in the experience than in where you are going, hitch along the *nationales.* Smaller *routes départementales,* with slower traffic, can also be good.

Try to look neat and respectable. Stand, don't sit. Look interested. Make eye contact with drivers. Sometimes doing a side-of-the-road "dance" or waving the flag of a popular country or state can get favorable results. The lighter you travel, the better your luck will be. Pick a place where the driver can stop easily and can get back on the road safely, like service stations and the stopping areas near toll booths. A destination sign may help you get longer rides and avoid 10-minute lifts, though short-distance hitching (village to village) is always easiest. Truckers may give you long rides, but will rarely stop at the roadside; approach them at gas stations, weigh stations, and roadside restaurants instead. It is illegal for truckers to pick up more than two passengers at one time.

It is not always safe to hitch alone in France. Two women are safer than one and often have better luck than a man and woman together, though this is also a safe and reliable combination. Two men may hitch more safely together, but may also have greater difficulty securing a ride. Always refuse rides in the back of a two-door car. Don't lock the door and keep your luggage handy—don't put it in the trunk if you can avoid it. In an emergency, open the car door. This usually surprises the drivers enough to make them slow down. If you feel uneasy about the ride for any reason, get out at the first opportunity or firmly demand to be let out.

You may be able to find rides (or hitching companions) by checking message boards in student travel offices or in student gathering places. **ALLOSTOP,** 84, passage Brady, 75010 Paris (tel. 42-46-00-66), with offices in many major cities, brings together drivers and riders to share the expenses of a car trip. Telephone or write a few days in advance if you can. For passengers, it costs 60F for long trips, plus 16 centimes per kilometer. Use of the service for six months costs 120F, unlimited service for one year 200F. ALLOSTOP also sells train tickets to people under 26 at a 25% discount.

By Bicycle

Cycling is an excellent way to see the countryside. French roads, with a wealth of well-paved minor routes, are generally fine: Ride in the morning or evening when it's cool and you have the road to yourself. Although you can ride on main roads (marked in red on Michelin maps), secondary roads (in yellow) or local roads (in white) are less traveled by cars and trucks. Cyclists should avoid major *autoroutes* (marked in red with a dotted line), and heed the round road sign bordered in red with a diagram of a bike: "Bikes Forbidden." The useful **Michelin green guides** are available in bookstores throughout France. Bikers may also want the larger-scale, more expensive (19-37F) maps from the **Institut Géographique National (IGN)**, 107, rue la Boëtie, 75008 Paris (tel. 42-25-87-90); Mo. St-Philippe du Roule. Outstanding touring regions include the Loire Valley (especially the route west of Tours to Villandry and Ussé), Normandy, Brittany, Provence, the Vosges, the Massif Central, and the somewhat mountainous Jura. In the Pyrenees and the Alps, you (and your bicycle) can catch a lift up the mountain on a train and then cycle down.

For touring information, first consult the tourist bureau annexed to most French embassies. The **Fédération Française de Cyclotourisme**, 8, rue Jean-Marie Jégo, 75013 Paris (tel. 45-80-30-21; Mo. Corvisart), is a non-profit, member-supported liaison between 2000 cycle-touring clubs. Although they are not a travel agency or tourist information bureau, they are friendly and will advise foreign cyclists on a limited basis. (Include 3 reply coupons for an airmail response.)

Most airlines will accept a boxed bike as one of your two pieces of luggage, provided that the total baggage weight does not exceed the given limit (for Air France in 1988, 70 lbs.). You can also count a bicycle as an extra piece of luggage on transatlantic flights; it will cost you US$60-80 each way, even if you have a round-trip ticket. Most airlines do not supply bike boxes; you can obtain one at bike shops, which often give away old cartons. Carry a wrench to the airport and know how to make adjustments on the spot if necessary.

French treads and rim sizes differ from English sizes, but spare parts in English sizes have become available in many towns. Even so, you should carry one or two extra inner tubes (*chambres à l'air*), a spare tire, and a pump if you plan on a long ride; tape a few spokes to the body. You can buy an excellent bicycle in France and have it shipped back home (see Paris: Shopping and Markets for information on sales tax rebates), but make sure you get one fitted for export—French parts are even harder to find in the U.S. than American ones are in France. Bikers will find it convenient to fly into Orly, since you can assemble your bike in the airport and ride it into Paris on the *piste cyclable*, a bike path that avoids heavy traffic the first few miles. If you arrive at the Roissy-Charles de Gaulle airport, take the Roissy Rail commuter train into Paris. Conductors will most likely not object to a bike in a box; when you reach your Métro stop you can liberate your faithful friend.

Once in France, you can easily combine biking with train travel. For information in advance, write to SNCF (see Useful Organizations above) for the brochure *Guide du train et du vélo*. Regardless of how far you go, it costs 42F to register a bicycle as baggage for transport. On some trains, you can load the bicycle into the baggage car (*fourgon*) yourself for free; in more than 20 stations, the SNCF provides cartons (10F) to protect the bike in transit. Look for the SNCF advertisements that say "*Dans certains trains votre vélo peut voyager avec vous, gratuitement.*" On trains thus advertised (sometimes called *trains omnibus*), your bike travels with you (on other trains, your bike may arrive up to 48 hours after you), and you save the registration fee. Bicycles are easily damaged in transit. All removable parts, such as headlights, should be taken off the frame, or padded and taped.

Experienced cyclists recommend a front bag with a transparent pocket for maps, as well as panniers, which can hold a sleeping bag.

You can also rent bicycles in many of the larger towns, and it is usually possible to get a serviceable 10-speed model. In Paris, try Bicy-Club de France, 8, place de la Porte Champerret, 75017 (tel. 42-27-28-82; Mo. Porte Champerret). The French National Railroad provides a service called *Train + Vélo* through 219 railroad stations in France.

By Foot

If you have more time than money and prefer countryside to cityscape, try hiking France's extensive network of long-distance footpaths. The **Fédération Française de la Randonnée Pédestre**, 8, av. Marceau (*entrée* 9, av. George V), 75008 Paris (tel. 47-23-62-32), provides topographical maps (*topo-guides*) with itineraries for 40,000km of footpaths. Huts or mountain hostels, which usually serve meals, are located along many of the suggested routes. The member organizations of the federation organize group trips through the countryside.

Proper **hiking gear** is essential: Lightweight leather hiking boots with sturdy rubber soles are best, though in summer you can get by with good sneakers, except in the mountains. You will also need a sweater, water-proof poncho, change of socks, long pants (in addition to shorts), and a comfortable pack with a hip belt (see Camping above for advice on backpacks). You may also want to carry a light butane or white gas stove and a mess kit. Remember that high altitudes and hot sun together make midday trekking unsafe; bring sunscreen, a hat, and plenty of water.

For more information, contact the **Club Alpin Français,** 9, rue la Boëtie, 75008 Paris (tel. 47-42-38-46). The club runs several centers in the Alps that provide instruction in Alpine technique.

The following books may help you plan: Spencer's *Walking in the Alps* (Hunter, 1986; US$8.95); Oaks's *Turn Right at the Fountain* (Holt, Rinehart, and Winston, 1981; US$9.95); Hunter's *Walking in France* (Haynes Publishers; US$9.95); and Jones's *Tramping Europe: A Walking Guide* (Prentice-Hall, 1984; US$7.95).

By Boat

France has more than 7000 miles of navigable rivers, canals, lakes, and sea coast. To float through the countryside or take better advantage of your time at the seaside, contact the **Syndicat National des Loueurs de Bateaux de Plaisance,** Port de la Bourdonnais, 75007 Paris (tel. 45-55-10-49). They'll set you up in whatever region and boat interests you, from dinghies and canoes to yacht cruiseboats. For information on waterways suitable for canoeing, contact the **Fédération Française de Canoe-Kayak,** 17, route de Vienne, 69007 Lyon (tel. 78-61-32-74).

Accommodations

Hostels

The **Fédération Unie des Auberges de Jeunesse (FUAJ),** the French branch of the **International Youth Hostel Federation (IYHF),** runs more than 200 youth hostels in France. To stay in an IYHF hostel, you must become an IYHF member. The **IYHF** card costs US$20 (CDN$18), US$10 (CDN$9) for those under 18 and over 54. **American Youth Hostels,** the U.S. affiliate of IYHF, dispenses the cards in most major cities; you can also write them at AYH, Inc., P.O. Box 37613, Washington, DC 20013-7613 (tel. (202) 783-6161). In Canada, write to the **Canadian Hostelling Association,** 333 River Rd., 3rd floor, Tower A, Vanier City, Ottawa, Ont. K1L 8H9 (tel. (613) 748-5638). Let's Go Travel Services, the Educational Travel Centre, and Travel CUTS dispense the cards as well (see Useful Organizations above). IYHF cards are available in France at the Paris office or at any hostel, although, according to international agreement, you should buy a membership in your home country. If you've lived in France for a year, a membership purchased in France costs 43F; otherwise, cards cost 80F. The *International Youth Hostel*

Handbook, volumes 1 and 2 (each US$8.45, CDN$6; postage included), details the locations of every hostel in Europe and includes a basic map. For a more detailed list of hostels in France, contact the FUAJ, 6, rue Mesnil, 75116 Paris (tel. 42-41-59-00; Mo. Victor-Hugo).

A night in an *auberge de jeunesse* costs roughly half the price of a hotel stay—prices average 24-60F, with breakfast (usually not obligatory) an additional 9F. Accommodations usually consist of bunk beds in single-sex dormitories, and most hostels either serve evening meals or have kitchen facilities you can use. Quality varies widely; some hostels are extremely well-kept and well-situated; others are in run-down barracks far from the center of town.

Hostel life has its drawbacks: an early curfew (usually 10-11pm, midnight-2am in Paris), lack of privacy, prohibitions against smoking and drinking, a 10am-5pm lockout, a three-day limit to your stay, hordes of vacationing school-children, and (sometimes) required household chores. But the prices compensate for these inconveniences, and many hostels fill quickly in July and August. Furthermore, lockout and curfew times are often flexible—many hostels leave a back door open most of the night. Some hostels accept reservations—it's worth calling ahead—but always arrive early if you can. Check-in times are uniformly 8-10am and 6-8pm or 10pm.

All hostels require **sheet sleeping sacks,** which they rent (usually 10F) or sell (about 100F). Some hostels will let you use your sleeping bag instead.

Hotels

French hotels can be a bargain. The French government publishes a comprehensive guide that classifies hotels with a star system: 4L (luxury), 4, 3, 2, 1. Most hotels we list are one-star or unclassified establishments, though sometimes we list two-star establishments offering inexpensive rooms. As a rule, French hotels charge by the room and not by the number of people staying in it, so two traveling together can sleep more inexpensively than a single traveler. Most rooms come with double beds. Expect to pay 65-80F for singles. Rooms for three or four can cost 45-55F per person. If your room has no shower, you'll have to pay extra (12-25F) or, especially in small hotels, go without.

When looking at hotels, remember that the French call the ground floor the *rez-de-chaussée,* and the second floor the *premier étage.*

Many hotels serve a *petit déjeuner obligatoire* (obligatory breakfast), which costs 12-18F. Since local cafes often serve croissants and coffee for less, you may want to opt out of breakfast if you can. Beware of hotels, usually in heavily touristed areas, that require *demi-pension* (one obligatory meal with each night's stay).

If you plan to visit a popular tourist area, especially during a festival, it is advisable to write ahead for reservations. Most hotels will confirm reservations only upon receipt of a check—not a credit card number—for the first night's rent. (Include an International Reply Coupon for a prompt reply.)

Inns and Gîtes

For a more pastoral experience, look for *logis* and *auberges de France,* hotels and restaurants roughly comparable to country inns. They serve excellent food and charge reasonable prices for comfortable rooms (although they usually charge more than the cheapest hotel). In any region, an *office de tourisme* will provide a list of them. To obtain this information by mail, write **La Fédération Nationale des Logis de France,** 25, rue Jean Mermosz, 75008 Paris (tel. 43-59-86-67).

Gîtes de Frances offer furnished lodgings in farmhouses, cottages, and even campsites that meet fixed standards of comfort and price. Intended for stays of two weeks or longer and located in areas where you might hike, sail, or ski, they range from fully-equipped houses to campgrounds near working farms. *Gîtes d'étape* are designed for cyclists, hikers, and other ramblers. For further information, contact the **Fédération Nationale des Gîtes de France,** 35, rue Godot-de-Mauroy, 75009 Paris (tel. 47-42-25-43). *Gîtes et refuges en France* lists over 1600 places to stay for hikers, climbers, cross-country and downhill skiers, and mountaineers. Order from Editions Créer, rue Jean Amariton, 63340 Nonette.

Student Accommodations

Short-term student housing is available in summer in the dormitories of most French universities. Contact the **Centre Régional des Oeuvres Universitaires (CROUS)** (see Study above). Travelers interested in summer housing—and students interested in year-long accommodations—can also contact the **Cité Internationale Universitaire de Paris,** 19, bd. Jourdan, 75690 Paris Cédex 14 (tel. 45-89-68-52). *Foyers,* youth residence halls, are a good bet in Paris; these single-sex dormitories require a three-night minimum stay. You can also find a bed through the **Accueil des Jeunes en France (AJF),** a central booking organization for youth accommodations in Paris. AJF has 8000 beds at its disposal year-round and more than 11,000 beds in summer. The following are AJF's four accommodation, welcome, and travel offices in Paris:

AJF Beaubourg, 119, rue St-Martin, 75004 Paris (tel. 42-77-87-80; Mo. Rambuteau/Hôtel de Ville/Châtelet-Les-Halles), opposite the Centre Georges Pompidou. Open Mon.-Sat. 9:30am-7pm.

AJF Gare du Nord, facing platform 19 in the arrival hall (tel. 42-85-86-19; Mo. Gare du Nord). Open June 1-Sept. 30 daily 8am-10pm; March-May and Oct. Mon.-Fri. 9:15am-6:15pm.

AJF Marais (Hôtel de Ville), 16, rue du Pont Louis Philippe, 75004 Paris (tel. 42-78-04-82; Mo. Hôtel de Ville/Pont Marie). Open March-Oct. Mon.-Fri. 9am-6:30pm.

AJF Quartier Latin, 139, bd. St-Michel, 75005 Paris (tel. 43-54-95-86; Mo. Port Royal). Open Mon.-Fri. 10am-7pm.

These offices guarantee every young traveler an immediate reservation for decent, low-cost lodging. Prices average 75-95F per night for bed and breakfast. However, some *Let's Go* readers have complained that AJF's rooms are occasionally substandard, and that its staff is reluctant to investigate complaints. Avoid buying AJF vouchers from travel agents, who sometimes charge high commissions; deal directly with the offices listed above. AJF provides train and bus tickets at reduced prices and also runs a youth center in Paris near place de la Bastille: **Résidence Bastille,** 151, av. Ledru Rollin, 75011 Paris (tel. 43-79-53-86; Mo. Voltaire/Ledru Rollin/Bastille). The center charges 75F for bed and breakfast.

Camping and Caravaning

Camping liberates you from hostel regulations and drab hotels. There are campgrounds all over France, many by lakes, rivers, or the ocean. Be aware, however, that the vacationing French often arrive at campgrounds with their trailers, radios, and a great deal of cooking paraphernalia—and there usually isn't much space between sites. In August you might have to arrive well before 11am to ensure yourself a spot.

French campgrounds, like hotels and restaurants, are classified by a star system. Three- and four-star sites are usually large, grassy campgrounds with hot showers, bathrooms, a restaurant or store, and often a lake or swimming pool nearby. Occasional **student discounts** are offered. Some campsites will ask for your passport: Resist giving it to them, and try to substitute a less vital piece of identification. The **International Camping Carnet** (membership card) is one highly acceptable substitute, and will save you a lot of time and money if you intend to do much camping. You may purchase it for US$23 from the National Campers and Hikers Association, 4804 Transit Rd., Bldg. 2, Depew, NY 14043 (tel. (716) 668-6242).

If you choose to camp unofficially, leave a site just as spotless as you found it. Within sight of a farmhouse, you should ask permission.

Let's Go lists campsites near the cities and towns that we cover; if you plan to camp extensively, though, you should buy the *Guide Officiel Camping/Caravaning.*

The book provides good maps and lists both ordinary campsites (including those available to caravans only—no tents), and *terrains à la ferme* (farm sites). It is available from the **Fédération Française de Camping et de Caravaning,** 78, rue de Rivoli, 75004 Paris (tel. 42-72-84-08). Michelin publishes a similar, but much less comprehensive guide, *Camping Caravaning,* geared to car-camping and designed to accompany the Michelin 1:200,000 scale maps.

International Host Organizations

Servas is an organization devoted to promoting peace and understanding among different cultures. Traveler members may stay free of charge in host members' homes in 90 countries. You are asked to be genuinely interested in sharing with your hosts, to contact them in advance, and to conform to the household routine. Stays are limited to two nights unless you are invited to stay longer. Prospective traveler members are interviewed and asked to contribute US$45 plus a refundable US$15 fee. To apply, write U.S. Servas Committee, Inc., 11 John St., #706, New York, NY 10018 (tel. (212) 267-0252). **Traveler's Directory** prints a semi-annual directory of members offering hospitality to other members. Annual membership is US$20 in North America, US$25 elsewhere. You must be willing to host others in your home. The directory's newsletter, *Vagabond Shoes,* available to nonmembers for US$10 per year, provides helpful advice on budget travel in Europe.

You might also want to try **Amicale Culturelle Internationale,** a non-profit organization that offers placements to visitors as paying guests in French families everywhere in France on a full-board basis, and in Paris and its suburbs on a half-board basis. Write them at 27, rue Godot-de-Mauroy, 75009 Paris (tel. 47-42-94-21). **Accueil France Famille** is a similar organization; it's address is 5, rue François Coppée, F-75015 Paris (tel. 45-54-22-39).

Worker's Accommodations

In many cities, rooms are available in **Foyers de Jeunes Travailleurs et de Jeunes Travailleuses.** These residence halls were founded for young workers with jobs in cities far from home. They are usually single-sex dorms with single rooms and a bathroom in the hall. They do accept foreign travelers if there's space available. At 50-60F per night, breakfast included, the *foyers* offer a fairly good deal to the single traveler; furthermore, they almost always have room because tourists don't know about them. For a list of *foyers* and more information, write the **Union des Foyers de Jeunes Travailleurs,** 46, rue Deschamps, 75116 Paris (tel. 45-03-12-00).

Retreats

Monasteries are ideal for those seeking a few days of peaceful contemplation. Reservations must be made well in advance. For a list of monasteries, *Repertoire de l'Hospitalité Monastique en France* (22F), write to **La Procure,** 3, rue de Mézières, 75006 Paris (tel. 45-48-20-25). For peace and quiet, **L'Accueil des Pèlerins de Chartres,** 9km from Chartres at 8, rue du Fossé-Bourg, JOUY, 28300 Mainvilliers (tel. 37-22-24-44), may be just the place. Light chores are expected and smoking is prohibited, but the five-day maximum stay comes with nightly slide presentations on Chartres and its previous pilgrims. Rooms are 35F per night, beds in dormitories 15F, and camping 5F. The obligatory member card is 5F. Meals are available.

Life in France

History and Politics

Dates in this book are given using B.C.E. (Before Common Era) and C.E. (Common Era), the historical equivalents of B.C. (Before Christ) and A.D. (Anno Domini).

The earliest people in France, the Gauls were an iron-using Celtic people. The Romans were the first in an age-long series of invaders who wanted to carve France, and the French, into pieces. Although Rome began its northward expansion early, it was not until 52 B.C.E., when **Julius Caesar** defeated the Celtic leader **Vercingétorix,** that the Romans gained control of French territory. A relatively stable period of social and economic growth came to an end with growing anarchy in the third century C.E., when Constantine transferred the imperial capital from Rome to Constantinople and the Empire in the West began to crumble. Torn by civil wars and barbarian invasions in the third and fourth centuries C.E., the Roman administration let Gaul slip from its grasp. Germanic invaders poured over Gaul's borders and divided the land into a number of small chiefdoms. By 415, Visigoths had established themselves in Spain and southern France, including the Loire Valley. Northern France was held by various tribes, among them the Franks, the Alamans, and the Burgundians.

The year 481 marked a new era, when 15-year-old **Clovis** acceded to the Frankish throne. A bright, ambitious, and thoroughly rapacious youth, he united the barbarian tribes and forged a new power, leading his army on to conquer all of Gaul. He gained more territory through conspiracy, assassination, and crude but persuasive diplomacy. After Clovis's death, his four sons split the kingdom, and under them the Merovingian line declined: They became known as the *rois fainéants,* the "do-nothing kings."

Power soon fell to aristocratic landholders, of whom the most prominent were the competing Neustrians and Austrasians. **Pepin II** won northern and western Gaul for the latter in 687, unifying all the Merovingian lands. Nonetheless, the Austrasian house was not yet royalty—its family held merely the office of mayor of the palace. **Charles Martel** (The Hammer) succeeded his father in 714, turned back the Muslims at Poitiers in 732, and thus won himself the title of defender and leader of western Christendom. His son **Pepin III,** also known as Pepin the Short, agreed to help Rome fight off the invading Lombards from northern Italy only if the Pope would decree that Pepin should wear the crown. This settled, Pepin came to the Pope's defense and came away with the Frankish crown, the last Merovingian puppet king having been neatly deposed.

Pepin's son, **Charlemagne,** conquered an empire and was crowned Emperor of the Romans by Pope Leo III on Christmas Day, 800, outdoing even his father. The Carolingian Renaissance, a rebirth of Latin culture, lasted from Charlemagne's accession in 768 to the death of Charles the Bald in 877. This era of emulation (not innovation) was short-lived, due partly to Norse raids during the second half of the ninth century, and the Empire floundered after Charlemagne's death.

His son **Louis the Pious,** the proverbial nice guy who finishes last, was imprisoned in a monastery by his own sons. Split into three once again by their squabbles, the entire Carolingian empire fragmented irreparably when the royal line began having inbreeding-induced genetic difficulties; names such as Charles the Simple, Charles the Fat, and Louis the Stammerer indicate the level of leadership at the time. During the age of French feudalism, noble families assumed all political and economic rights: When **Hugh Capet** became King of France in 987, founding the Capetian line, he wielded power only in his own domain, the Ile-de-France (the greater Parisian region).

The eleventh and twelfth centuries were a period of political consolidation and expansion: **William the Conqueror,** Duke of Normandy, brought his province under firm central government, rivaling the king of France in military power. **Philip II Auguste** was chiefly responsible for France's unification. In his 43-year reign, Philip married his way into the Artois, Valois, and Vermandois families, and conquered Normandy and Anjou. His statecraft contrasts sharply with the piety of his grandson **Louis IX,** who led two unsuccessful Crusades to liberate the Holy Sepulchre and was canonized after his death.

The reign of **Philip the Fair** (1285-1314) saw one of the most violent incidents of state in French history. Philip's determination to strengthen his secular government at the expense of Papal power led to a schism with the Papacy, the so-called second Babylonian Captivity. When Pope Boniface VIII expired (some say of shock, after Philip charged him with heresy), the king arranged the election of a French Pope—Clement V—and installed him at Avignon. French Popes ruled there while a separate line continued to sit in Rome until 1377, when the Conciliar movement began to heal the schism. But Philip the Fair's troubles were nothing compared to his successors'. **Philip VI Valois's** reign was afflicted with famine, the Black Death of 1348, and the outbreak of the Hundred Years' War, which began as a dispute over Edward III of England's right to the French throne. The French like to attribute their salvation from these threats to a peasant girl from Lorraine—and it is true that **Joan of Arc** bolstered France's sagging morale. Her career began with a vision instructing her to don armor and deliver France from the English. Leaving her village of Domrémy (which today has a population of 237), she confronted the Dauphin (Crown Prince) Charles with her dream at Chinon and marched victorious into Orléans a month later. Charles was crowned King **Charles VII** of France, asserting both the territorial integrity of France and the dynastic rights of the Valois.

The remaining Valois were faced with the task of rebuilding the nation. **Louis XI** suppressed the independent princes, including Philip the Bold, and strengthened the central power of the crown. Upon **Louis XII's** death in 1515, France was as strong as it had been in centuries, with monarchy, borders, and economy all secure.

French Catholics dissatisfied with their faith found new hope in the teachings of **John Calvin;** these French Calvinists (Huguenots) attacked church and state with equal fervor. **Catherine de Medici,** regent for her young son Charles IX, persuaded him to order the St. Bartholomew's Day Massacre (1572), in which 20,000 Parisian Huguenots were slaughtered—an event that made reconciliation between the Protestant and Catholic communities a rather remote possibility. In 1589 Charles IX was assassinated and the Protestant **Henry IV** Bourbon acceded. He calmed things down by converting to Catholicism himself. *"Paris vaut bien une messe"*—Paris is well worth a Mass, he reportedly said upon conversion. Issuing the Edict of Nantes in 1598, he guaranteed the religious and political rights of the Protestant community for nearly 100 years—until 1685 when Louis XIV violated it. This did not save Henry from assassination, however, and under his mother, **Marie de Medici,** and her ally **Cardinal Richelieu,** France saw an absolutist and Catholic revival at court. The Estates General (medieval parlement) were recessed until 1789.

Richelieu's reputation as a cunning statesman rested on his foreign policy and his strategies for suppressing aristocratic power. At the Cardinal's death, **Louis XIV** was five years old. During his 72-year reign, the Sun King continued Richelieu's work of constructing an absolute monarchy. Louis XIV forced the nobility to assemble around him at Versailles, his magnificent and costly château on the outskirts of Paris, and to engage in an assortment of elaborate court rituals, keeping them busy and out of mischief. A patron of artists and playwrights, among them Corneille, Racine, and Molière, Louis XIV glittered while his people starved. His death in 1715 again left a five-year-old heir, his great-grandson Louis XV. The aging Louis XV's prophetic words, *"Après moi, le déluge"* (After me, the deluge), ushered in the ill-starred reign of Louis XVI. As the financial situation of the overextended monarchy grew worse, an attempt was made to reform national finances with an Assembly of Notables, called in 1787. The group suggested that an Estates General be called to try to solve the crisis. The first Estates General since 1614 was convened at Versailles with all three estates—nobility, clergy, and members of the bourgeoisie. After several months spent struggling for more representative government, the Third Estate dramatically declared itself the National Assembly, and when the lower clergy, led by Talleyrand, joined them, the French Revolution began. Fearing a royal coup, the Paris mob seized the city and stormed the Bastille prison on July 14, 1789. On August 4, the assembly voted away all peasant obligations and rents and abolished all hereditary privileges. Three weeks later it adopted the Declaration of the Rights of Man. A new constitution was presented to Louis XVI on the first anniversary of Bastille Day. He appeared at the Hôtel de Ville and kissed the tricolor cockade, symbol of revolution. Now, the prime political battle was waged between the relatively moderate Girondins and the more radical Jacobins.

The First Republic, after the fall of the Girondin ministry, was scarred by the Reign of Terror. **Maximilien Robespierre** and his radical followers thinned the number of perceived enemies of the state with the guillotine. Robespierre too was toppled from power, and soon most of the original revolutionaries had gone the way of their victims. The subsequent power vacuum was filled by the Directorate, a corrupt oligarchy. The army was the biggest business in France in 1795, as well as the object of revolutionary idealism. The revolutionaries demanded careers based on merit rather than birth; the rise of a young Corsican artillery officer named **Napoleon Bonaparte** traced an exemplary trajectory. He used his prestige as a military strategist and dashing young géneral to snatch power from the Directorate in 1799.

Napoleon swiftly solved the problems of anarchy by naming himself First Consul and then Emperor. He drew up a new constitution, strengthened central bureaucracy, collected taxes, and instituted a draft. Taking advantage of new revenues and a strong military, Napoleon began a series of military campaigns, as remarkable for their daring as for their atrocious numbers of casualties. By 1809, Napoleon ruled all Europe west of Prussia. The imperial adventure screeched to a halt when Napoleon confronted an enemy no amount of French blood could conquer: the Russian winter. He abdicated in October 1814 and was exiled to the island of Elba, off Italy. While Talleyrand and Louis XVIII (the late king's brother) were negotiating a peace, Napoleon escaped to southern France and, in the strange footnote to his career known as the Hundred Days, marched on Paris with an increasingly large army. The British General Wellington met and defeated Napoleon at Waterloo in Belgium in June, 1815. The Emperor was then sent to the even smaller island of St. Helena, and the Congress of Vienna met and legislated an attempt to turn back time: The Bourbon dynasty was restored and the borders of France set as they were in 1792.

Although the new government was a constitutional parliamentary monarchy, it had its enemies. While the Revolution of 1830 could hardly be called a change of regime, the new "citizen king" **Louis-Philippe** extended suffrage and adopted a self-consciously bourgeois lifestyle. In 1848 Louis-Philippe was overthrown by a moderate Republic, which in turn crushed a more radical workers' uprising a few months later. The first president, elected by an overwhelming majority, was **Louis Napoleon,** nephew of the emperor.

Louis Napoleon outmaneuvered parliament, won over the army, found financial backing, and seized the government before the election of 1851. A year later he was proclaimed Emperor—Napoleon III—by national plebiscite. At home, Napoleon's forte was the economic sphere: He expanded credit and allowed France to move headlong into industrialization.

In foreign affairs, Napoleon III was himself outmaneuvered by the wilier and even more cynical Bismarck. Prussia's defeat of Napoleon in 1871 sent him into exile, and a third republic was born. The Republican regime that arose received its first challenge from the Paris Commune of 1871. Angry at the government for signing a humiliating peace with Germany (Alsace/Lorraine was lost), Parisians rioted and set up a communal government confined to Paris. Government forces regained control by pitilessly exterminating the Communards. The resulting Republican government would be the longest-lasting to date, falling only to the Nazis in 1940.

Severely weakened in 1871, France was saved from Germany in World War I only thanks to intervention first by Commonwealth and then by American forces. The country suffered during the inter-war years from financial problems (war debt and the international depression of the 1930s). Although England began to rearm in the 1930s, France did not, relying instead on the Maginot Line—a series of fortifications on the northeastern frontier begun in 1927. This barrier gave them a false sense of security and, together with the English, they declared war on Germany in September, 1939. However, the French military leaders were unprepared to meet the German military machine that simply marched *around* the Maginot Line, and in May, 1940, the Nazi *blitzkrieg* overwhelmed France. Fighting ended after a month, when a collaborationist government was set up at Vichy under **Marshal Pétain.**

In 1944 a provisional government was set up under **Charles de Gaulle,** leader of the Résistance, and in 1944 he became the first president of the Fourth Republic. While holding France's diverse political factions together, de Gaulle sought and eventually obtained greater powers for the presidency. In 1946 he resigned, partially to show how indispensable he was. After a series of unstable coalition governments and in the wake of a revolt of the army and French settlers in Algeria in 1958, de Gaulle returned and inaugurated the Fifth Republic, which has lasted to this day.

Under the 1958 Constitution, legislative power is held by Parliament, comprised of a 317-member Senate and a 491-member National Assembly. These representatives are directly elected by universal suffrage. Executive power is held by the president, who is elected by popular vote for a term of seven years. The president appoints a Council of Ministers, headed by the Prime Minister, which administers the country and is responsible to Parliament. In January, 1959, when de Gaulle became the Fifth Republic's first president, the newly-formed Gaullist party swept the National Assembly elections. De Gaulle favored an aggressive foreign policy, and U.S. NATO forces were ejected from the country. The Algerian crisis was resolved by granting that colony independence in 1962.

In May, 1968, Paris exploded with internal unrest. For two weeks, students fought to alter the authoritarian French university system: Demonstrations led to riots, and students occupied the Sorbonne and the Odéon. The students were joined by several million workers in a general strike against low wages and lack of social reform. They brought French industry to a halt and effectively paralyzed the country. The National Assembly was immediately dissolved, yet in the next general election, the Gaullist party received its greatest majority ever.

In April, 1969, de Gaulle resigned (again), and his successor **Georges Pompidou,** tried to combine Gaullist foreign policy with conservative domestic policy. The continuation of Gaullism and authoritarian policies was threatened, however, by the Union of the Left—an alliance of the Socialist and Communist parties. When Pompidou died in 1974, the Gaullists were split. A large segment refused to back the official party candidates and instead supported **Valéry Giscard d'Estaing,** nominee of the business-oriented Républicains Indépendants; he defeated the leftist candidate Mitterrand by a narrow margin. Giscard's term started with significant reforms (the voting age was reduced to 18, and abortion legalized), but gradually adopted a more conservative tone. Only the collapse of the Socialist-Communist coalition in 1977 saved Giscard's party from a major defeat in the 1978 elections. Unemployment dogged him during the 1981 presidential campaign, but the major issue was Giscard's personal style. To Europe's surprise, **François Mitterrand** was elected president by a comfortable majority, and the socialists swept 60% of the seats in the National Assembly.

Within his first two months of office, Mitterrand raised the minimum wage and instituted a mandatory fifth week of vacation. In March, 1982, he passed a law beginning the transfer of administrative and financial power from government-appointed prefects to locally-elected departmental assemblies and regional councils, thus dismantling the strongly centralized political system that had dominated France since the time of Napoleon. As a result of this decentralization, Corsica was made a *collectivité territoriale* with its own directly-elected 61-seat assembly. Even more importantly, Mitterand nationalized 36 banks, five key industrial groups, and two financial holding companies in the largest government takeover of private industry since World War II. The nationalization did not last, however: In 1987, steps were taken to re-privatize those industries taken over by the state.

Although social benefits and working conditions have substantially improved under Mitterand, the new government has had serious opposition. An economic recession in 1983 led to the adoption of deflationary policies, including reductions in public expenditures. Efforts to control inflation through wage freezes have caused a number of union strikes. The decreased support for Mitterand's government was reflected in the poor performance of Socialists in countrywide municipal elections. Right-wing parties gained a majority in the National Assembly as well. In the June 1984 elections to the European Parliament, Socialists again suffered serious setbacks, taking only 20 of the 81 seats allocated to France. The united Rassemblement pour la République and Union pour la Démocratie Française opposition, headed by **Simone Veil,** won 41 seats.

In 1984 Mitterand expressed his support for the deployment of US nuclear missiles in France, and his desire to strengthen France's own nuclear forces. In the summer of 1985, it was learned that French secret service agents were responsible for sinking the trawler *Rainbow Warrior,* flagship of the international environmental protection group Greenpeace, in the port of Auckland, New Zealand. Greenpeace had been monitoring French nuclear tests in the region.

Racism is another problem that plagues the government. More than 1.5 million Arabs came to France when the economy was prosperous and job prospects were good. But 2.5 million French were unemployed in 1987, and some French would like Arabs and other immigrants to return home. In the elections in March 1986, the National Front won more than 10% of the vote. This ultra-rightist party, headed by **Jean-Marie Le Pen,** has announced its desire to rid France of all Arab immigrants and their offspring.

In May, 1988, Mitterand was reelected president. He promptly appointed fellow socialist **Michel Rochard** prime minister, and dissolved the National Assembly, hoping that voters would choose a Socialist Party majority. In June, 1988, the right lost seats, the National Front dropped down to a single representative, and the Socialist Party gained some numbers (276); no party secured a majority. In any case, Mitterand appears to be setting a more conservative course for the next seven years.

To keep abreast of the latest in French politics, pick up one of the excellent daily papers. Most are more frankly partisan, and more free with their dissent, than American newspapers; *Le Figaro* leans to the right, *Le Monde* to the left.

Language

Language forcibly united France. The imposition of the *langue d'ouïl,* the dialect that evolved into modern French, was critical in forging the political unity of the nation, and in creating the image of a monolithic national culture that still persists. Yet France is not a country of one language. Breton (a Gaelic tongue) in Brittany, Flemish in Flanders, Alsatian in Alsace, Occitan in Languedoc, Catalan in Roussillon, Corsican in Corsica, and Basque in the Pyrenees are all spoken and are the source of a fierce regional pride that has recently begun to challenge the hegemony of French in the public school system.

Tourists themselves probably do the most to aggravate France's legendary linguistic snobbery towards visitors. Every summer Paris is besieged by hordes of monoglot tourists, many of whom expect to be addressed in English. Remember that people working in hotels, restaurants, and tourist offices are pressed hard enough just doing their job. Don't offend their culture by refusing to try even a few words of French. Buy a pocket dictionary and a phrasebook, but don't rely on them too much. Your best allies are an alert ear, good humor, sincere friendliness, a desire to learn, and a willingness to appear a little foolish in public and still laugh at yourself. And don't forget that the French are as shy about speaking English as you may be about speaking French.

Observing the conventions of French *politesse* will help immensely. Always address people in French first, using *Monsieur* or *Madame* (*Mademoiselle* for young women). Whenever you enter a store, restaurant, or hotel, greet the proprietor with "*Bonjour Madame/Monsieur.*" Only then should you ask, "*Parlez-vous anglais, Madame/Monsieur?*" Keep in mind, however, that the usual response to this question is negative. Never hesitate to struggle on in broken French, and always say "*Merci, au revoir.*"

France is gradually adapting to an ever-increasing number of tourists, and you will find multi-lingual signs in airports, train stations, and major tourist sites. In most towns, the tourist office staff speaks passable English, and at sites where the guided tours are in French, there is often a printed English translation available. In large cities and heavily touristed areas, hotelkeepers and waiters know enough

English for essential transactions. In the southwest, rural Brittany, and other rural areas, people speak less English, but are helpful and eager to understand. French Canadian travelers should be prepared to have their accents thought unusual—perhaps quaint, perhaps charming—but certainly odd.

Literature

Reading for Your Trip

Your trip is likely to afford you plenty of opportunities for reading: long train rides, waiting for buses, rainy days, and the flight there and back. The following is a slightly eccentric list of books that mixes masterpieces and less-acclaimed works. Most of the books mentioned are available in English translations and in paperback. The French department of any university or a librarian should be able to give you further guidance.

A towering monument for those who want a hefty book to last them through their journey, the eleventh-century *Chanson de Roland* (*The Song of Roland*) remains the most famous of French medieval texts. Set in the Pyrenees, this anonymous epic poem dwells on the gory battles between the French and the Muslims.

Known in English as *The Romance of Tristan,* or *Tristram, Tristran et Iseult* early established *l'amour* and *la mort* as the main raw material of French literature. Fragments of poems concerning the star-crossed, love-drugged pair have been found scattered across Europe, from England to Italy. For lighter medieval fare, read any of the about 150 extant *fabliaux,* short, narrative, usually baudy and amusing poems.

The genre of the modern reflective essay was largely invented by Michel de Montaigne in the sixteenth century. François Rabelais's *Gargantua and Pantagruel* is a rambling compendium of scurrilous humor.

If catching a play at the Comédie Française is a priority on your trip, consider reading a few of the plays in the classic repertoire. Pierre Corneille turned to Spanish history and literature for *Le Cid,* while Jean Racine reconsidered a plot from Greek mythology in his *Phèdre* (*Phaedra*), a verse tragedy dealing with a queen's forbidden love for her stepson. Molière's comedies include *Tartuffe,* the story of a hypocrite who lies his way into a gullible household; *Le Malade Imaginaire* (*The Imaginary Invalid*); and *Le Misanthrope.* They ridicule society, especially the medical profession and the *nouveaux riches. The Comédie-Française* in Paris still stages excellent productions of these classics. For a vivid portrayal of everyday life at the time, read Mme. de Sévignés *Lettres,* which comment on everything from kitchen recipes to palace intrigues. Mme. de La Fayette's *La Princesse de Clèves* broke ground for the genre of the psychological novel. It examines a married woman's *amour-passion* for a man who is not her husband, a perennial theme of French literature and film. Choderlos de Laclos's *Les Liaisons Dangereuses* is an epistolary novel in which a complex network of letters sustains and finally undoes a complex network of seductions.

The novels of nineteenth-century France are well-known. Victor Hugo's *Notre-Dame de Paris* (freely translated as *The Hunchback of Notre Dame*) is a must for those who like historical novels. Parisian life and the customs of the provinces are carefully dissected in Honoré de Balzac's *La Comédie humaine* (*The Human Comedy*), a series of some 90 novels which give an overview of all classes of contemporary French society. Henri Beyle, known as Stendhal, wrote *Le Rouge et le Noir* (*The Red and the Black*), the story of a passionate young man torn between love and ambition. Gustave Flaubert's *Madame Bovary* presents Emma, a doctor's wife literally dying of boredom in a small town in Normandy. Alphonse Daudet's *Lettres de mon moulin,* fictional letters written from a windmill-home in Provence, are filled with Provençal folklore.

If you like poetry that keeps you daydreaming and hallucinating, you may enjoy Gérard de Nerval. Geoffrey Wagner's *Selected Writings of Gérard de Nerval* is a decent translation of the works of Crazy Gérard, who eventually hanged himself.

Perhaps, as Baudelaire did, you lust for the the New and wish to be "Anywhere out of the world"; unlike you, Baudelaire remained ensconced at home (in Paris) penning such volumes of poetry as *Les Fleurs du mal* (*Flowers of Evil*) and *Petits poèmes en prose.*

Marcel Proust's *A la recherche du temps perdu* (*Remembrance of Things Past*), in several volumes and many, many pages, is a masterly evocation of upper-class life during the *belle époque,* though its deeper subject is the experience of time and memory, and an exploration of narrative methods for rendering them. Each of the volumes is self-contained, and *Du côté de chez Swann* (*Swann's Way*) is often read alone. Colette wrote on love with vitality, and her novels offer a woman's perspective (at times through a masculine character) of the sexual politics of her time; among her best known are *Cheri, La Vagabonde,* and *La Chatte.*

Those traveling in the Midi may wish to savor the autobiographical, fictional, and dramatic works of Marcel Pagnol, whose works *Jean de Florette* and *Manon des Sources* have recently been remade into films. Pagnol captures the whimsy and pathos of life in his native Provence at the turn of the century.

Less depressing than his novel *la Nausée* (*Nausea*), Jean-Paul Sartre's *Les Mots* (*The Words*) is a meticulously written account of his childhood. Simone de Beauvoir's *Mémoires d'une jeune fille rangée* (*Memoirs of a Dutiful Daughter*) deals with her upbringing in a narrowly bourgeois family whose values she rejects. New volumes of her autobiography keep appearing in English translation. In the novel *Les Mandarins,* Beauvoir writes of the temporary bewilderment of Parisian intellectuals after World War II. For lighter fare, you may want to flip through Raymond Queneau's fanciful novel *Zazie dans le métro;* precocious Zazie drives her Uncle Gabriel up the Eiffel Tower. Those of you traveling through Nevers on your way to Japan may enjoy one of Marguerite Duras's screenplays which was made into a film by Alain Renais; *Hiroshima Mon Amour* deals with the difficulties of communication between a man and a woman and the atrocities of World War II. Violette Leduc's classic novel *Thérèse et Isabelle* gives the reader a taste of what it might be like to be a lesbian in the French secondary school system.

The Visual Arts

Architecture

The most ubiquitous building in all of France is the church, the earliest of which date from the first few centuries of the second millenium, when building churches became a national obsession. Stylistically, churches fall into two main categories—the Romanesque and the Gothic.

The round arches and blunt, heavy walls of **Romanesque** churches resemble ancient Roman fortifications and developed from the remnants of Carolingian culture. During the Carolingian Renaissance, builders rediscovered Roman construction techniques and turned to fire-proof stone instead of wood. The need for solid masonry becomes evident in the square-ish, massive walls of Romanesque architecture. The **Basilique St-Sernin** in Toulouse exemplifies the extreme regularity and grand-scale precision of this architectural style. The church maps out an emphatic Latin Cross designed to accommodate large crowds of worshippers. The vaulted nave both averts the danger of fire and adds grandeur. But while St-Sernin's thick walls and barrel vaults provided ample space, they did not let in much light—a central problem in Romanesque architecture.

The second half of the twelfth century witnessed the decline of the Romanesque and the rise of the **Gothic.** Like Romanesque art, early Gothic style is feudal, founded on the ideal of the paternal baron as a staunch defender of Christianity. In Gothic art, however, this ideal has been softened. At the time, popular culture celebrated chivalric love rather than courageous deeds, and the cult of the Virgin Mary gave rise to an image of faith as mystical and intuitive. Architecture reflected this theology, stressing a purity of form conducive to meditation.

The main difference between Gothic and Romanesque architecture lies in the way the arches of the church support the roof. While the barrel-vaulted roofs in Romanesque structures rest on fortified pillars, Gothic structures utilize a system of arches that distribute weight outward rather than down. Flying buttresses counterbalancing the pressure of the ribbed-vaulting relieve the walls of the roof's weight, allowing for the installation of more windows. As a result, Gothic churches are taller and brighter than their predecessors.

The rebuilt **Church of St-Denis** in Ile-de-France is one of the earliest examples of Gothic style. The dimensions of this structure were dictated by an older church, but its circular string of chapels, luminous glass, and ribbed vaults proclaimed a new era. The windows here were enlarged from mere holes cut in thick walls to translucent walls in themselves. The outward pressure of the vaults is absorbed by heavy buttresses jutting out between chapels, so the bulk of the masonry is visible only from the outside. The interior remains airy and weightless. Other notable cathedrals are Amiens Cathédrale, Nôtre Dame de Paris, Nôtre Dame de Chartres, and Nôtre Dame de Reims.

The Italian Renaissance was slow to reach France, for French architects were reluctant to accept the cold intellectualism of the Florentine Quattrocento. In northern Italy (particularly Venice), however, the French found a style they could admire. Delegates of François I took home the profuse ornamentation and colored marbles of Milanese decoration and proceeded to blend these features with Gothic forms. Under the patronage of arts lover François, the wealthy built châteaux in the Loire Valley combining Italian ideas and medieval traditions in an enthusiastic hybrid. Notable are the châteaux at Chenonceau, Azay-le-Rideau, and Chambord (François I's country home).

In the latter half of the sixteenth century, royal palaces in the Ile de France took precedence over the luxurious châteaux of the Loire. In 1528 François I hired Italian artists to improve the original hunting lodge of **Fontainebleau.** The resulting Renaissance palace shows few traces of its medieval origins, and its great simplicity heralds the classicism of the next generation.

Painting

The Salon des Refusés was the first showing by a group of artists later collected under the rubric **"impressionism."** Once vilified innovators, the impressionists have become the most successful of bourgeois art movements. In various ways they began the dissolution of representational painting inherited from the Renaissance. They concerned themselves with the appearance of a scene at the instance of its observation, and paid special regard to light and shadow.

You'll have plenty of opportunity to see impressionist work in France. In Paris the impressionists are honored in a museum devoted to their work, the **Orsay Museum. Le Musée Rodin,** also in Paris, houses Rodin's sculptures, which, because of his emphasis on the effects of light on both the rough and polished surfaces of bronze, are sometimes linked to the work of the impressionists. Claude Monet's lily ponds, the subject of his final works, can be seen near his home at Giverny outside of Paris.

The impressionists are best understood in the context of the art that came before them. After the extravagance of the Baroque and the Rococo of the sixteenth and seventeenth centuries, a new style of art rose to prominence in the French Revolution—**neoclassicism.** Caught up in in the dawn of an empire, French culture turned to ancient Rome for inspiration. The official style of the Napoleonic era was neoclassical; the chief court painter and dominant propagandist was Jacques-Louis David (1748-1825). In David's patriotic *The Oath of the Horatii,* sons in antique costume swear allegiance to their country. In the same dignified epic style, David painted the coronation of Napoleon.

Jean-Auguste-Dominique Ingres (1780-1867), David's student, bridges the transition from neoclassicism to nineteenth-century **Romanticism.** While maintaining the emphasis on purity of outline and form, Ingres dresses his subjects in opulent materials, drawing attention to the sensual surface of his paintings. The Romantics who followed relied on vivid color and expressive brush strokes to create a similarly intense visual experience. Exemplified by artists like Théodore Géricault (1791-1824) and Eugène Delacroix (1798-1863), the Romantics reacted against the austerity of the Neoclassical movement. They asserted the right of individual sensibility over traditional rules. Delacroix's dramatic *Liberty on the Barricades* is an emotional and triumphant scene of revolution. In Géricault's *Raft of the Medusa,* the starving survivors of a shipwreck are given the muscular contours of Greek athletes and suffering is rendered majestic.

The mid-nineteenth-century **Barbizon school** turned from human figures to the sublime in nature. Jean-Baptiste-Camille Corot (1796-1875) and Théodore Rousseau (1812-1867) depicted landscape and rural subjects from direct observation. Their attention to light and atmosphere produces in their work a blithely idyllic feeling. These painters were realists by philosophy, but at times their sentiment overshadowed realistic technique; scenes appear to be remembered or dreamed, felt rather than seen.

The next generation of painters worked as **realists** in earnest. Gustave Courbet (1819-1877), Jean Millet (1814-1875), and Honoré Daumier (1808-1879) came forward as exponents of this style. They occupied themselves with presenting not only the heroic, but also the humble aspects of life.

You can view representative works of the neoclassicists, romantics, realists, impressionists, and post-impressionists at the **Louvre,** and city museums all over France showcase individual artists: the **Musée Picasso** in Antibes, the **Musée Matisse** and **Musée Marc Chagall** in Nice, for example.

For more background, consult H.W. Janson's *History of Art.* As an antidote to its scant attention to twentieth-century artists such as Rousseau, Gaugin, Matisse, Picasso, Léger and Braque, consult G. H. Hamilton's *Painting and Sculpture in Europe 1880-1940.*

In the early 1950s, after the devastation of Europe in WWII, the center of the art world (production, theory, and market) shifted decisively for the first time from Paris to New York. From abstract expressionism through pop, minimalism, conceptualism, and the other arcana of the '70s, American artists arose as leaders. While involvement in the contemporary scene still means contending with New York, there is now a digging into European tradition that bypasses recent American trends. While they once exhibited American work almost exclusively, Parisian galleries are once again showing French artists. Travelers interested in the current scene should visit not only the museums, but the galleries of Paris, especially the newer establishments near the Bastille and those in the chic Beaubourg area.

The new Parisian dynamism in painting, and its peculiarly complex relation to American art, is symbolized by the vogue for that most American of popular art forms, graffiti, for which there is no indigenous Gallic tradition. "IN PARIS LET'S GO NEW ART," shouted huge spray-painted letters in 1985 on a wall across from the Louvre (no reference to certain U.S. travel guides). The garish cartoons express both an acknowledgment of American fashion and a desire to transform it into something distinctively French.

Food

The French will only be united under the threat of danger. No one can simply bring together a country that has two hundred and sixty-five kinds of cheese.
—*Charles de Gaulle, 1951*

De Gaulle may have been wrong in his statistics (there exist over 400 kinds of cheese in France), but he understood the two most salient features of French cuisine: its variety and the seriousness with which it is taken. French cuisine involves not one tradition but many. The aristocratic tradition of extreme richness and elaborate presentation known as *haute cuisine,* originated in the 12-hour feasts indulged in by Louis XIV at Versailles, and is preserved today in a few expensive restaurants such as the Tour d'Argent in Paris. In their work and their writings, great nineteenth-century chefs such as Escoffier treated fine food as an essential art of civilized life. To learn something of the skills involved, leaf through the *Larousse Gastronomique,* a standard reference for chefs first compiled in the nineteenth century. A less elitist style of French cooking, and the one most familiar to Americans because of its successful popularization by Julia Child, is the *cuisine bourgeoise,* high quality French home-cooking. A glance through her books, *Mastering the Art of French Cooking I & II,* should give you a meter-long list of dishes to try while in France.

Both *haute cuisine* and *cuisine bourgeoise* rely heavily on the *cuisine des provinces* (provincial cooking, also called *cuisine campagnarde*) adapting hearty peasant dishes to their refined methods. All styles share the qualities of richness and freshness of ingredients. The richness results from butter, the chief cooking ingredient; the freshness is made possible by the ideal climate and efficient inland transport that makes France virtually self-sufficient in food production.

In the last few years a group of younger chefs, have invented *cuisine maigreure* (lean cooking), which, despite its simple presentation, has become chic and expensive, reaching such heights of over-refinement as desserts topped with a single blueberry. Food is a serious pleasure not just for professionals but for most French, who make the effort to create fine meals and take the time to enjoy them. Most families shop daily, and the idea of eating meals from bottles and cans raises a pitying eyebrow.

The French breakfast (*petit déjeuner*) is usually light, consisting of bread (*pain* and sometimes *croissants* or *brioches*—buttery breads almost like pastries) and *café au lait* (espresso with hot milk) or hot chocolate (*chocolat*). Many people still eat the largest meal of the day (*déjeuner*) between noon and 2pm, and most shops and businesses close for two hours at this time. Dinner (*dîner*) begins quite late and is also a meal to linger over.

Many restaurants offer a *menu à prix fixe* (fixed price meal), that costs less than ordering *à la carte,* and includes appetizer or soup, an *entrée* such as *pâté, crudités* (raw vegetables), or *jambon* (ham), a main course (*plat principal*), and dessert and/or *fromage* (cheese). Americans are usually disappointed with steak in France (*steak* or *bifteck*), which is not a French specialty, though other beef dishes such as *boeuf en daube* (braised beef) are. Chicken (*poulet*), duck (*canard*), veal (*veau*), lamb (*agneau*), and pork (*porc*) are generally the best-prepared meats.

When a salad is served, it usually follows the *plat,* to clear the palate for dessert, and generally consists of lettuce with a mustard vinaigrette. Finish the meal with espresso, which comes in lethal little cups. Look for *service compris* (service included) so you won't be surprised when you get the check (*l'addition*). Otherwise you should tip 15%.

Food should be among your budget priorities while in France. For an occasional US$10 spree you can have a marvelous meal; for US$15, an unforgettable experience. You needn't pay dearly to eat well, however: It's easy to find satisfying dinners for under 45F. An even better idea is to assemble inexpensive meals yourself with staples such as cheese, wine, and bread. The government controls the prices of bread, so you can afford to indulge with every meal, as do the French.

Since the French food industry has not conglomerated you will need to run from one specialty shop to the next to assemble a picnic (though you can often find all of the following shops in an outdoor market, or *marché*). A *charcuterie,* the French version of the delicatessen, offers cooked meats, *pâtés,* and sausages (such as *saucisson,* a dry salami). You can also find delicious prepared dishes here, though these sometimes cost as much as restaurant fare. *Crémeries* sell dairy products, and a street-corner *crémerie* will stock over 100 kinds of cheese. A *boulangerie* sells breads, including the *baguette,* the long, crisp, archetypal French loaf, and the round, soft, whole-wheat *pain de campagne,* along with pastries. A *pâtisserie* offers pastry and candy, and a *confiserie* stocks candy and ice cream. You can buy your fruits and vegetables at a *primeur.* For the adventurous, a *boucherie chevaline* sells horse-meat (look for the gilded horse-head over the door); the timid can stick to steaks and roasts from a regular *boucherie*. You can buy any amount of these foods; 100g of any given delicacy should be enough for one person.

You can also try a *supermarché*, American-style. Look for the small foodstore chains such as **Monoprix, Prisunic,** and **Félix Potin,** where prices are lower than most. *Epiceries* (grocery stores) also carry staples, wine, produce, and a bit of everything else. But the open-air markets, held at least once a week in every town and village, remain the best places to buy fresh fruit, vegetables, fish, and meat. Prices here are usually low, as there may be a half a dozen fruit-sellers trying to outdeal one another.

Each region has its specialties. Eat *Camembert, Pont L'Evêque,* and *Chèvre* cheeses, drink cider, and sample seafood in Brittany. *Crêpes* were first folded in Brittany, and are a real bargain there and elsewhere in France. Wine-based dishes are best in Burgundy (home of *boeuf bourguignon*), as are *escargots* (snails) and *grenouilles* (frogs). Look for local *pâtés* in Dordogne, and head for Alsace-Lorraine for heavier German foods. Provence offers excellent vegetable dishes such as *ratatouille* and dishes made with the pungent basil and garlic sauce called *pistou*, as well as seafood specialties such as *bouillabaisse,* a saffron-flavored fish stew. A Spanish menu prevails in the southwest and includes *cassoulet* and *paëlla,* while Alpine cuisine makes use of local cheese in its *raclette* and *fondue.*

Cafes in France, as in most of southern Europe, embrace a pleasant part of daily routine. The price of a cup of coffee gives you leave to sit and rest, converse, write, and read. When choosing a cafe, remember that you pay for its location. Those on a major boulevard can be much more expensive than smaller establishments a few steps down a side street. If you're simply thirsty, order your drink at the bar inside (the *comptoir*; the seating area is the *salle*)—prices are much cheaper. Coffee, beer, *Pernod* (a licorice-flavored cordial often served with mineral water or orange juice) and the anise-flavored *pastis* in the south, are the staple drinks; *citron pressé* (lemonade—*limonade* is a soda) and *diabolo menthe* (peppermint soda) are popular nonalcoholic choices. Cafes also offer Coke, but be prepared to pay twice what you would in the U.S. Coffee is almost always espresso; *à la créme* or *au lait* can be ordered large or small. If you order a *demi* or a *pression* of beer (same thing—the only size), you'll get a pale lager on tap (often Kronenburg or 33 Export). You can also order bottled imported beer: Heineken is popular in Paris, and Pelforth, a dark beer, in the south. A glass of red is the cheapest wine in a cafe (4-6F), with white costing about twice as much; southerners prefer rosé to white. Tips expected in cafes are small—usually only a few francs.

Cafes are not suited to cheap eating. A *croque monsieur* (grilled ham-and-cheese sandwich), a *croque madame* (the same with a fried egg), and assorted omelettes cost about 15F and rarely make a filling meal. Only occasionally is the food good and reasonably priced. Since the menu is always posted outside, check before you go in. You should avoid many places billed as *brasseries*—they often specialize in tough, minimal portions of steak or unspectacular chicken with fries.

Wine

The character and quality of a wine depend upon the climate, soil, and variety of grape from which it is made. Long, hot, and fairly dry summers with cool, humid nights create the ideal climate. Soil is so much a determining factor that identical grapes planted in different regions yield very different wines. **White wines** are produced by the fermentation of white grapes; **rosés** from the white-wine-style vinification of black grapes; and **reds** by the fermentation of the juice, skins, and sometimes stems of black grapes.

The major wine-producing regions are distributed throughout the country. The Loire Valley produces a number of whites, with the major vineyards at Angers, Anjou, Touraine, Tours, and, farther inland, Pouilly Sancerre and Quincy Reuilly. Cognac, farther south on the Atlantic coast, is famous for the double-distilled and blended spirit of the same name. Bordeaux, centered on the Dordogne and Garonne rivers, produces both the reds and whites of Médoc, Graves, and the sweet Sauternes. Côtes de Duras near Bergerac is also a Bordeaux. Armagnac, similar to Cognac, comes from Gascony (in the area around Auch), while Jurançon wines come from vineyards around Pau higher up the slopes of the Pyrenees. Southern wines include those of Languedoc and Roussillon on the coast, and Limoux and Gaillac inland. The vineyards of Provence on the coast near Toulon are famous for their rosés. The Côtes du Rhône from Valence to Avignon in the Rhône Valley are home to some of the densest viticulture and the most celebrated wines of France—red, white, and rosé. Burgundy is famous for both whites and reds, from the wines of Chablis and the Côte d'Or in the north of the region, to the Mônnais and Beaujolais in the south. There are also vineyards in the Jura and in Alsace. The *caves* (cellars) of Champagne centered at Reims on the Marne have bubbled merrily for centuries, and Normandy produces Calvados, an apple brandy distilled from cider in the area near Caen.

Since 1935, when France passed the first comprehensive wine legislation, the Appellation d'Origine Controlée (AOC or "controlled place of origin" laws), regulations have ensured the quality and upheld the fine reputation of French wines. All wines are categorized according to place of origin, alcohol content, and wine-making practices, and only about 16% of French wines are deemed worthy of the top classification. In general, the smaller the area controlling the appellation, the better the wine. Other categories include *Vins Délimités de Qualité Supérieure* (VDQS or "restricted wines of superior quality") and *Vins de Pays* (country wines), which each have restrictions on growing factors.

One way to discriminate among the bewildering range of wines in France is to examine the varieties of grapes that go into their production. All true Burgundies are made from only *Pinot Noir* grapes, while Bordeaux wines come from different mixtures of four varieties of grape, with *Cabernet-sauvignon* as the dominant variety. Whites are usually made from *Chardonnay* or *Chenin Blanc* grapes.

When shopping for a fairly expensive wine, study the label carefully. The majority of wines are matured by shippers who buy young wines from the growers and mix them to achieve the desired blend. In general, the label will indicate a product's region, but not its specific grower. Look for the term *mis en bouteille au domaine* (or *au château*) to ensure the wine was estate-bottled.

Wherever you go, drink the local wines. In wine country like Burgundy or Champagne, small local winemakers sell their product from *caves*—sometimes literally caves—and offer *dégustations* (tastings) to those who take the tour of their establishments. These brands tend to be cheaper, and often enjoy little fame only because they do not travel well. In many regions of France, you can fill a bottle from the kegs of wine in *épiceries* and *supermarchés*. These local wines are often both very cheap and of fine quality. Labels have little meaning for ordinary French table wines (*vins de table*), which are often artificially matured and adulterated with sugar and colorings. The real mongrels, such as *beaujolais villages* (blends of various bottlers' leftovers) or those made from the grapes of "various Common Market countries," can cost as little as 6F per bottle and give you memorable headaches. You can do much better, however, by seeking out a decent little regional vintage for around 24F to quaff with your *baguette* and *brie*.

Climate

The following information is drawn from the International Association for Medical Assistance to Travelers (IAMAT)'s *World Climate Charts*. In each monthly listing, the first two numbers are the average daily maximum and minimum temperatures in degrees Celsius; the numbers in parentheses represent the same data in degrees Fahrenheit. The lower numbers indicate the mean relative humidity percentage, and the average number of days with a measurable amount of precipitation per month.

	Jan.		April		July		Oct.	
Bastia	11/6	(52/42)	18/11	(65/52)	28/19	(82/60)	20/11	(68/52)
	69%	8	73%	7	65%	1	72%	9
Bordeaux	9/2	(48/36)	17/6	(63/43)	25/14	(77/57)	18/8	(64/46)
	87%	16	76%	13	76%	11	84%	14
Boulogne-sur-Mer	6/2	(43/36)	12/6	(54/43)	2 0/14	(68/57)	14/10	(57/50)
	87%	18	79%	14	83%	12	83%	14
Brest	9/4	(48/39)	13/6	(55/43)	19/12	(66/54)	15/9	(59/48)
	86%	22	82%	15	85%	14	85%	19
Lourdes	10/1	(50/33)	17/6	(63/42)	25/14	(77/57)	18/8	(65/46)
	84%	9	76%	8	80%	7	86%	9
Lyon	5/-1	(41/30)	16/6	(61/43)	27/15	(81/59)	16/7	(61/45)
	85%	15	70%	11	65%	10	81%	12
Nantes	8/2	(46/36)	15/6	(59/43)	24/14	(75/57)	16/8	(61/46)
	89%	18	77%	12	77%	13	85%	15
Nice	13/4	(55/39)	17/9	(63/48)	27/18	(81/64)	21/12	(70/54)
	68%	9	75%	9	72%	2	72%	9
Paris	6/1	(43/34)	16/6	(61/43)	25/15	(77/59)	16/8	(61/46)
	84%	17	68%	13	70%	12	81%	13
Strasbourg	3/-2	(37/28)	16/5	(61/41)	25/13	(77/55)	14/6	(57/43)
	84%	15	71%	13	71%	14	83%	12

Festivals and Sports

France blossoms with festivals throughout the year. In summer, almost every town celebrates a local *fête* that may include carnivals, markets, and folk dancing. The Cannes Film Festival, the Nice Jazz Parade, the Avignon Drama Festival, and the festivities in Aix-en-Provence occur in May, June, July, and August, respectively. In addition, there are at least a hundred smaller music festivals every year, as well as other events that combine music with dance or drama, such as the Paris Festival du Marais from mid-June to early July.

For a comprehensive listing by region of all festivals (music, dance, film, jazz, folklore, puppetry, *son et lumière,* theater, and literature) write for the catalog *Nouvelles de France,* available from the Ministère du Commerce, de l'Artisanat et du Tourisme, Direction du Tourisme, 17, rue de l'Ingénieur-Keller, 75740 Paris (tel. 45-75-62-16). The detailed catalog publishes a special summer issue in March (actually covering March-Nov.). The same ministry publishes *France in a holiday mood,* a highly condensed version of the catalog in English. For a list of music festivals, write to the French Tourist Office (see Useful Organizations above) and request *France Festivals '88;* for every other kind of festival, request *La France en fête 1989* from the European Association of Music Festivals, 122, rue de Lausanne, 1211 Geneva 21, Switzerland (tel. 22-32-28-03), for a booklet listing the dates and programs of major European music, dance, and theater festivals. In Paris, **AlloConcerts** maintains a 24-hour hotline in French that provides information on free open-air concerts in the parks (tel. 42-76-50-00). **FNAC,** the Fédération Nationale d'Achat des Cadres, is the main agency for buying tickets to anything in Paris. Their main office is at 136, rue de Rennes, 75006 Paris (tel. 45-44-39-12; Mo. Montparnasse-Bienvenue).

Try to be somewhere special for **Bastille Day** on July 14 (when the French celebrate the founding of the First Republic)—it's the one day each year when Parisians indulge in berserk but mainly harmless pyromania. May 1, **La Fête du Travail** (French Labor Day), marks a socialist celebration all over the country. For **Jeanne d'Arc Day** (the 2nd Sun. in May), Orléans has a commemorative celebration. The **Feux de St-Jean** is a rural holiday combining John the Baptist's Day (June 24) with the ancient Celtic summer solstice observance; bonfires are lit throughout the countryside. Brittany has become famous for its *pardons*—festivals held to honor a parish's patron saint.

The French are crazy about tennis (the French Open is in early June), skiing, sailing, windsurfing, and many other sports. The whole populace cheers on the rugby and soccer teams, among the world's best. Le Mans is a 24-hour car race on the second weekend of June, and the Tour de France, a three-week bicycle race in July traversing most of France. Check the itinerary to see if the participants will cycle past one of your stopovers.

Business Hours and Holidays

Banks, museums, and other public buildings close on the following public holidays: January 1, Easter Monday, May 1 (Labor Day), May 8, Ascension Day (a Thurs. 40 days after Easter), Whit Monday, July 14 (Bastille Day), August 15 (Assumption Day), November 11 (Armistice Day), and December 25. When a holiday falls on a Tuesday or Thursday, the French often take Monday or Friday off also (called *faire le pont*—to make a bridge). Note that banks close at noon on the day, or the nearest working day before, a public holiday.

Also keep in mind that most food stores close on Monday, though they remain open on Sunday mornings. Smaller stores (including groceries, shops, and even some banks) often close between noon and 2pm for lunch. Some stores and smaller businesses also close for a few weeks in July or August; they will post on their doors the names of similar stores open in the area. Almost all museums close on Tuesday.

Weights and Measures

> 1 kilogram (kg) = 2.2 pounds
> 1 meter (m) = 1.09 yards
> 1 kilometer (km) = about 5/8 mile
> 1 liter = 1.76 pints

Paris

Paris change! mais rien dans ma mélancolie
N'a bougé! palais neufs, échafaudages, blocs,
Vieux faubourgs, tout pour moi devient allégorie,
Et mes chers souvenirs sont plus lourds que des rocs.

Paris is changing! But nothing in my gloom has budged! New places, scaffold-
ing, blocks, old neighborhoods, everything becomes allegory for me, and my
precious memories are heavier than rocks.
                                        —Charles Baudelaire, Fleurs du Mal

Paris is a metaphor, a shrine, or a fantasy before it is anything so mundane as the hometown of three million people. Aside from the Seine, its heartbreaking beauty is entirely artificial, composed of monuments to the human desires to improve, please, and transcend.

Originally home of the Parisii on the Seine, the city was named Lutèce by Roman conquerors in 52 B.C.E. In 987, when Hugh Capet, count of Paris, became king of France, he inaugurated Paris as his capital, thus bringing prestige to the city that would grow in future centuries. King Phillipe Auguste (1180-1223) consolidated the crown's possessions and confirmed the basic segregation of functions that still characterizes the city: political and ecclesiastical authority on the Ile de la Cité, academic life on the Left Bank, and commerce on the Right Bank. The city plan reflects urban growth outward in three concentric ovals, marked by the *grands boulevards* encircling central Paris, the *boulevards exterieurs,* and the *boulevards périphériques,* corresponding to fortifications built in the fourteenth, eighteenth, and twentieth centuries.

Certainly there are slums in Paris, and many people find life hard here. But the city's facilities and physical layout embody the idea of a collection of individuals: Great spaces like place de la Concorde and the Arc de Triomphe glorify the idea of a public while innumerable alleys and courtyards preserve privacy. The huge city quickly becomes manageable for the visitor since each quarter, taken separately, is small with easily identified boundaries and points of reference. In addition, a superb transit system moves millions of Parisians of all classes safely and efficiently: It is said that no point in the city is more than five minutes' walk from a Métro station.

Parisians have learned that courtesy is the key to keeping life civilized. Behind closed doors, however, they believe in their right to think and do what they want. Discontent lurks beneath the beautiful facade, manifested by the graffiti on the subway and the swastikas adorning building walls.

But Paris seems to swallow extremes. Paris saw the first mass revolution in 1789, and has since witnessed many violent changes of regime: two empires, a monarchy, four republics, and two military occupations, not to mention the furious civil riots of 1968 and the more recent student protests of 1986 and 1987. Yet life always goes on, Parisians ultimately behave as they please, and the complacent observe from the cafés.

Intellectual and cultural life has always flourished here. From Villon to Curie to Cocteau to Kristeva, the number of Parisians whose ideas have influenced minds throughout the world is too large to count. And the number of foreigners who have left their mark here in turn is just as large. For Paris is also the capital of the exile, refugee, rabble-rouser, scholar, aristocrat, artist, and eccentric. At the beginning of this century, for example, the greatest Parisian artists, Picasso, Chagall, and Brancusi, were not French. Between the world wars, American "lost generation" writers helped fix Paris's reputation for modernity in the international imagination. The post-war period brought the city into the political spotlight as an asylum for

Paris

1 Accueil Central de France
   127 Champs Elysées
2 Transalpino: 16, rue La Fayette
3 American Express
4 Post Office

5   Sainte Chapelle and Palais de Justice
6   Notre Dame
7   Place des Vosges
8   Musée Carnavalet
9   Centre National d'Art et Culture
    Georges Pompidou
10 Musée and Palais de Louvre
11 Palais Royal
12 Comedie Française
13 Place Vendôme
14 Musée du Jeu de Paume
15 Orangerie
16 Petit Palais
17 Grand Palais
18 Opéra

19 Musée Rodin
20 Les Invalides
21 St-Germain-des-Prés
22 St-Severin
23 Musée de Cluny
24 Sorbonne
25 Pantheos
26 Palais du Luxembourg
27 Cité Internationale de l'Université de Paris
28 Sacré-Coeur
29 Tour Eiffel

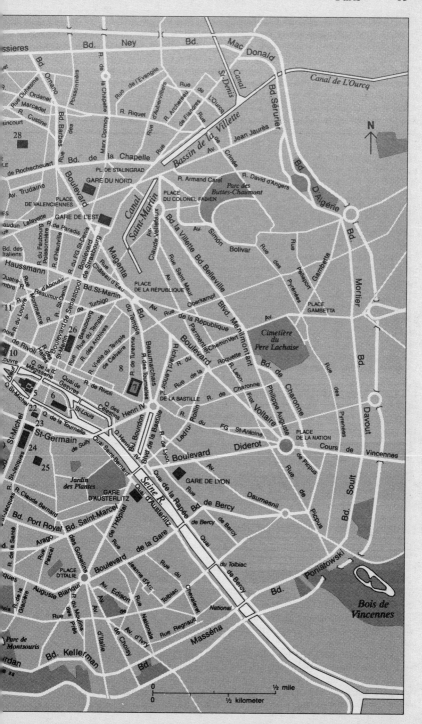

N

Bd.   Ney   Bd.   Mac   Donald

ssieres

Bd. Omano   Canal   Canal de L'Ourcq
R. des Poissonniers   St-Denis   Bd. Sérunier

Rue Duhesme   Rue de l'Evangile
Ordener   Rue de la Chapelle   Rue
Marcadet   R. d'Aubervilliers   Bd. D'Algérie
incourt   Custine   R. Riquet   Rue d'Armentes   Rue de Crimée
28   R. Barbès   Rue des Flandres   Av. Crimée   Jean Jaurès
Bd. de la Chapelle   Bassin de la Villette   R. David d'Angers
de Rochechouart   PL. DE STALINGRAD   R. Armand Carel
Av. Trudaine   GARE DU NORD   PLACE   Parc des
PLACE   Canal   DU COLONEL FABIEN   Buttes-Chaumont
DE VALENCIENNES   Saint-Martin   Bd. la Villette   Av. Simon   Bolivar
audun   GARE DE L'EST   Magenta   Rue   Bd. Belleville   des
Lafayette   Rue de Paradis   Av. Claude Vellefaux
R. du Faubourg   R. d'Hauteville   Rue Saint Maur   Gambetta
Bd. des   Poissonnière   Morlier
Italiens   Boulevard   PLACE   Pesson
Haussmann   Rue de Strasbourg   DE LA RÉPUBLIQUE   Rue   des
Quatre   R. d'Aboukir   Oberkampf   Pyrenées   PLACE
embre 4   R. Beaumur   Bd. St-Martin   Av.   Rue de la République   GAMBETTA
11   R. du Louvre   Turbigo   Bivd Ménilmontant
4   R. Montmartre   R. St-Martin   Parmentis   Chemin Vert   Cimetière
26   R. du Temple   Boulevard   du
nord   R. de Rivoli   R. Beaubourg   R. Vieille du Temple   Roquette   Père Lachaise
10   Q. de la M.   de Calvaire   Richard Lenoir   R. Léon
ouvre   Mégisserie   8   R. de Turenne   Beaumarchais   Charonne   Rue
5   Q. de Gesvres   R. de Rivoli   Q. des Célestins   PL.   R. de   Bd. de Charonne
6   Henri IV   DE LA BASTILLE   Philippe Auguste   des
St-Michel   St-Louis   Q. Henri IV   Rue   Voltaire
22   Q. de la Tournelle   Bourdon   Ledru Rollin   FG   St-Antoine   PLACE   Davout
23   St-Germain   Blvd de la Bastille   du   DE LA NATION
St-Jacques   de Sully   Q. Henri IV   Diderot   Cours   de
24   Quai Saint-Bernard   Boulevard   Vincennes
25   Jardin   Seine R.   GARE DE LYON   de Picpus
des Plantes   GARE   Qua de la Rapée   Rue   Bd.
R. Claude Bernard   D'AUSTERLITZ   Qual d'Austerlitz   Bd. de Bercy   de Picpus
Bd. Port Royal   Bd. Saint-Marcel   de Bercy   Daumesnil   Soult
Arago   des Gobelins   Qual   du Tolbiac   Bd.
de la Gare   du Bercy   Poniatowski
ques   Boulevard   Rue   du
PLACE   Jeanne d'Arc   Chevaleret   National   Bois de
D'ITALIE   Av. Edison   Tolbiac   Vincennes
Auguste Blanqui   de   Rue   Rue Regnault
Rue   Nationale   Masséna
Glacière   d'Italie   Av. d'Ivry
Parc de   de Choisy
Montsouris   Bd. Kellerman   Bd.
rdan

0   ½ mile
0   ½ kilometer

Ho Chi Minh, Khomeini, and East European emigrés such as authors Abram Tertz (Andrei Sinyavsky) and Milan Kundera. The flow of political refugees continued in the late 1970s with the arrival of Latin American emigrés; Chileans, in particular, including director Raul Ruiz.

Paris once presided over a domain embracing Algiers, Saigon, and Port-au-Prince, and has been adopted by many former subjects. Its universities and art and music institutes draw students from the world over. Witness the variety of North African and Caribbean restaurants, *pâtisseries,* markets, houses of worship, and neighborhoods (especially in the 10th, 19th, and 20th *arrondissements*), which recall Middle Eastern cities. In the last decade, the city has experienced an influx of Vietnamese and Chinese immigrants, and interest in Asian culture and cuisine is strong. However, the popular candidacy of Jacques Le Pen—proponent of expelling all immigrants and their offspring—and rumors of Arab, African, and Jewish conspiracy suggest that overt and covert racism still linger. A suspicion of outsiders continues—police may, at any time, ask for your identification and search your bags. Organizations such as SOS Racisme, however, work to alleviate the ignorance that economic discontent exacerbates.

Both Parisians and denizens of small communities agree, in whatever order they may put it, that there's Paris, and then there are the provinces. Province and capital are especially segmented in France due to the policies of a government that often ignored the welfare of the rest of the country. Although decentralization has been the trend since the war, Paris still monopolizes one quarter of France's manufacturing sector, and the bulk of the country's luxury and service trades.

Indeed, Parisians show little interest in improving their image in the rest of France or even the world. You, as an outsider ignorant of dress, manners, language, and history, can be made to feel like an alien from a different planet. Try to understand their position: Every summer, tourists more than double the city's population—most monoglot anglophones. It's easy to see why Parisians can feel overwhelmed by this recurrent invasion. Try to speak a little French—if you struggle a bit, your efforts will be all the more appreciated. And dress appropriately. Take the locals' lead: Avoid short shorts and other skimpy or loud sportswear, especially in houses of worship and restaurants.

In the spirit of its tolerance, forgive the Parisians' frequent pettiness and accept the city's great generosity. In you, as in millions of visitors, something of the city will strike an unforgettable chord.

Practical Information

Note: In Paris addresses "Mo." indicates the nearest Métro stop.

Getting Into and Out of Paris

By Air

Most transatlantic flights land at the Roissy-Charles de Gaulle Airport (tel. 48-62-22-80 or 48-62-12-12), 23km northeast of Paris. Charters usually fly into Orly Sud Airport (tel. 48-84-32-10), about 12km south, except during the airport's curfew hours, when they are diverted to Roissy. Paris's third airport, Le Bourget (tel. 48-62-22-80) handles only private flights within France. Signs in all three airports warn that packages or luggage left unattended may be destroyed by the police for fear of bombs.

The cheapest and fastest way to get into the city from **Roissy-Charles de Gaulle** is the **Roissy Rail** (tel. 42-61-50-50) bus-train combination to the Gare du Nord, Châtelet, St-Michel, and Luxembourg Métro stops. Take the free shuttle bus from Aérogare 1 arrival level gate 30, Aérogare 2A gate A5, or Aérogare 2B gate B6 to the Roissy train station, where you can board **RER** (Réseau Express Régional) line B to the Gare du Nord Métro stop (5:05am-11:50pm every 15 min., twice as frequent during heavy traffic periods; ½ hr.; 2nd class 26F, 1st class 39F).

Two other forms of public transportation can take you from Roissy to Paris, but at six Métro tickets costing 4.70F each, they are a bit more expensive. Bus #350 departs from Aérogare 2A gate A5, Aérogare 2B gate B6, or Aérogare 1 Boutiquaire level, and runs to Gare du Nord and Gare de l'Est (5:56am-11:38pm every 15 min., 50 min.). Bus #351 leaves from the same places for place de la Nation (6:16am-9:18pm every ½ hr., 40 min.). **Air France Pullman buses** (tel. 42-99-20-18) leave from Aérogare 2A gate A5, Aérogare 2B gate B6, and Aérogare 1 arrival level gate 34 (6am-11pm every 12 min.) and take you to Porte Maillot (17*ème*)in the northwest corner of Paris. (36F per person, 82F per 3 persons, 100F per 4 persons.) Taxis are only for the affluent: The trip will take about 50 minutes and cost around 200F (more in the evenings).

From **Orly Sud** gate H or Orly Ouest arrival level gate F, you can take the shuttle bus (5:40am-11:15pm every 15 min.) to the **Orly Rail Station** (tel. 42-61-50-50), where you can board the **RER** for a number of destinations in Paris. Buy 20F tickets from machines inside the airport at Orly Sud Gate H and Orly Ouest arrival gate F. To take the **Orly bus RATP** from Orly Sud, go to gate F (6:32am-11:30pm every 15 min., 6 Métro tickets); from Orly Ouest, stand at the arrival level gate D (6:34am-11:32pm every 15 min., 6 Métro tickets). This bus will take you to place Denfert-Rochereau in 25 minutes. The **Air France bus** (tel. 43-23-97-10) runs from Orly Sud gate J and Orly Ouest arrival level gate E every 12 minutes, and arrives at the Invalides and Gare Montparnasse 30 minutes later (29F per person, 75F per 3 persons, 91F per 4 persons). The cheapest, if slowest, way into Paris is Bus #285, which leaves from both the shuttle-accessible RER station and from the bus stop on the *autoroute* under Orly Sud. To get to the Orly Sud stop descend to the ground floor and follow the signs. (6.30F to Porte d'Italie, where you can transfer to the Métro; 55min.) Taxis cost at least 170F, and take about 35 minutes to reach the center.

If you happen to land in Paris in Le Bourget, take bus #350 (6:10am-11:52pm every 15 min., 2 Métro tickets) for Gare du Nord and Gare de l'Est. Bus #152 also makes these stops, and, for the same price, will take you to Porte de la Villette, where you can catch the Métro or a bus.

By Train and Bus

The arteries of France are made of steel. Generations of French people have entered and left their capital through the vast, bustling train stations. Each is a community of its own, with resident bums and policemen, cafes and restaurants, *tabacs,* and banks. Locate the ticket counters (*guichets*), the platforms (*quais*), and the tracks (*voies*) and you will be ready to roll. All train stations are reached by at least two Métro lines and the Métro station bears the name of the train station. For general train information and for the information numbers of individual stations, call 45-82-50-50 (8am-8pm). There is a free telephone with direct lines to the stations on the right-hand side of the Champs-Elysées tourist office.

A word on safety: Though full of atmosphere, each terminal is also full of thieves, and worse. Gare du Nord, for example, is safe during the day but becomes a rough area at night, with drugs and prostitution. As in all big cities, beware the characters in and around the stations; the unsuspecting may be invited out for a drink only to be doped up and ripped off.

For information about trains to other parts of Europe, inquire at most travel agencies or call the following train stations. Both alternatives are likely to have an English-speaking staff member.

Gare du Nord (tel. 42-80-03-03; for reservations 48-78-87-54). Trains to northern France, Belgium, the Netherlands, Scandinavia, USSR, northern Germany, and Britain.

Gare de l'Est (tel. 45-82-50-50; for reservations 45-65-60-60 for reservations). To eastern France (Champagne, Alsace, Lorraine), Luxembourg, parts of Switzerland (Basel also known as Bâle, Zürich, Lucerne), southern Germany, Austria, and Hungary.

Gare de Lyon (tel. 43-45-92-22; for reservations 43-45-93-33). To southern and southeastern France (Riviera, Provence), parts of Switzerland (Geneva, Lausanne, Bern), Italy, Greece, and points east.

Gare d'Austerlitz (tel. 45-82-50-50; for reservations 45-84-15-20). To southwestern France (Bordeaux, Pyrenees, Loire Valley), Spain, and Portugal.

Gare St-Lazare (tel. 45-82-50-50; for reservations 45-65-60-60). To Normandy, including the port at Le Havre, where ships leave for North and South America and England.

Gare de Montparnasse (tel. 45-38-52-29; for reservations 45-38-52-39). To western France (Versailles, Chartres, and Brittany).

Most buses into Paris arrive at **Gare Routière Internationale,** 8, place Stalingrad, 19ème (tel. 42-05-12-10; on 3 Métro lines; Mo. Stalingrad). The neighborhood is not the best. Métro line #7 (*direction* "Mairie d'Ivry") will take you directly, though slowly, into the 1er, 2ème, and 5ème *arrondissements* (1 Métro ticket), the center of Paris. Other buses have more bizarre ports of call. The Terminal City Sprint bus (tel. 42-85-44-55) that operates in conjunction with Hoverspeed from England, for example, drops its passengers in front of the Hoverspeed offices, 3 blocks from Gare du Nord. Find the nearest Métro stop, and extensive maps there can direct you from there. For information about buses to other European countries, call **International Express Eurolines Coach Station** (tel. 40-38-93-93).

By Thumb

The competition for rides out of Paris is overwhelming. Don't wait at any of the *portes* (city gates) where the major *autoroutes* radiate from the city: You'll inevitably get sucked into the long line of wayfarers, who all look as though they've been waiting for at least two days. (If you insist on standing at a *porte,* you'll be better off at Porte d'Orléans or Porte de Clignancourt.) Avoid this vacationer's purgatory and pull out your map of Paris public transportation. Figure out which *autoroute* leads to your destination, then trace the train or bus line until it approaches this highway—that's where you should start your hitching. The few extra francs you'll spend to get away from the city could save you hours of frustration. The following suggestions will help you get started:

Toward the east: Metz, Strasbourg, München. Take the Métro to Porte de Charenton and walk along bd. Massena, where you can catch the *Autoroute de l'est* A4. (This is the most expensive highway and the worst to hitch on.)

Toward the north: Lille, Brussels, Köln, Hamburg, Berlin, Scandinavia. Catch the Métro to Porte de la Chapelle, which is right next to the *Autoroute du nord* A1.

Toward the west: Rouen, Caen, Cherbourg, Mont St-Michel, St-Malo. Take the Métro to Porte de St-Cloud and walk up bd. Murat towards place de la Porte d'Auteuil, where *Autoroute de Normandie* A13 begins.

Toward the south: Take the Métro to Porte d'Orléans, walk down av. de la Porte d'Orléans, and turn left. You can get on to a number of *autoroutes* from Porte d'Orléans. **Southeast** A6: Lyon, Marseille, Cannes, Nice, Monaco, Switzerland, Italy, Barcelona. **Southwest** A10: Orléans, Bordeaux, Madrid, Galicia, Portugal. Also A11 branches off A10 towards Brittany: Chartres, Le Mans, Rennes.

In general, the more original and inventive your method of reaching an entrance to an *autoroute* outside of Paris, the fewer hitchhikers there will be to compete for rides. Hold up a sign that clearly states your destination, include the letters "S.V.P." (*s'il vous plaît*), and smile. Another option is to ask customers at gas stations or truck stops if they are going your way, but use discretion. The last two digits of every French license plate indicate that car's province of origin (i.e., Ile-de-France is 75). Consult a map of France for numbers, which correspond to the first two digits of the region's postal code; you may wish to wave your sign more energetically when a car looks like it's heading to your destination. It is not advisable for women to hitchhike alone.

If you have a little money and want to save some time, try **Allostop-Provoya,** 84, Passage Brady, 10ème (tel. 47-70-46-70; Mo. Strasbourg-St-Denis). They will try to match you with a driver going your way. The cost is 60F if your trip is longer than 300km, 30F if it is shorter. You must also pay your driver 16 *centimes* per kilometer. If you plan to use this service more than two or three times, it pays to spend the 120F for a year's worth of rides. If you buy the latter, you can pay 30F more for **Eurostop International,** which is good in Switzerland, Germany, Spain, France, Hungary, Italy, Holland, Belgium, Canada—76 cities total. If your home country is one of the nine listed above, you must purchase your card there. At Allostop-Provoya, you can also buy train and bus tickets to points throughout Europe. They sell BIJ/Transalpino tickets, as well as arranging special weekend tours in Europe. Several offices operate in other cities throughout France, including Bordeaux, Lyon, Strasbourg, and Toulouse. For their addresses check the respective city's practical information section, or call 47-70-48-71. For current Allostop information, call 47-70-46-70. (Open Mon.-Fri. 9am-7:30pm, Sat. 9am-1pm and 2-6pm.)

Getting Around

Paris is divided into *arrondissements* that spiral clockwise from the Louvre (1er) to Porte de Vincennes (20ème). All addresses in *Let's Go*'s Paris section are immediately followed by *arrondissement* numbers. If a postal code is given instead, the last two numbers are the *arrondissement* number. To formulate the postal code for addresses within Paris, add 750- or 7500- to the *arrondissement* number. The Métro and buses efficiently serve all *arrondissements,* but in the center (*arrondissements* 1-8), it is often more convenient and pleasant to walk. Experiencing Paris *à la parisienne* becomes increasingly difficult as mobs of tourists flow through the city. Strolling through an appealing neighborhood or eavesdropping for hours in a carefully selected cafe is often the best way to soak in atmosphere. Crowd lovers can try Les Halles (1er) with its modern cafes, elegant if tourist-ridden place de l'Opéra (2ème), Le Marais (4ème) with street shows outside Beaubourg, and Pigalle (9ème) with its bustling illicit nightlife. To discover lesser-known sides of Paris, wander along the peaceful St-Martin canal in the 10ème or down the *grands boulevards* of the 9ème and then veer towards the Gare du Nord (10ème), where you will find the closest thing the city has to a slum, a place where you should exercise caution and leave at nightfall.

Another important distinction is that between the **Right Bank** (*la rive droite*) and the **Left Bank** (*la rive gauche*) of the Seine. The Sorbonne area, the Latin Quarter (*Quartier Latin,* 5ème), and the student areas of Odéon and St-Germain (6ème) have earned the Left Bank, perhaps unjustly, a reputation for a bohemian lifestyle, student activities, and low costs. In fact, in much of the Left Bank (most of St-Germain and the 7ème), tourists have replaced locals, raising the cost of living. Many artists still take refuge from the mobbed St-Germain-des-Prés in the side streets of the Odéon. The 16ème, the Faubourg St-Honoré, and the rue de Rivoli make the Right Bank the more expensive and elegant side, or as the French would say, the BCBG (*bon chic bon genre*) area. Lower-class neighborhoods such as Belleville (20ème), with its large Arab population, and the area around Canal St-Martin (10ème), where you will find a bizarre mixture of artists, workers, and professionals, exist here too—usually without the tourists of the Left Bank.

By far the best guide to Paris is a *Plan de Paris par Arrondissements,* which includes a detailed map of each *arrondissement,* a wealth of up-to-date miscellany, and an essential index of streets and their nearest Métro stop. It costs 38-100F, depending on how elaborate an edition you buy: The 48F guide should suffice unless you're driving around Paris. Most bookstores, *papeteries* (stationary stores), and news kiosks sell a wide variety. The small map published by the RATP (Règie Autonome des Transports Parisiens), available free from the tourist office and at Métro stops, lists the stations alphabetically with cross-references to the map.

Métro

Safe and efficient, the Paris Métro can take you within walking distance of almost any spot in the city. Connections (*correspondances*) are easy and trains run fre-

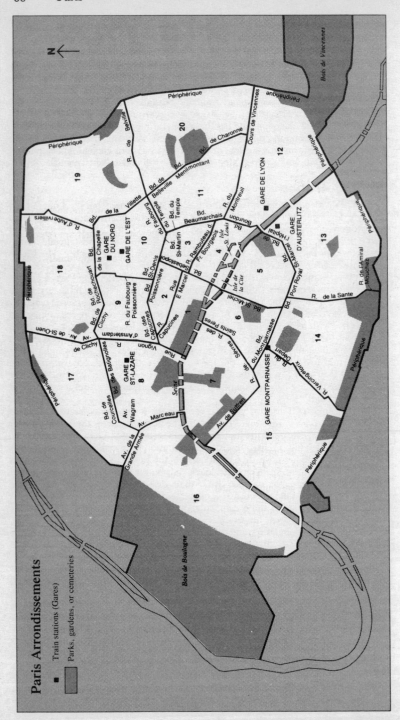

Paris Arrondissements

■ Train stations (Gares)

▨ Parks, gardens, or cemeteries

quently. A disabled Métro train is a rare sight. The first trains start running at 5:30am; the last leave the stations at the "*portes de Paris*" (i.e., Porte d'Orléans, Porte de Clignancourt, etc.) for the center between 12:40 and 12:55am. Remember this when making last-minute *correspondances*. The one exception is trains leaving from Porte de Balard, which do not go through to Porte Charentou, but stop at République. In the other direction, however, they go through the center to Balard. For the exact departure times of last trains from the *portes,* check the poster in the center of each station called "*Principes de Tarification.*"

All the train lines are well traveled at night, and Parisian women often travel alone. If you do this, use common sense—avoid empty cars and stay away from the most dangerous stations (Barbès-Rochechouart, Pigalle, and Anvers). The long, empty corridors of larger stations can be dangerous, and unsuspecting tourists make particularly appetizing targets. At night, many people choose to ride in the first car, where the conductor is only a door away. However, violent crime in the Parisian Métro is the exception, not the rule.

Free Métro maps are available at many stations, display maps are posted in all stations, and all have a *plan du quartier*—a detailed map of the surrounding neighborhood. Connections to other lines are indicated by orange "*correspondance*" signs, and the exits by blue "*sortie*" signs. All Métro lines are numbered but are referred to by their final destination.

Each trip on the Métro costs one ticket. Tickets can be bought individually (2nd class 4.70F, 1st class 6.80F), but purchase an economical *carnet* of 10 (2nd class 28.20F, 1st class 42F). First-class cars have a yellow stripe along the length of the car near the roof, and are located in the middle of the train, but the distinction exists only between 9am and 5pm. At other times, anyone can ride first class. These cars are generally less crowded than second-class ones, but that's about the only difference. No matter which you ride, hold onto your ticket until you pass the point marked *Limite de Validité des Billets;* you may be asked for it by a uniformed RATP *contrôleur* (transit inspector). If caught without one, you will be fined 12 times the price of the corresponding ticket if you are in first class with a second-class ticket, 24 times if you are in second class without a ticket, and 36 times if you don't have one in first. In addition, any *correspondances* you make to the RER (Réseau Express Régional, rapid train to the suburbs) require you to put your validated (and uncrumpled) ticket into a turnstile. Otherwise you may need to buy a new ticket to exit.

Tourist tickets (Billets Paris Sésame) are available for all RATP public transportation (Métro and bus), but they are overpriced at 57F per two days, 85F per four days, 141F per week. Better deals are available, even if you're staying in Paris for only one day. Métro passes vary in price according to zones—ever larger concentric areas whose center is Paris. The first zone is Paris-proper, the second and third zones encompass the surrounding suburbs, and the farthest fourth zone includes Versailles. "Formule 1" is valid for Métro, bus, and RER, and requires no ID photo. For two zones (the most you'll probably need), you'll fork over 19F, for three zones 24F, and for four zones 35F. If you're staying in Paris for a few days, get a Carte Orange, which comes in two varieties: weekly (*hebdomadaire*) and monthly (*mensuel*). Both allow you unlimited travel (starting on the first day of the week or month) on the Métro and buses in Paris and its immediate suburbs (zones 1 and 2; coupons for travel in zones 3, 4, and 5 are available at a higher cost). To get your *carte,* bring an ID photo (which can be purchased from a machine in many stations) to the ticket counter, ask for a Carte Orange complete with plastic case, and then purchase an orange *coupon mensuel* (2nd class 165F, 1st class 230F) or a yellow *coupon hebdomadaire* (2nd class 46F, 1st class 68F). Be sure to write the number of your *carte* on your *coupon* before you use it. There is also a *carte hebdomadaire* that allows you only two trips per day for a week, starting from the station in which the *carte* was purchased (25F). For more information, contact the **RATP** office, 53ter, quai des Grands-Augustins, 6ème (tel. 43-46-14-14; Mo. St-Michel); an English-speaking person is usually there during the week. (Open daily 6am-9pm.) You can also stop by the exceptionally friendly and useful **Services Touristiques de la RATP,** place de la Madeleine, 8ème (tel. 40-06-71-45; Mo. Madeleine; open

Mon.-Fri. 7:30am-7pm, Sun. and holidays 6:30am-6pm). RATP can also be reached 24 hours through Minitel (see Communications): 3615 RATP.

Buses

Because the Métro is so efficient and convenient, the Paris bus system is ignored by many visitors. It shouldn't be, as buses are often less crowded than the Métro, and bus rides allow cheap sight-seeing and greater familiarity with the city. The free bus map *Autobus Paris-Plan du Réseau* is available at the tourist office and some Métro information booths, and the routes of each line are also posted at each stop. Buses take the same tickets as the Métro (2nd class)—short trips cost one ticket, longer trips two. Enter the bus through the front door and punch your ticket by pushing it into the cancelling machine by the driver's seat. If you have a Carte Orange, flash it at the driver, but don't insert the ticket into the machine. As on the Métro, there are sometimes *contrôleurs* who will ask to see your ticket, so hold onto it until the end of the ride. For more information, call the RATP office (tel. 43-46-14-14).

Most buses run from about 7am to 8:30pm, although some, marked *Autobus du Soir,* continue until 12:30am, and others (*Noctambus*) run all night. Night buses (3 Métro tickets, 4 if you use 2 buses) start their runs from the Châtelet stop and leave hourly from 1:30 to 5:30am. At 5:30am, normal service resumes. Bus maps include an inset map of the *Noctambus* service. Buses with three-digit numbers come from or are bound for the suburbs, while buses with two-digit numbers travel exclusively within Paris. Buses in the #20s come from or are bound for Gare St-Lazare, in the #30s Gare de l'Est, in the #40s Gare du Nord, in the #70s Châtelet/Hôtel de Ville (with exceptions), in the #80s Luxembourg (with exceptions), and in the #90s Gare Montparnasse.

For more detailed diagrams of all bus routes, consult the *Plan de Paris par Arrondissements.* The pamphlet printed by the RATP, *Paris Bus Métro RER,* lists several bus routes that pass through interesting neighborhoods and by the main sights of Paris. It also lists directions to major museums, churches, and monuments. Some routes pass by enough sights to make them mini-tours in themselves. Buses worth riding from start to finish include:

Bus #20: From Gare St-Lazare to the Opéra, Montmartre-Poissonière, République, Bastille (50 min.). A trip down the *grands boulevards.* Open platform in back.

Bus #21: From Gare St-Lazare to the Opéra, Palais Royal, the Louvre, the Pont Neuf, St-Michel, Gare du Luxembourg, Porte de Gentilly (40 min.).

Bus #52: From Opéra to Concorde, Charles-de-Gaulle-Etoile, Auteuil, Pont de St-Cloud (50 min.).

Bus #56: From Porte de Clignancourt, Barbès, Gare de l'Est, République, Voltaire, Nation, St-Mandé, Vincennes (55 min.).

Bus #67: From Pigalle to Carrefour de Châteaudun, Louvre, Châtelet, Hôtel-de-Ville, Jussieu, place d'Italie, Porte de Gentilly (45 min.).

Bus #82: From Gare du Luxembourg to Gare Montparnasse, Ecole-Militaire, Champs-de-Mars, Tour Eiffel, Porte Maillot, Neuilly (45 min.).

Bus #83: From Place d'Italie, along bd. Raspail, Gare des Invalides, place des Ternes (50 min.). A glimpse of some of Paris's finest real estate and great views of the *quais.* Open platform in back.

Bus #95: From Montparnasse Tower past St-Germain-des-Prés, the Louvre, Palais Royal, the Opéra, and to Montmartre, near Sacré-Coeur (50 min.).

Bus #96: From Montparnasse past St-Michel, the Palais de Justice on the Ile de la Cité, Châtelet, Hôtel-de-Ville, Oberkampf, Ménilmontant, Porte des Lilas (50 min.).

Taxis

Taxi trips within Paris average 60-80F, but rates vary according to time of day and geographical areas. Tarif A, the basic rate, is in effect from 6:30am to 10pm

(2.49F per km); Tarif B, from 10pm to 6:30am and during the day from the airports (3.80F per km); Tarif C, the highest, is in effect from the airports from 10pm to 6:30am (5.10F per km). All taxis have lights on top indicating the rate being charged, so you can check to see that the driver is playing it straight. (Make sure the meter is on when you start the ride.) A 10-15% tip is customary (Parisians often round up to the nearest 5F). If you must take a taxi, try waiting at a stand (*arrêt taxis, tête de station*), hailing from the sidewalk (unless you are within 50m of a stand), or calling a radio-cab (tel. 42-02-42-02, 47-30-23-23, 42-70-41-41, or 47-39-47-39). The last is most expensive, since you must pay for the distance the cab drives to pick you up. For the going rates, call 42-02-22-22. Paris cabs normally cannot take more than three passengers, though drivers may be persuaded if you agree to take responsibility for any trouble with the police, including a potential 70F fine. If you have a complaint, write to Service des Taxis de la Préfecture de Police, 36, rue des Morillons, 75732 (tel. 45-31-14-80).

Bicycles

The center of Paris, with its narrow, congested streets and its ill-tempered drivers, is not the place for a leisurely afternoon pedal. Still, a few intrepid tourists do see Paris this way; the parks, especially the Bois de Boulogne and the Bois de Vincennes, can be explored on two wheels. For rentals, try **Paris-Vélo**, 2, rue de Fer-à-Moulin, 5ème (tel. 43-37-59-22; Mo. Censier or St-Marcel), an exceptionally friendly place with bikes from 60F per day, 240F per week (deposit 500F, including accident insurance). Try to book in advance and ask for any accessories you'll need. (Open Mon.-Sat. 10am-12:30pm and 2-7pm.) The **Bicyclub de France**, 8, place de la Porte-Champerret, 17ème (tel. 47-66-55-92; Mo. Porte de Champerret), also rents bikes but at higher rates (from 60F per day, 315F per week, deposit 1000F including insurance protecting only you, mandatory membership fee 25F). (Open Mon.-Fri. 9am-7pm, Sat.9am-1pm and 2-7pm.) For a high-class bike, try **Blyth & Co.**, 12, rue Dupetit Thomas, 3ème (tel. 48-87-97-97 or 48-87-94-94; Mo. République), which rents 15-speed Peugeots, equipped with kit, for 350F per week and 175F per additional week. Reservations are necessary. They also sell touring itineraries. (Open Mon.-Fri. 9am-5pm; in summer someone is around almost every day.) *Mobilettes* (mopeds) are no longer rented in the city because of insurance problems.

Cars

Paris is at best difficult to drive in. Parisian drivers are notorious for their "*système D*" (i.e., doing whatever works), which includes driving on the sidewalk in traffic jams, and passing in small streets at high speeds. *Priorité à droite* gives this right-of-way to the car approaching from the right, regardless of the size of the streets, and the Parisian driver makes it an affair of honor to take this right even in the face of grave danger. You are not allowed to honk your horn within city limits unless you are about to score by hitting a pedestrian. Flashing your headlights is the recognized sign for anger. If you do not have a map of Paris marked with one-way streets, it will be almost impossible to navigate, and you'll probably get lost. Street parking will be hard to locate, and garages are expensive. If you're still set on driving, you can rent a Renault 4 for 120F per day plus 1.30F per kilometer, or for 840F per week plus 1.30F per kilometer, liability insurance included; for full coverage pay 40F per day extra at **Inter Touring Service**, 117, bd. Auguste Blanqui, 13ème (tel. 45-88-52-37; Mo. Glacière; open Mon.-Sat. 8:30am-6:30pm). To rent a car for a week, one of the cheaper places is **Europcar**, 48, rue de Berri, 8ème (tel. 45-63-04-27; Mo. George V). You'll pay 2040F, including unlimited mileage, plus 94F per day for full insurance coverage. (Open Mon.-Sat. 8am-7pm.) Foreigners need an international license, passport, and credit card to rent in Paris.

Tourist Offices

Bureau d'Accueil Central: 127, av. des Champs-Elysées, 8ème (tel. 47-23-61-72; Mo. Charles-de-Gaulle-Etoile). Helpful English-speaking staff. Mobbed in summer. Fees for hotel-finding service: 1-star hotels 14F, 2-star 19F, 3-star 33F, hostels 5F. Referrals for hotels that belong to the Tourist Bureau. Will reserve rooms in any of 40 French cities no more than 7 days in advance (20F). Open daily 9am-8pm. There are 5 smaller *Bureaux d'Accueil*, also operated by the *office de tourisme*, located in the following train stations and at the Tour Eiffel:

Bureau Gare du Nord, 10ème (tel. 45-26-94-82; Mo. Gare du Nord). Open Easter-Nov. Mon.-Sat. 8am-10pm, Sun. 1-8pm; Nov.-Easter 8am-8pm.

Bureau Gare de L'Est, 10ème (tel. 46-07-17-73; Mo. Gare de l'Est). Open Easter-Nov. Mon.-Sat. 8am-10pm; Nov.-Easter 8am-1pm and 5-8pm.

Bureau Gare de Lyon, 12ème (tel. 43-43-33-24; Mo. Gare de Lyon). Open Easter-Nov. Mon.-Sat. 8am-10pm; Nov.-Easter Mon.-Sat. 8am-1pm and 5-8pm.

Bureau Gare d'Austerlitz, 13ème (tel. 45-84-91-70; Mo. Gare d'Austerlitz). Open Easter-Nov. Mon.-Sat. 8am-10pm; Nov.-Easter 8am-3pm.

Bureau Tour Eiffel, Champs de Mars, 7ème (tel. 45-51-22-15; Mo. Champs de Mars). Open May-Sept. daily 11am-6pm.

In summer, it's not unusual to wait up to three hours at any of these tourist offices. Lines are worse in the afternoon. Both international airports run reception offices where you can make hotel reservations (deposit required) and receive information about Paris.

Orly, South: Near gate H and **Orly West:** Near gate F (tel. 48-84-32-63). Both open daily 6am-11:45pm.

Roissy-Charles de Gaulle: Near gate 36 arrival level (tel. 48-62-22-81). Open daily 7am-11:30pm.

Also try the following:

Agence National pour l'Information Touristique (ANIT): 8, av. de l'Opéra, 1er (tel. 42-96-10-23; Mo. Palais-Royal). A friendly and efficient agency with information on vacations anywhere in France and its territories, tailored specifically to your budget. Prices for hotels and campgrounds but no reservations. Also tourist literature and information by mail (free). Open Mon.-Fri. 9am-6:45pm.

Tourist Information: Tel. 47-20-88-98. A tape-recorded message in English gives the major events in Paris. Updated weekly.

Budget Travel Organizations

Accueil des Jeunes en France (AJF): 119, rue St-Martin, 4ème (tel. 42-77-87-80; Mo. Rambuteau), across from the pedestrian mall in front of the Pompidou Center. Open Mon.-Sat. 9:30am-7pm. Also 16, rue du Pont Louis-Philippe, 4ème (tel. 42-78-04-82; Mo. Hôtel-de-Ville or Pont-Marie), near the Hôtel de Ville. Open Mon.-Fri. 9:30am-6:30pm. Also 139, bd. St-Michel, 5ème (tel. 43-54-95-86; Mo. Port-Royal), in the Latin Quarter. Open March-Oct. Mon.-Fri. 9:30am-6:30pm. Also Gare du Nord, arrival hall next to Agence de Voyages SNCF in the new building (tel. 42-85-86-19). Open June-Sept. daily 8am-10pm; March-May and Oct. Mon.-Fri. 9:30am-6:30pm. The Gare du Nord office does accommodations booking only. The other offices will give you free maps, sell ISICs (32F), and make room reservations in *foyers* in Paris, London, or Spain (72-85F per night). Unfortunately, they cannot book rooms in advance. Reduced-price student train tickets, charter flights, budget weekend holidays in Europe, and meal vouchers for Paris youth hostels. The office across from the Pompidou Center can be used as a mailing address but is so crowded that it pays to try one of the other branches—all friendly, centrally-located, and English-speaking.

Office de Tourisme Universitaire (OTU): 137, bd. St-Michel, 5ème (tel. 43-29-12-88; Mo. Port-Royal). A French student travel agency. Crowded and English-speaking. Offers summer accommodations in student residences around France. Singles 60F. You must buy vouchers here or at CROUS for each night of lodging. (See Accommodations.) Open Mon. 11am-6:45pm, Tues.-Fri. 10am-6:30pm, Sat. 10am-5:45pm.

Council Travel: 51, rue Dauphine, 6ème (tel. 43-26-79-65; Mo. Odéon). Take rue de l'Ancienne Comédie to rue Dauphine. Also at 16, rue de Vaugirard (tel. 46-34-02-90; Mo. Odéon). Take rue Monsieur-le-Prince from the carrefour de l'Odéon. Also at 31, rue St-Augustin, 2ème (tel. 42-66-20-87; Mo. Opéra). English-speaking, young people's travel service. Books international flights. Sells student train tickets, guidebooks, and ISICs (35F). BIJ/Transalpino rail tickets. If you have lost your CIEE charter ticket, go to the Opéra office and they will telex the U.S. to authorize a substitute, for which you will pay a penalty. All open Mon.-Fri. 11am-6:30pm, Sat. 10am-1pm and 2:30-5pm.

Council on International Educational Exchange (CIEE) and Centre Franco-Américain Odéon: 1, place de l'Odéon, 6ème (tel. 46-34-16-10; Mo. Odéon). The center has an agreement with the French work ministry that allows students enrolled full-time in an American university or foreign study program to work for up to 3 months. Anyone wishing to do this should contact CIEE's New York office *before* leaving the U.S. (see Useful Organizations in General Introduction). They cannot issue the papers if you have been in France a month or more. Once you have the papers, this office will help with housing and the like. Open Mon.-Fri. 9am-6:30pm.

Centre d'Information et de Documentation Jeunesse (CIDJ): 101, quai Branly, 15ème (tel. 45-66-40-20; Mo. Bir-Hakeim). A government-run information clearinghouse on French law, camping, touring, sports, employment, careers, and long-term accommodations. (The office is not too optimistic on jobs for non-French, but see Work in General Introduction.) Part-time jobs and housing listings are posted on the bulletin boards outside each morning at 9am. Pamphlets available include *Cours d'été pour étrangers en France, Placement au pair en France,* and *Tourisme en France* (a listing of various useful addresses pertaining to foreign exchange, housing, etc.). To check job listings or request brochures you can check listings on Minitel (see Communications below): 3615 CIDJ. Open Mon.-Fri. 9am-7pm, Sat. 10am-6pm.

Embassies

U.S.: 2, av. Gabriel, 8ème (tel. 42-96-12-02 or 42-61-80-75; Mo. Concorde), off place de la Concorde. For lost passports, go to the **Office of American Services,** 2, rue St-Florentin (tel. 42-96-12-02, ext. 2613), 3 blocks away. Passports replaced for US$36 or the equivalent in francs. Open Mon.-Fri. 9am-4pm.

Canada: 35, av. Montaigne, 8ème (tel. 47-23-01-01; Mo. Franklin-Roosevelt or Alma-Marceau). Open Mon.-Fri. 9am-11:30am and 2-4pm. New passport CDN$25.

U.K.: 35, rue du Faubourg-St-Honoré, 8ème (tel. 42-66-91-42; Mo. Concorde or Madeleine). Visa bureau open Mon.-Fri. 9am-1pm and 2:30-6pm. New passport 165F (must be paid in francs).

Australia: 4, rue Jean-Rey, 15ème (tel. 45-75-50-47; Mo. Bir-Hakeim). Open Mon.-Fri. 9:15am-12:15pm and 2-5pm. New passport 260F (must be paid in francs).

New Zealand: 7ter, rue Léonard-de-Vinci, 16ème (tel. 45-00-24-11; Mo. Victor-Hugo). Open Mon.-Fri. 9am-1pm and 2:30-6pm. New passport 200F (must be paid in francs).

Money

In summer, change money before the weekend, when many exchange offices close and lines are long. American Express and exchanges on the Champs Elysées are almost always crowded anyway, especially in the afternoon. Many post offices will change cash and AmEx traveler's checks at competitive rates and without commission, while bureaus at train stations tend to offer less favorable rates. Remember that even French traveler's checks are not accepted by most businesses. Count on three days to receive money wired from the U.S. to American Express, and even longer if the transaction is between banks. Banks close at noon or 1pm on the day before major holidays.

American Express: 11, rue Scribe, 9ème (tel. 42-66-09-99; Mo. Opéra or Auber), across from the back of the Opéra. No commission on AmEx traveler's checks, 5F commission on non-AmEx checks, 10F commission on cash. Don't forget to bring your passport. Mobbed during the summer, especially Mon., Fri., and Sat. They will hold mail for you free if you have either their card or traveler's checks; otherwise 5F per inquiry. Great place to use the washrooms or the public phones (through the brown door near window 9). Financial services open Mon.-Sat. 9am-5pm; other services, including mail inquiry, Mon.-Fri. 9am-5:30pm.

Currency Exchange: 154, av. des Champs-Elysées, 8ème (Mo. Etoile or George V). Open Mon.-Fri. 9am-5pm, Sat.-Sun. and holidays 10:30am-6pm. Commission 1%, or at least 10F. Across the street at #115, the **Crédit Commercial de France (CCF)** offers better rates and no commission. Open July-Sept. Mon.-Sat. 8:30am-8pm, Sun. 10:15am-6pm; Oct.-June Mon.-Sat. only.

Le Change de Paris: 2, rue de l'Amiral Coligny 1er (tel. 42-36-72-83; Mo. Louvre), across from the Louvre. No commission and good rates. Open daily 10am-7pm.

At Train Stations: Gare d'Austerlitz, 13ème (tel. 45-84-91-40). Open daily 7am-9pm. **Gare de Montparnasse**, 15ème (tel. 43-21-48-19). Open Mon.-Sat. 9am-8pm, Sun. 10am-8pm. **Gare de Lyon**, 12ème (tel. 43-41-52-70). Open daily 6:30am-11pm. **Gare de l'Est**, 10ème (tel. 42-06-51-97). Open Mon.-Sat. 7am-9pm. **Gare du Nord**, 10ème (tel. 42-80-11-50). Open daily 6:30am-10pm. **Gare St-Lazare**, 8ème (tel. 43-87-72-51). Open daily 7am-9pm.

At Airports: Orly-Sud (tel. 48-53-11-13). Open daily 6am-11:30pm. **Roissy-Charles de Gaulle** (tel. 48-62-24-92). Open daily 6am-11:30pm.

Communications

Post Office: 52, rue du Louvre, 75001 Paris (tel. 40-28-20-00; Mo. Louvre). All Poste Restante mail is held at this post office unless otherwise specified. Open 24 hours for **telephone** and **telegraph**, until 7pm for other services. Only urgent telegrams and calls, and no bulk mailings or packages over 2kg outside of normal business hours. Complete telephone book collection. Long lines Sat. and Sun. **Branch office**, 71, av. des Champs-Elysées, 8ème (tel. 43-35-60-00; Mo. George V). Open Mon.-Fri. 8am-11:30pm, Sat. noon-11pm, Sun. 2-8pm. Many more branches throughout the city; inquire at your hotel or hostel for the nearest one, or consult PTT signs. Generally open Mon.-Fri. 8am-7pm, Sat. 8am-noon.

Telephones: As soon as you arrive in Paris, buy a *télécarte*, available at ticket windows in all SNCF stations, Métro stations, post offices, or at *tabacs*. 50-unit card 40F, 120-unit card 96F. Few phones now accept coins, and the *télécarte* will save you from having to feed the phone frantically while you talk. When you insert the card, the digital display tells you how many units you have left. You can make collect ("*en PCV*") calls in Paris from post offices, from any of the newer telephone booths, and from any of the newest booths that accept only *télécartes*. For **international calls**, dial 19, plus the country code; for the international operator dial 19 33, plus the country code. If you have a U.S. telephone credit card, you can call the U.S. from France at operator-assisted rates (dial *France Dirècte*, 19 00 11, which connects you to an English-speaking operator). Calling overseas can cost as little as 5F, so you may wish to dial direct and ask your affluent friends to return your call at a booth that can receive calls. They should dial France's country mumber, 01, then the numbers posted inside on a sign that reads "*Cette cabine peut être appelée à*—" ("This booth can be called at—").

Telegrams in English: Tel. 42-33-44-11. Operators are not fluent, but they get the job done. Telegrams to the U.S., Canada, and Great Britain 5F per word (adress counts as text), to Australia 6F. Same price whether sent from post office or by telephone, but if by phone, you must have an address in Paris.

Minitel: This service is not essential if you are just passing through Paris; however, it is interesting to tap into this computer system that not only can provide the telephone numbers, addresses, and professions of Parisian telephone subscribers, but also offers newspapers on screen (including the *International Herald Tribune*) and train schedules. There are several coin-operated (2F per min.) Minitels for public use at the Bibliothèque Publique Information at the Centre Pompidou, where there is a superb collection of French and European telephone books, in better order than in many post offices in Paris.

Emergency, Health, and Help

Police: 9, bd. du Palais, 4ème (tel. 42-60-33-22 or 42-77-11-00; Mo. Cité). **Service des Etrangers** at the same address; call the first number and ask for the foreign service in case of visa problems, and so on. Open Mon.- Fri. 8:30am-4:00pm.

Police Emergency: Tel. 17.

Fire Department: Tel. 18.

Medical Emergency: SAMU ambulances, Tel. 45-67-50-50. Public service largely for resuscitation or other serious conditions. **Ambulances de l'Assistance Publique,** Tel. 43-78-26-26. Does much of the transportation from one hospital to another. **SOS Médecins,** Tel. 47-07-77-77. 24-hour emergency medical help. **Association des Urgences Médicales de Paris,** Tel. 48-28-40-09. Will send a doctor over in an emergency.

Poison Control: Tel. 42-05-63-29. French-speaking only.

Hospitals: Hospitals in Paris are numerous and efficient. They will generally treat you whether or not you can pay in advance. Settle with them afterwards and don't let financial uncertainty cause you to ignore a serious problem. **Cochin Hospital,** 27, rue du Faubourg St-Jacques, 14ème (tel. 42-34-12-12; Mo. Denfert-Rochereau), is very reliable, but not necessarily English-speaking. **Hôpital Américain de Paris,** 63, bd. Victor Hugo, Neuilly (tel. 47-

47-53-00; Mo. Sablons or bus #82), employs English-speaking personnel but is much more expensive than French hospitals. You can pay in dollars. If you have Blue Cross-Blue Shield, your hospitalization is covered as long as you fill out the appropriate forms first. They can also direct you to the nearest English-speaking doctor and provide dental services. **Hôpital Franco-Britannique de Paris,** 48, rue de Villiers, Levallois-Perret (tel. 47-58-13-12; Mo. Anatole-France), which is considered a French hospital and bills like one, also has some English-speakers, and a good reputation. Consultations 85F, with specialists 125F, Sun. and holidays 180F, 8pm-8am 222F.

All-night Pharmacies: Pharmacie Dhéry in the Galerie des Champs, 84, av. des Champs-Elysées, 8ème (tel. 45-62-02-41; Mo. George V). Open 24 hours. **Pharmacie Opéra,** 6, bd. des Capucines, 2ème (tel. 42-65-88-29; Mo. Opéra). Open Mon.-Fri. 8am-1am, Sat. 9am-1am, Sun. 8pm-1am. **Drugstore St-Germain,** 149, bd. St-Germain, 6ème (tel. 42-22-92-50; Mo. St-Germain-des-Prés or Mabillon). Open daily 9am-2am. Also, every *arrondissement* should have a *pharmacie de gard,* which, if not open 24 hours, will open in case of emergencies. The locations change, but your local pharmacy can provide the name of the nearest one.

Alcoholics Anonymous: 3, rue Frédéric Sauton, 5ème (tel. 46-34-59-65; Mo. Maubert-Mutualité). A recorded message in English will refer you to 3 numbers you can call for help. Open 24 hours.

Birth Control: Mouvement Français pour le Planning Familial, 4, square St-Irénée, 11ème (tel. 48-07-29-10; Mo. St-Ambroise). Also provides AIDS information. Open Mon.-Fri. 9am-noon and 2-6pm.

Down and Out: Services and aid for the desperate, drugged out, and destitute in Paris are provided by a number of organizations. If you are an American citizen and in real financial straits, the **American Aid Society** can help. Although their offices are in the U.S. Embassy, the society is an independent organization. (Embassy tel. 42-96-12-02 and 42-61-80-75, ext. 2717 and 2932 for the Aid Society.) You can borrow 50-100F interest-free for 48 hr., based on a personal interview. They will also help you find a cheap room. Open Mon.-Fri. 9am-1pm. For any sort of personal counseling (psychiatric or emotional, from pregnancy to homesickness), go to the 2 services based at the **American Church,** 65, quai d'Orsay, 7ème (Mo. Invalides or Alma-Marceau): the **International Counseling Service** and the **American Student and Family Service.** These 2 groups share the same staff and provide access to psychologists, psychiatrists, social workers, and a clerical counselor. Payment is usually 200-250F per session, but if you are truly in need, this fee is negotiable. The ICS keeps regular hours in the morning (Mon.-Sat. 9am-1pm), the ASFS in the afternoon (Mon.-Fri. 2-6pm). July-Aug., the office is staffed irregularly, but will respond if you leave a message on their answering machine. Call for an appointment (tel. 45-50-26-49 for both, at the Church) or call the **American Center,** 261, bd. Raspail, 14ème (tel. 43-35-21-50; Mo. Raspail), a cross-cultural center for students and artists in Paris that refers to a local social worker. Organizes concerts, art exhibits, theater, and art classes as well.

Drug Problems: Centre Marmottan, 17-19, rue d'Armaillé, 17ème (tel. 45-74-00-04; Mo. Argentine). Emergency line open 24 hours. Usually an English-speaker available. For consultations or treatments open Sept.-July Mon.-Sat. 9:30am-7pm; Aug. Mon.-Fri. only.

Psychiatric Problems: Le Centre Hôpital St-Anne, tel. 45-65-80-00. A 24-hour hotline. French-speaking only.**SOS Crisis Help Line: Friendship,** Tel. 47-23-80-80. English-speaking. Support and information for the depressed and lonely. Open daily 3-11pm. **SOS Amitié:** Tel. 42-96-26-26, 43-64-31-31, or 46-21-31-31. Willing to make the effort with non-French speaking people. Very helpful. Open 24 hours.

Gay and Lesbian Services: *Gai Paris* is not the haven for gay and lesbian activity that these words imply. In fact, closets are large and abundant here. Open gayness is tolerated, but still draws attention and sometimes harassment. Political activity has dropped since 1980, and the last Gay Pride march drew only 1000 people. The following services may be able to offer assistance or advice. **SOS Homosexualité,** 3bis, rue Clairaut, 17ème (tel. 46-27-49-36; Mo. La Fourche). Hardly just a crisis line. Pastor Doucé is a polyglot, author, activist, and friendly dispenser of information on various services, clubs, discos, bookstores, and other aspects of gay and lesbian life in Paris. Receptions Fri. at 8pm. Call to confirm time. Doucé or one of two English-speaking assistants is usually in the office daily 10am-1pm. Non-sectarian, non-denominational services Sun. at noon, followed by lunch. **La Maison des Femmes,** 8, Cité Prost, 11ème (Mo. Charonne), provides some information for lesbians and hosts Fri. dinners. **AIDES,** BP759, 75123 Paris CEDEX 03 (tel. 42-77-13-23), answers questions concerning AIDS. Though not officially a gay sevice, AIDES caters sensitively to the concerns of gay people.

Rape Crisis: SOS Viol, Tel. 05-05-95-95. Telephone service only. Call them from anywhere in France for counseling, medical and legal advice, and referrals. Open Sept.-June Mon.-Fri. 10am-7pm; July-Aug. irregular hours.

V.D. Clinic: 43, rue de Valois, 1er (tel. 42-61-30-04; Mo. Palais Royal). Free consultations, blood tests, and injection treatments. Plasma and chlamydia tests 175F each. AIDS test and consultation 120-150F. If you need to see a doctor, call for an appointment (also free). English-speaking. Open Sept.-June Mon.-Fri. 8am-7pm; July Mon.-Fri. 10:30am-6:30pm. In Aug. call noon-3pm to make an appointment.

Other

Métro and Bus Information: Tel. 43-46-14-14. Open daily 6am-9pm.

Lost Property: Bureau des Objets Trouvés, 36, rue des Morillons, 15ème (tel. 45-31-14-80; Mo. Convention). You can visit or write to them describing the object and when and where it was lost. Open July-Aug. Mon., Wed., and Fri. 8:30am-5pm, Tues. and Thurs. 8:30am-8pm.. No information given by phone.

Bookstores: See Shopping below.

Public Libraries: Bibliothèque Publique Information, at the Centre Pompidou (tel. 42-77-12-33; Mo. Rambuteau, Hôtel de Ville, Châtelet, or Les Halles). Many books in English. Record and video listening room. Novels are arranged alphabetically by century on the 1st floor (entrance to the library on the 2nd floor), so you'll have to hunt for those in translation. Open Mon.-Fri. noon-10pm, Sat.-Sun. 10am-10pm. **The American Library,** 10, rue du Général Camou, 7ème (tel. 45-51-46-82; Mo. Alma-Marceau or bus #92 from Montparnasse to Bosquet-St-Dominique). Primarily for Americans living in France or American students enrolled in French universities. Membership 265F per year (bring your passport and a photo). Summer membership 100F with 300F deposit. Nonmembers can read in the library for 25F per day. Open Sept.-July Tues., Thurs., and Fri. 2-7pm, Wed. and Sat. 10am-7pm; Aug. Tues.-Fri. noon-6pm, Sat. 10am-2pm. Much cheaper is the **British Council Library,** 9-11, rue de Constantine, 7ème (tel. 45-55-95-95; Mo. Invalides), which stocks only books originally published in England. 150F per year. Does not require British citizenship, but does require an address in France. One-day consulting fee 20F. Open Sept.-July 15 Mon.-Fri. 11am-6pm, Wed. until 7pm. If you need only a quiet place to read or write, the historic **Bibliothèque Mazarine,** 23, quai de Conti, 6ème (tel. 43-54-89-48; Mo. Pont-Neuf), stocks perfect silence, handsome old volumes in the walls, and scholars at work. You can obtain a *carte d'entrée* good for 6 visits by applying to the library (bring ID and 2 photos). Open mid-Aug. to July Mon.-Fri. 10am-6pm. Free to the public. For brief bibliographic information, call 43-26-39-16 (Mon. and Wed.-Fri. 1-5pm).

Alliance Française: 101, bd. Raspail, 6ème (tel. 45-44-38-28; Mo. Notre-Dame-des-Champs). Monthly French lessons for students at all levels of proficiency (or lack thereof). A note on the bulletin board upstairs tells when placement exams are given. After your exam you will need a photo, your passport, a 150F enrollment fee, and payment for the course (normal and conversational 900F, intensive 1800F). The office downstairs provides information on lodgings in Paris, including some with families. You can eat at the restaurant (6-9pm) for 26F. An excellent place to meet students of all nationalities. Open Mon.-Fri. 9am-6pm.

Religious Information Center: 8, rue Masillon, 4ème (tel. 46-33-01-01). Information about religious activities, concerts, and meetings in Paris. English-speaking. Open Mon.-Fri. 9am-noon and 2-6pm.

American Church in Paris: 65, quai d'Orsay, 7ème (tel. 47-05-07-99; Mo. Invalides or Alma-Marceau). As much a community center as a church. Bulletin board with notices about jobs, rides, apartments, etc. *Free Voice,* a free, English-language monthly specializing in cultural events and classifieds. After 11am interdenominational services on Sun., there is a ½-hr. coffee break and then a filling, friendly luncheon at 12:30pm (35F, students 25F). International counseling service. If you're down and out, you might come here for advice (tel. 45-50-26-49). Church open Mon.-Sat. 9am-11pm, Sun. 9am-8pm.

Synagogue: Temple de l'Union Libéral Israélite, 24, rue Copernic, 16ème (tel. 47-04-37-27; Mo. Victor-Hugo). Services Friday at 6pm, mostly in Hebrew, with a little French. Rabbi is English and stays after the service to speak with people.

Weather: Tel. 43-69-00-00 for Paris. Tel. 43-69-01-01 for all of France. In French.

Public Baths: 8, rue des Deux Ponts, 4ème (tel. 43-54-47-40; Mo. Pont-Marie). Shower, soap, and towel 4.35F. For the same price you can also go to 42, rue du Rocher, 8ème (tel. 45-22-15-19; Mo. St-Lazare), and to 40, rue Oberkampf, 11ème (tel. 47-00-57-35; Mo. Ob-

erkampf). They are clean, respectable, and quite popular in summer. Oberkampf open Fri.-
Wed: 7am-7pm, Thurs. noon-7pm. Others open Thurs. noon-7pm, Fri. 8am-7pm, Sat. 7am-
7pm, Sun. 8am-noon.

Swimming Pools: The office of the mayor of Paris runs 26 municipal pools. 8.20F per swim,
children and students 4.10F. 3-month pass 118.70F. The pools keep different hours during
the school year, but in summer all are open Mon. 2-7:30pm, Tues.-Sat. 7am-7:30pm, Sun.
8am-6pm. Topless is often an option. For more information, pick up the brochure *Les Pi-
scines,* free from the Hôtel de Ville or any *mairie,* which lists all the public pools and some
private ones as well. Or call the city's **Bureau des Sports,** 17, bd. Morland, 4*ème* (tel. 42-76-
54-54; Mo. Sully-Morland).

Laundromats: Check in the yellow pages under Laveries Automatiques to find one near your
hotel. The average price is 24F to wash and 6F to dry per 6 min. Most laundromats are open
until 10pm, last wash 9pm.

Publications About Paris

The green *Guide Michelin,* available in French or English (41F), is by far the
best source of information on the museums, history, and architecture of Paris. Providing detailed maps, the *Guide* features a number of interesting walking tours as
well. For the famous and respected restaurant stars, you must turn to the pages
of the red, hard-cover *Michelin* (90F) or its Paris section (11.50F), published separately in a thin paperback. W.H. Smith's *Blue Guide to Paris and Environs* (145F)
and the *Blue Guide to France* (239F) are easily found in Paris, more expensive and
less interesting than Michelin, but excellent references for history, art, and architecture.

The *Gault Millau* guide to Paris (French 139F, also in English), which comes
out every three years, is a consumer's guide to the city, listing restaurants, nightclubs, bookstores, and almost anything else you can think of. The restaurant guide
in French costs 49F. Though not aimed at the budget-minded, it will candidly tell
you what's a waste of money and what isn't. Patricia Wells's *Food Lover's Guide
to Paris* (Workman Publisher's, N.Y., 1984) reviews restaurants and cafes with a
wide range of prices (58F). An encyclopedic reference to history, restaurants, cafes,
practical information and more is *Paris: Guide Arthaud,* by Dominique Camus (Les
Editions Arthaud, Paris, 1987, 150F). It contains information on the changing win-
ing, dining, and dancing scene (in French only).

Pariswalks, by Alison Landes (New Republic Book Company, 83F), takes you
step-by-step on four walks around the Latin Quarter, and one around Place des
Vosges in the Marais, explaining odd street names and telling good historical stories
all the way. The prose is too cute, and the suggestions often ignore the privacy of
the occupants of interesting houses, but the paths are well-chosen and fun.

Paris Pas Cher (85F), a budget guide to Paris in French that is updated every
August (released in Sept.), is the best of its kind. It has listings for cheap restaurants,
hotels, and student agencies. It's also available in English as *The Good Value Guide
to Paris* (MA Editions, 80F). *Guide de France en Jeans* (Hachette) gives all the addresses and phone numbers you'll need to find anything—goods, services, entertainment, enlightenment—and is especially helpful for longer stays. Also by Hachette
is the *Guide de Routard,* which covers history, food, cafes, many very good and
cheap places, even where to sleep out. Unfortunately it's full of slang and not available in English (49F).

The weeklies (published every Wed.) *Pariscope* (3F), *Officiel des Spectacles* (2F),
and *7 à Paris* (5F) list current movies, theater, museum exhibits, festivals, clubs,
and bars. *Pariscope* is the most comprehensive while the articles and reviews in *7
à Paris* reflect *à la mode* Parisian tastes. Although in French, they are clear to everyone. The *Paris Free Voice,* a weekly newspaper published by the Cooperative for
Better Living at the American Church, is available there for free (65, quai d'Orsay,
7*ème;* Mo. Invalides), and also at many student centers. *Passion* (25F), a monthly
in English, includes short pieces of fiction, listings, and cinema. You can find it at
English bookstores, kiosks, and the tourist office on the Champs-Elysées. For gay
travelers, *Gai Pied* (regular yearly issue 14.50F; special summer issue 35F), is the

best source; the free monthly *Cinq Sur Cinq,* with listings for gay nightlife, is available in gay bars and bookstores. *Lesbia,* available at Mots à la Bouche (see bookstores) and some kiosks, is the best source for lesbian activities and listings of "in" bars.

Accommodations

Trying to find accommodations in Paris may be your most unpleasant experience in the city. In summer hotels fill quickly, and many of the inexpensive rooms are depressingly worn and often not too clean. There are four basic types of Parisian accommodations: hostels, *foyers,* bed and breakfasts, and hotels.

Since the IYHF hostels are either booked months in advance or far from the center of town, most people choose the hotels or *foyers,* which lodge tourists in the summer, but do not necessarily belong to an international hostel organization, since they serve primarily as student or young French worker lodgings during the academic year. If you are alone and enjoy meeting other solo travelers, the *foyers* are a better choice than hotels since they are economical for one person (with breakfast and shower included). Staffs of *foyers* are generally friendly, English-speaking, and prepared for the questions and demands of budget travelers. In a hotel, however, you will not have to observe the curfew often imposed in *foyers.* Couples will fare better economically in a hotel, and groups of three or four will do especially well in multi-bed rooms.

Bed and breakfast has just begun in France, taking the British system as a model. As a guest in a French home, you will have the best opportunity to experience French culture. The fledgling B&B organizations are eager to accommodate individual needs but sometimes require up to two months advance notice.

While *foyers* often limit stays to encourage a quick turnover, hotels welcome those staying long periods and may offer discounts. The less expensive, family-run hotels offer an opportunity to become more acquainted with Parisians, an advantage nonexistent in the more business/tourist-oriented hostels and *foyers.* Unfortunately, the families that manage their own hotels are often overburdened with maintenance and cleaning responsibilities; this forces them to require minimum stays and may account for crumbling plaster or stray cockroaches.

If you know when you will be in Paris, make reservations. *Hôteliers* usually accept reservations over the phone, although many require written confirmation and the first night's payment. When calling, remember that inexpensive doubles are furnished with a *grand lit* (double bed). Be courteous and don't make reservations you don't need, or you'll make life more difficult for the multitudes to follow. If you make reservations and don't need them, cancel at least one day in advance—even phoning the morning of your scheduled arrival is better than not at all.

Hostels

There are five hostels in Paris and its suburbs, but you probably won't be able to stay at any of them unless you arrive early in the morning. The friendly Auberge de Jeunesse on bd. Jules Ferry and its summer annex in the Cité Universitaire are booked months in advance. The d'Artagnan hostel is cozy and usually less crowded. The two hostels in the suburbs are inconvenient and often full of noisy children. Without the Carte Orange, transportation costs will make paying for a bed in a hostel more expensive than staying at a *foyer* or budget hotel in Paris. Remember that trains and buses travel infrequently at night, and that a hostel's curfew may restrict your nightlife.

If you forgot to buy an **IYHF card** at home, several hostel association offices in Paris sell them, as do CIEE, OTU, and other student travel agencies (see Budget Travel in Practical Information). The cards, valid throughout the world, cost 90F for foreigners of any age, and are available at the **Fédération Unie des Auberges de Jeunesse,** 6, rue Mesnil, 16*ème* (tel. 42-41-59-00; Mo. Victor-Hugo). With your card, you will get a *French Youth Hostel Handbook* free. Also a member of IYHF, **La Ligue Française des Auberges de Jeunesse, 38, bd. Raspail, 7ème** (tel. 45-48-69-84; Mo. Sèvres-Babylon; open Mon.-Sat. 9am-7pm), runs a smaller network of youth hostels in France and also sells IYHF cards. If you can prove that you've been in France for over three months and you are under 26, you can get the card for 50F.

Auberge de Jeunesse "Jules-Ferry" (IYHF), 8, bd. Jules Ferry, 11ème (tel. 43-57-55-60; Mo. République). Approximately 100 spots. Light rooms with plenty of space though not immaculate. Usually full by 8am in summer. To reserve (before May for the summer), send a letter and an international reply coupon 2 months in advance—no vouchers, no money. Phone reservations accepted when there is space. No groups accepted. Noisy party atmosphere and jovial management. Adequate kitchen facilities. 3-night maximum. 64F per night in 2- to 6-bed rooms, nonmembers 79F. Breakfast included. Doors and reception open 6am-2am.

Auberge de Jeunesse "Le d'Artagnan" (IYHF), 80, rue Vitruve, 20ème (tel. 43-61-08-75; Mo. Porte de Montreuil or Porte de Bagnolet). A popular, former *foyer* with renovated, unique, geometric rooms. Be sure to arrive before 9:30am, or reserve a week in advance. 400 beds, kitchen facilities, and friendly management. Rooms with 3-6 beds may accommodate families. 65F, nonmembers 80F. Breakfast included. No curfew.

Auberge de Jeunesse Cité Universitaire (IYHF), 27, bd. Jourdan, 14ème (tel. 45-80-00-07, but changes annually; RER: Ligne B to Cité Universitaire). Follow the signs into campus. During the school year a residence hall for students of *Arts et Métiers*. Usually booked; make reservations. Members only. Singles 60F. Sheets 13F. Showers included. Breakfast 11F. You can eat at the university restaurant in the park for 10F. Reception open July to mid-Sept. 6am-1am. Curfew 1am.

Auberge de Jeunesse Choisy-le-Roi (IYHF), 125, av. de Villeneuve-St-Georges, Choisy-le-Roi (tel. 48-90-92-30). From Austerlitz, St-Michel, Invalides, or Champ-de-Mars, take RER line C (7.40F, railpasses valid) to Choisy-le-Roi, then cross the bridge over the Seine. Take the road immediately to the right and follow the signs. A 30-min. walk from RER station. 280 beds mostly in rooms of 6. Not a top pick due to its location in a distant suburb. However, the immediate grounds are pleasant and the hostel is neat and modern, with TV, video games, restaurant, and bar. Reservations accepted by mail with voucher or by telephone 2-3 days in advance. 65F. Breakfast included. Optional *demi-pension* 95F. Meals in restaurant 36-40.50F. Reception open 7am-2am. Lockout 10am-4:30pm. Attractive camping from 24F (see Camping).

Auberge de Jeunesse "Butte Rouge" (IYHF), 444, av. de la Division Leclerc, Châtenay Malabry (tel. 46-32-17-43). Take RER line B2 to Robinson (7.80F, railpasses valid), then take bus #198 from in front of the station (1 yellow Métro ticket) to place Cyrano de Bergerac, and follow the sign about 200m to the hostel. A 20-min. walk from the RER station. In a pleasant suburb, this 39-year-old establishment (the "mother hostel" as it is called) may not be a showpiece, but it is small (36 beds in rooms of 1-6 beds) and pleasant since it takes small groups only. 32F. No breakfast. Kitchen facilities. 3-day minimum, 7-day maximum (flexible). Reception open 5-10am and 6pm-1am. No curfew, but the last bus from Robinson leaves at about 1am. Camping 14F; campers may use kitchen and showers only after other guests.

Foyers

Foyers don't belong to an international organization as IYHF youth hostels do. You don't need a membership card and they set their own rules, but in fact most of them function as youth centers. **AJF, BVJ,** and **CISP** are considered youth hostel organizations in France, though they are not internationally recognized. Parisian *foyers* are generally fun. French youth and a fairly international community of young travelers stay in them regularly. Often, however, the staff is non-Parisian—if meeting the natives is important, you may wish to try a small hotel or B&B. Some of the *foyers* are inconveniently located, but a few are in the center of town.

In summer, the best way to find a bed in a *foyer* is to go to the **Accueil des Jeunes en France (AJF), 119, rue St-Martin, 4ème** (tel. 42-77-87-80; Mo. Rambuteau), across from the Centre Pompidou, or, to avoid the long lines here, go to one of the other offices listed in Practical Information under Budget Travel Organizations. Even in the busiest months, the AJF guarantees you "decent and low-cost lodging with immediate reservation" for the same day only (they don't book rooms in advance). You must pay the full price of the *foyer* room when you make your reservation, so you don't get to see the room beforehand. AJF can also help you find a hotel room and doesn't charge a commission. Often, however, they cannot find you a room for the full duration of your stay, so you may have to come back in a few days and start again. (Open Mon.-Sat. 9:30am-7pm.) **L'Union des Centres des Rencontres Internationales de France (UCRIF),** whose network includes the BVJ hostels, doesn't book rooms, but will give you a pamphlet listing their hostels around France. Their office is at 4, rue Jean Jacques Rousseau, 1er (tel. 42-60-42-40; Mo. Louvre). (Open Mon.-Fri. 9am-1pm and 2-7:30pm.)

Hôtel de Jeunes (AJF): "Le Fauconnier," 11, rue du Fauconnier, 4ème (tel. 42-74-23-45; Mo. St-Paul or Pont-Marie); **"Le Fourcy,"** 6, rue de Fourcy, 4ème (tel. same as Fauconnier; Mo. St-Paul); **"Maubisson,"** 12, rue des Barres, 4ème (tel. 42-72-72-09; Mo. Hôtel-de-Ville or Pont-Marie). These 3 stars of the *foyer* system are all located in pleasant historic buildings in the Marais district, close to one another and to the sights. Rooms with their high ceilings, wood paneling, and breathing space often outclass those in cheap hotels. The largest (8-bed) rooms are attractive split levels. Le Fourcy is the only one with lockers, although all AJF residents can use them (5F per day, deposit 150F). Maubisson has an annex on rue François Miron, which means residents there are condemned to a 5-min. walk before breakfast. No lockout and no curfew. AJF gives priority to groups, which, unlike individuals, can make reservations. You can obtain a place through AJF or try showing up at the *foyer* 8-9:30am. You won't get keys until 4pm. 5-day maximum. 67F. Showers included. Breakfast 5F. The AJF also runs a restaurant, **La Table d'Hôte,** 16, rue du Pont Louis Philippe, 4ème, where family-style lunch and dinner cost a modest 40F. The restaurant is for AJF guests only, and you must reserve in advance for a meal. (Lunch noon-1:30pm, dinner 6:30-8pm.) The same people run the **Résidence Bastille,** 151, av. Lédru Rollin, 11ème (tel. 43-79-53-86; Mo. Voltaire), which costs slightly more and has a few singles. 75F in barracklike, multi-bed rooms. Singles 90F. Showers and breakfast included. Reception open 8am-10:30pm. Lockout noon-2pm. **Résidence Luxembourg,** 270, rue St-Jacques, 5ème (tel. 43-25-06-20; Mo. Luxembourg), is open July-Sept. only, and has the same prices. Reception open 24 hours. Key deposit 100F. Neither have curfews. Less snazzy than the Marais establishments, they nevertheless are well located and less crowded in summer. All limited to ages 18-30, though exceptions are made.

Centre International de Paris (BVJ): Paris Louvre, 20, rue Jean Jacques Rousseau, 1er (tel. 42-36-88-18; Mo. Louvre); **Paris Opéra,** 11, rue Thérèse, 1er (tel. 42-60-77-23; Mo. Pyramides); **Paris Les Halles,** 5, rue du Pélican, 1er (tel. 42-60-92-45; Mo. Palais Royal); **Paris Quartier Latin,** 44, rue des Bernadins, 5ème (tel. 43-29-34-80; Mo. Maubert). Right in the center of things, these 4 youth centers are friendly and comfortable. Rooms a bit crowded and small, but spotless. Large, cozy halls facilitate international friendships if your speaking abilities are up to it. No individual reservations accepted; arrive by 9am or go to the **UCRIF** office in Gare du Nord (arrival hall, next to AJF in the new building). Most will hold spots reserved by phone for an hour or two. You cannot occupy your room until 2:30pm. No families accepted. Paris Louvre has the least stylish common area and Paris Opéra the oldest rooms. Paris Les Halles is smaller than its neighbors and serves tasty food. Mostly multi-bedded rooms and a few singles. 75F. Showers and breakfast included. Paris Louvre has a restaurant with meals for 45F and *demi-pension* for 110F. 3-day maximum (flexible), except at Latin Quarter, which will let you stay for a few weeks (also flexible). A student foyer, Latin Quarter assigns singles only to students who are studying in Paris and who have applied to them in writing. Open daily 6am-2am.

Centre International de Séjour de Paris (CISP): CISP "Ravel," 6, av. Maurice Ravel, 12ème (tel. 43-43-19-01; Mo. Porte de Vincennes). Go right on bd. Soult, take a left on av. Courteline, and then a right on av. Vincent d'Indy, which turns into av. Maurice Ravel (10-15 min. from the Métro). A big place with excellent facilities, but on the edge of nowhere. Bar, restaurant, and access to a pool (use of pool 12-20F for CISP guests only). A few singles and doubles 110F. Rooms with up to 5 beds 90F. Beds in dormitory 77F. Breakfast and showers included. Meals 34F and 45F. **CISP "Kellerman"** at 17, bd. Kellerman, 13ème (tel. 45-80-70-76; Mo. Porte d'Italie), offers the same prices for beds and restaurant and also has facilities for the disabled. Its newer, cozier, airy white decor is complemented by its location in a park where you can go jogging. Both *foyers* give priorities to groups, but do accept families and individuals. Individual reservations by phone 1-2 days in advance only when there is space. Reception open 6:30am-1:30am. Curfew 1:30am.

Y&H Hostel, 80, rue Mouffetard, 5ème (tel. 45-35-09-53; Mo. Monge). Ideally located on a street crammed with restaurants, Y&H, as its name suggests, is staffed and frequented by the Young and Happy. Rooms are crowded with 2, 3, or 4 beds. The atmosphere is informal and pleasant. Though the building is old and run-down and the mattresses uncomfortably thin, the rooms are clean and the multilingual management bubbling with information. 63F. Showers included. Reserve by mail with 1 night's payment or arrive by 10am. After 10am they may be able to set up an extra bed in 1 of the bigger rooms, but you still pay the full price. Reception open 8-11am and 5pm-1am. Curfew 1am.

3 Ducks Hostel, 6, place E. Pernet, 15ème (tel. 48-42-04-05, Mo. Commerce), to the right of Eglise Jean Baptiste de Grenelle. In a quiet quarter, but expect a raucous crowd in this lively place. Party in the courtyard, but you'll receive a loud wake-up call by 10:30am. Renovations continue. Bar in reception. 63F. Showers included. Reserve by letter with 1 night's payment or arrive around 9am. If you're desperate, they'll give you a mattress on the floor. Lockout 11am-5pm. Reception open 9am-noon and 5pm-1am. Curfew 1am.

Foyer Franco-Libannais, 15, rue d'Ulm, 5ème (tel. 43-29-47-60; Mo. Cardinal-Lemoine or Luxembourg). Huge modern structure conveniently located near the Luxembourg and rue Mouffetard. Good chance of finding a room in July and Aug., when the students leave. Large, pleasant rooms and convivial atmosphere. Clean showers and W.C. in all corridors (don't pay extra to have them in your room). To reserve, write at least 15 days in advance; you must confirm with payment for the length of your stay. Singles 100F, with shower 110F. Studio 190F. Doubles 135-170F. Students pay 20F less on rooms, 15-20F less on rooms with shower. 10% less if you write in advance for month-long stays. Key deposit 20F. Open 7:30am-midnight, but guests can use the entry code to come in at any time.

Association des Etudiants Protestants de Paris (AEPP), 46, rue de Vaugirard, 6ème (tel. 46-33-23-30 or 43-54-31-49; Mo. Luxembourg or Odéon). Excellent location across from the Jardin du Luxembourg. Friendly atmosphere. Lots of international students and TV lounge, library (closed in Aug.), kitchen (open until midnight), table tennis, and a large open courtyard. 5-day minimum and 3-week maximum (flexible). No reservations although you can try calling 1 day ahead; arrive by 10am. The clean rooms with lockers are a bit noisy as they are on the street. Rooms with 4-6 beds 56F per person. Doubles 70F per person. Singles 72F. Showers and breakfast included. Reception open Mon.-Fri. 9am-noon and 3-7pm, Sat. 9am-noon and 6-8pm, Sun. and holidays 10am-noon. Curfew 10pm, but residents get a key.

UCJF (Union Chrétienne de Jeunes Filles), or **YWCA,** 22, rue Naples, 8ème (tel. 45-22-23-49; Mo. Europe-Villiers). In the summer accepts *passagères* (women only) for a 3-day minimum (no maximum). Otherwise 3-month minimum and obligatory *demi-pension* 2000F per month. All students must pay a 25F membership fee before enrolling and a 150F processing fee. Phone reservations accepted in summer. A very old-fashioned place, run by an engaging headmistress-type owner. Nice rooms and big dinner selection. Singles, doubles, and triples 90F per person. Quads 70F per person. Showers and breakfast included. New arrivals can't check in Sat.-Sun. unless they are desperate. Doors close Sun.-Thurs. at 12:30pm, Fri.-Sat. at 1am, but some exceptions are made. Reception open 8:30am-6:30pm.

Maison des Clubs UNESCO, 43, rue de la Glacière, 13ème (tel. 43-36-00-63; Mo. Glacière). Friendly, English-speaking staff. Clean and modern. TV in breakfast room. Group reservations only. Individuals show up 9:30-10am to check for vacancies. 5-day maximum (flexible). Singles 100F. Rooms with 2-4 beds 76F. Breakfast included. Doors close at 12:30am and don't open until 7am.

Maison Internationale des Jeunes, 4, rue Titon, 11ème (tel. 43-71-99-21; Mo. Faidherbe-Chaligny). 150 beds. Rooms with 2-8 beds for ages 18-30 and some family housing. Court views are nice, but rooms are dark. Co-ed showers and some co-ed rooms. Friendly manager speaks English. 3-day maximum (flexible). Reservations are not accepted, so come early in the morning. 75F, including a good shower and a meager breakfast. Open 8am-10pm. Loosely enforced lockout 10am-5pm. Curfew 1am.

Foyer International d'Accueil de Paris, 30, rue Cabanis, 14ème (tel. 45-89-89-15; Mo. Glacière), in a quiet area. Monolithic, modern, and clean—more like a high-rise apartment than a *foyer.* Families often stay here. Individual reservations not more than a month in advance. 15-day maximum, but only with reservations made a month in advance. The welcome here is hardly warm as the staff is harried. 3 rooms have facilities for the disabled. Singles 90F, with shower 105F. Doubles 78F, with shower 90F. Singles in the annex 140F. Breakfast 15F, meals 42F. Curfew 2am.

Cité Universitaire, 15, bd. Jourdan, 14ème (tel. 45-89-35-79; Mo. Cité-Universitaire). Like a large international campus; each country has its own foundation, which reflects the nation it represents. For housing in the **Fondation des Etats-Unis,** either write or go in person and ask for the *secretariat.* During the academic year students are required to apply to their country's foundation, but in summer you can stay in any of the other halls for a 10-day minimum. Write to M. le Délégué Général de Cité Universitaire de Paris, 19, bd. Jourdan, 75690 Paris CEDEX 14, or show up at the foundation where you wish to stay; usually room at the Moroccan house. The ice and laundry machines are in the American house. The Canadian, Swiss, and Norwegian houses are highly recommended. All singles 85F per night, 2200F per month. Must pay in full in order to book a room. Key deposit 150F in cash. Open 8am-12:30pm,

1:10-7:50pm, and 8:30pm-midnight. No curfew. Restaurant in Maison Internationale open Mon.-Fri. 11:45am-2pm and 6-8:30pm. 10 meal tickets 90F.

Foyer International des Etudiantes, 93, bd. St-Michel, 6ème (tel. 43-54-49-63; Mo. Luxembourg), across from the Jardin du Luxembourg. If you can get one of its 160 places, this is the *foyer* to stay in. From Oct.-June, it accepts only women connected with the University of Paris (including the Sorbonne's Cours de Civilisation Française); in June it accepts only female transients according to availability of space; July-Sept. it accepts both sexes. One of the best locations in Paris. TV lounge, piano, exquisite wood-paneled library (Oct.-June only), kitchenettes on floors (use own equipment), irons, hair dryers, and tennis courts. Lots of international students, and a *sympa* director. Reservations should be made 2 months ahead in writing, and followed by 150F and confirmation. Call ahead or arrive around 9:30am to check for no-shows. Singles 127F. Doubles (some quite small) 84F per person. Showers and breakfast included. Closed Sun.-Fri. 1:30am-6am; open all night Sat.

Maison d'Etudiants, 18, rue Jean Jacques Rousseau, 1er (tel. 45-08-02-10; Mo. Louvre). International students and professors stay in this somewhat subdued *foyer*. Rooms with 1-4 people are clean. 75F includes showers and breakfast. Reserve by mail with 1st night's payment or go to 2nd floor reception early in the morning. 3-day minimum. Open July-Sept. 8am-9pm. No curfew.

Bed and Breakfasts

Recently established in France, this system may offer the best prices for convenient locations, and, above all, a chance to participate in daily French life. After writing, or, in some cases, arriving in the office directly, you choose living conditions, location, and even the personality of your hosts. You may be required to pay the entire cost of your stay in advance.

Paris Rêveries Bed and Breakfast, 179, bd. Voltaire, 75011 Paris (Mo. Charonne). Run by 4 struggling students, this association offers lodging in some *péniches* (house boats) and apartments. Write well in advance to receive an application. Singles 120F. Doubles 180F. Breakfast and showers included.

Bed and Breakfast #1, 73, rue Notre-Dame-des-Champs, 75006 Paris (tel. 43-25-43-97; Mo. Notre-Dame-des-Champs). Businesslike, but if you arrive at the office in the morning, you may preview possible accommodations for that night. Write 1-2 months in advance for a larger selection. Include a 300F deposit, dates of your stay, number of people, bed required (single, double, or twin), location desired, and specify whether or not you want breakfast. Singles 150-190F. Doubles 170-210F. Breakfast 15F. Membership 100F per person, 150F per couple, 200F per family. 2-day minimum. Office open Mon.-Sat. 9am-7pm.

Café Couette (Coffee-Quilt), Bed and Breakfast (France), P.O. Box 66, Henley on Thames, Oxon, RC9 IXS England (tel. (44) 04-91-57-88-03). This British organization offers 65 rooms around Paris (about 400 in France) in comfortable, carefully selected homes. All a bit more expensive than other possibilities. Send £10 (£35 for families of less than 6), or the equivalent in francs or dollars, with your name, address, telephone, and age to become a member. You will receive a guide with names and descriptions of accommodations. The best choices include *châteaux*. £6.25-25 per person. Allow at least 35 days before the 1st night in order to reserve.

Bed and Breakfast Le Vesinet, 33, allée de la Meute, F-78110 Le Vesinet-Paris. (tel. (33) 130-71-45-60; RER Vesinet). A warm, friendly family offers 6 to 10 places in a comfortable home. Picnic in the large flowergarden. Single 110F. Double 140F. Breakfast 15F. Reserve by mail, or phone to check for space when you arrive in Paris.

Hotels

Seeking a hotel room in Paris in summer can be extremely disheartening. French hotel owners are sometimes rude, especially to those who don't speak French. Many are annoyed at the extra work that booming business creates. If *Let's Go* lists such a place, we do so because the location or price outweighs its drawbacks.

Fortunately, it is no longer necessary to run from one full hotel to the next, laden with all your gear; the **Accueil des Jeunes en France (AJF),** 119, rue St-Martin, 4ème (tel. 42-77-87-80; Mo. Rambuteau), will book you a room commission-free. (Open Mon.-Sat. 9:30am-7pm. See Budget Travel Organizations in Practical Information for less crowded branch offices.) You must, however, pay for the room in full on the spot in order to reserve, which means you can't see the room before committing yourself. **Tourist offices** offer a similar service, though they charge a small commission and make reservations only in hotels that are members of the tourist association (see Practical Information for locations).

If you prefer to arrange your stay before you leave, try to make reservations at least two weeks in advance (a number of hotels claim that they are fully booked 2 months in advance for the summer). Some hotels will hold a room for you if you merely ask for one in writing, but others require a deposit equivalent to the cost of one night's stay (*verser des arrhes*). Be sure to inquire whether you must arrive by a certain time, because some hotels hold rooms only until 6pm. Most large American banks can make out international money orders in French currency; enclose International Reply Coupons (sold at U.S. post offices). Never send more than enough to cover one night's stay, otherwise you might wind up stuck in a place you don't like and struggling to get the money back. Also, if you send the first night's payment and can't make it, call the hotel. If they can still rent the room (i.e., you cancel at least a day before), then you're entitled to your deposit back. Hotels are under no obligation to accept pets (and may charge a supplement), but they must accept children. Finally, an extra bed cannot cost more than 30% of the room's price.

If you're looking for a room on your own, or if you are unable to make a reservation, try to arrive as early in the day as possible (though before 10am many hotels won't know whether they will have space, as lodgers often decide to stay or check out in the morning). Hotels fill up quickly after morning check-out, and by late afternoon most rooms are gone. There is a high concentration of relatively inexpensive hotels in the **Latin Quarter** (Mo. St-Michel, Luxembourg, or Maubert-Mutualité). Streets radiating off **rue St-Jacques, rue Dauphine, rue des Ecoles, rue du Sommerard, rue Cujas** (Mo. Luxembourg), and **rue Victor-Cousin** (which becomes **rue de la Sorbonne**) are also all possibilities, but since this is such a popular neighborhood, these fill up quickly. Another possibility is to go to the area around **Gare du Nord** and **Gare de l'Est**, or near **place de la République**, where the hotels are plentiful and not as much in demand. The pleasant area between Pigalle and the top of Montmartre—especially around **place des Abbesses**—offers quite a few inexpensive, though slightly threadbare hotels. The hub of prostitution and other illegal activities, this neghborhood can be dangerous, but if you go to the Abbesses Métro stop (not Anvers) and avoid walking up from Pigalle, you should be safe. If you have a little more money to spend, you might try the area in the **Marais** around the Hôtel de Ville and **rue de Rivoli,** and also the adjacent streets such as **rue du Temple.** Always ask to see your room before you take it, even though most French hotel owners are not too keen on this. Also, the price of the kind of room may vary widely—a room with a nice view, or a few more square feet, may be priced higher—so always ask if there is anything *moins cher* (less expensive) before taking the first room offered.

The hotels below are listed geographically, beginning with the Left Bank (south) and moving to the Right Bank (north). They have been further grouped according to neighborhood and Métro stop. The Food section is divided into similar though not always corresponding districts, so check there for eateries once you've found a room. A word of warning: Because of renovations or a deluge of customers hotels may be upgraded from one to two stars. If prices have changed, keep hunting.

Rive Gauche (Left Bank)

Only one part of the Rive Gauche deserves a bohemian reputation: The Quartier Latin of the *cinquième,* bordered roughly by boulevard St-Michel, the Seine, and rue Monge, and intersected by rue St-Jacques and boulevard St-Germain. Even here, however, you must look through a throng of tourists to find relics of Bohemia. The Romans built some of this area's ancient streets, but the *Latin* in the *quartier*'s name refers to the language of scholarship spoken here until 1798. Traditionally home to many Parisian schools and scholars, the Latin Quarter has been transformed in the last 20 years, recent developments endangering its young, scholarly ambience. After the student uprisings of May, 1968, the University of Paris was decentralized, and in one blow the Quarter lost many of its inhabitants. Then a tidal wave of tourist gold swept over the area and crushed many of its small booksellers and cafes. Much of the area now resembles any other Parisian commercial center.

From September to June, the Quarter still swarms with students of the University of Paris at the Sorbonne and of the *grandes écoles,* prestigious exam-entry schools such as l'Ecole Nationale de Sciences Politiques (otherwise known as "Sciences Po") and l'Ecole Nationale Supèrieure. Now the intellectuals literally rub elbows with the hordes of tourists who invade the Quarter every summer. While much of the restaurant and bar business is geared to these mobs, the little cinemas, innumerable bookstores, and smaller cafes still cater to the scholars. And while the artists and hipper intellectuals have long since moved to the area around the Beaubourg and beyond, the Quarter retains an eternally youthful air.

Across St-Michel lies a different world. While just as full of tourists, St-Germain-des-Prés is hardly a budget or student area. After the nobility deserted the Marais in the beginning of the eighteenth century, they settled in St-Germain and have been there ever since. While the *hauts couturiers* may keep their headquarters on the Rive Droite, clothing boutiques line the streets stretching down from the Jardin du Luxembourg and the Théâtre de l'Odéon to the bd. St-Germain. Except for a slightly bohemian pocket around the Institut des Beaux Arts, the streets between the *boulevard* and the Seine sport a stylish collection of antique dealers and galleries. Perhaps significantly, one *grande école* that does make its home across St-Michel is "L'ENA," l'Ecole Nationale d'Administration, the training ground of government functionaries and ministers. (Giscard d'Estaing, François Mitterand, and Jacques Chirac are all alumni or *énarques*). Mitterand and a number of government ministers still live here, on anything but the wrong side of town.

Near the southern edge of the Jardin du Luxembourg, Montparnasse was once the home of artists and writers like Modigliani, Chagall, Cocteau, and Hemingway, and well known for its nightlife. Today the area is still filled with excellent restaurants but dominated by the **Tour Montparnasse,** which casts a shadow of respectable commerce over the surrounding area.

Near the Sorbonne

The Sorbonne area, fulcrum of the Latin Quarter, has been teeming with activity since Robert de Sorbon established a college here in 1253 for poor theological students. Through it runs the **boul-Miche** (boulevard St-Michel), with its cafes, bookstores, movie theaters, and ethnic restaurants. Inexpensive hotels abound on **rue du Sommerard, rue de Cujas,** and **rue Monge.** Farther east, the neighborhood around **place de la Contrescarpe** is more bohemian and less commercialized than much of the Latin Quarter by day. Rue Mouffetard resembles a large open food market, surrounded by inexpensive to medium-priced (though not always top-notch) restaurants. At night this area swarms with tourists in search of a high time. Many hotels in this quarter have converted from one to two stars in recent years and prices have doubled accordingly, so make sure to check prices before taking a room.

Hôtel Le Home Latin, 15-17, rue du Sommerard, 5*ème* (tel. 43-26-25-21; Mo. Maubert or St-Michel). An excellent choice. The management is friendly, concerned, and proud of its service. Most rooms have been attractively remodeled or are currently undergoing renovations. Singles 116F. Doubles 146-162F, with shower 216F. Triples 292F. Showers 10F. Breakfast included. Open 7am-2am. No reservations; arrive at 10am to get a space.

Hôtel du Commerce, 14, rue de la Montagne-Ste-Geneviève, 5*ème* (tel. 43-54-89-69; Mo. Maubert). Tiny rooms and narrow halls but cheap and in a great location. The old woman at the desk resembles a character from Balzac, and her animals are omnipresent. No reservations. Singles 71F. Doubles 82F, with shower 100F. Showers 13F. Baths 23F.

Plaisant-Hôtel, 50, rue des Bernardins 5*ème* (tel. 43-54-74-57; Mo. Maubert), in a dead-end street off rue Monge. More expensive than a budget hotel, it is still a good value for 2 stars, and it deserves its name. The rooms are very French: clean and pretty with sculpted plaster ceilings and lace curtains. English spoken. Phone reservations accepted with a letter of confirmation and 1 night's deposit. Singles or doubles 140-160F, with shower 240-270F. Showers 18F. Breakfast 20F.   —

Hôtel Marignan, 13, rue du Sommerard, 5ème (tel. 43-54-63-81; Mo. Maubert), on a quiet street between bd. St-Germain and rue des Ecoles. The rooms are large but hostel-like. The multilingual staff, varied in their tolerance of rambunctious clientele, provide a great deal of useful sight-seeing information, but keep strict limits on noise at night and during visiting hours, which end at 10pm. Laundry room and iron, but no washing machines. Popular, so reserve a month in advance by letter with 1 night's deposit—they will sometimes help you find another room if they are full. In summer, 3-night minimum. Singles 115F. Doubles 180-240F. Triples 280F. Quads 320-350F. Showers and breakfast included. Nov. to mid-March rates 20% lower.

Hôtel des Carmes, 5, rue des Carmes, 5ème (tel. 43-29-78-40; Mo. Maubert). 2-star hotel established in the early 1900s. Adequate, reasonably clean rooms and bathrooms with unusually firm mattresses and telephones. Singles 130F. Doubles 165F, with shower 205F, with W.C. 240F. Showers 15F. Breakfast included.

Hôtel de Cujas, 18, rue de Cujas, 5ème (tel. 43-54-58-10; Mo. Luxembourg). No reservations in summer. Singles and doubles 80F, with shower 105F. Rooms with two beds 155F, with shower 170F. Triples with shower 200F. Showers 10F. Open all night.

Grand Hôtel Oriental, 2, rue d'Arras, 5ème (tel. 43-54-38-12; Mo. Cardinal-Lemoine), on a gently sloping street. Newly redone, clean, comfortable rooms, and a curt, efficient management. Phone reservations accepted. Singles (usually rented by the month) 145F, with shower 195F. Doubles 150F, with shower 200F. Rooms with 2 beds and TV 240F. Showers 13F. Breakfast 16F.

Hôtel Studia, 51, bd. St-Germain, 5ème (tel. 43-26-81-00; Mo. Maubert), next to the Métro station. This 2-star's prices are comparable with those at the Plaisant's, but its rooms less attractive. Pleasant, professional manager speaks English. Make reservations about a month in advance for summer. Singles 152F, with shower 199F. Doubles 170F, with bath 298F. Showers 12F. Breakfast included.

Near the Jardin du Luxembourg

Still in the Latin Quarter, streets in this area are a little quieter than their neighbors north of the Panthéon. Hotels here generally give more for the money than those around place St-Michel, but they're not as plentiful. Possibly the oldest street in Paris, rue St-Jacques is lined with *charcuteries* and *boulangeries* past rue Soufflot.

Hôtel de Médicis, 214, rue St-Jacques, 5ème (tel. 43-29-53-64 or 43-54-14-66; Mo. Luxembourg). An excellent small hotel, especially for longer stays. Although the rooms are old and one of the showers smells, the prices are great and Mme. Rault, her husband, and their two big, moody Dalmatians make this a home. English spoken. All rooms with bidet and sink. 3- to 7-day minimum. Telephone reservations accepted Sept.-May, but it may be best to come around 10am to see what's available. Singles 70F. Doubles 85-100F. Triples 115F. Showers 10F. Reductions for extended stays.

Hôtel de Nevers, 3, rue de l'Abbé-de-l'Epée, 5ème (tel. 43-26-81-83; Mo. Luxembourg), on a quiet side street off rue Gay-Lussac. Simple, clean rooms overlook the Panthéon. Cheerful manager welcomes *Let's Go* readers. Phone reservations accepted. Singles 95F. Doubles 110F, with shower 185-250F. Extra beds 25F. Showers 20F. Breakfast included.

Hôtel de l'Avenir, 52, rue Gay-Lussac, 5ème (tel. 43-54-76-60; Mo. Luxembourg). Try to get one of the sunny rooms facing the street. Radio and television in the *salon,* and lots of friendly Americans. Spunky reception. Pleasant, cozy atmosphere. Singles 86-96F. Doubles 112F, with shower 127F. Showers 12F. Breakfast included. May be closed for renovations or reopened with higher prices in 1989.

Montparnasse

Montparnasse is conveniently located south of the Latin Quarter, where the 6ème, 14ème, and 15ème *arrondissements* meet. Known for its lively nightlife, the area is full of popular but expensive restaurants and movie houses. You will always find people here, especially on the Boulevard du Montparnasse. At night, the small, dark streets next to the cemetery harbor prostitutes or drug dealers. In general, avoid the small streets between Métro stops Gaité and Volontiers.

Celtik-Hôtel, 15, rue d'Odessa, 14ème (tel. 43-20-93-53; Mo. Montparnasse-Bienvenue or Edgar-Quinet), close to Tour Montparnasse. Comfortable, fairly clean rooms with marble fireplaces, kind reception, and not a bad price for the area. Usually rooms are taken only by reservation (by phone or written), and the 3 rooms without showers are almost always booked. Singles 120F, with shower 130F. Doubles with shower 160F, with 2 beds 210F. Showers 15F. Breakfast 15F.

Kenmore Hôtel, 37, bd. du Montparnasse, 6ème (tel. 45-48-20-57; Mo. Montparnasse-Bienvenue). Model boats fill up the glass cases in the lobby. Adequate rooms. Reception speaks English and Spanish. Conveniently located. Singles 117F, with shower 134F. Doubles 168F, with shower 195-224F. Showers 20F. Breakfast included.

St-Germain-des-Prés

Boulevard St-Germain, one of the greatest people-watching arteries of Paris and perhaps the world, enlivens St-Germain-des-Prés, which has made the sidewalk cafe into an art form. Jean Paul Sartre was a regular at one of the area's finest and most expensive establishments, the Cafe des Deux Magots. There *are* some affordable lodgings here, along with one of Paris's finest deals.

Hôtel Nesle, 7, rue de Nesle, 6ème (tel. 43-54-62-41; Mo. Odéon), off rue Dauphine. "You'll either love it or hate it" says Mme. Renée, the owner. Once a bastion of psychedelic '60s interior design, the Nesle has been overhauled in an eclectic mix of styles (Egyptian, Indian, Victorian. Most guests leave their doors open in the evening and mingle, although quiet is requested after 11pm. When the owner is not present, the reception staff can be either unhelpful or overly friendly. No reservations, so go early. Singles 80F. Doubles 160F, with shower and breakfast 210F. Showers 10F. Breakfast with incense and Arab music (Mon.-Sat. only) 18F.

Delhy's Hotel, 22, rue de l'Hirondelle, 6ème (tel. 43-26-58-25; Mo. St-Michel), on a tiny street between place St-Michel and rue Gît le Coeur. Rooms tend to be dark, but they all have direct-dial telephones and are reasonably priced given the excellent location. Since this 1-star is small, reservations in summer are recommended 1 month in advance, with deposit. If there is space you can reserve 1-2 days ahead by phone. Singles and doubles with shower 150-200F. Breakfast included.

Hôtel St-Michel, 17 rue Gît-le-Coeur, 6ème (tel. 43-26-98-70; Mo. St-Michel), near place St-Michel. Portuguese family offers warm welcome. Small, simple, clean rooms. Breakfast downstairs in stone cellar. Singles 110F. Doubles 145F, with shower 210F; with two beds 255F. Showers 12F. Breakfast included. Reception open 7am-1am.

Résidence St-Germain, 16, rue du Four, 6ème (tel. 43-54-60-61; Mo. St-Germain-des-Prés). A classic French *pension* in the heart of the city. Clean, correct, and highly recommended, though the proprietor does not accommodate non-French speakers. Singles 120F. Doubles 170F. Triples 300F. Showers 13F. Breakfast included. Call ahead to see if there's room. Since this is not a hotel, people are requested not to call after 10:30pm (although guests can return any time using the building code).

Seventh Arrondissement

Home to two of Paris's best-known landmarks, the Eiffel Tower and the Hôtel des Invalides, the *septième*'s prosperity is evidenced by the scores of fine antique stores and galleries lining the streets next to the Seine, and by La Varenne, the world-famous cooking school that, 10 years ago, introduced the world to the dubious blessing of *nouvelle cuisine*.

Hôtel du Quai Voltaire, 19, quai Voltaire, 7ème (tel. 42-61-50-91; Mo. Rue du Bac). A lovely, 3-star hotel with antique furniture in the rooms and a pretty room with *tapisseries*. Most rooms look out over the Seine to the Louvre. English spoken. Oscar Wilde lived in room #47. Reserve in writing at least 1 month in advance. Singles 150F, with shower 310F. Doubles with shower 450F, with bath 450F. Showers 30F. Breakfast included.

Ile de la Cité

Paris began on the Ile de la Cité, and today its narrow, winding streets, old houses, and monuments draw tourists in droves. As a result, cafe, hotel, and restaurant prices are inflated, yet there does remain one stalwart survivor.

Hôtel Henri IV, 25, place Dauphine, 1er (tel. 43-54-44-53; Mo. Pont-Neuf or Cité), on a lovely square behind the Palais de Justice. The lower floors are some 400 years old, and the building is deliciously beset with the problems of age. The rooms are spacious, but a bit faded, the walls thin and the washrooms and showers can be reached only by a little staircase that curls around outside. English-speaking management. In summer reserve 1-2 months in advance by telephone or letter. Singles 80F. Doubles 142F. Triples 160F. Showers 12F. Breakfast included.

Rive Droite (Right Bank)

The Right Bank calls to mind *grands boulevards, grands musées, grands magasins,* and, so many people assume, *grands prix.* But unexpected bargains and quiet hints of *le vrai Paris* still lurk behind the tourist-ridden Opéra and Louvre.

Le Marais

Le Marais, which extends from the Bastille to the Seine and northward to the Archives Nationales and rue Pastourelle, had modest beginnings as a swamp (*marais*), but later became a fashionable district of *hôtels particuliers* (townhouses). After the king left town for Versailles and fashion moved to the Right Bank in the eighteenth century, the Marais became a Jewish community, centered on rue des Rosiers and rue St-Antoine (formerly rue des Juifs). After World War II, the area was declared a historical district, and restoration began. More recently, the gay community has found a home here. Some claim that the Marais today is one of Paris's trendiest areas, and also one of its historically and ethnically richest. Rue des Rosiers houses an infinite variety of *kascher* (kosher) butchers, delicatessens, and felafel stands. Amidst superb architecture, nifty outfits, and good smells, the Marais offers some fine, affordable lodging possibilities.

Hôtel du Loiret, 8, rue des Mauvais Garçons, 4*ème* (tel. 48-87-77-00; Mo. Hôtel-de-Ville), near the Hôtel de Rivoli. Near many cafes, restaurants, and gay bars. Quiet, clean, and spacious rooms. Lots of foreign students. Reserve 2-3 days in advance by mail with 1 night's deposit, or arrive by 9am. Singles and doubles 80F, with shower 120F. Showers 15F. Obligatory breakfast 15F.

Hôtel Rivoli, 2, rue des Mauvais-Garçons, 4*ème* (tel. 42-72-08-41; Mo. Hôtel-de-Ville), on a small street off rue de Rivoli past the BHV department store. Nicely renovated. The rooms can be noisy since most face busy rue de Rivoli, but they are sunny, reasonably clean, and attractive. Helpful proprietor, cute children, and 3 tropical birds all run the place. No reservations. Singles 75-85F, with shower 90F. Doubles 110F, with shower 150F. Triples 140-180F. Showers 15F. Breakfast, usually in your room, 15F. Curfew 1am (flexible).

Hôtel de Nice, 42bis, rue de Rivoli, 4*ème* (tel. 42-78-55-29; Mo. Hôtel-de-Ville). Variety is key here as fragrant rooms range from aromatic to smelly, tasteful to tacky. Run by a charming family. Reserve 3 weeks in advance and confirm with a letter including 1 night's deposit. Rooms overlooking the square are the quietest. Singles and doubles 100-180F, with shower 195F. Triples with shower 270F. Showers 16F. Breakfast included and served in delightful *salon.* Curfew midnight or 2am.

Grand Hôtel Malher, 5, rue Malher, 4*ème* (tel. 42-72-60-92; Mo. St-Paul), well located on a small street connecting the Jewish quarter with rue de Rivoli. A picturesque hotel in an old building with lace curtains and blue decor. Rooms with telephones. Singles and doubles 100-130F, with shower 170F, with bath and W.C. 250F. Triples 150F, with bath and toilet 300F. Showers 12F. Breakfast, which can be brought up to rooms on the 1st 3 floors, 18F.

Hôtel Picard, 26, rue de Picardie, 3*ème* (tel. 48-87-53-82; Mo. République or Filles-du-Calvaire). Excellent 1-star hotel, run by an efficient and pleasant manager. Rooms are large, clean, and modern with telephones and often excellent views. Reserve at least 2 weeks in advance, or arrive early. If there's space, they'll accepte same-day phone reservations. If you're willing to pay a higher price your 1st night, the management will move you to a cheaper room as soon as one is available. Singles or doubles 120-150F, with shower 230F. 2 beds with bath and W.C. 250-300F. Extra beds half the room price. Showers 15F. Delicious breakfast with unlimited bread and coffee 20F.

Hôtel Chancelier Boucherat, 110, rue de Turenne, 3*ème* (tel. 42-72-91-28; Mo. Filles-du-Calvaire). Newly renovated rooms are tastefully decorated in cream and are in excellent condition. Attractive breakfast area. Extremely friendly, multilingual staff. The neighborhood, a bustling garment district by day, becomes uncomfortably quiet at night. Recommended for groups of 3 or 4. Singles 112F, with shower 228F. Doubles 135F, with shower 248F. Triples 237F, with shower 330F. Quads 257F, with bath 350F. Showers 12F. Breakfast 20F.

88   **Paris**

Tenth Arrondissement

The *dixième* is an interesting mixture of young professionals, bohemian artists, and workers. It extends from homely place de la République to the huge Gare du Nord and Gare de l'Est and encompasses picturesque Canal St-Martin. Accommodations here are plentiful and close to the stations.

Hôtel Kuntz, 2, rue des Deux Gares, 10ème (tel. 46-07-50-41; Mo. Gare du Nord or Gare de l'Est), on a side street off Faubourg St-Denis. Owner's motto: "Cleanliness above all." Peaceful and comfortable with impressive views of the train station. Singles 98F. Doubles 157F, with shower 175-195F, with bath 259F. Showers 10F. Breakfast 19F. Reserve by letter with deposit.

Hôtel Marclau, 78, rue du Faubourg Poissonière, 10ème (tel. 47-70-73-50; Mo. Poissonière), off rue La Fayette. Comfortable, modern rooms, and friendly if strict management. Hall bathrooms are unusually large. Reserve at least 1 week ahead of time in summer, or try calling on the eve before or the morning of the day you want to stay. Doubles 140F, with shower 170F. Triples 210F, with shower 294F. Showers 12F. Breakfast included.

Palace Hôtel, 9, rue Bouchardon, 10ème (tel. 46-07-06-86; Mo. Strasbourg-St-Denis), on a tiny street off rue du Faubourg St-Martin in a quiet mini-neighborhood. An extremely cozy and family-oriented place that welcomes *Let's Go*-ers. Large hall with a piano and tables at the entrance. Friendly management keeps it cleaner than most in the area. Spacious rooms though not in exemplary condition. Doubles 90F, with shower 140F. Triples 120F, with shower 170F. Quads 200F. Showers 15F. Breakfast in your room 15F.

Hôtel Little, 3, rue Pierre Chausson, 10ème (tel. 42-08-21-57; Mo. Jacques-Bonsergent). 2 stars are well earned here. Friendly atmosphere and lots of young people. Professional reception, direct dial telephones, and exceptionally good mattresses in newly-redone rooms. Singles 120F. Doubles with shower 200F. Triples with shower 250F. Quads with shower 300F. Breakfast 20F.

Hôtel du Progrès, 7, rue Pierre-Chausson, 10ème (tel. 42-08-16-55; Mo. Jacques-Bonsergent). Decent condition, decent decor, passably clean; if you can afford it, go next door. Singles 90F. Doubles 125F, with shower 160F, with bath 180F. Extra bed 30F. Shower 25F. Breakfast 17F.

Hôtel de Belfort, 22, bd. Magenta, 10ème (tel. 42-08-35-85; Mo. Jacques-Bonsergent). No groups here, so there's a good chance of getting a room. Check out the buddha in the reception area. English-speaking management, plain rooms. Singles 80F. Doubles 120F. Triples 150F. One of the rare places with 1- and 2-bed doubles for the same price. Showers 20F. Curfew 1:30-2am.

Hôtel de Nevers, 53, rue de Malte, 11ème (tel. 47-00-56-18; Mo. République), on a side street off av. de la République, near place de la République. Prettier and more luxurious than others in the neighborhood, though well-kept rooms are not too spacious. Strict but friendly manager. Singles 110F. Doubles 130F, with shower 180F, with bath, 230F. Showers 20F. Breakfast 20F. Reserve by letter with 1 night's deposit.

Hôtel des Grands Boulevards, 4, rue Gustave Goublier, 10ème (tel. 42-08-32-08; Mo. Château d'Eau), close to the station. Helpful manager. Large and usually clean rooms with carpeted walls. Singles 80F. Doubles 100F, with shower 150-200F. Showers 19F.

Hôtel La Fayette, 198, rue La Fayette, 10ème (tel. 46-07-44-79; Mo. Louis-Blanc). Not too attractive, but close to Gare du Nord and Gare de l'Est. On a noisy street; best rooms in back. Wooden floors and visible attempts at cleanliness. Singles 95F. Doubles 135F. Triples 162F. Showers 20F. Breakfast in bed included. To reserve, write with deposit.

Ninth Arrondissement

Most of this area is quiet and residential—once you are north of the *boulevards* or south of Pigalle. Inexpensive rooms are difficult to find, although the Trois Poussins is a good deal. During the day, Pigalle is overrun with pickpockets. At night, neither men nor women should go there alone. Parisians counsel foreigners not to go either to Anvers (use Abbesses Métro instead), or Barbès-Rochechouart.

Hôtel des Trois Poussins, 15, rue Clauzel, 9ème (tel. 48-74-38-20; Mo. St-Georges). Physically, this hotel is superior to its neighbors, but its real distinction is its management. The Desforges are a genuinely *sympathique* family who will go out of their way to make you feel at home. Reserve by writing; it's unlikely you'll find a room by just dropping in. Singles and doubles from 120F, with shower 180F. Singles 540F per week. The owners have remodeled

3 rooms themselves, complete with bathrooms and kitchenette (250F). Extra beds 35F. Showers 10F. Breakfast in your room 16F. Rates negotiable for extended stays (between 2300 and 4500F per month). Children accepted only with permission of the owner.

Hôtel Studios du Printemps, 32, rue Joubert, 9*ème* (tel. 48-74-04-20; Mo. Havre-Caumartin), between rue Caumartin and rue de la Chaussée d'Antin. A bland, rather pricey business hotel, but the sunny rooms have phones. Within walking distance of Paris's best-known department stores. Singles or doubles 130F, with shower 160F, with shower or bath and W.C. 220F. Doubles with 2 beds 250F. Showers 20F. Breakfast 18F. Animals allowed. Write with deposit for reservations.

Hôtel de Berne, 30, rue de Châteaudun, 9*ème* (tel. 48-74-37-66; Mo. Notre-Dame-de-Lorette). Another bland business hotel, but clean rooms and pleasant management. Some street noise. Singles 140F, with shower 170F. Doubles 160F, with shower 190F. Triples or quads 240-320F, with shower 290-440F. Showers 15F. Breakfast 15F. Group discounts.

Montmartre

The neighborhood between Pigalle and the butte of Montmartre is mainly residential and pleasant. Hordes of tourists traipse daily from the Moulin Rouge to place du Tertre. Because they never stop, the neighborhood remains peaceful and the prices low. Many of the side streets around place des Abbesses shelter small, inexpensive hotels. Even if the following are full you should not find it difficult to get a room elsewhere. Remember always to use the Métro Abbesses, and to stay away from the Métros Anvers, Pigalle, and Barbès-Rochechouart, where hotels are often brothels. The streets around place des Abbesses are safe.

Hôtel Tholozé, 24, rue Tholozé, 18*ème* (tel. 46-06-74-83; Mo. Abbesses), on a quiet (and steep) side street off rue des Abbesses crowned by a windmill. Although hardly picturesque, the recently remodeled rooms are attractive and clean, and have phones. The rooms on the street are sunny. Singles 70-90F. Doubles 100F, with shower 150F. Triples with shower and W.C. 220F. Showers 15F. Breakfast 15F.

Hôtel des Arts, 5, rue Tholozé, 18*ème* (tel. 46-06-30-52; Mo. Abbesses). Proprietor a bit truculent, but mellows with time. Rooms impeccably clean, if somewhat dark and spartan. Singles 75F. Doubles 85F, with 2 beds 95F, with 2 beds and shower 110-130F. Showers 15F. Breakfast 18F.

Hôtel Idéal, 3, rue des Trois-Frères, 18*ème* (tel. 46-06-63-63; Mo. Abbesses), down rue Le Tac from the Abbesses Métro entrance. Clean, dark rooms are adequate, but beds creak. Very correct manager. Singles 75F, with shower 130F. Doubles 90-100F, with shower 160F. Showers 20F.

Other Neighborhoods

A number of areas of Paris offer inexpensive accommodations precisely because they don't rub shoulders with the sights and nightlife of the city. Though far away, these hotels are well connected to the center by Métro and the city-weary may welcome the relief from the crowds. Also, these hotels are rarely full.

Hôtel du Ranelagh, 56, rue de l'Assomption, 16*ème* (tel. 42-88-31-63; Mo. Ranelagh), on a side street off leafy av. Mozart. Many professors stay here when studying at the Bibliothèque Nationale. Welcoming, warm manager. Newly redone, clean, and comfortable rooms. Dining room small but homey. Reserve by mail, preferably with 1 night's deposit. Singles 80F. Doubles 120F, with shower 175F. Showers 12F. Breakfast 18F.

Atlas Hotel, 12, rue de l'Atlas, 19*ème* (tel. 42-08-50-12; Mo. Buttes-Chaumont), off av. Simon Bolivar, in a quiet neighborhood with many high-rise apartment buildings. Quite close to the lovely Parc Buttes-Chaumont and to Belleville (the Chinatown of the 20*ème*). Extremely solicitous English-speaking owner who spent much of his life in the U.S. Price includes use of fully equipped kitchen, showers, and washer and dryer. Singles 130F. Doubles 150F. Rooms with 2 beds (for 2 or 3 people) 210F. Discounts for weekly stays.

Hôtel Moncey, 5, rue Lecluse, 17*ème* (tel. 45-22-25-59; Mo. Place Clichy). Somewhat dirty neighborhood, but the hotel, located on a quiet side street with many old houses, has a faded elegance and a lot of character. Singles 65-70F. Doubles 90-100F, with shower or bath 130-150F, with W.C. 170-180F. Showers 13F. Breakfast 13F.

Hôtel Beauséjour Gobelins, 16, av. des Gobelins, 5*ème* (tel. 47-27-83-91; Mo. Gobelins), on the border of the 13*ème* and 14*ème*. This newly refurbished hotel is likely to have space.

Ample rooms decorated in soft gray; friendly English-speaking reception. Singles 100F. Doubles 150F, with showers 220F. Triples 180F. Breakfast 18F. Showers 20F.

Camping

Camping will distance you from the city, and campgrounds near Paris get extremely crowded in summer. If you're determined to join the mob and pitch your tent, contact the **Camping Club of France**, 218, bd. St-Germain, 7ème (tel. 45-48-30-03; Mo. Bac), for a list of nearby campgrounds. The tourist office at 127, av. Champs Elysées, 8ème (Mo. George V), can usually provide campground information as well. Michelin map #96 is useful for locating the following sites. Note that all but the first site lie a considerable distance from the city.

Camping du Bois de Boulogne, allée du Bord de l'Eau, Bois de Boulogne, 16ème (tel. 45-24-30-00; Mo. Porte Maillot), off N185. A pretty, 3-star location in the middle of the woods on the banks of the Seine. The only campsite in Paris. From the station, take the Camping TCF bus (April-Oct., 12.40F) or take bus #244 from Porte Maillot (much cheaper but stops a few blocks away from the camp). Store, laundry, and warm showers. 1-month maximum. 55F per couple, 135F for 4 people with tent. 7F per tent, 6.50F per car. Open daily 6am-2am.

Camping du Tremblay (TCF), bd. des Alliés, 94500 Champigny-sur-Marne, Val de Marne (tel. 43-97-43-97). Take RER line A2 to Boissy-St-Leger; get off at the Joinville-Le-Pont station and take bus 108N (4.60F) directly to the camp. 14km east of Paris on N4 and A4, on the banks of the Marne River. 12F per person, 7F per tent, 3F per car. Open daily 6am-2am.

Camping Choisy-le-Roi, 125, av. de Villeneuve-St-Georges, Choisy-le-Roi (tel. 48-90-92-30). From Austerlitz, St-Michel, Invalides, Champs-de-Mars, take RER line C to Choisy-le-Roi, then cross the bridge over the Seine. Take av. Villeneuve-St-Georges immediately to the right and follow the signs. About a 30-min. walk from the station and about 1 hr. from St-Michel. An attractive site in a gritty suburb. Modern showers, toilet, and washing facilities. Disabled access. 13.50F per person, 12F per site, 12F per car.

Down and Out

If you are really down-and-out and need some help, contact the following:

The American Aid Society, in the U.S. Embassy, 2, av. Gabriel, 8ème (tel. 42-96-12-02, ext. 2717; Mo. Concorde). For Americans only. Can lend money interest-free. Open Mon.-Fri. 9am-noon. (See Emergency, Health, and Help under Practical Information for details.)

Armée du Salut (Salvation Army). Main office, 76, rue de Rome, 8ème (tel. 43-87-41-19; Mo. St-Lazare). Open Mon.-Fri. 9am-noon and 1-5:30pm. Free shelter for up to two weeks is available to the destitute. They have various facilities for men and women, including the **Cité de Refuge Hommes et Femmes,** 12, rue Cantagrel, 13ème (tel. 45-83-54-40; Mo. Porte d'Ivry or Chaveleret). Open daily 5am-midnight. These are social services for homeless people and not cheap accommodations deals. If you are not truly desperate, please don't disturb them.

In summer at the train stations, Gare du Nord and Gare de l'Est in particular, a long chain of sleeping-bag-cocooned travelers stretches out on the floor—its members have failed to find more luxurious lodging. Women alone should avoid this option, especially at Gare du Nord where drugs and prostitution abound late at night. (The area is usually safe during the day.) For the same reasons, Les Halles is not a place to linger after hours (although it's safe to change from or even leave the last Métro there). Otherwise, you might try the police, although they have been known to be rude.

Food

In a city that boasts some of the world's most famous and most expensive restaurants, you can still eat well cheaply. Try not to be lured by the fast-food burger places, which are unpleasantly flashy and more costly than their American models, or the impersonal convenience of *les selfs* (self-service cafeterias). Explore the small, family-owned establishments serving decent, sometimes excellent food for reasonable prices. You can eat well for 50F, and unforgettably for 80F. A number of restaurants in the lively Latin Quarter specialize in foreign fare—Greek, Italian, Vietnamese, and North African. Other quarters are known for ethnic or French provincial restaurants. Good Breton food abounds around Montparnasse, *lyonnais* food near the Gare de Lyon in the 11*ème*, and Alsatian in the 10*ème*. Caribbean and African restaurants occupy the 20*ème*, while the 18*ème* and 19*ème* enjoy innumerable North African places. Both the 13*ème* and 20*ème* support a large concentration of Asian restaurants. *Pariscope* lists restaurants regionally and ethnically. (See Publications about Paris.) While many of these are beyond the budget traveler's allowance, some serve 50-70F *menus*.

Remember that most restaurants are open for lunch (noon-2 or 3pm), and then close for the afternoon, reopening around 7pm for a dinner that lasts usually until 10pm. It is almost impossible to get a sit-down meal in the middle of the afternoon, so be sure to plan around the French schedule. Likewise, although many cafes and bistros stay open late at night, many of them stop serving food around 11pm or midnight. *Pariscope* lists a few restaurants at Les Halles that are open round-the-clock. Look for the sign "*Ouvert 24h sur 24.*" When you do sit down for a full meal, look for *menus à prix fixe* with *service et boisson compris* (fixed-price menus including tip and beverage). The cheaper *menus* will generally include an appetizer (*entrée*), main course (*plat*), and a choice of cheese or dessert. Drinks are extra unless *boisson comprise*—drinks included—is marked on the menu. The letters "S.N.C." stand for *service non compris*—service not included; a 15% tip is customary. Bread usually accompanies the meal for free. You are allowed by French law, if you choose, to order just one course from the *à la carte* menu, though the French are mystified by small appetites and sometimes show it. If you don't want a full meal, try a *crêperie, omeletterie,* or a vegetarian restaurant. Cafes also serve light dishes such as sandwiches, soups, and salads, though prices are often higher than in restaurants. All establishments are required to post their prices outside. If you don't want to pay for mineral water, remember to ask for a free *carafe d'eau.* Eating well is a form of entertainment for the French, and a satisfying meal including an appetizer, main course, cheese and/or dessert, as well as an apéritif, wine, and cognac with coffee, begins at 9pm and finishes at midnight just in time for the last Métro.

If you are serious about food but trying to save money, consider eating your main meal at lunch. Full *menus* often cost 15F less at lunch than at dinner. Many fine restaurants also offer *menus express* at lunch, usually just two courses, that can pull their pleasures down into your budget range. Wine lovers should frequent wine bars, where you can sample excellent *charcuteries* and *pâtés* as you sip your Sauternes or Saumur. Consider buying Patricia Wells's inspiring *A Food Lover's Guide to Paris* (see Publications about Paris), which points out extravaganzas along with bargains and discusses food and especially wine in more detail than possible here.

You'll get more out of your stay in Paris if you try some odd, very French tastes. *Tripes* cooked in herbs is loved by many. Made into sausage, *tripes* become *andouille* or *andouillette. Cuisses de grenouille* (frogs' legs) and *lapin* (rabbit, especially in a mustard sauce) are both tasty. *Raie* (skate) is an unusual fish that is sometimes bland and tough but can be delectable *au beurre noir.* Even more exotique, *cervelles* (brains) sautéed in butter is smooth and light if a little mushy. *Rognons* (kidneys) are a delicacy prepared in any fashion and surprisingly delicious considering what they've been through (or what's been through them). The ever infamous *hamburger à cheval* (horse-burger), often topped with a fried egg, continues to outclass its beefy cousin. Finally, try some *pâté.* Often a house specialty, it comes in hundreds of varieties, some highly seasoned with herbs. *Pâté de campagne* is chunky, while *pâté de foie* is soft and silky. (A *terrine,* not to be confused with a softer mousse, is also *pâté.*) Related to *pâté, rillettes* is very rich minced pork. Both *pâté* and *rillettes* are eaten on or with bread, and often garnished with *cornichons* (gherkins).

When fending for yourself, try the many specialty shops. *Crémeries* (dairy products), *charcuteries* (meats, sausages, *pâtés,* and *plats cuisine*—prepared meals), and *épiceries* (groceries) are open in the morning until noon (*boulangeries,* selling breads and pastries, stay open until 12:30 or 1pm) and then again from 2 to 7pm. Everything closes down on Sunday afternoons, as well as all day Monday, though *super-marchés* such as Prisunic and Monoprix are open Monday. In addition, some stores have an early closing day, often Wednesday. At any time of day, you can eat on your feet from vendors hawking *gaufres* (like Belgian waffles) or crêpes in all flavors from chocolate to cheese and egg, prepared hot on the spot for 10-20F. Fauchon (see Fast Foods) is a must for the gourmet and the gourmand. Its windows in place de la Madeleine, filled with tempting delicacies, may bring tears to your eyes as they make your mouth water.

Some argue that the best bread in Paris is not the popular *baguette,* but the *pain Poilâne,* a sourdough blend baked in wood-burning ovens and available from Poilâne stores in the Forum des Halles (1er) and at 8, rue Cherche Midi (6ème). Try the walnut or raisin bread made especially to accompany cheese. *Tartines* (plates of sliced bread spread with cheese, *pâté,* or *rillettes*) are served in wine bars and use *pain Poilâne.*

Vegetarians may have difficulty sampling French cuisine in Paris; Asian, African, and Indian restaurants offer better selections. However, Naturals (see Fast Food) offers not only cheap choices, but also distributes *Le Lien Diétique,* a free bimonthly newspaper for the microbiotic or vegetarian diner.

The restaurants listed below do not follow the same organization as our Hotels section. Restaurants sometimes cluster in neighborhoods where accommodations are lacking; *arrondissement* numbers should help you find eateries near your hotel. Assume that *service* is included and *boisson* is not, unless otherwise noted.

Rive Gauche (Left Bank)

Near Place de l'Odéon and Place St-Michel

As the walls of the Louvre exhaust the tourist with paintings, so too do the streets in this area bewilder the hungry with infinite choices. Nothing but rows of restaurants and cafes line **rue Grégoire de Tours** near carretour de l'Odéon, and **rue de la Harpe** and **rue de la Huchette** near place St-Michel. Pedestrian traffic, live music, and Greek cuisine flourish in the St-Michel area, while a more sedate atmosphere, conducive to digestion, reigns near place de l'Odéon. The Jardin du Luxembourg between the two areas is the ideal spot to take your *baguette.* If you are stricken with pangs of hunger in the wee hours, you can take out all kinds of sandwiches (15-25F), fresh croissants (5F), wine, and salads all night long at **Feri's,** 76, rue Mazarine, 6ème (tel. 43-26-77-35; Mo. Odéon; open daily 11am-6am).

Le Petit Vatel, 5, rue Lobineau, 6ème (tel. 43-54-28-49; Mo. Odéon or Mabillon), between rue de la Seine and rue Mabillon. What can you say about a restaurant with a lavender stove and hearty main dishes (35F) that is located only steps away from the Senate? An institution among students and artists, this place offers a changing *carte* (no *menu*) with dishes like black bean soup and curried rice (15F), main dishes like turkey or grilled beef (35F), a vegetarian plate (37F), and cheese or cake (13F). Cider, beer, or wine 6-8F. Open Mon.-Sat. noon-3pm and 7pm-midnight, Sun. 7pm-midnight. Closed 1 week in Aug.

Crémerie-Restaurant Polidor, 21, rue Monsieur-le-Prince, 6ème (tel. 43-26-95-34; Mo. Odéon), between bd. St-Michel and the Odéon Theatre. Decorated a la turn-of-the-century, this restaurant requires a card catalog to keep track of the literary greats, from Ionesco to Joyce to Hemingway, who've feasted on its ever popular home-style cooking. Try the *boeuf bourguignon* or the *sautée d'agneau* (lamb) for 40-56F. Prompt service and quality attract a line of hungry customers every night. Full meal including appetizer, main course, wine, and dessert or cheese 59F. Open daily noon-2:30pm and 7pm-1am.

Restaurant des Beaux-Arts, 11, rue Bonaparte, 6ème (tel. 43-26-92-64; Mo. St-Germain-des-Prés), across from the Ecole des Beaux-Arts and around the corner from where Oscar Wilde died and Jorge Luis Borges lived. Hearty, traditional food in large portions with quick service. Sit next to strangers—make a friend. 48F *menu* offers unusually wide selection. Open daily noon-2:30pm and 7-10:45pm.

La Mazarinade, 2, rue Jacques Callot, 6ème (tel. 43-54-88-19; Mo. St-Germain-des-Prés), well-hidden on a small street off rue de Seine. A delightful location. Avoid the dreary interior.

The menu is unoriginal but features a salad bar that must be followed by a main course. Lunch *menus* 55F and 69F, pasta 26-34F, salads 30F. Open Tues.-Sun. noon-2:30pm and 7-11pm.

Zéro de Conduite, 64, rue Monsieur-le-Prince, 6ème (tel. 43-54-50-79; Mo. Luxembourg), at bd. St-Michel. A favorite among Parisians, with checkered tablecloths and posters of old jokesters. A satisfying and extensive 55F *menu,* main courses 45-75F, *plat du jour* 38-52F. Open Sept.-July noon-2:30pm and 7-10:30pm.

Le Petit Mabillon, 6, rue Mabillon, 6ème (Mo. Odéon or Mabillon). A small restaurant on a quiet street near St-Sulpice. A few outside tables, lace curtains, and a wooden bar; otherwise, quite dark. Italian specialties. The 57.50F, 3-course *menu* offers a plate of *charcuteries, crudités,* or montanilla cheese with capers and anchovies, followed by *carpaccio,* a fresh pasta dish, or pork cooked with shallots. Finish with pie, sherbet, or pecan ice cream. Open Mon. 7-11:30pm, Tues.-Sat. noon-1pm and 7-11:30pm.

A la Bonne Crêpe, 11, rue Grégoire de Tours, 6ème (Mo. Odéon), off bd. St-Germain. Tiny place with wooden tables, lace curtains, and Quimper porcelain on the walls. You can have your crêpes stuffed with just about anything. Dinner crêpes 20-35F, dessert crêpes 25F. 40F *menu* served until 6pm. Have a traditional *bolée* (ceramic bowl) of *cidre* (slightly alcoholic apple cider, 8F). Open Mon.-Fri. noon-11:30pm, Sat. noon-12:30am, Sun. 5pm-midnight.

La Microbiothèque, 17, rue de Savoie, 6ème (tel. 43-25-04-96; Mo. Odéon). A health food restaurant serving walnut and apple yogurt, salad (18F), brown rice (24F), and more. Unfortunately, the servings are small for those accustomed to American health food. 39F and 65F *menus* with few choices. A small health food store at the front of the restaurant. Open Sept.-July Mon.-Sat. noon-2pm and 7-10pm.

La Cochonaille, 21, rue de la Harpe, 5ème (tel. 46-33-96-81; Mo. St-Michel), right in the middle of everything. Traditional food with, as its name implies, pink decor. An emphasis on pork dishes. The downstairs cellar is ideal for romance. The 3-course, 66.70F *menu* offers a wider selection than most. For 54F, you can choose an entree and main dish, or main dish and dessert, wine included. Open daily noon-2pm and 6:30-11pm.

Near Place de la Contrescarpe

Not far from the Panthéon and the Sorbonne, the restaurants here are some of the most interesting in Paris. **Rue Mouffetard,** a market street teaming with stalls and shoppers by day, is an international diner's paradise by night. **Rue Descartes,** the continuation of rue Mouffetard, and **rue Pot de Fer** prolong the exotic feast. There are many Greek restaurants, a few Vietnamese, some North African, and even a couple of French places.

Au Bistro de la Sorbonne, 4, rue Toullier, 5ème (tel. 43-54-41-49; Mo. Luxembourg). An orange sign with a large #4 marks the spot on a street off rue Soufflot. Foreign visitors receive a warm welcome from the non-English-speaking host at this popular restaurant. Hearty meals 25-75F. The unlimited salad and hors d'oeuvres bar is outstanding at 46F *à la carte* or included in the 57F (lunch) and 75F (dinner) *menus. A la carte quart poulet aux champignons* (30F) or a *galette* with salad (25-33F) are filling served with baked potatoes. Open Mon.-Sat. noon-2:30pm and 7pm-midnight.

Restaurant Astraea, 5, rue du Sommerard, 5ème (tel. 46-33-45-47; Mo. Maubert-Mutualité). A tranquil but truly *sympa* place, with a 3-course, 49F lunch *menu* and a 59F dinner *menu* including an excellent, generous salad bar and good Greek and French main dishes. Entrees 34-46F. Friendly owners speak English. Open Mon.-Sat. 11:45am-2:30pm and 6:30-11pm.

Le Tire Bouchon, 47, rue Descartes, 5ème (tel. 43-26-39-11; Mo. Cardinal-Lemoine). Tiny and crowded, this restaurant may have added an upstairs dining room by 1989 to accommodate all the *Let's Go*-ers. Eat delicious, simple French food to the strains of street musicians. Try the *steak au fromage* and *mousse au chocolat,* included in the 48F *menu* (*boisson comprise* only during lunch). Open Mon.-Thurs. 4pm-1am, Fri.-Sun. 10:30am-3pm and 6pm-1am.

Restaurant Perraudin, 157, rue St-Jacques 5ème (tel. 46-33-15-75; Mo. Luxembourg). The new owners of this old restaurant attempt to conserve the bistro atmosphere (and prices) of times gone by while offering home cooking and a large selection of country wines. Professional but courteous service. 59F lunch *menu.* Sunday brunch includes orange juice, coffee, toast, egg dishes with bacon and potatoes, and dessert pancakes (59F). Appetizers 20F, entrees 45-55F, desserts 15-20F. Try the *crème caramel.* Open Mon.-Fri. noon-2:30pm and 7:30-10:30pm, Sun. 11am-3pm.

La Mosquée, 39, rue Geoffroy-St-Hilaire, 5ème (tel. 43-31-18-14; Mo. Censier-Daubenton). Come here for a complete change of scene: tea in the courtyard or in the tea room. An institution since the 1920s. Behind the high white walls are a real mosque, turkish bath, and exquisite courtyard. 75F *menu*, served Mon.-Fri., includes *crudités, brik* (a thin dough with a fried egg inside), and a huge helping of chicken *couscous* (the best in Paris, according to expatriate Algerians). Huge 85F *menu*, served Sat.-Sun., offers more choice, more courses, and lamb *couscous*. No alcohol. End your meal with mint tea, but ask them to hold the sugar unless you want hot syrup. Tea room open Sept.-July 11am-9pm. Restaurant open 7-11pm.

Descartes Mandarin, 33, rue Descartes, 5ème (tel. 43-25-55-21; Mo. Cardinal-Lemoine). High quality Chinese and Vietnamese cuisine in large portions. 38F *menu* includes soup or spring roll, chicken or vegetarian dishes, rice, and dessert. 123 specialties 30-50F. Open Tues.-Sun. noon-2:30pm and 7-11pm. Also try **Elysées Mandarin,** 23, rue Washington, 8ème (tel. 42-25-71-20; Mo. George V), with more elegance and an excellent 70F *menu*. **St-Germain Mandarin,** 5, rue de Montfaucon, 6ème (tel. 43-29-07-14; Mo. St-Germain-des-Prés), offers a 55F *menu*.

Aux Savoyards, 14, rue des Boulangers, 5ème (tel. 46-33-53-78; Mo. Jussieu), on a twisting street. Homey place with a traditional 3-course, 55F *menu*, including potato or rice. Popular among students and professors. Open Sept.-July Mon.-Fri. noon-2:30pm and 7-10:30pm, Sat. noon-2:30pm.

Crêperie de la Mouff, 9, rue Mouffetard, 5ème (tel. 47-07-73-83; Mo. Cardinal-Lemoine). Enticing aroma draws you into this bit of Brittany. Crêpes prepared before your eyes. Crêpes of both *sarrazin* (buckwheat) and *froment* (wheat) flours 10-45F. *Bol* of cider 10F, half-pitcher 20F. *Apéritif* of Breton strawberry liqueur and cider 15F. Open daily noon-2:30pm and 7-10:30pm.

Restaurant Chez Léna et Mimile, 32, rue Tournefort, 5ème (tel. 47-07-72-47; Mo. Censier-Daubenton). Picturesque and elegant, overlooking a fountain. Tables inside and outside—you can take your time. 88F lunch *menu* and 140F dinner *menu* offer delightful French selections such as *sorbet d'avocat au crevettes, sauce cocktail* (avocado sherbet with shrimp and cocktail sauce), *apéritif* and wine included. A superb value despite the expense. Open Tues.-Fri. noon-2pm and 7-11pm, Mon. and Sat. 7-11pm.

Restaurant My-Vi, 6, rue des Ecoles, 5ème (tel. 46-33-30-66; Mo. Cardinal-Lemoine). 32.50F *menu*. Choice of hors d'oeuvres or soup, main dish, rice, and dessert. Portions are small and the food under-seasoned, but the price is right and the management friendly and English-speaking. Open Mon.-Sat. noon-2:30pm and 5:30-10:30pm.

Montparnasse, the Fifteenth Arrondissement, and the Thirteenth Arrondissement

The Bretons have brought their seafood specialties—crabs, oysters, and pretty *bigornots* (sea snails)—to Paris. Be sure to check the prices before you enter, as they are almost always high. Don't leave the area without walking along **rue d'Odessa,** where you'll find plenty of cheap, excellent *crêperies.* Vietnamese, Thai, and Chinese cuisine flourish around Métro Tolbiac and dominate avenue d'Ivry, avenue de Choisy, and avenue d'Italie—the 13ème's little Asia.

Théâtre de l'Arlequin, 13, passage du Moulinet, 13ème (tel. 45-89-43-22; Mo. Tolbiac), off rue Tolbiac. Identifiable by the Harlequin puppet on the wall, this is a remarkable place attached to a local semi-professional theater with unusually interesting 49.50F lunch and 59.50F dinner *menus* including *bisque de homard* (lobster bisque). Open Tues.-Sat. 7-11pm. Tickets to the off-beat and classical productions in the tiny theater 60F, students 40F.

Sampieru Corsu, 12, rue de l'Amiral-Roussin, 15ème (tel. 43-06-62-14; Mo. Cambronne). Run by a Corsican separatist and Marxist. They're operating in the red (not just politically), so be generous. French political propaganda serves as decoration. A 3-course meal of simple, rib-sticking food 31F, but pay according to your means. On most nights there is entertainment, and you should add something for the artist (about 10F). Open Mon.-Fri. 11:45am-1:45pm and 7-9:30pm.

Le Commerce, 51, rue du Commerce, 15ème (tel. 45-75-03-27; Mo. La Motte-Picquet), near the Tour Eiffel and the Musée Rodin. Traditional "business" food in a 2-tiered, spacious room. 49F *menu, boisson comprise.* An excellent value. *A la carte* features roast beef tongue (34F) and roast chicken (30F). Open daily 11:45am-2:45pm and 6:30-9:45pm.

Le Petit Parnasse, 138, rue de Vaugirard, 15ème (tel. 47-83-29-52; Mo. Falguière). Always crowded with businesspeople at lunch, and for good reason. 3 excellent *menus* 50F (lunch only), 70F, and 92F. Start with the assorted appetizers (they will leave the whole tray at your table) and finish with hot apple pie, fresh from the oven. Steaks and other meats 42-97F. Open Aug. 25-July Mon.-Fri. noon-2:15pm and 7:15-10:15pm. Closed last week in Dec.

L'Oiseau du Paradis, 44, rue du Javelot, 13ème (tel.45-83-46-17; Mo. Tolbiac), in the Centre Commercial "Mercure" in Paris's new Chinatown. Rather pricey, no *menu*. But the *canard lacqué* (glazed duck) is big, tender, and tasty (55F). Rice and noodle dishes 30-35F. Steamed specialties 13-30F. Seafood specialties 35-60F. 400 choices. Open daily 9am-2am.

Palais de Cristal, 70, rue Baudricourt, 13ème (tel. 45-84-81-56; Mo. Tolbiac), and **Tricotin,** 15, av. de Choisy, 13ème (tel. 42-85-51-52; Mo. Porte de Choisy), are both popular choices for Asian food that serve huge soups—a complete meal—for 30F. Both open noon-10pm. Palais closed Wed.

Les Jardins d'Hollywood, 55, bd. du Montparnasse, 6ème (tel. 45-44-19-18; Mo. Montparnasse-Bienvenue). A large and shiny California-style place with lots of choices, including many under-seasoned American dishes. *BCBG* crowd. The 64.50F *menu* features appetizers such as *mousse de canard* and *mousse de champignons* and main courses such as spare ribs and duck in peach wine. Brunch Sun. noon-3pm 64F. Open daily noon-3pm and 6:30pm-1am.

Taverne du Maître Kanter, 68, bd. du Montparnasse, 14ème (tel. 43-35-36-00; Mo. Montparnasse-Bienvenue). *Choucroute* (sauerkraut with sausages and other cuts of pork), the Alsatian house specialty, comes in 3 varieties (62F, 72.50F, and 82.50F; take-out 55F), all large enough to be shared. Sit at the outside tables. Open daily 11:30am-1am.

Rive Droite (Right Bank)

Les Halles and Le Marais

The Centre Pompidou is surrounded by fast-food restaurants and overpriced cafes. The Centre's own penthouse cafe offers a spectacular view of the city, but its prices are astronomical. Behind Beaubourg, toward the Marais around rue des Rosiers, you can find traditional Jewish food and felafel (an old and sizable Orthodox Jewish community lives there). On some of the small streets behind the Forum des Halles, new restaurants have opened with excellent chefs and almost affordable prices. Around Beaubourg, casual restaurants serve light meals. You can relieve your late-night hunger pangs at **As-Eco,** a supermarket in the mall area in quartier de l'Horloge, off rue Rambuteau, right across from the Centre Pompidou. (Open Mon.-Sat. 24 hours.) This area is not safe for women alone after dark.

Crêperie Colombine, 37, av. Duquesne (tel. 45-51-91-20; Mo. St-François Xavier). A cozy tea room awaits the hungry tourist with *galettes* and sweet crêpes (10-30F). Open Sept.-July Mon. and Wed.-Thurs. 6:30-11pm, Tues. and Fri.-Sat. 10am-2:30pm.

La Canaille, 4, rue Crillon, 4ème (tel. 42-78-09-71; Mo. Sully-Morland or Bastille), on a street parallel to bd. Bourdou. More a part of the Bastille scene than the Marais, this place serves remarkable food to a French business crowd. 55F *menu* (50F at lunch) includes items like a mind-expanding *sorbet aux trois legumes* or *coquelet à la crème de carotte et d'estragon* (chicken in an addicting carrot purée with tarragon). Abrupt but theatrical management asks you to write down your order. Popular, no reservations. Open Sept.-July Mon.-Fri. 11:45am-2:15pm and 7:30-11:30pm, Sat.-Sun. 11:45am-2:15pm.

L'Atelier Bleu, 7, rue des Prouvaires, 1er (tel. 42-33-74-47); Mo. Les Halles). Not blue as the name suggests, but light and spacious. Generous portions and reasonable prices. 70F *menu* (served until 10pm) offers unusual choices like gazpacho, beef with mint, and fish filet with orange butter. Main courses 66-78F, *à la carte* meals 90F. Open Mon.-Sat. noon-3pm and 7pm-6am.

La Coquillière, 12, rue Coquillière, 1er (Mo. Louvre or Les Halles). One of the big, slightly factorylike restaurants along this street (which turns into rue Rambuteau), but with a cheaper *menu,* elegant service, and umbrella-covered tables. Probably as close to Les Halles as you can afford. 62F *menu* includes *moules marinières.* Open 24 hours.

Chez Jo Goldenberg, 7, rue des Rosiers, 4ème (tel. 48-87-20-16; Mo. St-Paul). In this kosher-style deli, established in 1920, you can get corned beef on a baguette and goose pastrami. Jewish food from around the world at the restaurant and the take-out deli. Smoked salmon 80F, *foie gras* 69F, grape leaves 34F, and matzoh ball soup 32F. Friendly service; extensive wine list. Deli open daily 9am-1pm and 2:30-6pm. Tea room open 2:30-6pm. Closed during Yom Kippur.

Chez Marianne, 2, rue des Hospitaliers St-Gervais, 4ème (tel. 42-72-18-86; Mo. St-Paul), at rue des Rosiers. Choose a plate of 4 (50F) or 5 (60F) filling Middle Eastern specialties from *tarama* (smoked salmon purée) to felafel to stuffed grape leaves. Dessert strudels 18F. Outside tables. *Traiteur* sells all products. Open Sat.-Thurs. noon-11pm.

Le Kairouan, 55, bd. Sebastopol, 1er (Mo. Les Halles), behind an ice cream stand. Small and seedy-looking, but an excellent value. Generous *couscous* plates 25-38F. Mint tea 4F. "Oriental" pastry (including baklava) 6F. Open daily noon-midnight.

A la Perdrix, 6, rue Mandar, 2ème (Mo. Sentier or Bourse), off rue Montmartre. No surprises here, just traditional food at reasonable prices in a wooden, country-style setting. 3-course, 50F *menu; à la carte* is also affordable with *saumon poêlé* (fried salmon; 45F). Open Sept.-June Mon.-Fri. 11:45am-2:30pm and 6:45-9:30pm, Sat. 6:45-9:30pm; July for lunch only.

Mélodine, 42, rue Rambuteau, 3ème (tel. 42-74-74-91; Mo. Rambuteau), near the Centre Pompidou. Evidence that the French like their food to look good even in cafeterias. Salads, cheese, and desserts. 3-4 dishes that change daily 20-40F. *Steak-frites* with a tasty sauce 20F. Full meals 45F. Open daily 11am-11pm.

Naturals, 15, rue du Grenier St-Lazare, 3ème (tel. 48-87-09-49; Mo. Rambuteau). Popular, well-reviewed vegetarian fast food restaurant reminiscent of California. Pita sandwiches or tofu burgers 20F, sushi 15F, salads 25F, generous *plat du jour* with salad 40F, and vegetable or trout tarts 18F. Open Mon.-Sat. 10am-9pm.

Aquarius, 54, rue Ste-Croix-de-la-Bretonnerie, 4ème (tel. 48-87-48-71; Mo. Hôtel-de-Ville). Small vegetarian restaurant run by the Rosicrucians. Organically grown vegetables (*légumes biologiques*). Salads 10-24F, vegetable tarts 24F, and other prepared dishes such as *quenelles de soja* (soybean patties). 40F *menu* available noon-2pm and 7-10pm. No smoking and no liquor. Open Sept.-July Mon.-Sat. noon-10pm. Also at 40, rue de Gergovie, 14ème (tel. 45-41-36-88; Mo. Pernety). Similar *menu*. Open Mon.-Sat. noon-3pm and 7-10pm.

Sharakou, 4bis, place Ste-Opportune, 1er (tel. 42-33-70-47; Mo. Châtelet), just off rue des Halles. A Japanese restaurant specializing in do-it-yourself barbecue—the skillet is on the table. Sit on the floor in the tatami rooms or outside in the shade. Sashimi and a glass of sake 45F. *Menus* from 45F (3 dishes plus rice) to 115F (6 dishes plus rice). Open Mon.-Sat. noon-2:30pm and 7-11:30pm.

Near Place de l'Opéra and Place Vendôme

This is not a neighborhood of cheap eateries, but excellent values do crop up. More Japanese live in this neighborhood than elsewhere in Paris, and many expensive sushi restaurants line the streets. The best deals are the restaurants that cater to the business crowd.

Ma Normandie, 11, rue Rameau, 2ème (tel. 42-96-87-17; Mo. Pyramides), down from the Bibliothèque Nationale on pleasant place Louvois. A favorite among intellectuals. 42F lunch *menu* includes a promise of *service rapide*. 65F dinner *menu* offers many traditional choices. Wholesome country atmosphere with plenty of cheer. Eat downstairs, since only the most expensive *menu* is served upstairs. Open Aug.-June Mon.-Fri. 11:30am-2:30pm.

L'Incroyable, 26, rue de Richelieu, 1er (tel. 42-96-24-64; Mo. Palais-Royal). A tiny, lacy place away from the street. Regulars carouse with the jolly owner. Serves a changing *menu* of simple pleasures: pork chops, steak, and the like at an *incroyable* 44F, *boisson comprise*. Open Sept.-July Tues.-Fri. 11:45am-2:15pm and 6:30-8:30pm, Sat. and Mon. 11:45am-2:45pm, but get there early for the most choices.

L'Echalote, 14, rue Chabanais, 2ème (tel. 42-97-47-10; Mo. Pyramides), around the corner from Ma Normandie. Far from elegant. 63F *menu* (noon-2:30pm) with such delicacies as Breton *truite fumée* (smoked trout) and garlic sausages. Also a cozy bar with inexpensive wine (10F). Open Mon.-Fri. noon-2:30pm and 7:30pm-midnight.

Ninth Arrondissement

North of rue de Château Dieu and south of Pigalle is a lovely neighborhood on the sloping hillside of Montmartre, frequented by the French. Some popular restaurants lurk here, including the cheapest around.

Le Chartier, 7, rue du Faubourg-Montmartre, 9ème (tel. 47-70-86-29; Mo. Montmartre), at bd. Montmartre. The owner serves about 2000 meals per day in this beautifully preserved restaurant. Extensive selection; delicious, reasonably-priced food. *Menu, boisson compris,* 59F. Don't come here for a leisurely meal. **Le Drouot**, 103, rue de Richelieu, 2ème (tel. 42-

96-68-23; Mo. Richelieu-Drouot), and **Le Commerce,** 51, rue de Commerce, 15ème (tel. 45-75-03-27; Mo. Lamotte-Picquet), are under the same management and serve the same food in a less formal setting. Try the *steak haché au poivre vert* (chopped steak with green peppercorns). Both open daily 11am-3pm and 6-9:30pm.

Casa Miguel, 48, rue St-Georges, 9ème (tel. 42-81-09-61; Mo. St-Georges). Recently acknowledged by Guinness to be the cheapest restaurant in the *monde (occidental),* but much more than a gimmick. Started in 1949 by Maria and Miguel Lodina, refugees from Franco's Spain. Mme. Lodina has been serving cheap food since then as a labor of love in the small place (max. 32 people served per night). Small but acceptable portions. Appetizer, main course, and cheese 5F (no joke), service and wine included. Dessert 1.50F. Open Mon.-Sat. noon-1pm and 7-8pm, Sun. noon-1pm. Closed for 1 week late July- early Aug.

Restaurant Le Khayber Pass, 28, rue de Dovai, 9ème (tel. 45-26-72-34; Mo. Blanche), off rue Pigalle. Superior food, soothing atmosphere, and attentive service. Not exactly cheap, but worth it. Tasty *beignets de pommes de terre* (potato puréed with spices and fried) 14F, spicy goulash 65F, *poulet grillé* 40F, *riz* (saffroned rice with chicken and vegetables)—a huge plate—55F. Open daily 7pm-2am.

Haynes Restaurant-Bar, 3, rue Clauzel, 9ème (tel. 48-78-40-63; Mo. St-Georges), on a side street off rue des Martyrs. July 4 and you're homesick for spare ribs and American cocktails? Here's your answer—soul food in a friendly atmosphere. Hot hors d'oeuvres 35F, Nellie Bee's Barbecued Chicken 64F. Mixed drinks 35F, available only if you're eating. Open Sept.-July Tues.-Sat. 8-10:30pm.

L'Omeletterie, 48, rue Condorcet, 9ème (tel. 45-26-98-19; Mo. Anvers), at rue Rodier. 11 different omelettes and 2 *plats* that change daily, prepared with care and fresh ingredients. Omelettes (29-40.50F) are accompanied by a crisp green salad. The check is brought to you in an eggshell. Open Mon.-Sat. noon-2:30pm and 7-9:30pm.

Montmartre

Because Montmartre perseveres as a real neighborhood, despite the endless stream of pilgrims to the butte, its residents sustain quite a few inexpensive restaurants that are full of character. Place du Tertre is full of pricey choices, but nightly music and dancing in the cafes may make it worth the expense.

Au Grain Folie, 24, rue de la Vieuville, 18ème (tel. 42-58-15-57; Mo. Abbesses), at the top of rue des Martyrs. A tiny vegetarian restaurant with excellent thin crusted vegetable *tartes.* 55F *menu.* Get a *tarte garnie* (with salad, rice, and beans; 36-45F) or a salad (25-40F). Try the *brochette de poisson* with vegetable and grains (47F). Go elsewhere for dessert. English-speaking host. Open Tues.-Sun. noon-2pm and 7-10:30pm, Mon. 7-10:30pm.

Refuge des Fondus, 19, rue des Trois Frères, 18ème (tel. 42-55-22-65; Mo. Abbesses). The food is not fantastic, but a goofy gimmick makes this restaurant overwhelmingly popular: Customers are treated to a full baby bottle of wine with the *menu* (refills 5F). 60F *menu* includes cocktail or hors d'oeuvres, cheese and meat fondue, and pineapple in kirsh. Other desserts 6F. Open Sept.-July Tues.-Sun. 7pm-2am.

Restaurant l'Esterel, 8, rue Tardieu, 18ème (tel. 46-06-05-02; Mo. Abbesses). Barrel theme decor. This may be the ideal corner to dream the night away. 46F *menu;* try the house specialty *roule de jambon "Esterel."* A good place to try traditional food such as *lapin à la moutarde* (rabbit in mustard sauce, 49F). Open daily 7pm-1am.

Restaurant "Le Fait-Tout," 4, rue Dancourt, 18ème (tel. 42-23-93-66; Mo. Abbesses). Rue de Trois Frères turns into rue Dancourt. A quiet, less crowded place. Friendly young manager. 45F *menu* includes excellent choices such as *terrine lapin* (rabbit *pâté*) and *truite meunière.* 57F *menu* offers duck-orange *pâté,* skate in pepper sauce, and *profiteroles au chocolat.*

La Poutre, 10, rue des Trois Frères, 18ème (tel. 42-57-45-04; Mo. Abbesses or Anvers). A lovely, simple little restaurant across the street from Refuge des Fondus. Regional food of Périgord, including *pâté de campagne.* 48F *menu* (served until 11pm) includes a delicious broiled trout but is otherwise undistinguished. Open daily noon-3pm and 6pm-2am.

Restaurant Shehnaz, 10, rue Puget, 18ème (tel. 42-62-61-61; Mo. Blanche), on a tiny street off av. de Clichy. Indian specialties in an authentic atmosphere. No alcohol. 49F vegetarian *menu* and 65F meat *menu.* Open noon-2pm and 7-10pm.

Near the Arc de Triomphe

Most restaurants here are expensive or overpriced. You'll pay dearly for nostalgia at the two Burger Kings on the Champs-Elysées. Avoid that affluent thoroughfare and explore the side streets.

Cafétéria Monte Carlo, 9, av. de Wagram, 17*ème* (tel. 43-80-02-21; Mo. Etoile). This snazzy *self* features well-prepared food at reasonable prices. Pizza 15F, *canard à l'orange* 43.50F. A bit tourist-ridden because of its central location, but crowded with French as well. Open daily 11am-10pm, even July 14.

Le Conservatoire Rachmaninoff, 26, av. de New York, 16*ème* (tel. 47-20-65-17; Mo. Alma-Marceau). In the basement you can get the cheapest Russian food in Paris. If you have guts or speak Russian (signs are in French and Russian), you should be fine. Otherwise, you may be intimidated by the many signs warning that the restaurant is for students and professors only—avoid the table marked *reservé aux professeurs.* Appetizer and main course 45F. Open Sept.-July Mon.-Fri. noon-2:30pm and 7-9pm.

Tenth Arrondissement

Dominated by the massive railway yards of Gare du Nord and Gare de l'Est, and divided by the picturesque Canal St-Martin, the 10*ème* raises traffic jams, not the culinary arts, to new heights. The following two restaurants are convenient and reasonable.

New Delhi, 2, rue du Château Landon, 10*ème* (Mo. Château Landon), near Gare de l'Est. A modest Indian restaurant. 39F *menu, boisson comprise,* includes spicy potato pancake appetizer, choice of fish, beef, or chicken curry with rice, and dessert. Other main dishes 25-38F. They speak neither English nor French. Open Mon.-Sat. 11am-12:30pm and 6:30-10:30pm.

Restaurant Sizin, 36, Faubourg du Temple, 10*ème* (tel. 48-06-54-03; Mo. République), off a maniacally crowded street. Spicy individual Turkish pizzas 8F, salads 16-20F, main dishes 33-50F, and great baklava 15F. Open Mon.-Sat. noon-3pm and 7:30-11:30pm.

University Restaurants

Institutional food is poor even in France, but it's inexpensive. Students with an ISIC or a valid college ID card can buy *passager* meal tickets (18F). Some checkers don't even ask to see ID. Eating in one of the **Restaurant Universitaires (Resto-U)** is an opportunity to meet French students; those affiliated with CROUS pay only 9F per meal, and you may be able to buy a ticket from them.

Tickets are sold individually, or in *carnets* of 10, during lunchtime (11:30am-1:45pm). Dinner is served from 6 to 8pm. Most university restaurants are closed on weekends and in summer. To get a complete list with addresses, prices, and schedules, ask at **CROUS,** 39, av. Georges Bernanos, 5ème (tel. 43-29-12-43; Mo. Port-Royal; open Mon.-Fri. 9am-5pm). The most popular are the following:

Alliance Française, 101, bd. Raspail, 6*ème* (tel. 45-44-38-28; Mo. Notre-Dame des-Champs). Not CROUS-affiliated, but worth trying. Better-than-average student food for 20F (lunch noon-2pm) and 25F (dinner 6-9pm). A good place to meet students from all over the world, though usually not from France. Open Mon.-Fri.

La Table d'Hôte, 16, rue du Pont Louis-Philippe, 4*ème* (tel. 42-78-04-82; Mo. Pont-Marie). A cozy, family-style restaurant run by the Accueil des Jeunes en France. Full meals 40F, nonresidents 45F. Open Sept.-July Mon.-Fri. noon-1:30pm and 6-7:30pm.

Albert Châtelet, 10, rue Jean Calvin, 5*ème* (tel. 43-31-51-66; Mo. Censier-Daubenton). This CROUS-run restaurant has the best food and a very lively atmosphere. Excellent *couscous* Tues. nights. Open Sept.-June Mon.-Fri. 11:30am-2pm and 6:30-8:15pm.

Maison Internationale à la Cité Universitaire, 17, bd. Jourdan, 14*ème* (tel. 45-89-35-79; Mo. Cité Universitaire). Well-regarded but somewhat inconvenient unless you're staying in the hostel or one of the *maisons.* Carnet 90F. Open Mon.-Fri. 11:45am-2pm and 6-8:30pm.

Fast Food

If you don't feel like sitting down to two meals per day, but don't want to stand in the street clutching your *baguette* and brie, try French fast food restaurants—not hamburger joints, but places where you can consume real French food while standing up. Croissant places such as **La Brioche Dorée** on rue de Levis, **Tout Chaud** near Beaubourg, or **La Croissanterie** on bd. St-Michel are good for light pastry creations. A clever French McDonalds spin-off is **Asterix Burger,** 9, rue du Faubourg Montmartre, 9ème (tel. 47-70-50-52; Mo. Montmartre), with a basic Obélix burger (18.50F) and an Idéefix burger (9F). When the French use the American expression "Fast Food," they mean any meals that are quickly served—price is clearly a secondary consideration.

> **Fauchon,** 26, place de la Madeleine, 8ème (tel. 47-42-60-11; Mo. Madeleine), behind Eglise de la Madeleine. A shrine for the worship of good food for years and a must for window shoppers seeking the height of aesthetic indulgence. Fauchon's stand-up cafeteria is not cheap, but it does give you a chance to try dishes probably unaffordable in restaurants. 5 filling hot dishes, artistically presented (like everything at Fauchon) change daily (34-60F). Try the *oeuf Toupinet* (26F), the *crêpes Roquefort* (30F), and the *mousse au chocolat* (14F). Come before 2pm for the most choices. You may have to wait for a counter spot at lunch. Open Mon.-Sat. 9:40am-7pm.

> **Le Café de Paris,** 78, Champs-Elysées, 8ème (tel. 47-23-91-41; Mo. George V), in the Arcades du Lido, Paris's sophisticated answer to shopping malls. Don't sit down in the restaurant section where the food is mediocre and the prices high, but stand in the cafeteria section, where you can get a *feuilleté de jambon* (ham pastry puff) or a hot *tarte au fromage* (cheese pie; 13.50F each). Stick to the hot dishes; the sandwiches are unimpressive. Fine coffee 3.50-10F (more after 10pm). Very crowded at lunch. Open Mon.-Thurs. 8am-midnight, Fri.-Sat. and holidays 8am-2am.

> **Berthillon,** 31, rue St-Louis-en-l'Ile, 4ème (tel. 43-54-31-61; Mo. Pont-Marie), on Ile St-Louis. Everyone's favorite ice cream in Paris. Try caramel, nougat, white chocolate, pear, or rasberry (*quelle framboise!*)—expensive but worth it. If you're discouraged by the long lines, check the list posted in the window for other cafes selling Berthillon ice cream. Take your cone to the Seine, where between the view and the *saveur,* you'll discover *joie de vivre.* Open Sept.-July Wed.-Sun. 10am-8pm.

Cafes

Since the days when Voltaire drank 40 cups of coffee daily in Le Procope (Paris's first cafe, founded in 1686, and now a restaurant), cafes have been an integral part of Parisian social life. Ideal for light meals, they can provide the inexpensive high ground from which to watch the Parisian tide surge by. Cafes situated on fashionable thoroughfares, such as the Champs-Elysées, boulevard St-Germain, or rue de la Paix, cater to the extravagant (coffee 11-16F), but an intriguing crowd usually passes its sidewalk tables. Cafes near monuments also charge monumental prices, but for minimal atmosphere. In such lively places as place St-André-des-Arts, the Forum des Halles, place de la Sorbonne, and Montparnasse, you can get coffee for about 8F.

Indigenous crowds frequent more dilapidated, hidden spots, where coffee is only 4F and the use of *argot* (slang) makes eavesdropping an educational challenge. Choosing the perfect place to sip, read the paper, or write letters—*your* cafe, should not be taken lightly. The French don't pass the time just anywhere, so make sure the prices posted outside correspond to your budget, and be picky before you relax.

Prices in cafes are two-tiered, cheaper if you stand at the counter (*comptoir*) than if you sit at the tables (*salle*) inside or out. Both these prices should be posted. Remember that a *café* means a tiny black coffee; if you want a *café crème* (Parisians never say *café au lait,* though both names apply to milky espresso), you often have to pay up to twice as much for what the French consider a breakfast beverage.

In cafes, most beer on tap is lager, and a glass is called *une pression* or *un demi.* Bottled beers, foreign and domestic, are served as well. *Kir*—white wine with *crème de cassis* (black-currant liqueur)—is delicious and cheap. *Pastis* (a traditional, licorice-flavored aperitif that turns cloudy when water is added) comes in the popular brands Pernod, Ricard, and Pastis 51. Sometimes *cidre* (slightly alcoholic) is also available, either on tap or bottled. Mixed drinks, of the American cocktail-lounge variety, are almost never served in cafes. If you crave a Tom Collins or a Manhattan, you'll have to go to one of Paris's American bars (see Entertainment).

Cafes serve sandwiches for as little as 13F. Often they are a section of a *baguette* filled with ham, cheese (usually *camembert*), or *pâté.* A less-filling but tastier option is the *croque-monsieur* (a grilled ham-and-cheese sandwich) or *croque-madame* (the same with an egg on top) for about 15F.

In addition to serving drinks and food, cafes provide two other essential services: telephones and toilets. Calls from a public phone in Paris cost 1F, and you must often purchase a *jeton* at the counter unless the phone requires a *télécarte.* The toilets, are usually free and sometimes of the pit variety. In the fancier cafes, an attendant sits outside and expects a 1-2F tip. A red, diamond-shaped sign outside a cafe signifies that it is a *tabac* as well, and sells cigars, cigarettes, matches, postage stamps, and a selection of other useful items such as batteries, razor blades, and Métro and lottery tickets. Stamps are no more expensive in *tabacs* than in a post office.

La Coupole, 102, bd. du Montparnasse, 14*ème* (tel. 43-20-14-20; Mo. Vavin). One of the most famous cafes in Paris, cited by many authors, including Henry Miller. Still quite a "scene," full of Beautiful People who come to spend their monthly allowances eating oysters. Dancing in the basement. Sandwiches 16-30F, *plats* 45-96F, desserts 27-42F, coffee 8-29F. Open Sept.-July daily 8am-2am.

Café Costes, 4-6, rue Berger, place des Innocents, 1*er* (tel. 45-08-54-39; Mo. Les Halles). Opened in 1986 in the heart of Les Halles and designed by Phillipe Stark. A prime people-watching spot. Expect to be checked out—you should develop a sufficiently cold, critical return glance. Coffee 11F, beer 18F, sandwiches 18F. Open daily 8am-2am.

Café Beaubourg, 100, rue St-Martin, 4*ème* (tel. 48-87-63-96; Mo. Les Halles), across the way from Cafe Costes. This cafe was opened by the other Costes brother in spring 1987, with an even more modern, elegant interior (designed by Christian de Porzamparc of Cité de la Musique at la Villette fame). Check out the cavernous, art deco women's bathroom. Coffee 11F, beer and soda 18F, sandwiches 18-25F. Open daily 8am-2am.

Le Balto, 15, rue Mazarine, 6*ème* (Mo. Odéon). An honest cafe with honest prices. Mix of artsy students, working people, and interesting others, on a well-located but not hectic street. The service is glacial, in speed and spirit, in this otherwise perfect place for a cup. Coffee 5-8.40F. Wine by the glass 7-10F. Sandwiches 8.50-15F. Open Sept.-July Mon.-Sat. 8am-midnight.

La Palette, 34, rue de Seine, 6*ème* (tel. 43-26-68-15; Mo. St-Germain-des-Prés), at rue Jacques Callot. With an art gallery in the back, a name evoking turpentine and *ateliers,* and a model clientele, La Palette composes as artistic a coffee-sipping session as you're likely to find outside of a museum. Coffee 6-15F, wine by the glass from 11F. Open Sept.-July daily noon-2am.

Le Drugstore, many central locations, such as the *rond-point* (traffic circle) of the Champs-Elysées, St-Germain, and near the Etoile. A Parisian institution derived from the American version, encompassing an arcade of boutiques selling everything from tobacco to diamonds. The food isn't spectacular, but the locations are, especially those at the *rond-point* and St-Germain (with outside terraces). Stick to the *gourmandises* section, where you can get the best ice cream concoctions in the city. A Coupe Elysée (28.50F) comes with 3 flavors you choose. Cocktails 40F. Open daily 11am-1:30am.

Wine Bars

Sporting a history as long as that of French wine production itself, wine bars became increasingly popular a few years ago with the invention of a machine that pumps nitrogen into the open bottle, thus preserving the wine indefinitely. Now rare, expensive wines, exorbitant by the bottle, have become affordable by the glass. Enjoy your bottle or glass with a cooked dish or a *tartine* (cheese and/or *charcuteries*—the French equivalent of cold cuts—served on *pain Poilâne* or *pain de campagne*). Each place has its own flavor and specialty, from Bordeaux to Vouvray to Côtes du Rhône. Essential are the owners, who carefully select the wines in their *caves* (cellars) and set the tone for their establishments.

Over 100-strong, the wine shops in the **Nicolas** chain are reputed for having the world's most inexpensive cellars, while Nicolas himself owns the fashionable and expensive wine bar **Jeroboam**, 8, rue Monsigny, 2*ème* (tel. 42-61-21-71; Mo. Opéra).

Bistrot à Vins Mélac, 42, rue Léon-Frot, 11*ème* (tel. 43-70-59-27; Mo. Charonne). Cozy, lively atmosphere and full of Parisians. The charming owner Jacques Melac (easily recognizable by his moustache) matures 23 French wines in the cellar, specializing in Côtes du Rhônes. He has recently acquired his own label, identified by the moustache symbol. At his annual harvest party (last Sat. in Sept.), he picks the grapes that grow from the roof and keeps the wine flowing into the streets below. Wine by the glass (5.60F) and the bottle (54F). *Auvergnat* specialties, including pot of *rillettes* (pork) for 18F. Arrive early; no reservations accepted. Open Aug.-June Tues.-Sat. 9am-7:30pm, Tues. and Thurs. last dinner served at 10:30pm.

Taverne Henri IV, 13, place du Pont Neuf, 1*er* (tel. 43-54-27-90; Mo. Pont-Neuf). Robert Cointepas's traditional and friendly oak tavern long known to Parisians for its extensive wine list, and delicious *charcuteries* with *Poilâne* bread, served quickly but *à la française*. A plate of bread and *rillettes* 18F; a selection of *charcuteries* 46F. Wine by the glass 14-43.80F. Open mid-Sept. to mid-Aug. Mon.-Fri. 11:30am-9:30pm.

Le Beaujolais St-Honoré, 24, rue du Louvre, 1*er* (tel. 42-60-89-79; Mo. Louvre). As the name suggests, the specialty here is Beaujolais (from 16F per glass). A mural portrays the harvest. *Tartines* 25F, *menu* 57.50F. Open daily 6am-2am.

Le Brouet, 72, rue Vieille du Temple, 4*ème* (Mo. St-Paul), across from Hôtel Rohan. In a room like a wine barrel, aged and sturdy and decorated with antiques. The extremely knowledgeable owner will educate you on wine from the Juras. Most glasses 8-25F, some up to 55F. The food is expensive, but cheese plates are reasonable at 19-26F. Open Sept.-July Tues.-Sat. 12:30-2:45pm and 7:30pm-2am.

La Boutique des Vins, 33, rue de l'Arcade, 8*ème* (tel. 42-65-27-27; Mo. Madeleine). Elegant atmosphere. Select from among 125 personally-chosen wines (15-75F per glass). Food here is gracefully prepared, but a bit expensive; you can always get the *plat du jour* (68-125F). Open Mon.-Fri. 11am-3pm and 7pm-midnight.

Au Limonaire, 88, rue de Charenton, 12*ème* (tel. 43-43-49-14; Mo. Bastille). The owners' goal is to preserve a bit of the old Left Bank with nightly old Parisian-style singers and good prices. Wine by the glass 6-30F, *plat du jour* 42F, *charcuterie* plates 28F. Open daily noon-2:30pm and 8pm-midnight.

Sights

A monument to history and a patron of the avant-garde, Paris does not fear to superimpose centuries, thus inviting both the glee and dismay of critical observers. I.M. Pei's glass pyramid in the Louvre's courtyard exemplifies this penchant. Almost as many attractions as tour buses dot the immense city. The Marais's charming streets and ethnic neighborhoods, Beaubourg, the Louvre, the Arc de Triomphe, Opéra, and Montmartre are focal points on the Right Bank, while the Eiffel Tower, the Musée d'Orsay, Montparnasse, and St-Germain-des-Prés draw tourists to the Left. Notre-Dame on the Ile de la Cité, the queen of the hub, sits *à califourchon* on the forgiving Seine.

Both the monumental and intimate areas of Paris lie on two fairly narrow strips along the banks of the Seine (north to bd. Haussmann and beyond to Montmartre, south to Montparnasse, west to the Tour Eiffel, and east to place des Vosges and place de la Bastille). This inner sanctum of Paris is negotiable and most rewarding on foot, quickly introducing one to the style and layout of the city. If you're too rushed to amble, remember that the Métro traverses this area exhaustively, with many convenient stops.

Let's Go's Sights section is organized by neighborhood, and labeled by principal sight or quarter, each subdivision of which can be taken as a walking tour. The section is composed of two counterclockwise loops, both starting at the hub of Paris, the islands. The first spirals north and west through the Right Bank; the second spirals west, south, and east through the Left Bank. Montmartre and northeastern Paris are both on the Right Bank, but somewhat removed, and so are subsumed under The Periphery. A section is devoted to Paris's suburbs, which lie just beyond the *périphérique* and constitute, with Paris proper, the metropolitan area.

If you have a special interest, there's probably a museum in Paris devoted to it. The useful pamphlet *Musées de la Ville de Paris* (which lists the city, not the national, museums) and the comprehensive *Musées, Monuments, Expositions de Paris et de l'Ile-de-France,* published by the Musées Nationaux de la France, are available free from the tourist office. The latter can provide hours and prices for almost every museum in Paris. *Pariscope, 7 à Paris,* and *L'Officiel des spectacles* also list museums with hours and temporary exhibits. (See Publications about Paris.) In general, national museums are open Wednesday through Monday. Admission is free for ages under 18, half-price for ages 18-25 and over 60, and either free or half-price for everyone on Sundays. Remember, though, that such blanket discounts induce endless lines. City museums, on the other hand, are open Tuesday through Sunday and offer student rates (usually ½ the adult rate), so be sure to bring your ISIC. If you forgot to buy one, don't despair. Many checkers will accept current college ID as well. Frequent museum-goers, especially those ineligible for ticket discounts, may want to invest in a Carte 60, which allows entry into 60 Parisian museums as well as monuments in the suburbs and environs. The card is available at all major museums and Métro stations (1 day 50F, 3 days 100F, 5 days 150F). Photographic privileges are either free or cost 1F, the use of a tripod 5F; flash or other lighting is not permitted.

Remember that Parisian churches still function as places of worship (even Notre-Dame); many Parisians attend services, and those who don't expect to find quiet places for contemplation. When visiting be as quiet as possible at all times (especially during a service or mass), respect areas that are cordoned off for prayer, and observe the appropriate dress code (no shorts, low necklines, or bare shoulders).

The parks of Paris are an integral part of the city and are used extensively by young and old, by students and bums—and by dogs. You will learn to use them as the Parisians do, as a temporary refuge from the traffic and the cars. Each park has its *habitués* (regulars) who come to play *boules* or *pétanque* (a shuffleboardlike sport with metal balls), to feed their feathered friends, or to philosophize. On Sunday afternoons, you can watch all of Paris strolling in the gardens. Though walking is free, sitting down sometimes costs. The unauthorized chair franchise is run by tough old women who extort about 1F per seat. The benches are generally free.

Building the City

Stand by Notre-Dame on **Ile de la Cité,** where Paris began, and imagine a Roman temple in place of the twin-towered cathedral. To the north lies marshland or *marais;* to the south sit the Roman forum and baths of Lutetia, home of the Parisii, who worship Celtic and Roman divinities. As the years pass, Paris becomes the capital city of the Franks, but the Roman palaces will stand until the thirteenth century. Under Philippe Auguste, a wall springs up to protect the city; slender **Tour de Nesle** raises itself to the sky, reflected on the Right Bank by the first building of the **Louvre.** Soon **Notre-Dame,** conceived by Bishop Maurice de Sully, makes her grand debut and becomes the site of important crownings and weddings for the next five centuries. Meanwhile, hospitals and aqueducts appear all over the city and **Les Halles** becomes the central marketplace only to grow more food-oriented in the seven centuries following its establishment in 1110. Over on the Left Bank, students officially become members of the University of Paris in 1215, but another 40 years pass before they are granted their own building, the **Sorbonne.** On the middle of the island, a new **Palais de Justice,** the home of St-Louis, appears by midcentury, and within it the Gothic miniature **Ste-Chapelle,** its vaults seemingly suspended by the light streaming through its brilliant stained-glass windows.

The fourteenth century brings Charles V, who has the swamp drained and transforms **Le Marais** into a posh home. A little later, an old dump by the banks of the Seine becomes an elaborate garden and palace, the **Tuileries,** transformed by the cultivated Marie de Medici. In 1605, Marie's husband, Henry IV, equally determined to leave his mark on the city, builds the arcaded **Place des Vosges** as a symmetrical outpost of Le Marais.

Soon the new **Ile St-Louis** is constructed—an aristocratic neighborhood where Voltaire, Ingres, Baudelaire, Cézanne, and Georges Moustaki will all eventually live. The **Palais Royal** appears for the comfort of the implacable Richelieu; the **Palais de Luxembourg** for Marie de Medici. Suddenly, the sun rises over Paris, and under Louis XIV, *le roi soleil,* the city radiates with magnificent buildings and gardens. The **Champs-Elysées, place Vendôme, the Observatoire,** and, most impressive of all, the new royal residence of **Versailles** and its incomparable gardens take shape. Despite all this rich construction, a slum bubbles and seeps from Notre-Dame to the Palais de Justice. Class tension and elite privilege prove too much, and in the north the **Bastille** is stormed; the guillotine is erected and takes over 1300 lives, including those of the king and queen. Place de la Révolution (formerly place Louis XV), the scene of so many executions, is hopefully renamed **place de la Concorde** after the end of the Terror.

After a lull, as life settles down, arches are erected to Napoleon Bonaparte, who crowns himself emperor in Notre-Dame, then he crowns the city with Chagrin's grand **Arc de Triomphe** on the hill of Chaillot. Rue de Rivoli grows its arcades, and Parisians begin to bury their celebrities in elaborate tombs at growing cemeteries outside of town.

In the nineteenth century, Napoleon III lets Baron Haussmann loose on the city. He mows down the slums, replacing them with broad and elegant boulevards, much less suitable for anti-authoritarian resistance, more convenient for troops marching into small neighborhoods. The ornamental **Opéra** is born, **Bois de Boulogne** made into a park, the city divided into 20 *arrondissements,* and the celebrated sewers constructed. Also, the Louvre is finally completed in its present form. The 1870s bring turmoil and destruction once again. The newly elected commune is formed in response to the German invasion, and the Communard flames soon devour the Tuileries, the Palais de Justice, and the Hôtel de Ville. On May 28, 1871, the rebels are cornered and slaughtered at the cemetery of **Père Lachaise,** which becomes the site of an annual political pilgrimage. The Tuileries are never to regain their former glory, but a series of exhibitions sweeps Paris, leaving in its wake the **Tour Eiffel,** the **Petit Palais,** and flat-topped **Palais de Chaillot.** Playful art-nouveau gateways mark the entrance to the brand-new Métro stations. Add **La Défense** to the west and **Tour Montparnasse** to the south, and you can set your imagination to rest. All skyscrapers are relegated to the suburb of La Défense, and yet in 1977, right in the middle of the twelfth-century village of **Beaubourg,** springs up the futuristic **Centre Georges Pompidou,** a surrealistic steel arts complex, and in it the **Atelier Brancusi,** a faithful reproduction of the artist's 1917 workplace. Nearby the **Forum des Halles,** Beaubourg's companion, a tubular, steel-and-glass shopping mall, supplants the area's old market sheds.

In 1982, Mitterand decides to build a modern opera house "designed for the twenty-first century" at the **place de la Bastille.** Momentarily, this project became the victim of *cohabitation,* as Mitterand was joined as head of state by opponent Jacques Chirac, with the obvious result of intense squabbling. The Bastille project was scrapped with the arrival of Chirac, then resurrected in a reduced form, and is still scheduled for completion on July 14, 1989, the bicentennial of the French Revolution. I.M. Pei's **glass pyramid,** intended for the entrance of the Louvre was yet another football in one of *cohabitation*'s matches: its construction was delayed until the Ministry of Finance moved out of a wing in the Louvre to new quarters. However, the pyramid is well underway and should be completed by 1989.

The **Musée d'Orsay,** opened in December 1986, provides a home for Paris's late nineteenth-century art treasures in the Gare d'Orsay, itself an architectural masterpiece. Even this *chef d'oeuvre* was subject to the usual, intense public debate, and critics still complain that it's just too big. Finally, construction continues at **La Villette,** where the futuristic **La Géode** already screens movies on its hemispheric screen, and the **Cité des Sciences** houses a massive science museum. In the same complex, the Cité de la Musique, designed by the ultra-modern architect Christian de Porzamparc, will open after 1990 and include the new National Conservatory.

Ile de la Cité and Ile St-Louis

Paris was founded in the third century B.C.E., with the settlement of the Parisii tribe along the Seine, and although it is no longer the aquatic town it was in its early years, its center remains the almond-shaped Ile de la Cité. It and Ile St-Louis are the last two of eight original islands in this part of the Seine. The other six were destroyed by Henri III. Although only 4km long, Ile de la Cité is rich in history and points of interest. **Cathédrale de Notre-Dame** (tel. 43-54-22-63; Mo. Cité) was built from 1163 to 1330 according to the plans of Bishop Maurice de Sully. During the Revolution it was heavily vandalized and then rededicated to the cult of Reason, while its interior was used as a storage area. The cathedral found a patron in the Citizen King, Louis Philippe, and an able restorer in Viollet-le-Duc (1844-64), whose controversial work (he added a spire) changed, but saved, the cathedral. The interior height of the building and the grace of the interior supports are made possible by the external flying buttresses (best seen from place Jean XXIII, behind the church). The interior is dimly lit and devoid of the wealth of statuary and glass that graces Chartres, Amiens, or Laon. Guided tours in French only leave from the back of the church, by the main portals (Mon.-Fri. at noon, Sat. at 2:30pm, Sun. at 2pm; 22F, students 12F, ages under 17 3F). For a closer look at the gargoyles and griffins, as well as a view of Paris made famous by Victor Hugo in *Notre-Dame de Paris,* known in English as *The Hunchback of Notre-Dame,* climb the worn and winding stairs to the bell tower. (22F, students 12F, ages under 17 3F. Open daily 10am-5pm.) Or take a peek at the cathedral's archeological crypt (tel. 43-29-83-51; open daily 10am-5pm; admission 20F, students 10F). The cathedral (open daily 8am-7pm) is packed with tourists all day all summer. The courtyard (*parvis*) in front of Notre-Dame is the geopolitical heart of the country; all distances in France are measured from this spot.

Behind the cathedral, across from place Jean XXIII and down a narrow flight of steps, is the **Mémorial de la Déportation,** an abstract and hauntingly moving memorial erected in remembrance of the 20,000 French victims of Nazi concentration camps. Twenty thousand crystal spires represent the dead.

Another massive structure, given the size of the island, is the **Palais de Justice.** Built on the site of administrative buildings from the days of Roman governors and Capetian monarchs, the Palais began with a small chapel. It later grew to include a palace of kings, then the parliament, and finally, after the Revolution, the tribunal (hence its name). Inside, judges, lawyers, and prosecutors mill around, and clerks hurry from door to door. You can sit in on a public trial—the more inconspicuous you are, the better. (Open Mon.-Sat. 9am-6pm.) A small church inside the courtyard of the Palais de Justice, **Ste-Chapelle,** bd. du Palais, 4*ème* (tel. 43-54-30-09; Mo. Cité), is one of the oldest buildings in the city. Begun in 1246 to house the Crown of Thorns, it was finished in a record 33 months. It is said that St-Louis, King of France (1226-1270), gave away so many of the thorns as political favors that very few remain intact. Frequently hailed as the supreme achievement of Gothic architecture, Ste-Chapelle itself looks like a giant crown of thorns, suspended by the airy masonry that frames the windows. The building's lofty appearance is the clue to its two stories of chapels. The lower, darker one was intended for servants, the magnificently ornate upper one for nobles. This upper chapel is adorned with 15 partially-restored thirteenth-century stained-glass marvels portraying more than 1100 scenes from the Old and New Testaments. The chapel was reopened after major repairs in 1984, and is one of Paris's most impressive monuments. Check the weekly publications for occasional concerts here. (Open daily April-Sept. 9:30am-7pm; Oct.-March 10am-5:45pm. Admission 20F, ages 18-25 and over 60 12F, ages 7-18 5F.)

The fortified, turreted edifice at 1, quai de l'Horloge, is the **Conciergerie** (tel. 43-54-30-06; Mo. Cité), where the famous prisoners of the Revolution—Marie Antoinette, Danton, and Robespierre—were allowed their last glass of brandy before execution. A guillotine is on display in the chapel where prisoners went before their execution, as well as a facsimile of Marie Antoinette's last letter, written in pinpricks and addressed to her sister-in-law. The Conciergerie is still used as a temporary prison for those awaiting trial in the Palais de Justice, just as it was throughout much of France's history. Most of the rooms are remarkable for their heavy, stone-ribbed vaulting and their 2-meter-thick walls. The largest room, the **Salle des Gendarmes,** served as living and eating quarters for about 2000 people. The **Galerie des Prisonniers** is particularly memorable for the part it played in the Reign of Terror. From here nearly 2600 prisoners departed for the guillotine between January, 1793 and July, 1794. (Open daily April-Sept. 9:30am-7pm; Oct.-March 10am-5pm. Obligatory guided tours in French. Admission 22F, students 12F, ages under 17 3F.)

The minor sights of the Cité are equally enchanting. Lovely **place Dauphine,** a peaceful shaded area behind the Palais de Justice and the Conciergerie, is surrounded by houses dating from the early seventeenth-century reign of Louis XIII. The **Pont Neuf,** or New Bridge, is actually the oldest in Paris, built in the late sixteenth century. It connects the Cité to both the Right and Left Banks.

Residential **Ile St-Louis** lives in the shadow of the grand, public buildings of Ile de la Cité. Constantly ignored, forever in the wings, the inhabitants grew tired of the lack of press and proclaimed the island an independent republic in the 1930s. Nonetheless, Ile St-Louis has attracted its share of notables; here you'll find charming old houses where such luminaries as Voltaire, Mme. de Châtelet, Daumier, Ingres, Baudelaire, and Cézanne resided. Today the area is frequented by those in quest of Georges Moustaki's exact address or the excellent ice cream served at Berthillon. The *hôtels particuliers* along quai d'Anjou are particularly notable for their beauty and intimacy.

Rive Droite (Right Bank)

Le Marais

The district stretching from the Bastille to rue du Temple and from the Seine to rue Pastourelle was swamp (*marais*) until the thirteenth century, when Parisians drained it to provide land for convents and monasteries. Eventually, it was incorporated into the expanding city. In the seventeenth century, Henry IV commissioned the building of place Royale (now place des Vosges), which became the center of activity in the fashionable Marais. The *hôtels particuliers,* the elegant townhouses for which the area is famous, were erected during this period, and decorated by the famous artists of the time. Madame de Sévigné, who rented the Hôtel Carnavalet, was one of many hostesses who invited prominent literary and artistic figures to her *salon.* With the fall of the Bastille, however, the aristocracy fled, and members of the working class moved into the area's dilapidated mansions. For the most part, the *hôtels* continued to deteriorate until 1962, when a program to renovate Le Marais was undertaken. In the past few years, Le Marais has once again become fashionable, and the wealthy are taking up residence in the old houses. The area now harbors a strange blend of faded elegance, ethnic diversity, and youthful artistic and intellectual life. Architecture buffs will particularly enjoy strolling here.

In the Hôtel de Soubise you can visit the **Musée de L'Histoire de France,** 60, rue des Francs-Bourgeois, 3ème (tel. 42-77-11-30; Mo. Rambuteau), where important documents about French history, from Dagobert to Jean Moulin and the French Revolution, are well displayed. Definitely worth seeing are a letter dictated by Joan of Arc; the 1598 Edict of Nantes, which granted freedom of worship to the Protestants; the Declaration of the Rights of Man; and Napoleon's will. (Open Wed.-Mon. 2-5pm. Admission 12F.) Nearby is Hôtel Guénégaud, which houses the **Musée de la Chasse et de la Nature,** 60, rue des Archives, 3ème (tel. 42-72-86-43; Mo. Rambuteau). Lovers of venery will enjoy the animal trophies and paintings and tapestries illustrating the hunt and the hounds. You'll probably be alone in the beautiful rooms of the only Mansart *hôtel* left in Paris. (Open Wed.-Mon. 10am-12:30pm and 1:30-5:30pm. Admission 12F.)

In the Hôtel Salé, you can find the recently inaugurated **Musée Picasso,** 5, rue de Thorigny, 3*ème* (tel. 42-71-25-21; Mo. Chemin Vert or St-Paul). The Hôtel Salé was built by Pierre Aubert and finished in 1659 for one of the King's tax farmers, who collected and earned a commission on the hated salt tax; hence its name, meaning "Salty Mansion." In 1976 the architect Roland Simounet was chosen to redecorate the interior and to adapt this *hôtel particulier* to the needs of a modern museum. It now contains 203 paintings, 158 sculptures, 88 ceramics, 1500 drawings, and the artist's collection of primitive art, given to the government in lieu of inheritance taxes. Recent and generous donations continue to expand this thoroughly representative museum. Each room has been carefully arranged according to Picasso's different periods, and put into biographical context by comprehensive labels (in French and English). One room is dedicated to Picasso's set of Cézannes, Braques, Degas, Matisses, and Rousseaus. Be sure to examine the *vitrines documentaires* with manuscripts, books, and pictures pertaining to the paintings in question. A well-made audio-visual presentation introduces newcomers to some of Picasso's main works; ask for the times at the entrance (free). Tours are also available. (In French Mon., Thurs., Sat. at 2pm; price depends on exhibit. In English tours must be arranged in advance by groups of at least 30. Call 42-71-70-84.) Cassettes are available until 3pm (22F). Allow yourself a full day to see this wonderland properly. You can always take a rest in the cozy and inexpensive cafeteria or have a drink in the beautiful courtyard and sculpture garden. (Museum open May-Sept. Thurs.-Mon. 9:45am-5:15pm, Wed. 9:45am-9:45pm. Last admission ½ hr. before closing. Admission 21F, ages 18-25 and over 60 11F, ages under 18 free, Sun. and holidays 11F.)

One of the city's most interesting collections is in the **Musée Carnavalet,** 23, rue de Sévigné, 3*ème* (tel. 42-72-21-13; Mo. St-Paul), off rue du Parc Royal from place de Thorigny. Housed in a building where famous letter-writer Madame de Sévigné lived from the 1670s to the 1690s, this museum of the history of Paris includes paintings, objects, and letters dating from the sixteenth century to the present. (Open Tues.-Sun. 10am-5:40pm. Admission 20F, students 10F, Sun. free.) After the inauguration of Haussmann's urban renewal plans, the Marais was ignored by the upper class and subsequently became a home to immigrants, Jews in particular. **Rue des Rosiers,** near the Musée Carnavalet, is still the center of the Jewish community in Paris and is lined with kosher (*kascher*) restaurants, butcher shops, *boulangeries,* and synagogues. Across rue de Rivoli, the solemn 1956 **Mémorial du Martyr Juif Inconnu** (Memorial to the Unknown Jewish Martyr) at 17, rue Geoffrey l'Asnier, commemorates the Parisian Jews who died at the hands of the Nazis. During the war, thousands of Jews from the Marais were deported, but many also escaped into the quarter's baffling back streets.

Prior to its massive reconstruction, **Hôtel de Sens,** 1, rue du Figuier, 4*ème* (tel. 42-78-14-60; Mo. St-Paul), was one of Paris's two showcases of medieval residential architecture, the other being Hôtel de Cluny in the Latin Quarter. Built from 1474 to 1519, Hôtel de Sens has a lovely facade and pleasant front garden. The *hôtel* now houses a library specializing in local artisans' work. Call ahead for tours of the interior.

Don't miss the two courtyards of handsome **Hôtel de Sully,** 62, rue St-Antoine, 4*ème* (tel. 48-87-24-15; Mo. St-Paul). Built in 1624, it now airs numerous temporary exhibits, many of which are free. Here you can pick up the free brochure *Musées, Monuments, Expositions de Paris et de l'Ile-de-France,* with up-to-date listings of museum hours, and get the schedule for *visites-conférences* at Paris's sites. Reservations can be made here for any of their tours. (Wed. and Sat.-Sun. 25F, ages under 25 18F. *Hôtel* open daily 10am-6pm. Free.) Occupying a prominent position in Le Marais, **place des Vosges** is Paris's oldest square and one of its prettiest. Erected by Henry IV as place Royale to honor himself and his queen, Marie de Medici, the square is a masterpiece of seventeenth-century secular architecture. Part of its charm stems from its grassy enclosure, where Parisian children play and others savor the concoctions of nearby *pâtisseries.* Madame de Sévigné lived at 1bis; Cardinal Richelieu at #21; a favorite is the **Maison de Victor Hugo** at #6 (tel. 42-72-16-65; Mo. Chemin Vert), Hugo's home from 1832 to 1848. The collection includes photographs, manuscripts, letters, furniture designed by Hugo, and even his geometry notebook. One entire exhibit is devoted to nineteenth-century advertisements using Hugo's face: "Victor Hugo Clothes for Men," "Victor Hugo Stationer's," and so on. (Open Tues.-Sun. 10am-5:40pm. Admission 10F, Sun. free.)

A short walk away is **place de la Bastille** (Mo. Bastille), site of the riot of July 14, 1789, which kicked off the French Revolution. In reality, about 400 idealistic proletarians liberated a few petty criminals and social misfits, but the event quickly assumed huge symbolic significance. The Bastille had previously been home to such notables as Voltaire and the Marquis de Sade. Today, only the ground plan of the famous prison remains, marked by a line of stones. Rev up your imagination when you visit, or better yet, come when some sort of public demonstration is taking place. The Bastille has become Paris's newest trendy area, in particular the rue de Lappe. Mitterand's triumph in 1981, for example, was celebrated here with much fanfare. The President has since commissioned Canadian architect Carlos Ott to build an ultra-modern opera house here, but some Parisians assert that the **Bastille Opéra** will spoil the area. The inauguration date of Ott's project is, appropriately, July 14, 1989, the bicentennial of the French Revolution.

Les Halles

In the second half of the nineteenth century, Emile Zola, father of French literary naturalism, proclaimed the old market neighborhood of Les Halles "le ventre de Paris" (Paris's belly). In 1969, after 850 years of hawking chicken, carrots, and cabbages, produce-sellers were relegated to the less visible *banlieue* (suburbs) of Rungis, near Orly, and space-age architecture replaced their humble stalls. The Forum des Halles and the Centre Pompidou, two projects that have caused exemplary controversy, have nevertheless infused the district with new life.

The **Forum des Halles** is a mostly subterranean shopping complex with hundreds of stores and numerous fast-food joints, plus the RER and Métro station Châtelet-Les Halles. Unfortunately, maps inside the multilevel complex are hard to follow, and if you enter you can easily lose yourself among the overpriced and redundant boutiques. On the -1 *niveau* (subterranean level) sits the **Musée de l'Holographie** (tel. 42-96-96-83). Holographs on display seem to move; as you walk around a woman tosses you a kiss and a man winks. Jimmy Cliff sings a tune, Dizzy Gillespie blows his trumpet, and a talk-show host smokes a cigarette. A short film in English explains how holographs are made. (Open June-Sept. Tues., Thurs., and Sat. 10am-7pm, Wed. and Sun. 2-5pm; Oct.-May Tues.-Sun. 9am-noon and 2-6pm. Admission 25F, ages under 25 and over 60 19F.) The surrounding streets pulse with a number of popular student bars, old restaurants, cafes, and clothing stores. Be careful in this area at night: It is the recognized hangout of drug-addicts and is carefully patrolled by police with terrifying dogs. Also, at the new **Musée Grevin,** Forum des Halles, 1er (tel. 42-61-28-50; Mo. Châtelet-Les-Halles), appears *Paris Promenade 1900.* You'll see Hugo, Verlaine, Pasteur, Eiffel, and Zola in wax as you get a history lesson. (Mon.-Sat. 10:30am-6:45pm every 15 min., Sun. and holidays 1-7:15pm. Admission 34F, ages 7-15 22F. Tour lasts 35 min. and may be requested in English.)

The disparity between the ultra-modern design of the Forum and its Gothic and Renaissance neighborhood is most evident in a comparison of the Forum and **Eglise St-Eustache** (tel. 42-36-31-05), a cavernous, ramshackle beauty of a church begun in 1532. Enter on rue Rambuteau at rue du Jour. The Renaissance gilt of the small chapels contrasts sharply with the towering Gothic stone structure. A Rubens painting of 1611, *The Pilgrim of Emmaüs,* is housed in the eleventh north chapel. The organ is beautiful and less dusty than its peer at St-Sulpice. In the chapel next door, Jean-Baptiste Colbert was buried in 1683. Jean-Philippe Rameau also lies here.

The tubular **Centre National d'Art et de Culture Georges-Pompidou,** plateau Beaubourg (tel. 42-77-12-33; for recorded information in French on the week's events 42-77-11-12; Mo. Rambuteau, Hôtel-de-Ville, Châtelet, or Les Halles), commonly known as **Beaubourg,** has inspired architectural controversy since its opening in 1977. It's a building turned inside out: Piping, ventilation ducts, and escalators painted in primary colors run up, down, and sideways along the outside (blue for air, green for water, yellow for electricity, and red for heating). Anomalous as it is, Beaubourg has nonetheless become France's number-one tourist attraction (Versailles is second), serving as a repository of finished art and as a workshop for French and international artists in all media, from painting and architecture to video and television. The external escalator will take you up to each level, with a moving view of the city and festivities in Plateau Beaubourg below. From the fifth floor on clear days, the view is as fine as that from the Tour Eiffel. Between Pompidou and rue St-Martin, on the vast stone place, fire-eaters, jugglers, fortune-tellers, and dancers entertain masses of tourists.

The **Musée National d'Art Moderne** houses the center's main permanent collection, a rich selection of twentieth-century art, from the fauves and cubists to pop and conceptual art. Practically all the great names are represented: Matisse, Picasso, Braque, Kandinsky, Klee, Chagall, Miró, Giacometti, Calder, Dubuffet, Pollack, Warhol, Stella, and others. Since there are so many movable interior walls, shows can be mounted with a great deal of ease and creativity. Exhibits of post-1965 works are constantly changing. Past exhibits have been dedicated to Parisian art. In 1988, the '50s were commemorated with art, movies, and cultural mementos. The center is honeycombed with numerous exhibits and small shows that change frequently. Many are free, although the major ones charge 22F, children 15F (Sun. free). This ticket also admits you to the **Atelier Brancusi,** on rue Rambuteau at place Georges Pompidou, surprisingly unknown by most. Constantin Brancusi donated his sculptures to the Center under the condition that his 1917 *atelier* located at 8, impasse Ronsin, be exactly reproduced. The Romanian sculptor moved to Paris at the beginning of the century and was influenced by Rodin and the cubists here. His work makes use of the plastic abstraction that characterizes the evolution of modern art. Although quite small, the museum showcases Brancusi's main works and all his tools. (Open Mon. and Thurs. 12:30-6pm and Sat. 10:30am-6pm. Only 15 admitted at a time.)

A free noncirculating library, the **Bibliothèque Publique d'Information** has open stacks with a large selection of books in English (see Libraries under Practical Information for details). It also has a computer room; a sitting room with the latest newspapers from around the world; a free stereo center, where you can listen to popular or classical music; a free language-lab; and an Industry Gallery, **Centre de Creation Industrielle (CCI).** (Entire center open Mon. and Wed.-Fri. noon-10pm, Sat.-Sun. 10am-10pm. Admission varies: All-day pass—*laissez-passer 1 jour*—allows you to see everything in the center for 55F, ages 13-25 and over 60 50F; annual pass—*laissez-passer annuel*—170F, ages under 25 and over 60 130F. Temporary exhibits in the *grande galerie* 32F, in the *galeries contemporaines* 20F.)

Between the Pompidou Center and Eglise St-Merri, **place Igor Stravinsky** honors the Russian composer. The playful fountains by Jean Tinguely and Niki de St-Phalle are no doubt the most colorful in Paris, with mobile sculptures illustrating famous pieces by the great composer.

Paris's **Hôtel de Ville** (City Hall) was built after its predecessor went up in smoke during the Commune. An impressive 136 statues adorn its picturesque facade. The rich Renaissance and Belle Epoque decoration inside clearly shows the style of the times. Note the staircase by Delorme and the murals by Puvis de Chavannes. Make sure you drop by their information office, 29, rue de Rivoli, 4ème (tel. 42-76-40-40; Mo. Hôtel-de-Ville), where exhibits are sometimes held. (Open Mon.-Fri. 9am-5:15pm.) Place de l'Hôtel de Ville, with refreshing fountains and a great view across the Seine, is a welcome refuge from plateau Beaubourg when the fire-eaters become too insistent.

The tall belfry on rue de Rivoli is the **Tour St-Jacques,** a sixteenth-century flamboyant Gothic tower that surmounted a church destroyed during the Revolution. It was one of the starting points for the pilgrimage to Santiago de Compostela in Spain.

Palais-Royal and Opéra

North of the Louvre, this neighborhood in the 1*er*, 2*ème*, and 9*ème arrondisse-ments* harbors some of France's greatest cultural institutions amid a fast-paced business quarter.

The **Palais-Royal** (Mo. Palais-Royal) is a sedate collection of buildings, columns, and galleries opening onto a garden of roses and fountains. Cardinal Richelieu had a *palais cardinal* constructed in 1639; it became a *palais royal* when Anne of Austria, regent for Louis XIV, established residence there. Accessible by numerous passageways, this area was important as a meeting place during the Revolution, and the center of Parisian social life in the late eighteenth and early nineteenth centuries. On the southwestern corner of the Palais-Royal is the **Comédie Française** (see Entertainment), built in the late nineteenth century and later restored after a twentieth-century fire. Appropriately, a monument to Molière rises up not far from here on rue Molière at rue Richelieu. Continuing along the latter, you'll come to the **Bibliothèque Nationale**, 58, rue Richelieu, 2*ème* (tel. 46-03-81-26). Competing with the British Museum for the title of largest library in Western Europe, the Bibliothèque contains seven million volumes, including two Gutenberg Bibles and many first editions of famous French authors from the fifteenth century to the present, including Rabelais and Pascal. You must have two photos and college ID to use this massive resource, but the building's Mansart gallery is open to all for inspection (daily noon-6pm, admission 12F), and a small museum of antiques is contained within the halls (open daily 1-6pm).

For the best approach to the **Opéra** (tel. 42-66-50-22; Mo. Opéra), follow av. de l'Opéra, at the end of which Charles Garnier's grand edifice stands majestic and ornate. The interior of this Second Empire building is capped by Chagall's ceiling (1964). (Open daily 11am-4:30.) Opera buffs should visit the **Musée de l'Opéra,** in the rear at 1, place Charles Garnier, 9*ème.* The museum houses the ballet slippers of Nijinsky, the crown of Pavlova, portraits of Richard Wagner, sketches of famous costumes, and other operatica. (Open Mon.-Fri. 10am-noon and 2-5pm. Admission 12F.)

The **Musée Grévin,** 10, bd. Montmartre (tel. 47-70-85-05; Mo. Montmartre), is a˙wax museum representing mainly picturesque scenes from story-book history (Marie Antoinette in jail, for example), but also depicts such notables as Ronald Reagan. A magic show and a light show with mirrors are included. (Open daily 1-6pm. Admission 38F, ages under 14 26F.) Connecting bd. Montmartre with rue du Faubourg Montmartre are two lovely, nineteenth-century shopping arcades (*passages*), Jouffroy and Verdeau, full of antique book, print, and jewelry shops. Rue Richer, an old Jewish quarter lined with kosher butchers and good stores, cuts through Faubourg Montmartre.

To the south sprawl the busy and crowded **grands boulevards,** a trademark of the Right Bank, and the architectural achievements of Georges-Eugène Haussmann, a baron from Alsace, who from 1853 to 1870 transformed this part of Paris from a still partly medieval town into a modern business quarter of bustling thoroughfares. Lined with large department stores, airline offices, and a few cafes, the *grands boulevards* buzz with activity throughout the week. In this neighborhood stands **Eglise St-Roch,** a classic of French seventeenth-century architecture. The church is filled with eighteenth-century sculpture and paintings, including a Nativity by the Anguier brothers, and a memorable 1750 pipe organ. Pierre Corneille is buried in some unidentified spot in the church. A brochure (in French, 30F) in the sacristy describes the history and art of the church.

Place Vendôme and Place de la Concorde

The majesty of French urban planning becomes evident in the squares and buildings that dominate this area. **Place Vendôme,** with its uniformly dignified structures, is spectacularly beautiful. Construction took 33 years, and the square was completed in 1720. The column in the center was raised in 1810 to commemorate Napoleon's 1805 victory at Austerlitz. In the square, you will find the Ritz Hotel at #15 and the place where Chopin died at #12. The entire street shimmers with opulence; here are the well-known bankers, perfumers, and jewellers (Van Cleef & Arpels, Guerlain, and Rothschild, among others). Supposedly, Rothschild, instead of lending his friends money, would simply allow them to stroll with him around place Vendôme for a few minutes. The next morning the fortunate souls would be certain of credit at the most prestigious banks. Maybe you'll be so lucky.

The **Jardin des Tuileries,** where geometry prevails over nature, is probably the most famous of Paris's parks. Catherine de Medici missed the public promenades of her native Italy and so had the gardens built in 1564; a century later André le Nôtre gave them their present aspect. The Tuileries are sanctuaries for walking, reading, or resting. Sculptures by Rodin dot the manicured park.

At the far end of the gardens, the intimate and very Parisian **Musée de l'Orangerie** (tel. 42-97-48-16; Mo. Concorde) displays the Collection Jean Walter et Paul Guillaume. Mme. Guillaume, who married both of these private art collectors (at different times), donated to the French government a series of paintings ranging from impressionism to surrealism. The Orangerie hasn't the heavyweights of the Musée d'Orsay, nor as many, but neither does it have the crowds. Among its treasures are a series of Cézanne still lifes and works by Picasso, Matisse, Henri Rousseau, Modigliani, and Utrillo. Renoir's *Claude Renoir en Clown,* which has become the museum's trademark, depicts the painter's son wearing a bright orange costume. (Open Wed.-Mon. 9:45am-5pm. Admission 15F, students 8F, Sun. 8F. Last admission 15 min. before closing.) The Orangerie's mirror image at the end of the Tuileries, the **Jeu de Paume** has closed, signaling, perhaps, the end of an era.

Yoking the Tuileries with the Champs-Elysées is **place de la Concorde,** where the "nation's razor" was the centerpiece of free public sideshows during the Reign of Terror (1793-1794). The square had recently been consecrated to Louis XV. Louis XVI, Marie Antoinette, Danton, and Robespierre all lost their heads here. At the end of the Terror, the Directory optimistically relabeled the place *Concorde* (previously named *place de la Revolution* in 1792). The architectural grandeur of the square is now somewhat diminished by the constant flood of traffic. At the end of rue Royale stands **La Madeleine,** a church resembling a Greek temple. This church has a troubled past: It was almost chosen as Paris's first railway station in 1837.

Palais du Louvre

Because immensity and opulence often obscure simpler beauty, the **Palais du Louvre** (tel. 42-60-39-26; Mo. Louvre or Palais-Royal) draws more crowds than any other museum in Paris. As early as 1214, a fortress was built here to defend the city's west side. François I transformed the utilitarian building into a splendid Renaissance palace in 1546, and Catherine de Medici, Henry IV, Louis XIII, Louis XIV, and Napoleon III all added to their heart's content. Not until 1871 did the palace assume its present aspect. In the garden between the Pavillon de Marsan and the Pavillon de Flore stands the **Arc de Triomphe du Carrousel,** inspired by the Arch of Septimus Severus in Rome and built in 1806-08 to commemorate Napoleon's victories of 1805. At one time, the four bronze horses from St-Mark's in Venice graced this little arch; Napoleon "borrowed" them when he conquered the Veneto. The building spree continues into our own day; Mitterand seems compelled by some curse on French rulers to feed the Leviathan. He has commissioned American architect I.M. Pei to build a glass pyramid as the museum's main entrance. Opponents call the project an ultra-modern geometric extravagance that would clash with the Louvre's traditional architecture and claim that its 20-m height would interrupt the view that extends from the Palais and the Carrousel past the obelisk in place de la Concorde to the Champs Elysées and the Arc de Triomphe. Foes of the plan signed all the customary petitions. Construction started all the same, and of 100 tourists surveyed, only one approved the aesthetics of the modern eruption.

Visiting the **Musée du Louvre** requires time and a little skill to negotiate the vast size and the crowds. The most popular exhibition halls are packed in summer, especially on Sunday when admission is free; but some of the less popular galleries, such as Asian Antiquities on the ground floor, are often nearly deserted. If you insist on battling the crowds, you might come away with a peek at the skirt of the Winged Victory, or a glimpse of the bridge past Mona Lisa's shoulder. Get to the museum as soon as the doors open and run—do not walk—to your favorite painting. Several carefully planned trips to the Louvre are in order, each devoted to a few galleries. Better to enjoy a small part than to succumb to utter exhaustion while trying and failing to master all of it, even superficially. Invest in one of the museum guides sold near the entrance (10F). Some praise the green *Michelin* guide to Paris for background, while others prefer to rely on their senses.

Although the exhibits rotate, the layout of the museum remains basically immutable. Sculpture is found on the ground floor of the Pavillon de Flore in the Tuileries, extending across the street from the bulk of the Louvre. Representative pieces from France's Romanesque, Gothic, Renaissance, and neoclassical periods are exhibited here, as well as Italian sculpture of these periods.

Paintings are included in several parts of the museum according to school. The Spanish (El Greco, Goya, Ribera), Italian (Guardi, Botticelli, Bellini, Fra Angelico, Giotto), Flemish (Van Dyck), and Dutch (a few Rembrandts) schools are on the second floor of the Pavillon de Flore and Pavillon des Etats. The Medici Gallery contains a cycle of 21 paintings by Peter-Paul Rubens commissioned by Marie de Medici, Queen of France, and originally hung in the Luxembourg palace. The huge paintings display the corpulence and billowing garments for which the artist is renowned, while glorifying their patron's wealth. The *petits cabinets* of Flemish, Dutch, and German painting contain an excellent collection of works by Bosch, Brueghel, Van der Weyden, Dürer, and Holbein (these fringe the Medici Gallery, but are often unexpectedly closed, so check at the front desk). French paintings from the fifteenth to nineteenth century (Le Nain, de La Tour, Poussin, LeBrun, Watteau, Van Loo, Greuze, and David) extend the length of the second floor of the Grande Galerie (almost a quarter of a mile). Note the brilliant light emanating from La Tour's creations. Napoleon is immortalized here by David and Delaroch. Delacroix's *Liberty Leading the People* and Géricault's *The Raft of the Medusa* merit careful inspection as they represent the climax of French nineteenth-century Romanticism and embody French ideals of liberty, equality, and fraternity in the post-Napoleonic era. Also on the second floor is the Salle des Etats, which displays sixteenth-century painting, including Leonardo da Vinci's tempered-glass encased *La Joconde* (*The Mona Lisa*), yellowed with age, but still laughing complacently at the crowds fighting for eye contact. Even if you don't want to compete for a glimpse, the gallery is full of other treasures, such as da Vinci's *Virgin Mary and Child,* Titian's *Entombment,* and Veronese's *The Marriage at Cana.* The English school (seventeenth-nineteenth century) commands the third floor of the west wing. There you will find portraits by Reynolds and Gainsborough from the eighteenth century, and landscapes by Constable and Turner from the nineteenth. Temporary exhibits are displayed on the third floor of the Pavillon de Flore. The ground floor of the museum is occupied by antiquities. Follow the crowd to the *Winged Victory of Samothrace* (third century B.C.E.) on the landing of the Daru staircase, and the *Venus de Milo* (second century B.C.E.), located beyond the exhilarating *Winged Victory* in the Pavillon des Arts. The Greek, Roman, and Egyptian collections complete with mummies and Maltese falcons extend to the second floor of the museum as well.

Also on the second floor are objets d'art and furniture that re-create the lived-in palace atmosphere. The Louvre possesses a fine collection of Gobelins tapestries, along with the Maximilian tapestries. The Apollo-Gallery houses the crown jewels and the Regent diamond.

The Louvre runs an extensive, reasonably priced museum shop in the entrance foyer. You can also exchange currency here. An often overlooked area of the museum is the *Chalcographie* department located beyond the museum shop on the second floor. Here you can purchase up to five engravings from original plates, choosing from over 14,000 samples. Although they are more expensive than the reproductions in the shop below (200-1000F), they are considered genuine works of art. (Department open Wed.-Mon. 10am-1pm and 2-5pm.) Most people enter the Louvre through porte Champollion, on rue de l'Amiral de Coligny, the entrance closest to the Métro; for shorter lines, walk around to the *portes* on quai du Louvre. (Louvre open Wed.-Mon. 9:45am-5pm or 6:30pm—different rooms close at different times. All galleries open Mon. and Wed.; on other days call to inquire about specific galleries. Guided tours in English daily at 10:15am, 11:30am, and 3:30pm; in French at 11:30am and 3:30pm. 1½-hr. cassette tour 22F. Admission 20F, students 10F, Sun. free.)

Within the Palais, the **Musée des Arts Décoratifs,** Pavillon de Marsan, 107, rue de Rivoli, 1er (tel. 42-60-32-14; Mo. Palais-Royal), features furniture, objets d'art, china, and household items dating from the Middle Ages to the present, including an art-deco apartment, an exhibition room from the 1900 art-nouveau exposition, and art-nouveau jewelry. (Open Wed.-Sat. 12:30-6pm, Sun. 11am-6pm. Admission 25F, students 18F.) In the only unused portion of the Louvre, the **Musée des Arts de la Mode,** 109, rue de Rivoli, 1er (tel. 42-60-32-14; Mo. Palais-Royal), includes 8000 complete costumes and more than 30,000 accessories. The free opening presentation best highlights the collections. (Open Wed.-Sat. 12:30-6pm, Sun. 11am-6pm. Admission 25F, students 18F.)

Arc de Triomphe

You would have to be made of stone not to be moved by your first glimpse of the Arc de Triomphe, looming like destiny itself above the Champs-Elysées (tel. 43-80-31-31; Mo. Charles-de-Gaulle/Etoile). The world's largest triumphal arch and an internationally recognized symbol of France, its construction was ordered by Napoleon to honor the Imperial Army; work was completed in 1836. Since, in the first 50 years after its construction, no one could agree on what to put on top of the arch, it has kept its simple "unfinished" form. Since 1920 it has contained the Tomb of the Unknown Soldier. The eternal flame is rekindled every evening at 6:30pm, when veterans and small children lay wreaths decorated with blue, white, and red. Sculpted groups by different artists allegorically depict the history of France. Rude's *La Marseillaise* is to the right, on the Champs-Elysées side. Rather than risk an early death by crossing the busy traffic circle of place Charles-de-Gaulle to reach the Arc, use the underpasses on the even-numbered side of both the Champs-Elysées and av. de la Grande-Armée. For a stellar view, climb to the top. (Open daily 10am-5:30pm. Admission 22F, ages 25 and under 12F.)

Twelve perfectly symmetrical avenues radiate from the huge rotary of **place Charles-de-Gaulle,** the most handsome being shady **avenue Foch,** Haussmann's masterpiece, which runs west through the 16ème *arrondissement* to the Bois de Boulogne. The little dogs proudly parading along the tree-bordered sidewalks belong to the wealthiest households in Paris. Probably the only building here to which you can gain entrance is the **Musée d'Ennery,** 59, av. Foch, 16ème (tel. 45-53-57-96; Mo. Porte Dauphine), a small collection of Japanese and Chinese art in Ennery's nineteenth-century residence. (Open Sept.-July Thurs. and Sun. 2-5pm. Free.)

Avenue Foch might have solid money and classical good looks, but its neighbor **avenue des Champs-Elysées** enjoys glory and fame. Its reputation for fashionable cafes, luxurious shops, and spectacular views is deserved. Ever since Le Nôtre planted trees in 1667 to extend the Tuileries vista (and renamed it Elysian Fields, because of its shade), the avenue has been one of Paris's most appealing attractions. Crowded with tourists seeking entertainment in summer, it becomes a popular rallying point for Parisians in winter. (The march celebrating Général de Gaulle was held here in 1970.) Between rond-point des Champs-Elysées and Concorde on rue du Faubourg St-Honoré, the **Palais de l'Elysée** is home to the French President. Sorry, *pas de visites.* The **Grand Palais** (tel. 42-89-59-10) and **Petit Palais** (tel. 42-65-12-73; Mo. Champs-Elysées-Clemenceau), facing one another on av. Winston Churchill, were both built for the 1900 Exhibition and share the cavernous elegance of some English Victorian rail stations. They house temporary and permanent exhibits that most tourists overlook. (Grand Palais open Thurs.-Mon. 10am-8pm,

Wed. 10am-10pm. Admission 28F, Sun. 20F. Petit Palais open Tues.-Sun. 10am-5:40pm. Admission 20F, students 13.50F. Prices vary with temporary exhibits.) The wing of the Grand Palais facing av. de Franklin D. Roosevelt is given over to the **Palais de la Découverte** (tel. 43-59-16-65; Mo. Champs-Elysées-Clemenceau), a touch-and-feel science museum where you can turn wheels, pull levers, and push buttons to your heart's content. Demonstrations take place throughout the day—make sure to see the one with liquid air. (Open Tues.-Sun. 10am-6pm. Admission 15F, ages under 18 10F; **planetarium** 10F.)

Parc de Monceau

Parc de Monceau is to the vast Bois de Boulogne what chamber music is to Beethoven's Ninth. But Monceau is also one of the exclusive quarters of the French capital, and in its well-tended park you'll probably run into France's bourgeois youth jogging and relaxing. The park itself, designed by the painter Carmontelle for the Duke d'Orléans, in the 8ème (Mo. Monceau), has a duck pond and romantic ruins.

Nearby are several unusual museums. The elegant **Musée Nissim de Camondo,** 63, rue de Monceau, 8ème (tel. 45-63-26-32; Mo. Monceau or Villiers), recreates the atmosphere of an eighteenth-century domicile in an *hôtel* next to the Parc de Monceau. The Comte Moïse de Camondo turned his private collection into a museum in honor of his son Nissim, killed in World War I; the rest of the Comte's descendants died at Auschwitz. The opulent Louis XVI mansion houses a considerable collection of eighteenth-century art, including priceless Chinese vases, Aubusson tapestries, and Sèvres porcelain. (Open Wed.-Sun. 10am-noon and 2-5pm. Admission 15F, students 10F.) The **Musée Cernuschi,** 7, av. Vélasquez, 8ème (tel. 45-63-50-75; Mo. Villiers), set in a lovely villa just east of the park, specializes in ancient Chinese art. Don't miss the painted silk and the models of Japanese and Korean dress on the second floor. (Open Tues.-Sun. 10am-5:40pm. Admission 10F, students 5F, Sun. free.)

Russians have always had strong ties to France, and the **Eglise Russe,** 12, rue Daru, 8ème (tel. 42-27-57-34; Mo. Ternes), west of the park, attests to their happy sojourn here. Built in 1860 by the pre-*émigré* waves, the church exemplifies the vitality of Russian culture in Paris. (Services Sat. at 6pm and Sun. at 10:15am. Women should cover their heads.) Directly south of the park, the **Musée Jacquemart-André,** 158, bd. Haussmann, 8ème (tel. 45-62-39-94; Mo. St-Phillipe-du-Roule), displays a collection of Italian Renaissance (Uccello, Botticelli, Titian) and eighteenth-century French (Watteau, Boucher, Greuze) paintings. It also exhibits tapestries and antique furnishings. Occasional temporary exhibits replace the permanent collection so call or check weekly publications. (Open Wed.-Sun. 1:30-5:30pm. Admission 25F, students 12.50F.) Those interested in old instruments must visit the **Musée Instrumental du Conservatoire de Musique,** 14, rue de Madrid, 8ème (Mo. Europe), northeast of Jacquemart near place d'Europe. Lutes, lyres, harpsichords (one made for Marie de Medici), bagpipes, and many other vintage instruments are all on display. (Open Wed.-Sat. 2-6pm. Admission 10F, students 5F.)

Sixteenth Arrondissement and Bois de Boulogne

After a hard day strolling down the shady residential streets of the Passy quarter and visiting the many museums in the area, you can unwind in the huge Bois de Boulogne, which offers many great spots for a picnic.

If you're coming from the Tour Eiffel and the Left Bank, cross the Pont d'Iéna to the **Jardins du Trocadéro** with its powerful fountains, and the **Palais de Chaillot** (Mo. Trocadéro), built for the 1939 International Exposition. The Palais contains several museums. The **Musée de l'Homme** (tel. 45-53-70-60) captivates with its educational display of archeological finds. Illustrating human origins and various stages of tribal organization, the colorful exhibits include masks from Africa, Maori carvings from New Zealand, and pre-Columbian relics, along with helpful maps and occasional audio-visual presentations. There are also some French monuments, murals, and sculpture. (Museum open Wed.-Mon. 9:15am-5:15pm. Admission 15F, students 7F.) The **Musée de la Marine** (tel. 45-53-31-70), also here, displays ships, flags, exhibits on French naval history, and other things maritime. (Open Wed.-Mon. 10am-6pm. Admission 18F, students 9F.) Exhibitions of film paraphernalia are screened at the **Musée du Cinéma,** salle du Palais de Chaillot (tel. 45-53-74-39), including the most primitive of movie-making implements. The museum traces the history of sound and light in film, starting with magic lanterns and shadow theaters. (Open Wed.-Mon. 10am-1pm and 2-5pm. Guided visits in French only at 10am, 11am, 2pm, 3pm, and 4pm. Tour lasts 1½ hr. Admission 18F.)

Although not so flashy as its counterpart at the Centre Pompidou, the **Musée d'Art Moderne de la Ville de Paris,** 11, av. du Président Wilson, 16ème (tel. 47-23-61-27; Mo. Iéna), owns good selections of Modigliani, Dufy, and Roualt and frequently unveils exhibits of very recent, very bizarre works. Unfortunately, the sculpture outside the entrance has been covered with grafitti. (Open Tues. and Thurs.-Sun. 10am-5:30pm, Wed. 10am-8:30pm. Admission 32F, students 19F, Sun. free except for temporary expositions.) The Musée d'Art Moderne is just one of several museums constituting the **Palais de Tokyo,** 13, av. du Président-Wilson (tel. 47-23-36-53), which was built for the 1937 International Exposition. (Open Wed.-Mon. 9:45am-5:15pm. Admission 19F, Sun. 9F.) The nearby **Musée Guimet,** 6, place d'Iéna, 16ème (tel. 47-23-61-65; Mo. Iéna), exhibits one of the most extensive collections of Asian art in the Western world. (Open Wed.-Mon. 9:45am-5:15pm. Admission 15F, students and Sun. 8F.) It won't substitute for reading his novels, but the **Maison de Balzac,** 47, rue Raynouard, 16ème (tel. 42-24-56-38; Mo. Passy), is full of interesting memorabilia from the life and work of Honoré de Balzac, who penned the last part of *La comédie humaine* here from 1840 to 1847. (Open Tues.-Sun. 10am-5:40pm. Admission 15F, students 10F, Sun. free except for special exhibits.)

The **Musée du Vin,** rue des Eaux, 16ème (tel. 45-25-63-26; Mo. Passy), is in Abbey Passy's vaulted *caves,* dating from the thirteenth and fourteenth centuries. Exhibits on the distillation and fabrication of champagne and wine, the classification of wine, and a variety of old wines will compel you to taste at the exit. (Open Tues.-Sun. noon-6pm. Admission 25F, students 19F.)

After the Orsay, the **Musée Marmottan,** 2, rue Louis-Boilly, 16ème (tel. 42-24-07-02; Mo. La Muette), is Paris's impressionist specialist. Set inside the erstwhile *hôtel* of art historian Marmottan, this private collection originally concentrated on the First Empire Period (paintings of Napoleon, sculpture, furniture) and Renaissance *tapisseries,* but Marmottan received a substantial shot in the arm when he inherited works owned by Michel Monet, including many by Claude Monet. Descending into the underground Salle Monet is like diving into an aqueous, submarine world or wandering through Monet's private garden at Giverny (see Near Rouen). This uncannily silent gallery manages to catch the mood of Monet's mysteriously primeval *Nymphées* (*Water Lilies*). If you like paintings of Paris, don't miss Gustave Caillebotte's *Temps de Pluie à Paris* (*Raining in Paris*) and Pissarro's *Les Boulevards Extérieurs-Effet de Neige* (*Outer Boulevards-Effect of Snow*), two works on the ground floor for those who aren't yet fed up with the Parisian weather. (Open Tues.-Sun. 10am-5pm. Admission 18F, students and ages under 25 9F.)

The vast, wooded **Bois de Boulogne,** past the 16ème *arrondissement* (Mo. Porte Maillot, Sablons, Pont de Neuilly, Porte Dauphine, or Porte d'Auteuil), is as Parisian as late-night onion soup. Here you'll find lakes, restaurants, horse and bicycle races—even a baseball diamond in the corner of the Bagatelle soccer and rugby fields. In the past, the Bois was the private hunting ground of the king and his nobles. For a pleasant stroll, walk along **Lac Inférieur** (lower lake), down route de Suresnes from porte Dauphine (Mo. Porte Dauphine). The manicured islands in the middle of the lake can be reached only by rowboats rented by the hour (40F, deposit 100F). Across from the rowboat dock you can also rent a bike (14F per hr., 60F for 4 hr., leave ID as deposit). If you enjoy racing remote control cars, you may want to join in the Bois's mini Grand Prix. West of Lac Inférieur is **Pré Catelan,** a picture-perfect park. The pretty **Jardin Shakespeare,** in the center of the Pré Catelan, is a good example of life imitating art. Flowers mentioned in Shakespeare's plays have been grown here to reproduce scenes from *As You Like It, Hamlet, A Midsummer Night's Dream, Macbeth,* and *The Tempest.* In addition, the **Theater Shakespeare** (tel. 42-27-39-54; Mo. Porte Maillot; see Entertainment) produces a Shakespeare play every year. (Garden open Mon.-Sat. 10am-7pm. Admission 80F, students 40F.) The **Bagatelle** (tel. 40-67-97-00), once a private estate within the Bois, now sustains a well-preserved flower garden famous for its water lilies and a rose exhibition every June. (Open daily 8:30am-6:30pm. Admission 5F.)

In the north end of the Bois, the **Jardin d'Acclimatation** (tel. 40-67-90-82; Mo. Sablons) has a small zoo and amusement park that includes a small train, an enchanting river, and temporary children's exhibits. (Open daily 10am-6pm. Admission 6F.) Finally, be sure to visit the nearby **Musée National des Arts et Traditions Populaires,** 6, route du Mahatma-Gandhi (tel. 47-47-69-80; Mo. Sablons), one of Paris's newest, most innovative museums. It explores the roots and evolution of French cultural habits. The excellent collection of tools and everyday artifacts illustrates rural French life before the Industrial Revolution. (Open Wed.-Mon. 9:45am-5pm. Audio-visual presentation daily. Admission 15F, ages under 25 and over 60 8F, Sun. 8F.) When the moon comes out, so do the prostitutes—male, female, and transvestite, and a serious and extremely unsafe traffic jam ensues. Lone women should probably avoid the area unless they wish to discover their worth to the patriarchy.

Rive Gauche (Left Bank)

Quartier Latin (Latin Quarter)

The story of the Latin Quarter reads like a discourse on French intellectual history. The scholars of the Sorbonne, who chatted in Latin until the eighteenth century, have always cherished ideas—especially old ones. But the large student and bohemian population save the area from stuffiness. Steps away from the riotous, cosmopolitan boulevards, one can always find a drowsy park or square to soothe jostled sensibilities. The Latin Quarter makes such an impact that many visitors confuse it with the whole Rive Gauche. It actually occupies a small area confined to the 5*ème,* roughly including boulevard St-Michel and the area east to the Jardin des Plantes, bounded on the north by the Seine, and running south no farther than the end of rue Mouffetard.

Boulevard St-Michel, which divides the 5*ème* and 6*ème arrondissements* as it moves inland from the Seine, is synonomous with the Latin Quarter. The bookstores and cafes of Boul-Miche are among the most attractive in Paris, and the **Sorbonne** stands only a couple of blocks away. Reputedly the second-oldest university in Europe (after Bologna), dating from the first decade of the twelfth century, the Sorbonne has undergone numerous changes in its curriculum and organization in the last 800 years. Originally a center for theological studies, the university was decentralized into 13 autonomous campuses following the student riots of May 1968. The Sorbonne presently comprises Paris III and Paris IV Universities, two of the 13 campuses. Right behind the Sorbonne is the **Collège de France,** an institution created by François I in 1530 to contest the university's supreme authority. The free morning and evening courses given here are often outstanding; past lecturers include Henri Bergson, Paul Valéry, and Milan Kundera. (Courses run Sept.-May, schedule appears in Sept. For more information, call 43-29-12-11.)

Perched on the highest (65m) and most central point of the Left Bank is the **Panthéon** (tel. 43-54-34-51; Mo. Luxembourg), a church built by Louis XV in the shape of a Greek cross to fulfill a vow he made when ill that if he recovered he would replace the fallen Abbey of St-Généviève with such a building. In 1791, the Constituent Assembly started the practice of interring great patriots and figures of distinction in the former church and gave it the name Panthéon. The crypt of the Panthéon houses the heart of Léon Gambetta (in an urn) and the tombs of Victor Hugo, Voltaire, Rousseau, Louis Braille, and Emile Zola, as well as a host of Napoleon's flunkies. The rest of the cavernous, heavily neoclassical building is empty save for late nineteenth-century paintings of mythical scenes from Paris's early history, the most famous of which is by Puvis de Chavannes. (Open June-Sept. 9:30am-6:30pm; Oct.-May 10am-noon and 2-5:30pm. Admission 22F, students 12F.) The nearby **Lycée Henri IV** is one of Paris's most prestigious high schools, once the turf of intellectual Carrie Jaurès Noland.

At the intersection of boulevards St-Germain and St-Michel, in the center of the Latin Quarter, the **Musée de Cluny,** 6, place Paul-Painlevé (tel. 43-25-62-00; Mo. St-Michel), is Paris's museum of medievalia. The most famous of its treasures is the tapestry *La Dame à la Licorne (The Lady with the Unicorn)*; five of its six wall-length panels are supposed to represent the five senses. A group of tapestries such as this is called a *chambre,* or room; medieval rooms were tapestried primarily to retain heat. Recently unearthed and exhibited here is *La Galerie des Rois de Judas,* a set of statues of kings, which were sheltered above Notre-Dame's portals before the revolutionaries of 1793 shattered them in their battle against all Gothic or classical representation. Half of the museum is in a late Gothic *hôtel,* while the other half occupies the remains of the baths of Roman Paris. (Open Wed.-Mon. 9:45am-12:30pm and 2-5:15pm. Last entry 45 min. before closing. Admission 15F, students 8F, Sun. 8F.) Nearby, the Parisian police have their own museum, the **Musée des Collections Historiques de la Préfecture de la Police,** 1bis, rue des Carmes, 5*ème* (tel. 43-29-21-57, 336; Mo. Maubert-Mutualité). Historians may enjoy following the development of fire-fighters and police from the Middle Ages to 1870. The rest of us can review memorabilia from crime throughout the same period. (Open Mon.-Thurs. 9am-5pm and Fri. 9am-4:30pm. Free.)

Losing yourself in the streets between the Seine and bd. St-Germain is a pleasure. **Place René-Viviani,** next to Pont-au-Double, enjoys one of the best views of Notre-Dame. Across rue St-Jacques stands **St-Séverin,** a church noted for its flamboyant Gothic interior. Hidden away on nearby rue de la Huchette is Paris's smallest theater, **Théâtre de la Huchette,** 23, rue de la Huchette, 5*ème* (tel. 43-26-38-99; Mo. St-Michel), stomping ground of Ionesco's *La Cantatrice Chauve (The Bald Soprano)* since 1957. (Open Mon.-Sat. 5-10pm. Admission 80F, students 60F, Sat. no student rate.) Mitterrand did some remodeling when he moved into the Palais de l'Elysée. Still unsatisfied, he spends considerable time in his Latin Quarter apartment on **rue de Bièvre,** off bd. St-Germain. The *gendarmes* can often be seen blocking the street to cars; just in case, don't linger.

St-Germain-des-Prés and the Jardin du Luxembourg

This area of the 6*ème arrondissement* between the Seine and the Jardin du Luxembourg is as vibrant as any in the Latin Quarter. Moreover, some of the most famous cafes in Paris are located right on bd. St-Germain.

Located at the busy intersection of bd. St-Germain and rue de Rennes, **Eglise St-Germain-des-Prés** is Paris's oldest church, and one of the few Romanesque structures still standing in the area. Of special interest are the eleventh-century nave, the ornamented columns in the choir, and, in the second chapel on the right, the stone marking the interred ashes of Descartes. Perhaps the quaintest square in Paris is **place de Furstemberg,** off rue de l'Abbaye—tiny and romantic, with Victorian lampposts and lots of poetically inclined souls. Watch street musicians here on summer nights. The **Musée Eugène Delacroix,** 6, place de Furstemberg, 6*ème* (tel. 43-54-04-87; Mo. Saint-German-des Prés), commemorates the nineteenth-century romantic painter in his studio and home, where he died in 1863. (Open Wed.-Mon. 9:45am-5:15pm. Admission 10F, students and Sun. 5F.)

The streets around nearby rue de Seine are replete with expensive art galleries—the struggling artists' quarter of the past now belongs to wealthier individuals. To see what Parisian art students are doing, walk around the **Ecole des Beaux-Arts,** 14, rue Bonaparte at quai Malaquais, 6*ème* (tel. 42-60-34-57; Mo. St-Germain-des-Prés); it's Paris's best-known art school. For information about the changing exhibits, hours, and entrance fees, call or check any weekly publication (see Publications about Paris).

Near the Seine, across the Pont des Arts from the Louvre, the **Palais de l'Institut de France** sits solidly beneath an elegant dome. The *institut* is an umbrella association for five learned societies, the most famous of which is the **Académie Française.** Since its founding by Richelieu in 1635, the Académie's primary task has been to produce the official dictionary of the French language (officially ignored by most French speakers). It selects and squashes words and expressions, doing likewise with potential members—Molière and Proust never made it, and not until a few years ago was a woman, the novelist Marguerite Yourcenar (who now lives in the U.S.), accepted.

Coin collectors will enjoy the **Musée de la Monnaie de Paris,** 11, quai de Conti, 6*ème* (tel. 43-29-12-48; Mo. Pont-Neuf), with a display of medals as well as money. (Open Tues.-Fri. 9am-5:45pm, Sat. 9-11:45am. Free.)

The **Théâtre de l'Odéon,** at the handsome semicircular **place de l'Odéon,** rose from the dust in the late eighteenth century (see Entertainment). Reconstructed several times, **Eglise St-Sulpice** towers over the neighborhood. Inside, the murals by Delacroix, full of romantic zeal, are impressive but dim light often obscures their beauty. Don't miss the organ loft by Chalgrin, a bit dusty, but regarded as the most beautiful in the country. Far from austere, the church flaunts its abundance. Religious wealth yields to secular riches in *place St-Sulpice* with its extravagant fountain.

An eleventh-century crop farm later manicured by Marie de Medicis, the **Jardin du Luxembourg** is as integral a part of the Left Bank as the Sorbonne or the cafes. Trees and flowers—including some palms—are interspersed with statues of such poets as Baudelaire and Hérédia, modern sculpture, and even a mini Statue of Liberty. Rent a toy boat for 9F per hour and sail it on the pond with the kiddies, or attend a *guignol* (puppet show) daily at 4pm (tel. 43-50-25-00; admission 15F). The Luxembourg, planned in the seventeenth century, was destroyed in 1782 and again in 1867 and is now in its third incarnation. Inside the park presides the **Palais du Luxembourg,** commissioned by Marie de Medici and built from 1615 to 1627. After the death of her son, Henry IV, she tired of living in the Louvre, and had the Luxembourg palace built to remind her of the Pitti Palace in Florence, her birthplace. Architecturally, the palace is an interesting mix of French and Tuscan styles, and now houses the French Senate. Marie de Medici gave adjacent **Petit-Luxembourg** to Cardinal Richelieu in 1626; it now serves as the residence of the President of the Senate. The **Musée de Luxembourg,** next to the palace on rue Vaugirard, displays the works of the Dubufe family from 1840 to 1908, thus providing a manageable overview of art history. (Open daily 11am-6pm. Admission 15F, students 8F.)

Faubourg St-Germain and Tour Eiffel

The *septième arrondissement,* also part of the Left Bank, is more elegant and sedate than its neighbor, the Latin Quarter. Eighteenth-century French aristocrats lived in the **Faubourg St-Germain,** roughly between Invalides and rue des Sts-Pères. Embassies and ministries now occupy many of the elegant *hôtels,* but it remains an interesting area for a stroll. West of here looms the Tour Eiffel, and in between, the new Musée d'Orsay.

Perhaps the best-known landmark of the Faubourg St-Germain is the massive **Palais-Bourbon,** across the Seine from place de la Concorde, and its mirror image, **Eglise de la Madeleine,** seat of the French National Assembly. Commissioned by Napoleon in 1807, the palace is notable for the Delacroix paintings inside its library (tel. 40-63-60-00; open Sat. 10am-2pm). Close by, the **Musée National de la Légion d'Honneur et des Ordres de Chevalerie,** 2, rue de Bellechasse, 7*ème* (tel. 45-55-95-16; Mo. Solférino), sits in the handsome Hôtel de Salm. You might think the name more impressive than the collection, devoted to France's Legion of Honor and to foreign orders of chivalry, and teeming with medals, plaques, ribbons, and other decorations. (Open Tues.-Sun. 2-5pm. Admission 6F.)

Opened in December 1986, the **Musée d'Orsay,** 62, rue de Lille, 7*ème* (tel. 45-49-48-14; principal entrance at 1, rue de Bellechasse; RER Musée d'Orsay), is much more than a museum of impressionist painting. In addition to housing all the old favorites from the Jeu de Paume impressionist collection, the Orsay does nothing less than capture the artistic ideals of the second half of the nineteenth century in the Western hemisphere. The museum is in the old Gare d'Orsay, which, after its completion in 1840 as one of Paris's first rail stations, was as bold an expression of the modern era as the Eiffel Tower. The comprehensive collections from the 1848-1914 period include many international works and some unorthodox media such as film and photography. The museum lacks English documentation, and its historical exhibits are largely meaningless without a knowledge of French. Fortunately, the one-hour tours in English are good (Tues.-Sat. at 11:30am and 2:30pm; tours in French Tues.-Sat. at 11am and 1pm, Thurs. at 7pm). You must arrive for the tour 15 minutes in advance. (Open Tues.-Wed. and Fri.-Sat. 9:30am-6pm, Thurs. 9:30am-9:45pm, Sun. 9am-6pm. Last admission ¾ hr. before closing. Exhibits close ½ hr. before general closing. Admission 23F, ages under 25 and over 60 and Sun. 12F.) You may want to start your visit by ascending the staircase at the end of the first floor gallery opposite the entrance to get a knowledge of the layout and sculpture below. Architect Gae Aulenti designed this five-story, sunlit interior. The modern galleries each allow breathing space for a small collection of works while preserving the feeling of a turn-of-the-century train station. Critics maintain that the light is too dim for some paintings, too bright for others, or that the museum is simply too large for the collection, but some consider this one of the most beautiful museums in the world.

First floor exhibits cover sculpture from 1850 to 1870; paintings by Ingres and Delacroix through early Manet, Monet, Renoir, and Degas; architecture from 1850 to 1900; and temporary exhibits on photography up to 1870. Between Galleries B and D, the serene landscapes of the Barbizon school painters reflect the dominant trend of realism in painting before 1870. Here you'll find Jean-François Millet's famous *The Gleaners* and Gustave Courbet's *Burial at Ornans,* which shocked the art world in 1849-1850 with the mundaneness of its subject. Don't miss Charles Daumier's biting political caricatures *The Parliamentarians,* or his sympathetic *The Washerwoman,* eerily contemporary in its abstraction, and inspiration to both Degas and Toulouse-Lautrec. (In the 1st room, Gallery B.)

In 1863, the Academie des Beaux Arts Salon refused to exhibit many new painters, including Edouard Manet, whose *Déjeuner sur l'Herbe* shocked the academy both because of its subject—a contemporary orgy—and because of its flat, photographic quality. This and other jolting paintings such as *Olympia* and *Le Balcon* had a tremendous effect, as is evident throughout Gallery D. Look here for one of the Orsay's newest jewels: Monet's *The Magpie.* In the same gallery, you'll find American James McNeil Whistler's famous *Arrangement in Grey and Black: Portrait of the Artist's Mother.*

The shining strand of impressionist masterpieces that most visitors come to see stretches down the north side of the third floor (Gallery K). Monet turned his new techniques to the developing urban landscape, as in his series of the Gare St-Lazare, and Renoir to the human form, as in *Bal à la Moulin de la Galette.* Degas struggled to capture motion in his pictures, enlivening them with gestural surprises from the opéra (*Les Danseuses Bleues*) and the race track (*Cheveaux de Course Devant les Tribunes*). After 1880, Renoir returned to resolved lines and figures and painted works which became universally popular, such as *Danse à la Ville* and *Jeunes Filles au Piano.* Monet continued to experiment with paint and produced the magnificent series of the cathedral at Rouen and *Waterlilies.*

Vincent Van Gogh's brilliant, menacing pictures, such as *The Church at Auvers-sur-Oise;* his many self-portraits; and his interiors, such as *Van Gogh's Room at Arles* combined to inspire both the fauves and the expressionists of the next century. Paul Cézanne's renowned still-life *Apples and Oranges* is displayed here along with his *Bathers.* (All in Gallery K.) Henri Toulouse-Lautrec tried to capture moments and unfinished gestures, especially of theater people. (In the 2nd room after the corner, Gallery L.)

Self-taught Henri Rousseau painted in an evocative, primitive style like nothing seen before. Works such as *War* are in Gallery M, while later pieces such as *The*

Snake Charmer are in Gallery T. Before his voyage to Tahiti, Paul Gauguin worked in the Breton village of Pont Aven. Paintings from this period include *Beautiful Angel,* which betrays Gauguin's fascination with the primitive form. (In the 3rd room from the corner, Gallery M.) In the next room you'll find *Women of Tahiti* and *The White Horse,* typical of Gauguin's later works in Tahiti.

On the way down to the next floor are the Galleries of the Press and of Dates. These exhibits hold little interest for non-French speakers, but you'll probably spend more time than you intend in the Gallery of Dates. Once you find out that Monet painted *Femmes au jardin* in the same year that Karl Marx published the first volume of *Capital* (1867), you'll be hooked.

The movement for art nouveau in the late nineteenth century saw an outburst of creativity in all decorative arts. Look for examples of art nouveau in the jewelry of René Lalique and in the stained glass and furniture of the Nancy school. The flowing curves of art nouveau usually call to mind Hector Guimard, who in 1899 designed street-level entries for the Paris Métro, many of which still remain. Architect Koloman Moser's sketches for the decoration of the Viennese "Secession" group's famous cathedral in Steinhof, outside Vienna, are in Gallery X. With little European stimulus, American Frank Lloyd Wright developed increasingly abstract forms. You will find here a series of windows and examples of furniture from his early 1900s "prairie houses" (Gallery X).

The exhibits logically end with the early history of film-making. The new art form began with scientific research in photography, such as Edward Muybridge's well-known series on human and animal motion. The Orsay exhibits facsimiles of these along with a statue series of Degas to demonstrate the parallel developments in the two arts. Don't miss the continually showing film shorts of the Lumière brothers, particularly as the chairs offer a well-earned chance to sit down. If you wish to return to a particular exhibit after your tour, you may wish to buy a 10F pamphlet addressing a specific portion of the museum.

The top attraction of the Faubourg is no doubt the **Musée Auguste Rodin** at the Hôtel Biron, 77, rue de Varenne, 7ème (tel. 47-05-01-34; Mo. Varenne), off rue des Invalides. You'll know you've arrived when you see *The Thinker* in the subway. The works of France's greatest sculptor, who worked mostly in bronze and white marble, are displayed here in an elegant, eighteenth-century *hôtel.* The central foyer on the first floor houses some of Rodin's most famous: *The Kiss, The Hand of God,* and *The Cathedral.* Throughout the rose-filled gardens are such works as *The Thinker, The Gates of Hell,* and, in the middle of the basin, the *Ugolin Group.* The sculpture garden, frequented by nursemaids, small children, and young couples, welcomes picnickers as well. (Open July-Sept. Wed.-Mon. 10am-5:15pm; Oct.-June Wed.-Mon. 10am-4:30pm. Admission 16F, ages under 18 free, ages under 25 and over 60 and Sun. 8F.)

No building better exemplifies monumental architecture than the **Hôtel des Invalides,** 2, av. de Tourville, 7ème (tel. 45-55-92-30; Mo. St-François Xavier or La Tour-Maubourg). Constructed by Louis XIV as a shelter for war veterans, this red marble building holds Napoleon's remains in the crypt of one of its two chapels, in the innermost of six coffins. Napoleon's corpse was transferred here from Ste-Helena, his second island of exile, in 1840. Be sure to see his impressive tomb. War buffs will enjoy the **Musée de l'Armée,** located in one wing of the Invalides (tel. 45-55-92-30, ext. 33936). Napoleon fans will enjoy the memorabilia from his career. (Open daily April-Sept. 10am-6pm; Oct.-March 10am-5pm. Admission 23F, students 12F.) The same ticket admits you to the emperor's tomb in the church (open until 7pm). In the same area, near the Champs de Mars, is the **Ecole Militaire** (Mo. Ecole-Militaire), France's military academy, an interesting example of eighteenth-century, military-minded style. Across the street, on place de Fontenoy, 7ème is **UNESCO House** (tel. 45-68-10-00; Mo. Cambronne), one of Paris's most famous modern buildings (1958). Inside are works by Miró, Picasso, Calder, Giacometti, and others. (Open Mon.-Fri. 9am-6pm. Free.) You might enjoy the **Musée Seita,** 12, rue Surcouf, 7ème (tel. 45-56-61-50; Mo. Invalides), at rue de l'Université. The beautifully hung exhibit documents the history of tobacco, displaying Native American ceremonial pipes, Middle Eastern hookahs, and more. Temporary exhibits usually have nothing whatsoever to do with tobacco. (Open Mon.-Sat. 11am-6pm. Free.)

Upon completion of his impressive iron monument, Eiffel proudly declared in 1889 that "France will be the only country in the world with a 300m flagpole." Today, the **Tour Eiffel** (tel. 45. 50-34-56; Mo. Bir Hakeim) continues to symbolize Paris to much of the world. Yet Parisians hated the monstrosity, and it was almost torn down in 1909, until the French army discovered that it would make an excellent communications station. Only avant-garde artists and writers rallied around this symbol of modernity. Apollinaire, Seurat, and Pissarro loved it, and Vicente Huidobro, the Chilean poet, wrote a calligram on how to climb the tower. Critics still complain that the tower is not very attractive up close. Recently, renovations have removed excess weight and replaced rusty rivets. The top platform reopened in July, 1983, and now all three levels can be visited. (But you can climb the staircase only as far as the 2nd level.) On clear days the view from the third level will enchant you. Don't miss the free audio-visual documentary, *Cinemax*, about the tower's history. (Open daily 9:30am-midnight. Shows 9:30am-11pm. Admission: 1st level by foot 7F, by elevator 12F; 2nd level by foot 7F, by elevator 28F; 3rd level from 2nd level (if you've walked the 1st 2 flights) 7F, from ground 44F.)

Champ de Mars lies in the tower's shadow, and must forever serve as its doormat. A parade-ground in the eighteenth century, this park now features puppet shows (*guignols*) Wednesday, Saturday, and Sunday at 4:15pm.

To see what Paris is like where the sun never shines, visit **Les Egouts de Paris** (sewers of Paris), place de la Résistance, 7*ème* (tel. 43-20-14-40; Mo. Alma-Marceau). An interesting audio-visual presentation is followed by a tour conducted by an *égoutier* (sewer worker). Paris is proud of its 2100km of sewers: They can contain anything. Whole families used to live within them, and a small crocodile was discovered in the spring of 1984. Wear shoes with tread. (Open Mon., Wed., and the last Sat. of each month 2-5pm. Visits start when there are enough people, and last 1 hr. Admission 8F.)

Montparnasse

At the turn of the century, Montparnasse was the center of art and bohemian life; Picasso had his *atelier* at 242, bd. Raspail, and Hemingway frequented La Coupole and the swank Closerie des Lilas, of which Chagall and his group were also devoted fans. Now, however, it's metamorphasing into one of the most respectable business quarters in Paris. The 58-floor **Tour Montparnasse** (tel. 45-38-52-56; Mo. Montparansse-Bienvenue) broke the city's polished surface, but it's a sleek building nonetheless. Take advantage of its panoramic view from the 59th floor, the highest terrace in Paris. (Open daily in summer 9:30am-11:30pm; in off-season 10am-10pm. Admission 31F, students 23F.) Definitely more traditional is the **Cimetière Montparnasse**, bd. Edgar Quinet, 14*ème* (tel. 43-20-68-52; Mo. Edgar-Quinet or Raspail). It contains the graves of Baudelaire, Guy de Maupassant, Saint-Saëns, Saint-Beuve, Tristan Tzara, Henri Poincaré, Jean-Paul Sartre, Simone de Beauvoir, César Franck, and American singer Joelle Morgensen. (Open 9am-6pm. Free.)

The **Musée de la Poste**, 34, bd. Vaugirard, 15*ème* (tel. 43-20-15-30; Mo. Montparnasse-Bienvenue), leaves its stamp on exhibits of postal history, the modern post, and a complete collection of French *timbres* (stamps). Start on the fifth floor with the Middle Ages, and as you descend towards the present note the innovative, pre-automobile means of transport—balloons, for instance. (Open Mon.-Sat. 10am-4:45pm. Admission 10F, ages 18-25 5F.)

Parc Montsouris, farther south, 14*ème* (Mo. Cité-Universitaire), contributes an attractive, peaceful, hilly landscape to the neighborhood of the Cité Universitaire across the street. It encompasses rock falls, evergreens, a playground, and a nice pond.

Arènes de Lutèce and Jardin des Plantes

The spirit of the Latin Quarter spills eastward into this neighborhood, dominated by the Faculté des Sciences. Bookstores abound, and the restaurants around rue

Mouffetard and place de la Contrescarpe are some of the most rewarding in town (see Food). Located in a nearby park, the **Arènes de Lutèce**, an ancient Roman arena, still bears the original Roman appellation for Paris.

The **Jardin des Plantes**, 57, rue Cuvier, 5ème (tel. 43-36-19-09; Mo. Jussieu), contains a park, the National Natural History Museum, botanical gardens, and a small zoo. Here, post-impressionist Henri Rousseau found inspiration for his jungle fantasies. A lovely, shaded alleyway for strolling runs parallel to rue Bouffon. The remarkably varied flower beds are laid out in a grid—there's a rose labeled Hi-Fi, and a begonia accused of Hubris. Although parts of the park make for enjoyable meandering, you have to pay separately for each area. At the zoo don't miss the vivarium, which houses the axolotls, near-human creatures made famous by Julio Cortázar's short story, *Axolotl*. (Park open daily 7am-8pm. Museum open 11am-5:30pm. Zoo open daily in summer 9am-6pm; in off-season 9am-5pm. Admission for zoo and museum 25F, students 15F.) Outside the botanical gardens, on quai St-Bernard, lies the **Jardin Tino Rossi**, a park on the Seine named after a popular World War II singer. The park showcases modern sculpture and commands perfect sightlines to the barges on the Seine.

The **Mosquée**, 39, rue Geoffroy-St-Hilaire, 5ème (tel. 45-35-97-33; Mo. Monge), is Paris's Muslim mosque. The Alhambra in Granada, Spain, partially inspired this impressive Hispano-Moorish edifice, with carved wooden ceilings, mosaics, and hidden gardens. You can enjoy a *hamam* (Turkish bath) for 50F, but check the schedule since men and women go on different days. (Open Sat.-Thurs. 9am-noon and 2-6pm for guided tours. Admission 10F, students 6F.) A different kind of museum is the **Manufacture Nationale des Gobelins**, 42, av. des Gobelins, 13ème (tel. 43-37-12-60; Mo. Gobelins). The Gobelins tapestry factory, a state institution for over 300 years, still retains some of its seventeenth-century buildings. (Guided tours of the museum and factory Tues.-Thurs. at 2pm and 3pm; visits of the *ateliers* same days at 2:15pm, 3:15pm, and 5:30pm. Admission 22F, students 12F.)

At massive place Denfert-Rochereau, recognizable by Bertholdi's bronze lion sculpture, you can get under Paris's skin by way of the ancient **catacombes**, 2, place Denfert-Rochereau, 14ème (tel. 43-22-47-63; Mo. Denfert-Rochereau). At the close of World War II, it was revealed that the Resistance had set up headquarters with the old bones. Bring a flashlight. (Open Tues.-Fri. 2-4pm, Sat.-Sun. 9-11am and 2-4pm. Admission 15F, students 10F. Tours 20F.)

The Periphery

Montmartre

Some visitors expect all of Paris to be like Montmartre, so when they finally make it up this famed hill, they believe they have arrived at the City of Lights. To visit, walk north or take the Métro to Blanche or Abbesses. RATP shuttle buses from Pigalle or place des Abbesses run here, as does the funicular from rue St-Pierre. (Runs 10am-8pm every 5-10min.) The most visible areas of Montmartre are crowded and overpriced. Nonetheless, bona fide artists still starve in their garrets on the lovely, winding streets and steep staircases etched into the sides of the hills. **Place du Tertre**, just west of Sacré-Coeur, is a lovely marketplace full of cozy, open cafes, spontaneous musicians, and on-the-spot portrait artists. You may want to enjoy a leisurely drink only, as restaurants charge a bundle here. The **Musée de Montmartre**, 12, rue Cortot, 18ème (tel. 46-06-61-11; Mo. Lamarck-Caulaincourt), is located on a lovely side street behind Tertre in the old home of Rose of Rosimond, the actor who replaced Molière at the head of his troupe after the playwright's death. The museum idealizes to excess, but does have some fascinating early photographs of the heyday of the butte, as well as the original sign of the old (and now revived) folkclub **Au Lapin Agile**. (Open Tues.-Sat. 2:30-6pm and Sun. 11am-6pm. Admission 15F, students 8F.)

Even the area's history is unconventional. Montmartre, or *mont des martyres*, takes its name from the three saints beheaded here in 272 C.E.: Rusticus, Eleutherius, and St-Denis, Paris's first bishop. The latter promptly picked up his head, washed it off in a nearby fountain, and walked off. He ultimately expired 4 miles away, the legend tells us, on the spot where Basilique St-Denis stands today. The Paris Commune first assembled on the butte on January 28, 1871. The *communards* gathered 170 cannons on the hill to hold off both the Prussian invaders and the conservative French National Assembly that was trying to punish the rebellious city from its refuge in Versailles. The French army seized the cannons on March 18, but was unable to move them, as the *communards* captured and killed its generals, held elections, and on March 28 set up the Commune at the Hôtel de Ville, which lasted until May 23.

Basilique du Sacré-Coeur, 35, rue du Cheval de la Barre, 18ème (tel. 42-51-17-02; Mo. Château Rouge), the most visible landmark of the Montmartre area, is an impressive, exotic white church in Romanesque-Byzantine pastiche, seeming for all the world like the "stately pleasure dome" of Xanadu. Constructed after the Franco-Prussian War of 1870-71, Sacré-Coeur is complete with cupolas, a great dome, and a 112-m bell tower that commands a marvelous view of Paris far below. Many prefer the view to any in the city. (Church and dome open daily 9am-11:15pm. Church free. Dome 12F, students 8F. Crypt 20F, students 10F.) **Cimetière Montmartre,** 20, av. Rachel, 18ème (tel. 43-87-64-24; Mo. Place Clichy), rests on the north side of the butte. It is the final resting place of Dumas *fils,* Stendhal, Berlioz, Zola, Offenbach, and Nijinsky.

Throughout the past century, the picturesque bohemian lifestyle of **Pigalle** attracted inspired artists and writers such as Toulouse-Lautrec, Nerval, and Heine. When the artistic center moved to Montparnasse, however, the area's character changed radically. Today, the famous Red Light District along bd. Clichy is overrun with strange men who murmur "have good peep here" to random passersby. Women may prefer to avoid this area. Tourists cluster around the **Moulin Rouge** of Toulouse-Lautrec and *Can-Can* fame—you may have seen Renoir's film with José Ferrer.

For fans of nineteenth-century symbolist painting, the **Atelier of Gustave Moreau,** 14, rue de la Rochefoucauld, 9ème (tel. 48-74-38-50; Mo. Trinité), off rue Pigalle, has been turned into a museum. Pay a visit to the studio of the man who taught Matisse, Roualt, and many other fauvists. (Open Wed.-Mon. 10am-12:30pm and 2-5pm. Admission 15F, ages under 25 and over 60 and Sun. 8F.)

Northeastern and Eastern Paris

The sights in the 10ème, 19ème, and 20ème *arrondissements* are few and far between, hence the small influx of tourists. Some of these neighborhoods are inhabited by the *économiquement faibles*—a French euphemism translated as "financially weak" and equivalent to American "low-income groups." **Belleville,** in the 20ème, has become Paris's second Chinatown. If you keep a low profile and show caution, you should have no trouble, though rumors of mafia activity are frightening.

Not far from Montmartre, the **Musée de la Publicité,** 18, rue de Paradis, 10ème (tel. 42-46-13-09; Mo. Poissonnière), celebrates the art of the poster in a turn-of-the-century crockery shop. Exhibits have highlighted works by French masters of poster- and print-making, including Daumier, Toulouse-Lautrec, and Magritte. The tiled courtyard is also worth noting. (Open Wed.-Mon. noon-6pm. last admission 5:30pm. Admission 18F, students 10F.) Quite familiar to connoisseurs of Dubuffet's oil paintings is **Canal St-Martin,** which runs from place de Stalingrad, 10ème (Mo. Jaurès or Stalingrad), to place Frédéric-Lemaître, near place de la République (Mo. République), where it disappears underground, only to resurface near place de la Bastille. The area along the banks has been restored so that it makes a picturesque spot for a stroll or sunbathing. The canal continues on the north side of place de Stalingrad as the Bassin de la Villette in more industrial surroundings. Once crowded with barges, Paris's canals are now usually quiet, fished by hopeful anglers and sketched by art students. To get to this section, you can also take a boat from the Musée d'Orsay to the *écluses* (locks) on the canal (tel. 48-74-75-30). The 9:30am departure leaves from quai Anatole-France, the 2:30pm departure from 212, av.

Jean Jaurès (March-Oct.; 90F, ages 6-12 45F). Another option is to leave from Bas-sin de la Villette, 5bis, quai de la Loire, 19ème (Mo. Jaurès), at 9:15am or l'Arsenal, facing 50, bd. de la Bastille, 12ème (Mo. Bastille), at 2:30pm (tel. 46-07-13-13). (Tours last 3 hr. Tickets 70F, students 60F, ages under 12 45F.) The canal boat tours, though not as well known, may be more interesting than the *bâteaux mouches* on the Seine.

The **Parc des Buttes-Chaumont**, 19ème (Mo. Buttes-Chaumont or Botzaris), is the most picturesque of Paris's parks. Little gullies run down the hill, and high cliffs overlook the *lac*. The pont des Suicidés lends a sinister (or romantic) air to this site. Although out of the way, the park is ideal for a lakeside picnic far from the bustle of the city.

North of the Buttes-Chaumont, cross-sectioned by the canals St-Denis and de l'Ourcq, **Parc de la Villette** is a 150-acre green expanse under construction. Its **Grande Halle** (tel. 42-40-27-28) is a huge, converted nineteenth-century iron-and-glass slaughterhouse now used for concerts, art exhibits, and even boxing matches. (Open Wed.-Mon. 10am-5:50pm.) Behind the hall sits **La Géode** (tel. 42-45-66-00), an overgrown BB pellet that landed in a lake, where Disney-vintage, 3-D extrava-ganzas are screened on a 180-degree screen. (Admission 40F.) The **Zénith**, a 6,000-seat concert hall, hosts mainly rock groups. The newly opened **Cité des Sciences et de l'Industrie**, 30, av. Corentin-Cariou, 19ème (tel. 40-05-70-00 or 40-05-72-72; Mo. Porte de la Villette), is at least four times larger than the Beaubourg, and clearly the best science museum in the country. Because of the size, walking around inside can be exhausting. Innovative "hands-on" exhibitions, excellent audio-visual pre-sentations, and technological history are all included. You can sit in a space chair while your children take a tour of their senses. (Open Tues. and Thurs.-Fri. 10am-6pm, Wed. noon-9pm, Sat.-Sun. and holidays noon-8pm. Admission to whole "city" 30F, ages under 25 and over 60 23F, Sun. free. **Planetarium** 15F extra.)

Cimetière Père-Lachaise, 20ème (tel. 43-70-70-33; Mo. Père-Lachaise), is the grandfather of Paris's cemeteries and one of the city's most moving memorials to its rich past, with tree-lined promenades and lonely paths running between the graves. Many spots in the cemetery feel miles from civilization. On the tombstones are such names as Molière, Comte, Piaf, Colette, Balzac, Bizet, Apollinaire, and Proust. Some foreigners are buried here, too—Chopin, Oscar Wilde (with a Jacob Epstein memorial), Gertrude Stein, and Alice B. Toklas. The last members of the 1871 Paris Commune were killed in the northeast corner of Père Lachaise, against the **Mur des Fédérés**, and are buried beneath it. There is a view of the city from the terrace in front of the chapel there. The last scene of *Jules and Jim* was also filmed on that hill. The evidence of decay, particularly the smell, can be somewhat overwhelming. The guards distribute useful maps marked with the famous graves ("donation" 1-2F). (Open April-Oct. 7:30am-6pm; Nov.-March 8am-5pm.)

Less famous and less classy than the Bois de Boulogne, the **Bois de Vincennes**, 12ème (Mo. Porte Dorée or Château-de-Vincennes), is more interesting in many ways. The zoo and amusement park are bigger and better, and there is also the **Châ-teau de Vincennes**, a medieval fortress that long served as a prison. It's closed for renovation, but you can visit the dungeon. (Open daily 10am-6pm. Admission 5F.) The **Vincennes Zoo** (tel. 43-43-84-95; Mo. Porte Dorée) is considered the best in France; uncaged animals wander in relatively natural surroundings. In the center, wild goats make their homes on a 72-m high artificial rock. (Open daily 9am-5pm. Admission 30F, ages under 25 and over 60 15F.) To reach the horticultural displays of the **Jardins Floraux**, in blossom year-round, walk from the château down rue de la Pyramide. (Open daily 9:30am-8pm. Admission 7.50F.) Finally, **Lac Daumes-nil** spreads limpidly, a graceful, peaceful body of water.

Banlieue (Suburbs)

The **Cimitière au Chien et Chat** (Dog and Cat Cemetery), 4, Pont de Clichy, As-nières (tel. 47-93-87-04; Mo. Asnières), is about 30 minutes northwest from the cen-ter of Paris. Dating from the 1890s, this cemetery is the resting place of many a faithful pet. Tiny tombstones mark the passing of Zouzou, Phiphi, Zazie, Poupette, Loulette, Minou, and even, oddly enough, Iowa. A few birds are interred as well. On its own island in a lonely stretch of Seine, the cemetery has a kind of lugubrious beauty. (Open Mon.-Sat. 9-11:45am and 2-5:45pm, Sun. and holidays 2-5:45pm. Admission 15F.)

The town of **St-Germain-en-Laye** commands a stretch of the Seine 14km west of Paris, and was the birthplace of Claude Debussy, its château the birthplace of Louis XIV. The château is now given over to the essential **Musée des Antiquités Nationales** (tel. 34-51-53-65; RER St-Germain-en-Laye), which gathers prehistoric, Gallo-Roman, and Merovingian artifacts. There is also an apothecary with seventeenth- and eighteenth-century medicine jars from the Royal General Hospital. (Open Wed.-Mon. 9:45am-noon and 1:30-5:15pm. Admission 15F, students and Sun. 8F.) The town affords a remarkable rooftop view of Paris. Also in St-Germain-en-Laye is the **Musée Départemental du Prieuré**, 2bis, rue Maurice-Denis (tel. 39-73-77-87; RER: St-Germain-en-Laye), the former home of symbolist painter Maurice Denis and now a museum displaying his work and that of the Nabis. The building is a lovely seventeenth-century structure set in a large park. (Open Wed.-Fri. 10am-5:30pm, Sat.-Sun. 10am-6:30pm. Admission 20F, ages under 25 and over 60 10F.)

Napoleon and Josephine lived in lovely **Château de Malmaison,** 1, av. du Château, Rueil-Malmaison (tel. 47-49-20-07; RER: La Défense, bus 158A: Château or Malmaison), west of Paris. Although Napoleon divorced his first wife, a native of Martinique, he never evicted her. All visits are guided and leave on demand. (Open Wed.-Mon. 10am-12:30pm and 1:30-5:30pm. Last tours at noon and 5pm. Admission 20F, students and Sun. 10F.)

St-Cloud (tel. 46-02-24-20; bus #72 from Hôtel de Ville or #52 from Madeleine; Mo. Boulogne-Pont de St-Cloud; RER: Gare de St-Cloud), 3km southwest of Paris proper, was the scene of the assassination of Henri III in 1589 and the coup d'état of 18 Brumaire in 1799, among other notable occurrences. Nothing remains of the castle but the magnificent park, designed by Le Nôtre, which preserves lakes and 30-m fountains, statues, arbors, and an English garden. (Park open May-Aug. 7am-10pm; March-April and Sept. 7am-9pm; Oct.-Feb. 7am-8pm. Museum open Wed., Sat., and Sun. 2-5:30pm, with a short movie on its history. Free.)

St-Denis, 10km north of Paris (Mo. St-Denis-Basilique), is marked by **Basilique St-Denis,** containing the tombs of the kings of France (their bodies were tossed in unmarked graves during the Revolution). Suger, minister of Louis VII, built the twelfth-century Gothic church, which inspired the architects of Chartres and Senlis. Twelfth- to eighteenth-century French funerary sculpture imitated contemporary fashions, yielding a fascinating historical perspective. The underground archeological site reveals remnants of the sixth-century Franks. (Open Mon.-Sat. 10am-6:30pm, Sun. noon-6:30pm. Tombs open 10am-5pm. Admission 22F, students and Sun. 12F. Sunday organ concerts in summer 11:15am-noon.)

The peaceful suburb of **Sceaux** (Luxembourg RER: Sceaux, 10 min.), 10km south of Paris, is the site of the estate of Colbert (Louis XIV's finance minister), and includes the Château Perrault, built for him in the mid-1600s. Part of the château was destroyed in 1798, but the park remains in all of its splendor, with a waterfall and public promenades adorned with statuary. The more recent **Château de Sceaux** houses the **Musée de l'Ile de France** (tel. 46-61-06-71), dedicated to the history of the region encircling Paris—both its *haute culture* and its *traditions folkloriques.* (Open in summer Mon. and Fri. 2-6pm, Wed.-Thurs. 10am-noon and 2-6pm, Sat.-Sun. 10am-noon and 2-7pm; in off-season until 5pm. Park open 6:45am-9:30pm. Admission 8F, Sun. 4F.)

Charenton, at the southeastern corner of Paris, holds a unique treasure: the **Musée du Pain** (Bread Museum), 25bis, rue Victor Hugo (tel. 43-68-43-60; Mo. Charenton-Ecoles), where breads of all sorts are displayed. Considering the importance of bread in France, historians and bakers, not to mention dilettante lovers of that staple, will enjoy this excursion. (Open Sept.-June Tues. and Thurs. 2-5pm or by appointment.)

Mirapolis (tel. 34-43-20-00) is not really a suburb. Rather, it aspires to be a world in itself, composed of "lovely things to eat," "adventure land," "the scariest time of your life," and "the realm of make believe." Sounds great, but it's a disappointment if you're expecting Disney World. Nonetheless, amusement park buffs will enjoy the French version. To get there, take the train from Gare St-Lazare (*direction* "Cergy-Pontoise") to Cergy St-Christophe (20F), from where a bus will chauffeur you to the park. (Tickets Mon.-Sat. 75F, after 2pm 50F, Sun. 90F. Open May 12-Oct. 16 Sun.-Fri. 10am-7pm, Sat. 10am-9pm.

Entertainment

Paris after dark—you've heard a lot about it: The sun has gone down and now you're waiting for things to happen. Well, the city does have a lot to offer, but don't expect the offerings to swirl around you because a great deal of Paris is quiet and residential, and you may have to search for what you want. All-night crowds linger around Pigalle, St-Lazare, the Bastille, St-Germain-des-Prés, and Beaubourg, but omnipresent prostitution embellished by pimps and drug dealers will not stop at the lone tourist who happens to land in the wrong hands. Hide out in a club or bar from midnight to 6am (2am on weekdays), and you'll become absorbed in a private culture determined by the particular clientele and the night's spirit. After a long day's work, Parisians are able to ignore growing circles under their eyes, unbreathable smoky air, and mounting heat to boogie, clap, or stomp until dawn.

Unfortunately, most of Paris's after-dark attractions are expensive. Ticket prices for operas, concerts, and plays are almost as elevated as those in New York, and the *revues* for which Paris is famous cost a dazzling 350F. Still, there are ways of entertaining yourself without emptying your pockets. The area around Beaubourg (the Pompidou Center) fills with people who have come to observe fire-eaters, sword-swallowers, and to hear old men with guitars strumming the songs of Jacques Brel or Georges Brassens. Around place St-Germain, you can watch throngs of people parade past, garbed in a panoply of the latest fashions, and there are bars where the price of a drink permits you to listen to a jazz group for as long as you like. If you want to see a movie or just observe the more fashionable cafes, wander around Montparnasse and the touristy Champs-Elysées. For complete listings of evening activities, see Publications about Paris.

The student organization **COPAR**, whose ticket agency (Service des Activités Culturelles) is at 39, av. Georges Bernanos, 5*ème* (tel. 43-29-12-43; Mo. Port-Royal), sells discounted tickets and publishes a monthly list of plays for which these tickets may be obtained. The agency also sells reduced-priced concert tickets, even in summer. They will accept any student ID. (Open Sept.-July Mon.-Tues. and Thurs.-Fri. 9am-4:30pm, Wed. 9am-noon and 1-4:30pm.) Another useful service is that of **Alpha FNAC: Spectacles** at 136, rue de Rennes, 6*ème* (tel. 45-44-39-12; Mo. Montparnasse-Bienvenue); 26, av. de Wagram, 8*ème* (tel. 47-66-52-50; Mo. Charles de Gaulle-Etoile); and Forum des Halles, 1-7, rue Pierre Lescot, 1*er* (tel. 42-61-81-18; Mo. Châtelet-Les Halles). They sell tickets for theater and all sorts of concerts and festivals. Their Carte Alpha (50F for 1 year) or Carte FNAC (100F for 3 yrs., students 50F) entitles you to discounts of up to 40% on all classical music and theater tickets. (Open Tues.-Sat. 10am-7pm.)

A word about safety: Remember that while on the Left Bank the large crowds ensure relatively safety, elsewhere the city should be approached with care. For example, stay away from the quais and the Bois de Boulogne late at night.

Cinema

As well as screening the latest European and American big-budget features, Paris's cinemas show classics from all countries, avant-garde and political films, and little-known or forgotten works. Ever since the New Wave crested, French interest in American movies has been nothing short of phenomenal; in fact, many

American films play here that have not been shown in U.S. cinemas for years. First-run, big-studio films are screened in the large, sumptuous, expensive theaters on the Champs-Elysées, while more artsy offerings play in the little theaters on the side streets of the Left Bank.

The three entertainment weeklies give showtimes and theatres. Films are listed by several schemes: alphabetically under "new films," "first-run," and "others"; by genre; and by cinemas in each *arrondissement.* Film festivals are listed separately. The notation "V.O." (for *version originale*) after a non-French movie listing means that the film is being shown in its original language with French subtitles; "V.F." (for *version française*) means that it is dubbed. Occasionally during the peak tourist season, French movies will be shown with English subtitles. Almost all cinemas grant students a 10F discount off their regular 30-45F admission, but only on weekdays and sometimes only before 5pm. In many cinemas, prices are several francs lower on Mondays. In almost all Parisian theaters, you will be greeted by an usher who tears your ticket, escorts you to your seat, and expects a tip of 1F. Ushers who don't get tipped are liable to be nasty, and may even ruin the movie for you by telling you the ending.

Cinémathèque Française: At the Musée de Cinéma in the **Palais de Chaillot,** on av. Albert de Mun at av. Président Wilson, 16*ème* (tel. 47-04-24-24; Mo. Trocadéro). No screenings Mon. Answering machine lists all shows. A must for serious film buffs. This government-supported theater shows 3-5 films per day, many of them classics, near-classics, or soon-to-be classics. Foreign films almost always shown with French subtitles. Expect long lines. Admission 18F, members 9F.

Olympic, 7-9, rue Francis-de-Pressensé, 14*ème* (tel. 45-43-99-41; Mo. Pernety). Organizes festivals which run for about a week (the Marx Brothers and Richard Gere are 2 favorites). Two branches: the **Olympic Luxembourg,** 67, rue Monsieur-le-Prince, 6*ème* (tel. 46-33-97-77; Mo. Odéon), with three cinemas; and **Le St-Germain-des-Prés,** place St-Germain-des-Prés, 6*ème* (tel. 42-22-87-23; Mo. St-Germain-des-Prés), with one big, beautiful cinema. Both consistently screen high-quality independent, classic, and foreign films.

Action Ecoles, 23, rue des Ecoles, 5*ème* (tel. 43-25-72-07; Mo. Maubert); **Action Rive Gauche,** 5, rue des Ecoles, 5*ème* (tel. 43-29-44-40; Mo. Maubert), both on a large street parallel to bd. St-Germain, and **Action Christine,** 4, rue Christine, 6*ème* (tel. 43-29-11-30; Mo. Odéon), off rue Dauphine. Excellent festivals, from Marilyn Monroe to Marx Brothers.

George V, 144-146, av. des Champs-Elysées, 8*ème* (tel. 45-62-41-46; Mo. George V), and **Forum Horizon,** at the Nouveau Forum des Halles (Mo. Les Halles). Both have recently been endowed with ultra modern THX sound system.

Rotonde Montparnasse, 103, bd. du Montparnasse, 6*ème* (tel. 45-74-94-94; Mo. Vavin). Current imports and new French releases.

Theater

Theater in Paris is not just Molière, Corneille, and Racine. The classics are there if you want them, and so are the moderns, but there are also Broadway-type comedies and musicals, experimental plays, and political satires. Occasionally, you'll even see *commedia dell'arte* performed in the courtyard of the Bibliothèque Nationale, harlequin costumes glittering in the twilight. Aside from the intimate *café-théâtres* and *cafés chansonniers,* and the Las Vegas-style *revues,* theater in Paris exists in three main forms: the state theaters, such as the Comédie Française; the independent theaters, which concentrate more on newer works; and the surburban theaters, which have taken hold of Paris's avant-garde scene. In 1986-87, René González' **Maison de la Culture 39** in Bobigny rocked the town with wild productions of *Alcestis* (in English) and *King Lear.* The **Théâtre Gérard-Philippe** in St-Denis (tel. 42-43-00-59), along with the **Théâtre de Boulogne-Billancourt** in Boulogne-Billancourt (tel. 46-03-60-44), have also made news. The most acclaimed of these theaters is the **Théâtre des Amandiers de Nanterre** in Nanterre (tel. 47-21-18-81), whose renowned director Patrice Chereau brought American avant-gardist Robert Wilson back to Paris in the fall of 1987 for collaboration on an event called *Hamlet Machine.* In 1988, even *A Chorus Line* became international here. Children are not excluded from the Parisian theater world, and the famous *guignol* (giant puppet show) may offer the most comprehensible text for the Anglophone.

Theater tickets typically cost 150-200F, though there are also a few 17-60F tickets. Some theaters sell rush tickets to students at half-price; check half an hour before the performance. Most theaters close at least for the month of August, if not longer. For complete listings of current shows, see suggestions in Publications about Paris.

State Theaters

Comédie Française, 2, rue de Richelieu, 1er (tel. 40-15-00-15; Mo. Palais Royal). Founded by Molière, it stages the classics and some newer works. The actors here are famous for their superbly-articulated French, which helps comprehension. If you can't understand, the beautiful ceiling and chandeliers are adequately entertaining. Tickets go on sale daily 11am-6pm (40-150F). Rush seats 30 min. before curtain 17F. Open Sept. 15-July. Disabled access.

Théâtre de l'Odéon, place de l'Odéon, 6ème (tel. 43-25-70-32; Mo. Odéon), northeast of the Palais de Luxembourg. Productions of equally high caliber. Seats 30-150F. Rush tickets 40 min. before curtain 40F. The **Petit Odéon** in the same building produces new and experimental works. Tickets 45F, 30 min. before curtain 31F. Arrive at 6pm. Both theaters open Sept.-July.

Théâtre National de Chaillot, in the Palais de Chaillot, place du Trocadéro, 16ème (tel. 47-27-81-15; Mo. Trocadéro). New and avant-garde productions. Watch for its logo, since it sometimes performs in other theaters. Tickets 90F, 30 min. before curtain 55F. Open Oct.-July.

Lucernaire Forum Centre National d'Art et d'Essai, 53, rue Notre-Dame-des-Champs, 6ème (tel. 45-44-57-34; Mo. Notre-Dame-des-Champs). Part of an arts complex with a cinema, *dîner-spectacles,* restaurant, and children's theater. The theater presents only new productions in the *théâtre rouge* (red) or *noir* (black). Tickets 110F, students and often on Mon. 66F.

Independent Theaters

Théâtre de la Huchette, 23, rue de la Huchette, 5ème (tel. 43-26-38-99; Mo. St-Michel). Tickets are still hot for Eugene Ionesco's *La Cantatrice Chauve,* (*The Bald Soprano*) and *La Leçon* (*The Lesson*), which have been playing nonstop for 30 yrs. Tickets for both (short) shows 120F, with student ID 80F except Sat.; for 1 show 80F, with student ID 60F except Sat. Tickets on sale Mon.-Sat. 5:30-10pm. *La Cantatrice Chauve* at 7:30pm. *La Leçon* at 8:30pm. No shows Sun.

Théâtre Tourtour, 20, rue Quincampoix, 4ème (tel. 48-87-82-48; Mo. Châtelet). Watch for interesting new shows here and the annual song festivals in mid-June. Tickets 70-80F, students 60F, children 25F. Open Tues.-Sat. 2-8pm.

Jardin Shakespeare du Pré Catelan, at the end of the Bois de Boulogne (tel. 42-40-05-32). Take bus #244 from Porte Maillot. In summer, Shakespeare is performed here in English. Tickets can be purchased at the door or at FNAC: 80F, students 40F. Shows start at 8:45pm. Buses won't be running after the show.

Galerie 55—The English Theater of Paris, 55, rue de Seine, 6ème (tel. 43-26-63-51; Mo. Odéon). This 85-seat theater mounts contemporary productions in English. Tickets for chairs 100F, for stools 70F (students 60F). Box office and telephone reservations 1 week in advance 11am-7pm. Closed last half of Aug.

Experimental Theater Wing Studio, 14, rue Letelier, 15ème (Mo. Emile-Zola). 2-year-old extension of New York University's theater program. Productions in English.

Café-Théâtres

Continuing the European cabaret tradition, *café-théâtres* deliver caustic, often political, satire through skits and short plays; puns and double-entendres abound, so unless you are up on French *argot* (slang) and politics, you might miss a lot of the fun. Despite their name, in *café-théâtres* you do not necessarily sit at tables to be served as you watch the performance.

Au Bec Fin, 6, rue Thérèse, 1er (tel. 42-96-29-35; Mo. Palais Royal). Tiny (60 seats), usually with 2 different shows per night. Tickets 60F, students (except Sat.) 50F. 2 shows 115F. Dinner and 1 show 200F. Dinner and 2 shows 250F. Public auditions are sometimes held here (20F). Open daily.

Blancs Manteaux, 15, rue des Blancs-Manteaux, 4ème (tel. 48-87-15-84; Mo. Hôtel-de-Ville or Rambuteau). 3 different shows per night. Tickets 50F, ages 25 and under (except Fri.-Mon.) 40F. 2 shows and Fri., Sat., and holidays 100F. Mon. all tickets 35F. Reservations after 5pm. Open Mon.-Sat.

Le Café d'Edgar, 58, bd. Edgar-Quinet, 14ème (tel. 43-20-85-11; Mo. Edgar-Quinet or Montparnasse). Another small theater (80 seats). 3 different shows per night. Tickets 65F, students (except Sat.) 50F. 2 shows 100F, except Fri., Sat., Mon., and Tues., all tickets 50F. Reserve by phone 2:30-7:30pm. Open Mon.-Sat.

Le Point Virgule, 7, rue Sainte-Croix-de-la-Bretonnerie, 4ème (tel. 42-78-67-03; Mo. Hôtel-de-Ville). Often features gay subject matter. Tickets 60F, students (except Fri.-Sat. and holidays) 50F. Disabled access.

Théâtre de l'Arlequin, 13, passage du Moulinet, 13ème, (tel. 45-89-43-22; Mo. Tolbiac). Experimental and classic works and much laughter. Tickets 60F and 40F. Shows Tues.-Sat. at 8:30pm.

Chansonniers

Chansonniers are the musical cousin of the *cafe-théâtre*. French folk songs are performed, and the audience is invited to join in. Again, the better your French, the better you'll follow the proceedings. Admission usually includes one drink. You'll discover the old-style Paris that seems all but extinct.

Au Lapin Agile, 22, rue des Saules, 18ème (tel. 46-06-85-87; Mo. Lamarck-Coulaincourt). Picasso and his friends, among others, used to hang out here when Montmartre was Montmartre. Now you should get here before 7pm for a good seat, since it is usually crowded with tourists. Entry and 1st drink 90F, students 70F. Subsequent drinks 25F. Shows at 9pm. Open Tues.-Sun. until 2am.

Caveau de la République, 1, bd. St-Martin, 3ème (tel. 42-78-44-45; Mo. République). Also popular, but a more Parisian crowd fills the 100 seats. Tickets are sold 6 days in advance from 11am (100F). Shows daily at 9pm.

Guignols

This renowned Paris tradition of puppet shows entertains adults as much as children.

Guignol du Parc de Choisy, across from 149, av. de Choisy, 13ème (tel. 43-66-72-39; Mo. Tolbiac or Place d'Italie). Wed. and Sat.-Sun. at 3:30pm 7F.

Guignol du Square St-Lambert, square St-Lambert, 15ème (Mo. Commerce). Wed. and Sat.-Sun. at 3:30pm, Thurs.-Fri. and Mon.-Tues. at 5pm 5F. Consult weekly publications for more information.

Revues

Those bouncy, brassy cabarets for which Paris is famous are too expensive to think about. In any case, their attractions are dubious, with topless women and spectacles reminiscent of dancing routines in 1950s comedy shows.

Les Folies Bergère, 32, rue Richer, 9ème (tel. 42-46-77-11; Mo. Cadet or rue Montmartre). Tickets for a table and dinner go up to 341F, but you can stand at the bar (1st drink included) for 82F. Reserve by phone 11am-6:30pm. Show at 9pm.

Le Moulin Rouge, place Blanche, 9ème (tel. 46-06-00-19; Mo. Blanche). Once the haunt of Toulouse-Lautrec, now caters to busloads of instamatic-toting tourists. Dinner and show 510F. Champagne and show 350F.

Classical Music, Opera, and Dance

Classical music concerts in Paris can be extremely expensive, but you take advantage of the occasional free concert. In addition, box offices often sell a number of reduced (sometimes partial vision) seats if you inquire early enough. Sometimes rush tickets go on sale the morning of the concert for a fraction of the regular price.

Free concerts are often given in churches and parks, especially in summer, when festivals scatter music throughout the city. Concerts by well-known organists are given every Sunday at 5:45pm at **Notre-Dame,** as the setting sun illuminates the great rose window. The **American Church,** 65, quai d'Orsay, 7ème (Mo. Invalides or Alma-Marceau), sponsors free concerts (Sept.-July Sun. at 6pm). The **Eglise St-Merri** is also known for its free concerts; contact Accueil Musical St-Merri, 78, rue St-Martin, 3ème (Mo. Châtelet or Hôtel-de-Ville). Weather permitting, Sunday concerts are sometimes held in the kiosk (bandshell) in the **Jardin Luxembourg** (tel. 42-37-20-00, ext. 2023). For more information about free outdoor concerts, call 46-51-71-20. Infrequent concerts in the Musée d'Orsay are free with museum ticket.

Other churches, such as **Eglise St-Germain-des-Prés,** 3, place St-Germain-des-Prés, 6ème (Mo. St-Germain-des-Prés); **Eglise St-Eustache,** rue du Jour, 1er (Mo. Les Halles); and **Eglise St-Louis-en-l'Ile,** 19, rue St-Louis-en-l'Ile, 4ème (Mo. Pont-Marie), stage concerts that are either free or reasonably priced. For information about all church concerts, call 43-29-68-68. **Ste-Chapelle** hosts concerts a few times per week in summer (sometimes free on Sun.). Contact the box office at 4, bd. du Palais, 1er (tel. 43-54-30-94; Mo. Cité; open daily 10am-6pm; student tickets 60F). Check posters, any of the three Alpha FNAC offices (see Entertainment Introduction), and the entertainment weeklies for concert notices.

The Paris **Opéra,** place de l'Opéra, 9ème (tel. 47-42-57-50; Mo. Opéra), has reclaimed its position as a cultural leader over the past couple of years. In the 1986-87 season, the company broke ground performing Handel's hitherto forgotten *Julius Caesar.* And new director Rudolf Nureyev won acclaim for the ballet's innovative production of *Raymonda* and *Cinderella.* (Tickets 30-400F; on sale 11am-6:30pm at the Opéra, up to 2 weeks in advance. Discounts available for some productions.) Although you may not be able to see from the cheapest seats, the acoustics are fine, and you will be a lot closer to the enchanting Chagall ceiling.

Jazz

Some critics claim that Paris is no longer the jazz center it once was. True, the big names find it more profitable to play the huge summer festivals in the south of France and in Switzerland, and the small club scene has moved partly north to Copenhagen and Oslo. But Paris still nourishes dozens of interesting clubs. Not only do many fine, lesser-known American musicians play here, but the variety of music—including African, Antillean, and Brazilian—is fantastic. For the most complete listings, pick up a copy of the monthly *Jazz Magazine* or one of the three weeklies. At the following places, the cover charge includes the first drink, unless otherwise noted.

New Morning, 7-9, rue des Petites-Ecuries, 10ème (tel. 45-23-51-41; Mo. Château d'Eau). Probably Paris's premier jazz club. Stars like Taj Mahal play here, and you may even hear gospel. Prices vary with shows—not cheap. Open Sept.-July Tues.-Sat. from 9:30pm.

Caveau de la Huchette, 5, rue de la Huchette, 5ème (tel. 43-26-65-05; Mo. St-Michel). The one time Tribunal, prison, and execution rooms here were used by Danton, Marat, St-Juste, and Robespierre during the Revolution. It's sad that a place where the jazz greats came to play for 30 years is now overrun with middle-aged tourists looking for a bit of old Paris. Still, the music is generally good. Maxim Saury often whistles (and more) dixie. Cover Sun.-Thurs. 45F, students 40F; Fri.-Sat. 55F. Drinks from 18F. Open Sun.-Thurs. 9:30pm-2:30am, Fri. until 3am, Sat. until 4am. Must be at least 18.

Le Petit Journal, 71, bd. St-Michel, 5ème (tel. 43-26-28-59; Mo. Luxembourg). A *sympa* place—small jazz cafe with very French decor. Past performers include the Claude Bolling trio and Bill Coleman. 1st drink (required) 75F, 40F thereafter. Open Sept.-July Mon.-Sat. 10pm-2:30am.

Slow Club, 130, rue de Rivoli, 1er (tel. 42-33-84-30; Mo. Châtelet). Miles Davis's favorite Paris jazz club. Big bands, traditional jazz, and dixieland in a setting that hasn't changed in years. Cover 50F, weekends 62F. Women and students pay 5F less during the week. Drinks from 18F. Open Tues.-Thurs. 9:30pm-2:30am, Fri. until 3:30am, Sat. until 4am.

Le Petit Opportune, 15, rue des Lavandières-St-Opportune, 1er (tel. 42-36-01-36; Mo. Châte-let). Small, cozy, and well located. If very crowded, you can watch a video of the live band in the back for the same price. Jazz concerts nightly 11pm-2am. 1st drink 100F, 50F thereaf-ter. Upstairs, a more sedate crowd listens to jazz recordings for 25-50F per drink. Open daily 9pm-4am.

Chapelle des Lombards, 19, rue de Lappe, 11ème (tel. 43-57-24-24; Mo. Bastille), on the street it's in to be on. Jazz, African, and salsa in a *cave*. A bit snobby. Cover 68F, weekends 80F. Open Tues.-Sat. 10:30pm-dawn.

Le Furstemberg, 27, rue de Buci, 6ème (tel. 43-54-79-51; Mo. St-Germain-des-Prés). Large international bourgeois audience on weekends. Open weekends 6pm-3am with New Orleans jazz until 2:30am. A/C with comfortable leather booths. Live trio, but people come mostly to hear the pianist. Cover 75F, drinks 40-65F.

La Pinte, 13, carrefour de l'Odéon, 6ème (tel. 43-26-26-15; Mo. Odéon). Jean Claude, the friendly owner, manages a jolly local crowd upstairs while jazz groups play in the smoky cellar. Beer is the house specialty. Cover 75F, subsequent drinks 55F. Open Mon.-Thurs. 10pm-2:30am, Fri.-Sat. 10pm-4am.

Bird Land Club, 20, rue Princesse, 6ème (tel. 43-26-97-59; Mo. Mabillon or St-Germain). Small, friendly bar with cheap drinks and uncomfortable seats. Excellent jazz record collec-tion but no live music. No cover. Drinks from 25F. Open Sept.-July daily 7pm-7am. Will be renovated by summer 1989.

Also popular in France are clubs specializing in Brazilian samba.

Chez Felix, 23, rue Mouffetard, 5ème (tel. 47-07-68-78; Mo. Monge). On the top level, you can eat, and in the *caves* you can sway to the excellent Brazilian beat. Tues.-Thurs. 1st drink (required) 70F, 50F thereafter; Fri.-Sat. 1st 2 drinks 90F each, 50F thereafter. Bottle of wine 250F. Open Sept.-July Tues.-Sat. 8pm-5am. Music 11pm-dawn.

La Plantation, 45, rue Montpensier, 1er (tel. 42-97-46-17; Mo. Palais-Royal). Mostly African, Antillean, and salsa music. This friendly place has lots to offer: special Wed. evenings with special themes from funk and soul to reggae. Free Sun. bingo and a serious dancing crowd. M. Yaffa, the owner, is dedicated to improving race relations. Cover and 1st drink 75F, 2nd drink 40F. Open Tues.-Sat. 10:30pm-dawn, Sun. 4-10:30pm.

L'Escale, 15, rue Monsieur-le-Prince, 6ème (tel. 43-54-63-47; Mo. Odéon). Live Latin Ameri-can music—upstairs in spirited sing along, downstairs dance band. No cover. Drinks 60F. Open daily 11pm-dawn.

Jazz O Brazil, 38, rue Mouffetard, 5ème (tel. 45-87-36-09; Mo. Monge). Josette Hann wel-comes you with noisemakers to this lively place. Excellent samba guitarists and new groups. Try *caitirissa,* a lime juice and vodka, the house drink. No cover. Drinks 40F. Open daily 9:30pm-2am.

Discos and Rock Clubs

The discos that are "in" (or even in business) change drastically from year to year, though a few have been popular since the '60s, and the pace of change is slower than that in New York. Many Parisian clubs are officially private, which means they have the right to pick and choose their clientele. The handle-less front doors of the clubs are fitted with one-way peep holes through which the management can judge prospective customers. Many of the smaller places in the Latin Quarter admit almost anyone who is sufficiently decked out. Parisians tend to dress up more than Americans for a night on the town, but leather never goes out of style. To gain entry into one of the more exclusive places you must be accompanied by a regular. Many clubs reserve the dubious right to refuse entry to unaccompanied men. Women often get a discount or get in free. Private clubs are expensive—admission and a drink can cost more than 75F. Some of the following clubs take pride in the fact that they play no disco music; the French dance any way they please and often alone. Weekdays are cheaper and less crowded so you'll have a better chance of moving then, but most of the action (by force of inevitable body contact) happens on week-ends.

Les Bains, 7, rue de Bourg l'Abée, 3ème (tel. 48-87-01-80; Mo. Les Halles or Réaumur-Sébastopol). Popular, but hard to get in. Worth it though—Prince played a free concert here.

If the swimming pool is open, the sweaty may rip off their clothes to jump in. A turn-of-the-century facade conceals what used to be municipal baths. This is where Proust used to shower. You may see famous models and artists here. Mixed gay/straight crowd. 1st drink 120F, 2nd drink 100F. Open Tues.-Sun. midnight-5am.

Le Palace, 8, Faubourg Montmartre, 9ème (tel. 42-46-10-87; Mo. Montmartre). The funkiest disco in Paris; 2000 people a night on multi-level dance floors, moving to the beat of an awesome sound system. American cocktails. Dancing teas and rollerskating afternoons. Sometimes rock concerts are held here. Expensive restaurant. Cover Mon. 80F, Tues.-Thurs. 100F, Fri.-Sat. 120F, Sun. 120F for men, women free. Subsequent drinks 60-100F. Open Tues.-Sun. 11pm-dawn.

Scala de Paris, 188bis, rue de Rivoli, 1er (tel. 42-60-45-64; Mo. Palais-Royal). 3 balconies, dance floor, little sitting rooms, and video rooms. Cover Sun.-Thurs. 80F, women free; Fri. men 80F, women 60F; Sat. 80F for all. Sat.-Sun. 2:30-7pm reserved for ages 13-18 (no alcohol served), admission 40F. Open daily 10:30pm-dawn.

Charivari, 325, rue St-Martin, 3ème (tel. 42-78-80-29; Mo. Arts-et-Métiers). A huge new place that, in addition to a disco, holds 13 bars, 3 restaurants, and a cabaret. Cover 60F, drinks 20F. Open 11pm-dawn.

Club Zed, 2, rue des Anglais, 5ème (tel. 43-54-93-78; Mo. Maubert-Mutualité). Dancing sometimes to live bands. Disco kept to a minimum; enjoy Brazilian music, bebop, '60s music, and jazz instead. Wed. evening and Sun. afternoon rock only. 1st drink (required) 90F, 40F thereafter. Cover Wed. and Sun. afternoons 50F. Open Sept.-July Wed.-Thurs. 10:30pm-4am, Fri.-Sat. 10:30pm-5am, Sun. 4-8pm.

Le Balajo, 9, rue Lappe, 11ème (tel. 47-00-07-87; Mo. Bastille). The best place to go on Mon., when most others are closed. Full of middle-aged couples during the week. Music from the '70s and French songs from the '50s and '60s. The decor will remind you of your prom—or the prom you always imagined. Cover and drink 80F. Open Thurs.-Mon. 10pm-dawn.

Bars

The distinction between a cafe and a bar is subtle. You can order basically the same food in each. The visible difference is that a cafe is a room with plate-glass windows, open to the world, while a bar is usually closed and dim. Yet the essential nuance is cultural: While the French go to a cafe for a quick cup of coffee on their way to someplace else, a bar encourages planned *rendez-vous*. Historically, Paris has been the city of the *grands cafés* (Le Flore, La Coupole, La Closerie des Lilas), but the recent emergence of American bars has confused a once clear definition; the terms cafe and bar are now sometimes ambiguous. Café Costes is a cafe, Pub St-Germain is a bar, Café Pacifico is a bar, and La Closerie des Lilas is mostly a cafe during the day that becomes a bar as the sun sets.

Le Dôme, 108, bd. Montparnasse, 14ème (tel. 43-54-53-63; Mo. Vavin). Tiffany lamps and wicker chairs along with nostalgic old photos adorn the bar where Jean-Paul Sartre spent many an afternoon. Drinks 18-22F. Open 10am-2am.

La Closerie des Lilas, 171, bd. de Montparnasse, 6ème (tel. 43-54-21-68; Mo. Montparnasse-Bienvenue). Historically one of the most famous places in Paris. Frequented by young artists and writers throughout the nineteenth century—see their inscriptions on the tables. Also the former haunt of Mr. Hemingway—see the copper plaque. Fashionable, extremely beautiful, and crowded. Can be hard to find a spot. Excellent, large selection of drinks 17-70F. Open daily 10am-2am.

Pub St-Germain-des-Prés, 17, rue de l'Ancienne Comédie, 6ème (tel. 43-29-38-70; Mo. Odéon). Perhaps the largest pub in Europe with 7 rooms, 100 types of whisky, 450 different types of bottled beer, and 24 on tap. 3 underground rooms look like opium dens and are the most fun. Popular and '40s music is played and the place is generally packed with French youth. Drinks and ice cream only downstairs, full meals upstairs. Stick to the side dishes. *Dégustation* 35F: 8 small glasses of different beers (including Belgian cherry and apple). 4 different American beers 39F. Other beers from 36F per pint. Featured drink—*sein de Vénus* (29F). Open 24 hours.

Café Pacifico, 50, bd. de Montparnasse, 6ème (tel. 45-48-63-87; Mo. Montparnasse-Bienvenue). Rambunctious young people and lots of Americans, so you may have to stand to drink. British bartender. There are 3 such Mexican restaurants in Europe (Paris, London, and Amsterdam), and all are successful. Main dishes around 70F, *service non compris*. Brunch (noon-4pm) 80F and 100F. During the week (until 3pm) you get a free buck fizz (champagne and orange juice). Also a wide variety of cocktails from 29.50F. Tequilas from 27F, margarita 35F (pitcher 325F), sangria 30F (pitcher 125F). During Happy Hour (daily 6-7pm), you get snacks and drinks for half-price. Open Tues.-Sun. noon-2am, Mon. 3pm-2am.

New York, 68, rue Mouffetard, 5ème (tel. 43-36-61-43; Mo. Monge). Manager speaks several languages. Wide variety of cocktails 29-80F. *Pain Poîlane* sandwiches 26.45-40.25F. Pricey. Open Sept.-July daily 10am-2am.

La Rhumerie, 166, bd. St-Germain, 6ème (tel. 43-54-28-94; Mo. St-Germain-des-Prés). Still one of the most popular bars in Paris. Hard to find a seat here at any time, especially with a front-row view of the St-Germain evening scene, but try on stormy afternoons. Excellent daquiris 31F. Punch specialities 21-35F. Open Mon.-Sat. 11am-3am, Sun. 11am-2am.

The Mayflower, 49, rue Descartes, 5ème (tel. 43-54-56-47; Mo. Cardinal Lemoine). English-style with wood paneling and brass gleam. American license plates on the walls. French atmosphere with reasonable prices for Paris. Wide range of beers, including excellent Alsatians (25F) and Guinness on tap (22F for ½-pint). *Pain Poîlane* sandwiches 20-29F. Open daily until 2am.

Gay and Lesbian Entertainment

Separation of the sexes is a general rule, and men have many more options than women. Despite the growing epidemic, AIDs education has not, unfortunately, caught on here; safe sex may be your burden to enforce. Between the Métro stops Rambuteau and Hôtel-de-Ville, gay life flourishes with restaurants, cafes, and bars that fill nightly. Discos are spread throughout Paris, and change more rapidly than *hétéro* spots, so check *Gay Pied* (see Publications) for up-to-date information and an English introduction. *Lesbia*'s ads are a good gauge of what's hot.

Le Piano Zinc, 49, rue des Blancs Manteaux, 4ème (tel. 42-74-32-42; Mo. Rambuteau). Upstairs it's crowded, but the downstairs piano bar is popular, fun, and not too cruisy. Drinks from 10F; after 10pm from 16F. Mixed crowd. Open till dawn.

Le Bar Central, 33, rue Vieille du Temple, 4ème (tel. 42-78-11-42; Mo. Hôtel-de-Ville). Small and crowded but friendly and right in the middle of things. Mostly men. Drinks 9-27F. Open Mon.-Fri. noon-2am, Sat.-Sun. 2pm-2am.

La Champmeslé, 4, rue Chabanais, 2ème (tel. 42-96-85-20; Mo. Opéra). Romantic women's bar with comfortable couches, dim lighting, and varied music. Few men. Beer 15F, after 10pm 20F. Open Oct.-Aug. Mon.-Sat. 6pm-2am.

Le Petit Prince, 12, rue de Lanneau, 5ème (tel. 43-54-77-26; Mo. Maubert-Mutalité). Great for a romantic dinner with superb food. Light and tasty *quenelles* (baked fish mousse) included in the 69F *menu.* Delicious white-chocolate mousse 15F. Mixed crowd. Make reservations. Open daily 7:30pm-12:30am.

The Broad, 3, rue de la Ferronnerie, 1er (tel. 42-33-93-08; Mo. Châtelet). Huge place with dancing and a downstairs *cave* with intimate corners. No women allowed. Cover 45F, Mon.-Fri. free. Drinks 30-40F. Open Tues.-Sun. 11pm-dawn.

Studio de Nuit, 49-51, rue Ponthieu, 8ème (Mo. Georges V), in mall on Champs-Elysées. Good music and video. Women allowed in at doorman's discretion. Cover 45F, Sat. after 12:30am 65F. Drinks 40F. Open Tues., Thurs., and Sat. 10:30pm-6am.

Katmandou, 21, rue du Vieux-Colombier, 6ème (tel. 45-48-12-96; Mo. St-Sulpice). A chic bar that sometimes admits accompanied men. Some say it's the best lesbian bar in Paris. 1st drink 80F. Open 11pm-dawn.

Le New Monocle, 60, bd. Edgar Quinet, 14ème (tel. 43-20-81-12; Mo. Edgar Quinet). The newest lesbian bar in Paris. *Sympa.* Cover 60F. Open 11pm-dawn.

Chez Moune, 54, rue Pigalle, 9ème (tel. 45-26-64-61; Mo. Pigalle). Lesbian bar. Cabaret. Open 10pm-dawn.

La Péniche, a rocking lesbian boat bar with two levels. Advertised in *Lesbia.* Cover 60F.

Other Nightlife

Every evening after sunset and until midnight (1am on Saturday), Paris lives up to its reputation as the City of Lights. The Arc de Triomphe (Mo. Etoile), Notre-Dame (Mo. Cité), the Tour Eiffel (Mo. Bir-Hakeim), Place de la Concorde (Mo. Concorde), and the Hôtel de Ville (Mo. Hôtel-de-Ville) are illuminated and truly dazzling sights. In summer, the historic buildings of Le Marais (Mo. St-Paul) and some of the buildings and gardens of Montmartre (Mo. Abbesses) are lit up as well. A night ride on the **bateaux-mouches** (tel. 42-25-96-10) can be goofy and fun, but the high embankments on either side of the river obscure anything but the tops of most buildings. At night, spotlights attached to the side of the boat light up the buildings not already illuminated. (Boats leave 10am-noon, 1:30-7pm, and 8-11pm every ½ hr. from the right bank pier near pont d'Alma. 1¼-hr. rides 25F, ages under 12 10F.)

The French have developed a new art form: Take an impressive building, add a light show, superimpose a recorded message about the glorious history of the building, or the region, or the country, *et voilà:* **son et lumière.** It sounds tacky, and it is, but that's half the fun. In Paris, you can see one during the summer months at the **Hôtel des Invalides,** place des Invalides, 7ème (tel. 49-79-00-15; Mo. Invalides). The show is titled *Ombres de Gloire* (*Shadows of Glory*) and is given daily from April through October.

Festivals and Other Seasonal Events

French love of celebration is most evident in Paris, where the slightest provocation brings masses of people into the streets to drink, dance, and generally lose themselves in the spirit of the *fête* (festival) or *foire* (fair). Parisians like the size of a crowd to be in the hundreds of thousands. The gatherings in Washington on July 4, or in Times Square on New Year's Eve, are piddling in comparison to the assemblages of humanity on hand for Bastille Day fireworks, the coming of the New Year, or political demonstrations. The **Office de Tourisme,** 127, av. des Champs-Elysées, 8ème, (tel. 47-23-61-72; Mo. George V), provides a booklet in English that lists all the celebrations, large and small, that take place in Paris each month. The English information number (tel. 47-20-88-98) will give you the low-down each week on current festivals. *Pariscope* lists *fêtes populaires* for the coming week. You can also get a listing of festivals from the **French National Tourist Office** in New York at 610 Fifth Ave., New York, NY 10020 (tel. (212) 757-1125), or from the French Consulate nearest you.

March and April

Foire du Trône, Neuilly Lawn of the Bois de Vincennes (Mo. Porte Dorée). A gigantic amusement park with roller coasters, pony rides, fortune-tellers, funhouses, and enough caramel apples, cotton candy (*barbe à papa*), doughnuts, and waffles to keep the most gluttonous junkfood junkie happy for days. Jammed on warm weekends. End of March-May. Open 2pm-midnight.

Festival Internationale de la Guitarre (tel. 43-23-18-25). Concerts in many different Parisian churches. March 1-23 and April 15-22.

Festival des Instruments Anciens. Concerts in the churches of St-Germain-des-Prés, St-Julien-le-Pauvre, and the Conciergerie. March 4-April 1.

May

Festival de l'Ile-de-France (tel. 47-39-28-26). 100 free concerts in the châteaux and parks of Ile-de-France. May 10-July 14.

Festival de Versailles (tel. 49-50-71-18). Ballet, operas, concerts, and theater. Prices vary radically from one event to another. May 20-June 25.

Festival de Musique de St-Denis (tel. 42-43-30-97). Dance and music festival. May 15-June 23.

134   Paris

Foire du Trône continues.

June

Festival du Marais, 68, rue François Minon, 4*ème* (tel. 48-87-74-31 or 41-78-81-95; Mo. St-Paul). Classical and jazz music, theater, exhibits. Many of the events are outside, in courtyards, or in renovated Renaissance buildings in Le Marais. The classical concerts tend to be expensive, but other events are free. June 10-July 11.

Festival Foire St-Germain (tel. 43-29-12-78). Antique fair in place St-Sulpice, concerts in the Mairie du 6*ème,* sports events in the Jardin du Luxembourg. All events free. 2 weeks in mid-June.

Fêtes du Pont Neuf (tel. 42-77-92-26; Mo. Pont-Neuf), on the bridge. The bridge is closed to traffic and opened for dancing, music, street artists, and minstrels. A weekend in late June.

Foire du Trône, Festival de l'Ile-de-France, Festival de Musique de St-Denis, and **Festival de Versailles** continue.

July

Bastille Day (July 14). Big-time celebrations nationwide. *Vive la République* and pass the champagne. The day starts with the army parading down the Champs-Elysées and ends with fireworks at Montmartre, the Parc Montsouris, and the Palais de Chaillot. Traditional street dances are held on the eve of Bastille Day at the tip of the Ile St-Louis (the Communist Party always throws its gala there), the Hôtel de Ville, place de la Contrescarpe, and of course, the Bastille, where it all started. Dancing continues the next night. Avoid the Champs-Elysées on the eve of Bastille Day, when it becomes a nightmarish war zone of leering men cunningly tossing firecrackers under the feet of unsuspecting bystanders (and into the Métro). Check the newspapers a few days before to see where the main *bals* will take place.

Festival de France, 2, rue Edouard-Colonne, 2*ème* (tel. 42-33-44-44). Classical music at the Théâtre des Champs-Elysées. July 4-6.

End of the Tour de France (a few days after Bastille Day). Thousands of spectators turn out along the Champs-Elysées to watch the finish of the month-long bicycle race, which attracts as much attention in France as the World Series does in the U.S. Get there early and bring something to stand on and something to read as well.

Festival Estival (Paris Summer Festival; tel. 48-04-89-11; for reservations 45-62-40-80). Opera, chamber music, recitals in churches, palaces, and concert halls throughout the city. Tickets 25-40F. July 15-Sept. 21.

Festival de l'Orangerie de Sceaux. In the Orangerie of the Château de Sceaux (tel. 46-60-07-79). A mixture of chamber music, popular music, and piano recitals. Tickets 65-110F July 18-Oct. 11. Performances July-Aug. Sat.-Sun. at 5:30pm.

Versailles Display (tel. 39-50-71-81) Spectacular fountain effects every other Sun. starting the 1st Sun. in July at 4pm. Runs through Aug.

Festival du Marais and **Festival de l'Ile-de-France** continue.

August

Festival de Montmartre (tel. 46-06-50-48). Dancing, music, theater, and cinema. Last week of Aug.

Festival Estival, Festival de Musique de Sceaux, and **Versailles Display** continue.

September

Fête de Force Ouvrière, Bois de Vincennes. Speeches on defense of the workers. Wine tasting, food, amusement park on the same grounds as the Foîre du Thrône. 2nd or 3rd weekend in Sept.

Festival d'Automne (tel. 42-96-12-27). In the Pompidou Center and other museums and churches around Paris. Drama, ballet, expositions, and chamber music concerts. Late Sept.-Dec.

Fête de l'Humanité, parc de la Courneuve (Mo. Porte de la Villette, then special buses). The annual fair of the French Communist Party—like nothing you have ever seen. A million people show up to hear debates, ride roller-coasters, sample regional specialties, and collect

Marxist-Leninist leaflets. (*Humanité* is the French CP's newspaper.) Entertainers in recent years have included Charles Mingus, Marcel Marceau, the Bolshoi Ballet, and radical theater troupes. Communist parties from all over the world distribute literature and sell their native food and drink. A cross between a state fair, the Democratic Convention, and Woodstock; you don't have to be a Communist to enjoy it. 2nd or 3rd week of the month.

Festival de l'Ile-de-France (tel. 47-39-28-26). 2nd part. Another phase of the Ile-de-France festival, including concerts in churches and monuments in the area. Theme in 1988 is "Paris de l'Ecole de Notre Dame à 1789." Sept. 25-Dec. 20.

Festival de Musique de Chambre de Paris (tel. 42-60-31-84). Chamber music in St-Germain-des-Prés, St-Louis-à-l'Ile, and the Musée Carnavalet. 1 month.

Festival Estival, Festival de Sceaux, and **Festival de Montmartre** continue.

October

Festival de Jazz de Paris, 5, rue Bellart, 15*ème* (tel. 47-83-84-06). There's so much jazz in Paris anyway that this is hardly necessary, but it makes things official. Everybody on the European circuit (Nice, Antibes, Montreux, etc.) should be here. At the Théâtre Musical de Paris and the Théâtre de la Ville. Late Oct.-early Nov.

Festival International de Danse de Paris, 15, av. Montaigne, 8*ème* (tel. 47-23-40-84). In the Théâtres des Champs-Elysées, Théâtre Musical de Paris, the Centre Pompidou, and elsewhere. A 1st-class dance festival. 1988's riches included the Ballet de l'Opéra de Zurich and the Central Ballet of Peking. Late Oct. to mid-Nov.

Fête des Vendanges à Montmartre, rue Saules, 18*ème* (Mo. Lamarck-Caulaincourt). The celebration of the harvest of the vineyards on Montmartre. Though not France's best-known wine-producing region, Montmartre still bottles enough wine to warrant setting aside a day for celebrating its accomplishment. The 1st Sat. in Oct.

Festival d'Art Sacré, 4, rue Jules Cousin, 4*ème* (tel. 42-77-18-83). Sacred music at churches around Paris, including Notre-Dame, by the Radio France philharmonic orchestra and the Choir of Cologne. Oct. 1-Nov. 15.

Festival d'Automne and **Festival de Sceaux** continue.

November

Armistice Day (Nov. 11). Military parade from the Arc de Triomphe to the Hôtel des Invalides.

Festival d'Automne, Festival d'Art Sacré, Festival de Jazz de Paris, Festival de l'Ile-de-France, and **Festival International de Danse de Paris** continue.

December

Christmas Eve. At midnight, with the celebration of the Christmas Eve Mass, Notre-Dame becomes what it only claims to be the rest of the year: the cathedral of the city of Paris. Thousands of people fill the church. Many of the neighboring cafes stay open late for those who want to start celebrating Christmas early. Children's entertainment continues until the end of school vacation.

New Year's Eve. When the clock strikes midnight, the Latin Quarter erupts: Strangers embrace, motorists find people dancing on their hoods, and for an hour bd. St-Michel becomes a pedestrian mall, much to the dismay of the *agents de police* who are still attempting to direct traffic. A similar scene occurs on the Champs-Elysées.

Festival d'Automne continues.

Shopping and Markets

When in Paris, do as the Parisians do: Wear leather outfits, long-lasting perfumes, and Mixa Bébé cosmetics. You can often find these items at great prices, especially during the large sales (*soldes*) in January and August. Even if you don't plan to buy anything, note that Parisians have elevated window-dressing to an art form. Exploring the Left Bank boutiques near St-Germain-des-Prés or the fashionable designer shops in the Faubourg St-Honoré, rue de Rivoli, and the 16*ème* can be an interesting way to pass an afternoon. Visit the expensive but beautiful **Creeks** stores built by Philippe Stark, at 98, rue St-Denis, 2*ème* (tel. 42-33-81-70; Mo. Etienne Marcel), or at 155, rue de Rennes, 6*ème* (tel. 45-48-26-36; Mo. St-Germain-des-Prés). (Both open Tues.-Sat. 11am-7:30pm.) Then, if you're serious about getting the best deals, buy a copy of *Paris Pas Cher* at a kiosk, in which all stores are listed by merchandise and rated—the symbol of the foot represents the lowest prices. The logo "Paris Pas Cher" indicates that if you bring your book, you'll get a discount.

Toward the river on the Left Bank, rue Bonaparte is lined with antique stores containing furniture, books, and artwork. Place Vendôme and rue de le Paix are lined with famous jewelers: Cartier, Van Cleef & Arpels, and others. For bargains on large quantities of perfume, go to **Sylvia,** 1, rue Scribe, 9*ème* (tel. 47-42-26-64; Mo. Opéra); you'll get a 40% discounts on purchases over 1000F. (Open Mon.-Sat. 9am-7pm.) Also check **Raoul et Curly,** 47, av. de l'Opéra, 2*ème* (tel. 47-42-50-10; Mo. Opéra), and ask for foreigners' discounts—at least 20% off. (Open Mon.-Sat. 9am-6:30pm.)

Do not buy leather at the several Métro stations unless cost is no object. Instead wander along rue Dupetit-Thouars, 3*ème* (Mo. République), or rue Turenne, also in the 3*ème* (Mo. Filles-du-Calvaire), where you'll find the center of the leather wholesale business. Especially good deals await you at **Top Cuir,** 68, rue de la Chaussée d'Antin, 9*ème* (tel. 48-74-02-38; Mo. Trinité), and 41, av. du Général Leclerc, 14*ème* (tel. 43-27-26-68; Mo. Mouton Duvernet). (Both stores open Tues.-Sat. 10am-7pm, Mon. noon-7pm.) Also try **Au Marais,** 20, rue Dupetit-Thouars, 3*ème* (tel. 42-72-35-01, Mo. République; open Mon.-Sat. 10am-7pm), and **Mission Impossible,** 20, rue du Four, 6*ème* (tel. 43-25-05-87; Mo. Mabillon; open Mon.-Sat. 10am-7:30pm).

For silk, try **Le Jardin de Soie,** 10, rue St-Marc, 2*ème* (tel. 42-36-50-23; Mo. Richelieu-Drouot; open Mon.-Sat. 10:30am-7pm).

The *grands boulevards* around the Opéra and Gare St-Lazare, 9*ème* (Mo. Opéra or Havre-Caumartin), contain a number of large department stores. On bd. Haussman, 8*ème* and 9*ème* (Mo. Chausée-d'Antin), are the Macy's and Gimbel's of Paris: **Galeries Lafayette** and **Printemps,** located right beside each other and across from the British **Marks and Spencer.** All three rivals carry an extensive selection of merchandise. (Galeries Lafayette and Printemps open 9:30am-6:30pm.) For clothes, look at the stores on St-Germain, but buy on **rue St-André-des-Arts,** around **rue de Seine,** and the upper part of **boulevard St-Michel.** Rue de Rivoli and the little streets around (not in) Les Halles also offer some good deals.

At Galeries Lafayette and Printemps, foreigners can receive a **rebate** of 13% or 23% on purchases over 1200F (of perfume, precious jewelry, and cameras). In order to get this rebate, all purchases must be made in the same store within a period of six months, and the total amount spent must be greater than or equal to 1200F. Each time you make a purchase, tell the cashier to mark your sales slip for a *détaxe,* and save all the sales slips. When you have made your last purchase, take all your sales slips to the export discount desk. At this time you can also choose how you want your money (e.g., paid to you directly in francs or sent to a U.S. bank). You'll receive an export sales docket, and a stamped envelope to be presented to the French customs officials at the airport and then mailed back to the place of purchase. (Make sure you leave all the articles you have purchased near the top of your suitcase since the customs official might ask to see them). A *détaxe* savings may also be allowed when purchasing bicycles or cars, though the paperwork can be annoying. If your dealer is familiar with foreigners, you can get 17% back on bicycles purchased in France and 33% back on cars. Upon returning to the U.S., you must pay customs if purchases amount to over US$400, but often this is less than the rebate returned by French customs.

Along the Seine, the four buildings of **la Samaritaine** (named for the large pumphouse that once stood there and that supplied the Louvre and Tuileries with water; Mo. Pont-Neuf) and **Bazar de l'Hôtel de Ville** (Mo. Hôtel-de-Ville) carry everything you think you want and many things you know you don't.

TATI, 4-30, bd. Rochechouart (Mo. Anvers), is the cheapest department store in Paris, as the flood of humans spilling from its doors will attest. (Open Mon.-Sat. 9:15am-7pm.) Next door, you'll find the best prices on fabrics in the city. In the same neighborhood, on rue de la Goutte d'Or, 18ème, is the **Algerian market,** which looks just like Middle-Eastern *suqs,* where you can find some bargains. And if you're looking for a five-and-dime complete with a supermarket, go to any of the **Monoprix** or **Prisunics** that litter the city. For bargains on books and records, as well as audio and video equipment (and concert tickets), visit one of many FNAC locations (see Entertainment). FNAC also harbors a small collection of literary classics in English, all priced at about half the average elsewhere.

A large selection of English books can be found in several bookstores. The most famous is **Shakespeare and Co.,** 37, rue de la Bûcherie, 5ème (Mo. St-Michel), across the Seine from Notre-Dame, which has new and used books, a library upstairs, and a history that goes back to the likes of Gertie Stein and Ernest. Unfortunately, the selection is quirky, to say the least, and battered paperbacks can cost as much as 25F. (Open daily noon-midnight.) For a better selection, concentrating on American literature, and a large display of guide books at more reasonable price, seek out **Brentano's,** 37, av. de l'Opéra, 2ème (tel. 42-61-52-50; Mo. Opéra; open Mon.-Sat. 11am-8pm). The **Village Voice,** 6, rue Princesse, 6ème (tel. 46-33-36-47; Mo. Mabillon), is an excellent place with a small cafe in the back and poetry readings and lectures throughout the year. It has a good feminist literary collection. (Open Sept.-July Mon.-Fri. 11am-8pm; Aug. Mon.-Fri. 2-8pm.) **Les Mots à la Bouche,** 6, rue Ste-Croix-de-la-Bretonnerie, 4ème (tel. 42-78-88-30; Mo. Hôtel-de-Ville), is a serene bookstore with French and English titles, magazines, postcards, and newsletters of interest to both gay men and lesbians. Friendly English-speaking owner can be a fountain of information. (Open Sept.-July Mon.-Sat. 11am-8pm; Aug. Tues.-Sat. 11am-1pm and 2-7pm.) **Librairie des Femmes,** 74, rue de Seine, 6ème (tel. 43-29-50-75; Mo. Odéon), is a large, peaceful place to browse through the selection of women's literature. (Open 11am-6pm.) The best selection of magazines and British literature is at **W.H. Smith,** 248, rue de Rivoli, 1er, (tel. 42-60-37-97; Mo. Concorde), which even has a pleasant but overpriced English tea room upstairs. *Let's Go* sells for 150F here. (Open Mon.-Sat. 11am-7pm.) For guidebooks (including *Let's Go*), travel literature, and paperback Penguins, go to **Nouveau Quartier Latin,** 78, bd. St-Michel, 6ème (tel. 43-26-42-70; Mo. Luxembourg; open Mon.-Sat. 10am-7pm), or to **Calignani,** 224, rue de Rivoli, 1er (tel. 42-60-76-07; Mo. Tuileries), which also sells British hardbacks. (Open Sept.-June 9:30am-6:30pm; July-Aug. Tues.-Sat. 9:30am-5pm, Mon. 1:30-5pm.)

The largest flea market in Paris, and one of the largest in Europe, is the **Marché aux Puces de Saint-Ouen,** 17ème (Mo. Porte de Clignancourt; Sat.-Mon. 7am-7pm). Hundreds of stalls sell antiques and junk, old and new clothes, records, and food. Take av. Michelet into St-Ouen and turn left on rue des Rosiers for the antiques markets on your right. Continue and on your left you'll see bronze, furniture, and painting markets. Avoid the card games and junk vendors lined up in the middle of the streets or along av. Michelet. Since it's not always cheap, never pay the asking price and get there by 9am or else late in the day for bargains. The market can be extremely dangerous; organized bands of pickpockets can become violent while the police look the other way. You may be better off skipping it, and heading for the junkier, cheaper **Marché de Montreuil** (Mo. Porte de Montreuil; Sat.-Mon. mornings). Get here early or all the quality merchandise will be gone. Also visit the market at **Porte de Vanves** (Mo. Porte de Vanves; Sat.-Sun. 9am-7pm). Here too, you'll have to search for quality. Finally, the **Marché d'Aligre,** place d'Aligre near the Bastille, 12ème (Mo. Ledru Rollin), is the cheapest but least interesting of the flea markets (Tues.-Sun. until noon). The **Marché du Temple,** Carreau du Temple, 3ème (Mo. Hôtel-de-Ville), is not a fleamarket, but a beautiful building where new clothes are sold at wholesale prices. Sometimes overstock from the large store is vended in the open air as well. (Open Tues.-Sat. 9am-noon and 2-7pm, Sun. 9am-1pm.) Always be on guard for pickpockets.

Place Louis Lepine, close to the Ile de la Cité, 4ème (Mo. Cité), blooms with color as the **Marché aux Fleurs** takes over the small square (Mon.-Sat. 8am-7pm). On Sundays from 9am to 7pm, the colors really come alive as the plants are replaced by hundreds of birds for the **Marché aux Oiseaux** (be careful, they bite). Dogs are marketed at 106, rue Brancion, 15ème (Mo. Convention; Sun. 2-4pm); horses, donkeys, and an occasional mule are sold at the same place (Mon., Wed., and Fri. mornings). Every day, on quai St-Michel and quai Montebello, 1er (Mo. Pont Neuf), ferrets, chipmunks, and various other animals are sold, along with plants and horticulture equipment.

Stamp and postcard collectors congregate every Thursday, Saturday, Sunday, and holidays from 10am to nightfall at the **Marché aux Timbres**, on av. Gabriel at av. Marigny, 8ème (Mo. Champs-Elysées-Clemenceau). And if you're looking for **old books or posters,** don't forget to check out the *bouquinistes'* stalls on the quais of the Seine, starting at the Louvre and running up to the Hôtel de Ville, and across the river from quai de Conti to quai de Montebello. You might just come across a treasure, but you're more likely to find overpriced maps and postcards. For some real bargains and lots of free entertainment, stop by Paris's largest auction house, **Hôtel Drouot** 9, rue Drouot, 9ème (tel. 42-46-17-11; Mo. Richelieu-Drouot), which deals in everything from collectors' pieces to odd lots of toilet plungers. Auctions occur practically every day. (Open Sept.-July Mon.-Sat. 11am-6pm.)

Paris's **street markets** are special. Each neighborhood has its own, convening every day except Sunday afternoon and Monday. (Hours vary slightly, so ask the shop owner.) Early in the morning, merchants set up their stands; the care and attention that goes into the presentation extends far beyond cellophane wrapping. In the livelier markets, on rue Mouffetard, 5ème (Mo. Censier-Daubenton), and rue de Lévis, 17ème (Mo. Villiers), some merchants put on a real show by crooning their prices and begging you to come and buy. Most stands stay open until 6 or 7pm, and prices go down just before they close (this is especially true on Sun., right before they close for the afternoon). In August, most stores close, but posted on the window you will find the address of the next closest open *marché*.

Near Paris

Ile-de-France, the region of which Paris is the center, encompasses a rich concentration of spectacular châteaux, monuments, museums, and cathedrals. These sights are easily accessible from Paris by train, bus, or car and make excellent daytrips. *Pariscope* and other weeklies list the museums of the Ile-de-France, as does the free booklet on museums by the Hôtel de Sully (see Le Marais in Sights above). To make telephone calls out of Paris, you must dial 16.

Versailles

The magnificent palace of Louis XIV, Versailles embodies the Sun King's absolute power. Disliking Paris for its association with the power struggles of his youth, Louis XIV turned his father's small hunting château into his royal residence. The court became the center of noble life, where more than a thousand of France's greatest lords vied for the king's favor. Louis hoped to control the often wayward nobles by keeping them at Versailles—where he could keep an eye on them. Louis also destroyed the financial independence of the nobility by forcing them to pay crippling taxes to support his lavish expenditures. The ostentatious rooms and endless gardens were the climax of the Ancien Régime's economic drain on its citizens.

The guided tour of the interior of the **Château** leads through the apartments and halls that have been restored. These include the **Galerie des Glaces** (Hall of Mirrors), where the Treaty of Versailles was signed in 1919, ending World War I; the **Petits Appartements,** private royal chambers; **La Chapelle,** the setting for the marriage of the 16-year-old prince (future King Louis XVI) and Marie Antoinette in 1770; and **Les Grands Appartements du Roi et de la Reine,** the bedroom where

Marie Antoinette spent her last night at the Castle before attempting to escape from the rising tide of revolution.

The park still has many of its original *bosquets* (groves), first planted in the seventeenth century. The tourist office can provide a list of the times and dates of particularly spectacular water shows involving the elaborate fountains. (See Festivals and Other Seasonal Events above.) Generally, *les grandes eaux,* as these displays are called, take place from May through September every Sunday, but call the tourist office to confirm. (3:30pm. Free with admission, 15F if you don't go into the château.) The **Grand Trianon,** pink-and-white marble wings joined by a colonnade, is the royal guesthouse built for Louis XIV by Mansart. The **Petit Trianon,** built under Louis XV, was Marie Antoinette's play palace, and **Le Hameau** the hamlet where the Queen amused herself by pretending to lead a pastoral life. (Château open Tues.-Sun. 9:45am-5pm. Admission 23F, ages under 26 and on Sun. 12F. Grand Trianon open Tues.-Sun. 9:45am-noon and 2-5pm. Admission 15F, ages under 26 and on Sun. 8F. Petit Trianon open Tues.-Fri. 2-5pm. Admission 10F and 5F. Last admission 4:30pm. Combination tickets to both Trianons 18F, ages under 26 and on Sun. 9F, ages under 18 free. Gardens open sunrise-sundown.) For more information, call the **Musée National du Château de Versailles** (tel. 30-84-74-00).

Versailles also puts on a series of summer **Fêtes de Nuit** at Neptune's Pond. Fireworks, fountains, and lights combine for a fantastic extravaganza that serves the same purpose as a *son et lumière,* but on a scale to match the château. Derived from the Grandes Fêtes given in the park by Louis XIV, the 90-minute shows run regardless of weather (in summer, 8 on Sat.). Tickets (45-140F) go on sale one month before each festival at the Versailles tourist office and at some ticket agencies in Paris. Call the tourist office for information and reservations (tel. 39-50-36-29). Although the palace will almost certainly be mobbed by tourists, the edge of the river is usually relatively calm and an excellent picnic spot—buy provisions in town as you walk from the station to the château.

You can reach Versailles by RER Line C (4:53am-12:22am, every 15 min., 35 min. from the center of Paris, 20F) or more cheaply by taking the Métro to Pont de Sèvres and then transferring to bus #171. You can also catch the train at Gare St-Lazare (every 15 min., round-trip 20F) and arrive a half-hour later at Versailles Rive Droite where you can catch the special bus to the château. For more information on tours of the old section of Versailles, the town, and *visites conférences* on individual sections of the palace (15-30F), call the **Syndicat d'Initiative,** 7, rue des Réservoirs (tel. 39-50-36-22), a five-minute walk from the palace. (Open May-Sept. Mon.-Sat. 9am-noon and 2-6:30pm, Sun. 10am-noon and 2-6:30pm; Oct.-April Mon.-Sat. only.)

Chartres

Unforgettable **Cathédrale de Chartres,** spared by bureaucratic inefficiency after being condemned during the Revolution, survives today as one of the most sublime creations of the Middle Ages—worshipped by Henry Adams in print, Rodin in study, and by thousands of visitors in mute admiration. In the Middle Ages pilgrims came to admire a small cloth relic that legend says Mary wore while giving birth to Jesus. Today, most come to admire the dark vault's intricate stained glass (relating, in glowing "Chartres blue," all of biblical history from Adam and Eve to the Last Judgement), the statuary, and the outer buttressing.

Larger and more imposing cathedrals exist, but few reward time spent as generously as Chartres. A masterpiece of finely crafted details—architecture, sculpture, and glass—the cathedral is a statement of profound unity (in spite of the asymmetrical towers, the shorter surviving from an earlier structure), as well as an extraordinary fusion of Romanesque and Gothic architectural elements. Most of the glass is from the thirteenth century and was preserved through both world wars by the town authorities, who dismantled more than 3000 square meters and stored it piece by piece until the end of hostilities. See the films on stained-glass production, Chartres in the Middle Ages, and stained-glass history. They are shown free on request in the **Galerie du Vitrail,** 17, rue du Cloître Notre-Dame (tel. 37-36-10-03; open Feb.-Dec. Tues.-Sat. 10am-6pm, Sun. 10:30am-1pm and 2-6pm).

The structure stands on the site of a Romanesque cathedral that was destroyed in 1194 by a huge fire. All that survived was the holy relic, and clerics took advantage of the miracle to solicit funds for rebuilding on a scale befitting the Virgin, dedicating the cathedral to Mary. (Shroud displayed in the Treasury Feb.-April Mon.-Sat. 10am-noon and 2:30-5pm, Sun. 2:30-5pm; April-Sept. Mon.-Sat. 10am-noon and 3-6pm, Sun. 2-6pm; Oct.-Dec. Mon.-Sat. 10am-noon and 2-6:30pm; Sun. 2-5pm. Free. Cathedral open daily April-Sept. 7:30am-7:30pm; Oct.-March 7:30am-7pm.) You can also see the **crypt** (daily at 11am, 2:15pm, 3:30pm, and 4:30pm; in July-Aug. also at 5:15pm; admission 7F) and climb the (north) **Tour Jehan-de-Beauce** (open Oct.-Dec. and Feb.-Mar. 10-11:30am and 2-4:30pm, Sun. 2-4:30pm; April-Sept. 9:30-11:30am and 2-5:30pm, Sun. 2-5:30pm; admission 16F, students 9F). **Organ recitals** take place from July through October Sunday at 5pm (free); **Samedis Musicaux** are not only on Saturday so call the tourist office for a schedule. (Admission 50F, ages under 26 40F.)

No cathedral in the world has a tour guide quite like Malcolm Miller, Chartres's master of ceremonies, the man who, for the last 25 years, has brought the cathedral to life for Anglophone visitors. Miller's well-spun lectures call rapt attention to the wealth of symbolic detail in the glass and stone. Leave a tip or buy one of his self-proclaimed masterpieces and you'll make a friend. (Tours April-Jan. Mon.-Sat. at noon and 2:45pm; converts can catch both in 1 day.) Leave plenty of time for exploration on your own afterward.

Secular Chartres possesses quite a bit of elegance as well. Though the town lies on wheat-growing plains, its narrow, hilly streets climb and dip enough to afford moving glimpses of the cathedral. The international **Centre International du Vitrail** (stained-glass center), 5, rue du Cardinal Pie (tel. 37-21-65-72), hosts temporary exhibits on stained glass. (Open Tues.-Sun. 10am-12:30pm and 1:30-6pm. Admission 12F.) Also notable are the ancient collegiate **Eglise St-André,** a stately Romanesque structure by the Eure, and **Eglise St-Pierre,** a delicate Gothic masterpiece from the thirteenth century. (Both open July-Sept. 9am-7pm; Oct.-June 10am-5pm. Free.) Climb up rue St-Pierre to return to the *ville haute,* and spend some time here in the ancient city of Chartres. Tapes in English may be rented from the tourist office (35F, deposit 100F and passport, 1 hr.). A minitrain tours the old town, leaving from place de la Cathédrale. (40-min. ride departs daily 10am-6:30pm, every 50 min.). Tickets 20F, children 10F.)

The town itself, easily accessible from Paris, is a stop on frequent **trains** from Gare Montparnasse (7:19am-8:30pm, 20 per day; 50 min.; round-trip 108F). Bicycling and hitching are also possible, but getting out of Paris is a nuisance. The friendly **Office de Tourisme** (tel. 37-21-54-03), opposite the cathedral's main entrance, will find you accommodations (8F plus 50F deposit). Procure tickets and information for Samedis Musicaux here. (Open Nov.-April Mon.-Sat. 9:30am-12:30pm and 2-6:15pm; May-Oct. Sun. 9:30am-12:30pm and 1:45-6:45pm.) Consider taking a brief respite from Paris and staying the night. The pleasant **Auberge de Jeunesse (IYHF),** 23, av. Neigre (tel. (16) 37-34-27-64), is 2km south of the station, past the cathedral, and over the river by Eglise St-André. Follow the signs. The clean and comfortable rooms are 42F per night, sheets 14F, breakfast included. (Membership required. Open July-Sept. daily 8-10am and 6-11pm; Oct.-June 8-10am and 6-10:30pm.) Two lefts from the station puts you at the attractive **Hôtel St-Jean,** 6, rue de Faubourg St-Jean (tel. 37-21-35-69). (Singles 75F. Doubles 105F, with W.C. 140F. Showers included. Breakfast 20F. Open daily; closed Sun. until noon.) For delicious crêpes (14-30F) and salads, try **La Flambée,** 14, av. Jehan de Beauce (tel. 37-21-23-25). Near the train station, it's also a good place to relax while you wait for your train. The proprietor boasts of his *cuisine à l'ancienne* served in 45 and 57F *menus.* (Open daily 11:30am-11:30pm.) At **Au Pain de France,** place des Epars (tel. 37-21-48-80), a *salon de thé* in the center of town, you can sit outside and enjoy beautiful pastries, particularly the glazed fruit tarts (15F). (Open daily 10am-10pm.)

A 45-minute train ride from Chartres is **Illiers-Cambray,** onetime vacation home of Marcel Proust and setting for many of his works. The well-preserved town still looks much as it must have to Proust. The highlight of this literary pilgrimage, the **Maison de Tante Léonie,** 4, rue Docteur Léonie (tel. 37-24-05-40), is the home of his favorite aunt. Mementoes of Proust's life are displayed. (By tour only—daily at 3pm and 5pm.) To reach Illiers, take the *Micheline* (small train) from Gare de Chartres (tel. 37-28-50-50; 8:49am-7:41pm 6 per day, 19F).

Fontainebleau

Fontainebleau owes its existence to the royal passion for hunting: For eight centuries, this hunting lodge and royal residence was favored by some of France's most famous rulers, many of whom added a wing here or there and otherwise altered the château. François I transformed it into a Renaissance palace, importing Italian artists to decorate the interior with paintings and mosaics. Napoleon called the place La Maison des Siècles and lived there for much of his reign; cour des Adieux was the scene of his dramatic farewell in 1814. The resulting melange of styles enables you to follow systematically the evolution of interior decoration in France. Particularly worth seeing are the **Grands Appartements** (Galerie de François I) and the **Petits Appartements** (appartements de l'Impératrice Joséphine). (Both open Wed.-Mon. 9:30am-12:15pm and 2-4:15pm. Grand Appartements by guided tour only—4 times per day. Admission to the Grands Appartements 25F, students 14F; to the Petits Appartements 14F, students 10F.) Make sure to stop at the **Etang des Carpes,** an amazing pond with hundreds of carp, on your way from the **Jardin Anglais** to the **Jardin de Diane,** where royal peacocks still flaunt their feathers.

As splendid as the palace, **Forêt de Fontainebleau** is a thickly wooded 41,632-acre preserve with hiking trails and the famous sandstone rocks used for training alpine climbers. Much less crowded than Versailles, Fontainebleau, city of art and history, has two interesting museums: **Musée Napoléonien d'Art et d'Histoire,** 88, rue St-Honoré (tel. 64-22-49-80; admission 10F), and **Le Musée d'Art Figuratif Contemporain,** 43bis, rue Royale (tel. 64-22-60-23; admission 8F). (Both open Wed.-Mon. 9:30am-12:30pm and 2-5pm.) The train from Gare de Lyon leaves Paris every 15 minutes from 10am through midnight (40 min., round-trip 80F).

Melun and Environs

Between Paris and Fontainebleau is the commercial town of Melun, home of Brie cheese. Originally a Gallo-Roman village, Melun harbored Abélard's school of philosophy, established in 1101. Its oldest section is on a scenic island in the middle of the Seine and contains **Cathédrale de Notre-Dame,** first built in the ninth century and "remodeled" in the Gothic style. **Eglise St-Aspais,** on the mainland, dates from the sixteenth century and still has its original lovely windows. **Place St-Jean,** with its peculiar-looking fountain, is a great spot for a walk. Only a few blocks away, the town's excellent **Musée Municipal,** 5, rue du Franc Mûrier (tel. 64-39-17-91), has a good Greco-Roman collection and interesting documents about local history. (Open Mon. and Wed.-Sat. 10am-noon and 2-6pm.) Take the train from Gare de Lyon to Melun (10am-midnight every 15 min., ½ hr., round-trip 70F).

A masterpiece designed by Le Vau, decorated by Le Brun, and landscaped by Le Nôtre, **Château de Vaux-le-Vicomte** was built for Fouquet, the Minister of Finance under Louis XIV. The château's grandeur hastened its owner's downfall. Young King Louis, received for a feast here in 1661, became enraged at being outshone and stripped Fouquet of all his power, condemning him to life in prison. Astonished with the magnificence of Vaux, prototype of the classical style, the king appropriated Vaux-le-Vicomte's artists and eventually some of its works, and embarked on the construction of Versailles, where the style would reach full maturity. (Château open April-Nov. daily 9am-1pm and 2-6pm; Nov.-Dec. and Feb.-April 2-5pm. Fountains go on 3-6pm the 2nd and last Sat. of each month. Admission to château 40F and garden 15F, students 27F.) Unfortunately, there are no buses from Melun to the château. A cab (tel. 64-52-51-50) costs 40-58F, or try hitching up N36.

Chantilly

Set in beautiful surroundings at the edge of Forêt de Chantilly, Chantilly is a double château with a fine park and sumptuous museum. The château was in the hands of the Montmorency-Condé family from the seventeenth century until its bequest to the Institut de France in the late 1800s. The most renowned family member, the Grand Condé, celebrated victor of Rocroi and cousin of Louis XIV, commissioned the building of the Grand Château and enjoyed years of lavish living here. To get to the château from the train station, walk down rue des Otages and turn left in front of the tourist office (2km).

The **Musée Condé** (tel. 44-57-08-00) in the château testifies to the luxurious lifestyle of the princes. Magnificent furnishings and vast numbers of master paintings (Raphael, Delacroix, Corot) fill the chambers. The library holds 600,000 volumes and more than 1000 manuscripts, among them the exquisite *Très Riches Heures du Duc de Berry*. (Open Wed.-Mon. April-Oct. 10:30am-6pm; Nov.-March Mon.-Fri. 1-5pm and Sat.-Sun. 10:30am-5:30pm. Admission to park and museum 30F; to park alone 12F.)

Also visit the **Grandes Ecuries,** great stables that housed 240 horses and hundreds of hunting dogs until the Revolution. They were constructed in 1719 to satisfy Louis-Henri Bourbon, who hoped to occupy them when reincarnated as a horse. (Stables open Easter-Oct. Sat.-Sun. and holidays 2-6pm.) Visit a stallion in the **Musée Vivant du Cheval** (tel. 44-57-13-13), which has received awards for artistic merit and displays living horses as well as horse sculptures, paintings, and videos. (Open April-Oct. Wed.-Mon. 10:30am-6pm; Nov.-March Mon. and Wed.-Fri. 2-4:30pm, Sat.-Sun. 10:30am-6pm. Admission 35F, students 28F.) A 20-minute lesson in horse training occurs at 11:30am, 3:30pm, and 5:15pm in the Cours des Chenils (Nov.-March Sat.-Sun. at 3:30pm only).

More lavish and interesting than any château of the Loire, Chantilly is overrun with tourists, particularly on Sunday. Two of France's premier **horseraces** are held here in June—the Prix de Diane and the Prix du Jockey Club. The **Office de Tourisme,** av. du Maréchal Joffre (tel. 44-57-08-58), is in a small trailer. (Open Mon. and Wed.-Sat. 8:30am-12:30pm and 4-6:30pm., Sun. 9am-2pm.) Take the train from Gare du Nord (4:55am-12:49am, every ½-1 hr., 35 min., round-trip 60F). You can rent a **bicycle** outside the train station (20-36F per day).

Not far from Chantilly is **Senlis.** Its handsome Gothic **Cathédrale Notre-Dame's** influential sculpture and design shows the evolution of this style in the Ile-de-France. The spire, central portal, and galleries of the nave all date from the twelfth century, while the chapter house and cathedral windows were constructed during the fourteenth century. Especially remarkable is the Grand Portail consecrated to the Virgin Mary, later imitated in Chartres and Notre-Dame de Paris. Also worth seeing is the **Eglise St-Frambourg,** founded around 900 by the merciful Queen Adélaïde. It was reconstructed in 1177 by Louis VII, then destroyed in the Revolution. The great pianist Georges Cziffra restored the church once again a few years ago, and it now holds concerts and exhibitions throughout the year. Enter the park next to the *syndicat* to reach the **Château Royal,** a hunting lodge for kings from Charlemagne to Henri IV, now converted into a unique hunting museum. The remains of its Gallo-Roman fortifications, with 31 towers, still surround the town. (Open March to mid-Dec. Thurs.-Mon. 10am-noon and 2-6pm, Wed. 2-6pm. Admission 10F.) The old town is a network of medieval alleyways; several of the original gates of the old wall still stand. If you have a long wait, explore the city's cobblestone streets, unspoiled by tourists, for a refreshing change from Paris. Senlis's **Syndicat d'Initiative,** place du Parvais Notre-Dame (tel. (16) 44-53-06-40), can give you information on concerts and exhibitions. (Open April-Nov. Mon.-Fri. 2-6pm, Sat.-Sun. 10am-noon and 2-6pm.) Trains to Senlis leave from Gare du Nord usually every hour from 6:12am to 8:12pm. (Round-trip 69F. Change for a bus at Chantilly;

you can make a stop and continue your trip later.) It takes 25 minutes from Chantilly and one hour from Paris.

Beauvais

Cathédrale St-Pierre in Beauvais boasts the tallest Gothic chancel in the world, the product of architectural ambition pushed beyond reason. Begun in 1225, the chancel was completed in 1272, but survived only 12 years in its original state. Too top-heavy for the supporting columns, it collapsed in 1284. Rebuilding began immediately and continued until 1578, when the chancel and transept were completed. In the 1560s, however, an additional central spire was built above the intersection of transept and choir, again over-burdening the supporting pillars and resulting in the disastrous collapse of 1573. So much time and money was then spent on rebuilding and strengthening the chancel again (see the complex of flying buttresses around it) that the construction of the nave was never begun, and the opening from the transept has been bricked up for the last 400 years. Stand back from the cathedral and try to imagine its immense proportions—the largest of any Gothic church in the world—if the nave had been built.

Of interest as well are the stained-glass windows and the *tapisseries* from three centuries, spread out all around the cathedral. Also see the *Horloge Astronomique* with its 90,000 pieces, built by Vérité in the nineteenth century. Don't miss the older (1302) and smaller *horloge*, less obviously placed. (You can view them Tues.-Sat. at noon, 3pm, 4pm, and 5pm; Sun. at 3pm, 4pm, and 5pm.) To get there from the train station, walk straight ahead on bd. du Général de Gaulle and pass the garden on your left. At the first large intersection, turn left on rue de la Madeleine. Or simply head toward the sound of the bells.

The old bishop's palace is now the **Musée Départemental de l'Oise,** rue du Musée (tel. 44-84-37-37), with a permanent collection on the paleontological history of the area, as well as wood carving, ceramics, stoneware from fourteenth- to eighteenth-century Beauvais houses, local artwork, and temporary exhibits. (Open Wed.-Mon. 10am-noon and 2-6pm. Admission 10F, students 5F.)

Eglise St-Etienne, south of place de la Hachette, is a fascinating combination of a sober Roman nave and a richly-decorated Gothic choir, with some beautiful stained glass. Pay particular attention to the great sixteenth-century *vitraux* and to the magnificent *Arbre de Jessé*. (Open daily 9:30am-noon and 3:30-6pm.)

In 1664, the only branch of the great **Gobelins tapestry factory** of Paris was opened in Beauvais. It was concerned mainly with weaving tapestry for furniture, and its themes were pastoral rather than historical or mythological. Located next to the cathedral, the modern **Galerie Nationale de la Tapisserie** houses an interesting collection of tapestries, ancient to contemporary, historical to abstract, and a workshop for demonstrations where questioning the artists (in French) is encouraged. (Open April-Sept. Tues.-Sun. 9:30-11:30am and 2-6pm; Oct.-March 10-11:30am and 2:30-4:30pm. Admission 15F, students 9F. The *Atelier de demonstration* is open the same hours but is closed Sun. and holidays.)

The **Festival de Jeanne Hachette** (last weekend in June), celebrates, with medieval costumes and processions through the streets, the gallantry of the women of Beauvais in resisting the onslaught of the Burgundian army of Charles the Bold. Inexpensive accommodations are rare, but you can lunch reasonably at the cafes across from the cathedral; try specialties such as *quiche beauvaisienne* (30F) or *ficelle picarde* (ham-filled, rolled crêpe). Otherwise, pick up local *tuiles en chocolat* (curled cookies made with chocolate and nuts) at a *confiserie* or *pâtisserie*.

Beauvais has a **Syndicat d'Initiative** (tel. 44-45-25-26) opposite the cathedral (open April-Sept. Tues.-Sat. 9am-noon and 2-6:30pm) and another at 6, rue Malherbe (tel. 44-45-08-18), with the same hours year-round. Take the train from Gare du Nord (10 per day, 1 hr., round-trip 92F).

Meaux

Forty-five kilometers east of Paris is the ancient town of Meaux, capital of northern Brie and known, appropriately, for its cheese. They make three types of Brie: classic *Brie de Meaux; Brie de Melun,* thicker in texture and stronger in taste; and *Brie de Coulommiers,* which is less fully fermented. Meaux's tangy mustard is yet another claim to fame, not to mention the old fart Jacques-Bénigne Bossuet. **Cathédrale St-Etienne** has a mixed facade, as only the left tower was completed in the original, flamboyant Gothic style. The stained glass dates from the fourteenth century. The bishop's palace next door was made famous by Bossuet, nicknamed l'Aigle de Meaux (the eagle), who was bishop of Meaux from 1681 to 1704. Housed here now is the **Musée Bossuet** (tel. 64-34-84-45), filled with the theologian's memorabilia and otherwise a local folklore museum. (Open Wed.-Mon. 10am-noon and 2-5pm, Sun. 3-6:30pm. Free.)

For information, call the **Syndicat d'Initiative,** 2, rue Notre-Dame (tel. 64-33-02-26; open daily 10am-noon and 2-6:30pm). You can get to Meaux by A4 and N36, or by a half-hour train ride from Paris's Gare de l'Est (6:27am-12:59am every 35 min., round-trip 60F).

Normandy
(Normandie)

Inspiration to the impressionists, fertile Normandy encompasses rolling green hills, jagged coastline, and soaring cathedrals. This province has had a history separate from that of the rest of France. Seized by Vikings in the ninth century, Normandy was officially recognized as independent in 911, when the French king acknowledged the domination of the Norsemen (a name later corrupted to "Normans"). The great age of Norman independence, during which the Normans continued to expand their territory, lasted from the tenth to the thirteenth century. During this period, the Normans also created their greatest architectural monuments, a string of ornate cathedrals, each more impossible than the last, as if in hope that God would always favor the land that had so favored God.

During the Hundred Years' War, the English invaded and held Normandy—despite strong resistance. As a result of one such victory, Joan of Arc was captured by the English and burnt at the stake in Rouen for heresy. When the British were finally overthrown, they left behind a deep imprint on the customs, crafts, and cuisine of the area; Protestantism maintains its only French stronghold here. When the British returned, they were accompanied by their American and Canadian allies on D-Day, June 6, 1944.

Rouen, capital of upper Normandy, blends glorious Gothic architecture with the half-timbered houses of the old quarter. The city also serves as a base for touring the abbeys and parks of the Val du Seine and the coastal resorts of Dieppe, Fécamp, and Etretat. Caen, capital of Lower Normandy and William the Conqueror's favorite city, is a vibrant university town that has preserved its architectural heritage despite World War II bombings. It lies close to the faded but elegant seaside resorts of Deauville, Trouville, and Cabourg.

North of Bayeux are the Commonwealth D-Day landing beaches—there is a battle museum at Arromanches—and, farther west, the American landing beaches of Omaha and Utah. Here the rugged and tourist-shy Cotentin Peninsula begins; its magnificent crags battle with savage tides. On the other side of the peninsula stands Mont St-Michel, an eleventh-century abbey built on its own sea-encircled rock, where tourists outnumber the monks by 800,000 to one, and the tides are the highest in Europe.

Accessible by ferry from England and Ireland and by hovercraft from England, the Norman ports of Le Havre, Dieppe, and Cherbourg greet travelers coming to France. Within Normandy, major towns are connected by rail, but smaller towns are often connected only by bus. SNCF buses are covered by railpass; STN (Société de Transport Nationale) buses are not. Since many of the most memorable spots lie off the main roads, a bike or car is helpful for extended touring. Cyclists should keep in mind that the roads are hilly and the coastal winds blow roughly west-to-east.

Famous for its produce and dairy products, Normandy supplies a large percentage of the nation's butter. Try the creamy, pungent *camembert* cheese, but be sure it's ripe (soft in the middle). The province's traditional drink, *cidre,* is a hard cider that comes both dry (*brut*) and sweet (*doux*). *Calvados,* apple brandy aged 12 to 15 years, ranks with the finest, most lethal cognacs. In many places, you can buy from the farmers themselves; never offend the Norman's traditional sense of hospitality by turning down the offer of a cup of coffee that may greet you on such an occasion.

Like many of the provinces, Normandy is known for its conservatism. You might decide to leave your army pants in the backpack, especially if hitching. On the

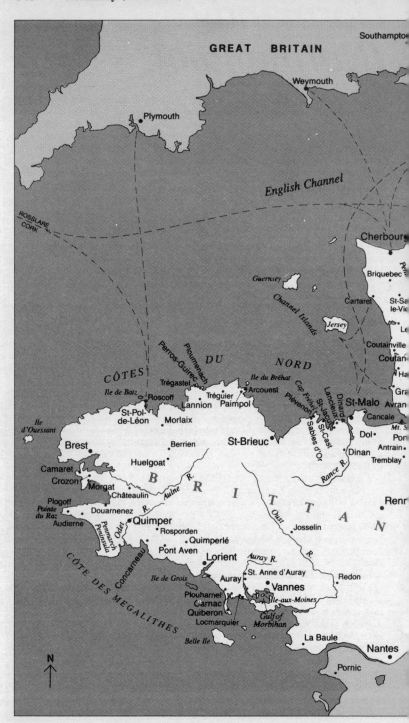

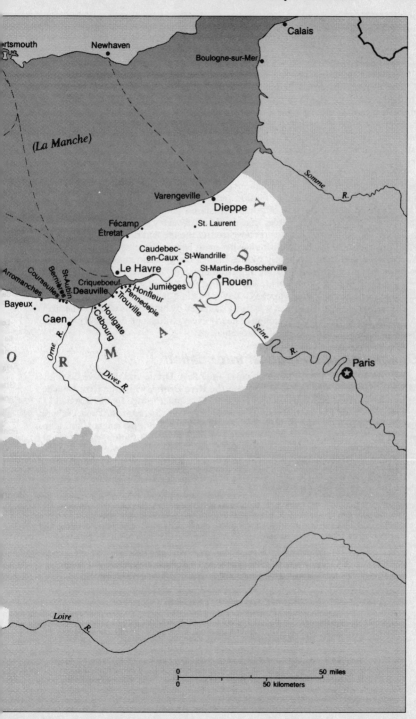

brighter side, women will encounter fewer hassles from men in proper, polite Normandy than in almost any other province.

Rouen

Joan of Arc was burned here, and Emma Bovary was bored here—but don't let the bad press deter you from visiting Rouen, one of France's most historically rich cities. Rouen has paid the highest tribute to its colorful past by building a flourishing present alongside it. Despite its bustling industry, the city's vital center is still the old town, a lively mixture of architectural styles. The businesspeople, students, tourists, and inflated prices, however, constantly remind you that this is no provincial town.

From the tenth through the twelfth century, Rouen enjoyed great prestige and power as capital of a large Norman empire that controlled much of France and spanned the channel to England. Gothic architecture blossomed at this time: Victor Hugo dubbed Rouen the city of a hundred spires, and visitors today still admire the towers, gargoyles, and gables that embellish Rouen's skyline.

Rouen's most famous legends revolve around the life and death of Joan of Arc. Held prisoner here by the English after her great campaign across France, she was interrogated and tried for heresy by the French clergy. Joan stood firm for three months and was sentenced to life imprisonment. Still not satisfied, the English pressed for a heavier punishment, and in May, 1431, Joan was burnt at the stake in Rouen's place du Vieux Marché, today a bustling marketplace.

During World War II, Rouen was badly damaged by both German and American bombing. The current reconstruction of nearly every church and dozens of medieval houses renders Rouen a haven for stonemasons.

Orientation and Practical Information

The Seine divides Rouen into two parts—the Rive Droite and the Rive Gauche. Most sights are located in the old city on the **Rive Droite,** while the **Rive Gauche** comprises modern buildings and wide avenues—a quiet refuge for the harried.

Rouen is served frequently by trains from Paris's Gare St-Lazare (70 min.). There are two train stations, the Rive Gauche and Rive Droite, but passenger trains stop only at the Rive Droite. To get to the center of town from that station, walk straight down rue Jeanne d'Arc for several blocks. A left on rue du Gros Horloge leads to place de la Cathédrale and the *syndicat;* a right leads to place du Vieux Marché. Continuing straight on rue Jeanne d'Arc will bring you to a bridge where you can cross the Seine to the Rive Gauche.

Syndicat d'Initiative: 25, place de la Cathédrale (tel. 35-71-41-77), opposite the cathedral. The friendly staff speaks English, and will book you a room for 9F. If you plan to stay for a while, pick up a free map and the restaurant and leisure guide, *Le P'tit Normand,* covering the Rouen area (40F). Open Easter-Sept. 15 Mon.-Sat. 9am-12:30pm and 1:30-7pm, Sun. 9am-12:30pm and 2:30-6pm; in off-season Mon.-Sat. 9am-noon and 2-7pm.

Student Travel: Voyage Wasteels, 111bis, rue Jeanne d'Arc (tel. 35-71-92-56). BIJ tickets. Youth railcards. Open Mon.-Fri. 9am-noon and 2-7pm, Sat. 9am-noon and 2-6pm.

Post Office: 45, rue Jeanne d'Arc (tel. 35-71-33-86). Poste Restante and **currency exchange.** Postal code: 76000. Open Mon.-Fri. 8am-7pm, Sat. 8am-noon.

Train Station: Rue Jeanne d'Arc (tel. 35-98-50-50). To Paris (at least 1 per hr., 70 min., 80F), Dieppe (every 1-2 hr., 40 min., 45F), Caen (every 1½-2½ hr., 2½ hr., 86F), and Le Havre (1 per hr., 50 min., 54F). Information office open Mon.-Sat. 8:30am-7:30pm, Sun. 9am-6pm.

Bus Station: SATAR, rue des Charettes (tel. 35-71-81-71), by the river, off rue Jeanne d'Arc. Outrageously expensive. Bus #163 to Dieppe (4 per day, 2 hr., 55F), #191/192 to Le Havre (every 1-2 hr., 3 hr., 65F), #261 to and from Fécamp (1 per day, 2¼ hr.). For more information, see Near Rouen. Information office open Mon.-Thurs. 8am-noon and 1:50-5:45pm, Fri. 8am-noon and 1:15-6pm, Sat. 8-11:30am.

Local Bus Service: TCAR, 79, rue Thiers (tel. 35-98-02-43). Information office open Mon.-Fri. 8-11:45am and 1:45-5:30pm.

Bike Rental: 21, rue des Bonnetiers (tel. 35-70-04-04). Bicycles 35F per morning (9am-noon) or afternoon (noon-7pm), 60F per day, deposit 300F. Scooters 100F per morning or afternoon, 180F per day, deposit 2000F.

Hitching: For Paris and Caen, take bus #12 to the end of the line. For Dieppe, take bus #2 or 8 to Déville. For Le Havre, get on autoroute du Havre, which starts in the center of town (you'll still have to wait). For destinations on the right bank of the Seine (Duclair, Jumièges, St-Wandrille), take bus #19 ("Mesnil-Esnard") to Cantelen, an easier hitch. **Allostop,** 70, rue d'Amiens (tel. 35-71-45-10), off rue de la République, matches riders with drivers for 40F per journey, plus 16 centimes per km. Open Mon.-Sat. 2-7pm.

Open Market: Tues.-Sun. 8am-2pm in place du Vieux Marché; Sun. 8am-noon in place St-Marc.

Laundromat: 79, rue Beauvoisine, fairly central. Wash 10F, dry 25F. Open daily 7am-10pm. Also near the hostel on rue Lafayette, off place St-Sever. Wash 10F, dry 2F per 7½ min. Stock up on 2F pieces.

SOS Amitié: Tel. 35-60-52-52. 24-hour counseling.

Hospital: Hôpital Charles Nicole, rue Edouard (tel. 35-08-81-81), or **Hôtel Dieu,** 51, rue de Lecat (tel. 35-89-81-30).

Medical Emergency: Tel. 15.

Police: 7, rue Brisout de Barneville (tel. 35-88-40-88).

Police Emergency: Tel. 17.

Accommodations and Camping

Surprisingly, finding a room in Rouen is more difficult in the off-season than in the summer. Because Rouen is more an industrial than a tourist city, accommodations are tight on weekdays from September to March. The cheaper lodgings are on the quiet side streets, which are actually more interesting than the busier areas. Most hotels lock their doors early; be sure to get a night key.

Auberge de Jeunesse (IYHF), 17, rue Diderot (tel. 35-72-06-45), on the Rive Gauche 2km from the station. Take bus #12 from the station or from rue Jeanne d'Arc and ride to rue Diderot. Or walk straight from the station down rue Jeanne d'Arc across the bridge, where the street becomes first av. Cartier and then av. de Bretagne; take the first left after rue Blaise Pascal onto rue Diderot (30 min.). Modern and chaotic; often full of schoolchildren. Dining room open late for socializing. Kitchen. 53F includes breakfast and linen. Lockout 10am-5pm. Curfew 11pm.

University Housing, available through **CROUS,** 3, rue d'Herbouville (tel. 35-98-44-50). Take bus #10 from the town center. Call before you arrive. The Cité Universitaire is 3km from the center of town, in Mont St-Aignan. You will need a student ID and an extra photo. 48F per night. Open June-Sept.

Hôtel Normandya, 32, rue du Cordier (tel. 35-71-46-15), between Tour Jeanne d'Arc and rue Beauvoisine. Very respectable and attractive rooms. Singles and doubles 80F, with shower 110F.

Hostellerie de Vieux Logis, 5, rue de Joyeuse (tel. 35-71-55-30). Classy, cozy rooms run by a friendly proprietor. May be full during the week. Great restaurant downstairs. Singles 66F. Doubles 75F.

Hôtel la Cache-Ribaud, 10, rue du Tambour (tel. 35-71-04-82), centrally located right off rue du Gros Horloge. Fairly elegant. Firm mattresses make this a rare find. Singles or doubles 70F. Singles with bath 95F. Rooms with 2 beds 100F. Breakfast 14F. Their *menu* (75-105F) is about the closest you'll get to Norman *haute cuisine* at a decent price—*mousse de foie gras, terrine de légumes, charlotte russe.*

Hôtel St-Ouen, 43, rue des Faulx (tel. 35-71-46-41), across from Eglise St-Ouen. Large, pleasant rooms. Singles and doubles 60-73F. Breakfast 13F. Curfew 10pm; get a key. Open Mon.-Sat.

Hôtel du Palais, 12, rue Tambour (tel. 35-71-41-40), next door to la Cache-Ribaud. Clean, carpeted, colorful rooms. Singles and doubles with shower 90F.

Camping: Camping Municipal at Déville, rue Jules Ferry in Déville-les-Rouen (tel. 35-74-07-59), 4km from Rouen. Take bus #2 from the ironworks museum (3 per hr., last at 9pm), or bus #161/163 from the *gare routière* (1 per hr., last at 8pm). Attractive sites with squeaky clean bathrooms.

Food

Local specialties include duck *pâté, sole normande,* and *tripe à la normandaise.* A mouth-watering range of fish, cheese, fruit, and vegetables is available from the *traiteurs* (food vendors) in and around place du Vieux Marché—go before noon to prepare your own food. On quieter side streets you'll find cheaper goods. If staying at the hostel, shop at Centre Commercial St-Sever, place de la Verrerie, better known as the *supermarché.*

Hostellerie du Vieux Logis, 5, rue de Joyeuse (tel. 35-71-55-30). Cozy with overstuffed chairs, candlelight, and a garden view. Lots of food and wine for only 60F. Make reservations for evening meals. Open noon-1pm and 7-8pm.

Bar des Fleurs, place des Carmes (tel. 35-71-93-30). One of Rouen's most animated and authentic gathering places, often with live music in the evening. Stick to the fish specialties. *Menus* 60F and 83F, *à la carte* 25-47F, *plat du jour* 34F. Seating 7-9pm.

La Galette, 168, rue Beauvoisine (tel. 35-71-91-64). *Galettes* (whole-wheat crêpes) 6-21F: shrimp 18F, mushroom 18F, salmon in cream sauce 34F. Open Sept.-July Mon-Fri. noon-2pm and 7:30pm-midnight, Sat. 7:30pm-midnight.

Crêperie Ty Briez, 5, rue du Père Adam, off rue d'Amiens near Eglise St-Ouen. *Galettes* 8.50-35F, 3-course *menu* with cider or beer 40F. Dessert crêpes 7-17F, gourmet dessert crêpes 22-30F. Open Tues.-Sat. noon-1:30pm and 7pm-midnight. *Menu* not served after 10pm.

Les Flandres, 5, rue des Bons-Enfants (tel. 35-98-45-16). Simple, filling *menu* 55F; *plats du jour* 32F. Friendly, unpretentious atmosphere. Open Mon.-Fri. noon-1:30pm and 7:30-9:15pm, Sat. noon-1:30pm.

Restaurant Le Lotus, 100, rue Gauterie (tel. 35-89-45-50). Vietnamese and French fare. *Menu* 65F. Open Mon. 7-11pm, Tues.-Sun. noon-2:30pm and 7-11pm.

Maison de Regime, 59, rue Ganturie. A health food store. Helpful proprietors. Good selection. Open Mon. 2-7pm, Tues.-Sat. 9am-7pm.

Sights and Entertainment

Rouen defines the word Gothic—around every corner buildings stand encased in filigreed stone carving. For efficiency, follow the sequence described below, and try to do your sightseeing from 10am to noon and from 2 to 6pm, the hours during which most of the sights are open. Churches open earlier. Admission to all attractions 12F, with student ID free. This includes the Gros Horloge, the Musée des Beaux Arts, the Ironworks Museum, and the newly opened Musée de la Céramique.

Its central spire piercing the sky, **Cathédrale de Notre Dame** dominates the center of old Rouen. Built between the twelfth and the sixteenth century, it incorporates nearly every intermediate style of Gothic architecture. Unfortunately, the facade that fascinated Monet is now black with soot, but current renovations should return it to a gleaming white. Inside, the four-story nave and lantern tower culminate in the pure line of the choir. The disturbing asymmetry is due to damage sustained early in World War II.

Behind the cathedral stands flamboyant **Eglise St-Maclou.** Dating from the fifteenth century, its curved west front incorporates one of the greatest collections of gables and sculpture of any Gothic church. Beyond the church, turn left into 186, rue de Martinville, where a small passageway leads to the **Aitre St-Maclou,** the church's former charnel house, which saw much use during the great plagues of the Middle Ages. Appropriately, its wooden beams bear a gory fifteenth-century frieze of the *danse macabre.* Today, in a happier incarnation, the building houses

Rouen's Ecole des Beaux-Arts. (Open daily 9am-6pm.) Up rue Damiette and rue Boucheries, next to the Hôtel de Ville, is **Eglise St-Ouen** (begun in 1318), the purest expression of Gothic architecture in Rouen. Its towering vaults are second in height only to those of Beauvais. The entrance, somewhat difficult to find, is on the side, through the Marmouset Portal.

The **Musée des Antiquités,** in Cloître Ste-Marie, 198, rue Beauvoisine, houses a collection of Egyptian, Gallo-Roman, Merovingian, and Renaissance relics, mostly from local sources. Mosaics, bronzes, earthenware, carvings, and the magnificent fifteenth-century tapestry *Cerfs Ailés* (*Winged Stags*) are among the exhibits. (Open Fri.-Wed. 10am-noon and 2-5:30pm. Admission 4F, ages over 65 2F, students and teachers with ID free.) The **Tour Jeanne d'Arc** on rue de Donjon is the last remaining tower of the château where Joan was imprisoned. The display inside contains material relating to the trial. (Open Fri.-Wed. 10am-noon and 2-5pm. Free.)

On rue Thiers is Rouen's superb **Musée des Beaux Arts.** (Open Wed.-Mon. 10am-noon and 2-6pm.) The galleries overflow with the works of artists from Rubens to Monet, including many local impressionist paintings and an entire room of Géricaults. **Place Verdrel,** in front of the Musée des Beaux Arts, offers some beautiful spots for a picnic, with a waterfall, sloping lawns, and lots of shade. Next to the Musée des Beaux Arts, housed in a fifteenth-century church, is the **Musée de Ferronnerie Le-Secq-des-Tournelles** (Ironworks Museum), rue Jacques-Villon, with an unusual collection of fancy grillwork, locks, keys, and other household objects in iron, dating from the third to the nineteenth century.

Walk along rue aux Juifs to find the elaborately decorated **Palais de Justice.** Though the interior was restored after World War II, the facade, crawling with gargoyles, still bears large pock marks inflicted by heavy shelling. Rouen's most mysterious attraction, the **Monument Juif,** was recently discovered during excavation around the Palais de Justice. Unfortunately, the tourist office has chosen an inappropriate day to open the underground, eleventh-century synagogue; you must arrange to take the tourist office's guided tour in French on Saturday at 2pm. (April-Sept. and Oct.-March only. Admission 22F, ages under 25 and over 65 17F.)

Rouen's most unusual church is **Eglise Jeanne d'Arc,** place du Vieux Marché, built on the site of her execution. Opened in 1979 by former president Giscard d'Estaing, its whimsical, modern structure resembles a hydrofoil. Avoid the slipshod Joan of Arc museum opposite the church.

Off place du Vieux Marché is the center of all tourist activity—rue du Gros Horloge, a crowded, noisy pedestrian zone crammed with shops and cafes. Halfway down the street, the **Gros Horloge** was built into a bridge spanning the thoroughfare and telling the time with charming imprecision. The platform above the clock overlooks the cathedral and the city.

Dramatist **Pierre Corneille's** home is at 4, rue de la Pie, off place du Vieux Marché. (Open Wed. afternoon-Mon. Admission 2F, students free.) Novelist **Gustave Flaubert** grew up at 51, rue de Lecat. (Open Tues.-Sat. 10am-noon and 2-6pm. Free.) **Croisset,** where Flaubert wrote *Madame Bovary,* burned down in 1986. It's not really worth a visit—all that remains is a museum commemorating Flaubert's father.

You may want to visit the newly-opened **Musée de l'Education,** rue Eau de Robec, as much for the tourist-free ancient quarter around it as for the annual exhibit on some aspect of the history of French education. (Admission 5F.)

And after a hard day's sightseeing, you can relax in the shade of the luxurious **Jardin des Plantes,** off rue St-Julien on the Rive Gauche, near the Auberge de Jeunesse. (Open May-July daily 9am-6pm.)

For nocturnal diversion, try the **Bar des Fleurs,** place des Carmes; **"Brasserie Bavaroise" Taverne Walsheim,** 260, rue Martinville; or **La Rotonde,** 61bis, rue St-Sever. **Exo 7,** 6km to the south of Rouen, is very popular among the youth of the city, and well worth the trek. In the past, this disco/club has welcomed such talents as Graham Parker and the Stray Cats, in addition to many reggae groups. Simply getting there is an adventure: Take bus #5, get off at place des Chartreux in Petit

Quévilly, and stick out your thumb. To return, you're on your own, as bus service stops at 10pm. Call ahead (tel. 35-72-28-92).

From the end of May through early July, Rouen celebrates the balmy days of summer in the **Festival d'Eté de Seine Maritime.** The fabulous program offers an unusual range of events including classical and Baroque music, theatre, and water ballet; there are the usual street exhibits and fireworks as well. For tickets and information, call 35-70-04-07, or write to La Maison du Festival, Chapelle St-Louis, Place de la Rougemare, 76000 Rouen.

Near Rouen

From Rouen to Le Havre, the Seine meanders through protected forest and apple orchards. In this undisturbed part of Normandy, Benedictine monks founded their great abbeys in the seventeenth century. Today, many exceptional ruins and spectacular abbeys still grace the countryside. Only 15 minutes away on bus #3 trembles the lush **Forêt Verte,** a perfect picnic spot.

Bus #191/192, leaving from the *gare routière* for Le Havre, will take you on the D982 along the Seine, through remote villages of half-timbered houses. Service is frequent (18 buses per day), but the price is exorbitant. (To Le Havre 2¾ hr., 58F.) You can get off at any of the villages along the way and get back on the next bus.

Twelfth-century **Abbaye St-Georges** in St-Martin de Boscherville, with its rounded arches and pyramidal towers, remains a masterpiece of Romanesque architecture, rarer than Gothic in this area. (Fare to St-Martin de Boscherville 15F.) The abbey lies a mere 10-minute walk from the bus stop (follow the signs). (Open April-Oct. Wed.-Mon. 10am-noon and 2:30-6:30pm. Admission 9F.) In **Jumièges,** about 4km off the D982, the gorgeous ruins of what was once a majestic eleventh-century Romanesque church, the **Ancienne Abbaye Notre Dame,** stand mysteriously in a half-forgotten pastoral landscape. (Open April-Sept. 10am-noon and 2-6pm; Oct.-March 10am-noon and 2-4pm. Admission 11F.) You will probably have to walk the 4km from Yainville, the closest bus stop. The only bus serving this region (still #191/192) goes all the way to Jumièges once per day (24F); the area is not served by train.

About 10km farther down D982 in the tiny village of St-Wandrille is the **Abbaye St-Wandrille** (tel. 35-96-23-11). There's no need to imagine the ancient setting here: The monks still live, work, and perform their devotions according to the 1500-year-old Benedictine rule. Mass is performed in Gregorian chant in a simple building next to the ruins of a Gothic church (Mon.-Sat. at 9:30am, Sun. 10am; vespers Mon.-Wed. and Fri.-Sat. at 5:30pm, Thurs. 6:45pm, Sun. and holidays 5pm). An amusing monk leads guided tours of the cloister and other buildings (12F). (Fare to St-Wandrille 33F.)

Both Jumièges and St-Wandrille are located within the **Parc Naturel Régional de Brotonne,** a protected area of forests and hills perfectly suited for camping, fishing, and riding. A picturesque campsite sits next to an outdoor recreational center at Jumièges-le-Mesnil: The **Camping Municipal** at **Base de plein air et de loisirs Jumièges-le-Mesnil** (tel. 35-91-93-84) is 3km down the hill on the main road from the ruins of l'Abbaye de Jumièges. (Open May-Aug. daily.) For more information on activities and licensing, contact Centre Administratif du Parc, 2, Rond-Point Marbec, 76580 Le Trait (tel. 35-37-23-16).

Caudebec-en-Caux is a few kilometers beyond St-Wandrille in the heart of the Parc de Brotonne, still on the #191/192 bus line. A large network of long and short hiking trails reaches out from here into the forested hills behind the town. As the town itself is not the most interesting, you'll want to start hiking as soon as possible. The Caudebec **Syndicat d'Initiative,** rue Thomas Basin (tel. 35-96-20-65), is up rue des Boucheries. (Open July-Aug. daily 10am-noon and 3-6:30pm; Easter-June and Sept. Sat. afternoon and Sun. only.) When it's closed, bring your inquiries to the *mairie* (tel. 35-96-11-12), a palatial building by the river and past the miniature golf course. A two-star **campsite** is about 1km beyond the town hall by the riverside (tel. 35-96-11-12; open April 13-Aug. 29). On the last Sunday in September, Caudebec hosts the **Festival du Cidre,** the region's largest folk festival, with cider flowing freely. (Fare to Caudebec-en-Caux 35F.)

Along the Seine south of Rouen lies **Giverny,** site of Claude Monet's pink-painted home and flowery garden, where the impressionist lived from 1883 to 1926. Monet painted his famous water lily series in the water garden here. The property was opened to the public as the **Musée Monet** (tel. 32-51-28-21) only five years ago. (Open April-Oct. Tues.-Sun. 10am-6pm; Nov.-March Tues.-Sun. 10am-noon and 2-6pm.) The gardens themselves are open all day and are a great place for a picnic. Giverny lies across from Vernon on the Rouen-Paris St-Lazare train line, and is not accessible by public transportation. Biking is a popular option.

Near the intersection of N182 and N138 in the Risle Valley sits **Notre-Dame du Bec-Hellouin.** The religious community here provided Canterbury with three archbishops, and the abbey boasts a fifteenth-century tower and Maurian-style cloister. **Le Bec-Hellouin** is 16km from Rouen, but perhaps the easiest way to reach it is to take the daily train from Paris to Evreux, and catch a bus from there.

Coast: Upper Normandy

Overlooking both the white cliffs along the coast and the fertile interior, the road from Dieppe to Le Havre passes through some of the most spectacular Norman countryside. Hitching is easier inland on D925, but the twisting coastal road offers spectacular panoramas. Trains frequently connect the larger towns of Dieppe, Fécamp, and Le Havre, but do not stop at any other towns along the upper coast. Cycling is best for exploring, though the CNA (Compagnie Normande d'Autobus) bus service will shuttle you up and down the steep hills more easily. Be prepared to spend the night wherever you disembark, because the next bus will probably arrive the next day. Buses do not run on Sunday, and depart in the afternoon only from Dieppe.

Eight kilometers south of Dieppe, but inaccessible by bus or train, is **Varengeville.** Because of the proximity, cycling is the way to go, but be prepared for some challenging slopes. Take a right off Varengeville's main road, and you'll come upon the **Parc Floral des Moutiers** (tel. 35-85-10-02), botanical gardens of unusual variety planted in 1900. (Open Easter-Nov. Mon. and Thurs.-Sat. 10am-noon and 2-7pm, Wed. and Sun. 2-7pm. Admission 4F.) Half a mile farther on, a beautiful twelfth-century Romanesque church surrounded by a thirteenth- to fifteenth-century maritime cemetery perches at the end of a rocky outcrop of coastal cliffs, commanding a sweeping view of the bay. Georges Braque, who designed the stained-glass windows for the church that replaced those destroyed in the war, was buried here. Also in Varengeville is **Manoir d'Ange,** a grandiose ensemble of Renaissance buildings, but it lies far from the main road and is a rip-off at 25F per person. (Open March-Oct. 2-7pm.)

A bit farther inland, toward Rouen, lies a tranquil beech forest. Guy de Maupassant was born August 5, 1850, in the nearby **Château de Miromesnil** (don't pronounce the s), which his mother rented to ensure him a noble birth, and in which he spent his first three years. Call ahead (tel. 35-04-40-30) and ask to be guided by Count Bertrand de Vogüé, the château's present inhabitant, who gives delightful tours when he is free. (Open May-Oct. 15 Wed.-Mon. 2-6pm. Admission 10F.)

Fécamp, two-thirds of the way to Le Havre from Dieppe, takes pride in being both an important deep-sea fishing port and a resort. The **bus station** on 8, av. Gambetta (tel. 35-28-16-04), behind Eglise St-Etienne, is served by two companies: **Auto-Car Gris,** which serves Le Havre via Goderville (8 per day) or via Etretat (5 per day), and **Compagnie Normande d'Autobus,** which runs to Rouen via Yvetot and Dieppe via St-Valéry-en-Caux. The **gare** on bd. de la République (tel. 35-28-03-11), down the steps from av. Gambetta, offers more frequent service. (Open Mon.-Fri. 5-6:30am and 8am-8pm, Sat. 8am-noon and 2-8:20pm.) Trains run from Dieppe (3 per day, 2 hr., 80F), Le Havre (6 per day, 1¼ hr., 34F), and Paris (7 per day,

21/3 hr., 112F). The town enjoys renown for its massive eleventh-century **Abbatiale de la Trinité.** The dimensions and harmony of the church are awe-inspiring: The nave is as long as that of Notre Dame de Paris, and the tower at the transept crossing rises some 70m. (Open May-Oct. Mon.-Sat. 11am-3pm, Sun. 11am-5pm.) To fully appreciate this "book in stone," you must rent two cassettes (10F and 15F) at the **Syndicat d'Initiative,** place Bellet (tel. 35-28-20-51), across from the theater. (Open in summer daily 10am-12:30pm and 2:30-6:30pm; in off-season Tues.-Sat. 9:30am-noon and 2-5:30pm.) In summer, a branch office operates on quai Vicomte (tel. 35-29-16-34) by the beach (same hours). Fécamp produces the celebrated Benedictine liqueur, distilled from aromatic plants that grow on the cliffs nearby. Guided tours of the factory, **Musée de la Bénédictine,** 110, rue Alexandre-le-Grand (tel. 35-28-00-06), last around 45 minutes and cost 15F, including a sample. (Open Easter-Nov. 11 daily 9:30-11:30am and 2-5:30pm. Without tasting ages 14-18 and over 65 6F, ages under 14 free.)

For accommodations in Fécamp, try **Hôtel du Commerce,** 28, place Bigot (tel. 35-28-19-28; rooms 65-90F, breakfast 17F), or the luxurious two-star **Hôtel de la Poste,** 4, av. Gambetta (tel. 35-29-55-11; doubles 118F). Fécamp's newly restored **Auberge de Jeunesse (IYHF),** above the town on rue du Commandant Roguigny (tel. 35-29-75-79), requires a short uphill climb from the station. (Open May-Sept. 1, but call before you go. 35F per person with IYHF card, camping 15F.) On the other side of town, **Camping Château de Reneville** (tel. 35-28-20-97), a nice two-star site with hot water, commands a good view over the beach. (8.20F per person, ages 4-7 4.10F. 2.70F per tent, 2.70F per car.)

Etretat, a much smaller coastal resort, stands guarded by its two famed portals of granite, the natural cliff arches of the **Falaise d'Amon** and the **Falaise d'Aval.** These breathtaking cliffs, which plunge undaunted into the tumbling surf, frame the town's beach and harbor perfectly. They inspired a dazzling Monet series and prove as spectacular in life. A walk around the base of the Falaise d'Aval (possible only at low tide) reveals that the whole cliff has been honeycombed with block houses and gun-emplacements now plastered with seaweed and barnacles. In town, **Eglise de Notre-Dame,** a twelfth-century Romanesque structure, has a magnificent, light-filled nave. The **Syndicat d'Initiative,** place de la Mairie (tel. 35-27-05-21), provides free help with accommodations and touring. You can pick up a table of tides in the office to find times for exploring the base of the cliffs. (Open daily 9:30am-12:30pm and 3-6pm, Sun. 10am-12:30pm.) For accommodations, try **Hôtel de la Poste,** 6, av. Georges V (tel. 35-27-01-34). Singles are 80F, with shower 112F, additional beds 20-30F. Breakfast is 13.50F. **Hôtel l'Escale,** place Maréchal Foch (tel. 35-27-03-69), offers rooms for 80F, with shower 99F, with bathtub 153F. Breakfast is 13F. A three-star **campground** lies about 1km from town on rue Guy de Maupassant (tel. 35-27-07-67; adults 7.50F, children 4.10F, 7.50F per car and tent). There is also an **Auberge de Jeunesse (IYHF)** in Yport (tel. 35-27-38-32), 12km north of Etretat and 7km south of the Fécamp rail station. (Open June-Sept. 1. 42F per person with hostel card, sheets 10F.) Bring your own food from town.

Dieppe

Dieppe seems to be the reflected image of Dover across the Channel; white chalk cliffs soar over a pebbly beach and port city. Far more inviting than Calais or Boulogne, it merits more than a cursory view through a ferry portal. Formerly a Victorian seaside resort, Dieppe seduced the likes of Ruskin, Beardsley, and Oscar Wilde. Today the city retains its popularity among English travelers.

Orientation and Practical Information

Dieppe is accessible by train from Rouen or from Paris's Gare St-Lazare. Service is most frequent on Sundays, when SNCF reduces the round-trip fare. Sealink runs ferries between Dieppe and Newhaven. The Sealink terminal is conveniently close to the center of town. **Grande Rue,** across from the terminal, is the main commercial street. The beach is 2 blocks to your right as you walk down Grande Rue. To get to the main train station, walk along quai Duquesne away from the Sealink terminal and the beach. The *syndicat* is to the right down bd. Général de Gaulle. From the train station, take the footpath to the left of the building across the street, and bear left through the gardens. When you get to bd. Général de Gaulle, turn right.

Syndicat d'Initiative: Bd. Général-de-Gaulle (tel. 35-84-11-77), in an annex of the Hôtel de Ville. Books rooms—a valuable service in this town—for 7F. Open May-Sept. 15 Mon.-Sat. 9am-noon and 2-7pm, Sun. 9am-noon and 2-6pm; Sept. 16-April daily 9am-noon and 2-6pm. **Annex,** by the beach, Rotonde de la Plage (tel. 35-84-28-70). Open July.-Aug. only.

Currency Exchange: Banks in Dieppe are open Tues.-Sat. 9am-noon and 2-5:30pm. Also at the **train station.**

Post Office: 2, bd. Maréchal Joffre (tel. 35-82-16-00). **Postal Code:** 76200. Open Mon.-Fri. 8am-6pm, Sat. 8am-noon.

Train Station: Bd. G. Clemenceau (tel. 35-98-50-50). To Paris St-Lazare (every 1-2 hr., 2½ hr., 82F), Rouen (every 1-2 hr., ¾-1¼ hr., 36F), Caen (change at Rouen, 104F), and Le Havre (change at Rouen, 73F). Ticket office open daily 6am-8pm. Information office (tel. 35-84-23-32) open Mon.-Sat. 9am-noon and 2-6:15pm, Sun. 9am-noon and 3-6pm.

Bus Station: Compagnie Normande d'Autobus, next to the train station (tel. 35-84-21-97). To Rouen (3 per day, 1¾ hr., 48F) and Fécamp (1 per day, 2½ hr., 51F). Also **Dieppe-Voyage** (tel. 35-84-21-61 or 35-82-31-01).

Ferries: Sealink, quai Henri IV, *gare maritime* (tel. 35-84-22-60). To Newhaven (late July-Aug. 6 per day, April-late July and Aug. to mid-Sept. 5 per day, mid-Sept. to March 4 per day, less frequent in Jan.; 4 hr.; one way 210F, with InterRail one way 151F, 60-hr. round-trip 216F).

Bike Rental: At the train station (tel. 35-84-20-71). 28F per ½-day, 33F per day, deposit 190F. Open daily 6am-8:30pm.

Laundromat: 46, rue de l'Epée (tel. 35-82-64-36), near the pedestrian district.

Hospital: Av. Pasteur (tel. 35-82-20-75).

Police: 68, quai Duquesne (tel. 35-84-87-32).

Police Emergency: Tel. 17.

Accommodations and Camping

Unless you have a reservation, it will be nearly impossible to find a room here in summer. Start early in the day, or better, call two or three days ahead, and make use of the *syndicat.*

Auberge de Jeunesse (IYHF), rue Louis Fromager (tel. 35-84-85-73). The "Janval" bus opposite the *syndicat* on bd. de Gaulle stops nearby, but makes only 3 trips per day. If you walk, turn left outside the station, turn right 4 blocks farther on rue de la République, then turn sharply left on rue Gambetta. Go approximately 300m up a hill, then turn right on av. Jean Jaurès, and left on rue Fromager. Continue straight and the hostel will be on the right (25 min.). A stopover for noisy English schoolchildren. Helpful and friendly management. Showers amd kitchen facilities. 40F. Closed 9:30am-5:30pm. Curfew 10:30pm.

Hôtel au Grand Duquesne, 15, place St-Jacques (tel. 35-84-21-51). Decent rooms and friendly proprietors. Singles 82F, with shower 99F. Breakfast 14F. Hearty meals available in their restaurant.

Hôtel de la Jetée, 5, rue de l'Asile Thomas (tel. 35-84-89-98), near the beach. Pleasant rooms, many with an ocean view. Exceptionally friendly management is fond of *Let's Go.* Singles and doubles 95F, with bathroom 140F.

Camping: Camping du Pollet, Tel. 35-84-32-87. A unique 2-star site east of the city, overlooking the ferry traffic of the port. From quai Duquesne, turn left to cross the port, then turn left again on the other side. The site is opposite the Sealink terminal. Bus-stop nearby. **Camping Pré-St-Nicholas,** route de Pourville (tel. 35-84-11-39), on top of the cliff 3km west of the city, and a 25-min. climb from the station. A 2-star site. Sells expensive hot food and groceries. Rather primitive showers.

Food

Stay away from the neighborhood around the Sealink terminal, and look for the local fish specialties: *sole dieppoise, harengs marinés* (marinated herring), *soupe de poisson* (fish soup), and *marmite dieppoise* (a fish and shellfish chowder). If you're cooking for yourself, buy fish at the port center. There are several **supermarkets** on rue Duquesne and rue Gambetta (near the hostel). Unlike Calais and Bologne, which bombard British visitors with *friteries,* Dieppe offers authentic fare at decent prices. For inauthentic fare, **Cafétéria le Viking,** near the hostel on rue Gambetta at rue Jaurès, will fill you up for 30F or less. **Crêperie,** 22, rue de la Morinière (tel. 35-40-01-71), flips up a mouth-watering selection of *galettes* for 17-30F *à la carte.* **Le Pacha,** 20, rue Parmentier (tel. 35-82-54-01), specializes in tantalizing your taste-buds with their *couscous* (45F). (Open Thurs.-Mon. noon-2pm and 7-10pm, Wed. 7-10pm.) Delight your palate and dismay your purse at **La Marine,** l'arcade de la Poissonerie (tel. 35-84-17-54), off Grande Rue; *soupe de poisson* and *sole dieppoise* are both delicious (*menus* 67F, 94F, and 119F).

Sights

While the only amphibious landing equipment on Dieppe's beaches today is commanded by windsurfers and the only invaders are tourists, the first German invasion is commemorated in the **Musée de Guerre,** 3km southwest along route de Pourville, near Camping St-Nicholas. The museum saw action as an underground radar base. (Open July-Aug. daily 10am-noon and 2-6pm; Easter-June and Sept. Tues.-Sun. 10am-noon and 2-6pm. Admission 15F.) Those staying at the hostel may want to visit the **Canadian Cemetery** in Hautot-Sur-Mer, where each identified gravestone bears an individual poem or inscription. Turn right out of the hostel, walk 15 minutes along a beautiful country road, then turn right at the cross and sign.

Dieppe's major attraction is still its beach. The pebbles scrape and prod naked backs, and the water will chill swimmers unless they venture in at the height of summer, but the view and salty air should restore fatigued backpackers. On the cliffs west of the city stands the fifteenth-century **Château,** now the civic museum, with its celebrated ivory collection, sampling of impressionist paintings, and permanent exhibit of George Braque's prints. (Open in summer daily 10am-noon and 2-6pm; in off-season Wed.-Mon. Admission 6F during special exhibits, otherwise 3F; students half-price.)

The gardens across from the station, near the *syndicat,* offer a soothing tranquility; peaceful and naturalistic, they oppose the French taste for geometric flower beds. Within, a waterfall tumbles into a meandering stream lined with willows and flower-covered banks.

Le Havre

Le Havre is France's largest transatlantic port. Most cruise ships from North America stop here as do the car ferries from Rosslare and Cork in Ireland, and Portsmouth in England. Whichever way you approach, the glut of refineries, warehouses, and factories that line the city's docks will engulf you: Still, the excitement of this brisk, bustling center is infectious.

Le Havre was bombed to rubble during World War II and since then has become an experiment in French civic design. The prevailing style is monolithic, with muscular war monuments, sprawling concrete buildings, and gaping squares—a refreshing contrast to the ornate detail characterizing the rest of Normandy. The interior of **Eglise St-Joseph,** designed by August Perret, merits examination; its thousands of glass squares refract colored light. The **Musée des Beaux Arts-André Malraux,** on bd. J. F. Kennedy (tel. 35-42-33-97), houses an airy, well-displayed collection of the canvases of Ernest Boudin and the Norman impressionists, and many works by Dufy, Pissarro, Monet, Sisley, and others. (Open Wed.-Mon. 10am-noon and 2-6pm. Admission 1F.) Most distinctive of all, the newly opened **Maison de la Culture du Havre** in l'Espace Oscar Niemeyer, place Gambetta, contains a state-of-the-art theater and cinema, which admits students into showings of classics and new films for only 20F. If post-modern architecture doesn't appeal to you, escape to the more sedate surroundings of the public park on av. Foch near the beach.

Orientation and Practical Information

Le Havre is located at the mouth of the Seine River, bordered by beach on one edge and port basins on the other. The large avenues of boulevard de Strasbourg and rue de Paris intersect at **place de Hôtel de Ville.** If you continue straight down avenue Foch, across from bd. de Strasbourg, you will arrive at the beach (10 min.).

The train station lies east of the center of town and is an easy walk down bd. de Strasbourg. The Townsend-Thoresen ferry terminal lies on the southern side of town. To get to the *syndicat* from here, take bus #3 from Perrey or walk straight down rue de Paris for about 10 minutes. The Irish Ferries terminal lies southeast and rather far from the center of town. Your best bet is to get a lift from fellow ferry passengers, or ask at the terminal for directions to the St-Nicholas bus stop on place Marion.

Office de Tourisme: Place de l'Hôtel de Ville (tel. 35-21-22-88). Turn left from the station onto bd. de Strasbourg, and walk straight for about 10 min., or take bus #1, 3, 4, 5, 6, or 12 from outside the train station. Accommodations service outside town 17F. English spoken. Open Mon.-Sat. 9am-12:15pm and 2-7pm.

American Express: 57, quai Georges V (tel. 35-42-59-11). Travel service will book anything from Transalpino to theater tickets. Open Mon.-Fri. 8:45am-noon and 1:30-6pm.

Post Office: Rue Jules-Siegfried (tel. 35-42-45-67). Poste Restante. **Currency Exchange. Postal Code:** 76600. Open Mon.-Fri. 8am-7pm, Sat. 8am-noon.

Train Station: Cours de la République (tel. 35-24-01-76). Information office open 9am-noon and 2-6pm. Ticket office open daily 7:30am-7pm. To Paris (10 per day, 2 hr., 120F), Rouen (8 per day, 45 min., 60F), and Fécamp (10 per day, 45 min., 34.50F). Baggage room open daily 5:30am-8pm (8F manual, 3F automatic).

Bus Station: Bd. de Strasbourg (tel. 35-26-67-23), across from the train station. **CNA.** To Rouen via St-Romain, Bolbec, Lillebonne, Caudebec, and Duclair. **Bus Verts.** To Caen, Deauville, and Honfleur via Pont Route de Tancarville. **Car Gris.** To Fécamp via Etretat, Yport, or Goderville, and to Etretat via Octeville. Local bus station **CGFTE,** 115, rue Jules Lecesne (tel. 35-41-72-22), and at the kiosk, place de l'Hôtel de Ville, next to the tourist office. One trip costs 10F; *carnet bleu* for 10 trips 27F. All bus service stops around 9pm.

Ferries: Pick up schedules at any travel agent or the tourist office. **Townsend-Thoresen Car Ferries,** quai de Southampton (tel. 35-21-36-50). Take bus #3 from the train station or the Hôtel de Ville. To Portsmouth, England (3 per day; 6 hr., 7 hr. at night; 272F, children 146F, same fares for round-trips within 60 hr.). Inquire about student discounts. You can reserve cabins on both day and night ferries. Information office open Mon.-Sat. 8:30am-noon and 1-8pm. Tickets available at those hours as well. **Irish Ferries,** quai du Môle Central (tel. 35-21-55-02). Take bus #4 from the Hôtel de Ville or the train station to stop Marceau. To Rosslare and Cork, Ireland (May-Sept. virtually daily; 400-580F, students 370-550F, children 126-400F depending on the day of departure; Oct.-April once every other day; 300F, students 270F, children 126F.) InterRail-holders receive a 50% discount; Eurail-holders sail for free, but must pay port taxes.

Laundromat: 23, rue Jean Fontaine. 12F per load, dry-cleaning 30F. Open daily 7am-9pm.

Hospital: 55bis, rue Gustave Flaubert (tel. 35-22-81-23).

Medical Emergency: Tel. 15. **SAMU,** Tel. 35-21-11-00.

Police: 30, place Jean-le-Brozec (tel. 35-25-22-55).

Police Emergency: Tel. 17.

Accommodations, Camping, and Food

If you find yourself in Le Havre, avoid the questionable areas around the station and the port. The **Union Crétienne des Jeunes Gens,** 153, bd. de Strasbourg (look for the triangular neon sign), is a centrally-located YMCA *foyer* for French workers that accepts anyone of either sex if it has space. Decent and dormlike, it is run by a warm and supportive staff. (Singles 37F, sheets 7F.) The cafeteria on the premises serves breakfast and lunch Monday through Saturday: *plats du jour* 15-25F. (Open daily 7am-11pm.) The pleasant **Hôtel Jeanne d'Arc,** 91, rue Emile-Zola (tel. 35-41-26-83), is also centrally located, off rue de Paris across the bridge from the tourist office. (Singles 70F. Doubles 80F. Toilet and bidet included. Breakfast 13F.) On the other side of the river sits friendly **Hôtel France,** 85, rue Louis Brindeau (tel. 35-41-79-96). (Singles 80F, with shower 100F, with bath 105-150F. Breakfast 18F. Open daily 7am-noon and 4:30pm-midnight.) Across the street at #86, the two-star **Hôtel Petit Vatel** (tel. 35-41-72-07) offers one-star prices. (Singles 100F, with shower 120F.) **Hôtel Séjour Fleuri,** 71, rue Emile Zola (tel. 35-41-33-81), has comfortable rooms for 85-95F. (Showers 20F. Breakfast 14F.) To get to Le Havre's **Camping Municipal** (tel. 35-46-52-39) from the station, take bus #5 (last bus at 9:05pm) or bus #71 (last bus at 8:30pm) to Jenner and walk the last 20 minutes. Hot showers, ping-pong, and a nearby grocery make your stay more pleasant. (10F per person, ages 4-14 5F. 7F per tent, 6.50F per car. Open Easter-Sept. 30. Gates closed 11pm-6:30am.)

Good food abounds in the small streets between rue de Paris and quai Lamblardie. **Le Tilbury,** 39, rue Jean de la Fontaine (tel. 35-21-23-50), serves an elegant 60F *menu. A la carte* dishes run 25-60F; an 80F *menu* is served Sat. night and Sun. (Open Tues. 7-10pm, Wed.-Sun. noon-1:30pm and 7-10pm.) On the same street at #17, the small **Crêperie Bretonne** (tel. 35-42-11-67) serves crêpes for 6-16F in a familial atmosphere. (Open Tues.-Sat. noon-2pm and 7-11pm, Sun. noon-2pm.) **Le P'tit Comptoir,** rue de la Fontaine and av. Faidherbe (tel. 35-42-78-72), right by the port, serves up a hearty *menu* for 55F. (Open daily 10am-2pm and 7-10pm.) Be sure to visit the **Maison des Jeunes et de la Culture,** av. Foch (tel. 35-42-66-97), across from the beach and 10 minutes from the Hôtel de Ville. Take bus #1 from the Hôtel de Ville to **Porte Océane** (every 20 min., last bus at 8:30pm). This lively restaurant enjoys a great view of the ocean. (*Plat garni* 20F, children's *menu* 18F. Open Mon.-Fri. 11:30am-1:30pm, Sat. 11:30am-1pm.) There's a cafeteria on the first floor with daily newspapers (open Jan.-July and Sept.-Dec. Tues.-Sat. noon-8pm), and a *cabaret de jazz* one Friday each month at 8:30pm. Call 35-42-61-90 for more information.

Coast: Lower Normandy

From Honfleur to Trouville stretches the **Corniche Normande.** The 14-km road threads a weaving, steep path flanked by characteristically large Norman hedges, thatched roof houses, and undisturbed green pastures sloping down to the water's edge. Tiny villages such as **Pennedepie** and **Criqueboeuf** appear to grow out of the convergent hillsides.

The best way to explore these harmonious hamlets and the Norman landscape is by bike, though with caution since the hills are astoundingly steep, and the roads sinuous. Because of the terrain, hitching may be difficult and even dangerous. **Bus Verts du Calvados** (tel. 31-44-77-44) serves the entire region from Caen to Le Havre. Bus #20 runs along the coast (3 per day from Le Havre to Caen, 7-12 per day from other places such as Honfleur and Deauville to Caen Mon.-Fri). The fare reflects the number of zones passed through; one zone currently costs 3.70F. Tickets are sold for a minimum of two-zone travel (7.40F); a *carnet* of five tickets buys travel through ten zones at a reduced price (29F). Bus service on Sunday is less frequent.

Honfleur's history can be traced to the eleventh century. The town launched some of the great French voyages of discovery to America in the sixteenth and seventeenth centuries, such as Samuel de Champlain's to Canada. Known as a *trésor des artistes* since the last century, the city drew numerous painters, who gathered around Eugène Boudin at the ferme St-Siméon.

A rich collection of pre-impressionist and contemporary paintings from the St-Siméon school is housed at the **Eugène Boudin Museum**, rue de l'Homme du bois (tel. 31-89-16-47). (Open March 15-Oct. 1 Wed.-Mon. 10am-noon and 2-6pm; Oct.-Dec. and Feb. 15-March 15 Mon. and Wed.-Fri. 2:30-5pm, Sat.-Sun. 10am-noon and 2:30-5pm. Admission 12F, students 8F.) That Honfleur's livelihood depends on the sea is evident in **Eglise Ste-Catherine**, unique in its use of wooden materials and parallel naves. The church was built by naval craftsmen schooled in shipbuilding techniques, and its vaulted roof resembles a ship's upturned hull. (Open daily 9am-noon and 2-6:30pm. Free.) The charming **Syndicat d'Initiative**, 33, cour des Fossés (tel. 31-89-23-30), by the bus station, will inform you about art exhibits and recommend accommodations. (Open Mon.-Sat. 9am-noon and 2-6pm; after Easter also Sun. 10am-noon.) The cheapest place to stay is the **Hôtel des Pèlerins**, 6, rue des Capucins (tel. 31-89-19-61), up rue des Lingots from Eglise Ste-Catherine. (Singles and doubles 100F, with shower 150F. Breakfast 16F.) The restaurant on the first floor is renowned, with prices to match its reputation—*menus* start at 87F. (Open Feb.-Dec.) Almost as good, but definitely cozier, is **Le Vieux Clocher**, 1, rue des Lingots (tel. 31-89-12-06), with a 85F *menu*. (Open Feb.-Dec. daily 1:30-10pm.)

A few kilometers farther down the road are **Deauville** and **Trouville**, twin playgrounds of the nineteenth-century's Beautiful People. Somewhat worn by the years, the two towns come alive in the summer when horse racing, casinos, and a thriving nightlife attract the flotsam of the European jet set. The budget traveler may have little use for the 350F purple umbrellas proffered by the glittering shops, but both towns offer ample opportunities to stroll and people-watch. Hotels are exorbitant, but **Camping Clairfontaine**, chemin de Clairfontaine (tel. 31-88-14-06), in Torquéville near the **Lion Supermarché**, is affordable at 20F per person, 20F per tent.

The seaside resorts west of Deauville, are less pretentious and more inviting. Houlgate is essentially a family resort, with a milelong, sandy beach—perhaps the most attractive in the area—and no gambling or nightclubs. This friendly, quiet village may prove more inviting than its blasé neighbors. An hour's walk eastward along the beach between Houlgate and Deauville takes you to the **Vache Noire** cliffs, crumbling limestone hills that contain important fossil deposits of ancient crustaceans, recently the subject of extensive scientific research. The cliffs can be reached only at low tide, but a tide chart is available at Houlgate's **Syndicat d'Initiative** (tel. 31-91-33-09), next to the town hall on bd. des Belges. (Open June 16-Sept. 30 daily 9am-1pm and 3-7pm; in off-season Tues.-Sat. only.) There is an annex just off the beach next to the casino (tel. 31-91-06-28; open in summer Sat.-Sun. 9am-1pm and 3-7pm). Most of the hotels in town have typical coastal resort prices, leaving **Hôtel Mon Castel**, 1, bd. des Belges (tel. 31-91-34-75), as the only affordable choice. (Singles 90F. Doubles 100F, with bath 115F.) Overlooking Houlgate beach is a 2-star campsite, **Camping de la Plage**, rue Henri Dobert (tel. 31-91-61-25), with hot showers. (Open daily April-Sept. Adults 14F, children 6F, 8F per tent, 7F per car.) At **Club Oasis** on the beach (tel. 31-24-41-96), you can rent windsurfers for 65F per hour. After a blistering day on the beach, settle down in the sedate restaurant of the **Hôtel Mon Castel** (see above), with *menus* at 68F, 90F, and 115F. (Open daily noon-2pm and 7:30-9:30pm.)

Cabourg

Just across the River Dives sits the lovely town of Cabourg, another faded nineteenth-century resort. Visit the impressive casino and the grand hotel facing the sea across promenade Marcel Proust, so named because the author frequently sojourned here. In fact, many scenes in his *A la recherche de temps perdu* take place in a Cabourg renamed Balbec. The town's street design follows an interesting semi-circular pattern: The myriad of roads converge on the grand hotel. Though Cabourg's beach may be its main attraction, a stroll down avenue de la Mer affords an interesting view of the commercial legacy of a summer boomtown. On the beach in front of the grand hotel, you can rent windsurfers for 65F per hour or 165F per day, no deposit required.

Cabourg is served by train from Paris-St-Lazare; Sundays only during the off-season. **Trains** go to Deauville (2 per day, 20F) and to Paris-St-Lazare via Deauville (2 per day, 120F). The *gare* (tel. 31-91-00-74) is located just across the River Dives from Cabourg. (Open Mon.-Sat. 8:15am-noon and 2-6pm., Sun. 10:30am-noon and 3-8:30pm.) **Bus Verts du Calvados** (tel. 31-44-77-44) has three stops in Cabourg and frequently serves Caen, Houlgate, Honfleur, Deauville, Trouville, and Le Havre. Check any covered stop for exact times; there is no station. Buy a ticket from the driver. The **Syndicat d'Initiative,** Jardins du Casino (tel. 31-91-01-09), is located in front of the grand hotel as you approach the beach. (Open Mon.-Sat. 9am-noon and 2-6:30pm, Sun. 10am-12:30pm and 3-6:30pm.) You can rent standard Peugeot 10-speed bicycles for 46F per day from the helpful *gare* (deposit 300F; open daily 8am-noon and 2-6pm), or you can lay down a 300F deposit for mediocre 3-speeds at **M. Delanoë,** 21, av. de la Mer (tel. 31-91-28-49; 45F per day, 200F per week).

The most reasonable place to stay is **L'Oie qui Fume,** 18, av. de la Brèche-Buchot (tel. 31-91-27-79), off the end of av. Georges Clemenceau. Pleasant rooms with sagging mattresses go for 85F, with shower 125F. Obligatory breakfasts (17F) are served in a flower-filled dining room. The overpriced **Hôtel au Bon Coin,** 23, av. du Commandant Levillain (tel. 31-91-03-64), across from the 8 Mai bus stop, offers similar beds. (Singles and doubles 100F, with bath 130F. Showers 10F. Breakfast 18F.) The three-star **Camping Plage,** rue Charles de Gaulle (tel. 31-91-05-75), has prices to match its high rating. (Adults 20F, children 10F, 30F per tent, tax 1F. Open April-Sept.) You can also try the smaller, 2-star **Oasis Camping,** rue Charles de Gaulle (tel. 31-91-10-62), farther down the road from Camping Plage. (Adults 10F, children 5F, 10F per tent, 5F per car. Open April-Sept.) For a good meal after a day in the sun, try **Le Champagne,** place du Marché (tel. 31-91-02-29), with *menus* from 68F, *à la carte* 40-70F. (Open in summer daily noon-2pm and 7-9pm.) **La Pépinière,** 10, av. Isabelle (tel. 31-91-17-46), off av. Brèche-Buchot, serves a filling 45F lunch *menu;* arrive before 1pm. (Open Mon.-Sat. noon-2pm.)

Caen

"One moment it was there; the next, the whole town—parks, churches, shops—dissolved into a pile of dust." So gasped an American soldier to reporters in 1944. Gutted in World War II, the capital of Lower Normandy has since been neatly rebuilt with a feeling for its history—William the Conqueror's favorite town retains a charm unmatched by others.

Caen served as William's ducal seat from 1035 to 1087. The red flag with two gold lions that flies above the château was the standard of the Dukes of Normandy, later incorporated into the English flag by the Plantagenet kings.

Smaller than Rouen, Caen has visibly become a university town. Political posters and graffiti cover all wall space, and students crowd the many small cafes around the château. These students have gained a reputation for radicalism, allying themselves with the Communist party, feminist groups, and the anti-nuclear movement.

Orientation and Practical Information

Caen is served frequently by trains from Paris's Gare St-Lazare (2 hr.). The station is far from the center of town and from the university. Walk to your right as you exit, and then make a right onto rue de la Gare, which continues as av. du 6 Juin. Any of the buses stopping at the station (except #4) will take you to the center of town (5F); you will be let off 1 block from rue St-Pierre and the tourist office.

The center of Caen is neatly enclosed in a parallelogram: The *gare* is outside the southern edge, and the château and Abbaye-aux-Hommes serve as adjacent northern corners. **Rue St-Pierre** and **rue de Strasbourg** flank the major pedestrian precincts and shopping centers.

Office de Tourisme: Place St-Pierre (tel. 31-86-27-65), by the church. English-speaking staff will help you find accommodations. Ask for regional information; they have itineraries covering all of Lower Normandy's "cheese-and-cider routes." Open July-Aug. Mon.-Fri. 8:45am-7pm, Sat. 8:45am-6pm, Sun. 10am-noon and 2-4:45pm; Sept.-June Mon.-Fri. 8:45am-12:15pm and 2-7pm, Sat. 8:45am-12:15pm and 2-6pm. **Branch office** on the pedestrian walk by Eglise St-Pierre. Open Mon.-Fri. 10am-1pm and 2-7pm, Sat. 10am-1pm and 2-6pm.

Currency Exchange: Crédit Agricole, 136, rue Falaise (tel. 31-52-04-92). Open Tues.-Fri. 8:30am-12:15pm and 1:30-5pm, Sat. 8:30am-12:15pm and 1:30-4:15pm.

Post Office: Place Gambetta. Poste Restante. **Postal Code:** 14000. Open Mon.-Fri. 8am-7pm, Sat. 8am-noon.

Train Station: Place de la Gare (tel. 31-83-50-50). Open daily 5am-9:30pm. To Paris (17 per day, 2 hr., 120F), Rouen (5 per day, 1½ hr., 87F), Cherbourg (8 per day, 1½ hr., 72F), Rennes (3 per day, 130F), Tours (5 per day, 135F). There are **baggage lockers** on the platforms (3F, 3-day max.); you can also store your bags with the office (9F per day).

Bus Station: Next to the train station (tel. 31-86-55-30). Open Mon. 6:40am-12:30pm and 1-7pm, Tues.-Fri. 7:30am-12:30pm and 1-7pm, Sat. 9am-12:30pm and 3-7pm. This is the central terminal for the **Bus Verts** covering the Calvados region from Le Havre to Carentan. Major service to Pont l'Eveque, Deauville, Bayeux, Corseulles, and Falaise, Le Havre, and Carentan.

Bike Rental: At the *gare.* 30F per half-day, 36F per day, deposit 200F.

Open Markets: Fri. 8am-1pm on place St-Sauveur. Sun. 8am-1pm on place Courtonne. Everything from fruit to frying pans.

Hospital: Hôpital Clemenceau, av. Côte de Nacre (tel. 31-44-81-12).

Medical Emergency: Tel. 15.

Police: Rue Jean Romain (tel. 31-86-08-34).

Police Emergency: Tel. 17.

Accommodations and Camping

Along with the youth hostel, Caen provides plenty of pleasant, reasonable hotels and student accommodations.

Auberge de Jeunesse (IYHF), Foyer Robert Reme, 68bis, rue Restout (tel. 31-52-19-96). It's a long walk. Take bus #3 (*direction* "Grâce de Dieu") to Armand Marie. A clean and recently-renovated hostel and workers' dormitory. Melvin, one of the directors, is an American basketball player. 50F per person. Breakfast included. Filling lunch and dinner 30F. Reception open daily 5-10pm. Open June-Sept.

Centre International de Séjour, la Cité (tel. 31-93-24-55), 5km north of town in Hérouville-St-Clair. Take bus #6 or 7 from the station. Spacious, carpeted singles 73F. IYHF members 62F per person. Triples available. Hot showers and breakfast included.

University Housing: CROUS, 23, av. de Bruxelles (tel. 31-94-73-37), a walk from town, north of the château. Call ahead. Student ID required. Adequate singles are a good value at 53F, hot showers included. No curfew. Office open Mon.-Fri. until 4pm, Sat. morning only. Open Feb.-Sept. Breakfast about 5F at **Restaurant B,** east of the track field. Dinner at 7:30pm with student's meal ticket about 10F.

Hôtel de la Paix, 14, rue Neuve-St-Jean (tel. 31-86-18-99), off av. du 6 Juin. Comfortable establishment with a helpful proprietor who offers sight-seeing advice. Singles and doubles 89F, with shower 122F. Breakfast 16F.

Hôtel Demolombe, 36, rue Demolombe (tel. 31-85-48-70), between place St-Pierre and the Abbaye-aux-Hommes. Low prices. Interesting shower. Singles 70-80F. Doubles 80-95F. Showers 15F. Breakfast 16F.

Hôtel St-Jean, 20, rue des Martyrs (tel. 31-86-23-35), near place de la Résistance. Quiet location, clean and modern. Private parking. View of the cathedral. Singles and doubles with shower 94F, with bath 107F. Breakfast 13.50F.

Camping: Terrain Municipal, route de Louvigny (tel. 31-73-60-92). Take bus #13 ("Louvigny"). Hot showers. 6F per person, 3F per tent. Open June-Sept.

Food

There are several inexpensive *crêperies* and *brasseries* near the château around rue du Vaugueux and avenue de la Libération. Fruit and vegetable markets spread their wares Tuesday through Saturday mornings under the trees on place Courtonne. For large quantities, bargain.

Restaurant Kouba, 6, rue du Vaugueux (tel. 31-93-68-47). Hearty *couscous* 27F. Open daily noon-2pm and 7-11pm.

Le Panier Naturel, 38, place Marcel Fouques. Vegetarian *menus* with a French touch 38F and 60F. Open Tues.-Thurs. noon-1:30pm, Fri.-Sat. noon-1:30pm and 7-9pm. Health food store attached. Open 10am-3:30pm and 5-8pm.

Grand Marnier, 13, rue Pierre Aimé Lair, off bd. de Strasbourg across from place de la République. A comfortable dinerlike *crêperie* serving basic crêpes (5-12F) and *galettes* (8-16F). Open daily 11am-7:30pm.

La Petite Marmite, 43, rue des Jacobins, not far from the theater. Some fine cooking. Dress nicely. 70 and 110F *menus* include Norman specialties such as *soupe de pêcheur* and *faux filet grillé au poivre vert.* Open Mon.-Fri. and Sat. evening.

Sights and Entertainment

Because of Caen's great prosperity in the late eleventh century, the contemporary city has inherited some of France's finest Romanesque architecture. William the Conqueror's reign coincided with a new acceptance of Christianity by Norman dukes. Persecution ended, monasteries re-opened, and new churches were built. William and his bride Matilda founded both of Caen's great abbeys in 1066.

In the center of town lies the ruin of William's imposing **château.** (Open in summer 6am-9:30pm; in off-season 6am-7:30pm.) Within the walls, the modern **Musée des Beaux Arts** (tel. 31-85-28-63) contains a few paintings by Perugino, Rubens, Van Dyck, and Monet, as well as the outstanding *La Vièrge à l'Enfant* by Van der Weyden and a collection of modern works. The **Musée de Normandie** (tel. 31-86-06-24), across the way, details Norman peasant life through the centuries and such local crafts as lace- and candle-making. (Both open March-Oct. Wed.-Mon. 10am-noon and 2-6pm; Nov.-Feb. 10am-noon and 2-5pm. Admission 5F, combination ticket 7F, students half-price, Sun. free.)

In the shadow of the château stands **Eglise St-Pierre,** whose famous bell tower rises majestically into the sky. The church's exterior shows the evolution of the Gothic style from the thirteenth through the sixteenth centuries. (Open daily 9am-6pm.)

Caen's most beautiful monument is probably **Eglise St-Etienne,** place St-Etienne, dating from the eleventh to the thirteenth centuries. The symmetry and elegant carving recommend the sober Romanesque facade; one tower is Romanesque, the other Gothic. (Open daily 8:15am-noon and 2-7:30pm.) The adjacent **Abbaye-aux-Hommes,** off rue Guillaume le Conquerant (tel. 31-84-81-25), was founded by William the Conqueror in atonement for the sin of marrying his cousin Matilda. Rebuilt in the eighteenth century, the abbey was used as a *lycée* and is now Caen's Hôtel de Ville. (Tours in French daily every hour 9am-noon and 2-5pm. Admission 4F, groups 2F per person. Call ahead.) The smaller and less ornate **Eglise de la Trinité** of the **Abbaye-aux-Dames,** off rue des Chanoines (Matilda's penance for her part in the same sin), has a Romanesque interior and two sixteenth-century towers. Particularly outstanding are the purple and cerise stained-glass windows in the east end, modern replacements for the original windows, destroyed in World War II.

To visit the crypt, enter through a low doorway in the south transept. (Open daily 9am-noon and 2-6pm.)

Try to make time for the short hike up to Caen's **Université,** north of the château (left along the ramparts to rue du Gaillon). Unlike most French universities, it is contained within a clearly defined campus. The iron phoenix at the entrance symbolizes the university's rebirth after its destruction in 1944. Although you can always meet students here, be aware that in summer Americans take over. Near the university, you can picnic or meditate in the expansive, pastoral **Jardin des Plantes** on place Blot (open 9am-8pm).

Caen supports a number of bars and discos, especially on the streets that wind around the château toward the university. In town on place St-Pierre, the **Taverne Flamande** reverberates to live jazz in a cafe setting (Tues.-Sun. after 4pm). The local crowd and jazz at the piano bar at **La Poterne,** 20, rue Porte au Berger (tel. 31-93-57-46), in the Quartier Vaugeux, set the mood for an intimate rendez-vous (Tues.-Sun.). If you'd rather go wild, head for **Le Jackspot,** 20, rue Vanquelin (tel. 33-86-36-02), between rue St-Sauveur and rue Ecuyère, where you can twist and turn on the disco floor until you drop (Tues.-Sun. after 10:30pm).

The **Théâtre Municipal de Caen,** off bd. Yves-Guillou (tel. 31-86-12-79), offers a yearlong calendar of concerts, musicals, dance, comedy, and vaudeville acts. (Tickets for theatre 60F-120F, for concerts 30-40F, students 30F.) The **Saison Musicale** includes a number of performances by Caen's chamber orchestra. In summer, the **Festival des Soirées de Normandie** schedules performances in churches, abbeys, and châteaux; ask at the tourist office for a complete listing.

Bayeux

A beautifully preserved, ancient town filled with worthwhile museums, Bayeux makes a convenient base for exploring the D-Day beaches, especially by bicycle. In search of Bayeux's famous tapestry, an eleventh-century linen embroidery depicting the Norman invasion of Britain, tourists flood this quiet town. The crowds gather around the cathedral and the tapestry, so take time to explore the tranquil side streets, lined with gray-brick Norman houses and bright flowers.

Orientation and Practical Information

Bayeux is on the Caen-Rennes and Paris-Cherbourg train lines. The station is about 10 minutes from the center. Turn left onto the highway (bd. Sadi-Carnot), then right, following the signs to the *centre ville*. Once there, continue up rue Larcher until it hits **rue St-Martin,** Bayeux's commercial boulevard. On your right, **rue St-Jean** marks the pedestrian zone.

Office de Tourisme: 1, rue des Cuisiniers (tel. 31-92-16-26), in a fourteenth-century wooden building. From the cathedral, turn right onto rue Bienvenue, which becomes rue des Cuisiniers. English spoken. You can book a room for the cost of the phone call. They'll rent you a tape recorder and headphones with a map describing a tour of the city (French only, and a bit long, 15F). Open July-Sept. 15 Mon.-Sat. 9:30am-12:30pm and 2-6:30pm, Sun. 10am-12:30pm and 3-6:30pm; in off-season Mon.-Sat. only.

Currency Exchange: Banks open Tues.-Fri. 9:15am-5:30pm, Sat. 9:15am-4:30pm, and the 1st Monday of each month. Change money at the **tourist office** when banks are closed.

Post Office: Rue Larcher. Poste Restante. **Postal code:** 14400. Open Mon.-Fri. 8am-7pm, Sat. 8am-noon.

Train Station: Place de la Gare (tel. 31-92-80-50; in Caen 31-83-50-50), 10 min. from the center of town. Open daily 8am-9pm. To Paris (2¼ hr., 125F), Lille (230F), and Caen (24F).

Bus Station: STDC, place de la Gare (tel. 31-92-02-92). No local bus service in Bayeux.

Taxi: Les Taxis du Bessin, Tel. 31-92-92-40. Open 24 hours. **Allo Taxi,** at the train station (tel. 31-92-04-10). Open 7am-9pm.

Bike Rental: At the **station** (tel. 31-92-80-50). 36F per day, 145F per week. Open daily 8am-9pm. Also **Family Home,** 39, rue Général de Dais (tel. 31-92-15-22). Rusty 3-speeds only; 35F per day. Open 7am-7pm.

Laundromat: 10, rue Maréchal Foch. Walk down the main street from the tourist office, and turn left at the traffic light.

Hospital: Rue de Nesmond (tel. 31-92-29-47), next to the tapestry building.

Medical Emergency: Tel. 15.

Police: Av. Conseil (tel. 31-92-94-00).

Police Emergency: Tel. 17.

Accommodations, Camping, and Food

Bayeux offers a wide range of accommodations options. The Family Home is a rare find, both for food and lodging. Wherever you stay, you should make reservations a day or two in advance or arrive here in the morning, because Bayeux is a popular destination.

Auberge de Jeunesse (IYHF)—Family Home, 39, rue Général de Dais (tel. 31-92-15-22). Follow the signs for the "Family Home" left from the train station; the signs for "Auberge de Jeunesse" have no arrows. Not a traditional hostel, but a converted sixteenth-century abbey extremely well kept, with eclectic decor and homelike bathrooms. Evening meal here is wonderful and huge (55F); "If you feel greedy," say the owners, "eat with us." If they have room at the table you can eat without being an overnight guest; just call ahead. Camping facilities available in nearby field. Bicycle rental 35F per day. Reservations accepted and often necessary. 65F, nonmembers 80F. Showers and breakfast included. Open daily 7am-11pm.

Centre d'Accueil, chemin de Boulogne (tel. 31-92-16-26), 10 min. from the town center. Walk left along bd. Sadi-Carnot, continuing straight as it becomes bd. Leclerc; the center is near the Musée de la Bataille de Normandie. Big, modern, comfortable, and noisy. A good deal. Groups welcome. Kitchen facilities. Single rooms 58F. No lock-out.

Hôtel de la Tour d'Argent, 31, rue Larcher (tel. 31-92-30-08), over a *brasserie* behind the cathedral. Decent singles and doubles 75F. Triples 105F. Showers 10F. Breakfast 14.50F.

Hôtel Notre-Dame, 44, rue des Cuisiniers (tel. 31-92-87-24), next to the cathedral. A luxurious establishment with high prices. Singles 95F. Doubles 130F, with bath 145 and 175F. Fancy restaurant downstairs posts 57-124F *menus.*

Camping: Municipal Camping, bd. Eindhoven (tel. 31-92-08-43), within easy reach of the town center and right next to RN13. Follow the signs left from the *gare.* Covered swimming pool. 7.70F per person, 4.20F per tent, 3.30F per car. Hot showers included. Open March-Oct.

Slide into the leather seats of **Les Arcades,** 10, rue Laitière, for its 50F *menu.* **Ma Normandie,** 41, rue St-Patrice, has a decent 60F *menu,* but the 60F *menu* at **Hôtel Notre-Dame** might be a better value. Two doors up the street, **Crêperie de la Notre Dame,** 8, rue de la Juridiction, folds surprisingly low-priced crêpes (5-18F) and *galettes* (8-18F) to eat in or take out. (Open Mon.-Sat. 11:30am-2pm and 5:30-9pm.) **Pizza Marsala,** 17, rue des Cuisiniers (tel. 31-92-47-60), serves good pizza and a fine variety of omelettes, plus spaghetti (22-36F) and *escalope bolognaise* (52F).

Sights

The **Tapisserie de Bayeaux,** actually a linen embroidery, was probably commissioned by Odon de Conteville, bishop of Bayeux, to illustrate the Norman conquest of England by his half-brother William at the Battle of Hastings in 1066. Despite the legend that it was embroidered by Queen Matilda herself, experts now believe that the tapestry is the product of an English workshop. At times strict chronology is abandoned in favor of symmetry as the Norman version of the defeat of the English King Harold gradually unfurls. If you can't tell a long bow (Norman) from a crossbow (English), note that the English are depicted with moustaches and the Normans without. The 70-meter-long tapestry was probably designed to hang in the cathedral, but it is now preserved in a spacious, renovated seminary on rue de Nesmond (tel. 31-92-05-84). Viewing is preceded by a brilliant slide show and various exhibitions, which, if overlong, will help you understand the tapestry's history. The 3F cassette explanation is worthwhile. (Exhibitions and audio cassette in French and English. Open daily June-Sept. 9am-7pm; Oct.-March 15 9:30am-12:30pm and 2-6pm; March 16-May 9am-12:30pm and 2-6:30pm. Admission 18F, students 9F.)

Bayeux's impressive **Cathédrale** stands nearby, a masterpiece of Norman design. Gothic spires top Romanesque towers, which squat on top of a small Roman church, now an underground crypt. You can visit the crypt on informal guided tours during the summer, or on your own when the tours aren't given. (Open daily in summer 8am-7pm; in off-season 8am-noon and 2-7pm.) Across the street, the **Musée Baron Gérard** (tel. 31-92-14-21), pushes a rather inconsequential collection of porcelain, but does contain some nice lacework and beautiful works by the painter David. In front of the entrance to the museum stands a firmly rooted *arbre de la liberté* (liberty tree), planted on March 30, 1797, and grown to magnificent height as if in testimony to the aspirations of the French Revolution. (Museum admission included in the ticket to the tapestry. Open same hours.)

Near the Centre d'Accueil and the British war cemetery, the **Musée Memorial de la Bataille de Normandie—1944,** bd. Fabian Ware (tel. 31-92-93-41), recalls the story of the Battle of Normandy through a large collection of uniforms, equipment, and photographs, and 100 life-size models and dioramas. The cost of admission includes an excellent, 40-minute film in English and French. (Open March-May and Sept.-Oct. daily 10am-12:30pm and 2-6:30pm; June-Aug. daily 9:30am-7pm; Nov.-Feb. Sat.-Sun. 10:30am-12:30pm and 2-6:30pm. Admission 15F, students 8F.)

The **Musée Diocésain d'Art Religieux,** 6, rue Lambert-Leforestier (tel. 31-92-73-80), at the Hôtel du Doyen, displays a limited collection of ecclesiastical dress, ceremonial banners, chalices, and ancient manuscripts. (Open July-Sept. 15 daily 10:30am-12:30pm and 2-7pm; Sept. 16-June Mon.-Sat. 10:30am-12:30pm and 2-7pm.)

Before investing in individual museum admissions, consider purchasing a ticket good for admission at all four museums at a slight savings (Musée Mémorial de la Bataille de Normandie, Musée Diocésain d'Art Religieux, Musée Baron Gérard, and the Tapisserie de Bayeux; 40F, children 20F; available at all museums).

The **Norman Craft Centre,** 5-9, place aux Pommes (tel. 31-92-90-33), offers exhibits and workshops on Norman-style furniture, wood-turning, porcelain, lithography, and silk weaving. (Open June-Aug. daily 10am-7pm; Sept.-May Tues.-Sun. 10am-12:30pm and 2-6:30pm.)

Near Bayeux: The D-Day Beaches

North of Bayeux are the British and Canadian D-Day landing beaches and, farther west, the American landing beaches of Omaha and Utah. Near the beaches, commemorative monuments, war cemeteries, and battle museums pay homage to the men and women who participated in military history's largest seaborne invasion. The drama began here at twilight on June 6, 1944, along a 50-mile stretch of coastline divided into lengths dubbed Utah, Omaha, Sword, Juno, and Gold. Operation "Overlord" dispersed over 16,000 troops of the American 82nd and 101st airborne divisions and the British 6th parachute brigade. The mission of the 82nd and 101st was to cut road and rail links between Paris and Cherbourg and to cover the Utah Beach landings; that of the 6th parachute brigade to capture bridges over the Orne River and protect the eastern flank of the invasion.

Most of the paratroopers' objectives were successfully carried out. The town hall in Ste-Mère-Eglise displays the American flag that paratroopers of the 82nd division planted to mark the liberation of the village. The **Voie de la Liberté** (Liberty Highway) begins at kilometer "0" in front of the town hall; similar milestones indicate each kilometer of the U.S. Army's advance to Bastogne in Belgium. The **Musée C-47** houses the C-47 that spilled U.S. paratroops over the Ste-Mère-Eglise district.

(Open daily June-Aug. 9am-7pm; Jan. 15-May and Sept.-Nov. 16 9am-noon and 2-7pm. Admission 12F, ages under 14 6F. For group tours call 38-41-41-35.)

At **Utah Beach,** near Isigny-sur-Mer, an exhibition on the landing is housed in a blockhouse near the American Commemorative Monument. A model of the operation shows how 836,000 men, 220,000 vehicles, and 725,000 tons of equipment were brought ashore. (Open Easter-Nov. 1 daily 9am-noon and 2-7pm; in off-season Sun. and bank holidays only. For group tours call 33-42-04-03 or 33-42-05-36.)

Following D514 from Isigny to Port-en-Bessin, you cross the landing point behind Omaha Beach. At **Colleville-St-Laurent** (19km from Bayeux) on the coast between Arromanches and Grandchamps, the American cemetery stands as a powerful memorial to the 70,000 men who gave their lives. More than 6000 American soldiers were killed on the first day alone. Row after row of white crosses and Jewish stars, many unmarked, form a dizzying pattern across the land. The **Pointe du Hoc,** a cliff 100 feet high, concealed six 155mm guns that commanded both Utah and Omaha beaches. The area is crisscrossed by underground German command tunnels winding between yawning craters, silent memorials to ferocious air and naval bombardments.

Ten kilometers north of Bayeux on D514 is **Arromanches,** a small town at the center of Gold Beach. Here the British built Port Winston in one day on June 6, 1944, using retired ships and mammoth blocks of concrete towed across the Channel at 1½mph and sunk in a wide semi-circle a mile out to sea. The harbor provided shelter while the Allies unloaded their supplies. Today, the hulks that remain indicate the enormous size of the artificial harbor. The **Musée du Débarquement,** right on the beach (tel. 31-22-34-31), houses fascinating relics and photographs of the British and Canadian landings. A film included in the price of admission is given in French, though English films can be arranged for groups. (Open daily 9am-5:45pm. Admission 15F, students 10F.)

Juno Beach, the landing site of the Canadian forces, lies east of Arromanches. The Canadian cemetery is located at **Bény-sur-Mer-Reviers,** near Courseulles, and there are commemorative monuments at Bernières, Courseulles, and St-Aubin. The second British beach, "Sword," continues east from Juno Beach. There are British cemeteries at **Hermanville-sur-Mer** and **Ranville.** Like their American counterparts, the British and Canadian paratroops spent the first hours of the June 6 invasion in confusion as they tried to organize at predetermined rallying points. War museums at **Benouville** and **Merville** recall the battles fought in the pre-dawn twilight.

You can find a fairly large, two-star municipal campsite at Arromanches, av. de Verdun (tel. 33-22-36-78). A three-star campsite, **Camping Reine Mathilde,** lies at Etreham, near Port-en-Bessin, 2½km from the sea, 7km from Omaha Beach, and 9km from Bayeux. Both are fully equipped—and densely packed. Squeeze your tent between the trailers and don't get run over. (12F per person, 10F per tent.)

Bus Verts serves Port-en-Bessin and other points west (bus #70; Mon.-Sat. 3 per day). Bus #74 serves Arromanches and other points east with two departures per day, at 11:45am and 5:50pm. However, infrequent service may preclude a long visit. Try instead to rent a bike for the trip to Arromanches from Bayeux (10km). All routes are relatively flat. Be sure to get a map at the tourist office in Bayeux. As restaurants in this area tend to be both substandard and *cher,* picnicking might be the best option. However, for those who simply can't exert themselves without the promise of reward, the country inn of **M. et Mme. Gerouard,** 14710 Trevieres, Asniers-en-Bessin, off N13 (tel. 31-22-44-14), beckons pooped travelers with savory and ample *menus* from 65F (reservations appreciated).

Cotentin Peninsula

The road from Cherbourg to Coutances passes through the rugged, hilly Cotentin countryside and a handful of picturesque, historic towns. Most are connected either by train, by SNCF bus (railpasses valid), or by an STN bus based in Cherbourg.

Since figuring out schedules and connections can be difficult, plan ahead. Hitching is often unsuccessful since most major roads are used by heavily-packed cars arriving by ferry and hurrying south to their final destinations. Biking may well be preferable to waiting in stations; however, the novice may end up spending more time pushing than riding.

Cherbourg

At the northern tip of the peninsula, Cherbourg, nicknamed "*Port de la Libération*" in World War II, is now a major port with numerous ferry and train connections. The tides of ferry passengers that wash in and out have sparked the development of an active nightlife featuring discos, casinos, and fine restaurants.

Normandy Ferries, Gare Maritime Sud (tel. 33-44-28-96), runs ferries to Rosslare, Ireland (17 hr.; in summer 496-500F, Oct.-April 400F; also served from Le Havre). Interail-holders receive a 50% discount, and Eurail-holders sail for free provided they pay a small port tax. (Information office open Mon. and Wed.-Fri. 9am-noon and 2-6pm.) **Townsend Thoresen Car Ferries** (tel. 33-44-20-13) serves Portsmouth, England. (Adults 310F, students 279F, children 175F. Motorists 288-672F, depending on size of vehicle. No reductions for Eurail- or Interail-holders. Also via Le Havre.) **Sealink** (tel. 33-20-43-88) offers ferries to Portsmouth and Weymouth in England (310F, students 263.50F, children 175F), as well as to Jersey or Guernsey (300F, students 255F, children 170F). SNCF buses provide transportation to and from the port to the *gare* for Sealink passengers only.

The **train station** (tel. 33-57-50-50) is a 10-minute walk from the ferry terminal, on the southern side of the Bassin du Commerce. Walk toward town along av. Aristide Briand, which turns into av. Carnot, turn right onto av. François Millet, and the *gare* is on your left. (Open Mon.-Fri. 6am-noon and 2-6:30pm, Sat. 9am-noon and 2-6pm, Sun. 9am-noon and 2-5pm.) There is rail service to Paris (7 per day, 3¼ hr., 178F), Rouen (3 per day, 3 hr., 150F), Caen (9 per day, 1¼ hr., 110F), Bayeux (9 per day, 1 hr., 107F), Avranches (3 per day, 3 hr., 85F), Rennes (3 per day, 4 hr., 138F, change at Lison). An **SNCF** bus also runs to Coutances (3 per day, 2 hr., 49F). **Lockers** for your baggage (5F) are at the train station, but there is no bike rental. Across the street from the station is **Autocars STN** (tel. 33-44-32-22), which serves shorter routes to Auderville, Les-Piex, Siouxville, Carteret, Barfleur, St-Vaast, and Carentan, though infrequently. (Open Mon.-Fri. 8am-noon and 2-6:30pm, Sat. 8:30am-noon.)

The Cherbourg **Syndicat d'Initiative** lies at the other end of the Bassin du Commerce (tel. 33-43-52-02) and has a plethora of brochures on the Cotentin. (Open June-Aug. Mon.-Sat. 9am-noon and 2-6pm, Sun. in an **annex** at the Gare Maritime; Sept.-May Mon.-Fri. 9am-noon and 2-6pm, Sat. 9am-noon.) The **post office** is located on rue du Val de Saire at av. Aristide Briand, about a 5-minute walk south from the ferries. Major banks such as **Crédit Lyonnais** and **Banque Nationale de Paris** are located on rue Gambetta, west of the Bassin du Commerce. You can also try the **Bureau de Change** at the ferry terminal.

A very friendly and helpful **Auberge de Jeunesse** is located at 109, av. du Paris (tel. 33-44-26-31), about 300m east of the train station, in the Centre Social et Culturel (40F per night, breakfast 14F). From the train station, take a right on rue Hallet to the end; the hostel is across the street to the right in a rather ominous looking building. (Curfew 11pm. Lockout 11am-6pm. Open March 17-Nov. 15.) The hostel rents **bikes** (35F per day). During July and August, you can also rent bikes at **LAMY,** 52, rue du Val de Saire (tel. 33-44-33-04), for a bit more (45F).

Along the canal and up many of the side streets are luxury hotels and seafood restaurants, plus various casinos, cafes, and discos. The **Café du Théâtre,** place du Théâtre, re-creates an almost *fin-de-siècle* elegance with its glass exterior and plush decor.

If you have time between connections, visit the **Musée de la Libération,** in the old citadel perched atop the Montagne du Route (tel. 33-53-03-58), about 1½km from the center of town. The strenuous hike will be worth it once you see the panoramic view of Cherbourg and its surroundings. The museum houses a large collection of German and American weaponry, photos, and documents. (Open April-Sept. 9am-noon and 2-6pm; Oct.-March 9:30am-noon and 2-5:30pm.) About 4km east of Cherbourg is **Château de Tourlaville,** a strikingly beautiful sixteenth-century structure in the Italian Renaissance style, whose history is marked by a somber incestuous love story. Take bus #1 and get off at Eglantines.

From an architectural point of view, the towns of **Bricquebec** and **St-Sauveur-le-Vicomte** south of Cherbourg are more typical of this area, composed of plain granite houses and Romanesque churches, with remains of medieval fortresses. These towns lie on the inland route down to Granville; they are not served by public transportation or by tourist offices, and are worthwhile primarily if you pass through by car. However, the semi-hardy may bike the 30-45km. In **Lessay** stands a fine Romanesque abbey, beautiful both for its architecture and setting. Visit on Sunday to hear the mass sung in Gregorian chant, but call the *mairie* in Lessay (tel. 33-46-46-18) to verify the mass time.

Coutances

Southeast of Lessay, Coutances, an attractive and peaceful town with three churches aligned on a hill, has long served as the region's religious center. Its thirteenth-century **Cathédrale,** which escaped wartime damage, is on rue Geoffroy Montbray (tel. 33-45-35-53). Note the 12 small, pointed towers tucked into the two main spires—a common feature of churches in the area—and the graceful flying buttresses. Though the intricate and dazzling French horticulture in the garden to the left of the cathedral may appear to be all that's worth seeing, an eighteenth-century Norman cider press stands remarkably intact. With a 400-liter capacity, the cider press is convincing testimony to Normandy's long love of *cidre bouché.* Outdoor speakers on every block of the main street downtown pipe loud and incongruous American rock 'n roll into the shopping area. **Eglise St-Pierre,** rue St-Pierre, is also open to the public.

The **train station** in Coutances (tel. 33-07-50-77) is a 15-minute walk from the cathedral (open Mon.-Fri. 5:30am-8:30pm, Sat. 5:30am-8pm, Sun. 6:30am-10pm): to Rennes (3 per day, 1¼ hr., 76F), Caen (8 per day, 1½ hr.), Granville (5 per day, 1 hr.), and Avranches (3 per day, 45 min.). You can rent **bikes** for 35F per half day or 45F per day, with a 250F deposit. **Buses** leaving from the train station connect Coutances with Cherbourg (2 hr., 56F), Granville (45 min., 65F), Mont St-Michel (1½ hr., 80F), and St-Lô (1 hr., 75F). Call **STN** (tel. 33-05-65-25) in St-Lô for departure times. Coutances's very helpful **Syndicat d'Initiative** is located at the public gardens (tel. 33-45-17-79), near **Les Unelles,** an abbey newly restored as a cultural center. (Open April-Oct. Mon.-Tues. and Thurs.-Fri. 9:30am-noon and 3:30-6:30pm, Wed. and Sat. 9:30am-noon; Oct.-April Mon.-Fri. 4-6pm.)

A 30-minute hike brings you to the **Foyer des Jeunes Travailleurs,** 20, rue Docteur Guillard (tel. 33-45-09-69), a dank lodging for rowdy, generally young male workers. Walk straight out of the train station and take a right at the end of the road, following the serpentine uphill route past the old town. Take a right onto the unmarked road at the large Codec supermarket, continue to the crest of the hill, bear right onto rue Docteur Guillard, and follow it left to the *foyer.* (Singles 49F, with breakfast 60F. Kitchen.) Otherwise, try the **Hôtel aux Trois Pilliers,** 11, rue des Halles (tel. 33-45-01-31), beside the cathedral. (Singles 80F, doubles 100F. Breakfast 15F.)

Fine *crêperies* line the cobbled streets of *centre ville,* and health food fans will note the **Diéthétique Coutançaise,** a well-stocked staples shop at 13, rue Geoffrey de Montbray. (Open Mon.-Sat. 9am-12:15pm and 2-7:15pm.)

Granville

Granville, a charming seaside town built on a rocky promontory, offers a little of everything: a bustling *ville basse* with narrow streets, an *haute ville* crowned by the massive fifteenth-century **Eglise de Notre-Dame,** and a lime beach. The town also claims the **Jardin Public Christian Dior,** off av. de la Libération, a piece of land donated by Dior about 100 years ago and made into an exquisite park overlooking the ocean. (Open daily 9am-9pm. Free.) Granville welcomes its share of tourists in the summer—don't expect solitude. In July and August weekly classical concerts take place in Eglise de Notre-Dame; contact the *syndicat* for dates and times.

Granville can be reached by car on D971, and hitching is no problem since the roads leading into and out of the city are well traveled during the day. **STN buses** (tel. 33-50-77-89) connect Granville to Coutances (3 per day, 45 min., 56F), Avranches (3 per day, 1¼ hr., 30F), and Mont St-Michel (1 per day, 2 hr., 55F). The buses share the **gare** (tel. 33-50-05-45) with SNCF trains. Walk 15 minutes from the center of town on av. Maréchal Leclerc to get to the station (open daily 9am-noon and 2-6pm). Trains run to Paris (4 per day, 3½ hr., 165F), Cherbourg (3 per day, change at Folliniers and Lison, 3 hr., 90F), and Avranches (3 per day, 1¼ hr., 28F). There are **lockers** in the station (3F, 3-day max.). From May through September boats leave daily for the Chausey Islands (2 per day; 50 min.; round-trip 68F, children under 14 42F). For more information, call **Vedettes** at the Gare Maritime de Granville (tel. 33-50-31-81), or contact Granville's **Syndicat d'Initiative,** 15, rue Georges Clemenceau (tel. 33-50-02-67), across from the casino. (Open daily June-Sept. 3-7pm; Oct.-May 9am-noon and 2-6pm.)

There is no youth hostel here, but **Hôtel Michelet,** 5, rue Jules Michelet (tel. 33-50-06-55), offers cheap beds and friendly reception. (Singles 60F. Doubles 70-85F, with shower 120F. Breakfast 16F.) Weary travelers arriving at the train station might opt for the two-star **Hôtel Terminus,** place de la Gare (tel. 33-50-02-05). The building has character, and the rooms are spacious. (Singles 75-115F. Doubles 83-113F. Showers in some rooms. Breakfast 15F.)

A few small coastal towns lie amidst pristine countryside and gorgeous beaches near Granville: **Hauteville-sur-Mer** and **Coutainville** are particularly worthwhile. These towns are not served by public transportation, but biking the hilly route is an option. **Bikes** may be rented at the shop of **M. Malorey,** 11, rue Clement de Maison (tel. 33-50-04-13; 40F per day).

Avranches

The most delightful of the peninsula's larger towns, Avranches lies southwest of Granville on D973 and on the Caen-Rennes train line. Perched atop a butte in a northern corner of Mont St-Michel Bay, this mountain town commands superb panoramas and is an invigorating uphill hike from the station. (Take the pedestrian path in front of the station, not the weaving highway to the left, and watch out for the elderly women who climb the hill daily—they may run you over.) Avranche's most seductive treasure is the **Jardin des Plantes** in the west end of the city. Even if you fail to be stirred by the delicately manicured gardens, the majestic view of Mont St-Michel should inspire you. Remember that from July to September, the Mont is illuminated at night, and what may appear from the garden as a fallen star is actually one of the world's most touristed sites. During the summer, the garden itself is lit at night to musical accompaniment. The **Musée de l'Avranchin,** on place St-Avril (tel. 33-58-25-15), houses the manuscripts and books written by some of the more prolific monks of Mont St-Michel. The literature was saved from destruction when the Mont's abbey was sacked during the French Revolution. (Open Wed.-Mon. 10am-noon and 2-6pm. Admission 10F, children 5F.)

The **Syndicat d'Initiative** on rue Général de Gaulle (tel. 33-58-00-22), next to the town hall, gives extremely helpful advice on visiting Mont St-Michel. In summer you can ask here about swimming in the **municipal pool.** (Adults 16F, children 10F. Open in summer daily 10am-noon and 2-6pm; in off-season Mon.-Fri. 10am-noon and 3-6pm.) The same building houses the **STN bus station** (tel. 33-58-03-07), which sends one bus per day to Mont St-Michel and back (July-Aug. only; leaves Avranches at 10:25am, returns from Mont St-Michel at 4:10pm; 30 min.; one way 25.50F, round-trip 38F). Buses also leave for Granville (Mon.-Fri. 4 per day, 1 on Sat.; 1¼ hr.) (Open Mon.-Tues. and Thurs.-Fri. 11:15am-12:15pm and 3:45-6:30pm, Wed. 10am-12:15pm and 3:45-6:30pm, Sat. 8:45am-12:15pm.)

Avranches has a wonderful **Auberge de Jeunesse,** 15, rue de Jardin des Plantes (tel. 33-58-06-54), near the Jardin des Plantes. However, you may not find space during the off-season, when the hostel houses primarily young workers. The hostel enjoys a TV room, ironing board, and superb kitchen facilities. (38F includes breakfast. Sheets 20F. Reception open Mon.-Fri. 5:30-9pm. Closed Sat. 2-6:30pm and after 8pm, closed Sun. 10am-6:30pm. Curfew 10pm, but you can get a key.) If the hostel is full, the **Hôtel la Renaissance,** rue des Fossés (tel. 33-58-03-71), is not far, behind the town hall. The young-at-heart, extremely friendly owners offer sunny rooms, and the jovial bar downstairs is always filled with neighbors. (Singles 55F. Doubles 95F. No showers. Breakfast 14F.) **Hôtel le Select,** 11, rue de Mortain (tel. 33-58-10-62), features an equally friendly proprietor, as well as nicely furnished rooms. (Singles 70F. Doubles 88F, with bath 105F. Showers 15F.) Across the street at #6, **Le Valois** (tel. 33-58-13-59), an enticing gourmet shop, sells take-out goulash and chicken for 10-15F per portion. (Open Jan.-June 20 and July 15-Dec. Mon.-Sat. 8am-1pm and 3-5:30pm, Sun. 3-5:30pm.) There are lots of cheap *brasseries* and restaurants around the *syndicat,* place Littre. **L'Express Bar,** rue des Fossés (tel. 33-68-35-64), has indoor and outdoor seating and plenty of appetizing *galettes* for 20-40F. (Open in summer Mon.-Sat. 9am-midnight, Sun. 5pm-midnight; in off-season Mon.-Sat. only.)

Mont St-Michel

No matter how many times you've seen it in pictures, you will be awed when you first glimpse Mont St-Michel. Shrouded in an immense and airy solitude, this dazzling structure soars over the swelling mass of land and sea. Built painstakingly over seven centuries on a tiny island (now connected to the mainland by a causeway), the stone buildings testify to both monastic solitude and Benedictine grandeur. The Mont today is understandably the victim of unrivaled tourist invasions. Try to get there in the morning; the crowds are as irritating as the Mont is unforgettable.

Orientation and Practical Information

Reaching Mont St-Michel is not a problem, although a little preliminary planning is necessary. **Trains** continue no farther than **Pontorson,** where STN buses (across from the Gare, tel. 33-60-10-97) shuttle passengers the remaining 10km to the Mont (6 per day, round-trip 25F, railpasses not valid); the last STN bus from the Mont to Pontorson leaves at 6:05pm. By train from Paris-Montparnasse, change at Dol for Pontorson (2 per day, 4¼ hr., 175F). The last train from Pontorson to Dol leaves at 9:12pm. **SNCF buses** (tel. 33-66-00-35) also connect Dol and the Mont but run on an inconvenient schedule. **Courriers Bretons et Normands** (tel. 33-60-11-43) offers regular service to Avranches, Granville, Villedieu, Caen, and St-Lô. For more information, stop in at the office by the train station in Pontorson. (Open Mon.-Fri. 8:30am-7pm.) Don't bother buying the museum tickets that the driver sells after the journey. The bus may be your best bet, though reliance on the bus precludes any evening prospect of the Mont. Hitching is difficult. You can rent a **bike** at the Pontorson train station (tel. 33-66-00-35; open daily 8am-noon and 2-8pm) for a half-day (35F), a day (45F), or a week (260F)—the road is straight and mostly flat farmland.

The Mont, a city unto itself, is structured around one central rampart, the Grand-Rue. Most hotels, restaurants, and sights are located along this thoroughfare.

Syndicat d'Initiative: Boîte Postale 4, 50116 Le Mont St-Michel (tel. 33-60-14-30), located behind the stone wall to your left after you pass through the Porte du Roi. The *syndicat* sells posters and books at lower prices than the stores. Ask about organized 2-hr. hiking expeditions over the sand to the **Ile de Tombelaine,** the other, much smaller outcrop in the bay

(April-June and Aug.-Sept., at the time of day when the tide is at its lowest). Avoid the **currency exchange** here—exchange rates at Mont St-Michel are badly inflated. Ask for the useful *Horaire des Marées,* a schedule of high and low tides. Open in summer Mon.-Sat. 9am-6pm; in off-season Mon.-Sat. 9am-noon and 2-6pm.

Post Office: Grand-Rue, near the Porte du Roi. **Postal Code:** 50116. Open Mon.-Fri. 9am-7pm, Sat. 9am-noon.

Bus Stop: All buses leave from the Porte du Roi. Tickets are available on board.

Medical Emergency: Tel. 15.

Police Emergency: Tel. 17.

Accommodations, Camping, and Food

Spending the night in Mont St-Michel may prove expensive, so you might consider staying in St-Malo, Avranches, or Pontorson instead. Most of the listings below are in Pontorson (**Postal code:** 50170), a small village reminiscent of old Normandy.

Pleine-Fougères (IYHF), rue de la Gare (tel. 33-48-75-69), about 5km from Pontorson. Count on walking both ways: Buses to Pleine-Fougères run only in the morning, and leave the town only in the afternoon. Members 57F. Open July-Aug.

Hôtel de la Croix Blanche, rue Grande Pontorson (tel. 33-60-14-04), in Mont St-Michel. Located in the thick of the souvenir shops and seething throngs of visitors. Not unreasonable, considering its location. Some rooms have a view. Reservations preferred. Singles 90F, doubles 110F. 47F *menu* in the restaurant downstairs. Open March 15-Oct. 15 7am-2am.

Hôtel de l'Arrivée, place de la Gare (tel. 33-60-01-57), near the station in Pontorson. Wildflower wallpaper and enthusiastic owners make this an excellent choice. Singles 52-82F, doubles 92-102F. Breakfast 14.50F. *Menu* downstairs 30F.

Hôtel de France, 2, rue des Rennes (tel. 33-60-29-17), across from the train station in Pontorson. A decent establishment. Singles from 50F. Open 7:30am-11pm.

Hôtel du Chalet, place de la Gare (tel. 33-60-00-16) in Pontorson. Enthusiastic owner. Clean singles 85F, doubles 120F. Big room for 6 215F. Breakfast 17F. Open June-Aug. 7am-2am; Sept.-May 7am-midnight.

Centre Equestre, 3km from Pontorson (tel. 33-60-27-73), toward Mont St-Michel. Take the STN bus to Mont St-Michel from the station and ask the driver to be let off. Sometimes accepts backpackers and cyclists. Call from the station to see if they have space.

Camping: Camping Pont d'Orson, rue de la Victoire (tel. 33-60-00-18), 10 min. from the station in Pontorson. A 1-star site by the river. Simple but adequate. 6F per person, 9F per tent. Showers included. **Camping du Mont St-Michel,** P.B. 8, 50116 Le Mont St-Michel (tel. 33-60-09-33). As close to the Mont as you will get (1.8km), at the junction of D275 and N776. Clean, pleasantly shaded sites. Next door is **Motel Vert** (doubles with shower 150F) and a supermarket. Best location for viewing the Mont at night, but fills fast. Reserve in advance. Adults 12F, children 6F, 8F per car, 10F per tent. **Camping St-Michel,** Route du Mont St-Michel (tel. 33-70-96-90), by the bay. A bit far from the Mont (9km), but the Granville bus stops 200m from the entrance. Buses go to the Mont at 10:30am and 5pm; ask the helpful proprietor for the return schedules. The sites are quiet and equipped with a common room and telephone. 12F per person, 6F per tent. Open May-Oct. 1. Gates open 24 hours.

Overpriced snackbars abound. The Mont's specialty is *omelette poulard,* a fluffy omelette like a soufflé (about 20F). Ask for a recipe at the *syndicat.* The best idea, however, is to pack a picnic and eat in the abbey gardens near the top of the hill (a few flights below the entrance to the abbey, admission 3F), or on the beach at low tide. Get your provisions at the **Shopi** supermarket at 5, rue Couesnon, in Pontorson. (Open Mon.-Sat. 9am-7:15pm, Sun. 9:30am-noon.)

Several cheap eateries line rue Couesnon in Pontorson, but the best is **Le Grillon,** a snack bar at 37, rue Couesnon, with crepes (5-25F), sandwiches, and a grill *menu.* **La Cave,** 37, rue de la Libération, is an overpriced hotel but has a particularly varied and tasty 42F *menu.*

Sights

In 708, the archangel St-Michel appeared in a glorious dream to the Bishop of Avranches. St-Michel told the bishop to build him a place of worship, the fruit of which was a rather modest oratory. Under the work begun by 30 monks from Jumièges, the structure expanded over the centuries with Romanesque and Gothic buildings on the top and sides of the rock, and fortifications surrounding them. As it grew to be one of the most influential spiritual bastions in northern Europe, visitors flocked behind the walls, inspiring the development of the *ville basse,* along with its proliferation of souvenir shops (medieval tourists took home chunks of the Mont as mementos).

Enter via the **Porte Bavole,** the only break in the outer walls, and then through the **Porte du Roi** onto Grand-Rue, a winding pedestrian street full of souvenir stands and restaurants. The overpowering crush may help you imagine what the Mont was like when a medieval pilgrimage passed through. After climbing several flights of stairs, you will arrive at the **abbey** entrance. In order to visit, you'll have to take an obligatory one-hour tour. (Open daily June-Sept. 15 9am-7pm; Sept. 15-June 9-11:30am and 1:30-5pm. Tours in English daily at 10:30am, noon, 2:30pm, and 4:30pm. Tours in French every 15 min. Admission 23F, ages 18-25 and over 60 13F, ages under 18 3F, Sun. half-price.) For a special treat, take one of the more detailed *visites conférences.* These two-hour tours allow you to walk atop a flying buttress and creep inside the darkest crypts. (Daily at 10am, 11am, 2pm, 3pm, and 4:15pm. 30F.)

The church balances on the highest point of the island, supported by some very cold crypts below and deliberately exposed to the skies for communion with the heavens. Passing through the refectory, you will descend into the dark and astonishingly chilly church foundations whose walls at some points are 2m thick. **La Merveille,** an intricately designed thirteenth-century cloister housing the monastery, encloses a seemingly endless web of passageways and rooms. If you're not impressed with its architectural complexities, the mechanical simplicity of the Mont's treadmill will surely catch your attention. Here, prisoners held in the Mont during the French Revolution would walk for hours without moving any distance. Their foot labor powered the elaborate pulley system that carried heavy stones up the side of the Mont.

Most interesting, however, may be the **Logis Tiphaine,** built in 1365 by the governor Bertrand du Guesclin to protect his young wife Tiphaine, an astrologer, from the English while he was fighting in Spain. After nine years here, Tiphaine died at the age of 39 "*d'une maladie de langueur.*" (Open daily 9am-6pm. Admission 15F, students 10F, children under 12 5F.)

After the tour, escape down the ramparts and into the abbey garden for some spectacular vistas of Normandy and Brittany. From here, you can reflect upon the soaring stone buttresses that wrap around the entire island to support the abbey—remember that each stone brought here was lifted by pulley. As you walk back through the *ville basse,* pause in the pretty parks off the ramparts, and circle the Mont's base along the sandy beach at the bottom. (You can use the ramparts to descend to the Porte du Bavole, thus avoiding the asphyxiating main street.) Do not wander off on the sand at any time of day. The bay's tides are the highest in Europe, shifting every 10 hours or so. During high-tide days, or *mascaret,* the water recedes for 18km and rushes in at 2m per second, flooding the beaches along the causeway. To see this spectacle, you must be within the abbey fortifications two hours ahead of time.

When darkness falls, Mont St-Michel is lit up, its brilliance reflected in the surrounding water. You can best see the glowing mount from the entrance to the causeway or from Avranches across the bay. (The Mont is illuminated at all church festivals and feasts, on high-tide nights, and July-Sept. nightly dusk-11pm.)

The beginning of summer at the Mont is celebrated in May at a spectacular folklore festival, **St-Michel de Printemps.** In July and August, a series of concerts, **Les Heures Musicales du Mont St-Michel,** takes place in the abbey. (Adults 70F per concert, students 35F.) Buy tickets at the door, or contact the *syndicat* in Avranches for more information.

Channel Islands (Iles Normandes)

US$1 = £0.58   **£1 = US$1.70**

The cliff-ringed Channel Islands are fertile, sandy, mild, and comfortable. Popular with the English and French, who swarm here on holiday in July and August, the islands are a pleasant interlude midway between France and England.

When King John lost the rest of the Duchy of Normandy to the French in 1204, the Channel Islands remained under the protection of the crown of England and have remained so through several French attempts to reclaim it. After the invasion of the islands by Hitler's troops, islanders evacuated to England and returned after the war with English ideas and slang. In return for fealty to the British, the islands enjoy favorable trade regulations and almost complete autonomy. Jersey has its own volunteer State Assembly, as does the Bailiwick of Guernsey, a federation of Guernsey and the smaller islands that surround it. Both stress democracy and moderation. As this home-rule suggests, the Channel Islands swear allegiance to neither one nor the other of their powerful neighbors. However, in speech, manner, custom, and cuisine, the Channel Islands appear ever so English.

Both Guernsey and Jersey issue their own currencies, of the same denominations and value as British sterling, but French currency is accepted by some and British currency by everyone. To avoid any difficulties, exchange your francs upon arriving.

Most ferry companies offer moderate round-trip fares to either Jersey or Guernsey, but one-way travel to and from either island is prohibitively expensive. It's most economical to visit only one island and explore its rolling countryside. Whichever island you visit, don't forget the hour difference in time.

Jersey

La Reine de la Manche (the Queen of the Channel), as the French call Jersey, harbors some surprisingly pretty coastal inlets behind the unattractive facade of its capital, St-Helier. Jersey is famed for sweaters, stamps, and packaged-tour holidays; unfortunately the last make the island seem like one cluttered duty-free shop. Since Jersey does not impose a sales tax, luxury goods are less expensive than they are in either France or England. Residents of both countries come in droves to clean up, leaving the island a little seamier in the process. Jersey's countryside, however, is rugged, green, and even more isolated than that of Guernsey. Try to avoid the built-up coast between St-Helier and Gorey. Instead, explore the cliff paths along Plemont and Bonley Bay, and relax on the sweeping, crescent-shaped St-Owen's beach.

Getting There and Getting Around

Reaching Jersey from either France or England is not difficult, but it can be expensive without a round-trip ticket. Most ferries from France leave the *gare maritime* in St-Malo and take roughly two hours to reach Jersey, with the exception of **Condor Hydrofoil**, Commodore Travel, 28 Conway St. and Albert Quay (tel. 721-63), in St-Helier, which makes the voyage in an unbeatable hour from St-Malo (2 each way per day 191F, same-day return 226F, 3-day return 328F, after 72 hr. 344F). **Vedettes Blanches** (tel. 744-58 or 788-46 in Jersey; 99-56-63-21 in St-Malo), runs once per day from St-Malo to Jersey (185F, 3-day return 309F, period return

174

324F). **Emeraude Ferries** (tel. 744-58 in Jersey; 99-82-83-84 in St-Malo), runs one or two ferries per day (191F, same-day return 196F, 3-day return 312F, after 72 hr. 327F). **Vedettes Armoricaines** (tel. 99-56-48-88 in St-Malo), makes the voyage to Jersey from St-Malo once or twice per day as well (rates vary with the days of the week; one way 170-180F, same-day return 200-216F, 3-day return 270-290F, after 72 hr. 295-315F).

Two ferry companies connect **Granville** to the Channel Islands. **Vedettes Vertes,** 1 and 3, rue Lecampian (tel. 33-50-16-36), has ferries leaving Granville for Jersey (April-Sept. at least 1 per day, 10 hr.), with an option to continue to Guernsey. **Vedettes Armoricaines,** 12, rue George Clemenceau (tel. 33-50-77-45 in Granville), sails to Jersey (May-Sept.). In addition, **Condor** and various companies in Britain offer ferries from the Channel Islands to **Weymouth,** England (one way 260F, round-trip 520F). All ferries offer reduced fares to children.

Cycling is the best way to see the unspoiled beauty of Jersey, although the long hills of the coast will almost certainly challenge you. If you're renting a bike, you'll have to make do with a 3-speed, as 10-speed rentals are not available. In general, most rentals charge £2.50 per day and £11 per week, with a £5 deposit. If you're over 21 and have an international driver's license, you can rent a moped for £6.50 per day, £33 per week from **Kingslea's,** 77, Esplanade (tel. 247-77). Hitching in Jersey can be difficult since most of the drivers are tourists.

St-Helier

The capital of Jersey, St-Helier exudes the rough-edged staleness of a port overrun by holiday tourism. The city is remarkably unattractive given the natural beauty of the island. Amid the duty-free shops and dingy bars, however, there are numerous inexpensive bed and breakfasts and a plethora of cheap restaurants. Don't let the town's gray atmosphere discourage you from viewing the rest of Jersey.

Practical Information

Tourist Office: The Weighbridge (tel. 780-00 for information and accommodations, 247-79 for information), near the docks. Open May-Oct. Mon.-Sat. 8am-9:15pm, Sun. 8am-noon and 6-9:15pm; Nov.-April Mon.-Fri. 8:45am-12:30pm and 1:45-5pm, Sat. 9am-12:30pm.

Post Office: Broad St. (tel. 262-62). You must use Jersey stamps on all mail. **Currency exchange. General Delivery.** No postal code. Open Mon.-Fri. until 5:30pm, Sat. until 1pm.

Telephone code: 534.

Airport: Tel. 461-11.

Bus Station: All buses leave from outside Weighbridge station, across from the tourist office. Service is frequent and fast. To Gorey Village (Mon.-Sat. every 20 min., Sun. every 40 min.; ½ hr.; 68p), Rozel Bay (every hr., ½ hr., 68p), the Zoo via La Hongue Bie (every 1-2 hr., last bus at 6:15pm, ½ hr., 68p), the German Underground Hospital (every hr., 15 min., 53p), St-Brelade's Bay (every hr., 25 min., 68p), St-Ouen's Bay (every hr., 40 min., 80p).

Ferries: Condor Hydrofoil, Commodore Travel, 28 Conway St. and Albert Quay (tel. 712-63). **Emeraude Ferries,** Tel. 744-58. **Vedettes Blanches,** Tel. 744-58 or 788-46.

Luggage Deposit: Across from terminal 2 in the Condor Hydrofoil office. 50p per day for as many days as your heart desires. Open 7:45am-6:30pm.

Laundromat: McClary's, 13 Burand St., near the center. Wash and dry about £1.60. Last wash 4:45pm. **Launderette,** 51 David Place, across from Royal Lives Assurance Co. Open daily 8am-8pm. Last wash 7:45pm.

Beach Guards: St-Ouen's Bay, Tel. 820-32. **Plemont Bay,** Tel. 816-36.

Hospital: General Hospital, Gloucester St. (tel. 710-00). Free clinic May-Sept. Mon.-Fri. 9am-12:30pm, Sat. 10-11:30am; Oct.-April Mon., Wed., Fri. 9-11am. Prescription charge £1.

Police: Rouge Bouillon, Tel. 755-11.

Emergency: Tel. 999 (no coins required).

Accommodations and Camping

If you think that finding a room in Jersey during the summer is a difficult task, you're wrong: It's nearly impossible. Luckily, you can take advantage of the free and efficient accommodations service at the tourist office (reservations for all of Jersey). Keep in mind that many B&Bs will take only visitors who stay for a few days or even a week. If you arrive late in the day during either July or August, be prepared to pay as much as £15. Many of the places listed below will be booked through September. You can ensure summer slumber under a roof only by reserving up to a year in advance. All of the following accept reservations by phone but may also require written confirmation and/or deposit. Meals are not obligatory and cost extra.

La Fontaine, 59 David Place (tel. 233-03). One of the cheaper B&Bs but a pleasant grade A. £10 per person. Doubles with shower £10.75 per person. Open May-Oct.

Bromley, 7 Winchester St. (tel. 239-48), near the center off Val Plaisant. Pleasant dining room; even the garrets are spacious and comfortable. Speak French, if you can; the proprietors do. B&B with dinner only: £14.75 per person, £16 with private shower.

Roselynne Guest House, 16 Roseville St. (tel. 732-23). Clean, modern rooms in an excellent location, but not very spacious. Pleasant proprietor and relaxed T.V crowd each night in the lounge. £15 per person.

Les Avenues, Les Platons (tel. 610-93), in Trinity. Follow the A9 north from St-Helier; at the A8, proceed straight onto the B63, and turn right onto the C97. The house is on your right, marked by a tiny wooden sign—take the bumpy dirt road to the B&B in the back of the farm. Or take bus #4 to Les Platons, and ask the driver to let you off near the radio towers (last bus at 5:45pm, 50p). Peaceful, pastoral, and spacious. Friendly proprietor. No singles. 3 doubles £7.50 per person, monstrous double for 1 person £11.

Les Ruettes, St-Lawrence (tel. 629-88), in the center of the island next to Carrefour Selons off the A10. Friendly guest house in the thick of pastures. Peaceful and quiet. £8 per person. Open July 30-Sept. 30.

Camping: Most of the island's campsites have facilities and services such as general stores with refrigerated goods, TV and game rooms, swimming pools, and hot showers. Reservations are necessary, so call ahead. **Beauvelande Camp Site,** in St-Martin (tel. 535-75), off route A6 from St-Helier. Take bus #3, debark at St-Martin's school, continue in the same direction, take the second right, and follow the signs; it's a 30-minute walk (last bus at 11:20pm). Quiet, secluded area; however, the site tends to attract families with extremely energetic children. Proprietor straight out of Mary Poppins. Excellent **bikes** £2 per day, £10 per week. Adults £4, children £3. Open April-Oct. **Rozel Camping Park,** just south of Rozel Bay (tel. 519-89). From St-Helier, follow the A6 all the way to St-Martin's church and continue straight through the intersection along the B38—the campsite is to the right on the B38. June-Sept. £3.50; April-May £2.70. Tent rental £2-4. Open April-Sept. 20. **St-Brelade's Camping Park,** just off route A13 (tel. 413-98), halfway between St-Aubin and St-Ouen's Bay. Quiet spot with inexpensive dinner and breakfast menus. Adults £4, children £2, £4 per tent, 50p per car. Open April-Sept. 15. **Quennevais Camping Site,** in St-Brelade (tel. 424-36), 100m south of the airport. A small grocery store and proximity to deafening jet airplane engines. Adults £3, children £1.50, £3 per tent. Open May-Sept.

Food

Jersey restaurants are adequate and inexpensive. Tea shops, featuring cream tea, a midday snack of sweet biscuits, clotted sweet cream, and jam, and wine bars are the best values. In St-Helier, many of these cluster around Bath St.; **Le Mesuriers** offers a ploughman's—salad with cheese or *pâté* and bread—lunch for 90p. Some B&Bs serve dinner for about £3, but you can usually do better in a restaurant. Ask the tourist office for a list of winners in the Good Food Festival (see Sights and Entertainment), many of which are reasonably priced. Be sure to visit the large open **market** held daily at Halkett Place. For a cheap meal, try one of the numerous pubs in the harbor area. Jersey dairy products are fresh and good—buy yogurt, ice cream, and milk, but avoid the vanilla milkshakes, which some Americans have likened to Kaopectate without the medicinal benefits.

Graham's Restaurant, 37 David Place (tel. 705-97). Filling 3-course menu £2.95 in a diner setting. Includes a choice of meat or fish large enough to curl up and go to sleep on, enough soup to dive into, and apple pie bobbing in fresh Jersey cream. Open daily 7am-2pm and 4:30-8pm.

Plates Restaurant, 24 Beresford St. (tel. 216-67). Light meal and sandwich shop bedecked entirely in—guess what. The moving window display is worth the visit. Great music. Tasty sandwiches 85p, ploughman's lunch £1.50. Scones and cream tea to suit the Mad Hatter. Children's menu.

Leaders Health Foods, 10-12 Beresford St. (tel. 715-88). Natural-foods shop and deli. The only soy milk connection around. Every kind of fresh juice imaginable. Wholesome sandwiches 80p. Wonderful whole-grain bakery. Vegetarian restaurant upstairs.

Broadway Restaurant, 24 Esplanade (tel. 795-03). A few theatrical names for some excellent food. Minelli or Streisand burger £2.40-3.65. Try the deep-fried rings of fresh squid £1.75. Open noon-2pm and 6-10pm.

The Waterfront, Chicago Pizza Restaurant, 10 Wharf St. (tel. 277-99). Curiously attired management. Soft rock music in a tavern-style ambience. Pizza £2.35-3.50. Apple pie £1.25. Open daily noon-11pm.

Albert J. Ramsbottom, 90/92 Halkett Place (tel. 787-72). A popular seafood restaurant with classical music in the background. Chicken or fish special with fries and ice cream £2.75. Open daily 11:30am-2pm and 5-10pm.

The Cobweb, St-Brelade's Bay. A good spot for refreshments if you're camping or swimming in the bay. Pleasant atmosphere. Homemade cakes, pots of tea, sandwiches. Not the cheapest.

Sights and Entertainment

At low tide, you can walk from St-Helier's grimy, gray, thin beach out to **Elizabeth Castle,** a Tudor fortress in the middle of the harbor. The castle is strong on anecdote, but weak on visual impact. On **Hermitage Rock** at the castle's south side, brooded Helier himself, a pious, sixth-century hermit decapitated by invading Vandals. (Open March-Oct. daily 9:30am-5:30pm. Admission 80p.) A second castle, Napoleonic **Fort Regent,** has been converted into an ultra-modern sports and entertainment complex that has almost destroyed the old character of St-Helier's center; it contains an aquarium, a shell museum, a postal museum, an exhibition hall, and carnival rides, in addition to a roller rink, swimming pool, weight-training room, and other sports facilities. The heated pool is open until 7:30pm during the week and until 5:30pm on weekends. The disco sponsors free vodka nights every night in March from 9:30pm. You pay only for the mixers. (Entire complex open in summer 10am-9:30pm; in off-season 10am-5:30pm. Admission in summer £3, in off-season £1.25.)

Bits of old Jersey history are preserved below the fort, in the **Jersey Museum,** 9 Pier Rd. The natural history exhibits are rather dull, but the museum is worth a visit for the **Lillie Langtry Room,** featuring memorabilia of "the Jersey Lily," a Victorian actress who was the reigning beauty of her time and one of Edward VII's mistresses. The **Barreau Art Gallery** on the second floor features a Gainsborough charcoal sketch, considered one of the earliest representations of a Jersey cow; Blampied watercolors for the first edition of Barrie's *Peter Pan;* a few works by Victorian portraitist Millais, a famous son of Jersey; and local oils of Jersey during the German occupation. (Open Mon.-Sat. 10am-5pm. Admission 80p, students 40p.)

A series of flower shows throughout the summer leads up to the **Battle of Flowers** each August. Some 30 floats covered with hundreds of thousands of blooms parade down the main thoroughfare. Festivities continue during the week with bands and entertainment. In days past, the procession of flower-decked floats would culminate in an orgy of destruction as people pulled the entries apart and pelted one another with petals. In the interest of order, however, the tourist office has decreed that winning floats should be preserved in a museum—hence the **Battle of the Flowers Museum** (in La Robelaine, Mont des Corvées St-Ouen), full of mummified blooms. (Open March-Nov. daily 10am-5pm. Admission 80p.) You must get bleacher seats in advance for the Battle Parade (£5-6). For tickets, contact the Jersey Battle of Flowers Association, Burlington House, St-Savior's Rd., St-Helier (tel. 301-78).

Nightlife abounds in Jersey, albeit of a rather honky-tonk nature. Nightclubs and discos fill the town; all are listed in the information guide available from the tourist office. **Thackery's** on the Esplanade specializes in trendy disco evenings that are popular with locals. Buy the *Evening Post* for a listing of current movies (£2.50-3) or shows at the Opera House. Free weekly concerts with brass bands or jazz groups take place throughout the summer in **Howard Davies Park.**

In the four-day **Jersey Good Food Festival** in May, local restaurants compete to tantalize the palate and delight the eye. While many gastronomic events cost upwards of £8-14 per person, there's plenty of free wine, crêpes, and seafood. A few restaurants and cafes offer live jazz music. Pick up a program at the tourist office. In June, the **Festival France and Jersey** celebrates the close ties between Jersey and Normandy with folk dancing, jazz and classical concerts, art exhibitions, cabaret, and theatre. During this festival, the entire French school system visits Jersey for their year-end spree. (For more information, call 267-88.)

Jersey Countryside

Gorey Village, Jersey's second largest town, consists of three stores and so few streets you may bump into yourself. The town's stellar attraction is **Mont Orgeuil Castle,** a massive and ruggedly beautiful thirteenth-century fort. Don't miss the Machicolated Bastion, whose name is as terrifying as its function. The slitted windows allowed defenders to shower unwanted visitors with boiling oil and rocks. (Open late March-Oct. daily 9:30am-6pm, last admission at 5pm. Admission £1.) The bay below the castle is lined with restaurants, souvenir shops, and expensive hotels. The **Oakleigh Guest House** (tel. 557-95) offers B&B for £10 in high season, £9 in middle season (open March-late Sept.), but there are more picturesque places to stay (see St-Helier Accommodations). To reach Gorey Village by bike, follow the A6 out of St-Helier, and turn right onto the B28, which winds its way to the castle. Buses to Gorey Village depart every 20 minutes Mon.-Sat., every 40 minutes Sun. (½ hr., 68p).

On the way to Gorey Village along the B28 is **La Hougue Bie,** an intriguing religious complex. At the base of a large hill lies the entrance to a 50-meter-long dolmen. You can crawl on your hands and knees down the four-foot-high tunnel and be damp and frightened. Outside, the tomb is covered by a 60-foot mound, capped by two medieval chapels. The tiny, twelfth-century **Notre Dame de la Clarté** has a simple eloquence and marvelous acoustics. Abutting this marvel is the dark and unexciting fifteenth-century **Jerusalem Chapel.** Nearby are the **Railway Museum, Agricultural Museum, Archeological Museum, Geological Museum,** and **German Occupation Museum.** All except the Occupation Museum are terribly dull. (Open March-Nov. Tues.-Sun. 10am-5pm. Last ticket issued at 4:15pm. Admission 80p, students 40p.)

To the north of La Hougue Bie on the B46 is author Gerald Durrell's **Jersey Zoo,** in Les Augres Manor. Protected by the Jersey Wildlife Preservation Trust, the 20-acre zoo is home to a variety of endangered species. Wallabies resembling giant gerbils, orangutans, a plumed basilisk that looks like a miniature creature from the black lagoon, snow leopards, and Chilean flamingoes meditate in exile. (Open daily 10am-6pm. Last ticket issued at 5pm. Admission £2.20, children under 14 £1.20. Closes at dusk in winter.) During the German Occupation, the Channel Islands became one of the most heavily fortified areas in Western Europe because of their strategic position near occupied Normandy. You can't avoid the bunkers and fortifications that crop up frequently along the coastline. Before the German seizure of the islands, Jersey had been completely demilitarized. At the **German**

Underground Hospital, Meadowbank, St-Lawrence, you can learn about the bombing of a fleet of potato lorries in St-Helier on June 28, 1940. The squadron of German bombers mistook the lorries for military vehicles. (Open March-Nov. daily 9:30am-5:30pm. Admission £2, children under 14 90p.) To reach the underground hospital from St-Helier, follow either the A1 or A2 out of town along St-Aubin's Bay, turn right onto the A11, and then continue straight onto the B99. Buses leave St-Helier for the hospital every hour (15 min., 53p).

Nearby, off A11, is the **Strawberry Farm** (tel. 836-24), in St-Peter's Valley. Avoid the dull museum, but don't miss the delicious strawberries and cream. You need not pay £1.25 for the ready-made desserts on the counter—just ask for a *punnet* of strawberries (50p); the cream and sugar are served free. (Farm open March-Oct. daily 9am-6pm.)

Three Jersey churches merit detours. In the **Fisherman's Chapel,** by the old parish church of St-Brelade, Norman murals still hang on the walls. **St-Matthew's Church,** in Millbrook between St-Helier and Coronation Park, is known as the "Glass Church" for its Lalique glass. **St-Saviour's Church,** near St-Helier, was administered 150 years ago by Deacon Le Breton, Lillie Langtry's father, and the Jersey Lily herself is buried in the family plot in the church graveyard.

Jersey has recently constructed several excellent cliff paths—all are satisfying day hikes, and some are illuminated at night. A vigorous mile separates romantic **Castle Grosnez** with its Cyrano de Bergerac-style promontory (open daily 9:30am-5:30pm; admisssion 80p), and Plemont Point. Other hikes take you from St-Aubin's to Corbière, and between Crabbe, Sorel, and Devil's Hole. The tourist office in St-Helier has details.

Jersey beaches come in all categories to suit all swimmers. But take care: Tides here are dangerous; the tourist board's list warns you about the danger spots. Beautiful **St-Brelade's Bay** is most popular, but **St-Ouen's Bay,** whose 5-mile sweep along Jersey's east coast receives the Atlantic surf, is the roughest and most spectacular. Surfboards are rented here. **Anne Port** and **St-Catherine** to the east are gentler, with small coves and little ripples of surf.

Guernsey

Never refer to Guernsey as part of the British Isles—despite its size, Guernsey is a country unto itself. The people of the Bailiwick (including Guernsey, Sark, Herm, and Alderney) have somewhat protected themselves from outside interference, including the grosser forms of tourism rampant in neighboring Jersey. By the gossip over shop counters and the joking familiarity of the pubs, the visitor is reminded that the pleasures of these islands are intended for the inhabitants themselves. Nonetheless, the sensitive visitor is more than welcome to share the Bailiwick's diversions and daily routine.

Western Guernsey is fringed with wide, sandy beaches; ominous gray bunkers and martello towers pepper the perimeter. The island's interior consists of a network of little roads, winding among grassy hills, wooded headlands, and cliffs. Cows and small cottages dot the landscape, while looming manor houses lend an element of mystery to the pastoral scenery.

Getting There and Getting Around

From France, **Condor Hydrofoil,** North Pier Stops, St-Peter Port (tel. 261-21), skims the water from St-Malo to Guernsey (2-3 per day, 2 hr., 223F, same-day return 242F, 3-day return 398F, after 72 hr. 414F). Condor also connects Guernsey to Jersey (3-4 per day; 1 hr.; 130F, open return 153F). **Emeraude Ferries,** New Jetty White Rock, St-Peter Port (tel. 71-14-14), connects St-Malo to Guernsey via Jersey daily (233F, open return 420F). Between Jersey and Guernsey, **Aurigny Air Services,** South Esplanade, Guernsey (tel. 234-74), makes 15-minute flights almost every half-hour (£16, same-day return £23.50). Guernsey is also accessible from Granville through **Vedettes Vertes** via Jersey (£231, same-day return £260, open return £304).

Since Guernsey comprises only about 24 square miles, you can walk almost anywhere on the island if you have enough time and patience. *Perry's Guide* (£1.50), with detailed maps and suggested walking paths for all the islands in the Bailiwick, is useful if you're planning to explore by foot or by bike. Hitching is almost impossible in St-Peter Port, but becomes somewhat more feasible away from the city. All buses leave from the terminal outside **The Picquet House** (tel. 246-77), which offers maps and details on the extensive bus system. An islandwide **Rover bus ticket** will give you unlimited bus travel for one day (£2) or one week (£10), but is only worthwhile if you plan to see all the sights. Though Guernsey is hillier than Jersey, cycling is still possible. For rental details, see Practical Information or ask at the information bureau.

St-Peter Port

The white-painted buildings of St-Peter Port climb the hillsides of the granite valley from which the town was hewn. Guernsey's capital is bustling and popular, offering delightful cobblestoned streets and some exceptional scenery. Constructed as the gateway to Guernsey, the town is perhaps most beautiful when seen from above, at Candie Gardens or the top of Constitution Steps.

Practical Information

Information Bureau: Crown Pier (tel. 235-52), 1 pier down from Sealink Dock. Free, efficient help with accommodations (necessary in high season). Free map and tourist guide, *What's On in Guernsey.* Open Mon.-Sat. 9am-8:30pm, Sun. 10:30am-1pm and 6-8:30pm.

Currency Exchange: Many banks in town, e.g., Lloyds, Barclays. Open Mon.-Fri. 9:30am-3:30pm, Sat. 8:30am-noon. **Thomas Cook,** La Pollet St. Open Mon.-Fri. 9am-5:30pm, Sat. 9am-4pm.

Post Office: Smith St. (tel. 262-41). You must use Guernsey stamps on your cards and letters. You can have your letter postmarked with an ornate collectors' stamp if you ask. **General Delivery.** No postal code; just address letters "Guernsey." Open Mon.-Fri. 8:30am-5pm, Sat. 8:30am-noon.

Telephone code: 481.

Airport: Aurigny Air Services, The Picquet House (tel. 234-74).

Buses: The Picquet House (tel. 246-77). Extensive service around the island with special coastal excursions in summer.

Ferries: Condor Hydrofoil, North Pier Steps (tel. 261-21). **British Ferries,** The Jetty (tel. 247-42). **Emeraude Ferries** and **Vedettes Blanches,** both at New Jetty White Rock (tel. 71-14-14).

Taxi: Central Taxi, Tel. 230-47.

Bike Rental: Get a complete list from the Information Bureau. Rentals are scarce in high season; call ahead. **T.G. Moulin & Co.,** St-George's Esplanade (tel. 215-81). Decent 3-speeds and a few 5-speeds £2 per day, no deposit if you give them the address of your hotel or B&B. Open Mon.-Sat. 9:30am-12:30pm and 2-6pm. **Millard's,** Victoria Rd. (tel. 207-77). 3-speeds £2 per day, £9.50 per week. 5-speeds £2.20 per day, £12.50 per week. Mopeds £5 per day, £22 per week. Motorcycles and scooters £6.50 per day, £27 per week. Open Mon.-Wed. and Fri.-Sat. 8:30am-12:45pm and 2-5:30pm, Thurs. 8:30am-12:45pm.

Sports: Beau Séjour Leisure Centre, Tel. 272-11. Swimming, saunas, squash, and roller-skating. Tourist membership (£1.50) allows you free admission to swimming, badminton, and table tennis Mon.-Fri. noon-2pm.

Laundromat: 59 Victoria Rd. Wash and dry about £1.60. Open daily 8am-7pm. Last wash 6pm. Also at Tudor House.**Samaritans,** 2 Forrest Lane (tel. 237-31). A suicide hotline.

Emergency: Tel. 999 (no coins required).

Accommodations and Camping

Guernsey controls its tourist industry carefully; all guesthouses are listed and graded in the official accommodations list available at the Information Bureau. Rooms are nearly impossible to find in July and August, so you should take advantage of the Information Bureau's free accommodations service. They'll try to find you a B&B in your price range if possible, but arrive early. There are no youth hostels, but plenty of camping spots.

5 Rozel Terrace, Mount Durand (tel. 240-50), in a residential neighborhood near the center and Victor Hugo House. £8 per person. Some rooms with shower. Open June-Aug.

Friends Guest House, 20 Hauteville (tel. 211-46). Luxurious rooms in a house where Victor Hugo and his family lived from 1855-56. Friendly proprietors. Back porch has a great view of the port. £10.50 per person.

Camping: Guernsey's 6 campsites are all accessible by bus from St-Peter Port, and most will rent equipment, especially if you book in advance. St-Sampson (bus H1 or H2) is nearest and has 2 sites: **Les Capelles Camping Centre,** route des Capelles (tel. 284-69). £2.20 per night. **Vaugrat Camp Site** (Mr. J. A. Lainé), Les Hougues, route de Vaugrat (tel. 574-68). £2.30 per night. Rents bikes. Near St-Sampson, in Guernsey's northern interior, Vale (bus J1 or J2) also has 2 sites: **L'Etoile Site** (Mr. A. M. Brache), Hougue Guilimine (tel. 443-25). £1.80 per night. Open June-Aug. **La Bailloterie** (Mr. H. A. Collas), (tel. 445-08). £1.50 per night. Open Easter-Sept. 14. In adjacent Castel (bus D1 or D2): **Fauxquets Valley Farm** (Mr. R. O. Guille) (tel. 554-60). £2 per night. Open mid-May to Sept. 14. Finally, in Torteval (bus C1 or C2): **Laleur** (Mr. G. O. Robilliard), (tel. 632-71). £2 per night.

Food

St-Peter Port restaurants offer good food for reasonable prices. For lunch, stick to the much cheaper pub grub of hotels and wine bars (usually under £1.75). For dinner, try the streets near La Pollet or above Mill and Mansell St. For baked goods and four o'clock tea, try **Maison Carré,** at the Arcade between Market and High St.

The **Golden Lion** on Market St. is a small, comfortable pub serving Guernsey's own potent Pony Ale on draught. The **Buccaneer** on Albert Pier opposite is loud, large, and smoky, but seems to be where the action is, with food (and baths for sailors) available. The **Brittania** in Trinity Square is small and friendly and serves real ale, which may be more bitter than you're used to, but that's because no gases or chemicals are added.

The Waterfront, Weighbridge (tel. 71-15-07). Deep-fried haddock £2.95. Vegetarian dishes £2.20-3.60. Open daily.

Peddles, High St. across from the town church. Filling and traditional. Tasty pub lunches for under £1.90. Open Mon.-Sat. 11:30am-2pm.

Royal Arms, St-Julien's Ave. (tel. 253-99). Cheap and delicious. Ham pie with vegetables £1.65. Open for lunch only.

Whistler's, Hauteville, near Pedvin St. The island's most famous restaurant, also one of its most expensive. Steak and mushroom pie £3.20, grills £5.10 and up. Try the "nearly mousse" (£1.30) for dessert. Make reservations.

Joker's Restaurant, next to the bus terminal. The cheapest place for dinner. Pizza £2.40-3.90, burgers £1.90-2.75, *spaghetti Bolognese* £2.50. Open Thurs.-Tues. noon-2pm and 6:30-10:15pm.

Sights

Up the hill from the town church, which incorporates twelfth- and thirteenth-century styles, the **market halls** display the abundant produce of Guernsey's soil and sea. The oldest portion, now known as the **French Halles,** was built in 1780 and restricted to the produce of Brittany after the Victorian meat market was erected. In the fish market, you may come across some ormer (from *oreille de mer,* "sea-ear") shells for sale, but they are now mysteriously rare. The animal itself is considered a delicacy, and the increasing shortage is something of a local sorrow. Along the Halles is a retail shop of the state dairy. You can sample the milk of the famous Guernsey cow, but avoid the medicinal-tasting milkshakes.

The **Guernsey Traditional Market,** held most Thursday afternoons on Market St., sells local specialties. Contrary to Guernsey's usual policy, the market and the evening entertainment are crowded and jazzed-up for tourists. (Open May-Sept.) Continuing up Cornet St. to 38 Hauteville, you'll come to Guernsey's most compelling attraction—the **Victor Hugo House** (the house now belongs to the city of Paris). Here Hugo spent 15 years, and wrote his greatest works, including *Les Misérables.* He wrote *Les travailleurs de la mer* (*Toilers of the Sea*) about the island. Exiled from France between 1855 and 1870, Hugo designed and decorated the interior; the house is preserved as the author left it. Gobelin tapestries cover the ceiling, the dining room contains the ancestral chair from which Hugo tried to speak to his forefathers, and symbols from various spiritual groups crop up in every room. The guides are encyclopedically knowledgeable and passionately interested; tours last from 15 minutes to an hour, depending on the group's mood. (Open Mon.-Sat. 10-11:30am and 2-4:30pm. Admission £1, students 50p, children and ages over 60 free.)

There is a statue of Hugo, cape and beard flowing, in the pretty **Candie Gardens,** Candie St. Also in the gardens, the **Guernsey Museum and Art Gallery** has a fairly interesting permanent collection on witchcraft and local archeology, and various temporary exhibitions. (Open daily 10:30am-5:30pm. Admission 70p, students 35p, ages over 60 25p.)

At 20 Smith St., near the post office, the **Channel Island Stamp Company** sells attractive local stamps to collectors. (Open Mon.-Sat. 9am-5pm.) By minting its own stamps and coins, Guernsey manifests its special relationship with Britain. The States of Guernsey, the governing body, meets at the **Royal Court,** at the top of Smith St., on the last Wednesday of every month except August. You can hear the formalities (in French) and the debate (in English) from the gallery. Proceedings begin at 10am; the opening ceremonies are particularly worth seeing. The queen sends a representative to the island parliament, but Guernsey sets its own laws and taxes; the island's only military obligation to England is to rescue the sovereign if he or she is captured and to help recover England if it is taken from the Crown.

Those of a military bent can visit the **Castle Cornet,** off the quay—a complex of fortresses dating from King John's day to that of the Nazis. (Open daily 10:30am-5:30pm. Admission 80p, ages under 14 40p, ages over 60 30p.) More Nazi memorabilia can be examined at the **German Occupation Museum.** (Open daily 10am-5pm. Admission 90p.)

The closest beaches to town are to the south on **Havelet Bay** (take the coast road). The tide-fed bathing pools here are interesting but overrun by crowds and inaccessible at high tide. Instead, take the cliff path up the stairs at the junction of Val des Terres, and in five minutes you will arrive at **Soldier's Bay,** a surprisingly peaceful, pebbly beach that was once reserved for the troops of Fort George, perched on the cliffs above.

In summer, concerts abound in St-Peter Port. Most feature classical music; check at the tourist office. The **Festival de Musique de Notre Dame** sponsors one concert per week in July and August. Contact the Information Bureau for exact dates.

Guernsey Countryside

Guernsey is shaped like a wedge of cheese that the sea has nibbled all around. The tiny bays that ring the island have a different character on each side. The east coast, facing France, is fortified with cliffs to the south and castles to the north. The south coast is a string of tiny, sandy bays, and the west coast is a series of sweeping curves, defined by rocks and headlands. The best way to explore the countryside is by bike, but be warned that the southeast corner of the island is marked by steep hills. Bus service, though extensive, is not very frequent, and hitching can be difficult and dangerous.

Once outside of St-Peter Port, the island turns medieval. Buildings, names, and legends constantly alert you to the Christian and pagan forces that still seem to do battle in the green countryside. The **cliff path** starting from Val des Terres south of St-Peter Port begins quite tamely, but the steep inclines aren't far off; beaches will stretch a mere 100 feet below you. By the end, near Torteval, the cliffs are nearly deserted, and if you wander from the path, you'll be wading through ferns and brambles shoulder-high. Early birds will get to see green **Fermain Bay** uncongested and will get to explore the German fortifications in solitude. Near the beginning of the path, Guernsey's **Aquarium** is housed in a set of tunnels that the Germans strengthened using Soviet and Eastern European prisoner labor during the Occupation. Look for the defiant hammer and sickle chiseled into a wall of the second tunnel. (Open daily 10am-9:30pm. Admission 70p.)

An hour and fifteen minutes by bike from St-Peter Port, you'll pass **Fermain Bay** and then reach **Telegraph Bay** and **St-Martin's Point.** If you're short on time, take the Jerbourg Road bus. One of the most beautiful spots on the island, St-Martin's Point's small grove of evergreens grows on land gently sloping down to the sea. Across Telegraph Bay, the peculiar rocks called "peastacks" protrude at the island's southern tip. Follow the path from here along the cliff to the **Doyle Monument,** which commands an especially good view of Herm.

Continuing around Jerbourg Point, you next reach **Moulin Huet Bay;** take your pick of the beaches here. **Petit Port** has perpendicular cliffs and white, crescent-shaped beaches. **Water Lane** at Moulin Huet, a lane with a stream in the middle, is typical of paths all over the southern bays.

As you continue around the bay to **Icart Point,** consider turning inland for cream tea at **Icart Tea Gardens,** one of the finest tea houses on the island. (Open daily 10am-5pm. Pot o' tea 35p, cream tea £1.) If you turn inland anywhere before Icart, you'll be near **St-Martin's,** the parish adjacent to St-Peter Port. The **St-Martin Parish Church Cemetery** is serenely guarded by *La Grande Mère du Climquière,* a stone lady dating from 700 B.C.E. One church warden who disliked pagans at his doorstep tried to chop her down, as the breaks in the stone attest.

Continuing inland toward the east, you'll soon come to the **German Underground Hospital** in St-Andrew's. It is preserved just as it was the day the Germans abandoned it: damp walls, rusted beds, and fetid atmosphere. (Open April-Oct. daily 10am-noon and 2-5pm. Admission £1, ages under 14 50p.) Also in St-Andrew's is the bizzare **Chapel of Les Vauxbelets,** which claims to be the smallest chapel in Europe. It's large enough only for the priest and two parishioners. The exterior is decorated with shells and bits of broken china—one monk dedicated his life to building it out of broken dishes sent to him by the faithful. About a mile south of the chapel is the **German Occupation Museum.** (Open daily April-Oct. 10:30am-5pm; Nov.-Dec. and Feb.-March 2-4:30pm. Admission 80p, children 40p.)

Rejoin the cliff path from the Occupation Museum and follow it to the end. In lovely, unspoiled **Torteval,** a few minutes from St. Peter Port, the **Imperial Hotel** on Pleinmont St. is anything but, serving excellent, cheap pub lunches (from £1.95) and good dinners. Continue all the way to **Pleinmont Point,** and wade through the ferns and shoulder-high brambles. Along the eastern coast, the grand sprawling expanses of the flat bays—**Roquaine, Vazon, Grand Havre**—are best seen at high tide. Low tide in Guernsey drops as much as 40 feet, which means a lot of walking over slippery rocks to reach knee-deep water. At low tide, however, you can walk across to **Lihou Island,** between Roquaine and Perelle Bays, and see the ruins of the **Priory of St-Mary.**

Legend has it that Guernsey witches based themselves in Perelle Bay at **Le Catri- orc,** one of the island's many ancient dolmens. The best place to discover their secrets is the **Dehus Dolmen** at the northern tip of the island, near the yacht marina in the Vale. Take the bus to Beaucette Marina from St-Peter Port. Though witchcraft has not made a popular resurgence in the island, as recently as 1914 a Mrs.

Lake was accused of weaving a spell over a Mrs. Outin and her husband. The husband fell ill and died, as did all of Mrs. Outin's cattle.

Sark and Herm

From the harbor of St-Peter Port, you can take ferries to two other islands of the Bailiwick. Farther away from St-Peter Port, the crown fief **Sark** is less touristed and more old-fashioned than nearby Herm. No cars are allowed on Sark; the only government is a feudal parliament, and Sark's feudal lord—the "Seigneur"—is still paid peppercorn tribute by 580 residents. His *droit du seigneur* (seigneurial privilege) includes the right to one-thirteenth of the profits from any land sale (a right he exercises even today, since he has no other income). Sark's is the smallest parliament in Europe; it meets in the tiny schoolhouse and consists of the leaseholders of the original 40 *tenements* (farms), 11 elected deputies, the *Seigneur,* the *Senescal* (magistrate), the *Prevot* (sheriff), and the *Greffier* (secretary). Until 1979, residents had to crank their telephones to reach the operator. During World War II, Dame Sibyl Hathaway ruled the island, made famous by her resistance to Nazi occupiers. Unlike the populace of most of the Channel Islands, Sark's residents chose not to evacuate; thus the island retains more of its original French character.

Isle of Sark Shipping Company, Ltd, White Rock (tel. 240-59 in Guernsey), runs ferries from Guernsey that arrive at Maseline and Creux harbor, the smallest free port in Europe. Regular day excursions give you about six hours on Sark (£9.40); long day excursions depart at 7:45am and return at 7pm (£4.75). In summer a ferry runs Tuesday, Thursday, and Saturday between Sark and Herm (1 per day, £6.30). Children ride all ferries for half-price. Details and tickets are available at Picquet House (see Practical Information) or from the kiosk near the clock tower.

The island is only 3½ miles long and 1½ miles wide. It is peaceful farmland sliced by a few dirt roads, awe-inspiring cliff paths overrun by bluebells and primroses, and isolated beach coves. From the harbor, a tractor will take you up to the center for 30p. The main drag (in fact, the only drag) is the Avenue, lined by a few grocery stores and teashops. If you can spare £3, take a horse-drawn carriage tour of the island's most interesting areas. There are also good, three-hour boat tours around the island, featuring local anecdotes and the interiors of some of the coastal caves (£3.50). Everything is within walking distance, but if you're in a hurry, you may want to rent a **bike** from **Jackson's,** at the crossroads on top of Harbor Hill (tel. (83) 21-61; open daily 8am-5:30pm). Rates are £1.50 per half-day, £2 per day, deposit £1. Jackson's also sells maps for 10p; you can get a smaller version free at the **tourist office** at the top of the hill. (Open Mon.-Sat. 10am-noon and 2-4pm; after hours call 23-45.) The most dramatic foot path is **La Coupée,** the steep bridge over Lamentation Caves, which connects Sark with **Little Sark.** Legend has it that before the present bridge was constructed by German prisoner-of-war labor after World War II, Little Sark schoolchildren had to cross above the 260-foot drop on a yardwide plank, crawling while buffeted by 100-mile-per-hour winds in winter. In low tide on Little Sark, gaze at the natural **Venus Pool.** On Wednesdays and Fridays, the lush **Seigneurie Gardens,** watered by the Seigneur himself, are open to the public (10am-5pm, 25p).

Cream teas are a real treat on the island, and the tea garden at **La Sablonnerie** is a lovely setting for munching on crumpets. Try the **Bel Air Tavern** for real Guernsey ale.

Accommodations on Sark are pleasant. Ask for the B&B rate without dinner (with dinner about £12). **Mrs. Sally Ann Brown,** Le Pelon (tel. (83) 22-89), advertises B&B for £8.50. Turn right just before the tourist office and right again after crossing the field; past the Mermaid tavern, turn left. Watch for a sign advertising haircuts. **Mrs. R. L. Wakely,** La Malouine (tel. (83) 21-25), is a particularly good French cook (£8, with dinner £12.50). Follow the directions above, but turn right at the sign for the lighthouse, after passing the tavern. The tourist office unofficially helps with booking.

Only 15 minutes from Guernsey by ferry, tiny **Herm** is essentially a strip of magnificent beach. Peculiarities of the tides sweep smooth shells from as far as 1000 miles away onto the island's shell beach, a long, flat expanse along the northeastern corner, where the swimming is excellent. Herm is very much on the beaten track. Not only is the cove of Belvoir Bay lined with sunbathers, but small yachts and motor boats use the water for a parking lot. Take to the cliff paths for more peace and quiet, but remember to pack a picnic from St-Peter Port, since provisions on Herm (from the 2 general stores and 3 beach cafes) are rather expensive and not very good. Walking around the entire island takes about an hour. The **White House Hotel** (tel. Herm 221-59) is the only one on the island; it is fairly expensive, but it also has a campground (£2.20 per night, ages under 16 £1; open July 13-Sept.).

Kiosks peddling **ferry** tickets to Herm line the St-Peter Port Quay. **Herm Seaways, Trident** (tel. 213-79 in Guernsey), and other ferries leave St-Peter Port in summer every hour from 8:30am, returning every hour until 5:30pm (round-trip £4, children £2.50).

Brittany (Bretagne)

The traveler who braves Breton souvenir shops can still reach the edge of a Breton cliff. Though the way of life in France's westernmost province has changed a good deal, Brittany seems ever to hover at land's end. The sea in all possible moods surrounds this rugged peninsula. In many little villages, customs and fascinating folktales endure. In some places Brittany women wear the traditional black dress and lace *coiffe* (elaborate headdress); most smaller towns support at least one bar animated with the Celtic lilt of *Breizh,* the old language. Unlike most of the French, the Bretons are a Celtic people, whose ancestors crossed over from Britain to escape Anglo-Saxon invaders in the fifth and sixth centuries. Their folk music most clearly reveals this heritage: The *biniou,* a musical instrument, is related to the Scottish warpipes and the Irish *uillean* pipes. The *vielle,* whose strings are sounded by means of a wooden disk attached to a crank, adds a scratchy, fiddlelike whine to the piper's jigs and reels.

Industrialization has come only recently to Brittany, not a wealthy province, and the traditional vocations of farming and fishing have become increasinly difficult to pursue. In the past, these economic difficulties have fueled a separatist movement. Recently, however, the French government has granted more autonomy to the local Breton leadership and has begun to support the preservation of Breton culture. In June, 1979, under Giscard d'Estaing's administration, students were allowed to replace one language section of the *baccalaureat* French exam with Breton. Mitterand's extensive road-building program during the 1980s opened up the region much more. In so doing, it diffused the bottled-up force of the Breton movement. The bilingual road signs in more isolated regions may be a thoughtful, or ironic, gesture on the part of the French government.

At village *pardons,* the annual festivals held in honor of local patron saints, the traditional black clothing, embroidered aprons, and headdresses come out of the closet. The best-known *pardons* take place at Tréguier in May; at Quimper's Festival de la Cornouaille between the third and fourth Sunday in July; at Ste-Anne-d'Auray in late July; at Perros-Guirec in mid-August; at Ste-Anne-La-Palud a week later; and at Josselin in early September. Also of note is Lorient's Festival Interceltique, held the first two weeks of August. For information, contact a *syndicat* in any larger town.

If the Celtic strain is growing harder to find in the people, it is still pervasive in the landscape. Brittany has its share of resorts and sandy beaches, but a wilder, more lonely beauty is never far away.

Ubiquitous *crêperies* fry up the famed regional specialty: crêpes of ground wheat flour (*froment*), with sweet fillings, and the darker buckwheat variety (*sarasin*) wrapped around eggs, cheese, or sausage. These are accompanied by *cidre brut* (the local cider) or by the sweeter *cidre doux,* while such delectable seafood dishes as *coquilles St-Jacques* (scallops), *saumon fumé* (smoked salmon), and *moules-marinières* (steamed mussels in a white wine-based broth) are served with *Muscadet,* a dry white wine from the vineyards around Nantes. Two distinctive pastries are *kouign amann* (flaky layers dripping with butter and sugar) and the custard-like *far breton.*

Practical Information

Getting to Brittany is hardly a problem. **Trains** leaving from Paris's Gare Montparnasse take 3½ hours to reach Rennes, and the Paris-Quimper connection averages a reasonably efficient 6½ hours. Getting around Brittany is a different matter. The three main train lines run between Rennes and Brest (passing through none of the most scenic towns); between Rennes, Redon, and Quimper; and between Redon and Nantes. Smaller, less frequent trains or SNCF **buses** connect such towns as St-Malo, Dinan, Paimpol, Roscoff, Camaret, Concarneau, and Quiberon to the main lines, but not directly to each other. The multitude of private bus lines is also a mixed blessing. Buses connect points that train lines miss, but their prices are high, their departures infrequent (once or twice per day), and their hours often inconvenient.

Cycling is the best way to travel, especially since the most beautiful sights are also the least accessible by public transportation. The terrain is relatively flat, though it gets a bit hillier in the Argoat region. Many IYHF youth hostels, including those at Dinan, St-Brieuc, Lannion, Lorient, and Quimper, rent bikes to their members at 30F per day plus a 200F deposit. An ever-growing number of train stations are also renting bikes for 37F per half-day or 47F per day (300F deposit or ID required). Most stations insist that you return the bike where you rented it, but it's worth asking about one-way rentals. You can transport your bike for free in many trains as well as on most ferries. The free pamphlet *Train et Vélo* contains a list of participating stations, fees, and regulations (available at any SNCF station). Avid cyclists who wish to "do Brittany" properly should by all means bring their own to France (see By Bicycle in the General Introduction).

Hikers can choose from a number of routes, including the long-distance footpaths ("Grandes Randonnées") GR341, GR37, GR38, GR380, and the spectacular GR34 along the northern coast. Many *gîtes d'étape* make this a particularly suitable region for hiking. ABRI offices in Rennes and Nantes, as well as the larger tourist offices, can help you coordinate your hiking or biking tour.

Hitching in Brittany is easiest along the major roads such as D786 from Morlaix to St-Brieuc. Smaller roads rarely secure you more than short lifts. The quickest hitching route to Paris is via Avranches in the north and Nantes, Angers, and Le Mans in the south, rather than the less-developed road through Rennes.

If you balk at crowds, beware visiting from mid-July through August, when those Parisians who don't depart for the Côte d'Azur descend on Brittany. In the off-season the beaches will be yours, though many of the coastal resorts, such as St-Malo, Quiberon, and Concarneau essentially shut down. Try to spend some time on the pristine islands off the mainland—Batz, Ouessant, and Bréhat, in particular—and in the smaller towns of the Argoat, where tourists are fewer and the calm peace of traditional Breton life less disturbed.

Rennes

In 1720, a drunken carpenter knocked over his lamp and set most of Rennes ablaze. Despite this calamity, the city has grown to be the administrative center of the Breton Peninsula. It provides excellent travel information: The *syndicat,* ABRI (Association Bretonne des Relais et Itinéraires), and the Centre d'Information Jeunesse Bretagne all can help you plan your journey in Brittany.

The city called "the gateway to the Breton Peninsula" is known to Bretons as the frontier. Ironically, prosperous, bourgeois Rennes, with its fancy chocolate shops and fashionable university students, lies at the outer limits of "true Brittany." Rennes is quite sedate during the summer, allowing the visitor plenty of space to discover its rich sights and curiosities. Unlike other towns in Brittany, it is most active during the school year, when the 36,000-strong student population livens things up.

Orientation and Practical Information

Rennes is three hours from Paris by train, and easily accessible from Normandy via Caen. The **Vilaine River** cuts the city in two, with the station to the south and most of the sights and shopping to the north. From the station, **av. Jean Janvier,** straight ahead, takes you to the river. Turn left along the river and walk 5 blocks to the Pont de Nemours for the tourist office. The *quais* which flank the Vilaine River are filled with shops and offices while the narrow streets behind the Cathédrale

St-Pierre and place St-Germain are full of antique and art shops housed in half-timbered buildings with overhanging stories or jetties.

Syndicat d'Initiative/Office de Tourisme: Pont de Nemours (tel. 99-79-01-98). Ask for the booklet *Camping, Caravanage Bretagne,* which lists all the IYHF youth hostels and almost all the campgrounds in Brittany (free); the list of hotels in Brittany (also free); and their city maps. For a list of Brittany's *gîtes d'étape,* visit ABRI (see below). Open June 15-Sept. 15 Mon.-Sat. 9am-7:30pm, Sun. 10am-noon and 2-5pm; Sept. 16-June 14 Mon. 2-6:30pm, Tues.-Sun. 9am-12:30pm and 2-6:30pm.

Association Bretonne des Relais et Itinéraires (ABRI): 9, rue des Portes Mordelaises (tel. 99-31-59-44). Devoted to helping you discover Brittany on foot or horseback, by bicycle or canoe. Topographical maps (20F each for the 1:100,000-scale maps appropriate for cyclists). Free lists of travel shelters (*gîtes d'étape*), hiking and biking routes. A 30% reduction on SNCF travel in Brittany is available to groups of 10 or more. 10-speeds 30F per day, deposit 600F. 3-speeds too. Open Mon.-Sat. 10am-12:30pm and 2-6pm.

Centre d'Information Jeunesse Bretagne: Maison du Champ de Mars, 6, cours des Alliés (tel. 99-31-47-48), on the 2nd floor. They can provide a comprehensive list of inexpensive hotels in Rennes, and information on cycling, cultural events, work opportunities, and more, for all of Brittany. Free babysitting service, and friendly staff. Open during school vacations and July-Aug. daily 10am-6pm.

Budget Travel: BIJ/Transalpino tickets and information. Must purchase tickets 24 hrs. in advance. Tickets also available at the train station, Allostop, and the **Organisation pour le Tourisme Universitaire** in the CROUS building, 7, place Hoche (tel. 99-36-46-11). Open Mon.-Fri. 9:30-11:30am and 1:30-4pm.

Post Office: Place de la République (tel. 99-79-50-71). **Currency exchange. Postal code:** 35000. Open Mon.-Fri. 8am-7pm, Sat. 8am-noon.

Train Station: Place de la Gare (tel. 99-65-50-50), at the end of av. Jean Janvier. To St-Malo (11 per day, 1 hr., 48F), Paris (10 per day, 3½ hr., 178F), Caen (3 per day, 3 hr., 127F), Nantes (7 per day, 2 hr., 80F), Dinan (7 per day, 1½ hr., 51F). Rents decent Peugeot 10-speeds locally and for one-way trips to Dinan, St-Malo, Dol, Combourg, and Messac. (37F per ½ day, 47F per day; 10F less for a bike with upright handlebars. Deposit 300F; you may leave the number of a major credit card instead of a cash deposit.) Information office open Mon.-Sat. 8am-7:30pm, Sun. 3-7pm. Telephone information daily 7:30am-10pm.

Bus Station: Bd. Magenta (tel. 99-30-87-80), off place de la Gare. To St-Malo (Mon.-Sat. 5 per day, 1 Sun.; 2 hr.; 42F), Nantes (3 per day, 3 hr.) Vannes (2 per day, 2¾ hr.), Dinard (Mon.-Sat. 4 per day, 2 hr.; Sun. 2 per day, 1½ hr.), Mont St-Michel (Mon.-Sat. 2 per day, change and buy a new ticket at Pontorson; 2 hr.). Service to tiny local towns is more frequent on weekdays during the school year. Information office open Mon.-Thurs. 8-11:30am and 1:30-5pm, Fri. 8-11:30am and 2:30-6pm, Sat. 8-11:30am.

Taxis: At the *gare* (tel. 99-30-66-45), and the *mairie* (tel. 99-79-59-69).

Car Rental: You can arrange for an auto rental at the **train station**'s information office. **François Location,** 89bis, av. de Mail (tel. 99-54-30-33), which runs westwards from place Mal Foch at the town's western end. **Hertz,** across the street (tel. 05-20-42-04), rents bikes as well as cars and trucks. Open Mon.-Fri. 8am-noon and 2-7pm, Sat. 8am-noon and 2-6pm.

Bike Rental: At the train station and the hostel. The train station is probably your best bet, but if they're all out, **Hertz** on av. du Mail (see above) rents bikes as well.

Hitching: Allostop, Maison du Champ de Mars, 6, Cours des Alliés (tel. 99-30-98-87), on the 2nd floor. Next to CIJB. Call for fees and hours.

Camping Store: Service Camping, 11bis, rue du Vieux Cours, off bd. de la Liberté. Sells equipment and does tent repairs. Also rents tents and trailers. Open Mon. 2-7pm, Tues.-Sat. 9am-noon and 2-7pm.

Lesbian Group: At the youth center MJC, rue de la Paillette (tel. 99-59-34-07), off av. de Mail. Meets Wed. 7-9pm.

Maison de l'Information des Femmes/Women's Center: 50, bd. Magenta (tel. 99-30-80-89). Information and free advice; welcomes individuals and groups. Open Tues.-Wed. and Fri. 10am-5pm, Thurs. 1-5pm.

Police: Bd. de la Tour d'Auvergne (tel. 99-65-00-22).

Hospital: **Hôpital de Pontchaillon,** rue Henri Le Guilaux (tel. 99-59-16-04).

Medical Emergency: SAMU, Tel. 99-28-43-15.

Anti-Poison Center: 24-hour hotline, Tel. 99-28-42-22.

Police Emergency: Tel. 17.

Accommodations and Camping

Accommodations shouldn't be a problem in Rennes, except in early July during the Tombées de la Nuit festival. The youth hostel is spacious and within walking distance. In addition, there are a number of small, moderately-priced hotels to the east of av. Janvier, between quai Richemont and the train station.

Auberge de Jeunesse (IYHF), 10-12, Canal St-Martin (tel. 99-33-22-33). From the cobblestoned *vieille ville,* take rue St-Malo, which leads north from place Ste-Anne straight to the hostel. If mapless or uncertain of your ability to navigate the *vieille ville*'s twisting streets, simply walk west from the *centre ville* along the Vilaine River until you reach canal d'Ile-et-Rance, and follow quai St-Cast/bd. de Chézy along the canal. The hostel is on the canal, just after rue St-Malo. Cyclists should follow the latter route to avoid the *vieille ville*'s cobblestones and feckless drivers. You can also take bus #20 or 22 (#2 on weekends) to Coëtlogon (every 20 min., 2.80F). From the bus stop, continue in the same direction to the intersection and then turn sharply right; look for signs. Newly renovated house in ideal location. Friendly management and bike rental (32.50F per day, 90F per 3 days, 200F per week; deposit 300F). Disabled access. Cafeteria and bar, 5 laundry machines (15F per token or *jeton.*) Also discount coupons (25%) for local cinemas (weekdays only). 4 beds per room max., some single rooms, excellent showers in every room, fluorescent bed lamps over every bed. 46F in 1- to 2-bed rooms, 34F in 3- to 4-bed rooms. Sheets 11F. Breakfast 11F. Doors close at midnight. Reception open Mon.-Fri. 8am-11pm, Sat.-Sun. 8-10am and 6-11pm.

Cité Universitaire, 94, bd. de Sévigné (tel. 99-36-10-21), for men, and av. Jules-Ferry (tel. 99-38-02-93), for women. To reach the men's dormitory, take av. Janvier from the train station and continue past the canal; the street is on the right just after place St-Melaine. The dormitory is a stone building, about 1km down on your right, fronted by a big courtyard with tennis and basketball courts. To reach the women's dormitory, go even farther along av. Janvier to rue Jean Macy and turn right; av. Jules-Ferry will be on your left after 1 block. Both offer comfortable university housing for 46F the 1st night, 28F per night thereafter. Because these dormitories may close at the end of June, when the university semester ends, you should first call or visit the **Centre Régional des Oeuvres Universitaires et Scolaires (CROUS),** 7, place Hoche (tel. 99-36-46-11). CROUS will tell you whether the Cités Sévigné and Jules-Ferry are open, and also whether other Rennes dormitories—such as the **Cités Maine** and **Normandie**—are accepting travelers for short stays.

Hôtel le Magenta, 35, bd. Magenta (tel. 99-30-85-37). A 5-min. walk from place de la Gare. Recently and tastefully remodeled. Singles 82F. Doubles 92F. Showers 25.50F. Breakfast 14.50F. Reception at the bar open Mon.-Fri. 7am-9pm, Sat. 7am-1pm, Sun. 7-9pm. Closed first 3 weeks in Aug.

Hôtel Riaval, 9, rue Riaval (tel. 99-50-65-58). Turn right as you leave the train station, and immediately turn right again onto the stairs just past the gas station. Follow the path over the railroad tracks to the end; when you emerge, quiet, somber rue Riaval will be in front of you, branching off slightly to the left (about 5 min.). The bridge over the tracks is perfectly safe during the day. Singles and doubles from 75F. Breakfast 15F.

Hôtel de Léon, 15, rue de Léon (tel. 99-30-55-28), near the Vilaine River off quai de Richemont. Large and comfortable rooms with comic strips decorating the walls. In a quiet industrial neighborhood. Singles 85F. Breakfast 18F. Closed 2 weeks in Aug.

Hôtel le Saint-Malo, 8, rue Dupont des Loges (tel. 99-30-38-21). Take av. Janvier from the train station and make a right on rue Dupont des Loges. Rooms are *propre* (clean) and *paisible* (quiet). Singles from 85F. Breakfast 18.50F.

Garden Hotel, 3, rue Duhamel (tel. 99-65-45-06), off of av. Janvier and a block from the museum. One petite, immaculate room, dressed up a bit drably in olive and brown, and named "Violette" (see doorway plaque). Wash cabinet and bedside telephone. 95F per night.

Camping: Municipal des Gayeulles, near Pare des Bois (tel. 99-36-91-22). Take bus #3 from rue de Paris, which is the southern border of the Jardin de Thabor, to parc Les Gayeulles. A grassy, scenic, 2-star site with beautiful flower beds. Isolated from the main road. Around 6F per person, 9F per site, 3F per car. Open Easter-mid-Oct.

Food

In Rennes, as in most of Brittany, *crêperies* are the cheapest places for a light meal; there are a number scattered about the old quarter, and on rue St-Melaine near the university and gardens. A covered **market** is held daily from 7am to 6pm, in the stone building at rue Jules-Simon and bd. de la Liberté. Some merchants close for lunch (1-3:30pm) or take Sunday and Monday off.

Restaurant des Carmes, 2, rue des Carmes (tel. 99-30-73-12), off bd. de la Liberté. 4 courses 36F, 5 courses 53F. Spare, elegant interior with lace curtains. Popular. Open Mon.-Fri. 11:45am-2pm and 7-10pm. Closed for a month in June-July at owner's discretion.

Au Jardin des Plantes, 32, rue St-Melaine (tel. 99-38-74-46). Good crowd and pretty half-timbered house. 4-course *menus* 39.50F and 52F. Open Sept.-July Mon.-Sat. noon-2pm and 7:15-9:45pm.

Le Boulingrain, 25, rue St-Melaine (tel. 99-38-75-11). Probably the best *crêperie* value in town. 3-crêpe *menu* 39F, *boisson comprise.* Try the *boulingrain,* which gives the restaurant its name: a crêpe stuffed with apples, caramel, and almonds (24.50F). Open daily 11:30am-2pm and 6:30-11pm.

Resto-Self, 5, rue Baudrairie (tel. 99-79-42-42), between the post office and the *mairie.* Serve yourself lunch. 9 hot dishes daily, including such favorites as grilled sardines (21.80F), *quiche Lorraine* (22F), and *couscous* (32.50F). Nonsmoking section. Children's menu 16F. Open Mon.-Sat. 11am-2:30pm.

L'Escale, rue St-Malo, near the youth hostel. Cross the bridge in front of the hostel, and walk down rue St-Malo. The restaurant is on your right. Smoky and cozy, with a local clientele. Entrees 50F, all kinds of *galettes* 6-20F. Open daily from 7:30pm.

Sights and Entertainment

Rennes offers entertainment ranging from that infamous band Alien Sex Fiend at the Maison de la Culture to marionette performances of *Peter and the Wolf* at the rue de la Paillette MJC. The pamphlet *Spectacles, informations* at the *syndicat* lists everything, even the blooming periods of Rennes's flowers, bushes, and trees. In either late June or early July, Rennes holds the festival **Les Tombées de la Nuit,** which promises non-stop music, dance, and theater by regional artists from noon to midnight. The **Festival International des Arts Electroniques** in early June sponsors events such as eventide illuminations of the canal. Hordes of madly pedaling cyclists zip through Rennes's streets in spring and summer, cheered on by avid locals and trailed by sag wagons blaring American rock music. Be sure to visit the gorgeous **Jardin de Thabor** (open daily 7am-9:30pm), behind the Renaissance **Eglise Notre Dame** and the **Cloître Ste-Melanie.** To reach the gardens, follow the continuation of rue Jean Janvier across the river and turn right at rue Victor Hugo. Go on a Sunday morning around 10am, when the din of the church bells (sometimes competing with the blare of bike race loudspeakers) hurries families toward mass. The **Musée de Bretagne** and the **Musée des Beaux Arts** are housed in the same building, at 20, quai Emile Zola (tel. 99-79-44-16), by the canal. The Musée de Bretagne introduces you to the region's history and traditions, while the Musée des Beaux Arts displays local landscapes. (Open Wed.-Mon. 10am-noon and 2-6pm. Admission 10F, families and Carte Jeune holders 5F. Admission to both 16F, families and Carte Jeune holders 8F.)

If you find the large, bland, modern buildings that dominate the Rennes skyline an eyesore, stroll through the narrow streets between place du Palais and Palais St-Georges for a view of half-timbered medieval houses with slanting frames and overhanging stories.

Summer nightlife in Rennes is less bustling than during the school year. If a cafe or drink is all you're after, stay within the picturesque *vieille ville.* But if you've got some extra energy (or crêpes) to dance off, head for pink-pillared and popular **L'Espace,** 43, bd. de la Tour d'Auvergne (tel. 99-30-21-95); Sun.-Wed. 50F, Thurs. 60F, Fri. 70F, Sat. 80F; open nightly 10:45pm-4:45am). **Pub Satori,** 82, av. du Mail (tel. 99-59-29-93), is around 60F. Entry to **Charleston Café Dansant,** 2, av. du Mail, costs 60F. At **Pym's Club Discothèque,** 27, place du Colombier (tel. 99-67-30-00), you must shell out 80F, unless you go from Sunday through Thursday, when you need part with only 60F.

St-Malo

Geographically isolated and economically prosperous, the original St-Malo was an island fortified with granite—proud, aloof, and fierce in its fight for independence. St-Malo was founded as a free city in the twelfth century, and for hundreds of years, it fought French domination as strongly as it did Norman and English invaders. The city's motto well suited its mood: "Neither French, nor Breton, I am from St-Malo." Now old St-Malo has surrendered itself to the mainland. An isthmus joins the *vieille ville* to its neighboring communities, and tourists swarm over the very walls that repelled their ancestors for so long. Most of the town was destroyed in the effort to retake it from the Germans in 1944, but it has been scrupulously reconstructed.

Today, as in the past, the sea's influence is inescapable in St-Malo, former strongold of shipbuilders, merchants, and privateers. Standing on the ramparts, surrounded by the ocean on three sides, you might well imagine that the distant cod trawler is setting sail for the New World under the *fleur-de-lis* and the command of *St-Malouin* Jacques Cartier. The city lends itself to romanticism; the poet Chateaubriand, buried at le Grand Bé, spent his youth roaming the port. Today, the *corsaires* are gone, but St-Malo, the only Breton city to have preserved its cod fishing fleet, hangs on to that sailor spirit with all the tourist brochures it can muster.

Orientation and Practical Information

St-Malo consists of the old walled city (called *intra muros*) and a complex of three former towns. **Paramé** and **Rothéneuf** lie to the southeast with long beachfront promenades; **St-Servan,** to the southwest, dates back to Gallo-Roman times. The *vieille ville* and the tourist office are a 10-minute walk from the station. Turn right, cross bd. de la République, and follow av. Louis-Martin. Various city buses make the trip to the walled city (the stop is porte St-Vincent), including the red-coded #2 and 3, and the purple-coded #4, which run every 20 minutes from the stop on bd. de la République (5.90F).

Office de Tourisme: Esplanade St-Vincent (tel. 99-56-64-48), near the entrance to the old city. They offer 2 city maps; request the one that indexes street names. Also pick up a free list of local campsites. The office has complete information on ferries to the Channel Islands and daytrips to Mont St-Michel and Dinard. Open July-Aug. Mon.-Sat. 8:30am-8pm, Sun. 10am-6:30pm; Sept.-June Mon.-Sat. 9am-noon and 2-6:30pm.

Budget Travel: BCE Voyage, in the building facing the tourist office (tel. 99-40-41-85). Train, boat, and plane tickets. This agency also provides **currency exchange.** Considering the 20F tariff per exchange, this news won't bring any joy to the traveler except on Sundays, when all other exchange places are closed. Open daily 9:30am-7pm.

Post Office: Main office, 1, bd. de la Tour d'Auvergne (tel. 99-56-12-05), at the intersection with bd. de la Liberté. **Currency exchange** at this office only. **Postal code:** 35400. Open Mon.-Fri. 8am-7pm, Sat. 8am-noon. **Branch office,** place des Frères Lamennais, in the *vieille ville.* Open July-Sept. 15 Mon.-Fri. 8:30am-6:30pm, Sat. 8:30am-noon; Sept. 15-June Mon.-Fri. 8:30am-12:30pm and 1:30-5pm, Sat. 8:30am-noon. To have mail held, address it: "Instance, Poste Restante"; "35401 St-Malo Principal" for the main office, or "35402 St-Malo *intra-muros*" for the old-city branch.

Train Station: Place Jean Coquelin (tel. 99-65-50-50 in Rennes only; 99-56-15-33 for reservations in St-Malo). To Paris-Montparnasse via Rennes (6 per day, 5-5½ hr., 208F), Rennes (12 per day, 1 hr., 48F), Caen (10 per day, 107F), Rouen (10 per day, 178F), Brest (4 per day, 158F), Morlaix (4 per day, 134F). For Caen and Rouen change at Dol; for Brest and Morlaix change at Rennes.

Bus Station: Information offices for citywide and long-distance buses are all located in the pavilion opposite the tourist office, esplanade St-Vincent. (Information on the St-Malo city buses tel. 99-56-06-06.) **Tourisme Verney,** Tel. 99-40-82-67. To Rennes (Mon.-Sat. 3 per day, 2 hr., 42F), Dinan (3 per day, 1 hr., 26.50F), Dinard (Mon.-Sat. 12 per day, 5 Sun.; 1 hr.; 15.50F), and Cancale (1-2 per day, none Sun.; 50 min.; 15F). Daytrips touring the Côte d'Emeraude 110F (includes crossing of the Rance by boat). Buses leave from the esplanade and stop briefly at the train station. Office open Mon.-Sat. 8:30am-noon and 2-6:30pm. **Courriers Bretons,** Tel. 99-56-79-09. To Pontorson (3 per day, 1 hr., 36F). Note there are no direct excursions to Mont St-Michel; you must change to a connecting **STN** bus at Pontorson. Round-trip tickets from St-Malo to the Mont via Pontorson 80F. The change at Pontorson takes a few minutes. To Cancale (Mon.-Sat. 7 per day; 3 Sun.; ½ hr.; 15.50F). Summer daytrips to other points along the Côte d'Emeraude and the Côte de Granite Rose. Reservations made free of charge. Office open May-Oct. Mon.-Sat. 8:30am-noon and 2-6:30pm; Oct.-May Mon.-Fri. 8:30am-noon and 2-6:30pm, Sat. 8:30am-noon.

Ferries: Voyages Pansart, esplanade St-Vincent (tel. 99-40-85-96), in the same pavilion where the bus offices are located. Information and booking for all ferries. Open July-Aug. Mon.-Sat. 8am-12:30pm and 2-7pm. Sun. 8:30am-noon and 4:30-6:30pm; Sept.-June Mon.-Sat. 9am-noon and 2-6:30pm. **Brittany Ferries,** Gare Maritime du Naye. To Portsmouth (1-2 per day; 8½ hr.; July-Aug. one-way 330F, round-trip 660F, Sept.-June one-way 300F, round-trip 600F). **Emeraude Lines,** Gare Maritime de la Bourse (tel. 99-82-83-84). To Jersey (April-Sept. 1-2 per day, Oct.-March erratic departures; 2½ hr., 191F) and Guernsey (May-late Sept. 1 per day, 4 hr., 223F). **Vedettes Blanches,** Gare Maritime de la Bourse (tel. 99-56-63-21). Same schedules and prices as Emeraude Lines. Note that the Vedettes Blanches office for round-trip excursions (Cap Fréhel, 82F; the St-Malo estuary, 45F) and one-way trips to the Côte d'Emeraude (Dinard, 16.50F; Dinan, 69F; the Ile de Cézembre, 42.40F; the Iles Chausey, 48F) is at Cale de Dinan (tel. 99-56-63-21). However, all information on Vedettes Blanches operations is available at the esplanade St-Vincent. **Condor Hydrofoils,** Gare Maritime de la Bourse (tel. 99-56-42-29). To Jersey (1-4 per day, 70 min., 191F), to Guernsey (May-Oct. 1-2 per day, 2½ hr., 223F), Sark (4-6 per week, 2 hr., 246F), Aurigny (mid-April to early Sept. 1 per week, 342F) and Weymouth (late March-Oct. 1-2 per day, 4 hr., 350F). **Vedettes Armoricaines,** Gare Maritime de la Bourse (tel. 99-56-48-88). Temporarily closed in June 1988; call for information.

Car Rental: Avis, Gare Maritime du Naye (tel. 99-81-73-24). **Europcar,** 16, bd. des Talards (tel. 99-56-75-17). **Thrifty Location,** 46, bd. de la République (tel. 99-56-47-60). Rents an Opel Corsa for 191F per day plus 1.91F per km, or 373F per day with unlimited mileage. Deposit US$100 per day or the estimated cost of the rental, to be adjusted upon return of the car. Will meet you at the *Gare Maritime* free of charge. Open daily 8am-12:15pm and 1-6:15pm. **Hertz,** 48, bd. de la République (tel. 99-56-31-61).

Bike Rental: Rouxel, 12, av. Jean Jaurès (tel. 99-56-14-90), near the train station. 40F per day, deposit 200F. Open Mon.-Sat. 8:30am-noon and 2-7pm. **Diazo,** place de l'Hermine (tel. 99-40-31-63), nearer the station. The **train station** rents 10-speeds at 47F per day, deposit 300F. Discounts for longer rentals. One-way rentals to certain stations in Brittany are possible.

Windsurfer Rental: Quai 34 Surf School, 7, rue Courtoisville (tel. 99-40-07-47). Walk along the Grande Plage until you see the signs. 50-70F per windsurfer. Deposit of passport or other identity card required.

Laundromat: 3, rue Ernest Renan, at bd. de la République, 2 blocks from the station. Open daily 7am-10pm.

Hospital: Centre Hospitalier de St-Malo, 2, rue Laennec (tel. 99-81-60-40).

Ambulance: Ouest-ambulance, 50, rue du Président R-Schuman (tel. 99-40-39-50).

Police: Place des Frères Lamennais (tel. 99-40-85-80).

Police Emergency: Tel. 17.

Accommodations and Camping

Not surprisingly, St-Malo is stuffed to the hairline in summer. People with rooms in the hotels in July and August most likely made reservations before you were born. To stay in the hostel, arrive early and often. Do not sleep on the beaches—even if the water is 350m away when you lie down, it will dash you against the wall within six hours.

Auberge de Jeunesse (LFAJ/IYHF), 37, av. du Père Umbricht (tel. 99-40-29-80). To avoid the 25-min. walk from the station, catch red bus #2 (3 per hr., 5F) on av. Jean Jaurès behind the station (3 right turns). Get off at Courtoisville. Pretty, ivy-covered building, fronted by tennis courts and a turreted dovecote. The beach is just 3 blocks away. In summer, you are more likely to find a bed in the annex. 34F. Sheet sacks 12F. Breakfast 12F. Lunch or dinner 32F (not served on weekends). Tennis equipment rental available. Reception open daily 9-10am, 5-6:45pm, and 7:30-8pm. Next door, the **Foyer des Jeunes Travailleurs** has color TV, a pool table, and a higher ratio of real French people. They will accept hostellers if there's no room at the hostel (32F).

Youth Hostel Annex, av. de Moka (tel. 99-56-31-55). From the station, take a right and then another onto bd. de la République. Turn right again on av. Jean Jaurès, then left on av. de Moka (10 min.). If you are turned away from the main hostel ignore their feeble map. Turn your back on the hostel, head right on av. du Père Umbricht/av. Pasteur, left at the store with the small turret (av. de Moka). The annex is far down the street on the right, a building with a chain-link fence that looks very much like the elementary school it is in the off-season. 65 beds in 4 rooms. Cold showers. Ill-equipped kitchen, no meals served. 30F per night. Sheets 11F. No curfew. Lockout noon-5pm. Reception open daily 8-10am, 5-7pm, and 8-10pm. Open mid-July to Aug. Call ahead.

Auberge de Jeunesse (IYHF), 13, rue des Ecoles (tel. 99-56-22-00), in Paramé. Dignified stone mansion with a greenhouse and friendly staff, but farther from town than the other hostels and often full. Take bus #2 from av. Jean Jaurès to Les Chênes (the last stop). If no one answers when you ring the cowbell over the door, go through the stone archway trellised with roses, and look for the staff in the kitchen—where, they say, the bell can't be heard. 34F per night in the house, 30F in fun bungalows with kitchens, 28F in the circus tents. Breakfast 12F. The price increases by 2.10F each night you stay on. Call before coming, and ask about the bungalows if they say there's no room.

Hôtel le Neptune, 21, rue de l'Industrie (tel. 99-56-82-15), on a drab side street, but right next to the beach. Cheerful rooms, and a scruffy bar. Slightly bizarre decor: A stuffed badger adorns the hallway, and another crouches on top of the refrigerator. Spacious, with good mattresses. Singles 86F, doubles 110F. Showers 15F. Breakfast 18F. Booked in July and August. Phone reservations accepted.

Hôtel Le Vauban, 7, bd. de la République (tel. 99-56-09-39). Tidy rooms and cheap meals. Singles and doubles 80-100F. Showers 8F. Breakfast 15F. 38-52F *menus.* Reception open May-Sept. daily; Oct.-April Mon.-Sat. Restaurant open noon-1:30pm and 7-8:30pm. Booked in July and August. Telephone reservations accepted.

Bar Hôtel le St-Maurice, 2, av. Père Umbricht (tel. 99-56-07-66), in Courtoisville on the same street as the hostel. Dark bar below and dingy, narrow staircase, but the rooms are clean. The street below gets noisy. Singles 85F.

Camping: Information on all municipal sights at the tourist office, or call 99-56-41-36. **Camping de la Cité d'Aleth,** near promenade de la Corniche in St-Servan (tel. 99-81-60-91), is the closest and most scenic campground. From July-Aug., you can take bus #1 to Aleth. Adults 7F, children 3F, 6F per car, 6F per tent. Open year-round.

Food

The outdoor **market** takes place from 8am to 1pm on Monday, Thursday, and Saturday, behind Eglise Notre-Dame-des-Grèves; on Tuesday and Friday, on place Bouvet in St-Servan and at the **Marché aux Légumes** *intra muros;* and on Wednesday, on place du Prieuré, in Paramé. There are cheap provisions at a number of supermarkets as well, for instance, **Intermarché,** bd. Théodore Botrel. You can buy fresh bread and just about any other conceivable edible at Brittany's supermarket chain. Try a bag of *craquelins de St-Malo,* which taste and look like enormous wheat puffs. Convenient for hostel- and annex-dwellers; just follow the signs. Open Mon.-Fri. 9am-12:30pm and 3-7:15pm, Sat. 2:30-7:30pm.

Crêperie Chez Chantal, 2, place aux Herbes, near the *intra muros* post office. They really stuff both crêpes and customers. Good reputation. Crêpes 9-35F.

Restaurant des Remparts, 17, rue Jacques Cartier (tel. 99-40-91-23), near the entrance to the *vieille ville.* Tourist-mobbed but not unreasonable (3-course *menu* 56F). Open daily noon-11pm.

Poulbots (tel. 99-40-86-95; open Thurs.-Tues. noon-2pm and 7-10pm) and **La Corvette** (tel. 99-40-15-04; open Tues. and Thurs.-Sun. noon-3pm and 6:30-11pm, Wed. 6:30-11pm), both down the street, have similar *menus* for 58F.

Restaurant L'Escale, 15, rue Jacques Cartier. 4-course *menu* 62F.

Sights and Entertainment

The best way to see St-Malo is to explore the ramparts—you'll have the old town at your feet on one side and a long stretch of sea on the other. Begin at the staircase marked *Accès aux remparts* near porte St-Vincent, which opens onto lively place Chateaubriand. Not far from the entrance (going counterclockwise), porte St-Thomas looks out onto the **Fort National,** accessible only at low tide. Farther along, at the **Tour Bidouane,** climb down to the beach and continue along the stone walkway to **Le Grand Bé.** This small island holds the unmarked grave of the Romantic poet Chateaubriand, who asked to be buried near the sound of the wind and the sea. Completely fenced in except for the side facing the sea, the stone cross on Chateaubriand's tomb seems to rebuff onlookers and embrace the sea. Nonetheless, the world's squabbles continue 3 yards behind him: On the plaque engraved with the words "*Un grand écrivain français a voulu reposer ici*" (a great French writer wanted to rest here), someone has drawn a line through the word "français" and scrawled above it "Breton." Don't set out for the island if the sea is within 10m of the submersible walkway, or you may be stuck with the wind and the wet for a good six hours until the tide recedes.

The old town is largely a reconstruction, but some seventeenth-century houses and tiny streets with curious names remain: rue du Chat qui Danse (Street of the Dancing Cat) and rue de la Pie qui Boit (Street of the Swilling Magpie). Intricate leaded windows adorn one facade along rue Pelicot, and the last house before the anti-car barricade is an example of fortified residential architecture. Farther down, you will see l'Escalier de la Grille (though the *grille* (gate) has been replaced with wooden doors), and to the right at 2, cour la Houssaye, lies the former residence of the Duchesse Anne de Bretagne. Gothic **Cathédrale St-Vincent** has also been extensively restored—the combination of dark, twelfth-century nave and fiery, modern stained-glass windows creates an eerie effect.

Near porte St-Vincent, built into the ramparts, is the tastefully curated **Musée de la Ville** (tel. 99-40-71-11). Each floor is dedicated to a period of *malouin* history. After inspecting the treasure chests, maps, and other pirate paraphernalia, climb to the turret, the highest public vantage-point on this part of the Côte d'Emeraude. (Open June-Sept. daily 9:30am-noon and 2-6:30pm; Oct.-May Wed.-Mon. 10am-noon and 2-6pm. Admission 10F, students 5F.) The **Musée International du Long Cours Cap-Hornier** (tel. 99-81-66-09) at the Tour Solidor in St-Servan offers nautical history and a view of the Rance estuary. (Guided visits July-Aug. daily 10am-noon and 2-6pm; Sept.-June Wed.-Mon. 10am-noon and 2-6pm. Admission 10F, students 5F. Bus #2 runs to St-Servan about every 20 min. from rue Jean Jaurès, behind the station, and from esplanade St-Vincent.) At place Vauban (tel. 99-81-64-34), you will find the **Aquarium** and the **Exotarium,** which houses snakes, lizards, and "wild insects of the tropical night." (Open July to mid-Sept. daily 9am-11pm; mid-Sept. to June 9am-noon and 2-7pm. Admission 12.50F, students 9.50F. Admission to both buildings 22F, students and ages under 16 19F.) Over 300 dolls and furnished dollhouses are preserved in the **Musée de la Poupée,** 13, rue de Toulouse (tel. 99-40-15-51), inside the walled city. (Open March 15-Nov. 15 daily 10am-noon and 2-7pm. Admission 12F, students 9F.)

Finally, for a dose of pre-packaged nightlife, drop by the large **Casino** on esplanade St-Vincent (tel. 99-56-00-05), just outside the walled city. For a minimum bet of 5F, you can gamble at *la boule,* a roulettelike game. (Open Wed.-Sat. 9:30pm-4am, Sun. 9:30pm-12:30am.)

Near St-Malo

St-Malo is a crowded but convenient base from which to explore the fascinating Côte d'Emeraude. To the east lies **Cancale,** which is famous for its oysters (serviced by Tourisme Verney buses; see Bus Station listings), and scenic **Pointe de Grouin.** Farther east, you will find **Mont St-Michel.** Given the dearth of cheap accommodations there, it makes sense to make Mont St-Michel a daytrip from St-Malo. The cheapest and most convenient round-trip is an excursion run by Courriers Bretons (June 3 per week, July to mid-Sept. 1 per day; 80F). Buses leave from esplanade St-Vincent at 9am and return at 6pm. Other bus and train connections require a change at Pontorson. **Bateaux de la Baie du Mont St-Michel,** Gare Maritime Le Vivier-sur-Mer (tel. 99-48-82-30), tours the bay of Mont St-Michel in an amphibious boat which rolls into the water on wheels (April-Sept. 4-5 per day, 74F). You may have trouble getting to Le Vivier-sur-Mer, 21km southeast of St-Malo. Ask at Voyages Pansart for bus information. Voyages Pansart can also inform you of other bus or boat excursions to Mont St-Michel and the Côte d'Emeraude. Vedettes Blanches cruises out to the 70m cliffs of Cap Fréhel, 50km to the west (May-June occasional departures, July-Sept. more frequent departures; 2½ hr.; 82F).

Dinard is the Breton haven for the Great Gatsby set. It is accessible by bus or a 15-minute boat ride. (Vedettes Blanches runs 9:30am-6:15pm, departing from the gare maritime complex; one-way 16.50F, round-trip 28.50F, bikes and mopeds 13F.) From Dinard's excellent beach, you can watch pedal boats, windsurfers, sailboats, and almost anything else you can think of. The town itself supports some ugly high-rises and amusement park-type fast food stands. Be sure to walk around both the **Pointe du Moulinet** and the **Pointe des Etetés,** where stone steps overgrown with rosebushes wind upward to mansions and vistas of the Côte d'Emeraude. Restaurants and hotels are expensive in Dinard, so make a daytrip of it. One reasonable hotel in Dinard is the **Hotel-Bar Beaurivage,** place du Général de Gaulle (tel. 99-46-14-34). Though not on the shorefront, the rooms are bright and spacious (singles 85F, doubles 110F). Reserve in advance. Vedettes Blanches also makes river trips up the Rance to Dinan, once per day with the tide (2 hr.; one-way 69F, round-trip 96F); boats stop in Dinard, but there's no time to get off.

Several ferries operate between St-Malo and the **Channel Islands.** (See Ferries under Practical Information.)

Dinan

Dinan prides itself on being the best-preserved town in Brittany. Less crowded than Dinard and St-Malo, its northern neighbors at the mouth of the Rance Valley, Dinan has preserved a quiet, medieval radiance. In the *vieille ville* 66m above the Rance, you can explore cobblestoned streets lined by half-timbered houses dating from the 1400s. Paths descend to the port, watched over by lazy cows—at sunset, you might see the cowherder, a spry old woman in an apron, leaping after them with a big stick.

Orientation and Practical Information

The tourist office in the *vieille ville* is a 10-minute walk from the station. Bear left across place du 11 Novembre 1918 onto rue Carnot, then right onto rue Thiers, which brings you to a large rotary intersection, place Duclos. Head up the hill to the left on rue du Marchix, which becomes rue Ferronnerie. Turn left at the sign for the tourist office, cross the square, take rue Ste-Claire, and turn left on rue de l'Horloge.

Office de Tourisme: 6, rue de l'Horloge (tel. 96-39-75-40). A granite-pillared sixteenth-century mansion next to a weeping willow. Walking tours of the town July-Aug. daily at 10am and 4pm (20F, children 10F). Excellent guide to the town's sights in French only 5F. Free map. Open daily Jan.-March 10:30am-1pm and 2-6pm; April-May 9:30am-12:30pm and 1:30-6:30pm; June-Sept. 9am-7pm; Oct.-Dec. 10:30am-1pm and 2-6pm.

Post Office: Place Duclos (tel. 96-39-25-07). **Currency exchange. Postal code:** 22100. Open Mon.-Fri. 8:30am-7pm, Sat. 8:30am-noon.

Train Station: Place du 11 Novembre 1918 (tel. 96-39-22-39, information 96-94-50-50). To Rennes via Dol (6 per day, 1½-2 hr., 51F), St-Brieuc (Mon.-Sat. 3 per day, 1 hr., 39F), Paimpol (1 per day, change at St-Brieuc and Guingamp; 4 hr.; 69F), Morlaix (Mon.-Sat. 3 per day, 2 Sun., change at St-Brieuc; 2 hr.; 80F), St-Malo (7 per day, change at Dol; 1¼ hr.; 39F). Information office open 8am-noon and 2-6:30pm; information tel. open Mon.-Sat. 8:30am-noon and 2-6pm.

Bus Station: CAT/TV, at the train station (tel. 96-39-21-05), on the other side of the *gare*'s baggage office. July-Sept. service to St-Malo only (3 per day; one-way 26.50F, round-trip 40F). Excursions to points along the northern coast, Mont St-Michel, and the Gulf of Morbihan in July and Aug. only. Information office open Mon.-Fri. 8am-noon and 2-6pm, Sat. 8am-noon. **TAE,** Tel. 99-50-64-17. Buses to Dinard and Rennes. Call for information.

Ferries: Vedettes Blanches, quai de la Rance (tel. 96-39-18-04). May-Sept. 1 excursion per day down the river to St-Malo, with the tide, returning by bus (2½ hr. down by boat, ¾ hr. back by bus; one-way 69F, round-trip 96F). Bikes 26F.

Bike Rental: M. Scardin, 30, rue Carnot (tel. 96-39-21-14). Cycles for around 40F per ½ day and 50F per day. Motorcycles for rent, too. Open Tues.-Sat. 8:45am-12:15pm and 2-4:20pm. The **train station** rents 3- and 10-speeds for 47F per day, deposit 300F. The **youth hostel** charges 25F per day, deposit 250F.

Canoe/Kayak Rental: Port de Dinan (tel 96-39-85-01 or 96-85-33-85). Look for the yellow sign. Canoe/kayaks 40F/30F per hr., 60F/50F per 3 hr., 100F/80F per 7 hr. Open July-Aug. Mon.-Fri. 10am-5pm.

Taxis: Place Duclos (tel. 96-39-06-00), outside the post office.

Laundromat: 33, Grand' Rue, opposite the Eglise St-Malo. Wash 12F, dry 2F. Open Mon.-Sat. 8:30am-8pm.

Hospital: Rue Chateaubriand (tel. 96-39-27-60), at Léhon.

Medical Emergency: Tel. 18.

Police: Rue de la Garaye (tel. 96-39-03-02).

Police Emergency: Tel. 17.

Accommodations and Camping

Dinan offers many campsites, a homey youth hostel, and a few cheap hotels that aren't always booked in summer. If you're camping outside the hostel's dormitory, bring along a life preserver: When it rains, the adjacent stream can become an instant river.

Auberge de Jeunesse (IYHF), Moulin du Méen in Vallée de la Fontaine-des-Eaux (tel. 96-39-10-83). Unfortunately, there's no bus to this wooded haven. However, the walk is pleasant whichever route you take. From the *gare*, turn left from the main exit, turn left again across the tracks, and follow the signs (a ½-hr. walk). A wonderful, friendly place by a stream and weeping willows. Good facilities, including a kitchen, common room with fireplace, books on Breton culture, 2 guitars, and a small record collection. Dorms are usually mixed. 36F per person. Breakfast 11F. Healthy lunch or dinner 36F ("we like to grill things," says one of the managers). Camping space nearby, but bring inflatable mattresses in case of rain. Cots in huge tent 28F. Decent bikes 25F per day. Lockers 5F. Reception open 8-11am and 5-11pm. Keys available for night owls.

Hôtel du Théâtre, 2, rue Ste-Claire (tel. 96-39-06-91), just around the corner from the tourist office in the *vieille ville.* Small but pleasant rooms. Singles and doubles 60-120F. Showers 5F (during limited hours). Breakfast 16.50F. Phone reservations accepted.

Hôtel-Restaurant de l'Océan, place du 11 Novembre 1918 (tel. 96-39-21-51), across from the station. Singles and doubles 80-120F. Open Nov.-Sept.

Hôtel de la Consigne, 40, rue Carnot (tel. 96-39-00-12), several hundred yards to the left of the station, on the way to the *vieille ville.* The tiny 60F single, with peeling wallpaper and narrow, frosted windows letting in the street noise, is rather oppressive. But it's cheap and convenient. Singles and doubles 60-120F.

Camping: The campsite at the **youth hostel** is in a beautiful location (12F per night). The tourist office provides a list of other sites, the closest of which is **Camping Municipal,** 103, rue Châteaubriand (tel. 96-39-11-96). If you face the post office in place Duclos, rue Châteaubriand is to your right. Unspectacular site with decent facilities. 8.60F per person, 7.50F per site, 5.35F per car. Open May-Nov.

Food

Place du Champ and place Duguesclin in the *vieille ville* have been the site of the town's outdoor **market** for a millennium. This food extravaganza is held Thursdays from 8am to 5pm.

> **Crêperie des Artisans,** 6, rue du Petit Fort (tel. 96-39-44-10). Featured in the *New York Times* and popular. Eat *galettes* and crêpes on the terrace. 50F *menu.* Open April-Sept. Tues.-Sun. noon-10:30pm.

> **La Kabylie,** 48, rue du Petit Fort (tel. 96-39-62-76). Excellent *couscous* 45-69F. Open June-Aug. daily roughly noon-2pm and 7-10pm; Sept.-May Wed.-Sun.

> **Le Connétable,** 1, rue de l'Apport (tel. 96-39-06-74), in the *vieille ville.* Reputedly the oldest *crêperie* in Dinan, in a fifteenth-century dark-timbered house. Wild pizza with ham, broccoli, and almonds 38F. House specialty *galette complète basque* (with ham, apricots, and more) 25F. Crêpes *arrosées* (with Grand Marnier, Kirsch, etc.) 18-20F. Open daily 11:30am-9:30pm.

> **Le Dauphin,** 11, rue Haute-Voie (tel. 96-39-25-66). Great food and pleasant atmosphere. Classy 3-course *menus* 43.50F and 54.50F. Open May-Sept. daily noon-2pm and 6:30pm on for dinner; Oct.-April Thurs.-Mon. lunch and dinner, Tues. dinner.

Sights

The **Promenade des Petits-Fossés** begins near the post office and follows the looming ramparts to the thirteenth-century **Porte du Guichet,** the entrance to the well-preserved and heavily fortified **Château de la Duchesse Anne.** Before you descend into the château's gloomy dungeons, pause to enjoy the antics of the **Jardin du Val Cocherel's denizens. In a grassy area sloping off to the right of the** *promenade,* goats prance, the rooster pretends not to notice the haughty white bird, and every now and then, a peacock lets out a honk. (Open daily 8am-7:30pm. Free.) Inside the castle's fourteenth-century *donjon,* the **Musée de Dinan** displays eighteenth-century polychromed statuettes and bas-reliefs, and a selection of medieval and Roman weapons and artifacts. Climb down the spiral stairs to the chilly air of the lowest room, the kitchen. The doorway on the left leads to an utter blackness best left unexplored—it was the toilet. The nearby **Tour de Coëtquen** houses additional galleries with temporary exhibits, and a small but memorable collection of *gisants* (tomb sculptures). (Chateau and museums open daily June-Aug. 9am-noon and 2-7pm; Sept.-Oct. and March-May 9am-noon and 2-6pm; Nov.-Feb. Wed.-Mon. 2-5pm. No admittance 40 min. before closing. Admission 6.20F.)

As you reenter the *vieille ville* through porte St-Louis, a right on rue Général-de-Gaulle will bring you to the **Promenade de la Duchesse Anne,** at the end of which stand the magnificent trees of the **Jardin Anglais.** Behind the trees rises **Basilique St-Sauveur.** The church blends a twelfth-century facade, a lovely buttressed apse, and a curvilinear three-tiered steeple from the seventeenth century, gray-tiled and sleek as an armadillo. The garden looks out over the Rance, the viaduct, and the port below. At the far end, a path and a tiny staircase lead down to the river. Across the small Gothic bridge and under the viaduct, the peaceful winding path leads to the cloisters and ruined priory at **Léhon,** about 40 minutes away. (You can also reach Léhon by road: Take rue Chateaubriand from the post office and turn left at the sign—roughly 3km altogether.)

From the port, reenter the walled city by **rue du Petit Port,** which becomes **rue du Jerzval,** one of Dinan's prettiest (and steepest) roads. Back in the center of town, on Grand' Rue, **Eglise St-Malo** contains a remarkable polychromed organ, built by the Englishman Alfred Oldknow in 1889. The church's interior is unusually well-lit by the flamboyantly colorful 1920s stained-glass windows. In the second window from the rear, on the right side, is a memorial to Dinan soldiers killed in WWI. For a schedule of live organ concerts, contact the *syndicat.* Finally, on rue de l'Horloge, the fifteenth-century **tower** commands a splendid view of Dinan's jumbled medieval streets and the surrounding countryside. (Open July-Aug. Mon.-Sat.

11am-12:30pm and 2-5:30pm.) Call the *syndicat* if you wish to tour the tower during the off-season.

After the revolution, ownership of Dinan's ramparts was divided up and titles were sold to the ascendant bourgeoisie. Now the town's rightist mayor wants them back and has launched a long-term repurchase and restoration project. As a result, access to the ramparts, now officially off-limits, should gradually improve.

Northern Coast

The northern coast's three principal geographic divisions—the Côte d'Emeraude, the Côte de Granite Rose, and the Ceinture Dorée—feature some of the most spectacular scenery in France, from rugged, windswept points of rock to serene coves and sandy beaches. Youth hostels and *gîtes d'étape* are conveniently located near the most worthwhile sites, ranging in quality from the rugged tent-camp near Cap Fréhel to the well-equipped hostel in Brest. (Remember that motorists cannot stay in most *gîtes d'étape*.)

Transportation will be your biggest problem. The Paris-Brest line assures frequent service (from east to west) to St-Brieuc, Guingamp, Plouaret, Morlaix, Landivisiau, and Landerneau, with the following connecting **trains** (or SNCF buses) running northward: from Guingamp to Paimpol (4 per day, 1 hr., 27F), for such sights as Pointe de l'Arcouest, Ile de Bréhat, Lézardrieux, and Tréguier; from Plouaret to Lannion (Mon.-Sat. 7-9 per day, fewer on Sun.; 15 min.; 12.50F), for Perros-Guirec, Trégastel, Trébeurden, Pointe du Château, Sept-Iles, and Ploumanach; from Morlaix to St-Pol-de-Léon and Roscoff (3-4 buses or trains per day; ½ hr., 15.50F to St-Pol-de-Léon; 45 min., 21F to Roscoff), for Ile de Batz. Private bus lines fill in some of the gaps between train stations, but hitching or cycling may be your best alternatives. All of these train stations (except Landivisiau, Landerneau, Plouaret, Paimpol, and St-Pol-de-Léon) rent three- and 10-speed bikes (47F per day, deposit 300F). Inquire about the possibility of one-way rentals. Several hostels rent bikes to IYHF members (roughly 30F per day, deposits up to 300F). Tourist offices have information on local rentals, and many stock the *Guide Touristique Côtes-du-Nord* (5F), which lists all bike and car rental concessions in the region and provides a wealth of information on outdoor activities. Even the main roads, which pass through fields edged by Queen Anne's lace, are well-paved, scenic, and relatively flat. Many trains will carry your bike for free, and some bus companies will do so for a small fee. Hikers can hoof the northern coast on the GR 34, which winds along the sea from Cancale, east of St-Malo, to Morlaix.

Tourisme Verney, located on esplanade St-Vincent in St-Malo (tel. 99-40-82-67), serves the following towns on the Côte d'Emeraude (from St-Malo east to west): Dinard, St-Lunaire, St-Briac, Lancieux, Ploubalay, and St-Jacut. Eleven buses per day run as far as St-Briac on weekdays; nine on Sunday. In July and August, two buses continue to St-Jacut (15F per bicycle).

Companie Armoricaine de Transports (CAT), with offices in St-Brieuc (tel. 96-33-36-60) and Lannion (tel. 96-37-02-40), runs service from St-Brieuc to (from east to west) Le Val-André, Sables d'Or, Le Vieux-Bourg, and St-Cast. A second line links St-Brieuc and Paimpol (6 per day, 1½ hr., 31.50F) with connections to Pointe de l'Arcouest and Lézardrieux.

Côte d'Emeraude

Between Dinard and St-Brieuc, high cliffs and rocky points alternate with long stretches of sand. As in most of Brittany, public transportation is scarce here, so you'll need to coordinate train and bus schedules in advance.

Perhaps the best place to begin excursions on the Côte d'Emeraude is **St-Brieuc,** on the Paris-Brest train line. Industrial St-Brieuc has few tourist attractions, though cyclists rolling into town from the Côte d'Emeraude may be tickled to know, as they take the D712 through the gray suburb of Yffiniac, that champion racer Bernard Hinault used to deliver mail there. The **Cathédrale St-Etienne,** built in the thirteenth and fourteenth centuries, is a stoutly buttressed building that originally served as a church fortress. The old woman who sits in front of the church and knits, sometimes wearing the Breton *coiffe* (lace headdress), knows all the local legends and is herself a legend among the townspeople. To get to the cathedral from the train station, take rue de la Gare to rue du 71*ème* Régiment d'Infanterie, and continue in the same direction on rue des Lycéens-Martyrs, bearing left at the fork. Bear right on rue de Rohan and take the next left.

St-Brieuc's new youth hostel, **Manoir de la Ville Guyomard (IYHF)** (tel. 96-78-70-70) is a former farm decorated with hot pink doors and black wood furniture. Singles and rooms with skylights and lofts are available, as well as individual rooms for couples and disabled persons. All beds have bed lamps, which stay on until you turn them off (the electricity's not cut). At reduced prices, 20 dormitory beds, 20 cots in a big tent, and 8 tent-sites for campers are also available. It rents bicycles at 25F per day (deposit 200F), as well as sea kayaks (to groups only). Ask about the ceramic studio. (34F per person. Sheets 12F. Breakfast 12F.) From the train station, take bus #1 from place du Champ de Mars/place Duquesclin, and follow the signs. You can also call the hostel from the train station and ask to be picked up. The walk takes about 30 min., but plenty of signs plaster the route. The **tourist office,** 7, rue St-Gouéno (tel. 96-33-32-50) is in the center of town, a 10-minute walk from the train station. Follow the signs toward the *centre ville* and then toward the *office de tourisme.* **Trains** link St-Brieuc to Dinan (3 per day, 2 Sun.; 1 hr.; 40.50F), Morlaix (10 per day, 1 hr., 54F), and Rennes (11 per day, 1 hr., 60F). There's an information office at the train station (tel. 96-94-50-50; open Mon.-Sat. 8am-noon and 1:30-7pm, Sun. 9am-noon and 2-7pm).

Northeast of St-Brieuc, **Cap Fréhel** is a windswept cape with enormous red and gray cliffs covered by ferns and yellow flowers. It provides little solitude in summer, when cars and tour buses bring armies to admire the view, but it is beautiful nevertheless. CAT (tel. 96-33-36-60 in St-Brieuc) runs buses from St-Brieuc to Vieux-Bourg (2 per day, 32.50F). From there, you're on your own; the Cap is 5km northeast on the D34A. Don't take the bus to Fréhel—it's nowhere near the Cap. Vedettes Blanches in St-Malo (tel. 99-56-63-21) runs a cruise that passes by but could not possibly dock at the 70m cliffs of the cape (departs in June 16 days, in July-Aug. daily from St-Malo and Dinard; 2½ hr.; round-trip 82F). A pioneer spirit prevails at the **Auberge de Jeunesse Plévenon (IYHF),** Kerivet, la Ville Hardrieux (tel. 96-61-91-87), a tent camp 4km from the Cap on the eastern coast of the peninsula. Take the D16 out of Plévenon toward Cap Fréhel, and watch for signs.

Across the bay to the southeast lies **Pointe de St-Cast,** only 2km outside the town of the same name. Point de St-Cast juts far out into the sea, and green fields descend all the way to the water; on a clear day, you can see St-Malo and the whole craggy coast in between. St-Cast may be reached by CAT bus from St-Brieuc (2 per day, 2 hr., 28F). SNCF buses run from Lamballe to St-Cast in July and August only (2 per day, 1½ hr., 24F). **Camping Municipal la Mare** (tel. 96-41-8-19), just to the west of the promontory on Plage de la Mare and **Camping Municipal les Mielles** (tel. 96-41-87-60), 100m from the Grande Plage, are both inexpensive and within easy walking distance. (Same rates at both: 6.55F per person, 3.90F per tent, 3.20F per car, 1.95F per bike.) About 4km from town on the east side of the *pointe* are the beach of **Pen Guen** and uncrowded **Camping de la Ferme de Pen-Guen.** Call the campsite's friendly owner (tel. 96-41-92-18), and he will momentarily stop feeding his geese and rabbits to fetch you from St-Cast for the cost of gas (roughly 6F). (5.20F per person, 2.60F per tent, 3F per car, 1F per bicycle.) At the **Office de Tourisme** in St-Cast (tel. 96-41-81-52), ask for information on other campsites. (Open July-Aug. Mon.-Sat. 9am-12:30pm and 2-7pm, Sun. 10am-noon and 3-5:30pm; Sept.-March Mon.-Sat. 9am-noon; April-June Mon.-Sat. 9am-noon and 2:30-5:30pm.)

There are several affordable hotels in St-Cast: **Hôtel du Commerce** in St-Cast Bourg (tel. 96-41-81-37) is the cheapest (doubles 80F, breakfast 16F). Others include **Hôtel de la Marine,** rue Frégate-Laplace (tel. 96-41-85-28), with doubles for

85F, breakfast 23f; one-star **Hôtel Angleterre et Panorama,** rue de la Fosserolle (tel. 96-41-91-44; open June10-Sept. 11), with doubles 86-100F, breakfast 19F; and **Hôtel de Paris,** bd. Duponchel (tel. 96-41-80-89), with doubles 85-130F, breakfast 18F. The tourist office's handy list of hotels, restaurants, and campgrounds locates all these hotels, as well as the aforementioned campgounds, on a map. Ask about boat trips to Cap Fréhel and Fort la Latte.

East of St-Cast, the coast is dotted with small resorts. **Lancieux** and **St-Jacut** are particularly pleasant; both are accessible by Tourisme Verney buses from St-Malo and Dinard. Buses run hourly to Lancieux (45 min. from St-Malo, 27F), continuing to St-Jacut in July and August only (2 per day, 35F from St-Malo).

Côte de Granite Rose

Paimpol anchors the eastern end of the Côte de Granite Rose, where the rocks are really rosy and the water is warm (warmer, at least, than the beaches around St-Malo). Historically a launching site for fishing expeditions to Newfoundland and Iceland, the city still retains the negligent, swaggering air of a seafarer's town. Tourism, though increasingly important, is not yet the main industry, as both the giant fish market (Tues. mornings on rue de l'Oise/place Gambetta, alongside the vegetable market) and the Breton-speaking clientele of the port's numerous bars can attest. Try **La Taverne** (open after 8:30pm) or **Le Pub** (open after 6pm), both on rue des Islandais, off quai Morand. You can buy provisions at the supermarket **Intermarche** across from the *gare.* (Open Mon. and Wed.-Thurs. 8:30am-12:30pm and 2-7:30pm, Tues. 8:30am-1pm and 2-7:30pm, Fri. 8:30am-12:30pm and 2-8pm, Sat. 8:30am-7:30pm.)

The best deal for both bed and board is the **Auberge de Jeunesse/Gîte d'Etape (IYHF)** at Château de Kerraoul (tel. 96-20-83-60), 25 minutes from the station. Turn left on av. Général-de-Gaulle, take a right at the first light and a left at the next light, then follow the signs to "Kerraoul." Take a left at the end of rue de Pen Ar Run. The hostel driveway will be on your right, just before the road bends sharply uphill to the right. The hostel sits in a large, peaceful park. (34F. Sheets 11F. Dinner 34F, including wine.) The *gîte d'étape* is located across the hall from the hostel's dormitory and has kitchen facilities and showers. (23F. Dinner 46F.) Options in town include the **Hôtel Berthelot,** 1, rue du Port (tel. 96-20-88-66), with clean, airy rooms and a friendly proprietor. (Singles 82F. Showers 15F. Breakfast 17F.) From place de la République, walk down to the port; rue du Port is off quai Morand, which will be to your left. The area has numerous campgrounds. Sunny **Camping Municipal de Cruckin,** near the Plage de Kruckin (tel. 96-20-80-15), is closest. From the *syndicat d'initiative,* follow schizophrenic rue du Général Leclerc as it twists along four identity changes: Général Leclerc to Prof. Jean Renaud to Commandant Charcot to Commandant le Conniat. Rue de Cruckin branches off to your left from rue du Commandant le Conniat. (5.40F per person, 4.50F per site, 3.80F per car. Showers 5F. Open mid-June to mid-Sept. Tues.-Sat. 8-11am and 6-8pm, Mon. 8-9am and 5:30-7:30pm, Sun. 10-11am.) A block farther down rue Commandant le Conniat lies **Camping de Beauport** (tel. 96-22-09-87; 5.60F per camper, 5F per site, 4.50 per car. Showers 4F. Open April-Sept.). The Abbaye de Beauport is just down the road to the left. **Rohou** (tel. 96-55-87-22) in Arcouest remains open year-round. You can also camp in the lovely park behind the youth hostel. Since everything in Paimpol—shops, tourist offices, train stations—shuts down for lunch, you might as well spend the time feasting on the excellent 54F seafood *menu* at the **Hôtel du Port,** quai Morand. Paimpol is connected by train to Guingamp (4 per day, 1 hr., 27F), which is the next stop over from St-Brieuc on the Paris-Brest line (8 per day, 20 min.). A ticket from St-Brieuc to Paimpol via Guingamp costs 43F. Taking your bike is no problem; the little red Guingamp-Paimpol railcar and most of the St-Brieuc-Guingamp trains have a baggage car where you can stash it for free. Six CAT buses run daily direct from St-Brieuc to Paimpol (1½ hr., 35F).

Paimpol makes a good starting point for exploring the coast. The **Office de Tourisme,** rue Pierre Feutren (tel. 96-20-83-16), has information on the surrounding area. From the train station, turn left, then right at the light; near the top of the hill, look for the sign and turn right again. (Open in summer Mon.-Sat. 9am-noon and 2-7:30pm, Sun. 9am-noon; in off-season daily 9am-noon and 2-7pm.) You can rent brand-new ten-speed **bikes** at **Cycles du Vieux Clocher,** place de Verdun (62F per day, deposit 1000F).

In Paimpol the **plage de la Tossen,** a small sandy beach, offers a lovely view of the bay. Just east of Paimpol, along the D786, are the ivy-covered ruins of the **Abbaye de Beauport.** Parts of the abbey date from 1202, when monks of the order of Prémontré escaped to Brittany from Normandy. The tour guide re-creates the daily life of the monks. (Open June 15-Sept.15 daily 9am-noon and 2-7pm. Admission 15F, students 11F.) Walk down the pebbled, primrose-bordered lane to the rear of the abbey for a vista of marsh and the Bay of Poulafret. The path winding along the coast is the European long-distance route G.R. 34, which you can take back to the Paimpol port.

If you're near Paimpol, you shouldn't miss pastoral, flower-laden **Ile de Bréhat.** The silence and the moss-covered rocks that rise out of the sea at low tide give Bréhat an eerie air. The western and northern sides of the island are almost totally uninhabited, punctuated by more wild, dolmenlike outcroppings. **Vedettes de Bréhat** (tel. 96-55-86-99) runs boats from Arcouest to Ile de Bréhat every hour in the summer, every two hours in the off-season. (Last boat from Bréhat departs at 7:30pm, 10 min., round-trip 23F.) To reach Arcouest, catch a bus from Paimpol or hitch the 6km north from Paimpol on the D789. Once there, you can also detour to **Pointe de l'Arcouest,** with its red and black cliffs and rocky shoreline. (10 buses per day from Paimpol, 20 min., 9F.) To the west, the D786 runs through artichoke fields to the enchanting town of **Lézardrieux** (5km). Guegan Voyages (tel. 96-22-37-05) runs 2 buses daily from the Paimpol gare SNCF (10 min., 7.50F).

The northernmost section of the Breton coast, from Lézardrieux to Perros-Guirec, is wild, sparsely inhabited, and low on public transportation. Breton farmers are known for letting people camp on their land in these parts, but campgrounds are also plentiful and two *gîtes d'étape* provide economical shelter near the coast. One is located at **Min ar Goas** (tel. 96-22-90-68), near the town of Lanmodez, about 7½km north of Lézardrieux on the D20 (23F per night, meals 46F). The bridge crossing the Jaud River into **Tréguier** has an interesting modern design: The road is aligned between two huge concrete rainbows spanning the banks. For architecture of a more ancient origin, visit the town's cathedral, built from the thirteenth through the fifteenth centuries, made luminous by two magnificent stained-glass windows in the transept and the back of the nave. On May 19, it is the site of a popular *pardon* honoring St-Yves, one of Brittany's favorite saints, patron (incongruously) of both lawyers and the poor; a priest and lawyer himself, St-Yves may well have invented free legal counsel in the fourteenth century. Inside the cathedral, at his tomb, one of the many plaques paying homage to the Breton saint comes from "the lawyers of the United States of America, in remembrance of their visit, August 21, 1932." From Tréguier, the D8 continues 10km north to **Pointe du Château,** another of the coast's scenic promontories. On your way, stop off at **Chapelle St-Gonéry** in Plougrescéant (17km), and the chapel at **Port-Blanc,** also the site of a small, white-pebbled beach. Tréguier's **Hôtel de l'Estuaire** (tel. 96-92-30-25) offers singles from 63F and doubles from 73F. It is served by the Guegan Voyages bus via Lézardrieux (2 per day, 20 min., 15F).

Twenty-one kilometers farther west is **Perros-Guirec,** a popular resort replete with a harbor and two gorgeous, well-protected, sandy beaches. Watch for the bilingual road signs along the D6 to Perros-Guirec/Peroz-Gireg. The first spelling is French, the second *Breizh* (Breton). A spectacular walk awaits those who try the **Sentier des Douaniers,** a cliff path that threads its way along the sparkling seacoast from Perros-Guirec's main beach to Pors Rolland in **Ploumanach,** a picturesque fishing resort. In Ploumanach, you'll find the massive red granite quarries that give the Côte de Granite Rose its name. The **Office de Tourisme** in Perros-Guirec, 21, place de l'Hôtel de Ville (tel. 96-23-21-15), has information on both Perros-Guirec and Ploumanach, as well as information on transportation and accommodations; ask for a list of *gîtes d'étape*. The office runs a **currency exchange** when the banks are closed on Monday. (Open July-Aug. daily 9am-8pm; Sept.-June 9am-noon and 2-7pm.) **Cycles Henry,** bd. Aristide Briand (tel. 96-91-03-33), rents bikes for 70F per day. Perros-Guirec has few cheap hotels, but many campgrounds. Try the two-star **West-Camping,** Carrefour de Ploumanach (tel. 96-91-09-19; 11F per site, 5F per car, 8F per tent, hot showers included; open June 15-Sept. 15). Three-star **Camping la Claire Fontaine,** rue de Pont-Hélé (tel. 96-23-03-55), lets you pitch your tent at similar prices (11F per person, 6F per car, 8F per tent; open June-Sept.). There is also a *gîte d'étape* at **Villa Stella Maris** (tel. 96-23-15-62), in the nearby town of Louannec. From Perros-Guirec's *centre ville,* head south toward Lannion for roughly 2km, then turn left onto the D6 for 3km to reach Louannec. (Dorm beds 23F. Kitchen facilities but no meal service.)

Three kilometers northwest of Perros-Guirec off the D788 stands the pretty rose-granite chapel of **Notre Dame de la Clarté,** where a *pardon* takes place August 15. Farther north, don't miss the collection of rocks called the **Château du Diable,** where extreme weathering has sculpted large stones into various shapes, some resembling animals. If you've always hoped to see a puffin, take a three-hour boat tour of the sea bird sanctuary on **Sept Iles,** a group of islands off the coast. There is a one-hour stop at the Ile aux Moines. (April-Sept. 2 per day from Trestraou; round-trip 70F, students 45F.) For information and tickets contact Vedettes Blanches, 1, rue Emile Bac (tel. 96-23-22-47).

The resort of **Trégastel** is also remarkable for the strange beauty of its rocks. Avenue de la Grève Blanche leads from the D788 to the white shore; a path follows the cliff to sandy **plage de Coz-Pors,** passing a series of rocks worn by wind and sea into fantastic shapes. Around to the right you'll find more rocks and a quiet, sandy cove. If you're continuing on to Trébeurden, take a few detours from the main road to see more deserted, yet no less spectacular coastline. Local campgrounds include **Le Golven** (tel. 96-23-87-77; 12F per person, 6F per car, 12F per tent, hot showers included; open May to mid-Sept.) and **Tourony** (tel. 96-23-86-61; 11F per person, 10.30F per tent, 5.80F per car; open May-Aug.), both three-star sites. Le Golven lies off the D788 between Trégastel and Trébeurden; Tourony off the same route as it approaches Trégastel from Ploumanach. Tidy, green-shuttered **Hôtel de la Corniche,** 35, rue Charles le Goffic (tel. 96-23-88-15), offers 65-85F rooms and a 55F *menu* in the restaurant downstairs. They charge 30% more per extra bed and 17F for breakfast. (Open June-Sept. 15. Rue Charles le Goffic is also kown as the D788 as it leaves town.)

Ceinture Dorée

Vegetables and tourists alike find the coast from Trébeurden to Roscoff agreeable. The mild climate encourages vegetating on the beaches, as well as in the artichoke fields. Ideal biking country, the terrain undulates—but not too violently—and in summer, you can ride behind vegetable-heaped wagons rattling off to market. (Beware of falling potatoes.)**Cars Verts,** 1, rue de Kergonan (tel. 96-23-50-32), in Trébeurden, sends four or five buses per day to Trébeurden from the rail station at Lannion (office open Mon.-Fri. 8:30am-noon and 2-6:30pm, Sat. 8:30am-noon). You can rent **bikes** from the station in Lannion (45F per day, deposit 250F). The **Auberge de Jeunesse Trébeurden (IYHF),** 4km north of Trébeurden on the D788 (tel. 96-23-52-22), isn't particularly clean or cheery, but it puts you in a better shorefront site than most hotels. In fact, it's right next to the Hôtel Toenot, whose big signs should help you find the hostel. (34F. Sheets 11F. Breakfast 11F.)

With its beautiful eighteenth- and nineteenth-century houses and narrow city canals, **Morlaix** deserves a brief visit. A graceful viaduct towers over the town, dwarfing the tiny river below. Look for **La Maison de la Reine Anne,** which exhibits a sixteenth-century oak construction unique to Morlaix. The staircase situated in the left-hand corner of the house looks as if it has collapsed, but it was actually designed this way in order to connect the opposite walls by a narrow indoor bridge. (Open Mon.-Sat. 10:30am-noon and 2:30-6pm.) The **Pavillon du Tourisme,** place des Otages (tel. 98-62-14-94), has a good walking tour (2F) called *Le circuit des Venelles.* (Open July 14-Aug. daily 9am-noon and 2-6:30pm; in off-season Mon.-Sat. only.) They also lead trips to the parish closes of **St-Thégonnec** and **Guimiliau,** two masterpieces of Breton church architecture only 10km to the west. You can rent bicycles at the station or at **Cycles Henri le Gall,** 1, rue de Callac (tel. 98-88-60-47), for 40F per day, with the deposit of a passport or other ID. Splendid all-terrain bikes are 50F per half-day, 80F per day, and 120F per three days. Ask about one-way rentals to neighboring towns. (Open Tues.-Sat. 8:30am-noon and 1:50-7pm, Mon. 2-6pm.) There's a currency exchange at **Crédit Agricole,** 6, rue Carnot (open Tues. and Thurs.-Fri. 8:20am-noon and 1:30-5:20pm, Wed. 8:45am-noon and 1:30-5:20pm, Sat. 8:20am-noon and 1:30-4:20pm).

Morlaix is on the main Paris-Brest line; seven to nine **trains** per day run to St-Brieuc (1 hr., 51F) and other points east. The same number of trains connect Brest to Morlaix (¾ hr., 37F). Call 98-80-50-50 for rail information. **CAT** buses (tel. 96-37-02-40 in Lannion) run once per day at 8:30am to Morlaix from Lannion. Morlaix is also the best starting-place for a trip to Brittany's lovely, wooded Argoat region (see Argoat Interior), and to the coastal towns farther north.

Good accommodations and cheap restaurants are not hard to find in Morlaix. The **Auberge de Jeunesse (IYHF),** 3, route de Paris (tel. 98-88-13-63), just manages to peep its roof over the inclined roadway. Step over the threshold like Alice into the rabbit hole, and find yourself in a ramblng building whose bottom drops two stories below the front door to the street below. From the train station, go straight, then down the many steps, and turn left to place Emile Souvestre. Go straight ahead on rue Carnot, right on rue d'Aiguillon, left on rue de Paris, and then left again on route de Paris. The hostel is around the curve to the right, about a 20-minute walk from the station. (34F. Sheets 11F. Breakfast 11F.) Three **gîtes d'étape** are within 10-15km of Morlaix: To the northeast in the town of **Garlan** (contact the mayor's office, tel. 98-88-19-04); to the southeast 11-12km along the D9 in Troyellou, near the town of **Plougonven** (contact Monsieur Kerharo, tel. 98-78-68-01); to the west in the town of **Penzé,** near Taulé (tel. 98-67-15-88). If you'd rather camp in town, try one-star **Camping Municipal de la Vierge Noire** in Ploujean (tel. 98-72-04-04), 1km north of the *centre ville.* (Open mid- June to mid-Sept.; 4.50F per person, 2.50F per tent, 2.50F per car.) For something a bit more luxurious, **Hôtel Les Arcades,** 11, place Cornic (tel. 98-88-20-03), has comfortable singles for 70F, breakfast 15.50F. Also try **Hôtel-Restaurant Ste-Melaine,** 77, rue Ange de Guernisac (tel. 98-88-08-79), which overlooks a quiet side street. (Singles 60-80F, doubles 110F. Breakfast 18F.) The restaurant below rustles up a 42F *menu* (open in summer Mon.-Sat. noon-1:30pm and 7:30-9pm, Sun. 7:30-9pm; in off-season Mon.-Fri. noon-1:30pm and 7:30-9pm, Sat. noon-1:30pm).

In the seventeenth century, the small resort **Roscoff,** to the northwest, marked the beginning of the feared Pagan Coast. Lawless inhabitants of the coast from Roscoff to Brignogan lit bonfires along the shore, pillaging the ships that mistook the fires for beacons and crashed on the rocks. Nowadays, you can beach yourself safely on Roscoff's sands or depart intact from the harbor for beautiful Ile de Batz, but most of Roscoff's hotels will still loot your stash of traveler's checks. However, clean and decent rooms (from 70F) are available at **Hôtel les Arcades,** rue Amiral Réveillère (tel. 98-69-70-45). You can dine on the terrace or in the elegant restaurant overlooking the bay toward Ile de Batz (59F *menu*). (Hotel and restaurant open mid-April to mid-Oct.) Campers can stake out a piece of Roscoff's two-star **Perharidy** (tel. 98-69-70-86; 4.60F per person, 2.70F per tent, 2.40F per car; open Easter-Sept). You can also base yourself in nearby St-Pol-de-Léon or Morlaix. SNCF trains and buses serve both St-Pol and Roscoff from Morlaix (4-6 per day; 25 min., 15F to St-Pol-de-Léon; ½ hr., 20F to Roscoff). While at Roscoff, don't miss the striking **Eglise de Notre-Dame de Croas-Batz,** whose Renaissance belfry resembles an Antoni Gaudí building more than a church tower.

Brittany Ferries (tel. 98-62-22-11) sails to Plymouth, England from Roscoff (5-6 hr.; Jan.-March and Nov.-Dec. 290F, April-July and Sept.- Oct. 290-300F, Aug. 290-322F). Round- trip discounts are available to students ages 18-26. Ferries also leave for Cork, Ireland (15 hr.; March, May, and Oct. 380F, April and June 380-480F, July 480-550F, Aug. 430-550F, Sept. 380-430F.)

Just south of Roscoff, the village **St-Pol-de-Léon,** local supplier of artichokes, potatoes, and onions, makes a good base for exploring the region. There are only two hotels in town, both attractive and reasonably-priced, but they may be full—call ahead. The more expensive **Hôtel de France,** 29, rue des Minimes (tel. 98-69-00-14), is an ivy-covered stone house with a small courtyard. (Singles and doubles from 95-130F, breakfast 19F. 55F *menu* in the hotel's restaurant.) **Hôtel Cheval Blanc,** 6, rue au Lin (tel. 98-69-01-00), also has pleasant, airy rooms. The friendly proprietor speaks English. (Singles and doubles 80-120F. Showers 15F. Breakfast 20F.) To reach the **Ancienne Cathédral,** which enshrines St-Pol's bones, follow av. de la Gare from the train station to Pen-ar-Pont and turn right; it becomes rue Cadiou and then rue Général Leclerc. After 10 minutes, you'll reach place de Guebriant, site of the cathedral. (Open daily 7-11:45am and 1-7:30pm.) (You'll pass **Breiz Bar** at 16, place au Lin, favorite haunt of Breton locals. Continue past the cathedral for the **tourist office.** The two-star **municipal campground,** Trologot (tel. 98-69-06-26), is open from June through September. (5F per person, 3F per tent, 3F per car.) There is a well-equipped private campground, **Ar Kleguer,** at Le Vrennit (tel. 98-69-05-39). (10F per person, 11F per site, 4F per car. Hot showers included, 7:30-11am and 6-8pm only.) The campgrounds are located 500m apart along the windy bay. To get to both campgrounds from place de Guebriant, take a right onto rue du 4-Août-1944 and follow the signs. At rue Vezen Dan and rue des Minimes is the **Crêperie Ty Korn** (tel. 98-69-25-14), whose crisp 4-20F crêpes are local favorites. Both hotels listed have reasonably-priced restaurants. St-Pol's pride is the magnificent belfry of its **Chapelle de Kreisker.** For 3F, you can crawl up 246 ft. of tiny, circular stairs to a magnificent view of the coast and surrounding towns. Leave all bundles below, since there's barely enough room for you. (Open 10-11:30am and 2-6pm; enter by the altar.)

There is a **gîte d'étape** in the town of Tréflaouénan, roughly 11km southwest of St-Pol-de-Léon, off the D788. (Contact the proprietor at Moulin de Kerguiduff, tel. 98-29-51-20.)

A study in bucolic bliss, **Ile de Batz** contains an attractive old town, just a smattering of tourists, and miles of wilderness and undiscovered beaches. Punctuated by natural rock jetties, its rugged shoreline presides over an emerald-green seascape. Along with Ouessant, Bréhat, and Groix, Ile de Batz is one of the handful of islands where the traditional Breton farming and seagoing lives still coexist harmoniously. A *pardon* honoring Ste-Anne takes place the last Sunday in July, with an open-air mass and a *fête.* Frequent **ferries** serve Ile de Batz from Roscoff (July-Sept. every hr. 8am-8pm, Oct.-June every 1½ hr.; round-trip 23F, no bicycles taken). For more information, check with the Roscoff *syndicat,* rue Gambetta (tel. 98-69-70-70; open mid-April to mid-Oct. Mon.-Fri. 10am-noon and 2-6pm) or with **Vedettes Blanches** (tel. 98-61-76-98). You may rent bicycles at the island dock from Monsieur Moncus (tel. 98-61-78-92). The island's **Auberge de Jeunesse (IYHF),** located straight up the hill from the pier at Créac'h ar Bolloc'h (tel. 98-61-77-69), has recently been remodeled. (Camping 15F, dorm rooms 34F, cots in tent 28F. Breakfast 11F, dinner 34F. Open April-Nov. 15. Call ahead to reserve a bed indoors.) Inquire about the associated *gîte d'étape,* (tel. 98-41-90-41). Also try the *syndicat* on the island (tel. 98-61-79-90.) You can buy food in town, but it's cheaper to bring it from the mainland. In July and August, the **Crêperie Ty Yann** bills a cheap *menu* of three crêpes, cider, and coffee (35F); it's just across from the hostel. (Open July-May 12:30-4:30pm and 7:15-10:30pm.)

Brest is a large, modern port with little to see, but you may have to stop here en route to beautiful Ile d'Ouessant. It also makes a convenient stop for cyclists, who can take a Vedettes Armoricaines ferry from the Port Maritime to the Crozon Peninsula (See Crozon Peninsula). At least the spacious, immaculate **Auberge de**

Jeunesse **(IYHF)** makes your stay painless, with a nearby beach to keep you amused. (34F in 4-bed rooms. Breakfast 11F. Bikes 30F per day.) The hostel is located at le Moulin Blanc, rue de Kerbriant (tel. 98-41-90-41), about 4km from the train station. From the stop across from the train station parking lot, take blue bus #7 (5.50F) to Port de Plaisance. After the bus stop, take the first left and turn left again at the first street (last bus at 7:10pm).

Brest also has numerous inexpensive hotels. Try one-star **Hôtel Le Ponant,** 20, rue de la Porte (tel. 98-45-09-32; singles from 52F, showers 10F, breakfast 15F). From the center of town, follow rue de Siam toward the water and cross the bridge to rue de la Porte. **Hôtel des Sports,** 4, rue du Vercors (tel. 98-02-01-65), just off rue Jean Jaurès, has singles from 58F. The **Syndicat d'Initiative,** place de la Liberté (tel. 98-44-24-96), has a complete list of the hotels in the region. For a good, cheap meal, go where many *Brestois* go: the tidy **Crêperie des Fontaines,** 44, rue Jean Macé (tel. 98-43-30-33). From the *gare,* take a right on bd. Clemenceau, a left on rue du Château, and a right onto rue Jean Macé. (3-crêpe *menu* 30F, substantial salads 20-30F. Open Mon.-Fri. 9am-9:30pm, Sat. 6-9:30pm.) The **post office** is 1 block away.

A mere boat ride from Brest is windswept **Ile d'Ouessant,** its green pastures dotted with sheep and stone crosses. Because of centuries of isolation, the island developed a Breton subculture found nowhere else. Fabled among sailors as the *Ile des Prêtresses* (Isle of Priestesses), it evolved a matriarchal agricultural society that exists even today; many women tend the sheep and farm, while the men voyage with the merchant marine. This unique culture includes elaborate ceremonies for those lost at sea and a tradition of women proposing to men. The intended man would, as custom dictated, take refuge under his bed covers. The aspiring fiancée would leave a platter of food by his bedside. If the man left the food untouched, the proposal was denied. If the man ate the food, then he consented to the marriage, and the couple would live together for a trial period.

Despite the many old customs, twentieth-century tourism has not bypassed Ouessant. Boats dock at **Port du Stiff,** on the northeastern shore; the main town of **Lampaul** is a 45-minute stroll across the island to the southwestern coast. You can also rent a bike at the dock (28F) or hop from the ferry into a bus (8F). In Lampaul, you'll find the **Syndicat d'Initiative** (tel. 98-48-85-83), where you can get a map. (Open daily July 7-Sept. 7 9:30am-12:30pm and 2:30-5:30pm; Sept.7-July 7 10:30-12:30pm and 3:45-4:45pm.) The cemetery adjoining the nearby church is bright with flowers, some fresh, others delicate porcelain.

At the **Ecomusée du Niou-Huella,** about 1km northwest of Lampaul, you can take a look at the interior of a traditional Ouessantine home. Take the D81 uphill out of town and watch for the sign indicating the turnoff. The guide will show you the beam where slaughtered pigs were hung and the blue-painted porcelain racks. The deceased porkers are gone, but rows of *faïencerie* still gleam on the porcelain racks. The stone house demonstrates an ingenuous spareness: A kitchen table opens to reveal a *laverie,* and windows positioned on both the eastern and western sides make the room a tunnel of light from dawn to dusk. (Open Wed.-Mon. 2-6pm, tours in French only 2:30-5:30pm every half-hour.) If you continue away from town on the road outside the museum, you'll come to kilometers of flowered heath. You can wander here for hours, mingling with the sheep. The heath overlooks a blue sea swirling around enormous rocks; even in calm sunlight, the sight is ominous.

Although exploring Ouessant on foot is enjoyable, cycling proves more efficient. Two shops in town rent **bicycles** to tourists: **Savina** (tel. 98-48-80-44) and **Malgorn,** just outside the church (tel. 98-48-83-44). Both send vans loaded with bikes to meet the ferries. (28F per day. No deposit.) If you have your own bike, leave it in Brest: The round-trip cost of taking it on the ferry (44F) far exceeds the rental fee. There are four hotels on Ile d'Ouessant; all are located in Lampaul and have comparable prices. **Le Fromveur** (tel. 98-48-81-30) has rooms from 85-105F, **Duchesse Anne** (tel. 98-48-80-25) from 75-82F, and **Roch ar Mor** (tel. 98-48-80-19) from 90F. The rooms at **L'Océan** (tel. 98-48-80-03) range from 55-105F, but their current attempt to get a star rating will probably jack up prices. You can camp at **Pen-ar-Bed** (tel.

98-48-84-65), a two-star site 2km from the port. (7.50F per person, 5F per tent.) From July to mid-September, **boats** leave Brest's Port de Commerce daily at 8:30am for Le Conquet, a 45-min. cruise by sea. At 9:30am, the boats then continue to the island. From the end of March through the first week of July, service is suspended on Friday. The return trip leaves Ile d'Ouessant at 5pm. (2-3 hr. from Brest, one way 65F, round-trip 106F; 1¼ hr. from Le Conquet, one way 52F, round-trip 88F.) **Cars de St-Mathieu** (tel. 98-89-12-02; at Brest's *gare routière* information office 44-46-73) buses landlubbers west along the D789 from Brest to Le Conquet (daily at 7:30am from the Brest *gare routière*, 80 min., 25F). In winter, the passage from Brest can get rough. Tickets are sold at both ports; it's best to make reservations a day or two in advance with the Service Maritime Départemental (tel. 98-80-24-68).

Crozon Peninsula

This rugged, cruciform peninsula has some of Brittany's finest seacoast. Brood over the ocean from the height of a towering cliff, or approach it more intimately from one of the fine, broad beaches. The peninsula's gentler inlets shelter small towns and modest resorts. Like much of Brittany, the area takes effort and perseverance to enjoy. **SNCF buses** (railpasses valid) run four times per day (twice Sun.) from Quimper to Crozon, Morgat, and Camaret. **Autocars Douguet** runs buses between Brest, Camaret, and Crozon. There is also a Vedettes Armoricaines **boat** from Brest to Le Fret, with a connecting bus to Crozon, Morgat, and Camaret. This is a good way for cyclists to avoid going all the way around on the coastal road, as the wind and the steep hills make cycling difficult. Tourist offices in Camaret, Crozon, and Morgat have a leaflet with all public transport timetables for the peninsula. The recent openings of two *gîtes d'étape* in Crozon and a youth hostel in Camaret renders the peninsula more accessible.

Camaret

Perhaps the best base for exploring the coast, Camaret is close to cliffs, beaches, and menhirs, a wealth of natural beauty. As the beached skeletons of old fishing boats can attest, the town has long passed its heyday as a major lobster port. Today, Camaret draws its livelihood from masses of sunbathers and tourists, but you can still find a drunken sailor or two.

Orientation and Practical Information

Camaret lies at the end of the SNCF bus line and the end of the Autocars Douguet bus line from Brest. For the most scenic approach from Brest, take the Vedettes Armoricaines boat to Le Fret, where a connecting bus brings you to Camaret, Crozon, or Morgat. The boat from Brest leaves from the same quay as do boats to Ile d'Ouessant. (See Brest and Ile d'Ouessant. 3 boats and buses per day, 45 min., one way 39F, round-trip 72F. Bikes 12F each way.)

Syndicat d'Initiative: Quai Toudouze (tel. 98-27-93-60), near the bus stop. You can't miss it. Ask for a list of *gîtes d'étape* in the area. Open July-Sept. Mon.-Sat. 9:30am-12:30pm and 2:30-7:30pm, Sun. 10am-noon; Oct.-June Tues.-Sat. 10am-noon and 2-5pm.

Currency Exchange: Crédit Agricole, place Charles de Gaulle (tel. 98-27-94-19), across from the tourist office. Open Tues.-Fri. 9am-noon and 2-5pm, Sat. 9am-noon and 2-4pm. The **post office** also changes currency.

Post Office: 2, rue de Verdun (tel. 98-27-92-51). From place St-Thomas, take rue de la Mairie, which becomes rue de Verdun. **Currency exchange. Postal code:** 29129. Open Mon.-Fri. 9am-noon and 2-5pm, Sat. 9am-noon.

Bus Station: SNCF and Autocars Douguet buses stop outside **Café de la Paix,** 30, quai Toudouze (tel. 98-27-93-05). Schedules posted outside; buy tickets inside. **SNCF** buses to Quimper via Crozon-Morgat (2 each morning, 1 each afternoon, with additional buses Mon. and Fri. during the school year; 41F to Quimper, 9F to Crozon-Morgat). **Autocars Douguet** (tel.

98-27-02-02) to Brest (Mon.-Fri. 1 each morning, 1 each afternoon, Sat. 1 each morning; 37F). **Vedettes Armoricaines** buses stop in place Charles de Gaulle to pick up passengers for the boat passage to Brest. The bus stops at Crozon, Morgat, and Le Fret (3 per day; the 39F boat ticket includes the bus service).

Bike Rental: Bidaut, 19, rue de Reims (tel. 98-27-80-57), parallel to quai Toudouze. Baggage bikes once again, but this time they're luminescent green. 40F per day, 200F per week, deposit 150F. Open Tues.-Sat. 9am-noon and 2-7pm.

Laundromat: Quai Toudouze. Wash 25F, dry 15F. Open daily 8am-6pm.

Medical Emergency: Tel. 18.

Police: Gendarmerie, Tel. 98-27-00-22.

Police Emergency: Tel. 17.

Accommodations and Camping

A night at the youth hostel costs only 25F. There are four hotels in Camaret, not nearly enough to accommodate the crowd of summer visitors. Cross your fingers or call in advance, and be prepared to spend lots of money.

Auberge de Jeunesse de l'Iroise (IYHF), route de Toulinguet. Take a left at the end of the quai (in front of the Hôtel Styvel), and bear right to get to the route de Toulinguet. Plain, with 18 beds and kitchen facilities. Open mid-June to Sept.

Hôtel Vauban, quai Styvel (tel. 98-27-91-36). A clean, 1-star spot with pleasant management. Singles and doubles from 115F. Showers 12F. Breakfast 18F. Open March 15-Oct. 15.

Hôtel du Styvel, quai Styvel (tel. 98-27-92-74). A posh, 2-star establishment with prices to match. Singles and doubles from 140F, with shower 200F. Showers 20F. Breakfast 20F. Open April-Sept.

Camping: Camping Municipal de Lannic, off rue du Gronnach (tel. 98-27-91-31), fairly close to town center. Go to the end of quai Toudouze, take a left at quai Styvel, ascend the hill, and take a right at the sign. 2-star site. 6.20F per person, 4.70F per site, 3.50F per car. Showers 5.70F. Open June-Sept. 15. **Camping de Lambezen** (tel. 98-27-91-41) is another 2-star site 5km away in Lambezen. Take a left off the road to Crozon just after you've ascended from Cararet. There's a sign at the turnoff, but it faces the other direction, so only those coming from Crozon can read it. From there on, follow the signs. 33F per site and 2 people, showers included. Open May-Sept. 15. There are also 6 campgrounds in the Crozon-Morgat area; ask at the *syndicat.*

Food

For seafood in Camaret, the best value is the three-course, 45F *menu* at **Les Crustaces,** 7, place St-Thomas. **La Licorne,** quai Toudouze (tel. 98-27-93-79), offers an elegant 55F *menu, boisson comprise.* (Open daily for lunch and dinner.) For those with smaller appetites and budgets, the town has several good *crêperies:* **Crêperie Rocamadour,** 11, place Charles de Gaulle, serves plump dinner crêpes (11-19F), an excellent seafood crêpe (30F), and a 30F *menu* including three crêpes. (Open Feb.-Nov. 15 daily noon-11pm.)

Sights

The seventeenth-century Tour Vauban at the end of the pier houses Camaret's **Musée Naval,** a small collection of engravings, paintings, and model ships. (Open daily June-Sept. 10am-7pm; Oct.-May 2-6pm; last entry 15 min. before closing. Admission 10F.) Nearby **Chapelle de Notre-Dame-de-Rocamadour** continues the marine theme; model boats hang from the ceiling, lifesavers from the walls, and the altar resembles a ship's stern. A *pardon* and a blessing of the sea are held here on the first Sunday in September.

The most spectacular sites, however, lie outside town. Just beyond the edge of town on the D8 stretches a circle of stone menhirs. The **Pointe de Penhir,** just 3½km away on the D8, is one of the finest capes in Brittany. A memorial to the Bretons of the Free French forces stands on the cliff; from there, it's a dizzying 76-m drop to the deep blue sea. Climb out onto the rocks for a superb view of the isolated rock masses of the **Tas de Pois.** Amazingly, there is a grassy plain on the leeward side of the point that leads down to a sheltered beach. Farther north, the road passes another stone circle, the **Alignements de Lagatjar,** some 100 menhirs arranged in intersecting lines and ending in a Stonehenge-like circle. These prehistoric stones are believed to have been installed in 2500 B.C.E., and apparently served in sun-worshiping rites. Whatever their purpose, they remain awe-inspiring. The D355 leads to the **Pointe des Espagnols,** another spectacular promontory with a view over Brest and the Plougastel Peninsula. South of Camaret is **Pointe de Dinan,** where you can cross a natural arch and look out at the Atlantic.

Morgat and Crozon

If it's a beach and an attractive resort you're after, stay at **Morgat.** Unfortunately, you'll pay for the pleasant surroundings. Windsurfers and sunbathers line the beach like armies, but the view of the surrounding coast is unspoiled. If you plan to spend the night, the cheapest place, pleasant **Hôtel Julia** (tel. 98-27-05-89) will gladly assist in the spending (singles and doubles from 80F). **A la Grange de Toul-Bass,** place d'Ys (tel. 98-27-17-95), will make your time in Morgat all the more worthwhile. The restaurant is an antique shop with a farmyard just outside. Sit on the terrace next to an antique harrow (surcharge 5F) and feast on enormous crêpes (6-23F) and seafood dishes (34-39F). The tomato-cheese crêpe (20F) tastes like a pizza hybrid. (Open April-Sept. daily 10am-midnight.)

The Morgat **Office de Tourisme** (tel. 98-27-07-92) is situated just before the town on bd. de la France-Libre. (Open July-Aug. Mon.-Sat. 9:30am-7pm, Sun. 10am-1pm; June and Sept. Tues.-Sat. 9:30am-noon and 2-6pm.) Two companies offer magical, mystical tours of Morgat's **marine caverns.** The boats glide past fantastic rock formations as twilight casts an eerie glow. **Vedettes Sirènes** (tel. 98-27-29-90 or 98-27-22-50) departs every 25 minutes, sometimes in the morning, sometimes in the afternoon (May-Sept. 15, 45 min., 34F). **Vedettes Rosmeur** (tel. 98-27-09-54 or 98-27-10-71) also offers tours (4 per day, 75 min., 46F). Tickets are sold on quai Kader, Morgat. Both companies operate additional voyages. Vedettes Sirènes sends boats out of Camaret on birdwatching trips to the Tas de Pois rock formations (1 per day, 1½ hr., 46F). On Sundays in July and August, Vedettes Rosmeur makes the one-hour crossing to Douarnenez at 6:15pm (one-way 45F, round-trip 60F).

Three kilometers north of Morgat, **Crozon** is smaller, but no less congested, despite being landlocked. From 8am to 2pm daily, an open **seafood market** takes place in place de l'Eglise. Marvel at the variety of crabs plucked from local shores. Should your stomach not howl for crab, try **Restaurant L'Océanic,** 24, rue du Camaret (tel. 98-27-02-70), which serves hot *pizza primavera* (32.50F) and other enticing pizzas (24-37F) in a breezy setting. (Open in summer Sun.-Mon. and Wed.-Fri. 7pm-midnight, Sat. 7pm-dawn; in off-season Wed.-Mon. noon-2pm and 7pm-midnight.) A number of supermarkets in town and the **Intermarché** off route de Camaret (open Mon.-Thurs. 8:45am-12:15pm and 2:30-7:15pm, Fri. and Sun. 8:45am-12:15pm and 2:30-7:15pm, Sat. 8:45am-7:15pm) will help you stock up for the road.

The Crozon **Office de Tourisme,** on rue St-Yves next to the *gare routière,* will give you a helpful map of the Crozon-Morgat area and information on accommodations. (Open July-Aug. Mon.-Sat. 9:30am-6pm; Sept.-June Tues.-Sun. 9am-noon and 2-6pm.) Crozon's **post office,** on rue Alsace-Lorraine. (Open Mon.-Fri 8:30am-noon and 2-5pm, Sat. 8:30am-noon.) The **postal code** is 29160. There are mediocre bicycles for rent at the **Peugeot Station,** 34, rue de Poulpatre, off the marketplace in Crozon. (Open Tues.-Sat. 8:30am-noon and 2-7pm.) Hikers, bikers, and other carless travelers can head for two new Crozon **gîtes d'étape: de Larrial** at Crozon and **St-Hernot** at Cap de la Chèvre, south of Crozon and Morgat. At 23F per night, they are the peninsula's cheapest roofed accommodations. (For de Larrial, call Mr. or Mrs. Le Breton, tel. 98-27-62-30; for St-Hernot 98-27-15-00.) At the two-star **Hôtel Moderne,** 61, rue Alsace-Lorraine (tel. 78-27-00-10), you'll find comfortable and clean rooms from 95F—they don't come any cheaper in Crozon. (Showers 18F. Breakfast 20F.) You can make long-distance phone calls on the **phone** downstairs and reimburse the concierge afterwards. If the Crozon *gîtes* are full, cyclists or ambitious walkers may want to take advantage of the **gîte d'étape** in Kerdilès, 4km outside of Landérennec (tel. 98-21-91-04). From Crozon, head east on the D887 for 5km, branch left onto the D791 for 7km, branch left again on the D60, and keep an eye out for signs after about 2km. The *gîte* sits near the bay and has 23F beds and kitchen facilities; call in advance for a prepared meal. A second *gîte* is scheduled to open in Le Faou in the summer of 1989. Call the *mairie* in Le Faou for details (tel. 98-81-90-44). Inquire at the **ULAMIR** (Union Locale des Animations de Milien Rural), in the SIVOM building on route du Camaret (tel. 98-27-01-68), for a list of local *gîtes* and hiking maps to get you from one to the other. If you have wheels, you should look into *chambres d'hôtes* (bed and breakfasts) in the region. Singles, including breakfast, range from 70-120F; doubles 100-190F.

Campgrounds abound near Crozon. The three-star **Les Pieds dans l'Eau** (tel. 98-27-62-43), 6km northwest of Crozon in St-Fiacre, lives up to its name with a magnificent view of the sea. (10F per site, 12F per person, 5F per car. Showers included. Fresh bread and croissant every morning. Office open daily June 15-Sept. 15 9am-noon and 2-8pm.) The two-star **Pen-Ar-Ménez** (tel. 98-27-12-36) is close to the Crozon SNCF station on bd. de Pralognan (*direction* Camaret). (10F per person, 10F per car, 6.50F per tent.)

Getting to Crozon and Morgat is not a problem. Vedettes Armoricaines **buses** from Brest or Camaret stop in Morgat, and Autocars Douguet run two buses per day between Crozon and Morgat. Buses to Crozon proper include SNCF's connection with Camaret (3 per day), and Vedettes Armoricaines's Camaret-Crozon-Morgat-Brest line. Also, the thrice-daily **boat** from Brest to Le Fret connects with thrice-daily buses to Crozon and Morgat. The two towns are only 3km apart. **Hitching** is incredibly easy; you shouldn't have to wait more than five or 10 minutes for a ride.

Argoat Interior

Argoat in Breton means "wooded country," and the Argoat Interior is just that: a rocky, wooded region encompassing the rolling hills of the Monts d'Arée, the Parc Régional d'Armorique, and one-car, two-cow villages surrounded by pastures. The bus ride from Morlaix to Huelgoat along the D769 is an hour-long introduction to the area's remarkable beauty. The bus threads its way between tall hedges that break now and then to reveal glimpses of stone houses and the ubiquitous hydrangea bushes with their rich blue, pink, and purple flowers. From a high point, the hills roll away like clouds seen from above.

The hilly terrain makes long-distance cycling difficult. You can't rush through the Argoat; this is the place for leisurely exploration of forests and small towns. The **Fédération Française de la Randonnée Pédestre** has excellent topographical maps of the region that include detailed hiking tours. The organization **ABRI** has designed routes that follow scrupulously marked trails from one *gîte d'étape* to the next (23F per night). These maps are available for 20-45F each at several *syndicats*, including those at Morlaix and Huelgoat, or from the ABRI (see Rennes Practical Information), which also suggests bicycle circuits. The walks take you through rock-strewn woods, past primitive stone churches, and through farming villages where the Breton language flourishes. Here in Brittany's interior, the people are friendlier, prices are lower, and the scenery no less inspiring than on the coastline.

Huelgoat

A small town on a lovely lake, Huelgoat lies within walking distance of many natural wonders. The Parc Naturel Regional d'Armorique, with its curious grottoes and rocks, stretches around the town, while the Arrée Mountains, megaliths, and parish closes are only a bike ride away. Huelgoat is one of the Argoat's more accessible towns; an early morning and an afternoon SNCF bus connect it to Morlaix to the north and Carhaix to the south (see Buses below). Morlaix is the better access point, since it is on the much-traveled Paris-Brest line. Hitching or cycling from Morlaix, take the D769 to Berrien and the D14 to Huelgoat (30km altogether). Reasonable accommodations are available in town, and the *gîte d'étape* makes a comfy base in Locmaria-Berrien, 6½km to the south, the stop right after Huelgoat on the bus line from Morlaix.

Orientation and Practical Information

Huelgoat's center flanks the eastern bank of the lake. All SNCF buses stop in place Aristide Briand, less than a minute's walk from both the lake and the tourist office.

Office de Tourisme: Off place Aristide Briand (tel. 98-99-72-32). Guides to local sights (2F) and hikes; topographical maps (22-25F), information on *gîtes d'étape;* guide to region (20F). Open June 15-Sept. 15 Mon.-Sat. 10am-noon and 2-6pm; Sept. 15-June 15 inquire at the *mairie* next door (open Mon.-Fri. 8:30am-noon and 1:30-5:30pm, Sat. 8:30am-noon).

Currency Exchange: All banks closed Sun.-Mon. No exchange at post office. **Crédit Agricole,** 14-16, rue des Cendres, off the main *place.* Open Tues. and Thurs. 9am-12:15pm and 1:30-5:30pm, Wed. and Fri. 8:30am-12:15pm and 1:30-5:30pm, Sat. 8:30am-12:15pm and 1:30-4:30pm.

Post Office: 22, rue des Cieux. **Postal code:** 29218. Open Mon.-Fri. 9am-noon and 2-5pm, Sat. 9am-noon.

Bus Station: Buses stop in front of the *boulangerie-pâtisserie* in place Aristide Briand. Schedules posted in the window. Mon.-Fri. 2 per day, 3 Sat., 2 Sun. to Morlaix (1 hr., 21.50F), Carhaix (13.50F), and Locmaria-Berrien (4.50F).

Pedalo Rental: In front of Crêperie de l'Argoat. Pedal-propelled boats 18F per hour. Open July-Aug. daily 1:30pm until owner feels like closing.

Medical Emergency: Call fire department (tel. 18).

Police: Route des Carrières (tel. 98-99-71-45).

Accommodations and Camping

Huelgoat is relatively secluded, and you can usually find a room here in the summer. But by no means should you count on it. If you're up for a 6km hike—lengthy but beautiful—cheap beds await you at the *gîte* in **Locmaria-Berrien.** (You can also take the bus, but try to look a little dusty when you arrive: *Gîtes* are intended for horseback riders, hikers and bikers.)

Gîte d'Etape, l'Ancienne Ecole, Locmaria-Berrien. Obtain key at the *mairie* Mon.-Fri. 8am-noon and 2-5pm (tel. 98-99-73-09). Mon.-Fri. after 5pm and Sat.-Sun. 9am-9pm, go to the green-shuttered house opposite the church and ask Mme. Morvan for the key. You can also inquire at the cafe across the street. If all else fails, try M. Blaize (tel. 98-99-95-08) or M. le Guern (tel. 98-99-70-75), or stop in at the bar just beyond the cafe. 2 buses per day go to the *gîte* from Morlaix (16F) via Huelgoat (3F); 1 extra bus goes early afternoon Sat. From the bus stop, follow the signs 1.2km up the hill to the cafe and church. Turn right; the *gîte* and *mairie* are on your right. Well-equipped kitchen and new toilets and showers. Peaceful location near pay phone. Women shouldn't go alone in June, as the *gîte* is likely to be empty and workmen carry keys to the building. 23F per person, 20F per horse. 2-night limit. Absolutely no cars.

Hôtel de l'Armorique, 1, place Aristide Briand (tel. 98-99-71-24), a stone's throw from the bus stop. Simple, fairly large rooms with comfortable mattresses. The bar below is sometimes noisy, but the proprietor is friendly. English and Spanish spoken. Singles 60F, doubles 70F, triples with 2 beds 120F, quads 130F. Showers 10F. Breakfast 18F. Reception open July-Aug. daily; in off-season Tues.-Sun.

Hôtel du Lac, 12, rue de Brest (tel. 98-99-71-14), on the waterfront. Decent rooms, but a little dingy. Owner speaks English. April 16-Sept. 14 singles and doubles 60-120F, Sept. 15-April 15 singles and doubles 50-110F. Showers included. Breakfast 20F. Seafood *menus* in restaurant below from 58F. Restaurant open daily noon-2pm and 7:30-9pm.

Camping: **Camping Municipal du Lac,** rue de Brest, (tel. 98-99-78-80), 5 min. from bus stop. Often crowded, but sunny and well-tended streamside location. 17F per person, 25F per 2 people, car and site included. Reception open June-Sept. Mon.-Fri. 7:30-11:30am and 4-8pm, Sun. 8-11am and 4-7pm. **Camping de la Rivière d'Argent,** 3km from town on the way to Carhaix (tel. 98-99-72-50 or 98-99-70-56). Quiet, woodsy spot on the river. 10F per person, 10F per site. Open June-Sept.

Food

Conveniently located for *gîte* dwellers, **Chez Anne,** at the Locmaria-Berrien bus stop (tel. 98-99-75-03), serves a filling 53F *menu* but no *à la carte* option. Breakfast is 15F. (Open daily 8:30-10am, noon-2pm, and 7-9pm.) Unfortunately, there is no grocery store near the *gîte.* Huelgoat's **market** takes place on the first and third Thursday of every month from 9am to 3pm in place Aristide Briand and along rue du Lac. Place Aristide Briand is also the location of two small supermarkets, bakeries, *crêperies,* but nothing is open much past 6pm.

At lunchtime the workers' restaurants on the outskirts of town pull out all stops. Skip breakfast, hike out to one of the following, and stuff your face.

Aux Amis Routiers, on the road to Carhaix at the intersection with the D769 (tel. 98-99-73-12), 3½ km from town. The restaurant's name—plural, predominantly masculine, and comradely—says it all. 3 consecutive entrees, *plat du jour,* vegetable, cheese, dessert, and obligatory bread—all yours for 45F. Open Mon.-Fri. noon-2pm, Sun. by reservation.

Restaurant Le Menez-Bras, route de Quimper (tel. 98-99-76-28), 2km from town. Every lunchtime, this stolid little house's parking lot fills up with trucks. The men sit around big, communal tables while the female cooks, who know them all by name, serve up steaming platters of food. Anyone—especially a woman—going into the restaurant alone might attract some surprised glances; don't worry. Chances are you'll get a table to yourself. Potato salad, cold meat platter, beef with carrots, steamed potatoes, cheese, dessert, coffee, wine, and a big basket of bread all for 40F. Open late Aug.-July Sun.-Fri. noon-1:30pm.

Crêperie des Myrtilles, place Aristide Briand (tel. 98-93-62-66). Crêpes 4.50-25F. *Menu* with 3 crêpes, including *crêpes myrtilles* for dessert, 32F. Open July-Aug. daily noon-9:30pm; April-June and Sept.-Oct. Tues., Wed., and Fri.-Sun. noon-9:30pm; Nov.-March Fri.-Sun. noon-9:30pm.

Sights

A terrible hurricane in October, 1987 destroyed many of the trees in Huelgoat's *forêt domaniale* (state forest). Huelgoat's forest still encloses enormous uprooted oaks under living, vine-twined ones, making the place look like the site of a troll fight.

The tourist office sells a map (2F) that indicates Huelgoat's best-known geological oddities. One footpath begins at the end of rue du Lac, where the lake empties into the Argent River. Twisting through piles of enormous granite boulders, the path leads to the **Grotte du Diable.** Descend the iron staircase into the dark, clammy chasm formed by overlying boulders. The footpath threads its way onto the **Roche Tremblante,** whose famed function is Huelgoat's greatest money-maker. If you can't budge the 137-metric ton boulder, ask any local 10-year-old (wearing a *syndicat* arm band) to show you. Although their tip dish is laced with 10F pieces, don't feel obliged to give to the rich; 2F is fine. Other sights in the immediate vicinity include the **Chaos de Moulin** and the **Ménage de la Vierge,** two imagination-stimulating piles of rock, the second of which is said to resemble the Virgin's house-cleaning equipment. The path **Allée Violette** (½ km) will bring you to the road from Carhaix, just past the bridge over the Argent River. You may either turn right and head back into town, or turn left and look for signs to the **Promenade du Fer-à-Cheval,** a half-hour stroll through more unbeatable woods. As the paths end, you are once more on the road to Carhaix. Turn left to head home, turn left to find the **Gouffre,** where the Argent River crashes into a deep cavity and disappears for some 150m. The **Allée du Clair Ruisseau** also starts on the D764 to Carhaix and leads to the **Mare aux Sangliers,** a pretty pond surrounded by, you guessed it, more rocks, said to resemble boars' heads (about 600m from the road). A 6-km journey brings you to **Locmaria-Berrien,** its sturdy eighteenth-century church surrounded by seventeenth-century oaks. Follow the directions to the *gîte*. Within 2km is the **Menhir de Kérampeulven,** a solitary obelisk. Take the D14 toward Morlaix, and turn left after roughly 1½ km from the edge of town. On July 13, don't miss the race of the *deux chevaux nautiques.* For one surreal afternoon, the lake swarms with Citroëns and farm tractors on pontoons.

Near Huelgoat

Many longer hikes and bike rides are possible in the area around Huelgoat. Hikers should inquire at the tourist office for topographical maps, and bikers may try taking the D764 out of town toward Brest. The road is well-traveled in places, yet very scenic, passing through the pretty little town of **La Feuillée** (8km). Back roads—especially the one from La Feuillée to Litiez—wind past isolated farmhouses and tiny villages, but you'll need a detailed map of the area and a very sturdy bike to take them. The roads grow less flat and the landscape more desolate as you approach the Arrée Mountains. Their craggy peaks and the strong wind from the sea give the impression of great altitude. One of the highest points is the **Roc Trévezel** (365m), which may be reached from La Feuillée by taking either the tiny road through Litiez or the larger D764, and turning left on the D785. The two routes are comparable in length; the Roc is about 14km from Huelgoat. Continue south on the D785 for roughly 8km, and turn right up a steep little road for 1km to reach **Montagne St-Michel.** From the back of the chapel at the summit, you can see the **Yeun Ellez,** a huge peat bog. In winter, the fog becomes so thick and the area so sinister that Breton tradition locates the entrance to hell at its center. The same spot is now occupied by an artificial lake, supplying a controversial thermonuclear station at Brennilis.

Brasparts lies 6½ km farther on the D785. The small **parish close,** typically Breton, includes the church, a fantastically detailed **calvary** carved in stone, and a charnel house that once stored exhumed bones to make room for newcomers in the overcrowded graveyard. **Les Cavaliers de Kerjean St-Michel** in Brasports will loan you a horse to go riding in the Monts d' Avrée (call 98-81-40-08 during mealtimes). Exit by the D21, then pick up the D14, which leads back to Huelgoat via the small parish closes of Lannedern and Loqueffret. The church at **St-Herbot** is a remarkably flamboyant square tower that you can ascend for an excellent view of the countryside. Outside stands the *calvaire,* a characteristically Breton ornament in the form of a wayside, trident-like cross dating from 1571. For an almost-home celebration, stop by the **Relais de St-Herbot,** next to the church (tel. 98-99-90-31), for a drink or an elegant 68F meal. (Open Thurs.-Tues. noon-2pm and 7:30-10pm, Wed. noon-2pm.) You are only 6km from Huelgoat; the entire circuit is roughly 52km.

The town of **Pleyben,** 26km southwest of Huelgoat, is the site of **Eglise St-Germain l'Auxerrois,** with its domed Renaissance bell tower and the magnificently ornate *calvaire,* a sort of four-way *arc de triomphe* depicting the life of Jesus. On the first Sunday of August the *calvaire* is the site of a *pardon.* Don't neglect to go inside the church. Delicately painted gargoyles gaze down from the beams with very human expressions. To reach Pleyben, leave Huelgoat via the road to Quimper, which becomes the D14. After 20km, turn left on the D785.

To the south of Huelgoat, **Carhaix** is a small town worth avoiding. However, you may find yourself stranded here because of infrequent bus service. **SNCF** buses (tel. 98-93-00-01) from Carhais run to Morlaix and Brest (2 or 3 per day; to Morlaix 1½ hr., 33F; to Brest 2½ hr., 60F), to Quimper (2 per day, 2 hr., 44F), to Chateaulin for a connecting bus to Camaret (2 per day, 1¼ hr., 58F), to Loudeac (3 or 4 per day, 1½ hr.), and to Guincamp (3 or 4 per day, 1¼ hr., 35F). Cheap beds and a familial environment await you at the **gîte d'étape** in **Port de Carhaix,** a 5-km hike out of town along the D769. With ample kitchen facilities, hot showers, and wonderful management, it makes a fine stopping point if you can put up with the trek. Call the *mairie* (tel. 98-93-00-13) or M. Kergona (tel. 98-99-54-42), and pick up the key at the Café Priol, on the D769 just across the road from the *gîte.* The bus to Quimper stops in Port de Carhaix, near the *gîte.*

Quimper

Historically the capital of La Cornouaille, the oldest region of Brittany, Quimper has managed both to grow and to retain its Breton flavor. Full of cheap hotels and restaurants, it makes a fine touring center for the surrounding countryside. Quimper holds the most important regional folk festival, the **Festival de Cornouaille,** on the fourth Sunday in July. The celebrations usually begin the preceding Tuesday and include concerts, films, parties, and plays in both Breton and French. Furthermore, Quimper makes a year-round effort to preserve its heritage: Some women wear traditional dress in the marketplace, one local high school conducts its classes in Breton, and stores prominently display Celtic records and books.

Orientation and Practical Information

To get to the center of town from the train station, which lies to the east, turn right and follow av. de la Gare to the river. Cross the bridge, turn left on bd. Amiral de Kerguélen along the river, and turn right on rue du Rois Gradlon for the cathedral, tourist office, and entrance to the old city. Once in the old city, Quartier St-Mathieu lies to your left and the Musée des Beaux Arts behind the cathedral to your right.

Office de Tourisme: Directions to the location during the summer of 1989 will be posted on the gates of the old site at 3, rue du Rois Gradlon, next to the cathedral. They'll locate rooms and on weekends, they'll tell you the name of the pharmacy open. (Pharmacies stay open Sundays on a rotating basis.) You can also find the pharmacy's name in the Sat. newspaper. Ask for the free booklet with public transportation timetables for Quimper and surrounding area. 1½-hr. guided tours in French (Aug. only Mon.-Sat. 2 per day, 20F). Information on all kinds of accommodations, including *chambres d'hôtes* and *gîtes d'étape.* The helpful, English-speaking office also sells bus excursion tickets to such nearby wonders as the Pointe du Raz. Open mid-June to Aug. Mon.-Sat. 8:30am-8pm, Sun. 9:30am-noon, longer during the festival; Sept. to mid-June Mon.-Sat. 9am-noon and 2-7pm.

Student Travel: Nord-Sud Voyages, 5, bd. Amiral de Kerguélen (tel. 98-95-40-79). Transalpino/BIJ. Open Mon. 10am-noon and 2-6:30pm, Tues.-Fri. 9am-noon and 2-6:30pm.

Currency Exchange: Banks in Quimper are open Tues.-Sat., except for **Crédit Agricole,** place St-Corentin, opposite the cathedral. Open Mon.-Fri. 8:30am-noon and 1:30-5pm. As usual, the best rates are at the **post office.**

Post Office: At bd. Amiral de Kerguélen and rue de Juniville. **Currency exchange. Postal code:** 29000. Open Mon.-Fri. 8am-7pm, Sat. 8am-noon. **Branch office,** rue du Calvaire, near the hostel. Open same hours. No currency exchange.

Airport: Brittany Air International, Tel. 98-62-10-22 or 98-94-01-28. To London's Gatwick Airport via Brest daily. **Air Inter.** Tel. 98-84-73-73 in Brest. 3-4 flights per day to Paris from Quimper's airport in Plugaffan (8km away, served only by taxi).

Train Station: Av. de la Libération (tel. 98-90-50-50 for information, 98-90-26-21 for reservations). To Paris (Mon.-Sat. 7-9 per day, 10-12 Sun.; 6½ hr.; 271F), Rennes (Mon.-Sat. 6-8 per day, 8-10 Sun.; 3 hr.; 123F), Nantes (5 per day, 3 hr., 127F), Brest (5 per day, 1½ hr., 57F). Information office open daily July-Aug. 8am-8pm; Sept.-June 8am-6:45pm. Inquire about one-way bike rentals. The station's *consigne* stores baggage for 10F per day.

Bus Station: Many private lines operate out of Quimper; ask at the tourist office or peruse the schedules posted around the parking lot/*gare routière,* next to the train station. At signpost #1: **Cars de Cornouaille** (tel. 98-87-40-05). Service south to Pont l'Abbée, Loctudy, and Lesconil (July-Aug. Mon.-Sat. 2 per morning and 3 per afternoon, Sun. 1 per morning and 3 per afternoon; Sept.-June Mon.-Sat. 3 per day; 1 hr.; 19.90F to Lesconil). At signpost #2: **Transports Départementaux du Finistère** (tel. 98-90-17-83). Their information office is in the small, squat building nearby (open Mon.-Fri. 9am-noon and 2:30-5:30pm). Service to Pont l'Abbée, Guilvinec, Penmarch, St-Guénolé (July-Aug. Mon.-Sat. 9 per day, 6 Sun., extra service during the school year; 28F to St-Guénolé). Buses also stop at the *syndicat,* near the cathedral. At signpost #3: **SNCF** buses to Douarnenez (4 per day, 17F) and Camaret (Mon.-Sat. 4 per day, 2 Sun.; 41F). Railpasses valid. Buy tickets at train station. Also at signpost #3: **CAT/TV,** tel. 98-95-02-36. Numerous excursions. In addition, service to Pointe du Raz via Douarnenez, Audierne, and Plogoff (2 per day, 37.50F), Brest (Mon.-Sat. 6 per day, 2 Sun.; 60F), Pleyben, Brasparts, and Morlaix (Mon.-Sat. 1 per day). All buses stop at, and

Sunday buses stop only at, 5, bd. Kerguélen. **Cars Caoudal,** tel. 98-56-96-72 in La Forêt-Fouesnant. Service to Concarneau (½ hr., 16.60F), Pont-Aven (1 hr., 24F), and Quimperlé (1¾ hr., 31F). Buses leave Mon.-Sat. 6 per day, 4 Sun., from Bar de l'Avenue, av. de la Gare (tel. 98-90-06-55), and stop downtown near the *syndicat* in place St-Corentin. Also service to La Forêt-Fouesnant. Buy tickets at the bar. No student discounts.

City Buses: Central station place de la Résistance (tel. 98-90-72-40). Tickets 5F. Schedules available in the office. Open Mon.-Sat. 10am-noon and 2-6pm.

Bike Rental: At the **train station** luggage department. 37F per ½-day, 47F per day, deposit 300F. The "½-day" is either 6:30am-1pm or 1-9:30pm. One-way rentals to Châteaulin, Douarnenez, Concarneau, and Rosporden. Office open daily 6:30am-9:30pm. **Velodet,** 4bis, av. de la Mer (tel. 98-57-04-60), out of town in Bénodet.

Medical Emergency: Tel. 18.

Police Emergency: Tel. 17.

Police: Rue Théodore le Hars (tel. 98-90-15-41).

Laundromat: Au Raton Laverie, 4, rue Jacques Cartier, just west of the train station. Wash 20F, dry 15F. Open daily 7am-10pm. **Lav' Seul,** 9, rue de Locronan, right off place de Locronan. Waste some more coins at the pinball place next door. Open daily 7am-9pm. Wash 18F, dry 2F).

Accommodations and Camping

Between July 15 and August 15, written reservations will make your life easier. Telephone reservations are not reliable, but it can't hurt to call. If you don't have reservations, start looking early in the day. In rare cases, the *syndicat* can put you up in a private home (no fee). For accommodations during festival week, make arrangements as early as you can—February, if possible.

Auberge de Jeunesse (IYHF), 6, av. des Oiseaux, Bois de l'Ancien Seminaire (tel. 98-55-41-67), 25 min. from the train station. Turn right as you leave the station and follow the road over the river. Follow the river to quai l'Odet from bd. de Kerguélen, then turn right on rue du Pont l'Abbée, and walk 300m up the hill—the hostel will be past the *lycée* on the left. You can also take the bus in front of the train station to place de la Résistance, where you change to bus #1 (*direction* "Penhars"); debark for the hostel at the "Chaptal" stop (Mon.-Sat. every 20 min., 5F). Clean but cramped quarters, with kitchen facilities. Friendly staff speaks English. 34F per night. Sheets 11F. Limited camping space 15F. Breakfast 11F, meal for groups of 10 minimum. During festival week, they'll try to squeeze you in. Telephone reservations not accepted. Office open 8-10am and 6-8pm. No lockout.

Hôtel de l'Ouest, 63, rue le Déan (tel. 98-90-28-35), near the train station. From the station, walk right on av. de la Gare and take a left on rue du Dr. Gaillard, just before the fork. Rue du Dr. Gaillard will lead you to rue le Déan (5 min.). Clean, cheery, spacious rooms on a quiet street. Friendly owner. Singles and doubles 70-130F. Showers 12F. Breakfast 16F.

Hôtel le Terminus, 15, av. de la Gare (tel. 98-90-00-63), on a noisy street across from the train station. Very clean, attractive rooms. Singles 80F, with shower 125F. Doubles 120F, with shower 145F. Breakfast 20F. Showers 15F. No phone reservations.

Hôtel Celtic, 13, rue de Douarnenez (tel. 98-55-59-35), on the edge of the old quarter, a block up from Eglise St-Mathieu. Musty, but nicely decorated with firm mattresses. Friendly management speaks English. Singles and doubles 65-85F, with shower 100F. Showers 12F. Breakfast 16F. Reception noon-midnight. Hotel closes for 3 weeks in Sept.-Oct. *Menus* from 50F in the restaurant below.

Hôtel de l'Odet, 83, rue de Douarnenez (tel. 98-55-56-75). Quite a hike from the station, but the rooms are tidy. Call first. Singles and doubles 85F, with shower 110F. Breakfast 18F. Phone reservations accepted. 50F *menu* in restaurant below.

Camping: Camping Municipal, a 2-star site in the Bois du Séminaire, right next to the hostel. You can pitch your tent in the woods, well away from the campers below. 3.75F per person, 2.10F per tent, showers 3.50F. Office open July-June 14 Mon.-Sat. 9-11am and 1-7pm.

Food

Quimper has the usual collection of *crêperies.* Try **Crêperie Victoria,** rue Ste-Catherine, or **Le Blé Noir,** right across the street. There is a large **covered market** in Les Halles in the old quarter along rue St-François (open Mon.-Sat. 8am-1pm and 3-7pm, Sun. 9am-noon). An **open market** takes place in the parking lot between the cathedral and the Musée des Beaux Arts (open May-Sept. Wed. and Sat. 9am-6pm; in off-season Wed. and Sat. 9am-2pm).

La Fringale, 4bis, av. de la Libération (tel. 98-90-13-12). The Breton specialty *L'ôte à l'Armorique* 21F, daily specials 24-40F, *couscous* 57F. Open June-Aug. daily noon-2:30pm and 7-10:30pm; Sept.-May Mon.-Sat. for lunch and dinner only.

La Vie en Rose, 10, rue du Guéodet (tel. 98-95-41-19). Develop your own 6-item salad for 40F, or choose from 20-30F entrees (including stuffed clams) and 50F *plats* (including curried pork with vegetables). Friendly management; the owner speaks impeccable English. Open Tues.-Sat. noon-2pm and 7-11pm, Sun. 7-11pm.

L'Escale, 44, quai de l'Odet (tel. 98-55-51-25). 47F, 3-course *menu, boisson comprise.* The restaurant is upstairs, not at the dingy bar area that opens onto the street. Open Mon.-Sat. noon-2pm.

Sights and Entertainment

The center of the old quarter is **Cathédrale St-Corentin,** dedicated to Quimper's patron saint, one of the many Breton saints unrecognized by Rome. St-Corentin was the spiritual advisor of Good King Cradlon, who ruled La Cornouaille from Quimper in the sixth century. (You can see the duo together in Luminais' dramatic *La Fuite du Roi Gradlon* at the Musée des Beaux-Arts.) A statue of the king, added in 1856, stands between the two distinctive spires.

The cathedral garden is a good point from which to study the elegant construction of the Gothic apse. From here, you can climb the old city ramparts for a good view of the cathedral and of the Odet River as it flows from Quimper. Also within the garden is the entrance to the **Musée Départemental Breton.** The Breton statues, furniture, and carvings in this small museum are interesting, but they are upstaged by the costumes and pottery upstairs, and the circular structure that leads to them. (Open June-Sept. Wed.-Mon. 10am-7pm; Oct.-March 10am-noon and 2-4:30pm; March-May 10am-noon and 2-5pm. Admission 10F, students 5F.)

The **Musée des Beaux Arts,** near the cathedral and the Hôtel de Ville, includes works by Rubens, Fragonard, Corot, and Boudin. It also houses a wonderful collection of Flemish still-lifes, another collection inspired by the Breton landscape, and a special room devoted to Quimper's own Max Jacob. (Open May-Sept. 15 Wed.-Mon. 9:30am-noon and 2-6:30pm; Sept. 16-April 9:30am-noon and 2-6pm. Admission 8F, students 4F, Sun. and Wed. free.)

As you walk along **rue Kéréon** in the old quarter, you'll glimpse the cathedral climbing high above the rooftops. Elaborate and handsome Breton furniture and pottery are displayed in the shop windows on rue du Salle. A browse through the shops here will give you a taste of contemporary Breton culture. The three record stores in the old quarter will play any selection of your choice—ask for the popular Breton group **Tri Yann.** You can also follow the flower-lined banks of the Odet River and climb **Mont Frugy** (on the south side of the river beyond the bus station) for a superb view of the city.

Pottery is a Quimper specialty and to fully appreciate the art, you should visit one of the two **Faïenceries** (porcelain studios) in town that are open to the public. **Les Faïenceries de Quimper H. B. Henriot** (tel. 98-90-09-36) is just across from Notre-Dame de Locmaria (open Mon.-Thurs. 9:30-11:30am and 1:30-5:30pm, Fri. 9:30-11:30am and 1:30-4pm; admission 12F). The **Faïenceries Keraluc** (tel. 98-90-25-29) is 1km out of town on route de Bénodet and offers free tours (open Mon.-Fri. 9am-noon and 2-6pm).

Those who miss the Festival de Cornouaille can still catch other celebrations of Breton culture. From late June to early September, festival week excluded, there is traditional **Breton dancing** in the cathedral gardens every Thursday at 9pm (15F). Accompanying the costumed dancers, *biniou* and *bombarde* players set the gardens on ear with traditional tunes. The first three weeks in August, Quimper holds its **Semaines Musicales.** Some of Europe's finest orchestras and choirs perform nightly. Some concerts are held in the cathedral, some in the Théâtre Municipal, and some in other churches. (Tickets 80F, students and children 50F, discounts for 3 or more concerts. Make reservations at the tourist office.) For a night of live music, try **Chez Paul,** 52, av. de la Libération (tel. 98-90-04-31), a bistro-cabaret and hotspot for local singers and musicians. (Open Wed.-Sat. 6pm-1am, Tues. and Sun. 8pm-1am.)

Near Quimper

Quimper is the approximate center of **Cornouaille,** so named because its original inhabitants came from Cornwall in England (supposedly from King Arthur's court at Tintagel). Biking here is arduous; luckily, bus connections from Quimper to nearby sights are good—just be sure to coordinate schedules in advance. **Vedettes de l'Odet** (tel. 98-57-00-58) will take you down the Odet River and back for 72F (July and Aug. only; buy tickets at the *syndicat*). The route down the east bank via the D34 leads to the tourist resort of **Bénodet,** 15km from Quimper; you're better off with the D20 and D144, which snake through tiny villages along the west bank and afford better views of the cliffs and forests. **Pont-l'Abbé,** 20km southwest of Quimper on the D785, is another popular beach town.

Halfway between Bénodet and Pont-l'Abbé on the D44 lies the **Jardin Botanique,** an extensive garden featuring a large rose bush section (admission 15F). A little farther along the D44 towards Bénodet is the **Musée de la Musique Méchanique,** a collection of organs, player pianos, and other mechanized musical instruments. (Open May-Sept. daily 2-7pm. Admission 20F, includes guided tour.) Buses in Quimper serve Bénodet, Pont-l'Abbé, and neighboring villages. Farther south, and also accessible by bus, the **Penmarch Peninsula's** tiny villages continue to practice many Breton customs.

Flatter terrain makes for easier cycling north of Quimper. Twenty-two kilometers northwest along the D765, **Douarnenez** is an active fishing port and fish-packing town. It's not spruced up for tourists, but it does have a magnificent view of the bay and is paradise to lovers of fresh seafood. The fishing boats come in at 11pm, and the fish are auctioned off at 6am. The big market occurs Mondays and Fridays, and is quite a sight. The best place to eat in town is **La Cotriade,** 46, rue Anatole France; the food is delicious, the decor and solicitous service amusing. Douarnenez is well-connected to Quimper by bus. In July and August, a ferry cruises from Douarnenez to Morgat on the Crozon Peninsula. (See Crozon Peninsula.)

The westernmost point of La Cornouaille and of all France is the **Pointe du Raz.** Nearby lies the tiny village of **Plogoff.** During the late '70s, when a nuclear power plant (now dismantled) was undergoing construction at Pointe du Raz, this community disavowed all government support and declared "independence" for nearly three weeks. The people actually imprisoned their mayor and swore in their own leader. CAT buses serve the Pointe du Raz. By bike take the D765/D784 35km to **Audierne,** and continue 15km to Pointe du Raz.

Concarneau

Those coming to Concarneau expecting St-Malo's seaside elegance will be disappointed. Although Concarneau is a popular summer resort, it remains a working, seafaring town. For every souvenir-seller trying to snag a tourist, there's a fisher trying to net and filet a tuna. This port's fishing identity is well-disguised, but you'll scent it along quai Carnot, lined by warehouses packing the daily catch. The *ville close* (walled city), connected to the rest of town by a drawbridge, gleams hazily at dawn and evening like the alleys of Venice. And at sunset, the harbor shifts with indigos, golds, and azures like a Seurat seascape.

Orientation and Practical Information

Rail service to Concarneau is limited to freight (and bicycles) only. You'll probably arrive by bus, if you use public transportation. The tourist office adjoins the bus station, in the little building overlooking the port's parking lot. To get to the freight station (should you need to pick up your bicycle or beach umbrella), take a right onto av. de la Gare for ½ km. The *ville close* lies beyond the tourist office in the other direction, accessible on the left by a small bridge.

Office de Tourisme: Quai d'Aiguillon (tel. 98-97-01-44), next to the bus station. Information on boat trips, bike rentals, and festivals. Good free maps and bus schedules. Ask about *gîtes d'étape* and *chambres d'hôte* in the area. Open July-Aug. daily 9am-8pm; Sept.-May Mon.-Sat. 9am-noon and 2-6pm; June Mon.-Sat. 9am-12:15pm and 2-7pm.

Student Travel: Sterne Voyages, 8, av. de la Gare (tel. 98-97-50-55). Sells Transalpino/BIJ tickets, and does all a travel agent should. Open Mon.-Fri. 9am-noon and 2-6:30pm, Sat. 9am-noon and 2-4:30pm. **Permanence d'Accueil Jeunes,** place Jean Jaurès (tel. 98-97-17-28). Information on sports and cultural activities, student travel, women's rights. Also advice for the disabled. Open Mon.-Thurs. 1:30-4pm, Fri. 8:30am-noon.

Currency Exchange: Crédit Mutuel de Bretagne, 1, rue des Ecoles. Open Mon.-Fri. 8:30am-noon and 1:30-5:30pm. On Sat. try **Crédit Agricole,** rue Général de Gaulle. Open Tues., Wed., and Fri. 8:15am-12:15pm and 1:45-5:15pm, Thurs. 8:45-12:15pm and 1:45-4:15pm, Sat. 8:15am-12:15pm and 1:45-4:15pm. Commission 17F. Also at the post office.

Post Office: 5, quai Carnot (tel. 98-97-04-00). **Currency exchange. Postal code:** 29110. Open July-Aug. Mon.-Sat. 8am-7pm; Sept.-June Mon.-Fri. 8am-noon and 1:30-6pm, Sat. 8am-noon.

Train Station: No service, but plenty of information at the **SNCF station,** av. de la Gare.

Bus Station: On av. Pierre Guéguin at quai Carnot, in the port's parking lot. SNCF information office next to the tourist office (tel. 98-50-63-42). To Rosporden (3-4 per day, 20 min., 10.50F) for rail connections on the main Paris-Quimper line. To Paris (3-4 per day, 6 hr.). Open July-Aug. only, Mon.-Sat. 9am-12:50pm and 2-5:30pm, Sun. 9am-12:50pm. All SNCF buses stop at the SNCF freight station, av. de la Gare, and at the port's parking lot near the tourist office. **Cars Caoudal** Information and Ticket office, across the parking lot near quai Carnot (tel. 98-97-35-31). To Quimper (Mon.-Sat. 6 per day, 4 Sun.; ½ hr.; 16.60F), Quimperlé via Pont-Aven (Mon.-Sat. 6 per day, 4 Sun.; to Pont-Aven 20 min., 11F; to Quimperlé 1 hr., 21.40F). Backpacks or suitcases cost 6F extra, even when bus is empty. Bikes 10F. Open Mon.-Fri. 8:45am-1:20pm and 2:45-6:45pm.

Bike Rental: At the **SNCF station.** 37F per ½-day, 47F per day, deposit 300F. Lower rates after 2nd and 10th days. Also at the **hostel.** 30F per day, deposit 200F.

Medical Emergency: Tel. 18.

Police: Av. de la Gare (tel. 98-97-17-17).

Police Emergency: Tel. 17.

Accommodations and Camping

Finding a hotel room in summer is difficult, but not impossible. Fortunately, Concarneau has numerous campgrounds and an excellent hostel. In July and August, make phone reservations—even at the hostel.

Auberge de Jeunesse (IYHF), quai de la Croix (tel. 98-97-03-47), beside a little chapel. From the bus station follow the main street, av. Pierre Guéguin, which becomes quai Peneroff, toward the water and around to the right, where it becomes quai de la Croix (10 min.). Superb location next to the beach and town. Through the bedroom and kitchen windows you get a salty wind and a view of rocks and the bay. Easy-going atmosphere; co-ed bathrooms without locks on the shower doors. Multilingual staff. 34F per night. Breakfast 11F. Filling dinner or lunch *menu* 34F. Office open daily 8-10am and 6-8pm. Kitchen and bathroom areas stay open during the day, but bedrooms are locked.

Hôtel des Voyageurs, 9, place Jean Jaurès (tel. 98-97-08-06). Otherwise known as "Chez Francine," the name of the excellent restaurant below. Clean, airy, centrally-located rooms. Noisy street below. Rooms from 85F.

Brittany (Bretagne)

Hôtel Renaissance, 56, av. de la Gare (tel. 98-97-04-23). Take a right from the bus station and walk 5 min. Clean rooms near the station, reasonably priced. Nothing fancy. Doubles from 90F, 145F with shower. 40F per extra bed. Breakfast 18F.

Hôtel de la Crêpe d'Or, 3, rue du Lin (tel. 96-97-08-61), just off quai Carnot. Well-lit rooms near the station. Restaurant downstairs offers a 45F *menu.*

La Bonne Auberge, plage du Cabellou (tel. 98-97-04-30). Far away, but worth it. Take bus #2 from the *gare routière* (18 per day; last bus at 6:40pm), and get out at Le Cabellou, the last stop. In a peaceful rural area overlooking a sandy beach, this stopping place resembles a country home more than a hotel. Comfortable rooms. Doubles 90-145F, with shower 140F. Breakfast 17.50F. Open June-Sept.

Les Filets Bleus, plage du Cabellou (tel. 98-97-06-86). Also on the beach at Cabellou. Follow la Bonne Auberge's bus directions. Open June-Sept.

Camping: Camping du Dorlett, near Plage des Sables Blancs (tel. 98-97-16-44). Take bus #1 from the *gare routière* to Le Dorlett (13 per day, last bus at 6:20pm). 9.20F per site, 6F per person, showers included. Open mid-June to Sept. **Camping de Kersaux,** about 2km out of town (tel. 98-97-37-41), next to Plage du Cabellou. Take bus #2 from the *gare routière* to Le Cabellou, and backtrack along the route you came. The campground will be on your right, shortly after the beach ends. 10.55F per person, 6.35F per site, 3.55F per car. Showers included. Open June-Sept. 15. **Camping Rural de Lochrist,** about 4km out of town (tel. 98-97-25-95). Take bus #1 from the *gare routière* to La Maison Blanche, and follow route de Quimper farther away from town. Also rents tents. 9F per site, 8F per person. Showers 4F. Open June 15-Sept. 15. Ask at the tourist office for a list of other area campgrounds.

Food

The cost of food in Concarneau is discouraging. Seafood *menus* start at 45F and run quickly up to 80-100F. As usual, you'll probably resort to *crêperies.* Some good ones crop up near the youth hostel. **Ty Clementine** (tel. 98-97-21-05) serves 8-35F crêpes. For 33F, try an apple crêpe flambéd with the Breton apple liquor *calvados.* Seafood crêpes including squid and smoked salmon cost 29-35F, large salads 32F. (Open Thurs.-Tues. noon-3pm and 6:30pm until they decide to close.) Just across from the hostel, the **Crêperie de la Croix** serves crêpes (5-18.50F) in a pleasant garden. If you'd rather buy your own food, absolutely fresh (but not especially cheap) **fish** is sold Monday through Friday from 8am to noon near the port by the tourist office. There's a covered **market** daily from 9am to noon in place Jean Jaurès, as well as an open-air market outside on Monday and Friday mornings. Provisions are cheaper at **Intermarché,** quai Carnot. (Open Mon.-Fri. 9am-7:15pm, Sat. 9am-7pm.)

Taverne de la Ville-Close, 42, rue Vauban (tel. 98-50-71-39). 57F *menu* includes choices such as *moules marinières,* pork in mustard sauce, and grilled steak. A hefty, healthy *salade paysanne* (peasant salad) 30F. Open July-Sept. 15 daily 12:30-2pm and 7:15-10:30pm; Sept. 15-May Fri.-Sun.; June Wed.-Mon.

Chez Francine, 9, place Jean Jaurès (tel. 98-97-08-06). Great 30-42F salads (the most expensive includes mussels, clams, *calamari,* crab, and more). Open Tues.-Sat. 8am-7:30pm, Thurs. 8am-2:30pm.

L'Escale, 19, quai Carnot (tel. 98-97-03-31). Full dinner *menu* 34F. Fine food, if you can put up with the dim, dirty look and the loud music.

Sights

The usually deserted ramparts of the old town command a fine view of the harbor. Entrance to the most extensive section of ramparts costs 3.40F, but at the Tour du Havre (a short walk down rue Théophile Louarn) and at the Tour du Passage you can ascend for free.

The **Musée de la Pêche,** rue Vauban (tel. 98-97-10-20), in the *ville close,* houses a large exhibit on the fishing industry, but only fishing fanatics would want to pay the admission. (Open daily July-Aug. 9:15am-8:30pm; Sept.-June 10am-12:30pm and 2:30-7pm. Admission 20F, ages 5-18 12F.) Between midnight and about 6am, the quays by the large warehouses on the port come alive as fishing boats unload their catch and buyers bid for it. Try to catch the spectacle if you're out late or up early. At 7am and 10am, you can bid for the big ones yourself, at *la criée* (auction).

Concarneau's beaches are somewhat overrated, as the extensive tides deposit heaps of seaweed and muck on the rocks. The best beaches for swimming are the **Plage des Petits Sables Blancs** and the **Plage des Grands Sables Blancs.** Take bus #1 from av. Pierre Guéguin near the port to either of these beaches, or to Cabellou, the resort on the other side of town. (18 per day, last bus from beach leaves at 6:40pm.) The "beach" in front of the youth hostel is mainly a pile of barnacle-encrusted rocks, but it has an unforgettable view over the port to the sea—enough to inspire the impressionist in anyone.

The last week in July, Concarneau holds its annual **Festival International,** with music, dance, and parades in ethnic costume. A more local folk festival, **Les Filets Bleus,** ("The Blue Nets") was first held in 1905 to aid Concarneau's sardine fishermen. Though the extravaganza now benefits the tourist industry more than the fishing trade, the tradition continues: During the next to last week in August, the entire city turns into a giant playground, complete with four platforms of dancers, food sampling, and evening celebrations. On the last day of the festival, the next to last Sunday in August, it costs 30F to enter the gates.

Quimperlé

Two rivers, L'Ellé and L'Isole, meet at Quimperlé to form La Laïta, which winds south some 15km through the unspoiled Forêt de Carnoët and on to the sea. This confluence of rivers gives the city its name: The Breton word *"kemper"* means "junction." The city's *basse ville* sits on the island created by the three-way intersection. Ancient bridges (note lovely pont Fleuri, rue Ellé, behind Eglise Ste-Croix) span slow-moving waters, and fifteenth-century houses line rue Brémond d'Ars. The jewel of the *basse ville* is the eleventh-century Eglise Ste-Croix. Up the hill (and it's quite a hill), Quimperlé's *haute ville* is the site of the fourteenth- to fifteenth-century Eglise Notre-Dame, so tightly wedged into its surroundings that the steep streets pass under its arched buttresses. With these architectural highlights and an uncrowded, relaxed atmosphere to boot, Quimperlé makes an ideal spot to unwind after an overdose of hasty traveling.

Orientation and Practical Information

If you arrive by bus from Quimper or Concarneau stay on past the SNCF station to the stop by the rivers of the *basse ville.* The *syndicat* is on rue de Bourgneuf, on the east bank of the Laïta River, just across the Ellé from place Charles de Gaulle. Otherwise, the walk from the station to the *basse ville* takes about 15 minutes and serves as a good introduction to the town. From the station take a left on bd. de la Gare, then a right on rue de l'Hôpital Fremeur. Cross place St-Michel diagonally to the right, pass the church on your left, and take rue Brouzic (which becomes rue Savary) to the jumble of cobblestones that passes for a staircase on rue Jacques Cartier. Cross the bridge to place Charles de Gaulle and turn right for the *syndicat.*

Syndicat d'Initiative: Rue du Bourgneuf (tel. 98-96-04-32), in the *basse ville.* Solicitous staff, helpful maps, and a brochure describing architectural highlights. Open for 15 days around Easter and June-Sept. 15 Mon.-Sat. 9:15am-noon and 2:15-6:30pm.

Currency Exchange: Société Générale, 2, place Carnot (tel. 98-96-09-14). Open Mon.-Fri. 8:25am-12:05pm and 1:35-5:10pm. Crédit Agricole, 2, place Charles de Gaulle (tel. 98-96-02-10). Open Tues.-Sat. 8:30am-12:15pm and 1:30-5:15pm, Sat. 8:30am-12:15pm and 1:30-4:15pm.

Post Office: Place Charles de Gaulle, in the *basse ville.* **Postal code:** 29130. Open Mon.-Fri. 8am-noon and 1:30-5:30pm, Sat. 8am-noon.

Train Station: Bd. de la Gare (tel. 98-39-24-24), in the *haute ville*. On the main Paris-Quimper line. To Paris (7 per day, 5½ hr., 252F), Lorient (5 per day, 15 min., 15.50F), and Quimper (10 per day, ½ hr., 32F). Information desk open daily 6am-noon and 1:30-6pm.

Bus Station: City buses are hopeless, but 2 lines connect Quimperlé to nearby towns. **Cars Caoudal,** Tel. 98-56-96-72. Information and tickets at Café de la Gare, across from the train station. 6 buses per day, 4 Sun., go to Pont Aven (¾ hr., 14.60F), Quimper (1¾ hr., 31F), and Concarneau (1 hr., 21.40F). All buses stop outside the SNCF station and in the *basse ville*, next to the cafe Au Retour de Toulföeh, across the Isole River from the post office. Luggage 6F. **Ellé Laïta,** 19, rue Brémond d'Ars (tel. 98-96-13-77). To Lorient (Mon.-Sat. 3 per day, ½ hr., 11F), Le Pouldu (Mon.-Sat. 3 per day, ½ hr., 15F), Le Faouët (Mon.-Sat. 2 per day, 45 min., 13.50F). Buses stop at the SNCF station only. Office open Mon.-Fri. 9am-noon and 2-6:30pm, Sat. 9am-noon.

Bike and Moped Rental: Cycles Peugeot, 5, rue de la Tour d'Auvergne (tel. 98-96-05-18), in the *basse ville*. Decent 5- and 10-speeds 26F per day, 165F per week, deposit 250F. Mopeds 45F per day, 252F per week, deposit 650F. Open July-Sept. 15 Tues.-Sat. 8:30am-noon and 2-6:30pm. **Fontaine Sports,** 2, rue de Pont-Aven. Bikes 35F per day, 65F per 2-day period, and 180F per week. 850F or ID deposit required.

Canoe Rental: Take rue Audran to the banks of the Ellé River, or contact M. Reveillere (tel. 98-06-16-81).

Laundromat: Bd. de la Gare, just opposite the station. 20F per 7kg, dry 2F. Open daily June-Aug. 7am-11pm, Sept.-May 7am-9pm.

Public Baths and Showers, 6, rue Mme. Morvan. Showers 5.80F, baths 9.30F. Open Fri. 3-8pm, Sat. 8am-noon and 3-8pm, Sun. 8am-noon.

Medical Emergency: Tel. 18.

Police: Gendarmerie, place Charles de Gaulle (tel. 98-96-00-58).

Police Emergency: Tel. 17.

Accommodations and Food

Gîte d'Etape, Pors- (or Porz-) en-Breton (tel. 98-96-16-56), 2-3km out of town on rue de Moëlan/D16. By bus from Quimper/Concarneau, ask the driver to stop at Pors-en-Breton, a right turn off D16. From the SNCF station, turn right, and right again at the bottom of the hill towards Moëlan. Turn left at the sign for the *gîte;* the farm is at the end of the road. If there isn't a *porcelet* (roasted young pig) on the table and wine in your glass the night you arrive, you should stay until there is. Friendly farm life with horses, visitors, and a pervading, persuasive philosophy. Live Celtic music on occasion. Not-so-clean facilities and mattresses are the only drawbacks. Beds 23F. Excellent lunches and dinners on request 46F. Complete kitchen. Rides into town are easy. All other accommodations in town pale by comparison.

Hôtel-Restaurant Moderne, 22, place St-Michel (tel. 98-96-01-32), in the *haute ville*. Clean and bright 1-star singles and doubles from 75F, with shower 110F. Showers 12F. Breakfast 15F. Restaurant downstairs offers a 50F *menu*.

Hôtel-Restaurant de l'Europe, 32, bd. de la Gare (tel. 98-96-00-02). The huge, pale pink facade across from the train station hides red and green hallways. The proprietress wears the Breton lace headdress and black clothing. Dimly lit rooms 60F, with shower 75F, with bath 80F. Phone reservations accepted.

Hôtel-Restaurant Les Tilleuls, 23-25, rue du Bourgneuf (tel. 98-96-07-97), in the *basse ville*. Doubles 65-70F, with 2 beds 90F. Showers 7.50F. Excellent restaurant below offers a 39F *menu*.

Camping: Camping municipal de Quimperlé, just out of town on the N165 (tel. 98-39-31-30). 2-star site with showers, swimming, and TV. 10F per person, 7.70F per site, 3.80F per car.

In Quimperlé, *crêperies* and pizzerias are everywhere. Halfway up the lovely, crumbling staircase of rue Jacques Cartier is **La Vache Enragée** (The Raging Cow), 5, rue Jacques Cartier, with a tasty 52F *menu*. (Open June-Oct. Wed.-Mon. for lunch and dinner; in off-season Tues.-Sun. afternoon.) **Crêperie Croqu' Odile,** 16, rue l'Hôpital Fremeur, serves crêpes (3.30-21F), salads (26-39F), omelettes (17-31F), and sandwiches (13-19F). There are also two **markets:** one Monday to Saturday from 8:30am to 1pm, with fresh fish sold on the premises opposite Eglise Ste-

Croix; the other Friday from 9am to 6pm and Sun. from 9am to noon at place St-Michel in the *haute ville*. Get supermarket grub at the **Intermarché** on bd. de la Gare. (Open Mon.-Thurs. 9am-12:15pm and 2:15-7pm, Fri.-Sat. 9am-7pm.)

Sights

Round-shaped **Eglise Ste-Croix's** design, copied from the Holy Sepulchre in Jerusalem, resembles a symmetrical Greek cross rather than the traditional, elongated Latin cross. Three chapels are superbly ornamented and the fourth branch of the cross, the altar, rises majestically above the rest. Below it, the crypt sports low, solid Romanesque arches and austere tomb sculptures. Look for the light switch above your head at the entrance. Tucked away in a corner, back on the ground floor, stands the *Mise au Tombeau,* a sixteenth-century sculpture of 10 mourners grouped around Christ's body.

Built between 1470 and 1500, the **Maison des Archers,** 7, rue Dom Morice, just off rue Brémond d'Ars, housed the town's crack commando squad of archers, equivalent to Breton *gendarmes.* Now a museum of local lore, it includes the room of Théodore Hersart de la Villemarqué, who wrote the famous **Barzas Briez,** the traditional Breton chorus. (Open July-Aug. 31 daily 10am-noon and 1-6pm. Admission 11.40F.) The tourist office supplies a complete list of cloisters and abbeys found in and around the town.

Near Quimperlé

As you head west toward Quimper, the countryside becomes a colorful mass of yellow genets. **Pont-Aven,** a small town in a lovely valley, was Gauguin's residence before he left France for Tahiti. Today local artists' galleries line the streets, displaying works by painters who have no desire to move to the tropics. The **Office de Tourisme,** place de l'Hôtel de Ville (tel. 98-06-04-70), suggests walks along the river Aven, through the **Bois d'Amour** that inspired many impressionist landscapes, and out to the sixteenth-century **Chapelle de Trémalo,** whose impressive crucifix inspired Gauguin's *Yellow Christ.* Tourist office open July-Aug. Mon.-Sat. 9am-1pm and 2-7:30pm, Sun. 10:30am-12:30pm and 3-6:30pm; April-June and Sept. Mon.-Sat. 9am-12:30pm and 2-6:30pm, Sun. 10:30am-12:30pm and 3-6:30pm; Oct.-March Mon.-Sat. 9am-12:30pm and 2-6:30pm). Each year the **Musée Municipal,** in the Hôtel de Ville, features the works of a contemporary Breton painter or of a different painter in Gauguin's Pont-Aven group. The museum's permanent collection includes Gauguin's drawings and letters and a number of paintings by Breton artists from 1860 to 1940. (Open from late March-Dec. 10am-12:30pm and 2-7pm. Admission 12-15F depending on the exhibit, students 8F.) The town may disappoint those hoping to see an extensive exhibition of Gauguin's paintings: There are a few here, but the great ones are scattered at museums in better-known towns than Pont-Aven. However, Gauguin-buffs will be entranced by the traces of the artist's work in and around Pont-Aven. In addition to the museum's documents and the Trémalo crucifix, there's a calvary next to the fifteenth-century church at **Nizon,** about 1.5km northwest of Pont-Aven, that inspired Gauguin's *Green Christ* (now at the Musées Royaux des Beaux Arts in Brussels). The *syndicat* suggests a scenic bicycle route to Nizon that returns along the rue des Grands Chênes—more inspirational landscape. Rent bikes at the BP service station (tel. 98-06-02-77).

Despite the number of struggling, starving artists in town, hotel prices are geared to the wallets of the rich. Two-star **Ajoncs d'Or,** next to the tourist office at 1, place de l'Hôtel de Ville (tel. 98-06-02-06), offers lovely rooms for nasty sums (105-240F). The stone tablet over the hotel entrance announces that the English poet Ernest Dowson, "author of *Cynara* and other beautiful poems," lived in the very same building in 1896. (Breakfast 22F. Open May-Sept.) You can **camp** at the beautiful beach at **Raguenes,** 7km to the south off the D77. Closer to Pont-Aven is the luxurious **Roz-Pin** (tel. 98-06-03-13; open May-Sept.). Take the rue des Abbés Tanguy to the intersection at Kergoz, take a left (*direction* "Nevez"), and follow the signs.

Cyclists should pedal to the bucolic *gîte d'étape* in Riec-sur-Belon (23F per night). Signs to the *gîte* appear on the D783 to Quimperlé. The tourist office will also locate private rooms in town. Prices range from 80-180F for doubles.

Lorient, on the coast to the south, was founded in the eighteenth century as the main post of the powerful French East India Company. Still a major port today, it shows little trace of its colorful history. The town was a submarine shelter during World War II, and the constant shellings almost destroyed it. Nevertheless, Lorient retains pride in its heritage, and holds the **Festival Interceltique** every year during the first two weeks in August, with dancing, music, and films from the Celtic cultures of Ireland, Scotland, Wales, and the Isle of Man. There is a superb **Auberge de Jeunesse (IYHF)** by the ocean at 41, rue Schoelcher (tel. 97-37-11-65), about 3km from the train station. Built into the side of a hill overlooking a lake, the hostel is a modern bunker with excellent kitchen facilities, hot showers, and clean, comfortable rooms. Television, game rooms, a bar, and facilities for disabled travelers are available. (34F per person, sheets 13F, camping 15F. Breakfast 11F, dinner 34F.) From the train station take bus C (*direction* "Kerroman," every ¼ hr., 5.50F, last bus to hostel at 8pm); debark at the stop marked *Auberge de Jeunesse,* and then follow the signs for 5-10 min.

Lorient is also the departure point for ferries to **Ile de Groix,** another of the small, spectacular islands off the Breton coast. (In summer 4-8 per day, round-trip 66F.) Although it lacks the popularity of its closest rival, Belle-Ile, Ile de Groix remains uncrowded and less touristed. Most of the interesting sights can be reached by foot—many of the paths along the coast are too narrow and the terrain too rough for even a bicycle. Luckily, the island is only 8km long and 4km wide. It's small enough to explore in a day, although you'll probably end up wanting to stay longer. If you lose your way while hiking, don't panic: There are numerous signposts scattered throughout the island. The **Ecomusée de l'Ile de Groix,** 50 yds. from the port where the ferry docks, has maps outlining hiking paths of 13-14km, but you're better off exploring on your own. The museum itself merits a visit. It's devoted to explaining every detail of the island's history, and contains geological, aquatic, and costume exhibits. (Open Tues.-Sun. 10am-12:30pm and 2-5pm. Admission 10F.)

A night on the island is both relaxing and inexpensive. Two kilometers from Port Tudy is an **Auberge de Jeunesse** (IYHF; tel. 97-05-81-38) that makes an excellent base for exploration. From the ferry dock, turn left, follow the signs up the hill, and turn left again. (30F per night. Hot showers 5F. Office open 8:30-11:30am and 6-11pm. Open May 20-Sept. 20.) A little closer to the port and consequently less peaceful is a *gîte d'étape* (tel. 97-05-89-87). Turn left from the port and walk for two minutes; you can't miss it. (23F per night; 6F extra if you stay during the day. Showers and kitchen facilities included.) Campers should head for **Camping des Sables Rouge** (tel. 99-64-13-14), a 3-star site at Port Coustic, near the Pointe des Chats on the southern tip of the island. (16F per site, 12F per person, 5.40F per car. Open April-Sept.) Bike rentals and food supplies are available in Port Tudy and Le Bourg, 1km south. Don't expect to find civilization anywhere on the island other than these two towns.

Quiberon and Belle-Ile

In summer everyone comes to Quiberon to find a quiet beach and escape the crowded cities—with the obvious results. Nonetheless, it's difficult to avoid Quiberon altogether. It's too close to sandy Grande Plage, rugged Côte Sauvage, and spectacular Belle-Ile, which is easily accessible by ferry. If you head north along the peninsula, you'll find groves of windblown pines and jagged, rocky coastline. Quiberon also has huge fishing and canning industries that, in summer, are obscured by the throng of pleasure boats and windsurfers. Walk by the canneries on quai de l'Océan for a look at a different facet of Brittany's southern coast. Cycling is a popular and convenient means of touring the area. Unfortunately, train service to Quiberon operates only in July and August; off-season, it's buses only.

Practical Information

Office de Tourisme: 7, rue de Verdun (tel. 97-50-07-84). A hefty tourist brochure with a detailed street map of the southern half of the peninsula suggests a cycling tour of the Côte Sauvage. The enthusiastic staff will help book accommodations for the price of a phone call. Open July-Aug. Mon.-Sat. 9am-7pm, Sun. 10am-noon and 5-7pm; Sept.-June Mon.-Sat. 9am-12:30pm and 2-6:30pm.

Currency Exchange: Crédit Agricole, rue de la Gare, opposite the SNCF station. Open Tues.-Fri. 8:30am-12:30pm and 2-5:15pm, Sat. 8:30am-12:30pm and 2-4:15pm. Commission 20F. Change at the post office to maximize bananas.

Post Office: Place de la Duchesse Anne, near the church. **Currency exchange. Postal code:** 56170. Open July-Aug. Mon.-Fri. 9am-7pm, Sat. 9am-noon; Sept.-June Mon.-Fri. 9am-noon and 2-5pm, Sat. 9am-noon.

Train Station: Rue de la Gare (tel. 97-50-07-07). Open July-Aug. only. Trains to Plouharnel (near Carnac) are most frequent (10 per day; ½ hr.; local service 6F, "express" 11F). All connections elsewhere go via Auray (6 per day, 40 min., 21.50F). To Paris (4 per day, 6-7 hr., 241F), Vannes (4 per day, 1½ hr., 32F), Nantes (4 per day, 2¾ hr., 94F). Tickets sold daily 7:10am-8pm and 10-10:45pm. Information office open daily 8:30am-noon and 12:45-6:45pm. **Baggage check** (10F per bag per day) open 6am-noon, 1-1:30pm, 3-8pm, and 10-10:45pm.

Bus Station: All buses stop at the train station, Port Maria (the ferry dock), and Place Hoche. **Transports le Bayon,** Tel. 97-24-26-20 in Auray. To Plouharnel (7 per day, ½ hr., 10F), Carnac or Carnac *plage* (6-7 per day, ¾-1¼ hr., 15F), and Auray (7 per day; 1½-2 hr.; 29.50F, 30F on Sun.). To get from Auray to Locmariaquer, take the last bus to Auray—around 5pm—and a bus or taxi from there (1 per day, 1¾-2½ hr.). **TTO** to Plouharnel (4 per day, ½-1 hr., 13F), Carnac or Carnac *plage* (4 per day, ¾-1¼ hr., 15.50 to Carnac *ville,* 16F to the *plage*), Auray (4 per day, 1½-2 hr., 29F), and Vannes (4 per day, 2-3 hr., 45F).

Ferries: Port Maria (tel. 97-31-80-01 in Belle-Ile). To Belle-Ile (Oct.-late March Mon.-Fri. 4 per day, Sat.-Sun. 6 per day; late March-June 8:30am-8:45pm 6-10 per day; July-Aug. 6:15am or 8am-8:45pm 10-12 per day; Sept. 8-10 per day; 45 min.; round-trip 66F; bikes 28F). Information and ticket office open late March-Sept. 6am-9pm; in off-season 7:15-11am and 1-8:30pm.

Bike Rental: Cyclomar, 17, place Hoche (tel. 97-50-26-00). 3-speeds 31F per day, 134F per week, deposit 200F. Mopeds 94F per day, 432F per week, deposit 350F. 10-speeds for rent as well. Open daily July-Aug. 8am-midnight; March-June and Sept.-Dec. 8am-12:30pm and 2-7:30pm. **Cycles Lenoble,** 4, rue de la Poste (tel. 97-50-18-11). 34F per day, 152F per week. Open 9am-12:30pm and 2-6:30pm. **Cycles Loisirs,** 3, rue du Manémeur (tel. 97-50-10-69), behind the tourist office. 3-speeds 28F per day, 156.10F per week; 5-speeds 46F per day, 196.70F per week, deposit 200F.

Medical Emergency: Tel. 17 or 18. **Auray-Hôpital Général le Pratel,** Tel. 97-24-15-51.

Police: Av. Général de Gaulle (tel. 97-50-07-39).

Police Emergency: Tel. 17.

Accommodations, Camping, and Food

As in all popular seaside resorts, food and lodging are expensive. Quiberon has the additional disadvantage of being small. You will not find a hotel room here in July or August without reserving months in advance. Camping is a better option, but even the campgrounds (and there are dozens) fill up in summer. With a little luck, a few beds will be available at the *auberge.*

Auberge de Jeunesse (IYHF), 45, rue du Roch-Priol (tel. 97-50-15-54), a 1½-km walk from the station. Turn left and follow the signs. Small and pleasant. Picnic tables and a communal feeling. Kitchen, but no meals. Make reservations for July-Aug. 34F, on cot under tent 28F, in your own tent 15F. Abused bikes 30F per day. Office open 8:30-10am and 6-10pm; don't count on finding anyone there at dinnertime.

Au Bon Accueil, 6, quai de l'Houat (tel. 97-50-07-92). Don't let the dingy hallways fool you—the rooms are clean and comfortable. *Pension* required only for stays of 3 days or longer. Singles and doubles from 85F, with showers 96F, 100F for 3 beds. Showers 15F. Breakfast

16F. A popular 54F *menu* downstairs in restaurant. Open April-Nov.; always booked July-Aug.

Le Corsaire, 24, quai de Belle-Ile (tel. 97-50-15-05), at Port Maria. Comfortable rooms, though a bit moldy on the edges. Dried-up corsaires haunt the hallway wallpaper. Singles 88F. Doubles 120F. Breakfast 16F. No showers. Telephone reservations accepted.

Roch Armoz, 1, rue des Dauphins (tel. 97-50-29-19), a few blocks down from the hostel off rue du Roch-Priol. Rooms on a long-term basis, but sometimes has space for itinerants. 80F per night (rooms may be shared at no extra cost) includes showers and kitchen use.

Camping: Most of the campsites are located on the east side of the peninsula, where the beaches are broader and more spacious than in Quiberon proper. Most of the nine campgrounds fill in summer. 2-star **Camping du Goviro,** bd. du Goviro (tel. 97-50-13-54). 7F per person, 4F per tent, 3.80F per car, showers 5F. Right behind is the slightly more spacious **Camping Bois d'Amour** (tel. 97-50-13-52). 2-star, same prices. Open May 15-Sept. 15.

Even the *crêperies* are overpriced here, so try to cook for yourself. In the morning, fishing boats bring their catch to rue de Verdun and sell it right from the basket. Or go to quai de l'Océan at any time of the day and see which of the canneries are open—many sell fish on a retail basis. Buy groceries at **Super-Rallye supermarket** on rue du Port Haliguen, near the youth hostel; at **Stoc** on rue de Verdun; or at **Intermarché** on rue de Port de Pêche. A local specialty is *niniches,* tasty caramel-type candies; look for the signs on the Grande Plage. Delectable **Patisserie Riguidel** is on quai de Belle Ile at rue du Port-Maria. Their traditional Breton pastries, such as buttery *kouign amann,* are hard to resist. The **Restaurant La Goursen,** on the quai, usually offers a seafood *plat du jour* (45-60F), but their other dishes exceed the modest budget.

Sights

The town's beaches are the most popular attraction. Although crowded, Quiberon's **Grande Plage** is smooth, sandy, and surprisingly clean, considering its location in the heart of town. Near the campgrounds, smaller, rockier **Plage du Goviro** evades the congestion of the port area. From the port, follow bd. Chanard east along the water as it becomes bd. de la Mer and then bd. du Goviro (15 min.).

To appreciate the beauty and unique landscape of the region, you must get out of the town itself. The beautiful Côte Sauvage, the length of the Quiberon Peninsula's western side, stretches a wild and windy 10km. Barren heaths and isolated menhirs evoke a Celtic splendor, and overlook jagged cliffs and promontories. The sandy coves along the route may tempt you to try swimming, but heed the signs marked "*baignades interdites*" (swimming forbidden); people have drowned in these treacherous waters.

Frequent boats depart from Quiberon's Port-Maria for **Belle-Ile,** an island off the coast that lives up to its name. The island's coast is a magnificent mixture of high cliffs, small creeks, and crashing seas, while farther inland, thick patches of heather and gorse color the fields. The crossing takes 45 minutes, and you can take a bike with you. (See Ferries under Practical Information for schedules and fares.)

The best way to see the island is by bicycle. **Louis Banet** (tel. 97-51-50-70) rents sturdy bikes for 32F per day, plus a 300F deposit. The garage is located on quai Gambetta just before the bridge to the citadel. (Open daily 9am-12:15pm and 2-7pm.) Three francs buy you a helpful map from the **tourist office** (tel. 97-31-81-93) near the gangplank. (Open July-Aug. Mon.-Sat. 9am-noon and 2:30-7:30pm, Sun. 9am-noon; Sept.-June Mon.-Sat. 9am-noon and 2-6pm, Sun. 9am-noon.) The terrain along the coast is flat enough for easy cycling, but formidable hills plague the inland routes. Watch for "*cyclistes ralentir danger*" (cyclists, slow down; danger) signs that indicate a steep descent.

One good cycling route begins with the 6-km ride northwest from **Le Palais,** the island's largest town, to **Sauzon,** a tiny fishing port with a picture-book facade. The town maintains a serene beauty that even the tour buses can't disturb. The ocean laps gently on the tree-covered shores, and white houses with brightly colored shutters line the winding streets. From Sauzon, a 4-km jaunt takes you to the **Pointe**

des Poulains, at the northernmost tip of the island. This wind- and sea-battered spot, surrounded by water and rock, may just convince you that you've reached land's end.

Four kilometers southwest lies the breathtaking **Grotte de L'Apothicairerie** on the Côte Sauvage. The grotto took its name from the cormorants' nests that once lined the rocks like the bottles in an apothecary's shop. You can climb down into the cave (heed the signs warning you of the treacherous waters) to where the sea washes into the chasm, taking on a strange aqua tint. From the grotto, follow the D25 south to the rough **Aiguilles de Port-Coton,** which Claude Monet captured in an 1886 painting, and the nearby **Plage de Port-Donnant,** where waves crash onto the sandy beach between high stone cliffs.

Inexpensive accommodations on the island include two campgrounds, *gîtes d'étape,* and an **IYHF youth hostel.** The hostel (tel. 97-31-81-33) is located in Le Palais, about a 20-minute hike from the port. Turn right from the port and follow the quai to the citadel; cross the bridge and walk up the hill. Here you'll pass popular **Camping Les Glacis** (5.10F per adult, 4F per tent), which also offers **municipal showers** (open Mon.-Sat. 9-11:30am and 5-7:30pm, Sun. 9-11:30am). Continuing on to the hostel, turn left at the top through a residential area, then right at the *gendarmerie,* and look for signs. Formerly a military barracks, the building served only recently as a juvenile prison. Needless to say, the hostel is not the most comfortable lodging on the island. But its location is convenient and the kitchen facilities acceptable. (34F per night. Sheets 11F. Breakfast 11F. Office open 8:30-10am and 6-10pm.) For more appealing accommodations, the *gîte d'étape* in **Port Guen** (tel. 97-31-55-88), about 3km south of Le Palais, offers 23F beds and fresh vegetables in a colorful barn. A second *gîte* in **Locmaria** (tel. 97-31-70-92), 11km from Le Palais, is neither as pleasant nor as accessible. Heading south on the D25, continue past the sign indicating that you've entered Locmaria and then take the first left. Stop at the pink house 1km down the road to pick up the key from M. or Mme. Cario. (23F. Open March-Nov. Arrive after 6pm.) Campers can pitch their tents in a rural setting at the farm **Trion Guen** (tel. 97-31-85-76).

Near Quiberon

Superb stretches of countryside lie northeast of the Quiberon Peninsula, with great pine forests and open heaths. This is one of the oldest settled parts of Brittany; the menhirs and dolmens scattered throughout the area are ever-present reminders of ancient Breton ways.

Just a few kilometers east of Plouharnel in **Carnac** stand the mysterious **Alignements du Ménec.** Here, more than 1000 menhirs, some over 10 feet high, stretch in a line over 2km long toward the horizon. The purpose of this 10,000-year-old megalithic arrangement remains a sublime mystery. Also in Carnac lies the **Tumulus de St-Michel,** a great burial chamber within an earthen mound. Most of the decorations have been removed, but you can take a tour of the internal passageways. (Open 10am-6pm. 15 min. 3.50F, students 1.70F.) The top of the tumulus offers a fine view of the coast and surrounding countryside. One way to introduce yourself to the history and materials that went into building the tumulus and other dolmens scattered around Brittany is to visit the **Musée Miln le Rouzic** with its collection of *moulages,* large stones incorporated into dolmen constructions. (Museum open July-Aug. daily 10am-noon and 2-6:30pm; Sept.-June Wed.-Mon. Admission 16F, students 8.50F.) For more information on the various druidic sites, try the **Syndicat d'Initiative** in Carnac *ville,* place de l'Eglise (tel. 97-52-13-52; open Easter-June Tues.-Sat. 9am-1pm and 3:30-7pm; July-Aug. Mon.-Sat. 9am-1pm and 2-7pm, Sun. 10am-12:30pm and 5-7pm; Sept. Mon.-Sat. 9am-noon and 2-7pm), or the *syndicat* on the beach, 74, av. des Druides (same tel.; open Tues.-Sat. 9am-noon and 2-6pm).

To get to Carnac, take the bus from Quiberon (15.50F, see Buses), or from the Auray SNCF station (16F). You can also take the train to Plouharnel and catch a bus from there (see Trains, Buses). The bus stop Carnac-ville puts you close to the sites and the museum. The museum is a five-minute walk from the Tumulus de St-Michel just up rue du Tumulus. The Alignements du Ménec are 10-15 minutes from either the museum or the Tumulus: Go north on rue de Courdriec, rue de Poul Person, or rue des Korrigans until you see the menhirs on route des Alignements.

In Carnac, **Robert Lorcy,** 6, rue de Courdriec (tel. 97-52-09-73), rents bicycles for 16F per half-day, 23F per day, 100F per week, with a 500F or passport deposit. (Open July-Aug. Mon.-Sat. 8:30am-12:30pm and 2-7pm, Sun. 8:30am-12:30pm; Sept.-June Tues.-Sat. and sometimes Sun. 8:30am-12:30pm and 2-7pm.) On the beach, **Agence ABC/Cyclo-Loisirs,** 62, av. des Druides (tel. 97-52-02-33), charges 17-25F per hour, 33-42F per half-day, 48-55F per day. **BMX,** 20, av. des Druides, offers comparable prices. All of the above are often short of bikes in July and August.

If you're serious about the prehistoric Bretons, you can stay in any one of a dozen campgrounds around Carnac, including three on the route des Alignements. The two-star **Alignements de Kermario** (tel. 97-52-16-57) is just across the road from the megaliths. (8.45F per person, 12.75F per tent, 3.45F per car. Open June-Sept.) **Camping Kerabus** (tel. 97-52-17-89) is about three minutes away from the druidic wonders on allée des Alouettes off route d'Auray. (7.30F per person, 5.20F per tent, 4F per car. Hot showers 4F. Open June-Sept. 15.) Inquire at the *syndicat* for a complete list of campsites. Hotels in Carnac are outrageously overpriced, but many local families rent rooms. You can ask at the *syndicat,* but they may not be very helpful because these operations compete with the hotels that sponsor the *syndicat.* You will probably have to wander around town a little, but "**chambres à louer**" (rooms for rent) signs appear everywhere. More can be found in the nearby village of **La-Trinité-sur-Mer,** which enjoys one of the largest pleasure ports in France and a wonderful view across the Bay of Quiberon.

Another base for exploring the area's megaliths is **Auray,** with its handful of affordable hotels. The Auray River meanders south from Auray through gentle, wooded terrain dotted by châteaux. The river passes by several oyster-fishing villages and empties into the lovely Gulf of Morbihan. Auray itself has a picturesque bridge spanning the river, a tiny port, and a lovely old quarter. A few kilometers north is the village of **Ste-Anne-d'Auray,** which holds one of the largest *pardons* in Brittany on July 26 and 27. (Hotels fill up at this time.) Smaller, less-touristed *pardons* take place from March on. **Transports le Bayon** runs one bus every Monday to Ste-Anne-d'Auray from the Auray train station (15 min.). In Auray, **Hôtel le Moderne,** 20, place de la République (tel. 97-24-04-72), is a faded, cavernous place that can't live up to its name—it's agreeable nonetheless. It offers a few singles and doubles for 80-105F, showers 15F, breakfast 18.50F. (Open March-Nov. 15.) **Crêperie Quintin,** rue du Père Eternel, off place de la République, serves delicious *moules marinières* for 18F as well as filling crêpes and *galettes* (5-22F) in a cozy atmosphere. (Open daily noon-midnight.) The **Syndicat d'Initiative,** place de la République (tel. 97-24-09-75), will gladly help with accommodations. (Open July-Aug. Mon.-Sat. 8:45am-7pm, Sun. 9am-noon; Jan.-June and Sept. Mon.-Fri. 9am-12:30pm and 2-6:15pm, Sat. 9:30am-12:30pm.) The train station (about a 20-min. walk from town) rents **bikes** (37F per ½-day, 47F per day, deposit 300F). The Quiberon-Auray train runs only in July and August, but frequent buses run year-round (see Trains, Buses). Auray lies on the main Brest-Bordeaux, Brest-Toulouse, and Paris-Quimper train lines.

Vannes

Vannes, host of flotillas of ferries and affordable hotels, is an excellent base for touring the Gulf of Morbihan. Though the islands of the gulf are the main reason for stopping here, the city itself is not without interest. Partly because it is quieter, Vannes's walled *vieille ville* has more "atmosphere" than the old districts of St-Malo or Concarneau. Toward evening, its twisted streets make for meditative strolling.

Orientation and Practical Information

The train station lies north of the center of town. Turn right out of the station, follow the road to the bottom of the hill, and turn left on av. Victor Hugo. After several blocks, a right on rue J. le Brix and a left at the *mairie* on rue Thiers will bring you to the post office in place de la République (15-min. walk). From there, the *vieille ville* lies to your left, and the port lies straight ahead. Alternatively, take pink bus #4 ("Calmont") or purple #7 ("République") from the train station to place de la République. Between the two you shouldn't have to wait more than 20 minutes (4.60F; no service Sun.).

Syndicat d'Initiative: 1, rue Thiers (tel. 97-47-24-34). From the train station, follow the signs to *centre ville* and then to the *syndicat*. Information on the Gulf of Morbihan, and a booklet with all public transport timetables for the area. In July and Aug., 1½-hr. guided tours of the city leave twice per day (at 10:30am and 3pm; 18F, ages under 25 10F). Open July-Aug. Mon.-Fri. 9am-7pm, Sat. 9am-12:15pm and 2-6:15pm, Sun. 10am-noon; in off-season Mon.-Sat. 9am-noon and 2-6pm.

Student Travel: Dubreuil Voyages, 18, rue Billault (tel. 97-47-41-76). Transalpino/BIJ tickets. Open Mon.-Sat. 9am-noon and 1:30-6pm.

Bureau d'Information Jeunesse: At the *mairie*, place Maurice Marchel (tel. 97-54-13-72). Information on jobs and schools, drug counseling, contraceptives, and vacation strategy. Open Tues. and Thurs.-Fri. 1:30-6pm, Wed. 10am-12:30pm and 1:30-6pm, Sat. 10am-noon.

Currency Exchange: Crédit Agricole, 9, place Henri IV (tel. 97-63-35-44). Open Tues.-Fri. 8:45am-5:45pm, Sat. 8:45am-4:15pm.

Post Office: Place de la République. Label Poste Restante mail "Recette Principale" to direct it here. American Express and Visa checks changed. **Postal code:** 56000. Open Mon.-Fri. 8am-7pm, Sat. 8am-noon.

Train Station: Av. Favrel et Lincy (tel. 97-42-50-50), north off av. Victor Hugo. To Paris (Mon.-Sat. 8 per day, 11 Sun.; 5 hr.; 232F), Rennes (7 per day, 1¼ hr., 71F), Quimper (12 per day, 1¼ hr., 69F), Nantes (9 per day, 1½ hr., 75F). July-Aug. to Plouharnel (near Carnac) and Quiberon, via Auray (6 per day; 1½ hr.; 26F to Plouharnel, 33F to Quiberon). Information office open July-Aug. daily 8am-7pm; Sept.-June 8am-noon and 2-7pm.

Bus Station: Transports et Tourisme de l'Ouest (TTO), rue du 116e R.I. (tel. 97-47-29-64). Line 20bis: to Muzillac (Mon.-Sat. 2-4 per day, ½ hr., 22F), La Roche-Bernard (Mon.-Sat. 2-4 per day, 1 hr., 33F), and Nantes (Mon.-Sat. 1-2 per day, 2¾ hr., 85F). Line 16: to Rennes and points in between (Mon.-Fri. 2 per day, 3 hr., 78F to Rennes). Line 23 (4-5 per day): Auray (½ hr., 15.50F), Carnac (1 hr.; 32F to the *ville*, 34F to the *plage*), Quiberon (2 hr., 45F). Line 22: to Larmor-Baden (Wed. and Sat. 3 per day, ½ hr., 15.50F). Office open Mon.-Fri. 8am-noon and 1-6:30pm, Sat. 8:30am-noon and 2-6:30pm. Buy tickets on bus; buses stop in front of office. **Tourisme Verney/Compagnie des Transports Morbihan,** place de la Gare (tel. 97-47-21-64), opposite SNCF station. Line 3: to Pontivy and points in between (Mon.-Sat. 2-3 per day, 1½ hr., 36.50F). Line 5: to Muzillac and points in between (Mon.-Sat. 2 per day, 1 hr., 20F). Line 7: slow boat to Port-Navalo (Mon.-Sat. 4-5 per day, June-Sept. 3 Sun. also; 1 hr.; 28F). Buses stop behind office and at the *préfecture* in town. Numerous excursions throughout Brittany. Office open for tickets Mon. 6am-noon and 2-6:30pm, Tues.-Fri. 9am-noon and 2-6:30pm, Sat. 9am-12:30pm. **Transports du Pays de Vannes (TPV),** Tel. 97-47-21-64 city buses. Information and schedules at the Tourisme Verney window. Connections to *centre ville*, train station, and nearby suburbs. Basic fare 4.60F. Central stop at place de la République in front of the post office.

Ferries: Oodles and oodles. The most useful are **Vedettes Vertes,** Gare Maritime (tel. 97-63-79-99), 1½km from town toward Conleau. To Belle-Ile (Easter-June and Sept. Sun., holidays, and Thurs. 1 per day; July-Aug. 1 per day at 7:45am; you get 7½ hr. on the island; round-trip 115F). Tour of the Gulf of Morbihan, including stop on Ile aux Moines (Sept. 15-30 and late March-May 2 per day, June 1-15 3 per day, June 15-Sept. 15 4 per day; 4-9 hr.; 70.40F). Tour of Gulf and the River Auray, with up to 3 stops, at Ile aux Moines, Bono, and Locmariaquer (June-Sept. 15 4 per day, 6½-9 hr., 90.40F). Plenty of other services from neighboring ports. **Vedettes Blanches Armor,** Tel. 97-57-15-27. From Larmor-Baden to Gavrinis (March-Sept. 25 9-11:30am and 1:30-5:30pm every ½ hr.; 20 min.; round-trip 16F). Office open daily 8:30am-noon and 1:15-6pm. J. Pasco's **Vedettes l'Angelus,** Tel. 97-57-30-29. From Locmariaquer's Port du Guilvin. Tour of Gulf (June-Aug. 4 per day, 35-65F), Belle-Ile (July-Sept. 21 1 Sun., 2 hr., 6½ hr. on island, round-trip 90F). All ferry services request reservations.

Laundromat: 5, av. Victor Hugo, just opposite the Foyer des Jeunes Travailleuses. Wash 20F, dry 2F. Open daily 7am-9pm.

Rape Crisis Counseling: Foyer Ker Anne, Tel. 97-63-48-22.

Hospital: Centre Hospitalier Chubert, place Docteur Grosse (tel. 97-42-66-42).

Medical Emergency: Tel. 18.

Police: Commissariat, 13, bd. de la Paix (tel. 97-47-19-20).

Police Emergency: Tel. 17.

Accommodations and Camping

Hotels in Vannes fill quickly, but student accommodations are never hard to find. The two *foyers* offer clean, comfortable, and cheap rooms with real French people.

Foyer des Jeunes Travailleuses, 14, av. Victor Hugo (tel. 97-54-33-13). Clean, pink-and-peach-colored singles for women, although the friendly staff will never turn anyone away even if they're male. 40F per night. Sheets 20F. Showers included. Breakfast 9F. Dinner (Sun.-Fri. only) 28.50F. *A la carte* entrees 25.50F each. Register before 10pm. Curfew 11pm, keys available.

Foyer du Jeune Travailleur, 2, rue Paul Signac (tel. 97-63-47-36). Take bus #1 or 2 from the bridge at the corner of av. Favrel et Lincy and av. Victor Hugo (near SNCF station) to Kerizac (*direction* "Menimeur"). By foot, turn right outside the station, and right again at the bottom of the hill onto av. President Wilson, which becomes av. 4 Août. After 1½km, turn left onto av. Dégas and watch for the signs (20 min.). Dormitory singles primarily for men, though women occasionally find rooms here, too. 45F per night. Sheets, showers, and breakfast included. Dinner 30F. Office open Mon.-Fri. 8am-12:30pm and 2-8pm, Sat. 11am-12:30pm.

Hôtel-Restaurant Le Mirage, 19, rue de la Boucherie (tel. 97-47-17-16). Not very clean, but overpoweringly cheap. 10 singles or doubles 50F, showers included. Breakfast 10F. Restaurant (see below) is a bargain too. Arrive by 8:30pm.

Hôtel la Chaumière, 12, place de la Libération (tel. 97-63-28-51). From the train station, turn right off av. Victor Hugo onto bd. de la Paix and walk 3 blocks. Colorful and clean rooms with outdoor bathrooms 65F. Rooms with more convenient facilities 110-120F. Showers 15F. Breakfast 18F. Lively bar downstairs. Phone reservations accepted.

Hôtel au Relais Nantais, 38, rue Aristide Briand (tel. 97-47-15-85). From the station head straight onto rue Olivier de Clisson, and then left on av. St-Symphorien/bd. de la Paix to rue Aristide Briand. Uninspired decor and dark hallways, but rooms are clean. Centrally-located. Doubles 94F, with shower 105-110F. Breakfast 18F. Busy bar downstairs with pool table. Telephone reservations accepted.

The Gulf area is crawling with campgrounds, and in summer each and every one is crawling with campers. Nearest to town, **Camping Municipal de Conleau** (tel. 97-63-13-88) is a three-star wooded site near the beach. From the Hôtel de Ville, take blue-coded bus #2 (*direction* "Conleau") and get off at stop Camping. On foot from place Gambetta at the head of the port, or rue Thiers, follow rue du Port along the harbor for 3km. (9.70F per person and per tent. Open March-Oct.)

Food

For a feast of your own making, there's a **Stoc** supermarket that sells fresh bread on 19, rue du Mené (open Mon.-Sat. 9am-12:30pm and 2:30-7:15pm), as well as an enormous **open market** (Wed. and Sat. 8am-noon) that fills place Lucien Laroche, place du Poids Public, and place des Lices. *Crêperies* line practically every street in the old quarter, but this is one town where you might want to skip the crêpes for the following reasons:

La Paillote, rue des Halles (tel. 97-47-21-94), in the *vieille ville.* A bustling place to which young locals are loyal. Salads 13-30F, Creole dishes 27-44F, big pizzas 26-45F. The 45F "Super Paillote" pizza contains mussels, *Coquilles St-Jacques,* and cognac. Open Mon.-Fri. noon-2pm and 7-10:30pm, Sat. 7-10:30pm. Next door, the cozy **Crêperie Kalon Breiz** (tel. 97-54-27-20) offers a 31F, 3-crêpe *menu.*

Hôtel-Restaurant le Mirage, 19, rue de la Boucherie (tel. 97-47-17-16). Falls into the un-abashed category of *restaurant ouvrier* (workers' restaurant), which means cheap, huge meals. 30F buys soup, appetizer, bread, pork and potatoes, noodles, cheese or fruit, and ice cream. For 40F, they throw in a steak. Open noon-2pm and 7-8pm.

Chez Carmen, 17, rue Emile Burgault, near the cathedral in the *vieille ville. Couscous* 42-65F; try the lamb varieties. 62F for the spectacular seafood *paella.* Open Tues.-Sat.

Cafeteria les Arcades, in the mall facing the *préfecture* (tel. 97-42-57-73). A comfortable and cavernous self-service restaurant with *plats du jour* (19-39F), pizza (18F), steak (21.50F), des-serts (12F). Open Mon.-Fri. 11:30am-3pm and 6:30-10pm, Sat.-Sun. 11:30am-10pm.

Sights and Entertainment

In the center of the old district stands the half-Romanesque, half-Gothic **Cathé-drale St-Pierre.** Notice the solid, grounded buttresses, asymmetrical facade, and dog, dragon, and naked woman gargoyles. On one side of the cathedral is a pretty park with the remains of the cloister's **arcade.** On the other side, **rue Saint-Guénahel** is lined with overhanging half-timbered houses, their second stories braced by diago-nal timbers that rest on sculpted heads (look for #17-19). At the bottom of this street sits the heavily fortified and still intimidating fourteenth- and fifteenth-century **Porte Prison.** Here too is the entrance to the ramparts (open daily until 7pm). The fortified medieval gates at the other end of the old city were replaced in 1704 with ornate **Porte St-Vincent** (at the end of the street bearing the same name). In front of the ramparts, a stream flanks the pleasant **Jardin de la Garenne.** The view from outside the walls is lovely. In July and August, the ramparts are illuminated at night, making them pleasant for an evening stroll.

The **Musée de Préhistoire** (Archaeological Museum), at 2, rue Noé, exhibits a collection of artifacts from the megaliths at Carnac and other sites nearby. (Open Mon.-Sat. 9:30am-noon and 2-6pm. Admission 10F.) The new **Musée des Beaux Arts** is around the corner on rue des Halles, in a beautifully restored sixteenth-century house. The museum has several works by Rodin, but its special collection is of art inspired by the Breton landscape and inhabitants. (Open June Wed.-Sat. 10am-noon and 2-6pm; July-Aug. daily 10am-noon and 2-6pm; Sept.-May Tues.-Sat. 10am-noon and 2-6pm. Admission 10F, students 5F.) Avoid the overpriced (30F) and much-touted **Aquarium;** a few small tanks of tropical fish make it about as exciting as an overgrown pet shop. In the first half of August look for the four-day **Jazz Festival** held in the Jardins de Limur (tickets 65F per night, 250F per 4 nights; for more information, call 97-47-47-30).

Near Vannes: Gulf of Morbihan

Vedettes Vertes (tel. 97-63-79-99) will take you around the Gulf of Morbihan (60F), and up the River Auray (an extra 20F). Your ticket allows you to get off at any stop and pick up a later boat (make sure you have a timetable). Boats leave four times per day in late June, July, and August, less often in the off-season. (For all ferry information, first see Ferries above, then drop by the *syndicat* for the whole truth.) The largest island in the gulf, **Ile-Aux-Moines,** is only 6km long, a combina-tion of soothing pine groves and pleasant beaches. Try to make it to the other end of the island, where there are dolmens, beautiful heather moors, and deserted little roads. Bike rentals on the quay are well-worth the price (20F per ½-day); pick up a map at the *syndicat* (tel. 97-26-32-45). Breton life has changed little here; there are few cars, and fishing is still the main source of income. The island's tiny town contains some very typical Morbihan thatched-roof cottages and the ever-present granite church. In the summer, the island becomes a family resort, but this quiet invasion does little to disturb the tranquil atmosphere.

Vedettes Vertes also bypasses, but doesn't stop at, the **Tumulus de Gavrinis,** an ancient burial mound 100m in circumcision, made of stone and covered with earth-works. An archeological dig continues to explore the mound and its artifacts, esti-mated to be 7000 years old. To reach the tumulus, take a TTO bus from Vannes to Larmor-Baden (Wed. and Sat. 3 per day, ½ hr. 15.50F). From there, **Vedettes**

Blanches Armors (tel. 97-57-05-31) runs boats (March-Sept. 25 9-11:30am and 1:30-5:30pm every ½ hr., 20 min., round-trip 16F). A stop at Port Navalo will put you on the less tourist-infested Presqu'Ile de Rhuys, which has a fine campground practically at the tip of the peninsula: Camping Municipal de Port Navalo is a two-star site right up from the ferry stop. The peninsula also has its own supermarché.

Across from Port Navalo, Locmariaquer remains one of the prettiest villages in Brittany; white houses line the port and a solitary church steeple breaks the skyline in the distance. Just beyond are the Grand Menhir and Table du Négociant, the broken remains of a 347-ton menhir and a ritual tomb with remains of rare drawings. The Merchant's Table is composed of three huge "tables" suspended on points to form the galleries. Both the Grand Menhir and the Table rank among Brittany's most important archaeological sites. The less massive Dolmen des Pierres-Plats, 1km out of town in the opposite direction, is not half as spectacular as the beach here—on a good day you'll get a wide view of the coast toward Quiberon and of Belle-Ile in the distance. You may want to spend the night at one of several campsites on this mild and breezy land's end. J. Pasco's Vedettes Angelus (tel. 97-57-30-29) sails from Locmariaquer's Port du Guilvin around the gulf (50F), around the gulf and up the River Auray (65F), and to Belle-Ile (round-trip 90F; you get 6½ hr. on the island). A whole fleet of ferries leaves from other ports near Vannes. Try the *syndicat,* but even they cannot keep them all straight.

The formation of the gulf makes for unpredictable tides and for some of the strongest currents anywhere. A whole lot of ocean tries to squeeze into a very small gulf—these waters are treacherous for both swimmers and small sailcraft. If you're experienced and if the tide is coming in toward the gulf, the waters of the eastern part may be manageable. Ask at the *syndicat* about sailing schools that can give you advice.

Nantes

"*Nantes, ça bouge!*" is the slogan here, and even a short stay proves that this is indeed a city on the move. Nantes bears much resemblance to Paris: Wide boulevards mark the boundaries between administrative *arrondissements,* and opulent architecture testifies to a wealthy past. As does Paris, Nantes changes color in summer when the students leave and the tourists arrive.

Nantes is either at the southern tip of Brittany or on the western edge of the Pays de la Loire, depending on whom you ask. (The *Nantais* falsely affirm the former, note indisputably true Bretons with proud disdain.) Under the rule of the great Ducs de Montfort, François I and II, Nantes was firmly established as the administrative center of Brittany. But it was also in this city, in 1532, that Brittany was finally ceded to the French crown, ending its independence forever.

Orientation and Practical Information

Nantes spreads for miles on both sides of the Loire with a 40-story skyscraper (amusingly named the Tour Bretagne) at its center. The city's major axes are cours John Kennedy, which becomes cours Franklin Roosevelt, running west from the train station, and cours des 50 Otages, which runs north to the tower. To get to the center of town and the tourist office, turn left out of the station onto boulevard de Stalingrad, which becomes cours John Kennedy. After 1km, turn right onto rue de Gorges, which takes you to place du Commerce, where you'll find the tourist office. The hostel is a 10-minute walk in the other direction.

Maison du Tourisme: Place du Commerce (tel. 40-47-04-51), in the 19th-century building of commerce. Helpful staff speaks English and drops a 200-page guide to the city and its architecture into your hands for free. Guided tours of Quartier Feydeau (at 10am) and Vignoble (at 2pm). Open Mon.-Fri. 9:30am-7pm, Sat. 10am-6pm.

Travel Information: CROUS, 14, rue Santeuil (tel. 40-73-73-84). Information on student travel. BIJ tickets. Many other branches. Open Mon.-Fri. 10am-12:30pm and 1:30-5:30pm.

Voyages Wasteels, 6, rue Guépin (tel. 40-89-70-13). BIJ tickets. Open Mon.-Fri. 9am-noon and 2-6:30pm. **ABRI,** 7, rue de la Clavurie (tel. 40-20-20-62). Organizes cycling tours of Brittany, complete with good topographical maps. Ask about the 120 *gîtes d'étape*. Open Tues.-Sat. 9am-12:30pm and 2:30-6pm.

Centre Régional d'Information Jeunesse, 28, rue du Calvaire (tel. 40-48-68-25). Youth travel information and a babysitting service to boot. Open Mon.-Fri. 10am-1pm and 2-7pm, Sat. 10am-12:30pm and 2-5pm.

Currency Exchange: Crédit Agricole, 2, place Ladmirault (tel. 40-73-06-64), and 6, rue de Gorges (tel. 40-89-46-03). Open Sat. until 4pm. The post office also changes foreign currency.

Post Office: Place de Bretagne. **Currency exchange. Postal code:** 44000. Open Mon.-Fri. 8am-7pm, Sat. 8am-noon.

Train Station: Gare d'Orléans, 27, bd. Stalingrad (tel. 40-50-50-50). To Paris-Montparnasse (11-14 per day; 3-4 hr., overnight trains 5 hr.; 185F), Bordeaux (5-8 per day, 4 hr., 178F), Poitiers (5 per day, with change at Tours, 3-4 hr., 145F; via Cholet, longer trip, 104F), Quimper (7-10 per day, 3½ hr., 127F), Rennes (7 per day, 2 hr., 80F). Quiberon (July-Aug. 4 per day, with change at Auray and sometimes Redon, 2¾ hr., 94F). Information office open Mon.-Sat. 8:30am-7pm, Sun. 9:30am-12:45pm and 2:15-7pm.

Bus Station: TTO, Tel. 40-89-27-11. Buses leave from the station on rue de Mayence near Champ de Mars. From the Duchesse-Anne tram stop near the château, take av. Carnot south, turn right on rue Jenmapes, and left onto rue de Mayence (5 min.). Or take bus #26, 27, 28, or 29 to Champ de Mars. To La Baule (Mon.-Sat. 2 per day, 1 Sun.; 2¾ hr.; 53F), St-Nazaire (same departures as above, 1¾ hr., 44F), Rennes (2-3 per day, 2½ hr., 84F), Vannes (Mon.-Sat. 1-2 per day, 2½ hr., 85F). Information office open Mon.-Sat. 8:15am-12:15pm and 3:30-6:30pm. Buy tickets on the bus when office is closed. Buses also stop opposite the branch office, 4, allée Duquesne (tel. 40-20-45-20), which parallel to cours des 50 Otages. A host of smaller companies stop at the *gare routière* behind place Elisa Mercoeur, near allée Baco. Schedules posted at information office (tel. 40-47-62-70), near the *tabac*. To La Plaine (2-3 per day, 2 hr.), St-Brévin (3 per day, 1¾ hr.), St-Gilles (2-3 per day, 2 hr.), Fromentine (7 per day, 1½ hr.), Les Sables d'Olonne (4 per day, 3¾ hr.). **Cars Brisseau** (tel. 40-48-03-21) runs 2 buses per day to Montaigu (24.50F) and Les Herbiers (39F). **Car Groussin** takes care of St-Philbert and points in between (Mon.-Sat. 2-3 per day, 45 min., 21F). Service is more frequent during the school year. Central stop for **city buses** is place du Commerce. One ticket buys you unlimited travel on both buses and tram for a 1 hr. (5.50F).

Car Rental: Hertz, 6, allée du Commandant Charcot (tel. 40-74-18-29), just off the train station. Cheapest model 200F per day plus 2.69F per km. Open Mon.-Fri. 7:30am-12:30pm and 1:30-7pm, Sat. 8am-12:30pm and 2:30-6pm.

Hitchhiking: Allostop-Provoya, at the CRIJ, 10, rue Lafayette (tel. 40-89-04-85). Give them 3-4 days notice and 60F, and they'll find you a driver entitled to charge you 0.16F per km for gas and tolls. Rides under 200km 20F; 6-month subscription 180F. Open Mon. 2-6pm, Tues.-Fri. 10am-1pm and 2-7pm, Sat. 10am-noon and 2-5pm.

Centre d'Information Féminin et Familial, for counseling, and **Délégation Régionale aux Droits des Femmes,** for crisis intervention, 5, Maurice Duval (tel. 40-48-13-83). Open Mon. 2-5:30pm, Tues. 9:30am-noon and 2-5:30pm, Thurs. 9:30am-5:30pm, Fri. 9:30am-12:30pm and 2-5:30pm.

Hospital: Centre Hospitalier Régional, place Alexis Ricordeau (tel. 40-48-33-33).

Medical Emergency: Tel. 18. **SAMU,** Tel. 40-48-35-35.

Police: Commissariat Central, place Waldeck-Rousseau (tel. 40-74-21-21).

Police Emergency: Tel. 17.

Accommodations and Camping

Nantes supports plenty of cheap hotels, and in summer lots of student dormitory space becomes available, including the beds at the hostel, tastefully remodeled in primary colors. The city is also stocked with *foyers,* although they all try to send you to the hostel (and why not?).

Auberge de Jeunesse (IYHF), 2, place de la Manufacture (tel. 40-20-57-25). From the station, turn right onto bd. de Stalingrad, left into the Manufacture complex opposite the tram stop, and right to the farthest corner of the complex (10-min.). Or take the tram from the train station to stop Manufacture (5.50F). Lots of space, a few 2-bed rooms, new facilities, kitchen, and TV. Warm, English-speaking staff. 37F. Sheets 11F. Breakfast 11F. Office open 7-10am and 6-11pm. Notify the staff if you wish to leave early or stay out late. Open July-Aug.

Centre Jean Macé, 90, rue du Préfet Bonnefoy (tel. 40-74-55-74), a 15- to 20-min. walk from the station. Turn left onto cours John Kennedy (also called bd. de Stalingrad), then right at place de la Duchesse Anne onto rue Henri IV, which becomes rue Sully. The center is on rue Sully at rue du Préfet Bonnefoy. Or take bus #12 from the SNCF station to place Maréchal Foch, and continue up rue Sully. Clean if dimly-lit rooms with 2 or 3 beds. 42F. Showers included. Breakfast 10F. Plain but filling meals 30F, Sunday meal 32F. Reception open 8am-8pm.

Foyer Nantais de la Jeune Fille, 1, rue du Gigant (tel. 40-73-41-46). From the train station, take the tram to place du Commerce, walk up cours des 50 Otages to either stop St-Nicolas or Cathédrale. From there, catch bus #21, 22, or 23, and get off at stop Edit de Nantes. The foyer is directly across the street. Both men and women accepted. Private rooms with showers 52.50F. Lunch or dinner 29F. Office open daily 9am-7pm.

Foyer des Jeunes Travailleurs, Beaulieu, 9, bd. Vincent Gâche (tel. 40-47-91-64). From the train station, take the tram to place du Commerce and from there, take bus #24 (*direction* "Beaulieu") to Albert (5.50F). Co-ed showers and 2-bed rooms. Kitchen facilities and 30F meals. Both men and women accepted. 50F, with sleeping bag 42F. Breakfast included. Doors never close; office open 8am-10pm. **Other location,** 1, rue Porte Neuve (tel. 40-20-00-80). From the train station, take the tram to place du Commerce and catch bus #40, 41, or 36 from across the street on cours des 50 Otages to stop place Viarme. Reception open 8am-8pm.

Hôtel Roosevelt, 28, rue des Petites Ecuries (tel. 40-47-17-00), 15 min. from the train station. Turn left on cours John Kennedy, bear right on cours Franklin Roosevelt, and right onto rue des Petites Ecuries. A great bargain. Rooms are a bit small, but clean and pleasant with firm mattresses. Singles 65F. Rooms with 2 beds 85F. Showers 10F. Breakfast 12F.

Hôtel Calypso, 16, rue de Strasbourg (tel. 40-47-54-47), just off cours John Kennedy. Comfortable, clean rooms. Friendly, chatty manager. Rooms with double bed 80F, with shower 92F. 2-bed rooms 108F and 130F. 10F per extra bed. Showers 10F. Breakfast 15F.

Hôtel d'Orléans, 12, rue du Marais (tel. 40-47-69-32), just off cours des 50 Otages. Nice, spacious rooms. 1-star. A few rooms 55F, most 78F, with shower 99F, with color TV 78F. Hedonist dens with color TV and shower 112F. Showers 16F. Breakfast 15F. Open Aug.-July 23.

Camping: Camping du Val de Cens, 21, bd. du Petit Port (tel. 40-74-47-94), 3km from town. Take bus #42, 43, 54, or 55 from place du Commerce to Petit Port. A 4-star site with all the extras. 11F per site, 7.30F per person.

Food

Nantes's specialties are its white wines *Muscadet* and *Gros Plant,* and its delicate white fish, prepared *au beurre blanc* (with butter sauce). **Markets** occur Tuesday through Sunday from 9am to 1pm in place du Bouffay and at the **marché de Talensac,** along rue de Bel Air near place St-Similien. A supermarket, **Decré,** sits in the basement of Nouvelles Galeries, rue du Moulin, in *centre ville.* (Open Mon.-Sat. 9am-7pm.)

Crêperie Jaune, 1, rue des Echevins (tel. 40-47-15-71), just off place du Bouffay. Popular with students. Come early for a seat. *Plat du jour* 46F, but everyone comes for the house specialty, a delicious and immense crêpe called *pavé nantais* (32-36F depending on the ingredients); vegetarian versions available. Doors open at noon.

La Mangeoire, 16, rue des Petite Ecuries (tel. 40-48-70-83). Cozy and attractive, with welcoming young owners. Well-prepared *menu* 46F, *plat du jour* 32F. Open Mon.-Sat. noon-1:30pm and 7:30-9:30pm.

Friterie de la Gare, 22, bd. Stalingrad, between train station and hostel. A *restaurant ouvrier* (workers' restaurant) in the "grease it, salt it, and serve it" style. *Menus* 37F and 39F. Open Mon.-Fri. 11:45am-2pm and 7:30-10pm, Sat. 11:45am-2pm.

La Brasserie des Sportifs-Chez Rémi, rue de la Bâclerie (tel. 40-47-98-68), off place du Bouffay. Huge servings of delicious *couscous* 48-90F. The 120F *paella* serves 2 people. 48F *menu.* Open Tues.-Sat. noon-2pm and 7-11pm.

La Brocherie, 13bis, rue Beauregard (tel. 40-47-72-37). Cozy. Specializes in *brochettes.* House aperitif, Le Zébulon, 9F. 39F lunch *menu.* 49F *menu* doesn't include dessert; choose the 59F, 75F, or 85F *menu* to pile on the calories. Open Mon.-Fri. until 11pm, Sat. dinner only.

Sights and Entertainment

Nantes's **Cathédrale St-Pierre** exemplifies the full-scale construction found only in large and prosperous cities. Its Gothic vaults soar some 37m above the worshipers' heads (higher than the arches of Notre Dame in Paris), thanks to the lightweight, white Vendée stone of which they are made. The original church took over four centuries to build (1434-1893), and its fascinating facade, loaded with narrative sculpture, is crowned by plain towers from the 1930s. (Cathedral open daily 8:45am-noon and 2-7pm.) Behind the cathedral, on rue Malherbe (off rue Henri IV), **Chapelle de L'Immaculée** utilizes an eerie aerial Virgin in place of a spire. To the right of the chapel, at 4, rue Malherbe, a smaller iron Virgin prays from a flamboyant perch.

Nearby, Nantes's heavily fortified fifteenth-century **château** was built by François II. The best of three museums inside the château, the **Musée des Arts Populaires Régionaux,** may allow you your closest look at traditional Breton culture; it houses an excellent collection of colorful costumes and *coiffes,* period rooms, and some fine carved-oak furniture. The **Musée des Arts Décoratifs** sponsors temporary exhibits, often devoted to Breton subjects, in a beautiful, converted tower. The **Musée des Salorges** is a nautical museum. Note also the ornate windows overlooking cours John Kennedy. (Château and museums open July-Aug. daily 10am-noon and 2-6pm; Sept.-June. Wed.-Mon. 10am-noon and 2-6pm. Entry to the courtyard and ramparts free; admission to all 3 museums 15F, students 7F, Sun. free.)

Two blocks from the cathedral, at 10, rue Clemenceau, is Nantes's **Musée des Beaux Arts** (tel. 40-74-53-24). The collection includes some fine paintings by Rubens, Courbet, and de la Tour, as well as Ingres and early Italian painters. (Open Wed.-Mon. 10am-noon and 1-5:45pm, Sun. 11am-5pm. Admission 5F, students 2.50F, Sat.-Sun. free.) The **Musée Thomas Dobrée,** place Jean V (tel. 40-89-34-32), contains a library of rare books and manuscripts. (Open Wed.-Mon. 10am-noon and 2-6pm. Admission 7F.) The **Musée Archéologique,** place Jean V (tel. 40-89-34-32), displays Neolithic and rare Merovingian artifacts. (Open Wed.-Mon. 10am-noon and 2-6pm. Admission 7F.) The **Musée d'Histoire Naturelle,** 12, rue Voltaire (tel. 40-73-30-03), features reptiles and insects from the region. (Open Tues.-Sat. 10am-noon and 2-6pm, Sun. 2-6pm. Admission 5F, students 2.50F.) Take your imagination for a walk at the **Musée Jules Verne,** 3, rue de l'Hermitage (tel. 40-89-11-88), near the river in square M. Schwob, which tries to recreate, through a collection of the author's novels, letters, and old photographs, the imaginative world of Captain Nemo and other Jules Verne characters. (Open Mon. and Wed.-Sat. 10am-noon and 2-5pm, Sun. 2-5pm. Sat.-Sun. free.) The nearby **planetarium** at 8, rue des Acadiens (tel. 40-73-99-23), off square Moysan, completes Nantes's museum possibilities with vistas of the galaxies. (Showings Tues.-Sat. at 10:30am, 2:15pm and 3:45pm; Sun. at 2:15pm and 3:45pm.)

West of the château are many elegant buildings dating from the city's period of wealth and expansion in the eighteenth century. **Ile Feydeau,** between allée Turenne and allée Tuouin, was at one time an island; here prosperous sea merchants spent the spoils of the slave trade on lavish houses. Walk down **rue Kervegan** for the best view. Even more stately is eighteenth-century **place Royale** and **rue Crébillon,** leading to **place Graslin.** Off this street, the **Passage Pommeraye,** a nineteenth-century gallery in iron and glass, is executed with typical Victorian exuberance.

Often overlooked, Le Corbusier's **Cité Radieuse** is a place of pilgrimage for architecture and Corbu buffs. It embodies a unified conception of suburban life. Take bus #31 from the Commerce stop on cours Franklin Roosevelt.

The students at **Université de Nantes** do their share for the Breton regionalist movement, but they seem largely intent on continuing the city's strong cosmopolitan tradition. Fine bookstores cluster near place St-Pierre. Although university buildings are scattered through the city, the area north of rue Crébillon is most popular in the evening, and rue Scribe has a multitude of bars and cafes to catch the late-night crowd. Every evening at 10pm you can hear a live jazz ensemble at **The Break Club,** 1, rue des Petites Ecuries. (Open Mon.-Sat. 10pm-3:30am.) At disco **Le Samba,** 8, rue Fouré (tel. 40-20-09-32), off the Champs de Mars, dance to the music of Africa and the Antilles. The tourist office provides a complete list (a long one) of Nantes's discos and piano bars.

Near Nantes

La Baule boasts that it has the most beautiful beach in Europe, and it may well be true. One smooth curve of sand stretches for miles along the coast, washed by gentle, warm waves. Relaxation seems to be the town's main industry. Naturally, like Pornic to the south, La Baule is densely populated in summer, and expensive. **Trains** connect Nantes to La Baule (July-Aug. 6 per day, Oct.-June 8-10 per day; 1 hr.; 48F). Buses from Nantes (change at St-Nazaire) are half as fast and more expensive. There are two train stations: La Baule-les-Pins, east of the center in a quiet area close to camping, and La Baule-Escoublac, close to the busy center. From this station, take av. Serbie to av. Georges Clemenceau, and turn right to reach the **Office de Tourisme** (tel. 40-24-34-44; open July-Aug. daily 9am-7:30pm; Sept.-June Mon.-Sat. 9am-12:30pm and 2:15-6:30pm). From here, av. du Général-de-Gaulle runs down to the beach. You'll probably want to also.

La Baule has very few inexpensive hotels that don't require *pension,* so it's best to book in advance. The **Almanzor,** 17, av. des Pétrels (tel. 40-60-28-93), near place de la Victoire, is a small hotel with clean and attractive rooms. (Singles and doubles from 105F, with shower 125F. Extra beds 20F. No hall shower. Breakfast 18.50F.) The **Violetta,** 44, av. Georges Clemenceau (tel. 40-60-32-16), close to the station, is neither so clean nor so attractive. (Singles 115F. Doubles 120F, with wash basin 90-135F. Showers 20F. Breakfast 18F.) The **Camping Municipal,** av. P. Minot (tel. 40-60-17-40 or 40-60-11-48), is a three-star site. (48.50F per tent and 2 people, 11F per additional person. Open March 25-Sept. 30.) A peaceful *gîte d'étape* lies 6km from St-Nazaire, approximately 12km from La Baule. Call M. Burban (tel. 40-22-56-76 or 40-66-05-66) for directions. The *gîte* is a dusty old stone farm building with two fireplaces and a complete kitchen (23F includes hot showers). For groceries, a large and lively **market** is held in the afternoons on av. Marché at av. des Pétrels. Otherwise, count on spending a lot of money for food.

A sunny crescent of rocky coast curving south from the mouth of the Loire through **Pornic,** the so-called **Côte de Jade,** enjoys the breakers, the beaches, and even the menhirs you'd expect from the rest of Brittany, but all an easy one-hour train ride from Nantes. Trains run from Nantes to Pornic on their way to St-Gilles-Croix-de-Vie (Sat.-Thurs. 4 per day, 6 Fri.; 1¼ hr.; 39F). Make this a daytrip: After 24 hours the souvenir shops selling Donald Duck inner tubes might get on your nerves. For bike rental, **Cycles Becquet** at 24, rue de la Maine (tel. 40-82-26-80), charges 30F per day, deposit 250F. (Open Mon.-Sat. 8:30am-12:30pm and 2:30-6:30pm.)

The **Syndicat d'Initiative,** place de Môle (tel. 40-82-04-40), is a five-minute walk from the station in a pavilion on the harbor. From the station, go right, head straight across the canal, and turn left on quai Leray. The friendly staff will give you loads of pamphlets and suggest walks, but aren't much help with accommodations. (Open Mon.-Sat. 9am-12:30pm and 2-6pm, Sun. 9:30am-12:30pm.) The town lacks inexpensive hotels, and the moderate ones are packed for the entire season. **Relais St-Gilles,** 7, rue Fernand de Mun (tel. 40-82-02-25), has rooms with a double bed and wash cabinet for 111F. (Showers 13F, breakfast 15F.) Ask at the tourist office about *chambres meublées,* boardinghouse rooms for one or two people (70-100F). Food in Pornic is mostly crêpes. **La Sarrasine,** 28, rue des Sables, behind the casino, is better than most and also serves seafood.

To leave Pornic is to love it. The canny will head quickly for one of the lovely beaches west of town. As you depart, notice the ninth-century château, restored in 1830. It's entirely a prop for the harbor—you can't go in. A promenade on the townward side of the new harbor, **Port de Plaisance,** was a favorite of Flaubert and Michelet. Rising on the high ground behind the castle, the druidic stones, known as the **Mousseaux** are somewhat disappointing for Brittany but not bad for a stroll within city limits. More magnificent views of the bay and ocean await you as you walk west along the coast toward Ste-Marie, and the beaches—**Grandes Vallées, Sablons, Porteau,** and **Gordière**—get smaller and somewhat less crowded farther away.

Loire Valley (Pays de la Loire)

Once a trade route, no longer navigable because of accumulated sand, the Loire shares its fertile valley, vineyards, history, and châteaux with less well-known rivers, including the Indre, the Cher, the Vienne, and the Maine. The proverbial châteaux of the Loire Valley can be anything from grim medieval military ruins to elegant country mansions. Rather incongruously, the foundations of these dignified buildings are firmly entrenched in a historic sewer of mischief, genius, promiscuity, and dirty-dealing.

Henry II and Richard Coeur de Lion mobilized two of the oldest communities, Chinon and Beaugency, to defend the region from the French crown in the eleventh century. The English and French played hot potato with the Loire until Joan of Arc helped procure it for the latter during the Hundred Years' War. During the Renaissance, the region was consolidated under the French monarchy through coercion and marital alliances. Under the Valois kings, a united France entered a period of unparalleled prosperity during which fortresses were transformed into the country residences of the nobility. Strongholds sprouted more decorative features and were filled with works of the Italian masters. Some of the finest châteaux, notably Blois and Chambord, were built in this era of court scandals and infamous mistresses. The construction of two superb châteaux, Azay-le-Rideau and Chenonceau, were directed by women. The valley today valiantly mingles thriving vineyards, industrial complexes, sedate villages, and two nuclear power plants.

As one would expect from so fertile a region, delicacies abound. Specialties include *rillettes* (a cold minced pork *pâté*), *fromage de chèvre* (goat cheese), and the creamy, sweet *Port Salut* cheese. Freshwater fish, especially salmon, trout, and pike, will please the palate. After a long day of biking, sit down to *veal escalope, coq au vin, champignons* (mushrooms) marinated in wine, and *asperges* (asparagus) steeped in butter. The Loire is most famous for its light white wines, such as *muscadets,* Touraine, Montlouis, and Vouvray, and fragrant reds Chinon, St-Nicolas-de-Bourgueil, and Saumur—nearly every town has a local wine worth sampling. On rural roads, look for signs marked *cave/dégustation,* which indicate tours and free samples.

Oddly, the grandeur of the region's attractions seems to inspire badly proportioned itineraries. Those who confine their exploration to daytrips from large industrial cities such as Tours and Orléans will leave ill-informed. Those favoring daily three-châteaux blitz bus tours will leave tapestries yawning from boredom and exhaustion. The excellent hostels in Blois, Chinon, and Saumur are comfortable bases, but pose daunting logistical challenges since public transportation routes fan out of the larger cities, and infrequent service can strand you in these havens of rural beauty.

Trains don't reach many châteaux, and when they do, they are scheduled at inconvenient hours. Tours (connected by rail to 12 châteaux) is best if you plan to travel only by train. Every train station distributes the useful booklet *Les Châteaux de la Loire en Train Eté '89,* with train schedules and information on SNCF bike and car rental. Buses are not much better. Ussé, Villandry, and Chambord can be reached only by bicycle, car, or tour bus. At least five or six days should be set aside for a train tour of the major châteaux. Generally, a group of four renting a car can beat tour bus prices. Bikes, however, seem most suited to the region. Distances between châteaux and hostels tend to be short, and the terrain hilly enough to be challenging but not impossible. Rent bikes in almost any Loire town; if you rent from the Tours, Langeais, Amboise, Chinon, Loches, Onzain, Blois, or Asay-le-Rideau train stations, you can return them to any other station on this list. Also think about buying or renting *panniers* (saddle bags) and leaving your backpack and other luggage in a locker. Even hardcore Eurailpass users should consider biking to the least accessible châteaux. Hitching can be hard work along the less-traveled routes; don't expect quick lifts since many of the cars traveling between châteaux are fully packed with families and luggage. Whatever the form of locomotion, take it slow: One or two châteaux per day is a healthy dose.

In the last century, the châteaux have been renovated, and many have been opened to the public. Chambord, Blois, and Cheverny are notable for their interiors, while other châteaux, especially Azay-le-Rideau, are renowned for their splendid setting. Only ruins of Chinon and Saumur remain, but their delightful towns recommend them, while feudal Angers guards many celebrated tapestries.

In 1952 M.P. Robert-Houdin gave the first *son et lumière* at Chambord. This man conceived and inflicted upon pioneering tourists a bombastic, melodramatic history lesson accompanied by darting floodlights. Although possibly a tiresome form of torture, some *son et lumière* shows, including the original, scintillate with wit, anecdotes, and theatrics. The best of the bunch takes place at Château Le Lude, which coordinates a terrific water, firework, and costume spectacle. (Mid-June to early Sept. Fri.-Sat. night, 45-80F. English translation available. Call 43-94-62-20 for more information. For bus transportation, see Tours Practical Information.)

Orléans

In 1429 Joan of Arc went to battle to deliver Orléans, then the most important city in France after Paris. Whether she would do the same for the modern city is anybody's guess. It is somehow appropriate that Orléans distills vinegar instead of wine as much of the rest of the Loire Valley does—an encounter with its inhabitants may well leave a sour taste in your mouth. As the city continues to grow as a rich industrial and commercial center, Orléans is becoming undeniably *embourgeoisé.* The "best" nightclubs are often tacitly all-white, and the Le Pen contingent is strong here. However, many exceptions exist, especially outside of the posh *centre ville,* among the university populations, and because of numerous recent immigrants from Vietnam, Pakistan, and Africa. Although devastatingly bombed during 1940, industrial Orléans still maintains many mementoes from its non-industrial past: Churches and buildings from the sixteenth, seventeenth, and eighteenth centuries line the narrow byways of the old city, where almost every street has some architectural rarity. A central location and low hotel prices render it a good base for exploring the upper part of the Loire countryside, the Loiret.

Orientation and Practical Information

The train station, the bus station, the tourist office, and most of the inexpensive hotels lie on the north side of the old city above the Loire. To reach the main square, **place du Martroi,** cross the large intersection at place Albert 1er and walk down rue de la Républic for five minutes. Southward between place du Martroi and the Loire, the streets are lined with shops and cafes. One block south of the square, **rue Jeanne d'Arc** runs east-west between the cathedral and the museum. The restaurant-rich pedestrian area of **rue de Bourgogne** lies 1 block south of rue Jeanne d'Arc and 1 block north of the river. Across the Loire is the university and the Parc Floral (easily accessible by bus "S").

Office de Tourisme: Place Albert 1er (tel. 38-53-05-95), next to the new shopping center connected to the train station. Energetic staff will book hotel rooms (6F) and load you with brochures. A walking tour in French leaves from the office July-Aug. Wed. and Sat. at 2:30pm (22F, students 11F). Cassette rentals detailing a visit to the city are available in English (36F, deposit 250F). Open July-Aug. Mon.-Sat. 9am-7pm, Sun. 9:30am-12:30pm and 3-6:30pm; Sept.-June Mon.-Sat. 9am-7pm.

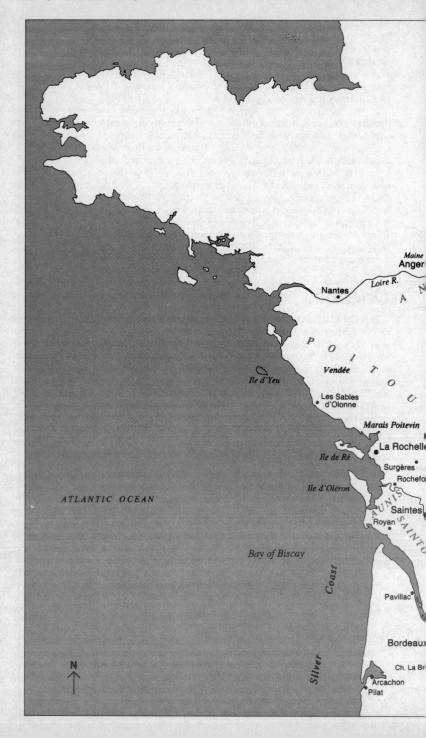

Maine
Anger

Nantes   *Loire R.*

A N

P O I T O U

Vendée

Ile d'Yeu

Les Sables
d'Olonne

Marais Poitevin

La Rochelle

Ile de Ré
Surgères

Rochefo

Ile d'Oléron

AUNIS

Saintes

Royan

SAINTO

ATLANTIC OCEAN

Bay of Biscay

Silver Coast

Pavillac

Bordeaux

Ch. La Br

Arcachon
Pilat

N
↑

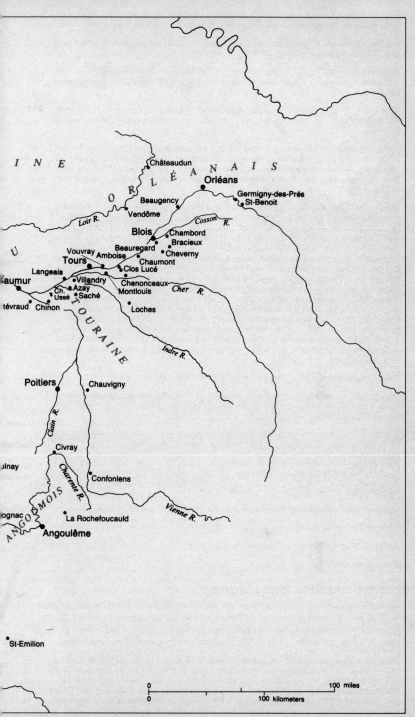

Student Travel: Arlina Voyages, 116, rue Faubourg Bannier (tel. 38-62-13-49). BIJ tickets. Also tickets to destinations in Asia. Open Mon. 2-7pm, Tues.-Sat. 9am-noon and 2-7pm.

Currency Exchange: All banks in Orléans close Mon., but you can change money at the main post office or its branch office.

American Express, 12, place du Martroi (tel. 38-53-84-54), 5 min. from the train station along rue de la République. Changes most traveler's checks for a 5F commission. Amex checks commission-free. Open Mon.-Fri. 9am-12:30pm and 1:45-6pm.

Post Office: Place du Général de Gaulle (tel. 38-41-35-14). *Recette Principale.* **Postal code:** 45000. Open Mon.-Fri. 8am-7pm, Sat.-Sun. 8am-noon. **Branch office,** next to the train station with same hours.

Train Station: Place Albert 1*er* (tel. 38-53-50-50). To Paris-Austerlitz (25 per day, 1¼ hr., 67F), Tours (15 per day, 1¼ hr., 64F), Blois (10 per day, ½ hr., 37F), and Amboise (5 per day, ¾ hr., 53F). Connections from Tours to Poitiers (109F) and Bordeaux (211F). Information office open Mon.-Sat. 7:15am-7:45pm, Sun. 9am-noon and 2-7pm. Ticket booths open 3:30am-1:30am.

Bus Station: Halte Routière, 300m behind the train station. The starting point for most local routes serviced by **SEMTAO.** For schedules and information try the booth here (open Mon.-Sat. 8:30am-12:30pm and 3-6:30pm) or on place du Martroi (open Mon.-Sat. 9am-12:30pm and 2:30-6pm). Operates 5:30am-9pm every 15 min. The "S"-line, which goes from place Albert 1*er* to the university and beyond to Parc Floral and the Loire, operates until midnight. SEMTAO runs a mini-train, 45-min. tour of Orléans in French June 15-Sept. 15 daily at 2:30pm, 3:30pm, and 4:30pm (20F, ages 14 and under 5F). For information, call 38-84-41-11. Individual bus tickets 6.50F, *carnet* of 10 44F. Ticket is good for corresponding bus lines up to 1 hr. after initial use. **Les Rapides du Val de Loire,** av. du Münster (tel. 38-53-94-75), a block away from the train station. Follow the signs that read *gare routière.* To Beaugency (16 per day, ½-1 hr., 22F), St-Benoit-sur-Loire (5 per day, 1 hr., 27F), Germigny-des-Prés (5 per day, 1 hr., 23F), Chateauneuf-sur-Loire (11 per day, ¾ hr., 21F), Blois via Beaugency (7 per day, 1½ hr., 37F), and Chartres (4 per day, departure times vary each day of the week, 1½ hr., 52F). No direct service to Châteaudun from Orléans; you must change at Chartres. Information office open Mon.-Sat. 6:30am-12:30pm and 3:45-7:30pm, Sun. 10:30am-12:30pm and 4:15-7:35pm.

Taxis: Taxi Radio Orléans, place Albert 1*er* (tel. 38-53-11-11).

Bike Rental: Societé Alexis, 14, rue des Carmes (tel. 38-62-63-50). 45F per day, deposit 300F. Open Tues.-Sun. 8:30am-noon and 2-7pm. Also at the **train station.** 32F per ½-day, 47F per day, deposit 300F.

English Bookstore: La Foire Aux Images, 200, rue Bourgogne (tel. 38-62-26-40). A couple of shelves of cheap, used classics. Open Tues.-Sat. 10am-12:30pm and 2:30-7pm.

Laundromat: Lav Club, 95, rue Faubourg Bannier, around the corner from Hôtel Coligny and near the station. Open daily 8am-9pm.

SOS Amitiés: Tel. 38-62-22-22. For a friendly voice.

Hospital: Centre Hospitalier Régional, 1, rue Porte Madeleine (tel. 38-51-44-44).

Medical Emergency: SAMU, Tel. 38-63-33-33.

Police: 1, place Gambetta (tel. 38-54-08-71).

Police Emergency: Tel. 17.

Accommodations and Camping

Several inexpensive hotels cluster on rue Faubourg Bannier, north of place Gambetta. The youth hostel is pleasant and relaxed and not far from the center of town. Rooms fill by early evening, so schedule your arrival carefully or call ahead (3 days is enough for most hotels, even in the busiest times); a deposit is unnecessary.

Auberge de Jeunesse (IYHF), 14, rue du Faubourg Madeleine (38-62-45-75), on the west side of town. Take bus B (*direction* "Paul-Bert") from in front of the train station (6.50F, last bus at 8:20pm). Or walk: Turn right outside the station onto place Gambetta; follow bd. Rocheplate, which becomes bd. Jean Jaurès; turn right onto rue du Faubourg Madeleine, and the hostel will be on your right (15 min.). Surprisingly serene, given its proximity to the city. 50-bed establishment with friendly management and decent kitchen facilities. 38F per night. IYHF card required. Sheets 6F. Bike rental 32F per day, deposit 300F. Lockout 9:30am-5:30pm. Curfew 10pm; keys available. Office open daily 7:15-9:30am and 5:30-10pm; in winter Sun.-Fri. only. Open Feb. 16-Nov.

CROUS, 17, av. Dauphine (tel. 38-63-68-57), in Les Hêtres. Take bus S from place du Martroi or from the front of the train station to La Source-Université (6.50F). Students 32F. Sheets 12F. Open late June-Sept.

Hôtel Coligny, 80, rue de la Gare (tel. 38-53-61-60), in the north section of town. From the station, take av. de Paris to rue de la Gare. A little dark but well-kept; pleasant proprietor is working to make rooms even more pleasant. Singles 65F, with shower 85F. Doubles 70F, with shower 95F. Showers 6F. Breakfast 13F.

Hôtel Touring, 142, bd. de Châteaudun (tel. 38-53-10-51), northwest of town. Walk or take bus A (not the "Olivet" bus) to rue Trannier at rue Châteaudun. A little farther out than Coligny. Clean and comfortable with welcoming owner. Singles 66F, with shower 85F. Doubles 79F, with shower 102F. Triples 107F, with shower 136F. Showers 15F. Breakfast 15F. Call 3-4 days in advance for a weeknight.

Hôtel de Paris, 29, rue Faubourg Bannier (tel. 38-53-39-58), a 3-min. walk across place Gambetta from the train station. Pretty pastel rooms and a proprietor who enjoys speaking English. A good bet if you arrive in town too exhausted to walk very far or to speak French. Singles 68F, with shower 80F. Doubles 80F, with shower 140F. Showers 10F. Breakfast 16F.

Hôtel Charles Sanglier, 8, rue Charles Sanglier (tel. 38-53-38-50), off rue de Bourgogne. Right in the center, near the river. Tiny, clean hotel with nice wooden floors, but watch out for the cleaning lady. Singles 78F. Doubles 100F. Showers 10F.

Château de Bel-Air, 501, rue Hème, Olivet (tel. 38-63-56-53). From Orléans, take bus A from place Albert 1er 5km out of town. Here's your chance to hold court in a small, aging château that's fronted by a carriage house and lawn and backed by a garden and river. Clean rooms furnished with antiques but without showers or toilets. Spooky if you're alone. Singles 67F. Doubles 95-137F. Closed Wed. until 6:30pm.

Camping: Campers can choose between 3 nearby sites. **Camping Municipal Olivet,** rue du Pont-Bouchet (tel. 38-63-53-94), the closest. A 2-star site open June-Oct. 15. Take bus N, O, or S to Aumône. **St-Jean-de-la-Ruelle,** rue de la Roche (tel. 38-88-39-39 or 38-43-00-44), a 2-star site. Take bus B from place Albert 1er to the Roche aux Fées stop. Open June-Nov. **La Chapelle-St-Mesmin,** rue des Grêves (tel. 38-43-60-46), the municipal campsite of the châteaux. Take bus D and ask for the campground stop on the riverbank. Open June-Nov.

Food

Orléans' local cheese is *frimault cendré,* a savory relative of *camembert;* the local wine is *Gris Meunier,* available at any local shop, the Monoprix on rue Jeanne-d'Arc, or the one at 47, Faubourg Bannier. Several medium-priced restaurants serve varied ethnic cuisine along rue de Bourgogne. The **market** is held daily, but the location changes. Check at the tourist office.

Le Viking, 235, rue de Bourgogne (tel. 38-53-12-21), just west of the cathedral. Unpretentious *crêperie* with delicious *gratin* dishes for 20-26F and a 39F *menu* (not available Sat. night) that includes *crudités,* dinner crêpe, drink, and dessert. Open Tues.-Sat. noon-2pm and 7-11pm.

Dany Grill, 22, rue Général-Sarrail (tel. 38-62-32-69), on a side street in a residential area north of place Gambetta. The street is off rue du Parc, which is off bd. de Châteaudun, not far from the train station. Bring a map, but the search is worth it. Possibly the most entertaining and delicious meal you'll eat in France. Gourmet 92F *menu,* but they'll let you order individual items from it. Open Tues.-Sat. 8pm until last customer leaves.

Le Picotin, 1, rue Pothier (38-53-89-36), a block from the cathedral. High-quality *crêperie* with reasonable prices. Crêpes from 20F, big mixed salad 25F. Open Mon. 7-10:30pm, Tues.-Sat. noon-2pm and 7-10:30pm.

La Tour d'Auvergne, 55, bd. Aristide Briand (tel. 38-53-21-84), at carré St-Vincent near the tourist office. Popular, no-nonsense 47F *menu.* Open Tues.-Sat. noon-2pm and 7:30-10pm, Sun. noon-2pm.

Fleurs d'Asie, 154, rue de Bourgogne (tel. 38-53-60-91). The most varied *menu* among those offered by a string of Vietnamese and Chinese restaurants. Excellent cuttlefish. Fish sautéed in coconut milk 30F. 42F *menu*, service and drink not included (not available Sat. night). Open Wed.-Mon. noon-1:30pm and 7-10pm, Tues. 7-10pm.

Sights

Tours sponsored by the tourist office are a sound introduction to the city and include places you would not otherwise get to see, such as the crypt of **Eglise St-Aignan**, which dates from the early fifteenth century. (See Practical Information.) If you decide to explore on your own, stroll through the Renaissance back streets to see Orléans's entry in France's unanimous tribute to Joan of Arc: **Cathédrale de Ste-Croix,** which stars a Joan of Arc chapel with monuments and a series of stained-glass windows depicting events from her life. Badly damaged by the Huguenots in 1568, the cavernous cathedral was rebuilt in Gothic style. (Open daily 9am-noon and 2-7pm.) The remains of the cathedral's fourth-, eighth-, and eleventh-century incarnations include fragments of a Carolingian floor mosaic (the only one in France) and a fourth-century Roman baptismal font. (Admission 8F.) The older gent who will guide you (in French, English descriptions available for the subterranean excavations) is a riot.

The **Maison de Jeanne d'Arc,** 3, place de-Gaulle, off place du Martroi, commemorates the shepherdess's contribution to Orléans and France. Joan of Arc stayed on the site in 1429, and the house was lovingly reconstructed after the 1940 bombing. The period costumes on display and the audio-visual recreation (in English upon request) of the siege of Orléans are well worth the admission price. (Open May-Oct. Tues.-Sun. 10am-noon and 2-6pm; Nov.-April Tues.-Sun. 10am-noon. Admission 6F, students 3F, ages under 13 free.) The nearby **Centre Jeanne d'Arc,** 24, rue Jeanne d'Arc (tel. 38-42-22-69), has tons of documents on Orléans's savior, and you can watch movies on her for free. They have the Ingrid Bergman version. (Open Mon.-Thurs. 9am-12:15pm and 2-5:30pm, Fri. 9am-12:15pm and 2-4:15pm.) On May 7 and 8, the town breaks into a tremendous celebration honoring Joan of Arc who, on May 7, 1429, delivered Orléans from the hands of the English. Street musicians, flower sellers, mimes, a big parade, and fireworks all contribute to the festivities.

Situated next to the *cité universitaire* and the new high-rise city of Orléans-la-Source, bordering Olivet and Orléans, the **Parc Floral** cultivates extensive fields of purple and white iris and a potpourri of tulip beds in the spring. It harbors peaceful spots for a picnic or some solitude. The park surrounds one source of the Loire River, a branch of which flows (replete with haughty pink flamingos on its banks) through the village of Olivet, a few kilometers to the west. (Parc Floral open April-Nov. 11 daily 9am-6pm, admission 14F; Nov. 12-March daily 2-5pm, admission 7F.) Take bus S from place Albert 1*er* in Orléans (6.50F; last bus back to Orléans at 11:45pm).

Near Orléans

Beaugency's picturesque setting with its vaulted bridge over the Loire alone merits a short visit. The vestiges of twelfth-century Beaugency, badly damaged during the Wars of Religion, cluster around place Dunois. **Château Dunois,** not very interesting in itself, houses an appealing **Musée Régional de l'Orléanais,** containing exhibits of local lacework, costumes, furniture, and children's games. (Open 10am-noon and 2-4pm; June-Nov. until 6pm. Admission 11F, students 5F.) Walk down rue de l'Evêché and turn onto rue Ravelin for a glimpse of medieval Beaugency. On place Dunois, twelfth-century **Eglise Notre-Dame** is noteworthy for its gently sloping Romanesque architecture.

The **Syndicat d'Initiative,** 28, place du Martroi (tel. 38-44-54-42), distributes information on the surrounding region. (Open Mon.-Sat. 9:30am-12:30pm and 2:30-7pm, Sun. 9:30am-12:30pm.) There's an **Auberge de Jeunesse (IYHF)** 3km out of town on route de Châteaudun (tel. 38-44-87-38). (34F per night. IYHF card required. Breakfast 11F, brunch and dinner 34F. Often crowded in summer—call ahead. Office open March-Dec. 8:15-9:30am and 5-9pm.) The cheapest, pleasant hotel in town is **Hôtel des Vieux Fossés,** 4, rue des Vieux Fossés (tel. 38-44-51-65). (Singles or doubles 55F, with shower 70F. Showers 10F. Breakfast 15F.) There's **camping** on the bank of the river from April to November (tel. 38-44-50-39). The **Crêperie de la Tour,** 26, rue de la Cordonnerie (tel. 38-44-83-93), serves up a 38F lunch *menu.* (Open Tues.-Sun. noon-2pm and 7pm-midnight.) Beaugency is easily accessible from Blois and Orléans by train, and 10 buses per day run between Beaugency and Orléans. Fares for all these trips is between 20-25F. The train station rents **bikes** (47F per day).

About 35km southeast of Orléans stands **St-Benoît-sur-Loire,** an ancient Benedictine monastery and basilica. This cloistered church is a lovely diversion for those tired of châteaux tours, and the tranquility is enough to make you consider joining the order. The open porch tower, with scenes from the Book of Revelation depicted on its columns, is one of the purest examples of Romanesque architecture in France. Nearby, on 65, rue Orléanaise, the **Hôtel de la Madeleine** (tel. 38-35-71-15) has rooms from 75F. The municipal campground **Le Port** (tel. 38-35-70-92) is close to town and open April through November.

The tiny Carolingian church of **Germigny-des-Prés,** founded in 806 by Théodulfe, Bishop of Orléans and friend to Charlemagne, sits 3km from St-Benoît in a tiny village of under 400 people. The church's Byzantine mosaic, the only one in all of France, depicts the Ark of the Covenant with dazzling glass cubes transported from Italy by Charlemagne. The curator will take you on a guided tour through this largely reconstructed church, believed to be the oldest in France. (Tours Mon.-Sat. at 11am and 3pm, Sun. 3:15pm and 4:30pm.)

Both Germigny and St-Benoît are accessible by bus from Orléans (5 per day from the *halte routière,* 1 hr., 23F to Germigny, 27F to St-Benoît). You can also hitch from Orléans to Châteauneuf-sur-Loire, 25km east along the N60; from there you can thumb to Germigny and St-Benoît, though this last leg will require a bit more patience, as the traffic falls to a trickle on tiny D60.

South from Chartres en route to the Loire is **Châteaudun.** Dominating the valley, the fortress walls merge with sheer cliffs, together an imposing and impregnable front. (Open daily April-Sept. 9-11:45am and 2-6pm; Oct.-March 10am-11:45am and 2-4pm. Admission 22F.) The **Syndicat d'Initiative,** 3, rue Toufaire (tel. 37-45-22-46), shares a building with a **Musée Ornithologique,** which houses a unique collection of stuffed birds crammed together in great display cases—along with a few minerals. There's a small, simple **Auberge de Jeunesse (IYHF),** av. des Martineaux (open mid-March to Sept.; kitchen available; 34F per night). The municipal campground, **Moulin à Tan,** a two-star site, lies 2km from town on rue de Chollet (tel. 38-45-05-34; open mid-March to mid-Oct.). To hitch from Orléans, head northwest on D955. Châteaudun is 55km from Orléans. Buses to Châteaudun leave from Chartres only.

Blois

Blois feverishly guards what most of its Loire neighbors can never possess: its own château right in the middle of town. The intriguing exterior of the château gives the city the flavor of lost centuries. You will probably never forget the winding staircase crawling with stone salamanders (Francois I's emblem, a symbol of immortality) in the château's courtyard. For a town of 50,000, the explosion of shops and large stores is surprising; Blois's old quarter struggles for breathing space amid an unappealing onslaught of urbania. The best feature of Blois, however, is its proximity to the beautiful châteaux of Chambord, Cheverny, and Chaumont, which all repose in unadulterated settings nearby. Unfortunately, Blois is smaller than other centers for châteaux-hunting and so has the highest tourist-to-local ratio around.

Orientation and Practical Information

On the north bank of the Loire, Blois is a major stop on the railway line between Orléans and Tours. The station is north of the château and the center; take av. Jean Laigret five minutes south to the tourist office. Continue in the same direction past the château on your left and almost immediately you will be in *centre ville.* Take the store- and cafe-lined rue Denis Papin to the Loire and cross the bridge. On the other side, **avenue Wilson,** a more serene street, contains a number of cheaper hotels and restaurants. On Monday all banks are closed, and most stores are closed Monday mornings.

Office de Tourisme: 3, av. Jean Laigret (tel. 54-74-06-49 or 54-78-23-21), in the lovely Renaissance Pavilion of Anne de Bretagne. Will find you a room for 5F plus a deposit of half the price of 1 night's stay. Changes cash (except $100 bills) and traveler's checks (commission 22F). Complete information on châteaux and how to get to them. Sells tickets for bus tours to nearby châteaux and the various shows at the Blois château. Open April-Sept. Mon.-Sat. 9am-7pm, Sun. 10am-1pm and 4-7pm; Oct.-May Mon.-Sat. 9am-noon and 2-6pm.

Bureau d'Information Jeunesse de Loir-et-Cher, 7, av. Wilson (tel. 54-78-54-87), on the other side of the Loire from *centre ville.* Eager staff. Information on travel throughout France and work (mostly babysitting) in the Blois area. Open Mon. 2-7pm, Tues.-Sat. 10am-7pm.

Post Office: Rue Gallois (tel. 54-78-08-01), near place Victor Hugo in front of the château. Changes cash and traveler's checks (commission on checks 1%). **Telephones. Postal code:** 41000. **Branch office,** rue Ronceraie, across the river, the 3rd left after the bridge. Both open Mon.-Fri. 8am-7pm, Sat. 8am-noon.

Train Station: On top of the hill on bd. Daniel Dupris at av. Jean Laigret (tel. 54-78-50-50), a 10-min. walk from the tourist office, up av. Jean Laigret. Trains to Paris via Orléans (1 hr., 92F), Tours (1 hr., 37F), Amboise (40 min., 25F), and Angers via Tours (3 hr., 85F). Information and reservation booth open Mon.-Sat. 8am-noon and 2-7pm, Sun. 9:30am-noon and 2-7pm.

Bus Station: Autocars STD, 2, place Victor Hugo (tel. 54-78-15-66), 2 min. from the tourist office. Conducts frequent ½-day trips combining châteaux Chambord and Cheverny (April 3-Oct. 2 Sun.-Mon., Wed., and Fri.; 90F, students 75F) and Chenonceaux and Amboise (April 2-Sept. Tues., Thurs., and Sat.; 90F, students 75F). Pleasant trips include commentary in English and admission into the châteaux. Tickets also sold at the tourist office or on the bus itself. Buses leave from the train station at 1:45pm and return around 6:45pm. Also regular bus service to Vendôme (3 per day, 4 hr., 28F), Cheverny (Mon.-Sat. 5 per day, 2 Sun.; ½ hr.; 14.70F, get off at Scierie), and Montlivault (2 per day, ¾ hr., 7.50F). Office open July-Aug. Mon.-Sat. 7:45am-12:15pm and 1:30-6:15pm, Sun. 8am-noon and 2-6pm; in off-season Mon.-Sat. only.

Bike Rental: Call a week in advance mid-July to mid-Aug. At the station (tel. 54-74-24-50). 47F per day, deposit 300F or a major credit card. Open daily 6am-9pm. **Atelier Cycles,** 44, levée des Tuileries (tel. 54-74-30-13). Decent 5- and 10-speeds 40-50F per day with passport as deposit. Open daily 9am-10pm. **S.M.C. S.A.R.L. Sports Motos Cycles,** 6, rue Henri Drussy (tel. 54-78-02-64). 40F per day, deposit 250F. Open Tues.-Sat. 9am-noon and 2-7pm.

English Bookstore: Livr' Images, 53, rue Denis Papin (tel. 54-78-01-10). A few shelves of vacation or junk reading. Open Mon. noon-7pm, Tues.-Sat. 9am-7pm.

Laundromat: 1, rue Jeanne d'Arc, near the river. Wash 20F, dry 2F. Open Mon.-Sat. 7am-8:30pm, Sun. 9am-8:30pm.

All-night Pharmacy: *Pharmacie de garde* changes nightly. Consult newpapers, the door of any pharmacy, or call the police.

Hospital: Centre Hospitalier de Blois, Mall Pierre Charlot (tel. 54-78-00-82).

Medical Emergency: SAMU, Tel. 54-78-78-78.

Police: 30, rue Christophe Colomb (tel. 54-43-15-58).

Police Emergency: Tel. 17.

Accommodations

The summer throng of visitors makes finding a room in Blois an arduous task. In July and August, travelers stay usually only one or two nights, but their vacated rooms are taken in the afternoon by the next wave. Call a few days in advance to reserve a place or you may end up on the granite banks of the Loire.

Auberge de Jeunesse (IYHF), 18, rue de l'Hôtel Pasquier (tel. 54-78-27-21), 4½km outside of Blois in Les Grouets. Take bus #70 (*direction* "Les Grouets") and get off at Eglise des Grouets. A secluded and rambling building with 2 single-sex dorm rooms. Excellent kitchen facilites, hot showers, and a relaxed evening atmosphere. Only 48 beds and often full in summer; call ahead. 34F per person. Sheets 11F. Breakfast 10F. Closed 10am-6pm. Open March-Nov. 15.

Hôtel de la Croix Blanche, 24, av. Wilson (tel. 54-78-25-32), a few blocks after you cross the bridge. Comfortable rooms above a bar are kept spick-and-span by the young couple who run this pleasant hotel. Singles or doubles 75F, with shower 88F. Triples 115F, with showers 165F. Showers 10F. Breakfast 18F. You will pass 2 other hotels of similar quality before you get to this hotel. First, **Le Pavillon,** at #2 (tel. 54-74-23-27), has 1- to 3-bed rooms for 70F, with shower 115F. Showers 10F. Breakfast 12.50F. **La Sologne,** at #20 (tel. 54-78-02-77), offers singles or doubles for 70F, with shower 100F. Triples 120F, with shower 130F. Showers 6F. Breakfast 12F.

Saint-Jacques, 7, rue Ducoux (tel. 54-78-04-15). Orderly and professionally run, with spacious and bright rooms. Lounge with color TV. Singles 75F, with shower 100F. Doubles 130F, with shower 160F. Bath 15F. Delicious breakfast 18F.

Hôtel St-Nicolas, 2, rue de Sermon (tel. 54-78-05-85). Clean rooms. Rooms 75F and 90F. Showers 10F. Breakfast 18F.

Camping: La Boire, 2km out of town (tel. 54-74-22-78). 8F per person; showers included. Open March-Nov. A little farther out, but nicer is **Lac de Loire,** Tel. 54-78-82-05. Open June-Oct.

Food and Entertainment

Restaurants in Blois serve up high prices for the town's active tourist industry, but you may want to luxuriate in the ambience at those near the château. Restaurants cluster around **rue St-Lubin** and along the Loire banks. Several *très* chic bars front rue Foulérie. One amusing way to spend an evening is to go to **place de la Résistance** by the river, choose a sidewalk café, and sit and watch the locals watch the tourists.

La Scala, 8, rue des Minimes (tel. 54-78-70-49), a few blocks from the post office. Hearty Italian specialties in a quaint atmosphere. Pizza and pasta 28-50F, varieties of *risotto* 48F, ice cream 21-40F. Open Mon. 7-11pm, Tues.-Sat. 11am-2pm and 7-11pm. For more gourmet pizza, try **Le San Remo,** 9, rue Anne de Bretagne, which also serves elegant desserts for 18-27F.

Packman, 25, rue Denis Papin (tel. 54-74-11-88), right in the center of town. There are 3 good things about this cafeteria: It's cheap, it's clean, and every salad (10-15F) comes with a free roll. Open Sun.-Thurs. 6am-11pm, Fri.-Sat. 6am-1am.

La Manhattan, 39, Jean-Laigret (tel. 54-78-97-86), a few blocks from the train station on the way into *centre ville.* By far the best of the restaurants near the station. Treat yourself to a surprisingly tasty 52F *menu* or, if you're impecunious, try the *salade verte* (lettuce only), which comes with tons of bread (9F). Open daily noon-2pm and 7-9pm.

Les Glycines, 54, rue Foulérie (tel. 54-74-17-95). A bit more sedate and slightly cheaper than others of its kind on the street. 62F *menu* is good but has only 3 courses; pizza 30-42F, salads from 26F. Open Mon.-Fri. noon-2pm and 7-11pm, Sat. 7-11pm.

Salsa, 4, impasse Ronceraie (tel. 54-78-28-67), across the river. Take a left off av. du Wilson onto rue Dupré, then take the 1st right onto ruelle Ronceraie, and follow the signs (5-10 min. from the river). A fantastic way to spend an evening: Have one of their filling tropical platters (35-60F). Open daily 8pm-2am.

Sights

Home of French monarchs Louis XII and François I, the **Château de Blois** was a seat of power during the Renaissance, comparable to Versailles in subsequent ages. Walk through the streets and terraces outside the château and around the courtyard inside to appreciate the differences among the three major architectural styles. Inside, the rooms reek of intrigue. Hidden panels are opened by foot pedals, and doors are concealed by tapestries. You can either take the interesting but lengthy guided tour (in English or French, with frequent departures) or walk through on your own. Start with the Aile François I, fronted by a grand, ornamental staircase, with several rooms furnished in fine Renaissance style. In 1588, the Protestant king Henri III had the Catholic Henri, Duc de Guise, assassinated here in an attempt to eliminate opposition to the crown. The king himself was murdered eight months later. The basement of this wing houses the **Musée Archéologique**, with funerary urns and other artifacts from the Loire Valley. Continue into the **Salle des Etats,** the only part of the château (along with one tower) surviving from the thirteenth century. The fifteenth-century Aile Louis XII next door houses the small **Musée des Beaux Arts** and the **Musée d'Art Religieux.** (Château and museums open daily June-Sept. 9am-6pm; Oct.-May 9:30am-noon and 2-6pm. Admission includes entrance to museums 21F, students 10F.) Beware of the attractively advertised *son et lumière* show almost every evening in French (at 10:30pm) and English (at 11:15pm). While the château stonework is beautiful when illuminated at night, the show is uninformative and histrionic (20F, ages 5-12 and 65 and over 15F).

South of the château lies the impressive **Abbaye St-Lomer.** A dark blue ceiling caps the fine, broad ambulatory with its radiating chapels, typical of the late Romanesque style; the Gothic nave was added more than a century later. A pleasant garden leads from the church to the river through what was once the cloister of a Benedictine abbey. Blois's **Cathédrale St-Louis** is a seventeenth-century reconstruction of a Gothic church. It stands just north of the old quarter, a wonderful place for wandering among half-timbered houses and ancient archways. You'll get both a perverse pleasure at seeing how the food of the gods is made from a disgusting brown sludge and a sample of the finished product at the **Poulain Chocolate Factory.** The big orange-brick building is visible as you leave the train station; just follow your nose. (Tours Mon.-Thurs. at 8:45am, 10am, 11:15am, 1:15pm, and 2:45pm; Fri. 8:45am, 10am, and 11:15am. Admission 4F, children 2F.)

Near Blois

The woods and fields across the river south of Blois shelter some of the most remarkable châteaux of the region—all but Chaumont inaccessible by train from Blois. Eurailpass holders should go to Tours, connected by rail to several châteaux. However, the cheapest bus tours leave from Blois (see Practical Information). You can take a half-day, two-châteaux extravaganza (either Chambord and Cheverny or Chenonceau and Amboise); the price includes an English commentary during the bus ride and admission to the châteaux. More independent travelers might opt to take buses between the châteaux. In Blois, STD offers reduced rates to students and ages 10 and under. Best of all, the châteaux are all within easy bicycling range of Blois. Bicycle trails are beautiful and largely flat; the ambitious can combine several châteaux in one daytrip. Hitching is also viable; from Blois to Chambord you'll have about an hour's wait, while the trip from Blois to Cheverny is quicker since it's just 2km off D956.

The largest and most extravagant of the Loire châteaux, **Chambord** is so enormous that not even summer's daily deluge of sightseers clutters its grand halls. A remarkable architectural undertaking, Chambord's mix of dormers, turrets, and arcades seems a bit haphazard; yet viewed from afar, a definite harmony appears. Chambord was built by François I for his frequent hunting trips to the nearby forests; some claim Leonardo da Vinci played an important role in its construction; others, agreeing with Henry James, credit the lesser-known artist and architect

Pierre Trinqueau. The river Cosson was diverted to improve the setting, and visitors approach the château along a magnificent kilometer-long, tree-lined avenue. Indeed, much of the château's appeal lies in its isolation; only one hotel (doubles from 190F) and a few souvenir shops violate the verdure. Period wallpapers and fabrics decorate the rooms, and tourist traffic is efficiently and artfully routed on a path that circulates from airy balconies to splendidly furnished rooms. There are several ways to see Chambord. The cheapest is wandering around on your own; rooms are adequately labeled in English. The pamphlet in English will help with its detailed plan (3F). An excellent guided cassette tour is designed primarily for architecture or history buffs (22F, 32F per 2 listeners). The lengthy, guided tour in French concentrates on the building's creation; you do see a few rooms not normally open to the public. Chambord is also a hunting reserve whose grounds are surrounded by a 32-km wall, one of the longest in France. (Château open daily July-Aug. 9:30am-6:30pm; Sept.-June 9:30am-11:45am and 2-4:45pm. Admission 22F, students 12F, children 6F.) Campers can head to **Camping Huisseau-sur-Cosson,** 6, rue de Châtillon (tel. 54-20-35-26), about 5km southwest of Chambord on D33. (8.50F per person includes tent. Showers 4F. Open June-Nov.) There is another campground in **Bracieux** on route de Chambord (tel. 54-46-41-84) with a swimming pool, tennis court, and free showers. (8.50F per person, 4F per tent; gate open Mar. 26-Oct. daily 7:30am-10:30pm.) To bike or hitch to Chambord from Blois, take D956 south for 2-3km and turn left onto D33 for 11km.

Cheverny preserves a rare and sumptuous dignity; its symmetrical late Renaissance exterior conceals an impressive and comfortably furnished interior, including a bed slept in by Henri IV. You can wander with the free pamphlet in English through chambers with painted ceilings, portraits, antique furniture, and tapestries (notably a Gobelin of the *Abduction of Helen*). On the grounds a compound houses purebred bloodhounds; you can see all 70 gulp down their bins of ground meat, which takes 60 seconds, daily at 5pm. The park around the château, with its formal gardens, is also attractive, but an electrified fence ensures that tourists see nothing without paying. (Open daily June-Sept. 15 9:15am-6:45pm; Sept. 16-May 9:30am-noon and 2:15-at least 5pm. Admission 20F, students 12F.) In town, the Cheverny **Syndicat d'Initiative** (tel. 54-79-95-63) can guide you to the **Camping-Cour Cheverny du S.I.** (tel. 54-79-90-01; 8.50F per night, open June 2-Sept.). The *syndicat* is located on av. de la République. (Open July-Aug. Mon.-Sat. 10am-noon and 3-7pm, Sun. 10am-noon; April-June and Sept. 3-6pm.) To hitch, go south along the D956. Bikers will want to take a less direct and less busy route.

Only 9km south of Blois towers **Beauregard,** a smaller, less-touristed château that conjures up the aura of sixteenth- and seventeenth-century French royalty. Although difficult to reach by public transportation (the only bus runs infrequently and stops several km away), Beauregard makes an interesting and not too challenging daytrip by bike from Blois. The most direct route takes you along a busy four-lane highway, so ask at a bike rental shop for touring routes. Hitching is also possible: Head south on D956. Beauregard is most notable for the upstairs portrait gallery, the largest in all of Europe, with over 350 portraits from 1328 to 1643. The tour guide gives an amusing rundown of European history in French, pointing out bloodlines between the royalty and using the portraits and a flashlight as props. (Open July-Aug. daily 9:30am-6:30pm; Sept. and June daily 9:30am-noon and 2-6:30pm; Oct.-May Thurs.-Tues. 9:30am-noon and 2-5pm. Admission 16F, students 10F. Tours given frequently each day.)

Perhaps the most underrated of all the châteaux in the area, **Chaumont-sur-Loire** is a good reminder that châteaux were first built to defend rather than to entertain. A compact feudal fortress, its towers, battlement, and small drawbridge dominate the valley below. Catherine de Medici lived here with her astrologer until the death of her husband, Henri II. She then forced Henri's mistress, Diane de Poitiers, to vacate the more desirable Chenonceau in exchange for Chaumont. Obviously, Diane didn't make out too badly. The château is best known for its luxurious *écuries* (stables); the horses were fed from porcelain troths in private stalls. Electricity was installed in the stables in 1906, even before it was installed in the château—the power is used to light elegant lamps that hang just above the stalls. (Château open daily June-Sept. 9:15-11:35am and 1:45-5:35pm; Oct.-May until 4:50pm. Admission 22F, students 12F.) A sheltered campsite is close by at **Camping "Grosse Grève,"** just off the bridge on the southern bank of the Loire (tel. 54-20-93-95; 7.20F per night). Chaumont is accessible by train from Blois (8 per day, 10 min., 11F) and Tours (8 per day, ½ hr., 28F). The **train station** (tel. 54-78-50-50) lies in Onzain, 2km north of Chaumont, across the bridge.

Vendôme, a small Loiret city, is surrounded by gently rolling farmland. The abbey-church of **La Trinité** sports an impressive facade, designed in the sixteenth century by Jean de Beauce, architect of the north tower of Chartres's cathedral. Inside, look for majestic arches and the *Vitrail Notre Dame de Vendôme,* the oldest existing stained-glass image of Mary as the Virgin Mother. Try to come around 5pm, when you can climb the tower and watch the evening bells ring. Walk up the hill to the ruined **château,** dismantled by Henri IV in 1589. The fragments of the defending walls and the half-standing towers enclose a lovely garden and terrace with a delightful view of the church and countryside. (Open July-Aug. Tues.-Mon. 9am-noon and 2-6pm; in off-season Wed.-Mon. only. Admission 6F, students 4.60F; admission to the grounds only 2F.) The **office de tourisme,** place St-Martin (tel. 54-77-05-07), is at the base of the ramp leading to the castle on the banks of the Loire. **Camping Municipal des Grands Prés,** rue Geoffrey Martell (tel. 54-77-00-27), is a large three-star site with a swimming pool, pleasantly situated on the banks of the river just outside of town. (8F per night.) Buses to Vendôme leave daily from Blois, but cost a steep 28F. To hitch, take D957 northwest from Blois; Vendôme lies 32km away.

Amboise

Set on a steep hillside over the Loire in unspoiled countryside, Château d'Amboise enjoys both scenic and historic prominence. Though the château itself is neither as ornate as Chambord nor as graceful as Chenonceau, its view of the Loire is well worth the uphill hike. The small town beneath defers to the château, but the old quarter, a stone bridge, and riverside banks lend it a quiet dignity.

The dearth of cheap accomodations render Amboise a daytrip only, unless the peacefulness entices you to stay.

Orientation and Practical Information

Several trains per day stop in Amboise, which lies midway between Blois and Tours. The **train station** (tel. 47-57-03-89) is a 15-minute walk from the center of town, on the opposite side of the river, and rents **bikes** for 47F per day plus a 300F deposit. To reach either the château or the tourist office, walk south from the station along rue Jules Ferry and cross the first bridge onto the tiny **Ile d'Or,** an island neighborhood of which a quarter is devoted to camping facilities. Continue straight, cross the next bridge, and you're in *centre ville.* On your left is the château and down the quai to your right is the **Office de Tourisme,** quai Général de Gaulle (tel. 47-57-09-28), which provides a much-needed accommodations service for 3F. (Open July-Aug. Mon.-Sat. 9:45am-7pm, Sun. 10am-noon and 3-6pm; Sept.-June Mon.-Sat. 8:30am-noon and 1:30-6pm.) All banks in Amboise charge a commission for currency exchange and are usually closed Sunday and Monday. Try **Crédit Lyonnais,** 34, rue Nationale (tel. 47-30-52-52; open Tues.-Sat. 8:35am-noon and 1:35-4:45pm). The **post office** is just down the street from the tourist office on quai Général de Gaulle (open Mon.-Fri. 8:30am-12:15pm and 1:30-6:30pm, Sat. 8:30-noon) and will also change currency for a commission. The **postal code** is 37400.

Accommodations, Camping, and Food

For a small town, Amboise's accommodations are expensive and, with few exceptions, lack charm. Beware of hotels that require you to eat their overpriced meals.

In summer it's a good idea to call at least a few days in advance. In July and August the youth hostel is usually booked to the gills by groups you probably would want to avoid anyway, such as your hometown's high school glee club.

Maison des Jeunes—Centre Charles Péguy, Ile d'Or (tel. 47-57-06-36), a 10-min. walk from the train station. After the 1st bridge turn right. Nice location. If office is closed, go around to the back of the building, ring the bell, and ask for the warden. Kitchen has an oven but no stove-top. Beds in doubles, quads, or sixes. 40F. Sheets 15F. Breakfast 13F, only for groups. Reception open 3-10pm. No lockout. Closed in summer Mon.; in off-season Sun.-Mon., but management may let you in if you call ahead. In summer, come early.

Hôtel à la Tour, 32, rue Victor Hugo (tel. 47-57-25-04), across from the château. 6 well-kept rooms with wood floors above a bar. Mild-mannered owners, but you'll begin to wonder when you see their hot-red hall bathroom. Often full in summer. Call 1 week in advance. Singles 80F. Doubles 110F. Triples 150F. Breakfast 18F. Open Dec.-Oct.

Hôtel le Chaptal, 13, rue Chaptal (tel. 47-57-14-46), off rue Nationale in the center. Adequate rooms 72-82F, with shower 107-157F. Extra bed 30F. No hall shower. Breakfast 17F. In summer, call in advance. Reception open in summer daily; in off-season Tues.-Sun. The large family restaurant has 52 and 75F *menus.*

Hôtel Platanes, route de Nazelles (tel. 47-57-08-60), in a drab neighborhood behind the train station. Rooms are quiet and immaculate. Singles 85F. Doubles 125F. Showers 15F. Breakfast 18F. *Menu* with regional specialties 52F, required of 1-night hotel guests.

Camping: The best place to stay in Amboise is the fine campsite on the Ile d'Or (tel. 47-57-23-37), across from the château. Showers and hot water. 12F per person, 15F per tent. In summer, crowded swimming pool 8F. Call in advance, but there's usually a spot.

Amboise has an excess of overpriced street cafes but redeems itself by having the best restaurant in the Loire Valley: **Chez Roger,** 7, rue du Général-Foy (tel. 47-57-61-53), not far from the château. Roger puts on lunch and dinner every weekday, and all the locals show up for the 39F lunch *menu* which includes five generous, simple but tasty courses and all the bread and wine you want (coffee 2.50F). If Roger's mess-hall dining room just doesn't appeal to you, you can dine in a sixteenth-century house at **L'Ecu,** 7, rue Corneille (tel. 47-30-58-95), off rue Nationale. Salads, crêpes, *galettes,* and most items on the menu are 20F or less. (Open Mon.-Sat. noon-3pm and 7pm-midnight, Sun. 7pm-midnight.) An elegant, traditional meal is available at **Restaurant de la Poste,** 5, rue d'Orange (tel. 47-57-01-88), near the postal museum (58F *menu*). (Open daily noon-2pm and 7-9pm; Nov.-Easter Tues.-Sun.)

Sights

Having spent the last three years beautifying the **Château d'Amboise,** where he was born and raised with Italian treasures and a fanciful garden, Charles VIII died here in the sixteenth year of his reign: He struck his head on a doorway while hurrying to watch a game of cards being played in the moat. The château was finished by Louis XII and François I in a luxurious, highly decorative style influenced by the Italian Renaissance and by Leonardo da Vinci, who came to help. What remains of the castle is only one wall of the original rectangular set of fortifications; three of the walls were demolished at the beginning of the nineteenth century. This portion, the **Logis du Roi,** is lavishly furnished in a late Gothic style with fine tapestries. In 1560 La Renaudie and other protestants were condemned to death in the great hall, and 275 years later, for a period of five years, the great Algerian leader Abd el-Kader was exiled here. Best of all, however, is the **Tour des Minimes,** a giant five-story ramp for bringing horses and carriages into the château, complete with central ventilation. (Château open daily July-Aug. 9am-6:30pm; Sept.-June 9am-noon and 2-5pm. Admission 20F, students 10F. Obligatory tour in French only, with a printed English summary.) From June through August, an extravagant Renaissance show called *A La Cour Roy François,* involving over 400 characters dressed in period costumes, occurs in the evenings. Lighting effects, fireworks, and sixteenth-century music are thrown in for the price of 45F per person. Information and reservations (5F) are available at the ticket booth on the ramp ascending to the château (tel. 47-57-14-47).

From the château, walk alongside the cliffs on rue Victor Hugo among centuries-old *maisons troglodytiques,* hollowed out of the hill and still inhabited today. A half-kilometer down the road is the **Clos Lucé,** the gracious manor where Leonardo da Vinci, under the patronage of François I, spent the last years of his life. The generally unsatisfying museum displays some fine furnishings and tapestries, but most highly touted are three rooms of models based on the master's drawings. Unfortunately, the models don't measure up to da Vinci's visionary plans, and the obligatory guided tour in French goes a bit too fast. (Tours July-Aug. only; in off-season you're on your own.) The various gardens behind the house afford a fine view of the château and chapel. (Open daily June-Sept. 9am-7pm; Oct.-Dec. and Feb.-May 9am-noon and 2-5pm. Admission 26F, students 18F, ages 7-15 13F.)

The unassuming **Musée de la Poste,** 6, rue Joyeuse (tel. 47-57-02-21), in the Hôtel de Joyeuse, presents the history of mail delivery in France. The eclectic exhibit ranges from the uniforms worn by Napoleonic mail carriers to the first stamp printed in France. (Open April-Sept. Tues.-Sun. 9:30am-noon and 2-6:30pm; Oct.-Dec. and Feb.-March Tues.-Sun. 10am-noon and 2-5pm. Admission 7F, students and ages under 10 3F.)

Near Amboise

Sheltered by an ancient forest, graceful **Chenonceau** cultivates an intimacy with its natural surroundings that resists even the most ferocious of crowds. Arching effortlessly over the Cher River, tons of white stone appear suspended in air, capped with slate-gray peaks. The gallery served as a military hospital during World War I and as a passageway from occupied France to the free zone during World War II. You need not take a guided tour and can admire the interiors leisurely; just pick up a pamphlet in the language of your choice and wander around. From the end of spring until late summer, the château is packed with sightseers and kids, who see it all as a glorious playground. On hot and crowded summer days you will probably get little sense of Chenonceau as a former royal residence. But it doesn't really matter—the stunning exterior (viewed from the spacious garden or explored by rowboat, 10F) is Chenonceau's most impressive aspect. (Open daily March 16-Sept. 15 9am-7pm; Sept. 16-Sept. 30 9am-6:30pm; Oct. 9am-6pm; Nov. 1-Nov. 15 9am-5pm; Nov. 16-Feb. 15 9am-noon and 2-4:30pm; Feb. 16-Feb. 28 9am-5:30pm; March 1-March 15 9am-6pm. Admission 30F, students and ages 7-15 20F.)

The **Musée de Cires,** a collection of wax figures in period costumes, illustrates the history of the château. (Museum open same hours as château, and only with admission to château. 8F.) The *son et lumière* presentation at Chenonceau is a nice diversion if you're staying nearby, but not worth making the elaborate transportation plans necessary otherwise. Although not immune from hokey historical narration, it wisely concentrates on the beauty of the grounds. Bring bug repellent. (Shows May-June on selected evenings; July-Sept. nightly at 10pm and 10:45pm. Admission 30F. Call the château for information, tel. 47-23-90-07.)

Four **trains** per day (1 on Sun.) connect the village of Chenonceaux to Tours (¾ hr., 25F). The station is 2km from the château; walk straight up the road from the station, turn left onto rue Bretonneau, and then left again onto rue du Château. **Les Rapides de Touraine** (tel. 47-46-06-60 in Tours) runs five buses per day (2 Sun.) from Tours to Chenonceau (1 hr., 31F) via Amboise (½hr., 19.50F). Unless you have a bike or car, your only other option is to hitch from Amboise (8km south on D31, then 5km east on less-traveled D40) or Tours (27km east on N76).

Because the *son et lumière* ends at 11:30pm, you'll have to stay in or near Chenonceau to see it. The only reasonable prospect in town is the comfortable, two-star **Hostel du Roy,** 9, rue Docteur Bretonneau (tel. 47-23-90-17), minutes from the château. (Singles 75F. Doubles 95F. Showers included. Obligatory breakfast 20F, dinner from 50F. Open Feb.-Nov.) Otherwise, try **La Taverne,** 2km away on the route to Tours (tel. 47-29-92-18), or **Chez Madeleine Badier,** a little farther on the route to Tours (tel. 47-29-92-48). Both hotels have rooms for about 100-150F and inexpensive restaurants. In Chenonceau itself, **Le Gâteau Breton,** 16, rue Bretonneau (tel. 47-29-90-14), cooks up both *à la carte* dishes and 42F *menus.* The tiny **campsite** in Chenonceau is located a few streets left of the entrance to the château (tel. 47-23-90-21; 5.80F per person and per tent). Camping is also available in nearby **Civray,** about 1km away (tel. 47-23-92-13), and a one-star site in **Chisseaux,** about 2km from the château (tel. 47-23-86-18; 8F per person, 10F per tent).

Tours

Straddling both the Loire and the Cher, Tours is within 60km of some of the loveliest châteaux, and right on the doorstep of the fine wine-growing towns of the Touraine, Vouvray, and Montlouis. Bus and train connections to the châteaux are delightfully frequent, and the plentiful, cheap hotels and wonderful *foyer* make Tours a fine base for visiting the surrounding region.

Tours itself includes everything from a glitzy pedestrian zone crammed with haughty, high-priced boutiques and cafes to demure residential areas, august public buildings, and tree-lined boulevards, not to mention an old quarter with buildings dating from the Renaissance. Since the Middle Ages, Tours has been a center of education; a large, lively, and international student population mingles with and somewhat mitigates the stodgy bourgeoisie, some of whom never miss a chance to size up an outsider's apparent shortcomings.

Orientation and Practical Information

Tours lies only 2¼ hours from Paris-Austerlitz. The train station, bus station, and tourist office are all located in **place Maréchal Leclerc.** The city's focal point is **place Jean Jaurès,** a two-minute walk west from the tourist office along bd. Heurteloup. From here, numerous sidewalk cafes stretch southward along av. Grammont, while rue Nationale, Tours' answer to the Champs Elysées, cuts a northward path to the Loire. To the left of rue Nationale along rue du Commerce and rue du Grand Marché lies the *vieille ville,* while about 1km to the right, the cathedral and the Musée des Beaux Arts stand off rue Colbert.

Office de Tourisme: Place Maréchal Leclerc (tel. 47-05-58-08), in the pavilion across the parking lot from the train station. Diligent staff, some of whom speak English, with brochures on just about every aspect of Tours and the Loire Valley. Will book accommodations (6F plus 50-100F deposit) and arrange bus tours to the châteaux. A general bus tour including only the exteriors of sites (at 10am, 2½hr., 45F) and a detailed historical tour on foot (at 3pm, 2½ hr., 25F) both depart daily from the office mid-June to early Oct. Open June-Aug. Mon.-Sat. 8:30am-8pm, Sun. 10am-noon and 3-6pm; Sept.-May Mon.-Sat. 9am-noon and 2-6pm. After hours, information on hotels and a map (1F) available from a machine outside the office. **Services for Handicapped People:** The tourist office provides guides for people in wheelchairs staying in Tours, *Tours en Fauteuil Roulant* and in all France *Touristes Quand Même.*

Services Touristiques de Touraine: Inside the train station (tel. 47-05-46-09). Full-day and ½-day excursions to nearby châteaux, complete with guide. Day tours, which depart at 8:45am from outside the *gare* on platform 20, blitz 3 châteaux, such as Blois, Chambord, and Cheverny (ticket 115F, entrance fees 44F), or Loches, Chenonceau, and Amboise (Ticket 100F, entrance fees 45F), and return around 6:45pm. Half-day tours average 69F, entrance fees 45F, leaving at 1:15 from platform 20 and returning at 7pm. In summer, *son et lumière* trips available too; prices include admission. To Azay-le-Rideau (85F), Le Lude (110F), and Amboise (100F). There are 2-3 departures per week late March-early Oct. French and English commentary from guide on bus. Office open Mon.-Sat. 8-11am and 3:30-7pm, Sun. 8-11am. Reservations here or at the tourist office a day in advance recommended. Another option, with similar prices and châteaux, but that also include a *cave* and *dégustation,* is **Touraine Evasion,** which has a fleet of minibuses. (Contact the tourist office or call 47-66-52-32 Mon.-Fri. or 47-66-63-81 Sat.-Sun.) Groups of 5-7 can create their own itineraries.

Budget Travel: Frantour, in the train station (tel. 47-05-68-45). BIJ and plane tickets with student and youth discounts. Open Mon.-Fri. 9am-noon and 2-6pm. **Wagon-Lits Tourisme,** 9, rue Marceau (tel. 47-20-40-54). The same services. Also organizes charter flights, but without any semblance of friendliness. Open Mon.-Fri. 9am-12:15pm and 2-6:30pm, Sat. 10am-12:30pm and 2-6:30pm.

Currency Exchange: In the **train station** at SOS Hôtels France (see below), you can change all brands of traveler's checks for 10F. Best deal is at the **Crédit Agricole** booth, next to the tourist office, which charges no commission except Sun.-Mon., when most banks are closed. Open June 15-Sept. 15 Tues.-Sat. 8:30am-1:30pm and 5-9pm, Sun. 9am-6pm, Mon. 8am-9pm. **Crédit Lyonnais** charges a 24F commission and changes traveler's checks at competitive rates. Branch office at 71, rue Nationale. Open Tues.-Fri. 8:30am-noon and 1:30-5pm, Sat. 8:30am-noon.

Post Office: 1, bd. Béranger (tel. 47-21-50-15). The *recette principale* is here for general delivery. **Postal code:** 37000. Open Mon.-Fri. 8am-7pm, Sat. 8am-noon.

Train Station: 3, rue Edouard Vaillant (tel. 47-20-50-50 24 hours). Many long-distance trains require you to change at St-Pierre-des-Corps, a station in a Tours neighborhood 5 min. away, so check the schedule carefully. To Chinon (3 per day, 1 hr., 33F), Angers (7 per day, 1½ hr., 60F), Poitiers (12 per day, 1½ hr., 57F), Bordeaux (12 per day, 2½ hr., 167F), and Paris (1-2 per hr., 2 hr., 118F). Châteaux served by train include Azay-le-Rideau (Mon.-Sat. 3-4 per day, 2 Sun.; ½ hr.; 21.50F), Chenonceau (Mon.-Sat. 3 per day, 1 Sun.; ¾ hr.; 25F), Loches (Mon.-Sat. 3 per day, 1 Sun.; 1 hr.; 32F), Langeais (Mon.-Sat. 6 per day, 2 Sun.; ½ hr.; 17.60F) and Blois (10 per day, 35 min.; 37F). Train information available at friendly **Acceuil** desk by tracks (open 24 hours). Next to this is the **SOS Hôtels France** (tel. 47-66-74-37), which will help orient you, book hotels anywhere for the price of the call, and change money. Open daily 7am-8:30pm.

Bus Station: Place Maréchal Leclerc (tel. 47-05-30-49), across from the tourist office. **Les Rapides de Touraine** (tel. 47-46-06-60) runs 4-5 buses per day (service less frequent Sun.) to Amboise (½ hr., 19.40F) and then on to Chenonceau (1 hr., 31F). **Cars Coudert** (tel. 47-59-06-23 in Loches) runs 4 buses per day to Loches (1 hr., 22.50F). **Eurolines** (tel. 47-66-45-56), offers amazing deals on travel throughout Europe, North Africa, and the U.K. (Tours-London round-trip 720F, students 650F. Tours-Casablanca round-trip 1500F.) Most buses with bar and video. Information office at the *gare routière* open Mon.-Sat. 9:30-11:30am and 1:30-6pm.

Bike Rental: At the train station (tel. 47-44-38-01). 47F per day, deposit 300F or ID. **Au Col de Cygne,** 46, rue du Docteur Fournier (tel. 47-46-00-37), 1½km from the tourist office and train station. Walk straight on rue Edouard Valliant off to the side of the station and turn left onto rue Docteur Fournier. Decent 3- and 5-speeds 45F per day, deposit 350F. 10-speeds 52F per day, deposit 350F. Open Tues.-Sat. 9am-noon and 2-7:15pm, Sun.-Mon. 9am-noon. **Grammont Cycles,** 93, av. de Grammont (tel. 47-66-62-89), and **M. Barat,** 156, rue Girandeau (tel. 47-38-63-75) both have cheaper rates. It may prove easier to rent bicycles in smaller towns such as Azay-le-Rideau, since rentals in Tours are often cleaned out July-Aug. However, phone reservations a week in advance will almost ensure you a bike even in summer.

English Bookstores: Bouquinerie du Centre, 20, rue Marceau (tel. 47-05-81-47). Flexible owners are willing to buy, exchange, and sell (10F) used books. Wide selection. Open Mon. 2-7pm, Tues.-Sat. 9am-7pm. For one of the most complete collections of Penguin classics, try **La Boîte à Livres de L'Etranger,** 2, rue du Commerce (47-05-67-29). Open Mon. 2:30-7pm, Tues.-Sat. 9am-noon and 2-7pm.

Laundromat: 20, rue Bernard Palissy (tel. 47-28-64-34), 5 min. from the station. Modern and convenient. Wash 13-20F, dry 2F for 5 min., detergent 3F. Open daily 7am-9pm.

SOS Amitié: Tel. 47-54-54-54. For a friendly call.

Medical Emergency: Tel. 18. **SAMU,** tel. 47-28-15-15. **Hôpital Trousseau,** av. de la République (47-47-47-47).

Police: 14, rue de Clocheville (tel. 47-05-66-60). All-night doctor and pharmacy information.

Accommodations and Camping

Hotels in Tours are both cheap and plentiful, especially, and conveniently, right next to the train station. If you arrive before noon, and it's not a holiday, reservations are never needed. Though the hostel is packed in summer, the *foyer* provides cheap, often private rooms and usually has space in the morning because it accepts neither groups nor reservations.

Auberge de Jeunesse (IYHF), av. d'Arsonval, Parc de Grandmont (tel. 47-25-14-45), 4km from the station. Take bus #2 or 6 from place Jean Jaurès (about 5.50F). Large and dusty rooms, 10-12 beds in each. Adequate kitchen facilities. Lively atmosphere. 45F. Sheets 11F. Breakfast (8-9am) included. Small dinner 33F. Bike rental includes a whopping 2 bikes for 42F per day, deposit 200F. Curfew 10:30am. Reception Feb.-Dec. 14 open 5pm-midnight. Reservations recommended in summer.

Le Foyer, 16, rue Bernard Palissy (tel. 47-05-38-81), across bd. Heurteloup from the tourist office and straight down rue Bernard Palissy. Probably a better deal than the hostel. Centrally located with singles (50F) or doubles (45F), some with terrific views of the cathedral illuminated at night. Good and cheap cafeteria. Accepts both sexes ages 16-25, but they rarely check for age. Breakfast 7F. Office open Mon. afternoon-Sat. morning. Very crowded in July, less so in Aug.

CROUS, Parc de Grandmont (tel. 47-05-17-55). Take bus #1 to Parc Sud (last bus 8:30pm). Rooms available July-Sept. at the university. You must appear in person at Bâtiment A (9am-1pm or 2-5pm). Call ahead. With the steep price (50F), you're better off in a hotel, unless you want to sample student life. You must obtain tickets in advance to eat in the cafeteria (14F).

Hôtel Bretagne, 8, rue Blaise Pascal (tel. 47-05-41-43). The nicest, cleanest of the cheap hotels lining a street west of the station. Singles 65F, Doubles 75F, with shower 75F-108F. Showers 10F. Breakfast 15F.

Mon Hôtel, 40, rue de la Préfecture (tel. 47-05-67-53). From the station, cross bd. Heurteloup to rue de Buffon, and turn right onto rue de la Préfecture. Extreme cleanliness (you can smell the disinfectant from the street) and quaintness. Singles and doubles 80F, with bath 100-120F. Showers 12F. All-you-can-eat breakfast 15F.

Hôtel Grammont, 16, av. de Grammont (tel. 47-05-55-06). *Let's Go* has received rave reviews, and with good reason. Clean and quiet rooms, cozy atmosphere, and friendly English-speaking management. Singles 85F. Doubles 90F, with shower 120F. Breakfast 18F. Often booked in advance in summer. Call for reservation at least 2 days in advance.

Hôtel Vendôme, 24, rue Roger Salengro (tel. 47-64-33-54), 1 block off av. Grammont. Four generations of family make this a homey place. Extensive renovations should be finished by fall 1988 so that rooms will be even more comfortable and so guests will no longer have to take showers separated only by a sheer curtain from the curious teenaged son's bedroom. Singles 68F. Doubles 90F, with shower 95-130F. Showers 15F. Breakfast 18F.

Olympic Hôtel, 74, rue Bernard Palissy (tel. 47-05-10-17). Dark entrance, but rooms are clean. Singles 65-80F. Doubles 72-85F, with shower 110-115F. Breakfast 15F.

Hôtel Le Comté, 51, rue Auguste Comté (tel. 47-05-53-16), just off rue Blaise Pascal. Rooms are haggard. Nonetheless, very agreeable management and quiet location. Singles 56-67F. Doubles 70-96F. Showers 8F. Bath 12F. Breakfast 15F.

Camping: There are dozens of campgrounds within a 20-mile radius, most near châteaux and along the Loire. Pick up a list from the tourist office. **Camping Tours Edouard Peron,** on N152 (tel. 47-54-11-11), is closest to the city. Take bus #6 ("Ste-Radégonde," 5.50F). For information, call 47-54-11-11 or the mayor's office at 47-66-29-94 (*poste 46*). Open May 21-Sept 11.

Food

The Touraine region, the garden of France, is famous for food and wine, but not for bargains. Fortunately, and probably thanks to the large student population, Tours has scores of cheap, but by no means always good, restaurants. Try some of the local fish, especially salmon or trout, with one of the light white wines from Montlouis, Vouvray, or Touraine. Appetizing restaurants line rue Colbert and dot the old quarter, around place de la Lampraie. In summer you can venture to the pedestrian district of Les Halles and explore the wide variety of somewhat pricey restaurants with outdoor seating. For *cuisine tourganelle* that is kinder to the budget, investigate the *traiteurs* who sell prepared food. Every Monday, Tuesday, Thursday, Friday and Sunday from 8 to 9:30am, there is a small fresh produce market at place des Halles. Many other such markets offer flowers, clothing, used goods, etc.

Le Foyer, 16, rue Bernard Palissy. Lively and local, frequented by young French workers who occasionally bring a tape player and broadcast French and American tunes in the cafe section. You *must* purchase a membership card at the foyer office (2F). 4-course menu 29.50F; meat and vegetables 21.50F. Open Sept.-July Mon.-Fri. 11:45am-1:15pm and 7-8pm, Sat.-Sun. 11:45am-1:15pm; Aug. Mon.-Fri. only.

Le Point de Jour, 38bis, av. de Grammont (tel. 47-05-34-00). From the train station, follow rue Gilles and turn left on av. de Grammont. Cordial couple are serious about your eating healthily and cheaply. 3-course vegetarian *menus* at lunch (49F) and dinner (59F) will fuel you all day. Vegetarian *pâté* in pastry (8F). Chemical-free fruit and wine. Store open daily 10am-11pm, meals daily 11:30am-2pm and 7-10pm.

Le Continental, 17, rue Blaise-Pascal, near the train station. An unassuming place with a particularly filling 40F *menu*. Diet/health platter of *crudités* and ham 28F. Open daily noon-2pm and 7-10pm.

Aux Trois Canards, 16, rue de la Rôtisserie (tel. 47-61-58-16), in the *vieille ville*. Elegant, candlelight dinners complete with classical music 25-50F. 4-course *menu* 42F, *boisson comprise*. Open Mon.-Fri. noon-2pm and 7:30-10pm, Sat. 7:30-10pm.

Self-Service Restaurants: Plenty along rue Gilles and near the train station. **Le Marest,** 35, rue Charles Gilles, is more authentic than most with a good selection of entrees, but it is not cheap. Open daily 8:30am-10pm. **Le Ferry,** just around the corner on rue de Bordeaux, is somewhat cheaper. But do yourself a favor and avoid the hot entrées. Open daily 10am-10pm. **Flunch,** Galerie du Métrople, 1, rue Bordeaux, is a shameless chain cafeteria in a pedestrian mall near the station. Filling meals 24-37F.

Sights

Though the old quarter was seriously damaged during World War II, several buildings in the area around rue Briconnet and rue du Change have been preserved. Renaissance houses, some open to the public, dot the quarter. (Pick up an annotated plan from the tourist office.) The **Hôtel Goüin,** 25, rue du Commerce (tel. 47-66-22-32), presents one of the finest examples of a Renaissance facade; don't bother paying to see the archeological collection inside. Flanking rue des Halles, the **Tour de l'Horloge** and the **Tour de Charlemagne** are fragments of the eleventh-century Basilique St-Martin, a huge Romanesque masterpiece that stood on the pilgrimage route to Spain. Enter at 3, rue Descartes. The **Nouvelle Basilique St-Martin,** a turn-of-the-century church of Byzantine inspiration, overlaps the foundation of the old structure, allowing the tomb of St-Martin to remain unmarred. (Open daily 7:30am-noon and 2-6:30pm.) Some of the roads north of the church are lined with fifteenth-century half-timbered houses graced with decorative details.

Just to the east soars **Cathédrale St-Gatien,** possibly Tours's most compelling sight. Just off the south transept, you'll find the tomb of the infant children of Charles VIII, whose stone effigies are guarded by small angels. Farther back, thirteenth-century windows in the chancel portray the gospels in a subtle blue. Be sure to walk around the church to appreciate the exterior details and the flying buttresses—one of which plants itself in the courtyard of a neighboring house, providing a setting for Balzac's cruel novel *Le Curé de Tours*. With the attendant's permission, you can see the graceful cloister adjoining the cathedral. (Open in summer daily until 8pm; in winter until 5:30pm. Closed noon-2pm. Admission 5F.)

A short walk down rue Jules-Simon, the **Musée des Beaux Arts** is housed in the former episcopal palace at 18, place François Sicard (tel. 47-05-68-73). The collection includes works from the Italian Renaissance, several paintings by Delacroix, and one by Rembrandt. The museum's lovely courtyard and gardens make a nice retreat from the rest of town. (Museum open Wed.-Mon. 9am-12:45pm and 2-6pm. Admission 10F, students 5F. Gardens open in summer Fri.-Sun. 9am-noon.) More interesting, the unique **Musée de Compagnonnage,** 8, rue Nationale, Clôitre St-Julien (tel. 47-61-07-93), commemorates the forerunner of the trade union and displays a truly engrossing array of pre-industrial artisan craftworks, including a chocolate violin and wooden shoes large enough for a child to sleep in. (Open Wed.-Mon. same hours as Beaux Arts. Admission 5F, students 2.50F.) Downstairs, the **Musée des Vins de Touraine** (tel. 47-61-07-93) occupies an ancient wine cellar, but you won't get any free samples for your 5F entry fee (students 2.50F). A 15- to 20-minute bus ride from the *centre ville* (bus #7 from place Jean Juarès, 5.50F) will bring you to **Plessis-Les-Tours** (tel. 47-37-22-80), Louis XI's favorite address. The austere brick-and-stone manor does not soar, swoop, or otherwise inspire, but you can see the king's furnished bedroom and examine documents on the castle's history. (Open Feb.-Dec. Wed.-Mon. 10am-noon and 2-5pm.)

Châteaux Near Tours

Something interesting awaits you in every direction from Tours, but you must be flexible. Hitching may be difficult, but if you take bus #2 or 6 out of town to the hostel (near N751), you could get lucky. The best way to visit the châteaux is to combine trains, buses, and bikes with your thumb (see Tours Practical Information). The best way to ease tension when things go wrong is to take advantage of the many *dégustation* opportunities. There are five *caves* in **Vouvray,** just off N152, 9km east of Tours, which is accessible by bus #61 from place Jean Jaurès (Mon.-Sat. 5 per day, 20 min.). **Montlouis,** across the river to the south, is an 11-km hike out of Tours.

Lush **Loches,** 40km south of Tours, once struck fear into the hearts of the enemies of the French kings. Today it makes a nice daytrip for those tired of the tapestries-and-bedrooms châteaux tours. Here, the grim dungeon shares the hilltop with the delicate Renaissance *logis* (residence); both command supreme views of the well-preserved medieval town between. Climb the four walls of the towering eleventh-century **donjon** for the views and an encounter with cawing, defecating birds. Then take the 40-minute tour of the sinister dungeons. Ludovico Sforza, Duke of Milan, spent his captivity here covering every inch of his cell with mystic messages and symbols. Be glad that you're only a visitor. From June to September, you can visit the apartments and the *donjon* with or without a guide; at other times a tour is required. (Open July-Aug. daily 9am-6pm; March 15-June and Sept. 9am-noon and 2-6pm; Oct.-March 14 Thurs.-Tues. 9am-noon and 2-5pm. Admission to castle and dungeon 13F, students 10F.)

The friendly **Office de Tourisme,** in a pavilion near the station on place de la Marne (tel. 47-59-07-98), will help with accommodations. (Open in summer daily 9:15am-8pm.) In July and August they sponsor walking tours of the illuminated medieval city. (Mon.-Wed. at 9:30pm. Tickets 15F.) **Tour St-Antoine,** 2, rue des Moulins (tel. 47-59-01-06), is a two-star with a few less-expensive rooms (80F and 95F). The **Camping Municipal,** rue Guintefol (tel 47-59-05-91), is a beautiful site with an indoor swimming pool. Take N143 south, then follow route de Châteauroux to Stade Général Leclerc. (8F per person. Open May-Sept.) For lunch or dinner try the refreshing and shaded terrace of **La Gerbe d'Or,** 22, rue Balzac (tel. 47-59-06-38), below the castle on the way into town (4-course *menu* 52F; a more elegant and varied *menu* begins at 72F). **Le Turlupin** (tel. 47-59-05-91) serves omelettes (20-30F), salads (25F), and wonderful dessert crepes (15-20F; open Mon.-Sat.).

Verdant **Villandry** maintains fantastic formal gardens—three terraces of sculpted shrubs and flowers. Most interesting is the intermediate terrace, where knee-high hedges are arranged in various patterns: a Maltese Cross, a Croix de Lorraine, and a charming reproduction of the **Carte du Tendre** with its four types of love (tender, courtly, passionate, and flighty). You may wish to take the uninteresting 40-minute tour just to view the 15-minute slide show presented at the end. The 140-plus slides include some spectacular shots of the castle and its gardens during all four seasons. (Open March 15-Nov. 15 daily 9am-noon and 2-6pm; gardens open year-round 9am-7pm. Admission to gardens 17F, students 11F; admission to the castle an additional 7F, students 6F.)

Ussé's pointed towers, white turrets, and chimneys inspired the story of *Sleeping Beauty.* Surrounded by the thick woods of the Forêt de Chinon, the fifteenth-century château rises above terraced gardens and the Indre River. You don't have to take the tour to see models of the Sleeping Beauty story (complete with wicked queen) in eighteenth- and nineteenth-century French costume. (Château open May

3-Sept. daily 9am-noon and 2-7pm; March 15-May 2 and Oct. 9am-noon and 2-6pm. Admission 31F, students 19F.) The fields opposite the cathedral make a great riverside picnic spot.

In its gracious pastoral setting, raised on one of a series of islands in the Indre River, **Azay-le-Rideau** rivals Chenonceau in beauty. Built according to the whims of François I's corrupt financier (who was away embezzling in Italy), the château embodies the purity and vigor of the Renaissance. Italian influence shaped the open loggia on the court and the parallel staircases. The interior glistens with light from the reflecting pool. Unfortunately, the only way to see the rooms is to take the obligatory tour in French that is given by guides faint from boredom and the abominable crowding. Go early, especially in high season, to catch them in their prime. (Château open daily July-Aug. 9:15am-6:30pm; March 28-June and Sept. 9:15am-noon and 2-6:30pm; Oct.-March 27 9am-noon and 2-5pm. Admission 18F, students 10F.) The *son et lumière* performance, like Chenonceau's, allows for nocturnal garden-wandering but is jazzed up with costumed actors in boats. (Shows May-July at 10:30pm; Aug.-Sept. at 10pm. 25F, children 20F. Information tel. 47-61-61-23, *poste* 3162.)

The château is a 2-km walk from Azay-le-Rideau's train station. Turn right outside the station, then left on D57 for 2km. Azay's **Syndicat d'Initiative,** 26, rue Gambetta (tel. 47-43-34-40), will help with accommodations, few of which are cheap. Ask about buses to **Saché,** Balzac's home, located 7km east of Azay. (Open March 14-Sept. daily 9am-noon and 2-6pm; Oct.-March 15 Thurs.-Tues. only.) **Camping Parc du Sabot** (tel. 47-45-42-72) is a large, two-star site with tennis courts and kayak and canoe rentals on the banks of the Indre, across from the château. (8F per person, showers included; 5F per tent. Open May-Nov.) Rent 10-speed bikes to visit Ussé and Villandry at the station or at **Le Provost,** 13, rue Carnot (tel. 47-43-30-94; 20F per ½-day, 32F per day; open Tues.-Sat. 8am-noon and 2-7pm).

Langeais, feudal and forbidding, was one of the last medieval fortresses built for defense. Constructed from 1465 to 1469 for Louis XI, Langeais guarded the route from Brittany. Brittany's union with the crown was celebrated here in 1491 with the marriage of Charles VIII of France and Anne de Bretagne. The tour includes a walk along the upper fortifications, whose stone slabs, when drawn back, reveal holes for hurling the proverbial boiling oil, pitch, and stones at attackers. In the small château courtyard stand the ruins of the original eleventh-century fortress.

Several trains per day stop in Langeais on their way to either Saumur or Tours. The **train station** (tel. 47-20-50-50) is a ¼-km walk from the château; signs will point you in the right direction. You can rent **bikes** at the station for 47F per day, with a 300F deposit. Langeais is a fairly easy 10-km hitch northward from Azay-le-Rideau on D57. The *syndicat* is at place du 14 Juillet (tel 47-96-58-22). The town is small and has little in the way of indoor accommodations, but there is a **Camping Municipal** on N152, 1km from the château (tel. 47-96-85-80; 4.50F per person, 4.70F per tent; open June-Sept. 15).

Chinon

Built into the side of a hill, Chinon spins cobblestone and rutted-dirt streets up and around the hillside to its château's ruins. Having ducked both heavy tourism and heavy industry, Chinon's intrigue lies in its streetlife. The tree-lined Vienne glides peacefully through the middle of town; the restored *vieille ville,* birthplace of the great sixteenth-century comic writer François Rabelais (in whose *Gargantua* and *Pantagruel* Chinon's white wine is celebrated), presents a delightful maze of alleyways, chimneys, and medieval timber-frame houses, some with fine sculptural detail. Chinon's hostel is one of the best in France. You will find good camping, and an ideal spot for repose. Plus, Chinon has train connections and bike rentals to get you to Azay, Ussé, Villandry, and even Saumur—in the unlikely event that you feel like leaving.

Orientation and Practical Information

From the train station, walk west along rue du Docteur Labussière, bear left onto rue du 11 Novembre, and continue straight along quai Jeanne d'Arc for the center of town, which will be on your right before the bridge. Chinon's shopping square is place Général de Gaulle, a small affair that gives onto rue Voltaire to the west and the unparalleled *vieille ville*. The château perches atop the medieval reverie of rue Haute St-Maurice, a continuation of rue Voltaire.

Office de Tourisme: 12, rue Voltaire (tel. 47-93-17-85), about 15 min. from the station. Go west along the river to the Rabelais statue, north through place Général de Gaulle, and then right on rue Voltaire. Wonderfully helpful, scatterbrained staff, presided over by a woman who loves to arrange daytrips by bus to nearby châteaux. Will suggest out-of-the-way destinations, book hotel rooms for the price of the call, and change money when banks are closed. Rents a few bikes. Open June 15-Sept. 15 Mon.-Sat. 9am-7pm, Sun. 10am-12:15pm; Sept. 16-June 14 Mon.-Sat. only.

Currency Exchange: Crédit Lyonnais, quai Jeanne d'Arc (tel. 47-93-02-65), just before the bridge. Open Tues.-Fri. 8:35am-12:25pm and 2-5:30pm, Sat. 8:35am-12:25pm and 2-4pm.

Post Office: 10, quai Jeanne-d'Arc (tel. 47-93-12-08). **Postal Code:** 37500. Open Mon.-Fri. 8am-noon and 1:30-5:45pm, Sat. 9am-noon.

Train Station: Av. Gambetta (tel. 47-93-11-04), at av. du Docteur Labussière. To Tours (2 per day, 1 hr., 33F). SNCF buses, not trains, connect Chinon to Thonars (2 per day, 1¼ hr., 33F); Eurailpasses are valid.

Bus Station: Place Jeanne-d'Arc (tel. 47-46-04-96 in Tours). From the train station, walk west on av. du Docteur Labussière to quai Jeanne d'Arc. To Tours (Mon.-Sat. 2-3 per day, 1 hr., one way 33F, round-trip 48F), Ussé (1 per day, SNCF railpasses valid), and Azay-le-Rideau (2 per day).

Bike Rental: At tourist office. 25F per day, deposit 100F. At train station. 47F per day, deposit 300F or credit card. You can return to Tours or Langeais. Free transport of bikes on many trains. Open daily 10am-7:30pm.

Medical Emergency: Clinique Jeanne d'Arc, rue du Pavé Neuf (tel. 47-93-17-78), off rue de Tours. If you can't make it there, call tel. 18, and the paramedics will stop by.

Police: 1, rue Voltaire (tel. 47-93-08-30, *poste* 320). Can tell you the location of the nightly *pharmacie de garde.*

Police Emergency: Tel. 17.

Accommodations, Camping, and Food

Bargains are scarce among Chinon hotels so arrive early, call ahead, or plan on staying in the youth hostel. The quiet hostel is uncrowded, relaxed, and worth a try even if you don't have an IYHF card.

Auberge de Jeunesse (IYHF), rue Descartes (tel. 47-93-10-48 or try 47-93-21-37), about ½ km from the center of town and only a 5-min. walk from the train station. Turn left onto av. Gambetta and then right onto rue Descartes. A combination youth hostel, *foyer,* and youth cultural center, this large, modern building has clean rooms with 4-6 beds apiece. Not at all crowded like most Loire hostels in summer. Good kitchen facilities and quiet atmosphere. 33F. Sheets 11F. Lock-out 2-6pm. Reception open 6-10:30pm. Curfew 10:30pm, easily negotiable.

Hôtel le Point du Jour, 102, quai Jeanne-d'Arc (tel. 47-93-07-20), 5 min. from train station. Shuttered rooms are fairly clean but dark. Singles and doubles 80F, with showers 120-140F. Showers 12F. Breakfast 16F.

Hôtel du Progrès, 19, rue du Raineau (tel. 47-93-16-40), a 15- to 20-min. haul from the center, across the river. Picturesque flower-boxed house is clean, airy, friendly, but a little more expensive. Singles and doubles from 90F. Showers 10F. Breakfast 19F.

Le Jeanne-d'Arc, 11, rue Voltaire (tel. 47-93-02-85), above a cafe opposite the tourist office. Surprisingly quiet and extremely clean. Singles and doubles with shower 120F. Triples and quads 210F. Showers 10F. Exceptionally buttery croissants at breakfast 18F. Call 2 days in advance in summer.

Camping: **Camping Municipale de Chinon,** right across the river at Ile-Auger (tel. 47-93-08-35), off RN749. Pleasant sites in an excellent location 10-15 min. from the tourist office. Almost worth a visit solely for its view of the château on moonlit nights. 6F per person, 4.50F per tent. Hot showers 5F.

The old quarter wins it hands down for style and ambience, though prices can be high. Not just another flash-in-the-pan *crêperie,* **Du Grand Carroi,** 30, rue du Grand Carroi, just off rue Voltaire, fries up great crêpes for the price (20-30F) in a suitably dim setting. (Open Tues.-Sun. noon-2pm and 7:30-11pm.) If you'd rather eat on a shaded terrace, try **Les Années 30,** 78, rue Voltaire (tel. 47-93-37-18), for authentic French cuisine. (4-course *menus* 65 and 95F. Open Thurs.-Tues.)

Sights

You can let your imagination recreate the forlorn **Château de Chinon,** now a cliff top of ruins. This hulking château was never destroyed but fell into ruin through neglect under Cardinal Richelieu and later Napoleon. It was originally built by Henry II of England to protect his holdings in France, but passed into French hands when King John (Lackland) lost it to King Philippe in 1205.

There were three parts of this eminently defensible château: the main **Château de Milieu, Château du Coudray** to the west, and **Fort St-Georges** to the east. The last no longer exists; it once stood on the hill next to the present-day entrance. An optional guided tour (in French or English) leads through the **Logis Royaux,** partially reconstructed since 1970. The *logis* contain some medieval tapestry and sculpture, but the focus is on history: In almost every room, a genealogical chart or official document is on display. The ruined great hall contains a plaque marking the site where Joan of Arc prophetically recognized Charles VII, then the beleaguered Dauphin, in 1429.

After the tour, you are free to wander around the impressive fortifications. Note the king's secret entrance, a narrow staircase leading into the *logis* from the ravine separating the châteaux. The only other entrance was through the fifteenth-century **Tour de l'Horloge,** which now houses a rather uninspired Musée Jeanne d'Arc. (Château open daily March 15-April 9am-noon and 2-6pm; May-Sept. 9am-6pm; Oct.-March 14 9am-noon and 2-5pm. Admission 15F, students 10F.)

Chapelle St-Radagonde, a twelfth-century ruin, is about a 25-minute walk from the center. Follow rue Jean-Jacques Rousseau onto a mountain road lined with *maisons troglodytiques,* comfortable caves cut in the chalk where families live year-round. Behind is an elaborate complex of caves now containing regional art, tools, and utensils. The proprietor, who speaks inspired English, will spend 40 minutes guiding one visitor. The chapel is open only when the proprietor is there (usually throughout all school vacations—about July-Aug. 15), so check with the *syndicat* before hiking. (Open daily 10am-7pm. Admission 8F.)

The **Musée du Vieux Chinon,** rue Voltaire, has collections of local pottery, model boats, and lace bonnets, among other things. (Open 10am-noon and 3-7pm. Admission 10F, students 5F.) The **Cave Plouzeau,** 94, rue Voltaire (tel. 47-93-16-34), conducts tours and pours out some of their superb Chinon white wine. (Open Tues.-Sun. 10am-noon and 2-6pm.) You may also want to visit the kitschy but entertaining **Musée Animé de Vin,** 12, rue Voltaire, which illustrates the wine-making process with "automatons" who lace their speech with Rabelais quotations and end with the exhortation "drink always and never die." Shows are given in both English and French. (Open Fri.-Wed. 10am-noon and 2-6pm. Admission 12F, including a glass of Chinon wine.) There is a large, all-day **market** every Thursday in place Hôtel de Ville. On the first weekend of August, Chinon holds its popular **Marché Médiéval** with persons in period costume—medieval peddlers and artisans crowd the streets, bars offer food and drinks under the trees, and those in period costume may explore the château and town museums at will. A ticket for various activities costs 35F but the tariff is waived if you're dressed for the occasion (anything vaguely evoking the Middle Ages).

Saumur

Immortalized in Balzac's novel *Eugénie Grandet,* Saumur bears few traces of the provincial haven from which Eugénie watched life go by. The vines that made old Grandet rich, along with mushrooms, still provide the town's main source of income, but the heavy traffic on the cobblestone streets, brought by urban sprawl, adds a distinctly modern clang to the city. Saumur offers a variety of sights and museums, many of them of a horsey bent because of the resident *Cadre Noir* equestrian corps. This agreeable town merits a couple of days' exploration.

Orientation and Practical Information

Frequent trains running between Nantes and Tours serve Saumur; destinations father away often require changes, usually at Tours. The station is on the northern bank of the Loire, and most of the town is on the southern bank. From the station, turn right, cross the bridge to Ile d'Offard, and continue across a second bridge (the old pont Cessart) to the city center, or take local bus A to place Bilange, where the tourist office is. From there, rue d'Orléans runs south to rue Maréchal Leclerc. To the right of place Bilange, off rue Dacier, lies place St-Pierre. Rue St-Nicolas stretches westward, parallel to rue Beaurepaire, where the second tourist office is located.

Office de Tourisme: Place de la Bilange (tel. 41-51-03-06). Helpful staff will book beds (3F), change money (commission 4%), and give information on tours of châteaux and vineyards. Most speak English. Open June 15-Sept. 15 Mon.-Sat. 9:15am-7pm, Sun. 10:30am-12:30pm and 3-6:30pm; Sept. 16-June 14 Mon.-Sat 9:15am-12:30pm and 2-6pm. **Branch office,** 25, rue Beaurepaire (tel. 41-51-03-06), in *centre ville.* Same services. Equally warm staff. Open June 15-Sept. 15 Mon.-Sat. 9am-7pm; Sept. 16-June 14 Mon.-Sat. 9:15am-12:30pm and 2-6pm.

Currency Exchange: Crédit Lyonnais, rue de Gaulle (tel. 41-67-64-01). Accepts all forms of traveler's checks (commission 24F). Open Mon.-Fri. 9:20am-12:30pm and 2:30-6:30pm.

Post Office: Rue Volney (tel. 41-51-22-77). Have your Poste Restante mail addressed to "Saumur Volney," or it will be delivered to the main office on rue des Près (tel. 41-50-13-00), ½ hr. out of town. **Postal code:** 49400. Open Mon.-Fri. 8am-7pm, Sat. 8am-noon.

Train Station: Av. David d'Angers (tel. 41-67-50-50). From place Belange in *centre ville,* take bus A toward St-Lambert or Chernin Vert. 11 trains per day to Tours (¾ hr., 39F) and Angers (20 min., 30F). The station can arrange connections to more distant destinations such as Sables d'Olonne (1 per day, 3-5 hr., 123F).

Bus Station: Place St-Nicolas (tel. 41-51-27-29), on the southern banks in front of the church. Go 2 blocks west of pont Cessart, then 1 more block south. To Doué-la-Fontaine (2-3 per day, ½ hr.), Angers (4 per day, 1½ hr.), and Fontevraud (3 per day, 35 min.). 3 or 4 buses per day to Thonars, Chinon, Angers, and Tours. **Local buses** depart from place Roosevelt (tel. 41-51-11-87); tickets 8.40F, in carnet 4.20F.

Bike Rental: At the train station. 37F per ½-day, 47F per day, deposit 300F. **Jaquet,** 4, rue St-Nicholas. 35F per day with ID as deposit. Open Tues.-Sun. 9am-12:15pm and 2:15-7pm. **Brison,** 49, rue Maréchal Leclerc (tel. 41-51-02-09). 25F per ½-day, 35F per day. Open Tues.-Sun. 8am-noon and 2-7pm.

Laundromat: 12, rue Maréchal Leclerc. Modern and efficient. Wash 15F, dry 2F per 5 min. Open daily 7am-9:30pm.

Hospital: Centre Hospitalier, rue Seigneur (tel. 41-53-25-00).

Medical Emergency: SAMU, Tel. 41-48-44-22. Ambulances.

Police: Rue Montesquieu (tel. 41-51-04-32), just after the Hôtel de Ville.

Police Emergency: Tel. 17.

Accommodations and Camping

Good values are painfully scarce, and calling ahead in summer is wise.

Auberge de Jeunesse (IYHF), rue de Verdeu (tel. 41-67-45-00, on Ile d'Offard. From the train station, turn right onto av. David d'Angers, turn right again onto rue de Rouen, cross the bridge, and take the 2nd left onto rue Montcel, which becomes rue de Verdeu. The hostel is located on a delightful island at the end of the road next to a 3-star campsite. Good kitchen facilities and washing machine. Reception open 8-10am and 5-10pm. 38F per night. Sheets 17F. Breakfast 12F. Lockout 10am-5pm. Curfew 10pm; ask for a key if you plan to be out late. Reservations recommended in summer.

Hôtel de Volney, 1, rue Volney (tel. 41-51-25-41). Quaint, pretty rooms near *centre ville.* Singles and doubles 100F, with shower 155-175F. Showers 10F. Breakfast 20F.

Hôtel Bretagne, 55, rue St-Nicholas (tel. 41-51-26-38). Noisy location but attractive rooms with wood floors and firm mattresses. Rooms 85F-120F, with shower 150F. Showers 15F. Breakfast 15F. Open Sept. 16-Aug. Mon.-Sat.

Camping: Camping Municipal de L'Ile d'Offard, at the end of rue Verdeu (tel. 41-67-45-00), on Ile d'Offard next to the hostel. A 3-star rapidly becoming a 4-star. 11F per person, 25F per site, vehicle included. Open Mon.-Fri. 8am-noon and 2-10pm, Sat.-Sun. 8-10am and 5-10pm.

Food

Saumur's proud name graces a fine white, a delicious rosé, and an earthy red wine. The *caves* are just outside town; ask the *syndicat* about tours and *dégustations.* Thinly sliced *champignons* (mushrooms) marinated in wine are a local specialty. Good restaurants peep out from the streets around place St-Pierre. Small fresh produce markets line place de la République (Sat. morning), and av. de Gaulle (Thurs. morning). A modern, covered market, **Les Halles,** place St-Pierre, opens daily (7am-12:30pm and 3-7pm).

Auberge St-Pierre, 6, place St-Pierre (tel. 41-51-26-25), 2 blocks northwest of the château. A warm and popular place that serves up 42F and 100F *menus,* both with a wide variety of entrees. Open daily noon-10pm.

Le Pullman, 52, rue d'Orléans (tel. 41-51-31-79). Made to look like a train car to remind you of those long-distance journeys; the booths even have overhead luggage racks. The place specializes in fish, with good 50F and 120F *menus,* and fish or meat *à la carte* (32-55F). Open Tues.-Sat. noon-2pm and 7-10pm, Sun. noon-2pm, Mon. 7-10pm.

Le Calèche, rue St-Nicolas. Popular and crowded at night. Salads 25-40F, omelettes 20-30F, *galettes* 11-32F, crêpes 11-30F. Open Tues.-Sun. noon-1:30pm and 7-9:30pm.

Le Quichenotte, 41, rue Fourrier, hidden away on the other side of place St-Pierre. Imaginative crêpe combinations at low prices. The 45F *menu* includes 2 crêpes, meat, and salad. Open Thurs.-Tues. noon-2pm and 7-9:30pm.

Sights

The picture-book fourteenth-century **château** cuts a pretty profile above the city. Designed for defense, it has fewer fine touches than its Loire Valley counterparts although it is better preserved. Duke René of Anjou tried to make it more comfortable in the fifteenth century, and it proved useful to the Protestant governor of the town during the Wars of Religion and to the members of Saumur's cavalry school, who resisted the German army in 1940. Although the castle lacks grace, plain and simple, the museums within more than compensate.

The **Musée des Arts Décoratifs** has assembled a fascinating collection of medieval painting and sculpture, fifteenth- and sixteenth-century tapestries, and faïence. The **Musée du Cheval** upstairs will interest equestrian enthusiasts. The guided tour, in English by special request, blitzes through both museums in an hour, locking doors behind it; ask the guide if you want to see anything in more detail afterwards. If you don't mind shaky staircase steps, climb the **Tour de Guët** for a view of the environs. (Château and museums open June 15-Sept. 15 daily 9am-6:30pm; Sept. 16-June 14 9am-11:30am and 2-6pm. Admission 18F, students 10F.)

Saumur's tradition as an equestrian center goes back to its establishment in 1763 as the royal training ground for the cavalry. The French cavalry still trains here, though in 1943 the school was enlarged to house "modern cavalry," or artillery. About 10 minutes from the center of town stands the palatial **Ecole de Cavalerie,** founded in 1814, where the nation's elite equestrian order, the Cadre Noir, resides. Competitions and public presentations are held periodically throughout the summer. Contact the *syndicat* for dates. Nearby, the **Musée des Blindés** (tank museum) amuses only artillery buffs. (Open Mon.-Fri. 9-11:30am and 2-5:30pm, Sat. 10am-noon and 3-6pm. Admission 17F.) Real French soldiers drive real tanks around the buildings near the museum like bumper cars.

Every year in late July, the cavalry school shows off in the celebrated **Carrousel,** featuring jumping, dressage, and stunts. A chilling three-hour military revue follows the two-hour horse show. (Tickets 35-75F.) Every week in July and August various performances occur at place de l'Hôtel de Ville.

Near Saumur

Abbaye de Fontevraud enjoyed quiet fame as a monastic center for royalty and nobility from its founding in the eleventh century until the Revolution. More than half of the governing abbesses were of royal blood. The guided tour leads through the cupola-capped abbey church with the remains of the tombs of the Plantagenets: Henry II, Eleanor of Aquitaine, Richard Coeur-de-Lion, and Isabelle of Angoulême, the wife of King John of England. The original tombs were destroyed during the Revolution; afterwards the British government repeatedly but unsuccessfully sought the transfer of the royal remains to Westminster. The Plantagenets, the French government maintains, were Dukes of Anjou first and kings of England second. The church is a superb Romanesque structure with two cloisters alongside. As elaborate as the tombs and church is the enormous, octagonal, tower-capped kitchen, the twenty-chimneyed **Tour Evraud.** For a decade, the abbey has also hosted during the month of July the **Centre Culturel de l'Ouest de la France,** an institute that brings art and architecture exhibits, concerts, and plays to this historic setting. Call 41-51-73-52 for reservations and tickets (30-100F). (Abbey open June-Sept. 15 Wed.-Mon. 9am-7pm; Sept. 16-Oct. Wed.-Mon. 9:30am-12:30pm and 2-6pm. Admission 14F, students 8F.) Three **buses** per day run from Saumur to Fontevraud (about 15km); there are also buses from Saumur and Chinon to Montsoreau (4km away).

A daytrip to the countryside allows you to visit the local wine and mushroom *caves.* Most are located 3km west of Saumur on D751 in St-Hilaire-St-Florent; pick up a list at the *syndicat.* (Most *caves* open Mon.-Sat. 9-11:30am and 2-5:30pm.) A bit farther along D751, the **Musée du Champignon** organizes tours through some of the *caves* where mushrooms are grown. Originally mined for stone to build the nearby châteaux, the *caves* now grow 70% of France's mushrooms in about 500km of underground tunnels. (Open mid-March to mid-Nov. daily 10am-12:30pm and 2-5:30pm. Admission and obligatory tour 11F, students 8F.) Take the local bus from place Roosevelt to St-Hilaire-St-Florent, and walk the 1km from the last stop.

Angers

Guarding the western gateway to the château region, the massive stone walls of Angers once daunted potential attackers of the Dukes of Anjou; today they cringe in the face of an urban assault fueled by some 200,000 inhabitants. Angers retains little more than its château and cathedral from its illustrious past as the center of the flourishing duchy of Anjou. Today, this bland, boulevard-marked city has little to captivate the visitor except a multitude of cheap hotels.

To get to the marvelous château, follow rue de la Gare to rue Talot onto bd. du Roi-René, on which you continue left for a few blocks. The **château** was built by the dukes of Angers at the beginning of the thirteenth century. It narrowly escaped destruction during the Wars of Religion, when Henry III ordered its demolition; fortunately, he died before his plans were carried out. The 3- to 5-meter gray walls are collared by a deep moat that has been drained and planted with a formal garden. Most of the buildings on the inside were constructed during the fifteenth-century reign of Anjou's last and greatest duke, René le Bon, who not only commanded an empire that included Sicily, Piedmont, and Lorraine, but also found the time to write several romances and volumes of poetry. An exhibition of his work is housed in the small Gothic chapel.

Angers' richest attraction, the **Tapisseries de l'Apocalypse,** a 75-panel representation of the Book of Revelation, was woven of wool and gold thread from 1375 to 1380. Recognized as a masterpiece of European medieval art, the tapestry is noted for the consistency of its figures, the flamboyance of its multi-headed lions and serpents, and the graphic dialogue attributed to its characters. (Château open April-June 9am-noon and 2-6:30pm; July-Sept. 9am-6:30pm; Oct.-May 9:30am-noon and 2-5:30pm. Admission 24F, students 12.50F.) The tapestry was originally housed in the **Cathédrale d'Angers,** on rue St-Maurice in *vieille ville,* and several of the works still remain here. Inside, notice the Angevin vaults and the two rose windows that seem to unify the cathedral's interior as they reflect each other across the transept. (Open daily 6:45am-7pm.)

The **train station,** rue de la Gare (tel. 41-88-50-50), accommodates many trains traveling to and from Saumur (½ hr., 31F), Tours (1 hr., 60F), Orléans (2¼ hr., 248F), and Paris-Austerlitz (2¾ hr., 150F). **Bikes** can be rented at the train station (47F per day, deposit 300F). **Buses** leave about twice per day for many nearby locations from the *gare routière* at place de la République (tel. 41-88-59-25). In front of the station is the **Office de Tourisme** (tel. 41-87-72-50), which organizes trips to châteaux, changes money (commission 15F for cash, 20F for traveler's checks), and makes hotel reservations (5F). (Open June-Sept. Mon.-Sat. 9am-8pm; Oct.-March Mon.-Sat. 9am-noon and 2-7pm.) The **main office,** place Kennedy (tel. 41-88-69-93), performs the same services and employs an English-speaking staff. (Open June-Sept. Mon.-Sat. 9am-7pm, Sun. 10:30am-6:30pm; Oct.-March 9am-noon and 2-7pm.) The **post office** is at rue Franklin-Roosevelt (tel. 41-88-45-47), near the cathedral. Poste Restante mail should be addressed "Angers-Ralliement"; otherwise it will be delivered to the rue Bamako office, a half-hour walk south of town. Angers's **postal code** is 49000.

Even in summer, unless you happen to arrive on a holiday, getting a place for the night is not a problem. Space-age accommodations and extensive sports facilities make the bus ride (#6 to Accueil Lac de Maine, 5F) worth it at the **Centre d'Accueil du Lac de Maine,** route de Pruviers (tel. 41-48-57-01), which offers singles for 50F and breakfast for 13F. Call ahead to see if there's space (open June 15-Sept. 15). To reach the **Foyers des Jeunes Travailleurs,** rue Darwin (tel. 41-48-14-55), take bus #6 (*direction* "Val-de-Maine") or #10 (*direction* "Beaucouze") to Bill. There are cheaper prices (34F per night), but not as many amenities (open July-Aug.). Near the bus station are clean rooms at family-run **Les Négociants,** 2, rue de la Roë (tel. 41-87-70-03). (Singles and doubles 80F, with shower 100-125F.) Just across the street from the train station is **La Coupe d'Or,** 5, rue de la Gare (tel. 41-88-45-02), with small but comfy rooms for 80-90F, with shower 130F. Call ahead in summer. There are two campgrounds close to Angers. The best, with a lake and sandy beach, is **Camping du Lac de Maine** (tel. 41-73-05-03), right next to the Centre d'Accueil. Almost as nice is **Camping du Parc de la Haye** (tel. 41-69-33-63), 4km out of Angers by bus #3 to Val d'Or, with a pond and riding facilities close by (open June 15-Sept. 15).

The pleasant pedestrian district around place Romain has many enticing sidewalk cafes, *pâtisseries,* and *charcuteries.* Angers offers many inexpensive dining options. Try **La Treille,** 12, rue Moutault (tel. 41-88-45-51), for an original 52F *menu* near the château. (Open Mon.-Sat. noon-2pm and 7-9pm.) The best of the restaurants near the train station is **Le Signal,** rue de la Gare (tel. 41-87-49-41), which serves salads (25-35F) and a 49F *menu.* (Open daily noon-2pm and 7-9pm.)

Poitou-Charentes

From the wide, flat expanses of Les Sables d'Olonne to the mountainous, sandy slopes of the Dune du Pilat, the beaches of Poitou-Charentes are blessed with more hours of sun per year than any other part of France except the Mediterranean coast. In summer, hordes of Anglophones invade the shores of the region that once struggled to keep the English at bay, while other determined tourists stalk the wineries of Bordeaux and Cognac in quest of the ideal free sample.

Inland, the Charente River lazily threads its way through medieval hilltop towns, past red-tiled roofs and fertile vineyards. Superb Roman ruins, including an amphi-theater, grace Saintes, one of the Empire's most important outposts. It was during the eleventh and twelfth centuries, however, that the region attained its greatest prosperity and acquired its most distinctive architectural profile—its Romanesque churches.

During this period, medieval pilgrims, shepherded by Cluny's Benedictine works, traveled through the region on their way to the shrine of St-Jacques de Compostelle in Spain. The pilgrims required abundant sanctuaries in which to rest their weary feet and revitalize their devotion, hence the myriad churches that dot the country-side.

The conical towers and closely ornamented facades of Poitiers and Angoulême and the dark crypt of Saintes's Eglise St-Eutrope prove that round arches lack only the elevation, not the elegance, of their pointed Gothic successors. In Bordeaux, Romanesque gives way to a scarcely surpassable Gothic style: Eglise St-Michel, for instance, unfurls a virtual catalogue of flamboyance.

Possession of medieval Aquitaine was batted from one side of the stormy channel to the other at the behest of the beautiful, powerful, and canny Eleanor of Aquitaine. Troubadours' songs, legends, and historical documents record the remarkable life of this heiress, who first married France's Louis IX and then divorced him to marry young Henry Plantagenet, the new King of England. Henry brought Maine, Anjou, and Normandy to the union and their newly aggrandized realms exceeded those of the rival French king. Aquitaine, one of the finest and most contested dowries in history, did not fall into the hands of Philippe Auguste during the reign of Henry's incompetent son, King John. For more than a hundred years the region remained in English hands—long enough for the English to acquire a taste for claret (their name for red Bordeaux wine). Aquitaine served as an English base during the Hundred Years' War, before Joan of Arc indirectly secured it for France. In the seventeenth century, after the Wars of Religion, the Protestant Huguenots of the port city of La Rochelle sought English help against the machinations of the Catholic Cardinal Richelieu, who, in spite of an English fleet nearby, besieged the city and reduced it to obedience and a century of obscurity. The coastal cities re-vived only in the eighteenth century, when trade with the Canadian colonies brought unparalleled wealth. The ties with French Canada still remain: This area actively supported the Québécois independence movement a few years back. Though the port industry remains important, tourism has now become a major con-cern for the coastal towns and islands, and travelers throng the beaches and camp-grounds all summer long.

Trains in Poitou-Charentes run efficiently and frequently to all major towns. Hitching and cycling are enjoyable ways of seeing the countryside, and local tourist offices can advise you on rural accommodations. For a vacation of a different sort, consider traveling by boat down one of the region's main rivers, the Clain or the Charente. (Daytrips average 65F; inquire at the *syndicats* in Saintes and Bordeaux.)

An intriguing array of food awaits the visitor. Shellfish comes fresh from the coast; *farci* (a stuffed-meat dish), *canard* (duck), and *chabichou* (a rich goat cheese) are inland specialties. The most famous drink here is not wine but blended brandy from Cognac. You might also try *pineau,* an aged mixture of cognac and either grape or pear juice.

Poitiers

A city on a hill above the rivers Clain and Boivre, Poitiers has attracted invaders, settlers, and visitors for centuries. From the ramparts of this "balcony" town, you can see much of Poitou, including Poitier's twentieth-century sprawl. The center of town, however, preserves the flavor of the *ancienne ville;* recent archeological excavations have unearthed a Bronze Age fortress here. Poitiers eventually became a major outpost of the Roman Empire. From the tenth to the fifteenth century, it was ruled by the rich and powerful Counts of Poitou and Dukes of Aquitaine. A university was established by Charles VII in 1432, and subsequently Poitiers's artistic and intellectual life flourished. Today, the city bustles with the activity of 16,000 university students, and retains the grandeur symbolized by its old Romanesque architecture.

Orientation and Practical Information

Poitiers is neatly enclosed by train tracks to the west and a semi-circular formation of the River Clain to the east. The city's vitality is centered around the stores and cafes about **place Maréchal Leclerc** and **place Charles de Gaulle,** 3 blocks north. The center of town is a 15-minute hike from the train station. The snazzy, mechanical billboard across the street from the station dispenses excellent maps for 2F. Buses #1,2,3,7,8 and 16 run from the station to the Hôtel de Ville in the center of town. From the station, cross the street to bd. Solférino, which curves off the hill to the left. Climb the stairs, take rue Arthur Ranc to the post office, and cross the street, heading up where rue Arthur Ranc becomes rue de la Marne. Turn left on rue Claveurier (no street sign; just take the first left away from the store Aux Printemps), and left again on rue des Grandes Ecoles for the *syndicat.*

Syndicat d'Initiative: 8, rue des Grandes Ecoles (tel. 49-41-21-24). Guided walking tours of the city in summer at 10am and 3pm (20F, students 10F). Helpful staff and plenty of free brochures, including a city map. Hotel-hunting service 10F in town, 10F in the *département.* Open Mon.-Fri. 9am-noon and 1:30-6pm, Sat. 9am-noon and 2-6pm.

Office Départemental du Tourisme: 11, rue Victor Hugo (tel. 49-41-58-22), near place Maréchal Leclerc. Very helpful for information on the town and its surroundings. Open Mon.-Fri. 9am-noon and 2-5:30pm, Sat. 9am-noon.

Centre d'Information Jeunesse (CIJ): 64, rue Gambetta (tel. 49-88-64-37), near the Hôtel de Ville on a pedestrian street. A veritable gold mine of clues on places to stay, cultural activities, sports, and employment, even a ride board for hitching. Free maps. If you're under 26, bring photo, ID, and 60F for your *carte jeune* (discounts on everything everywhere). Open Mon.-Fri. 10am-7pm, Sat. 10am-noon and 2-6pm.

Student Travel: Agence Touristique de l'Ouest, 2, rue Claveurier (tel. 49-01-84-84). Open Mon.-Fri. 9am-noon and 2-6:30pm, Sat. 9am-noon and 2-6pm.

Currency Exchange: On Sat. try the **post office** or **Crédit Agricole,** 65, rue Gambetta (tel. 49-41-02-34). Open Tues.-Fri. 9am-12:30pm and 2-6pm, Sat. 9am-12:30pm and 2-4pm.

Post Office: 16, rue Arthur Ranc (tel. 49-01-83-80). **Telephones** and **currency exchange.** Poste Restante. **Postal code:** 86000. Open Mon.-Fri. 8:30am-9pm, Sat. 8:30am-noon.

Train Station: Bd. du Grand Cerf (tel. 49-58-50-50 for information, 49-58-29-53 for reservations). To Angoulême (12-16 per day, 1-1½ hr., 62F), Saintes (4-8 per day, 1½-2 hr., 98F), La Rochelle (7-9 per day, 1½-2 hr., 78F), Bordeaux (12-16 per day, 2 hr., 123F), and Paris (10-14 per day, 2½-3½ hr., 162F). Information office open Mon.-Sat. 8am-7pm, Sun. noon-4pm.

Bus Station: Parc de Blossac (tel. 49-41-14-20). To Chauvigny (Mon.-Sat. 4 per day, 2 Sun.; 1 hr.; 22F) and St-Savin-sur-Gartempe (Mon.-Sat. 3 per day, 2 Sun.; 1½ hr.; 31F). Buses run to most of the smaller towns in the area. All buses stop at the train station.

Local Buses: Convenient city routes. Ask for a schedule at the *syndicat*. Tickets 6F.

Bike Rental: Cyclamen, 49, rue Arsène Orillard (tel. 49-88-13-25). 10-speeds for serious bikers. Open Tues.-Sat. 9am-noon and 2-7pm; Sat.-Tues. counts as only 2 days.

Bookstore: Librairie de l'Université, rue Gambetta off rue de la Marne. Excellent selection of maps. Open Mon.-Sat. 9am-noon and 2-7pm.

Laundromat: Rue de René Descartes Philosophe at place de la Liberté. Wash 2F, dry 2F per 5 min., soap 2F. Open daily 8am-7pm.

Medical Emergency: Tel. 15. **Ambulance,** Tel. 49-88-33-34.

Police: 45, rue de la Marne (tel. 49-88-94-21).

Police Emergency: Tel. 17.

Accommodations and Camping

The hostel, university housing, and campgrounds are all far from the center of town. Fortunately, you will find many reasonable hotels downtown. It's a good idea to call ahead, although accommodations are generally available in the summer.

Auberge de Jeunesse (IYHF), 17, rue de la Jeunesse (tel. 49-58-03-05), 3km from the station. Take bus #3 from the station or the Hôtel de Ville, or turn right at the station, walk along bd. du Pont Achard until it becomes av. de la Libération, and follow the signs. Large building with pool (5F a swim) next door. Clean, but somewhat cramped dormitory space. In summer 45F per night, breakfast included; in off-season 30F per night, breakfast 9.50F. Lunch or dinner 34F. Reception open 8-9am and 6-11pm.

University Housing, 42, rue du Recteur Pineau (tel. 49-46-26-80), at the Résidence Descartes. Take bus #1 from the Hôtel de Ville. Clean dormitory singles with bed, sink, and desk. Call during the day if arriving late. 63F per night; several nights, 57F per night. Breakfast 5F at the university restaurant across the street. If closed, the **Résidence Rabelais** at 38, rue de Recteur Pineau will be open.

Hôtel le Carnot, 40, rue Carnot (tel. 49-41-23-69). On a commercial street—plead for a room that faces the back. Four rooms at 65F. No showers. Breakfast 14F. The bar-restaurant on the ground floor is frequented by locals. The *à la carte* selections are good buys; 5-course *menus* 47-50F. Meals served Mon.-Sat. noon-2:30pm and 7-10:30pm.

Hôtel Jules Ferry, 27, rue Jules Ferry (tel. 49-37-80-14), near Eglise St-Hilaire on a pleasant street. From the station, turn right and follow bd. de Pont Achard for 5 min. to a staircase on your left. At the top, go straight on rue La Cesve and immediately turn right onto rue Jules Ferry. Renovated interior; clean rooms and big beds. The personable manager speaks English and Spanish. Singles and doubles from 82F, with shower 100F. Showers 12F. Breakfast 15F. Garage 12F.

Hôtel du Poitou, 79, bd. Grand Cerf (tel. 49-58-38-06), close to the station on the left. Rooms not too clean, and walls a dingy faded pink, but the prices are the best near the station. Often full June-July. Singles and doubles 70F. Bath 16F. Breakfast 15F. Restaurant downstairs posts a 50F *menu.* Open Sept.-July.

Camping: Le Porteau, on a hill 2km out of town (tel. 49-41-44-88). Take bus #7 and ask to be dropped off *"devant le terrain"* (in front of the field). Clean bathrooms, showers, and a patch of grass on which to pitch a tent. 4.10F per person; parking 1.85F, electricity 3.25F. **Camping St-Benoît,** route de Passelourdin (tel. 49-88-48-55), 5km from Poitiers. Take bus #2 from the train station, transfer to bus #10, and get off at St. Benoît.

Food

Poitevin cuisine draws on northern and southern traditions. Try the *fromage de chèvre,* the local *andouillette* (spicy sausage), and, if you're up to it, the *anguilles* (eels). Baked goods are also superb, from the *brioche* and *clafoutis* (a cherry tart) to the local *macarons.* The **outdoor market** at place du Marché open until noon on Tuesday, Thursday, and Saturday is a real spectacle—they sell just about anything you could consider eating, dead or alive. **Monoprix,** a supermarket and department store on rue des Cordeliers at rue du Marché Notre Dame, offers everything from inexpensive lingerie to anchovies. The nut-berry-megavitamin fan will find bliss at **Santé et Vie,** 68, rue de la Cathédrale. (Open Tues.-Sun. 9am-12:30pm and 3-7pm.)

Most hotel-bars in Poitiers post five-course *menus* for around 55F. Avoid the overpriced cafes on place Maréchal Leclerc; you need only wander out a block or two to find more reasonable values. Few places open Sundays (when a *Poitevin* or *Poitevine* says "every day" he or she usually means Monday through Saturday).

> **University Restaurants: Restaurant Roche d'Argent,** 1, rue Roche d'Argent (tel. 49-88-04-13). Decent meals with unlimited seconds. The best deal in Poitiers. Price 18.60F, unless you buy a ticket from a student (9.30F). Open Mon.-Fri. 11:30am-1pm and 6:45-7:45pm. A **brasserie** at the same location is open periodically in summer; Sat.-Sun. 11:30am-1pm and 6:45-7:45pm during the school year. **Restaurant Champlain,** 117, av. Recteur Pineau, is also open in summer. Take bus #1 to Champlain.

> **Le Roy d'Ys,** 51, rue de la Cathédrale (tel. 49-88-81-47). A plain but friendly *crêperie* with great *galettes* (10-30F). If you like mushrooms, try the *pavé nantais* (28F) or any of the other 15-odd mushroom selections. Also try the *flambées* and a killer peach melba (25F). Open Tues.-Sat. noon-2pm and 7pm-midnight.

> **Flunch,** rue de Petit Bonneveau at rue Carnot, 1 block south of the Hôtel de Ville. A slick, modern cafeteria totally devoid of atmosphere. Steak and potatoes 25F. Open daily 11am-2:30pm and 6-10pm.

> **Le Poitevin,** 76, rue Carnot (tel. 49-88-35-04). Hedonistic budget buster. Authentic regional cuisine. 68F *menu.* Open Mon.-Sat. noon-2pm and 7-10pm.

> **Le Regal Bar Brasserie,** rue de la Regratterie in *centre ville.* 3-course lunch 35F, foot-long sandwiches 9.50F. Play a game of football with the lively crowd that frequents the place. Open Mon.-Sat. for lunch.

> **A la Crêpe d'Or,** place Charles VII, north of Notre Dame. The owner will enthusiastically describe how Charlemagne defeated the Arabs right on the site of her *crêperie.* Try the crêpe with apricots (10F). Open Mon.-Sat. noon-2pm and 7pm-midnight.

Sights and Entertainment

The churches that pepper the old part of town are the most compelling reason to visit Poitiers. After experiencing the hustle and bustle of *centre ville,* follow rue Gambetta to twelfth-century **Notre Dame la Grande.** Its three-tiered western facade, considered one of the finest examples of Romanesque bas-relief in France, portrays various biblical episodes, including the Annunciation, the Visitation, the Nativity, and Joseph's meditation. Inside, gentle, diffuse light reveals wall-frescoes and columns decorated with geometric patterns. (Open daily 8am-7pm.)

Many tourists mistake impressive Notre-Dame for "the Cathedral," but this appellation rightfully belongs to the larger **Cathédrale St-Pierre,** a few blocks down rue de la Cathédrale. Remarkable for its sheer size, and for the strength of its horizontal lines, the cathedral was constructed in the twelfth century on Eleanor and Henry Plantagenet's orders. Above the central door, irreverent pigeons hop from heaven to hell and back during the Last Judgement. (Open daily 8am-7:30pm.)

Just west of the Cathédrale St-Pierre, the Mediterranean **Baptistière St-Jean** dates from the sixth century—the oldest existing Christian building in France. The octagonal font built into the floor dates from the fourth century, and recent diggings have uncovered aqueducts used to transport water. The original frescoes are barely visible in some of the chapels, but on the whole, the stone-and-brick structure is in remarkable condition. The baptistery serves as a museum of Roman and early Christian decoration, with many carved sarcophagi and friezes. (Open April-Sept. Wed.-Mon. 10:30am-12:30pm and 3-6pm; Oct.-March Wed.-Mon. 2-4pm. Admission 4F.)

Next to the baptistery, the **Musée Ste-Croix** contains innumerable relics from Poitiers's Bronze Age and Roman settlements, as well as a fine collection of Dutch and Flemish paintings. (Open Wed.-Mon. 10-11:30am and 2-5:30pm. Free.)

Heading east on rue Jean Jaurès from the *baptistière,* cross pont Neuf and turn left on bd. Coligny, which becomes bd. du Colonel Barthal. Follow the road as it curves (near the golden statue of the Virgin) and pause for a breathtaking view of

Poitiers. Turn right on bd. de la Digue, right on rue du Père de la Croix, and go straight until you reach chemin de l'Hypogée and the **Hypogée Martyrium** (a 20-min. walk). A vestige of antiquity, this seventeenth-century underground chapel was built on a site where 72 Christian martyrs were buried by the Romans. (Ask for the key next door at 101, rue du Père de la Croix. Open daily May-Sept. 10am-noon and 2-6pm; Oct.-April 10am-noon and 1-4pm.) Secular Romanesque architecture is represented by the **Palais de Justice,** place A. Lepetit in the *centre ville,* the former palace of the Dukes of Aquitaine. The vast twelfth-century timber-roofed King's Hall once echoed with the ballads of troubadours, plans of crusading knights, and the verse of Eleanor of Aquitaine's *Courts of Love.* (Open May-Sept. Mon.-Sat. 9am-12:30pm and 2-7pm; Oct.-April Mon.-Sat. 9am-noon and 2-6pm.)

Eglise Montierneuf, in the northern end of the city, has a plain Romanesque front hidden by trees, the towers that seem to be *de rigueur* in Poitiers, and a simple barrel-vaulted interior. But if you walk around it on bd. Chassaigne, you'll be surprised by its elegant, soaring apse supported by the lightest of flying buttresses. (Open Mon.-Sat. 9am-noon and 2-6pm. Closed to visitors Sun. during services.)

Poitiers is taking pains to attract the communication technology industry with two ambitious projects: Futuroscope and Devenir. **Futuroscope** is a science-oriented amusement park 10km north of Poitiers (tel. 49-62-30-00). Take bus #16. (Open May-Oct. daily 8am-7pm. Admission 70F, children 40F.) **Devenir,** a new museum of technology, across the street from the Baptistière St-Jean, will open September, 1988.

During the first two weeks of May, Poitiers hosts **Le Printemps Musical de Poitiers** (tel. 49-41-58-94, M. Zlatiev), a festival of concerts, exhibits, and debates. (Tickets 25-50F.) The concert series, **Rencontres Musicales de Poitiers,** features mostly classical works in biweekly concerts from late October through late April. (Tickets 55F, ages under 26 38F; tickets available at kiosk in place Maréchal Leclerc; schedule at *syndicat.*) *L'Affiche Hebdo,* available at the *syndicat,* has a comprehensive list of cultural events.

Near Poitiers

About 20km east of Poitiers lies the town of **Chauvigny,** typical of the Vienne region, with its medieval walls rising from a spectacular hilltop site. Inside the town's defenses stands the Romanesque **Eglise St-Pierre,** notable for its intricate sculpture depicting episodes from the Bible. **Abbaye St-Savin-sur-Gartempe,** 10km to the east, displays a remarkable collection of frescoes even finer than those of Notre-Dame-la-Grande in Poitiers. Chauvigny and St-Savin are each accessible three to five times per day by bus (see Bus Station above). You can also easily hitch along N151. In Chauvigny, the **Hôtel du Chalet Fleuri** (tel. 49-46-31-12) sits by the river and offers singles from 65F, doubles 80-150F.

Halfway to Angoulême on D1, the town of **Civray** claims one of the finest Romanesque churches in France, **Eglise St-Nicholas.** The sculptural work on its classically ordered west facade is remarkable. For information on transportation, see Bus Station above.

Les Sables d'Olonne

If you like education with your leisure, don't stop at Les Sables d'Olonne. An uninteresting pile of stones constitutes the town's church, there's not a château in sight, and the alleged local folk culture survives only in postcards and a few farm houses. What Les Sables does have is sand. Magnificent stretches of the stuff have made this town one of the busiest resorts in the Vendée. Les Sables is a good place to play truant from culture and dip your toes into clean blue water.

Orientation and Practical Information

The train station lies off av. de Gaulle, which leads to place Liberté in the northern section of town. From the fountain and trees of place Liberté, rue de l'Hôtel de Ville branches west towards the port and quai Dingler; rue Travot plunges south to the crescent beach and to sweltering, crowded promenade Georges Clemenceau.

All aspects of your stay in Les Sables are covered by the witty guide *L'Eté Branché,* available from July through December at bookstores (French only).

Office de Tourisme: Rue Maréchal Leclerc (tel. 51-32-03-28). From the station take a right onto av. de Gaulle, which leads to place Liberté, and bear diagonally right across the square onto rue Leclerc. Remarkably patient staff (even in high season) will outfit you with a map and list of hotels. Open July-Aug. daily 9am-12:30pm and 2-7pm, Sat. 9am-12:30pm and 2-6:30pm, Sun. 10:15am-12:30pm and 3:30-6:30pm; Sept.-June Mon.-Fri. 9am-12:15pm and 2-6:30pm, Sat. 9am-noon and 2-5:30pm.

Point Information Jeunesse: Rue Eugène Nauleau (tel. 51-90-71-30), in Olonne-sur-Mer 5km north of Les Sables. Information on social and cultural activities. Open Wed. and Sat. 9am-12:30pm and 2-6:30pm.

Agence de Voyages: 12, av. du Général de Gaulle (tel. 51-32-02-54), a stone's throw from the train station. Transalpino/BIJ tickets. Helpful staff. Open Mon.-Fri. 9am-noon and 2-7pm, Sat. 9am-noon and 2-5pm.

Post Office: Rue Nicot, behind the train station. Photocopy machine 1F per page. Open Mon.-Fri. 8:30am-6:30pm, Sat. 8am-noon. **Postal code:** 85100.

Train Station: Av. Général de Gaulle (tel. 51-62-50-50). More than 8 trains per day to La Rochelle (2 hr., 76F) via La Roche-sur-Yon (27F). Also to Nantes (1½ hr., 60F) and Paris (5 hr., 250F). Rents 4 mediocre bikes 37F per half-day, 47F per day, deposit 300F. Open Mon.-Thurs. 5:45am-8pm, Sat. 5:45am-9pm, Sun. 6am-9:15pm. Information office open daily 8:30am-noon and 2-6:30pm.

Bus Station: The *gare routière* is to the left of the train station. **CFIT**, Tel. 51-32-08-28. Line #8 provides early morning service to the ports in St-Gilles-Croix-de-Vie (22F), St-Jean-de-Monts, Fromentine (44F), and to other small towns. Office open Mon.-Fri. 8-11:30am and 3-6:30pm, Sat. 8-11:30am. **Sovetours,** Tel. 51-95-18-71. To La Rochelle (52F) and La Roche-sur-Yon (22.60F). Office open daily 8am-noon and 2-6:30pm, Sat. 9:30am-noon.

Bike and Moped Rental: Le Cyclotron, 66, promenade Clemenceau (tel. 51-32-64-15). Bikes 33F per day, 150F per week, deposit 300F. 10-speeds 35F per day, 170F per week. Beat-up mopeds from 150F per day, deposit 1500F. Free helmet. Open daily July-Aug. 9am-midnight; April-June 10am-noon and 2-6:30pm. Inquire at the *syndicat* for other rental agencies.

Surfboard Rental: Pacific Surf Shop, 13, promenade Clemenceau (tel. 51-95-96-94). Surfboards 100F per day.

Windsurfer and Sailboat Rental: At la Base des Dériveurs (tel. 51-21-16-50), on the west end of the beach. Windsurfers 39F per weekend, 65F per week. Sailboats 146F per week. Open daily 9am-7pm.

Laundromat: Rue Castelnau. Wash 20F, dry 2F per 5 min. Open 7am-8:30pm.

Ambulance: Tel. 51-95-32-52 or 51-21-86-30.

Police: Rue de Verdun (tel. 51-21-14-43).

Police Emergency: Tel. 17.

Accommodations, Camping, and Food

Masses descend on Les Sables in July and August. By the beginning of June, most hotels are booked solid. The hostel is rarely booked by groups, unlike many hostels in this region, but it is small and has no telephone. To reserve a space, send payment for one night's stay well in advance, or try reserving a hotel room by phone. From October through May, finding a room shouldn't be difficult.

Auberge de Jeunesse (IYHF), rue du Sémaphore (no phone), in neighboring La Chaume. Don't attempt the dusty 50-min. walk from the station—take the bus from place Liberté (*direction* "Côte Sauvage," 1 per hr., 4F), get off at Armandeche, and walk up rue de Sémaphore.

The hostel will be on your left. Or walk to quai Guiné on the western edge of town, catch a ferry to La Chaume (non-stop service until 12:30am, 2.80F), head south on quai Georges V, turn right at place de l'Ormeau, and follow rue l'Ormeau, which becomes rue du Village Neuf. Turn left onto rue du Sémaphore. The hostel—a cross between a Spanish church and a medieval barn— will be on your right at the end of a driveway. Small and dusty cabin space with outside showers and toilets, but a beautiful view of the rocky Côte Sauvage and a refreshing, low-key atmosphere. Great kitchen facilities. 22F per night. You can also camp outside. No lockout; doors are never closed. Open July-Aug.

Hôtel le Merle Blanc, 59, av. Aristide Briand (tel. 51-32-00-35), a block away from the beach. Clean as a whistle, with a touch of class and paper-thin walls. The supermarket is only 5 steps away. English spoken. Singles 62-65F. Doubles 82-85F. All with bidet and sink. Breakfast 15F. Open March 15-Sept. 31.

Hôtel Les Olonnes, 25, rue de la Patrie (tel. 51-32-04-12). Decent doubles 76F. Showers included. Breakfast 15F. Open mid-June to Aug.

Le Relais des Voyageurs, 84, av. Alcide Gabaret (tel. 51-95-15-96). Slightly cramped doubles from 100F. Showers 10F (large bathtub and great shower). Breakfast 20F. Hearty 4-course *menu* served downstairs (45F).

Le Majestic Hôtel, 24, quai Guiné (tel. 51-32-09-71), near beaches and center of town. Singles and doubles 100F. Breakfast 15F. Guests received until 11pm. Also offers 4-course 55F *menus* in the restaurant downstairs.

Hôtel Beauséjour, 96, rue Léon David (tel. 51-32-05-88), a 15-min. walk from the center of town. Decent rooms and polite management, but tiny bathrooms. Singles and doubles 100F. 5-course *menu* 59F.

Camping: There are dozens of sites in and around Les Sables—camp your heart out. The most convenient are always booked: **Le Lac,** bd. Kennedy (tel. 51-95-13-35). 2-star, booked in season. **Les Dunes,** L'Aubraie-La Chaume (tel. 51-32-31-21). 2-star, on top of a dune. Open June 15- Sept. 15. No reservations accepted. **Les Roses,** rue des Roses (tel. 51-95-10-42). 4-star with a 7-month waiting list. The *syndicat* has a list of many more sites nearby.

Le Bon Soleil, 90, rue Printanière (tel. 51-95-12-63), serves one of the best 37F meals you'll ever have. (Open daily 7am-8pm.) **Le Théâtre,** 20, bd. Roosevelt, serves good local seafood and 40-120F *menus.* If you're staying at the hostel, **Restaurant Rosemonde,** 10, quai George V (tel. 51-95-25-81), in La Chaume, is convenient and cheap with a filling 40F *menu* that includes *moules.* A daily **market** takes place in Les Halles just south of the church. (Open Mon.-Sat. 8am-1pm. Big market days are Wed. and Sat. 7am-1pm.) **Arôm' Café,** 94, rue National, just off place de la Liberté, sells innovative homemade ice cream (5F per scoop).

Beaches

The town lives up to its name with its great arc of beach, which, in spite of the encroachment of high-rises, remains clean and pleasant. At low tide the extremely gentle slope of the beach becomes an immense playing field. **Plage de Tanchet,** farther east near the lake campground, is the first of several along the east road. To the northwest lies the seaside reserve, **Forêt d'Olonne,** where huge dunes tumble down from dry woodlands to the sea.

The Islands

Ile d'Yeu

Reclusive monks christened the island Ile Dieu (God's Island) in the ninth century. Although in recent years this seclusion has been marketed, the beauty that inspired the first monks remains unspoiled. This tiny island of farms and hedges ringed by a splintered coast concerns itself with fishing most of the year and receives tourists only in summer. The island even has a microclimate: One coast might be sunny when the opposite coast is soaked with rain, and palm trees thrive with no threat of frost.

The island stretches roughly northwest to southeast. Ferries to the island land at **Port-Joinville,** a fishing port on the north coast. About 3½km south of Port-Joinville, **Vieux Château** perches precariously on rocks in the port. Built by monks in the ninth and tenth centuries, the château has been occupied by the Romans, the English, and the Spanish. The cross opposite the château was erected in 1934 after five ships were lost off the island during a violent tempest. Close to the cross and the château is a nudist beach.

Farther east on the island in **Port de La Meule,** climb up large rocks, feel the sea breeze on your face, and listen to the cry of sea gulls as they glide smoothly over the blue expanse of earth and sky. From your rocky perch, you can see **Notre Dame de Bonne Nouvelle** (dating back to at least 1520), a white church compliment-ing the rugged shoreline with its dignified simplicity.

Moving east from Port de la Meule, you will find **L'Anse des Vieilles** with its soft sand beaches. The *anse* (cove) was not named after old women; "*vieilles*" refers to a species of fish found in the area. Northwest of Les Vieilles stands **St-Sauveur,** the oldest church on the island.

Ile d'Yeu remains isolated because only the determined and undaunted ever reach the island, thanks to problematic public transport. Ferries to the island leave from Fromentine, St-Gilles-Croix-de-Vie, and Les Sables D'Olonne. **Fromentine** is acces-sible by bus from Nantes (see Nantes Practical Information) and Les Sables d'Olonne (4 per day, 40F). One or two ferries per day make the trip to Ile d'Yeu, but it is not always possible to return on the same day. (One-way 50F). Call 51-68-52-32 for information. It's best to make reservations and arrive at the port 30 min-utes before departure time. **St-Gilles** is accessible by train from Nantes (5 per day, 51F) or La Roche-Sur-Yon (2 per day, 35F) and by bus from Les Sables. From Les Sables, ask the driver to drop you off at the *embarcadère.* From May through September, ferries from St-Gilles make three to six round-trip sailings per week to Ile d'Yeu (100F, 1 hr. 40 min.). Call for reservations (tel. 51-55-45-42) or drop by the offices of **Garcie-Ferrande,** bd. de l'Egalité. The **Office de Tourisme,** bd. de l'Egalité (tel. 51-55-03-66), 500m east of the port, can help you with accommoda-tions and with the details of your trip. The ferries from **Les Sables** cost 170F round-trip. For information, call 51-90-80-80.

Once on the island in Port-Joinville, you can rent bikes at **Loca-Cycles** (tel. 51-58-40-31), **Vélo Plein 'Air** (tel. 51-58-36-08), or **Vélo-Prom'nade** (tel. 51-58-43-22). The bike shops are all located at the port and all open daily 8:30am-7pm. The **Office de Tourisme** is on place du Marché (tel. 51-59-32-58; open Mon.-Sat. 10am-12:30pm and 4-6pm).

The island makes room for a few expensive hotels and one **municipal campground** (tel. 51-58-34-20), located at **Pointe de Gilberge,** about 1km from the ferry landing close to the beaches. If you don't stay overnight, you'll have only six or seven hours on the island, so make the most of it. Food is deplorably expensive, so you may want to buy supplies on the mainland before departing. In Port-Joinville, try the **supermarket** five minutes away from the port on rue de Calypso. Take a left from the port, then a right at the first stoplight (rue de Calypso). (Open Mon.-Sat. 8:45am-12:45pm and 3:30-7:30pm, Sun. 9:30am-12:15pm.)

Ile de Ré

The islands off the coast near La Rochelle provide a compelling excuse to hit the beach. The nearest island, **Ile de Ré,** is connected to the town of La Pallice by a newly constructed 3-km bridge (tolls 82F per car, 18F per person, 4.50F per bike). Hike over the bridge or take one of the buses that run from the bus station several times per day. The island is a 30-minute bike ride from the center of town. The bridge lands you in the town of **Rivedoux.** Go straight for about 10 minutes. On your left you will see the **Office de Tourisme,** more of a shack than an office, place de la République (tel. 46-09-80-62), which will supply you with information on the island's numerous villages, beaches, and campgrounds. (Open in summer 9am-noon and 5-7pm.) Between the tourist office and the bridge is **Camping Municipal** (tel.

46-09-84-10), a huge campground that doesn't take reservations. (8.30F per person, 7.70F per site, plus 1F tax. Hot showers included. Office open Mon.-Sat. 9-11:30am and 2-9:30pm.) For other campgrounds, call 46-09-80-04.

Sand covers most of the island's 60km of beach. Beginning in July, French youth descend upon the island for sun and surf. You can find people up and ready to party at any time of the day or night. Nightclubs pop up all over the island, but they charge at least 50F and are generally not worth it. Better to stick to a midnight swim *à la française* or a clambake on the beach. **Locasport** (tel. 46-09-65-27) rents bicycles for 65F per day with a 100F deposit or a passport.

Ile d'Aix

South of Ile de Ré lies tiny **Ile d'Aix,** barely 2km long but big enough to have sheltered Napoleon I for a week in July, 1815, the emperor's last days on French soil. Mediterranean-style cottages line dusty streets on this island, which only 200 permanent residents call home. During the summer, hordes of beach-fanatics occupy the tiny island. The **Musée Napoléon** houses a fairly substantial collection of Napoleon memorabilia, including various of the emperor's clothes. (Open Thurs.-Tues. 10am-noon and 2-6pm.) Ramparts encircle the southern tip of the island; drawbridges are the only entrances. **Ferries** run from **Pointe de la Fumée,** 3km west of Fouras and 14km west of Rochefort. (June 20-Sept. 22 daily 8am-8pm every ½ hr., round-trip 41F; Sept. 23-Dec. 22 and March 20-June 19 6-8 per day, round-trip 27F; Dec. 23-March 19 4-6 per day, round-trip 15F.) Call 46-84-60-50 for information. Buses leave Rochefort for La Fumée four to five times per day (½ hr., 13.10F). Two or three buses per day connect La Rochelle and Fouras (45 min., 44F; see La Rochelle Practical Information). In season round-trip cruises leave from La Rochelle almost every day. 72F purchases about five hours on the island. Inquire at **Océcar's** main location, 14, cours des Dames (tel. 46-41-78-95; open Mon.-Fri. 8:30am-noon and 2-7pm, Sat. 9am-noon). The island has but one, expensive hotel.

The campground on the island, **Camping Municipal de Fort la Rade** (tel. 46-84-50-64), has some superb campsites on the ramparts.

Ile d'Oléron

The larger **Ile d'Oléron,** affectionately dubbed "luminous island" by its inhabitants, claims no fewer than 20 fine sand beaches along a 70-km coastline, a thriving oyster industry, a château, and an animated summer beach crowd. The **citadel,** in the town of **Le Château d'Oléron,** now sprouts grass but still conveys an impression of stalwartness. The low (6-10m) ramparts and the slanted walls that deflect rather than absorb cannonball blows were innovations in fortress building. The island is connected to the mainland town of **Le Chapus** by one of the longest toll bridges in Europe (3-km long; tolls 21-41F, depending on the season). Citram bus connections to Le Chapus from La Rochelle are lousy; round-trip excursions by Océcar start at 86F, including a stop at Ile d'Aix. Better bus service runs from the towns of Rochefort (4-5 per day, 1½ hr., 35F) and Saintes (4-5 per day, 1¾ hr., 42F).

Le Château d'Oléron is just across the bridge, 3km from the main road. Hotel accommodations start at 100F, so you might consider staying at the hostel in Saintes and making Oléron a daytrip. For **camping** in Le Château, try **Les Ramparts,** bd. Philippe Daste (tel. 46-47-61-93), or **La Brande,** rue des Huitres (tel. 46-47-62-37). Campsite fees range from 15-20F per person. The **Office de Tourisme,** on place de la République (tel. 46-47-60-51), distributes free maps and brochures on all the sights, including a list of campgrounds and bike rentals. (Open July-Aug. daily 9am-12:30pm and 3-7pm, Sun. 10am-noon; Sept.-June Tues.-Sat. 10am-noon and 2:30-6pm.) For bike rental, try **Lacellerie Cycles,** 5, rue Maréchal Foch (tel. 46-47-69-30; bikes 40F per day, deposit 600F; open daily 8:30am-12:30pm and 2-7:30pm). For picnic provisions, try the **Supermarché Bravo** on rue des Antioches (open Mon.-Sat. 9am-12:30pm and 3-7:30pm). The *Syndicat d'Initiative* in St-Pierre d'Oléron, the administrative center of the island, is located at place Gambetta (tel. 46-47-11-

39; open July-Aug. Mon.-Sat. 9am-8pm, Sept.-June Mon.-Sat. 2:30-6pm). The **postal code** of Le Château d'Oléron is 17480.

La Rochelle

Named after the "soft rock" on which the earliest settlers built their homes (1132), La Rochelle later became the coastal power of Aquitaine and profited from its position as a port city vital to both France and Britain. In the seventeenth century, the powerful and unscrupulous Richelieu saw La Rochelle as an obstacle to uniting France, and convinced Louis XIII to besiege the town. After a large portion of the population had starved to death, the city finally surrendered. It did not regain its former wealth until the twentieth century, when its white sand beaches and elegant old buildings were rediscovered by vacationers. Now, throngs of visitors crowd the picturesque harbor, and the city endures more backpacking students than any other in France. La Rochelle used to boast that it kept the English out of Aquitaine; today it heartily welcomes Anglophones.

Orientation and Practical Information

The main seaport of Charentes-Maritimes, La Rochelle lies about halfway between Nantes and Bordeaux on the main railway line. The public information computers outside the train station and at place de Verdun will give you a printout of the best route to your destination. To get from the train station to the center of town, follow the directions given for the tourist office below, or take a short ride on bus #1 (6F).

The city stretches north from its old port, where **Tour de la Chaîne** and **Tour de la Lanterne** stand undaunted by the surging tides of tourists. **Rue du Palais** bisects the town longitudinally with its numerous arcaded galleries and shops. Place de Verdun lies north of the old port and to the left of rue du Palais, but the more colorful pedestrian district is just a block up from quai Duperré to the right of rue du Palais.

Office de Tourisme: 10, rue Fleuriau (tel. 46-41-14-68). From the train station, walk down av. du Général de Gaulle, cross a square, continue on quai Valin, turn left on quai Duperré, and right at the clock tower. Follow rue du Palais/rue Chaudrier, and turn right on rue Fleuriau. Hotel-booking service 10F. Good free maps. Open mid-June to mid-Sept. Mon.-Sat. 9am-7pm, July-Aug. they may stay open until 8pm; mid-Sept. to mid-June 9am-12:30pm and 2:30-6pm.

Office Départemental de Tourisme de la Charente-Maritime: 11bis, rue des Augustins (tel. 46-41-43-33), next to Maison Henri II. Information on the area surrounding La Rochelle and on festivals and other activities. Cordial staff. Open Mon.-Fri. 9am-noon and 2-5pm.

Centre Départemental d'Information Jeunesse (CDIJ): 14, rue des Gentilshommes (tel. 46-41-16-36 or 46-41-16-99), near Hotel Henri IV. Sells BIJ/Transalpino tickets and the *carte jeune* (60F). Ad boards for lodging, sales, and jobs. Ride/rider matching service 12F, list of rides free. Open Mon.-Fri. 10am-noon and 2-6pm, Sat. 10am-noon.

Post Office: Place de l'Hôtel de Ville (tel. 46-41-92-88). **Currency exchange. Main office,** av. Mulhouse, by the train station. Poste Restante. **Postal code:** 17000. Open Mon.-Fri. 8am-7pm, Sat. 8am-noon.

Train Station: Bd. Maréchal Joffre (tel. 46-41-50-50). To Poitiers (more than 6 per day, 1½ hr., 78F), Bordeaux (4-5 per day, 2 hr., 101F), Paris-Austerlitz (7 per day, 5 hr., 215F), Nantes (4-5 per day, 2 hr., 94F), and Rochefort (21.50F). To Nice and Lyon (about 3 per day). Maps of town 15F. Office open daily 8am-6:40pm.

Bus Station: There are 3 bus services in La Rochelle; all staff offices at the new *gare routière* in place de Verdun. **Local buses** (tel. 46-41-32-93) run to campgrounds, the *centre ville* (bus #1 from the train station), and La Pallice (also bus #1). Fare about 6F. **Citram,** 30, cours des Dames (tel. 46-41-04-57), runs 2-3 buses per day to Surgéres (50 min., 22F) and Angoulême (3 hr., 76F). Office open Mon.-Fri. 9am-noon and 2-6pm, Sat. 10am-noon. **Océcars** (tel. 46-41-20-40) serves Châtelaillon, Fouras, of Rochefort, Royan, and points in between. Service varies with school hours; passengers are mostly children. Buses leave from cours des Dames.

Office open Mon.-Fri. 8am-noon and 2-7pm, Sat. 9am-noon. Both Citram and Océcars run a multitude of tours and excursions.

Ferry: Bus de Mer, near the youth hostel (tel. 46-41-32-93). Runs from the old port to port de Plaisance des Minimes every 30 min. (6F). Easter-Oct. daily 8am-8pm.

Bike and Windsurfer Rental: Vélos Municipaux, Quai Valin. Will lend (for free) 1-speed bikes for 2 hr.; 3F per hr. thereafter. ID held as deposit. Open daily 9am-12:30pm and 1:30-7pm. At **train station,** 37F per half-day, 47F per day, deposit 300F. **Locasport,** Plage de la Concurrence (tel. 46-41-66-33, M. Salaun). From the port, walk south past the Tour de la Chaîne and follow the shoreline until you reach the beach. Bikes 27-48F per day, with passport as deposit. Also rents windsurfers by the hour or by the day. Open daily 9:30am-noon and 1:30-6:30pm; in off-season shorter hours.

Laundromats: 20, rue de la Pépinière, or rue St-Jean du Pérot, near the Tour de la Lanterne. Wash 24F, dry 16F. Open daily 9:30am-7:30pm. Also at the modern hostel. Wash 12F, dry 6F. Open daily 8-10am and 3-11pm.

Medical Emergency: Tel. 46-41-31-31 or tel. 18. **SAMU,** Tel. 46-27-15-15.

Police: 2, place de Verdun (tel. 46-41-92-44).

Police Emergency: Tel. 17.

Accommodations and Camping

Hotel prices run high in sophisticated, popular La Rochelle; it's a good idea to call ahead. Reservations are usually required from July through August, and the few available rooms usually fill by early afternoon. Cheaper places line the east side of the harbor, from the train station to just above place du Marché.

Centre International de Séjour, Auberge de Jeunesse (IYHF), av. des Minimes (tel. 46-44-43-11), 2km south of the station. Walk straight on av. de Gaulle, turn left on av. Colmar, and turn left again all the way along the fish market—follow the signs. You can also take bus #10 from place de Verdun or the train station. Beautiful, modern building with great facilities, including a laundry room. Often filled in summer; arrive by 3pm to secure a room. To reserve, write with 1 night's payment. Beds 50F, breakfast included. Singles 70F, singles for nonmembers 130F. Filling lunch or dinner 35F. Bike rental 30F per day. Open until 2am. Reception open daily 8-11am and 3-11pm. Lockout 10am-3pm.

Hôtel Printania, 9-11, rue du Brave Rondeau (tel. 46-41-22-86), off rue Thiers, near place du Marché. Husband and wife management firmly reminds you to eat a good breakfast (14F). Small living room for guests. Call ahead. 15 decent singles and doubles 90F. Triples 100F, with shower 110F. 5 persons 180F. Rooms without windows 60-80F. Showers 5.50F. Open all day.

Hôtel le Florence, 2, rue Marcel-Paul (tel. 46-41-17-24), 10 min. north of the *centre ville.* A bit of a hike, but the best prices you'll find in La Rochelle. Singles 75F. Doubles 90F. Breakfast 19F.

Hôtel de Bordeaux, 43, rue St-Nicolas (tel. 46-41-31-22), off quai Valin about 5 min. from the station. Faces a pleasant street, closed to traffic. Spanish- and English-speaking management. Call ahead. 9 renovated doubles with phones 100F. Showers included. Breakfast 15F.

Hôtel Henri IV, place de la Caille (tel. 46-41-25-79), at rue St-Saveur and rue du Temple, in the *centre ville.* 3-4 respectable doubles 100F. No communal shower. Breakfast 18F. Open Feb.-Dec. until 11pm.

Camping: Camping Municipal, bd. A. Rondeau (tel. 46-43-81-20). Take bus #1 from place de Verdun to Port Neuf. 2-star site surrounded by factories with space for 500. 10F per person, 6F per tent, 4F per car. Open year-round. **Camping des Minimes,** av. Marillac (tel. 46-44-42-53). 2-star site only 15 min. from the center of town, served by bus #10 from place de Verdun. 10F per person, 4.50F per small tent, 5F per big tent, 4F per car. Open June-Sept. 15. The *office de tourisme* has a list of other sites—all more distant. Camping outside official campgrounds is prohibited.

Food

Daily until 1pm, the **market** in place du Marché sells fresh fish, fruit, and vegetables. Buy mussels, oysters, and shrimp at the numerous outdoor fish stands near the harbor. Restaurants specializing in *les fruits de mer* (seafood) abound. The outdoor restaurants near place de la Chaîne will gladly relieve your wallet of at least 90F; better bargains exist on the other side of the harbor and near place du Marché. You will usually pay 20-30F more at any restaurant with a view of the harbor.

Le Pilote, 18, rue du Port (tel. 46-41-38-08), just off quai Dupérré. A tiny seafood restaurant near the action on a crowded street. 3-course *menu* 55F; more ambitious *menu* 90F. Open Sat.-Thurs. noon-2pm and 7:30-10pm.

Le Cordon Bleu, 20, rue du Cordonan (tel. 46-41-22-48), north of place du Marché. Intimate and distant from portside prices. 38F and 50F *menus.* The *plat du jour* comes with wine.

Pizzeria-Grill Don Arturo, 46, rue St-Nicolas. Largely local clientele and large local owner. *Menus* 35F and 50F, pizzas 23-30F. Open noon-2pm and 7:30-10pm.

Il Vesuvio, 24, cours des Dames. Pizza (25-35F) and Italian cuisine. Outside seating by the port. Open daily until midnight.

Café de L'Arsenal, 12, rue Villeneuve (tel. 46-50-53-75). The cheapest, most filling deal of all. Self-service, American-style cafeteria. Try the *poulet basquaise* (21F) or *rôti de veau* (20F). Don't leave without a taste of the *mousse au chocolat.* Open daily 11:30am-1:30pm and 6-9:30pm. Other location: **Café Bravo,** 30, bd. Santel (tel. 46-27-25-94). Same food, just farther away.

Sights

The famous towers that guard La Rochelle's port date from the late fourteenth century. Because of its defense system, the city thrived as a commercial center over the next two centuries, renowned for its wealthy bourgeoisie and immortalized in Alexandre Dumas's *The Three Musketeers.*

Originally, a chain was passed between the forbidding **Tour St-Nicholas** and the **Tour de la Chaîne** to seal off the harbor whenever the town was threatened; today the chain stretches between low stone pylons in place de la Chaîne. Tour de la Chaîne features a rather hokey *son et lumière* and a model of the town in Richelieu's day. (Tour de la Chaîne and its miniature village open April-June 15 Tues.-Wed., Sat.-Sun., and holidays 10am-noon and 2-7pm; June 16-Sept. daily 10am-noon and 2-7pm; Oct.-Nov. Sun. and holidays 10am-noon and 2-7pm. Admission 12F, students 8F.) A low rampart runs from Tour de la Chaîne to **Tour de la Lanterne,** also known as **Tour des Quatre Sergents.** Topped by a flamboyant Gothic steeple, the tower rises to more than 45m; in 1822 during the Restoration Monarchy, four sergeants were imprisoned here for the heinous crime of crying *"Vive la République."* From the top of the tower, you have a panoramic view of the city, and on a clear day, you can see across to the Ile de Ré. (Tour de la Lanterne and Tour St-Nicholas open April-Sept. Wed.-Mon. 9am-noon and 2-6pm; in off-season shorter hours. Admission to either tower 17F, ages 18-25 and over 60 6F. Admission to both towers 24F.)

Beyond the picturesque harbor with its whitewashed townhouses stretch La Rochelle's elegant arcaded streets, built during the city's eighteenth-century heyday. Walk underneath the fourteenth-century **Grosse Horloge** (clock tower) and up rues du Palais and Chaudrier. At 10, rue du Palais, is the renovated **Palais de Justice,** originally completed in 1789. Step into the *chambre correctionnelle* and watch lawyers and judges go through their paces and cases. The ornate Renaissance **Hôtel de Ville,** on rue Gargolleau, is rumored to have more chandeliers per square foot than any building in Europe. (Open April-Sept. Mon.-Fri. 9:30-11am and 2:30-5pm, Sat. 2:30-5pm; Oct.-March Mon.-Fri. 2:30-5pm.) La Rochelle is home to the largest **aquarium** in France at port des Minimes (tel. 46-44-00-00), near the youth hostel; take bus #10. (Open daily July-Aug. 9am-7pm; Sept.-June 10am-noon and 2-7pm.) Sailing buffs will be blown away by **Musée de la Voile,** next to the aquarium (tel. 46-45-40-77). (Open July-Aug. daily 10:30am-7pm, in off-season shorter hours. Admission 20F.) The **Musée des Automates,** rue de la Désirée (tel. 46-41-68-08), houses 300 mechanical dolls, both modern and historical. (Open Feb.-Dec. daily 10am-noon and 2-7pm. Admission 20F.)

For a quiet walk or picnic, take allée du Mail and choose a spot from the benches under the shady trees facing the beach, or the adjacent park and well-kept gardens.

Niort and the Marais Poitevin

About halfway between Poitiers and La Rochelle sits the pleasant town of Niort. Henry Plantagenet II and Eleanor of Aquitaine left a few noteworthy legacies here; the town makes a convenient base for daytrips to the Marais Poitevin.

Directly east of Niort lies the Marais Poitevin, 100,000 hectares of marshland. The slow-moving canals and waterways that crisscross the marsh have earned the area the sobriquet "Green Venice." This oasis of tranquility remains undisturbed by the frenzied holiday activity of the Atlantic coast. Here sunflowers color the landscape a dazzling yellow and ancient hamlets sleep along meandering roads. The "grand canal" of the area outlines a triangle whose vertices are **Marans, Fontaines,** and **Coulon.** At the center of this triangle lies the county seat, **Maillezais.**

Orientation and Practical Information

Niort is accessible by train from La Rochelle (6-7 per day, ¾ hr., 41F), as well as from Poitiers (6-8 per day, 1 hr., 48F) and Paris (8 per day, 4 hr., 193F). The center of town lies about place de la Breche and the pedestrian zone and is a 10-min. walk northwest from the train station. From the **train station,** head straight up rue de la Gare, and the tourist office will be on your right.

Unfortunately, Maillezais and the other towns along the grand canal are not easily accessible by public transportation. Furthermore, hitching is hardly possible, as the roads see very little traffic. Your best bet is to rent a bike in Niort. To reach Maillezais by car or bike from La Rochelle, head straight out on the N11 for 5km, turn left onto the D137 for 15km, and right onto the D938 for 14.5km. Turn right onto the smaller D25; in the small town of Maillé, turn left onto D15; and continue for 5km. From Niort, take rue du Ribray out of town, following the signs to Marais Poitevin. At Coulon, head straight through the only intersection with a stoplight. After passing through the village of **Glands,** turn left at the first intersection; go straight until **Le Mazeau;** and then follow the signs to Maillezais. It is extremely easy to lose your way on these back roads; don't hesitate to ask directions from locals along the way.

Syndicats d'Initiative: **Niort,** Place de la Poste(tel. 49-24-18-79). Will gladly load your pack with wads of information. Open Mon. and Sat. 9:15am-noon and 1:30-6pm, Tues.-Fri. 9:15am-noon and 1:30-7pm. **Coulon,** Place de L'Eglise (tel. 49-35-90-26). Open June 15-Sept. 15 Mon.-Sat. 10am-6pm. **Maillezais,** inside the Camping Municipal (see below). Open July-Aug. Mon.-Sat. 11am-noon and 3:30-6:30pm.

Post Office: Place de la Poste (tel. 49-24-84-03), in Niort. **Currency Exchange. Postal code:** 79000. Open Mon.-Fri. 8am-7pm, Sat. 8am-noon.

Train Station: Rue de la Gare (tel. 49-80-50-50). 2 SNCF buses per day leave for Coulon. Information office open daily 8am-noon and 2-7pm.

Bike Rental: At the **train station,** mediocre bikes 37F per half-day, 47F per day, deposit 300F. **J.F. Maingeneau,** 105, av. des Limoges (tel. 49-28-20-38). Better bikes 60F per day. Open Tues.-Sat. 9am-noon and 2-7pm.

Accommodations, Camping, and Food

Unfortunately, Niort has no youth hostel, and cheap accommodations are difficult to find. The **Foyer des Jeunes Travailleurs,** 8, rue St-André (tel. 49-24-50-68), in Niort, usually full in July and August, is available only for stays of 2 weeks or more. If you have no luck here, try the *foyer*'s other location: 147, rue du Clou Bouchet (tel. 49-79-17-44). **Hôtel St-Jean,** 21, av St-Jean d'Angély (tel. 49-79-20-76), has clean singles for 67F, doubles 85F. (Showers 14F. Breakfast 16F.) **Modern Hôtel,** 113, rue de la Gare (tel. 49-28-13-34), sits conveniently next to the train station. The rooms are simple but clean. (Singles and doubles 75F). Also try **Hôtel de la Paix** next door. (Singles 70F. Doubles 75F. Breakfast 15F.) The **Camping Municipal,** bd. de l'Atlantique (tel. 49-79-05-06) in Niort is next door to the stadium. Take bus #6 from place de la Breche. (6F per person.) **La Cloche d'Or,** 7, rue Brisson (tel. 49-24-01-32), next to place des Halles, bills a filling 55F *menu*.

In Coulon, the **Camping Municipal** (tel. 49-35-90-26) is your best option. (Open June-Sept. In June or Sept., register at the *syndicat*.) In Maillezais, the **Hôtel des Etrangères** (tel. 51-00-70-15) offers decent rooms for 80F. The restaurant downstairs serves 40F and 50F *menus*. (Open in summer daily noon-2pm and 8-9pm; in off-season Mon.-Sat.) Campers may want to head for the **Camping Municipal de Maillezais** (tel. 51-00-70-79), also in town. (6.80F per person, 4F per tent. Open April-Sept.)

Sights and Entertainment

Niort is graced by its well-preserved **donjon,** which affords a remarkable view from atop its battlements. Under the order of Henry Plantagenet II, the construction of the dungeon included plans for a 700-meter-long rampart wall. Destroyed during the Wars of Religion, these ramparts once enclosed a small city within the borders of rues Brisson, Thiers, l'Abreuvoir, and the river Sèvre Niortaise. Today, the dungeon holds an unremarkable collection of local relics, tools, and costumes. (Open Wed.-Mon. 9am-noon and 2-6pm. Admission 6F, students free.)

In **Maillezais,** take the 45-minute boat tour past poplar-lined marsh banks and peacefully grazing cows. The tiny plants on the water are so profuse that the canals appear to be paved with lime-green paint. Boat tours Easter-Oct. daily 9:30am-12:15pm and 1:30-6:30pm. The boat seats six and charges a flat 55F: You pay 9F if the boat is full, 55F if you're the only passenger. Tours are also available in Coulon (70F per boat) and Le Mazeau (55F per boat).

Before you step off firm ground, visit the ruins of **Abbaye St-Pierre** (tel. 51-00-70-11). Built on the site of a castle belonging to the Duke of Aquitaine, the abbey rose to prominence under the direction of the Benedictine Order. The abbey has a stormy history, having also been a bishopric under the charge of 22 abbots and then a Protestant stronghold complete with garrison. Confiscated by the state in 1791 (a result of the French Revolution), the abbey was sold to mercenary demolition agents who tore it to pieces. One family began to preserve what was left in 1840. Excavations carried out in the 1960s have revealed an intricate cellar system (inaccessible to the public) connected to the foundations of the cloisters by means of narrow stairways. (Open daily 9am-8pm. Admission 8F, students 5F.)

The **Saintonge** region southeast of Niort has numerous Romanesque remains—ruined abbeys and country churches grace the tiniest villages. About 40km southeast of Niort lies the town of **Aulnay** (inaccessible by train or bus) with its dazzling **Eglise St-Pierre.** In town, Hôtel-Restaurant **Le Donjon,** rue Porte-Matha (tel. 46-33-17-31), offers attractive, clean rooms. **Camping** is allowed on the grass next to the stadium, just across the street from the church.

Rochefort

Rochefort originally boomed because of the arsenal and naval base which Louis XIV commissioned here. Today the military presence has diminished—only the husk of the once bustling **Arsenal** remains—and the town no longer has a strong identity. Largely industrial, Rochefort has become a vacation resort only by virtue of its proximity to the sea. The town remains a convenient stopover for trips down the coast and excursions to Ile d'Aix or Ile d'Oléron, but unless you are an avid Loti reader, Rochefort doesn't have much to offer.

Rochefort's most curious treasure is **La Maison de Pierre Loti,** 141, rue Pierre Loti (tel. 46-99-16-88); formerly the home of gadabout and writer Pierre Loti (1850-1923). A museum that displays Loti's almost limitless vision of interior decoration now occupies the house. The novelist's playrooms include a mosque upstairs (reconstructed from materials of a mosque torn down in Damascus), an Arab room where Loti kept a harem (make-believe and otherwise), and a sharply contrasting, minimally decorated room where Loti contemplated death. You must take the tour to see the house. (Tours July-Aug. Tues.-Sat. at 10am, 11am, 2pm, 3pm, and 4pm, Sun.-Mon. at 2pm, 3pm, and 4pm; Sept.-June Wed.-Sat. 10am, 11am, 2pm, 3pm, and 4pm, Sun. 2pm, 3pm, and 4pm. 20F, students 10F.) The exhibit at **La Corderie Royale** (the royal ropeworks) will reveal everything you've ever wondered about rope. (Open daily 9am-7pm, guided tour at 3pm. Admission 15F.) The **Musée Naval,** place de la Gallissonière, houses an unspectacular collection of models of eighteenth- and nineteenth-century vessels. (Open Nov.15-Oct.15 Wed.-Mon. 10am-noon and 2-6pm.)

Orientation and Practical Information

The Charente River borders Rochefort to the south, east, and west. Place Colbert marks the center of town. To get to the tourist office from the train station, go straight on av. Wilson, turn right on av. Pelletan, left on rue Denfert Rochereau, and left on av. Sadi Carnot.

Office de Tourisme: Av. Sadi Carnot (tel. 46-99-08-60). Good free maps and plenty of free brochures. Open July-Aug. daily 9am-8pm; Sept.-June Mon.-Sat. 9:30am-12:30pm and 2-6pm.

Office Municipal de la Jeunesse, 97, rue de la République (tel. 46-87-16-42). From the tourist office, go 3 blocks down rue Audry de Puyravault and turn left on rue de la République. Free information on jobs, cultural events, and accommodations. Friendly office with a rideboard for hitching. Open Mon.-Fri. 9am-noon and 2-6:30pm.

Post Office: Rue du Docteur Peltier (tel. 46-99-07-00). **Postal Code:** 17300. Open Mon-Fri. 8am-7pm, Sat. 8am-noon.

Train Station: Bd. Aristide Briand (tel. 46-99-15-11). More than 6 trains per day to La Rochelle (20 min., 23F), Saintes (½ hr., 31F), and Royan (10 per day, change at Saintes, 1 hr., 50F). **Lockers** 3F. Information office open Mon.-Sat. 8:30am-6:50pm, Sun. 9:30am-noon and 1:30-6:30pm.

Bus Station: Océcars, place de Verdun (tel. 46-99-23-65). To Royan (3 per day, 1½ hr., 39F) and La Rochelle (3 per day, 1¼ hr., 21F). Office open Mon.-Fri. 8:30am-noon and 2-7pm, Sat. 8:30am-noon. **Citram,** place de Verdun (tel. 46-99-01-36). To Ile d'Oléron (6 per day, 35-45F) and Le Chapus (6 per day, 25F). To La Fumée for connecting ferries to Ile d'Aix (4-5 per day, ¾ hr., 13.10F). Office open Mon.-Fri. 9:15am-12:15pm and 2-6:30pm.

Bike Rental: Héline, 30, rue Gambetta (tel. 46-99-08-56). 33F per day, deposit 500F. Open Tues.-Sat. 9am-12:30pm and 2-7pm. Also at the **train station** (37F per half-day, 47F per day, deposit 300F.)

Medical Emergency: SMUR, Tel. 46-99-37-43.

Police: 42, av. Jean Jaurès (tel. 46-87-26-12).

Police Emergency: Tel. 17.

Accommodations and Food

The overspill of vacationers from La Rochelle tends to fill Rochefort in July and August. You should reserve a room in June or even earlier. However, in the off-season Rochefort is quite tranquil.

The **Auberge de Jeunesse (IYHF),** 20, rue de la République (tel. 46-99-74-62), is antiseptically clean and cheap (34F per night). Camping in the yard costs 15F. The hostel has kitchen facilities and rents bikes for 6F a day. Reservations are required from July through August; send in a 30% deposit. The **Hôtel Colbert,** 23, rue Audry de Puyravault (tel. 46-99-08-28), offers clean doubles for 80F. The **Hôtel Roca Fortis,** 14, rue de la République (tel. 46-99-26-32), is a bargain at 85F per double. The unremarkable **Camping Municipal,** av. de la Fosse aux Mats (tel. 46-99-14-33), requires a 15-minute walk from the center of town (6.10F per person, 4.10F per tent).

The local **market** takes place at the intersection of av. Charles de Gaulle and rue Jean Jaurès on Tuesday, Thursday, and Saturday mornings; take your bread and cheese to the gardens near the *corderie* for a picnic. **Chez Nous,** 72, rue Jean Jaurés (tel. 46-99-07-11), popular with the *Rochefortais,* serves a filling 39F *menu.* **Le Galion,** 38, rue Toufaire (tel. 46-87-03-77), a self-service cafeteria, is not at all interesting, but a substantial meal will put you back only 25F.

Saintes

Saintes stretches peacefully along the banks of the green Charente River, amid flat expanses of fields that extend 30km to the sea on one side and 38km to Cognac on the other. Originally the Roman capital of southwest France, Saintes adopted Christianity in the third century, and spent much of its time thereafter fending off flame-throwing barbarians. The pyromaniacal invaders succeeded in burning Saintes to the ground several times. When things calmed down in the eleventh century, the citizens of this provincial town breathed a sigh of relief—and set about building churches. Today, this Saintonge capital invites you to bask in its atmosphere of "simplicity, harmony, and sweetness." In Saintes you will find what is often obscured in seaside resorts: the relaxed rhythm of a small yet beautiful town.

Orientation and Practical Information

Saintes is on the main railway line, about halfway between La Rochelle and Bordeaux, and about 20 minutes by train from the coast. The Charente River slices Saintes in half from north to south. Life centers around the **Arc de Triomphe** and the **Pont Palissy.** The center of town is a simple 15-minute walk from the station. As you leave the *gare,* take a left, follow av. de la Marne 2 blocks south, turn right on av. Gambetta, and take it to the river. You will see the arch on your left. Cross the bridge and continue straight for about 5 blocks. The tourist office will be on your right.

Office de Tourisme: 62, cours National (tel. 46-74-23-82). Friendly office helps with accommodations (fee 5F in town, 10F in the region), provides guided tours of the city (Mon.-Sat. 10am and 3pm, 27F), and organizes cruises on the Charente (May Sun.; June weekends; July-Aug. daily; 30-50F). Open June 16-Sept. 19 Tues.-Sat. 9am-7:30pm, Sun.-Mon. 10am-noon and 2-6pm; Sept. 20-June 15 Tues.-Sat. 9am-noon and 1:30-6pm.

Post Office: 8, cours National (tel. 46-93-05-72), near the bridge. Sells traveler's checks. Poste Restante costs 2.20F a piece. **Postal Code:** 17100. Open Mon.-Fri. 8:30am-7pm, Sat. 8:30am-noon.

Train Station: Av. de la Marne (tel. 46-92-50-50). To La Rochelle (6 per day, 1 hr., 45F), Bordeaux (4 per day, 1¼ hr., 67F), Cognac (6 per day, 20 min., 20F), Angoulême (6 per day, 1 hr., 47F), Royan (10 per day, ½ hr., 27F). Information office open daily 8:30am-12:30pm and 2:30-7:50pm.

Bus Station: Autobus Aunis et Saintonge, 1, cours Reverseaux (tel. 46-93-21-41). To Cognac (3 per day, 1 hr., 17F). To points along Ile d'Oléron: Le Château (3 per day, 1½ hr., 40F), centre St-Pierre d'Oléron (3 per day, 2 hr., 46F), and St-Denis (3 per day, 2¼ hr., 58.50F). To Royan (3 per day, 1 hr., 22F). Open Mon.-Fri. 8am-noon and 2-6pm. **Branch** at rue Jean Moulin across from the train station. Open Mon.-Fri. 8am-noon and 2-6pm.

Bike Rental: Héline, 177, av. Gambetta (tel. 46-92-04-38). 33F per day, 110F per week; deposit 400F or passport. Open Tues.-Sat. 8:30am-12:30pm and 2-6:30pm. **Grolleau Cycles,** 9, place Blair (tel. 46-74-19-03). 33F per day, 58F per 2 days. Open Tues.-Sat. 8:30am-12:15pm and 2-6:45pm.

Laundromat: At rue Gambetta and av. Marne. Wash 13F, dry 2F per 8 min. Open Mon.-Sat. 8am-9pm.

Centre d'Information sur les Droits des Femmes: 4, rue St-Michel (tel. 46-93-06-69). Information and counseling. Open 2nd and 4th Mon. of month 2-5pm or by appointment.

Hospital: Tel. 46-93-00-95.

Ambulance: SAMU, Tel. 46-27-15-15.

Police: Tel. 46-93-01-19.

Police Emergency: Tel. 17.

Accommodations and Camping

A few hotels fill up during the mid-July festivals, but rooms are not generally hard to find. The youth hostel usually has space.

Auberge de Jeunesse (IYHF), 6, rue du Pont Amilion (tel. 46-92-14-92), near the center of town next to the Abbaye-aux-Dames. From the train station, take av. de la Marne to rue Gambetta, walk down rue Gambetta to rue Ste-Claire, turn left on rue St-Pallais and right on rue Pont Amilion. Quiet, relaxed atmosphere. With kitchen, ping-pong table, and slightly musty bathrooms. Cook your own meals. 34F per night. Office open 7-10am and 6-9:45pm. No lockout. Open Jan.-Nov.

Hôtel le Parisien, 35, rue Frédéric-Mestreau (tel. 46-74-28-92), just west of the train station. Simple and clean. Animated 11-year-old will show you to your room. Singles 70F, doubles 75F. Breakfast 16F. Open April 16-March.

Hôtel St-Palais, 1, place St-Palais (tel. 46-92-51-03). Great location in the abbey's courtyard. Lively bar downstairs, clean rooms, and cheap to boot. Manager speaks English. Singles 65F, doubles 75F. Showers 5F. Breakfast 15F. Call ahead.

Hôtel de la Gare, 46, rue Frédéric-Mestreau (tel. 46-93-06-12). Yellowed walls in fairly large rooms. Doubles 70F. 40F *menu* in restaurant downstairs. Open Nov.-Sept.

Le Gambetta, 72, av. Gambetta (tel. 46-93-02-85). Small, close to center, and cheap. The *brasserie* downstairs is a local hangout. Doubles 70-90F, some with showers. Hall showers 15F. Breakfast 18F. Open Oct.-Aug. until 1:30am.

Camping: Camping Municipal, 6, route de Courbiac (tel. 46-93-08-00). 2-star site spreading over green fields along the banks of the Charente, next to the municipal swimming pool. A healthy ½-hr. walk from the train station. Follow av. Gambetta across the river, and turn right on quai de l'Yser. 6.50F per person, 4.50F per tent, 2.40F per car. Open May 15-Oct. 15 7am-10pm.

Food

A boisterous **market** takes place Tuesday through Sunday at different places around town: on cours Reverseaux Tuesday and Friday, at the base of Cathédrale St-Pierre Wednesday and Saturday, and at av. de la Marne and av. Gambetta near the station Thursday and Sunday. Prices are low, and the vendors will let you sample their fat oysters and little shrimp. *Escargots* cooked in garlic and parsley are the specialty here. The supermarket **E. Leclerc** is located to the east of the hostel, 2 blocks up rue Pont St-Emilion. (Open Mon. 3-7:15pm, Tues.-Thurs. 9am-12:30pm and 3-7:15pm, Fri. 9am-8:15pm, Sat. 9am-7:15pm.) You might take your goodies to the pleasant **Jardin Public,** just south of the tourist office, for an aesthetic lunch on the green banks of the Charente.

Café Germanicus, 10, rue Arc-de-Triomphe (tel. 46-74-55-36). Self-serve cafeteria with a Roman air. *Spaghetti boulognaise* 19.50F. Open Mon.-Sat. 11:45am-10pm, Sun. 11:45am-3pm.

Pension St-Michel, 28, rue St-Michel (tel. 46-93-08-51). Where the market people themselves eat after their morning's work. Well-prepared food and family-style service. 38-48F *menus.* Open Mon.-Thurs. 11:45am-1:30pm and 7-8:15pm, Sat. 11:45am-2:30pm.

Crêperie Victor Hugo, 20, rue Victor Hugo. Whole-wheat crêpes 9-28F, dessert crêpes 8-24F, *galettes* 11-26.50F; 50F *menu* includes 2 crêpes and a *mousse.* Open Tues.-Sat. noon-2:30pm and 4:30-10pm.

Les Iles, 17, rue Désiles (tel. 46-93-72-17). 49F seafood *menu* includes a duck entree and trout; the 67F *menu* is more elegant. Open Tues.-Sat. noon-2pm and 7:30-9:30pm.

Pizza-Bojo/Pizzeria Grill, 17, rue de la Poste (tel. 46-93-10-35). Pizzas 20-35F. Open Mon.-Fri. noon-2pm and 9pm-midnight, Sat. 9pm-midnight.

Sights and Entertainment

Rising incongruously between street and river in the *centre ville,* the Roman **Arc de Triomphe** was originally erected in the first century on a bridge linking the two sides of town; an inscription still visible along the top dedicates it to Tiberius, Germanicus, and Drusus. Today, pigeons roost comfortably in its chipped columns. The **Abbaye-aux-Dames,** one of the most beautiful of the many Romanesque churches in the region, was for centuries administered by women from the best families in France. The interior was redone with Angevin vaulting in the twelfth century, but the west facade and the Poitou-style central tower are particularly fetching. (From the arch, take rue Arc de Triomphe/rue St-Pallais.) The **Musée Archéologique,** on esplanade André Malraux, next to the arch, is an intriguing forest of Roman columns, friezes, and cornices piled into two buildings and across a small square. Most of the works date from the demolition of the town's ramparts during the third century. (Open June-Sept. Wed.-Mon. 10am-noon and 2-6pm; Oct.-May Mon. and Wed.-Sat. 2-5pm, Sun. 10am-noon and 2-6pm.)

Just across the river from the arch stands the fifteenth-century **Cathédrale St-Pierre,** its imposing, unfinished bell tower capped not by a spire but by a small dome. Inside, the the massive 350-year-old organ is impressive. From the cathedral, walk up rue des Jacobins, climb the stairs, and work your way up to cours Reverseaux. Take a left and then a right on rue St-Eutrope towards **Eglise St-Eutrope.** This split-level Gothic-Romanesque hybrid is one of the many churches built in the eleventh century on the pilgrimage routes to St. Jacques de Compostelle in Spain. The cold, dark Romanesque crypt to the side can make even the bravest travelers shudder.

As you leave St-Eutrope with your back to the *centre ville,* you will see signs for the most magnificent of Saintes's Roman remains, the **Arènes Gallo-Romaines,** a crumbling amphitheater overgrown with grass that has retained its power to intimidate (a 15-min. walk west of the river). Built in 40 C.E., the tunnel entrance and several of the supporting arches still stand; at one time the structure could seat 20,000 people. Plant yourself center stage, address the emperor, and await the tigers.

Saintes hosts several summer festivals, notably the **Jeux Santons,** a weeklong celebration of folk music from around the world (the 2nd week in July; some events free, others 50-80F). Call 46-74-47-50 for exact dates, or inquire at the tourist office. The **Fête de Musique Ancienne** takes place the first two weeks of July (tickets 80F, students 60F). For information, call the Institut de Musique Ancienne de Saintes (tel. 46-92-51-35) or stop by the *syndicat.* Tickets are usually available at the door.

Near Saintes

Royan, a half-hour train ride from Saintes, is the principal resort on the Côte de Beauté. If murky waters that toss dead oysters onto crowded shores aren't your cup of tea, then avoid the five beaches lining the Côte Sauvage, especially La Palmyre and La Courbre. Royan's bustling harbor offers no bargains and little else.

German bombs leveled the city during World War II. Reconstruction yielded a slew of staid, modern buildings and one of the more provocative buildings in Aquitaine, **Notre-Dame de Royan,** designed by Guillaume Gillet and built from 1955 to 1958. Instead of columns or piers, internally strengthened walls support the ultrathin (8cm) ceiling. The design gives every member of the congregation an unobstructed view of the main altar. The exterior, despite its unorthodox steeple, still manages to resemble an airport terminal.

The **Office Municipal de Tourisme** is at the rond-point de la poste (tel. 46-05-04-71; open July-Aug. daily 9am-7pm, Sept.-June Mon.-Sat. 9am-12:30pm and 2-6pm). From the **train station** (tel. 46-05-20-10), you can get back to Saintes. **Buses** (tel. 46-05-03-81) run to neighboring towns and, with changes, to Ile d'Oléron. Cheap rooms are scarce. **Hôtel le Grand Soleil**, 21, bd. Clemenceau (tel. 46-05-13-07), has decent singles and doubles for 80F. **Chez Maria**, 75, bd. de la République (tel. 46-05-22-98), bills an excellent four-course meal for 55F. Inquire at the *syndicat* for a list of campgrounds that includes three-star **Clairefontaine,** av. Louise, in nearby Pontaillac.

Cognac

A half-hour train ride from Saintes or Angoulême brings you to the unprepossessing town that has given its name to one of the most celebrated distillations of all time. Cognac sits serenely among carefully tended fields where strictly-regulated soils bear white gold, the grapes used to distill each generation of cognac brandy. The city itself preserves a small-town atmosphere, but within its confines stand the distilleries of Hennessy, Martell, Rémy-Martin, and every other world-famous exporter of cognac. The very air reeks of the stuff, but not the bars—nearly all of the local specialty is exported, and the residents stick to less expensive wine or to *pineau,* a combination of cognac and grape juice, aged at least three years and costing at least 35F per bottle. *Pineau* comes in white or rosé, whereas cognac comes only in amber, the color resulting not from the grape but from the tannins of the Limousin oak casks used to age it. No other wood will do, just as no other process could replace the centuries-old double distillation. It would take a strong stomach to drink very young cognac: The aging and the blending of different vintages creates the softer, smoother, sweeter drink. Cognac is categorized by age: VS (very special) or VSOP (very special old pale) cognac is at least eight years old; *Paradis* blends brandies between 50 and 180 years old.

Cognac lies aging behind many a blank wall of the town, and on those walls live possibly the happiest little organism in the world—a sooty black fungus that subsists exclusively on the vapors that escape from the pores of the wooden casks. Think of them and weep.

Orientation and Practical Information

On the northern bank of the Charente, Cognac is within easy range of a daytrip from Angoulême, Saintes, and even La Rochelle if you plan your trains ahead. The center, place François 1er, near shopping, hotels, and the *syndicat,* is a 15-minute walk from the train station. Head straight out of the train station on rue Général Leclerc for 4 blocks, bear right on rue de Barbezieux/rue Elisée Mousinier, and bear right again on rue Bayard (following the signs to the *centre village* and the *office de tourisme* all the way). The tourist office will be on your left.

Office de Tourisme: 16, rue du 14 Juillet (tel. 45-82-10-71). Pleasant staff will find you a room for the price of a phone call. When the banks are closed, they will exchange foreign currency with a smile and a free nip-bottle of *pineau.* Free maps with all the cognac houses clearly marked. Open June 15-Sept. 15 Mon.-Sat. 8:30am-7pm; Sept. 16-June 14 Mon.-Sat. 9am-12:30pm and 2-6:15pm.

INFO 16: 53, rue d'Angoulême (tel. 45-82-62-00). Information on youth activities (including **Allostop** and nearby *foyers*). Smaller city maps free. There's also a ride board and baby-sitting services. Sells BIJ tickets and Carte Jeune (60F). Open Mon.-Fri. 10am-noon and 2-7pm, Sat. 10am-noon and 2-6pm.

Budget Travel: Agence de Voyages, 28, rue du 14 Juillet (tel. 45-82-00-87). BIJ/Transalpino tickets. Open Mon.-Fri. 8:30am-noon and 2-6:30pm; Sat. 9am-noon.

Post Office: Place Bayard (tel. 45-82-08-99), at the other end of rue du 14 Juillet from place François 1*er*. **Currency exchange. Postal Code:** 16100. Open Mon.-Fri. 8am-7pm, Sat. 8am-noon.

Train Station: Place de la Gare (tel. 45-38-50-50), off bd. de Paris. A quiet spot, since your travel options are not plentiful. To Angoulême (5 per day, 1 hr., 37F) and Saintes (6 per day, 20 min., 20F). Station open Mon.-Sat. 6am-8pm, Sun. 8am-midnight.

Bus Station: Autobus Citram, place Gambetta (tel. 45-82-01-99). To La Rochelle (1 per day, 3 hr., 54F) and Angoulême (Mon.-Sat. 6 per day, 2 Sun.; 1 hr.; 33F). Information office open Mon.-Fri. 7:45am-noon and 2-6:15pm, Sat. 9-11am.

Car Rental: Transatco, 28, rue du 14 Juillet (tel. 45-82-00-84). Friendly staff will contact any rental agency for you.

Bike Rental: J.F. Dupuy, 18, rue Elisée Mousnier (tel. 45-82-10-31). Good 10-speeds 50F per day, deposit 400F. Open Mon.-Fri. 8:30am-noon and 2-6:30pm, Sat. 9am-noon.

Medical Emergency: Ambulance Tel. 45-32-19-30.

Police: 8, rue Richard (tel. 45-82-01-86). **Emergency:** Tel. 17.

Accommodations and Camping

Because there is no hostel, and not all that much here besides cognac, you may want to make Cognac a daytrip from Saintes or Angoulême. In July and August, call at least two weeks in advance to make reservations.

Hôtel du Cheval Blanc, 7-9, place Bayard (tel. 45-82-09-55), across from the post office. Adequate, with good prices for a 1-star hotel. 6 singles 68F each. 4 doubles 80F. Doubles with 2 beds 100F. Showers 12F. Breakfast 18F. Reception open Mon.-Fri. until 9:30pm. Closed 3-6pm, Christmas, and the 2nd half of Aug. Call ahead in summer.

Tourist Hotel, 166, av. Victor Hugo (tel. 45-32-09-61); 10 min. from the train station. Take bd. de Paris to the right. Spacious and friendly. Attractive courtyard in the back. Private parking. 10 doubles 70F. 2-bed rooms 100F. Showers usually included. Breakfast 15F. Closed Sun. and the first 3 weeks of Aug.

La Résidence, 25, av. Victor Hugo (tel. 45-32-16-09). Comfortable, clean 2-star hotel with lots of reasonable rooms. English spoken. 6 singles 90F. 11 doubles 100F. Showers usually included. Breakfast 18F. Reservations advisable in July.

Foyer Sainte-Elizabeth, 20, rue Saulnier (tel. 45-82-04-90), close to the *centre ville.* Pretty run-down but the cheapest you'll find. Travelers (ages 16-25) accepted. 40-45F per night.

Camping: Camping Municipal de Cognac, bd. de Chatenay (tel. 45-32-13-32), 15-min. walk from place François 1*er.* Follow rue Henri Fichon to the campground. 4.60 per person, 2.10F per tent, 2.10F per car, and 4.30F for electricity. Open May 15-Oct. 15.

Food

To taste the stuff that made this town famous, you can go to the cognac houses, take their tours, and get a free dégustation at the end. The cheapest place to buy a bottle of cognac or *pineau* is probably **Prisunic,** place François 1*er* (cognac 70F and up, *pineau* 35-40F; open Mon.-Sat. 8:30am-7pm.) If you are a bit more picky, go to **La Cognathèque,** place Jean Monnet, and ask for guidance. (Open Mon.-Sat. 9am-noon and 2-6pm.)

There is an indoor **market** Monday through Friday from 7am to 1pm, at place d'Armes.

Le Sens Unique, 20, rue du 14 Juillet (tel. 45-82-06-50). A cozy little place with a barrel-shaped bar. Decent *menu* 44F, including oysters for appetizers. 5 excellent courses 55F. Tasty fish dishes *à la carte* 42-56F. Open Mon.-Fri. noon-2pm and 7:30-10pm.

La Couscousserie, 30, allées de la Corderie (tel. 45-82-76-54, near Martell). An off-beat restaurant near the center. 48F *menu,* and—surprise—*couscous* 38F. Open Tues.-Sun. 10am-2pm and 6pm-midnight.

Pizza Le Bojo, 42, rue Henri Fichon (tel. 45-32-35-39), just off place François 1er. Popular place, quick service, with water served in goblets and lots of good English music to enjoy over lunch. Good-size pizza or pasta 16-35F.

Le Central, 55, bd. Denfert Rochereau (tel. 45-82-01-44). Local spot behind the *marché*. Hearty 4-course 46F *menu,* beer or wine included. *Plat du jour* 30F. Open Thurs.-Mon. noon-2pm and 7-9pm, Tues. noon-2pm.

Le Chantilly, 146, av. Victor Hugo. A local spot with a simple restaurant-bar. Eat whatever the boss feels like serving: 60F includes *plat du jour,* coffee, and a bottle of wine. Lunch is served at noon, dinner at 8pm; don't be late. Open Sun.-Fri.

Sights

The joy of visiting Cognac lies in making your way from one brand name to the next, touring the warehouses, listening to the films about the history of each house, and collecting your nip bottles of golden brandy. More informative and less brand-inculcating than the others, **Hennessy**'s tour merits being seen, and you are treated to a (short) boat ride across the narrow Charente. (Open June 15-Sept. 15 Mon.-Fri. 9am-5:30pm; Sept. 16-June 14 Mon.-Fri. 8:30-11am and 1:45-4:30pm. Tours in English. Free.) **Martell** is open July-Aug. Mon.-Sat. 8:30-11am and 1:30-5pm; June and Sept., Mon.-Fri. 8:30-11am and 2-5pm; Oct.-May Mon.-Thurs. 8:30-11am and 2-5pm, Fri. 8:30-11am. On Sunday, **Otard,** bd. Denfert Rochereau, is the only major house open, but even though you get a tour of the first home of François I, the tour is downright hokey. (Tours April-Sept. daily at 10am, 11am, 2pm, 3pm, 4pm, and 5pm; Oct.-March Mon.-Fri. 10am, 11am, 2pm, 3pm, 4pm, and 5pm. Free.) Get a complete list of *chais* (distilleries and storehouses) from the tourist office.

Cognac has a few claims to fame besides drink. By the second half of the fourteenth century, the city was a bustling port, trafficking in wine and salt, and in 1448, a certain Charles d'Angoulême brought his new wife, Louise de Savoie, to stay for a while. Their son François was born in the château here—the same François who later became King François I of France. His statue stands in the center of town, and the château in which he was born now serves as the *chais* of **Baron Otard.**

The **Musée du Cognac,** located in the Jardin Public, provides a welcome respite from dank storehouses. Examine the collection of late nineteenth-century liquor bottles. Also on display is a wooden boat discovered on the banks of the Charente in 1979; it dates back to 2590 B.C.E., the neolithic age. (Open June-Sept. Wed.-Mon. 10am-noon and 2-6pm; Oct.-May Wed.-Mon. 2-6pm. Free.)

Among the city's fifteenth-century half-timbered houses, **Eglise du Sacré Coeur,** rue de Bellefonds, stands out as Cognac's most impressive architectural work. Look behind you as you enter the church at the little gothic spires in the back of the nave.

When you tire of trudging through the fragrant warehouses, where it is said that 22,000,000 potential bottles of cognac evaporate through the pores of the barrels each year, venture out into the countryside where the actual distilling takes place. There are six regions (called *crus*) in which official cognac grapes grow. The *cru* closest to Cognac, Grande Champagne, is the most prestigious, while the most distant bears the prosaic title Bois Ordinaire. Numerous small distilleries also operate in the region (for example, on the *routes* to Saintes or Angoulême); in many you can look around and taste the cognac and *pineau* produced on site. Unfortunately the *chais* are spaced far enough apart (at least 6km) to make a walking tour difficult. If you are on wheels and wish to explore, head for rue Gande in the *vieille ville,* follow it downhill to the gates of the city (porte St-Jacques), and turn right on quai Papin. Take the bridge across the Charente, and look to your right for the D731, in the direction of St-Jean-d'Angély. You will be in the region of vineyards known as the Borderies; several distilleries lie within 5km of Cognac. Unfortunately, none is accessible by bus.

Angoulême

From its dignified perch above the Charente River, Vieil Angoulême surveys not only modern Angoulême but much of the Charente Valley as well. The fortified ramparts command a view of miles of vineyards and red-roofed houses. Within the confines of the ramparts, seventeenth-century houses battle it out for breathing space along cobblestoned streets. Today Angoulême serves as an industrial, commercial, and administrative center, retaining the majesty with which it once presided over the surrounding countryside.

Orientation and Practical Information

In the upper Charente Valley, Angoulême is about halfway between Bordeaux and Poitiers on the main rail line and is also accessible from Saintes via Cognac. The old town, the most interesting part of Angoulême, sits high on a plateau just south of the Charente and southwest of the train station. As you leave the station, stop in at the tourist information booth for an excellent free map; then turn right and climb av. Gambetta (which turns into rampe d'Aguêsseau) to place Marengo. Continue up the pedestrian street, rue Marengo, towards the Hôtel de Ville. From the Hôtel de Ville, take av. Georges Clemenceau to the ramparts and turn right. The tourist office is across from the Cathédral St-Pierre.

Office de Tourisme: 2, place St-Pierre (tel. 45-95-16-84). Decent free maps, lists of hotels, and self-guided walking tours of the city. Open July-Aug. Mon.-Sat. 9am-7pm; Sept.-June Mon.-Sat. 9am-noon and 2-6pm. **Information kiosk** at place de la Gare (tel. 45-92-27-57). Maps and everything you need. Open Tues.-Sat. 9am-noon and 2-6pm.

Centre d'Information Jeunesse: 6, place Bouillard (tel. 45-92-86-73), next to the Hôtel de Ville. Information on just about everything, ride-board, Carte Jeune, BIJ tickets, coffee, temporary job information, and someone with whom you can discuss your problems. Open Tues.-Sat. 10am-7pm.

Post Office: Place du Champ de Mars (tel. 45-95-23-11). **Currency Exchange. Postal code:** 16000. Open Mon.-Fri. 8am-7pm, Sat. 8am-noon. **Branch office,** place Francis Louvel. Open Mon.-Fri. 8am-6:45pm, Sat. 8am-noon.

Train Station: Place de la Gare (tel. 45-38-50-50). More than 6 trains per day to Bordeaux (1½ hr., 78F), Poitiers (1 hr., 65F), Saintes (via Cognac, 1 hr., 48F), and Royan (1½ hr., 65F). 3 per day to La Rochefoucauld (22.50F). Information office open Mon.-Sat. 8:30am-7pm, Sun. 9am-7pm.

Bus Station: Autobus Citram, place du Champ de Mars (tel. 45-95-58-68). 1 per day to Confolens (2 hr., 39F) and Niort (87F). 3-4 per day to Cognac (1 hr., 33F). Office open Mon.-Fri. 5:45am-1pm and 1:30-8:45pm. **STGA,** place du Champs de Mars (tel. 45-91-55-22). Urban buses cost 6F. Ask for schedule at the tourist office.

Car Rental: Clustered around the train station; follow the signs. **Avis** and **Europcar** have the best deals.

Bike Rental: M. Pelton, 5, rue des Arceaux (tel. 45-95-30-91). Bike and motorcycle sales, but rents some bikes for about 34F per day, deposit 300F. Sat.-Tues. counts as 1 day. Open Tues.-Sat. 9:15am-noon and 2-7pm.

Laundromat: 3, rue Ludovic Trarieux in Vieil Angoulême. Wash 12F, dry 2F per 6 min. Open daily 7am-8pm. Also at 11, rue St-Roch. Wash 20F, dry 8F per 15 min. Open Mon.-Sat. 8am-7pm.

Ambulance: SAMU, Tel. 45-91-91-33 or 45-91-56-57.

Police: Place du Champs de Mars (tel. 45-38-05-55).

Accommodations and Camping

Finding cheap accommodations in Angoulême will not present any problems in summer. Decent and affordable hotels cluster near the intersection of av. Gambetta and the pedestrian precinct which leads down the hill from the *vieille ville.* The hostel is an especially good deal.

Auberge de Jeunesse (IYHF), on Ile de Bourgines (tel. 45-92-45-80), next to the campsite, 2km from the station. Turn right from the station, turn right across the bridge, bear left onto rue de la Rochefoucauld, right on rue de Paris, and left on rue Vinière across the bridge. The hostel will be to your left. Or take bus #7 from place du Champ de Mars and Cathédrale St-Pierre. Nice 85-bed hostel in a modern building on a small, forested island. Obliging management. Free passes to outdoor, Olympic-sized municipal swimming pool next door; free use of canoes and kayaks on the Charente, as well as a TV and iron. Kitchen facilities. 34F per night. Sheets 12F. Breakfast 11F. Good meals 35F. Ask for a key if out past 11pm. Often booked by groups in summer.

Hôtel du Cheval de Bronze, 7, rue St-Roch (tel. 45-95-02-74), just off av. Gambetta. 1-star. A bit noisy. A pleasant proprietor, and lots of clean, comfortable doubles 70F. Rooms with 2 beds 110F. Showers 10F. Breakfast 15F. Open Sept.-July.

Hôtel de l'Eperon, 68, rue de la Corderie (tel. 45-95-20-41), off av. Gambetta. Simple, clean, and pleasant. Singles 65F, doubles 75F, triples 110F. Showers 17F. Breakfast 15F.

Hôtel Le Palma, 4, rampe d'Aguesseau (tel. 45-95-22-89). Always full, so call ahead. A handful of singles 65F. Doubles (1 or 2 beds) 90F. Showers included. Breakfast 15F. Open Aug. 18-July 25. Excellent restaurant downstairs.

Hôtel les Messageries, place de la Gare (tel. 45-92-07-62), just a few steps to the right from the train station . Kind manager. Singles and doubles 80F. Showers 10F. Breakfast with croissant 15F. Open Sept.-July.

Hôtel de l'Ile, rue de Périgueux (tel. 45-95-03-01), near Eglise St. Martial. The bathrooms smell and the corridors haven't seen light for years, but the cheapest hotel in Angoulême. Singles 55F, with shower 65F. Doubles 80F.

Camping: Camping Municipal, on Ile de Bourgines (tel. 45-92-83-22), very near the youth hostel. Great location. 20F per person, showers included.

Food

Angoulême's specialty is *fromagier,* a cake filled with goat cheese. Ask for it at the local *boulangeries.* They also sell *clafoutis,* a peasant-style cherry flan, and delectable chocolate *marguerites* and *duchesses.* Don't miss the cheapest freshest food in town, at the **covered market** on place des Halles Centrales, 2 blocks down rue de Gaulle from the Hôtel de Ville. (Open daily 7am-12:30pm.) Excellent but sometimes expensive restaurants crowd the winding streets of Vieil Angoulême just west of the market. The finest places for a picnic are on the ramparts by the streams of the **Jardin Vert,** or behind the hostel by the small dam.

La Sicilia, 7, rue des 3 Notre Dames, in Vieil Angoulême. Dodge waiters racing around at top speed. Pizzas 21-42F, big salads 10-31F; also varied ice creams and dessert crêpes. Try the *pizza du chef* (40F). Open Tues.-Sat. noon-2pm and 7-10:30pm, Mon. 7-10:30pm.

Le Palma, 4, rampe d'Aguesseau. A pretty restaurant under a hotel (see Accommodations). Decent food at decent prices: 40F, 60F, and 90F *menus.* Open Mon.-Sat. 8am-2pm and 6-10pm.

Brasserie Alsacienne, place du Champ de Mars (tel. 45-92-91-44), near the post office. Mountains of sauerkraut. Hearty 55F *menu.* Wide variety of special desserts. Open Tues.-Sat. noon-2:30pm and 7-11pm.

Le Boeuf, 28, rue des 3 Notre Dames (tel. 45-92-60-96), near Eglise St-Andre. A little of everything. Try the smoked salmon (35F). Open Tues.-Sun. 12:15-2pm and 7:15pm-midnight.

Sights and Entertainment

Begin your tour of Angoulême with a stroll along the ramparts. Rumor has it that on a clear day you can see Cognac. If you follow the ramparts long enough, you will eventually come to the **Cathédrale St-Pierre.** Its dome and the square *campanile* may make you think you're in Italy, but the facade is pure Aquitaine, with distinctive bee-hive towers and close-packed decoration in a Romanesque frame.

The doorway and its flanking arches teem with lively scenes of hunting parties and jousting. Above, the false tympanums depict a more sober scene: Christ surrounded by the symbols of the four evangelists.

Behind St-Pierre, the **Musée Municipal** in the restored bishop's palace displays sixteenth- and nineteenth-century paintings, pottery, and Romanesque art. (Open Tues.-Sun. 10-11:45am and 2-5:45pm. Admission 10F.) The **Musée Archéologique,** 44, rue Montmoreau, displays regional treasures from the Gallo-Roman era to recent centuries. (Open Wed.-Mon. 10am-noon and 2-6pm. Free.) The center of Vieil Angoulême is **Eglise St-André,** redone in a Gothic style but retaining the original Romanesque tower and entrance. A step away on place F. Nouvel is the **Palais de Justice,** enclave of the Jacobins during the Revolution. Such luminaries as Calvin, Flaubert, Hugo, and Balzac have all graced the hall with their presence. Nearby, the staff of the **Hôtel de Ville** gives a tour of the rooms where Marguerite de Valois was raised. Other churches in town include Gothic **Eglise St-Martial,** in the center of town near the pedestrian zone. The extraordinary **Maison St-Simon,** 15, rue de la Cloche Verte (tel. 45-92-34-10), a sixteenth-century building with walls 2-feet thick, houses expositions of avant-garde art. (Open Tues.-Fri. 10am-noon and 2-6pm, Sat. 2-7pm. Free.)

From the end of June to the end of August, Angoulême hosts **Les Nuits d'Eté**—weekly theater, dance, and jazz. Most events are free; tickets to the other events start at about 30F. During the festival, restaurants open Sundays. The second week in May, Angoulême hosts the **Festival International de Jazz et Musiques Métisses** with groups from France, South Africa, Jamaica, Nigeria, Italy, Great Britain, and the United States. Call 45-95-43-42 for information.

La Rochefoucauld

A half-hour train ride from Angoulême (*direction* "Limoges," 21F) lies the unspoiled town of La Rochefoucauld, the site of a splendid sixteenth-century château, complete with dungeon, chapel, and galleries. (Open late June-early Sept.) The town's simple but handsome **Cathédrale Notre-Dame-de-l'Assomption** was built in the thirteenth century, attacked three times by Huguenots, and repeatedly reconstructed in one style or another. The tranquil cloisters of the **Couvent des Carmes** have calmed many a troubled mind.

In summer, the *syndicat* in Angoulême showers tourists with ads for La Rochefoucauld's *son et lumière* spectacle, with a costumed cast of 500 and plenty of horses. The historical hoopla is presented at least a dozen times from the tail end of June through the end of July, and begins in the château's courtyard at 10:30pm (55F).

Hôtel de France, 13, Grande Rue (tel. 45-63-02-29) is tasteful and tidy. (Doubles 75-100F. Breakfast 15F. Open March-Jan. Sun.-Thurs. until 10pm.) La Rochefoucauld also has a clean, two-star **camping municipal,** just around the corner from the château, next to the municipal pool. (4.80F per person, 2.90F per tent, 2.90F per car. Showers 3.20F. Open May-Sept.)

The town's attractions are a short walk from the train station. Look to your right for av. de la Gare, and take a left on rue Porte Marillac, which becomes rue des Halles. (Driving or biking from Angoulême, turn left on rue des Halles at the signs for the château.) From rue des Halles, turn left at the ivy-covered wall for the cathedral or right at the two large stone flower boxes for the cloisters; for the château and the serene waters of **La Tardoire,** continue straight. The **Syndicat d'Initiative,** rue des Halles (tel. 45-63-07-45), is next to the cloisters. (Open late June to mid-Sept. Mon.-Sat. 9am-noon and 3-6pm.) A cheery fruit and vegetable **market** takes place daily at 18, rue des Halles (Mon.-Sat. 8am-12:30pm and 2:30-7:30pm, Sun. 8am-12:30pm). The **postal code** is 16110.

North of La Rochefoucauld is **Confolens,** a well-preserved medieval town with intriguing houses, an ancient bridge, and a twelfth-century church. Confolens hosts a well-known **International Folklore Festival,** held around the second week of August. Fifteen countries send dance groups in picturesque garb. For information, contact the Confolens **Syndicat d'Initiative,** place des Marronniers (tel. 45-84-00-77; open Mon.-Sat. 9am-noon and 2-4pm). The **Hôtel de Vienne,** 4, rue de la Ferrandie (tel. 45-84-09-24), offers fine rooms. (Singles and doubles from 72F. Showers 12F. Breakfast 14F. Open until 10pm.) There's also a two-star municipal **campground,** route de St-Germain. (4.50F per person, 3.50F per tent, 2.20F per car; open April-Oct.) Confolens is accessible only by bus. Check with Citram in Angoulême.

Bordeaux

When Eleanor of Aquitaine married Henry Plantagenet in the twelfth century, her sizable dowry included the port city of Bordeaux. The marriage soured Anglo-French relations for three centuries but sweetened the pot of *Bordelais* merchants. The English developed a taste for Bordeaux red wine, and the mighty grape rose to power. Modern Bordeaux is far from idyllic—a thin layer of grime covers the grandiose remnants of its prosperous past, and the Garonne River flows a delicate shade of brown. Beyond the showy boutiques, you will find a city at once magnificent and polluted, crowded and diverse, but never boring. Bordeaux has some of the most acclaimed High Gothic churches in all of France. If you've been traveling through small towns seeing small-town churches, Bordeaux's cathedral will remind you of what big money can buy. Meals and accommodations in Bordeaux are cheap; the city is a good stopping point for travelers as well as a springboard to the awe-inspiring Dune du Pilat at Pyla-sur-Mer.

Orientation and Practical Information

Bordeaux's train station is a healthy half-hour walk to the center of town. First, pick up a decent map at the information booth in the station or a better map from the information panel with rotating advertisements (2F). Take cours de la Marne to place de la Victoire, turn right on the pedestrian street rue Ste-Catherine, and follow it into town. The *syndicat* will be on the right next to the Grand Théâtre. You can also catch either bus #7 or #8 (every 5-10 min., 6F) to the corner of cours de l'Intendance and cours du 30 Juillet for the *syndicat*. The neighborhoods around the hostel and the train station are depressed but not dangerous during the day. Many a *Bordelais,* however, will warn you to watch your valuables, as theft is rampant. The area around the center of town and rue Ste-Catherine is filled with expensive boutiques.

Syndicat d'Initiative: 12, cours du 30 Juillet (tel. 56-44-28-41). Take bus #7 or 8 from the train station. Large office, usually crowded. Can help you get a winery tour. Decent but not very detailed map, lists of hotels, camping information hotline (July-Aug.), and lots more. Sells Carte Jeune (60F). Runs a worthwhile bus tour of nearby wineries, with several *dégustations* (mid-May to mid-Oct. daily at 1:45pm; admission 90F, students 70F). Open June-Aug. Mon.-Sat. 9am-7pm, Sun. and holidays 9am-3pm; Sept.-May Mon.-Sat. 9am-12:15pm and 1:45-6:30pm. **Information booth** at train station (open daily 9am-1pm and 2-6pm).

Travel Agency: Havas Voyages, 54, cours du Châpeau Rouge (tel. 56-90-93-00), near the Grand Théâtre. Open Mon.-Fri. 9am-6pm, Sat. 9am-noon.

Centre d'Information Jeunesse d'Aquitaine: 5, rue Dufour Dubergier (tel. 56-48-55-50). Reams of information about campgrounds, hostels, activities, jobs, etc. BIJ and train tickets. Pick up your Carte Jeune (60F). Open Mon.-Fri. 9am-6pm.

CROUS: 18, cours du Hammel (tel. 56-91-98-80). Very little help to tourists; they can tell you which university restaurants are open but can't sell you tickets. Open Mon.-Fri. 9am-12:30pm and 1:30-4pm.

Consulates: U.S., 22, cours Maréchal Foch (tel. 56-52-65-95). Passports US$35 with 3 photographs, US$20 for ages under 18. Open Mon.-Fri. 9am-noon and 2-4:30pm. Visa section open Mon.-Fri. 9am-1pm. **U.K.,**15, cours de Verdun (tel. 56-52-28-35). Open Mon.-Fri. 9am-noon and 2:30-5pm.

Currency Exchange: On Sat. try the **post office** or the **Banque Franco-Portugaise,** 10, rue Claude Bonnier (tel. 56-98-73-93). Open Tues.-Fri. 9am-12:30pm and 2-6:30pm, Sat. 9am-

12:30pm and 2-5:30pm. On Sun., go to **Thomas Cook,** at the train station (tel. 56-91-58-80). Open daily 8am-8pm.

American Express: 14, cours de l'Intendance (tel. 56-81-70-02). Both a travel agency and a money exchange bureau. Open Mon.-Fri. 8:45am-noon and 1:30-6pm.

Post Office: Main office, 52, rue Georges Bonnac (tel. 56-48-87-48). Letters must be marked "Recette Principale" to be held at this branch by Poste Restante. **Postal code:** 33000. **Branch office,** on cours de la Marne, 5 blocks from the train station. Open Mon.-Fri. 8am-7pm, Sat. 8am-noon.

Train Station: Gare St-Jean, rue Charles Domercq (tel. 56-92-50-50). A huge, modern station, with marble floors so shiny you won't need a mirror. Information upstairs and ticket sales downstairs. City maps available at the information desk. Showers 13F. To Paris (10-14 per day; 4½-5½ hr. by day, up to 8 hr. by night; 267F), Angoulême (8-12 per day, 1 hr., 78F), Poitiers (10-14 per day, 2½ hr., 128F), Saintes (5-8 per day, 1-1½ hr., 70F), Nantes (5-8 per day, 4 hr., 186F), Toulouse (9-11 per day, 2½ hr., 135F), Nice (4-5 per day, 9-10 hr., 387F), Arcachon, with bus connections to the Dune du Pilat (12-16 per day, 45 min., 38F), St. Emilion (3-6 per day, 45 min., 32F). Information office open daily 8am-8pm.

Bus Station: Citram, 14, rue Fondaudege (tel. 56-81-18-18). To Libourne (Mon.-Sat. 15-18 per day, ¾ hr., 23F), Blaye via St-Gervais (Mon.-Sat. 20-25 per day; ¾ hr., 22F to St. Gervais; 1¾ hr., 33F to Blaye), Pauillac (1 hr., 35F), St-Emilion (5-7 per day, 1¼ hr., 32.50F), and Labrède (1-2 per day, ¾ hr., 18F). Information booth open Mon.-Sat. 9am-noon and 2-6:15pm. Buy tickets on board. Many smaller lines serve Bordeaux: Inquire at the *syndicat* for schedules. **CGFTE,** 25, rue du Commandant Marchand (tel. 56-24-23-23). City buses. Tickets 6.50F, *carnet* of 10 25F. Get a schedule at the *syndicat.*

Car Rental: Avis, in the train station (tel. 56-91-65-50). Open Mon.-Sat. 8am-7pm.

Bike Rental: The **train station** rents bikes for 45F per day with 300F deposit. Inquire at the baggage desk. Open 24 hours.

Hitching: Allostop, 13, cours de la Somme (tel. 56-94-58-49). Give them 3-4 days' notice and a 55F subscription fee, and they'll find you a ride for 0.16F per km for gas. 30F subscription for journeys under 300km. Open Mon.-Fri. 2-7pm, Sat. 10am-noon. To get a head start on hitching to Bayonne and Biarritz, take bus #6 to its terminus on N10; to Toulouse, take bus B or L to N113; to Périgneux, take bus #4 to N89.

Harvest Work: A small number of jobs picking grapes are available for 3-4 weeks starting Sept. 1. Pay is roughly 28F per hr. plus room and board. Contact the employment offices in Langon (tel. 56-62-34-88), Pauillac (tel. 56-59-07-51), or Libourne (tel. 57-51-18-08) well ahead of time.

Agence Nationale pour l'Emploi; 1 terrasse Front-du-Médoc (tel. 56-90-92-92). Information on temporary jobs. Open Mon.-Fri. 8:15am-12:15pm and 1:30-4:30pm.

Bookstore: Mollat, 87, rue Porte Dijeaux. Novels in English. Open Mon.-Sat. 9am-6:45pm.

Entertainment Hotline: Tel. 56-48-04-61. In English. Lines open 24 hours.

Laundromat: Take your pick. The most convenient is on cours de Marne, 5 min. the from station and hostel. Wash 12F, dry 2F per 5 min. Open daily 7am-10pm. Also at 27, rue de la Boëtie. Wash 15F, dry 2F per 5 min. Open daily 7am-9pm.

Centre d'Information sur les Droits des Femmes, 5, rue Jean-Jacques Rousseau (tel. 56-44-30-30). Information and counseling. Open Mon. noon-4pm, Tues. 2-7pm, Thurs. 10am-noon.

Medical Emergency: Tel. 17 or 18. **SAMU** ambulances, Tel. 56-96-70-70.

Hospital/Clinic: Hôpital St-André, 1, rue Jean Burguet (tel. 56-96-83-83). 24-hour emergency room. Free VD treatment Mon., Tues., Thurs.- Fri. 5-6pm.

Police: 87, rue Abbé de l'Epée (tel. 56-90-92-75).

Police Emergency: Tel. 17.

Accommodations and Camping

Between the hostel (a 10-min. walk from the station) and the Maison des Etudiants (a 30-min. walk or 6F bus ride), you shouldn't have trouble finding a reasonably priced bed, although calling ahead in July and August is a good idea. Hotels come in two categories: near the station (crowded, grimy) and not-so-near (better). Hotels near the station are likely to be full, but one day's advance notice, or a little footwork, should suffice. Some university dorms are available from July through mid-September at village #5 on the university campus in Talence (tel. 56-80-74-34). Take bus F from place de la Victoire.

Auberge de Jeunesse (IYHF), Foyer Barbey, 22, cours Barbey (tel. 56-91-59-51). Only 10 min. from the station: Bear right, then left onto cours de la Marne, then left again to cours Barbey. Huge (250 beds), but still fills up frequently. Kitchen facilities. A couple of washing machines. Sleeping bags allowed. 33F, nonmembers 36F. Breakfast 15F. Reception open 7-9:30am and 6-11pm. Lockout 9:30am-6pm. Strict curfew 11pm.

Maison des Etudiants, 50, rue Ligier (tel. 56-96-48-30). Take bus #7 or 8 from the station to Bourse du Travail, and continue in the same direction on cours de la Libération to rue Ligier. The Maison is on the righthand corner. On foot from the station, bear right onto cours de la Marne to place de la Victoire, cross the *place,* pick up cours Aristide Briand/cours de la Libération, and look to your right for rue Ligier (30 min.). Single rooms, quiet, clean, and closer to the center of town than the hostel. Warm and friendly. Ping-pong and TV downstairs. Kitchen lacks pots, pans, and silverware, but you might be able to borrow some. Has a few beds for women only Oct.-June. Accepts men as well July-Sept. Plenty of beds during summer 50F; with student I.D. 41F. Sheets and showers included.

Hôtel Huguerie, 67, rue Huguerie (tel. 56-81-23-69), in the *centre ville.* Tidy, tasteful singles and doubles 63-84F, with shower 100F. Showers 8F. Extra bed 15F. Breakfast in bed 14F.

Hôtel d'Amboise, 22, rue de la Vieille Tour (tel. 56-81-62-67), in the *centre ville.* Attractive rooms overlooking pedestrian streets. A few singles 65F, doubles 75F, with shower 95F. No communal shower. Breakfast 15F. Open 8am-9:30pm.

Hôtel la Boëtie, 4, rue de la Boëtie (tel. 56-81-76-68), a quiet street between place Gambetta and the Musée des Beaux Arts. Comfortable, spacious rooms and friendly management. Singles 75F, doubles 90F. Breakfast 15F. Reception open 8am-11pm.

Hôtel-Bar-Club Les 2 Mondes, 10, rue St-Vincent-de-Paul (tel. 56-91-63-09). Turn left from the station and right onto rue St-Vincent de Paul (3 min. on foot). One-star. Spacious, clean, bright rooms. Singles 72F, doubles 86F, with shower 84-100F. Triples 135F. No communal showers. Breakfast 15F.

Hôtel Cazassus, 35, rue du Temple (tel. 56-81-69-54), 3 blocks south of place Gambetta, off cours de l'Indépendance. Singles and doubles 67-75F. 2 beds 85-94F. Showers 13F. Breakfast 15F.

Camping: There are no campgrounds in the city itself, but several lie in the immediate vicinity. **Camping Chemin Long,** 108, rue Henri Vigneau (tel. 56-34-07-58), in Merignac. **Camping les Gravières,** Pont-de-la-Maye in Villenauve d'Ornon (tel. 56-87-00-36). A 2-star campground in a forest by the river. 200 sites. 14F per person, 12F per tent, 16F with car. Hot showers. Reception open 8am-11pm. Both are surrounded by countryside.

Food

Known in France as *la région de bien boire et de bien manger* (the region of fine drinking and dining), Bordeaux welcomes you with a variety of specialty restaurants. Along with the celebrated wine, you'll find fat oysters, tender *confits* of duck and goose (meat preserved in its own fat, and often fried up with potatoes—a delicacy), and *champignons* (mushrooms) as light as truffles. Bordeaux has restaurants in all price ranges, including some of the cheapest in France (30F *menus,* including wine). These cluster around pleasant **place St-Michel,** a multi-ethnic neighborhood located at a safe distance (but a short walk) from downtown madness. The restaurants near the **Grosse Cloche** in rue St-James offer just slightly more expensive (35-45F) *menus.* The area around place Général Sarrail, especially along rue des Augustins, also has some moderately priced establishments. For a look at more costly *menus,* walk along **rue des Faussets,** right off place St-Pierre. This ancient, newly renovated pedestrian street is lined with restaurants, each more atmospheric and elegant than its neighbor; most offer main dishes and *menus* for under 65F.

A cheap **supermarket** (close to Maison des Etudiants) is open Monday through Saturday from 9am to 10pm at the huge **Centre Meriadeck,** rue Claude Bonnier, near the post office. **Markets** are all over town. The market on allées de Tourny (moving to place de Grands Hommes in 1990) is upscale and expensive; the **marché des Capucius,** off cours de la Marne at the end of rue Clare, is a mad house—cheap and much more fun (open Mon.-Sat. 6am-1pm). There are markets near Eglise Notre-Dame, at the foot of rue Montesquieu (open Mon.-Sat. 6am-1pm), and on cours Victor Hugo at place de la Ferme de Richemont. On Sundays, try the grocery stores along cours Victor Hugo.

During the academic year, Bordeaux vibrates with student cafes. Many cluster around place de la Victoire. The "popular" places change every month. Be adventurous. Animated **Le Colorado,** 104, cours Aristide Briand, encourages mingling. (Open Tues.-Sat. noon-2pm and 6pm-2am.) The **Alligator,** place Général Sarrail, is a popular jazz club.

University Restaurants: If you figure out which branch is open, you can find an 18F, all-you-can-eat meal of respectable quality. Better yet, buy a ticket with your ISIC or your Carte Jeune and eat for 10F. Tickets are easily bought from students at the door and officially obtained at the restaurant. Tickets sold Mon., Wed., and Fri. 11:30am-1pm. **LEBEC,** rue de Cursol (tel. 56-91-79-96), is usually open July-August and Oct.-May Sun.-Fri. 11:40am-1:30pm and 6:40-8:10pm. Call CROUS (tel. 56-91-98-80) for an update, or stop by any location and look for posted schedules.

La Perla, 3, rue Gaspard Philippe (tel. 56-91-04-05). Looks out on the tower in the center of place St-Michel. 30F buys soup, *hors d'oeuvres,* vegetable, meat, dessert, and wine. Spanish specialties. Open Mon.-Sat. 10:30am-1:45pm and 6:30-8:45pm. Other restaurants with similarly designed international *menus* may be found on side streets off place St. Michel; some are even a few francs cheaper.

L'Athenee, 44, rue des trois Conils (tel. 56-52-18-18), 1 block east of the cathedral. A cozy place with appetizing 40F and 65F *menus.* Delicious desserts 15-22F. *Plat du Jour* with cheese and dessert 33F. Open Mon.-Fri. afternoon.

La Bouche Rit, 11, rue des Augustins. A lively joint with a sense of humour. Pizza and other dishes 21-38F. Open Tues.-Sat. noon-2pm and 7-10pm.

La Flambée, 26, rue du Mirail (tel. 56-92-71-02). Friendly management. For a memorable feast, try the 100F *menu* including *fruits de mer gratinée* (seafood with melted cheese). Or try the Burgundy fondue. Open Mon.-Sat. noon-2pm and 7:30-10pm.

Sights and Entertainment

Bordeaux's prosperous past is unambiguously indicated by two full-scale, whole-hog High Gothic masterpieces, **Cathédrale St-André** and **Eglise St-Michel.** The cathedral, built between the eleventh and the sixteenth centuries, is remarkable for its extravagant facade, its numerous and well-preserved grimacing gargoyles, and, above all, for its strange assortment of flying buttresses. Just to the right of the main portico sits a sixteenth-century buttress composed of a string of slender columns; the one next to it resembles a ribbon of flames. (Free organ recitals are held here every other Tues. evening mid-June to mid-Sept. Call 56-81-78-79 for information.) Across town, Eglise St-Michel is accompanied by an immense, free-standing bell tower of the fifteenth century, an imposing, flamboyant, hollow shell. Even if such architectural overstatements leave you cold, investigate the St-Michel neighborhood for its atmosphere and its phenomenally cheap restaurants. Nearby, **Eglise Ste-Croix,** a twelfth- and thirteenth-century Benedictine abbey, has a facade laden with Romanesque arches and statuettes. Another of Bordeaux's showpieces is its **Grand Théâtre.** The vestibule and staircase, sadly in need of refurbishing, influenced Garnier's Opéra in Paris. The regular season runs from mid-October to June (closed in summer); performances cost 45-150F, with occasional student discounts. (Tours July-Aug. Mon.-Fri. at 10:30am, 3pm, and 4:30pm, Sat. at 3pm and 4:30pm. Adults 10F, students 5F.)

Bordeaux's **Jardin Public** was vandalized during the Revolution and subsequently used as a target range by the army, but from 1856 on, it was gradually renovated and redesigned in the English style. Today these lovely 25 acres of green in the center of Bordeaux support botanical gardens. (Open daily 7am-10pm.) The

Musée des Beaux Arts, near the cathedral, houses a fine collection of French art, including works by Délacroix, Corot, Renoir, and Matisse. (Open Mon.-Sat 10am-noon and 2-6pm. Admission 12F, students 6F, free Wed.) In place du Colonel Raynal, **Galerie des Beaux Arts** shows refined temporary exhibits. (Open Wed.-Mon. 10am-7pm, Wed. 9-11pm. Admission 20F, students 15F.) **Musée d'Aquitaine,** on cours Pasteur, houses a collection of archeological treasures from the area, including the 2000-year-old *Vénus à la Corne.* (Open Wed.-Mon. 10am-6pm. Admission 5F, students 3F, free Wed.) The museum also oversees archeological sites throughout the city. (Ask at the tourist office for details.) Bordeaux is making a great effort to restore the city around place du Parlement, and you may be interested in a walking tour through some of these lovely seventeenth- and eighteenth-century streets.

Wine and Wineries

There are three main families of red Bordeaux wine: Medocs and Graves; St-Emilion, Pomerol, and Fronsac; Bordeaux and Côtes de Bordeaux. All except Graves are named after the region from which they come; Graves takes its name from the small pebbles in the soil on which its vines grow. The white wines are a different story: The dry (sold in a green bottle) and the sweet *liquoreux* (in a clear one), are each made by a different process. The dry are harvested and fermented like most wines, but grapes (such as the Sauternes) for the *liquoreux* gain their aroma from "the noble rot," a microscopic fungus that attacks the over-ripe grape.

Opposite the *syndicat,* the **Maison du Vin/CIVB,** 1, cours du 30 Juillet, 33075 Bordeaux (tel. 56-52-82-82), disseminates lots of information. They are the only house within Bordeaux proper that offers free tastings. (Open Mon. 8:30am-12:30pm and 1:30-6pm, Tues.-Fri. 8:30-6pm, Sat. 9am-12:30pm and 1:30-5pm.) Both **Magnum,** 3, rue Gobineau (tel. 56-48-00-06; open Mon.-Sat. 9am-7:30pm), and the **Vinothèque,** 8, cours du 30 Juillet (tel. 56-91-66-70; open Mon.-Sat. 9am-7pm), next to the *syndicat,* have knowledgeable salespeople and will gladly sell you a bottle of Bordeaux red in the 10-10,000F range.

A visit to the major wine-producing châteaux requires, at the very least, a preliminary phone call. Many huge houses, such as **Château Haut-Briond** (tel. 56-98-33-73), manage to sell their wines with no help from backpack-laden small-fry. Ask them how they may be reached by bus and they are likely to suggest you take a cab; hesitate, and it's all over. Enlist the support of the *syndicat* to help you make reservations. Many smaller houses, however, accept walk-in visitors. Get a list of smaller châteaux from the *syndicat.*

Bus tours of châteaux in the region leave from the *syndicat* and are a good way to see many wineries quickly. (Mid-May to mid-Oct. 90F per person, students 70F.)

About 35km east of Bordeaux is the village of **St-Emilion,** with beautiful cloisters and a splendid hillside view of the vineyards of more than 1000 wineries, which cultivate some of the world's best-known grapes. St-Emilion defines the word idyllic. There are over 29 wine-producing châteaux in St-Emilion that bear the mark of highest distinction—*Grand Crus.* Trains run to St-Emilion three to six times per day (¾ hr., 32F). Take a right on the main road from the station and walk the 2km to St-Emilion. The *Syndicat d'Initiative,* place des Créveaux (tel. 57-24-72-03), sits at the foot of the church tower. (Open daily 9:30am-12:30pm and 1:45-6pm.) The *syndicat* organizes tours (some in English) of the different châteaux (July-Sept. 15 Mon.-Sat., 2½ hr., 40F). These include a round-trip bus ride to the winery, a guided tour of the château, and a free *dégustation.* If you feel like striking out on your own, ask the *syndicat* for a list of châteaux that offer tours in English. The medieval town merits as much attention as its famed wineries. From atop the **donjon** (3F, open daily 9am-12:30pm and 2:30-6:45pm), the scenic panorama begs to have its photograph taken. St-Emilion's intriguing **Eglise Monolithe** takes its name from its unorthodox construction. The entire structure was painstakingly carved from a single, massive piece of rock. The guided tour passes through the ancient catacombs adorned with open sarcophagi and an occasional bone or two, lending an eerie atmosphere to the unassuming village. Tours leave daily from the *syndicat* about every

45 minutes beginning at 10am (45 min., last tour at 5:45pm, 20F). Don't get too caught up rushing from winery to winery; instead, secure a patch of grass, a jug of wine, and the view.

Near Bordeaux

Southeast of Bordeaux, toward Leognan, lies the beautiful thirteenth-century **Château de la Brede** (tel. 56-20-20-49; in theory open Wed.-Mon. 9:30-11:30am and 2:30-5:30pm), former home of the philosopher Montesquieu (1689-1755). The château is accessible by **Citram** bus (1-2 per day, ¾ hr., 20F).

North of Bordeaux in the **Pauillac** commune, the wine museum at **Châteaux Mouton-Rothschild** provides a vicarious thrill, but visits are made by arrangement only (tel. 56-59-22-22). Pauillac is served by frequent Citram buses (10-15 per day, 1 hr., 32F).

About every hour, trains leave Bordeaux for **Arcachon,** a 45-minute ride away (39F). Do not fail, under any circumstances, to get on one of these trains. Arcachon, a bustling seaside resort with a beautiful sandy beach, is not the main attraction. The real reason to visit lies 10km south of town. It is one of the most sublime beaches in the world: the **Dune du Pilat** at **Pyla-sur-Mer.** At 117m above sea level, the spectacular dune is the largest in Europe, massive enough to absorb the summertime throngs effortlessly. In the late afternoon especially, you'll have plenty of room to ski down the forgiving but steeply-raked slopes, and to slog painfully back up. This golden alp is more than just a pile of sand; it's a million intersecting curves, textures, and shadows. Buses leave for Pyla (a short walk from the Dune) from the Arcachon station (about 24 per day, last return at about 7:45pm, 40 min., one way 7F). From the stop at Hôtel Haïtza, continue straight on foot, climbing to the left (10-15 min.).

Arcachon's **Syndicat d'Initiative,** place Roosevelt (tel. 56-83-01-69), is a stone's throw south from the station (turn left from station; open Mon.-Fri. 9am-noon and 2-7pm, Sat. 9am-noon and 2-6pm.) Pyla's *syndicat,* rond-point du Figuier (tel. 56-54-02-22), provides lists of hotels, but you almost certainly won't be able (or willing) to afford a single one, especially in July and August, when prices are inflated 50-80%, and the cheapest rooms top the 100F mark. (Open July-Aug. 10am-1pm and 3-7pm; Sept.-June 9am-5pm.) Instead, try the three-star municipal campground (tel. 56-83-24-15) in Arcachon, **Camping les Abatilles,** allée de la Galaxie (open April to mid-Oct.), or choose from four campgrounds in Pyla, including a three-star site on the Dune, **Camping de la Dune** (tel. 56-22-72-17; open May-Sept.). Camping off campsites is prohibited in the area. Across the bay from Arcachon in **Cap-Ferret** is an **Auberge de Jeunesse,** 87, av. de Bordeaux (tel. 56-60-64-62; open July-Aug.). Cap-Ferret is accessible by ferry from Arcachon's **Jetée Thiers** (9am-noon and 2-7pm every ½ hr.; one way 24F, round-trip 32F; tel. 56-54-83-09). Arcachon oysters are delightful when washed down with a bottle of Graves—but most of the restaurants here are as expensive as the hotels. Across from Arcachon's station, the **Coquille,** 63, bd. du Général Leclerc, includes oysters (*huitres*) and mussels (*moules*) in its five-course 55F *menu.*

Périgord-Quercy

The French spend their vacation month in the provinces of Périgord and Quercy, and wealthy British purchase country homes here. Winding roads pass through extraordinarily green fields brushed by tall, graceful trees that perhaps hide truffles waiting to be sniffed out by a plump pig. Outside the farms, geese peck innocently as their livers fatten for *foie gras*. Despite the animated markets selling live trout and rabbits, enough gloomy gargoyles glare down from the rooftops to make you realize the age of the town. The region's deeply etched history is studded with stories, such as the tale of the Sarlat abbot who was accidentally killed by one of his own monk's arrows, or the saga of the construction of the Tour de Mataguerre in Périgueux—built largely by lepers.

Hovering about Périgord and Quercy's many rivers are dramatic cliffs, some of which hide prehistoric cave art. The 20,000-year-old bison drawings at Les Eyzies are among the last in Europe still open to the public. In the Gouffre de Padirac, boatmen pole tourists down an icy subterranean river.

Above ground, there's also plenty to discover: Dramatic castles tower over golden cliffs at Beynac and Rocamadour. Every now and then you'll come across a village built *into* a cliff side, such as La Roque-Gageac. Isolated châteaux such as Hautefort recall an era of elegance, but most of the châteaux and the feudal *bastides* were built for defense during the Hundred Years' War.

Bus and train connections in the region are neither frequent nor convenient. Driving, hiking, and biking are the most rewarding means of getting around. Many *sentiers de grandes randonnées,* clearly marked long-distance footpaths, form an extensive network connecting such cities as Limoges, Les Eyzies, Sarlat, Souillac, and Cahors, passing through remote areas. Hitching can be a problem on the perilous slopes and bends of the area's small roads. In summer, tourist buses travel from the larger towns through the valley and to more secluded spots, such as Rocamadour and Les Eyzies. Excursions range from 95-220F, with 10% discounts for students.

From late July through August, tourists compete frantically for hotel rooms, tickets, and breathing space. Sarlat, Rocamadour, Padirac, and Les Eyzies are especially crowded. Oddly, Périgueux is more peaceful, despite its many architectural attractions.

Périgueux

In Périgueux the Isle River winds lazily past scattered Roman ruins, a massive Byzantine-Romanesque cathedral topped with an outrageous number of domes and spires, and a *vieille ville* of Renaissance *hôtels particuliers* and narrow pedestrian streets. With plenty of moderately priced accommodations, and wooded countryside within walking distance from *centre ville,* Périgueux is also a good base for daytrips to the cave paintings of Les Eyzies and the fortified *bastides*.

Orientation and Practical Information

The *vieille ville* and *syndicat* are a 10- to 15-minute walk from the train station. Turn right on rue Denis Papin and left on rue des Mobile-de-Coulmiers, which becomes rue du Président Wilson. On your right, you'll pass rue Lafayette, which leads to the Roman ruins clustered around the train tracks. Continuing straight on rue du Président Wilson, the *syndicat* will be on your left up av. d'Aquitaine and the *vieille ville* will be directly ahead, perched on the western banks of the Isle River and enclosed by cours de Tourny, bd. de M. Montaigne, and rue Taillefer.

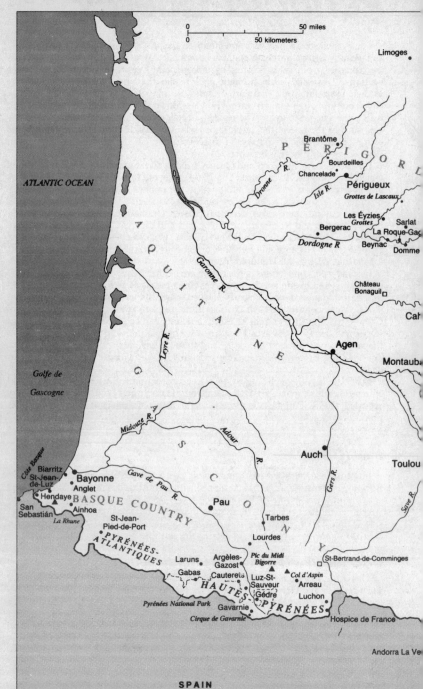

0   50 miles
0   50 kilometers

Limoges

ATLANTIC OCEAN

PÉRIGORD

Brantôme
Bourdeilles
Chancelade   Périgueux
Grottes de Lascaux

Dronne R.
Isle R.

Les Éyzies
Grottes
Bergerac   La Roque-Gac
Dordogne R   Beynac
Domme
Sarlat

AQUITAINE

Garonne R.

Château
Bonaguil

Cah

Agen

Montauba

Golfe de
Gascogne

Leyre R.

GASCO

Midouze R.
Adour R.

Auch

Toulou

Gers R.

Save R.

Côte Basque
Biarritz
St-Jean-
de-Luz   Bayonne
Anglet
Hendaye
San
Sebastián   Ainhoa
La Rhune

Gave de Pau R.

BASQUE COUNTRY

St-Jean-
Pied-de-Port

Pau

Tarbes

Lourdes

St-Bertrand-de-Comminges

PYRÉNÉES-
ATLANTIQUES

Laruns   Argelès-
Gazost
Gabas   Cauterets
Luz-St-
Sauveur
HAUTES   Gèdre
Pyrénées National Park
Gavarnie
Cirque de Gavarnie   PYRÉNÉES

Pic du Midi
Bigorre
Col d'Aspin
Arreau
Luchon

Hospice de France

Andorra La Ve

SPAIN

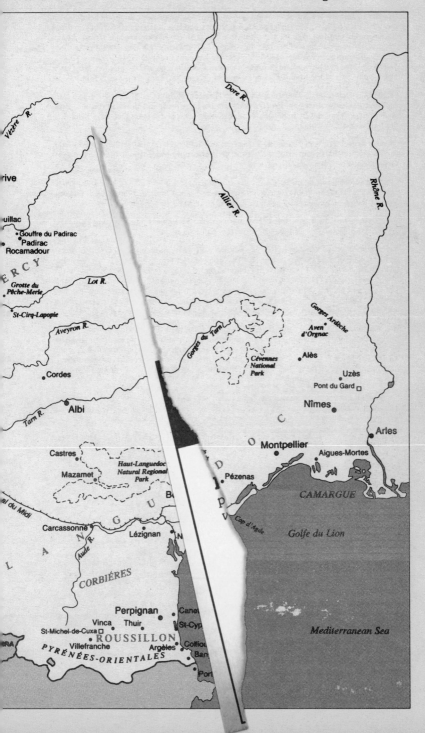

Syndicat d'Initiative: 1, av. d'Aquitaine (tel. 53-53-10-63). English-speaking and helpful, with bus schedules, topographical maps and hiking guides, and lists of alternative accommodations (farms and campsites). Ask for the invaluable brochure *La Fête en Périgord* (free). Guided tours of town, sometimes in English, July-Aug. (14F, students 8F). Organized bus tours of surrounding towns in summer (140-175F, reservations obligatory; see Near Périgueux). Open July-Aug. Mon. 9am-noon and 2-7pm, Tues.-Fri. 8:30am-noon and 1-7pm, Sat. 9am-noon and 2-5pm; Sept.-June Mon.-Fri. 9am-noon and 2-7pm, Sat. 9am-noon and 2-5pm.

Office Départemental de Tourisme: 16, rue du Président Wilson (tel. 53-53-44-35). Information on the Dordogne region. Brochures on camping, festivals, and shows in the city. Busy staff—be persistent. Open June-Sept. Mon.-Fri. 9am-noon and 2-6pm; Oct.-May Mon.-Fri. 9am-noon and 2-4:30pm.

Student Travel: HAVAS Agence de Voyages, av. d'Aquitaine (tel. 53-08-12-62), across from the post office. BIJ/Transalpino tickets. Student discount airfare tickets (non-refundable). Open Mon.-Fri. 8:30am-noon and 1:30-6pm.

Centre d'Information Jeunesse (CIJ): 1, av. d'Aquitaine (tel. 53-53-52-81), next to the *syndicat*. Tons of information on concerts, excursions, and other youth activities. Helps you find student lodging (free). Open Tues.-Fri. 2:30-6:30pm, Sat. 2:30-5:30pm.

Post Office: Rue du 4 Septembre, near the *syndicat*. **Telephones** and **currency exchange.** Postal code: 24000. Open Mon.-Fri. 8am-7pm, Sat. 8am-noon.

Train Station: Rue Denis Papin (tel. 53-09-50-50 daily 4am-midnight; 53-03-23-00 for reservations). To Paris (6-7 per day, 5-6 hr., 222F), Lyon (4 direct per day, 7-8 hr., 226F), Toulouse (6-8 per day; 4 hr.; 141F via Brive, 137F via Agen), Limoges (10-13 direct per day, 1-1¾ hr., 55F), Bordeaux (11-13 direct per day, 1½-2 hr., 69F), Sarlat (3-4 per day, 1½ hr., 53F), Les Eyzies (4 per day, ½-¾ hr., 29F; take the 7:15am train to see the cave paintings), and Brive-la-Gaillarde (6 per day, 1-1½ hr., 44F). Information office open Mon.-Thurs. 8:30am-7:45pm, Fri. 9am-7:40pm, Sat. 9am-noon and 2-7:45pm, Sun. 10am-noon and 2-7:45pm.

Bus Station: Place Francheville (tel. 53-08-76-00). Disregard the abandoned lower part of the building; the offices are upstairs. Schedules are confusing and fluctuate often. **Gonthier Nouhaud** (green and white buses) goes to Mussidan and Hautefort. Other lines run to Riberac, Verteillac, Payzac, Limoges (2½ hr.), Excideuil, Sarlat via Montignac (2 hr. to Sarlat), Brantôme, and Bergerac (1-1½ hr.). Check at the *syndicat* or station for schedules; most lines also stop at the SNCF station.

Car Rental: Europcar, 14, rue Denis Papin (tel. 53-08-15-72), across from the train station. The most reasonable rates in town and a special weekend rate. Drive to the *bastides* and smaller towns, but avoid the jammed streets of Les Eyzies and Rocamadour.

Bike Rental: Au Tour de France, 96, av. du Maréchal Juin (tel. 53-53-41-91). Open Mon.-Sat. 8:30am-12:30pm and 2-7:30pm. **Huot Sports,** 41bis, cours St-Georges (tel. 53-53-31-56).

Hospital: Centre Hospitalier, 80, av. Georges Pompidou (tel. 53-07-70-00).

Medical Emergency: Tel. 18. **SAMU,** Tel. 53-08-81-11.

Police: Commissariat, rue du 4 Septembre (tel. 53-08-17-67).

Police Emergency: Tel. 17.

Accommodations and Camping

Several inexpensive hotels cluster beside the train station. A few more are scattered on the way into the *vieille ville* and in the pedestrian area. In summer, reserve a few days in advance.

Foyer des Jeunes Travailleurs Résidence Lakanal, off bd. Lakanal (tel. 53-07-83-61). From the station, turn right and follow the tracks as closely as you can; when you reach bd. Lakanal, turn right to find the tracks, and look to your right for the *foyer* (20 min.). Located just behind Club Municipal, Loisirs et Culture. Dormitory rooms with bunk beds for short stays. 42F. Sheets, showers, and breakfast included. Cafeteria lunch 30-35F. Dinner 30F. Reception open Mon.-Fri. 6-8pm, Sat.-Sun. after 8pm.

Hôtel du Midi et du Terminus, 18-20, rue Denis Papin (tel. 53-53-41-06), opposite the train station. Run by a kindly manager and his family. Comfortable, attractive rooms on a noisy street. Some are small. TV lounge. A "room in the turret" single with a small sky window 70F. Doubles 80F, with shower 90F. 2 big, comfortable beds 115F. Hall showers included.

Breakfast with *croissant* 18F. 1-day advance notice suffices. Excellent *menus* from 55F daily noon-2pm and 7:30-9:30pm. Reception closed Sun. 2-6:30pm. Open Oct. 7-Sept. 25.

Hôtel des Voyageurs, 22, rue Denis Papin (tel. 53-53-17-44), across from the station. No-frills accommodations; definitely cheap. Station announcer and trains clearly audible. Doubles 55-60F. 2 beds 75F, with shower 80F. Showers 8F. Breakfast 15F. 1-day advance notice is wise. Reception open Mon.-Sat. Closed 3 weeks in summer.

Hôtel des Arènes, 21, rue du Gymnase (tel. 53-53-49-85), between Eglise St-Etienne-de-la-Cité and Tour de Vésone. Convenient, comfortable, and quiet 2-star. Airy doubles with telephone 70F and 90F, with shower 120F. 40F per extra bed. Showers 22F. Breakfast 17F, 20F, and 27F. Reception open until 11pm. Closed Sun. noon-6pm.

Camping: Barnabé-Plage, 80, rue des Bains (tel. 53-53-41-45), 1½km from Périgueux in Boulazac. Take the city bus (*direction* "Cité Belaire") from cours Montaigne or from the SNCF station. 2-star site on the river with canoe rentals. 9.80F per person, 8.50F per tent, 5.50F per car. Open daily 8:30am-midnight. **Camping de l'Ile,** route de Brive (tel. 53-53-57-75), 3km from town in Boulazac. 1-star. 12.75F per person, 9.40F per tent, 9.40F per car. Open April-Sept. daily until 11pm. **Farms** in the region sometimes let rooms or camping space. The *syndicat* has a list.

Food

The most notable of *périgourdin* specialties are truffles and *pâtés*. *Charcuteries* along rue Limogeanne are palaces of *pâté de foie gras* and other delicacies. You can buy fresh produce at the daily morning **market** in place du Coderc, and meat in the adjacent, covered **Halles**. There is also a market near the cathedral on Wednesdays and Saturdays. **Monoprix**, dominating place de la République in *centre ville,* has a supermarket on the second floor. (Open Mon.-Tues. and Thurs. 9am-12:30pm and 2:15-7pm, Wed. and Sat. 9am-1pm and 2-7pm.) The garden bordering the ruins of the Arènes Romaines, or the more central place St-Louis, are pleasant picnic spots. Most hotels serve 50-60F *menus;* the Hôtel du Midi's is particularly delicious.

Lou Campagnard, 2, rue Lammary, just off place St-Louis. A workers' restaurant full of rowdy regulars. Lunch only, but you won't need dinner. 40F buys soup, entree, meat, vegetable, salad, dessert, and wine. Open Mon.-Sat. noon-2pm.

Febus, 11, rue Notre-Dame (tel. 53-53-20-75). Somewhat obscure, but casual bar-restaurant with young, regular crowd. Light but savory 40F *menu,* good salads 20-30F, chili and *plats du jour* 25F. Specializes in Mexican cuisine. Exotic cocktails and beers. Open for meals May to mid-Oct. daily noon-midnight; open for drinks year-round.

La Belle Epoque, 1, place du Général Leclerc (tel. 53-09-51-99), beside the Palais de Justice off bd. Montaigne. Indulge in authentic *périgourdin* cuisine in an elegant setting. *Menus* 90F and up. Open Tues.-Sun.

Pizzeria Les Coupoles, rue de la Clarté (tel. 53-08-22-97), near Cathédrale St-Front. Good-sized pizzas 23-37F. Open Tues.-Sun.

Café-Bar Le Gambetta, 18bis, rue Gambetta (tel. 53-53-73-70). Light lunches and interesting salads (30-35F). *Plat du jour* 37F. Open Mon.-Fri. noon-2pm and early evenings.

Sights and Entertainment

As you face the station on rue Denis Papin, look to your left for the narrow, three-humped footbridge across the train tracks to av. Maréchal Juin. Turn left, then take rue du Président Wilson for the *vieille ville* and the tree-lined waters of l'Isle and its canal. The river flows through the old town, and the great white domes and 70-meter-high belfry of **Cathédrale St-Front** float above it. Built in the shape of a Greek cross, the cathedral successfully combines Sacré-Coeur's Byzantine domes, the Abbey of Cluny's Romanesque arches, and the stylish turrets of a reformed fortress. In 1852, the architect of Paris's Sacré Coeur, Abadie, added more Byzantine turrets than conservative critics deemed decent, creating a cathedral that doesn't know when to quit. (Free tours of the cavernous interior in summer daily 9am-noon and 2-5pm. Admission to the ninth-century cloisters and crypt 10F.)

One kilometer southwest, just across the tracks, is the massive, cut-away cylinder of the **Tour de Vésone.** Once the sacred temple of an important Gallo-Roman city of the first century, but now shorn of its marble encasement, it looks like a crumbling smokestack. Legend has it that the break in the tower was made by St-Front chasing away the last demons of paganism. Farther on stands the Romanesque **Eglise St-Etienne-de-la-Cité,** with its unmistakable Aquitaine dome resembling a helmet in the sky. St-Etienne's first cupola dates back to the eleventh century. Up from St-Etienne is the **Jardin des Arènes,** where both children and couples find recreational space. Here you can see the remains of the first-century Roman stairwells and the ancient arena's vomitorium (exit area). (Open May-Aug. 7:30am-9pm.) From the garden, take av. du 50*ème* R.I., and turn right on rue Turenne for **Château Barrière,** a fortified medieval residence of modest proportions with jazzy Renaissance doors and windows (unthinkingly used by some as a dump). In the *vieille ville,* rue Limogéanne and rue de la Miséricorde in particular are graced by lovely Renaissance houses.

On allée de Tourny, Neanderthal Man and his ancestors await you at the **Musée du Périgord.** Not the amusing death notice on the glass case enclosing the Chancelade Man's remains. The ornate script announces that the death occurred 15,000 years ago, and is signed by "his tribe and old Cro-Magnon cousins of Les Eyzies, DE PROFUNDIS." The museum's collection also includes Stone Age implements and Roman artifacts. (Open Wed.-Mon. 10am-noon and 2-5pm. Admission 5F, Wed. free.)

On summer evenings, join the local youth in the sidewalk cafes along **boulevard Montaigne.** The **Café St-Louis,** 26bis rue Eguillerie, sometimes features live jazz. (Open Mon.-Sat. 8pm-2am.) If you crave disco, try **L'An des Roys,** 51, rue Aubarede (tel. 53-53-01-58), or **L'Ubu,** 3, rue des Jacobins, a *club privé* that might not let you in. (L'An des Roys open Wed.-Sat. from 10:30pm and Sun. from 2:30pm. L'Ubu open Tues.-Sun.)

Near Périgueux

Twenty-five kilometers north of Périgueux lies **Brantôme,** a beautiful village whose setting is sublimely pastoral: One glance takes in the stone bridge, weeping willows, and weir on the river—ideal for a lazy afternoon or roadside picnic. The Dronne River encircles the town, reflecting the old houses and their flower-covered balconies. Brantôme's architectural highlight, its ancient **abbaye,** was founded by Charlemagne in 769. Take the fascinating tour of the monastic buildings and the grottos, where the earliest inhabitants scratched out a chapel and a mill. (Tours in French only, with a poor English translation available. 10-11am and 2-5pm on the hour, ½ hr., 10F.) The monks took refuge in the **Grotte du Jugement Dernier** whenever the abbey was attacked; the eerie medieval reliefs depicting the Last Judgment are especially striking. The rest of the abbey buildings are now the town hall and the **Musée Fernand-Desmoulin,** named after the local painter whose works it exhibits, along with a collection of prehistoric artifacts discovered near Brantôme. (Open 1 week around Easter and June 16-Sept. 15 Wed.-Mon. 10am-noon and 2-6pm. Admission 5F, Wed. free.) You can also climb the splendid eleventh-century bell tower by the church. (Tower tours at 10:45am, 11:30am, 3:15pm, 4:15pm, and 5:15pm. Admission a steep 10F.)

Brantôme's **Syndicat d'Initiative,** on av. de Pierre de Bourdeille near the abbey (tel. 53-05-80-52), sells maps suggesting walking circuits of Brantôme and the surrounding region (2F). (Open daily 10:30am-noon and 3:30-6pm.) The **Hôtel de la Poste,** rue Gambetta, posts a four-course *menu* with wine for 40F. Rooms upstairs range from 60-100F. The pedestrian streets of Brantôme have a good number of *boulangeries, pâtisseries,* and *charcuteries* that can supply your picnic lunch.

Getting to Brantôme is not so pleasant: One bus per day runs on Fridays and Saturdays during the school year (45 min., 19.30F). During July and Aug., the *syndicat* organizes bus tours of the Dronne Valley (including Bourdeilles and Brantôme) that depart Wednesdays at 8am and return at 6pm. Check with the *syndicat* or call the station (tel. 53-08-43-13) for details. As the bus tour costs 140F (student discount 10%), the budget option—biking—appears even more attractive. Though there are sometimes too many cars for comfort, the route passes through peaceful countryside and gets hilly only toward the end. Hitching is impossible as the road weaves a narrow, twisted path.

Seven kilometers southwest of Brantôme lies **Bourdeilles,** where a fortified medieval castle, bridge, and town sit on the Dronne. In July and August, daily canoe and kayak rentals at Porte des Réformés, Brantôme (tel. 53-05-80-46) enable you to paddle your way to Bourdeilles. (80F includes the return to Brantôme by van.) You can also walk from Brantôme, and CFD buses connect Bourdeilles to Périgueux erratically. On the same line as Brantôme lie **Chancelade,** a once great but now crumbling abbey, with a museum of its own tenth- to twelfth-century art, and **Villars,** where there are several cave paintings. In **Excideuil** are the ruins of a twelfth-century castle; the town is a one-hour bus ride from Périgueux (1-2 per day). The fully intact château at **Hautefort,** with medieval towers and Renaissance facades, is more impressive but just as difficult to reach by bus. (See Bus Station in Périgueux.)

South of Périgueux, between Bergerac and Agen, are the feudal **bastides.** Some of these small fortress-towns were built by the English, some by the French, when both countries claimed sovereignty over the area during the Hundred Years' War. The *bastides* share a common design: rows of rectangular blocks, cut at right angles by narrow streets and surrounded by square ramparts. The English fortress of **Monpazier** is the best preserved, retaining its church, arcaded town square, and fortifications. It is also quite close to the intimidating medieval castle of **Biron.** Other *bastides,* including **Lalinde, Villeneuve, Villeréal,** and **Puylaroque,** can be visited by bike or car in a day.

In addition to the excursion to Brantôme and the Dronne Valley, Périgueux's *syndicat* arranges **bus tours** from mid-June to mid-September to the following points: Sarlat, Domme, La Roque-Gageac, and Beynac (Tues. at 9am, return 6:50pm; 140F); the *bastides* and the château in Biron (Thurs. at 7:50am, return 7:20pm; 155F); and the Thot museum, the re-created Lascaux II caves, and the museum in Les Eyzies, but not the caves and paintings (Fri. at 7:50am, return 7pm; 175F). Call the day before to confirm departures. Buses leave from outside the *syndicat* and 5-10 minutes later from the *gare.* (Students get a 10% discount.)

Brive

Since 1437 Brive has proudly borne the name *Brive-la-Gaillarde* (Brive the Bold). The days of danger have passed, however, and modern Brive, surrounded by the countryside of Périgord and Quercy, has comfortably adapted to its role as regional center. With 54,000 inhabitants, the city tolerates its share of dull residential areas, but nonetheless makes a pleasant stopping point en route to such destinations as Rocamadour, Padirac, Cahors, Lascaux, and Hautefort.

The center of Brive is dominated by the twelfth-century **Collégiale St-Martin,** named after the Spaniard who, after introducing Christianity to Brive in the fifth century, was murdered and martyred. His decapitated bust in the left transept is still venerated by locals. In 1986, excavations made at St-Martin uncovered ancient walls and a bell foundry. Photos of the discoveries are exhibited just inside the church's main portal. (Tours July-Aug. Sun. at 4pm; or call 55-24-10-82 at least 1 day in advance to request a tour.) **Musée Edmond-Michelet,** 4, rue Champanatier, close to place de la Liberté, is a 5-minute walk northwest from the train station. The building was the home of a local leader in the Resistance and commemorates the fight against the Nazis. (Open Mon.-Sat. 10am-noon and 2-6pm. Free.) An excellent collection of archeological finds from southern France, formerly housed in the **Musée Ernst-Rupin,** rue Massenal (tel. 55-74-90-15), has been transferred to **Hôtel de la Benche,** 2 blocks away on rue Blaise Raynal. The archeological archives, however, remain on display at the old museum site. (Open Wed. 3-6pm, Sat. 4-6pm.)

You should come to Brive for the wonderful **market,** if nothing else. One of the biggest in the area, it occupies a huge chunk of place du 14 Juillet and comprises both indoor and outdoor markets. Inside, live hens and rabbits and fresh fruit and vegetables are sold right next to each other. (Open Tues., Thurs., and Sat.—Sat. is the big day—6am-noon.)

Another delight in Brive is the **Auberge de Jeunesse,** 56, av. du Maréchal Bugeaud (tel. 55-24-34-00). From the train station, take av. Jean Jaurès on your right for 2 blocks, and turn right on bd. Clemenceau, which changes into bd. Brune, bd. Amiral Grivel, and finally bd. Voltaire—all this in 1½km. The hostel will be on your left at bd. Voltaire. Located in a beautifully renovated building, the hostel enjoys extensive facilities (including a kitchen) and its own yard. (42F. Breakfast included. Lockout 11am-6pm. Curfew after 11pm.) If the hostel is full, plenty of other inexpensive options exist. The cheapest hotels line av. Jean Jaurès, which starts at the train station. **Hôtel l'Avenir,** 39, av. Jean Jaurès, is a bargain with clean, good-sized singles for 55F, doubles 70F, and quads 100F. (Showers 10F. Breakfast 16F.) The friendly owner speaks English and keeps a bar downstairs. (Reception open Mon.-Sat. 7am-11pm.) **De La Gare** (tel. 55-74-14-49), a bit closer to the station, has equally good rooms. (Singles 55-60F. Doubles 70F. Quads with 2 big beds 85F, with shower 95F. Breakfast 16F.) The three-star **Camping Municipal,** bd. Michelet (tel. 55-24-34-74), charges 8F per person and 5F per tent. (Showers included. Open daily 7am-10pm.)

Le Champanatier, 15, rue Dumyrat (tel. 55-74-24-14), slightly to the left from the train station, serves a 110F *menu* including veal cooked the local way (*veau fermier corrèzien à la crème*). (Open July-Aug. daily noon-1:45pm and 7:15-8:45pm; Sept.-June open Sat. noon-Fri. afternoon.) If you'd rather be frugal, **Le Quercy,** 3, place du 14 Juillet (tel. 55-24-26-92), cooks up 30-60F entrees and 50-65F *menus.* (Open Tues.-Sun.) **Brasserie Le Molière,** at place Molière (tel. 55-24-00-68), just behind the tourist office, serves a 35F *plat du jour* and omelettes for 15-25F. (Open Mon.-Thurs. 11am-2pm and 7-8:30pm, Fri.-Sat. open later.)

The **Office de Tourisme** is in Immeuble Château d'Eau, place du 14 Juillet (tel. 55-24-08-80). From the train station, follow av. Jean Jaurès to St-Martin, continue on av. de Paris slightly to your right, and the tourist office, a high tower, will be on your right. The friendly, well-informed staff speak English. (Open July-Aug. Mon.-Sat. 9am-12:30pm and 2:30-7pm, Sun. 10am-1pm; Sept.-June Mon.-Sat. 10am-noon and 2:30-6pm.) The **Gare Routière,** newly relocated to av. Léo Lagrange, opposite the municipal sports complex, is a 20-minute walk from the youth hostel. Avenue Léo Legrange branches eastwards off bd. Voltaire, away from the town center. Buses shuttle from the *gare routière* (often making stops at the SNCF *gare* and other points in Brive) to such nearby towns as Tulle (5 per day, 1 hr.), St-Privat (2 per day, 2 hr.), Perpezac-le-Noir (Mon.-Sat. during the school year 3 per day, 1½ hr.), Thiviers with stops at Excideuil and Hautefort (1 per day Tues. and Thurs. only, 2½ hr.). One bus per day runs to Montignac from the train station (Mon.-Sat. at 6pm, 1 hr., 22.40F). The only return bus leaves the Montignac depot at 6:45am. To see Lascaux II, you'll have to spend two nights and a full day in Montignac or try your luck hitching (there is no train connection within 10km of the town). From the **train station** (tel. 55-23-50-50), you can get to major cities and many towns in Périgord-Quercy; trains go to Rocamadour (4 per day, 45 min., 32F), Souillac with 4-5 connecting buses to Sarlat (4 per day, ½ hr., 28F), Cahors (9 per day, 1½ hr., 60F), Paris (18 per day, 4 hr., 225F), Toulouse (10 per day, 2½ hr., 112F), Aurillac (6 per day, 1 hr., 60F), Montauban (9 per day, 5 hr., 89F), and Bordeaux (6 per day, 3 hr., 107F).

Les Eyzies

Some of the world's best-preserved prehistoric cave paintings hide in the limestone cliffs above Les Eyzies-de-Tayac. The town itself can get unpleasant when too many tourists assemble, but the dank caves preserve a carefully monitored solitude. A visit requires an early start—ideally from Périgueux—and killing a few hours between buying your ticket and starting your tour. You may pass this time pleasantly on the banks of the rivers Vézère and Dordogne, which quietly join forces about 1½ km southwest of the caves. All the caves at Les Eyzies are closed on Tuesday.

Orientation and Practical Information

Les Eyzies is linked by train to Agen, Périgueux, and, with a change at Le Buisson, Sarlat. There are also weekly tourist buses from Sarlat and Souillac. To get to the center of town from the train station, turn right and walk 1km down the village's only street; the Grotte de Font-de-Gaume lies 2km down D47.

Syndicat d'Initiative: Place de la Mairie (tel. 53-06-97-05), 5 min. from the train station. Helpful. Excellent list of nearby caves, advice on getting scarce tickets, **currency exchange** (traveler's checks fee 5.48F), and, in summer, tours of the museum and outlying area. Tours to Sarlat, Domme, La Roque-Gageac, and Beynac (Tues. at 8:45am, 120F); Lascaux II, Thonac, Thot, La Madeleine, Les Eyzies (Fri. at 8:45am, 155F). Also rents bikes (see below). Information on car and canoe rentals, horse trails, and camping. Sells guides to cycling and hiking in the area. Open July-Aug. Mon.-Sat. 9am-7pm, Sun. 10am-noon and 2-6pm; March-June and Sept.-Nov. Mon.-Sat. 9am-noon and 2-6pm; Jan.-Feb. Tues. and Thurs. 9am-noon and 2-6pm.

Currency Exchange: Crédit Agricole, just beyond the post office. Open Tues.-Fri. 9am-12:30pm and 1:30-4pm, Sat. 9am-noon. Also at the post office and the *syndicat*.

Post Office: Down the street from the *syndicat*. **Currency exchange. Postal code:** 24620. Open Mon.-Fri. 9am-noon and 2-5pm, Sat. 9am-noon.

Train Station: Tel. 53-06-97-22. To and from Périgueux (6-7 per day, 30-45 min., 29F) and Sarlat (2-3 per day with a change at Le Buisson, 1 hr., 35F). Information office open in summer daily 4:45am-noon, 2-6pm, and 7-11pm.

Bike Rental: At the train station. 47F per day, deposit 279F. At the *syndicat*. 20F per ½-day, 30F per day, 180F per week, deposit 50F plus ID.

Hospital: Tel. 53-59-00-72 in Sarlat.

Police: Tel. 53-29-20-17.

Police Emergency: Tel. 17.

Accommodations, Camping, and Food

Les Eyzies would be a pleasant place to stay if its hotels didn't empty your purse and guests didn't have to reserve months in advance. Fortunately, you can avoid all this aggravation by stepping 3km out of town to the idyllic *gîte d'étape*. Another option is to look for a bed in a private house in town (120-150F; economical only if two people share a room). The *syndicat* has a list of such private homes, or you can look for signs that say *chambres*.

Gîte d'Etape: Ferme des Eymaries, route de St-Cirq (tel. 53-06-94-73). From the tourist office in Les Eyzies head out of town on route de Périgueux, cross the train tracks and the river Vézère, look for the route de St-Cirq immediately on your left, take this for 1½ km, then turn right just before more train tracks, and follow the signs for 1km (25 min.). Cozy buildings at the base of cliffs with a superb view of farmland and more cliffs. The stone wall of one room dates back to medieval times; the toilets and showers, in agreeable contrast, are new. Kitchen facilities. A blissful break from crowded Les Eyzies. 29F. Breakfast 13F. Dinner 45F with advance notice (Mon.-Fri. only). Open April-Oct. daily 6am-10pm. Call for reservations July-Aug.

Hôtel du Périgord, on D47 near the Grotte de Font-de-Gaume (tel. 53-06-97-26). Singles and doubles 85-120F. Breakfast 20F. Reservations necessary. Open March 20-Oct. 14 daily 8am-9pm.

Hôtel de France, rue du Musée (tel. 53-06-97-23). A 2-star place. Beautiful rooms 77-127F, with shower 127-190F. Breakfast 25F. Open mid-March to mid-Nov. 7:15am-midnight.

Camping: Luckily the area is ideal for camping and there's usually plenty of room. **La Rivière,** just out of town on route de Périgueux (tel. 53-06-97-14). Take a left at the fork of the train station and continue just past the river. 12F per person, 10F per tent and car, electricity 10F. Also has 8 rooms 80-100F. Breakfast 15F. Reasonable snack bar and canoe rental. Open March 15-Oct. daily 8am-9pm. **Camping Le Pech,** 3km from the train station (tel. 53-06-95-84), mostly uphill. Walk to the end of the main street, and follow the signs. Call ahead and the kind managers will come and pick you up. 8F per person, 7.50F per tent and car, electricity 7.50F. Hot showers 1.50F. Open July-Aug. daily 8:30am-midnight; in off-season 8:30am-10pm.

Most hotels serve expensive, well-prepared meals. The **Café de la Mairie** (tel. 53-06-98-26) purveys affordable but rather meager snacks, while the **Auberge du Musée** (tel. 53-06-97-23), the restaurant of the Hôtel de France, serves an adequate 70F *menu* indoors or outdoors. Lunches (called *snacks*) are also served (25-35F). A more imaginative option is the **Halle Paysanne des Eyzies** (tel. 53-06-94-20), just out of town on route de Sarlat. This rural shopping mall is full of tempting local produce on the ground floor and arts and crafts upstairs. Samples are occasionally available—you can taste *foie gras* for free. (Open June-Sept. 15 daily 9am-1:30pm and 2:30-7pm.) A small **market** is held in town on Monday mornings; the fourth Monday of the month brings the **general fair,** a larger market. Just past the Halle Paysanne is **Resto Mentalo,** with outdoor tables and pizzas for 26-35F. If you'd like to eat by prehistoric caves, go to **Restaurant de Laugerie-Basse,** on D47 towards Périgueux. (*Menus* 42.50F, 47.50F, 52.50F, and 75F.)

Sights

By far the most important sight is the **Grotte de Font-de-Gaume** (tel. 53-06-97-48), 2km down D47. Inside the legendary cave are silhouette drawings of horses, deer, and bison—faint, but still amazing. During peak season, 20 people are admitted at half-hour intervals in closely monitored groups. Because of these restrictions, and because many of the limited tickets are bought in advance by tour groups, the road to the famous cave is paved with hard-luck stories. In summer, you must come as early in the day as possible; the 7:14am train from Périgueux arrives at 7:50am. If you arrive by 8am, you'll probably get a late-morning or afternoon ticket—at the very least, you'll have a few hours to wait. You should return at least 10 minutes before your 45-minute tour begins. Each group is led by an enthusiastic guide armed with a flashlight. (Open April-Sept. Wed.-Mon. 9-11:15am and 2-5:15pm; Oct.-March Wed.-Mon. 10-11:15am and 2-4:15pm. Admission 22F, ages 18-25 and over 60 12F, ages 7-18 5F, ages under 7 free.)

The **Grotte des Combarelles,** 2km farther down the road (tel. 53-06-97-72), contains dazzling prehistoric carvings. Visitors are admitted in groups of six; the slightly rambling tour lasts one hour. Tickets are available at 9am for morning tours, 2pm for afternoon tours, and sell quickly. (Same hours, dates, and prices as the Grotte de Font-de-Gaume.)

In the town of Les Eyzies, the **Musée National de Préhistoire** (tel. 53-06-97-03) exhibits a vast collection of weapons, tools, bones, cave drawings, and carvings. (Open April-Nov. Wed.-Mon. 9:30am-noon and 2-6pm; Dec.-March Wed.-Mon. 9:30am-noon and 2-5pm. Admission 10F, ages 18-25 and over 60 5F, ages under 18 free, Sun. 5F.) A two-minute walk from the train station is **Eglise de Tayac,** a church with slate-roofed bell towers and narrow fortress windows.

Near Les Eyzies

The hills around Les Eyzies are pock-marked with caves and rock formations, and as you travel northwest from the village along D47, you'll run across a series of roadside attractions. Most interesting is the **Grotte du Grand Roc** (tel. 53-06-96-76), 1½km from town, which lies halfway up the chalk cliffs and commands a splendid view of the Vézère Valley from its mouth. It has no cave paintings, just impressive stalactites and stalagmites. Take the 25-minute tour. (Open daily July-Sept. 8 9am-7pm; March 15-June and Sept. 9-Nov. 15 9am-noon and 2-6pm. Admission

24F, ages 6-12 11F.) Next to the Grand Roc, the **Laugerie-Basse** (tel. 53-06-97-12) and the **Laugerie-Haute** (tel. 53-06-92-90) display cross-sections of geological strata containing human remains and showing various epochs of habitation in the caves. (Laugerie-Basse open June-Sept. daily 9am-6:30pm. Admission 16F, ages 6-12 10F. 35-min. tour. Laugerie-Haute open daily July-Aug. 9am-7pm; Sept.-June 9am-noon and 2-6pm. Admission April-Sept. 15F, ages 18-25 and over 60 9F, ages 7-18 5F; Oct.-March 7F, 4F, and 3F, respectively.) Bison and groups of horses are carved into the stone walls of the **Abri du Cap-Blanc** (tel. 53-59-21-74 or 53-29-66-63), in Marquay, 6km from Les Eyzies. (Open daily July-Aug. 9:30am-7pm; late March-June and Sept.-early Nov. 10am-noon and 2-5pm. Admission 17F, ages under 12 7.50F.)

The town of **Montignac,** 20km northeast of Les Eyzies on N704 (*direction* "Brive"), preserves the twentieth century's most elaborate salute to the artistic cave-dwellers: a complete re-creation of the caves of **Lascaux,** called simply **Lascaux II** (tel. 53-53-44-35). The exhibit, inaugurated in 1983 (20 years after the caves were closed to prevent the deterioration of their paintings by breathing tourists) is the work of painter Monique Peytral and a team of a dozen sculptors. Peytral's creative art is interesting in its own right and is shown infrequently in the area. (Open July-Aug. daily 9:30am-7:30pm; Feb.-June and Sept.-Dec. Tues.-Sun. 10am-noon and 2-5:30pm. Tickets sold at place Tourny in Montignac, starting at 9am. Admission 35F, ages under 12 15F. 40-min. guided tour.) Montignac may also be reached by train from Brive (Mon.-Sat. 1 per day, 1¼ hr.).

Sarlat

Despite the tourist-besieged main street, lined with vendors of *foie gras,* t-shirts, and switchblades, Sarlat remains a town with an uncommon medieval atmosphere. After all, as early as the eighth century, Sarlat was a prosperous commercial center. In the *vieille ville,* narrow, deserted streets wind past old stone doorways and gargoyles wear wretched expressions. Thanks to the 1965 renovations, most of the old quarter looks as if it were carved from a single block of golden sandstone.

Orientation and Practical Information

Sarlat's *vieille ville* is neatly bisected by the modern commercial thoroughfare, **rue de la République,** known locally as *la Traverse.* To the east lie most of the sights and all the tourists. The old streets on the west side of the main drag are just as interesting and infinitely less crowded.

Office de Tourisme: Place de la Liberté (tel. 53-59-27-67). A busy but helpful office housed in the sixteenth-century Hôtel de Maleville. Free maps of the *vieille ville.* Information on excursions, camping, and bike tours; suggestions about walks and hikes; an accommodations service (5F plus 100F deposit); and a currency exchange on days when the banks are closed. Their free booklet, *Informations Générales,* includes transport schedules and excursions. Guided tours of the town (in French and English) July-Aug. Mon.-Fri. 4 per day, 2 Sat., 1 Sun.; June and Sept. Mon.-Sat. 2 per day, 1 Sun. Tours 17F, students 10F. Open June-Sept. Mon.-Sat. 9am-noon and 2-7pm, Sun. 10am-noon and 4-6pm.

Currency Exchange: Banks open Tues.-Sat. On Mon. go to the post office. To change traveler's checks that the post office won't accept (e.g., checks in British pounds sterling), try Périgord Tourisme, 12, place Pasteur (tel. 53-59-05-48), or the tourist office.

Post Office: Place du 14 Juillet (tel. 53-59-12-81). **Telephones** and **currency exchange. Postal code:** 24200. Open Mon.-Fri. 8am-noon and 1:30-6:30pm, Sat. 8am-noon.

Train Station: Route de Souillac (tel. 53-59-00-21). Ticket booths open daily 5:45am-9pm. To Bordeaux (3-4 per day, 2¾ hr., 87F), Brive (4 per day, 40F), Périgueux (4 per day, 1½ hr., 53F) via Les Eyzies (3 per day, 1 hr., 35F) and Le Buisson (1½ hr., 27F). Les Eyzies and Le Buisson are both connections to Paris, but connections are ill-timed and indirect. Much simpler is the route via Souillac, served by SNCF bus. To Paris (Mon.-Sat. 3 per day, 2 Sun.; 6½-7 hr.; 240F). The same buses to Souillac connect with trains to Toulouse (2-3 per day, 3 hr., 104F). The ride from the station to *centre ville* is free.

Bus Station: SNCF buses (SNCF discounts valid) and **Trans-Périgord** buses (SNCF discounts sometimes valid) stop at the station and in place Pasteur. Trans-Périgord to Souillac (4-5 per day, 45 min.). SNCF to Le Buisson (2-3 per day, 1 hr.). **Cars Pezin,** with offices in a funeral parlor in place Pasteur (tel. 53-59-21-25), to Domme (1 Sat, ½ hr.). **Cars Canitrot** (tel. 65-41-07-20) to Gourdon (1 Sat., 45 min.) from place Pasteur. Complete schedules printed in *Informations Générales,* available free at the tourist office.

Bike Rental: At the train station. 37F per ½-day, 47F per day, 279F per week, deposit 300F. **Garage Matigot,** 52, av. Gambetta (tel. 53-59-03-60). 3- and 10-speeds 30F per day, 180F per week, deposit 100F. Mopeds 60F per day, 350F per week, deposit 200F. Open July-Sept. Mon.-Sat. 8:30am-noon and 2-7pm; Oct.-June Tues.-Sat. only.

Hospital: Centre Hospitalier, Jean Le Claire (tel. 53-59-00-72).

Medical Emergency: Tel. 17 or 18.

Police: Commissariat, place Grande Rigandie (tel. 53-59-05-17).

Police Emergency: Tel. 17.

Accommodations and Camping

Sarlat has a youth hostel, but it operates only June 15 through September. Hotels tend to be expensive, and reservations in summer are recommended. The tourist office keeps track of vacant hotel rooms and can also find you a room in a local home (5F charge if they make the reservation).

Auberge de Jeunesse (IYHF), 15bis, av. de Selves, route de Périgueux (tel. 53-59-47-59), 30 min. from the station but only 5-10 min. from the *vieille ville.* From the station, follow av. de la Gare and signs to *centre ville.* Take rue de la République, which becomes av. Gambetta, through the town center and bear left at the fork onto av. de Selves. The hostel is on the right, just before the supermarket. Easy-going atmosphere and a sympathetic owner. Somewhat cramped dorm space, clean exterior toilets and showers, well-equipped kitchen. Rarely full. 30F. Camping space 15F. Sheets 11F. Bicycles 30F per day, 40F per 2 days. Office open 9am-1pm and 6pm-midnight. Lockout 10:30am-6pm, but someone might be there in the afternoon. Lockouts abandoned when it rains. No curfew. Open June 15-Oct.

Hôtel Marcel, 8, av. de Selves (tel. 53-59-21-98), opposite the youth hostel. The cheapest rooms in town—clean, musty, and comfortable—on a noisy street. 1-star. Singles and doubles 65-75F, with shower 110F. Showers 8F. Breakfast 22F. Well-respected restaurant downstairs serves a 5-course, 50F *menu.* Reception open until 10pm.

Hôtel des Récollets, 4, rue Jean Jacques Rousseau (tel. 53-59-00-49), up the little ramp after rue Papucie. Great location in the quiet half of the *vieille ville.* Clean rooms. Doubles 105F, with shower 115F. Breakfast 20F. 1 week's notice is wise July-Aug. Phone reservations accepted.

Camping: Les Perières, ¾km out on D47 (tel. 53-59-05-84), the closest to town. A 4-star site with its own swimming pool, tennis courts, game room, library, and bar. Usually full July-Aug. The minimum price is 98F per 3 persons, including tent and electricity. Open 9am-noon and 2-7pm. **Les Accacias,** at La Canéda (tel. 53-59-29-30; for information 53-59-15-56). Slightly farther away (2½km) and slightly less expensive (1-star), with hot water and food. 15F per person, 15F per tent, electricity 15F, tax 1F per person per day. Open Easter-Sept. **Rivaux,** on D47 (tel. 53-59-04-41), off D6 north of Sarlat, 2½km away. A 2-star site with hot showers. 9.50F per person, 9F per tent, electricity 7.50F, tax 1F per person per day. Open daily 7am-11pm.

Food

Pick up groceries at the enormous **Intermarché** supermarket, just across from the youth hostel. (Open July-Aug. Mon.-Sat. 9am-7:30pm; Sept.-June 9am-1pm and 3-7:30pm.) *Boulangeries* and *charcuteries* line rue de la République. For a treat, ask for the *specialité de la maison* (a layered pastry with cream and raspberry filling, 6.50F) at **Patisserie Mertz Roland** on rue de la République. Abandon your unreasonable diet with a rich slice of chocolate walnut cake for 7F. Most restaurants in the *vieille ville* offer *menus* for about 50F. The celebrated Saturday **market,** full of truffle and *foie gras* bargains, is an all-day affair; a smaller market takes place Wednesday mornings.

Restaurant du Commerce, 4, rue Albéric Cahuet (tel. 53-59-04-26). Lots of outdoor seating and satisfied customers. 35F *menu* includes delicious soup, meat and potatoes, salad, and dessert. 50F entitles you to tender *confit de canard* (duck in aspic); 70F, a truffle salad. Try the *gâteau noir* (chocolate cake). Open daily April-Nov. noon-2pm and 6:30-10pm; Jan.-March noon-2pm.

Auberge du Bon Chabrol, 2, rue des Armes (tel. 53-59-15-56), off rue de la République. Authentic Périgordin cuisine. Local dishes served either inside an old *hôtel particulier* or outside. 40F lunch *menu* Mon.-Fri.; 66F dinner *menu* (service 10%). Open June-Sept. daily noon-2pm and 7-9pm; Oct.-May Thurs.-Tues. noon-2pm and 7-8:30pm.

Hostellerie Marcel, 8, av. de Selves (tel. 53-59-21-98), opposite the hostel. Well-known and well-liked. 5-course, 50-64F *menu* includes *poulet basquaise.* Open Jan. to mid-Nov. daily; mid-Nov. to Dec. Tues.-Sun.

Le Relais de la Poste, rue de l'Albusse, by the Lanterne des Morts. The romantic, light-strung terrace overlooks a steep passageway. 3-course *menu* 50F.

Sights and Entertainment

The well-written, English guide to **Cathédrale St-Sacerdos** describes the interior of each chapel, including some lovely gilded statuettes. The elevated terrace behind the cathedral overlooks the rough-hewn but elegant stone roofing. Here you will also notice a beehive-shaped monument, called **La Lanterne des Morts.** Built in the twelfth century, its full significance baffles even the experts. No one can understand why the architects left no access to the second-story chamber, in the conical part of the structure.

Next to the cathedral are the **Palais Episcopal** and the **Maison de la Boëtie,** birthplace of Etienne de la Boëtie, the friend celebrated by Montaigne in his *Essais.* Built in the sixteenth century, the Maison's pointed gable and highly decorated windows exemplify the Italian Renaissance style. Now it serves as the Chambre de Commerce et d'Industrie, and its ground floor common room frequently houses small exhibitions. On the other side of the main thoroughfare, the **Musée de la Chapelle des Pénitents Blancs,** on rue de la Charité at rue Jean Jacques Rousseau, maintains a small but impressive collection of polychromatic statuettes and ecclesiastical garments. Of note are the primitive, seventeenth-century statue of the Virgin holding a leper's skull and the mannequin clothed in a penitent's white robes and pointed hat. If you ask, the friendly manager will explain the historical connections between the Crusades, the plague, the penitents, the Spanish explorers of the New World, and the white costumes, similar to those of the Ku Klux Klan. (Museum open Easter to mid-Oct. daily 10am-noon and 3-6pm. Admission 10F, students 5F.) The **Musée Aquarium** features fish from the rivers of the Dordogne basin. (Open daily June-Sept. 10am-7pm; Oct.-May 10am-noon and 2-6pm. Admission 18F, students 15F.)

From July 27 through August 9, Sarlat hosts the **Festival des Jeux du Théâtre,** a series of plays in the open-air theater in place de la Liberté. (Tickets 80-150F, with Carte Jeune 10% discount.) For reservations, write Festival des Jeux du Théâtre de Sarlat, B.P. 53, 24200 Sarlat. For information, call Hôtel Plamon at 53-31-10-83. Frequent concerts are held in the cathedral in July and August. (Tickets 30-80F. Consult the brochure *La Fête en Perigord* for exact dates.)

Near Sarlat

If you have a bike, Sarlat makes an ideal base for touring the area's remarkable attractions; if you have more patience than energy, try your luck with the buses. Some 14km from Sarlat, the fortified village of **Domme** perches high on a cliff overlooking the Dordogne Valley. From the **Belvédère de la Barre,** you can see the plain and its poplar-lined river, the villages of Beynac and La Roque-Gageac, the châteaux of Montfort and Giverzac, and cows the size of cockroaches. You can also visit the caves where Domme's inhabitants took refuge during the Hundred Years' War and the Wars of Religion. **Cars Pezin,** place Pasteur (tel. 53-59-21-25), in Sarlat, runs buses to and from Domme on Saturday. (See Bus Station under Sarlat Practical Information.)

SNCF buses to Le Buisson (Mon.-Sat. 2-3 per day) stop at the village **Beynac,** whose golden castle on a golden cliff surveys an entire region: The wonderful view from the top includes the castles of Marqueyssac, Castelnaud, and Fayrac. If you decide to bike, try to stop in **La Roque-Gageac,** huddled between the river and a high cliff and considered one of the most beautiful villages in France. Trans-Périgord buses bound for Souillac (see Bus Station in Practical Information) also stop at **Carsac,** whose eleventh-century, golden-toned Romanesque church merits a brief visit. More convenient than SNCF or Trans-Périgord buses, the SNCF excursion bus stops at Carsac, Domme, and La Roque-Gageac. (From Sarlat June 14-Sept. 13 on Tues., returning the same day. Tickets, including a guide's commentary, 120F, students 110F. Reserve at the tourist office.) To swim in the Dordogne, head for **Vitrac Port,** 7km from Sarlat (*direction* "Bergerac"; turn left at the edge of town onto D46).

Souillac

Souillac is like a hole in a doughnut: Though there's nothing much in the town itself, the surrounding countryside reveals Dordogne at its finest. Unfortunately, while Souillac is relatively accessible, hotels are booked solid in summer, and cheaper accommodations are nonexistent: Souillac in season is for campers only. Cyclists have many scenic rides to choose from. Rocamadour is a challenging 20-km trip, relieved by plenty of opportunities to swim in the Dordogne River.

Orientation and Practical Information

The train station is a 20-minute walk from the *centre ville.* Go straight from the station exit, left on av. Jean Jaurès, and right on av. du Général de Gaulle. The *syndicat* and *vieille ville* are on the right. To reach the Dordogne, keep going for 1½km on av. de Toulouse.

Syndicat d'Initiative: Bd. Louis-Jean Malvy (tel. 65-37-81-56). Information on summer SNCF excursions to Les Eyzies (120F); Rocamadour and the Gouffre de Padirac (120F); and Domme, La Roque Gageac, Beynac, and Sarlat (95F). Decent maps available from animated staff. Also inquire about *gîtes d'étape* in the *département* of Lot, *chambres d'hôte,* and hiking tours. Open June-Sept. Mon.-Sat. 9am-1pm and 2-7pm, Sun. 9am-noon and 2-6pm; Oct.-May Mon.-Sat. 9am-noon and 2-6pm.

Currency Exchange: Banque Populaire, 31, av. Gambetta. Open Mon.-Fri. 8am-noon and 1:30-5pm. Currency exchange until 4pm only. On Sat., try the post office.

Post Office: 11, bd. Louis-Jean Malvy. **Postal code:** 46200. Open Mon.-Fri. 8am-12:30pm and 2-5:30pm, Sat. 8am-noon.

Train Station: Tel. 65-32-78-21. Souillac is on the Paris-Toulouse rail line. To Toulouse (6-8 per day, 2 hr., 92F) via Gourdon (15 min., 17F) and Cahors (1 hr., 39F). To Paris (4-6 per day, 5-6 hr., 237F) via Brive-la-Gaillarde (15-30 min., 27F) and Limoges (2 hr., 73F).

Bus Station: Information tel. at the train station. Trans-Périgord buses (railpasses sometimes valid) to Sarlat Mon.-Sat. stop first at train station and then 4 min. later on av. de Sarlat (Mon.-Sat. 5 per day, 3 Sun.; ¾ hr.; 20.50F). SNCF buses to St-Denis-Près-Martel stop first at the station and then 2 min. later at Hôtel Renaissance (Mon.-Sat. 3 per day, 1 Sun.; ¾ hr.; 15.50F).

Bike Rental: SNCF station. 37F per ½-day, 47F per day, 279F per week, deposit 300F or ID. **Au Vélo Dingo,** on rue de la Halle at rue de Paliès (tel. 53-31-00-93 in Sarlat). 3-speeds 35F per ½-day, 45F per day, 200F per week, deposit 200F plus ID. Light 10-speeds 40F per ½-day, 50F per day, 220F per week. Open July-Aug. Mon.-Sat. 9:30am-1pm and 2-7pm.

Medical Emergency: Tel. 18, or call the police.

Police: Gendarmerie, route de Sarlat (tel. 65-32-78-17).

Accommodations, Camping, and Food

The only way to find a hotel here in July or August is to start early, cross your fingers, and go down the list provided by the *syndicat*. The attractive, one-star **Auberge du Puits,** place du Puits (tel. 65-37-80-32), provides comfortable doubles from 95F, with shower 115F or 125F. (Showers 10F. Breakfast 19F. Reception open 7:30am-10:30pm. Restaurant *menus* from 47F.) In a noisy area, the less attractive, two-star **Nouvel Hôtel,** 21, av. du Général de Gaulle (tel. 65-32-79-58), lets simple doubles from 70F, with shower 90F. There are no cockroaches in the rooms, at least—or else they're quicker than the ones in the hallway. (Breakfast 20F. *Menus* from 45F.) Quieter, smaller, and cheaper is the **Hôtel Beffroi,** place St-Martin (tel. 65-37-80-33). Singles and doubles are 65-120F; breakfast 17F. Another option is **Hôtel L'Escale,** 36, av. Louis-Jean Malvy, in the center of town. (Singles 65F. Doubles 80F. Showers included.). The bar downstairs is a lively hang-out.

Campers can head for nearby **Camping Municipal Les Ondines,** av. de Sarlat (tel. 65-37-86-44), on the banks of the Dordogne. (8F per person, 6F per tent. Open July-Sept. 7am-8pm.) Quieter **Camping de Lanzac** is a 20-minute walk farther on the other side of the river, next to pont de Lanzac (8F per person, 6F per tent). Another possibility is the 4-star **Camping La Paille Basse,** route de Borrèze (tel. 65-37-85-48 or 65-32-73-51; 22F per person, 28.50F per tent; open July-Aug. 8:30am-12:30pm and 1:30-9pm, May 15-June and Sept. 1-15 shorter hours).

Most of Souillac's hotels offer reasonably filling 50-60F *menus.* You'll get the best deal at the **Hôtel Beffroi** (tel. 65-37-80-33), called Chez Jeanette by loyal locals. (Delicious *menus* 46F, 68F, and 85F.) Service is informal and unhurried—count on spending at least an hour over your meal. (Open Mon.-Sat. noon-1:30pm and 7-9pm.) **La Crêperie,** 33, rue de la Halle, serves crêpes and *galettes* in a quiet atmosphere (8-34F). Decent salads 17-23F. (Open daily noon-midnight.) Every first and third Friday of the month, the **farmer's fair** comes to town, with its booths selling nuts, herbs, flowers, honey, live trout, and ducklings. The principal location is place de la Halle (open roughly 9am-4:30pm). A smaller **market** is held each Monday and Wednesday morning from about 8am to 12:30pm.

Sights

The town itself has only a few intriguing features. The **Eglise Abbatiale,** an extravaganza of domes and octagonal chapels, is crowned by three cupolas similar to those of the Byzantine-Romanesque cathedrals of Périgueux and Cahors. Devils and fantastic monsters devour one another on the portal columns. Above the door, another bas-relief depicts the legend of Théophile, who after selling his soul to the devil is redeemed by the Virgin. Near the cathedral in place St-Martin stands the partially demolished **beffroi,** a twelfth-century bell tower now reduced to a cut-away of its massive stone walls.

In the third week of July, Souillac hosts a **jazz festival** with nightly concerts and general hoopla in the streets. Tickets run 80-120F, or 220F for three nights (no student discount), and may be purchased at the *syndicat,* or by mail after July 1. Write to Festival de Jazz, B.P. 99, 46200 Souillac.

The D43 winds its way southeast through the lovely Dordogne Valley. About 5½km from Souillac, you can stop for a swim near the village of Pinsac. Farther along, you'll come to a breathtaking view of the **Château de Belcastel,** clinging tenaciously to an outcrop above the town of Lacave. Although the château itself is not open to the public, you can wander freely around the terrace and chapel beside it. In **Lacave,** the petrified **Grottes de Lacave** (tel. 65-37-87-03) are covered by one-hour guided tours (25F, children 14F), complete with elevator and electric train through "twelve fairyland halls," stalactites, mirages, and some prehistoric remains. (Open daily July 9am-noon and 2-6:30pm; Aug. 9am-7pm; April-June and Sept.-Oct. 15 9am-noon and 2-6pm.) The 7-km stretch of D23 between Lacave and the village of Meyronne follows the Dordogne and passes several swimming spots. Contact the Souillac *syndicat* for details on excursions through the area.

Copeyre (tel. 65-37-33-51) rents canoes and kayaks at 12 locations along a 130-km stretch of the river. (2-person canoe 35F per hr., 130F per day; 1-person kayak 25F per hr., 90F per day, insurance and bus transport back up river included.) Arrive at 8:30am to pick up your rental with least hassle. To make reservations, call 65-32-72-61. (Open daily 9am-6pm.) The site nearest Souillac is **Camping Municipal des Ondines,** off av. de Sarlat.

Rocamadour

Built into the face of a sheer cliff above the Alzou Canyon, Rocamadour enshrines the object of countless pilgrimages: the small chapel of Notre-Dame-de-Rocamadour. In the twelfth century a perfectly preserved body was unearthed near the chapel—supposedly that of a hermit who lived out his life on the cliff. This discovery gave the town its name, derived from *roc amator* (lover of the rock). Since then, even before the elevator was installed, saints (Domenic and Bernard), kings (Henry Plantagenet of England, Philippes IV and VI and Louis XI of France), and heretics seeking absolution have all grovelled up to the chapel on their knees.

Orientation and Practical Information

The train station lies 5km out of town. You can take a taxi or hitch, which is difficult since passing cars are often stuffed with tourists. Alternatively, you can walk; it's a pleasant trek through quiet fields and farmland. Just make sure the train schedule leaves you time for the sights, as the walk takes almost an hour each way. When you reach the intersection near the campground and the **Hôspitalet** (where the van stops and where you should leave your car), take the pedestrian route through porte de l'Hôpital for a view of the city.

The only thing harder than getting to Rocamadour is getting lost once you're there—the town has only one curling, crowded street, running parallel to the cliff and defended at either end by two thirteenth-century fortified gates.

Syndicat d'Initiative: Hôtel de Ville (tel. 55-33-62-59). Reluctant to communicate historical information on the pilgrimage, but happy to orient visitors and provide **currency exchange**—particularly helpful since there's no bank. (No currency exchange Wed.) Look for interesting exhibits in the *syndicat*'s exhibition room (free). Office open daily July-Aug. 10am-noon and 3-7pm; April-June and Sept. 10am-noon and 3-7pm.

Office de Tourisme: At L'Hôspitalet (tel. 65-33-62-80), on the road to town from the train station. The sign outside says that they handle only hotel reservations, but they may be more helpful than the *syndicat.* Open July-Aug. 9am-noon and 3-8pm.

Post Office: Rue Roland le Preux. **Postal code:** 46500. Open Mon.-Sat. 9am-noon and 2-5pm.

Train Station: Tel. 65-33-63-05. Rocamadour is most easily reached via Brive (5 per day, 45 min., 31F). From the south, catch a bus at Sarlat or Souillac for St-Denis-Près-Martel (Mon.-Sat. 3 per day, 45 min. from Souillac, 15.50F). Trains from St-Denis to Rocamadour are infrequent (3-4 per day, 15 min., 14F). The station also rents bikes for 37F per ½-day, 47F per day, deposit 250F. Open Mon.-Fri. 8:30am-10:30pm and Sat.-Sun. 10am-noon and 1:30-7:30pm.

Taxi Service: A briskly efficient woman (tel. 65-33-62-12) will run you to and from the train station in her van. Go to the left of the courtyard as you exit the train station. Fare each way about 8F.

Police: Commissariat: Tel. 65-33-60-17.

Accommodations, Camping, and Food

Rocamadour is small and congested, better suited to daytrips than overnight stays. Hotels are not cheap and are booked solid in summer. You might try **Hôtel du Lion d'Or,** Porte Figuier (tel. 65-33-62-04), which offers doubles for 80F (1 bed) and 90F (2 beds). If you snag one of these, feel lucky—their other rooms go for 100-200F. (No hall shower. Breakfast 22F. Open April-Oct.) **Hôtel Terminus,** place de la Carretta (tel. 65-33-62-14), lets two rooms at 75F (85F for 2 people) and two more rooms at 100F and 105F. (Showers 10F. Breakfast 24F. Open April-Oct.) Several campgrounds exist, and some campers set up in nearby fields. **Relais du Campeur,** above Rocamadour at L'Hôspitalet (tel. 65-33-63-28), has hot showers, a food store, and a free pool. (13F per person, 13F per site, electricity 8F, tax 1F per person per day. Hot showers included. Open April-Sept.) Reception is at the *épicerie* next to the campground. To camp closer to the train station, try **Camping Les Tilleuls,** a three-star campground with a free pool and a generous manager. Turn left from the station, cross the tracks, and take a right on the main road (10 min.). (11F per person, 11F per tent, electricity 8F. Open daily 7am-noon and 7:30-11pm.)

Food in Rocamadour is not particularly cheap or well-prepared, but several restaurants serve 45-60F *menus.* One of the better is **Le Bellevue,** at L'Hôspitalet (tel. 65-33-62-10), with a 54F, four-course *menu,* a 68F gourmet *menu,* quick service, and a flower-lined terrace overlooking the Alzou Canyon. On Rocamadour's main street by the *syndicat* beams **Chez Anne Marie,** with a pleasant ambience and a 47F *menu.* Just outside the train station, 5km from town, **Restaurant des Voyageurs** serves a 40F *menu,* including *plat du jour, crudités,* and ice cream. Crêpes and sandwiches are sold all along the street in Rocamadour, and there is one small *épicerie.* A store by Porte Hugon sells fresh fruits and vegetables.

Sights

Ascending steeply beside the town's main street is the **Escalier des Pèlerins;** some pilgrims still kneel at each of its 216 steps. At the top of the **Cité Religieuse,** also accessible by elevator (6.80F, round-trip 9F; 7:45am-10pm every 3 min.). The *cité* encompasses the impressively fortified **Evêché,** once the palace of the bishops of Tulle, and the eleventh-century **Basilique St-Saveur,** housing an eloquent sixteenth-century sculpture of Christ. Several small chapels also huddle in the *cité,* most notably the **Chapelle Notre-Dame,** to which generations of pilgrims have come. A beautiful fresco of the Annunciation adorns the chapel's outer wall, and above the door is an ancient sword thrust into a rock—reputedly the legendary sword of Roland. **Chapelle St-Michel** opens only for guided visits (given free throughout the summer, starting at the basilica—tip the guide 1-2F). Around and in between the chapels are free exhibitions, crypts (open only to guided tours), and the **Trésors Musée,** housing items related to the sanctuaries. (Museum open April-Oct. daily 9am-noon and 2-6pm. Admission 8F. Tours of the crypts in French only daily 9am-noon and 2-6pm.)

Still higher up—accessible by the zigzagging pathways through the trees—presides the **château,** first built in the fourteenth century to protect the pilgrims below and now inhabited by the chaplains of Rocamadour. Its buildings are private, but the public may walk on its **ramparts,** which command exceptional views of the valley below. (Open July-Aug. 9am-7pm; April-June and Sept.-Oct. 9am-noon and 1:30-8pm. Admission 5.50F, students 3.50F.) Try to see Rocamadour early in the morning, when you will have it almost to yourself, or late at night, when the town's sheer rock face is lit up by stars and spotlights.

The annual *pèlerinage* to Rocamadour takes place during the week of September 8, and dates back to the early Middle Ages. Pilgrims from the region used to gather here for shelter, and from 1170 on, both kings and popes came to Rocamadour to worship. The site's sanctity increased with the spread of a rumor that Amadour, the hermit who lived in the cliffs of Rocamadour, was in fact the Zacchaeus of the gospel. In the later Middle Ages, Rocamadour and its oratory became associated with the grandiose Benedectine order, and the little church of Notre-Dame became increasingly popular as a center for organized pilgrimages. The Wars of Religion stunted Rocamadour's growth, but in 1853, local clergy rekindled the pilgrimage that today draws thousands on their way to Lourdes.

For more unorthodox diversion, visit the 150 friendly monkeys who inhabit the **Forêt des Singes,** outside the Hôspitalet. The monkeys roam freely and some of them belong to rare species. (Park open June 15-Aug. 3 9am-7pm; April-June 15 and Sept.-Oct. 15 10am-noon and 2-6pm. Call 65-33-62-72 for more information.)

Fifteen kilometers from the village of Rocamadour, 10km from the train station, and 100m underground is the astounding **Gouffre de Padirac,** which lives up to any subterranean realm imagined by Jules Verne. At the end of the nineteenth century, a speleologist explored Padirac's enormous sinkhole or *gouffre*—held by local superstition to be the entrance to hell—and discovered these enormous underground caverns. A 1½-hour tour descends to the bottom of the *gouffre* and below it, to the underground river that carved out the dank passageway. The voyage continues in klunky aluminum boats poled along by jolly gondoliers. Bring a raincoat, as it rains incessantly in one of the vaults. (Open daily April-July and Sept.-Oct. 11 8:30am-noon and 2-6:30pm; Aug. 8am-7pm. Admission 27.50F.) From July 9 through August 22, excursions to the *gouffre* from Rocamadour leave from the train station every Wednesday and Friday at 9am (3 hr., 54F). To make it a daytrip, take the early train to Rocamadour from Brive, which puts you there at about 8:45am; then take the excursion, explore the town, and take the train back to Brive at 7:02pm (no evening train on Sat.). For information, call **Arcoutel et Cie** (tel. 65-33-62-12). You can also take the excursion bus from Brive, which leaves the city bus station in place du 14 Juillet at 1:30pm (July-Aug. daily), tours Martel, the *gouffre,* and Rocamadour, and returns to Brive at 7pm (95F). Contact the Brive *syndicat* (tel. 55-24-08-80) for reservations. Group excursions to the *gouffre* leave from Souillac once per week from June 22 to September 7 (120F; contact the Souillac *syndicat* at tel. 65-37-81-56). Cyclists may consider heading for the **Auberge de Jeunesse (IYHF),** place du Monturu (tel. 55-91-13-82), 30km northeast of Padirac in Beaulieu-sur-Dordogne. (Open Easter-Sept.)

Cahors

Situated in the green hills of Quercy, Cahors's red-tiled houses and scorching summer afternoons may make you think of Spain. But the *vieille ville*'s narrow alleys, where shirts sway on clotheslines, faintly suggest Venice. Cahors too is surrounded by water—on three sides at least: The lazy Lot River loops round it to the east, south, and west.

Orientation and Practical Information

From the train station, a 15-minute walk takes you to the center of town. Turn right onto av. Jean Jaurès, then take the third left onto rue Wilson. (A right would take you away from the center and to the medieval bridge.) Continuing straight on rue Wilson toward *centre ville,* you arrive at **boulevard Gambetta,** Cahors's liveliest thoroughfare, which runs north-south. In front of you lies the *vieille ville* between the Lot and bd. Gambetta; 1 block south, on the right, is the *syndicat.*

Syndicat d'Initiative: Place Aristide Briand (tel. 65-35-09-56), near rue Wilson at bd. Gambetta. Free map, information on camping and canoeing, a book of suggested routes for hiking and bicycling, and a guide to regional wines. Tours of the *vieille ville* leave here daily in summer (at 10am and 3pm, 15F). Minibus tours also offered at these times (from 60F, depending on which circuit you choose); they end with a wine-testing session if you go to the *caves.* The newspaper *Vacances et Loisirs* lists dates and addresses. Open July-Aug. Mon.-Sat. 9am-12:30pm and 1:30-6:30pm; Sept.-June Mon.-Sat. 9am-noon and 2-6pm.

Voyages Belmon: 2, bd. Gambetta (tel. 65-35-59-30). Excursions to Rocamadour, the Gouffre de Padirac, Sarlat, and Domme (July-Aug., 110F). Reserve at their office, the train station, or the *syndicat.* Open Mon.-Fri. 9am-noon and 2-7pm, Sat. 9am-noon.

Maison de Jeunes et de la Culture (MJC): 42, impasse de la Charité (tel. 65-35-06-43), behind and to the right of the cathedral. Canoe trips, occasional concerts and films, arts and crafts. A friendly hang-out for ping-pong and card playing. Open Tues.-Thurs. and Sat. 2-7pm, Fri. 2-7pm and 8:30-11:30pm. Bar open 10am-7pm and during *soirées.*

Currency Exchange: A number of banks line bd. Gambetta, but the only exchange offices open on Mon. are the post office and **Crédit Agricole**, 22, bd. Gambetta (tel. 65-30-10-35). Open Mon.-Fri. 8:30am-noon and 1:30-5:30pm; exchange 8:30-11:30am and 1:30-4:30pm.

Post Office: Rue Wilson, between pont Valentré and the *syndicat*. **Telephones** and **currency exchange. Postal code:** 46000. Open Mon.-Fri. 8am-7pm, Sat. 8am-noon.

Train Station: Av. Jean Jaurès (tel. 65-22-50-50). Cahors is on the Paris-Toulouse line. To Paris (7 per day, 5-6 hr., 279F), Brive (8 per day, 1¾ hr., 59F), Souillac (6 per day, 1 hr., 41F), Montauban (11 per day, ½ hr., 41F), and Toulouse (12 per day, 1¼ hr., 69F). Information booth open 5:30am-12:30am.

Bus Station: SNCF buses (railpasses valid) in front of the train station. To Capdenac (3-4 per day, 2 hr.) via St-Cirq-Lapopie and the Figeac *gare*. To Monsempron-Libos (4-6 per day, 1¼ hr.) via Puy L'Eveque and Fumel (near the Château de Bonaguil).

Car Rental: Europcar, 26, av. Jean Jaurès (tel. 65-30-19-20), across from the train station. Open Mon.-Sat. 8am-noon and 2-6pm.

Bike Rental: Combes, 117, bd. Gambetta (tel. 65-35-06-73). 30F per day, 160F per week, deposit 200F plus ID. Open Tues.-Sat. 8:30am-noon and 1-7pm. Also at the **train station** (inquire at *syndicat* desk in the station). 28F per day, deposit 200F.

Laundromat: Laverie Laveco, on rue de la Prèfecture at rue Cathala, which becomes rue Co-ture. Wash 20F, dry 1F per 3 min., soap free. Open daily 8am-8pm.

Centre d'Information sur les Droits des Femmes, 2, rue Frédéric Suisse (tel. 65-30-07-34), next to the *foyer*. Free advice on all concerns, including traveling as a woman in France. Open Mon.-Fri. 9am-noon and 2-6pm.

Hospital: Centre Hospitalier, rue Wilson (tel. 65-35-47-97).

Police: Rue St-Gery (tel. 65-35-27-00).

Police Emergency: Tel. 17.

Accommodations and Camping

Finding a room shouldn't be a problem if you start looking early in the day.

Foyers des Jeunes Travailleurs Frédéric Suisse, 20, rue Frédéric Suisse (tel. 65-35-64-71), 10 min. from the train station. Spacious dorm, usually with a few beds July-Aug. Some of the rooms are almost elegant, and popular with the mosquitoes as well. TV and ping-pong. Singles and doubles 34F, showers included. Sheets 11F. Breakfast 11F. Lunch (noon-1pm) or dinner (7:15pm) 36F. Tell them in advance if you'll be eating there. Reception open Mon.-Fri. 9-11:30am and 2-7pm, Sat. 10-11:30am. No lockout, no curfew.

Hôtel l'Escargot, 5, bd. Gambetta (tel. 65-35-07-66). Cheerful owners and reasonable rooms. Rooms 69-115F. Breakfast 16F. Reception open Tues.-Sat. Pleasant restaurant downstairs with a 48F *menu.*

Hôtel de la Paix, place St-Maurice (tel. 65-35-03-40), overlooking the covered market. Ade-quate rooms, flimsy decor but clean. Singles and doubles 80F, with shower 100F. Showers 15F. Breakfast 20F. Reception open Mon.-Sat. 7am-9pm.

Hôtel de la Bourse, 7, place Rousseau (tel. 65-35-17-78), off a stone, spiral staircase. Elegant old rooms. Often full with regulars during the week; try weekends when they've gone home. Doubles 65-70F. Triples 115-120F. Showers 15F. Breakfast 16F. The restaurant serves a meat, vegetable, and dessert 35F *menu.* Reception open Aug. 28-July 26 7am-10pm.

Camping: Camping Municipal St-Georges (tel. 65-35-04-64), 5 min. from the *syndicat.* Follow bd. Gambetta across pont Louis Philippe—it's right on the river bank. Behind the camp-ground, an alley leads to a path up Mont St-Cyr. 4.50F per person, 4.50F per tent.

Food

The big **markets** take place Wed. and Sat. until 12:30pm in front of the cathedral, though there are usually fruit, vegetable, and flower stands other days of the week as well. There's a big covered market nearby (open Tues.-Sat. 7:30am-12:30pm and 3-6pm, Sun. 9am-noon). Stroll behind the *syndicat* to reach the supermarket **Pri-sunic** (open Tues.-Fri. 9:15am-12:15pm and 3-7pm, Mon. and Sat. 9:15am-12:15pm and 2:30-7pm). Local *boulangeries* and *pâtisseries* offer *pastis,* a flaky pastry. Be sure to sample the town's famous, full-bodied red wine, advertised as "the wine of kings and of the Russian Orthodox Church" and referred to simply as "vin de Cahors." Visit local restaurants and wine stores, or get a list of *caves* from the *syndicat* and go yourself.

> **Le Procopio,** 163, quai Champollion (tel. 65-30-12-09). Huge pizzas and delicious salads with tomato-ricotta dressing. 3 dining rooms and a vine-ensconced terrace. Pizza 25-45F, salads 16-35F, pasta 26-30F, lasagne 28F. Open Mon.-Sat. noon-1:45pm and 7:30-11:30pm, Sun. 7:30-11:30pm.

> **Marie Colline,** 173, rue Clemenceau (tel. 65-35-59-96). Chic vegetarian restaurant with low prices, but small portions. *Plat du jour* 28F, good soups and salads 16F, desserts 15F. Open Tues.-Sat. noon-1:45pm.

> **Le Champ de Mars "Chez Piche,"** 17, bd. Léon Gambetta (tel. 65-35-04-80). Standard *brasserie* with a filling 42F *menu.* Open Mon.-Fri. 9:30am-9:30pm, Sat. 10am-4pm.

> **Le Melchior Bar-Restaurant,** place de la Gare (tel. 65-35-03-38), across from the train station. Satisfying *plat du jour* 34F, *boisson comprise;* without wine 28F. 51F *menu.* Open daily 12:15-2:30pm and 7:15-9:30pm.

> **Restaurant de la Préfecture,** 64, rue de la Préfecture (tel. 65-35-12-54), tucked away in a quiet alley to the left of the cathedral. Delicious regional fare in an elegant setting with a 65F *menu.* Open daily noon-1:30pm and 7:30-9pm.

Sights

Though the fourteenth-century Pont Valentré's three towering turrets seem fantastic and impractical (except, perhaps, for picnics), they helped repel invaders during the Hundred Years' War and the Siege of Cahors in 1580. Legend holds that the architect bargained with the devil to hurry the bridge's construction. He tricked the devil of his due, however, and in revenge, Satan repeatedly toppled the central tower. When a nineteenth-century architect replaced the tower, he added a small carving of the devil struggling to pull it down, visible from the middle of the bridge. (Be careful of traffic; the narrow span is still in use.) To get a good view of the town and the river, climb the steps of the first turret to the open landing halfway up. If you have the time and energy, cross the bridge and climb any of the hills that encircle Cahors for a more panoramic view.

Like the church at Souillac, **Cathédrale St-Etienne** is topped by three domed cupolas of Byzantine inspiration, though its austere facade suggests—rightly so—a fortress: The church served as a refuge for monks during the religious wars. The northside Romanesque portal, formerly the front entrance on the west side, was moved in the fourteenth century to allow the construction of the fortresslike facade. The northern wall's beautifully sculpted tympanum, dating from 1135, depicts Christ's Ascension. To the right of the choir, a door leads to the **cloître,** built around 1500. The cloister overlooks the cathedral domes and gives on to the **chapelle musée,** containing a remarkable fresco of the Last Judgment. The gaping monster's maw to the far right of the left panel represents the entrance to hell, subject of the righthand panel. (Cathedral and museum open Tues.-Sun. 10am-1pm and 3-6:30pm. Free.)

For three or four days around July 14, Cahors hosts its **Festival de Blues,** bringing together prominent blues artists such as Magic Slim and B.B. King. Tickets cost 60-100F and can be reserved at the *syndicat.* A free concert (in 1988 featuring Import-Export and Otis Rush) is sometimes held on the last day.

Near Cahors

To paddle your way down the Lot River, stop by the MJC (see Practical Information), which rents canoes and kayaks. **Safaraid** (tel. 65-36-23-54) at Bouziès, where the river Célé joins the Lot, arranges more expensive trips lasting up to two weeks (mid-May to mid-Sept. only). The *syndicat* provides more information on canoe routes and rentals.

Within comfortable biking range of Cahors sits the exquisite village of **St-Cirq-Lapopie,** which sits high atop a cliff overlooking the river. Beautifully restored medieval houses line the steep and narrow streets, and the view from the ruins of **Château Lapopie** sweeps over the village, river, cliffs, and broad plains below. A bus leaves three to four times per day from Cahors's *gare routière* (35 min., 22.50F) to a point at the base of the hill, 4km away from the castle.

Several kilometers north of St-Cirq-Lapopie and inaccessible by public transport is the **Grotte du Pêche-Merle,** a vast cave decorated with prehistoric carvings and engravings. The artists left their mark by exhaling moist, powdered pigment—primitive spray paint. (Open Easter-Sept. daily 9:30am-noon and 2-6pm; in off-season call 65-31-27-05.)

Farther from Cahors, down the Lot Valley to the west, stands sixteenth-century **Château de Bonaguil.** Though it only partially escaped the fury of the Revolution, what remains is an immense and commanding fortress. (Open March-Sept. 10am-noon and 2:30-6pm.) Through July and August, a series of concerts and stage productions (in 1988 featuring Beethoven's symphonies, Gershwin's *Porgy and Bess,* Molière's *L'Avare,* and contemporary French comedies) take place at the castle. Tickets (40-100F, with Carte Jeune 20% discount) can be reserved at the Fumel *syndicat* (tel. 53-71-13-70). To get to Bonaguil from Cahors, take the SNCF bus to Fumel (Mon.-Sat. 6 per day, 4 Sun.; 1 hr.; 37F), and follow D673 for 4½km and D158 for 3½km. Inquire at Cahors's *syndicat* for bus schedules and more information.

Basque Country (Pays Basque)

The French Basques, although less militant than their Spanish cousins, are equally nationalistic. They believe that Euzkadi (the Basque country) is one nation, now divided between France and Spain. Unlike the Spanish Pais Vasco, which was linguistically liberated after the death of Franco, the Pays Basque has watched its language disappear at an alarming rate. While beachfront Basques rake in tourist money, the mountain enclaves of Euzkadi have steadily lost younger Basques to the big cities and are losing ground in the wool market. The nationalist movement, promoted by several political parties in the 1960s, lost much popular support owing to alleged connections with the ETA (the militarist Spanish Basque Liberation Front). All the same, comparatively inactive French Basques who identify more with France than with Euzkadi still harbor their militant cousins from French police investigations and threatened Spanish extradition. In past years, arrests and acts of violence have scared visitors away, leaving the beaches and hotels less crowded. However, tourists are never the targets—and extremely rarely the victims—of this terrorism.

Visitors to the coastal towns may acquire suntans, Basque berets, and a bellyful of *gâteau basque* and *poulet basquaise*. For a more profound understanding of Basque culture, visit hustling Bayonne, where the Musée Basque houses a fine collection of Basque artifacts. Farther inland, smaller towns in the Pyrenean foothills keep the traditional way of life and the language.

The region is poorly served by rail, though St-Jean-Pied-de-Port is accessible from Bayonne. Trains run from Bordeaux in the north and from Pau in the east. Excursion buses travel to a few towns in the area. Hitchhiking and cycling are still the best ways to penetrate the hills.

The people of this region don't enjoy great material wealth—note the simplicity of their timber-framed houses and farm equipment. Yet the Basques are known for being fun-loving and exuberant. The regional sport, *pelote* (known as jai-alai in the U.S.) is the fastest game played with a ball. A hard ball is hurled at a wall by means of a *chistera* (basket appendage) laced to the wrist. Try to get to a *fronton* (arena) to appreciate the speed and skill of the local players. (Tickets to the world cup matches in St-Jean-de-Luz, which are played all summer, start at 30F.) Basque *fêtes* involve several days of drinking and dancing. The most famous festival occurs in Bayonne in the first week of August. For a complete list of festivals and events, pick up the free guide, *Fêtes en Pays Basque,* at tourist offices all over the region. It is extremely difficult to find accommodations in August because of the popularity of these festivals. However, reservations are possible as late as July.

Basque cuisine is distinctive—and inexpensive. Dense Bayonne ham (pressed and cured), renowned throughout France, may not be delectable to those averse to almost-raw meat. Basque fish stew rivals *bouillabaise. Pipérade,* an omelette, is made with tomatoes, green peppers, and ham. Deceptively simple *gâteau basque* (Basque cake) can rival France's most elegant *pâtisseries.* Once a major wine-producing region, the Pays Basque is making a comeback with some vigorous reds, notably *vin d'Irouleguy.* The local liqueur Izarra, distilled in Bayonne, is an herbal liqueur similar to chartreuse, though sweeter.

Bayonne

Capital of the Pays Basque, Bayonne is an exhilarating city to stroll through—perhaps because it exists at the edge of a different culture. Kilometers away from surf beaches, the Pyrenees, tiny Basque villages, and the Spanish border, Bayonne enjoys all the cosmopolitan accoutrements without seeming blasé. Lively markets crowd narrow streets, and rivers lead to two wonderful museums, a citadel, and a Gothic cathedral, while a big breezy bridge flutters with flags and fishermen's lines. After the first Tuesday in August, Bayonne drops its facade of cool charm for the festival: Five days of concerts, dances, bullfights, and fireworks erupt. And why not? Crisscrossed by the Adour and Nive Rivers, Bayonne has served as a major port, military base, and industrial center since the twelfth century. Chocolate first came to France through its port, and the martinets of the city invented the bayonet.

Orientation and Practical Information

A little more than six hours from Paris, Bayonne is linked by bus to the nearby towns of Anglet and Biarritz, both directly west. The merging rivers split Bayonne into three main areas. On the northern side of the Adour, **St-Esprit** contains the train station and place de la République. Pont St-Esprit arches across the Adour to **Petit-Bayonne,** home of Bayonne's two museums, several inexpensive hotels, and some lively bars. Five small bridges cross the Nive River and connect Petit-Bayonne to **Grand-Bayonne,** on the west bank of the Nive. The oldest part of town, Grand-Bayonne has a pedestrian zone lined by alluring shops and *pâtisseries.* The center of town is easily manageable on foot, while the excellent bus system covers the outskirts and beaches.

Syndicat d'Initiative: Hôtel de Ville, place de la Liberté (tel. 59-59-31-31), in Grand-Bayonne under the arcade on the side facing the river. Provides excellent maps of Anglet and Bayonne, but won't find you a room. Be sure to pick up the *Programme des Fêtes en Pays Basque.* Guided tours of the city Mon., Wed., Fri. at 10am or Tues., Thurs., Sat. at 3pm (10F). Open in summer Mon.-Sat. 9am-noon and 2-7pm; in off-season Mon.-Fri. 9am-noon and 2-6:30pm, Sat. 9am-noon.

Budget Travel: Pascal Voyages, 8, allée Boufflers (tel. 59-25-48-48), in Petit-Bayonne. Kind and helpful staff. BIJ/Transalpino tickets. Airline student discount tickets. No credit cards or checks accepted. Open Mon.-Fri. 8:30am-noon and 2-6:30pm, Sat. 9am-noon.

Post Office: Rue Jules Labat, in Grand-Bayonne. **Telephones** and **currency exchange. Postal code:** 64100. Open Mon.-Fri. 8am-6:30pm, Sat. 8am-noon. **Branch office,** on bd. Alsace-Lorraine, closer to the train station. **Telephones.** Open same hours.

Train Station: Off place de la République (tel. 59-55-50-50). To Paris (7 per day, 5½-6½ hr., 330F), St-Jean-Pied-de-Port (6 per day, 1¼ hr., 36F), Hendaye (11 per day, 45 min., 27F), St-Jean-de-Luz (11 per day, ½ hr., 17F), and Bordeaux (6 per day, 2 hr., 101F).

Bus Station: STAB, place du Réduit (tel. 59-59-04-61), on the riverside. Pick up bus-route map here or at the *syndicat.* Also outside the Hôtel de Ville in Grand-Bayonne (tel. 59-63-20-89). Lines #1 and 2 go to Biarritz. Line #2 also goes to Anglet (25 min.) and Biarritz's gare la Négresse (45 min., 6F). Buses leave every 30-40 min. Tickets 6F, *carnet* of 10 47F.

Taxi: At the **train station** (tel. 59-55-13-15). 24-hour service (tel. 59-63-17-17).

Bike Rental: Location Vélos, at the train station (tel. 59-55-05-88, ask for *service des bagages*). 47F per day, discounts after 3 days, 279F per week, deposit 250F plus ID. Open 6am-midnight.

Laundromat: 16, rue Pointrique, in Petit-Bayonne. Wash 12F, dry 2F per 8 min. Open daily 7:30am-9:30pm.

Hospital: Rue Jacques Loeb, St-Léon (tel. 59-63-50-50). Take bus #3.

Medical Emergency: SAMU, Tel. 59-63-33-33.

Police: Rue Jacques Laffitte (tel. 59-25-77-00), in Petit-Bayonne opposite the Musée Bonnat.

Police Emergency: Tel. 17.

Accommodations and Camping

Bayonne has more cheap hotels than any other city; they cluster mostly in St-Esprit around the train station. The hotels in Grand-Bayonne are generally more expensive; in Petit-Bayonne look around **rue Pannecau** and **place Paul Bert.** Reservations are advisable.

Hôtel du Moulin, 12, rue Ste-Catherine (tel. 59-55-13-29), 2 blocks from the station. A small hotel in a quiet location but passing motorcycles on the nearby main street may keep you awake. A geriatric but fun bar downstairs. Simple but clean singles 55-65F. Doubles 70-75F. Showers 6F. Breakfast 15F. *Demi-pension* for stays of 8 days or longer 110F, including breakfast and one full meal.

Hôtel des Basques, 4, rue des Lisses (tel. 59-59-08-02), in Petit-Bayonne off place Paul Bert, facing Caserne au Château-Neuf. Noisy during the festival, but there are quieter rooms that do not overlook the square. Singles and doubles 67-108F, with shower 83-130F.

Hôtel des Arceaux, 26, rue Port Neuf (tel. 59-59-15-53), in Grand-Bayonne's charming pedestrian district. English, German, Spanish, and Swedish spoken. Clean and pleasant singles and doubles 80-85F. Triples and quads 130F. Breakfast 18F.

La Cremaillère, 1, rue Ste-Ursule (tel. 59-55-12-35), across from the station. Cheap. Dark, noisy bar downstairs. Simple doubles 62F, with shower 68-72F. Rooms with two double beds and shower 108F.

Camping: Barre de l'Adour, 130, av. de l'Adour (tel. 59-63-16-16), in an unpleasantly industrial setting at the mouth of the river in Anglet. Take the bus (*ligne verte*) from Bayonne's Hôtel de Ville. 9F per person, 11.60F per tent, 3.80F per car. Reception open 8am-9pm. No campers after 11pm. Open June-late Sept. Camping de la Chêneraie, RN117 (tel. 59-55-01-31), north of town behind St-Esprit. A 4-star facility with everything. 12.50F per person, 22F per tent and car. Open March 15-Oct. 15 8am-8pm, but reservations not taken until noon.

Food

Food in Bayonne is varied and affordable. The streets of Petit-Bayonne have a number of small restaurants and cafes, most of them offering 50-60F *menus.* There are also some good, cheap restaurants on the side streets of St-Esprit. Sardines and anchovies are always fresh and unlike anything you've ever had from a can; Basque fish stew is a spicy treat, though be warned that anything can go in your soup—seashells and bones included. The *charcuteries* hold their own, too, with *farci* (stuffed pork) and zesty salads of all types. Bayonne is known for its hams, marzipan, chocolate, and its local liqueur Izarra. Your best bet, economically speaking, is the **marché municipal,** on the Nive by the Pannecau bridge, under the parking area. (Open Thurs.-Sat. 5am-1pm and 3-7pm, Mon. 5am-noon.)

Restaurant Koskera, rue Higues, just to the right of the chapel facing the station. Cheap local food, big servings, and a family atmosphere. *Truite meunière* 22F, *poulet basquaise* 25F. Open for lunch and dinner.

Restaurant Dacquois, 48, rue d'Espagne (tel. 59-59-29-61), in Grand-Bayonne. Regional specialties, local clientele, and a filling 47F *menu.* Open Mon.-Sat. noon-2pm and 7:30-10pm.

Restaurant Irintzina, 9, rue Marengo, in Petit-Bayonne. The bargain 45F *menu* includes omelette, meat, vegetable, and dessert. Open Mon.-Sat. noon-2pm and 7-8:30pm.

El Mosquito, rue des Augustines, in Petit-Bayonne. Eat mounds of chili (38F) in a cozy den decorated with Persian rugs. "Pancho" plays authentic South American music on Fri. and Sat. nights (extra charge 10F). Open daily from 7:30pm.

Pizzeria Carina, 41, rue Maubec (tel. 59-55-39-02). Follow the street to the left of the train station. In a dead part of town, but the pizzas are decent (27-39F) and so is the steaming *paella*-for-two (100F).

Hotel-Restaurant-Bar, rue Neuve. From the train station, walk to the bridge and look to your right for the dilapidated Hôtel-Restaurant-Bar sign. The food is cheap. 32F *menu* includes meat, soup, and cheese or dessert. It can't hurt to ask, but the hotel is always booked by regulars.

Restaurant Côte Basque, 3, place de la République, near the station. Local food for territorial locals. *Plat du jour* 30-35F. 50F *menu* includes *poulet basquaise.* Ice cream for dessert an additional 8F. Open daily noon-2pm and 7-9pm.

Bar des Amis, 13, rue des Cordeliers (tel. 59-59-30-58), in Petit-Bayonne on a street parallel to rue Pannecau. Nothing fancy, but a tasty 40F, 4-course *menu* served 8-10pm.

Crêpes Au Grand Marnier, Au Gourmet, rue Ste-Catherine, 2 blocks from the train station. Like discovering gold. Crêpes from 3.50F. Delicious ice cream 15-18F, including *pêche melba, coupe mambo* (vanilla ice cream, pineapple, coconut, whipped cream, hot fudge, and a cookie on top), and *coupe iceberg* (mint-chocolate chip ice cream, mint and chocolate topping, and whipped cream). Open Tues.-Sat. 8am-7pm.

Sights and Entertainment

Cathédrale Notre-Dame looms over Grand-Bayonne's gourmet shops and wood balconies. Built in the thirteenth century, the church didn't acquire its golden stone and twin spires until the nineteenth century. The narrow nave, constructed in the purest Gothic style, is remarkable for its soaring vaults and graceful lines. The sacristie contains a few paintings and carved stone portals, but is usually closed. Nearby is the lineup of stone Bayonne bishops and a door leading into the cloître.

Petit-Bayonne may be *petit,* but it holds two of the finest museums in this region. The **Musée Basque,** at quai des Corsaires and rue Marengo (tel. 59-59-08-98), by pont Marengo, has fine exhibits concerning every aspect of Basque life: costumes, furniture, fishing boats, and a room devoted to *pelote.* Modern women can compare the present social situation to the iron cage used from 1215-1789 to dip quarrelsome women into the Nive. On the bottom level, note the unique, rounded Basque tombstones, which have the same form as giant keyholes. This primitive cruciform shape reappears in the decorative arts as well as in the front wall of *pelote* arenas. (Open July-Sept. Mon.-Sat. 9:30am-12:30pm and 2:30-6:30pm.; Oct.-June Mon.-Sat. 10am-noon and 2:30-5:30pm. In summer tickets sold until noon and then until 6pm. Admission 10F, students 5F.) The library downstairs houses over 10,000 volumes, including just about everything published concerning the Basques, and is open to the public during museum hours Monday through Friday.

Bayonne's recently renovated museum of fine arts, the **Musée Bonnat,** 5, rue Jacques Lafitte (tel. 59-59-08-52), in Petit-Bayonne is small but elegant. Bonnat, a native of Bayonne, was a celebrated nineteenth-century painter who bequeathed his extensive collection to the city and even directed the construction of the museum. Rich in English, Italian, French, and Spanish paintings from the thirteenth through nineteenth centuries, it includes an impressive collection of Rubens and a few works by Delacroix, Dégas, and Antoine Bayre. Several rooms are devoted to the art of Bonnat himself; his grandiose, classical style bears comparison with the major schools of French nineteenth-century painting. (Open June 15-Sept. 10 Wed.-Mon. 10am-noon and 3-6pm, Fri. 3-9pm; in off-season Mon. and Wed.-Thurs. 1-7pm, Fri. 1-10pm, Sat. 10am-noon and 3-6pm, Sun. 10am-noon and 3-7pm. Admission 10F, students 5F, seniors free.)

Free tours and tastings of Izarra, the heavy Basque liqueur, are offered at **Izarra Distillery,** 9, quai Bergeret (tel. 59-55-09-45), in St-Esprit just off place de la République (entrance on rue de Belfort). Izarra is sold cheaply here; the sweet *framboise* (raspberry) liqueur goes for 75F per 70-centiliter bottle, while the yellow (32 herbs used) and green (48-herb) liqueurs cost 75F and 95F, respectively. Only three people in the entire distillery possess the secret herbal recipe for Izarra. (Open July-Aug. Mon.-Sat. 9-11:30am and 2-6:30pm; Sept.-June Mon.-Fri. 9-11:30am and 2-4:30pm.)

In August and early September, Bayonne holds four **corridas** (bullfights) in the large Plaza de Toros. A bullfight is also held on Bastille Day. Tickets cost 50-300F and sell out fast. For ticket information, write or call **Bureau des Arènes Municipales,** 5, rue du 49ème, Bayonne (tel. 59-59-25-98). The **Utopia Cinema,** 7, rue Denis Etcheverry (tel. 59-55-66-55), offers relatively less violent entertainment—undubbed American films (tickets 25F, students and Carte Jeune holders 20F).

Throughout the year, bare-handed *pelote* matches can be seen at 4pm Thursdays in the Trinquet St-André (*pelote* court). Thursdays at 8pm in July and August, the orchestra Harmonie Bayonnaise gives free concerts in the place de Gaulle gazebo.

Anglet

Wedged between Bayonne and Biarritz, suburban Anglet (hard T) can most charitably be thought of as a spacious passage between two crowded cities. Less charitably, it must be admitted that the town is pretty bland. Nonetheless, Anglet does possess some fine beaches, a youth hostel, and a 370-acre pine forest with hiking paths along the coast. Plenty of buses run to Bayonne and Biarritz.

Although there are a number of reasonable hotels in Anglet (singles in the 50-90F range), the well-equipped **Auberge de Jeunesse (IYHF),** 19, rue de Vignes (tel. 59-63-86-49), is the least expensive place to stay. Bus #6 (*direction* "La Barre") runs approximately every 40 min. from the Biarritz Hôtel de Ville to the hostel. (Service Mon.-Sat. 7:23am-7:52pm, Sun. 9am-7:35pm; 6F.) From Bayonne, take bus #4 (6:45am-8:20pm every 20 min.; 6F) from the *gare* SNCF to La Barre, and switch to bus #6 (*direction* "Arcadie"). Located amid suburban split-levels, the hostel is clean, relatively new, large (95 beds), and equipped with laundry facilities (17F includes wash, dry, and soap). (48F. Camping 28F. Breakfast included.) The hostel provides a cot in one of five circus-style tents for those with an aversion to curfews (44F). Lunch and dinner are served in the summer but you must purchase tickets before 10am (34F). Daylong rentals of surfboards (50F), boogie boards (30F), or wetsuits (20F) may be arranged at the reception between 9-9:30am and 6-6:30pm. The hostel is usually packed—try to make reservations or arrive at least an hour before opening. (Open 9-10am and 6-10pm. No lockout.) The basement snack *brasserie,* open only after 6pm, serves generous portions of *spaghetti à la bolognaise* (23F), *poulet basquaise* (25F), and steak and fries (25F).

Three of Anglet's campgrounds are two-star sites. **Chambre d'Amour,** route de Bouney (tel. 59-03-71-66), has 800 places and is open from April through September. (11F per camper, 12F per tent, 5.50F per car, tax 1F. Showers included.) **Barre de l'Adour,** 130, av. de l'Adour (see Bayonne) has 600 sites and is open mid-June through mid-Sept. (9.40F per person, 12F per tent, 4F per car, tax 1F. Showers included. Reception open 7am-10pm.) **Fontaine Laborde,** av. de Fontaine Laborde (tel. 59-03-89-67), near the hostel, has 300 sites. (Open June-Sept. 10.50F per person, 10.50F per site, 4.80F per car; no caravans.) All are well-situated and fully equipped. Chambre d'Amour is a five-minute walk from Cinq Cantons, down rue Chambre d'Amour (follow the signs). To reach Camping de la Barre, take the green bus from Bayonne or the "Navette des Plages" shuttle bus (#4) to the northern end of its line. Camping Laborde is on av. de Fontaine Laborde, down the hill toward the beach from the hostel.

The main **Office de Tourisme,** place du Général Leclerc (tel. 59-03-77-01), has information on accommodations and prices (open July-Aug. Mon.-Sat. 9am-12:30pm and 1:30-7:30pm, Sun. 10am-noon; Sept.-June Mon.-Fri. 9am-noon and 1:30-7:30pm, Sat. 9am-noon), and is situated near the post office (open Mon.-Fri. 9am-noon and 2:30-5pm, Sat. 9am-noon).

The primary reasons to come to Anglet are its beaches; the 4km of fine sandy stretches are reputedly patrolled by the highest concentration of lifeguards anywhere on the coast. Beneath the lighthouse, in a bay surrounded by large perpendicular cliffs, is **Chambre d'Amour** beach. Larger waves and more beachfront shops attract the surfing elite to adjacent **Sables d'Or** beach. Here you can rent a surfboard from **Waïmea Surf Shop** (tel. 59-03-81-18; 30F per hr., 70F per 4 hr., 100F per 8 hr., 360F per week, deposit 500F; open daily 9:30am-noon and 2-7:30pm). Farther north lie the beaches of **Les Corsaires** and **Les Cavaliers.** Swimmers should be wary of the cross-current pull in the waters off any of the beaches. It can drag you a considerable distance along the shore. All the beaches are within walking distance of the hostel and Cinq Cantons, and are accessible by the **Navettes des Plages** (beach shuttles), which run between Biarritz and La Barre. Part of the STAB system, the *navettes* depart 12 times per day (July-Aug. Mon.-Fri. 7:23am-7:52pm, Sun. 9am-7:35pm; 6F).

Biarritz

The Basque name "Biarritz" has become a cliché, synonymous with "Jet Set," "Beautiful People," "the Rich and the Famous," "the Proud and the Tanned." Part of the fun of Biar-"ritz" is that everyone tries to look the part of a jet-setter. Big surf, big rocks, and lovely warm water could make even the Grinch join the frolic. Ritzy resort ambience aside, Biarritz *is* accessible to budget travelers. The town where Napoleon III, Bismarck, and Queen Victoria and her retinue summered has now acquired snack bars and California-style surf shops. This is a Basque town in name only.

Orientation and Practical Information

Getting to Biarritz is not as easy as it was in the grand old days, when trains ended their journeys in the now-deserted station. Today, trains run through **Biarritz-la-Négresse,** 3km out of town. To get to the center, take blue bus #2, which travels to Bayonne via Biarritz and Anglet (6:30am-8pm every 20-40 min.). As most Paris-Bayonne trains don't stop in Biarritz, it's better to go to Bayonne and take a bus to downtown Biarritz. Red bus #1 runs regularly from the Bayonne to the Biarritz Hôtel de Ville (July-Aug. daily 6:35am-11:20pm; in off-season Mon.-Sat. 6:35am-8:45pm). Bus #2 leaves from the Bayonne train station (Mon.-Sat. 6:25am-8:10pm). All buses cost 6F.

Office de Tourisme: Javalquinto, square d'Ixelles (tel. 59-24-20-24), off av. Edouard VII. Friendly staff supplies free map and loads of brochures. They'll track down a room for you, but there's no guarantee you can afford it. Open June 15-Sept. 15 Mon.-Sat. 9am-7:30pm, Sun. 10am-12:30pm; Sept. 16-June 14 Mon.-Fri. 9am-12:30pm and 2:15-6:15pm, Sat. 10am-12:30pm and 3-6pm.

Student Information Center: Hôtel de Ville, av. Edouard VII (tel. 59-24-52-50). Babysitting placement services available, as well as information for women and families.Open Mon.-Thurs. 8:30am-12:30pm and 2-6pm, Fri. 8:30am-12:30pm and 2-5pm.

Currency Exchange: The post office and most banks are open Mon.-Sat. **Bureau de Change,** rue Mazagran, in the heart of town. No commission. Open daily 10am-8pm.

Post Office: Rue de la Poste (tel. 59-24-23-71). **Postal code:** 64200. Poste Restante. Open Mon.-Fri. 8am-7pm, Sat. 8am-noon.

Train Station: Biarritz-la-Négresse, 3km out of town (tel. 59-55-50-50), accessible by frequent buses. To Bayonne (11 per day, 10 min., 8F), Hendaye (11 per day, ½ hr., 21F), St-Jean-de-Luz (11 per day, ¼ hr., 10F), Bidart (7 per day, 5 min., 5.50F), and Guéthary (9 per day, 10 min., 5.50F).

Bus Station: ATCRB, rue Joseph Petit (tel. 59-24-36-72), a 3-min. walk from the beach, in the same building as the tourist office. To St-Jean-de-Luz (12 per day, ½ hr., 11.60F), with ill-timed connections to Hendaye (you'll have to wait 45-60 min., 21.60F). Half-day excursions to la Rhune (70F), St-Jean-Pied-de Port (80F), and other regions in the southeast of France. Full-day excursions to the Iraty Forest and the Kakonette Gorge (120F), Gavarnie (125F), and St-Sebastian (100F).

Car Rental: At the *gare* SNCF (tel. 59-23-58-97). Open 6am-11pm. **Avis,** 25, av. Edouard VII (tel. 59-24-33-44). Opel Corsa 202F per day plus 2.64F per km and gas. Open Mon.-Sat. 8am-noon and 2-7pm.

Bike Rental: SOBILO, 24, rue Peyroloubilh (tel. 59-23-39-52). Bikes 35F per day, mopeds 80F per day, deposit 300F plus ID. Rents cars too. Open Mon. 9:30am-noon and 2-7pm, Tues.-Sat. 9am-noon and 2-7:30pm, Sun. 2-7pm.

English Bookstore: Bookstore, on rue Gardère at av. Edouard VII. An elegant shop with a small, mixed selection of English books. For literary junk food, head down the street to the English rack at **Maison de la Presse,** av. Edouard VII, across from the Hôtel de Ville.

Laundromat: 5, rue du Port-Vieux, towards the beach. Wash, dry, soap 34F. Open 9am-10pm. Another at 4, av. Jaulerry, across from the post office. Wash 24F, dry 2F. Open daily 7am-10pm.

Medical Emergency: SAMU, Tel. 59-63-33-33.

Police: Av. Joseph Petit (tel. 59-24-68-24), opposite the tourist office.

Police Emergency: Tel. 17.

Accommodations and Camping

The cheaper hotels are spread all over town, but in July and August most are booked solid, so call ahead. The tourist office can provide a comprehensive list of hotels. A better option is to stay in Anglet or Bayonne and commute. From the hostel in Anglet, take bus #6. From Bayonne, take red bus #1 from the Hôtel de Ville, or take blue bus #2 from the *gare.*

Hôtel Berhouet, 29, rue Gambetta (tel. 59-24-63-56). Clean and pleasant, with somewhat expensive restaurant downstairs. Singles and doubles 90-130F. Breakfast 18.50F.

Hôtel Barnetche, 5bis, rue Floquet (tel. 59-24-22-25). Take rue du Helder from place Clemenceau. Rooms from 115F. Obligatory breakfast 15F. In summer 12 dorm beds 70F, breakfast and showers included.

Hôtel Franco-Belge, 2bis, rue Gardague (tel. 59-24-27-10). Quiet, clean, and near the center. Single 72F. Doubles 95-100F. Breakfast 12.50F.

Hôtel Arokenia, 15, rue Gardague. Nothing fancy, but quiet and close to the center and beaches. Singles and doubles from 86F.

Hôtel de la Marine, 1, rue des Goélands (tel. 59-24-34-09), off rue Mazagran. Friendly owners, hall showers free. English spoken. Singles with shower 80F. Doubles with shower 100-120F. Often full July-Aug.

Hotel Beau Soleil, 6, rue du Port-Vieux (tel. 59-24-26-51), 50m from the beach. Cramped doubles 82F.

Camping: The coast is lined with campgrounds. In Biarritz there are three campgrounds within walking distance of the train station. **Municipal,** av. Kennedy, quartier de la Négresse (no phone), nearest the station and least expensive. 9F per person, 11F per tent, 4F per car. Open June-Sept. **Splendid,** rue d'Harcet (tel. 59-23-01-29). 10F per person, 12.80F per tent, 4.50F per car, tax 1F. Hot showers included. Open April-Sept. 9am-10pm. **Biarritz,** 28, rue d'Harcet (tel. 59-23-00-12). 10F per person, 13F per tent, 4.20F per car. Showers included. Open April 22-Oct. 15 8am-9pm. Slendid and Biarritz are closer to the beach and about 2km from the station. To get to all 3 campgrounds, take av. Kennedy from the station and follow the signs.

Food

Forget those Basque feasts unless you're in the money. The self-reliant should check out the **marché municipal** on rue des Halles (open daily 6am-1pm).

Le Sully, place d'Ixelles, av. Joseph Petit (tel. 59-24-16-47). Fresh *moules marinières* (mussels) 35F, Basque specialties, and 50-75F *menus* in a bohemian atmosphere.

Le Zoulou, 6, rue du Port-Vieux. Colorful African masks hang on the walls. Lively atmosphere. Seafood 32-49F, *plats* 35-55F. Open daily noon-2am.

Le Jardin, 3, rue du Port-Vieux. Cheerful red, white, and green decor. Enjoy your meal in alcoves livened by artificial vines, electric candles, and top-40 radio. *A la carte* dishes from 30F. Ask for *repas complet* (choice of a huge vegetarian plate or *rôti de porc*) 40F. Wide choice of salads 15-35F.

Snack Bar Couscous Royal, 26, rue Gambetta. Dingy bar, cheap food. *Moules marinières* with fries 35F. *Poulet basquaise* with fries 38F. Steak, fries, and salad 35F. *Couscous Royal* 55F.

Hôtel-Restaurant Atlantic, 10, rue du Port-Vieux (tel. 59-24-34-08). The atmosphere is pleasant, slightly staid, and the food is excellent. *Moules marinières* 34F. *Poulet basquaise* 38F. *Riz basquaise* 17F.

Epicerie Fauchon, 41bis, rue Mazagran. This gourmet shop isn't a restaurant, but you can put together a cheap, tasty beach meal from the homemade specialties. The *gâteau basque* (9F per slice, cherry or cream filling) is tops, and the peppery squares of Spanish potato omelette (9F) are tasty and filling. Open until 7pm.

Patisserie Paries, 27, rue Gardère. Specializes in *mouchous basques*—dense, pasty, and delicious almond macaroons the size of an infant's fist (3.20F).

Sights

Biarritz's warm, sandy beach and grand casinos set the scene for promenading and intense people-watching. Off-season *voyeurs-voyageurs,* however, might find the town a shadow of its summer self. With only one open casino, chilly Atlantic surf, and far fewer fireworks and festivals, Biarritz sinks into an off-season slumber.

With the first blossoms of blue and pink hortensia, however, the garden boulevards and promenades regain their postcard splendor. Dominated by two casinos, **Grande Plage** attracts armies of bathers and surfers. Snack shops, cafes, and postcard stands line the beachfront. Just north is **plage Miramar,** nestled against the base of the cliffs, and **Pointe St-Martin,** where bathers escape the crowds and peacefully repose *au naturel.* Protected by jagged rock formations from the violent surf, the old **Port des Pêcheurs** harbors colorful small craft and little bistros. The scuba diving school (near the steps to the Plateau de l'Atalaye) offers scuba initiation excursions for 70F.

From the **Plateau de l'Atalaye,** the **Rocher de la Vierge** juts out into the sea, providing spectacular views of the coastline stretching north to the lighthouse and southward along the **plage des Basques,** located at the foot of more beautiful cliffs. Directly below, embedded in the half-sunken rocks, are iron crosses for sailors lost at sea. Just inland from the crags, the **Musée de la Mer** offers a simple display of North Atlantic marine life and documentation on various methods of fishing and boat models. (Open in summer daily 9am-7pm. Admission 20F, students 10F.) East of the Musée is the small, crowded **plage du Vieux Port,** whose cliff walls harbor a calm bit of Atlantic and a family-beach atmosphere. Bathers remain undaunted by the filthy water.

Rent surfboards at the Anglet hostel (see Anglet); the pavilion overlooking the plage des Basques (40F per hr., boogie boards 20F; deposit 200F plus ID); or **Plums,** 5, place Clemenceau (tel. 59-24-08-24; 50F per ½-day, 90F per day).

The guide *Programme des Fêtes,* published each year by the tourism and festival committee in Biarritz, lists the multitude of daily activities from July through October. Events range from firework displays to triathlons and acrobatic water-skiing, with concerts, cocktail soirées, dancing, and just about everything in between. A series of frisbee, beach bum, and beach volleyball tournaments justify Biarritz's currently-touted nickname: "Californie de l'Europe." Look also for free art exhibits at the Hôtel du Palais. Basque culture isn't totally absent from Biarritz, at least not during the tourist season. In July and August, *pelote* and folklore exhibitions take place in Parc Mazon Mondays at 9pm, *cestapunta pelote* matches at the Jaï Alaï arena on Wednesdays and Saturdays at 9:30pm, and bullfight-parodying *courses de vaches* (cow races) in Parc Mazon Thursdays at 9:15pm. Tickets start at 30F.

Near Biarritz

Biarritz and Anglet don't have a monopoly on fine beaches in the area. Some of the most spectacular sand and scenery lies farther south along the Côte Basque. The frequent trains running to the Spanish border also stop at the smaller towns on the way, as do ATCRB buses (about 10 per day to Hendaye, near the border; Mon.-Sat. 4 per day to San Sebastian, fewer Sun.; all leave from place d'Ixelles in Biarritz, outside the ATCRB office).

Superb beaches await you at **Bidart,** a small, picturesque town perched on top of a cliff. Here, a hard-sand promontory commands one of the highest vantage points on the Côte Basque. Just to the south, less rocky and more crowded beaches are graced with fine sand, fine waves, and fine bronzed youths clasping surfboards. The town itself, though crowded in summer, maintains a charming facade. Loudspeakers outside the Hôtel de Ville keep the air musical, or at least lively—the radio station they're tuned to favors the latest American hits. Rue de la Grande Plage stretches steeply down the cliffs to the popular **plage du Centre.** The friendly **Office de Tourisme,** rue de la Grande Plage (tel. 59-54-93-85), will try to help you find a room in July and August, but success is never guaranteed as most of the hotels are booked solid. (Open in summer Mon.-Fri. 9am-12:30pm and 2-7pm, Sat. 9am-noon and 2-7pm, Sun. 9am-noon; in off-season Mon.-Fri. 9am-noon.) The **post office** is nearby on place Sauveur Atchoarena (open Mon.-Fri. 9am-noon and 2-5pm, Sat. 9am-noon). You may call for a **taxi** from the train station (tel. 59-54-90-03).

There are 10 one-star hotels in Bidart, a few of which charge two-star prices. **Hôtel Itsas-Mendia,** rue de la Grande Plage (tel. 59-54-90-23), offers the best rooms for prices that reflect their high standards (singles and doubles from 95-135F, showers included). A classy restaurant downstairs serves a 60F *menu.* **Hôtel Fronton,** in the center of town (tel. 59-54-90-63), provides cheaper rooms that are perfectly pleasant, provided you don't mind the bopping-ball sounds (from the next door *pelote fronton* court) and radio music (non stop from the town hall loudspeakers). (Rooms 70-120F. Showers included. Breakfast 18F. No phone reservations.) Campsites are plentiful and may just be the best way to spend the night. Reservations are a good idea. Try the two-star **La Plage** (tel. 59-54-92-69; open June-Sept.), off N10 near plage de l'Uhabia, or the nearby two-star **Le Parc** (tel. 59-26-54-71; 9F per person, 9F per tent, 5F per car, electricity 8.50F, tax 1F per day; open mid-June to mid-Sept. 7:30am-10pm).

Bidart lies on the Bayonne-Hendaye rail line with more than 10 trains per day to Biarritz and Bayonne in the north and 10 trains to St-Jean-de-Luz and Hendaye in the south. **ATCRB** buses from Biarritz (see Biarritz Practical Information) also stop in Bidart on their way to St-Jean-de-Luz (about 10 per day).

From Biarritz it is more convenient to take a bus to Bidart, since the train stops 1½km outside of town. In fact, the tiny Bidart train station may be no more by the time this book is published, thanks to efforts to phase out stations that see little traffic. (Train station open May-Sept. 5:40am-9:40pm.) From the **train station** (if it's still there), it's a 15-minute walk to town. Take the small tree-shaded path to your right, across a wooden bridge, and walk through the field of corn. Make a quick left on the main road, then a right on the street by Camping Ur-Onea. Make a quick right at the top of the hill, then a left on rue des Ecoles. Cross rue Nationale, then take rue de l'Eglise (where the church is). This will bring you to the center of Bidart.

St-Jean-de-Luz

Well-protected by a narrow approach, St-Jean-de-Luz, at the mouth of the Nivelle River, was once the home port of daring privateers, feared by the English and admired by their fellow French. Despite the annual tourist onslaught, the town has preserved more of its Basque character than rival Biarritz.

Orientation and Practical Information

Framed by outdoor cafes and the Maison Louis XIV, **place Louis XIV,** next to the port, is the center of town and the beginning of **rue Gambetta,** the crowded pedestrian artery. To get here from the train station, go up av. de Verdun and continue straight for five minutes until you see the *syndicat,* the bus station, and *centre ville* just a few steps away.

Syndicat d'Initiative: place Foch (tel. 59-26-03-16). Maps and information on events and excursions. Accommodations booking service. Open July-Aug. Mon.-Sat. 9am-noon and 2-7:30pm, Sun. 10am-noon; Sept.-June Mon.-Sat. only.

Currency Exchange: Banks closed Sun. and, except for the **Crédit Mutuel,** 2, bd. Thiers (tel. 59-26-21-40), on Mon. as well. You can also exchange currency at the post office on Mon. On Sun. use the exchange office at the train station in neighboring Hendaye (tel. 59-20-65-57; open 7-9:15am, 9:45am-noon, 2-8pm, and 8:45-10:30pm) or the bank across the street, **Banque de l'Aquitaine** (tel. 59-20-69-22; open 8am-7pm), which also accepts traveler's checks.

Post Office: Bd. Victor Hugo (tel. 59-26-01-95). **Telephones** and **currency exchange. Postal code:** 64500. Open Mon.-Fri. 9am-6pm, Sat. 9am-noon.

Train Station: Av. de Verdun (tel. 59-26-02-08). To Biarritz (11 per day, 9.50F), Bayonne (11 per day, 17F), and Bidart (8 per day, 6.50F).

Bus Station: Place Foch, by the *syndicat.* **ATCRB** sends 12 buses per day to Biarritz (11.60F) and Bidart (8.20F). Also to Bayonne and St-Jean-Pied-de-Port. Office open Mon.-Sat. 8am-noon and 1:30-6:30pm.

Bike and Moped Rental: Next door to the train station. 37F per ½-day, 47F per day, deposit 300F. Open 5:40am-11:30pm. **Peugeot,** 5-7, av. Labrouche, 1 block from the station. Bikes and mopeds.

Police: Route de Bayonne (tel. 59-26-08-47).

Police Emergency: Tel. 17.

Accommodations, Camping, and Food

Hotels fill up rapidly in summer, and reservations might be hard to make, as most budget places save their rooms for regular, long-term guests. Especially in August, you should arrive early. In emergencies, the two sailing school dormitories in Ciboure might have space. **Club Léo Lagrange,** impasse Okineta (tel. 59-47-04-79), or **Center UCPA,** Socoa Point (tel. 59-47-18-17), which lies just west of St-Jean-de-Luz's port.

Hôtel Toki-Ona, 10, rue Marion Garay (tel. 59-26-11-54), 1 block from the station. Probably the best deal in town. Generally packed; reserve ahead. Singles 80F. Doubles 95F. Triples 115F. Tax 2F. Showers 7F. Breakfast 15F.

Hôtel de Verdun, 13, av. de Verdun (tel. 59-26-02-55), across from the train station. Singles 90-115F, with shower 125F. Doubles 110-150F. Showers 10F. Breakfast 15F. Restaurant next door serves 4-course *menus* for 39-50F.

Hôtel Kapa-Gorry, 9, rue Paul Gélos (tel. 59-26-04-93), a short walk out of town along the beach. Might have room when the other hotels are filled. Rooms 90-120F. Showers 10F. Breakfast 17F.

Hôtel de Paris, bd. Commandant Passicot (tel. 59-26-00-62), next to the train station. Singles from 110F, with shower 140F. Doubles from 130F, with shower 160F. Showers 10F. Breakfast 21F.

Camping: There are 13 sites in St-Jean-de-Luz proper and 13 more within 13km, most of them 3-star. Their combined capacity is in the thousands. Incredibly, most are filled, but the tourist offices in Biarritz and St-Jean-de-Luz will find you a free camping spot where possible. **Camping International** (tel. 59-26-30-32), **Camping Chibaou Berria,** chemin de Chibaou (tel. 59-26-11-94; 12F per person, 17F per tent and car, electricity 8F; open 8am-9pm), and **Camping de la Ferme** (tel. 59-26-34-26; 10.50F per person, 17F per tent and car, tax 1F) are all in Quartier Erromardie north of downtown. To get there, board the ATCRB bus from place Maréchal Foch (*direction* "Biarritz"; every hr. 7am-8pm except 8am and 1pm).

The Basque and Spanish specialties in St-Jean de-Luz are the best north of the border, although most *menus* are nothing to crow about. One exception is **Restaurant Ramuntcho,** 24, rue Garat (tel. 59-26-03-89). The 66F *menu* includes two substantial and tasty dishes as well as dessert. You can wash down a steaming heap of mussels with the unorthodox red wine Corbières (15F per ½-bottle). (Open noon-2pm and 7-9:30pm.) Bustling **La Vieille Auberge,** 22, rue Tourasse, serves a popular 60F *menu* that also features dessert and two dishes (*moules marinières, soupe de poisson,* or *salade Luzienne* for the first course; Basque specialities such as *poulet basquaise* with rice for the second). **La Banquise,** 34, bd. Thiers, serves a small but flavorful 56F *menu* and a hearty 45F *soupe de poisson.* (Open daily 12:15-2pm and 7:15-9:30pm.) Neighboring **Restaurant Le St-Jean,** 30, bd. Thiers, also offers a 3-course, 56F *menu.* You may order in German, English, Spanish, or French. The best place for fresh seafood is the little stand with the sign **Crustacés Sardines Grillés,** at a corner of the covered market's *poissonerie* on bd. Victor Hugo. Eat engulfed in fishy aroma at the outdoor tables. (Tuna *pipérade* 34F. *Moules marinières* 22F. *Soupe de poisson* 25F.) Plenty of shops where you can buy your own fare and do it yourself front bd. Victor Hugo and rue Gambetta. If you're at the beaches, **Les Vagues Snack Bar** in the beachfront pavilion offers a 35F *menu* (pizza, salad, and cheese). The market on **place des Halles** is the place to shop on Tuesday and Friday mornings (open daily 7am-1pm), and the town's many small squares are excellent picnic spots.

Sights

The museum in the **Maison Louis XIV** has been redone in seventeenth-century style, but the 25-minute guided tour is not worth the admission price. (Open June 8-Sept. 15 Mon.-Sat. 10:30am-noon and 3-6:30pm, Sun. 3-6:30pm. Admission 15F, students 12F.) Louis XIV stayed at this house, owned by the Lohobiague family, for 40 days in 1660, when the 22-year-old monarch came to St-Jean-de-Luz to sign the Treaty of the Pyrenees. The house hosted the king again when he returned to marry Marie-Thérèse of Spain. In the nearby **Eglise Ste-Jean Baptiste,** where the marriage ceremony took place, you can see the portal that was ceremoniously sealed forever after the newlyweds exited the church—look to the right of the main entry. In the naval, a gold tabernacle reaches from altar to domed ceiling; 21 life-size apostles, angels, and saints stand between the tiered gold columns. Note the bilingual prayer books in French and Basque.

Despite an ugly concrete pavilion packed with snack bars and souvenir shops, the stretch of sand along **promenade Jacques Thibaud** retains a festive air. Watch a volleyball match or rent a James Bondish catamaran pedalboat. (20F per ½-hr., 35F per hr.) The summer season abounds with Basque festivals, bullfights, concerts, and the world cup of *Cesta Punta.* Ask at the tourist office for the free guide, *St-Jean-de-Luz en Fêtes.* Tickets to *pelote* matches cost 30F and up. Matches are played Monday, Thursday, and Saturday evenings (at 5:30pm, 7:30pm, and 9:30pm) throughout the summer and well into September. Bullfight parodies involving clowning matadors, cows, and a swimming pool occur Wednesdays at 9:30pm in the Erromardie Arena. The biggest annual festival is the **Fêtes de St-Jean,** which lasts for three days beginning on the weekend closest to St-Jean's Day (June 21). The **Nuit de la Sardine** sounds like a horror movie but is actually a night in mid-July at the Campos-Beri Jaï Alaï stadium that features up to 2000 participants (who've paid 20F each), one orchestra, lots of fireworks and Basque singers, and one giant sardine. At the **Fêtes du Thon,** the whole town gathers around the harbor to eat tuna fish. Complete with street musicians, dancing in the thoroughfares, confetti, and fireworks, this festival takes place on the Saturday closest to July 7 (4pm-midnight).

Near St-Jean-de-Luz

Ten kilometers southeast of St-Jean-de-Luz lies the miniscule town of **Col de St-Ignace,** which isn't a town so much as a welcoming center for **La Rhune,** the most spectacular lookout point in all the Basque Country. Stop in Col de St-Ignace only to board the wooden, two-car cog-train that scales the mountainside to La Rhune at a snail's pace. At each turn you will be confronted with dazzling views of the mountain's plunging forest line and the quilted farmland below. You might also see herds of wild Basque ponies ("pottok" horses) and a daring mountain biker navigating the rocks. Once you reach the top at La Rhune, 900m above sea-level (it can be chilly, even in July), you can take in a fabulous panorama of the ocean, the Forêt des Landes, and the Basque Pyrenees.

La Rhune lies on the Spanish side of the French-Spanish border, and you will hear shop-owners and workers rambling in both French and Spanish. Because of its duty-free status, the shops here overflow with liquor bottles at reduced prices, but it's probably best not to indulge if you're planning to descend the mountain by foot. The only way to return directly to Col de St-Ignace is to follow the train tracks—not dangerous, as the train rumbles along not much faster than you will. To descend by a different route, take the well-marked path to the left of the tracks down to Ascain, and walk the tortuous 3 km on D4 back to Col de St-Ignace. You might be able to get a ride from hikers returning to their cars at the foot of the path. Plan on spending an hour to an hour-and-a-half on your descent. From July 1 through September 30, the two trains ascend and descend daily every half-hour from 9am to noon and from 1:30 to 5:30pm. From May through June and October through November 15, trains depart on Sunday only at 10am and 3pm. Purchase tickets from the **VFDM** office (tel. 59-54-20-26) at the end of the tracks in Col de St-Ignace (one way 18F, round-trip 27F). In summer, expect a half-hour wait. Col de St-Ignace is accessible by bus from St-Jean-de-Luz. **Le Basque Bondissant** (tel. 59-26-25-87 or 59-26-23-87) runs four buses to the departure point for La Rhune, one of which is too late in the evening (Mon.-Sat., 20 min., 6.50F). Catch the bus in St-Jean-de-Luz from opposite the Hôtel du Commerce by the train station.

Buses stopping in Col de St-Ignace from St-Jean-de-Luz continue 3km farther down D4 to the tiny Basque village of **Sare** (10 min., 2.50F). The Pyrenees rise in the distance and the small roads fanning out of town are shaded by evenly spaced trees. Almost everything is clustered around the **Syndicat d'Initiative,** in the *mairie* in place de Sare (tel. 59-54-20-14), which will help you look for a room. (Open Mon.-Fri. 9:30am-12:30pm and 2:30-6:30pm.) But as in most of the Basque region, hotels in town are often booked solid in August. You might try **Hôtel de la Poste,** place de Sare (tel. 59-54-20-06). (Nice rooms with firm mattresses 85F, with shower 110F. Showers 10F. Breakfast 16F.) There are also three campgrounds in Sare, and although reservations are recommended in August, you should not have a problem finding a spot. **Camping de la Petite Rhune,** 2km from town (tel. 59-54-23-97), has a tennis court and 100 spaces at 7.50F per person, 9.50F per site, 4F per car; hot showers included. (Open June-Sept. 8am-10pm.)

To profit most from Sare's beautiful setting, take a delicious meal on the terrace of **Restaurant Mendi-Bichta.** The terrace overlooks rolling Basque countryside, and the 50F *menu,* including *pipérade* and *gâteau basque,* is just as good as the view. **Hôtel-Restaurant Lastiry,** next to Hôtel de la Poste in place de Sare (tel. 59-54-20-07), boasts a cozy, oak-beamed dining room and a three-course, 60F *menu* consisting of a large salad, excellent *poulet basquaise,* and dessert. Try some of the cheapest and best-tasting *gâteaux basques* from the stands on place de Sare. While you're waiting for the bus to St-Jean-de-Luz, visit the church by the *syndicat.* The interior unmistakably resembles the one in St-Jean-de-Luz. Interestingly, its courtyard is a cemetery; note the circular Basque tombstones. On September 13, Sare paints itself red during an all-day and all-night *fête* featuring musicians and merrymaking in the streets, food and drink, and a large ball. Should you be in Sare in October, ask the *syndicat* about opportunities to watch a Basque ring-dove-hunt (*chasse à la palombe*). The **Fête de la Palombe,** held on a Sunday in mid-October, is a festival still dedicated to solemn ritual rather than antics for tourists. It begins in the morning, with a convocation of ring-dove hunters, a mass in the church, and a parade in which the hunters wear their gear.

St-Jean-Pied-de-Port

Narrow, cobblestoned **rue de la Citadelle** climbs up through the *haute ville* of St-Jean-Pied-de-Port to the old fortress. In the opposite direction from Porte de Notre Dame, **rue d'Espagne** leads across the calm Nive River and beyond, toward

Spain. Rounded by the footsteps of pilgrims on their way to Santiago de Compostela, these cobblestones today bear the weight of rubber-soled tourists. In the past few years, St-Jean-Pied-de-Port seems to have become everyone's favorite daytrip. Once you do reach this town, you'll do well to venture into the mountains nearby. Situated at the foot (*pied*) of the Ronceveaux mountain pass (*port,*) this ancient capital of the inland Pays Basque gives you access to some lovely, less- trodden territory.

Orientation and Practical Information

St-Jean-Pied-de-Port is 8km from the Spanish border, 55m from Bayonne and 76km from the Navarese capital Pamplona. Although buses occasionally climb up here (mainly for group excursions), the village is most easily reached by train from Bayonne (1 hr., 24F).

The picturesque *haute ville* spreads behind the ramparts below the *citadelle*. The more modern *basse ville* lies even farther down, of no particular interest unless you want to take a dip in the municipal swimming pool on rue de Ste-Eulalie.

Syndicat d'Initiative: 14, place Charles de Gaulle (tel. 59-37-03-57), in the center just outside the old city walls, to your right as you enter the old city. Free maps and walking and hiking itineraries. Ask for hiking information on the nearby Forêt d'Iraty. Also pick up a free copy of *Programme des Festivités* July-Aug. Open in summer daily 8:30am-12:30pm and 2-7pm; in off-season Mon.-Fri. 8:30am-noon and 2-5:30pm, Sat. 10am-noon.

Currency Exchange:Crédit Agricole, rue de la Poste. No commission and excellent rates. Open Mon.-Fri. 9am-12:15pm and 1:45-5:45pm.

Post Office: Rue de la Poste. **Telephones. Postal code:** 64220. Open Mon.-Fri. 9am-noon and 2-5pm, Sat. 9am-noon.

Train Station: Av. Renaud (tel. 59-37-02-00). To Bayonne (Mon.-Sat. 4-6 per day, 5 Sun.; 1¼ hr.; 24F). The friendly station master may let you leave your pack here free of charge.

Bike Rental: Chez Steunou, place du Marché (tel. 59-37-25-45), in the center near the *syndicat.* 35F per day; deposit 300F and ID. Open daily 8am-7:30pm.

Hospital: Fondation Luro, Ispoure (tel. 59-37-00-55). For taxi-ambulance, call 59-37-05-70 or 59-37-05-00.

Police: Rue d'Ugagne (tel. 59-37-00-36).

Police Emergency: Tel. 17.

Accommodations and Food

Finding a room is generally not a problem, but prices are on the high side. **Hôtel Ramuntcho,** above the old city walls and porte de France (tel. 59-37-03-91), offers rooms with pleasant views and a terrace to stretch out on. (Singles and doubles 105-130F. Showers included. Breakfast 18F.) **Hôtel Itzalpea,** place du Trinquet (tel. 59-37-03-66), outside and just opposite the old walls, has plain rooms. Tell the proprietors if you plan to leave early in the morning, so they can chain the prowling watchdog. (Singles and doubles 70-80F. Triples 90-100F. Showers 10F. Breakfast 14F.) You can also rent rooms in private homes from 70F; get a list in the tourist office. St-Jean-Pied-de-Port has a nice **Camping Municipal** on the Nive riverbank, a *pelote*'s throw from the municipal *fronton*; cross the bridge from the *syndicat* and continue straight. (7.50F per person, 4.30F per tent.) **Camping Bidegainia** (tel. 59-37-03-75 or 59-37-09-09) is a popular 3-star site with trout-fishing 1km away from St-Jean-Pied-de-Port. (4.70F per person, 5.50F per tent. Showers 2.70F. Open April-Aug. daily 8am-9:30pm.) Try also **Europ' Camping** (tel. 59-37-12-78), a 4-star site 1km from St-Jean on D918 to Bayonne, complete with restaurant, free pool, and sauna. (18F per person, 25F per tent and car, electricity 12F. Showers included. Open Easter-Oct. 8am-10pm.) The *syndicat* will help with lodgings; when closed, it posts an accommodations board outside.

St-Jean is a good place to sample Basque specialties, especially trout. **La Vieille Auberge** (also known as **"Chez Dédé"**), just outside the city walls on rue de France, serves a delicious 50F, four-course *menu estival* (summer menu) featuring *truite meuniére* and *poulet basquaise,* wine, coffee, and service included. Young locals come here to avoid tourists. Just up the street, the **Ramuntcho** serves excellent three-course *menus* from 60F on a balcony with a view of the mountains. The **Restaurant Hillion,** on place du Trinquet as you enter the *haute ville* from the train station cooks up a 35F *menu* that consists of *crudités* and *gâteau basque,* with *truite de pays, poulet basquaise,* or *pipérade* (a soft omelette with tomatoes and ham) as the main course. It also serves bigger 55F and 70F *menus.* **Hôtel Itzalpea's** restaurant assembles a generous 35F *menu* with vegetable soup, *pipérade,* and delicious chocolate ice cream or *gâteau basque.* **Market** day is Monday, when many Basques come in to town from the country: The wives shop, while the husbands sit in cafes with their black berets and shoot the breeze. Mock bullfights (*courses de vaches*) are held on market day throughout the summer at 9:30pm in the jai-alai stadium.

Sights

St-Jean's streets and picture-book location are the main attractions. The ancient *haute ville,* framed by **Porte d'Espagne** and **Porte St-Jacques** (gates to the *rue pié-tonne* open daily 11am-7pm), consists of one narrow street, rue de la Citadelle, bordered by houses made from the dark red stone of the region. Check out the sixteenth- and seventeenth-century dates carved above the front portals. Along the Nive, at the bottom of rue de la Citadelle, stands **Eglise Notre-Dame-du-Pont,** a church that once doubled as a fortress. The church is a fourteenth-century structure possessing a large nave and tiny choir but altogether lacking cruciform plan or chapels.

At the top of rue de la Citadelle is the paved ramp leading to the fortress. The fortress is now closed to the public, but you can walk around its steep walls. From atop the colossal arch, there's a sweeping mountain and valley panorama. To the left as you face the valley, a postern staircase of 269 steps descends to the Porte de l'Echangette behind the church near the Nive. Farther down rue de la Citadelle, the **Prison des Evêques** stands at #41, in a building dating from 1584 with a dark, vaulted underground cell. (Open 10am-12:30pm and 2-7pm. Admission 5F.) A pleasant and wooded walk leads from the church along the Nive to the **pont Romain.** The area around the Roman bridge on allées d'Eyheraberryis ideal for orgiastic picnics. Wash off afterwards in the fast-flowing stream (waders should wear shoes and avoid rusted metal objects).

For pizzas (24-32F) and salads (15-28F), hit **Pizzerie Hortzadarra,** 3, rue de la Citadelle (open daily noon-2pm and 7-10pm). Get your appetizer two doors down at the gourmet shop **Laurent Petrocorena,** 1, rue de la Citadelle, where regional specialties (*foie gras, pâté,* ham) can be sampled for free. Soft ice cream fans should not miss the *glace maison* at the **Pâtisserie Barbier Millox,** 17, rue d'Espagne (5F per generous single cone, 10F per double cone).

In summer, St-Jean-Pied-de-Port celebrates. Music is played over the loudspeakers daily, and, though evenings can be slow as donkeys, dances and concerts are frequent. A different kind of pelote is played almost daily at the fronton. (Tickets 30F, but you can easily watch a match from the fence.) In July and August, St-Jean-Pied-de-Port promises an event every day, ranging from folk dancing to choral concerts, street parties, mock bullfights, and more *pelote.* For schedule information, pick up the *Programme des Festivités* (free) at the tourist office.

St-Jean is still part of the grand footpath from Paris to Santiago de Compostela. Each weekend one of the region's villages holds a festival that includes public dancing (until as late as 3am) on Saturday and Sunday evenings. Around August 15, St-Jean-Pied-de-Port celebrates its patron, St-John the Baptist, with fireworks, late-night revelry, and a fair of local edibles.

Near St-Jean-Pied-de-Port

Superb and easy hiking awaits you at the **Forêt d'Iraty,** 28km southeast of St-Jean-Pied-de-Port along D18. Unfortunately, no public transportation runs to this forested valley in the Pyrenees near the Spanish border. Furthermore, hitchhiking is difficult along the area's narrow, tortuous roads. The tourist office in St-Jean offers pamphlets and guides that map out 5- to 28-km excursions in the surrounding mountains and villages, including one path leading to the Forêt d'Iraty. These excursions may be more realistic alternatives for those without wheels since they begin in St-Jean-Pied-de-Port. The road leading to the Forêt d'Iraty passes beautiful and undisturbed Basque farmland and rises steeply through the mountains where spectacular panoramas await you at every twist of the road. Exercise caution at all times while driving here.

Serious hikers should buy a *Carte de Randonnées, 1/50,000 Pays Basque Est* (47F), which provides the most complete and detailed hiking map for the Basque Pyrenees (travel shelters are indicated on the longer paths, such as GR10 and GR65). These large trails fan out of St-Jean-Pied-de-Port. Once in the **Pointe d'Iraty,** consider taking the 9-km **Larreluche** trail, which ascends a breathtaking slope of green mountains sometimes topped by blond Pyrenean cows or pottok horses (Basque ponies) let loose for the summer. Located at the end of most of the trails, **Chalet Pedro,** with their 90F *menu,* will remind you always to bring a picnic. If you don't have your own provisions, try their trout (30F), caught from the stream behind the restaurant. Campers may pitch a tent along any of the stream's shaded banks, just off D18 between Chalet Pedro and Chalet d'Iraty. For mountain lodgings, hikers should pick up the guide *Randonnées Pyrénées* (available for free at tourist offices), which lists the *gîtes d'étape* indicated on the *Carte Randonnée.* In winter, the trails in the Forêt d'Iraty are frequented by cross-country skiers. Red signs posted on trees are for skiers only; you can ignore the warning *access interdit* if you are hiking in summer.

Gascony (Gascogne)

In the south of Gascony rise the High Pyrenees, challenging hikers and rock climbers, experienced and novice alike. The Pyrenees were probably created by the shifting of the Iberian Peninsula, a process that gave the peaks their jagged profile and still causes rockslides and avalanches. Some valleys in the region are filled with multicolored granite—the most famous of these is the massive face of the snowy Cirque de Gavarnie.

In addition to beautiful landscapes, these slopes offer refuge for a wide range of rare wildlife and fauna. Climb high enough and you might see the renowned *ibards* (mountain antelope). Since the creation of the Parc National des Pyrénées in 1967 (1 of only 5 national parks in France), their once-endangered population has doubled. The Pyrenees also shelter the last colonies of brown bears, eagles, and vultures in France, species still threatened by extinction.

Most of the region's larger towns are accessible by train, and buses serve the more remote areas, which are the best bases for hiking and skiing. Make sure you coordinate train and bus schedules before venturing out on daytrips.

Once in the mountains, accommodations are inexpensive: the Club Alpin Français (CAF), the Comité des Sentiers de Grande Randonnée, and the Parc National all maintain simple *gîtes* along major trails, and shepherds' cabins are available in summer along wilder routes. The **Grande Randonnée No. 10 (GR10)** runs across the length of the Pyrenees, past its finest scenery. If you plan to follow any part of this, pick up the guide *GR10* (47F) in a bookstore—it provides good trail directions and up-to-date listings of refuges along the route. Also essential is at least one of the four detailed purple 1:25,000 maps (44F) of the Parc National.

Whether or not you hit the trail, you will have the chance to sample the mild *fromage des Pyrénées* (or *fromage du pays*), made either from cow's or sheep's milk. When you stop in a village, try to sample some of the fine *béarnaise* cuisine: duck and goose *pâté,* fresh fish, and the superb rosé wines called *vins de Béarn*. You will find the *béarnais* themselves as expansive and hospitable as the region they inhabit.

Hiking

Exercise caution. Trails may be well traveled, but you'll still be hours away from emergency services in town. Sneakers are not wise, as trails can become very slippery. Go slow when descending; the uneven terrain and loose rocks can easily cause a fall. Your daypack should be light—keep it down to the bare essentials: map, compass, army knife, trail food, sweater, matches, and first-aid kit. You should also bring a container filled with water, as many sources in the hills contain *giardia,* a serious parasitic disease transmitted by sheep. Never drink the mountain water directly from its source. You are allowed to pitch a tent anywhere in the mountains, but camp close to a refuge and far away from possible rolling stones. Travel with somebody, try to leave a copy of your itinerary with the local CAF or police station, and check the local weather report before you leave. (Storms often rush through the valleys with amazing swiftness.) Once on a trail, stick to it; something that looks like a short cut may end up being a dangerous slope. On a first trip, it is certainly worthwhile to join a guided hike. Contact Club Alpin Français (office in Pau) for details, or the Parc National offices in St-Lary, Luz St-Sauveur, Gavarnie, Cauterets, Anens-Marsous, Gabas, and Bedous.

Pau

A graceful city of gardens set against the Pyrenees, Pau prides itself on having produced two kings. Henry IV was born in the château here and during his reign as King of France, kept Béarn an independent country and Pau its capital. Under Henry's son Louis XIII, however, Béarn was annexed to the kingdom of France and reduced to the status of a province. Another *Pauan,* J.B. Bernadotte, took off from bourgeois origins to become the king of Sweden in the early nineteenth century. Simultaneously, Pau's decline was reversed, and the city became a popular winter vacation paradise for the English well-to-do. When Queen Victoria took her 1889 winter holiday in Biarritz instead, Pau once again slipped out of the international limelight. Vestiges of the town's old glory remain: the château, the boulevards, and the extensive resort facilities created for the English colony. Now you can enjoy them without the regal prices they once commanded. Never lacking in concerts and cultural events, Pau makes a good place to stock up on civilization before hitting those lonely mountain heights.

Orientation and Practical Information

Pau lies 156km and 2½ hours by train west of Toulouse. A steep uphill walk separates the train station from the center. You (and your bicycle) can also take the free funicular across the street. The funicular climbs to bd. des Pyrénées every five minutes (Mon.-Sat. 7am-9:40pm, Sun. 1:30-9pm). It's difficult to orient yourself in Pau; get the free map from the tourist office.

Office Municipal de Tourisme: Place Royale (tel. 59-27-27-08), next to the Hôtel de Ville. From the funicular station, walk straight across the park. A cheery, well-equipped office with free maps and plenty of information on the Pyrenees region, hiking and camping, and Pau itself. Pick up a free copy of *Les Fêtes du Béarn* for a calendar of the region's summer activities. Open daily July-Aug. 9am-12:30pm and 2-7pm; Sept.-June 9am-noon and 2-6pm.

Comité Départemental de Tourisme des Pyrénées-Atlantiques: Parlement de Navarre, rue Henri IV (tel. 59-83-92-37). Information on trips into the Pyrénées. **Service des Gîtes Ruraux,** 124, bd. Tourasse (tel. 59-80-19-13), in the Cité Administrative, is also helpful with trails and trail lodgings.

Budget Travel Aquitaine Tourisme, 84, rue Emile Guichenné (tel. 59-27-88-82). BIJ/Transalpino tickets. Open Mon.-Fri. 9am-7pm, Sat. 9am-noon.

Student Lodging Service: Service Mutuel Pour le Logement des Jeunes, 2, rue de Craonne (tel. 59-84-38-84). Accommodations service for long stays in Pau—can get you a room for as little as 20F per night. Open Mon. and Wed. 5-8pm, Tues. and Thurs. noon-2pm.

Post Office: On cours Bosquet at rue Gambetta (tel. 59-27-76-89). **Currency exchange** and **telephones. Postal code: 64000.** Open Mon.-Fri. 8am-6:30pm, Sat. 8am-noon.

Train Station: Av. Gaston Lacoste (tel. 59-30-50-50), at the base of the hill dominated by the château. To Bayonne (8-10 per day, 60F), Bordeaux (6 per day, 118F), Lourdes (14 per day, ½ hr., 28F), Nice (3 per day, 359F), Paris (4 per day, 341F), and Toulouse (7 per day, 109F). Station open 5am-11:30pm. Information desk open in summer Mon.-Sat. 9am-6:25pm.

Bus Station: CITRAM—Courriers des Basses Pyrénées, 30, Palais des Pyrénées, av. de Tassigny (tel. 59-33-27-39). To Oloron-Ste-Marie, site of a major folk festival during the 1st week of Aug. (2 per day); Aubisque via Laruns (27.50F), a good starting point for hikes into the Pyrenees (4 per day, 27.50F). Buses leave from place Clemenceau and the base of the funicular. **Société TPR,** 2, place Clemenceau (tel. 59-27-45-98). Regularly to Lourdes and Biarritz. Although both companies run excursions, they tend to be expensive (95-130F). Opt for the trips arranged by the tourist office (65F per ½-day, 80-100F per day; destinations include Cauterets and Gavarnie). **STAP,** rue Gachet (tel. 59-27-69-78), has information on city buses. Tickets 4.50F, *carnet* of 10 20F. Open July-Aug. Mon.-Fri. 8:50am-noon and 2-5:30pm; Sept.-June also Sat. 8:50am-noon.

Taxi: Tel. 59-02-22-22.

Laundromat: Lavo Self, 11, rue Castetnau (tel. 59-80-03-34). Open Mon.-Fri. 8:30am-noon and 2-7pm, Sat. 8:30am-noon and 2-5pm. **Lavomatique Foirail,** 3, rue de Bordeu. Wash 12F, dry 5F. Open daily 7am-10pm.

Maison des Femmes, 12, rue René Fournets (tel. 59-82-82-54). Open Sun.-Tues. and Thurs.-Fri. 2-5pm.

Comité pour les Homosexuels, complexe de la République, place de la République, #603.

Hospital: 145, av. de Buros (tel. 59-32-84-30).

Medical Emergency: SAMU, Tel. 59-27-15-15.

Police: Rue O'quin (tel. 59-27-94-06).

Police Emergency: Tel. 17.

Accommodations and Camping

A number of cheap hotels dot the busy downtown area. The hostel is the best deal but is a long walk from the train station (30 min., no buses).

Auberge de Jeunesse/Foyer des Jeunes Travailleurs (IYHF), 30, rue Michel Hounau (tel. 59-30-45-77). From place Clemenceau, follow rue Maréchal Foch that becomes cours Bosquet. Take a left to rue Lespy, then a right on rue St-François d'Assise, and finally a right (about 15 min.). A friendly place with a bit of luxury at low prices: hot showers in every 2nd floor room, laundromat, kitchens, a lively bar and self-service cafeteria, and a game room. Singles 45F. Breakfast included, Mon.-Fri. until 8:15am, Sat. until 9:30am, Sun. until 11:30am. 4-course meals (served 11:45am-1:15pm and 7-8:15pm) 32F. No meals Sat. evening or Sun.

University Housing: CROUS, av. Poplanski (tel. 59-02-88-46), at the Cité Universitaire Gaston Phoebus. Take bus #4 from *centre ville*. Rooms around 30F with student ID. Open 9am-11:30am and 2-6:30pm. Available July-Sept. only. Call 59-02-73-35 for reservations.

Hôtel Bernard, 7, rue de Foix (tel. 59-27-40-28). From Hôtel des Balances, cross place Reine Marguerite, past Hôtel Mon Auberge. Big, airy, comfortable. Singles 60F. Doubles from 85F. Breakfast 13F.

Hôtel Le Béarn, 5, rue Maréchal Joffre (tel. 59-27-52-50), on the side street opposite Cinéma Béarn. Well-kept rooms, a charming dining room, and an elevator. Singles and doubles 60-75F, with showers 100-110F. Breakfast 15F.

Hôtel de la Pomme d'Or, 11, rue Maréchal Foch (tel. 59-27-78-48), on a main boulevard off place Clemenceau. The hotel has a courtyard that blots out the bustle. Rooms are plain but well-kept, and the management is cheerful. One single 50F. Other singles and doubles 70-80F, with shower 85-100F. Triples and quads 110-160F. Breakfast 17F.

Camping: There are several campsites on the outskirts of town. **Camping Municipal de la Plaine des Sports et des Loisirs** (tel. 59-02-30-49) is a 6-km trek from the station, but bus A takes you right there. **Camping du Coy,** a 2-star site in Bizanos (tel. 59-27-71-38), is a 10-min. walk east of the train station. Open daily 8am-10pm.

Food

Rue Léon Daran and other streets leading up to the university have inexpensive fare, but in Pau a little extravagance may be justified. The region that brought you Béarnaise sauce has many other specialties: salmon, pike, *oie* (goose), *canard* (duck), and *crudités,* a cold vegetable platter that includes such delicacies as baby asparagus and eggs *béarnaise*. Elegant little restaurants serving regional dishes fill the side streets around the château.

Chez Olive, 9, rue du Château (tel. 59-27-81-19). Tasty, 60F *menu;* an even better 78F one. Friendly and unpretentious; the food is simple but well prepared. Try the *bouchées aux fruits de mer* (seafood in a puff pastry) and *truite pochée au beurre blanc* (poached trout). Open Mon. 7-10pm, Tues.-Sat. noon-1:30pm and 7-10pm.

Restaurant O'Gascon, 13, rue du Château (tel. 59-27-64-74), next to Chez Olive. Friendly restaurant in a fancy setting serving good food. 4-course, 60F *menu.* Open Mon. noon-2pm, Wed.-Sun. noon-2pm and 7-10pm.

La Goulue, 13, rue Henri IV (tel. 59-27-72-83). 3-course, 55F *menu,* with superb cuts of meat and well-prepared sauces (served until 9pm). Open daily 10am-1:30pm and 6pm-midnight.

Au Fruit Défendu, 3, rue Sully. Small and fancy. 60F *menu* with *soupe de poisson, fondue bourguignonne,* and cheese or dessert (served until 9pm). *Raclette* 85F.

Le Palmarium, 10, rue des Cordeliers (passage du Hédas, tel. 59-27-41-40), halfway down a narrow stone staircase off rue des Cordeliers. An airy, pink-and-green place with a skylight and flowery branches decorating the walls. Excellent food. Trout filet poached with herbs 32F. 60F *menu* features the *plat du jour* and fish soup. Open Tues.-Sun. for lunch and dinner.

Sights

On a clear day the view from **boulevard des Pyrénées** stretches some 50km over the vineyards and hills to the distant, jagged heights. An exceptionally beautiful French garden blooms immediately below the walkway; adjoining the boulevard is **Parc Beaumont,** filled with bright flowers, a lake, and a small waterfall.

The **château,** a rambling structure with six square towers, overlooks the river from the highest point in Pau. Built by the viscounts of Béarn in the twelfth century, the castle later was occupied by the kings of Navarre. Fifty glorious Gobelin tapestries, several ornate chandeliers (some weighing over 300kg), well-preserved royal chambers, and artistically decorated ceilings grace the castle. In Henry IV's bedroom, the guide will show you the tortoise shell that served the royal infant as a cradle. It was believed that the tortoise would bestow its fabled longevity on the toddling monarch. (Open in summer 9:30-11:45am and 2-5:45pm; in off-season 9:30-11:45am and 2-4:45pm. Last guided tours ½ hr. before closing. Admission 21F, students 11F, ages under 18 free.) The **Musée Béarnais** on the third floor has an exhibition of local traditions and crafts, as well as displays of preserved butterflies, birds, and bears. (Open in summer 9:30am-12:30pm and 2:30-6:25pm; in off-season 9:30am-12:25pm and 2:30-5:30pm. Admission 6F.)

The **Musée des Beaux-Arts,** rue Mathieu Lalanne, possesses a small but engaging collection of paintings, including notable works by El Greco, Ribera, Zurbarán, Miranda, Rubens, and Degas, as well as an impressive collection of contemporary art. (Open Wed.-Mon. 10am-noon and 2-6pm. Free.) For those interested in Scandinavia and in the anomalies of history, the **Musée Bernadotte,** 8, rue Tran, is a fascinating way to spend an afternoon. J.B. Bearnadotte was born in this house in 1763 and, after a thriving military career, became king of Sweden in 1818. Well-informed, English-speaking guides make the museum even more interesting. (Open Tues.-Sun. 10am-noon and 2-6pm. Free.) From the last week of June to the first week of July, Pau holds its **Festival de Pau,** with classical plays, concerts, recitals, and ballet performances—some of which are staged in the château courtyard. Pick up a free brochure from the tourist office. (Tickets 45-125F per event. No student discounts.) As soon as the festival ends, a program of free concerts and spectacles begins. Organized by the Pau Festival Committee, the program includes firework displays, *pelote* tournaments, poetry readings, a leg of the Tour de France, and jazz, rock, ballet, and reggae performances. Ask for the free schedule at the tourist office.

Pau serves as a good departure point for trips into the mountains. The **Club Alpin Français (CAF)** office in Pau at 5, rue René Fournets (tel. 59-27-71-81; open Mon.-Wed. and Fri. 5-7pm, Thurs. 5-8pm), provide information on hiking. SNCF and private buses link the town to Laruns, north of the Parc National. From here you can catch a local bus, hike, or hitch to Gabas, a good base with camping and a CAF refuge. Other accessible sights—some of the finest in the Pyrenees—include the Col d'Aubisque mountain pass, the Pic du Midi d'Ossau peak (2884m), and the Lac d'Artouste, all with CAF mountain refuges nearby. Laruns is also a good departure point for hitchhiking and biking; via Argèles-Gazost (south of Lourdes) and Luz to Arreau, steep, narrow roads lead past beautiful mountains. In between, you may also be able to take advantage of local transportation and make side trips to mountain villages such as Cauterets and Gavarnie. During the last two weeks of July, convoys of **Etoíle Bus** (tel. 59-02-45-45) leave place de Verdun at 5:30pm for the Festival des Pyrénées at Gavarnie, returning to Pau at 1:30am (see Near Cauterets).

Lourdes

A town of just over 18,000 inhabitants, Lourdes is overrun each year by 4,500,000 pilgrims. Since the 1858 apparitions of the Virgin to Bernadette Soubirous, a young girl of the town, the miracle of Lourdes has blossomed into a pre-packaged tourist industry. Special trains, buses, and charter flights from all over the world bring entire parishes to the sacred site, and the streets are jammed with souvenir stands selling empty Virgin-shaped water bottles, kitschy statues, and plastic rosary beads. Yet the **Caverne des Apparitions,** where Bernadette had the vision that transformed the town, is still conducive to mystic feelings. Next to it, the modern **Basilique Pius X** is a concrete monstrosity that looks like a cross between Madison Square Garden and a parking garage—fortunately, most of it is underground. It can accommodate up to 20,000 people. (Purportedly the building was also designed for use as an atomic bomb shelter.)

Practical Information

Since Lourdes is a major train stop, getting there is no problem. The train station is located on the northern edge of town; the *centre ville* is 10 minutes away. If you arrive by plane from Paris, head directly for the waiting bus, as it is usually the only one (26F for the 10-km trip). The grotto, basilica, and souvenir shops are all clustered in the northeastern section of town, 10-15 minutes from the tourist office. (No shorts allowed when visiting the grotto and basilica.) The arcades to the right of the basilica house the information booth **Touristes et** *Pélerins Isolés* (open 7am-noon and 2-6pm), where you can obtain all necessary information for a pilgrimage visit.

Municipal Tourist Office: Place Champ Commun (tel. 62-94-15-64). From the train station turn right and then left down the hill. A comprehensive list of the 380 hotels in Lourdes. Good maps and a free brochure describing all the attractions in town. Open Easter-Oct. 15 Mon.-Sat. 9am-noon and 2-7pm, Sun. 10am-noon; in off-season Mon.-Sat. 9am-noon and 2-6pm.

Post Office: At rue de Langelle and chaussée Maransin. **Telephones** and **currency exchange.** **Postal code:** 65100. Open Mon.-Fri. 8am-7pm, Sat. 8am-noon.

Train Station: Av. de la Gare (tel. 65-94-35-36). Lourdes is one of the terminal points for train routes in the Pyrenees. To Pau (7 per day, ½ hr., 28F), Paris (5 per day, 7-9 hr., 356F), and Toulouse (9 per day, 2½ hr., 92F). Information desk open daily 8:30am-noon and 2-6pm. Excursions leave from the SNCF excursion booth outside.

Bus Station: Gare Routière, place Capdevielle (tel. 62-94-31-15), just below the tourist office. All departures from the train station. To Argelès and Pierrefitte (9-10 per day; 8.30F to Argéles, 12.80F to Pierrefitte). Open Mon.-Fri. 10am-noon and 2-6:45pm, Sat. 10am-noon.

Taxi: Tel. 62-94-31-30.

Hospital: 2, av. Alexandre Marqui (tel. 62-94-78-78).

Medical Emergency: SAMU, Tel. 18.

Police: 7, rue Baron Duprat (tel. 62-94-02-08).

Police Emergency: Tel. 17.

Accommodations and Camping

Lourdes is an easy daytrip from many towns, so you shouldn't have to stay overnight. If you do, however, you won't have trouble finding a place—there are so many hotels that residents have started putting up signs on their doors saying "This is *not* a hotel" to deter unwelcome intruders. The best place to look is around **rue Basse** in the center of town (from the train station turn right after you've crossed the bridge). Also try the **route de Pau.** Two lower-priced alternatives, both Christian organizations, are designed with the pilgrim rather than the tourist in mind. The first, **Centre des Rencontres "Pax Christi,"** 4, rue de la Forêt (tel. 62-94-00-66), is a 10-minute walk up the road behind the basilica and has hostellike accommodations for 36F per night, showers and breakfast included. Complete *pension* (bed and 3 meals) costs 100F. (Open July-Aug.) Reserve a month in advance through Les Amis de Pax Christi, 44, rue de la Santé, 75014 Paris (tel. 34-36-36-68). If you're under 25, stay at **Camp des Jeunes, Ferme Milhas,** rue Mgr-Rodhain (tel. 62-94-03-95), a 10-minute walk uphill out of town. Dorm accommodations cost 22F; camping in your own tent is 15F. You'll need a sleeping bag, but showers are included. You are strongly encouraged to participate in evening services and community activities. Ask for directions and reserve a place at the Service Jeunes booth in the big plaza by the sanctuaries. (Open April-Sept.) You can also try the **Foyer des Jeunes Travailleurs (IYHF)** in nearby **Tarbes** (accessible by train from Lourdes, 15F) at 88, rue Alsace-Lorraine (tel. 62-36-63-63). Take bus #2 from the Tarbes train station to place Verdun, and change to bus #1. (Hostel open July-Sept. daily 8am-noon and 3-10pm, July-Sept.)Mon.-Sat. 7:30am-7pm.)

Cauterets

Set 1000m up in a breathtaking valley on the edge of the **Parc National des Pyrénées Occidentales,** Cauterets makes the best base for exploring nearby towns and mountains. In winter, some of the best skiing in the region rises just a gondola, chairlift, or T-bar ride away. Long, white runs drop hundreds of meters down the slopes, while cross-country ski trails lead into the heart of the national park past mountain refuges and spectacular vistas. In summer, green pastures and an extensive network of hiking paths roll through the mountains.

There isn't much to see in Cauterets itself. A considerable number of visitors come for treatment in the *thermes* (hot springs). For entertainment, visit the **Palais des Attractions** on esplanade des Oeufs, where you'll find lots of youth, loud music, a game room, exhibits, a swimming pool, library, and a club upstairs that you can enter for free after 10:30pm.

Practical Information

Cauterets is most accessible by bus from Lourdes (1 hr., 18F).

Municipal Tourist Office: Place de la Mairie (tel. 62-92-50-27). List of all hotels in town (with prices) available. **Currency exchange** on July-Aug. weekends. Information center open July-Aug., Christmas, and French winter holidays Mon.-Sat. 9am-7pm, Sun. 9am-noon and 4-7pm; in off-season Mon.-Sat. 9am-12:30pm and 2-6pm, Sun. 9am-noon. **Maison de la Montagne,** next door, arranges guided hiking tours in the evenings (6-7pm).

Parc National des Pyrénées: Maison du Parc, place de la Gare (tel. 62-92-52-56). Hiking trips, nature films, a Pyrenean flora and fauna exhibit, and information on the park and its trails. Open April-Sept., Dec., and Feb. daily 9am-noon and 3:30-7:30pm.

Régie Municipale des Sports de Montagne, av. Docteur Domer (tel. 62-92-58-10). Mainly ski information.

Currency Exchange: Crédit Agricole, 16, rue de Belfort. Open Mon., Wed., and Fri. 9:30am-12:30pm and 2-4:30pm; Tues and Thurs. 9:30-12:30pm. Also at the post office.

Post Office: Rue de Belfort (tel. 62-92-54-00). **Telephones** and **currency exchange. Postal code:** 65110. Open Mon.-Fri. 9am-noon and 2-6pm, Sat. 8am-noon.

Bus Station: Place de la Gare (tel. 62-92-53-70), in a wooden chalet. Cauterets is served by Lourdes Les Pyrénées buses (tel. 62-94-22-90), which also run to Gèdre and Gavarnie. To Gavarnie via Pierrefitte (2 per day), and Lourdes (6 per day, 18F). From Lourdes, change buses at Pierrefitte to Gèdre, Gavarnie, and Luz St-Sauveur. Open Mon.-Fri. 9am-noon and 3-6:30pm and Sat. 9am-noon.

Bike Rental: Skilys, route de Pierrefitte at av. de la Gare. 10-speeds 35F per day. Mountain bikes plus guided tour 50-100F, depending on the duration of tour (3 hr.-1 day). Open daily 9am-12:30pm and 2-7pm.

Sports Equipment Rental: Tony Sport, 10, av. du Mamelon Vert (tel. 62-92-56-18). Downhill skis 50F per day, cross-country skis 40F per day, hiking shoes 20F per day. Open daily 8am-7pm. Several other equipment rental shops operate on rue Richelieu.

Weather Update: Tel. 62-32-97-77 for High Pyrenees, 59-27-50-50 for Atlantic Pyrenees. 24-hour recording. For a forecast specifically for those venturing into the mountains around Cauterets, call **Météo-Montagne** (tel. 62-32-90-01).

Mountain Rescue Service: Tel. 62-92-54-69.

Accommodations and Food

Make reservations in summer, avoiding the hotels that require *pension*. The **Center UCJG "Cluquet,"** av. Docteur Domer (tel. 62-92-52-95), is friendly and affordable. From the SNCF station, walk up the hill along the path that starts in front of the cable car station, then turn left past the tennis courts. (27F per night in 14-bed tents, including sheets, showers, and use of excellent kitchen. Pitch your own tent for 14F, or take a bed in a cabin for 35F. Open June 15-Sept. 13.) In town, the *gîte d'étape* **Le Pas de l'Ours**, 21, rue de la Raillère (tel. 62-92-58-07), warmly receives hikers, climbers, and skiers, and also functions as a youth hostel. Co-ed accommodations in big, communal rooms with bunkbeds are 33F including showers. From the bus station, take rue Richelieu to place Foch and continue in the same direction on rue de la Raillère. Good cooking facilities are available and they even have a sauna (45F, 70F per 2 people). **Hôtel du Béarn**, 4, av. Général Leclerc (tel. 62-92-53-54), offers unadorned singles and doubles for 60-110F. (Breakfast 15F. Open Dec.-Sept.) **Hotel Restaurant Christian**, 10, rue Richelieu (tel. 62-92-50-04), also has pleasant rooms. (Singles and doubles 80-100F, with shower 110-130. Open April-Sept.)

Pick up your trail food at the covered **market** in the center of town. (Open daily 8:30am-12:30pm and 2:30-7:30pm.) On Fridays during July and August, check out the open-air **market** held all day in front of the cable car station on place de la Gare. You can also shop at the supermarket **CODEC**, on av. Général Leclerc. (Open daily 8:30am-12:30pm and 4-7:30pm.) **La Flore**, 11, rue Richelieu (tel. 62-92-57-48), not only lives up to its name with window-box flowers but also concocts a 48F *menu* featuring *escalope à la crème* (veal in cream sauce). (Open daily noon-2pm and 7pm-2am.) At #10, **Restaurant Christian** (tel. 62-92-50-04) serves good 49F and 58F *menus*. (Open April-Sept. daily noon-2pm and 7-9pm.) Take in a four-course, family-style meal at **Hotel du Lac,** 7, rue du Raillère, or order a whole roast ring dove (130F) down the street at **Le Silver Tree**, #8 (tel. 62-92-56-50), and share it with a friend. Opportunities for quicker meals abound. For 30F, create your own salad (4 ingredients) at **Restaurant Exotique,** 7, av. de l'Esplanade. Or try the 39F lunch express *menu* at **Jules César Brasserie/Restaurant**, rue du Mamelon Vert. A meal can be as quick as a flash in the pan at **Royalty Crêpes,** esplanade des Oeufs (4 crêpes 11-17F, 15-20F for 6).

Near Cauterets

Before taking off for the mountains, read the general advice in the Gascony introduction. There are trails from Cauterets to suit both the amateur and the most experienced hiker. Be sure to pick up one of the purple 1:25,000 maps of the Parc National des Pyrénées (44F); for the Cauterets region use *Balaîtous*. The *Promenades en Montagne* series on the Vallée des Cauterets (available at the tourist office and the Parc National, 25F) is also invaluable, detailing numerous itineraries and listing area refuges. **La Civette**, a bookstore opposite the tourist office in Cauterets, sells a complete selection of maps. (Open daily 9am-noon and 3-7pm.) The **GR10** passes through Cauterets and continues to Luz St-Sauveur by two different paths. The easier one crosses the plateau of Lisey, while the other leads past **Lac de Gaube,** glaciated fields of the Vignemale 3200m up, Gavarnie, and the village of Gèdre.

A good way to start your mountain ramblings is with the easy hike to **Col d'Ilhéou** (1198m), just about 1½ hours away. You can refuel at the **Refuge d'Ilhéou** and then continue along the path to **Col de la Haugade** (2311m), another 1½ hours away, but already a more difficult hike. From there descend to **Plant du Cavan** (1625m), a plateau with plenty of wildlife and good camping. The route leading southwest from here to **Refuge Wallon** is very touristy.

Another good base for trips to the mountains is the **Hôtellerie Fruitière** (1371m), a 10-minute drive or a one-hour walk from Cauterets. Hike 1½ hours to **Lac d'Estan** (1804m), and then continue along the more difficult route to **Lac de Labas** (2281m), where the combination of lakes and mountains exemplifies the beauty of the Pyrenees. From here you should continue only if you are a serious hiker. If you hike past Lac Glacé, you will come to **Col Gentianes** (2729m), from where you go down—and pay close attention while you do it—to **Refuge Baysellance** (2651m). (42F per night. Open July-Sept.) This area is close to the **Pique du Vignemale,** the highest mountain in the French Pyrenees (3298m). The hike down to Cauterets from here is quite difficult. Stay overnight in one of the refuges unless you are in very good shape. Furthermore, outside of August and September, snow on the steep slopes can make this path treacherous. Proper equipment and a thorough knowledge of hiking are indispensable.

Gavarnie is a picture-perfect mountain village set in the **Massif du Marboré.** In the winter its ski slopes are less packed than those of nearby resorts, and during the rest of the year, its spectacular scenery draws adventurers from all over France. From **Col de Boucharou** in Gavarnie, hike the 11km to the **Brèche de Roland** (2800m); this half-day's route is less frequented than the rest of the area's paths, but you'll need some hiking experience. A **refuge** (tel. 62-92-48-24) awaits you in the forest of the Brèche de Roland. The grandiose, snow-covered **Cirque de Gavarnie** and its mist-wreathed *cascade* are also nearby. Hordes of tourists heave themselves onto horses for the trip to the Cirque (round-trip from the village about 60F, 2-3 hr.). To avoid being trampled, take the path marked *rive droite.*

During the last two weeks of July, the **Festival des Pyrénées** occurs at the foot of the Cirque de Gavarnie. The nightly performance begins as the sun sets over the mountains; afterwards, torches are distributed to light the way back to the village. Last year's festival featured Shakespeare's *Macbeth* and *A Midsummer's Night Dream,;* the latter, complete with pyrotechnics and galloping horses, took place in three different settings. Instead of a conventional stage rearranged in three different ways, this performance called for a mobile audience. Tickets cost 90F and are sold at tourist offices, bookstores, banks, and hotels throughout the region.

Some 8km from Gavarnie in the opposite direction is the pretty town of **Gèdre,** also within walking distance of spectacular scenery. The **tourist office** here (tel. 62-92-48-26) will be happy to help you plan your itinerary . Contact also Gèdre's **Parc National des Pyrénées** (tel. 62-92-48-83). Ten kilometers back along the road to Lourdes lies **Luz St-Sauveur,** another base for mountain excursions. The **Maison du Parc National et de la Vallée** (tel. 62-92-87-05 or 62-92-83-61) here can give you mountains of valuable information. (Open Mon.-Fri. 10am-noon and 2-7pm, Sat.-Sun. 2-7pm.) In **Camping les Cascades,** at the edge of town, a *gîte d'étape* (tel. 62-92-82-15) welcomes the weary. Alternatively, you can pitch a tent at the campground (tel. 62-92-85-85).

The region is accessible by SNCF **Lourdes les Pyrénées buses** (tel. 62-94-22-90) from Lourdes. Two buses per day go to Luz-St-Sauveur (45 min., 28F); there, you can change to a bus bound for Gèdre and Gavarnie (35 min., 20F).

Auch

Auch rhymes with *gauche* but isn't at all. A graceful town with a golden, castle-like cathedral, a crumbling tower, and an illuminated fountain, Auch is an ideal setting for fairy tales and tourist brochures. You can see Auch's sights, the Tour d'Armagnac and the Cathédrale Ste-Marie, in one day, but the narrow streets and meditative pace of this hilltop town are best appreciated during a prolonged stay.

Moreover, Auch makes a good base for excursions into the duchy's emerald pastures.

Cycling is superb along the tree-lined roads, although some mean hills will test your mettle. You'll pass sunflower and rose fields, vineyards, windmills, châteaux, pigeon houses, and quiet green hills. You can see all this equally well on foot; the hiking paths GR 65, 652, and 653 pass through Auch.

Orientation and Practical Information

Auch makes a pleasant daytrip from Toulouse (1½ hr. by train). The Gers River divides the city into the *basse* and *haute villes*. From the train station in the *basse ville*, turn left down av. de la Gare, then right down rue Voltaire to get to the *syndicat* and the *vieille ville*. For a particularly impressive approach, turn right after crossing the river and climb the steep steps to the cathedral. A bus leaves from the train station for the cathedral (every ½ hr., 3.70F).

Syndicat d'Initiative: 1, rue Dessoles (tel. 62-05-22-89), on place de la République in front of the cathedral. Friendly and efficient. Free tours of the museum and cathedral, and a brochure that lists all the events. Open July-Aug. Tues.-Sat. 9am-noon and 2-6:30pm, Sun.-Mon. 2-6:30pm; Sept.-June Tues.-Sat. only.

Youth Information: AJIR, 9, rue Espagne (tel. 62-05-07-63). Well-organized and enthusiastic. Information on sight-seeing, transportation, sports, and cultural activities. Open in summer Mon.-Fri. 1-6pm; in off-season Mon.-Sat.

Currency Exchange: On Sun. and Mon., when the banks are closed, you can change currency in the Hôtel de France, place de la Libération.

Post Office: Rue Gambetta. **Telephones. Postal code:** 32000. Open Mon.-Fri. 8am-7pm, Sat. 8am-noon.

Train Station: Av. de la Gare (tel. 62-05-00-46), in the *ville basse*. Information, reservations, and ticket service open Mon.-Sat. 5:15am-9:45pm, Sun. 6:15am-9:45pm. To Toulouse (6 per day, 1½ hr., 53F), Montauban (1 SNCF bus per day, 1½ hr., 53F), and Agen (7-8 SNCF buses per day, 46F).

Bus Station: Allées Baylac, place du Forail (tel. 62-05-76-37). To Condom (3-4 per day, 1 hr., 22.50F), Bordeaux (1 per day, 4 hr., 91F), and Toulouse (2 per day, 1¼ hr., 43F).

Bike Rental: In summer from the Maison de Gascogne. 25F per day, 150F per week, deposit 300F. Also at the train station. 37F per ½ day, 47F per day.

Taxi: Tel. 62-05-00-48 or 62-05-66-25.

Medical Emergency: Av. des Pyrénées (tel. 62-05-11-10).

Police: Tel. 62-05-24-01.

Police Emergency: Tel. 17.

Accommodations and Camping

Although there are only about 10 hotels in Auch, many are inexpensive enough to justify your stay. In addition, the youth hostel usually has plenty of space, and a *gîte d'étape* 4km from town sits in the shadow of a château.

Auberge de Jeunesse, Foyer des Jeunes Travailleurs, in the building complex Cité Grand Garros (tel. 62-05-34-80). From the station, walk left on av. Pierre Mendés, cross the train tracks at rue du 11 Novembre, and turn right immediately on rue Jean de la Fontaine, which becomes rue du Bourget and leads to the *foyer* (20 min.). Or, catch bus #1 or 2 from the station and get out at Grand Garros (last bus 6:45pm). Almost always has space, but call before making the trek. Luxurious for a youth hostel. Singles 34F. Sheets 11F. Breakfast 11F, lunch or dinner 34F. No curfew.

Gîte d'Etape, Château St-Cricq, on the route de Toulouse (tel. 62-63-10-17), 4km from Auch. Sleep in the castle annex. 30 beds available to hikers, horseback riders, and cyclists. 33F. Call before 5pm.

Hôtel de la Gare, 2, av. Pierre Mendés France (tel. 62-05-23-81), a short walk from the station. Slightly shabby rooms, but pleasant owner. Singles 80F. Doubles 110F. Showers included. Restaurant downstairs serves a family-style, filling 43F *menu, boisson comprise.*

Hôtel de Paris, 38, av. de Marne (tel. 62-63-26-22). Turn left at the train station and left on av. de la Marne (5 min.). Carved wood furniture and quiet halls. Singles from 90F, with showers 120F. Doubles from 110F, with shower 150F. Breakfast 17F.

Hôtel des Trois Mousquetaires, 5, rue Espagne (tel. 62-05-13-25), off place de la République near the cathedral. Flowered rooms with solid furniture. Doubles from 80F. Showers included. Good for families; rooms for 3 people (120F with shower) and 5 people (100F without shower). Breakfast 15F.

Fermes d'Accueil: You can pitch your tent at a local farm and help with the chores for about 13F per night or 70F per week. Also look for **chambres d'hôte,** singles or doubles with a farming family at rates comparable to a hotel's. As the nearest such place is 7km from town, only the mobile should bother to call 62-63-16-55 for more information.

Food

Looking for budget food in Auch is fruitless, so you might as well resign yourself to paying a little more than usual and eating heartily. Look for the regional specialties: *crêpes aux champignons* (with mushrooms), *poule-au-pot* (stewed chicken), *tourins à l'ail* or *à l'oignon* (garlic or onion soup), *garbures* (tripe), *palombes* (ringdoves), *confits* (conserves—of goose, etc.), *maigrets* (lean duck), and *pastis gascon* (layered apple or plum cake). Alternatively, you can sample some of the cheaper *pâtés* at the *charcuteries* and some of the local melons and prunes at fruit vendors. Or you can visit the open **market.** The *basse ville* holds one on av. Hoche (Thurs. until 3pm); the *haute ville* holds another adjacent to place de la Libération in front of the cathedral (Sat. until 6pm). In Grand Garros, a **Codec** supermarket makes shopping easy for hostel dwellers.

Resto Quick Seguin, 6, rue Dessoules (tel. 65-05-26-93), across from the tourist office. Wood-beamed *salon de thé* that doubles as a cafeteria. Small pizzas 7F. Hamburgers 9F and 15.50F. Chicken 15.50F. 10% surcharge to eat in restaurant. Open Tues.-Sat. noon-6:30pm.

Les Trois Mousquetaires, 5, rue Espagne (tel. 62-05-13-25), off place de la République. 45F *plat du jour* comes with salad, vegetables, and bread. Open Tues.-Sat. noon-2pm and 7-9:30pm.

Le Rimbaud, 7, rue des Grazes (tel. 62-05-63-54). Go down rue Gambetta and turn right on rue du Sénéchal; turn right on rue du Pony and rue au Mirabeau, then left on rue Champrouet. Exotic dishes and original twists on French standards. Can be expensive, but salads (apple-hazelnut salad 25F) and quiche slices (spinach *tarte* 30F) are filling. The 52F *menu indien* includes salad, chicken curry, and rice. Sit on terraces outside or in rustic booths inside. Open daily noon-2pm and 7-9:30pm.

Les Grenadines, 165, rue Victor Hugo (tel. 62-05-48-96). The 20-min. walk ascends to a nice view of the surrounding hills. Fish specialties and a 49F lunch *menu* featuring grilled beef and *salade humeur du chef.* Young crowd. Open Tues.-Sat.

Sights

Cathédrale Ste-Marie, an elegant example of Gothic construction in the late fifteenth and early sixteenth centuries, bears a west facade and square towers in classical style. These were added a century later, but with such care and elegance that they harmonize perfectly with the rest of the structure. Try to catch the west facade at dawn or sunset, when the cathedral shimmers like a golden mosaic. The masterworks of the cathedral are the ornately carved choir stalls, made of oak soaked in the Gers, then dried for 30 years and carved by monks who doubled as local craftsmen. Supposedly, the soaking process hardened the wood and made it resistant to termites, worms, and woodpeckers. The stalls are, in fact, in remarkable condition. The carvings total over 1500—the large upper figures (labeled) depict biblical characters, the lower ones mythological beings, and the scenes on the short stairways the life of Christ. (Choir open daily in summer 9am-noon and 2-6pm; in off-season 9am-noon and 2-5pm. Admission 5F.) The creator of the 14 stained-glass windows of the apsidal chapels is well known: Arnaut de Moles, a local sixteenth-century painter. Admission to the cathedral's treasure is free, but you have to ask to see it. If you're taking one of the five free daily tours, try to convince your guide to take you up the winding stairs for an aerial view of the cathedral. While you're at it, request a walk on the roof. (Cathedral open daily in summer 7:30am-noon and 2-8pm; in off-season 8am-noon and 2-6pm.)

Near the cathedral, the **Tour d'Armagnac,** now a weathered monolith, once served as a prison. Leading down to the river from the tower is the **escalier monumental,** a formidable staircase that poses a challenge to your legs but offers expansive views of the *basse ville* and countryside below. In the middle stands a statue of the most famous of Louis XIV's musketeers, d'Artagnan, who was born near Auch in 1615 and later immortalized by Alexandre Dumas and Hollywood alike. From place Salinis, you can also follow the road leading under medieval **Porte d'Arton** to the *pousterles,* steep and narrow ancient stairways.

The **Maison de Gascogne,** rue Gambetta, is a mall where regional crafts and specialties (largely culinary and alcoholic) are exhibited and sold during July and August. (Open daily 10am-12:30pm and 2:30-7:15pm.) You can sample (mostly free) baked goods such as the flaky *croustade* (3F), practically dripping with sugar, and the fiery *armagnac,* the Gascon answer to cognac, somewhat sweeter and a trifle more herbal. By making the entire tour of the lower level, you should be able to get about eight free tastes of *armagnac* and *floc d'Armagnac,* the local version of *pineau.* Upstairs, from July to September, there are exhibitions of regional art, and each one of the 20 local towns occupies a small booth in which it seeks to seduce tourists into buying. The **Musée des Jacobins,** place Louis Blanc, has temporary exhibits of contemporary art, a collection of regional arts and crafts, and a selection of rare furniture from Auch, all set in a former convent. (Open July-Sept. Tues.-Sun. 10am-noon and 2-6pm; Oct.-June Tues.-Sat. 10am-noon and 2-4pm. Admission 5F, students 2.50F.)

The tourist office provides extensive information on Auch's environs. If you're tempted to visit wine cellars ask for a list of local *caves.* **Condom,** a town to the north, contains the **Musée de l'Armagnac,** which demonstrates the production of the regional liqueur. In late October a large antique show takes place in the **Halle des Expositions** next to the municipal campground (admission 15F). The first week in June brings a group of international musicians to the **Festival de Musique.** (Tickets 45-100F, students 20% less.

Languedoc-Roussillon

Languedoc has never been comfortable with Parisian rule, and it's easy to see why. In this a rugged southern land, the people are as much Spanish as they are French in origin, language, and architecture. Once a formidable autonomous state, Languedoc stretched from the Rhône all the way to the foothills of the Pyrenees, including the Catalan coastal region of Roussillon in the south, and in the west, the area around Toulouse now called the Midi-Pyrénées. The regime's independence ended, however, when the Albigensian War brought the yoke of Parisian rule to Languedoc. Pope Innocent III wished to wipe out the numerous Manichean heretics living in the area, the Cathars and Albigensians. An opportunistic baron from the Ile-de-France, Simon de Montfort, and his northern armies embarked on a campaign of conquest against all of Languedoc. Regional sentiment solidified around the persecuted Cathars. The citizens of Languedoc fought valiantly, but the area eventually succumbed to the superior forces of the Church and the north. In the centuries that followed, policies decided in the northern capital often disrupted local traditions, leading to poverty, resistance, and homegrown leftist ideology. Languedoc has proudly maintained its socialist tradition, and the newspapers on the stand today, such as *L'Humanité* and *La Dépêche du Midi*, are direct descendants of the nineteenth-century journals founded by Jean Jaurès and other leftist politicians.

From the ninth to the thirteenth centuries, a magnificent popular and literary culture grew up in the southern *langue d'oc*. Tales of adventure and poems of courtly love were written by troubadours employed by the southern courts. However, when the French kings dominated the province, the language faded, and in 1539 the Edict of Villiers-Cotterets imposed the northern *langue d'oïl*. Today, the *langue d'oc* is struggling to survive. High school students may now take one of their university qualifying exams in it and traditional societies keep the language vital.

Long the political, educational, and cultural center of Languedoc, Toulouse is convenient to several attractive towns: Cordes, a fortified medieval city restored by modern artists; Albi, with its giant basilica, charming medieval town, and a superlative museum of the works of Toulouse-Lautrec; and Castres, birthplace of Jean Jaurès and home of the Musée Goya. Farther south are Carcassonne, the double-walled thirteenth-century fortress city restored by Viollet-le-Duc, and Perpignan, capital of the once-Spanish province of Roussillon and gateway to some of the finest beaches in France. Moving east, you'll reach Montpellier, a university center like Toulouse with the largest old quarter in Europe, and finally, Nîmes, an erstwhile Roman city near the enchanting Rhône Valley, spectacular gorges, and the monumental Pont du Gard.

Be adventurous in sampling southwestern cuisine, and it will reward your palate without breaking your budget. The most popular local dish is *cassoulet*, a hearty ragout of white beans, sausage, pork, mutton, and goose. *Roquefort* and *St-Nectaire* are tangy, fermented cheeses, and all sorts of luscious fruits come from the Garonne Valley. Don't forget to wash your meals down with a glass of one of the region's full-bodied red wines such as Minervois or Corbières. For dessert or as an aperitif, sip the sweet white wines of Lunel, Mireval, and St-Jean-de-Minervois.

The major towns in Languedoc are linked by frequent trains. The Canal du Midi also links the towns of the region; its locks are visible in the centers of Toulouse and Perpignan. The hilly countryside makes cycling a bit difficult, and the sparse traffic reduces hitching possibilities, but it is still relatively easy to explore both city and country by means of your own locomotion. The people of the southwest are generally more generous and helpful than their counterparts elsewhere in France, and Languedoc remains less expensive than more popular vacation areas in the south of France.

Toulouse

Largely constructed out of brick, *la ville rose* glows pink in the morning, red at noon, and mauve at dusk. Perhaps the colors reflect the town's progressive politics, actively supported by its large student population. Toulouse is the capital of France's Leftist Belt, known as *le midi rouge,* and has traditionally voted for left-wing candidates—François Mitterand, for example.

The city's *gauche* penchant reflects a tradition of cultural and economic independence from Paris. After becoming a major commercial center for the Roman Empire in the fifth century, Toulouse entered an era of cultural splendor in the ninth century. France's fourth largest city, modern Toulouse crackles with a heterogeneous energy. Always packed with young people, the city has recently absorbed huge waves of immigrants: Spaniards in the 1930s, Central European Jews in the 1940s, North Africans since the 1950s, and Portuguese in the 1970s. Of all these influences, the Spanish prevails, asserting itself in the dress and accents of Toulouse's people and in the architecture of many of the city's buildings and squares. This foreign influx has triggered the growth of a reactionary Nationalist Front fringe party; graffiti reading *la France aux Français* is directed at immigrants, not imperious tourists. Outside the central core of the city, you may be unnerved by Toulouse's patches of squalor and its seeming neglect of historic areas. Those who come here simply to change trains are missing some of the most distinctive architecture in France. As polished as Paris in some neighborhoods, its picturesque suqares and lively cafes still impart the intimacy and warmth of a small town.

Orientation and Practical Information

Toulouse sprawls on both sides of the Garonne Valley, but the museums, churches of interest, and important sights are located within a compact section east of the river in the center of town, near place Wilson and place du Capitôle. From the train station, walk down broad allée Jean Jaurès to place Wilson and turn right on rue Lafayette to reach the *syndicat.*

Syndicat d'Initiative: Donjon du Capitôle, rue Lafayette (tel. 61-23-32-00), in the little park behind the Capitôle. Brisk, efficient office. Makes accommodations reservations in other cities, including Aix, Paris, and Marseille (May-Sept., free). Walking tours of the old city (27F) and bus excursions to places of interest nearby (110F). Sells train tickets. **Currency exchange** May-Sept. Sat.-Sun. and holidays (500F limit). Open Mon.-Sat. 9am-7pm, Sun. 9am-1pm and 2-5:30pm; Oct.-May Mon.-Sat. 9am-6pm. Also an information service at the station. Open July-Sept. Mon.-Fri. 8-11:45am and 1:30-5:15pm.

Student Travel: Wasteels, 1, bd. Bonrepos (tel. 61-62-67-14), across the canal and to the left from the train station. BIJ tickets and Cartes Jeunes. Open Mon.-Sat. 9am-noon and 2-7pm.

Centre d'Information Jeunesse, 17, rue de Metz (tel. 61-21-20-20). Information on sports, leisure, travel, and education. Open Mon.-Fri. 10am-6:30pm, Sat. 10am-noon.

Currency Exchange: Banque Populaire, at the station. Open Tues.-Sat. 9am-12:45pm and 2:15-5:40pm. Also at the *syndicat,* the post office, any number of banks around place du Capitôle, and the airport **Toulouse-Blagnac.**

Post Office: 9, rue Lafayette (tel. 61-22-33-11), opposite the *syndicat.* Poste Restante, **currency exchange,** and **telephones. Postal code:** 31000. Open Mon.-Fri. 8am-7pm, Sat. 8am-noon.

Train Station: Bd. Pierre Sémard (tel. 61-62-50-50; for reservations 61-62-85-44). To Paris (9 per day, 8 hr., 304F), Bordeaux (10 per day, 2¾ hr., 127F), Lyon (6 per day, 6 hr., 252F), Marseille (11 per day, 4½ hr., 197F), Albi (14 per day, 1 hr., 46F), Castres (8 per day, 1½ hr., 51F), and Montauban (every hr., ½ hr., 35F).

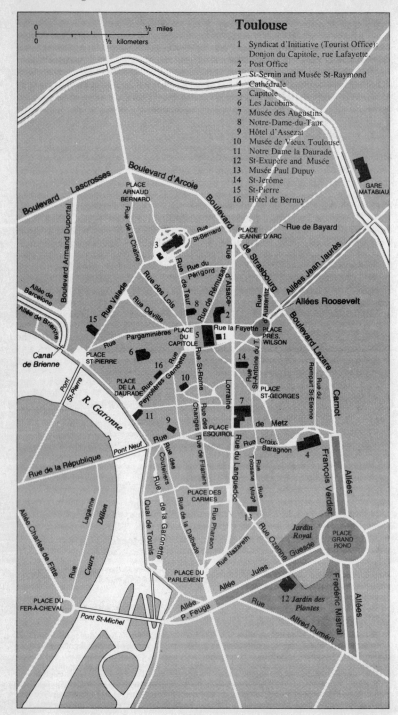

Toulouse

1 Syndicat d'Initiative (Tourist Office);
  Donjon du Capitole, rue Lafayette
2 Post Office
3 St-Sernin and Musée St-Raymond
4 Cathédrale
5 Capitole
6 Les Jacobins
7 Musée des Augustins
8 Notre-Dame-du-Taur
9 Hôtel d'Assezat
10 Musée de Vieux Toulouse
11 Notre Dame la Daurade
12 St-Exupère and Musée
13 Musée Paul Dupuy
14 St-Jérôme
15 St-Pierre
16 Hôtel de Bernuy

Bus Station: 68, bd. Pierre Sémard (tel. 61-48-71-84), next to the train station. Frequent connections to Albi (10 per day, 1½ hr., 40F) and Castres (8 per day, 1½ hr., 40F). Less frequent to Auch (2 per day, 2½ hr., 43F), Carcassonne (2 per day, 2½ hr., 50F), Moissac (3 per day, 32.50F), and other regional towns. **City Buses,** place du Capitôle (tel. 61-23-1-02). Tickets cost 4.70F (1 zone) and 7F (2 zones), while a *carnet* of 10 costs 34F (1 zone) and 50F (2 zones). Route maps are available at the bus station's ticket booths and the tourist office.

Hitching: For Carcassonne, take bus #2 to RN113. For Paris, take bus #10 to start. For Auch and Bayonne, take bus #64 to RN124. For Albi, take bus #16 or 19. **Allostop,** 17, rue de Metz (tel. 61-22-68-13), matches passengers with drivers for 40F per ride, 1-yr. subscription 120F. Open Mon.-Fri. 3-6:30pm, Sat. 10am-noon.

English Bookstore: The Bookshop, 17, rue Lakanal (tel. 61-22-99-92), down from Les Jacobins. An attractive, friendly store with an impressive selection of novels and non-fiction. Trade in your used paperbacks. Comic books and dictionaries also. Open Tues.-Sat. 10am-noon and 2:30-7pm.

Laundromat: Laverie Self-Service, 20, rue Cujas. Wash 10F, dry 2F per 7 min. Open daily 7am-9pm. Another at 14, rue Emile Cartailhac, just near St-Sernin. The same prices. Open 6:30am-10pm.

Public Showers: At the train station. Bath 14.50F, shower 9F. Open 4:30am-9pm.

All-Night Pharmacy: Commissariat de Police, 17, rue de Rémusat (tel. 61-21-81-20).

Medical Emergency: Tel. 61-49-33-33.

Police: Rempart St-Etienne (tel. 61-29-70-00).

Accommodations and Camping

There are plenty of inexpensive hotels near the train station, especially on rue Caffarelli, off allée Jean Jaurès. However, this neighborhood is unpleasant, and the *concierges* tend to be suspicious and inhospitable. (Be sure to ask about curfews.) Following allée Jean Jaurès from the station past place Wilson, you'll find numerous small hotels scattered around the stylish shops of the old city center.

Auberge de Jeunesse (IYHF), Villa des Rosiers, 125, rue Jean Rieux (tel. 61-80-49-93). Call ahead before making the trek. Take allée Jean Jaurès from the train station, turn right on bd. de Strasbourg, go to the 1st bus stop on the far side, and take bus #22 (*direction* "Gonin-La Terrasse") for 10 min. The hostel will be on your left. Otherwise, a ½-hr. walk. Small, somewhat run-down, and remote, but very friendly. Sometimes allows camping in the garden. Members only, 34F per night. Sheets 11F. Breakfast 11F. Kitchen available. Curfew 10am, but flexible.

Hôtel des Arts, 1bis, rue Cantegril (tel. 61-23-36-21), at rue des Arts off place St-Georges. Run by a delightful young couple who speak English. Each room is a discovery, and the owners are constantly redecorating. Lively, student neighborhood. If they don't have space for you, they'll find you a room in one of the nearby hotels. Singles 60-80F, with shower 100F. Doubles 90F, with shower 110F. Quads with shower 160F. Showers 10F. Big continental breakfast 20F.

Nouvel Hôtel, 13, rue du Taur (tel. 61-21-13-93), off place du Capitôle. Ideal location and adequate rooms. Doubles 90F, with shower 110F.

Hôtel du Pays d'Oc, 53, rue Riguet (tel. 61-62-33-76), off allée Jean Jaurès to the left, 10 min. from the station. Bright, neat rooms. Singles 70F. Doubles 75F, with shower 90F. Showers 5F. Breakfast 15F.

Hôtel de l'Université, 26, rue Emile Cartailhac (tel. 61-21-35-69), near place St-Sernin. Decent rooms 76-82F, with shower 90-105F. Showers 8F. Breakfast 16F.

Hôtel St-Antoine, 21, rue St-Antoine (tel. 61-21-40-66), off place Wilson. Adequate rooms in an upscale neighborhood. Indoor courtyard functions as lounge area. Singles or doubles 75-87F, with shower 110-130F. Breakfast 20F.

Camping: There are excellent campgrounds outside the city. The municipal site is **Pont de Rupé,** av. des Etats-Unis (RN20 north), chemin du Pont de Rupé (tel. 61-70-07-35). Take bus P. 20.50F per person, includes site. **Les Violettes,** on RN113 (tel. 61-81-72-07), after Castanet (Deyme). A 4-star extravaganza. 32F per person, including everything. **La Bouriette,**

201, chemin de Tournefeuille (tel. 61-49-64-46), at St-Martin-du-Touch along RN124. A 2-star site.

Food

Largely because of student and immigrant populations, inexpensive restaurants of all varieties crowd the city. The outdoor markets can supply your picnics in the luxuriant Jardin Royal or Jardin des Plantes. Many budget restaurants are located on narrow pedestrian streets off rue St-Rome. **Les Halles**, on the ground floor of the Parking Victor Hugo, is open daily with an overwhelming number of food stands.

Auberge Louis XIII, 1bis, rue Tripière. Tucked away in a quiet street off rue St-Rome. Enter through a lovely tangled garden. Interesting, mostly student crowd. 37F and 46F *menus* feature appetizing choices. Open Sept.-July noon-2pm and 7-9:45pm.

Place du May, 4, rue du May (tel. 61-23-98-76), off rue St-Rome next to the Auberge Louis XIII. A stylish terrace, soft background music, and a creative 48F lunch *menu* (without dessert or appetizer 38F). 75F dinner *menu*. Open Mon.-Sat. noon-2pm and 7-11pm, and Sun. dinner.

Au Coq Hardi, 6, rue Jules-Chalandre (tel. 61-21-61-01), off rue St-Rome. Popular with students. Traditional family-style meals. 3-course, 49F *menu*. Open Mon.-Fri. noon-2pm and 7-10pm, Sat. noon-2pm.

Le Ciel de Toulouse, Nouvelles Galeries, 6, rue Lapeyrouse (tel. 61-23-11-52). Not typically French, but fun. On the 6th floor of a department store, this place serves hundreds of people in 5 bar-like units. Pizza 12F, big *plats du jour* 24-35F. Open Mon.-Sat. 11:30am-3pm; serves as a *salon de thé* 3-6pm.

Cafétéria Casino, place Wilson. Looks like the other expensive cafes on the *place,* but the prices here are some of the lowest in town. Entrees 20-36F. Rib-steak with fries 32.50F. Functions as a *salon de thé* in the afternoon. Open daily 11am-11pm.

Les Caves de la Maréchale, 3, rue Jules-Chalandre (tel. 61-23-89-88), off rue St-Rome on a narrow pedestrian street. An ideal spot for lunchtime indulgence. Pamper yourself with some of Toulouse's most refined food—the 60F lunch *menu* resembles their dinner menu at nearly half the price, including hors-d'oeuvre buffet, *plat du jour,* dessert, wine, and coffee. Warm lighting and sophisticated setting in an old wine cellar. Open Mon. night-Sat.

Sights

Toulouse encompasses several of the country's most architecturally distinctive and historically important religious monuments. Start your ecclesiastical tour by heading up rue du Taur from place du Capitôle. You will reach the majestic **Basilique St-Sernin,** the largest Romanesque cathedral in France and one of the most magnificent. Its octagonal tower, symbol of Toulousain power, overflows with graceful double arches; the oldest part of the church, the brick west facade, is deceptively dull. Inside you'll find a cradle-vaulted nave of exquisitely simple lines, surrounded by unusual double aisles. You can enter the ambulatory, which leads to the seventeenth-century choir, Byzantine marble reliefs, and the shrines and relics of the crypt. Useful guided tours of the basilica are given (in summer daily at 2:15pm and 3:15pm, 26F), but you can just wander around on your own. (Open daily 8am-6pm. Crypt open 10am-6pm. Admission to the crypt 8F.)

Just down rue du Taur is **Eglise Notre-Dame-du-Taur,** originally known as St-Sernin-du-Taur after St-Saturnain, the first Toulousain priest, who was martyred in 250 C.E. Legend has it that he was tied to the tail of a wild bull that dragged him to death in the city's streets; the building marks the site where they say his corpse finally fell. His name was corrupted over the years to St-Sernin, and his remains were long ago moved to the crypt of the cathedral.

If Basilique St-Sernin is one of the finest examples of a southern Romanesque church, **Les Jacobins,** rue Lakanal, holds the honor for southern Gothic, or *gothique du Midi.* (The name of the church derives from a monastic order founded some eight centuries earlier, whence the designation for French revolutionary sympathizers, who first met in a Jacobin monastery.) A row of thin columns divides the single nave into two unequal aisles; amber colonettes run up the columns and from the light vaults, creating a beautiful multicolor effect against the light stone. The *salle capitulaire* repeats the decor of the main church with its many colors and thin columns; piano concerts are held here weekly on summer evenings (tickets from 60F available at the *syndicat*). (Church open June-Sept. Mon.-Sat. 10am-6:30pm, Sun. 2-6pm; Oct.-May 10am-noon and 2:30-6:30pm. Admission to cloister 6F, Sat.-Sun. free; chapel 10F.)

Four different efforts to transform a simple eleventh-century Romanesque church into a grander cathedral based on northern models resulted in **Cathédrale St-Etienne.** In the thirteenth century, the rose window (copied from Notre-Dame in Paris) was added. Even later additions include a flamboyant Gothic choir. Occasional concerts on the seventeenth-century organ are given—information is available at the *syndicat.* (Open June-Sept. 7:30am-7:30pm; Oct.-May 2-7pm.)

The **Musée des Augustins** (tel. 61-23-55-07; entry on 21, rue de Metz, off rue Alsace-Lorraine) not only houses an unsurpassed depot of Romanesque and Gothic sculpture, but also a sumptuous and clearly presented collection of Romanesque capitals. Note especially the 15 gargoyles from Les Cordeliers, another abbey that burned to the ground in the nineteenth century and was largely pillaged. (Museum open Mon. and Thurs.-Sat. 10am-noon and 2-6pm, Wed. 10am-noon and 2-10pm, Sun. 2-6pm. Admission 6F, Sun. free. Concerts Oct.-June Wed. 8:30-9pm.) Cozy **Musée de Vieux Toulouse,** rue de May, houses disorganized exhibits on Toulouse's history and popular culture. (Open June-Sept. Mon.-Tues. and Thurs.-Sat. 3-6pm, Wed. 2:30-5:30pm. Admission 6F.)

Slicker and more organized, the small **Musée Paul Dupuy,** 13, rue de la Pleau, shows an extensive collection of popular arts, including *faïences,* arms, instruments, and costumes. (Open Wed.-Mon. 10am-noon and 2-6pm, Sun. 2-6pm. Admission 6F, Sun. free.) The **Musée St-Raymond,** place St-Sernin, next to the church, houses the town's archeological finds and organizes interesting exhibits on specific topics, such as Roman gladiators. (Open daily 10-11:30am and 2-6pm, Sun. 2-6pm. Admission 6F, with exposition 10F; Sun. free.)

Also take a look at Toulouse's secular buildings. Toulouse was a prosperous city before the pastel-blue dye produced here lost its popularity to indigo imported from the Indies. Every dye merchant built his own mansion and over 50 of these have survived. Many date from before the seventeenth century; some are restored and still inhabited. Perhaps the finest is the **Hôtel d'Assezat,** place d'Assezat, on rue de Metz. Other *hôtels* are scattered throughout the city. You can do well just by walking the narrow streets of Vieux Toulouse and ducking into the courtyards of the various buildings—invariably elegant brick constructions with pleasant gardens.

The **Jardin des Plantes** and the more formal **Jardin Royal,** across the street, offer shady havens with plenty of benches and even a few drinking fountains. For bicyclists seeking a bit of greenery, the **Grand Rond** unrolls into allée Paul Sabatier, which takes you to the Canal du Midi.

At some point in your visit to Toulouse, take the time to linger on the pleasant brick seas of **place du Capitôle,** where Spain, France, and Italy seem to meet. Every morning but Monday and all day Wednesday a vast **market** unfolds here. Vendors of eclectic wares also set up shop around Basilique St-Sernin on Sunday mornings.

Entertainment

Whatever beat you dance to probably throbs in one of Toulouse's late-night *caves* or bars. The least expensive and most off-the-wall places lie along rue des Blanchers, but the city center is also full of rhythmic hideaways. Place St-Georges is the center of student life. Gay bars are concentrated on rue de Colombetta.

Le Broadway, 11, rue des Puits-Clos (tel. 61-21-10-11). Popular with both gay and straight people. Regarded as the city's leading nightclub. Open daily 11:30pm-6 or 7am.

L'Ubu, 16, rue St-Rome. The place for the jet-set crowd for over 20 years. The doorman will let you in if you have "the look." Plan on coming late, then arrive even later. With 70F drinks and the inevitable stuffiness, it might not even be worth it.

Le Florida Café, place du Capitôle. Beautifully-decorated old interior. Same crowd as at l'Ubu.

Pick up a copy of *50 festivals de musique en Midi-Pyrénées* from the tourist office. From July to September, Toulouse hosts its **Musique d'été,** with classical concerts, jazz, and ballet in a variety of outdoor settings, concert halls, and churches. (Tickets 40F and 60F sold at the *syndicat* and on location before the performance.)

Montauban

The sleepy town of Montauban was born out of the townpeople's twelfth-century struggle against the oppressive abbey at Montauriol ("golden mountain"). In 1144 Alphonse Jourdain, Count of Toulouse, helped the enraged population sack the abbey, found Montauban (originally Montalban, "white mountain"), and build it with bricks stolen from the abbey. Hence, the *Montalbanais'* proud assertion of their right to commerce and independence, a spirit that was translated architecturally into the irregular brick arcades of the old market center, place Nationale.

Orientation and Practical Information

Montauban is 50km north of Toulouse, a half-hour away by train. Place Nationale is the center of the city, bordered by pedestrian shopping streets. From the train station, walk down av. Mayenne and across pont Vieux; continue on côte de Bonnetiers, and turn right on rue Gillaque. From place Nationale to the *syndicat,* walk down rue de la Résistance and turn right on rue Bessières; the *syndicat* is in the second courtyard on the left.

Syndicat d'Initiative: 2, rue du Collège (tel. 63-63-60-60). Will help you find a room. Information on the city and environs, including a list of *hôtels particuliers,* some of which are open to the public. A city guide gives detailed walking tours. If you understand French, take their lively, free guided tours of the city (July-Aug. Mon.-Sat. at 10am). Open July-Aug. daily 9am-noon and 2-7pm; Sept.-June Mon.-Sat. only.

Post Office: Bd. Midi-Pyrénées. **Currency exchange** and **telephones. Postal code:** 82000. Open Mon.-Fri. 8am-7pm, Sat. 8am-noon.

Train Station: Rue Robert Salengro (tel. 63-63-50-50). On the Paris-Toulouse line. To Paris (9 per day, 5½-6 hr., 288F), Cahors (6 per day, ½ hr., 41F), and Toulouse (every hr., ½ hr., 37F). On the Nantes-Bordeaux-Toulouse line. To Bordeaux (9 per day, 2 hr., 107F), Moissac (6 per day, ½ hr., 22.50F), and destinations on the Côte d'Azur usually via Toulouse.

Bus Station: Gare Routière, place Lalaque, down av. Mayenne from the train station. To Albi (1 per day, 3 hr., 40F), Auch (2 per day, 2½ hr., 41F), Moissac (2 per day, 1 hr., 43F), Toulouse (7 per day, 1 hr., 23F), Villefranche (2 per day, 1¼ hr., 32F), and Bruniquel (3 per day, 45 min., 12F). Fewer buses on Sun. **City buses,** at rue du Collège, next to the tourist office (tel. 63-63-52-52). Bus maps and tickets 3.90F each, *carnet* of 10 32F.

Car Rental: Harle, 17-18, place Lalaque (tel. 63-63-15-80). 157F per day plus 1.55F per km, 2248F per week with unlimited milage.

Bike Rental: Gury, 26, av. Gambetta (tel. 63-63-19-10). 20F per day, deposit 800-1000F . Open Tues.-Sat. 8am-noon and 2-7pm.

Hitching: For Toulouse or Castres, take bus #6 (*direction* "Rouges") from the train station or in front of Eglise St-Jacques, along Faubourg Toulousain. For Moissac or Agen, take bus #4 (*direction* "le Paturin") from bd. Midi-Pyrénées along cours Foucault to Albarèdes. For Rodez or Cahors, take bus #7 along av. Moulin.

English Bookstore: Deloche Librairie, 21, rue de la République.

Laundromat: 15, rue d'Elie, off place Nationale. Open July-Aug. Mon.-Tues. and Thurs.-Sat. 9am-8pm., Sun. 10am-8pm; Sept.-June Mon.-Sat. 8am-10pm, Sun. 10am-8pm.

Accommodations and Camping

Hôtel du Commerce, 9, place de la Cathédrale (tel. 63-63-03-31), by the cathedral. A tightly run ship with adequate rooms. Stylish lounge downstairs. Singles 70-75F. Doubles 95F. Showers 10F. Breakfast 15F.

Hôtel de la Poste, 17, rue Michelet (tel. 63-63-05-95), off place Nationale. Clean and simple rooms. Singles 70F. Doubles 75F. 3- to 4-person room 130F. Showers 10F. Breakfast 18F.

Camping: The closest is in Albias (tel. 63-31-00-44), 8km north of Montauban. Also in Montech (tel. 63-64-82-44), 8km west, and Lamothe-Capdeville (tel. 63-31-32-29), to the northeast.

Food

The **market** is held Tuesday through Saturday mornings until 12:30pm in place Nationale. Many inexpensive restaurants line **rue d'Elie** and **rue d'Auriol,** off place Nationale.

Restaurant Toulousain, 2, rue Gillaque (tel. 63-63-20-66). Friendly, working-class establishment with a good, robust 45F *menu. Cassoulet* with vegetable 22F. Open Sept.-July Mon.-Sat. noon-1:30pm.

La Clef des Champs, 3, rue Armand (tel. 63-66-33-34). Like a country picnic brought indoors. Pressed wildflowers on the walls and fresh vegetarian *plats* (30F) and salads (14F). Desserts 13F. Open Tues.-Sat. 11:45am-2pm.

Don Quichotte, 8, place de la Cathédrale. Serves *tapas.* Collect several appetizers to make a meal, but be careful—prices add up quickly. Squid with lemon 15F, deep fried calamari rings 15F, omelettes 14F, and salads 18F. Open and still hopping at 2am.

Le Temps des Cerises, 10, rue d'Auriol (tel. 63-63-20-68). Traditionally furnished beer room. Delicious 44F lunch *menu,* or a 65F dinner *menu.* Interesting salads 24-29F. Open daily noon-2pm and 7:30-10pm.

Sights

Place Nationale is the centerpiece of town, once officially called place Commune, then place Royal under Louis XIV, and place Impériale under Napoleon. But it's always been *les couverts* to the townspeople, for the triple row of covered arches that girdle it. The shops have gradually moved into the arches so that today only the first row is free for cafe tables and the daily market. The town grew organically, without structure; thus arose the irregularity of arch width—the thicker, more ornate arches corresponded to the wealthier shop keepers who took shelter under them.

A prosperous port on the Tarn river, with a thriving textile and silk industry, Montauban was a regional center of Protestantism in the sixteenth century. The belfry of **Eglise St-Jacques** shows holes gouged out by Louis XIII's cannon shots during an unsuccessful siege in 1621. When neighboring towns surrendered to royal forces, Montauban was at last overcome, and in 1629 Catholicism was reimposed. After the revocation of the Edict of Nantes (which had guaranteed religious freedom) in 1685, Louis XIV ordered the construction of the **cathédrale.** Robert de Cotte, architect of the royal chapel at Versailles, insisted the stone for the facade be transported from distant quarries. Inside hangs Ingres's large, dramatic *Le Voeu de Louis XIII.*

Though no longer navigable, the Tarn river was once a gateway to the Atlantic. **Pont Vieux** stretches across the river, connecting the center of town to the train station. The diamond-shaped pattern of the bridge's pavement alternates between black basalt from the volcanoes of Auvergne, transported by the Tarn, and granite from the Pyrenees, brought by the Garonne; the two rivers converge 30km west at Moissac. To the left of the bridge stand the monasteries where women who refused to convert were imprisoned until they agreed to take Catholic husbands.

To the right of the bridge as you face town, the Palais Episcopal is now the **Musée Ingres.** The *Montalbanais*'s corpus is remarkable not only for the exotic lustre of the canvases such as *Jesus et les médecins, la Rêve d'Ossian,* and the *Portrait de Madame Gonse,* but also for the drawings and preparatory studies on rotating display, which reveal a great deal about Ingres's technique. Many works of the well-known native sculptor, Bourdelle, are displayed on the ground floor. His works modify his mentor Rodin's style, leaning toward a modernistic treatment of the subject. A visit to the museum also includes the **Palais des Evêques** (bishop's palace), with partially furnished rooms, painted walls, and a damp basement displaying torture instruments. (Open Tues.-Sun. 9:30am-noon and 1:30-6pm. Admission 10F, students 4.50F.)

Near Montauban

Sumptuous **Abbaye de Moissac** lies on the train line between Bordeaux and Toulouse. Founded in the sixth century, and later a pilgrimage center en route to Santiago de Compostela, the church was reduced to a portal and cloister during the French Revolution. The famous Romanesque tympanum illustrates chapter IV of the Apocalypse: Christ, enthroned, gazes straight ahead serenely, surrounded by two angels and four animals symbolizing the evangelists.

The **cloître's** 76 column heads are each different, and in three different styles: an oriental style depicting fantastic animals, approaching the delicacy of Byzantine ivory carvings; a classical style in palm, rose, and scroll patterns; and a narrative style unique to Languedoc, especially notable for its biblical scenes. During the French Revolution, government supporters methodically knocked off the heads of the statues, missing only three. (Cloister open daily 9am-7pm. Admission 11F, students 6F.) Treasures taken from the abbey are now contained at the **Musée Moissagais,** behind the cathedral. Housed in the former home of the nuns, the museum also displays popular art and objects of nineteenth-century Moissac. The collection includes *faïences* and handmade lace bonnets for every age and occasion.

The small town of **Moissac** is clean, quiet, and harmonious with the abbey. From June through August, it holds a small series of classical concerts in the church and cloister. (Tickets 60-80F, students 30-60F. Available at the *syndicat* next to the cloister.) **Les Récollets,** place des Récollets (tel. 63-04-03-64), off place des Halles, lets simple doubles for 64.50F, with shower 78.50F. (Hall shower included. Breakfast 16F.) Downstairs, the cheap restaurant serves a 45F *menu, boisson comprise,* and pizzas from 26F. **Camping Beauséjour,** 53, av. Jean Jaurès (tel. 63-04-01-28), is a three-star site with a small supermarket, 15 minutes from the center and 1km from the train station in the direction of Montauban. (15F per person. Showers 4F. Office open 8am-7:30pm.)

The tiny hill village of **Bruniquel,** east of Montauban and accessible by bus, shimmers in an imposing setting and an air of remote tranquility. Its thirteenth-century **château** overlooks the confluence of the Aveyron and Vere Rivers. Bruniquel has attracted both troubadour poets and nineteenth-century literati of Romantic persuasion, including poet Charles Nodier.

Residents themselves are fascinated by their village's history. The local chronicler Pierre Malrien, who has written three books on the village and its neighbor, Penne, conducts tours of the castle (in summer 10am-noon and 2-6pm; in off-season 3-6pm; admission 6F). It's best to call him (tel. 63-67-25-18) a day in advance to arrange a visit. Although visitors flow through the castle daily, the village is not crowded with tourists. The discreet hotel **Etape du Château** (tel. 63-67-25-00) offers basic doubles with shower for 100F. For **camping,** call **Le Payssel** (tel. 63-67-25-95), less than 1km outside of the village. (11F per person, 14F per site.) The **Restaurant l'Etage,** rue droit de la Peyre (tel. 63-67-25-41), near the entrance of the castle, serves a four-course, 65F *menu* in a comfortable dining room. In the afternoon, it becomes a *salon de thé.* The **syndicat** (tel. 63-67-24-91) is open afternoons: Tuesday through Saturday in the *mairie,* and Saturday through Monday in place des Gedes.

Also on the *circuit des bastides,* a collection of fortified villages in the Tarn region, are the imposing ruins of the château in **Penne.** The village is still intact, and commands regal views over the Aveyron valley. The tiny **syndicat** (tel. 63-56-00-52), left of the access to the old town, sells maps of walking tours that start in the village (1F). Guided walking tours of the castle and village leave Sunday and Thursday at 4pm from the *syndicat* (10F). The office also has information on canoeing and kayaking daytrips in July and August (50F per person, 90F for 2 people). Call M. Denis Lacombe at the Café la Terrace (tel. 63-56-35-03). The **Camping à la Ferme Auri Feuilles** (tel. 63-93-05-17) is on the route des Bastides, in the direction of Vaours (16F per night, 110F per week). Buses leave Montauban twice per day for Bruniquel (18F) and once per day for Penne (13F), but don't return until the following morning. Call the *gare routière* in Montauban (tel. 63-63-88-88) for more information.

Agen is a busy industrial town along the Garonne River, between Montauban and Bordeaux. Known for its plums and rugby team, Agen warrants a visit only for its museum. Housed in four sixteenth- and seventeenth-century *hôtels,* the collection is effectively and tastefully displayed. Among its Gallo-Roman antiquities is a lovely marble *Vénus* found in the Mas d'Agenais. Five works by Goya, including a self-portrait, highlight a strong collection of paintings. (Open Wed.-Mon. 10am-noon and 2-6pm. Admission 5F, during special exhibitions 10F.) **Eglise de St-Caprais,** built between the eleventh and sixteenth centuries, is graced with beautiful Romanesque capitals depicting the life of the structure's namesake.

The **Syndicat d'Initiative** (tel. 53-47-36-09) is down bd. Carnot from the train station. This helpful office will give you information about the region, including transport. It also dispenses a city guide and gives free tours of the *vieille ville* on Mondays and Thursdays. The **Auberge de Jeunesse (IYHF),** 17, rue Lagrange (tel. 53-66-18-98), is 1½km outside of town. Take the bus from the station (*direction* "Lalande") to Léon Blum, or walk. Turn left on bd. Dumon, left again on av. Barbusse, cross over a bridge, and turn right on bd. du Docteur Messines. The hostel is quite comfortable and equipped with a kitchen. (Members only, 34F. Closed 10am-6pm. Curfew 11pm.) The **Camping Municipal** (tel. 53-66-18-98) is next door, with access to all hostel facilities. (2.40F per person, 1.50F per tent.) In town, **Hôtel Moderne,** 96, bd. Carnot (tel. 53-66-05-33), is decent. (Singles 65F. Doubles 75F.) A **market** is held every morning and all day Saturday at **Les Halles,** on place des Laitiers.

Albi

Albi gave its name to the Albigensian Crusade, the bloody regional conflict; Pope Innocent III scourged the heretical Cathars, or Albigensians, through inquisition and crusade. Centered in Albi, these Manichean heretics believed the mind and soul to have come from God, the body and the material world from Satan. Their doctrines contradicted the Church by advocating anti-social and anti-reproductive practices, and their ascetic, non-clerical lifestyle was an early objection to Roman corruption. Today, not heretics, but those interested in the works of *Albigeois* Henri de Toulouse-Lautrec come to Albi, a quiet town nestled in a forested valley.

Orientation and Practical Information

Albi lies only one hour by train northeast of Toulouse. From the station bear left to reach the *syndicat* and the center of town. Make another left on av. Général de Gaulle, and then bear left over place Laperouse to the cobbled pedestrian streets of the *vieille ville.*

Syndicat d'Initiative: Place Ste-Cécile (tel. 63-54-22-30). **Currency exchange** (commission 20F) on Sun.-Mon., when banks are closed. Will reserve a hotel room for 10F. Detailed map of the city 12F. Open July-Aug. daily 9am-7pm; Sept.-June Mon.-Sat. 9am-noon and 2-6pm.

Post Office: Place du Vigan (tel. 63-54-17-85). **Telephones** and **currency exchange. Postal code:** 81000. Open Mon.-Fri. 8am-7pm, Sat. 8am-noon.

Train Station: At the end of av. Maréchal Joffre (tel. 63-54-50-50). To Toulouse (14 per day, 1 hr., 45F), Rodez (5 per day, 1½ hr., 47F), and Brive (6 per day, 4 hr., 137F). Many other destinations with a change at Toulouse. **Bike rental.**

Bus Station: Gare Routière Halte des Autobus, place Jean Jaurès (tel. 63-54-58-61), is the stop for private bus companies with service to Toulouse (7 per day), Pedez (2 per day), and Castres (4 per day). **Cars Bécardit,** rond-point du Lude (tel.63-54-03-79), organizes round-trip excursions to nearby towns: Castres (1 per day, 40F) and Cordes (1 per day, 30F). Make reservations at the *syndicat.*

Taxis: Albi Taxi Radio, Tel. 63-54-85-03.

Bike Rental: At the train station. 35F per ½-day, 45F per day, deposit 300F. **Rey,** bd. Soult (tel. 63-54-08-33). Open Mon.-Sat. 8am-noon and 2-5pm.

Laundromat: 8, rue Emile Grand. Wash 12F, dry 2F.

Medical Emergency: Centre Hospitalier, rue de la Berchere (tel. 63-54-33-33).

Police: 23, rue Pompidou (tel. 63-54-12-95).

Accommodations and Camping

Albi attracts droves of tourists, so its few hotels fill quickly. Reserve in advance if you wish to stay here, or commute from more accommodating Toulouse.

Maison des Jeunes et de la Culture, 13, rue de la République (tel. 63-54-53-65). Clean, hostel-like lodging, but without lockouts and curfew, and open to all at rock-bottom prices. Overflows with activities and bulletin boards. Newly-redecorated rooms. Co-ed bathrooms and a largely male clientele. No kitchen. Dorm bunks 21F. Breakfast 12F. Filling homecooked meals 34.50F. Check-in Mon.-Sat. at 6:30pm, Sun. at noon. You can leave your backpack until 2pm. Closed 3-6pm.

Hôtel la Regence, 27, av. Maréchal Joffre (tel. 63-54-01-42), 1 block from the train station. Large, pretty rooms with carpeting and old furniture. Cozy living room. Rooms 75-100F, with shower and TV 160F. Extra bed 30F. Shower 10F. Large breakfast 18F.

Hôtel Le Vieil Alby, 25, rue Toulouse-Lautrec (tel. 63-54-14-69), in the *vieille ville.* Very proper rooms. Owner is friendly but picky about upkeep of rooms (no eating in them). Owner almost requires that you eat in his excellent restaurant unless you arrive Sat. or Sun., when it's closed. 60F *menu,* wine included. Breakfast 22F. Hotel and restaurant open Tues.-Sun. afternoon. Call Fri. if you're coming Mon. Singles 100F. Doubles from 110F, with shower 135F.

Hôtel du Parc Rochegude, 6, place Edmond-Canet (tel. 63-54-12-80), on the edge of the *vieille ville* near a park. Exceptionally clean, with generous owners. Rooms 110F. Showers included. Breakfast 22F.

Camping: Parc de Caussels, 2km east of Albi on D99 (route de Millau; tel. 63-54-38-87). 300 sites. Swimming pool nearby. 25F per 2 people. Hot showers included.

Food

Treat yourself to some of the typically hearty dishes of this region: *cassoulet* and *tripes.* Albigensian stew should be washed down with the local Guillac or Cunac red wine. Provisions are available at the large indoor **market** on place St-Julien held Tuesday through Sunday mornings until noon, or at the well-stocked supermarket **Casino,** 39, rue Lices Georges Pompidou. A large, open-air market occurs on place Ste-Cécile Saturday mornings. Slightly more expensive, health food stores, **La Vie Claire,** 23, rue Séré-de-Rivières, and **Les Aliments Naturels,** 1, rue Puech Bérenguier, in the *vieille ville,* both have small selections of wholesome pizzas, pastries, and quiches. The Parc Rochegude and the banks of the Tarn are good spots for a picnic.

Auberge St-Loup, 26, rue de Castelviel (tel. 63-54-02-75), behind the cathedral. Local specialties served in a medieval inn with an intimate atmosphere. The adventurous eater might want to try the *gras double* (made with sheep tripe). 60 and 70F *menus.* Open Tues.-Sun.

La Pastacoutta, 11bis, rue de la Piale (tel. 63-54-40-30), across from the cathedral in a sunken old street. Good homemade pasta with subtle sauces. Attentive staff and thoughtful owner. Pasta 30F, grills 50F. Open Mon.-Sat. noon-2pm and 7pm-1am. Best to reserve for Sat. night.

Restaurant Couronne, 77, rue Croix Verte, off rue Lices Georges Pompidou. Less expensive than the restaurants in the tourist area. Simple, unpretentious family cooking for local pensioners. Filling 40F *menu* includes wine but not service. *Plat du jour* 25F with dessert and a glass of wine. Open Mon.-Fri. noon-2pm and 7:30-9pm, Sat. noon-2pm.

La Tartine, 17, place de l'Archevêché (tel. 63-54-50-60), across from the tourist office. Specializes in tea, salads, and desserts. Try the filling *salade tartine* (18F) or the *sorbet citron* (16F). Perfect for a light lunch in the sunshine. Open daily 10am-1am.

Sights and Entertainment

Born to an aristocratic family, Toulouse-Lautrec turned poster-painting into an art form and created storms of controversy with his unique interpretation of form and color and his candid view of French life. Until his early death at the age of 37 in 1901, he kept his distance from the impressionist circle and the public's taste—for this reason, the collection of works gathered by the artist's assiduous mother and housed in the **Musée Toulouse-Lautrec** is the best anywhere. Located in the **Palais de la Berbie,** the museum contains not only all 31 of the famous posters of Montmartre nightclubs, but also dozens of oils and pastels and rooms full of the master draftsman's sketches and drawings.

Toulouse-Lautrec is known for his paintings of prostitutes, whom he observed by renting a room in a brothel, as well as his portraits of the day's biggest cabaret stars. You need only see portraits of this squat, sadly comic aristocrat to speculate on his self-exile to the sidelines of Parisian society, his interest in the passions of the isolated individual behind the facade of a *nouveau riche, gai Paris.*

Upstairs is a fine collection of contemporary art, including sculpture and paintings by Dégas, Dufy, Matisse, and Rodin. The museum also contains a chapel and a few archeological exhibits. (Museum open July-Sept. daily 9am-noon and 2-6pm; Oct.-June Wed.-Mon. 10am-noon and 2-5pm. Admission 12F, students 6F; with special exhibition 15F, students 8F. Guided tours every 15 min., 10F.) Toulouse-Lautrec fans can also visit the artist's birthplace, the **Maison Natale de Toulouse-Lautrec,** in Vieil Albi. (Open in summer only 9am-noon and 3-7pm. Admission 15F, students 10F.)

Next to the Musée Toulouse-Lautrec, **Basilique Ste-Cécile** towers mightily but gracefully over the entire town. Built in 1282 after the papal crusaders quashed the heretical Albigensians, the structure was designed to serve as a fortress as well as a basilica. Inside, almost every square meter of the large single nave has been covered with bright yet never restored sixteenth-century Italianate frescoes, mostly decorative except for a gigantic and well-preserved mural of the Last Judgment, depicting gruesome and fearful scenes of life in hell. The *choeur* (choir, admission 2F) is decorated on the outside with a chronological procession of 30 life-like stone statues of Old Testament figures. In summer, lighted and guided tours of the basilica take place at 9pm (the church is illuminated 8:45-10:30pm); regular guided tours are frequent (15F). The vast organ, the largest in France, was restored in May, 1981. Wednesday late afternoons in July and August bring free concerts to Albi.

In intimate **Eglise St-Salvy,** the radiant violet light of the stained-glass windows fills the humble pews. While the fragrant garden of the cloister is usually accessible, the church is often closed.

A pathway next to the entrance to the cathedral leads to the narrow pedestrian streets of **Vieil Albi,** where craftspeople exhibit their trades and wares in a somewhat touristy atmosphere. Prices are steep, but you can always watch, or look at the timber-framed houses. For a different picture of working Albi, cross the Tarn over the **Pont Vieux,** a soaring, eleventh-century bridge with dramatic views of the river and town.

Albi entertains with a number of summertime festivals and celebrations. The **Feu de la St-Jean** around June 20 kicks off the season with dances and a giant log fire;

the **Festival du Théâtre** takes place during the last week of June and the first week of July. Albi is also a center for film: The six-day **Festival International du Film 9.5-16mm** features a busy agenda of screenings and banquets during the first week of August (tickets free at the tourist office), and another festival in October runs short films (about 20F per night). The **Festival de Musique,** a fine series of concerts, opera, ballet, and even flamenco guitar recitals resounds from July 25 to the first week in August. The **Bureau de Festival** (tel. 63-54-26-64), just opposite the syndicat, sells tickets (60-160F); buy in advance.

Near Albi

Albi perches at the western tip of the Tarn Valley, a large, outstretched district of cliffs, forests, and quiet little towns. **Château du Bosc** (tel. 65-69-20-83), where Toulouse-Lautrec spent a happy childhood, hides in a forest 45km from Albi. (Open Easter-Nov. 1 9am-noon and 2-7pm.) At the eastern end of the valley is **Millau,** gateway to one of France's most overwhelming natural wonders, the **Gorges du Tarn.** Ask the Albi *syndicat* for information on visiting the region by excursion buses in July and August (90-110F). Slow public buses also ply the route (3 per day, 2½ hr.). Experienced equestrians can follow a trail through the heart of the valley, while novices can hire horses by the hour. Contact the **Centre Equestre Albigeois** (tel. 65-54-46-91) about horse rentals.

Twenty-four kilometers from Albi, the small walled city of **Cordes,** founded in 1222, served as sentinel on the frontier of the Cathar territories during the thirteenth-century Wars of Religion. Jutting out high above the fertile valley of the Cerou River, the fortified city has been extensively renovated, largely due to artist Yves Brayer, who arrived in 1940. **Eglise St-Michel,** at the summit, has a glorious rose-colored window that illuminates the shadowy interior in the afternoons. The *syndicat* is on place de Halle (tel. 63-56-00-52; open June-Sept. daily 10am-12:30pm and 2:30-6pm; in off-season weekends only). The central square, **La Bride,** commands a marvelous view of the valley. French writer Albert Camus often came here to meditate. Cordes is a center for artisanry, and the *syndicat* provides a list of the addresses of craftspeople in residence. The **Musée Yves Brayer** is only worth visiting for its colorful and fanciful renditions of the town (admission 3F). The **Musée Charles Portal** exhibits clear and interesting presentations on local customs and life, and a reconstructed farmhouse interior. (Open July-Aug. daily 1-6pm; Sept.-June Sun. and holidays only 2-5pm. Admission 10F, students 6F.) If you're in the region on Bastille Day, don't miss the **Fête du Grand Fauconnier,** which sends Cordes back 500 years. Townspeople wrap their homes in garlands and medieval bunting and parade as queens, princes, knights, and fair damsels, celebrating with a banquet and a torchlit procession in a festival unrelated to the French national holiday. (Entrance is 40F, unless you're in costume.) The church and place des Halles reverberate with classical music performed by international groups during a music festival in July and August. (Tickets 30F, with reductions for students, available at the *syndicat.*)

Cordes is prohibitively expensive. The least expensive hotel, the **Auberge de la Bride** (tel. 63-56-04-02), on place des Halles, offers clean, airy singles and doubles for an exorbitant 160F. (Breakfast 20F.) For slightly less expensive rooms, try the handful of hotels in the lower town. **Camping le Moulin de Julien** (tel. 63-56-01-42) is a three-star site with a swimming pool, lake, and miniature golf, 1km out of town. The *syndicat* can give you information on *chambres d'hôte* in the area (singles or doubles 115-200F, including breakfast).

To get to Cordes, you must take a train via Gaillac to Vindrac. At the station in Vindrac, you can rent a bicycle and ride the 5km to Cordes. Alternatively, you can hitch from the junction of bd. de Strasbourg, av. Deusbourg, and rue Albert Thomas, or call a day before you arrive and schedule to be picked up by a mini-bus (tel. 63-56-14-80; 24F). Use the same number to call a taxi.

Castres

Celebrated journalist and politician Jean Jaurès put his hometown on the map. Leaping into prominence in 1896 as leader of the striking glass-workers of Carmaux, Jaurès vociferously joined other socialists, notably Emile Zola, in defending Captain Dreyfus, the Jewish officer framed as a traitor by French generals. The sensational and divisive case exposed the anti-Semitism that afflicted nineteenth-century France. After the turn of the century, Jaurès fought a losing battle against rising militarism in France and sought in vain to avert war by organizing an agreement between the French and German working classes. In 1914, his fate as a beleaguered martyr was sealed when he was assassinated in a Parisian cafe. His name is given to a prominent street, it seems, in every city in France.

Today, Castres is a quietly touristed town with a large museum of Spanish art, an uninteresting *vieille ville,* and a cluster of Venetian-style buildings on the banks of the Agout River.

Orientation and Practical Information

Castres lies 60km from Toulouse and 50km north of Carcassonne. To reach the center of town from the station, follow av. Albert 1er to the left and continue to bd. Henri Sizaire. Bear right until you reach the Jardin de l'Evêché. The pedestrian streets of the old city are clustered near the river. The Hôtel de Ville, museums, *syndicat,* and place Jean Jaurès with its clothes stores and banks are on the west side. Rue Alquier Bouffard, and its continuation, rue Villegoudon, cross the pont Neuf and lead to **place Soult,** a center of cafes.

Syndicat d'Initiative: Place de la République (tel. 63-59-92-44), in the Théâtre Municipal. Information on the national park nearby. Suggests walks and excursions by car in the Tarn region. Open July-Aug. daily 9am-noon and 2-7pm; Sept.-June Tues.-Sat. 9am-noon and 2-6:30pm.

Post Office: Bd. Alphonse Juin (tel. 63-59-28-54), near the *syndicat.* **Telephones** and **currency exchange. Postal code:** 81100. Open Mon.-Fri. 8am-7pm, Sat. 8am-noon.

Train Station: Av. Albert 1er (tel. 63-54-50-50). To Toulouse (8 per day, 1 hr., 50F), Carcassonne via Toulouse (8 per day, 2½ hr., 103F), and Albi via St-Sulpice (7 per day, 2 hr., 50F). Open daily 7:45am-12:30pm and 2-9:30pm.

Bus Station: Place Soult (tel. 63-35-37-31). To Carcassonne (2 per day), Toulouse (4 per day), and Albi (4 per day).

Bike Rental: At the train station. 33F per day, deposit 190F and ID.

Taxis: Tel. 63-59-99-25 or 63-59-96-44.

All-Night Pharmacy: Call the Commissariat de Police (tel. 63-34-40-10).

Medical Emergency: Bd. Maréchal Foch (tel. 63-59-24-00).

Police: Tel. 63-35-40-10.

Accommodations, Camping, and Food

The train station is a 20-minute hike from the center in a lonely neighborhood, so stay in this area only if you're too exhausted to walk. There is no youth hostel, but the *syndicat* prodvides information on *gîtes d'étape.*

Hôtel du Perigord, 22, rue Emile Zola (tel. 63-59-04-74), in *centre ville.* Large, unusually fine rooms in an old hotel, with high ceilings and good furniture. Most with 2 beds. Singles and doubles 70F, with shower 80F. Quads 104F. Breakfast 15F. Restaurant downstairs posts a 50F *menu,* wine included. Open Sept.-July Sun.-Fri.

Hôtel Carcassés, 3, rue d'Augue (tel. 63-35-37-72), off place Soult. Family establishment and gigantic rooms with sloping floorboards. Many rooms can accommodate families. Room prices based on the number of double beds (each 60F). Showers included. Breakfast 15F.

Splendid Hôtel, 17, rue Victor Hugo (tel. 63-59-30-42). Basic rooms in the center of town. Doubles 76F, with shower 96F. 2 beds 150F. Breakfast 17F. Closed Nov.-May Sat.-Sun.

M. and Mme. Piquot, Parisot, 81110 St-Avit (tel. 63-50-30-57), 15km out of town on the road between Soval and Dourgne. Take the morning bus to Carcassonne. Also served by buses from Carcassonne (leaving from Hôtel Bristol) and Albi. Get off at the Coulon stop. English-speaking owners will pick you up at the train station if you pay for gas (about 50F). 14-room château surrounded by 27 acres of land near a lake (9km away). All meals are vegetarian. Full board 140-170F. Reserve well in advance July-Aug.

Camping: Camping Municipal, av. de Roquecourbe (tel. 63-59-56-49), near *centre ville.* Cross the canal and turn left on av. Luicien-Coudert. 17F.

A large **market** convenes on place Jean Jaurès Tuesday through Thursday until about 12:30pm. Picnic in the shady Jardin de l'Evêché beside the Hôtel de Ville. Try the local *roquefort* and *bleu* cheese, both of which are very sharp.

Les Sarrasines, 34, rue Villegoudou (tel. 63-35-77-50). Crêpes 10-26F, salads 11-25F. Lavender and lace decor, and art exhibitions on the wall—perfect for a slow afternoon. Open Tues.-Sat. noon-midnight.

Restaurant Carcassés, 3, rue d'Augue (tel. 63-35-37-72), off place Soult. Working-class establishment with local clientele and dedicated staff. Filling but no frills 45F *menu, vin compris.* Open noon-2pm and 7-9pm.

L'Eau à la Bouche, 6, rue Malpas (tel. 63-72-28-33). Turn left at place Jean Jaurès before the Banque Nationale Populaire. Soothing atmosphere with white wicker furniture and soft-blue decor. Refined 60F *menu.* Open noon-2pm and 7-10pm.

Sights

Castres's two greatest monuments overlap in theme. One commemorates a pacifist, while the other exposes the atrocities of war. The **Musée Jaurès,** place Pélisson (tel. 63-72-01-01), is packed with pamphlets, trenchant political cartoons, old photographs, and faded newspaper articles that catch the flavor of Jean Jaurès's spirited, often bitter rhetoric, and revealing as much about turn-of-the-century France as about the man himself. (Open July-Aug. daily 9am-noon and 2-6pm; April-June and Sept. Tues.-Sun. 9am-noon and 2-6pm; Oct.-March Tues.-Sun. 9am-noon and 2-5pm. Admission 10F.)

Next to the beautiful, impeccably-manicured **Jardin de l'Evêché** in the Hôtel de Ville stands the **Musée Goya,** housing a fine collection of early Spanish paintings by Catalonian and Aragonese masters. The museum's collection of Goyas spans a period of over 50 years. *Los desastres de la guerra* depicts the pathos and horror of the Napoleonic Wars, while the 40 etchings of *Tauromaquia* document the shift in bullfighting from knightly engagement on horseback to democratic combat on foot. (Museum open same hours as above. Admission 20F, students 15F, free Wed. in winter.)

The **Centre d'Art Contemporain,** 35, rue Chambre de l'Edit, is the only small modern art museum to be recognized by the national Ministry of Culture. Daily guided tours help you understand the avant-garde photography, painting, and sculpture. (Open Mon.-Sat. 9am-noon and 2-6pm, Sun. 10am-noon and 2-6pm. Admission 5F, ages under 20 free.)

Castres was once a major textile center, and the **Quai des Jacobines** presents a fine view of the medieval merchants' houses across the Agout River. The wooden galleries were used for drying, while the arched entryways opening onto the river allowed easy shipment. Today little of the industry remains; the dilapidated houses are undergoing extensive renovation.

The **Festival Goya** in the latter half of July features Spanish music, dance, art, and theater (tickets available at the Théâtre Municipal). Castres also stages a small folkloric **Festival Occitan** with music and dance on June 24.

The countryside south of Castres is well worth visiting. The town of **Mazamet** (*syndicat* tel. 63-61-27-07) has several restaurants and hotels and is accessible by train from Castres (6 per day, 20F). Mazamet is the most convenient base for visiting the rugged **Montagnes Noires,** located in the **Parc Natural Régional du Haut Languedoc,** a seldom visited but starkly beautiful reserve, full of lakes and well suited for campers and hikers. In the northwest corner of the park sits the **Sidobre,** one of the many famous granite quarries near Castres, known for its weird, irregular boulders, especially the wobbly Roc de l'Oie. You can make the 15-km trip along av. de Sidobre by biking or hitching. Both the Castres and Mazamet *syndicats* can provide information on hiking, camping, rural lodgings, riding, tennis, and water sports in the area.

Carcassonne

The Cité de Carcassonne is a child's toy castle grown to adult proportions, a thirteenth-century Disneyland, a double-walled, fortified city with towers and turrets rising from a precipitous plateau. One of the most extravagant fortresses in all of Europe, its towers and battlements bristle over an impossibly long expanse of hilltop. An agglomeration of fortifications from Gallo-Roman times to the thirteenth century, Carcassonne fell into disrepair after the Wars of Religion, and soon, villagers so rapaciously pillaged the walled town in search of building materials that for centuries little more than a few crumbling walls remained. In 1844, Viollet-le-Duc, famous architect and chief of the newly created government section of historic monuments, decided to restore the ancient fortress. Although Viollet's grandiose visions were not matched by his attention to historical detail, he created a living museum of medieval urbanism.

Orientation and Practical Information

The Cité, nicknamed *la pucelle du Languedoc* (the maiden of Languedoc), is perched above the *ville basse,* the ordinary town of modern Carcassonne. Most shops, offices, and hotels—as well as the train station—are situated in the modern town. To reach the Cité, you can catch the black #4 bus from the train station (every ½ hr. until 6:53pm, 15 min.), or from place Gambetta (every ½ hr. until 7:02pm, 5 min.). You can also walk the 3km from the station: Cross the canal du Midi, turn left onto bd. Omer Sarraut, turn right onto bd. Jean Jaurès, then turn left at place Gambetta (a central park), cross pont Neuf, and follow the signs to the entrance of the Cité.

Syndicat d'Initiative: 15, bd. Camille Pelletan, place Gambetta (tel. 68-25-07-04). From the train station, follow bd. Jean Jaurès . **Currency exchange** on weekends when the banks are closed (commission 5F). Open in summer Mon.-Sat. 9am-7pm, Sun. 10am-noon; in off-season Mon.-Sat. 9am-noon and 2-6:30pm. **Annex** in the porte Narbonnaise (tel. 68-25-68-81), to your right as you enter the Cité. Open July-Aug. daily 9am-7pm.

Post Office: Rue Jean Bringer. **Currency exchange, telephones** and Poste Restante. **Postal code:** 11000. Open June 15-Sept. 15 Mon.-Fri. 9:45am-12:30pm and 1:45-5:45pm, Sat. 9:45am-12:30pm; Sept. 16-June 14, Mon.-Fri. 9:15am-noon and 2:15-5pm. **Branch office,** rue Vicomte Trencavel, in the Cité right down the street from the youth hostel. Open Mon.-Fri. 9:45am-12:30pm and 1:20-5pm, Sat. 8:45-11:45am.

Train Station: Behind Jardin St-Chenier (tel. 68-47-50-50). Carcassonne is a major stop between Toulouse (11 per day, 48 min., 54F) and points north and east, such as Montpellier (10 per day, 2 hr., 84F), Nîmes (7 per day, 2½ hr., 108F), Lyon (3 direct per day, 5½ hr., 226F), Marseille (every 2 hr., 3 hr., 160F), Toulon (5 per day, 4 hr., 196F), and Nice (5 per day, 6 hr., 252F).

Bus Station: Bd. de Varsovie (tel. 68-25-12-74). To Lezignan (in summer 5 per day, in winter 2; 50 min.), Saissac (Tues., Thurs., and Sat. 2 per day), Quillan (2 per day), Castelnaudary (4 per day, 45 min.), Toulouse (3 per day, 2½ hr.). Offices of 3 smaller companies across the street from Café Bristol in front of the train station. To Albi, Lagrasse, St-Hilaire, Latours, and other nearby towns.

Taxis: Tel. 68-71-50-50 or 68-25-14-79.

Bike Rental: Castilla, 12bis, rue Auguste Comte (tel. 68-25-66-64). Open Sept.-July Mon.-Fri. 8am-noon and 2-6pm. Also at the **train station** (tel. 68-25-30-00).

All-night Pharmacy: Call the *commissariat de Police* (tel. 68-25-19-01) after 8pm.

Medical Emergency: SAMU, Centre Hospitalier, route de St-Hilaire D342 (tel. 68-25-60-30).

Police: 40, bd. Barbes (tel. 68-25-19-01).

Accommodations and Camping

The youth hostel is located (miraculously) in the very middle of the Cité, and is large and comfortable. When the hostel is full, find a hotel in the *ville basse*—those in the Cité are exorbitantly expensive. The **M.J.C. Centre Internationale de Séjour,** 91, rue Aimé Ramon (tel. 68-25-86-68), is strictly for groups, but you might call them as a last resort.

Auberge de Jeunesse (IYHF), rue de Vicomte Trencavel (tel. 68-25-23-16). Friendly and extremely clean dormitory accommodations. Hostel cards and sheet sleeping sacks required or 15F surcharge. Bed and obligatory breakfast 45F. Showers included. Open July-Aug. daily 8-11am and 6-11:30pm; Sept. and June until 11pm; April until 10:30pm; Nov., Feb., and March until 10pm. Call in advance.

Hôtel de l'Octroi, 106, av. Général Leclerc (tel. 68-25-29-08), at the foot of the Cité on a boulevard serviced by bus #4 (stop: Leclerc). Clean and appealing with kind owners. Singles 64-68F. Doubles 70-88F, with 2 single beds 97F, with shower and W.C. 140F. Triples 115F. Showers 11F. Breakfast 17F.

Le Cathare, 53, rue Jean Bringer (tel. 68-25-65-92), near the post office. Well-decorated rooms. 2 singles at 75F and 80F. Doubles 95F, with shower 125F. Showers free. Breakfast 18.50F. Downstairs restaurant has a 41F *menu.*

Hôtel St-Joseph, 81, rue de la Liberté (tel. 68-25-20-94), just 5 min. from the station. Clean, frilly, large rooms and friendly management. Singles 62F. Doubles 65-75F, with shower 110F. Triples 110F. Quads 130F, with shower 150F. Showers 10F. Breakfast 12F.

Hôtel Bonnafoux, 40, rue de la Liberté (tel. 68-25-01-45), near the station. Simple, bright rooms. The owner is an expert on ancient Mediterranean peoples, an ardent humanist, and an inspired conversationalist. Singles 60F. Doubles 76F, with shower 110F. Showers 10F. Breakfast 15F, obligatory July-Aug.

Hôtel de la Poste, 21, rue de Verdun (tel. 68-25-12-18), also near the post office. Worn rooms above a bar, but friendly management. Singles and doubles 95F, with shower 125F. Quads 150F, with shower 190F. Breakfast 18F. Open Mon.-Sat.

Camping: Camping de la Cité, across the l'Aude from the modern town (tel. 68-25-11-77), and accessible from the Cité. 36F per person including tent.

Food

The restaurants within the Cité are surprisingly inexpensive. Most serve the regional specialty *cassoulet,* a stew of white beans, herbs, and some form of meat, usually lamb in Carcassonne. Popular wisdom has it that whatever the ingredients, every good *cassoulet* produces gastric agony the morning after. For provisions, visit the **market** in place Carnot (also known as place aux Herbes; open Tues., Thurs., and Sat. until 1pm), or the **covered market** at place d'Eggenfelden, off rue Aimé Ramon (open daily until 5:30 or 6pm). For seeds, berries, and whole food, shop at **Nature et Santé,** 103, rue Dr. A. Tomey, at rue de la Liberté. (Open Tues.-Sun. 9am-12:30pm and 2:30-7:30pm.)

In the *ville basse,* simple but affordable restaurants line bd. Omer Sarraut. Restaurants in the Cité tend to shut down in winter.

Au Bon Pasteur, 29, rue Armagnac (tel. 68-25-46-58), in the *ville basse* near Eglise St-Vincent. A friendly, English-speaking owner and a 55F *menu* that has many choices, and generous portions of *cassoulet, vin compris.* Open Tues.-Sat. noon-2pm and 7:15-9:30pm.

La Taverne Médiévale, 4-7, rue Cros Mayrevieille (tel. 68-71-04-82), on the Cité's main thoroughfare. A cafeteria serving decent food, though not as cheap as others. Pleasant, wood-beamed room. *Menu* 50F, *cassoulet* 35F. Open daily 11:30am-3pm and 6:30-10pm.

L'Ostal des Troubadours, 5, rue Viollet-le-Duc (tel. 68-47-88-80). A fun place for coffee or drinks amid an animated crowd and lively musicians. Provençal songs, Irish ballads, blues, rock. The restaurant serves some of the cheapest *menus* (39F and 59F, service not included).

La Rotonde, 13, bd. Omer Sarraut (tel. 68-25-02-37), in the *ville basse* across from the train station. A late-night *brasserie* and cafe, with a quick 44F *menu* and an unlimited hors d'oeuvre bar. Open daily 6:30am-2am.

Le Sénéchal, 6, rue Viollet-le-Duc (tel. 68-25-00-15). The dinner *menu* is somewhat expensive, but it's a small price to pay for excellent food and a beautiful courtyard setting. 65F *menu* includes wine. Open Wed.-Mon. noon-2pm and 7-9:30pm.

Sights and Entertainment

Occupying a strategic position on the road between Toulouse and the Mediterranean, the original fortifications at Carcassonne date back to the Roman Empire in the first century and the Visigoths in the fifth century. An early fortress here withstood Clovis, King of the Franks, in 506 C.E., and other invaders, but Carcassonne fell with Languedoc during the Albigensian Crusade in 1209. When the Cité passed to the control of the French King Louis IX (St-Louis), the monarch ordered the construction of the second outer wall, copying the double-walled fortress design French crusaders had seen in Palestine. The city's military importance later lapsed and was neglected until Viollet-le-Duc re-imagined it.

You can detect the different epochs of construction by walking through the grassy *lices* (formerly used for jousting tournaments) between the two sets of walls. The bottom layers of brick and stone date from the earliest period, while the oddly-shaped towers and rounded fronts and flat backs date from the Visigothic era. The upper layers of thicker, flatter stones and the taller towers date from the thirteenth century, as does the entire outer wall of fortification. Massive arches and buttresses and the intricate arrangement of wooden beams supporting the turrets exemplify Viollet-le-Duc's mastery of medieval engineering. The blue slate roofs used for the towers of the inner ring of fortresses are so out of place amid the red-tiled roofs of the Midi that local authorities here recently embarked on a scheme to re-roof using local materials.

Entrance to the *lices* and outer walls is free, but to visit thirteenth-century **Château Comtal** and the inner towers you will have to take the guided tour in either French or English (tours in French run continuously, in English at 10am amd 2:30pm only; 40 min.). Alternatively, take the more detailed *visite conférence* (in French only, continuously, 1½ hr.). Both tours start at the château gates within the city. Since its construction in the twelfth century by Philippe the Bold, the château has served as armory and barracks for several regimes, including that of Napoleon. (Château open April-Sept. 9am-noon and 2-6:30pm; Oct.-March 10am-noon and 2-5pm. Admission 22F, ages 18-25 and over 60 12F, ages under 18 5F.)

At the other end of the city, the apse of **Basilique St-Nazaire** basks in the glow of its variegated stained-glass windows (the coolest place in Carcassonne on a hot summer's day). Viollet idiosyncratically restored the tower with crenellations in a Visigothic style that clashes with the rest of the structure. Outside, the narrow streets of Carcassonne, despite their tourist shops, exude a medieval atmosphere. About a thousand people live here in a sort of thirteenth-century time warp.

It is hard for the ordinary *ville basse* to compete with the romp of the Cité. Built as a *bastide* under St-Louis in 1260, the city streets meet at prosaic right angles. The flower-lined **boulevard de Varsovie** and **Jardin à Chevier,** in front of the train station, provide pleasant promenades. The banks of the Aude offer ideal spots for strolling or picnicking, and vistas of the Cité. **Cathédrale St-Michel,** a fourteenth-century Gothic church, has a round steeple, octagonal tower, and luminous rose windows. A prime example of fourtheenth- to fifteenth-century *gothique languedocien* **Eglise St-Vincent** contains a large single nave. Pilgrims flocked to **Notre-Dame**

de Santé, a tiny, sixteenth-century chapel. It stands to the right of pont Vieux, on the way back to the Cité.

Carcassonne stages an eclectic **festival** in the restored theater of the Château Comtal and the Basilique St-Nazaire throughout July, with performances of international theater, dance, and music as well as art shows in the **Tours Narbonnaises.** Last year's schedule included Miles Davis, French recording-star Michel Jonasz, the Toulouse symphony orchestra, and *Hamlet* performed in French. (Tickets 60-150F.) For information, contact Festival de la Cité, Théâtre Municipal, 11005 Carcassonne (tel. 68-71-30-30). In June, the city celebrates its medieval history with the **Troubadours festival** featuring period music and theater. In August, the entire Cité returns to the middle ages during the **Médiévales.** People dressed as medieval townspeople talk to visitors, display their crafts, and pretend nothing has changed in 800 years. At night, the Cité stages an elaborate sound and light show. (Tickets 70F; call the *syndicat* for reservations.) A spectacular fireworks display illuminates the city on July 14, **Bastille Day.**

Near Carcassonne

From Carcassonne to Perpignan, the road (unfortunately, neither the train nor the bus) leads through the starkly beautiful region known as **Les Corbières,** past ruined châteaux sitting above multicolored limestone cliffs. This sparsely populated, hot, dry region may deter travelers (especially hitchhikers), but those who venture out will be rewarded. The Carcassonne tourist office can arrange taxi service between villages in the region for groups of no more than four. Round-trip prices start at 350F. **Lezignan** (35km from Carcassonne), ugly and inconvenient itself, harbors a lavish camping center, **La Pinède,** only 100m from the center of town. The fine **Château de Peyrepertuse,** on the D14, is actually two ruined thirteenth-century castles perched impossibly over sheer, rocky cliffs. Five kilometers away and 730m up, **Quéribus** is so well-protected that it was never taken by force, but given in exchange for the freedom of its captured owner Chabert de Barbaira. This transaction was the last military act in the anti-Cathar crusades. **Fort de Salse,** 16km north of Perpignan on the flat coastland, has dauntingly massive brick walls and Spanish towers. Smaller but no less impressive châteaux dot this once hotly contested land, and in many little towns you can visit *caves* where the region's celebrated wines are painstakingly prepared including the full, rich Minervois reds. Accessible by bus from Carcassonne, **Lagrasse** is the site of a once-flourishing Benedictine Abbey, dating from the eighth century and one of the oldest in France. Contact **Voyages Bourdier** (tel. 68-25-09-06) for information on exact departure times to Lagrasse (Wed. and Sat. 2 per day, 1 hr., round-trip 75F).

The Carcassonne tourist office distributes copious information on the surrounding areas. Pick up the booklets *Châteaux cathares* and *Carcassonne et sa région.* They also offer information on camping, as well as a complete listing of local festivals, concerts, and markets in the *Département de l'Aude.*

Perpignan

Perpignan's strategic location between the Mediterranean and the Pyrenees was used to military advantage between 1276 and 1344, when the kings of Majorca established their royal residence here. A part of France only since 1659, Perpignan is still considered the northern capital of the Catalan, with Barcelona as its southern counterpart. Though friendlier and less pretentious than vacation destinations on the Côte d'Azur, Perpignan remains a quiet and dull spot despite the summer deluge of backpackers. More worthy of exploration is the surrounding Catalan region. The city serves as a gateway to white-sand beaches 13km east, picturesque fishing villages 25km south, and the Pyrenees, whose foothills begin 30km west.

The **Palais des Rois de Majorque** is still the city's most impressive sight, especially now that it has been restored. Bask in the immense arcaded courtyard, and note the two curiously superimposed chapels. The **citadelle** was used as an arsenal in the last century, and restoration has only recently begun; its forbidding walls still surround the palace. (Gates open Wed.-Mon. 9:30am-noon and 2:30-6pm. Admission 10F, students 5F, ages under 10 free.)

Worth seeing if only for its enchanting setting is **La Casa Païral**, place de Verdun (tel. 68-35-66-30, ext. 6042), a museum of Catalan culture and folklore, with exhibits on local music, dress, dance, agriculture, and religion. It is housed in **Le Castillet**, another impressive brick castle with a fine view of the city—for those who manage to climb all the steps to the top. (Open July-Sept. Wed.-Mon. 9:30-11:30am and 2:30-6:30pm; Oct.-June Wed.-Mon. 9am-noon and 2-6pm. Free.)

Orientation and Practical Information

From the train station, walk straight up av. Général de Gaulle, and turn right before the large *place* onto cours Lazare Escarguel, which crosses the canal. Turn left immediately after crossing the bridge; the regional tourist office is on your right on quai de Lattre de Tassigny (15 min.). Place Arago and place de la Victoire lie farther along the canal from the regional tourist office.

Syndicat d'Initiative: Bureau Municipal du Tourisme de Perpignan, in the Palais des Congrès, place Armand Lanoux (tel. 68-34-13-13). Don't come here for information: It's too far from the train station (a ½-hr. walk), and disorganized, unhelpful, and understaffed to boot. Guided tours of the city daily at 3:30pm. The **Comité Départemental du Tourisme,** quai de Lattre de Tassigny (tel. 68-34-29-94), is better prepared to distribute information on the city as well as on the entire Roussillon region. Information on hotels, camping, *gîtes d'étape,* restaurants, walks, train and bus schedules, and festivals. City maps. Open daily June 15-Sept. 15 9am-8pm; Sept. 16-June 14 9am-noon and 2-7pm.

Currency Exchange: At the train station on weekends and holidays. No commission, but rates are deplorable. Open Mon.-Fri. 8am-noon and 5-7pm, Sat. 8am-noon and 3-7pm, Sun. 8-11am and 6-7pm.

Post Office: Quai de Lattre de Tassigny. **Telephones. Postal code:** 66020. Open Mon.-Fri. 8am-7pm, Sat. 8am-noon.

Train Station: Rue Courteline (tel. 68-35-50-50). To Narbonne (30 per day, ½ hr., 42F), Paris (6 per day, 10 hr., 385F), Villefranche (7 per day, 50 min., 34F), Prades (7 per day, 40 min., 31F), and Collioure (12 per day, ½ hr., 23F).

Bus Station: Gare Routière, 17, av. Général Leclerc (tel. 68-35-29-02), near place de la Résistance. To Narbonne (Mon.-Sat. 2 per day, 1½ hr.), Béziers (Mon.-Sat. 1 per day, 2 hr. 20 min.), l'aéroport (Mon.-Sat. 3 per day, 15 min.), Vinça (8 per day, 50 min.), Argelès-sur-Mer (Mon.-Sat. 8 per day, 4 Sun.; 25 min.), Collioure (Mon.-Sat. 8 per day, 4 Sun.; 40 min.), Port-Vendres (Mon.-Sat. 8 per day, 4 Sun.; 45 min.), and Banyuls-sur-Mer (Mon.-Sat. 5 per day, 4 Sun.; 1 hr.). **Car Inter 66,** 17, av. Général Leclerc (tel. 68-35-29-02). 4 buses per day to all the beaches from le Barcarès to Cerbère. 10 buses connect individual beaches. Schedules available at both tourist offices.

Municipal Buses: Tel. 68-61-01-13. City bus #1 goes to Canet-plage Mon.-Sat. 22 times per day (last bus at 7:30pm, last return from Canet-plage at 8pm, 25 min.). Buses leave from place des Platanes (10F, day pass 30F). Intra-city bus tickets 5F, *carnet* of 6 25F.

Medical Emergency: Tel. 18.

Police: Tel. 17.

Accommodations, Camping, and Food

Auberge de Jeunesse (IYHF), La Pépinière, off av. de la Grande Bretagne in parc de la Pépinière (tel. 68-34-63-32). From the train station, turn left on bd. du Conflent, then right on av. de la Grande Bretagne. Lively and cramped, with friendly management. Dormitory rooms and spartan kitchen facilities. 45F per night. Sheets 11F. Breakfast included (served 7:30-8am). Lockout 9am-6pm. Curfew 11pm. Call ahead in July and Aug.

Hôtel de la Poste, 8, rue Fabrique Nabot (tel. 68-34-42-53), near place de Verdun. Friendly management and refreshingly clean rooms. Singles 85-90F, with shower 125F. Doubles 90-95F, with shower 135F. Triples and quads 180-215F. Showers 10F. Breakfast 17.50F.

Hôtel le Bristol, 5, rue Grande des Fabriques (tel. 68-34-32-68), just off place de Verdun. Adequate rooms in a good location. Singles 65F. Doubles 70-80F, with shower 100F. Triples 100F, with shower 130F. Quads 120F. Showers 15F. Breakfast 15F.

Hôtel le Berry, 6, av. de la Gare (tel. 68-34-59-02), in front of the train station. Large, clean doubles 55F, with shower 90F. Triples with shower 120F. Extra bed 30F. Showers 15F. Breakfast 15F and 17F.

Camping: La Garriogle, rue Maurice Levy (tel. 68-54-66-10), is a 1-star site. Take bus #2 from the station (4.80F). Camping Le Catalan, route de Bompas (tel. 68-63-16-92), is much larger with 240 sites and a swimming pool. Cars Tixador (tel. 68-63-29-70) runs 5 buses per day Mon.-Sat. (last at 6:15pm), 3 Sun. (last at 2:15pm). The tourist office has a list of the campsites with vacancies and can make you a reservation.

Place de la Loge and place de Verdun in the *vieille ville* are filled with restaurants and cafes that stay lively at night. More expensive restaurants line the canal's quai Vauban. An open-air market is held daily at place de la République from 5am to 6pm.
Le Perroquet, 1, av. Général de Gaulle (tel. 68-34-34-36), a stone's throw from the train station, offers surprisingly cheap, excellent food. Their 47F *menu* features a wide range of choices, such as *escargots* and *lapin* (rabbit), both prepared with a Catalan twist. Open Sat.-Wed. noon-1:45pm and 7-9:30pm, Thurs. for lunch only. Ideal for light snack or quick meal, Le Palmarium, place Argo (tel. 68-34-51-35), wears the guise of a new and spiffy cafeteria with a fashionable terrace overlooking the canal. Grills are 30-35F. Open daily 11:30am-2:30pm and 6:45-9:30pm. Finally, Le Canneton, 12, rue Victor Hugo, offers a bland 30F *menu*, wine included. Open Mon.-Sat. for lunch and dinner.

Near Perpignan

Buses depart from promenade des Platanes in Perpignan for Canet-Plage (*syndicat* tel. 68-80-35-88), a popular resort with a long, wide beach and 10 campsites that are usually full. (2 or 3 buses per hr., 25 min., one way 10F.) You should make this a daytrip. Farther south along the coast are two other resorts, St-Cyprien-Plage (*syndicat* tel. 68-21-01-33; 6 campsites and a long, sandy beach), and Argelès-sur-Mer (*syndicat* tel. 68-81-15-85; 61—count 'em—campsites). There are buses to St-Cyprien from the *gare routière* on av. Général Leclerc in Perpignan (Mon.-Sat. 5 per day, 3 Sun.; ½ hr.), and to Argelès-sur-Mer (Mon.-Sat. 8 per day, 4 Sun.; ½ hr.), Collioure (Mon.-Sat. 8 per day, 4 Sun.; 45 min.), and Banyuls-sur-Mer (4 per day, 70 min.). Also, Cars Inter 66, 17, av. Général Leclerc (tel. 68-35-29-02), has 4 buses per day connecting the beaches from le Barcarès to Cerbère; schedules are at the *syndicat*.
South of Argelès, the Pyrenees come right to the shore, creating magnificent coastal scenery along the Côte Rocheuse (Rocky Coast), also known as the Côte Vermeille. The rocks and the sea here are more memorable than the crowded beaches. Collioure, on the train and bus lines, merits a visit for the old village itself. Matisse came here in 1905 as an unknown and was followed by Derrain, Gris, Dufy, Dali, and Picasso. The bright colors that were the trademark of the Fauve painters can still be found here. The Hôtel des Templiers, quai de l'Amirauté (tel. 68-82-05-58), is wallpapered with paintings that many artists left behind as gifts to the former proprietors or as payments for their meals. Today, less-known painters still live in Collioure. No fewer than 13 art galleries line the streets of the town. The village's new Musée de Collioure, on the road to Port-Vendres, displays the work of artists who painted here. (Open July-Sept. daily 3-8pm; Oct.-June Wed.-Mon. 2-7pm. Admission 12F, students 8F.) Collioure's centerpiece, the thirteenth-century Château Royale now serves as a museum for contemporary painting and sculpture and exhibits on regional history. The castle has been occupied by Spanish, Catalonian, and French forces, and each wave of rulers has added to the architecture. In 1679, the French strategist Vauban fortified the castle and the village against future takeovers by building towers on the surrounding hills. (Castle open April-Oct. daily 10am-1pm and 2:30-7:30pm. Admission 16F.) At the other end of the crescent-

shaped village is the seventeenth-century **Eglise St-Vincent.** Its dark interior is brightened by a gilded altar crafted by Catalonian sculptor Joseph Sunyer in 1698. (Open 8am-noon and 2-6pm.)

If you plan to spend the night, be warned that hotels are expensive. You can try the **Hôtel des Templiers** (tel. 68-82-05-58) to see if they have room in their annex (doubles 135F). **Hôtel Le Majorque,** 16, av. Général de Gaulle (tel. 68-82-29-22), provides simple, clean rooms (doubles 130F, with shower 150F; quads with shower 200F). **Hôtel l'Arapède,** 3km from Port-Vendres (tel. 68-82-05-86), offers fresh, luxurious rooms for slightly less than in the village (doubles with shower 140F; open Easter-Oct.). Near the quiet Port-Vendres train station, 3km from Collioure, the **Hôtel Béar,** place de la Gare (tel. 68-82-01-59), has a pink 1930s facade (doubles 130F, with shower 150F; triples with shower 165F; big breakfast with eggs 21F). The friendly owners like Americans and students. (Open March-Nov.)

Food is somewhat more affordable. **L'Albatros,** 48, rue de la Démocratie (tel. 68-82-35-33), in the *basse ville* facing the port, has a small, bright interior that is decorated like a Matisse paper collage. (*Moules* 30-38F, pizza 30-40F. Open Thurs.-Tues. noon-3pm and 7pm-midnight, Wed. 7pm-midnight.) **Le Chiberta,** 18, av. du Général de Gaulle (tel. 68-82-06-60), also in the *basse ville,* is a family restaurant where the owner does the cooking. (*Menu* 57F. Open June-Sept. 7-9pm.) The Collioure **Syndicat d'Intiative,** place de la Mairie (tel. 68-82-15-47), near the port, has plenty of information on the area, including campsites. (Open Mon.-Sat. 9:30am-noon and 3:30-7pm, Sun. 10am-noon.)

From Perpignan, you can also take the train to its other terminus in the Pyrenees. The train stops first in **Prades** (7 per day, 40 min., 31F), where the 1000-year-old **Abbaye de St-Michel-de-Cuxa** reposes 3km away. At the end of July and beginning of August, the abbey hosts the **Festival de Prades,** held in honor of Pablo Casals, the Spanish cellist who lived here the last 23 years of his life. (Tickets 100-130F.) The bureau du Festival, rue Victor Hugo (tel. 68-96-33-07 or 68-96-50-95), can give you more information. The **postal code** for Prades is 66500.

If you don't have much time, it's best to stay on the train all the way to **Villefranche** (7 per day, 50 min., 34F). A fortified village founded in 1092, it occupies a prized location at the confluence of the Cady and Têt Rivers and at the base of three mountains. The town's civic architecture (22 thirteenth- and fourteenth-century facades are registered as historical monuments) is as well preserved as its military ramparts. Built into the mountainside high above the town, **Fort Liberia** was designed by chief French military architect Vauban in the seventeenth century to protect the valuable position of Villefranche after the 1659 "Treaty of the Pyrenees" established the new Franco-Spanish border close by. Although never attacked, the three separate levels of fortification formed an elaborate defense system that guarded Villefranche from every possible angle. More impressive still, the fort's entrance extends 1000 steps underground. (Open 9am-8pm. Admission 25F, children 10F.)

Although the **Syndicat d'Initiative,** place de l'Eglise (tel. 68-96-22-96), can help you find lodging, the friendly, knowledgeable staff at the **Association Culturelle,** 38, rue St-Jean (tel. 68-96-25-64), can answer more detailed questions on hiking and camping in the area. (Open 9am-noon and 2-7pm.) The association manages a **Point Accueil Jeunes,** a simple, unheated cabin where you can stay (with a sleeping bag) for 5F. The *mairie* (tel. 68-96-10-78) operates another small campground where you can stay for one or two nights. The association also organizes guided tours of the village, the eleventh-century church, and the towers. (Mon.-Fri., 20F.) Hotels in Villefranche fill quickly in summer. **Hôtel Le Terminus,** outside the village next to the train station (tel. 68-96-09-85), offers rooms for 80F. **Hôtel Le Canigou,** 90, rue St-Jean (tel. 68-96-12-19), provides adequate rooms for 75F. (Showers 10F. Breakfast 14F. Open July-Aug.) There are several *gîtes d'étape* in this region, but many require that you stay for a week. There is also farm housing available: Contact Famille Tublet, Mosset (tel. 68-05-00-37) for details.

From Villefranche, you can catch the charming, open-air *petit train jaune* through the Pyrenees all the way to **La Tour-de-Carol** (2½ hr., 69F), where trains connect to Toulouse and Barcelona. Six trains daily make the climb through the mountains, stopping at small villages along the way. The spectacular views of plunging mountainsides and steep gorges are worth the somewhat nauseating train ride accompanied by the wild shrieks of children. The Association Culturelle distributes a pamphlet describing each town on the rail line. Most are too small to support any hotels.

Montpellier

Montpellier has already celebrated its first millennium but remains a youthful town, removed from the blasé sophistication of the Côte d'Azur. Its renowned universities attract 45,000 students each year, keeping the average age of the population under 35. This university town stands close enough to the beach to keep its students in a state of exquisite torture all through spring exams. During the summer, thousands of foreign students flock here to learn French painlessly at the university by the sea (4- to 6-week programs; write CERAVUM, 11, rue St-Louis, 34000 Montpellier). The newly restored areas of town and many of the old streets lined with eighteenth- and nineteenth-century mansions are pleasant places for strolling and window-shopping. However, the real attraction here is the city's vibrant rhythm, which reverberates in place de la Comédie and in the *vieille ville*'s myriad squares, cafes, and restaurants. Now that municipal dance and drama companies, as well as an orchestra, have been established, Montpellier has become a major cultural center.

Orientation and Practical Information

Trains run directly to Paris, Avignon, Nîmes, Marseille, Nice, and Perpignan. Place de la Comédie is the modern town center, a combination of slick office buildings, nineteenth-century hotels, and a large open space that comes alive at night with street musicians, dancers, and strolling entertainers. To get here from the station, follow rue Manguelone uphill (5 min.) or wait for city bus #16 (free), which makes a complete circuit of the city along bd. Victor Hugo and bd. du Jeu de Paume.

Bureau Municipal de Tourisme: Palais des Congrès (tel. 67-58-26-04), near place de la Comédie. Information on Montpellier and the Languedoc-Roussillon region. Knowledgeable, English-speaking staff. **Currency exchange** on weekends and when banks are closed. Guided tours of the city in French (1-2 per day, 18F, students 10F) and in English (1 per week, 22.50F). Open June 15-Sept. 15 Mon. 9am-noon and 2-7pm, Tues.-Sat. 9am-8pm, Sun. 10am-1pm; in off-season Mon.-Sat. 9am-6pm. Address may change in 1989.

Budget Travel: Atoll Voyages, 1, rue de l'Université (tel. 67-66-03-65). BIJ/Transalpino tickets. Information on hitching. Open Sept.-June Mon.-Fri. 8:30am-12:30pm and 1:30-6:45pm, Sat. 9:30am-12:30pm and 1:15-3:15pm; July-Aug. closed Sat. afternoon.

Post Office: Place Rondelet (tel. 67-92-48-00). **Currency exchange** and **telephones. Postal code:** 34000. Open Mon.-Fri. 8am-7pm, Sat. 8am-noon.

Train Station: Place Auguste Gilbert (tel. 67-58-50-50). A small tourist office and an exchange desk in the station. To Agde (hourly, 20 min., 38F), Avignon (hourly, 1 hr., 58F), Arles (8 per day, 1 hr., 46F), Carcassonne (16 per day, 2 hr., 83F), Marseille (8 per day, 2 hr. 10 min., 92F), Béziers (44F), Narbonne (hourly, 50 min., 54F), Nîmes (almost hourly, ½ hr., 36F), Nice (8 per day, 4½ hr., 187F), Sète (hourly, 1 hr., 20F), Toulouse (hourly, 3¼ hr., 123F), Perpignan (10 per day, 1 hr. 50 min., 86F), Toulon (8 per day, 3 hr., 122F), and Paris (9 per day, with change in Lyon, 5 hr., 355F plus 13F TGV reservation).

Bus Station: Gare Routière, rue Jules Ferry (tel. 67-92-01-43), next to the train station. Line #17 to Palavas (2-3 per hr., 7F), Aigues-Mortes (by coastal route daily, 1½ hr., 27F; by land and Camargue daily, 2 hr., 32F), Béziers (hourly, 1½ hr., 41.50F), Carnon (2 per hr. 20 min., 14F), Sète (10 per day, 1½ hr., 16.50F), Pézenas (15 per day, 1 hr., 38F), Nîmes (hourly, 1¾ hr., 50.50F), Alès (4 per day, 1¾ hr., 52F), Vailhauques (3 per day, 45 min., 5.50F), La Grande Motte (2 per hr., 45 min., 17.80F), Le Grou-du-Roi (hourly, 1 hr., 23F), Ganges (5 per day, 1½ hr., 34F), Le Vigan (3 per day, 2 hr., 44.50F), Rodez (2 per day,

4-5 hr., 103F), Millau (3 per day, 2½ hr., 65F), Lamalou-les-Bains (3 per day, 2 hr., 49F), and Gignac (8 per day, 35 min., 20F).

Taxis: Tel. 67-41-37-87.

Bike Rental: At the **train station.** The 12 bikes here are usually rented, but there are no other rentals in town.

Hitching: Allostop Provoya, 9, rue du Plan de l'Olivier (tel. 67-59-65-79). Matches riders with drivers. Annual membership 130F. Trips under 300km 30F; over 300km 60F. Open Mon.-Fri. 4:30-7:30pm, Sat. 10:30am-12:30pm. Call for information 10am-noon.

Laundromat: Le Lavoir, 30, rue de Candolle. Lively, cozy cafe-laundromat with bright decorations, comic strips on the walls, generous management, and good music. Wash 16F, dry 8F, soap 3F per 5kg. 38F if you want your wash done for you. Sit in the little cafeteria while waiting. Coffee 4F. Open Mon.-Fri. 8am-8pm, Sat.-Sun. 9am-7:30pm. **Laverie,** 36, rue du Faubourg du Courreau. Centrally located. Wash 20F per 7kg, dry 2F per 5 min., soap 2F. Open daily 7am-9pm.

Crisis Lines: SOS Amitié, Tel. 67-63-00-63. 24-hour crisis line. **SOS Femmes,** Tel. 67-66-12-80. Helps women in need. **Disabled Travelers:** To report problems, call the *mairie* at 67-34-71-77.

Hospital: St-Eloi, 2, av. Bertin Sans (tel. 67-63-90-50).

Medical Emergency: SAMU, Tel. 67-63-00-00.

Police: 22, av. Georges Clemenceau (tel. 67-58-07-07).

Police Emergency: Tel. 17.

Accommodations and Camping

You don't have to worry about finding a place to stay in Montpellier. In addition to the youth hostel and *foyer,* there are many one- or no-star hotels. During the summer festivals, find a hotel room in the morning, since they may all be full by afternoon.

Auberge de Jeunesse (IYHF), 2, impasse de la Petite Corraterie (tel. 67-79-61-66), a 15-min. walk northeast of the train station. Plain dormitory accommodations in big room. 45F per night. Sheets 11F. Obligatory breakfast included with IYHF card; without, 20F. Open 8am-noon and 6pm-1am.

Foyer des Jeunes Travailleuses, 3, rue de la Vieille (tel. 67-52-83-11), 10 min. from the train station past place de la Comédie and left off rue de la Loge. In a renovated fourteenth-century mansion with clean, modern facilities, including a TV room and washing machine. Accepts travelers of both sexes year-round. Friendly management. Singles 65F. Doubles and quads 50F per person. Breakfast included. Lunch (noon-1pm) and dinner (7-8pm) 32F. Lovely terrace dining above the street. Reception open daily until 8pm.

Hôtel Majestic, 4, rue du Cheval Blanc (tel. 67-66-26-85), off Grand' Rue, 3 blocks down rue des Etuves from the tourist office. Good location. May not be majestic, but clean. Singles 60F. Doubles 70F, with shower from 85F. Triple 100F. Showers 20F. Breakfast 15F. Arrive early July-Aug.

Hôtel Plantade, 10, rue Plantade (tel. 67-92-61-45). From the train station, bear left on av. de la République, which becomes bd. du Jeu de Paume. Turn left on rue du Faubourg du Courreau; it's the 1st right. Friendly English-speaking proprietor; interesting decor. Singles and doubles 80F, with shower 103F. Showers 12F. Breakfast 13.50F.

Hôtel Fauvettes, 8, rue Bonnard (tel. 67-63-17-60). The street runs by the Jardin des Plantes, and the hotel has its own garden. Basic singles 65F. Doubles 80F, with shower 100F. Breakfast 13F.

Nova Hôtel, 8, rue Richelieu (tel. 67-60-79-85), down the street from the Majestic. Rather stuffy and faded rooms. Singles 70-78F. Doubles 78-98F, with shower and toilet 148F. Showers 15F. Breakfast 16.50F; obligatory July-Aug.

Food

The **university restaurants** are open during the term from 11:30am to 1:30pm and 6:30 to 8pm. Check at **CROUS**, 2, rue Montreil, to see which are open in summer. You must show an ISIC to buy a meal ticket. University restaurants are **Arceaux**, rue Gustave; **Boutonnet**, rue Emile Duployé; **Triolet**, 1061, rue du Truel; and **Vert-Bois**, 209, rue de la Chênaie. Several *charcuteries* and food stores line Grand' Rue Jean Moulin. You'll find groceries and a department store in **Monoprix**, place de la Comédie. A morning **market** is held daily around the *préfecture*.

Pasta Factory, 10, rue St-Firmin (tel. 67-52-70-05). Bright, geometric, new-wave Italian decor. As much *franglais* slang in the menu as there is pasta. 34.50F lunch *menu* and 71F dinner *menu* with wine (tequila cocktail and after-dinner drink included). Loud music free also. Open daily noon-2:30pm and 7pm-midnight.

Taverne du Peyrou, 17, rue Terval (tel. 67-60-56-73). Refined, unlimited hors d'oeuvre bar with seafood specialties, but save room for the *moules farcies* (hearty sausage-stuffed mussels). 58F *menu*. Friendly, attentive owners. Open Mon.-Fri. noon-2:30pm and 7pm-midnight, Sat. 7pm-midnight.

Au Voilier Nommé Désir, 10, rue du College Duvergner (tel. 67-66-34-15), on place de la Chapelle Neuve. Beautiful, flowered balcony terrace popular in summer; inside seating is light and pleasant. Fish specialties. 59F *menu* is not served on terrace, but try the *brochette de poisson au citron* for 43F if you want to be outside. Open Mon.-Fri. noon-2pm and 7-10pm, Sat. 7-10pm. Reserve for dinner Fri.-Sat.

Le Petit Mickey, 15, rue du Petit St-Jean (tel. 67-60-60-41). Cheap and filling *menu* appreciated by locals. Open Mon.-Fri. 11:30am-2pm and 7:30-9:45pm, Sat. 11:30am-2pm.

Crêperie Tou Pourlou, 3, rue Ste-Anne, near the Cathédral Ste-Anne. Dark and warm, with kind owners. Open Thurs.-Tues 7:30pm-1am.

La Tomate, 6, rue Tour-des-Flammes (tel. 67-60-49-38). A cozy restaurant in the pedestrian quarter.

Le Viel Ecu, 1, rue des Ecole Laïques (tel. 67-66-39-44), on place de la Chapelle Neuve. Good food served in a sixteenth-century chapel or on the popular terrace. A favorite with locals. 85F *menu*. Open Mon. 7-11:30pm, Tues.-Sat. noon-2:30pm and 7-11:30pm.

Sights and Entertainment

Montpellier is best appreciated by a leisurely walking tour. Its expansive, renovated place de la Comédie is at the heart of the pedestrian district, and boutiques and interesting bookstores line the *vieille ville*'s cobbled streets. Often obscured in the medieval streets are *hôtels particuliers* from the seventeenth and eighteenth centuries. The *syndicat* can locate them for you on a map, but if you explore the large, arched doorways, you might discover beautiful interior courtyards on your own.

The upper part of town is also conducive to strolling. The seventeenth- and eighteenth-century **Promenade du Peyrou** links a large **Arc de Triomphe**, erected in 1691 to honor Louis XIV, to the lush and peaceful **Jardin des Plantes**, France's first botanical garden. It was designed in 1593 to allow the botany school to study medicinal herbs. Dating from 1839 (the original was destroyed in the Revolution), the monumental equestrian statue stands midway along the promenade leading toward **Château d'Eau**, the arched terminus of the exquisitely preserved aqueduct that supplied the city with water. Walk here in the evening, when the arch and pool are lit up.

The lower side of place la Comédie leads to the most recent architectural additions to the city: **Antigone** is an exceptional neo-classical housing complex designed by Catalonian architect Ricardo Boffil. The pride of Montpellier, these buildings were designed as low-cost housing for people of all income groups.

The airy, light **Musée Fabre**, 13, rue Montpelliéret, near the tree-lined esplanade, presents an important collection of works by Courbet, Géricault, and seventeenth-century Dutch and Flemish painters. The top floor exhibits contemporary and local art. (Open Tues.-Fri. 9am-noon and 2-5:30pm, Sat.-Sun. 9am-noon and 2-5pm. Admission 13F, Wed. free.) The **Collection Xavier-Atger,** at the Faculté de Médecine, rue de l'Ecole-de-Médecine, is housed in the library next to the cathedral. The collection contains drawings and preliminary sketches by several Renaissance and baroque masters, including Fragonard, Watteau, and Caravaggio. (Open Sept.-July Mon.-Fri. 10am-noon and 2-6:30pm, Sat. 10am-noon. Free.)

The **Théâtre Municipal,** place de la Comédie (tel. 67-66-31-11), mounts drama and concerts year-round; it also hosts a **dance festival** of international performances, workshops, and films from late June through early July. (Tickets 65-120F.) During the last two weeks of July, a **jazz festival** takes place at Château d'O, outside of Montpellier. Past performers include the Pat Metheny Group, Herbie Hancock, and Jeau-Luc Ponty. For more information, contact the Centre Culture du Caugnedoc, 20, rue Lakanal (tel. 67-79-65-51). Throughout the year, Café Doyen, 13, rue du Grand-St-Jean, presents folk music and theater (Mon.-Sat. at 9pm).

The **Centre Culturel Irlandais,** 10, rue du Berger, off des Ecoles Laïques, sponsors classical guitar concerts and real Irish singing, but actually doubles as a friendly, unpretentious bar with Guinness on tap.

During the summer, Montpellier's clubs and cafes are less active than during the academic year, when students make for a pulsating nightlife. The **Bar du Musée,** 1, rue Montpellerain, attracts a regular crowd of students with cheap beers (7F) and loud music. **Rockstore,** off place de la Comédie on rue Verdun, emulates the Hard Rock Cafe's decor with a red car coming out of the wall, Springsteen posters, pool tables, a big dance floor, and loud music. (Open until 4am.) **Les Deux Verseaux,** 3, rue Voltaire (tel. 67-60-66-40), is a bar and dance spot for gay men. (Open daily 7pm-2am.) The **Sax'aphone,** 24, rue Ernest Michel (tel. 67-58-80-90), 1km south of the train station, plays Caribbean music from 11pm to 3am.

Near Montpellier

West of Montpellier lies **Cap d'Agde,** with long, busy beaches bordered by pine groves and condominiums. Take the frequent trains (½ hr., 32F) to the town of Agde, then catch the shuttle bus to Cap d'Agde, 7km away. Try to get off a little past the Cap d'Agde town center. At the last stop is a nude beach (*plage naturiste*). The cathedral in Agde, with its crenellated roof, resembles a castle from a distance. Buses also leave Montpellier regularly for both towns. Northwest of Montpellier, the spectacular **Gorges de l'Herault** stretch for 50km along the Herault River, running parallel to D4 and close to **St-Guilhem-le-Desert** and its interesting ruins of an abbey, castles, and fortifications.

Narbonne

Although its history extends back to the Roman era, Narbonne encourages more contemporary activities. Narbonne offers the visitor Roman and religious monuments, while new beach developments at **Narbonne-plage** and **Gruisson-plage,** less than 12km away, attract hordes of tourists every year.

The city's main attractions are clustered together in the *vieille ville*. The **Cathédrale St-Just et St-Pasteur,** an imposing Gothic structure, surprised its builders by turning out only half as large as it was supposed to be. It is the fourth-tallest cathedral in the south of France; however, had it been completed to original measurements, it would have been the largest in France. Construction began in 1272 but stopped in 1340 due to a long, bitter zoning dispute between town authorities and the archbishops; the church, surprisingly, lost out. During this time, Narbonne served as an important religious center in the south as the archbishopric for all of Lanquedoc.

The opulent **Palais des Archevêques,** next to the cathedral, testifies to the wealth and power of the former archbishops of Narbonne. Inside, the **Musée Archéologique** displays prehistoric and Gallo-Roman artifacts. Across the courtyard, the **Musée d'Art et d'Histoire** is housed in the old apartments of the archbishops.

The collection includes seventeenth-century paintings from the French and Flemish schools. **L'Horreum,** an uncovered Roman grain warehouse, now stores some Roman sculpture. Try not to get lost in the maze of dark caves. The **Maison Vigneronne** is a seventeenth-century powderhouse restored to explain wine-production, with displays of maps, photographs, and traditional tools. The church of **Notre-Dame de LaMourguier** has a lapidary museum with Roman stones, in-scriptions, sculptures, and sarcophagi found in the area. (All museums open July-Sept. 15 daily 10-11:50am and 2-6pm; Sept.-May 10-11:50am and 2-5:15pm. Global ticket 5F, students 2.50F.)

Take time to walk around the old neighborhoods on your own, or take the city's walking tour, which leaves from the town hall in the *palais* (July-Sept. 15 Mon.-Sat. at 10am and 4pm; 10F, less for students).

In Narbonne, try to stay at the **Foyer des Jeunes Travailleurs "Le Capitole,"** 45, av. de Provence (tel. 68-32-07-15). Large and clean, it contains luxurious rooms and private bathrooms. (Singles 69F. Doubles 115F. Quads 48F. Key deposit 50F or ID. Breakfast included. Meals 33.50F, served Mon.-Fri. noon-1pm and 7:15-8pm. Open daily.) **Hotel de la Gare,** 7, av. Pierre Sémard (tel. 68-32-10-54), has large, clean rooms from 90F (quads with W.C. and shower 140F). The owner will tell you the hotel is full if you show up with a backpack, so leave it in a locker at the *gare.* (Large breakfast 17F.) Managed by its generous owner, **Hôtel le Novelty,** 33, av. des Pyrénées (tel. 68-42-24-28), offers affordable rooms and a filling 49F *menu.* Both the restaurant and hotel are popular with truck drivers. (Singles and doubles 80F. Triples 110F. Quads 145F, with shower 170F.) **Chez Feliz,** 20, bd. Général de Gaulle (tel. 68-32-10-67), has simple cabin-like rooms and a brisk owner. (Singles 60F. Doubles 70F. 30% extra per additional person. Breakfast 13F.) The restaurant serves a family-style 48F *menu.* (Open daily noon-2pm and 7:30-9pm.) There are also several campgrounds in the Narbonne area. Those on the coast are usually full and always crowded. Try **Camping le Languedoc** (tel. 68-65-24-65), 1km southeast.

L'Escargot, 9, rue Corneille (tel. 68-32-14-70), on a small street off rue de l'Ancien Courrier near Monoprix, is the best bet for well-priced, hearty food. (41F *menu* with unlimited hors d'oeuvre bar. ¼ liter of wine 3.50F. Open Tues.-Sat. noon-2pm and 7-9pm, Sun. noon-2pm.) **La Paillote,** passage de l'Ancien Courrier (tel. 68-32-25-21), has a pleasant outdoor terrace for afternoon snacks or a more expensive meal. (69F *menu.* Open Mon.-Sat. noon-11pm.) A covered **market** occurs every morning at Les Halles. An open **market** takes place all day Thursday on quai Victor Hugo.

Narbonne's **Syndicat d'Initiative,** place Salengro (tel. 68-65-17-52), is a 10-minute walk from the train station. Turn right onto bd. Frédéric Mistral, then left onto rue Chennebier (after 5-10 min.), which leads directly into place Salengro—the *syndicat* will be on your left. The staff exchanges currency and offers information on beaches, campsites, hotels, and restaurants. (Open June 16-Sept. 14 daily 8am-7pm; Sept. 15-June 15 Mon.-Sat. 8:30am-noon and 2-6pm.) The **post office,** 25, rue Gambetta, has **telephones** and a **currency exchange.** (Open Mon.-Fri. 8am-7pm, Sat. 8am-noon.) The train station lies close to the main sights and the downtown area. **Trains** go to Perpignan (14 per day, ¾ hr., 39F), Toulouse (13 per day, 1½ hr., 81F), Béziers (12 per day, 15 min., 20F), Nîmes (12 per day, 1 hr. 20 min., 73F), and Montpellier (12 per day, 55 min., 56F). In addition to bus service to the beaches, the *gare routière* also sends **buses** to Béziers, La Nouvelle, Perpignan, and Carcassonne.

Beaches near Narbonne

Gruisson is an old Roman fishing village that has expanded into a modern vaca-tion spot complete with restaurants, cafes, a disco, and nightlife. Jean-Jacques Beineix's film *37°2 le matin* (*Betty Blue*) was filmed here. Take the bus directly to the beach (5 per day, 40 min., last departure 6:05pm, 15.80F). There's an **informa-tion office** in the new port on bd. Pech Maynand (tel. 68-49-09-00). Hotels in Gruisson are expensive, but the **Motel de la Clape,** residence Barberousse (tel. 68-49-02-30), in the new port, occasionally has a free studio that can be affordable if shared by several people. Campers have more options: The **Camping Municipal** (tel. 68-49-07-22 or at the mairie 68-49-01-02) is a two-star site 1km from the beach with 600 sites. (Open June 15-Sept. 15.) **Presqu'iles II** (tel. 68-49-08-49),Gruisson's **bike rental** service, doubles as a laundromat.

Ten kilometers north of Gruisson, Narbonne-plage has three campsites: the two-star **Camping Côte des Roses** (tel. 68-49-83-65), with a food store; the three-star **Camping Soleil d'Oc** (tel. 68-49-83-65), with sports facilities and a snack store; and the four-star **Camping la Falaise** (tel. 68-49-80-77), with restaurant and store. Buses leave from quai Victor Hugo in Narbonne for the town beach (8 per day, 20 min., 15F).

Béziers

Despite the crowds of tanning tourists, the *Biterois* have preserved their own identity over their 2000-year history. Once a liberal religious center, Béziers stood solid when Pope Innocent III tried to purge it of Protestant *cathars* (heretics) in 1209. The entire population was slaughtered, and the buildings were burned. Not until wine production revitalized the local economy did the town begin to rebuild itself. Today this city of 90,000 is the world's largest producer of wine, albeit mostly table wine.

Any of the nearby *caves cooperatives,* central outlets for local wines, or private *vignobles* (vineyards) will give you a tour and let you taste the St. Chignon, Bourlou, and St-Saturnin wines. The **Syndicat d'Initiative,** 27, rue du 4 Septembre (tel. 67-49-24-19), distributes a pamphlet of suggested routes for visiting the producers, as well as information on area beaches. (Open July-Aug. Mon.-Sat. 9am-7pm, Sun. 10am-noon; Sept.-June Mon.-Fri. 9am-noon and 2-6pm, Sat. 9am-noon and 3-6pm.) Pleasure boats are now the main traffic on the **Canal du Midi,** and you can see them patiently maneuvering a series of nine locks (*écluses*), at the foot of the city. The **Cathédrale St-Nazaire,** a Roman church built on the ruins of a pagan temple, was destroyed with the rest of the city in 1209, and rebuilt and enlarged until the fourteenth century. The functional fortified towers at the top of the cathedral are characteristic architectural features of the region. Climb to the top for a view of the surrounding mountains and sea. The **Fabrégat des Beaux Arts,** place de la Révolution, and its annex, **Hôtel Fayet,** 9, rue des Capuces, house a medium-sized collection of nineteenth-century paintings, including works by Dufy, Soutine, Delacroix, and Corot. (Open Tues.-Sat. 9am-noon and 2-6pm, Sun. 2-6pm. Free.) Béziers's public garden, **Plateau des Poètes,** in front of the train station, is a delightful spot for picnicking or for escaping the sweltering sun (open 7am-10pm).

Béziers's favorite spectator sports include rugby (the city's famous team has won 10 world championships). The important **feria** at the end of August features dancing, parades, and *corridas de torros* (bullfights). A less frenetic festival at the end of July features classical music in the city's church (tickets 60F; sold at the *syndicat*).

Béziers has no youth hostel but a handful of inexpensive, simple hotels. **Hôtel Métropole,** 16, rue des Balances (tel. 67-28-45-50), offers incredibly cheap rooms in the center of the *vieille ville.* The young owners are attentive. From allée Paul Riquet, take rue 4 Septembre—the hotel is on the second small street on your left. (Singles 40-50F. Doubles 37-55F. Quads 75-108. Showers 10F.) **Hôtel Angleterre,** 22, place Jean Jaurès (tel. 67-28-48-42), has quiet simple rooms in the center. (Singles 70F. Doubles 85F, with shower 140F. Quads with shower 220F. Showers 15F.) **La Dorade,** 10, rue André Nougaret (tel. 67-28-83-11), off place du Général de Gaulle, is run by a kind Spanish mother and daughter. Rooms are clean and affordable. (Doubles 55F, with shower 60F. Quads 90F, with shower 115F. Breakfast 15F.) The restaurant downstairs serves 45F and 60F *menus.* Up the street from the train station, the **Hôtel de Paris,** 70, av. Gambetta (tel. 67-28-43-80) has crisp, clean-smelling rooms. (Doubles 70-95F, with shower and W.C. 140F. Extra bed 25F. Quads 125F. Showers 15F. Breakfast 17F.)

A bright, neoclassical Greek restaurant, **Le Uy konos,** 5, rue Bagatelle (tel. 67-28-28-38), near the top of Plateau des Poèts, serves a delicious 55F house-sampler *assiete,* which includes mild cheese purées and fish mousse with egg. Or try their 80F *menu. A la carte,* moussaka is 40F, baklava 20F. (Open Mon.-Sat. 7:30pm-midnight.) On rue Viennet down from the cathedral, **Le Thé Retrouvé** serves tea and light meals. (Open Tues.-Sat. noon-7pm.)

The **gare routière,** place Jean Jaurès (tel. 67-28-23-85), does not operate service to local beaches, but does serve Narbonne (5 per day, last bus 7:05pm, 40 min., 21.50F), Pezenas (10 per day, last bus 6:50pm, 40 min., 18F), and Montpellier (15 per day, 1 hr. 35 min., 40F). Frequent **trains** connect Béziers to Narbonne and Montpellier.

Beaches near Béziers

City buses (tel. 67-28-36-41) leave place du Général de Gaulle for **Valras** beach (11 per day, last return 8pm, round-trip 19F). Valras was a fishing village that developed into an all-purpose family entertainment beach resort complete with waterslide and ferris wheel. In the evening, you can join a game of *boules* or enjoy seafood caught by the returning fishing boats. Five kilometers away, **Serignan** beach is calm and wide (accessible by bus from Béziers).

Nîmes

Nîmes, like Rome, was built with Roman labor on seven hills; 2000 years later it still competes with Arles for the title *la Rome française.* Visible throughout the city, an emblematic, enchained crocodile commemorates Emperor Augustus's victory over Anthony and Cleopatra in Egypt. Arriving in France, Augustus made the pathetic figure a symbol of Egypt's demise and gave Nîmes to his troops as a Rome away from Rome. In addition to the well-preserved *arènes* (Roman arena), where summer bullfights and a prestigious jazz festival take place, Nîmes also possesses an elegantly articulated Roman temple and the Maison Carrée.

Despite its rather unclean facade, the city is acquiring a slick, prestigious image, due mainly to the efforts of right-wing mayor Jean Bousquet. Bousquet has planned a new center of contemporary art and media, **Mediathèque.** Similar in function to Paris's active Georges Pompidou Center, this is scheduled to open in 1989.

Orientation and Practical Information

The arena marks the center of the city. Most of the interesting sights lie within the area bordered by bd. Victor Hugo, bd. de la Libération, and bd. Admiral Courbet. The first two fan out from the arena. To get to the tourist office from the train station, go up av. Feuchères, veer left around the small park, and go around the arena; then continue straight onto bd. Victor Hugo—the tourist office is 5 blocks down, up the street from the Maison Carrée.

Office de Tourisme: 6, rue Auguste (tel. 66-67-29-11; recorded announcement in French 66-67-86-86). Free accommodations service. Information on bus and train excursions to pont du Gard, the Camargue, and nearby towns. Guided tours of the city July-Aug. daily (in English at 9am, 42F). Exhaustive festival information. **Currency exchange** on weekends and after 5pm. Open July-Aug. Mon.-Sat. 9am-7pm, Sun. 10am-3pm; Sept.-June Mon.-Sat. 9am-7pm, Sun. 10am-noon.

Comité Départemental du Tourisme du Gard: 3, place des Arènes (tel. 66-21-02-51 or 66-21-08-11). Visit this place before wandering beyond Nîmes. Information on sights and festivities in the region. Open Mon.-Fri. 8am-7:30pm, Sat. 9am-1pm.

Post Office: Bd. de Bruxelles, near place de la Libération at the end of av. Feuchères. **Telephones** and **currency exchange. Branch office,** bd. Gambetta. **Postal code:** 30000. Open Mon.-Fri. 8am-7pm, Sat. 8am-noon.

Train Station: Av. Feuchères (tel. 66-23-50-50). Nîmes is on the major line between Bordeaux and Marseille. Direct service to Toulouse (16 per day, 2 hr. 50 min., 142F), St-Raphäel (137F), Sète (hourly, 1 hr., 45F), Arles (29F), Montpellier (1 or 2 per hr., ½ hr., 34F), Paris (6 per day, 4½ hr., 329F plus obligatory 13F TGV reservation), Orange (6 per day, 1¾ hr., 45F), and Marseille (67F). Trains and SNCF buses (railpasses valid) for Aigues-Mortes (6 per day, 50 min., 50F) and the beaches at Le Grau du Roi (1 hr., 31F). Also bike rental (see below).

Bus Station: Rue Ste-Félicité (te. 66-29-54-00), behind the train station (tel. 66-29-54-00). Frequent buses to Alès, Aigues-Mortes, and other regional towns. Friendly, professional staff. Open Mon.-Fri. 8:30am-noon and 2-6:30pm. Société des Transports Départementaux du Gard (STDG), Tel. 66-29-27-29 or 66-84-96-86. To Vers (3 per day, 50 min., 23.50F), Uzès (8 per day, 55 min., 23.50F), Pont St-Esprit (4 per day, 1¼ hr., 52.50F), Pont-du-Gard (8 per day, ½ hr., 22.50F), Avignon (7 per day, 1¼ hr., 31F). Les Courriers du Midi, Tel. 66-29-52-00. To Montpellier (hourly, 1½ hr., 35F). SNCF Buses to Aigues-Mortes (6 per day, 55 min., 28F), Le Grau du Roi (6 per day, 1 hr. 5 min., 31F), and La Grande Motte (5 per day, 1¼ hr., 34.50F). Les Rapides de Camargue to St-Gilles (4 per day, 35 min., 13.80F). City buses: Transports Commun Nîmes, Tel. 66-38-15-40. Tickets 4.70F, *carnet* of 5 15.70F.

Bike Rental: At the train station (tel. 66-29-72-41). 15 bikes, often all rented. 35F per ½-day, 47F per day, 330F per week. Deposit 300F.

Bookstore: Librairie Anglaise, 8, rue Dorée (tel. 66-21-17-04). A collection of English-language books.

Laundromats: 4, place de la Cathédrale. Also at 47, rue de la République, near the *arènes*.

Droits de la Femme, 1, rue Raymond Marc (tel. 66-67-70-21, ext. (*poste*) 1746 and 1743), in the *préfecture*.

24-Hour Doctor and Pharmacy: Tel. 66-67-96-91. The commissariat has a list.

Medical Emergency: Tel. 66-21-60-01. SAMU, Tel. 66-67-00-00.

Police: Tel. 66-67-96-91.

Police Emergency: Tel. 17.

Accommodations and Camping

You should be able to find a fairly inexpensive room in Nîmes if you arrive early in the day. Many hotels cluster around the arena, and others off bd. Admiral Courbet.

Auberge de Jeunesse (IYHF), chemin de l'Auberge de Jeunesse, a continuation of chemin de la Cigale (tel. 66-23-25-04), 3½km from the station. Take bus #6 (last at 7:45pm, 4.70F) from the train station to the Cigale stop, then walk 500m uphill. To walk, go past the *jardin*, take route d'Alès, and follow the signs. 78 beds and camping space available. Friendly informal hostel in a peaceful setting with a well-equipped kitchen. Beds 45F. Sheets 11F. Breakfast included. Snack bar (dinner 32F) open 6am-11pm. No curfew.

Hôtel de France, 4, bd. des Arènes (tel. 66-67-47-72), in front of the arena. Courteous proprietor. Oddly shaped singles 70F, with shower 75F. More conventional doubles 92F, with shower 110-120F. Triples and quads with shower 140-180F. Breakfast 15F.

Hôtel Majestic, 10, rue Pradier (tel. 66-29-24-14), off av. Feuchères near the train station. 2-star hotel with big, simple rooms and fresh-smelling sheets. Singles and doubles 100F, with shower 120F. Breakfast 18F.

Nouvel Hôtel, 6, bd. Amiral Courbet (tel. 66-67-62-48). Centrally located with warm, English-speaking owners. Doubles 85F, with shower 135F. Triples and quads with shower 190F. Breakfast 18F.

Le Lisita, 2, bd. des Arènes (tel. 66-67-62-48). 2-star hotel. Redecorated rooms. Singles 85F, with shower 100F. Doubles with shower 150-180F. Breakfast 18F.

La Couronne, 4, square de la Couronne (tel. 66-67-51-73). Clean, basic singles 85F. Doubles 110F, with shower 135F. Triples and quads 165-182F. Showers 10F. Breakfast 14F.

Camping: Domaine de La Bastide, route de Générac (tel. 66-38-09-21), about 4½km from the train station. In summer, take bus #4 from bd. Gambetta or av. Feuchères, near the train station (about every 45 min.; last bus Mon.-Fri. at 7:28pm, Sat. at 7:13pm; 5F). A 3-star site with a cafeteria and a summer food store. 42-50F per 2 people and tent.

Food

Specialties include *brandade de Morue* (a delicious puree of codfish with olive oil and spices) and *herbes de Provence* (a mixture of herbs and olive oil used on *canapés* as hors d'oeuvres). For dessert, try a *croquant villaret* (a dry almond cookie) or a *caladon* (a cookie with almonds and honey). In the summer the gardens are the perfect place for a picnic. Buy your fruits and vegetables in the **market** in the Halles, rue Général Perrier, near the Maison Carrée (open Mon.-Sat. 8am-1pm); in the **Prisunic** off bd. de la Libération; or in the open-air **market** (Mon. morning) along bd. Gambetta.

Les Persiennes, 5, place de l'Oratoire (tel. 66-67-80-22). Refined food, an excellent unlimited hors d'oeuvre bar, and attentive service. 61F *menu* has interesting choices (wine included). Open Sept.-July Tues.-Sat. noon-2pm and 8-10pm.

L'Oeuf à la Côte, 29, rue de la Madeleine (tel. 66-21-88-55), in the *vieille ville*. High ceilings and clean, white stone walls. Terrace seating also. 42F *plat du jour* with entree. *Salon de thé* between meals. Open daily noon-midnight.

Les Hirondelles, 13, rue Bigot (tel. 66-21-38-69), at rue Porte de France. A lunchtime restaurant with a local crowd and a 45F *menu,* wine included. Open Mon.-Sat. noon-3pm.

Pizzeria Cerutti, 25, rue de l'Horloge (tel. 66-67-64-69), behind the Maison Carrée. Pizza and pasta 38F. For night-owls. Open daily noon-2pm and 7pm-1am.

Les Centurons, 5, rue Porte de France (tel. 66-76-29-39). A working-class restaurant with a boisterous clientele and a 40F *menu.* Open Mon.-Sat. 11:30am-2pm.

Sights

Most of the Roman monuments in Nîmes are concentrated in two areas—near the *arènes* and near the *jardins*—these are within easy walking distance of each other. Admission to all the monuments is covered by a 23F global ticket (students 13F).

Start your visit in the **Jardins de la Fontaine.** (Take bd. Victor Hugo from the *arènes,* and turn left along the canals.) Climb **Tour Magne,** one of the towers on the Roman city walls, built by Augustus in 15 B.C.E. (Open July-Aug. daily 9am-7pm; April-June and Sept. 9am-noon and 2-7pm; Oct.-March 9am-noon and 2-5pm.) From the top, you can see at least five churches in different parts of the city; of these, the most interesting is **Cathédrale St-Castor,** with a spacious but short Romanesque nave and an elaborate, sculpted facade depicting scenes from the Old Testament. When you descend from the tower, inspect the ruins of the Roman **Temple of Diana,** uncovered during the construction of the garden in 1745. Maréschal, a military engineer who designed the gardens, was criticized by contemporaries who thought his masterpiece looked more like a soldiers' parade ground than an ornament for the city. Nonetheless, the park makes a quiet retreat from the town, especially on summer evenings when the ponds are illuminated. (Park open July-Aug. 7am-11pm; April-June and Sept. 8am-9pm; Nov.-March 8am-7pm.)

The **Amphithéâtre Romain** is Nîmes's most famous Roman monument. Smaller than the one in Arles, it is preserved in frayed but magnificent entirety. During the summer, the jazz festival is held here, as are bullfights. (Open 8am-8pm.) Nîmes's **Maison Carrée** (Square House) is unique in its proportions—actually rectangular, its length (26.5m) is almost exactly twice its width (13.5m). Built in the first century B.C.E., it was dedicated to the grandsons of the Emperor Augustus. The Greek-style portico of this Roman temple is accented by fluted Corinthian columns and exquisite decorations. Closed for restoration in 1988, **Musée des Antiquités,** inside, displays statues of Venus of Nîmes and of Apollo with a quiver full of arrows, as well as several superb Roman mosaics. (Open July-Aug. 9am-6pm; Sept.-June 9am-noon and 2-5pm. Admission 12F, students 7F.)

Currently under renovation, the **Museée des Beaux Arts,** rue Cité Foulc, will exhibit shows of international contemporary art until the new art center is built. Its permanent collection includes ancient art. (Open daily 10am-7pm.) The **Galerie des Arènes,** next to the arena, also displays contemporary art. The **Musée du Vieux Nîmes,** Palais de l'Ancien Evêché, place aux Herbes, displays regional, popular arts including seventeenth- and eighteenth-century furniture, textiles, and ceramics. (Open in summer Mon.-Sat. 9am-noon and 2-6pm; in off-season Mon. and Wed.-Sat. only.)

Only ancient history buffs will want to see the **Castellum,** the brief and unremarkable remains of the Roman plumbing system that distributed water from the Eure to different parts of the city. The only relic of this kind in the world, the basin has 10 small holes that were used to divert water into five different canals leading to every quarter of the village.

Entertainment

In the second week of July, the arena resounds with the sounds of the **International Jazz Festival.** The event regularly features stars such as Miles Davis, Dizzy Gillespie, Sarah Vaughan, and B.B. King. Tickets cost 120-140F, and reservations can be made through the *règle des arènes* (tel. 66-67-28-02) or through Jazz Club, 21, rue Porte de France, 30000 Nîmes (tel. 66-21-34-02; open Mon.-Fri. 3-7pm, Sat. 4:30-6:30pm). Before the start of the jazz festival, the arena stage is used for one major opera production (tickets in the stands 60F) and usually a large rock concert (tickets 150F). In the first half of July, various concerts fill the city, including some at the Temple of Diana (seats from 50F, tickets at door). For a complete listing of summer events, ask at the *syndicat* for the leaflet *Rendez-vous à Nîmes.*

Nîmes is the home of France's major school of **bullfighting,** l'Ecole Française de Tauromachie. The most important bullfights are held at the end of May or the beginning of June (tickets from 50F), but some occur in the last week of September. "Courses Camarguaises" offers more humane entertainment; the aim of the fighters is to strip the bull of the decoration on his horns and forehead, rather than to kill him.

Café-Théâtre le Titoit de Titus, 6, rue Titus (tel. 66-67-64-73), off the canal, sponsors innovative drama, comedy, and concerts throughout the year. **Musique en stock,** 28, rue Jean Reboul (tel. 66-21-73-73), is another good place for live music. The excellent cinema **Le Sémaphore,** 25a, rue Porte de France (tel. 66-67-88-04), 1 block over from bd. Victor Hugo, mounts a great summer film festival during July and August. They also host occasional concerts and lectures by filmmakers.

Near Nîmes

Twenty kilometers towards Avignon, the **Pont du Gard** reaches across the Gardon Valley. A wonder of engineering and aesthetics, this mortarless Roman aqueduct was built 2000 years ago to bring water from the Eure into the Nîmes's Castellum. In the nineteenth century, Napoleon tried to restore the grandeur of the past empire by repairing the monument. Three levels of graceful arches support the water canal, enclosed except for periodic breaks that allow for ventilation and maintenance. You can walk across the narrow top of the aqueduct—an exhilarating experience since no guardrails separate you from the rock-filled river 50m below. **Buses** from Nîmes's bus station leave frequently for the Pont du Gard (Mon.-Sat. 8 per day, 4 Sun.; 40 min.; 22.50F). You can also come by bus from Avignon (6 per day, 23.50F) or from Uzès (6 per day, 23.50F).

Leave yourself a few hours to hike the rocky hills around the aqueduct, to soak up sun on the rocks lining the Gardon, and even to take a swim in the clear, sand-bottomed river. You can rent canoes and kayaks by the hour (45F and 30F) from **Kayak Vert** (tel. 66-22-84-83), on the rocky beach in front of the *syndicat.* The **syndicat** (tel. 66-37-00-02) is on the left after crossing the bridge from the Hôtel de Vieux Moulin. The staff exchanges **currency** (in summer daily 9am-7pm) and provides information on the four campgrounds nearby, including the least expensive, two-star **Camping International** (tel. 66-22-81-81), with restaurant (open March-Oct. 15; 40F for 2 people).

On the same bus line as the Pont du Gard is the town of Uzès, which former resident André Gide recalled in his poems. Standing formidably in the center of town, the **Duché d'Uzès** has been inhabited for 1000 years by the royal family of the Crussol d'Uzès. The family is at home when the flag flies from the castle tower. Inside the *duché,* there are paintings, tapestries, Louis XIII and Louis XIV furniture, and a fourteenth-century Gothic chapel. (Open Tues.-Sun. 9:30am-noon and 2:30-6pm. Admission 30F.)

Uzès is a relaxed town, ideal for idle walks. Pass by the **Tour Fenestrelle,** a six-story bell tower unique in France, but very common in northern Italy. Cylindrical, it looks like the tower of Pisa without the lean. **Place aux Herbes,** at the center of the *vieille ville,* next to the castle, is the site of a lively **market** on Saturdays. If you can come for the summer **feria,** or **fête votive** (patron saint's day), usually at the beginning of August, you will be greeted by bulls running through the streets and free-flowing pastis. The town is one of few allowed to serve the strong alcoholic drink during its festivals. A high-quality international music festival, the **Nuits Musicales d'Uzès,** takes place the second half of July. Tickets (from 70F-140F) are available from the **Syndicat d'Initiative,** av. de la Libération (tel. 66-22-68-88). The friendly office distributes information on transportation and the region, changes money, and can help with lodging. It can also provide you with a list of nearby farms for camping. (Open Mon.-Fri. 9am-6pm, Sat. 9am-noon and 3-5pm.) **La Taverne,** 4, rue Sigalon (tel. 66-22-13-10), has doubles for 85F (showers included). Breakfast is 19F. If the hotel is locked, try knocking at #1 across the street. The restaurant downstairs posts a delicious 50F *menu.* **Camping Municipal Vallée de l'Eure** (tel. 66-22-11-79) offers sites not far from Uzès. (19.40F per person includes tent. Open June-Sept.) Uzès can easily be reached by bus from Nîmes (Mon.-Sat. 7 per day, 4 Sun.; 55 min.; 28.50F) or from Avignon (3 per day, 1 hr., 28.50F).

To get away from it all, head for the unspoiled, spectacular territory north of Nîmes. In the **Gorges de l'Ardèche,** between Vallon Pont d'Arc and Pont-St-Esprit, the sparkling Ardèche River winds between precipitous white cliffs and buttes. The spectacular, rugged canyon is sparsely forested with scrub pine. For challenging driving, follow the *route touristique* (D290), which twists above the cliffs along the northern bank, with views (and space to park) at every turn. Whether you hike or drive, stop to admire the panorama at the **Belvédères du Serre de Tourre,** almost directly above the river near a ruined castle. Canoeing and kayaking are the most exciting means of taking in the rocky scenery. The **Grotte de la Madeleine** also lies on the *route touristique,* and is considerably less tourist-thronged than the Aven d'Orgnac. (Open April-Sept. 9:30am-noon and 2-6:30pm, by tour only; July-Aug. tour also at 1pm. Admission 19.50F, students 15F.)

There is no bus service along the D290. However, buses run between Nîmes and Pont-St-Esprit (4 per day, 1½ hr., 51F). There are many **boat rental** agencies, with standardized prices of 120F for a one-person kayak, 200F for a two-person canoe, including life jackets and the return trip from Sauze to Vallon. Try **Ardèche Bateaux,** Camping la Rouvière, on the river at Vallon Pont d'Arc (tel. 75-37-00-44 or 75-88-00-61 in summer or tel. 75-37-12-97). For a one-day descent into the gorge, you must leave before 9am. You can also do a mini-descent of 6km. All boat trips start from the riverhead at Vallon Pont d'Arc; you'll be brought back by minibus or taxi. Mild rapids punctuate the Ardèche, and the water level varies.

The place to start any tour of the Gorges de l'Ardèche is **Vallon Pont d'Arc,** although the town itself is an ugly tourist trap. The town lies a few kilometers from the natural bridge that spans the gorge, and is accessible by bus from the town of Alès, which is well-connected by rail and bus to Nîmes and Avignon. The **Syndicat d'Initiative** (tel. 75-88-04-01) provides useful trail maps and other information. For boating trips from March to November, call **Jean-Louis Tourre,** Ferme de la Vallee du Tioure (tel. 75-88-02-95), on route des Gorges. (3-4 hr. on the river. Leaves 8am, downstream by 3pm, return by taxi. 1-4 people 600F, picnic included.) Campgrounds abound near Vallon; two sites are on the river at **Gaud** and **Gournier** (5F per night). **Camping Pont d'Arc** (tel. 75-37-00-64) is at the foot of the natural bridge, with a sand beach, restaurant, and canoe rentals. **Camping les Tunnels** (tel. 75-37-00-22) and **Mondial Camping** (tel. 75-37-00-44) are both near Vallon on route des Gorges.

While in the Ardèche Valley, visit the outstanding caverns of the **Aven d'Orgnac** (tel. 75-38-62-51). Its chambers are immense—the vault called the Grand Chaos reaches 50m. Try to ignore the guides' theatrical stunts, such as switching off the lights. (Open March-Nov. 9am-noon and 2-6pm. Admission 27F, students 23F, ages 6-14 17F.) Unfortunately, neither trains nor buses stop nearby.

Alès is an industrial town, with a unique **mining museum**, chemin de la cité Ste-Marie (tel. 66-30-45-15), in an old coal mine. Put on a hard hat, descend underground, and get a realistic impression of the job. (Open April-Sept. 9-11:30am and 2-6pm. Admission 20F.) The town makes an easy trip from Nîmes (12 trains per day, 45 min., 32F); you can also take the bus (6 per day, 1 hr., 28F). Situated immediately west of the **Parc National des Cévennes,** it makes a good base for forays into this region of close-packed mountains. *Sentiers de grandes randonnées* (hiking trails) lace the park. Grapes have grown on the hills of the Gard region since Roman times, and friendly winemakers will welcome you into their *caves*.

Alès's **Chambre de Commerce,** rue Michelieu (tel. 66-52-21-15), can give you information on the town and its surroundings and can help with student lodgings. (Open Mon.-Fri. 8am-noon and 1:30-5:30pm.) From July through September an **annex** operaties in the pavilion, place Gabriel Péri (tel. 66-52-32-15), in the center of the town. (Open Mon.-Sat. 9am-noon and 1:15-7pm, Sun. 10am-noon and 1-4pm.) The **Foyer Mixte de Jeunes Travailleurs,** 2, rue Jean-Baptiste Dumas (tel. 66-86-19-80), accepts travelers during the summer. **Hôtel de Flore,** 23, bd. Victor Hugo (tel. 66-30-09-84), has pleasant doubles for 70F (with shower 100F). **Camping Les Châtaigniers,** chemin des Sports (tel. 66-52-53-57), is right in town. (Open May-Sept.)

In the wild swamps of the Camarague, **Aigues-Mortes,** city of the "dead waters," broods in medieval invincibility, completely surrounded by ramparts built in the time of Louis IX (St-Louis), who launched his crusades from here. Although it was never attacked, the remarkable fortress **Tour de Constance** is equipped with the latest in medieval warfare. Its 6-meter-thick walls also prevented dozens of Huguenots from escaping (1692-1768). From the fortress begins the 1½-km walk along the town ramparts. (Open April-Sept. daily 9am-7pm; Oct.-March 10am-noon and 2-5pm. Entrance closes ½ hr. before closing time. Admission 22F, ages 18-24 and over 60 12F, ages 7-17 5F; Sept. 15-May 15 ages 7-18 free.) The **Office Municipal de Tourisme,** Cloître des Capucins, place St-Louis (tel. 66-53-73-00), has information on walking, cycling, and horseback-riding (50F per hr.) in the Camargue region. (Open 9am-8pm.) There is a **bike rental** at 8, bd. Gambetta (tel. 66-53-78-65), for 40F per ½-day, 60F per day. (Open Mon.-Sat. 9am-noon and 2-7pm.) The tourist office organizes tours of the salt beds and refinery near the town (July-Aug. 2 per week; 3½ hr.; 40F, children 20F). **Companie des Salins du Midi** produces 400,000 tons of salt per year—enough for all of France and large exports. The marshes also contain a **bird reserve.** Sporadic tours visit the **Chapelles des Pénitents,** two elaborate fifteenth-century chapels belonging to a religious order committed to social service. The name derives from their practice of self-punishment after sinning, such as walking barefoot around town dressed in cloak and hood. The private chapels are still used by the 20 members in Aigues-Mortes.

The city sponsors a festival of new and classical French theater and dance during the last week of July and the first week of August. (Tickets 68F and 85F, available at the tourist office.) During the **fête votive** the first two weeks of October, the town organizes harmless bullfighting games in makeshift arenas built for the occasion. More *courses Camarguaises* (bull games) are held from June through September (Wed. and Fri. at 9:30pm, 20F).

Aigues-Mortes is well served by bus from Nîmes (7 per day, 55 min., 27.50F) and Montpellier (2 per day). If you want to stay, check out the relatively inexpensive accommodations at **Hôtel l'Escale,** av. Tour de Constance (tel. 66-53-71-14), just outside the town walls. (Doubles with shower 100F. Triples 175F. Quads 180-220F. Breakfast 18F.) The restaurant serves large, family-style meals for 60F, wine included. **La Petite Camarque,** Quartier le Môle (tel. 66-53-84-77), offers camping in a luxurious four-star setting. (Open May-Sept.) A **market** is held Wednesday and Sunday mornings along the outer walls.

Provence: Rhône Valley

In this favored province of the Romans, the hills are colored with lavender, mimosa, and grapevines, and the air is redolent of the *herbes de provence*—thyme, rosemary, and sage. The enchanting qualities of the region inspired medieval troubadours in their fanciful verses of courtly love; later they inspired local artist Cézanne and attracted Picasso and Van Gogh, who spent years struggling to capture the too-blue light. The landscape varies enormously with undulating mountains in the east, haunting rock formations along the Delta, flat marshlands in the Camargue, and gentle hills and rocky cliffs in the Vaucluse.

The cities of Provence mix ancient splendor and ebullient entertainment. With their impressive Roman remains and cobblestoned grace, Orange and Arles recline near the Rhône as it flows toward the Mediterranean. Home to the medieval papacy for a brief period, Avignon still possesses the formidable white Palais des Papes, and today it hosts an arts festival that unites masses of people in celebration. Revel in the elegant style and nightlife of Aix-en-Provence, or relax in the Virgilian tranquility of Vaison-la-Romaine in the idyllic Vaucluse. If the crowds that descend upon Provence in search of its summer festivals press the limits of your toleration, the wildlife preserves of the Camargue marshes and the long beaches nearby provide respite, though Les Stes-Maries-de-la-Mer also overflows with French and German vacationers seeking Riviera waters at lower prices.

Life plays itself out gently along the shaded promenades, next to fountains, and in endless glasses of *pastis* at sidewalk cafes, just as Marcel Pagnol describes in his plays and novels. Remnants of Provençal customs and dress still appear, and nineteenth-century regional poet Frédéric Mistral has a large following here. The Provençal dialect that he tried to revive, however, is heard less and less.

In summer, even the smallest of Provence's hamlets comes alive, with music, dance, theater, or outdoor antique markets. For a fairly complete listing of the summer's events, ask for *Provence, terre des festivals '89,* a thick booklet available at most *syndicats.*

Ever since Julius Caesar exalted the Provençal wines in his *Commentaries,* this region has been exporting the sun-soaked nectar. Vintage wines include Châteauneuf-du-Pape, Gigondas, and Côtes-du-Rhône. In certain regions of Provence you can follow the *route de vin* and stop in at the local *caves* for samplings. The area's temperate climate yields a cornucopia of fruits and vegetables—dozens of types of olives, cherries, sweet figs, asparagus, garlic, and herbs. Eat the Cavaillon melons fresh before they grace the *haute cuisine* restaurants of Paris. Try *ratatouille* (a rich blend of eggplant, zucchini, and tomatoes); *bouillabaisse* (an often-expensive fish soup), served with toasted bread and *rouille* (a saffron-flavored mayonnaise); and *soupe au pistou* (soup made with *pistou,* the Provençal equivalent of the Italian *pesto,* a fragrant basil-garlic sauce). There's also *aïoli,* a mayonnaise-like sauce made from olive oil and garlic, and served with hors d'oeuvres, vegetables, and fish soup. Honey here is made from lavender and other flowers.

Provence is also a major transport center, with quick connections to Languedoc and the Côte d'Azur. Within Provence, rail and bus service to cities and most towns is excellent. Hitching is fine along the country roads but can present difficulties out of such cities as Aix and Avignon. To see the region properly, rent a car and take only the smallest roads or, even better, bike along them. Bicycle rentals are available at almost all train stations, as well as in many shops. Only a few kilometers from cities, even at the height of the season, you can be alone with the scent of lavender. During festivals, reserve hotel rooms or arrive early in the day. Also be prepared

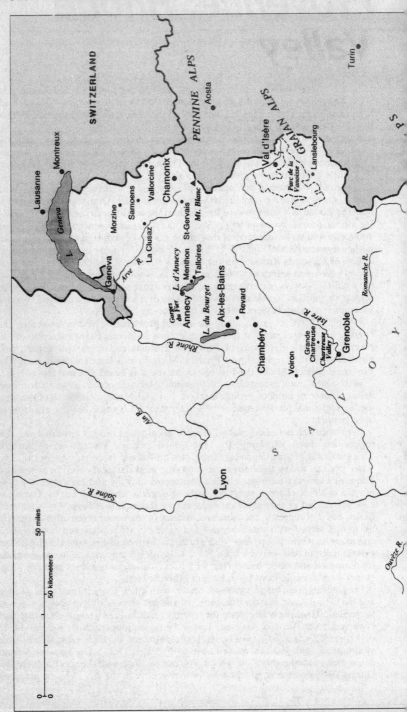

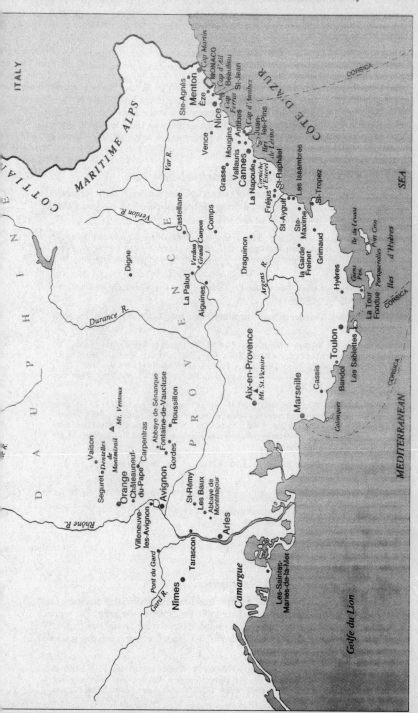

for higher prices, as restaurants often serve only one *menu,* or none at all during dinner hours.

Orange

Once the Roman town of Aurasio, Orange was built by Julius Caesar as a reward for his soldiers after they had conquered Gaul. The Roman homes, streets, arena, and city walls have disappeared, but the theater is still the town's centerpiece. In July, it is used to its best advantage when Orange puts on the Choregies, a prestigious opera and choral festival. Attending a performance in the theater is unforgettable.

Orientation and Practical Information

Avenue Frédéric Mistral, in front of the station, becomes rue de la République, the main drag leading more or less directly to the tourist office. As you walk this way, the Roman theater stands to the left.

Office de Tourisme: Cours Aristide Briand (tel. 90-34-70-88). Maps, a booklet listing hotels and restaurants, and **currency exchange** when banks are closed, including weekends. Hotel reservations 10F for 1-star hotels. Open June-Sept. Mon.-Sat. 9am-7pm, Sun. 9am-1pm; Oct.-May Mon.-Sat. 9am-5pm.

Currency Exchange: Banks (open Mon.-Fri.) line rue de la République. On weekends, the tourist office changes money.

Post Office: Bd. E. Daladier on cours Portoulles. **Postal code:** 84104. Open Mon.-Fri. 8am-7pm, Sat. 8am-noon.

Train Station: Av. Frédéric Mistral (tel. 90-34-17-82). Direct to Avignon (15 per day, 20 min., 21.50F), Arles (7 per day, 40 min., 40F), Marseille (9 per day, 80 min., 78F), Cannes (7 per day, 4 hr., 162F), Nice (7 per day, 4½ hr., 178F), Valence (12 per day, 1 hr., 55F), Lyon (12 per day, 2 hr., 104F), Dijon (11 per day, 3½-6 hr., 185F), and Paris (8 per day, 4½ hr., 304F plus 13F TGV reservation).

Bus Station: Cours Portoulles (tel. 90-34-15-59), in front of the post office. To Avignon (Mon.-Sat. 7am-6:45pm about every hr., 5 Sun.; ¾ hr.; one way 20F, round-trip 36F), Vaison-la-Romaine (Mon.-Fri. 4 per day, 3 Sat., 2 Sun.; 25F), Séguret (Mon.-Fri. 3 per day, Sat.-Sun. 2 per day; 20F), Carpentras (5 per day), and other regional towns. Office open Mon.-Fri. 10:30am-noon and 2-6:30pm.

Bike Rental: Hertz, 11, bd. Daladier (tel. 90-34-00-34). 3- and 10-speed bikes. 45F per day, deposit 400F.

Laundromat: Lavomatique, 5, rue St-Florent. Open daily 8am-8pm. Wash 12F, dry 2F per 10 min.

Hospital: Cours Portoulles (tel. 90-34-46-33).

Police: Place Clemenceau (tel. 90-51-77-95).

Police Emergency: Tel. 17.

Accommodations and Camping

On festival weekends in July and August, hotels are booked well in advance. During the week, however, you should be able to find inexpensive lodging. The region's **youth hostels** are located in Séguret (20km away; bus service from Orange, tel. 90-46-93-31) and Fontaine de Vaucluse (tel. 90-20-31-65). Campgrounds are scattered throughout the area.

Hôtel Freau, 3, rue Ancien-College (tel. 90-34-06-26), off place aux Herbes. In an old converted house. Kindly management and old, homey furniture. Likely to have rooms during the week. Doubles 75F, with shower 90F. Triple 125F. No hall shower. Breakfast 16F. Open Sept.-July.

Arc Hôtel, 8, place aux Herbes (tel. 90-34-09-23). Small and central, but usually booked during festival weekends. Single 75F. Doubles 85F, with shower 120F. Triple with shower 160F. Showers 10F. Breakfast 17F.

Hôtel St-Florent, 4, rue du Mazeau (tel. 90-34-18-53), near place aux Herbes. Cramped singles 70F. Doubles 90F, with shower 100F. Hall showers 10F. Breakfast 15F.

Hôtel le Français, 21, av. Frédéric Mistral (tel. 90-34-67-65), next to the train station. Well-kept, with proud owner. Doubles 100F, with shower 130F. Triples 160F, with shower 190F. Obligatory breakfast 20F.

Camping: St-Eutrope, colline St-Eutrope (tel. 90-34-09-22), up a steep hill. From cours Aristide Briand, walk up to montée Prince d'Orange and keep on climbing. 5F per person, 6F per tent. Open March 15-Oct. **Le Jonquier,** rue Alexis Carrel (tel. 90-34-19-83), in the other direction off RN7 to Lyon. 17F per person, ages under 7 6F, 20F per tent.

Food

Orange's many squares make outdoor eating enjoyable. In the cafes in place aux Herbes and place de la République, you can order a *pain bagna,* the traditional salad-filled sandwich of the Midi. Gather your supplies at the open **market,** place Clemenceau (Thurs. until noon).

Ma Cuisine, 4, rue du Renoyer (tel. 90-34-49-67), off place Clemenceau. 55F *menu* with outdoor seating. Friendly owners. Open Mon.-Sat. noon-2pm and 7-9:30pm.

Le Provençal, 27, rue de la République (tel. 90-34-01-89). Elegant atmosphere. Open Thurs.-Tues. noon-2pm and 7:30-9:30pm.

Arausio, 15, cours Aristide Briand (tel. 90-34-13-06). Outdoor eating. Avoid the expensive tourist menus, and ask for the 55F *menu du jour.* Open April-Sept. daily noon-2pm and 7-9:30pm; Oct.-March noon-2pm.

Au Goût du Jour, 9, place aux Herbes (tel. 90-34-10-80). A so-called "English" *salon de thé* with French pastries and quiches. Pleasant garden atmosphere. *Plat du jour* (wine and coffee included) 43F. Open 9am-10pm, but only tea and pastries are served between meal hours.

Le Yaca, rue de Tourre (tel. 90-34-70-03), next to the theater. Polished, calm atmosphere. Dishes include *brochettes* and *truite* (trout). Reservations necessary during the festival. Open Thurs.-Tues. noon-2pm and 7-10pm or later.

Sights and Entertainment

Orange's **Théâtre Antique** is the best-preserved in France. Its stage wall, the only one in Europe still intact, is the theater's main attraction. A few majestic columns and friezes hint at the facade's former splendor. A statue of the Emperor Augustus, discovered and reconstructed in 1931, presides over the entire scene from above the central royal doorway. (Open daily April-Sept. 9:30am-6:30pm; Oct.-March 10am-noon and 1:30-5pm. Admission 15F, students 12F.) The ticket to the theater also admits you to the **Musée Lapidaire** across the street, which houses an interesting collection of stonework unearthed from the theater site, and seventeenth- and eighteenth-century artwork from the region. (Open April-Sept. Mon.-Sat. 9am-6:30pm; Oct.-March Mon.-Sat. 9am-noon and 2-6:30pm.)

Orange's other Roman monument, the **Arc de Triomphe** stands on the ancient via Agrippa, which once connected Arles to Lyon. Take rue Victor Hugo to av. de l'Arc de Triomphe. The arch testifies to Roman vanity and power. Its well-preserved northern facade depicts Caesar's gory victory over the Gauls.

From mid-July to early August, the theater reassumes its ancient function as the setting for the **Choregies,** a series of celebrated opera and choral productions. In 1989, the program will feature three classical operas: Mozart's *La Flute enchantée* on July 9, Beethoven's *Fidelio* on July 22, and Verdi's *Nabucco* on August 5 and 8. Information is available from the Maison des Choregies, place Sylvain, 84100 Orange (tel. 90-34-15-52 or 90-34-24-24), across the street from the theater. (Open Mon.-Fri. 9am-noon and 1-6pm; after June 10 Mon.-Sat. 9am-noon and 1-6pm.) Tickets start at 145-290F for the entire series. You can often get an expensive ticket at a lower price by buying it from someone at the entrance on the evening of the performance.

The area around Orange swells with vineyards; for a view over the orange roof-tops of the city to the neighboring towns of the Vaucluse, climb to the top of St-Eutrope hill. This beautiful area between the Rhône and Durance Rivers abounds in fragrant fields of lavender and spices, and small villages sit perched among the rocky hills. Scattered throughout the region, *caves* produce red and rosé Côtes du Rhône wines.

Vaison-la-Romaine

Tucked away along the remote western border of the French Alps, Vaison-la-Romaine cultivates a langorous charm. This sleepy town preserves a lovely medieval quarter capped by a ruined twelfth-century fortress. The extensive ruins of an important Gallo-Roman settlement lie across the l'Ouvèze river in the contemporary town. A youth hostel accessible by bus lies only 8km away in Séguret, and Vaison-la-Romaine makes a refreshing respite from the larger, more tourist-thronged towns along the Rhône.

Orientation and Practical Information

The bus leaves you in place de Montfort, a center of cafes and late-night *brasseries*. To get to the tourist office and the Roman ruins, take Grand' Rue for 2 blocks, through place de la Poste. To reach the *haute ville,* take Grand' Rue in the other direction, across the l'Ouvèze River.

Office de Tourisme: Place du Chanoine Santel (tel. 90-36-02-11). **Currency exchange** and hotel reservations. Maps and historical information on the town. Guided tours in French of both the Puymin area (mid-July to mid-Sept. Wed.-Sat. and Sun. afternoon-Mon. at 10am and 3pm; 19F, students 12F) and the Villasse area (Wed. and Sat., 14F). Also tours of the *haute ville* (Mon. and Thurs., 14F) and the Cloître Cathedrale (Tues. and Fri.).

Post Office: Place de la Poste, next to the mairie off Grand' Rue. **Telephones. Postal code:** 84110. Open Mon.-Fri. 8am-noon and 2-5pm, Sat. 8:30am-noon.

Bus Station: Cars Lieutand, Tel. 90-36-05-22; in Avignon tel. 90-86-36-75. To Avignon (Mon.-Fri. 4 per day, 3 Sat., 2 Sun.; last at 5:35pm; 28F) and Orange (Mon.-Fri. 4 per day, 3 Sat., 2 Sun.; last at 4:10pm; 21.50F). There is no train station in Vaison.

Hospital: Centre Hospitalier de Vaison-la-Romaine, Tel. 90-36-04-58.

Ambulance: Fire department, Tel. 18 for emergency, or call 90-36-26-10.

Police: Quai de Verdun and rue Gevandau (tel. 90-36-04-17).

Police Emergency: Tel. 17.

Accommodations and Camping

The few hotels in Vaison tend to be expensive and full during the summer. Fortunately, you will probably find room at the youth and cultural center 1km outside town or at the exceptional youth hostel in Séguret, 8km away on the bus line.

Auberge de Jeunesse (IYHF), 8km away in Séguret (tel. 90-46-93-31), on route de Sablet toward Orange. Tell the bus driver to drop you off. The last bus from Vaison leaves at 5:35pm, but you might try to hitch the short distance. Bed and breakfast 42F. Doubles 55F. Dinner 42F, wine included. Open May-Sept.

Centre Culturel à Coeur Joie, av. César Geoffroy, (tel. 90-36-00-78). A huge center with all kinds of sports and cultural facilities. Bed and breakfast in rooms with 2 or 3 beds 87F.

Hôtel du Théâtre Romain, place de la Poste (tel. 90-36-05-87), near the tourist office. Large, comfortable, clean rooms. Friendly owners. Doubles 106F, with shower 156F. Triples 196F. Pleasant, 5-person converted apartment 236F. Showers 18F. Breakfast 20F. Restaurant offers a 56F *menu.*

La Piscine, 9, av. du Général de Gaulle (tel. 90-36-05-95). Large, spotless rooms, each with a shower. Singles 110F. Doubles 140F. Triples 150F. Breakfast 20F.

Camping: Le Moulin de César, next to the Centre Culturel (tel. 90-36-06-91). Large campground on the banks of two rivers. 14.50F per person, 9F per tent. Open March-Oct.

Food

In 1483, Pope Sixtus II gave Vaison the right to hold a weekly **market.** Vaison exercises that privilege every Tuesday morning. The lively market fills the entire town center with sweet-smelling herbs and inexpensive fruits, vegetables, clothes, and pottery.

Many of the *caves* in town offer *dégustations* of the local wines, so you can taste the Ventoux rosés and the strong reds of Gigondas free if you show an interest in buying. Regional specialties include *tapenade* (an olive paste) and honey from Ventoux.

La Grasihado, place de la Poste (tel. 90-36-05-75). Pleasant terrace and *menus* at 54F and 73F. Pizza 32-36F, spaghetti 28-36F. Open July-Aug. daily noon-2:30pm and 7-10:30pm; Sept.-June Wed.-Sun. only.

Auberge des Platanes, 12, place Susauze (tel. 90-36-02-16), off place Montfort. Cheap and satisfying 3-course, 40F *menu;* 5-course *menu* 50F. Open Easter-Oct.

Le Bacchus, 9, cours Taulignan (tel. 90-36-19-85), between the Puymin ruins and place Montfort. A *crêperie* and grill combined. Meal crêpes 16-29F, dessert crêpes 9-26F, and a classic *menu* without crêpes 70F. Open July-Aug. daily noon-2pm and 7-9:30pm; Sept.-June Sat.-Thurs. afternoon only.

La Taverne Alsacienne, 1, Grand' Rue (tel. 90-36-31-05). Cuisine isn't local, but the *choucroute* (sauerkraut with meat) is tasty and filling. 55F *menu.* Open July-Aug. daily noon-2:30pm and 7-10:30pm; Sept.-June Tues.-Sun. only.

Sights and Entertainment

In **Quartier de Puymin** and **Quartier de la Villasse,** the foundations and columns of Roman houses alternate with elaborate baths and remarkable mosaics. The ruins stretch over hills carpeted with roses, pine trees, and cypresses. The Puymin excavations reveal the evocative ruins of a **théâtre.** You can still see faint details such as the pits for stage machinery and the curtain holes. To see all the ruins and the adjoining museum, you can take a scheduled tour from the tourist office (see Practical Information). (Ruins open June-Sept. daily 9am-7pm; Oct. and Dec.-May 9am-6pm; Nov. 9am-5pm. Admission to all monuments 16F, students 8F.)

Near Quartier Villasse, **Cathédrale de Notre Dame** mixes styles and eras, and the adjoining eleventh-century **cloître** displays a unique, double-faced Gothic cross. Across the l'Ouvèze and up the hill, narrow streets wind through the gardens of the **quartier féodal.** The tower of the twelfth-century **fortress,** built under Count Raymond VI of Toulouse, affords a panorama of the new town, the vine-covered Ouvèze Valley, and **Mont Ventoux** (1912m), about 15km from Vaison.

Just east of Vaison stretches a line of conical mountains, the **Dentelles de Montmirail,** which constitute the diminished western border of the Alps. Wrapped around one of them, 8km from Vaison, the picturesque fifteenth-century village of **Séguret** has a friendly youth hostel that organizes excursions and activities and has detailed hiking information (see Accommodations).

From early July to early August, Vaison holds an impressive **summer festival.** Almost nightly performances of ballet, opera, drama, and classical music are held in the Roman theater. (Tickets 85-225F.) For information, contact the Bureau du Festival, 84110 Vaison-la-Romaine (tel. 12-61-81-03; after April 1 90-36-06-25 or 90-36-24-79). Every three years (next in early August 1989), Vaison holds its **Choralies,** bringing together several choral groups from around the world. (Tickets for evening performances 70-130F.) Music fills the streets, singers practice in cafes and parks, and informal concerts brighten street corners. For festival information, write the Bureau du Festival (see above) or stop by the festival office, place de la Villasse (tel. 90-36-25-50).

Avignon

Like most of Provence, Avignon took its inspiration from Italy—not from the Romans but from the medieval popes. In 1309 Pope Clement V, a Frenchman, moved the papacy to his native country, partly to escape the regional warfare and corruption of feudal Italy, partly to oblige the more powerful French king Philippe le Bel, who had ruthlessly thwarted the Church's political ambitions. During the "second Babylonian captivity," seven French popes reigned; the last, Gregory XI, transferred the seat back to Rome in 1377. In this short period the Palais des Papes was built, a sprawling Gothic fortress of white stone, and Avignon became a chapel-filled stronghold surrounded by battlements and towers.

Today, Avignon is the seat of emphatically secular, even bacchanalian activities during its famous festival. From early July to early August, people from all over Europe congregate for hundreds of plays, concerts, dance performances, and general excitement. In turn, hotel and restaurant prices skyrocket, accommodations become scarce, and authorities crack down on visitors sleeping in the streets. If you're not intent on experiencing the festival, consider visiting Avignon for its varied religious and architectural attractions. Moreover, Avignon makes an excellent base for exploring the Rhône Valley.

Practical Information and Orientation

Situated on a bend in the Rhône River, Avignon lies on the TGV line between Paris (4 hr.) and Marseille (1 hr.). Enclosed within fourteenth-century ramparts, the city itself is a maze of endless alleyways, small streets, and public squares. To reach the tourist office from the train station, walk straight ahead through porte de la République on cours Jean Jaurès, which becomes rue de la République, the main thoroughfare. The tourist office is on your right (5 min.). At night, lone travelers should avoid the area around rue Thiers and rue Philonarde.

Office de Tourisme: 41, cours Jean Jaurès (tel. 90-82-65-11), 3 blocks from the station. Their free brochure *Avignon pratique* lists restaurants, hotels, useful addresses, hostels, *foyers,* and campgrounds. **Currency exchange** Sat. 9:30-11:45am and 2-5pm. Guided tours of town July-Sept. Mon.-Sat. (15F, students 7.50F). The **branch office** in the train station (tel. 90-85-56-68; for reservations 90-82-05-81) will book you a hotel room the same day (5F). Both offices open July-Aug. Mon.-Sat. 9am-8pm, Sun. train station office open 10am-5pm, city office open 11am-6pm; in off-season Mon.-Sat. 10am-6pm.

Festival Information: All theater is in French, but movies are often in English. Tickets sold at the tourist office 11am-6pm, or by telephone (tel. 90-86-24-43) at least 48 hr. before the event. After 1pm, no tickets are sold for that day's performances, but you can often get a seat at the theater 1 hr. before showtime. Tickets are usually 50-120F. For "Off" events, you can buy tickets at the door (50-80F), or a card (about 50F) that saves you 30% and allows you to make reservations. Contact the "Off" bureau, Conservatoire de Musique (tel. 10-82-29-95), opposite the Palais des Papes. (Open during the festival daily 11am-8pm.) A kiosk at the far end of place de l'Horloge gives out festival information and a schedule of free street performances. For more information, write the **Bureau du Festival,** BP 92 84006 Avignon.

Post Office: Av. du Président Kennedy (tel. 90-82-99-40), inside the walls across from the train station. **Currency exchange** and **telephones. Postal code:** 84000. Open Mon.-Fri. 8am-7pm, Sat.-Sun. 8am-noon. **Branch office** in place Pie. Poste Restante (specify which office on letters) and **telephones** upstairs. Open same hours.

Train Station: Porte de la République (tel. 90-82-56-29). TGV to Paris (12 per day, 4 hr., 328F plus obligatory 13F reservation). Trains to Arles (7-8 per day, 25 min., 28F), Marseille (15 per day, 1 hr., 70F), Toulon (8 per day, 2 hr., 100F), Cannes (8 per day, 3½ hr., 160F), Nice (8 per day, 4 hr., 173F), Nîmes (20 per day, 25 min., 36F), Montpellier (15 per day, 1 hr., 59F), Valence (13 per day, 1 hr., 72F), Orange (13 per day, 15 min., 23F), Dijon (5 per day, 4 hr., 205F), Carcassonne (7-8 per day, 3 hr., 133F), and Toulouse (7-8 per day, 4 hr., 165F).

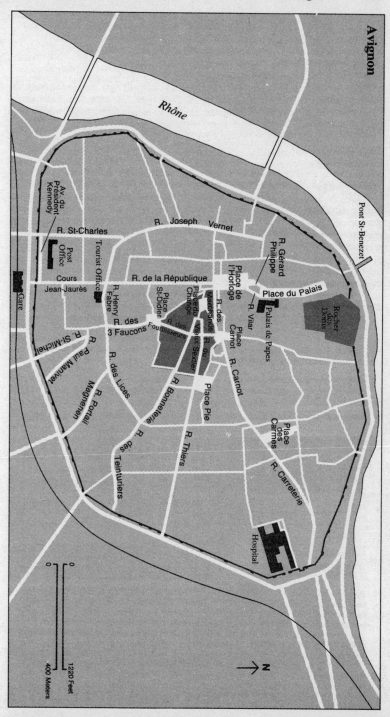

Bus Station: Efficient *gare routière* east of the train station. Departure times for buses are synchronized with train arrivals, especially the TGV. The branch of the tourist office in the train station can provide schedules and prices. Cars Lieutaud, Tel. 90-86-36-75. To Vaison-la-Romaine (Mon.-Sat. 5 per day, 2 Sun.; 1½ hr; 26.50F) and Orange (15 per day, 1½ hr., 21.50F). Rapides Sud-Est, Tel. 90-82-51-75. To Orange (10 per day, 1½ hr., 19.50F) and Châteauneuf-du-Pape (4-5 per day, ½ hr., 17F). Société des Transports Départementaux de Gard (STDG), Tel. 66-29-27-29. To Uzès (4 per day, 1 hr., 34F), continuing to Alès (2 hr., 57F). Also to Pont du Gard (July-Aug. 5 per day, 40 min., 27F). Midi-Bus, Tel. 90-82-68-95. To St-Rémy (7 per day, 40 min., 22F), Les Baux (2 per day, 1 hr., 33F), and Châteaurenard (every hr., 20 min., 11F). Cars Arnaud, Tel. 90-38-15-58. To Fontaine-de-Vaucluse (in summer 3 per day, 1 hr., 20.50F). Nice is served once per day by Cap Phocéen (5 hr., 84F). Buses to Spain also leave from the ramparts to the left of the station; IBERBUS, across the street, has schedules. Public transport line #10 goes to Villeneuve-les-Avignon (every ½ hr., 20 min., 4.80F); for information, inquire at the booth (tel. 90-82-68-19) across the street from the train station, next to porte de la République.

Bike Rental: At the train station (tel. 90-82-62-92, ext. 1183). 20 bikes. 35F per ½-day, 45F per day, 294F per week. Deposit 250F. Open 6am-8pm. Better bikes at Cycles Peugeot, 19, rue Florence (tel. 90-82-32-19). 40F per day, 219F per week. Avoid Dopieralski, 84, rue Guillaume Puy; the bikes are in extremely poor condition. Ride at your own risk and expense.

American Center: Centre Franco Americain de Provence, 23, rue de la République (tel. 90-85-50-98). Organizes various cultural exchanges, *au pair* stays, language courses, and the well-publicized French-American Film Workshop held the week before the official start of the Avignon festival. Has library and bookstore and shows films in English.

Laundromats: Lavomatique, 9, rue du Chapeau Rouge, off place Pie. Wash 15F, dry 2F per 10 min. Open daily 7am-8:30pm. Another at 27, rue Portail-Magnanen. Same prices. Open daily 7am-8pm.

Women's Center: Vaucluse Information Femmes, 9, rue Carnot (tel. 90-86-41-00). Open Mon.-Wed. 9am-noon and 2-6pm, Thurs. 9am-6pm.

Hospital: Ste-Marthe Hôpital, porte St-Lazare (tel. 90-82-99-28). Hôpital de la Durance, 305, rue Raoul Follereau (tel. 90-89-91-31).

Medical Emergency: SOS Médecins, Tel. 90-82-65-00.

Police: Tel. 90-85-17-17.

Police Emergency: Tel. 17.

Accommodations and Camping

Hotels in Avignon become scarce and expensive during the festival, and the handful of reasonable ones are reserved long in advance. Expect to pay at least 80F for a single. The tourist office has a list of organizations that set up inexpensive dormitory accommodations during the festival. If you are sleeping outside, buy some insect repellent and use it generously; the Rhône River breeds bloodthirsty bugs. You might consider staying in Nîmes, Orange, or Arles, and commuting by the frequent, speedy trains.

Foyers: You can reserve beds at the *syndicat*. Foyer Bagatelle, Ile de la Barthelasse (tel. 90-86-30-39), across the river in the camping compound. Take bus #10 from the post office or walk (25 min.). 250 beds. 37F per night. Sheets 11F. Breakfast 18F. *Demi-pension* 98F, *pension complète* 139F. The Squash Club, 32, bd. Limbert (tel. 90-85-27-78). A 30-min. walk along the walls from the train station, or take bus #2 from the station. 40F per night, with sheets and breakfast 60F. Foyer YMCA, 7bis, bd. de la Justice (tel. 90-25-46-20), in Villeneuve, across Pont Daladier and the 1st left after the train bridge. A ½-hr. walk, or take bus #10 from the post office across from the train station. Has a pool. 35-85F per night. Breakfast included. *Pension complète* 120-170F. Open March-Nov. Office closed at lunch. Centre Pierre Louis Loisil, av. Pierre Sémard (tel. 90-25-07-92), in Villeneuve *centre ville*. Take bus #10 from the post office across from the train station. Dormitory-style quarters with 3-4 beds per room. 46F per night. Sheets 18F. Breakfast 10F. *Demi-pension* 84F, *pension complète* 105F.

Hôtel le Parc, 18, rue Agricol-Perdiguier (tel. 90-82-71-55). Clean, pleasant, and highly recommended. Doubles 80F, with shower 110F. Quad with shower 140F. Breakfast 15F.

Hôtel Saint-Roch, 9, rue Paul-Mérindol (tel. 90-82-18-63), outside porte St-Roche. A 10-min. walk left of the train station. Clean and cared for, with garden. Singles with shower 85F. Doubles with shower 135F. 3-4 persons 170-200F. Breakfast 23F.

Pacific-Hôtel, 7, rue Agricol-Perdiguier (tel. 90-82-43-36). Large, airy rooms and friendly, English-speaking management. Singles 85-90F, with shower 110-120F. Doubles 120F, with shower 150F. Triples and quads with shower 200F. Breakfast 15F.

Hôtel Innova, 100, rue Joseph Vernet (tel. 90-82-54-10). Worn, bungalow-like rooms. Singles 75F, with shower 95F. Rooms with 2 beds 140F, with 3 beds 180F. Showers 10F. Breakfast 15F.

Hôtel Central, 31, rue de la République (tel. 90-86-07-81). Clean rooms. A small terrace shielded from the central street. Singles 86F, with shower 100F. Doubles 104F, with shower 162F. Triples 137F, with shower 246F. Quads 140F, with shower 249F. Showers 10F. Breakfast 19F.

Festival Accommodations: CEMEA. Organizes 4- to 21-day stays at various locations during the festival. 620F for 4 days includes *pension complète* and various activities. Many festival performers and workers take part in seminars and discussions in order to give students a sense of what happens backstage. Reservations for all programs should be made in advance through CEMEA, 76, bd. de la Villette, 75940 Paris CEDEX 19 (tel. 42-06-38-10), but if you just show up, you may find a place. Office during the festival, 8, rue Frédéric Mistral (tel. 90-86-50-00). **Centre de Rencontre International Pax Christi (IYHF)**, rue Porte-Evêque (tel. 90-85-13-34). An exceptionally warm and relaxed place organized by a Christian charity and run by a group of cheerful volunteers. 5-day maximum stay. Open only during the festival. You can reserve through Pax Christi's main office, 44, rue de la Santé, 75014 Paris (tel. 43-36-36-68). Membership 5F.

Camping: The closest to town is **Bagatelle**, across the river on Ile de la Barthelasse (tel. 90-86-30-39). An immense campground in the shade. Over 1200 places. Hot showers, cafeteria, laundromat, and supermarket. 15.40F per person, including tent and tax. **Camping Municipal St-Bénezet** (tel. 90-82-63-50). Nearby and more of a family campground. 11.50F per person, 10.50F per tent, 1F tax. **Les Deux Rhône.** Difficult to reach without a car or bike, but quiet and cheap. 18.50F per person, including tent and tax. Open May-Sept. **Camping du Parc des Libertés**, Ile de la Banthelasse (tel. 90-85-17-73). Even more difficult to reach on this huge island. Cafeteria, bike and canoe rental. 12F per person, 8F per tent. Open June-Sept. 15.

Food

Cafes fill place de l'Horloge. These are better suited for coffee after dinner, when the clowns, musicians, and mimes have appeared on the streets. **Parc de Rocher des Doms,** overlooking the Rhône, offers many scenic spots for a picnic, and has an outdoor cafe near the pond. Buy provisions in **Les Halles,** the large indoor market in place Pie (open Tues.-Sun. 5:30am-12:45pm) or at the less expensive open-air **market** on Saturday outside the city walls near porte St-Michel. The tourist office provides a list of restaurants with meals for 60F or less. The shaded, old rue des Teinturiers has small, interesting cafes and restaurants that are popular meeting places during the festival.

Arrête tes Salades, 4, rue Pavot (tel. 90-85-24-34), in a narrow alley off rue des 3 Faucons midway between place des Corps Saints and place St-Didier. Incredibly cheap and delicious food: the best bargain in Avignon and, perhaps, in all of Provence. 29.50F *menu* includes salad, *plat du jour,* and exquisite chocolate cake. Run by a friendly French-American couple who are genuinely interested in your dining pleasure. Open daily in summer 11:30am-2:30pm and 6:30pm till the last customer leaves.

Tapas, 10, rue Figuière (tel. 90-82-65-99), off place St-Didier. Tasty, though the small dishes are ideal only for a light lunch or snack. Wide variety of hot and cold foods and salads, including fried squid, pork, gazpacho, and other dishes with a Spanish twist. 10F per serving. Open daily during the festival noon-2pm and 7pm-1am.

Le Pain Bis, 6, rue Armand-de-Pontmartin (tel. 90-86-46-77). A small place with some outdoor seating, pastel colors, and contemporary art. All the ingredients are *biologique* (organic), and most dishes are vegetarian. Sandwiches and cold plates for lunch, and a 54F *menu.* Open Mon.-Fri. noon-2:30pm and 7pm-midnight.

Tache d'Encre, 22, rue des Teinturiers (tel. 90-85-46-03). A pleasant *café-théâtre* with live piano music Wed.-Fri. at 8:30pm. 52F and 79F *menus.* Open daily noon-2pm and 7pm-midnight.

Le Saboly, 4, place Nicolas Saboly (tel. 90-85-58-93), off place de l'Horloge. Popular, with terrace seating. 55F *menu* includes *moules marinières,* trout, pork, steak, or squid, with your choice of dessert. Open daily noon-2pm and 7-9pm.

La Ciboulette, 1bis, rue du Portail Magnanen (tel. 90-85-09-95), off rue des Lices. Fresh indoor garden decor, and outdoor tables as well. 50F lunch *menu* includes wine. Dinner *à la carte* (most dishes 50-70F). Pizza 35F.

Le Magnanen, 19, rue St-Michel (tel. 90-82-21-66), not far from the station, near porte Magnanen. Tiny and popular with locals. Open Mon.-Sat. 11:45am-2pm and 6:45-8:30pm.

Sights

The **Palais des Papes** sprawls along a clear, sloping square, and every vantage point brings surprises. Smooth granite unifies the towers and battlements; spires and high-pointed arches suggest a Gothic cathedral. The palace gleams with sunlight by day and lamplight by night. (Open July-Aug. daily 9am-6pm; Sept.-June 9-11:30am and 2-5:30pm. Oct.-March tours in French 9-11am and 2-4pm every hr.; April-June tours in English at 10:45am and 3:30pm; July-Sept. at 10:45am and 3:45pm. Admission 20F, students 12F. You must pay a supplement when there is an exposition.) Warmly colored frescoes grace the interior of **Chapelle St-Martial,** noted for its vast dimensions. Adjacent to the Palais sits **Cathédrale Notre-Dame-des-Doms,** a rather heavy, Romanesque church with a richly decorated interior. Since its founding in the twelfth century, it has been considerably restored and rebuilt. One of the two popes responsible for its construction now lies ornately entombed under the cathedral. At the far end of place du Palais is the austere **Petit Palais,** once home to cardinals and now to fine Italian primitive, Gothic, and Renaissance paintings and sculpture. (Open Wed.-Mon. 10-11:50am and 2-6pm. Admission 14F, students 7F; March-Oct. Sun. free.)

The **Musée Calvet,** 65, rue Joseph Vernet, houses an excellent collection of seventeenth- and eighteenth-century French and Flemish paintings. A fascinating exhibit of ironwork (locks and gates) from the region is also on display. (Open Wed.-Mon. 10am-noon and 2-6pm. Admission 14F, students 7F; March-Oct. Sun. free.)

Le Rocher des Doms (open daily 7:30am-9pm), a lovely park with a pond full of ducks and fish, has a panoramic view of Mont Ventoux, the fortifications of Villeneuve-les-Avignon, and twelfth-century **Pont St-Bénezet.** The bridge ends abruptly halfway across the Rhône, resembling a gangplank with only four of the original 22 arches intact. This is the "Pont d'Avignon" of nursery-rhyme fame. Legend has it that the bridge was constructed on the advice of a shepherd boy, St-Bénezet, who was told by visiting angels to build a bridge across the Rhône. If you want to *"danse sur le pont d'Avignon,"* you'll have to pay 5F in a souvenir shop under the bridge. (Open daily 9am-noon and 2-7pm.) Newer **Pont Daladier** is a good vantage point from which to see both the broken bridge and the towering Palais des Papes—and it doesn't cost a red centime.

Across the river rises **Villeneuve-les-Avignon,** guarded by the the **Tour de Philippe le Bel,** a fourteenth-century fortification standing where pont St-Bénezet used to end. (Open April-Sept. Wed.-Mon. 10am-12:30pm and 3-7:30pm; Oct.-March Wed.-Mon. 10am-noon and 2-5pm. Admission 5.90F, students 3.80F.) When Avignon was Italian, Villeneuve was France's southeastern outpost. **Fort St-André** is celebrated for its magnificent view of Avignon, especially at sunset. (Open daily 9am-noon and 2-6:30pm. Admission 17F, ages 18-25 and over 60 9F.) You'll have to pay an extra 4F to enter the attractive terraced gardens, graced with wildly twisting olive trees, on the site. **Chartreuse du Val de Bénédiction,** a monastery founded in 1352 under Pope Innocent VI, is now being restored, but during the year it gathers various artists-in-residence. (Open July daily 9am-6:30pm; April-June and Aug.-Sept. 9am-noon and 2-6:30pm; Oct.-March 10am-noon and 2-5pm. Admission 22F,

ages 19-25 and over 60 12F, ages 7-18 5F.) Bus #10 runs between Avignon and
Villeneuve every half-hour in summer (4.80F).

Entertainment

The **Festival d'Avignon,** held from early July through early August, is a riot of
activities, a nonstop explosion of plays, dance, mime, and everything else from Gregorian chants to an all-night reading of the *Odyssey*. Hardly a cloister, church, or
basement stands without a play occupying its innards, or an archway without a si-
tarist or puppeteer. The official festival has at least 12 different venues, the courtyard
of the Palais des Papes and the municipal theater being the most impressive. (Events
start 9:30-11pm.) The "Off" fringe festival has at least 35 different locations. For
film fanatics, the movie houses in town have rotating schedules and show an average
of five different movies each day. Afternoon and midnight showings are usually
cheaper. During the festival, there is also a lot of good music (jazz around place
Grillon) and theater in the streets (place de l'Horloge). On Bastille Day, Avignon
ignites an impressive fireworks display.

Avignon calms down the rest of the year, but it is still full of theater, films, and
people. Regular performances of opera, drama, and classical music are held in the
Théâtre Municipal, place de l'Horloge (tel. 90-82-23-44). (Box office open daily
11am-6pm. Tickets 40-150F, students 20-75F.) The **Centre d'Action Culturelle,**
8bis, rue de Mons (tel. 90-82-67-08), provides information on jazz clubs and theater
groups. The **Utopia Cinema,** 15, rue Galande (tel. 90-86-59-94), off rue de la République, is an avant-garde movie theater that screens a wide variety of films throughout the year (30F). The **Maison Jean Vilan,** 8, rue de Mous (tel. 90-85-59-64), shows
videos free (Mon.-Sat. at 3pm).

For more improvised nightlife, **Pub Z,** place Pie, is a raucous, but enjoyable wa-
tering hole for French and American students with outside seating. Place des Corps
Saints (Saints' Bodies—ironically, Avignon's prostitutes' working turf) is also the
unlikely location of three lively bars: The popular **Grand Siècle** offers outside seating and live music; **Célestins** attracts a more punkish crowd; and **4 Coins** is another
avignoinnais hotspot.

Near Avignon

Buses link Avignon to several attractive towns (schedules at the tourist office or
near porte St-Michel), but bus service can be erratic. **Carpentras,** where Petrarch
spent his childhood, is graced with a small triumphal arch, a magnificently decorated fifteenth-century **synagogue** (the oldest in France), and **Cathédrale St-Siffrein,**
with both Flamboyant Gothic and classical elements. From mid-July to mid-August
the town sponsors the lighthearted **Festival Offenbach et son Temps,** with
nineteenth-century operettas, ballet, drama, and classical music in its open-air theater. (Tickets 40-150F, students from 30F.) For information contact (before June
30) Festival, BP 113 84200 Carpentras (tel. 90-63-46-35). After July 1, the festival
office is at place d'Inguimbert (tel. 90-63-05-72). If you plan on spending the night,
the Carpentras **Syndicat d'Initiative,** 170, allées Jean Jaurès (tel. 90-63-00-78 or 90-
63-00-68), can help you find a room. Try **Hôtel La Lavende,** bd. Alfred Roger (tel.
90-63-13-49). Buses to Carpentras leave hourly from Avignon.

Isolated on a hill, the stone village of **Gordes** was mostly in ruins 40 years ago,
but the combined efforts of the permanent population of 1600 and the summertime
vacationers have transformed Gordes into an attractive town with shaded outdoor
cafes, restored buildings, and high-quality artisan work. Gordes's calm, understated
atmosphere has made it a fashionable retreat for Avignon festival directors and actors. The village puts on a **festival** of its own the first week of August, with a variety
of music and theater. (Tickets 50-120F, ages under 18 40-90F.) Free side shows
by international performers also take place in the squares. An exhibit of Vasarely's
vibrant geometric paintings is in the **Château de Gordes,** a medieval castle restored
during the Renaissance. (Open July-Aug. daily 7am-7pm; in off-season Wed.-Mon.

10am-noon and 2-6pm. Admission 15F.) Two kilometers south of Gordes is the **Village des Bories,** a cluster of strange, dome-shaped stone huts built around 200 B.C.E. (tel. 90-72-03-48; open daily 10am-sunset). Enclosed in its own peaceful valley only 3km north of Gordes, the **Abbaye de Sénanque** is one of the purest examples of twelfth-century monastic architecture. Founded in 1148 by monks from central France, the abbey has not been inhabited since 1969. Although the monks will move back in 1989, the abbey is still open to the public. (Open daily July-Aug. 10am-7pm; April-June and Sept. 10am-1pm and 2-7pm; Oct.-March 10am-noon and 2-6pm.) Consider reaching the abbey from Gordes by way of the **Chemin des Bilais,** a 4-km footpath that begins just outside the town center after the Hôtel du Domaine de l'Enclos on route de Sénanque.

The Gordes **Syndicat d'Initiative,** place du Château (tel. 90-72-02-75), has information on Gordes, the Village des Bories, and the Abbaye de Sénanque, as well as camping and lodging in the Vaucluse region. However, it does not change money, and there are no banks in Gordes. (Open May-Sept. 9am-noon and 3-7pm.) The only affordable hotel is **Le Provençal,** place du Château (tel. 90-72-01-07), with luxurious rooms. (Doubles with bath 170F. Triples 220F.) Unfortunately, the closest campsite to Gordes is the **Camping Municipal des Chalottes,** 9km away in Murs (tel. 90-72-05-38; 25F per night).

Roussillon, the little town Wiley took as a model for his *Village in the Vaucluse,* is as richly colored as the ochre paint it produces. Synthetic production has stopped large-scale mining, but the town continues to export 3000 tons of ochre per year. The one-room **Musée des Arts et Traditions,** place de l'Arcade (tel. 90-75-66-66), explains ochre's artistic uses, and the way it's mined, particularly the trying conditions under which miners must work. (Open May-Nov. Sat.-Sun. 2-7pm; call to make an appointment anytime.) **Camping l'Arc en Ciel** (tel. 90-05-67-17), 2½km away, is 7F per person and 7.50F per tent. (Open April-Nov.) Roussillon is 7km from Gordes and 14km from Cavaillon. Buses from Apt (17km away) serve the town on Wednesday and Saturday. Call **Cars Apt** at 90-74-20-21.

The tiny village of **Fontaine-de-Vaucluse,** one hour by bus from Avignon (3 per day, 22.50F), is the site of one of the largest natural springs in the world and the largest in Europe. Even Jacques Cousteau has yet to explore the 400-meter-deep pool at the source of the spring just below the cliffs. You can fish for trout in the dazzling green water here. The site lured fourteenth-century Italian poet Petrarch, who spent 16 years here. But today the village attracts more tourists than it knows what to do with, and hotel and restaurant prices are correspondingly high. Fortunately, **Camping Municipal Les Prés** (tel. 90-20-32-38) is only ½km out of town. Reserve in advance. A tranquil, relaxed **Auberge de Jeunesses (IYHF),** chemin de la Vignasse (tel. 90-20-31-65), occupies an idyllic setting 1km out of town. Cross the bridge and follow the road; you'll see signs at the town limit. (34F in dorm rooms. Breakfast 10F. Kitchen facilities. Lockout 10am-5pm. In winter no heating. Open Jan.-Nov. Mon.-Sat.) Fontaine-de-Vaucluse has a **Syndicat d'Initiative** (tel. 90-20-32-22; open Easter-Oct. Mon.-Sat. 9am-noon and 2-6:30pm).

The village of **Châteauneuf-du-Pape** was named after the castle built for Pope John XXII from 1316 to 1333. This castle was destroyed by four escaping German soldiers in August, 1944. One wall remains intact and is still visible on the outskirts of town. The castle grounds overlook the vineyard-carpeted valley below. To understand what drew the popes here, visit the **Musée des Vieux Outils de Vignerons,** a small museum of winemaking in the Père Anselme *cave,* on av. BX Pierre de Luxembourg, down the hill from the center of town. You might even get lessons on proper wine-tasting techniques. (Open daily 9am-noon and 2-6pm. Free.) The **Syndicat d'Initiative,** place du Portail (tel. 90-83-71-08), in the center of town, provides a long list of *caves* accepting visitors. (Open in summer Mon. 3:30-8pm, Tues.-Sat. 9:30am-12:30pm and 3:30-8pm; in off-season daily 9:30am-12:30pm and 2-6pm; closed Nov.) Tasting the famous grape is free at all of these, but small *caves* will give you more personal attention. One such place is the **Crouzet-Feraud** *cave,* chemin Bois de la Ville (tel. 90-39-72-30). For more information on area *caves,* contact the Fédération des syndicats de Producteurs de Châteauneuf-du-Pape, route d'Avignon (tel. 90-83-72-21). Four buses per day leave Avignon for Châteauneuf-du-Pape (17F).

If you are too groggified at the end of the day to move, you can stay at **La Mère Germaine,** place de la Fontaine (tel. 90-83-70-72), next to the *syndicat.* (Doubles 100F, with shower 130F.) Two kilometers away lies the two-star campground **Islon St-Luc** (tel. 90-83-76-77; 10.90F per person, 6.65F per site; open June 15-Sept. 15). All of Châteauneuf's restaurants consider themselves gastronomic and charge accordingly. You'll find less expensive but good regional cooking at **Le Pistou,** 15, rue Joseph-Ducos (tel. 90-83-71-75; open Thurs.-Mon. noon-2pm and 7:45-9:30pm, Tues. noon-2pm).

Arles

Arles has a little of everything for which Provence is famous. The sturdy arches of its *Arènes Romaines* have survived the centuries beautifully and now watch over summer bullfights, just as the Roman *Théâtre Antique* accomplishes its original purpose, elegantly housing dance performances and concerts. The lighting and landscape of Arles drew the likes of Van Gogh, who spent several years here though little commemorates his sojourn, and Picasso, who loved Arles so much he donated the collection of drawings now on display. Provence lives on in Eglise et Cloître St-Trophime, in monuments bearing Provençal inscriptions, and in other efforts to preserve the regional language and culture. Beaches are an hour away at Stes-Maries-de-la-Mer, as is the intriguing marshland of the Camargue. Most appealing of all, ruins, religious and secular art, beaches, and festivities come together in a town both relaxed and welcoming.

Orientation and Practical Information

Arles is a 20-minute train ride from both Nîmes and Avignon, and makes a better base for exploration since its prices are lower. The interesting sections of town lie between the Rhône and bd. des Lices. To get from the station to bd. des Lices and the tourist office, veer left through place Lamartine (1st square after the station), follow bd. Emile Combes for 1km as it bends between high walls and railroad tracks, then turn right onto bd. des Lices at the end of the ancient city wall on your right.

Office de Tourisme: Esplanade Charles de Gaulle (tel. 90-96-29-35), off bd. des Lices and across from the Jardin d'Eté. Follow the signs from the station to the *centre ville.* Guided tours of the city (2 per day), and Van Gogh tour (in summer 1 or 2 per week); both 2 hr., 20F, students 10F. Accommodations service 4F. Open July-Sept. daily 8am-8pm; Oct.-March Mon.-Sat. 9am-6pm; April-June daily 9am-8pm. **Currency exchange** open same hours.

Post Office: 5, bd. des Lices. **Currency exchange** and **telephones. Postal code:** 13200. Open Mon.-Fri. 8am-7pm, Sat. 8am-noon.

Train Station: Av. Tallabot. Arles is on the Paris-Marseille and Bordeaux-St-Raphaël lines, with frequent service to Avignon (hourly, 20 min., 28F), Nîmes (16 per day, ½ hr., 31.50F), Orange (10 per day, ½ hr., 41F), Montpellier (16 per day, 1 hr., 56F), Sète (16 per day, 1½ hr., 67F), and Toulouse (6 per day, 3½ hr., 169F), Tarascon (16 per day, 10 min., 12F), Marseille (13 per day, 50 min., 54F), and Aix-en-Provence (13 per day, 1¼ hr., 70F). Information office open Mon.-Sat. 8-11:50am and 2-6:30pm.

Bus Station: Modern and efficient terminal across from the train station. Schedules for all companies and destinations posted outside. All buses leave from in front of the station. **Carts Verts de Provence,** 16, bd. Georges Clemenceau (tel. 90-93-74-90), sends buses to Les Baux (Mon.-Sat. 4 per day, ½ hr., 23F), St-Rémy (Mon.-Sat. 1 per day, ¾ hr., 26F), Aix (Mon.-Sat. 3 per day, 2 on Sun.; 2 hr.; 53F), Marseille (Mon.-Sat. 4 per day, 2 on Sun.; 2½ hr.; 62F). **Compagnie des Chemins de Fer de la Camargue,** Tel. 90-96-36-25. To Stes-Maries-de-la-Mer from the station or place Lamartine (5 per day, ¾ hr., 28F). To Nîmes (Mon.-Sat. 4 per day, 3 on Sun.; 1 hr.; 24F). **Cars du Delta,** 26, bd. Georges Clemenceau (tel. 90-96-01-90). To Aix (2 per day, 1¾ hr., 54F) and Marseille (2 per day, 2½ hr., 62F). This company also organizes weekly excursions that are no more expensive than regular bus tickets. To Les Baux-St-Rémy (52F), Uzès-Pont de Gard (60F), La Camargue traditionelle (85F), La Camargue sauvage (56F), Abbaye de Senanque-Gordes-Fontaine de Vaucluse (85F). These are full-day and afternoon trips April-Sept. only.

Bike Rental: The train station rents bikes only to groups, so try **Dall' Oppio**, 10, rue Portaguel. Open Tues-Sat.

Hitching: To hitch north to Les Baux, follow av. Lamartine 2km out toward Avignon to the D17. For the Camargue, cross the Rhône and take av. de la Camargue. For Nîmes, follow the N113.

Laundromat: Washmatic, rue Jouvène (tel. 90-96-20-93). Wash 12F, dry 2F. Open Tues.-Sat. 8:30am-12:15pm and 2:30-7pm.

Swimming Pool: Off av. Maréchal Foch, near the Auberge de Jeunesse. Admission 7F. Open in summer daily 10am-8pm.

Medical Emergency: Centre Hospitalier J. Imbert, Quartier Fourchon (tel. 90-96-64-10).

Police: Bd. des Lices (tel. 90-93-98-34).

Police Emergency: Tel. 17.

Accommodations and Camping

Inexpensive hotels are numerous and densely packed around place du Forum and place Voltaire. During the first two weeks of July, when the photography festival is in full swing, you must call in advance.

Auberge de Jeunesse (ALAJ), av. Maréchal Foch (tel. 90-96-18-25), 5 min. from the center and 20 min. from the station. Buses run infrequently. Take the bus to Hôpital from bd. Stalingrad near the station. To walk, take bd. Emile Combes to place de la Croisière, and follow the signs. Next door to the municipal swimming pool. Clean and modern with a friendly staff. Bar with good music. Dorms with 8 beds. No sleeping bags allowed. 45F per night, including sheets, shower, and breakfast. Supper 40F. No kitchen facilities. Office open 7-10am and 5:30-10pm. Curfew 11:30pm. Open March-Oct.

Hôtel de Provence, 12, rue Chiavary (tel. 90-96-03-29), off rue du 4 Septembre, on a straight line into town from the train station. Fine place, kind proprietor. Small but clean singles 80F. Doubles 90F, with shower 115F. Showers 12F. Breakfast 17F.

Hôtel Camarguais, 44, rue Amédée-Pichot (tel. 90-96-01-23), off rue du 4 Septembre. Gracious owner speaks English. Rooms are clean and pleasant but small. Above a neighborhood bar. Doubles 90F, with shower 120F. Extra bed 40F. Showers 7.50F. Breakfast 17F.

Terminus Van Gogh, place Lamartine (tel. 90-96-12-32), 1 block from the train station. Small rooms but charming decoration and owners. Singles 70F. Doubles 90F, with shower 120F. Showers 11F. Breakfast 16F.

Hôtel de France, place Lamartine (tel. 90-96-01-24), next door. Often filled by afternoon with train travelers. Well-kept. Singles 70F. Doubles 88F, with shower 120F. 2 beds 110F, with shower 130F. Showers 9F. Breakfast 18F.

Le Petit Hôtel de l'Arlésienne, 75, rue Amédée-Pichot (tel. 90-96-11-36), off rue du 4 Septembre. 10 rooms, many of them with a glorious view of the arena. Owners like to speak English. Doubles 100F, with shower 120F. Breakfast 18F.

Le Galoubet, 18, rue du Docteur Fanton (tel. 90-96-25-34). Large, clean rooms with firm mattresses. Winding staircase and elegant restaurant downstairs. 46F *menu* includes wine. Doubles 100F, with shower 140F. Showers 10F. Breakfast 14F.

Hôtel-Pizzeria de Studio, 6, rue Réattu (tel. 90-96-33-26), by the Musée Réattu. Another faded bargain. Adequate rooms. Doubles 50F, with shower 90F. Triples and quads with shower 140F. Breakfast 20F.

Camping: There are several sites in the area, but none within walking distance. The closest is **Camping-City,** Route de Crau (tel. 90-93-08-86). A 2-star with 75 sites. Open April-Sept. 23.50F. Two other 2-star campgrounds in nearby Raphile on the RN113: **Le Gardian** (tel. 90-98-46-51), 13F per person, 12F per tent; and **La Bienheureuse** (tel. 90-98-35-64), 10F per person, 10F per tent.

Food

Arles supports many small restaurants featuring *cuisine provençale:* fish, rabbit, and veal dishes. One local specialty is *fougasse,* a pretzel-shaped bread that often contains bits of ham. Compared to those in most other cities in Provence, the restaurants in Arles are quite inexpensive (3-course meal with wine 50F). Wednesday mornings, a colorful **market** is held along bd. Emile Combes, and on Saturday mornings, an all-purpose market takes over the town along bd. des Lices, in front of the tourist office.

The best cafes for watching and sipping are on **place du Forum,** where everyone comes for breakfast armed with croissants from nearby *boulangeries,* and where, come nightfall, everyone seems to know everyone else. You'll also enjoy the cafes on **place Voltaire,** by the arena, strung merrily with colored lights and alive with rock or jazz music on Wednesday nights in summer. As a rule, cafes on bd. des Lices are noisy, crowded, and overpriced.

> **Lou Gardian,** 70, rue du 4 Septembre (tel. 90-96-76-15). Excellent, family-run place serving Provençal specialties. Attracts more hungry tourists than locals but food is good. Large portions served in large tureens. 46F, 56F, and 75F *menus* all bargains, including both wine and service. Crowds pour in as soon as the doors open, so make reservations or come late. Open Mon.-Sat. 11:45am-2pm and 6:45-10pm.

> **Le Criquet,** 21, rue Porte-de-Lauve (tel. 90-96-82-08), on the hill behind the Jardin d' Eté. One of the cheapest restaurants in Arles with a filling and appetizing 50F *menu, service non compris* but wine included. Tiny (seats 25), but air-conditioned. Open Sat.-Thurs. noon-2pm and 7-9:45pm.

> **Le Poisson Banane,** 6, rue du Forum (tel. 90-96-02-58). Enter from rue de Barreme opposite Hôtel du Trident. Any place that takes its name from a J. D. Salinger story is off to a good start. Warm, youthful atmosphere. *Menu* 65F. Fish and meat dishes *à la carte* 45-60F. The desserts are extravagant (try the banana mousse, 20F). Open Wed.-Mon. 7:30pm-late.

> **Le Passage,** quai Max Dormoy (tel. 90-93-44-44). Appetizer: leafing through books. Main course: local specialties. Dessert: watching a movie. Nightcap: looking at photography. You can spend an entire evening at this movie theater-bookstore-gallery-restaurant. Films in original language. Open for meals noon-2pm and 7-10pm.

> **Magali,** rue du 4 Septembre (tel. 90-96-03-29). Run by same management as Hôtel de Provence. 48F *menu* includes *salade niçoise,* choice of veal, beef, or chicken dishes, and dessert. Terrace seating.

Sights

If you plan to visit all the monuments and museums in town, buy the economical global ticket sold at most of the attractions (33F, students 22F).

The elliptical **Arènes,** one of the largest remaining amphitheaters in France (seating up to 26,000 people), dates from Augustan times. In the eighth century it was converted into a fortified stronghold; three of the four original towers still stand. As in the past, the arena features cruel, bloody entertainment—bullfights take place here sporadically from Easter through September. The top of the structure commands a fine view of the Rhône, the Camargue, and surrounding plains. (Open daily May-Sept. 8:30am-7pm, except on bullfight days; Oct.-April 9am-noon and 2-5pm. Admission 10F, students 5F.) The **Théâtre Antique** nearby retains the plan, if little of the elevation, of the original Augustan construction. Of the original stage wall, only two admirable marble columns remain, though these alone lend an eerie effect to summertime drama and dance spectacles. (Hours and admission same as for the arena.) The **Jardin d'Eté,** behind the theater on bd. des Lices, provides pleasant places to have lunch, but don't even consider sitting on the manicured lawns. The beautiful capitals of **Cloître St-Trophime** merit a visit. (Admission 15F, students 10F.) The **Thermes Constantin,** now in ruins, once served as public baths for the Romans. Patrons chose from three baths: the *frigidarium, tepidarium,* and *calidarium.* (Baths open same hours as arena. Admission 10F, students 5F.)

The **Musée Réattu** houses a collection of contemporary art, as well as watercolors and oils of the Camargue by Henri Rousseau, and two rooms of canvases by the neoclassical painter Réattu. The museum takes most pride, however, in the 57 drawings that Picasso tossed off not long before his death in 1971, and donated to this town, whose cafes and bullfights he adored. Be sure to check the backs of the drawings for whimsical doodles. Upstairs are temporary exhibits by noted European photographers and artists. (Open May-Sept. daily 9am-7pm; Oct.-April 9am-noon and 2-5pm. Admission 13F, students 7F.)

The **Musée d'Art Chrétien** possesses one of the world's richest collections of early Christian sarcophagi. Many of the more interesting ones come from the Alyscamps, an ancient Roman burial ground later consecrated for Christian use by St-Trophime. In the Middle Ages, this cemetery, referred to by Dante in his *Inferno,* enjoyed such fame that bodies were brought to it from great distances. Beneath the museum lie four extensive, forbidding galleries, the **crypto-portiques,** dating from the Roman era. (Museum open May-Sept. daily 8:30am-7pm; Oct.-April 9am-noon and 2-5pm. Admission 4.80F, students 3.70F.) The *Musée Arlaten,* curiously bypassed by most tourists, houses an extraordinary folk museum, with everything from a stuffed bull to kitchen utensils. The museum strives to preserve Provençal traditions, which are fast disappearing: The attendants wear regional dress, and the signs are in the local dialect. (Open April-June Tues.-Sun. 9am-noon and 2-6pm; July-Sept. daily 9am-noon and 2-6pm; Oct.-March Tues.-Sun. 9am-noon and 2-5pm. Admission 8F, students 5F.)

The *syndicat* organizes guided tours of the city in French and German (Mon.-Sat. at 10am and 5pm; 1 hr.; 10F, students 5F), and of specific monuments such as the arena (Mon.-Sat. at 10am and 11am), cloister (at 10:30am and 11:30am), and Alyscamps (at 4pm and 5pm; 15F, students 10F). There is also a tour for "Tracing the steps of Van Gogh" (Tues. and Fri. at 5pm; 2 hr.; 20F, students 10F). Tours depart from the *syndicat,* except those for monuments, which meet at the specific site.

The **Rencontres Internationales de la Photographie** in July is a slick and exciting festival. During the first two frenetic weeks, undiscovered photographers swarm aroung town with their portfolios under arm, trying to attract agents. More established photographers give shows in some 15 sites (including parked train cars and a salt warehouse), conduct nightly slide shows, and offer workshops. When the festival crowd departs, you can still see the remarkable exhibits they leave behind (5-15F per exhibit, but a global ticket in an economic 80F, students 60F). In 1988, the themes of the exhibition were China, dance, and advertising. For more information, visit the *syndicat* or contact "Rencontres," 16, rue des Arènes, BP 90 (tel. 90-96-76-06). After the photography festival ends, the city doesn't miss a beat, starting up its **dance and music festival** in the Théâtre Antique and other sites. Dance performances feature the works of young choreographers. The events are accompanied by a fair amount of dancing in the streets. For more information, contact ADCA, la Mairie, place de la République, 13200 Arles (tel. 90-93-98-10; *poste* 4479). Tickets are 180F.

Every year on May 1, the ancient *Confrèrie des Gardians* (the men who herd the Camargue's wild horses) parade through town and then gather in the arena for the **Fête des Gardians,** a traditional but tame version of a rodeo. On July 2 and 4, bonfires blaze in the streets, and locals dress in traditional provençal costume for the beautiful and fascinating **Fête de la Tradition.** The **Reine d'Arles,** a young woman chosen to represent the region's language, customs, and history, is crowned at the end of the festival. Celebrating the 100th anniversary of the painter's arrival in Arles on September 6, 1988 a **Van Gogh exhibition,** including many original works, is scheduled to be shown January 18 to April 30, 1989, and then may be moved to a permanent location in town. For more information, contact the tourist office.

Near Arles

Les Baux, 15km from Arles, is a conspicuously restored village cut into rock overlooking a forlorn valley. Souvenir shops, overpriced cafes, and tourists by the busload choke the former home of powerful provincial counts, today transformed into a tourist trap. To avoid the clutter and crowd, walk through **Porte Eyguières** ("water door" in Provençal), once the only entrance to the town, to the valley below, or walk up to the **Cité Morte,** the ancient city, which dominates most of the hill. (Open July-Aug. 8am-8pm; Sept.-June 9am-7pm. Admission 15F.) The top of the château commands an extraordinary view of the **Val d'Enfer,** and, to the south of Arles, the Camargue and (on clear days) the sea.

The Syndicat d'Initiative, in the Hôtel de Ville (tel. 90-97-34-39), about halfway up the hill between the parking lot and the Cité Morte, operates a **currency exchange** and can book you a room. Don't make plans to stay here, however. The 100 hotel rooms almost always fill in summer, and few cost less than 170F. The most affordable hotel, **Le Mas de la Fontaine,** at the foot of the village (tel. 90-97-34-13), has old furniture, a garden, and a pool. (Doubles showers 120F. Breakfast 16F.) Most backpackers bring picnics to eat in the Cité Morte; you can buy supplies at the small *épicerie* in the parking lot, or better yet, at the Monoprix in Arles before you leave.

To reach Les Baux, take the bus from bd. Clemenceau in Arles, outside the Cars Verts de Provence office (tel. 90-93-74-90), or on bd. Stalingrad, across from the *tabac* (April-Oct. Mon.-Sat. 2 per day, ½ hr., 23F). Buses also travel from Avignon (July-Aug. 2 per day, 55 min., 31F) and from St-Rémy (2 per day, 15 min., 10F).

Almost everyone needs to take a summer vacation, and the Popes of Avignon took theirs at the **Abbaye de Montmajour,** 2km from Arles in the direction of Les Baux. The rectangular twelfth-century towers, Romanesque church, cloisters, and nearby **Chappelle Ste-Croix** all perch serenely above the surrounding fields of sunflowers. (Open in summer Wed.-Mon. 9:30am-7pm; in off-season 9am-noon and 2-5pm.)

St-Rémy has two well-preserved Roman monuments. One kilometer south of town on avenue Pasteur, the **Mausolée,** virtually intact and decorated with bas-reliefs of battles, contains statues of Gaius and Lucius Caesar, grandsons of the emperor Augustus. The **Arc de Triomphe,** ornamented with fine sculpture, is the oldest in the region. You should not miss the **Ruines de Glanum,** across the road. First established in the sixth century B.C.E. by Phocaean traders from Asia Minor, the city was destroyed in the second century B.C.E., restored by the Romans around the turn of the century, and sacked once and for all in the third century. Only fascinating ruins of old houses, temples, and baths remain. (Open April-Sept. daily 9am-noon and 2-6pm; Oct.-March 9am-noon and 2-5pm. Admission 22F, ages 18-26 and over 60 12F.) Van Gogh devotees can make the pilgrimage to the **Monastère de St-Paul-de-Mausole,** the tranquil twelfth-century monastery where he was treated from May 1889 to May 1890. (Open daily 9am-noon and 2-6pm.)

The **Grand Hôtel de Provence,** 36, bd. Victor Hugo (tel. 90-92-06-27), is an old hotel with airy, well-furnished rooms overlooking a garden. (Singles 80F. Doubles with shower 100-165F. Triples and quads 145-240F.) **Camping Monplaisir,** on chemin de Monplaisir (tel. 90-92-22-70), is just outside of town. (Open March-Oct. 9F per person, 13F per tent.) The **Office de Tourisme,** place Jean Jaurès (tel. 90-92-05-22), provides a free guide to walks in the region, including a three-hour trek to Les Baux. (Open June-Sept. Mon.-Sat. 9am-noon and 3-7pm, Sun. 9am-noon; Oct.-May Mon.-Sat. 9am-noon and 2-6pm.) To get to St-Rémy, take the bus from Arles (Mon.-Sat. 1 per day, ¾ hr., 25F) or Avignon (7 per day every 2 hr., 40 min., 23F).

Midway between Arles and Avignon, **Tarascon,** a remarkable, sprawling castle, dominates the banks of the Rhône. In town, there's a relaxed and friendly **Auberge de Jeunesse (IYHF),** at 31, bd. Gambetta (tel. 90-91-04-08), with kitchen facilities. (34F per night. Sleeping bags allowed. Bike rental 30F. Lockout 10am-5pm.) On the last Sunday in June, Tarascon holds a traditional Provençal parade with regional costumes, dancing, and music; the mythical green dragon *Tarasque,* symbol of Tarascon, is wheeled rapidly through the streets. To reach Tarascon, take the bus from St-Rémy (3 per day) or Avignon (3 per day). Tarascon also has a train station with frequent connections to Avignon and Arles.

The Camargue

Imagine the Florida Everglades combined with a vast desert, and you'll conjure up the wild, flat marshlands of the Camargue. As the sun bakes vast expanses of sand and tall grass, and parboils the shallow waters, the whole scene grows desolate and oppressive. The bleak landscape of the Camargue makes an unlikely setting for the exotic wildlife that graces these wetlands. Pink flamingos, black bulls, and the famous white horses roam freely here, and chances are strong you'll see some of these semi-legendary animals.

Many of the area's inhabitants are *gardians,* rugged herdsmen with wide-brimmed hats, and large numbers of gypsies, who pass through intermittently. Rice is grown in the northern sections of the marshland, supplying the tables of Provence with the *riz de Camargue.* Much of the region, however, remains unpeopled and uncultivated, protected as a national park. A small zone is accessible to tourists without a permit, but entry into the **Reserve Naturelle Zoologique et Botanique de la Camargue,** one of Europe's most celebrated natural sanctuaries, is limited to keepers, scientists, and researchers. Fortunately, there is plenty of wildlife to see outside the preserve, whose borders are marked by biking and hiking paths.

The best way to see the Camargue is on horseback—you will feel more like a part of the landscape than a tourist. Rides are organized mainly for beginners and follow fairly limited routes. However, advanced riders can have more freedom. The *syndicat* in Les Stes-Maries-de-la-Mer will give you a list of all the horse rentals in the area (60F per hr., 150F per ½-day, 260F per day). Rates do not vary from one establishment to another. Touring by bicycle is also a good way to see much of the area, as trails within the preserve are open only to cyclists and pedestrians. (See Les Stes-Maries for bike rentals.) Get a trail map from the *syndicat.* A two-hour ride will reveal some of the area, but you'll need a whole day if you plan to stop on the miles of wide, deserted white-sand beaches near the bike trail. Boat tours leave from the mouth of the Petit Rhône and promise views of the horses and bulls. (Tours July-Aug. daily every 2 hr., Sept.-June 2 per day; 75 min.; 46F.) Inquire at the *syndicat* for details. Avoid the "Safari" tours of the Camargue; the best trails are closed to both cars and tour jeeps.

Les Saintes-Maries-de-la-Mer

As Camargue's main settlement, Les Stes-Maries preserves a medieval quarter and distinctive church that are now surrounded by the white cottages and tourist stores of a beach resort. According to legend, the town was founded by the three Marys, accompanied by the risen Lazarus and their Egyptian servant Sarah. Sarah became the patron saint of the gypsies, and on May 24 and 25 each year (also a smaller version in mid-Oct.), the **Pèlerinage des Gitans** is held here. Nomadic people assemble from all over Europe and carry Sarah's statue, amid flowers and fanfare, down from the church to the sea. The statue of Sarah sits in the crypt of the medieval fortified church, haloed by candles. (Free, but dress conservatively.) The church-tower has a magnificent view of town, sea, and Camargue. (Open May 15-Sept. 30 daily 8am-noon and 2-7pm; April 1-May 15 and Oct. 1-Nov. 15 Fri.-Wed. 10:30am-12:30pm and 2-6pm.)

Despite its saintly origin, people now come to "the poorman's Riviera" to swim, sunbathe, windsurf, and explore the area around the preserve on foot, horse, or bicycle. Topless hordes fill the town's pebbly beaches. If you continue past the camping area east of town, you'll have 25km of beach and dunes to explore. A 15-minute bicycle ride along the coastal trail will take you to fine white sand where you won't see another soul. Six kilometers out of town you can bask in the nude in the *zone naturiste*.

A series of Camargue-style bullfights (performed without killing the bull) enlivens the modern arena on summer evenings (tickets 50-200F, available at the *syndicat*). Those interested in the area's flora and fauna should stop in at the **Centre d'Information de Ginès,** along the D570 (tel. 90-97-86-32; open April-Sept. daily 9am-noon and 2-6pm, Oct.-March Sat.-Thurs., free). If birds interest you, go next door to the **Parc Ornithologique de Pont de Gau,** 4km from Les Stes-Maries (tel. 90-47-82-62; open Feb.-Nov. 8am-sunset; admission 15F).

Practical Information

Syndicat d'Initiative: 5, av. Van Gogh (tel. 90-47-82-55), next to the arena. Information on camping and maps for walking tours. Open daily July-Aug. 9am-8pm; Sept.-June 9am-12:30pm and 1:30-7pm.

Currency Exchange: Société Marseillaise de Crédit, av. de la Plage (tel. 90-97-86-09). No commission. Open Mon.-Fri. 9am-12:30pm and 3-6:15pm. Also at the **tourist office** July-Aug. daily 10am-1pm and 2-7pm.

Post Office: Av. Gambetta. **Telephones** here and in the phone company's trailer near the beach, or near the cluster of campsites. **Postal code:** 13752. Open Mon.-Fri. 9am-noon and 2-5pm, Sat. 8:30-11:30am.

Bus Station: Buses run regularly from Arles to Les Stes-Maries (5 per day, 1 hr., 28F). Buses leave from the area opposite the Station Bar on bd. des Lices in Arles, and from the intersection of rue Jean Jaurès and av. d'Arles at the entrance to Les Stes-Maries. Come at least 20 min. early to secure a seat. **Delta Cars** and **Arles Voyages** (both on bd. Clemenceau) conduct bus tours of the Camargue (April 2-June 30 Thurs. and Mon., July 2-Sept. 15 Wed.-Thurs. and Sat., Sept. 17-Oct. 1 Thurs. and Sat.; 40F). Tour buses also leave from outside the train station in Avignon; buses leave daily for Les Stes-Maries from Nîmes; and a bus runs from Montpellier to Les Stes-Maries (July-Aug. 3 per week). Call **Les Courriers du Midi** (tel. 67-92-05-00 or 67-92-01-43) for more information.

Bike Rental: Le Vélociste, place de l'Eglise (tel. 90-97-83-26), next to the church. The friendly folks here rent the best bikes and will point you in the right direction. 18F per hr., 38F per 4 hr., 55F per day. Open daily 9am-8pm. **LOCA Sports,** 30, av. d'Arles. 38F per 4 hr., 55F per day. Windsurfers 70F per ½-day, 100F per day. Open daily 9am-7:30pm. **Camargue Vélo,** 37, rue Frédéric Mistral (tel. 90-47-94-55). 55F per day. Open April-Oct. daily 8am-8pm. **Hôtel Méditerranée,** rue Frédéric Mistral (tel. 90-97-82-09). 55F per day.

Taxi: Tel. 90-97-82-09 or 90-97-80-74.

Police: Route d'Arles 570 (tel. 90-47-80-04).

Police Emergency: Tel. 17.

Accommodations and Food

The best and almost the only way to spend the night here is to camp. Sleeping on the beaches is illegal, but rows of sleeping bags decorate the sand at night. Hotels fill up quickly in summer, and you'll be hard pressed to find any with rooms for under 100F. You can always base yourself in Arles and make the town a daytrip.

Auberge de Jeunesse (IYHF), 10km along the road to Arles at Pioch Badet (tel. 90-97-91-72), a regular bus stop between Les Stes-Maries and Arles. In summer fills up early in the day. Take the 8am bus from Arles, or arrive earlier. 49F per night. Sheets 11F. Breakfast included. Open 8-10am and 5-11pm.

Hôtel de la Plage, av. de la République (tel. 90-97-84-77), right in the center. Old hotel with clean rooms. Doubles 104F, with shower 124F. Showers 15F. Breakfast 20F.

Hôtel Méditerranée, 4, bd. Frédéric Mistral (tel. 90-97-82-09). Plush place with a few rooms. Doubles 100F, with shower 135F. Breakfast 17F.

Les Salicornes, 5, av. d'Arles (tel. 90-97-85-13). 10 rooms, each with shower and private toilet, 160-180F. Breakfast 18F.

Camping: La Brise, Tel. 90-47-84-67. A large site 5 min. from the center of town and right by the ocean. Reservations accepted, but if you arrive before noon July-Aug., you will generally find room. 33F per person, includes tent and tax. **Le Clos du Rhône,** 2km on the other side of town (tel. 90-97-85-99). Quieter 4-star site on the banks of the Petit Rhône. 45F per person, includes tent and tax. Open June 15-Sept. 15. Reservations accepted.

One of the Camargue's main crops is rice, and you will find it in gelatinous cakes sold at *pâtisseries.* Buy your provisions at **Express,** 12, av. Victor Hugo (open daily 8am-12:30pm and 4-7:30pm), at the somewhat cheaper **UNICO,** av. d'Arles (open daily 7am-12:45pm and 4-7:45pm), or at the **market** on place des Gitanes (Mon. and Fri. 9am-noon). The restaurants in town ask too much for too little. The self-service cafeteria **Les Amphores,** 2, av. Van Gogh, on the second floor, offers palatable main courses (20-36F; open 11:45am-3pm and 7-10pm). **Les Flamants Roses,** 49, av. F. Mistral, has an eccentric bright pink interior and terrace. Local specialties such as *riz provençal, Moules Marinières,* and melon grace its 58F *menu.*

Aix-en-Provence

At the base of montagne Ste-Victoire, elegant Aix (pronounced Ecks), the ultimate *ville bourgeoise,* takes pride in its tranquil fountains and stately *mansions.* Five centuries ago the capital of Provence under King René, Aix still radiates the *joie de vivre* infused by "*le bon roi.*" In fact, were it not for the king, muscatel grapes never would have made it to Provence. The boulevard bearing his name girds the city to the south, and many restaurants and shops have also assumed his title.

The inhabitants of Aix are also proud of their local painter, Cézanne; eight small paintings of his hang in Musée Granet. The *atelier* (studio) in which Cézanne painted toward the end of his life was restored by American patrons and is now open to the public.

Every summer in July and early August, Aix hosts a characteristically grand music festival. While Avignon's events are informal, concerts in Aix are refined and expensive, with ushers in tuxedos. In the streets, however, and particularly in and around cours Mirabeau, electric guitars and amplifiers resonate as open-air painters hawk their watercolors and Aztec pipes mingle with children's choruses and conch shells.

During the academic year, some 40,000 students maintain the festive and youthful spirit of Aix in the cafes, restaurants, and clubs of the *vieille ville.*

Orientation and Practical Information

The main axis of Aix is **cours Mirabeau,** a wide promenade that sweeps through the center of town, linking the tourist office at the west end with the churches and university at the east end. The streets to the north in the sprawling *vieille ville* are, by contrast, random and narrow, starting and stopping at large and small squares and leading to unexpected fountains of water-spouting boars or elegant dolphins. **La Rotonde,** at the west end of cours Mirabeau and just north of the train station, is the central terminus for city buses. To get here from the train station, bear left onto av. Victor Hugo (5 min.).

Office de Tourisme: 2, place du Général-de-Gaulle (tel. 42-26-02-93). A busy office with the usual services: hotel reservations (20F, 2F nonrefundable), **currency exchange** (Mon.-Sat. 9am-noon and 2-5:30pm, Sun. 9am-noon), and guided tours of the city (daily at 10am, 3:30pm, and 9pm; tours in English Wed. at 10am; 20F, students 10F). Pick up a plan of Aix with suggested walking tours. The monthly guide to events in Aix, *Le Mois à Aix* (2F), is useful during the festival. Open July-Sept. Mon.-Sat. 8am-10pm, Sun. 8:30am-12:30pm and 6-10pm; Oct.-June 8am-7pm.

Festival Information: For the music festival only, go to the Palais de l'Ancien Archevêché (tel. 42-23-11-20 or 42-23-37-81). Reserve tickets by mail or phone before July 1. Open Feb.-June 9am-noon and 2-6pm; July-Jan. 10am-1pm and 3-7pm. The green booth in the courtyard outside sells tickets during the festival Mon.-Sat. 9am-1pm and 3-7pm, Sun. 10am-noon. Just outside the tourist office stands a kiosk that distributes information on the dance festival only.

Budget Travel: Council Travel, 12, rue Victor Leydet (tel. 42-38-58-82), off place des Augustius. The only Council branch in France outside of Paris. Books international and domestic flights at reduced student prices. Check out Air Inter prices for domestic flights: Some are as cheap (if not cheaper) than 2nd-class train tickets. Open Mon.-Sat. 9am-1pm and 2-6:30pm. **Transalpino**, 3, rue Lieutaud. Books international and long-distance domestic train rides at reduced prices (30% off) for ages 25 and under and students under 27. Air Inter flights (with up to a 62% reduction for special "blue" period travel) available here as well. Open Mon.-Fri. 10am-1pm and 2-6pm.

Currency Exchange: The post office has the best rates, smallest commission (only 1%), and longest hours (same as those for the central office on rue Lapierre). The large banks on cours Mirabeau keep ridiculously short hours and slap on a steep commission.

Post Office: 2, rue Lapierre (tel. 42-27-68-00), across La Rotonde from the tourist office. **Postal code:** 13100. Open Mon.-Fri. 8am-7pm, Sat. 8am-noon. The **annex**, place de l'Hôtel de Ville (tel. 42-23-44-17), provides the same services and is less crowded, closing at 6:30pm.

Train Station: At the end of av. Victor Hugo (tel. 42-27-51-63; 91-08-50-50 in Marseille), off rue Gustavo Desplace. To get just about anywhere from Aix, you have to go to Marseille, via the hourly trains (45 min., 28.50F). To Nice (3 hr., 132F), Cannes (2½ hr., 118F), and Monaco (4 hr., 136F). Direct to Briançon (6 per day, 4½ hr., 136F).

Bus Station: Rue Lapierre (tel. 42-26-01-50), behind the post office. A very confusing place. To Avignon (4 per day; 1½ hr.; one way 53F, round-trip valid for 2 months 79F) and Marseille (every ½ hr.; ¾ hr.; one way 17.50F, round-trip 19.50F). By autoroute to Cannes (2 per day; 1½ hr.; 79F, ages under 20 with Carte Jeune 63F), and Nice (2 per day; 2 hr.; 86F, ages under 20 with Carte Jeune 63F). By N7 to Cannes (2 per day, 2½ hr., 63F), Nice (4 per day, 3½ hr., 67F), and Arles (5 per day, 1½ hr., 60F).

Taxi: Tel. 42-27-71-11.

Bike Rental: Avis, 11, cours Gambetta (tel. 42-21-64-16). 60F per day, 315F per week.

Hitching: The autoroute A8 swings right through Aix, but hitching can be tricky. You're better off waiting for the long haul rather than taking a short ride and being dropped off on the highway. For Avignon, follow bd. de la République until it becomes A8. For Nice, follow cours Gambetta.

Bookstore: Paradox, 2, rue Reine-Jeanne (tel. 42-26-47-99), behind the Roi René Hôtel on bd. du Roi René. Sells works in English. Open Tues.-Sun. 9am-noon and 3-7pm.

French-American Center: Centre Franco-Americain de Provence, 24, place de l'Archevêché (tel. 42-23-23-36). Organizes exchanges, *au pair* stays, and 3- to 4-week crash language courses. Unofficial flat-finding service for members only (membership 100F). Membership and services open to all nationalities.

Laundromat: Off La Rotonde on the corner of rue Bernadines and rue de la Fontaine. Wash 12F, dry 2F. Open daily 7am-8pm. Also near the University at 60, rue Boulegan. Open Sept.-July. **Le Laver**, rue Aumone Vieille. Wash 12F, dry 2F. **Laverie Lou Lavadou**, Centre de Service ZAC du Jas de Bouffan, bd. de la Grande Thumine, near the youth hostel. Wash 14F. Open Mon.-Sat. 9am-7pm.

Women's Center: Information Femmes, 24, rue Mignet (tel. 42-20-69-82), in the *sous-préfecture*. Open Mon.-Tues. and Thurs. 9am-noon and 2-4pm.

Medical Emergency: Centre Hospitalier, chemin des Tamaris (tel. 42-23-98-00).

Police: Tel. 42-26-04-81.

Police Emergency: Tel. 17.

Accommodations and Camping

There are few inexpensive hotels near the center, and during the festival they are all booked in advance. Do likewise, or arrive early and hope for cancelations. The youth hostel is a 25-minute hike outside of town, but buses run until 8pm.

Auberge de Jeunesse (IYHF), 3, av. Marcel Pagnol (tel. 42-20-15-99), quartier du Jas de Bouffan, next to the Fondation Vasarely. A 25-min. walk from the center of town, or take bus #12 or 8 from La Rotonde (every ½ hr., last at 8pm, 5F). A modern hostel in a newly-developed neighborhood. Strict proprietor. Call ahead to make sure there's room. Bed and obligatory breakfast 45F. Sheets 11F, no sleeping bags. Meals 35F. No kitchen facilities. Curfew 11pm. Lockout 10am-5:30pm.

CROUS: Cité des Gazelles, 38, av. Jules Ferry (tel. 42-26-33-75), outside the center. July-Aug. the university occasionally offers 51F singles with a 2-night minimum stay.

Foyers: The tourist office will supply you with a list of foyers, some of which do not accept individuals. Try **Foyer des Abeilles,** av. de Maréchal Leclerc (tel. 42-59-25-75), a 10-min. walk from the hostel towards town. No reservations from individuals accepted. Dorm rooms 50F. Singles 70F. Doubles 65F per person. Filling dinner 43F.

Hôtel Pax, 29, rue Espariat (tel. 42-26-24-79), on a busy street. Reasonable prices. Singles from 58F. Doubles from 75F, with shower 135-160F.

Hôtel des Quatre Dauphins, 54, rue Roux Alphéran (tel. 42-38-16-39), near place des Dauphins, down from the Musée Granet. Full of old furniture and character. Clean and fairly inexpensive. Owner prefers longer stays. Singles 70F. Doubles 90-110F, with shower 145F. Quad with shower 205F. Showers 8F. Obligatory breakfast 19F. Tax 1F per person.

Hôtel Vigouroux, 27, rue Cardinale (tel. 42-38-26-42), near place des Dauphins. English-speaking owner. Doubles 90F, with shower 150F. Showers 6F. Breakfast 17F.

Hôtel Sully, 69, bd. Carnot (tel. 42-38-11-77), opposite the Ecole d'Arts et Métiers and 2 min. from place des Prêcheurs. Opposite a cafe and near several *boulangeries* and a laundromat. Charming, warm, and hospitable; fills quickly. Doubles 90F, with shower 100F. No reservations accepted.

Camping: All campsites lie outside of town, but there are 3-star sites relatively close by, all of which cost around 34F per person and tent. The last one is likely to have room even in summer. **Arc en Ciel,** Pont des Trois Sautets, route de Nice (tel. 42-26-14-28), 3km from the center of town. **Chantecler,** val St-André, by route de Nice (tel. 42-26-12-98), 3km from the center. **Le Felibrige** in Puyricard, off the RN7 or the RN de Manosque (tel. 42-92-12-11), also 3km from Aix. Take the bus to Puyricard from cours Sextius (Mon.-Sat. every ½ hr.). A pleasant campground conveniently located next to a pool.

Food

Although the restaurants in Aix serve delicious regional specialties made with fresh vegetables and seafood and sometimes seasoned with the garlic *aïoli* sauce, the city's culinary reputation comes from its *confiseries* (confections). In France, prepared almonds used in cakes and cookies originates in Aix; its most famous confection is the *calisson d'Aix* (a small iced almond cookie). Other regional specialties include the soft nougat and the hard praline candy. Ask for these in any of the *pâtisseries* or *salons de thé* along rue d'Italie or rue Espariat. For provisions, visit the **market** near the Palais de Justice in place Verdun (open Tues., Thurs., and Sat. mornings).

The cafes on cours Mirabeau often serve bland and overpriced meals, and are better suited for after-dinner drinks and people-watching. Affordable restaurants with terrace seating cluster in the area around place des Cardeurs.

Hacienda, 7, rue Mérindol, west of place des Cardeurs. Outdoor seating, quick service, and an excellent value. The 47F *menu* includes steak, veal, or fish; fries or vegetables; dessert; and wine. 15% surcharge for terrace seating. Open Sept.-July Mon.-Sat. noon-2pm and 7-10pm.

Djerba, rue Rifle-Rafle (tel. 42-21-52-41), on a tiny street off place des Prêcheurs. Busy outdoor restaurant with North African specialties. 40F lunch *menu* features pork or steak. 85F dinner *menu. Couscous* 40-55F, *plat du jour* 30F. Open Mon.-Fri. 11am-2pm and 6-10pm.

La Tour de Pise, 10, rue Victor Leydet (tel. 42-26-06-36), 1 block from cours Mirabeau. Popular and small. Italian food *à la carte* (spaghetti 30F). 58F *menu* has French classics. 44F *menu* for lunch only. Open Mon.-Sat. noon-2pm and 7-11pm.

Le Tipaza, 6, rue des Matheron (tel. 42-96-38-75), 3 blocks from place des Cardeurs, off rue Paul Bert. Very friendly. 40F lunch *menu.* Excellent *couscous* 40-55F, salads 25F. 50F and 75F *menus* with North African specialties.

La Fourchette, 40, Forum des Cardeurs (tel. 42-63-02-16). French classics served in a crisp, new interior. Outdoor tables. Interesting salads 26-45F. *Plat du jour* with dessert or appetizer

49F (lunch only). *A la carte* is too expensive. Open Mon.-Fri. noon-2pm and 7:30pm-midnight, Sat.-Sun. 7:30pm-midnight.

Alimentation Nguyên-Thành, 16, rue Gaston de Saporta. A take-out with appetizing southeast Asian specialties. Makes a wonderful picnic. Beef with vegetables 12F. Shrimp with vegetables 14F. Saja salad 7.50F. Open Tues.-Sat. 10am-2pm and 4-8pm.

Sights

If you can rouse yourself from the cushioned, wicker cafe chairs, Aix does have some museums of note. A fine collection of Beauvais tapestries from the seventeenth and eighteenth centuries hangs in the **Musée des Tapisseries.** The back room of the museum often houses contemporary weavings as well as a collection of looms from various eras. (Open in summer Wed.-Mon. 9:30am-noon and 2-6pm; in off-season Wed.-Mon. 10am-noon and 2-6pm. Admission 9F, students 6F.) The **Musée Granet,** place St-Jean-de-Malte, displays a collection of Roman sculptures and Egyptian mummies. It also houses a large number of Dutch and classical paintings, as well as exhibitions of contemporary art. The current pride and joy of the museum is the recent acquisition of eight small paintings by Cézanne. (Open July-Aug. daily 10am-noon and 2-6pm; Sept.-June Wed.-Mon. only. Admission 12F, students 7F.)

The **Musée du Vieil Aix** contains an eccentric collection of exhibits on local history and popular customs. Some displays look like a pack rat went wild, but others are highly informative. See the sections on the *jeux de Fête-Dieu,* a town pageant-tournament-puppet show invented by King René to bolster the traditions of chivalry, which he thought threatened by the invention of powder weapons. A guidebook printed in English, available at the entrance, explains the exhibits. (Open May-Oct. Tues.-Sun. 10am-noon and 2-6pm; Nov.-Jan. and March-April Tues.-Sun. 10am-noon and 2-5pm. Admission 10F, students 5F.)

Cathédrale St-Sauveur is an architectural melange of additions and carvings from eleventh-century Romanesque to late Flamboyant Gothic. The main attractions, beautiful sixteenth-century carved panels of the main portal, remain in perfect condition, thanks to their protective wooden shutters. The interior's claim to fame, the *Triptych du Buisson Ardent,* depicts King René and his queen in odd juxtaposition with the Virgin and Child and the burning bush of Moses. This work is usually closed away, but for a small tip, the guard will show it and the front panels to you, complimentary lecture included. Adjoining the church, the delicate thirteenth-century **Cloître St-Sauveur** has a wooden roof over the galleries instead of the usual heavy arches. During the festival, mass is held every Sunday at 10:30am. (Church open Mon.-Sat. 8am-noon and 2-6pm, Sun. 2-6pm.) **Bibliothèque Méjanes,** in the Hôtel de Ville, displays an impressive collection of illuminated manuscripts and, often, works of contemporary artists. (Open Tues.-Thurs. and Sat. 10am-noon and 2-6pm, Sun.-Mon. and Fri. 2-6pm. Free.) The **Fondation St-John Perse** stores materials and manuscripts related to this Nobel prize-winning poet.

A perfect response to bourgeois Aix, the defiant **Fondation Vasarely,** 1, av. Marcel Pagnol, Jas de Bouffan, can be found outside town near the youth hostel. Take bus #12 or 8 from La Rotonde to Vasarely. The black and white pattern of the building makes an apt backdrop for the artist's gigantic, vibrant op-art murals—hypnotic experiments with color and shape that reach almost from the floor to the domed ceiling high above the hexagonal-shaped rooms. (Open Wed.-Mon. 9:30am-12:30pm and 2-5:30pm. Admission 20F, ages 7-18 10F.) After this visual stimulation, you can relax in the park outside, one of the quietest spots in Aix.

Cézanne's Atelier, 9, av. Paul Cézanne, requires a 5-minute walk out of town. It remains much as he left it in 1906, with his easel, a smock, and an unfinished canvas. Some of his paintings, as well as a few etchings and drawings, remain here. Unless you are a true Cézanne devotee, you may find the visit not worth the effort. (Open June-Sept. Wed.-Mon. 10am-noon and 2:30-6pm; Oct.-May Wed.-Mon. 10am-noon and 2-5pm. Admission 7F, students 5F.)

Entertainment

Aix is famous for its **International Music Festival,** held from mid-July to early August, and drawing first-rate musicians and renowned orchestras from around the world. Tickets run very high, since the festival isn't subsidized. Seats are scarce, and student discounts rare. The program features opera in the **Théâtre de l'Archevêché** (tickets 220-620F); concerts in **Cathédrale** and **Cloître St-Louis,** 60, bd. Carnot (tickets 140-240F); and recitals by advanced music students at **Cloître St-Sauveur** (*Une heure avec . . .* tickets 70F). Strictly speaking, the festival begins and ends with these concerts, but in practice everyone else takes the opportunity to celebrate. There are many exhibitions all over town and some improvised youth activities—strange dances around the fountains, all-night rock concerts, reggae performances. In preparation for the music festival, Aix holds a less formal, but no less interesting, two-week jamboree of big-band jazz, classical quartets, and wind ensembles beginning the second week of June. Most concerts are free, and each evening *concerts dans la rue* feature conservatory music students playing everything from rock fusion to classical music in the *vieille ville.* For a list of concerts and locations, ask at the tourist office for the program *Aix en Musique.*

For the first two weeks of July, Aix holds its international **Dance Festival,** with performances ranging from classical ballet to modern and jazz. Tickets cost 60-150F (students 45-85F). For information on both the Music and Dance Festivals, contact the Comité Officiel des Fêtes, 2bis, av. Victor Hugo (tel. 42-26-23-38).

Although Aix's primary source of entertainment is the never-ending parade on the *cours,* excellent jazz clubs, frequented by a lively, appreciative crowd go bop in the night. Addresses change from year to year, so check the posters on the streets or inquire at the tourist office. The cinema **Studio 24,** cours Sextius (tel. 42-27-63-32), shows the manager's favorite films; during the summer six or seven play daily. **Le Mazarin,** rue Laroque (tel. 42-26-51-31), also shows good *version originale* (undubbed) films. **Théâtre de Verdure,** parc Paysage du Jas de Bouffan (tel. 42-59-38-30), runs an inexpensive outdoor theater that goes into high-gear during the music festival with classical concerts, theater, and dance performances. For some prefabricated nightlife, **Le Mistral,** 3, rue Frédéric Mistral (tel. 42-38-16-49), next to the restaurant Gu et Fils, attracts a mature student crowd. **La Chimère,** Montée d'Avignon (tel. 42-23-36-28), quartier des Plâtrières, outside the town, attracts a sizable gay crowd to its bar and disco. (Open Tues.-Sun. 10pm-6am.)

Near Aix

As you walk toward the Montagne de Ste-Victoire, you can retrace Cézanne's easel stops along the D17, now called **route de Cézanne.** The road winds its way to the hamlet of **Le Tholonet** (5km from Aix), where you can pause for refreshment before heading back to town. Ten buses per day run from Aix to Le Tholonet (Mon.-Sat. on the hr.). From the town, you can hike up to the ridge-top of the Montagne de Ste-Victoire (about 1½ hr. each way). Passing medieval abbey buildings, the trail arrives at the summit, called **Croix de Provence,** where a huge cross presides over a panorama of the entire mountainous region. Trail maps are available at the tourist offices in Le Tholonet and Aix. A minibus excursion around the Montagne Ste-Victoire and Cézanne's sites leaves Monday from the tourist office. Call the tourist office or Tylene Transports Tourisme (tel. 42-26-26-28) for information. (Tours in English and French, 165F.)

Picasso devotees can find him buried in **Vauvenargues,** just 16km east of Aix. Three or four buses per day run from Aix; you can also hitch. Although visitors are not allowed entrance to the nineteenth-century château where Picasso lived, some of the artist's sculptures are on display in the park.

Provence: Côte d'Azur

The Côte d'Azur has been lost, not to tourists, but through its own paradisiacal qualities. Shrewd developers have turned its beauty to big business and its pleasures to profit. Today, as many low-budget tourists as high-handed millionaires throng the Riviera. Lodging can be hard to find in July and August, and hotel and restaurant prices in the better-known resort towns are steep. During the summer, you may feel that you have come to a cultural wasteland where only a desire to tan unites the masses.

Still, the Côte d'Azur remains a beloved holiday spot for many people. Away from the coast, farming villages lie strewn every few miles across a splendidly varied hinterland; wooded ridges spring suddenly from expanses of flat farmland. Traces of the Roman rule established by Caesar can be seen at Fréjus, Antibes, and Digne. Nearly every town along the eastern part of the Côte boasts a chapel, room, or wall decorated by Matisse or Chagall, and excellent museums abound throughout the entire area. Every spot hosts its own festival, many of them world renowned. In addition to countless summer jazz festivals, the Cannes Film Festival is held in May, Nice's *Carnaval* in February, the Monte Carlo Rally in January, and the Grand Prix in May. Delicious regional food specialties include *bouillabaisse* (a hearty fish soup), *salade niçoise, soupe au pistou* (laced with garlic, fresh basil, and pine nuts), and other dishes flavored with local herbs, garlic, tomatoes, and olive oil. Take advantage of the fresh seafood; if you love garlic, you'll have lots of company. Near Marseille, Cassis (no relation to *crème de Cassis*) is the tiny home of a flavorful white wine, and Côtes de Provence has achieved worldwide fame for its fruity rosé. In short, the French Riviera is not to be missed. And if you visit in the off-season, you might see a shadow of the former Côte, unobstructed by cars and people. An alluring, uncommonly beautiful area, its colors alone are spectacular: Dazzling white villas rim a remarkably blue sea, while silvery olive trees shelter fragrant roses and mimosa.

Inland, the inhabitants, usually shorter, sturdier, and darker than their northern compatriots, make their living by growing grapes, oranges, and olives, and cultivating silk. However, the long, dry summer that produces a tan harms cattle and crops and causes devastating forest fires. As people are forced to find livelihood elsewhere, farming village populations have severely diminished.

The coast from Marseille to Italy is well served by frequent, inexpensive trains and buses. Most of the famous attractions lie along the coastal rail line from St-Raphaël to Menton, a two-hour stretch. Trains for the Côte leave Paris (Gare de Lyon) every hour in summer, and the trip takes 7-8 hours on the TGV to Marseille. You might want to base yourself in one of the larger cities (Nice, for example) and make daytrips to quieter beaches and smaller coastal retreats. Groups should consider renting a car to explore the spectacular coast—firms will often waive the 500F deposit if you have a credit card. Mopeds rent for about 60-80F per day (plus a 1000F deposit); larger firms have better machines. Helmets are required. Hitching is average between smaller towns, but fairly bleak along the main *autoroute*.

Beaches

Familiarize yourself with the Côte before you stalk the perfect tan. If you've come just for the sun, try to arrive in early June or in September, when the warm air and water aren't obscured by fashionable droves of beached lemmings. In summer, optimal swimming tends to be during the two-hour period before the 9pm sunset.

Always bring a towel: Even the sand beaches are a bit rocky, and you'll want something to sit on. Nearly all the beaches are topless.

It can be difficult to distinguish between the little beach towns; they all claim to be the "jewel" or *"perle"* of the Riviera, to have a slightly warmer *microclimat* (perfect for growing champion citrus fruits) than neighbors five minutes away, and to be the original *cité des arts.* However, all beaches were not made equal. The largest towns have the worst beaches. Marseille has an artificial beach, while the beaches at Nice are pebbly. At Cannes, they are private, and at Monte Carlo, remote. Seek out the quieter beaches between towns: Cap Martin, between Monaco and Menton, and Cap d'Ail—and to a lesser extent, Eze-sur-Mer—between Nice and Monaco. St-Raphaël has smooth, public, and fairly crowded stretches of sand right off the train line, and equally fine but less peopled beaches nearby. West of Nice, Antibes and Juan-les-Pins both have long, white-sanded *plages* with clear water and fine swimming, and around the *calanques* (mini-fjords), accessible only by moped, the privacy of the beaches is rarely enforced. Some of the finest sandy expanses stretch *between* St-Raphaël and St-Tropez. Since almost all of the towns on the Côte lie along one local rail line, it may be worthwhile to hop on and off at small stations to see what you can find.

Accommodations are extremely tight in high season; youth hostels and hotels are often booked months in advance. Although it is illegal, many travelers end up sleeping where they lay their towels during the day. A number of beaches provide showers, toilets, and even towels for a small fee (7-12F). It is not always safe to spend the night on the beaches at Nice, Cannes, and Juan-les-Pins. Wherever you are, make use of the lockers (5F and 10F) available at most train stations—and hide the key. Even in stations where lockers have been closed because of vandalism, you can always store your luggage for 10F.

Marseille

Its most crowded streets a riotous confluence of ethnic, national, and social variety, Marseille truly is, as Dumas declared, "the meeting place of the entire world." For here, unlike most of France, black, white, and brown, rich and poor, live side by side, if not always amicably. Home of the French Mafia, Marseille wallows in grime and danger. If you take precautions, however, it is unlikely that you will ever be at risk, even if you are a woman alone. The beaches here are artificial, sandy, and, for the most part, public.

Orientation and Practical Information

The center of town is the **Vieux Port,** which hums with sounds—from the first throaty calls of the morning fish sellers on quai des Belges, to inebriated goodnights shortly before dawn. The adjacent streets comprise the **vieille ville.** At night in both the Vieux Port and *vieille ville,* a lone woman is an easy target, but groups are safe. Coming straight out of the port is Marseille's main artery, **La Canebière,** affectionately known to English sailors as "Can o' beer." Jammed in the day but empty after 10pm, La Canebière can also be dangerous. Avoid the streets adjoining La Canebière (especially cours Belsunce and bd. d'Athènes) for the same reasons. Between the train station and La Canebière twist the narrow, dusty streets of the **North African quarter.** In the day, the stores and restaurants are exotic and inexpensive, but at night the streets' beggars are replaced by muggers. Finally, the area in front of the opera (near the port) is the meeting ground for prostitutes and their customers. Nevertheless, Marseille is no more dangerous than Paris, London, or New York. When in doubt, stay in a group or call a cab; they operate 24 hours.

As you leave the train station, turn left and descend the majestic steps. Continue straight down boulevard d'Athènes until you arrive at La Canebière—and the tourist office and port—on your right.

Office Municipal de Tourisme: 4, La Canebière (tel. 91-54-91-11), near the Vieux Port. English spoken. Information on boats, festivals, and youth activities. Free accommodations service. Bus tours leave in summer daily at 10am (85F). SNCF information and reservations. Open July-Sept. daily 9am-9pm; Oct.-June Mon.-Sat. 9am-6:30pm, Sun. 9am-noon and 2-6pm. **Annex,** at the train station. Open June 20-Aug. Mon.-Sat. 8am-8pm; Sept.-June 19, Mon.-Sat. 9am-5pm.

Student Travel: Vovac, 8, rue Bailli-de-Suffren (tel. 91-54-31-30), at quai des Belges in the Vieux Port. BIJ/Transalpino tickets. Open Mon.-Fri. 9:30am-12:30pm and 2:30-6:30pm, Sat. 9:30am-noon. Also at **Voyages Wasteels,** 87, La Canebière (tel. 91-50-89-12).

Centre d'Information Jeunesse: 4, rue de la Visitation (tel. 91-49-91-55). Information on sports and activities, including climbing excursions to the *calanques.* They also have a *Guide des Loisirs* designed exclusively for disabled persons (10F). **CROUS,** 38, rue du 141e R.I.A. (tel. 91-95-90-06), has information on housing, work, and travel for students.

Consulates: U.S., 12, bd. Paul Peytral (tel. 91-54-92-00). Open Mon.-Fri. 8:30am-noon and 1-5:30pm. **Canada.** Now under the auspices of the U.S. consulate. **U.K.,** 24, av. du Prado (tel. 91-53-43-32). Open Mon.-Fri. 9am-noon and 2-5pm. All other consulates can be reached through the **Secretariat du Corps Consulaire,** 15, rue Beavau (tel. 91-54-91-54).

Currency Exchange: Change de la Bourse, place Général de Gaulle, off La Canebière. A percentage commission. Open Mon.-Fri. 8:30am-6:30pm, Sat. 8:30am-noon and 2-5pm. **Thomas Cook,** at the train station, is open daily 8am-6pm and will change everything but French franc traveler's checks. Commission 10F.

Post Office: 1, place Hôtel des Postes (tel. 91-90-31-33), at the intersection of rue Colbert and rue Barbusse. Poste Restante in same building, around the corner at 8, rue du Colonel J.B. Pétré. **Currency exchange** at this branch only. **Postal code:** 13001. Open Mon.-Fri. 8am-7pm, Sat. 8am-noon. **Branch offices** at 11, rue Honnorat, near the train station (open Mon.-Fri. 8:30am-7pm, Sat. 8:30am-noon), and place de Stalingrad, at the end of La Canebière (open Mon.-Fri. 8am-7pm, Sat. 8am-noon).

Airport: Aéroport Marseille-Provence, Tel. 42-78-21-00. Flights to Corsica, Paris, and Lyon. Buses connect the airport with Gare St-Charles (5:30am-9:50pm every 20 min., 25 min., 33F). **Air France,** place de Gaulle (tel. 91-54-92-92), off La Canebière. Open Mon.-Fri. 9am-noon and 1:30-6:30pm.

Train Station: Gare St-Charles, Tel. 91-08-50-50. Nearby *bureau d'accueil* (reception desk) open 24 hours. Main information and reservation desk open daily 8am-8pm. Marseille is a major rail center with connections to nearly all major towns in the south, including Aix (every hr., 35 min., 28F), Arles (every ½-1 hr., 45-60 min., 54F), Avignon (every ½ hr., 1 hr., 70F), Nîmes (every 1-2 hr., 75 min., 72F), Montpellier (every 1½-2 hr., 1¾ hr., 96F), Toulon (every ½ hr., 1 hr., 43F), and Nice (every hr., 2½ hr., 118F). Also to nearby Cassis (every ½ hr., 20 min., 21F). To Paris (9 TGV per day, 5 hr., 372F plus 13F required reservation) and Lyon (every 2 hr., 3½ hr., 178F). **SOS Voyageurs,** in the train station (tel. 91-64-71-00). Cheery retirees will help orient you and find you lodgings. Open Mon.-Sat. 8am-8pm.

Bus Station: Place Victor Hugo (tel. 91-08-16-40), behind the train station. Open Mon.-Sat. 8am-6:30pm, Sun. 8:30am-6pm. **Société Varoise de Transport (SVT),** Tel. 91-62-24-19. To Nice (2 per day by *autoroute,* 2 hr., 100F; 1 by the *nationale,* 4 hr., 74F) and Toulon (Mon.-Sat. 5 per day, 4 Sun.; 1½ hr., 35F). **Les Cars Verts de Provence,** Tel. 90-93-74-90. To Arles (4 per day, 2½ hr., 58.50F). **Les Rapides du Sudest,** Tel. 91-64-53-52. To Avignon (8 per day, 2½ hr., 68F). The **Société Cars et Autobus de Cassis,** Tel. 42-73-18-00. To Cassis (12 per day, 1 hr., 21F). **Cars Phoceens,** Tel. 91-50-57-68. To Cannes (2 per day by *autoroute,* 2 hr., 90F; 1 per day by *nationale,* 3 hr., 100F). Most bus companies offer reduced rates to students.

Ferries: SNCM, 61, bd. des Dames (tel. 91-56-32-00). Information and tickets for boats to Corsica and North Africa. To Tunis (in summer 4 per week; 22 hr.; 675F, ages 2-12 390F, students and large families 545F, plus 95F for *couchette*). To Tangiers in Morocco from Sète in France (2 per week; 48 hr.; 900F, children 450F, students and ages under 26 700F). To Sardinia from Marseille or Toulon (1 per week; 11 hr.; 450F, ages 2-12 315F). To Corsica from Marseille or Toulon (2-3 per day; 10 hr.; 220F, ages 4-12 117F). Prices are cheaper and boats less frequent Oct.-April. Round-trip tickets are sometimes less expensive than 2 one-ways. Office open Mon.-Fri. 8am-6:30pm, Sat. 2-5:30pm, Sun. 8am-6pm.

Municipal Transportation: A practical network of buses and metros run by **RTM,** 7, rue Reine-Elizabeth (tel. 91-91-92-10). Both take the same **tickets** (6.50F; 6 for 28F), which are sold at metro and bus stops. You can also pay for the bus with exact change. The ticket is good for 70 min. after first use for further rides on either bus or metro. Metro lines #1 and

2 both have stops at the train station. The former ("M2") will take you to the Vieux Port (*direction* "Castellane"). The tourist office has a free *RTM Plan-Guide du Réseau*.

Taxis: At taxi stands throughout the city (at the train station and on the Vieux Port) or by phone request. Available 24 hours. Prices are based on zone and time of day, and drivers have been known to overcharge. **Maison du Taxi,** Tel. 91-95-92-50. **Marseille Taxi,** Tel. 91-02-20-20. Call the mayor's office in case of complaints (tel. 91-77-16-00).

Hitchhiking: Allostop, 1, place Gabriel Péri (tel. 91-56-50-51). Matches riders with drivers. Open Mon.-Fri. 2-4pm, Sat. 10am-noon.

English Bookstore: Diffusion Générale de Librairie, 21, rue Paradis (tel. 91-33-57-91), off La Canebière. Reasonable prices, large selection. Open Mon.-Fri. 9am-noon and 2-6pm.

Laundromats: Laverie Libre Service, 27, bd. National (tel. 91-95-93-00). Wash 15F per 5kg, dry 2F per 6 min. **Laverie Automatique,** 18, rue de la Grande Armée (tel. 91-95-79-95), off square de Stalingrad. Run by a delightful manager. Wash 16F per 6kg, dry 2F per 6 min, soap 2F. Open daily 8am-7pm.

Special Services: SOS Amitié is a 24-hour crisis line (tel. 91-76-10-10). **CORPS** is a gay center at 48, rue de Bruys (tel. 91-94-19-91). Open in summer around 8pm. **CODIF,** 81, rue Sénac (tel. 91-47-17-05), has information for women. **Office Municipal pour Handicapés et Inadaptés,** 128, av. du Prado (tel. 91-81-58-80). An excellent center for disabled persons. Open Mon.-Fri. 9am-noon and 2:30-6pm. Transportation service for the disabled. Call 91-78-21-67 (8am-noon and 1-6pm) 1 day ahead of time. Service operates daily 6am-midnight.

All-night Pharmacy: The *pharmacie de garde* changes nightly. Call the police (tel. 91-91-90-40), consult a newspaper, or look on any pharmacy's door for the address.

Medical Emergency: For a home visit call 91-52-84-85. **SAMU** ambulances, Tel. 91-49-91-91.

Police: 2, rue Antoinne Becker (tel. 91-91-90-40). Also in the train station on Esplanade St-Charles (same tel., ask for *poste* 4017).

Police Emergency: Tel. 17.

Accommodations and Camping

Marseille has a profusion of inexpensive hotels, especially near the station on bd. Maurice Bourdet, place des Marseillaises, and for more central two-stars, rue Breteuil. Unfortunately, both hostels lie far from the center of town. Even in summer, with the help of the tourist office or the kindly SOS Voyageurs staff, you can almost always find space. Do not be tempted by the cheap prices and proximity of the hotels in the North African quarter. These are unsafe.

Auberge de Jeunesse de Bois-Luzy (IYHF), 76, av. de Bois-Luzy (tel. 91-49-06-18). Take bus #6 or 8 from cours Joseph Thierry (6.50F). A former château, located on a hill with a view of the *calanques* and the sea. Relaxed atmosphere. Proprietor speaks English, Finnish, and Dutch. Cooking and camping facilities (15F per night). Hot showers. The rooms and office close 10am-5pm, but the outside gate stays open 24 hours. There is a second hostel at **Bonneveine,** 47, av. J. Vidal (tel. 91-73-21-81), a short walk from the long, pebbly beach. From the station, take the metro to place Castellane (6.50F), then bus #19 to Les Gatons Plage or bus #44 to place Bonnefon (same ticket). Very large, but often filled. Cooking facilities. Office open 7:30-9:30am and 5-11pm. Both hostels charge 34F per night. Breakfast 11F. Other meals 34F. Hostel card required but can be purchased at both locations.

Hôtel Edmond Rostand, 31, rue Dragon (tel. 91-37-74-95), in the center of town off rue Paradis. A charming, intimate hotel run by two real gentlemen. Singles with shower 72F. Doubles with shower 99F. Triples 154F. Quads with shower 154F. Showers 10F. All-you-can-eat breakfast, served in your room if you wish, 16F. Reservations necessary in summer.

Hôtel Gambetta, 49, allées Léon Gambetta (tel. 91-62-07-88). Centrally-located and near the train station. Spotless modern rooms. Attentive couple give a good welcome to all. Singles 70F, with shower 100F. Doubles with shower 120F. Extra bed 30F. Showers, TV in room, and breakfast each 15F.

Hôtel Moderne, 11, bd. de la Libération (tel. 91-62-28-66). Follow La Canebière to rue de Monsabert, which becomes bd. de la Libération. Guests rave about this small but grand hotel and its manager. Singles 60F. Doubles 120F, with shower 140F. Triples 157F, with shower 177F. Showers and breakfast both a costly 20F. Fills early.

Hôtel de la Bourse, 4, rue Paradis (tel. 91-33-74-75), near the Vieux Port on an upscale street. Big, clean but slightly deteriorated rooms. One single 70F. Doubles 90F, with shower and TV 120F. Triples 140F. Quads with shower 190F. Showers 25F. Breakfast 20F.

Hôtel Azur, 24, cours Franklin Roosevelt (tel. 91-42-74-38), about 15 min. from the train station. Take allée Gambetta from bd. d'Athènes and go straight. Clean and pleasant rooms overlooking a small garden. Friendly multi-lingual receptionist. Recently renovated. Singles 100F, with shower 130F. Doubles 100F, with shower 150F. Showers 15F. Breakfast 20F.

Hôtel Moderne, 30, rue Breteuil (tel. 91-53-29-93). From the train or bus station, take bd. d'Athènes, which becomes bd. Dugommier, to right on La Canebière to the Vieux Port, which rue Breteuil feeds into. Immaculate rooms decorated with spunk. Singles or doubles 75F, with shower and TV 180F. Triples with shower and TV 180F. A few doors down is **Hôtel le St-Charles,** 26, rue Breteuil (tel. 91-37-78-86). Big rooms and nice management. Singles or doubles 95F, with shower 115F. Triples 125F, with shower 145F. Showers 10F. Breakfast 15F.

Hôtel Beaulieu, 1, place des Marseillaises (tel. 91-90-70-59). A little more expensive but just to the right after you descend the stairs from the train station. Small, clean, modern rooms, some of which can be noisy. Singles 112F, with shower 152F. Doubles 164F, with shower 184F. Triples with shower 246F. Showers 15F. Breakfast included. In summer, preference is given to those who pay for *demi-pension* (i.e., 1 meal besides breakfast).

Camping: Marseille's campsites are away from the urban pollution, south of the central city near the Parc Borely, a large, densely-wooded park with an English garden. Take bus #44 from the Castellane metro stop (6.50F). Try **Les Vagues,** 52, av. de Bonneveine (tel. 91-73-76-30), which is not far from the sea. (32F per 2 people and tent.) The **Auberge de Jeunesse de Bois-Luzy** allows camping in tents as well (15F).

Food

Marseille is the home of the celebrated *bouillabaisse,* a fish stew cooked with saffron and a meal in itself. Mussels, eel, and (at extra cost) lobster are often included in this special melange of local seafood, all of which *must* be fresh. For the real thing, expect to pay 60-100F. The restaurants on quai de Rive Neuve in the Vieux Port all serve their own versions of the famous stew at reasonable prices but of a lower quality. The slightly more expensive restaurants opposite, on quai du Port, serve better *bouillabaisse* and include a view of Notre Dame de la Garde. To prepare your own *bouillabaisse,* buy the ingredients directly from the fishers on quai des Belges at the base of La Canebière. Come early for the best quality and the most colorful scene. Bargain *couscous* restaurants abound near **rue Longue des Capucins,** but the neighborhood is dangerous at night.

Le Mondial, 68, rue Tilsit, off rue de Lodi near cours Julien. Cheap hole-in-the-wall, much favored by locals. 4-course 28F *menu,* has French classics, 33F with wine. Open Sept.-July Mon.-Fri. noon-2pm and 7-10pm.

Chez Soi, 5, rue Papere (tel. 91-54-25-41), off La Canebière. Quality family cooking and Provençal specialties. 45F *menu* with plenty of choice. Open mid-Aug. to mid-July Tues.-Sun. 11am-11pm.

Restaurant le St-Charles, 26, rue Breteuil (tel. 91-37-78-86), in the hotel of the same name. A neighborhood place with good food. 50F *menu* includes *hors d'oeuvre,* entree, and dessert. Thurs.-Sat. *couscous* 38-48F. Open Mon.-Sat. noon-2pm and 7-9pm.

La Dent Creuze, 14, rue Sénac (tel. 91-42-05-67), off La Canebière. Spirited staff in this popular, rustic restaurant cook up a storm, and **fast.** 50F *rapide menu* for lunch includes all-you-can-eat salad bar. Open Tues.-Fri. and Sun. noon-2pm and 7pm-midnight, Sat. 7pm-midnight.

Le Jardin d'A Côté, 65, cours Julien (tel. 91-94-15-51). Large outdoor parasols and appetizing salads are ideal for lunch, and the blue and white interior is pleasant when the *mistral* wind picks up. *Plat du jour* with wine 35F. Large salads 25-42F. Open noon-2:30pm and 8pm-1am.

Le Vaccares, 64, rue de La République (tel. 91-56-16-76), west of quai des Belges. Amiable staff and ample portions. 43F *menu* with tasty lamb and wine. Open Mon.-Sat. 11:30am-1pm and 7:30pm-midnight.

Sights and Entertainment

The **Jardin du Pharo,** at the mouth of the Vieux Port, contains a castle built by Napoleon III for Empress Eugénie, with excellent views of the harbor and city. The nineteenth-century **Basilique de Notre Dame de la Garde,** crowned with a gilded Virgin and lined with multicolored marble, could be considered fussy, but the main attraction is the view from the top of the Pomègues and Ratonneau Islands, Château d'If, the city, and its surrounding mountains. To get there, take bus #60, or follow rue Breteuil, turn right down bd. Vauban, and then turn onto rue Fort du Sanctuaire.

North of the port, on av. Robert Schumann, reigns the **Ancienne Cathédrale de la Major,** which has a Romanesque altar reliquary from 1122, a delicate ceramic relief by Luca Della Robbia, and a fifteenth-century altar dedicated to Lazarus. (Open Wed.-Mon. 9am-noon and 2-6:30pm.) At the end of quai de Rive Neuve, the **Abbaye St-Victor** evokes the ascetic beginnings of Christianity. The catacombs and basilica, constructed in the fifth century, contain an extensive array of both pagan and Christian relics, including the third-century remains of the two martyrs over whose tomb the abbey was originally built.

Gaudy **Palais Longchamp,** at the eastern end of bd. Longchamp, was built in the late nineteenth century and contains the eclectic **Musée des Beaux-Arts.** The museum is particularly strong in Provençal painting, but also exhibits paintings of Marseille's early history and devotes one room to Honoré Daumier (1808-1879), the satirical caricaturist from Marseille. Works by Ingres, David, and Rubens, and some early landscapes by Raoul Dufy are also displayed. (Open Thurs.-Mon. 10am-noon and 2-6:30pm, Wed. 2-6:30pm. Admission 6F.)

Marseille's many small museums appeal to individual interests. **Musée Cantini,** 19, rue Grignan, contains primarily Provençal ceramics but also has changing contemporary art exhibitions. The house alone, a seventeenth-century mansion with an elegant courtyard, merits a visit. (Open daily noon-7pm. Admission 3F, during exhibitions 12F.) **Musée Grobet-Labadié,** 140, bd. Longchamp, is also in a lovely mansion and displays musical instruments, some medieval sculpture, tapestries, Flemish paintings, and even a few Corot landscapes. (Open Thurs.-Mon. 10am-noon and 2-6:30pm, Wed. 2-6:30pm. Admission 5F.) **Musée du Vieux Marseille,** Maison Diamantée, 2, rue de la Prison, is a historic museum that features *santons,* tiny clay figures characteristic of the Provençal region, displays of maritime history, and maps. (Open Thurs.-Mon. 10am-noon and 2-6:30pm, Wed. 2-6:30pm. Admission 6F.)

Motorboats run from the Gare Maritime on quai des Belges (tel. 91-55-50-09; open daily 7am-7pm) to **Château d'If** (15 min., round-trip 32F), which was immortalized by Alexandre Dumas in *The Count of Monte Cristo.* The tour guides are willing to play along with the tale and will point out the hole through which the Count escaped. Originally designed to defend Marseille, the fortress was later used as a prison and confined Mirabeau and many Huguenots. Boats will also take you to **Ile de Frioul** (round-trip 32F), a large, parklike island. In summer, boats can take you around the *calanques.* All boats run more or less every hour from 7am to 7pm. Combined trips to Château d'If and Ile de Frioul cost 50F round-trip.

Along bd. Michelet (en route to the *calanques*) is Le Corbusier's **Cité Radieuse,** designed in the early 1950s. It embodies many of the architect's theories on modern, efficient, moderately priced housing.

Music festivals resound throughout the summer in Marseille. From late June to early August, internationally known singers perform beneath the stars in the Jardin du Pharo. In 1988 Ray Charles and Glenn Miller gave free concerts here. Call for information (tel. 91-55-29-92). There is also classical music at **Eglise du Sacré Coeur** and **Cathédrale de la Major.** (Tickets 100F.)

Cours Julien and rue Vian, 1 block up, are choice areas for promenades. You can watch the passersby in the early evening from **Il Caffe,** 63, cours Julien (tel. 91-42-02-19), an ideal spot for coffee or fresh juices (12F). (Open Mon.-Sat. 9am-9:30pm.) **L'Avant Scene,** 59, cours Julien (tel. 91-42-19-29), is a *café-théâtre* with a gallery, newsstand, and restaurant. (No theater in Aug.) **Septime Severe,** 8, rue Vian (tel. 91-42-10-19), has music, art, and salads late into the night. Down the street at **Les Thés Tard,** 2, rue Vian (tel. 91-42-29-74), an intriguing mix of *très* cool black Africans and mellow Gauls gathers. (Open daily noon-2pm and 7pm-2am.)

Place Thiers hides a good number of nightclubs, such as **Ascenseur,** with late-night jazz or Brazilian music. (Open nightly. Free.) You might also try the **Rose Bonbon,** 7, rue Venture (tel. 91-33-10-63), an upbeat nightclub between rue St-Ferreol and rue Paradis. Good gay clubs include **Boots,** 5, rue Haxo (tel. 91-54-41-15), and **Les Nuits Blanches,** 22, place Thiers. (Both open 11pm-daybreak.) For complete nightlife information, pick up *Marseille Poche* at the tourist office.

Near Marseille

Between Marseille and Toulon zigzag the **calanques,** inlets of clear blue water surrounded by walls of jagged rock. Splendid views greet the traveler all along the coastal route, with the most impressive *calanques* at **En Vau.** At **Port Miou,** the craggy rocks cradle blooming heather, and a small, tree-studded beach lies between the angular walls of **Port Pin.** During July and August, the **Société des Excursion-nistes Marseillais,** 16, rue de la Rotonde (tel. 91-84-75-52), conducts free walking trips of the *calanques* once or twice per week. Or, you can take bus #22 (*direction* "Les Baumettes") to the end of the line—near *calanques* Morgiou and Sormiou.

Twenty-three kilometers (and as many minutes by train) from Marseille is **Cassis,** an idle, rich, and beguiling resort town. (**Syndicat d'Initiative,** Tel. 42-01-71-17.) Immaculate white villas are clumped around the hills above Cassis, while the town itself—a network of winding staircases, slender alleyways, and gardens thick with flowers—rests beside a bright port and the deep blue sea. Getting there takes deter-mination, as the train station is 4km out of town. However, several **buses** from Mar-seille run to Cassis (1 hr., 18F). Call Société Cars et Autobus de Cassis (tel. 42-01-70-41) for schedule information. The only affordable lodging is the **Auberge de Jeu-nesse La Fontasse (IYHF),** 10km away on the B559 (tel. 42-01-02-72), toward Mar-seille. The hostel is open year-round (34F per night), but has no hot water, and even the nearest bus leaves you 5km away (*direction* "Les Calanques"). You might prefer to try **Camping Les Cigales** (tel. 42-01-07-34), 10 minutes away.

Toulon

Although more modest in size than Marseille, Toulon is hardly tame, with its salty, sassy port and an enigmatic Arab quarter. In this, the second largest port in France, uniformed sailors, looking like children on a school outing, wander the streets. Because Toulon is small, a good neighborhood rapidly blends into an unsafe one, and people alone should exercise care after 7pm on the streets between rue Jean Jaurès and the port.

Orientation and Practical Information

Toulon is connected by frequent trains to Marseille, St-Raphaël, and St-Tropez. The center of the city lies between the train station and the shore. A pedestrian zone cuts across the city, creating ideal spots for relaxed evenings in cafes. To get to the *syndicat* and the center of town, walk left out of the train station for 3 blocks, then turn right down av. Colbert.

Syndicat d'Initiative: 8, av. Colbert (tel. 94-22-08-22), at rue Victor Clapier. Makes free reser-vations for hotels in the city and knows which campsite has space—a valuable service, espe-cially in July and Aug. English-speaking staff exceedingly able and kind. Open July-Aug. Mon.-Fri. 8:30am-6:30pm, Sat.-Sun. 8am-6pm; Sept.-June Mon.-Sat. 8:30am-noon and 2-6:30pm. **Annex** in the train station (tel. 94-62-73-87) open daily July-Aug. 8am-7pm; Sept.-June 8:30am-6pm.

Student Travel: Voyages Wasteels, 3, rue Vincent Courdouan (tel. 94-92-93-93). Open Mon.-Fri. 9am-noon and 2-6:30pm, Sat. 9am-noon.

Currency Exchange: Aux Reflects de Provence, 15, quai Stalingrad, by the port. Competitive rates. Open July-Aug. daily 9:30am-10pm; Sept.-June Mon.-Sat. 9am-8pm.

Post Office: Place Liberté, at the western end of the pedestrian zone. **Postal code:** 83000. Open Mon.-Fri. 8am-7pm, Sat. 8am-noon. The *recette principale* is at the post office on rue Raymond Poincaré, about 15 min. east from the center of town.

Train Station: Bd. Toesca (tel. 94-22-90-00). Open daily 4am-12:30am; tickets and information daily 8am-7:30pm. To Marseille (every ½ hr., 1 hr., 43F), St-Raphaël (every hr., 1 hr., 56F), Nice (every hr., 2 hr., 87F), Cannes (every hr., 1½ hr., 72F), and Bandol (10 per day, 20 min., 13F). Buses and boats leave for St-Tropez from St-Raphaël. Three trains per day go to Hyères (16.50F) in summer.

Bus Station: Across from the train station (tel. 94-93-11-39). Open daily 8:30am-7pm. Buses depart from in front of the train station, except for the green bus to Bandol (every hour, 55 min., 12F), which leaves from the corner of av. du Maréchal Leclerc and av. Vauban. **Autocars Raynaud,** Tel. 94-93-07-45. **Sodetrav** (tel. 94-65-21-00) runs buses to St-Raphaël, with stops in several beach towns. To Hyères (every 15 min., 35 min., 28.50F), Le Lavandou (13 per day, 1¼ hr., 46F), Cavalaire (7 per day, 1¾ hr., 62F), La Foux, and St-Tropez (7 per day, 2 hr., 72F). To Ste-Maxime (5 per day, 2¾ hr., 80F), Fréjus (5 per day, 3 hr., 95F), and St-Raphaël (5 per day, 4 hr., 95F). In summer, trips may be much longer due to traffic. Less frequent connections Sept.-March.

Ferries: SNCM, 21 and 49, av. de l'Infanterie-de-Marine (tel. 94-41-25-76 or 94-41-01-76). To Corsica (2 per day; 10 hr.; 2nd-class round-trip 600F, ages 4-12 300F). In the "blue" period (Oct.-April), reductions for married couples on cabin tickets; ages 12-25 30% off; ages over 60 50%. Twice a day in summer boats go to Porquerolles (70F), Port Cros (100F), and Ile du Levant (120F). For general information, call the **Gare Maritime**(tel. 94-41-18-38).

Bookstore: Les Kiosques, rue Paul Ferrero (tel. 94-92-29-88), next to the Place Liberté post office. Good selection of cheap used books in English. Will buy books, tapes, and records. Open Mon.-Sat. 7:30am-8pm.

Laundromat: Laverie, 25, rue Baudin. Cheerful murals and best prices. Wash 10F per 7kg, dry 2F per 5 min. Open daily 7am-9pm.

Gay Center: Centre Homosexual d'Accueil Toulonnais (CHAT): 22 or 169, av. du. Dr. Fontan (tel. 94-62-60-78).

All-night Pharmacy: Call the police *commissariat* (tel. 94-22-90-30), or look on any pharmacy door for the name of that night's *pharmacie de garde.*

Medical Emergency: SAMU, Tel. 94-27-07-07. **SOS Medecins,** Tel. 94-62-50-50.

Police: Rue Xavier Savelli (tel. 94-22-90-30).

Police Emergency: Tel. 17.

Accommodations and Camping

Although finding an inexpensive hotel here is easier than elsewhere along the Côte d'Azur, you should still make reservations in July and August. Call a week in advance; some hotels will request a deposit by mail. You can send a traveler's check or *mandat* (money order) from the post office. Head for the areas of the upper *vieille ville,* safer than some questionable neighborhoods near the port.

Auberge de Jeunesse, rue Ernst Renan, Quartier Mourillon (tel. 94-46-59-59), south of downtown close to the beaches. Take bus #3 from av. de Maréchal Leclerc to the Lamalgue stop (7.80F). Walk up rue Castel; the hostel is on the right. Simple dormitory accommodations. Room doors not locked when the office is closed. 30F per night. Sheets 10F. Breakfast 10F. Dinner 42F. Curfew 11pm. Office open at 6pm. Hostel open July-Aug.

Hôtel Lutetia, 69, rue Jean Jaurés (tel. 94-93-07-75), right in the center. Big, rambling hotel and garrulous management welcome you with an excellent price. Singles and doubles 68F, with shower 115F. Triples 85F, with shower 115F. Quads 95F, with shower 150F. Showers 15F. Breakfast 15F.

Hôtel de Strasbourg, 10, rue Leblond St-Hilaire (tel. 94-92-84-78), near the end of rue Jean Jaurés, a 10-min. walk straight down from the station. Comfortable, large rooms with a gentle family in charge. Several singles 65F. Doubles with shower 110F. Triples with shower 160F. Hall showers included. Breakfast 16F.

Hôtel Lux, 52, rue Jean Jaurès (tel. 94-92-97-46), in the pedestrian zone. Sunny, cheery management and rooms. Den with TV. Singles 80F, with shower 110F. Doubles 90F, with shower 110F. Triples 125F, with shower 155F. Quads with bath tub 180F. Room for 5-6 215F. Showers 15F. Breakfast 18F.

Little Palace, 6-8, rue Berthelot (tel. 94-92-26-62), in the pedestrian zone. Old-fashioned rooms and friendly proprietor. Singles 70F. Doubles 80F, with shower 80-100F. Showers 10F. Breakfast, which can be served in your room, 15F.

Camping: There are many campgrounds around Toulon, but none in the city proper. Inquire at the tourist office about which sites have room. **Camping Beauregard** (tel. 94-20-56-35) is 6km from Toulon and 400m from the sea.

Food

You will find plenty of restaurants in and around the pedestrian zone. For seafood, look around the Vieux Port, but remember that the places on the waterfront charge for the view. Also try rue du Pomet and rue Poncy near the opera. Be careful at night, when sailors and prostitutes take control of the streets nearby. A fruit and vegetable **market** takes place every morning from 6am to noon on cours Lafayette.

Restaurant Riny, 52, rue Jean Jaurès (tel. 94-92-89-17). Here you're invited to see chef Bernard do his thing in the kitchen. At lunch, try *coq au vin* with wine (37F) or a traditional French *menu* (49F). Open Fri.-Sat. and Mon.-Wed. noon-1:30pm and 7-10pm, Sun. noon-1:30pm.

Piano Crêperie, 45, rue Victor Clapier (tel. 94-91-93-04). Over 50 crêpes (26-52F) and as much variety in the jazz played. Open nightly 7pm-1am.

Le Jardin des Delices, 2, rue Peliourier (tel. 94-93-19-30), in the middle of the pedestrian zone on Place Puget. Pleasant both inside and out (but eating on the terrace will cost 10% more). Appetizing veal 40F. Open Mon.-Sat. 7am-8:30pm, but full meals served noon-3pm only.

Al Dente, 30, rue Gimeli (tel 94-93-02-50), a few blocks from the *syndicat* at rue Dumont d'Urville. Fresh homemade pasta in an incongruously slick environment. Ravioli Roman-style (heavy on the cheese and herbs) 38F. On weekdays lunch *menu* 40F. Open Mon.-Fri. noon-2pm and 7-10:45pm, Sat.-Sun. until 11pm. Closed Sun. lunch.

Le Monarque, 2bis, place Gambetta (tel. 94-92-26-72), parallel to the port. Abundant 66F *menu* starts with choices from a cart with 18 hors d'oeuvres. Open Wed.-Mon. noon-2pm and 7pm-late.

Sights

Toulon's small, relatively isolated, and uncrowded beaches at **Mourillon** are accessible by bus #3 (stops in front of the train station and Galleries Lafayette on bd. Leclerc, 7.80F). You can visit the **Musée Naval,** place Ingénieur Général Monsenergue, to get your fill of models and replicas of old ships. (Open in summer daily 10am-noon and 1:30-6pm; in off-season Wed.-Mon. only. Admission 16F, students 8F.) From the sixteenth-century **Tour Royale** at the museum, you have a good view of the coast. (Admission 10F, children 5F.) For a wider view of the coast and city, take a *téléphérique* (suspended cablecar) to the top of Mont Faron from bd. Perrichi, several blocks behind the station. (Open in summer Mon. 9:15am-noon, Tues.-Sun. 9:15am-noon and 2:15-6pm; in off-season Tues.-Sun. only. One way 15F, round-trip 24F, children 16F.) The **Musée du Débarquement,** at the top, exhibits displays of the 1944 Allied landing. (Open daily 9:30-11:30am and 2:30-6:15pm. Admission 15F, children 7F.) Boat tours of the port leave from quai Stalingrad, as do one-hour boat trips to **St-Mandrier,** an isthmus with a fort and ancient prison (admission included in the 15.50F tour). From late May to mid-July, Toulon hosts an **international music festival** that attracts renowned groups from as far away as Moscow and a wide range of non-classical performers. Tickets (20F and up) are sold at the *syndicat* (tel. 94-93-52-84).

The Centre Culturel Châteauvallon, 5km from Toulon, hosts the **Festival de la Danse et de l'Image** in late July. Movies and musical performances are featured. (Festival tickets 30F for movies, 105F for performances.) Call 94-24-11-76 for information, or ask at the Toulon *syndicat*.

Bars galore, both gay and straight, line the streets around **rue Pierre Semard** and **rue des Riaux.** Although the police patrol these streets, lone visitors will feel uneasy as early as 7pm. A disco in a safer neighborhood is **Le Hi-fi Club,** 44, bd. de Strasbourg (tel. 94-92-31-14), near the *syndicat.*

Near Toulon

The islands off the coast of Toulon are known as the **Iles d'Hyères,** or the Golden Isles, a reference to the color of the sun's reflection off the mica rock. Reaching these treasured isles can be expensive, but few regret the trip. **Porquerolles,** the largest island, possesses the most colorful history. Inhabited first by a religious order, the island was declared a criminal's colony by royal mandate. Left to their own devices, the convicts soon transformed the island into a base for pirate forays all along the coast. Louis XIV finally ended their raiding decades later. If you have lots of time to spend in this national park, replete with sandy beaches, pine trees, and purple heather, "to the lighthouse" should be your resolve. Perched on the island's south side, the structure looks on panoramas of rocky cliffs plunging into blue waves. You can get there by walking straight through town from the port and continuing directly through the dry but pleasant interior of the island. Or turn right just outside the port (look for signs), and go to **Plage d'Argent.** Here a rambling pine grove gives way to a crescent of white sand, transparent water, and a yacht-filled cove. You can rent **bikes** outside the port; go left 100m towards town (35F per day, deposit 50F). As you disembark, you can't miss the **office de tourisme;** they distribute a list of accommodations on yachts (100-125F per night). The neighboring **Ile du Levant** harbors one of Europe's most famous nudist colonies, **Héliopolis,** which is rather ironic since monks also originally settled this island. Except for the western tip where ferries land, the entire island goes *au naturel.* The nudists enjoy massive, jutting cliffs, long *calanques* (rocky inlets), and lush vegetation. Rugged, peaceful **Port-Cros** is hilly and the least cultivated of the islands. The natural springs nourish greenery and flowers, and the entire island bursts with color—it is often referred to as the "Island of Eden." Although a wildlife preserve, it is privately owned and camping is prohibited. The tranquil "Solitude Walk" is precisely that, unless you come on a weekend in high season. The rewarding hike to **Port-Man** requires more time and energy. Fine beaches and well-equipped **campgrounds** grace **La Capte** on the **Glens Peninsula.** On Ile du Levant, you can camp at **Le Colombéro** (tel. 94-05-90-29) or **Les Eucalyptes** (tel. 94-05-91-32).

Boats for the islands (tel. 94-41-18-38 or 94-92-96-82) depart from quai Stalingrad in Toulon. Boats go to Porquerolles (round-trip 70F), Port Cros (round-trip 100F) and Ile du Levant (round-trip 120F) twice per day in the summer, once in off-season. The trips last between 1½ and 2 hr. Boats also depart for the islands from Port d'Hyères. (Infrequent trains from Toulon; bus every 15 min., 50 min., 27.50F.)

If you find yourself back on the mainland in **Hyères,** savor the carefully coiffed elegance of this oldest of Riviera resorts. The **Syndicat d'Initiative** in Hyères at Roton de Jean Salusse, av. de Belgique (tel. 94-65-18-55), will provide lists of campgrounds and hotels (open Mon.-Sat. 8:30am-noon and 2-6pm). The town holds a weeklong **Jazz Festival** in mid-July with international groups. Tickets (80F) are available at the Théâtre Denis, cours Strasbourg (tel. 94-65-22-72), or in Toulon at the Phonothèque, place de la Liberté (tel. 94-32-27-30).

Inland, two excellent wine-growing regions, small Bandol and Côtes de Provence, nudge Toulon from west and east. They produce mostly rosé, but also some white and red wines. **Bandol** has been a refuge for many literary figures, including Bertolt

Brecht and Thomas Mann. The resort has become popular with Germans, and even more so with the French. The hills around Bandol are filled with new holiday homes, but the town center retains hints of a traditional Mediterranean village. Its white, twisting streets surround a delightful town square, which doubles as market-place and nighttime dance floor. Bandol's **Office de Tourisme,** allées Vivien (tel. 94-29-41-35), near the bus station, will change money in summer. (Open in summer daily 9am-7pm; in off-season daily 9am-noon and 2-6pm.) Bandol is also a recreational center with tennis and sailing. In May and June you can watch regional regattas from the port. Rent a windsurfer at Hookipa Beach (tel. 94-29-53-15) for 55F per hour, with discounts for longer rentals. To hit a few, inquire at the Tennis Club Bandol (tel. 94-29-55-40). Just west of town are some delightful stone beaches snuggled up against steep coves. Be bold in your search; you may have to cut between private condominiums to get to these perfectly public beaches, but this is common practice. (Buses to Bandol leave the Toulon train station July-Sept. every 55 min. Call **Littoral Cars** at 94-29-46-58 for schedule information.) Trains stop in Bandol on the way to Marseille 10 times a day in summer (25 min., 13F).

About 10km north of Bandol lies the village of **Le Castellet,** quite tourist-ridden but pleasant, with plenty of handicraft stores where you can see artisans at work. On your way there, don't forget to sample the local wines in the many vineyards you will pass. You should have plenty of time to do this, since the best way to get to Le Castellet is to drive, hitch, or bike. You can rent a bicycle in Bandol at **Kit-Provence,** 118, av. du 11 Novembre (tel. 94-29-60-40), for 30F per half-day, 60F per day, 175F per week. Small roads from Le Castellet lead to **La Cadière-d'Azur,** a small village with three chapels and a view of the Provençal valley.

St-Tropez

St-Tropez is preceded—and exceeded—by its risqué reputation. Images are transmitted by the media of the wealthy and the beautiful flaunting themselves on the beaches, of celebrity-studded streets, and of decadent living. You can see the supposed *crème de la crème* of St-Tropez striking pretty poses on the decks of their jumbo yachts, which crowd the tiny port. However, remember Edward Lear's answer to St-Tropez decades ago: "Bosh!" St-Tropez is best seen on a day-trip because of high restaurant prices, a paucity of cheap hotels, and above all, because St-Tropez is just another pretty beach. Try finding something to do here on a rainy day: Eyeing the Signac and Matisse works in the museum will occupy all of 30 minutes.

The famous beaches are all 3-8km from the center of town. **Plage de Pampelonne** (6km away) has the most sand, **Plage de Tahiti** (4km) the most wealth, and **Plage des Salins** (4km) the most public space. (Some readers have reported, however, that the last is unsafe.) A city-run minibus leaves from place des Lices every 20 minutes for the beaches (daily except Mon. afternoon, 8F, last leaves at 5:25pm). Sodetrav buses also run to Pampelonne (5-6 per day, 15 min., 12-15F) and Tahiti (3 per day, 10 min., 12F). Hitching remains a popular form of transportation, so you may have some competition. You can rent your own wheels from **Louis Mas,** 5, rue Quaranta (tel. 94-97-00-60). Bicycles go for 42F per day, deposit 500F; mopeds start at 71F per day, deposit 1500F, gas 20F. (Open Mon.-Sat. 9am-7pm, Sun. 9:30am-12:30pm and 6:45-7:15pm.) Great swimming and good climbing rocks can be found at **Plage de l'Escalet,** 15km away (the Sodetrav beach bus from St-Tropez stops at the village of l'Escalet twice per day). Otherwise, you can walk to **Les Canoubièrs,** a smaller, quieter beach 10 minutes out of town, or the small **Plage des Graniers,** just east of town past the incongruous marine cemetery. You needn't worry about being underdressed at any of these beaches, but be prepared to have your body critically assessed by all.

It is worth strolling around St-Tropez itself, and climbing up the **citadelle** to enjoy a panoramic view of the entire gulf. The dungeon of this sixteenth-century fortress houses a naval museum with paintings of scenes from the village's history and other artifacts. (Open June 15-Sept. 15 Wed.-Mon. 10am-6pm; Sept. 15-Oct. and Dec.-

June 14 Wed.-Mon. 10am-5pm. Admission 14F.) In the serene confines of an ancient chapel, the **Musée de l'Annonciade,** rue de la Nouvelle Poste, exhibits a wild, impressive collection of fauvist and neo-impressionist paintings by Signac, Derain, Van Dongen, Vlaminck, and Matisse. Temporary shows occupy the ground floor. (Open June-Sept. Wed.-Mon. 10am-noon and 3-7pm; Oct. and Dec.-May 10am-noon and 2-6pm. Admission 10F, students 4.50F.)

Each year from May 16 to 18, St-Tropez goes all out with its *bravade* (act of defiance) in honor of its patron saint—a Christian martyr beheaded by Nero. The martyr's body was set adrift with a cock and a dog aboard only to arrive intact in this town, which to this day takes good care of its bodies.

The **Syndicat d'Initiative,** quai Jean Jaurès (tel. 94-97-41-21), can give you information on sports and can try to help you find a room. (Open June-Oct. Mon.-Sat. 9am-8pm, Sun. 10am-1pm; in off-season Mon.-Sat. 9am-7pm.) There is a small **American Express** bureau, 23, av. du Général Leclerc. (Open for financial services Mon.-Sat. 9am-9:30pm.) The **postal code** is 83990.

Even by mid-June the few affordable hotels are generally booked. Call ahead or hope for the best at **Les Chimères,** quartier du Pilon (tel. 94-97-02-90), on the edge of town a few blocks beyond the bus station off av. Leclerc. (Singles 100F, doubles 160F. Breakfast included.) **Lou Cagnard,** 18, av. Paul Roussel (tel. 94-97-04-24), a two-star hotel, offers doubles with shower from 160F. Camping is by far the cheapest option, but again, you should make reservations. The tourist office will tell you which sites have space, but you probably won't have much luck in July and August. **Camping Courban,** route de la Belle Isnarde (tel. 94-97-11-84), is pleasant. (21F per person, including tent.) You might also try **La Croix du Sud,** route de Pampelonne (tel. 94-79-80-84; 17F per person, 30F per tent), or **Les Tournels,** route du Phare de Camarat (tel. 94-79-81-38; 34F per person, including tent). There are no youth hostels nearby—the closest is the **Auberge de Jeunesse (IYHF)** in La Garde-Freinet (tel. 94-43-60-05), 20km away. This relaxed hostel hides in a tiny village in the mountains. (43F per night. Breakfast included. Meals 32F. Open March 15-Oct.15. No reservations accepted, but call before you leave to make sure there's room.) Take the bus from the *gare routière* near the port (1 per day).

High prices are part of St-Tropez's trademark. Find a less expensive restaurant for dinner, but don't skip the ritual coffee at the portside **Café Senequier** or **Café des Arts** on place des Lices. Pasta (*spaghetti carbonara* 35F) waits to be devoured at the **Trattoria di Roma,** av. du Général Leclerc (tel. 94-97-51-97), near the bus station. (Open daily noon-10pm.) **Mario,** 7, rue de la Miséricorde, offers French and Italian dishes on an extravagant lavender terrace for 25-60F. (Open daily 7pm-late.)

The town lies well off the rail line but can be reached by **bus** from St-Raphaël (8 per day, 1½ hr. but twice as long in traffic, 38.50F), Toulon (8 per day, 2½-4 hr., 76.60F), or Hyères (6 per day, 2-3 hr., 60F). Call **Sodetrav buses** (tel. 94-97-62-77), or ask the tourist office for more information. A faster, no more expensive, and much more enjoyable alternative is to go by boat from the port in St-Raphaël (mid-June to mid-Sept. 3-4 per day, April-June and Sept.-Oct. 1-2 per day; 50 min.; one way 40F, round-trip 80F). Boats also leave from July to the beginning of September from Ste-Maxime and Port-Grimaud (about every ½ hr., 20 min., one way 16.50F, round-trip 32F). Contact **Gare Maritime de St-Raphaël** (tel. 94-95-17-46) for more information. (Open daily 9am-noon and 2-6pm.)

St-Tropez to Cannes

Known to the French as the "land of blue, green and gold," the Var, the coast and the hinterland between St-Tropez and Cannes, makes a wonderfully varied sojourn for tourist-weary tourists. Here the sky and sea, the inland forests, and the sun and sand (rarer as you move east) form particularly rich and enticing hues.

When the glitter and crowds become intolerable, head to one of the nearby hill towns, such as **Grimaud,** with its shady lotus trees, old fortress, and eleventh-century, barrel-vaulted church. It is on the St-Raphaël-Toulon bus line, with a connection at La Foux (from St-Raphaël 8 per day, 1½-3 hr., 37F; from Toulon 1 direct line per day and several with a change, 2½-4 hr., 78F). The bus from Toulon goes on to the less frequented, more picturesque village of **La Garde-Freinet** (15 min. from Grimaud), with a small but exceptional youth hostel (see St-Tropez Accommodations) and a good campground, **Camping Municipal St-Eloi** (tel. 94-43-62-40), with free hot showers and a snack bar. (Open June to mid-Sept.; 7.50F per person, 8.50F per tent.) Camping is one of the best ways to take advantage of the dazzling landscape; pick up a copy of *Campings du Var* at area *syndicats*. The friendly **Syndicat d'Initiative** is next to the youth hostel in **Chapelle St-Eloi.** (Open Wed.-Mon. 9:30am-12:30pm and 5:30-7:30pm; tel. 94-43-67-41 in summer; 94-43-62-86 in off-season.)

The alluring beauty of some French towns does not come without effort. In the early 1960s, striving to recreate a typical Mediterranean fishing village, **Port Grimaud** let the sea flow into canals dug throughout town, creating avenues of water. The original goal has been partially attained: Boats have replaced cars, which must be left outside the town limits. However, Port Grimaud's wealth renders it fundamentally different from its humble ideal. In any case, the artificial beaches are clean and uncrowded. There are large campgrounds just outside town, including **Les Prairies de la Mer** (tel. 94-56-25-29), a three-star site open from April through October. (50F per 2 people, tent included.) You can reach Port Grimaud from St-Tropez by ferry and bus (8 per day, 7F). The hitching back from Port Grimaud is said to be best from the parking lot at the town exit. Nearby **Ste-Maxime** is another tourist-mobbed center with a sandy beach (8 buses per day from St-Raphaël, 45 min., 23.50F). The **Syndicat d'Initiative**, av. Général de Gaulle (tel. 94-96-19-24), can help you navigate your way. (Open July-Sept. daily 9am-7pm; Oct.-June Mon.-Sat. 9am-noon and 1:30-6pm, Sun. 10am-noon and 3-5pm.) **Les Issambres** (½-1 hr., 12-15F from St-Raphaël on the same bus line) and **St-Aygulf** (20 min., 5.50F) offer perhaps slightly more appealing beaches.

You'll probably land in **St-Raphaël** if you arrive by train and want to travel around the Côte by bus. A resort for the rich since prominent Romans came for the fresh air, St-Raphaël is still host to the affluent. However, the expanse of public beaches, relatively cheap hotels, and the refreshingly unassuming locals await those on the other side of the financial spectrum. Buses for St-Tropez (8 per day, 1½-3 hr., 37F) and other coastal towns, as well as for Toulon (8 per day, 3-5 hr., 102F), leave from the other side of the train tracks. (Go down the hill, through the underpass, and turn right.) Boats for St-Tropez (see St-Tropez) depart from the Gare Maritime, a 5-minute walk to your right from the station. (Turn left when you see the harbor.) You can also, on certain days, travel by boat to Port-Grimaud and the Iles de Lérins. The **Comité Départemental de Tourisme**, (tel. 94-40-49-90) in the train station, provides useful hotel and transportation information for all of the Var, including booklets of suggested bike and car routes. (Open Mon.-Thur. 8am-noon and 2-6pm, Fri. 8am-noon and 2-5pm, Sat. 8:30am-noon.) The good-natured woman who runs this office is more knowledgable than the staff at the *syndicat,* place de la Gare (tel. 94-95-16-87), across from the train station. However, the *syndicat* staff can tell you about room availability, a significant problem in July and August. (Open June-Aug. Mon.-Sat. 8:30am-noon and 2-6pm, Sun. 8:30am-noon; Nov.-May Mon.-Sat. only.) **Les Templers**, place République (tel. 94-95-38-93), is a large, jolly hotel and restaurant with singles for 90F, doubles 120F. **Hôtel des Pyramides**, 77, av. Paul Doumer (tel. 94-95-05-95), is a two-star hotel with singles for 90F, doubles 150F (breakfast included). By the ocean is **Centre International du Manoir (IYHF)**, in Boulouris (tel. 94-95-20-58), a plush, modern youth hostel, with dormitory rooms in the annex and a bar and disco. (75F per person. Rooms with 1-5 beds 100F per person. Breakfast included. Meals 45F.) A bus makes the 5-km trip to the hostel from St-Raphaël approximately every half-hour until 6:30pm (4.60F). A daily morning market occurs behind the train station under the overpass, but Les Templers restaurant nearby is a good deal with 45F, 55F, and 60F *menus* and pizza for 30-35F. (Open daily noon-1:30pm and 7-11:30pm.) The scene at the bar, patronized by aged and young locals alike, is a riot.

The town of **Fréjus,** founded by Julius Caesar in 49 B.C.E., lies 10 minutes away from St-Raphaël by bus (every ½ hr., 4.50F). Small and sedate, Fréjus can either be very relaxing or quite dull. The partially reconstructed Roman **amphithéâter** (open June-Sept. Wed.-Mon. 9-11:45am and 2-6:15pm; Oct.-May Wed.-Mon. 9-11:45am and 2-4:15pm; admission 6F) is unremarkable until the bullfights begin on July 17 and Aug. 15. Fréjus's **cathédrale** has a baptistry, probably built at the end of the late fourth century, making it one of the oldest buildings in France; the original mosaics merit a visit. Surprisingly, Fréjus puts on mammoth rock concerts each summer (tel. 94-53-44-95 or 94-52-26-60; tickets from 100F); George Michael came in 1988. The **Syndicat d'Initiative** is in place Calvani (tel. 94-51-53-87; open Mon.-Sat. 9am-noon and 3-6pm). Along **Corniche de l'Estérel,** there is the cheap but usually full **Auberge de Jeunesse Le Trayas/Théoule-sur-Mer (IYHF),** av. de la Veronese (tel. 94-44-14-34), a 2-km bus ride from Le Trayas's train station. There are five trains per day from St-Raphaël (about 12.30F) and Cannes (10F), the last one leaving each station about 6:30pm; there are also eight buses per day from Cannes (½ hr., 9.30F) and St-Raphaël (35 min., 13.50F).

The *massif* (rock mass) between St-Raphaël and La Napoule has the most spectacular scenery on the Côte. Blood-red rocks are splattered with the rich green of olive trees and the brilliant yellow of mimosa blossoms. Forming a series of *calanques* (coves), the rocks plunge abruptly into the glowing blue of the Mediterranean. You can catch only a glimpse from the train or bus, since most tracks pass through tunnels; the best way to see the stunning *corniche* (cliffs) is to rent a minibike.

The village of **La Napoule** has a peculiarly intriguing **museum,** set in a medieval château, which houses the bizarre works of American sculptor Henry Clews. His art features a grotesque menagerie of scorpions, lizards, and gnomes. The museum is generally open in the late afternoon, but you should call beforehand as the hours vary (tel. 94-49-95-05; admission 9F). Traffic-ridden La Napoule is not the place for a long visit. Fortunately, it lies on the train and bus lines between St-Raphaël and Cannes (by bus from St-Raphaël 17.50F, from Cannes 6.10F).

About 80km northwest of Cannes reigns the **Grand Canyon de Verdon,** 630m deep and 20km long, said to be the deepest canyon in Europe. Here, massive cliffs streaked with yellow and pink plunge to swift rivers and forested valleys. A rented car will simplify the visit immensely; good roads with spectacular views twist through this unspoiled territory. You can get hiking maps and information on shelters and camping in the canyon from the **Syndicat d'Initiative,** in the mairie at **Les Salles-sur-Verdon** (tel. 94-70-20-01). Les Salles sits just outside Aiguines, which is connected daily by bus with **Draguignan,** in turn accessible by infrequent bus from Cannes, and by almost hourly buses from St-Raphaël (65 min., 20.50F). The *syndicat* at Draguignan, av. Georges Clemenceau (tel. 94-68-63-30), also has information on the Verdon Canyon. Bus tours of the canyon leave from St-Raphaël's train station on Thursdays from June through September (departing 8am and returning around 7pm, 105F). Reservations are advised; contact **Forum Cars,** place de la Gare (tel. 94-95-16-71). Similar tours leave twice per week (April-Sept.) from Antibes (107F) and Cannes (107F), and weekly from Nice (150F). However you travel through the canyon, seek out the vertiginous views at Point Sublime and at the Balcons de la Mescla. Buses run once per day from Draguignan to Comps and Castellane at the eastern end of the canyon. Midway between Aiguines and Castellane is the **Auberge de Jeunesse (IYHF)** at La-Palud-sur-Verdon (tel. 92-74-68-72), accessible by bus from Castellane. (33F per person. Camping 15F. Open March-Nov.) Pleasant lodging is also available at the **Auberge du Point Sublime,** 17km from Castellane (tel. 92-83-60-35). Call before hitching or taking a taxi. (Doubles with shower 100F. Breakfast 16F.)

Cannes

Cannes, the costliest, most gaudy jewel in the Riviera's collection, sparkles with opulent villas, expensive boutiques, and cafes serving 18F lemonades. Yet the plebeian traveler can still do reasonably well here once ensconced on Cannes's public, sandy beach. Apart from perfecting your tan, there's little to do except window-shopping or attending bizarre events such as the recent Clairvoyancy and Hairdressing Festivals. Every May, 350 films are unveiled at the **Festival International du Film,** as directors, actors, producers, and star-gazers gather around the Palais des Festivals. Some screenings are open to the public, but normally all you can do is stand outside and gape. Tickets go on sale a week in advance at the *billetterie* (ticket office) of the Palais des Festivals. Cannes, the sister city (and appropriately so) of Beverly Hills, also holds a **Festival Américain.** The gala begins on July 4 and ends on July 14, Bastille Day, thus celebrating revolutions on both sides of the Atlantic; tickets for the football game and the jazz and country music concerts are available at the ticket office.

Orientation and Practical Information

The heart of town is **boulevard de la Croisette,** a long and lavish promenade that runs beside the sea. On one side of the road stand palatial luxury hotels; on the other stretch private beaches, owned by the hotels and studded with parasols. Don't despair, though; if you walk far enough westward down la Croisette, you will come to a small block of public beach. There are other sandy public beaches past Port Canto and past Palm Beach (on place Franklin Roosevelt)—windsurfing lessons are offered at the one near Palm Beach.

The *syndicat* in the train station will give you a map for 2F; otherwise, just walk straight ahead out of the station towards the ocean for 5 blocks. You'll pass **rue d'Antibes,** a major street with many boutiques; you should head down rue Belges to boulevard de la Croisette. Turn right on la Croisette for 1 block and you'll see the smoked glass **Palais des Festivals** set on the waterfront. The main tourist office is on the ground floor.

Syndicat d'Initiative: 1, rue Jean-Jaurès (tel. 93-99-19-77), upstairs in the train station. Plenty of brochures, but the staff is patronizing and inept. Will make hotel reservations free of charge and suggest bike and car rentals. English spoken. Open July-Aug. daily 9am-8pm; Sept.-June Mon.-Sat. 9am-1pm and 2-6pm. **Branch office,** 1, bd. de la Croisette (tel. 93-39-24-53). Also handles parking spaces and sells rail tickets. Open Mon.-Sat. 9am-6pm.

Budget Travel: Tourisme SNCF, in the train station (tel. 93-39-20-20). BIJ/Transalpino tickets. Open Mon.-Fri. 9am-noon and 2-6pm, Sat. 9am-noon.

Cannes Information Jeunesse: 7, rue Georges Clemenceau (tel. 93-68-50-50). General youth information. For more details on various water sports and activities, go to **OMJASE,** the Municipal Youth Office, at 2, quai St-Pierre (tel. 93-38-21-16).

Currency Exchange: Office Provençal, 17, rue Maréchal-Foch (tel. 93-39-34-37), across from the main train station. Open Mon.-Fri. 8am-7pm; in off-season Mon.-Fri. 9am-noon and 2-7pm.

American Express: 8, rue des Belges (tel. 93-38-15-87). Open Mon.-Fri. 9am-noon and 2-6pm, Sat. 9am-noon. **AmEx Bank,** 3, bd. de la Croisette (tel. 93-39-84-67), will also exchange money. Open Mon.-Fri. 9am-noon and 2-5pm.

Post Office: Main Office, 22, rue Bivouac Napoléon (tel. 93-39-14-11). **Branch office,** 37, rue Mimont (tel. 93-38-30-79), behind the train station. **Postal code:** 06400. Both branches have **telephones** and are open Mon.-Fri. 9am-6pm, Sat. 9am-noon. In July and Aug. there is a mobile **telephone office** on quai St-Pierre. Open daily 9am-10pm.

Train Station: 1, rue Jean-Jaurès (tel. 93-99-50-50). Cannes lies on the major coastal line, with connections approximately every ½ hr. to St-Raphaël (½hr., 24F), Juan-les-Pins (10 min., 6.50F), Antibes (15 min., 8F), Nice (40 min., 25F), Monaco (1¼ hr., 32F), and Menton (1½ hr., 35F). Also hourly to Toulon (1¼ hr., 69F), Marseille (2 hr., about 90F), and many other towns. Station open 6am-midnight. Information desk open 8:15am-noon and 2-6pm. Ticket sales until 11pm.

Bus Station: Two locations. Next to the train station (tel. 93-39-31-37). Open daily 9am-noon and 2-6:15pm. To Grasse (every ½ hr., 45 min., 14.70F), Mongrins (every hr., 15 min., 6.80F), Golfe-Juan (5 per day, 6.20F), and Vallauris (every hr., 8F). Most buses leave from place de l'Hôtel de Ville (tel. 93-39-18-71). Every 20 min. to Juan-les-Pins (½ hr., 9.10F), Antibes (10.10F), Nice (1¼ hr., 24.60F). Also to St-Raphaël (7 per day, 70 min., 21F), stopping along the way at La Napoule (6.10F), Le Trayas (9.50F), Grasse, and Vallauris. **Local buses** 5.40F, 6 tickets 18.60F.

Taxis: Tel. 93-38-30-79.

Bike Rental: 2 Roues, 5, rue Allieis (tel. 93-39-46-15), off place Gambetta in front of the train station. Bicycles 42F per day, deposit 1000F. Mopeds from 95F per day, deposit 2000F. Open Mon.-Sat. 9am-noon and 3-7pm.

Hitching: Call **Allostop** in Marseille (see Marseille Practical Information) or visit Cannes Information Jeunesse (see above) to register in person.

Showers: Rue Jean Hibert (tel. 93-68-52-13), in the *vieille ville.* Open mid-Sept. to mid-Aug. Wed.-Fri. 3-6pm, Sat. 8-11am and 3-6pm, Sun. 8-11:30am.

All-night Pharmacy: The location of the night's *pharmacie de garde* is printed in the daily *Nice Matin* in the Cannes section, and affixed to the door of every Cannes pharmacy.

Hospital: Pierre Nouveau, 13, av. des Broussailles (tel. 93-69-91-33).

Medical Emergency: Tel. 93-38-39-38 or 93-99-12-12.

Police: Tel. 93-39-10-78.

Police Emergency: Tel. 17.

Accommodations and Camping

Although most of Cannes's hotels have more stars than you can afford, there are some good bargains centrally located just off rue d'Antibes, and close to the beach. Be sure to book ahead, but if you arrive early in the day, the tourist office can usually find you a room.

Hôtel National, 8, rue Maréchal-Joffre (tel. 93-39-91-92), a few blocks to the right as you leave the station. Tired management and tired rooms, but clean, cheap, and conveniently located. Singles 90F. Doubles 110F. Triples 180F. Showers 12F. Breakfast 18F.

Hôtel de Bourgogne, 13, rue du 24-Août (tel. 93-38-36-73), a small street 1 block to the right from rue des Serbes as you leave the station. Adequate rooms and gruff owner. Centrally located. Singles 75F. Doubles 90F, with shower 140F. Showers 14F. Breakfast 15F. Open Jan.-Nov.

Hôtel Chanteclair, 12, rue Forville (tel. 93-39-68-88), a few streets from the western end of rue Félix-Fauré. Nice rooms on a quiet, sheltered courtyard. Lovely women just took over. Singles 100F. Doubles 130F, with shower 160F. Triples 150F, with shower 180F. Showers 10F. Breakfast 17F.

Hôtel des Roches Fleuries, 92, rue Georges-Clemenceau (tel. 93-39-28-78), a 10-min. walk from the center of town. Sumptuous split-level rooms. Captivating terrace garden. Budget-demolishing luxury. Singles 132F, with shower 182F. Doubles 150F, with shower 200F. Triples with shower 270F. Showers 15F. Breakfast included. Open Dec. 27-Nov. 14.

Hôtel Régence, 13, rue St-Honoré (tel. 93-39-05-42), 1 block from bd. de la Croisette near the public beach. Tidy and simple rooms. Doubles 144F. Triples 226F. Quads 268F. Showers 10F. Breakfast included. Open Dec.-Oct.

Hôtel du Nord, 6, rue Jean-Jaurès (tel. 93-38-48-79), across from the train station. Outgoing owner loves the USA and has traveled there extensively. Eat breakfast among pictures of the Grand Canyon. Pleasant rooms but some let in a lot of street noise. Singles 145F. Doubles 210F, with showers 250F. Triples with showers 320F. Hall showers included. Breakfast 16F. Open Dec. 16-Nov. 14.

Robert's Hotel, 16, rue Jean Jaurès (tel. 93-38-66-92), in front of the train station. Doubles 165F, with shower 200F. Triples with shower 260F. Showers 12F. Breakfast included. Open March-Dec.

Camping: Le Grand Saule, 24-26, bd. de la Frayere (tel. 93-47-07-50), in nearby Ranguin. Take the bus from place de l'Hôtel de Ville or the local train (hourly, 12 min.). A 3-star site with hot showers and pool, but sometimes crowded. 99F per 2 people, tent included. Open Easter-Oct. In Cannes-La Bocca, try **Caravaning Bellevue,** 67, av. M. Chevalier (tel. 93-47-28-97), with 211 spaces. 55F per person, tent included. Open March-Oct. Also, **Aire Naturelle Clos St-Hubert,** quai de la Badie (tel. 93-48-67-32), has 25 spaces. 45F per 2 people. Open June-Sept. For more breathing space, try the 11 campgrounds around Mandelieu. **Camping Les Pruniers,** la Pinède, av. de la Mer (tel. 93-49-92-85 or 93-49-99-23), 8km away, isn't gorgeous, but you'll get in. 80F per 2 people. To get to Mandelieu, take the St-Raphaël bus to La Napoule (8 per day, 10 min., 6.80F); the campgrounds are within easy walking distance. Infrequent trains run to La Napoule from Cannes (6F).

Food

The elegant sidewalk cafes on bd. de la Croisette, Cannes's center of conspicuous consumption, are very expensive. Stock up on packaged provisions at the **Casino Supermarket,** 55, bd. d'Alsace (open Mon.-Sat. 8:30am-10pm), which also has a characterless cafeteria upstairs, good for a quick bite (entrees 15-35F; open daily 11am-11pm). Better yet, go to the outdoor markets in place Gambetta and rue Forville, held every morning until about 12:30pm. Rue Meynadier, a scenic pedestrian street, is lined with many inexpensive restaurants with outdoor seating.

Chez Mamichette, 1, rue St-Antoine (tel. 93-39-49-62), off the western end of rue Félix Fauré. A cozy, cheerful Savoyard restaurant up a hill near the Vieux Port. Try the *fondue savoyarde* (45F), the *menu* (60F) or, if you're really hungry, the *raclette* (85F). Open Mon.-Sat. noon-2pm and 7-11pm. Several other attractive restaurants line the same street.

Au P'Tit Creux, 82, rue Meynadier (tel. 93-38-94-95). Tiny restaurant serving hearty *couscous* (45F) and a *menu* with French classics (55F). Outdoor seating. Open daily noon-2pm and 6pm-midnight.

Manhattan, 3, rue Félix-Fauré (tel. 95-39-74-00). The restaurant that never sleeps. Pizza 32F, loud music and videos from 7pm-7am.

La Lorraine, 36, bd. de Lorraine (tel. 93-38-51-39), a 10-min. walk to the left from the train station. *Choucroute* and other Alsatian (despite the name) specialties in a large, elegant room. 55F *menu.* Open daily 11am-1pm and 6:30-10pm.

Le Bouchon, 10, rue de Constantine (tel. 93-99-21-76), around the corner from La Lorraine. Varied 58F and 85F *menus* feature *canard à l'orange* (duck with orange sauce, 70F) and *aïoli* (Provençal garlic mayonnaise dip with raw vegetables, 50F). Open Jan.-Nov. Tues.-Sun. 7-10pm.

Entertainment

While it may not have much in the museum department, Cannes certainly does know how to entertain its guests at night. Popular with locals, **Le Blitz,** 22, rue Massé (tel. 93-39-31-31), has both disco and video bar. (Open daily 11pm-4am. 50F per person.) *Au pairs* and other international types favor the **Bar du Port,** quai St-Pierre. (Open daily 8pm-2:30am.) The **Mendigotte** bar, 22, rue Mace (tel-93-39-31-31), is a favorite of lesbians and gay men. (Opens 11pm.)

Cannes to Nice

If you are based in Cannes or Nice, many a daytrip, by rail or by boat, awaits you. Both the **Iles de Lérins** off the coast of Cannes have small inlets for swimming and relaxing. Owned by a Cistercian order of monks, the smaller **St-Honorat** still harbors an active monastery (open daily 10am-2:30pm), and its quiet pine forests are a welcome change from fast-paced Cannes. **Ile Ste-Marguerite,** also pleasantly forested, is best-known for its fort, open to visitors. This was the home of the Man in the Iron Mask, immortalized by Dumas. Twelve boats per day leave from the harbor across from the Cannes tourist office on bd. de la Croisette. (Round-trip Cannes to St-Honorat ½ hr., 30F; Cannes to Ste-Marguerite 15 min., 25F.) Boats also leave from Golfe-Juan and Juan-les-Pins to both islands. (Round-trip to both islands 50F, ages 4-10 ½-price.)

Mougins, set on a hill only 8km from Cannes, is one of the most peaceful towns on the coast. Picasso came here to find inspiration among the rambling hills, olive trees, gentle streams, and valleys. Walk through the streets of this old fortified town, and climb to the top of the monastery tower for an unrivaled view of the coast. Buses leave from near the train station in Cannes (every 20 min., 15 min., 7.50F).

Grasse, in the hills outside Cannes, is the perfume capital of the world, and the *parfumiers* lead free tours around their factories. The **Fragonard Parfumerie** is the largest (open daily 8:30am-6:30pm). Grasse may be fragrant, but unless you're a cologne-freak there's not much to see. Even its local hero, the eighteenth-century painter Fragonard, became bored and left for Paris. The **Villa-Musée Fragonard,** 23, bd. Fragonard, exhibits some of his work as well as that of other members of his family. (Open July-Sept. Mon.-Fri. and the 1st and last Sun. of each month 10am-noon and 2-6pm; Oct.-June Mon.-Fri. 2-5pm. Admission 6F, children free.) Buses leave from near the train station in Cannes and pick up passengers at the bus station at place de l'Hôtel de Ville (every 20 min., 45 min., 15F).

Most towns on the Riviera stay up late, but no place hops like **Juan-les-Pins.** Boutiques remain open until midnight, cafes until 2am, and nightclubs until 4 or 5am. Every year, in the second half of July, the **Festival International de Jazz** arranges an outstanding music program (tickets 130-200F). If you are male, your best bet might be to leave your pack at the station, stay at a club (cover 60-100F) until 5am, and then stake out a spot to nap on the beach at dawn. One such dance club is **Les Pêcheurs** on Port Gallice. (Open June-Sept. 11pm-5am.) The beaches are unsafe for women at night. Unless it is July or August, a good room is not impossible to find in Juan-les-Pins. The **Syndicat d'Initiative,** 51, bd. Guillaumont (tel. 93-61-04-98), will provide restaurant and hotel lists but will not make reservations. (Open in summer Mon.-Sat. 9am-noon and 2-6pm, Sun. 10am-noon and 3-6pm; in off-season Mon.-Sat. only.) **Hôtel Eden,** 16, av. Louis Gallet (tel. 93-61-05-20), is a two-star, homelike establishment with kind owners, spotless rooms, and winding staircases. (Singles with shower 180F. Doubles with shower 240F. Triples with shower 280F. Breakfast included.) Also try the friendly **Hôtel Trianon,** 14, av. de l'Estérel (tel. 93-61-18-11). (Doubles 186F, with shower 236F. Triples 244F, with shower 284F. Shower 12F. Breakfast included.) Located on the same sunny peninsula as Juan-les-Pins is **Cap d'Antibes,** or "Le Cap," accessible by foot (along bd. de la Garoupe) and by a mini-train (9am-6pm, leaves from Hotel des Postes), but not by SNCF train. The **Relais International de la Jeunesse,** bd. de la Garoupe (tel. 93-61-34-40), sits among the villas and pines of Cap d'Antibes. (45F, breakfast, at 8am sharp, included.) Sheets 8F. Meals 37F. Lockout 10am-5:30pm. Curfew midnight. Open June-Sept.)

An agreeable walk or a four-minute SNCF train ride will take you from Juan-les-Pins to **Antibes,** a busy, glamorous resort by the sea that is a bit less frenetic than some of its Riviera neighbors. Antibes is also the hometown of Graham Greene, the celebrated English writer, as well as of numerous artists and posh galleries. Preeminent here is the **Musée Grimaldi-Picasso,** place du Château (tel. 93-34-91-91). Itself a work of art, the museum perches on a cliff beside the sea, overlooking a sculpture garden. Several small rooms display drawings, paintings, and ceramics by Picasso, most of them the work of a single season. The top floor features his *atelier* (studio) and paintings by young comtemporaries, such as de Staël, Hartung, and Mathieu. (Open in summer Wed.-Mon. 10am-noon and 3-7pm; in off-season Wed.-Mon. 10am-noon and 2-6pm. Closed Nov. Admission 15F, students 8F, Dec.-May Wed. free.) The **Musée Archéologique,** in the Bastion St-Andrée sur les Rempart (tel. 93-34-48-01), illuminates archeological digs of the area and the history of Antipolis (the ancient Greek name for Antibes), and sponsors rotating art exhibitions next door in the municipal art gallery. (Open July-Aug. 9am-noon and 2-7pm; Sept.-Oct. and Dec.-June Mon. and Wed.-Sun. 9am-noon and 2-6pm. Admission 6F, students 3F.)

The **Syndicat d'Initiative,** 11, place de Gaulle (tel. 93-33-95-64; from the train station go right towards *centre ville* for 10 min.), will help with accommodations and supply a list of the 12 campgrounds in the area. (Open July-Aug. Mon.-Fri. 9am-8pm, Sat. 9am-noon and 2-7pm, Sun. 10am-noon and 3-6pm; Sept.-June Mon.-Fri. 9am-noon and 2-6pm, Sat. 9am-noon.) **Modern Hôtel,** 1, rue Fourmillière (tel. 93-34-03-05), has a tiled staircase from the 1930s and fresh, cool rooms. (Singles or doubles 130F, with shower 150F. Triples with shower 250F. Showers 12F. Breakfast 17F.)

In Antibes, restaurants will, as a rule, eat up your budget. However, at **Le Tire Bouchon,** on place Nationale (tel. 93-34-76-14), tasty salads are only 26F. (Open daily noon-midnight.) Better yet, grab a fresh sandwich (12-18F) to go from the snackbar of **Cameo Restaurant,** located around the corner on rue de la République. Otherwise, try the morning **open market** at Cours Masséna, near the beach. In the afternoon, the marketplace grows lively with craftsellers and performers. In August, Antibes holds a music festival, **Eté Musicale,** in front of the château. Tickets (50-110F) are available at the tourist office.

Vallauris has always been known as the pottery capital of France. Picasso was fascinated by the town's ceramics and came here to work shortly after World War II. Most of the stores sell mass-produced, low-quality ware, but the **Galerie Madoura** (tel. 93-63-74-93) stocks high-quality reproductions. At 1500F a plate, though, you might opt just to look. (Open Mon.-Fri. 9:30am-12:30pm and 2:30-6pm.) Vallauris hosts a bi-annual exhibition of ceramics and modern art from over 30 countries. To get to this world's fair of pottery, take a bus from Cannes (from near the train station or from place de l'Hôtel de Ville, hourly 8am-7:30pm, ½ hr., 8F), from Antibes (5 per day), or from Golfe-Juan (6:35am-8:15pm every ½ hr., 15 min., 5.20F). The **Syndicat d'Initiative** is on 84, av. de la Liberté (tel. 93-63-73-12).

Biot, east of Antibes, is the home of the **Musée National Fernand Léger** (tel. 93-65-63-61). Housed here are large canvases of Léger's cubist renditions of mechanized modern life; even his human figures are composed of bolts and tubes. (Open in summer Wed.-Mon. 10am-noon and 2-6pm; in off-season 10am-noon and 2-5pm. Admission 15F, students 8F.) Take the bus from place Guynemer, Antibes (every 2 hr., 20 min.), as the train stop is a good 3km from the museum. Biot is also known for its fine glassware. Many glass-blowing shops are open to the public.

Nice

Nice weathers its influx of tourists each summer with all the usual accoutrements of a Riviera town—casual affluence, an ample beach, museums, flowery avenues—but without the affected aloofness of its neighbors. Furthermore, Nice is blessed with all the conveniences of a big city—reasonably priced hotels, good public transport within the town and to all points on the coast, and a population accustomed to visitors. Carry as little cash as possible here, as Nice's big-city appeal is coupled increasingly with big-city crime; lone women in particular may be targets. Be careful at night near the train station and in Nice's *vieille ville.*

Nice sustains a spontaneous charm often lacking in more poised Riviera towns. Tucked untidily into the southeastern pocket of the city and limited to pedestrians, the *vieille ville*'s labyrinth of tiny streets hides restaurants and bars, and creates much of the city's distinctive Mediterranean flair. You can enjoy this flavor at the flower, fish, and vegetable markets in cours Saleya Tuesday through Sunday from dawn until noon, when this section of the *vieille ville* erupts with color and confusion. On the opposite side of the château, raised 92m on the hill where Nice's fortress once stood, and below the *vieille ville,* lies Port Lympia, a warren of alleyways, boulevards, *brasseries,* and *tabacs.*

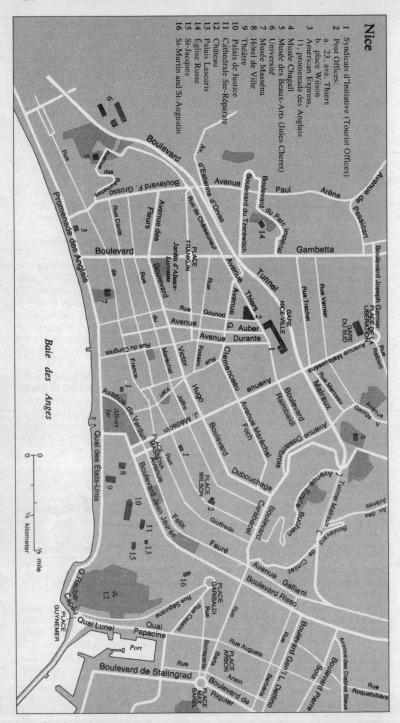

Nice

1 Syndicats d'Initiative (Tourist Offices)
2 Post Offices:
   a . 23, ave. Thiers
   b. place Wilson
3 American Express,
   11, promenade des Anglais
4 Musée Chagall
5 Musée des Beaux-Arts (Jules Chéret)
6 Université
7 Musée Masséna
8 Hôtel de Ville
9 Théâtre
10 Palais de Justice
11 Cathédrale Ste-Réparate
12 Château
13 Palais Lascaris
14 Église Russe
15 St-Jacques
16 St-Martin and St-Augustin

Arrive in Nice early in the day in the summer, or you'll almost certainly be forced to join the legion of visitors who camp outside the train station. Because of its convenient location, Nice is annually invaded by students, and the station moonlights as one of the largest bedrooms in France. Groups of young people check their baggage at the concierge and head for the rocky waterfront, but police do sporadically enforce a law that prohibits sleeping on the beach.

Orientation and Practical Information

The SNCF train station (gare Nice-Ville) sits right in the center of town, next to the *syndicat,* on **avenue Thiers.** To the left, **avenue Jean-Médecin** runs toward the water to **place Masséna.** The pedestrian zone west of place Masséna swarms with boutiques, overpriced restaurants, and English-speaking bodies. Heading right from the *gare,* you'll run into **boulevard Gambetta,** the other main street running directly to the water. Sweeping along the coast, the majestic and festive **promenade des Anglais** is crowded, noisy, and rock-covered. You may want to find a room in Nice and then travel elsewhere for swimming and sunbathing.

Syndicat d'Initiative: Av. Thiers (tel. 93-87-07-07), beside the train station. English spoken. After 10am they will book you a room. Stake out a place in line early, because there are a limited number of rooms available (10F for a reservation in a one-star hotel and 20F for two-star hotels, of which 10F will be deducted from your hotel bill). Information on car rentals and on every activity from flying to snorkeling. Ask for their detailed map (2F), extremely helpful in the *vieille ville.* Open July-Aug. daily 8:45am-7pm; Sept.-June Mon.-Sat. 8:45am-12:30pm and 2-6pm. Another office at **5, av. Gustave V** (tel. 93-87-60-60), near pl. Masséna. Very helpful. Open June-Aug. Mon.-Sat. 8:45am-12:30pm and 2-6pm; Sept.-May Mon.-Fri. 8:45am-12:30pm and 2-6pm.

Centre d'Information Jeunesse, 19, rue Delille (tel. 93-80-93-93), not far from the outermost edge of promenade du Paillon. Posts a bulletin board with summer jobs for students of any nationality. Jobs include baby-sitting and bartending. Open Mon.-Fri. 9:45am-6:45pm, Sat. 9:45am-5pm.

Currency Exchange: Office Provençal, 17, av. Thiers (tel. 93-88-56-80), across from the train station. No commission. Open 7am-midnight. The banking district is along av. Jean-Médecin, off pl. Masséna.

American Express: 11, promenade des Anglais (tel. 93-87-29-82). Be prepared for long lines. Open for financial services May-Oct. Mon.-Fri. 9am-6pm, Sat 9am-noon; Nov.-April Mon.-Fri. 9am-noon and 2-6pm. **BEMO,** 7, av. Gustave V (tel. 93-82-11-48), next to the downtown *syndicat.* No commission and much shorter lines than at American Express. Open April-Sept. Mon.-Sat. 9am-5pm; Oct.-March Mon.-Fri. 9am-5pm.

Post Office: Main office (*Recette Principale*), 23, av. Thiers (tel. 93-88-54-41), near the train station. **Telephones** here. **Postal code:** 06000. Open Mon.-Fri. 8am-7pm, Sat. 8am-noon. **Branch office** (*Poste Restante Principale*), pl. Wilson (tel. 93-85-98-63), off rue de l'Hôtel des Postes. **Telephones** here as well. Open Mon.-Fri. 8am-7pm, Sat. 8am-noon. Poste Restante mail may be sent to either post office.

Airport: Aéroport Nice-Côte d'Azur, Tel. 93-21-30-30. Take bus #9 from pl. Masséna or the port. **Air France,** 10, av. Félix-Faure (tel. 93-21-32-32). Open 9am-12:45pm and 2-7:35pm. **Air Inter** is nearby at 4, av. de Suède (tel. 93-87-83-32). One-way flights to Paris 483F, New York 5770F, Istanbul 3355F. An SNCF minibus runs between the train station and the airport 8:18am-5:58pm (8 per day, 15 min., 20F baggage included).

Train Stations: Gare SNCF, av. Thiers (tel. 93-87-50-50). Information office open Mon.-Sat. 8am-7pm, Sun. 8am-noon and 2-7pm. About every 20 min. (5:45am-11:59pm) to Cannes (40 min., 22F) and Antibes (25 min., 15.20F); about every 30 min. (6:20am-12:25am) to Monaco (25 min., 11.80F) and Menton (35 min., 16.20F). Also to other coastal towns, northern France, Italy, Spain. In summer, 4 per day connect with the TGV express from Marseille to Paris (7½ hr. in all; 441F plus 13F required reservation, ½-price in "blue" period for holders of the Carte Jeune or Carte Couple/Famille). Showers at the station 14.10F; towels 6.30F; soap 4.50F. Open daily 5:45am-9pm, showers not allowed after 7pm. Toilets 2.20F. Next door at the **Cafétéria Flunch** (open daily 10:30am-2:30pm and 5:30-10pm), the bathrooms are uncrowded and clean. **Gare de Sud,** 33, av. Malausséna (tel. 93-88-94-88 or 93-88-28-56), on the upper continuation of av. Jean-Médecin. Special trains, the *chemins de fer de la Provence,* leave for Digne through the southern Alps (5 per day, including 1 with guide; 3 hr., 85F; 50% off with InterRail, free with Eurail or France Vacances passes). Information booth for this service at the main train station (tel. 93-88-94-88). Open daily 7:45am-12:15pm and 2:15-6:15pm.

Bus Station: Gare Routière, promenade du Paillon (tel. 93-85-61-81), off av. Jean Jaurès across from the *vieille ville*. Open Mon.-Sat. 8am-6:30pm. Every 20 min. (6:30am-7:30pm) to Villefranche (7.20F), St-Jean (9.40F), Eze (11.30F), Cap d'Ail (13.80F), Monaco (15.90F), Monte-Carlo (17.40F), and Menton (45 min., 24F); last return bus leaves Menton at 8pm and Monte-Carlo at 8:30pm. Every 15 min. (6:15am-7:30pm) to Antibes (19.50F), Juan-les-Pins (21.50F), and Cannes (1½ hr., 24.60F). To St-Paul (1 per hr., 45 min., 15F) and Vence (1 per hr., 55 min., 16.50F). Also to La Turbie (4 per day, 15.90F).

Public Transportation: Station Centrale, the TN (Transports Urbains de Nice) bus system at 10, av. Félix Fauré (tel. 93-62-08-08), near pl. General Leclerc and pl. Masséna. Information on city buses. Bus #12 from the train station goes to pl. Masséna and the beach (Mon.-Sat. 6:05am-1:30am, Sun. 7:45am-1:30am). Fare 6.50F. Buy *carnets* of 5 tickets at av. Thiers *syndicat,* or at kiosks and *tabacs* all over Nice (27.50F).

Ferries: SNCM, 3, av. Gustave V (tel. 93-89-89-89), perpendicular to promenade des Anglais and opposite the tourist office. Another office on quai du Commerce, from which the boats sail. Buy tickets at least 1 hr. before departure, particularly on weekends. Passage to and from Bastia, Caloi, Ile Rousse, Propriano, and Ajaccio, all on Corsica (5-8 hr.; one-way 176F, ages 4-12 94F); the cheapest and shortest route to Corsica from any French port. Throughout the year, from Nice only, ages under 26 get a 30% discount during specific hours. In the "blue" period (Oct.-early May), ages over 60 get 50% off. Special rates for couples. Open Mon.-Fri. 8am-noon and 2-6pm, Sat. 8am-noon.

Bike and Moped Rental: Nicea Location Rent, 9, av. Thiers (tel. 93-82-42-71), near the station. Friendly owners will help you with directions. Bikes 70F per day, deposit 1500F; mopeds 100F per day plus 25F for gas; motor scooters 215-300F per day, motorcycles 325-600F per day, deposit for scooters and motorcycles 6500F. Reduced rates on 3-day and weekly rentals. **Ets Arnaud,** 4, pl. Grimaldi (tel. 93-87-88-55), near the pedestrian zone and beach. Tips on tours for hard-core cyclists. Mopeds 105F including enough gas to go round-trip to Monaco, deposit 1900F; bikes 50F, deposit 700F. Reductions for longer periods. Open Mon.-Sat. 8:30am-noon and 2-7pm.

Bookstores: Riviera Bookshop, 10, rue Chauvain (tel. 93-85-84-61). Extremely friendly and well-stocked with English-language books; even carries a few second-hand books. Open Mon.-Sat. 9:30am-12:30pm and 2-6:30pm. **The English Bookshop,** 4, rue de Congrès (tel. 93-87-08-93). Larger but far more expensive. *Let's Go: Europe* 190F. Open Mon.-Sat. 9:30am-12:30pm and 2-6:30pm.

Laundromat: Laverie Self-Service, 18, rue de Belgique, near the train station. The winsome West African manager does it for you in 90 min. Wash, dry, and soap 28F per 5kg. Least crowded from noon-4pm. Open daily 6am-11pm. Several others in the vicinity of the train station. Try the one at 16, rue Berlioz, near rue Verdi. Wash 14F. Open daily 8am-9pm.

SOS Amitié: Tel. 93-26-26-26. 24-hour friendly ear.

SOS Femmes en Détresse: Tel. 93-52-17-81. 24-hour line for victims of sexual assualt.

Women's Center: Centre d'Information Droites des Femmes Tel. 93-72-22-84. For legal issues, walk-in service Mon.-Thur. 9am-3pm, Fri. 1-3pm. For professional concerns by appointment only.

Accueil de Nuit, rue Jules Gilly, in the *vieille ville* nears cours Saleya. This homeless shelter is open only to the truly desperate. No hostel wonderland.

All-Night Pharmacy: 7, rue Masséna (tel. 93-87-78-94). Free parking. Open 7:30pm-8:30am.

Hospital: St-Roch, 5, rue Pierre Devoluy. From av. Jean Médecin, turn left on rue Pastorelli, which turns into rue P. Devoluy.

SOS Medical Service: Tel. 93-53-03-03. Available 24 hours.

Police: Tel. 93-53-53-53.

Police Emergency: Tel. 17.

Accommodations

Rooms in summer are like tickets to a great concert: gone as soon as they're on sale. So arrive at the av. Thiers *Syndicat d'Initiative* early for help in finding a room (see Practical Information), or call individual hotels in advance. Managers are usually reluctant to accept phone reservations without a deposit through the mail. The greatest concentration of hotels is just outside the train station, on the west side of av. Jean-Médecin. Most are pleasant, fairly inexpensive, and accustomed to English-speaking guests. If the ones we list are full, try the area north of the train station, between bd. Gambetta and av. Malausséna. There are also several hotels, some more expensive, on the other, more desolate side of av. Jean-Médecin; head away from the station. University dorms are vacant in the summer (50F). Call **CROUS** (tel. 93-96-73-73) for reservations.

International House for Young People, 22, rue Pertinax (tel. 93-80-98-00), only 200m from the train station next to a corner laundromat and a flight up. Young, bearded British manager sincerely cares about guests. A bohemian delight: the rules on silence after 8pm and protection of personal belongings are based entirely on trust. Coed rooms 40F, private quads 45F, and doubles 50F. The 30 spaces fill up early. If you can't find lodgings elsewhere, you can sleep on the floor or perhaps next door, where a Spaniard sometimes has space. Bring your own sheets. Showers and use of large kitchen included. No curfew.

Auberge de Jeunesse (IYHF), rte. Forestière du Mont-Alban (tel. 93-89-23-64), 4km away. Take bus #5 from the train station (6.50F) or walk to place Masséna, then take #14 from bd. Jean-Jaurès (every 25-40 min., 6.50F). You'll have to walk after the last bus leaves Nice at 7:30pm (about 45 min. from the station). A small hostel (62 beds). Bed, breakfast, and shower 45F. Required sheet rental 10F. Lockout 10am-6pm. Curfew 11pm; in summer 1am.

Relais International de la Jeunesse "Clairvallon", 26, av. Scudérei (tel. 93-81-27-63), in Cimiez 10km out of town on bus #15 from pl. Masséna (every 10 min., 20 min., 6.50F). Inconveniently located. A large, unofficial hostel in an old villa with a swimming pool (free). Run by students. Luggage must be kept in a common storage room. Bed and breakfast 45F. Check-in 6pm. Curfew midnight.

Hôtel Belle Meunière, 21, av. Durante (tel. 93-88-66-15), near the station. This quasi-villa was a gift from one of Napoleon's generals to his mistress. Large garden to relax in. Run by a friendly, loquacious, and accommodating family. In summer, the atmosphere of a school dorm. Singles 57F. Doubles 94-114F, with shower 139F. Triples 156F, with shower 216F. 52F per person in dorm. Showers 10F. Breakfast 13F. Free, ample parking. Open Feb.-Nov.

Hôtel les Orangers, 10bis, av. Durante (tel. 93-87-51-41), a 3-min. walk from the station. Well-worn but clean, spacious rooms. Stoves and refrigerators are available for a fee based on the size of the room. Sometimes women can share rooms with other women travelers. Singles 55F. Doubles 120F. Triples with shower 210F. Showers 10F. Breakfast 13F. Reduced rates on longer stays. Open Dec.-Oct.

Hôtel Novelty, 26, rue d'Angleterre (tel. 93-87-51-73), near the station. Devoted owner enjoys welcoming student to his slightly frayed rooms, which he keeps promising to modernize. Singles 88F, with shower 158F. Doubles 132F, with shower 222F. Triples 186F, with shower 288F. Showers 10F. Breakfast included.

Hôtel du Centre, 2, rue de Suisse (tel. 93-88-83-85), off av. Jean Médecin near the train station. Native-Californian owner and exceedingly cordial staff will pamper weary travelers and bring breakfast in bed. Immaculate, if sparse rooms. Singles 95F, with shower 120F. Doubles 110F, with shower 140F. Triples with shower 240F. Hall showers included. Breakfast 15F. Black-and-white TV rental 15F, color 20F.

Hôtel Montreuil, 18bis, rue Biscirra (tel. 93-85-95-90), off av. Jean Médecin. A small establishment, but the price is right and the manager friendly. All rooms with TV. Singles 100F. Doubles 130F, with shower 160F. Hall showers included. Breakfast 15F.

Hôtel Clemenceau, 3, av. Georges Clemenceau (tel. 93-88-61-19), off av. Jean Médecin near the train station. Recently renovated rooms are stately, and some boast floor-to-ceiling windows. Gracious, English-speaking management. Singles 90F, doubles 120F, triples 150F, quads 180F. Hall showers included. Breakfast 17F.

Hôtel St-François, 3, rue St-François (tel. 93-85-88-69), in the *vieille ville* near the morning fish market and across from the *gare routière*. Lively Corsican manager speaks English. Singles 125F. Doubles 125-165F. Triples 165-180F. Showers 15F. Breakfast 12F.

Hôtel Rialto, 55, rue de la Buffa (tel. 93-88-15-04), 2 long blocks from the sea at rue de Rivoli. Rooms equipped with kitchenette and refrigerator, many with private showers. Singles 95F, doubles 120F, with shower 125-150F. No breakfast, but there are several excellent *boulangeries* nearby.

Hôtel Mono, 47, av. Thiers (tel. 93-88-75-84), a few blocks west of the train station along the same road. Removed from the concentration of hotels south of the station. Might have room after the others are filled. Adequate rooms. Friendly owner. Singles or doubles 100F, with shower 150F. Triples 140F, with shower 180F. Showers 8F. Breakfast 12F.

Hôtel Central, 10, rue de Suisse (tel. 93-88-85-08), off rue d'Angleterre. Small and clean with modernized bathrooms. Singles 105F, with shower 140F. Doubles 120F, with shower 160F. Triples with shower 240F. Showers 15F. Breakfast 17F. Hôtel Select Serraire, in the same building. Owner has two dogs straight out of *Call of the Wild*. Singles or doubles 95-130F, with shower and kitchen 150F. Showers 15F. Breakfast 16F. 1-week minimum stay.

Hôtel Regency, 2, rue St-Siagre (tel. 93-62-17-44), off rue Pertinax near train station. Upscale management and cozy rooms. Discount with fridge for longer stays. Singles 75F, with shower 100F. Doubles 95F, with shower 130F. Triples 140F, with shower 170F. 10-min. shower 10F. No breakfast but stoves available for rent.

Food

The area around the train station specializes in fairly inexpensive but mediocre fare. Though seafood restaurants in Nice are expensive, they are worth the francs invested. Boulevard Jean Jaurès, opposite the fountain, or cours Saleya, in the *vieille ville,* are fountains of savory *bouillabaisse,* the Mediterranean fish medley. The **fruit market** just to the east of pl. Masséna bustles each morning, as does the **fish market** in pl. St-François. Complete your picnic at the bakeries, cheese shops, and wine stores throughout the city. *Pissaladière,* an onion, olive, and anchovy pizza, is a Niçois specialty. Avoid eating a meal at the overpriced tourist haunts on rue Masséna; they are more appropriate for people-watching, which can be enjoyed for the price of a drink or dessert. Few restaurants open before 7pm, and most stay open late.

CROUS, 18, av. des Fleurs (tel. 93-96-73-73), lists the addresses of student cafeterias. The cafeteria at Montebello, 96, av. Valrose (tel. 93-52-56-59), near the Musée Matisse, is usually open until mid-Aug. Buy a ticket if possible from a student (9.30F), or else pay the *passager* rate (29.50F). Open daily 11:30am-1:30pm and 6:30-8pm.

Chez Davia, 11bis, rue Grimaldi (tel. 93-87-73-67), a short walk from pl. Masséna off bd. Victor Hugo. Excellent food at excellent prices. Run by a charming Italian woman whose family has owned the establishment for 30 years. Wide selection. 4-course, 45F *menu* and 5-course, 62F *menu*. Try the *coq au vin.* Sun. specialty is duck or rabbit. *Plat du jour* with dessert 38F. Open Thurs.-Tues. noon-2pm and 7-10pm.

Restaurant de Paris, 28, rue d'Angleterre (tel. 93-88-64-29), near the train station. Recommended by locals, this popular restaurant offers a variety of specialties at affordable prices. *Menus* 28F, 38F, and 49F. Open Dec.-Oct. daily 11:30am-2:15pm and 5:15-11:30pm.

Le Saëtone, 8, rue d'Alsace-Lorraine (tel. 93-87-17-95), off rue d'Angleterre near the train station. An engaging, cozy restaurant serving traditional regional dishes. Fills up quickly. Try the *soupe au pistou* and their special dessert *mousse au café. Menus* 39F and 45F. Open Thurs.-Tues. 11:45am-2pm and 6-10pm. La Petite Biche, across the street at 9, rue d'Alsace-Lorraine (tel. 93-87-30-70), is not as distinctive, but offers a varied 49F *menu.* Open daily 11:30am-2pm and 6-10pm.

Le Grillardin, 1, Descente du Marché (tel. 93-62-34-90), on the steps going into the *vieille ville* from the outermost edge of square Leclerc. This spacious pizzeria's portly portions will leave you begging for mercy. Delicious *menu* 48F. Open daily noon-2:30pm, 7pm-2:30am, and 4-9am.

La Gitane, pl. Rosseti (tel. 93-62-06-77), in the center of the *vieille ville* next to a beautiful fountain. Filling, family-style fare. *Menu* 59F. Open noon-2pm and 7-11pm.

Le Dalpozzo, 33, rue de la Buffa (tel. 93-88-97-06), 2 blocks from promenade des Anglais. A white-tablecloth-and-marble affair without pretension. Dinner *menu* with wine 70F. You can order *bouillabaisse* if you call a day ahead. Pizza 28-32F, pasta 30-36F. Open daily 11:30am-2:30pm and 6:30-11pm.

La Fontaine, 22, rue Benoit Bunico (tel. 93-80-58-99), in the *vieille ville.* Refined local fare in an intimate atmosphere. *Menu* 59F. Open Tues.-Sun. noon-2:30pm and 7-11pm.

Il Palio, 5, rue de la Boucherie (tel. 93-80-06-25), in the heart of the *vieille ville.* Whimsical mural on front beckons you to sample Italian delights. Pasta *menu* 45F. Meals served at noon and 8pm exactly. Open Mon.-Sat., except Wed. noon seating.

L'Entracte, 5, rue de la Poissonierie (tel. 93-80-55-53), near cours Saleya. Although a bit cramped, a friendly, moderately-priced crêperie on a lively street. Crêpes 15-25F. Open 11am-2am.

Festival des Glaces, 15, rue Masséna (tel. 93-87-70-78), in pl. Magenta. Ice cream in the latest styles. Strictly dessert, but you will probably pay as much here as you would for a whole meal elsewhere (28-50F); for sweet tooths that love kissing franclets goodbye. Open Feb.-Dec. daily noon-1am.

Sights

The most confirmed museum-haters will have a hard time resisting Nice's collections, ranging from modern art and paleontology to natural and maritime history. Since most of the city's museums are hidden among attractive houses in quiet suburbs, visiting them gives you a respite from the beach and place Masséna as well as a glimpse of the luxurious residential areas. Furthermore, virtually all the museums are municipal and free of charge. The *syndicat*'s leaflet "Museums of Nice" provides more detailed information.

Among the best, but closed for renovations until February, 1989, is the **Musée Matisse,** 164, av. des Arènes de Cimiez (tel. 93-81-59-57). Take bus #15 (6.50F) from the Station Centrale (place Masséna) to av. des Arènes de Cimiez. Housed in a villa overlooking the ruins of a Roman bath complex, the collection spans Matisse's career, from the impressionist-inspired oils of the 1890s to the simpler line drawings of the 1950s. The museum exhibits Matisse's sculpture as well as his studies for the famous chapel at Vence. (Open May-Sept. Tues.-Sat. 10am-noon and 2:30-6:30pm, Sun. 2:30-6:30pm; Oct. and Dec.-April Tues.-Sat. 10am-noon and 2-5pm, Sun. 2-5pm. Free.) While in the area, wander around the beautiful gardens of the Franciscan monastery nearby.

Also by bus #15 to stop Docteur Moriez (or a 20-min. walk from the station) is the **Musée National Marc Chagall,** av. du Docteur Ménard (tel. 93-81-75-75). Like many museums on the Côte, this is an elegant modern building that makes radiant use of glass, space, and light. The 17 oil paintings devoted to Old Testament themes, including the vivid *Song of Songs,* are full of Chagall's inventiveness and color. The collection contains many lithographs and engravings—works, according to Chagall, in which he could put all his sadness and happiness. (Open July-Sept. Wed.-Mon. 10am-7pm; Oct.-June. Wed.-Mon. 10am-12:30pm and 2-5:30pm. Admission 22F; students, seniors, and on Sun. 11F.)

The **Musée des Beaux-Arts Jules Chéret,** 33, av. Baumettes (tel. 93-44-50-72), is an absolute must for lovers of the grotesque. From the Station Centrale take bus #38 or 40 to Chéret (6.50F). Among the artists whose works are displayed here is Gustave Albert Mossa (1883-1971), an undeservedly unknown Niçois painter. His best works employ expressionist techniques to depict classical themes; the resulting symbolism is frighteningly bizarre. The collection also includes works by Dégas, Monet, Sisley, Renoir, and Bonnard, as well as a good showing of Raoul Dufy. Visit the lovely sculpture garden with works by Rodin and Carpeaux. (Open May-Sept. Mon.-Fri. 10am-noon and 3-6pm; Oct.-April 10am-noon and 2-5pm. Closed 2 weeks in Nov. Free.)

In town, visit the **Musée Masséna** (tel. 93-88-11-34), housed in an elegant villa at 65, rue de France, near promenade des Anglais. Take bus #12 from train station to Meyerbeer. It is furnished and decorated in the Napoleonic style of the First Empire, and canvases by Renoir, Dufy, and Sisley are displayed upstairs. (Open May-Sept. Mon.-Fri. 10am-noon and 3-6pm; Oct.-April Mon.-Fri. 10am-noon and 2-5pm. Free.) The **Musée International de Malacologie,** 3, cours Saleya (tel. 93-85-18-44), has two aquariums and a collection of over 15,000 shells. Open May-Sept. Tues.-Sat. 10:30am-1pm and 2-6:30pm; Oct. and Dec.-April Tues.-Sat. 10:30am-1pm and 2-6pm. Free.) Other museums include an **Archeological Museum,** 167, av. des Arènes de Cimiez (tel. 93-81-59-57). Take bus #15, 17, 20, or 22 to Arènes and visit the Gallo-Roman site for 1F (guided visits July 1-Sept. 15 daily at 5pm). The thermal sites contain bathing pools and hot and cold rooms. (Open May-Sept. Tues.-Sat. 10am-noon and 2:30-6:30pm; Oct. and Dec.-April Tues.-Sat. 10am-noon and 2-5pm.) On the other end of the spectrum, the **Gallery of Contemporary Art,** 59, quai des Etats-Unis (tel. 93-62-37-11), exhibits works from the 1960s to the present, and always has room for new talent. (Open Tues.-Sat. 10:30am-noon and 2-6pm, Sun. 2-6pm. Free.)

If you've had your fill of Gothic and Romanesque churches, take a look at the **Cathédrale Russe,** 17, bd. du Tsarévitch, a 5-min. walk from the train station. Before the Revolution, Nice was a favorite resort for wealthy Russians. Built between 1903 and 1912 in the style of the Iaroslav church in Moscow, this intimate church is dominated by six onion domes. The typically Niçois tiles, however, give the building a hybrid feeling. Visitors wearing shorts or sleeveless shirts will not be allowed inside. (Open in summer Mon.-Sat. 9am-noon and 2:30-8pm; in winter 9:30am-noon and 2:30-5pm. Admission 5F.)

Nice maintains many parks and public gardens, the largest of which is the **Jardin Albert 1er.** Located at promenade des Anglais and quai des Etats-Unis, it is a quiet, shady refuge with benches, fountains, and leafy nooks. Be sure to look at the ornate, eighteenth-century Triton fountain. Jardin Albert also contains a bandstand where evening concerts are frequently performed.

The ruins of a **château** rest on the hills above the *vieille ville.* Climb the stairs as medieval pilgrims did, or take the lift. At the top you'll come upon a park with exotic pines and unusual cacti, as well as a view of the port and the Baie des Anges (Bay of Angels).

Entertainment

Nice's **Parade du Jazz,** July 9-19 at the Parc et Arènes de Cimiez (tel. 93-21-22-01) near Musée Matisse, attracts some of the most commercially successful European and American jazz musicians; music plays simultaneously on the three stages from late at night until early in the morning. Tickets (100F) are available at the door or at the FNAC in Nice Etoile shopping center, on av. Jean-Médecin. The **Festival de Folklore International** and **Batailles des Fleurs,** pageants of flowers and music along promenade des Anglais, bloom in the heat July 23-Aug. 6 (reserved seats in the stands 60F). In December there is an Italian film festival, and February 11-24 fireworks fan across the city's skies as parades create a living garland throughout Nice's **Carnaval.** The *Semaine des Spectacles,* published every Wednesday (5F), carries entertainment listings for the entire Côte and is available at newsstands.

Most of Nice's bars along the waterfront cater to the piano-bar set and are expensive. Bars around place Masséna lean toward the jukebox sort. There are several smoky *bars américains* (bars that open late and close early the next morning) around Pier Lympia, but most are unmarked so they might be hard to find. Try **The Hole in the Wall,** rue Place Vieille, or ask in a cafe or on the dock. Clubs can be expensive and disappointing. **Findlater's,** rue de Lepante, 2 blocks east of av. Jean-Médecin, once popular, is now on the decline. (Open Tues.-Sat.) For gay men, **Bar Charlot,** 8, rue St-François de Paule, in the *vieille ville,* is, for now, the most inviting place to go. (Open daily 11pm-3am.) **The Quartz Discotheque,** 18, rue Congrès (tel. 93-88-88-97), with a long bar, comfy chairs, and a small dance floor, attracts a crowd of mixed sexual orientation. (Opens 11pm.) **L'Expobouffe,** 24, rue Benoit Bunico (tel. 93-80-75-40), is a *café-théâtre* with performances Friday and Saturday nights (100F).

Nice to Monaco

Nice is ideally suited for daytrips, either to the big cities on either side of it, or to smaller coastal villages on the coast. You can leap on and off the train to Monaco, visiting the small towns en route, or take buses circumscribing the towns of St-Paul-de-Vence and Vence. **Buses** leave Nice's *gare routière* about every hour (7am-7:30pm) for St-Paul-de-Vence (45 min., 15F) and Vence (55 min., 16.50F). The same bus also stops at the train station at Cagnes (hourly 7:25am-7:55pm; 20 min. to St-Paul, 30 min. to Vence). Keep in mind that the last bus returns from Vence at 6:30pm and that prices and times change frequently. Special loop tickets (*billets circulaires*) are available in Nice (35F) and allow you to get on and off the buses all day.

The neighboring villages of St-Paul-de-Vence, whose fourteenth century fortifications still exist (if only to keep out cars), and Vence, a former Roman market town, are two communities whose inland beauty makes a pleasant respite from the surfocentric coastal towns. The pride of **St-Paul-de-Vence** is the **Fondation Maeght** (tel. 93-32-81-63), a 1-km walk from the center of town. Get off at the second St-Paul bus stop, just outside the center of town on the way to Vence, and follow the signs up a steep, winding hill. The museum, designed by Josep Sert, is actually part park, with fountains, wading pools, and split-level terraces. Works by Miró, Calder, Arp, and Zadkine are arranged with such care that, despite their abstractness, they seem natural in their garden setting. Stained-glass windows by Braque and Ubac are set in the garden chapel. Inside is an excellent permanent collection, as well as rotating exhibits usually devoted to a single artist. (Open daily July-Sept. 10am-7pm; Oct.-June 10am-12:30pm and 2:30-6pm. Admission depends on the exhibition 21-26F, students 16-21F.) St-Paul itself is among the best-preserved hill towns in France. Walk along the ramparts, virtually unchanged since the sixteenth century, for a panoramic view of the hills and valleys of the Alpes-Maritimes. The village has become an artists' colony, and *ateliers* (studios), galleries, and expensive boutiques fill the lower floors of the houses. Restaurants are overpriced, so go on to Vence, where food is cheaper. The St-Paul **Syndicat d'Initiative** (tel. 93-32-86-95) is open Monday, and Wednesday to Saturday (10am-noon and 2-6pm).

The most notable building in **Vence** is **Chapelle du Rosaire**, 1½km from the bus stop on av. Henri Matisse. The chapel's tiny interior was designed by Matisse, who considered it his masterpiece. Two of the walls are dominated by green, yellow, and blue stained-glass windows. (Open Dec. 15-Oct. Tues. and Thurs. 10-11:30am and 2:30-5:30pm, also by appointment if you call 93-58-03-26 a day ahead. Free.) The **Syndicat d'Initiative** in Vence is in a booth in place du Grand Jardin (tel. 93-58-06-38), beside the bus stop. It provides maps. (Open Mon. 9am-noon, Tues. and Thurs. 9am-noon and 2-6:30pm, Wed. and Fri.-Sat. 9am-noon and 2:30-6:30pm.) Also remember to inspect the elegantly crafted pottery for which the town is famous.

For a relaxed view of the countryside of Alpes-Maritimes and Haute-Provence, consider the special trains running from Nice's Gare du Sud to **Digne.** (See Nice Practical Information.) Another full and varied daytrip from Nice includes Villefranche-sur-Mer, St-Jean-Cap-Ferrat, and Beaulieu-sur-Mer. Villefranche and Beaulieu are on the rail line between Nice and Monaco (about every ½ hr., 10 min., 9F), and buses connect both of them to Cap-Ferrat, current haunt of the beautiful people. St-Jean and Cap-Ferrat can also be reached by bus from Nice. (Mon.-Sat. 2 per hr. 6:30am-7:30pm, Sun. 1 per hr.; to St-Jean ½ hr., 10F; to Cap-Ferrat 11F.) On the way to St-Jean-Cap-Ferrat stands the **Fondation Ephrussi de Rothschild** (tel. 93-01-33-09), a pink Italianate villa built at the turn of the century to house the superb furniture and art collection of the Baroness de Rothschild. Works by Monet and Fragonard, Chinese vases, and Beauvais tapestries are complimented by spectacular gardens surrounding the villa. (Open July-Aug. Tues.-Sun. 3-7pm; Sept.-Oct. and Dec.-June Tues.-Sun. 2-6pm. Admission including guided tour 26F, students 16F. Gardens open 9am-noon, 11F.)

Villefranche-sur-Mer overlooks a crescent-shaped bay full of sailboats and has attracted many artists, including Aldous Huxley and Katherine Mansfield, to its narrow streets and pastel houses. **Rue Obscure,** a climb, is one of the most peculiar streets in France; its small, cramped houses are huddled with their backs to the elements. Jean Cocteau decorated the fourteenth-century **Chapelle St-Pierre** with boldly executed scenes from the life of St. Peter and of the Camargue gypsies of Stes-Maries-de-la-Mer. (Open July-Sept. Sat.-Thurs. 9:30am-noon and 2:30-7pm; Oct.-Nov. 15 Sat.-Thurs. 9:30am-noon and 2-4:30pm; Dec. 15-March Sat.-Thurs. 9:30am-noon and 2:30-6pm; April-June Sat.-Thurs. 9:30am-noon and 2-6pm. Admission 5F.) The **Syndicat d'Initiative,** Jardin François Binon (tel. 93-01-73-68), has information on the small villages of the region, and can suggest excursions by foot, bus, or train. They do not make hotel reservations but will direct you to hotels or, for stays over a week, apartments. (Open daily June 15-Sept. 15 9am-7pm; Sept. 16-June 14 Mon.-Sat. 9am-noon and 2:30-6pm.) **Hôtel L'Amiraute,** 6, av. Foch (tel. 93-01-72-68), is a small hotel with doubles for 150F. (Breakfast an exorbitant 30F.)

Another haven from the sun-crazed bustle of the Riviera's cities is **Beaulieu,** also along the train line between Nice and Monaco. The gravel beaches are somewhat less crowded, and Beaulieu's casino is smaller and less pretentious than Monaco's. By the sea, Greek villa **Kérylos** has been reconstructed with ivory-and-marble mosaics and frescoes. (Open July-Aug. Tues.-Sun. 3-7pm; Sept.-Oct. and Dec.-June Tues.-Sun. 2-6pm. Admission 15F.) Near the colorful *marché* (Mon.-Sat. 6am-1pm) at place Général de Gaulle, the **Selecte,** 1, Montée des Myrtes (tel. 93-01-05-42), offers wall-to-wall carpeting in airy rooms. (Singles 100F, with shower 150F. Doubles 130F, with shower 160F. Triples with shower 220F. Shower 15F. Breakfast 18F.) The **Office de Tourisme,** place de la Gare (tel. 93-01-02-21); makes reservations for free. (Open in summer Mon.-Sat. 9am-12:20pm and 2:30-7pm, Sun. 10am-noon; in winter Mon.-Sat. 9am-noon and 2:30-6pm.)

The finest beach east of Antibes is unquestionably at **Cap d'Ail,** 20 minutes by train from Nice (about every ½ hr., 14F). From the station walk down the stairs, under the tracks, and turn right. You'll find small, rocky coves to the east—perfect for sunning or fishing, but dangerous for swimming. A ½-km walk west leads to a pebbly beach sheltered by cliffs; swimming is safe here. The **Relais International de la Jeunesse,** bd. de la Mer (tel. 93-78-18-58), is a bed and breakfast on the way to the beach. Situated right on the sea, it's an old villa in an exclusive neighborhood. Since there's a midnight curfew (Fri.-Sat. 1am), don't stay here if you plan to gamble the night away at the casino. (Dinner 35F.) After four days you are expected to take dinner; in summer longer stays are discouraged. (Open March 15-Oct., but check beforehand; lock-out 9:30am-5:30pm.)

Monaco/Monte-Carlo

The Monaco of legend glitters with majestic wealth and jet-set glamour. In reality, Monaco is clogged with unsightly high-rises and gaudy new hotels. However, the sun and excitement will eventually win over even reluctant visitors and resolute critics. Travelers will find it difficult not to succumb to the liberating, self-indulgent atmosphere (an indulgence is often expressed in the form of hideously conspicuous consumption).

Monaco is ruled by a hereditary Prince (now Ranier III, whose late wife American actress Grace Kelly is buried in the Monaco Cathedral), but there is not much to reign over. The *Monégasques* (citizens of Monaco) number only 4500; the territory occupies under one square mile (1.95 sq. km). The currency, electricity, and tap water are all French. In fact, stamps and tobacco are about all that Monaco does not sponge off France. This does not mean that state functions are not performed with comic self-importance. Whether through the street-cleaners' zealousness or the pomp of the changing of the palace guard, Monaco is eager to prove and practice its statedom.

Orientation and Practical Information

Place d'Armes is a good starting point from which all other areas can be reached. From the train station go right on av. Prince Pierre and continue for 2 blocks. Then follow av. de la Porte Neuve into Monaco proper: **Monaco-Ville.** Here, above the fetching old city, the *vieille ville,* rises the Palais Princier; historical and tourist sights abound near the citadel. Or, again from place d'Armes, take rue Grimaldi to the **Monte-Carlo** of casino fame. The tourist office is also here. Another street, av. du Port, takes you down to the sea from place d'Armes. These pleasant walks take no more than a half-hour each.

Office National de Tourisme: 2a, bd. des Moulins (tel. 93-50-60-88), near the casino. Staffed by socialites who, if pushed, will be helpful and make reservations free of charge. You can also call hotels from a special phone at the train station. Open July-Aug. Mon.-Sat. 9am-7pm, Sun. 10am-noon; Sept.-June 9am-noon and 2-6pm, Sun. 9am-noon.

Currency Exchange: Crédit Lyonnais, 7, av. Prince Pierre (tel. 93-30-28-73), near the train station. Open Mon.-Fri. 8:30am-noon and 1:30-4pm. **Compagnie Monégasque de Change,** parking des Pêcheurs (tel. 93-25-02-50), in the parking complex connected to the Musée de l'Océanographie. No commission except on French travelers checks. Open daily 9am-7pm. Also, inside the **train station.**

American Express: 35, bd. Princesse Charlotte (tel. 93-25-74-45). Open Mon.-Fri. 9am-noon and 2-5:30pm, Sat. 9am-noon. Financial services stop at 5:30pm weekdays.

Post Office: Square Beaumarchais, Monte-Carlo. Monaco issues its own stamps, but unless you mail your postcards here, you'll have to start a stamp collection. For Poste Restante specify Palais de la Scala, Monte-Carlo. **Postal code:** MC 98000 Monaco. Open Mon.-Fri. 8am-7pm, Sat. 8am-noon. 7 postal annexes throughout the city.

Train Station: Av. Prince Pierre (tel. 93-87-50-50). Monaco lies on the St-Raphaël-Ventimiglia line, with direct connections to Nice (every ½ hr. 5:30am-11pm, 20 min., 12F), Antibes (1 hr., 26F), Cannes (70 min., 33F). Service is less frequent to other towns along the coast. To Menton (every ½ hr. 6:40am-12:55am, 10 min., 5F). To and from Annot, Digne, and Lyon (4 per day). Information desk open daily 9am-7pm. Currency exchange open 8:30am-5pm.

Bus Station: Buses to other cities leave from many locations in Monaco. Destinations include Italy and small neighboring villages. Call tourist office for information.

Local Buses: Tel. 93-50-62-41. 5 routes link the entire town 7am-9pm, and with all the steep hills and staircases, you may want to use them. Bus #4 connects the train station to the Casino in Monte-Carlo. Tickets 5.50F.

Bike and Moped Rental: Auto-Moto Garage, 7, rue de la Colle (tel. 93-30-24-61), near the station. Mopeds 80F per day, deposit 1000F; 5-speed bikes 50F, deposit 1500F. Open 8:30am-12:30pm and 2-9:30pm.

Bookstore: Scruples, 9, rue Princesse Caroline (tel. 93-50-43-52), near the train station. Sells books in English, including that summer classic *Let's Go: France.* Open 9am-noon and 2:30-7pm.

Hospital: Centre Hospitalier Princesse Grace, av. Pasteur (tel. 93-25-99-00).

Police: Tel. 93-30-42-46.

Police Emergency: Tel. 17.

Accommodations, Camping, and Food

Monaco's accommodations are crowded, almost impossibly so in summer, and expensive. Near the station, however, especially on rue de la Turbie, relative values can be unearthed. Reservations are a must from mid-June through August. You might choose to exile yourself and go to **Beausoleil** (officially outside the borders of Monaco), a five-minute walk from Monte-Carlo, where there are many cheaper hotels, especially along bd. du Général Leclerc.

Centre de Jeunesse Princesse Stéphanie, 24 av. Prince Pierre (tel. 93-50-75-05), 100m from the train station. Built to accommodate the festival swarms of bedless youth, this otherwise excellent facility fails because it is only open as a hostel July 1-Oct. 1, and the 40 beds are lotteried off at 2pm to the crowds who begin gathering at 10am. No reservations accepted. 35F per night, breakfast included. 1-night maximum stay. Open 7-10am and 2pm-1am.

Hôtel de France, 6, rue de la Turbie (tel. 93-30-24-64), near the train station. Simple, but with elegant details. Singles 110F, with shower 180F. Doubles 135F, with shower 220F. Triples 215F, with shower 350F. Breakfast 23F.

Hôtel Villa Boeri, 29, bd. du Général Leclerc (tel. 93-78-38-10), in Beausoleil. Owner loves TVs: regular and cable in the rooms and in the lobby. Some rooms with balconies overlooking the sea. Singles 85F, with shower 115F. Doubles 165F. Triples 290F. Showers included. Discount for *Let's Go* readers. Breakfast 20F.

Hôtel Cosmopolite, 4, rue de la Turbie (tel. 93-30-16-95), very near the train station. Homey and clean. Singles 114F, with shower 170F. Doubles 150F, with shower 225F. Showers 12F. Breakfast 24F.

Hôtel Cosmopolite, 19 bd. du Général Leclerc (tel. 93-78-12-70), in Beausoleil. Modern bathroooms and bright wallpaper. Renovated by a young couple that just took over. Singles and doubles 140F, with shower 160F. Triples 170F. Showers 10F. Breakfast 17F.

Camping: There are no campgrounds in Monaco, but there are two sites between Roquebrune and Cap Martin, on the N7 toward Italy. **La Toracca,** 14, av. du Général Leclerc (tel. 93-35-62-55), is a 3-star site with 120 sites and a restaurant. Open March-Sept. You can also camp in Menton at **Municipal du Plateau St-Michel** (tel. 93-35-81-23), or ask at the tourist office.

Undistinguished but inexpensive sustenance can be found among trellises of plastic flowers near the station at **Le Biarritz,** 3, rue de la Turbie (tel. 93-30-26-17), where the 30.50F and 65F *menus* reflect an Italian influence. (Open 9am-11pm.) Also near the station, **Le Périgordin,** 4, rue de la Turbie (tel. 93-30-06-02), serves a 52F *menu* and French duck specialities in a refined atmosphere. The manager force feeds ducks for three weeks in order to get a liver large enough for his special *pâté.* (Open Mon.-Sat. noon-2pm and 5:30-10:30pm.) **Garden Burger,** 22bis, rue Grimaldi (tel. 93-25-20-80), on the way to Monte-Carlo from the station offers filling hamburgers (14.50-21F). (Open Mon.-Sat. 10:30am-9:45pm.) Up the street from the youth hostel is **Le Soleil d'Or,** 20, bd. Ranier III (tel. 93-25-46-60), where you can devour anything from ice cream to sandwiches (15-20F) or their daily special (40F). The staff may look a little haggard due to the long hours. (Open Mon.-Fri. 24 hrs.) **L'Aurore,** 8, rue Princesse Marie de Lorraine (tel. 93-30-37-75), in Monaco-Ville, is often glutted with tourists, but there's plenty of room at the long tables and a fortifying lunch of chicken, fries, and a salad (43F). (Open daily 8am-5pm.) For a picnic lunch, try the fruit and flower **market** at place d'Armes (open daily 6am-1pm).

Sights and Entertainment

The **Casino** is an extravagant folly, worth visiting even if you're not a gambler. Surrounded by gardens and overlooking the coast, the old casino building was designed by Charles Garnier and resembles his Paris Opera House. The interior is an example of late nineteenth-century rococo at its best, with red velvet curtains, gold and crystal chandeliers, and gilded ceilings. Here Mata Hari once shot a Russian spy; here in 1891 the Englishman Charles Deville Wells broke the bank repeatedly and turned 10,000 gold francs into a million; and here Richard regaled Liz with the huge diamond. Today, the rooms teem with backpackers and tourists. The slot machines open at 10am, and the *salle américaine* (for blackjack, craps, and roulette) at 4pm, but the hardcore veterans don't arrive until after 10pm. Admission to the main room—or "kitchen"—is free (you must be over 21), but it costs 50F to enter the *salons privés,* where French games such as *chemin de fer* and *trente et quarante* begin daily at 3pm.

The casino also houses the sumptuous **Théâtre** that was the occasional stage for Sarah Bernhardt and the long-time venue of Diaghilev's Ballets-Russes. You can visit only by attending a ballet or opera performance; tickets cost 140F (students 70F), but here at least you are guaranteed a return for your money. Outside the theater, just across the main lobby from the casino rooms, is an extensive display of costumes from the theater's opera productions.

For a taste of Monaco's new and democratic vulgarity, visit the **Loews American-style Casino,** as garish and brash as the older casino is elegant. Like a Vegas palace, the place has a haphazardly mythical theme (large Tarot-like cards adorn the wall). (Tables open daily at 5pm. Free. Minimum age 21.)

Monaco-Ville is full of stately "sights." At 11:55am each day, you can see the changing of the guard outside the **Palais Princier,** a ritual which, given the size of this principality, resembles a Marx Brothers' routine. Skip the uninteresting state apartments and the **Musée du Palais.** You can have a much better time at the excellent **Musée de l'Océanographie,** directed by Jacques Cousteau, but you'll have to fish in your pockets for 42F (students 21F) to get in. (Open daily July-Aug. 9am-9pm; June and Sept. 9am-7pm; Oct.-May 9:30am-7pm.) Connected to this museum, in parking des Pêcheurs, is the new **Monte Carlo Story,** a creative, colorful film on Monaco's exotic history. Admission 25F, students and ages over 65 16F, children 6-14 12.50F. (Open May-Sept. daily 9am-8pm; Oct.-April daily 9am-6pm.) The **Jardin Exotique,** with its outstanding cactus collection, is privy to sweeping panoramas of the coast, as well as grottoes with stalagmites and stalactites. (Open May-Sept. 9am-7pm; Oct.-April 9am-6pm. Admission 25F, students 16F.)

Monaco becomes a real circus in May when the Grand Prix automobile race roars to a finish through its winding streets. The drama and excitement lie as much in the dynamics of the crowd as the race itself. The **Orchestre Philharmonique de Monte-Carlo** performs evening concerts in July and August at the Cours d'Honneur of the Palais Princier (tickets 60-250F). The royal family usually attends these concerts. (Up-to-date program information is available at the tourist office.) One of the highlights of the summer season is the **Fireworks Festival,** an explosive international competition which lights up the sky in late July and early August. If you're in the area in winter, try to go to a night of **Festival International du Cirque,** which features the world's best circuses. A gala performance on the last night features the best acts from all the circuses (late Jan.-early Feb).

Menton

Bought by France in the nineteenth century, Menton has done quite well for itself in the shadow of its neighbor and former owner Monaco. Residents claim Menton is the hottest part of France, weatherwise. But Menton's serenity and civility contrast with the action on other parts of the Riviera. They result in part from the preponderance of retirees who spend their golden years in the *perle* of the Riviera. Moreover, the embrace of the verdant mountains (upon which Menton's celebrated lemons grow) inspires a relaxing peace. Even the crowds of summer, who make accommodations difficult to find, can't entirely disrupt the gentle pace. Follow rue de la Gare from the train station, turn right on av. Boyer until you reach the grandiose Palais d'Europe. Inside is the **Office de Tourisme,** 8, av. Boyer (tel. 93-57-57-00), with a refreshingly irreverent staff who will direct you to available rooms. However, they make no reservations except in especially busy times.

Accommodations, Camping, and Food

Auberge de Jeunesse, plateau Saint-Michel (tel. 93-35-93-14). Follow rue de la Gare, cross under the train tracks at the bridge, continue in the same direction and up the steep cascade of steps. Or take the SNCF minibus that departs from the train station (9am-7pm, 20F). A recently modernized hostel. Soul-stirring view of Menton's bay. Be sure to call ahead to see where you'll be sleeping if you mind being shunted to a sturdy, clean but cramped tent without electricity. No reservations accepted. Curfew 11pm. Open 5-11pm. Lockout 9:30am-5pm. 46F per person; in tents 42F. Breakfast included, dinner 34F. Open Jan. 16-Dec. 14.

Hôtel Mondiale, 12, rue Partouneaux (tel. 93-35-74-18), around the corner from the tourist office. Clean rooms and cafe downstairs. Singles 110F. Doubles 150F. Triples 240F. Open Dec.-Oct.

Le Terminus, place de la Gare (tel. 93-35-77-00), opposite the train station. Genial, English-speaking management welcomes you into their slightly frayed, but satisfactory hotel. Singles or doubles 93F, with shower 153F. Showers included.

Hôtel Beauregard, 10, rue Albert 1er (tel. 93-35-74-08), behind and below the train station. A peach-painted wonder with a pretty garden in front. Well-kept rooms. Singles 130F, with shower 200F. Doubles 150F, with shower 200F. Triples with shower 250F. Breakfast included.

Camping: Campground Municipal du Plateau St-Michel, route des Ciappes de Castellar (tel. 93-35-81-23). Convenient and open from March to mid-November. 8.50F per person, children and dogs 4F, cars extra. Fleur de Mai, 67, route de Gorbio (tel. 93-57-22-36). 200 sites. St-Maurice, 49, route de Gorbio (tel. 93-35-79-84).

Restaurant de la Poste, 1 impasse Bellecour (tel. 93-57-13-79), off rue Partouneaux, bills a simple chicken or steak 55F *menu.* (Open Thurs.-Tues. noon-1:30pm and 7-8:30pm.) Opposite the station, Le Terminus, place de la Gare (tel. 93-35-77-00), serves its 38.50F and 50F *menus* outdoors. (Open Nov. 16-Oct. 14 Sun.-Fri. lunch and 7:15-9pm.) Off rue St-Michel, in an area of expensive little restaurants, La Chaumière, 7, rue Piéta (tel. 93-57-80-70), posts a 3-course 54F *menu.* (Open Tues.-Sun.)

Menton has its own modest casino at the end of av. Boyer (open daily 4pm-4am; admission 53F), but its prize possession is the Musée Jean Cocteau. Next to the *vieille ville* on promenade du Soleil, the museum is located in a seventeenth-century stronghold. Cocteau, best-known for his brilliant work in film and fiction, was skilled in all the plastic arts, and the museum houses a representative collection of his work, which is rarely displayed elsewhere. (Open June 15-Sept. 15 Wed.-Sun. 10am-noon and 3-6pm; Sept. 16-June 14 Wed.-Sun. 10am-noon and 2-5:30pm. Free.) Devoted Cocteau fans should also visit La Salle des Mariages, a room completely decorated by the artist and located in the Hôtel de Ville, rue de la République. (Open Mon.-Fri. 8:30am-12:30pm and 1:30-5pm. Admission 5F.) The municipal market is across the street in the *vieille ville.* Choose from a selection of quail, rabbit, goat, horse, cheese, fruits, and *pâtés.* (Open Tues.-Sun. 5am-1pm.)

Rising above the *marché* is the bell tower of Eglise St-Michel, a fine seventeenth-century baroque church. Some of the ornate sculpture and painting inside dates from the sixteenth century, the side chapels having been decorated by local artists. In August, the Festival de Musique takes place in the square in front of the church. In September, there are piano recitals at the Théâtre du Palais de l'Europe. (Tickets 30-180F, available at the Palais de l'Europe, av. Boyer, tel. 93-35-82-22.) Every Sunday from January 28 to February 12, Menton celebrates its Fête Internationale du Citron, an exaltation of the lemon, which includes a Corso des Fruits d'Or in which floats in various shapes and forms made of lemons are paraded through town.

Corsica (Corse)

Stubbornly and wisely, Corsica is set in its ways and doesn't want to be disturbed. Travel here is an adventure unrivaled by sallies to other parts of France. You'll explore unmatched coastal scenery and mountainous wilderness. You'll brave Corsica's infrequent, expensive buses and trains along their slow, twisting routes. As equipment for your expedition, bring along time and patience, and if you're a creature of comfort, be ready for a different standard of living. Corsica may compel you to forget conveniences; for the adventurous lover of the outdoors, the island may well prove to be an unspoiled paradise.

Corsica's heartland features steep, sometimes rocky mountains, divided by creeks and covered with vineyards, grazing sheep, and *maquis* (underbrush). Around them winds a jagged coastline, blessed with dazzlingly clear water, idyllic inlets, and long, sandy beaches. The air, too, is astonishingly clear, and is bathed almost year-round by brilliant (often scorching) sunshine.

Underdevelopment has been the island's curse as well as its saving grace. While the Côte d'Azur is cultivated and opulent, Corsica is untamed; life here, especially in the mountains of the interior, is as robust and unadorned as the land itself. Cars, good roads, plumbing, television, and telephones are only recent developments. In the small villages just a few kilometers inland, families continue to live in the homes of their ancestors. Although more than half the island's population now resides in the large towns of Bastia and Ajaccio, most Corsicans uphold the tradition of returning to the small villages of their families on weekends. Younger generations have started leaving for the cities, the mainland, and beyond only within the last 40 years.

For most people, the island's history begins and ends with Napoleon, who, as Emperor of France, did little to improve the conditions of his birthplace—but the island knew an earlier history of colonialism. First a Greek and later a Roman and Pisan colony, Corsica became a Genoese protectorate in the thirteenth century. Enjoying only brief independence from 1755 to 1769, the island has been under French rule ever since.

Corsicans themselves shrug off connections to the mainland, and while most Corsicans speak French, they much prefer their own language, an unwritten Romance dialect related to Italian. Corsican was recently reinstituted in the public school system, a sign that the island is gaining more autonomy. Referring to themselves proudly as Corsicans, some groups, notably the outlawed Front Libéral National Corse, whose initials adorn every graffiti-marked surface, continue to try to bomb their way to independence. Visitors are not in any real danger, as the bombs have been targeted only at abandoned government buildings.

It is best to visit Corsica before June 14, the day inaugurating high season. Services are more widely available between then and September 15, but prices soar. August 15, the **Fête de l'Assomption,** celebrating the Virgin Mary, is an important religious holiday in all of France. However, because it is also Napoleon's birthday, the date has special significance in Corsica and has become its unofficial "national" holiday. Every town on the island erupts with fireworks and dancing in the streets.

A single brochure lists all of Corsica's hotels, another lists all campsites, and still another contains useful addresses and telephone numbers, including organizations to contact for horseback-riding, hiking, sailing, and other sports. The train schedule for the entire island comes on a single sheet of paper, and one booklet lists all bus schedules. You can pick up these brochures at most Corsican *syndicats;* the Bastia branch is particularly well-stocked. Most banks, such as the Crédit Agricole, open only weekdays.

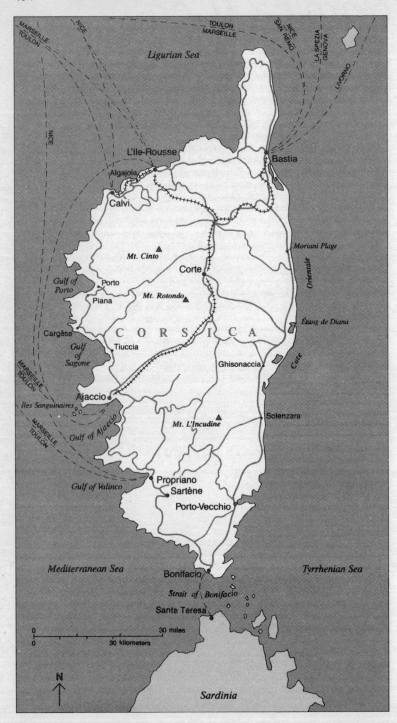

MARSEILLE
TOULON
NICE
TOULON
MARSEILLE
NICE
SAN REMO
LA SPEZIA
GENOVA
LIVORNO

Ligurian Sea

NICE

L'Ile-Rousse

Algajola

Bastia

Calvi

Mt. Cinto ▲

Corte

Moriani Plage

Gulf of Porto

Porto

Piana

Mt. Rotondo ▲

Orientale

Étang de Diana

Cargèse

C O R S I C A

Gulf of Sagone

Tiuccia

Ghisonaccia

Cote

MARSEILLE
TOULON

Ajaccio

Iles Sanguinaires

Mt. L'Incudine ▲

Solenzara

MARSEILLE
TOULON

Gulf of Ajaccio

Propriano
Sartène

Gulf of Valinco

Porto-Vecchio

Mediterranean Sea

Bonifacio

Tyrrhenian Sea

Strait of Bonifacio

Santa Teresa

0   30 miles
0   30 kilometers

N
↑

Sardinia

Getting There and Getting Around

Air France and **Air Inter** fly to Bastia, Ajaccio, and Calvi from Paris (953F, with discount 523F), Nice (303F, with discount 203F), and Marseille (354F, with discount 247F). Discounts, offered on several "blue" flights each week, apply to ages 25 and under, students under 27, seniors, and families of at least three. All flights from Paris to Corsica leave from Orly airport (west terminal). Air France has offices at 6, av. Emile Sari, Bastia (tel. 95-32-10-29), and at 3, bd. du Roi-Jérôme, Ajaccio (tel. 95-21-00-61). In Calvi, contact Agence Tramar, quai Adolphe Landry (tel. 95-62-01-38). Air Inter's offices are at the airports in Bastia (tel. 95-36-06-59 or 95-36-02-95), Ajaccio (tel. 95-21-91-92 or 95-21-63-06), and Calvi (tel. 95-65-20-09).

The **Société Nationale Maritime Corse Méditerranée (SNCM)** operates car ferries from Marseille, Toulon, and Nice, to Bastia, Calvi, and Ile Rousse in the north, and Ajaccio and Propriano in the south. Allow 5-10½ hours for the crossing. There are about six trips per day in summer, three otherwise. From Marseille or Toulon, a second-class ticket costs 220F, from Nice 176F. In the "blue" period (roughly Oct. to mid-May), travelers over 60 are eligible for a 50% discount, and students under 26 for a 30% discount. InterRail passholders receive a 33% discount. A 30% discount for travelers under 26 is offered year-round on ferries to and from Nice. Crossings to Corsica from Italy are shorter and sometimes cheaper. **Corsica Ferries** runs mid-June through early September to Bastia from Livorno (daily, 4 hr., 155F), La Spezia (daily, 5 hr., 155F), and Savona (daily, 8 hr., 195F); service is less frequent in the off-season. The company also serves Calvi from Savona four times per week from mid-June to the beginning of September, less often at the beginning of June and end of September (5½ hr., 195F). From April to mid-October **NAV.AR.MA.** Lines runs to Bastia from Livorno (4 hr.), La Spezia (4½ hr.), and Piombino (3 hr.), providing daily service in summer (Mon.-Fri. 138F, Sat.-Sun. 156F).

To visit any area but the main towns, you will need a car. Hitching is difficult on the narrow roads between villages, and public transportation is slow and infrequent, even between important tourist centers. However, renting a car is very expensive: 160-200F per day for the least expensive models, plus 1.60-2F per kilometer, although there are discounts and unlimited free mileage after a few days' rental (from 1800F per week). You may have to return the car to your point of origin if the agency operates only one or two offices. Mopeds (*mobilettes*) run about 125F per day or 665F per week (deposit 1000F). Renting a bike costs about 70F per day and 400F per week (deposit 500F); it's cheaper to rent a bike on the mainland and bring it with you. Note that biking is difficult on the island since the curving mountain roads are either too narrow or dangerous to manage. Do not attempt cycling here unless you are confident of your abilities. Even drivers should be very careful, especially on the mountain roads, where you're safest plodding along at a cow's pace. Accept the fact that the roads get crowded in summer and travel can be painstakingly slow. (The bus from Ajaccio to Bonifacio, for example, takes 4 hr. to cover 145km.) Gas is cheaper here than on the mainland and in Italy, but remember to fill up your tank when you can, since gas stations are few and far between. If you do run out of gas, call the local **Brigade de Gendarmerie.**

Public transportation is slow and infrequent. Four **trains** per day travel each way between Bastia and Ajaccio (4 hr., 91F), via Corte and Ponte Leccia; two per day run between Bastia and Calvi (3½ hr., 70F), via Ponte Leccia; and two per day between Ajaccio and Calvi (5 hr., 107F), via Corte and Ponte Leccia. A special service connects Calvi and Ile Rousse (in summer 10 per day, 50 min., 21F). The Corsican rail system accepts no passes save InterRail (50% off), and does not connect with Bonifacio or Porto-Vecchio. **Buses** connect the island's major towns, but are neither cheaper nor more frequent than trains. The route from Bastia to Ajaccio, for example, is served only twice per day in summer (3½ hr., 86F), and may prove unpleasant to those with queasy stomachs. If you hitchhike, be patient and expect to get only short rides. Remember that most summer drivers are tourists. You might increase your chances by offering to pay for gas. (Write "je vous offre l'essence" on a sign. 10 liters (about 50F) usually covers 100km on flat roads.)

A majestic way to see Corsica is to backpack the **Grande Randonnée-20,** a superb 15- to 21-day trail that takes you high into the mountainous interior. Do not try this trail on your own, and be prepared for cold, snowy weather, even in early summer. For further information, contact the **Parc Naturel Régional** in Ajaccio (tel. 95-21-56-54).

One tip for finding addresses: Because of the vague numbering and nomenclature in Corsica, you're better off asking for who or what you're looking for instead of the street name.

Accommodations, Camping, and Food

Hotels on Corsica are rare. Those that exist are expensive, and, despite their high prices, most fill up by early morning in high season. Camping, however, is an enjoyable option, and there are many campgrounds all over the island. The government has outlawed unofficial camping (*camping sauvage*), because it causes brush fires as well as tension between locals and tourists. The measure has had little effect, however, and some claim that sleeping on a remote beach is perhaps the most enjoyable way to bed down in Corsica. Those who do camp on their own should be unobtrusive.

Ask for the brochure *Auberges de Jeunesse en France* at the *syndicat;* there are about 30 hostels on Corsica, mostly inland, and only a handful are located near the major towns. You rarely, if ever, need a hostel card to stay at one, and most hostels don't impose an age restriction.

Corsican cuisine is hearty, fresh, and pungent. Seafood is excellent along the coast; try *calamar* (squid), *langouste* (lobster), *gambas* (prawns), or *moules* (mussels). In fall and winter you can order *nacres* (pink-shelled mollusks) and *oursins* (sea urchins). Other delicacies include *pâté de merle* (blackbird *pâté*), *saussison* (pork sausages), *truite* (river trout), and *sanglier* (wild boar). Excellent cheeses include *brucciu* (a white cheese made from goat's milk that can be eaten soft, with sugar or in an omelette, or hard), and *chèvre* (also made from goat's milk); both keep without refrigeration.

Corsican wines are heady, flavorful, and as inexpensive here as on the mainland (10-15F per bottle in a market). The *syndicat* can provide a leaflet of all the vineyards open for visits. Worth tasting is the sweet *Muscat,* as well as several potent *eaux de vie,* flavored with Corsican berries. The unofficial official drink, here as in Provence, is *pastis,* a wickedly strong brew flavored with anise and imbibed at all hours.

Ajaccio

Despite its growing congestion and size, Ajaccio still has the air of a small town where old men pass the time in quiet cafes or play *boules* on the dusty squares. The best way to enjoy this town is to slow down to its residents' pace, although you may get bored after a day or two. The town's fate was determined in 1769 when Napoleon was born here. Even if you don't visit his natal home, you'll be constantly reminded of his name and face—tourist stores sell an incredible variety of Napoleon ashtrays and statues, and half the streets are named after one Bonaparte or another.

Orientation and Practical Information

Cours Napoléon, which stretches from place de Gaulle (formerly place du Diamant) to the train station, contains most of the city's services. The pedestrian **rue Fesch** starts at place Maréchal Foch (formerly place des Palmiers) and runs parallel to cours Napoléon. It is a livelier street, with smaller, more interesting stores and some restaurants. The *vieille ville* is bound by place Foch, place de Gaulle, and the Citadelle.

From quai l'Herminier, where the boat leaves you, bear left and walk toward the *citadelle* to place Foch and the tourist office. To reach cours Napoléon, walk through the *place,* and up av. du 1*er* Consul. Avoid visiting the town on a Sunday, when everything is closed.

Syndicat d'Initiative: Hôtel de Ville, place Maréchal Foch (tel. 95-21-40-87). Does not make hotel reservations, but will tell you where there's room. Well-stocked with pamphlets listing all of the island's youth hostels, campsites, and hotels, as well as bus and boat excursion schedules. Pick up *Corsica, the holiday island,* a good brochure with practical information. Open June 15-Sept. 15 daily 8:30am-8pm; Sept. 16-June 14 Mon.-Fri. 8:30am-6pm, Sat. 8:30am-noon.

Currency Exchange: Caisse d'Epargne, 9, cours Napoléon (tel. 95-21-11-13), or at the post office.

Post Office: Cours Napoléon (tel. 95-21-13-60), at rue Ottavy. **Telephones** downstairs. **Postal code:** 20000. Open Mon.-Fri. 8am-7pm, Sat. 8am-noon.

Airport: Campo dell'Oro (tel. 95-21-07-70), 7km away. Take bus #1 ("Ricanto") from cours Napoléon (10F). Flights to Nice (2-3 per day, 303F), Marseille (3-4 per day, 354F), and Paris (5-6 per day, 953F). "Blue" period discounts for students under 27 and families: Nice 203F, Marseille 247F, Paris 523F. Also to London, Lisbon, Geneva, Brussels, and Amsterdam. **Air France** offices at 3, bd. du Roi-Jérôme (tel. 95-21-00-61). **Air Inter** at the airport (tel. 95-21-91-92 for flight schedules, tel. 95-21-63-06 for reservations).

Train Station: Rue Jean-Jérôme Levie (tel. 95-23-11-03), between cours Napoléon and bd. Sampiero. To Corte (4 per day, 2½ hr., 49F), Calvi (2 per day, 5 hr., change in Ponte Leccia, 107F), Ile Rousse (2 per day, 4½ hr., 94F), and Bastia (4 per day, 4 hr., 91F).

Bus Station: On quai l'Herminier, part of the Gare Maritime (tel. 95-21-28-01). Several firms located here organize excursions to nearby sights. **Autocars Roger Ceccaldi,** Tel. 95-21-38-06. Excellent 1-day tour (every Tues.) of Calanche de Piana and the mountains in the interior (110F). **SNCF,** 16, place Foch. Organizes tours to Calvi, Bonifacio, the inland countryside, and Filitosa. **Autocars Arrighi** runs the same excursions. Given all the companies, you should be able to visit what you want on the day you want. Arrighi also operates a daily round-trip to Soccia, a 1½-hr. walk from the Lac de Creno. The bus passes through Tiuccia, Sagone, and Vico. **Ollandini** also has an agency here and is the only company that offers regular bus service (tel. 95-21-06-30). Open Mon.-Sat. 7-11am and 3-7pm, Sun. 7-8am and 3-7pm. To Bonifacio (June 16-Sept. 15 2 per day, in off-season Mon.-Sat. only; 4 hr.; 88F), Calvi (July 1-Sept. 15 daily, mid-March to July 1 and Sept. 15 to mid-Oct. Thurs. and Sun. only; 10 hr. with a 3½-hr. stopover in Porto; 96F, luggage 5F), Propriano (June 16-Sept. 15 2 per day, in off-season Mon.-Sat. only; 2 hr.; 46F), Sartene (June 16-Sept. 15 2 per day, in off-season Mon.-Sat. only; 2 hr.; 54F), Porto-Vecchio (June 16-Sept. 15 2 per day, in off-season Mon.-Sat. only; 4 hr.; 93F), Corte (April 15-Oct. 2 per day, in off-season 1 per day; 2 hr.; 47F), and Bastia via Corte (April 15-Oct. 2 per day, in off-season 1 per day; 3½ hr.; 87F.)

Municipal Buses: TCA, Tel. 95-50-04-30. Take bus #1 from place de Gaulle to the train station and airport; #5 from place de Gaulle to Marinella and the beaches on the way to Iles Sanguinaires.

Ferries (SNCM): quai l'Herminier (tel. 95-21-90-70), across from the bus station. 2 boats to France per day. Toulon and Marseille 169F, Nice 148F. Open 8-11:45am and 2-6pm.

Taxi: Tel. 95-21-00-87.

Car Rental: Balesi, 5, rue Stéphanopoli (tel. 95-21-05-49). 166.75F per day plus 1.81F per km; 2000F per week with unlimited mileage (all taxes included). **Locafab,** at the airport (tel. 95-22-76-11). 150F per day plus 1.68F per km; 1870F per week with unlimited mileage. Drivers be at least age 23.

Bicycle Rental: SARL, alas, all the way out at the airport (tel. 95-20-14-15). 70F per day, 400F per week, 1500F deposit.

Parc Naturel Régional: Rue Général Fiorella (tel. 95-21-56-54). Maps for the Grande Randonnée-20 and other mountain trails, as well as information on shelters and trail conditions. Open Mon.-Thurs. 8:30am-noon and 2-6:30pm, Fri. 8:30am-noon and 2-5:30pm.

Hospital: Av. Imperatrice Eugénie (tel. 95-21-90-90).

Medical Emergency: Tel. 15.

Police: Tel. 95-21-19-17.

Police Emergency: Tel. 17.

Accommodations and Camping

Hotels in Ajaccio are more numerous and pleasant than in most Corsican towns, but you can still expect to pay as much for mediocre lodgings here as you would for a plush den on the mainland. In July and August, call ahead to make reservations.

Hôtel Bonaparte, 1-2, rue Etienne-Conti (tel. 95-21-44-19). Neat, small rooms with a view of the port. Doubles with shower 130F, triples 170F. Breakfast 20F.

Hôtel Belvédère, 4, rue Henri Dunant (tel. 95-21-07-26). Walk up the flight of stairs at the corner of rue de Sergent Casalonga and rue Maréchal Ornano. A large, old hotel surrounded by a lovely garden with a view of mountains and sea. Singles 112F, doubles 134-154F, triples 166F. Showers 10F. Breakfast 20F. Reservations recommended.

Hôtel du Palais, 5, av. Beverini (tel. 95-23-36-42), off cours Napoléon and 5 min. from the station. Courteous owner in a tidy 10-room hotel. Singles with shower 120F, doubles with large bed and shower 130F, with twin beds, 144F. Breakfast 20F. Oct.-March lower rates.

Hôtel Colomba, 8, av. de Paris (tel. 95-21-12-66). A small hotel in the center of town. You might need to get your breakfast elsewhere. Singles 110F. Doubles 120F, with shower 130F. Triples 160F. Breakfast 20F.

Camping: The closest to town is **Pech Baretta** (tel. 95-21-36-74 or 95-52-01-17), 3km away. Take bus #5 from av. Docteur Ramaroni just past place de Gaulle (last bus at 7pm). 15.50F per person, 7F per tent. Open May 31-Sept. 30. **U Prunelli** (tel. 95-25-19-23) is near the bridge of Pisciatello, next to Porticcio, which is accessible by ferries from Ajaccio (every ½ hr.) and by bus (6 per day; tel. 95-25-40-37). Friendly and cheerful. 18F per person, 6F per tent. Other campgrounds are more than 10km away.

Food

The morning **market** on bd. Roi Jérôme in place César Campinchi behind the *syndicat* can provide you with a beautiful picnic lunch. After dinner, the cafes along the port allow you to gaze at the fishing boats and the passersby.

La Serre, 91, cours Napoléon (tel. 95-22-41-55). Cheery, stylish cafeteria popular with families. *Plats du jour* and pasta from 35F. Complete the meal with *crudités* (10F) and ice cream (10F). Open daily 11:30am-10:30pm.

Les Liserons, 50, cours Napoléon. Family-style food at excellent prices. 4-course *menu* 35F, including wine. Open noon-2pm and 7-10pm.

Chez Pardi, 60, rue Fesch (tel. 95-21-43-08). Frequented by locals. A fine restaurant upstairs serves Corsican specialties. *Menus* 55F, 70F, and 120F, *vin compris.* Open July-Aug. Mon.-Sat. noon-2pm and 7:30-9:30pm.

U Fucone, 1, rue Général Campi (tel. 95-21-13-85), near place de Gaulle. Well-prepared local dishes in a snug setting. The owner is also the cook, and the 55F *menu* includes wine. Open Mon.-Sat. noon-1pm and 7:30-9:30pm, but try to arrive early.

Restaurant Pech, near the campground (tel. 95-52-00-90), in front of the bus stop. Saves campers the trouble of going back to town. Open Wed.-Mon. noon-2pm and 7:30-10pm.

Sights and Entertainment

If you cherish the Little Corporal as much as his hometown does, you can visit the house where he was born, just off rue Bonaparte. The house is furnished in period style, and Napoleon's mother's bedroom is still intact. On the second floor is a family tree and a collection of portraits and arms. (Open Mon. and Wed.-Sat. 9am-noon and 2-6pm, Sun. 9am-noon. Admission 10F, students 5F.) Next to the *syndicat,* the **Salon Napoléonien** features busts, portraits, and a bronze death-mask. (Open in summer daily 9am-noon and 2:30-5:30pm, in off-season Mon.-Sat. 9am-noon and 2-5pm. Admission 2F.) On rue Fesch, 11F (students 5F) will admit you to **Chapelle Impériale,** where most of the Bonapartes are interred. (Open April-Sept. 9-11:45am and 2:30-6pm; Oct.-March 2-5pm.) **Musée Fesch,** next door, houses paintings by fifteenth- and sixteenth-century Italian Renaissance masters; it will re-open some time in 1989 after extensive renovations. Only recently opened to the public, the **Musée du Capitellu,** opposite the *citadelle* at 18, bd. Danielle Casanova (tel. 95-21-50-57), is an intriguing collection of Corsican paintings and *objets d'art* from the eighteenth and nineteenth centuries. (Open Tues.-Sat. 10am-noon and 2-6pm, Sun. 10am-noon, Mon. 2-6pm. Admission 20F.)

Southwest of Ajaccio at the mouth of the gulf are the **Iles Sanguinaires** (the Bloody Islands), where dramatic grottoes glow a gory scarlet at sunset. Many private entrepreneurs organize boat excursions for about 70F per person. M. Costiera (tel. 95-25-04-03) runs two trips per day in summer (at 8:30am and 2:30pm, 3 hr.). Alternatively, take the bus marked "Parata" from place de Gaulle to the mouth of the gulf, 14km away, and view the islands from the mainland. The **Tour de la Parata** (1608), a Genoese watchtower found here, is in better condition than most; take a careful look at its engineering. To get off shore and walk up into the mountains, consult the *syndicat,* which will help map out some good hikes.

The most convenient, but least appealing beach is the **plage St-François,** next to place de Gaulle. Don't be satisfied with the dirty sand and rocky ocean bed. The beaches on the way to the Iles Sanguinaires are intimate, clean, and accessible by bus #5 (6.50F). The beaches in **Porticcio** are sandy and wide, but crowded. Take a shuttle boat to the resort, on the other side of the bay. **Vedette Silene** (tel. 95-51-05-56) leaves from the port (Mon.-Sat. 1 per hr.; 15 min.; one-way 20F, round-trip 35F; last boat returns at 7:30pm). **Tahiti-plage** in front of the airport is long, relatively empty, and easily accessible via bus #1 from cours Napoléon (6.50F).

Ajaccio has a surprising number of clubs and discos; several are open all night and are located on or around cours Napoléon. If you're looking for high stakes, elegance, or glamour, you won't find them at Ajaccio's **Casino,** bd. Lantivy (tel. 95-21-41-14). It costs only 1F to play. (Open until 3am.) You can also go next door to **l'Octogone,** the disco where the casino's clientele refuels. Quai Napoléon along the port has many lively cafes with outdoor seating, and the restaurants along rue des Glacis, 1 block behind quai Napoléon, are perfect for romantic, late-night dining, if a bit expensive.

Ajaccio to Calvi

The most heart-stopping of all Corsica's roads runs between Ajaccio and Calvi, sweeping past beaches and small resorts, then ascending steeply through wooded gorges and mountain villages. Exercise extreme caution when driving along the tortuous, single-lane N199 (there are no guard rails). Some of the cleanest and most beautiful beaches in Corsica line the coast along the **Golfe de Sagone.** Tiuccia, 25km from Ajaccio, is a small beachside village, notable for its ruined castle. **Camping Le Calcatoggio** (tel. 95-52-28-31), 3km from Tiuccia is a shady site with direct access to the beach (13F per person, 12F per tent). **Cargèse,** at the end of the Gulf of Sagone, is a small Greek Orthodox community. The Greek Mass still echoes in **Eglise Grècque** every Sunday, and the traditional chants, incense, and candlelight contribute to an unearthly, haunting beauty. You can spend the night here at the **Hôtel de France** (tel. 95-26-41-07), which offers large rooms for 115F. (Triples 125F. Breakfast 18F.) The rooms at the **Hôtel Bel'Mare** (tel. 95-26-40-13) are expensive, but you can afford the luxury of a meal on the restaurant's terrace, overlooking the ocean. (Simple *menu* 48.40F, pizza 22-30F, omelettes 24-28F. Open daily noon-2:30pm and 7pm-midnight.)

Near the southern tip of the Gulf of Porto, **Piana** is a sedate and picturesque village with rose-colored roofs, granite cliffs, eucalyptus trees, and a view of the sea. Far more spectacular than the town itself is the panoramic view of Piana from the surrounding mountains. **Hôtel Continental** (tel. 95-26-82-02) is the oldest hotel in the village and is still run by the same charming family. The original house has large rooms with old furniture. The annex, across a large garden, has modern doubles with showers and W.C. Between Piana and Porto, the road runs through the area called the **Calanche (Calanques) de Piana.** Here the scenery is even more spectacular—huge red mountains plunge into little bays filled with black and emerald water. The calanques often form lifelike shapes—a dog's head, a turtle, and an eagle, for instance. Guy de Maupassant called the shapes "a menagerie of nightmares." If you are here early in the morning, you might catch a glimpse of the rare African fish-eagle; this area is its only known European habitat.

The bus between Calvi and Ajaccio usually stops in **Porto** for about 3½ hours—just long enough for the driver to steady his nerves and for riders to hike along the cliffs above the spectacular bay and go swimming. A bare, dusty **Camping Municipal** (tel. 95-26-17-76), 10 minutes away, has the advantage of a beachside location. Four kilometers away in **Ota** is a family-like **youth hostel** (tel. 95-26-10-05), with dorm rooms, good kitchen facilities, and a mountain view. (No hostel card required and no age restriction. 42F per night. Breakfast 20F.) Porto's hotels are overpriced and usually full. The Porto **Syndicat d'Initiative**, up the main road leaving the port (tel. 95-26-10-55), can help with camping and transportation, including motorboat rentals for exploring the coast. (Open Mon.-Sat. 9am-noon and 4-7pm.) If you are taken aback by the commercialism and the crowds at Porto, you might consider hitchhiking to the calmer beach at **Serriera**, 8km away.

After Porto, the road becomes more tortuous until **Fango**, a small village named for a clear river that passes by. Turn right on the road to Manso for about 1km to the old stone bridge on the left. The river passes underneath it, and the warm pool there provides a beautiful, peaceful place to swim. The river ends at the beach at **Galeria**, 1km farther down the road to Calvi.

Hitchhiking along coastal route D81 between Ajaccio and Calvi can be successful, but it's best to make it a two-day trip since cars travel slowly on the mountain road. The D81 begins 6km outside of Ajaccio off the N194; to get there, take bus #2 from the *préfecture* in Ajaccio and ask the driver to let you off at the beginning of the D81. Start early to avoid the competition for rides at midday. Slow buses leave Ajaccio for Calvi and return daily, but you won't have time to stop at the attractive beaches and small villages along the way if you plan on getting to Calvi the same day. **Cars Ollandini** (tel. 95-21-14-08 or 95-21-07-53) leaves Ajaccio and Calvi at 8am and arrives at 6pm (96F). **S.A.I.B.** buses (tel. 95-21-53-74) run as far as Porto (at 7:20am and 3:30pm, return at 2:15pm). **Autocars Arrighi** (tel. 95-21-09-90) runs inland to the village of Vico, where there's a **youth hostel** (tel. 95-26-60-55; 27F) in the Couvent St-François. The bus continues to Soccia, a 1½-hour walk from the Lac de Creno. (Mon.-Sat. 1 afternoon bus to Tiuccia, Sagone, Vico, and Soccio. Returns the following morning.)

Calvi

Calvi is a distillation of all that is loveliest in Corsica—an indolent town stretched beside the blue sea, with snow on red mountains behind its bright port, and long white beaches. But Calvi knows how to use its beauty for a profit; it's a chic resort with prices that will make your eyebrows rise and your heart sink.

Within the *citadelle,* the fortified part of town high above the rest, there is shelter in the silent, winding streets and in **Oratoire St-Antoine,** a fifteenth-century building that is now a museum of ancient and medieval religious art. The view from the ramparts, of the sea and the mountains, of sailing vessels and waves, merits poetry and fanfare.

Orientation and Practical Information

Avenue de la République runs parallel to the port and leads from the train station to the *syndicat,* then on to the citadel.

Syndicat d'Initiative: Place de la Gare (tel. 95-65-05-87), next to the station. Maps, hotel lists, and information on trains and excursions. Will not make hotel reservations, but will tell you where there's room. Has a list of rooms in private homes. Open June-Sept. Mon.-Sat. 9:30am-noon and 3-6:30pm; Oct.-May Mon.-Fri. 9am-noon.

Currency Exchange: The accommodations and restaurants in Calvi will lighten your wallet considerably, but you can lose your money just as easily by exchanging it at banks. **Société Generale,** bd. Wilson, levies a steep commission, and **Credit Lyonnais,** also on bd. Wilson, offers abominable rates.

Post Office: Route de Santore. Take the 1st right after the youth hostel on av. de la République, and then the 1st left. **Telephones** here. **Postal code:** 20260. Open Mon.-Fri. 8am-noon and 2-6pm, Sat. 8am-noon.

Train Station: Place de la Gare (tel. 95-65-00-61). To Bastia (3 per day, 3 hr., 70F), Corte (2 per day, 3½ hr., 59F), and Ajaccio (2 per day, 6 hr., 106F). Open until 8pm.

Buses: Ollandini, 6, av. de la République (tel. 95-65-06-74), near the youth hostel. To Porto (1 per day at 8am, 3½ hr., 48F), Ajaccio (10 hr., including a 3½ hr. stopover in Porto; 96F), Fango (1 hr., 18F), Piana (8 hr., including stopover; 51F), Cargèse (8¾ hr., 62F), and Sagone (11 hr., 70F). **Santini** (tel. 95-37-02-98) runs a bus from the citadel to St-Florent (Mon.-Sat. 4pm, 2 hr.) **Canavar** buses run to Galeria from the citadel (Mon.-Sat. 5pm, 45 min.). **Gazzo,** 40, bd. Paoli, runs buses to Bastia (Mon.-Sat. 6:10am, 3 hr.), from place de la Porteuse d'Eau. More bus schedule information at the tourist office.

Ferries: Agence Tramar, quai Adolphe Landry (tel. 95-65-01-38). Handles SNCM boat trips to mainland France. Open Mon.-Fri. 9-11:30am and 2-5:30pm, Sat. 9-11:30am. **Corsica Ferries,** next to the SNCM booth on quai de Commerce (tel. 95-65-10-84). Sails for Savona in northern Italy (late May to mid-Sept. approximately 3 per week, 5½ hr., 195F). Open Mon.-Fri. 9am-noon and 2-6pm.

Taxi: Tel. 95-65-03-10. To the airport, 7km outside of town, about 40F.

Bicycle Rental: Balagne Cycles, av. de la République (tel. 95-65-12-44), on the way out of town past the train station. 10-speeds 70F per day, deposit 600F. Mopeds 150F per day, gas 30F, deposit 1200F. Open daily 8:30am-noon and 3-7pm.

Accommodations, Camping, and Food

BVJ Corsotel, av. de la République (tel. 95-65-14-15), opposite the train station. Billed as a "youth center" for travelers age 15-35. Cheery atmosphere, big common rooms including a TV lounge. 75F per person in rooms of 2-5 people, with private bathrooms. Breakfast included. Dinner (7:30-8pm) 50F. Open March-Nov.

Hôtel Laeticia, rue Etienne Millie (tel. 95-65-09-63), on a small street off rue Joffre. Clean rooms. Doubles 150F.

Camping: La Clé des Champs, Tel. 95-65-00-86. Follow the road from the train station to Ile Rousse and watch for the sign on your right (15-min. walk). Or, get off the train at the last stop before Calvi and cross the road to Ile Rousse (5 min.). Clean with lots of shade. 15F per person, 6F per tent. Tax 1F. Many other campgrounds at the entrance to the town and along the coast. Take the train to Ile Rousse or follow the road to find them. Open Easter-Oct.

The old pedestrian streets above the port are filled with moderately-priced restaurants with outdoor seating; the restaurants along the port are more expensive; the streets of the citadel are serene and contain few restaurants. **Le Poème** in the *citadelle* is an intimate restaurant with delicious pastries and breads, but full meals are expensive. (*Plats du jour,* including *entrée,* 70-80F. Open April-Oct. 9am-1am.) On a terrace off bd. Wilson, **Restaurant Minigola** and **U Fornu** both serve local fare and 55-65F *menus.* (Minigola open noon-2:30pm and 6:30pm-midnight; U Fornu open June 30-Sept. 31 5:30-11pm.) Most of Calvi's **clubs** are prohibitively high-priced, so spend the evening on the lively waterfront. Cafes and bars stay open into the wee hours.

Near Calvi

Ile Rousse is one of Corsica's oldest resorts, devoted primarily to a middle-aged clientele. The town dates from 1758, when Pascal Paoli, leader of independent Corsica, built it to compete with Calvi, which he wanted to punish for its allegiance to Genoa. Paoli's name is given to the town's main square. The stretch of coastline here is among the most heavily touristed on the island, luring crowds with its seductive white-powder sand beaches and calm, shallow water. Boats travel from here to the Côte d'Azur; buy **SNCM** tickets from **Agence Tramar**, av. Joseph Calizi (tel. 95-60-09-56; open Mon.-Fri. 8:30am-noon and 2-5:30pm, Sat. 8:30am-noon).

In town, the **Hôtel Select "Chez Marie,"** 9, place Paoli (tel. 95-60-01-74), is an old-fashioned, family-run establishment. The owner expects you to take full *pension* in the summer (290F per person), unless you stay only for one or two days. (Doubles with shower 120F. Breakfast 15F.) Since restaurants are expensive on Ile Rousse, you should plan on shopping at the morning **market** off place Paoli. **La Cave** is the least expensive restaurant on place Paoli (*menu* 55F, pizza 22-40F). A train covers the coast between Calvi and Ile Rousse (June to mid-Sept. 10 per day, May and mid-Sept. to Oct. 5 per day, Nov.-April 2 per day; 50 min.) The line is divided into three sections, at 7F per section; you can save money by purchasing a *carnet* of six tickets for 28F. Another train links Ile Rousse and Bastia (2½ hr., 54F). Several **campgrounds** lie along the route—just hop off the train when you see a beach or campsite that suits your fancy. Prices usually run 16F per person, 10F per tent. Ile Rousse's **Syndicat d'Initiative**, at the foot of place Paoli (tel. 95-60-04-35), can brief you about camping. (Open Mon.-Fri. 10am-noon and 3-6:30pm.)

Algajola (2 stops, 14F from Calvi) illustrates how a village can grow up inside and around a ruined fortress, using the walls as protection against the sea. Algajola has no *syndicat*. **Hôtel l'Esquinade** (tel. 95-60-70-19) lies at the edge of the village facing the beach. (Singles 92-112F; doubles with shower and toilet 144F, with beach view 164F; triples 176-196F; quads 208F. Breakfast 15F.)

A trail (20-30 min.) from Cantaretti City, a "ranch camping" site in Algajola, leads to the commune of **Pigna**. Founded in 800 C.E. in the hills away from the sea, the village was rejuvenated in the 1960s by the arrival of shepherds, organ and lute makers, potters, and engravers who came here to work exclusively with their hands. Every July 13 marks the **Paese in Festa,** a daylong celebration blending traditional poetic events with improvised musical and theatrical productions.

Calvi is ringed with **vineyards** whose *caves* are open to the public. Many are quite accessible, and all are listed in the *syndicat*'s brochure on Corsican wines. Opening hours increase in September, when much of the wine is made.

Corte

Huddled against a mountainside and crowned by a fifteenth-century *citadelle,* this sleepy town provides welcome relief from the tourist-choked coastal towns. Corte (pronounced Court-AY) is the largest town in the Corsican interior, and for this reason (as well as its impregnable location), it was made the capital of the embattled eighteenth-century Corsican Republic. Barely touched by tourism, Corte remains one of the most traditional Corsican towns. Located only a short distance from Corte are some of Corsica's most beautiful hiking trails, both daytrips and longer journeys (see Near Corte below).

The town has retained one feature from its glory days. The University of Corsica reopened in 1980, more than 200 years after its predecessor, founded by the "enlightened despot" Pasquale Paoli, was closed.

Corte is accessible by train from Bastia (4 per day, 2 hr., 43F), Ajaccio (4 per day, 2½ hr., 49F), and Calvi (change at Ponte-Leccia, 2 per day, 3½ hr., 59F). **Ollandini** buses (tel. 95-46-25-54) ply the same stretch right into town. (To Bastia Mon.-Sat. 2 per day, 1½ hr., 41F and to Ajaccio 2 per day, 2 hr., 47F.) Buses depart from in front of the agency on place Xavier Luciani. The **train station** is 1km out of town; to get to the center, turn right, cross the bridge, and continue along av. Jean Nicoli past the university and up the hill.

For **tourist information** (tel. 95-46-26-20 in summer, 95-46-20-77 in winter), climb to the entrance of the *citadelle.* The guides there are friendly and well informed about Corte and its surroundings. (Open May-Oct. Mon.-Sat. 9am-8pm.

Admission 5F.) Tours of the *citadelle* leave on the hour from 9 to 11am and 3 to 5pm. You can enjoy an excellent view of the island peaks from this point.

From July through September, you can stay in student dorms at the university. (49F per night. No breakfast. ISIC required.) Contact the **CROUS** office at the university, av. Jean Nicoli, 20250 Corte (tel. 95-46-02-61; open Mon.-Fri.). You might also try the **Hôtel du Nord,** 22, cours Paoli (tel. 95-46-00-68); an amiable owner and recently renovated wood interior make you feel at ease, but avoid rooms overlooking noisy cours Paoli. (Singles 120F. Doubles with shower 150-170F. Triples 196F. Quads 250F. Breakfast included.) Otherwise, **Hôtel de la Poste,** 2, place du Duc du Padoue (tel. 95-46-01-37), offers singles for 112F and doubles for 129F (breakfast and shower included.) There are three **campgrounds** near town, in the direction of the Restonica Valley. Take a left from the train station to the center of town (5-10 min.). From there follow av. du Président Piérucci. **U Sognu** (tel. 95-46-09-07) is pleasant and quiet with clean facilities. **Restonica** and **Alivetu** (tel. 95-46-11-09), facing each other, are a little less expensive. (Both 14F per person, 7F per tent. Open April-Oct.) You can also rent a tent at Restonica. Seven kilometers from Corte off the N193 in the direction of Ajaccio is a tiny, 10-bed **auberge de jeunesse** at **Casanova** (tel. 95-47-03-17). The coed sleeping quarters are cramped and hovel-like, but chances are you'll be alone in this tranquil spot. (Hot shower and excellent kitchen facilities, including refrigerator. 37F per person.)

Restaurant le Bip's, 14, cours Paoli (tel. 95-46-06-26), is a relaxed place, with a 55F *menu.* The entrance is off the parking lot. (Open daily noon-3pm and 7:30pm-midnight.) **U Spanu,** av. Xavier Lucciani, just off place Paoli (tel. 95-46-07-85), offers a 59F *menu,* a *menu Corse* at 85F, and pizza from 30F. (Open daily noon-1:30pm and 7-11pm.)

Near Corte

Southwest of Corte, a tiny road stretches 15km through the **Gorges de la Restonica,** one of the more sparsely populated areas on the island. The scenery is magnificent: A crystal-clear, trout-filled stream, its banks lined with fig, poplar, and chestnut trees, cascades down the mountain. Camping here is excellent, and there are several official sites. As the road climbs above 1600m, it becomes lined with gnarled pines, and you can see snowy peaks as late as June. From the end of the road, follow the direction of the river to the **Lac de Melo** (1-hr. hike), a snow-fed beauty at almost 2000m, surrounded by mountains that reach up to 2700m (Mt. Cinto). You can continue to the **Lac de Creno** and join the **Grande Randonnée-20,** the challenging trail that winds its way across the entire breadth of Corsica. In summer you can swim in these lakes, although the water is fairly cold (18°C). There are many other excellent trails in this area. Wear good hiking shoes (not running shoes), and always hike in company. Also be prepared for cold, even snowy weather as late as June. For more information, contact the **Parc Naturel Régional** in Ajaccio (tel. 95-21-56-54). The guides at the *citadelle* in Corte can help map out trails suited to your abilities.

Bastia

Busy, traffic-clogged, and industrialized, Bastia is Corsica's least characteristic city but also the island's largest port—your boat may well deposit you here. The city was Corsica's capital until 1811, when Napoleon designated Ajaccio as its successor. Today, Bastia is the island's economic center.

If you get stuck here waiting for a ferry, you can walk around the fourteenth-century *vieille ville,* which dates from the Genoan occupation. The **Musée d'Ethnographie** in the fifteenth-century **Palais des Gouverneurs Génois** above the port (tel. 95-32-16-99), presents a retrospective account of daily Corsican life, region by region. (Open in summer Mon.-Sat. 9am-noon and 3-6pm; in off-season Mon.-Sat. 9am-noon and 2-5pm. Admission 4F.) To get the best view of the **Vieux Port,** walk to the end of the Jetée du Dragon. The city's most popular attraction is **place St-Nicolas,** a wide and dusty 300m esplanade lined with cafes and always busy with fanatic *boules* players.

Orientation and Practical Information

The new port and the train station are connected by **av. Maréchal Sebastiani,** where you'll find the tourist office kiosk and the post office. The commercial bd. Charles de Gaulle, bd. Paoli, and rue César Campinchi run parallel to place St-Nicolas and lead to the old port and old town.

Syndicat d'Initiative: 35, bd. Paoli (tel. 95-31-02-04). Information on the entire island. Pick up the indispensable booklet *Transports Collectifs en Haute-Corse* for bus schedules to destinations on Cap Corse and around the island. Open June-Aug. Mon.-Fri. 8am-noon and 2-6pm, Sat. 8am-noon; Sept.-May Mon.-Fri. 9am-noon and 3-6pm.

Tourist Office: Place St-Nicholas (tel. 95-31-00-89). Information and guided tours. Open in summer Mon.-Fri. 8:30am-noon and 2-6pm, Sat. until 4pm; in off-season Mon.-Fri. only.

Currency Exchange: There are several banks on bd. Paoli. Most open Tues.-Fri. 8:15-11:45am and 2:15-4:30pm. The post office offers competitive rates (1% commission).

Post Office: Av. Maréchal-Sebastiani. **Telephones** and **currency exchange** here. **Postal code:** 20200. Open Mon.-Fri. 8am-7pm, Sat. 8am-noon.

Airport: Bastia-Poretta (tel. 95-36-02-03) 23km away. A bus leaves from place de la Gare, in front of the Préfecture, and is timed for airplane departures (½ hr.). Flights to Marseille (3 per day, 50 min., 354F), Nice (2-3 per day, 40 min., 303F), Paris (5-6 per day, 1½ hr., 953F). In the "blue" period, students under 27, ages 25 and under, families, and seniors are eligible for discounts: to Marseille 247F, to Nice 203F, to Paris 523F (each rate normally 718F). Daily flights to London via Paris, Geneva via Nice, and Amsterdam via Nice. **Air France,** 6, av. Emile-Sari (tel. 95-31-99-31). **Air Inter** at the airport (tel. 95-36-02-95).

Train Station: Place de la Gare (tel. 95-32-60-06), just off av. Maréchal Sebastiani. Corsica's most modern station. Quiet and empty. To Calvi (2 per day, 3½ hr., 70F), Corte (4 per day, 2 hr., 43F), and Ajaccio (4 per day, 4 hr., 91F). You can leave your **luggage** at the *consigne* for 10F per day, but remember that the station is closed 8pm-6:30am.

Bus Stations: Gazzo, 40, bd. Paoli. To Calvi via Ile Rousse (1 per day, 3½ hr.). **Rapides Bleus,** 1, av. Maréchal Sebastiani (tel. 95-31-03-79). To Porto-Vecchio along the Côte Orientale (Mon.-Sat. 8:30am and 4pm, Sun. 8:30am; 3 hr.). **Ollandini,** Tel. 95-31-44-04. To Corte (Mon.-Sat. 8:15am and 3pm, 1½ hr., 41F) and Ajaccio (3½ hr., 86F). For excursions around Cap Corse, inquire at the bus stop on rue du Nouveau Port (service runs July-Aug. only).

Ferries: SNCM, Hôtel de la Chambre de Commerce (tel. 95-31-36-63). Open daily 8-11:15am and 2-5:30pm. 2 boats per day to Marseille and Toulon (10 hr., 220F) and Nice (6 hr., 193F). 30% reduction for passangers 25 and under to Nice only; 30% reduction for all passengers in off-season. **Corsica Ferries,** 5bis, rue Chanoine Leschi (tel. 95-31-18-09). To Italy: Livorno and La Spezia (4-5 hr., 155F) and Savona (8 hr., 195F). **NAV.AR.MA. Lines,** 40, bd. Paoli (tel. 95-31-01-79), or 4, rue Commandant Luce (tel. 95-31-46-29). To Italy: Livorno (4 hr.) and Piombino (3 hr.). One-way to both ports 138F.

Car Rental: Budget, 35, rue César Campinchi (tel. 95-31-09-02). Citroën AX 171F per day plus 2.42F per km, 2241F per week with unlimited mileage (prices include insurance). **Mattei,** 5, rue Chanoine-Leschi (tel. 95-31-57-23). 198F per day plus 1.90F per km (insurance not included). Deposit 1200F.

Bike Rental: Locacycles, 40, rue César Campinchi (tel. 95-31-02-43). 10-speeds 60F per day, 363F per week, deposit 500F. Mopeds 100F per day, 560F per week, deposit 1000F. 10% discount in off-season.

Hospital: Falconaja, Tel. 95-33-73-83.

Medical Emergency: Tel. 15.

Police: Tel. 95-33-51-69.

Police Emergency: Tel. 17.

Accommodations and Camping

Stay in town only if you're so exhausted from the ferry ride that you can't move on. There are several cheap hotels near the port and the train station, but most are dingy. The tourist office has a complete list.

Riviera-Hôtel, 1bis, rue du Nouveau Port (tel. 95-31-63-04). Airy, respectable rooms near the port. Doubles 100F, with shower 140F, extra bed 40F. Breakfast 18F.

Hôtel de l'Univers, 3, av. Maréchal Sebastiani (tel. 95-31-03-38), down the street from the train station. Cheerful rooms and management. Singles 90F. Doubles 100F, with shower 140F. Triples 140-160F.

Hôtel Gatti, 7, rue Miot (tel. 95-31-06-83), off rue César Campinchi. Large, spotless rooms in quiet area of town. Doubles 90F, with shower 120F, with two double beds 140-160F. Obligatory breakfast 20F.

Camping: Les Sables Rouges, closest to town (tel. 95-33-36-08). From the train station, take the small train which follows the coast (every ½ hr., last train 8pm). 8F per person, 10F per tent. **Camping San Damiano,** route de la Lagune de Pinette (tel. 95-33-68-02), 15km south of Bastia. Closer to the airport. Open June-Oct.

Food

Several small restaurants are situated between the train station and place St-Nicholas. For about 50F, you should be able to get yourself a good dinner.

Chez Gino, 11, av. Emile Sari (tel. 95-31-41-43), 5 min. from the ferry terminal. A lively neighborhood eatery, ideal for a pre- or post-ferry snack. Pizzas 17-38F, huge ice cream concoctions 11-40F. 45F will fill you to the hatches. Open until 1am. Closed 2-4:30pm.

Le Dépot, 22, rue César Campinchi (tel. 95-24-09-64). A cozy, intimate place with winding wooden staircase and brick walls. Fire-cooked pizza 22-40F, *plats du jour* 50-70F. No fixed-price *menu*. Open daily noon-2pm and 7pm-midnight.

Saint-Georges, 35, av. Emile Sari (tel. 95-31-24-33), down the street from Gino's and near the port. Traditional, family-style food. *menu* 60F, *plats du jour* from 50F, pizza 30-42F. Open daily 10am-3am.

24-Hour Bread Distributor, rue Miot. Go just to look at this machine, a cultural anachronism distributing traditional country-style loafs with an ultra-modern apparatus (4F).

Near Bastia: Cap Corse

From Bastia, you can explore the string of fishing villages and quiet inlets of Cap Corse, a 48-km peninsula north of the city that points toward France. The road (113km) around the Cap passes sheltered coves and high, forest-covered mountains. Sprinkled amidst these hills of chestnut and lime trees and olive groves are fortified old towns such as **Cagnano,** 5½km inland from the port of **Porticciolo,** built in the period of Genoese rule. On the coast you can see several Genoese towers, including the restored **Tour de Losse,** part of an elaborate system that could once warn every Corsican within two hours of an impending attack by barbarians or pirates.

Macinaggio, 40km from Bastia, is one of the few port towns where you can find services and supplies (including gas and a large supermarket). The attentive **Syndicat d'Initiative** (tel. 95-35-40-40) has information on hotels, campsites, and bus transport. (Open daily 10am-noon and 6-8pm.) The **post office** has **currency exchange.** (Open Mon.-Fri. 9am-noon and 2-5pm, Sat. 9am-noon.) **Hôtel des Iles** (tel. 95-35-43-02) is your only choice in this small town. Its friendly owners offer clean rooms with a view of the port. (Doubles with shower 180F. Breakfast 20F.) If you spend the day here, you can take a motorboat trip to **Ile de la Giraglia,** which has a lighthouse, or to **Santa Maria,** the site of a beach and Roman chapel. Six-person zodiac boats leave from the port every half-hour from 10am to 12:30pm. You can bring a picnic, and the boat will pick you up in the afternoon. Call **Testamora** (tel. 95-35-05-92) for more information. If you want to walk to Santa Maria (1½ hr.), ask the *syndicat* for directions.

Rogliano, Macinaggio's sister village 2.5km inland, is solemn and undisturbed by tourism or modernization. Shaped like an amphitheater, it contains the ruins of a Genoan castle, as well as a restored and inhabited Genoan square tower and a large sixteenth-century church, **San 'Agnello.** You can walk from Macinaggio to Rogliano, or take the shuttle truck to the **Restaurant u Sant Agnellu** (tel. 95-35-40-59) and stay for a meal (*menu* 80F).

In the unspoiled port of **Centuri,** on the other side of the peninsula, 57km from Bastia, fishing boats bring in the daily catch of *langoustes, moules,* and fish. Sublimely picturesque, Centuri is often photographed as a pure example of an authentic fishing village. **Camping l'Isoluttu** (tel. 95-35-62-81) is near the beach. (12F per person, 10F per tent, 7F per car.) In town, three one-star hotels all have high prices. **Le Pêcheur** (tel. 95-35-60-14) is the most rustic. **Le Centuri** (tel. 95-35-61-70) is a modern hotel with large rooms, all equipped with shower and private bath or toilet. (Doubles 190F.) Since Centuri's handful of restaurants all offer approximately the same mid- to high-priced meals, you should stroll about and compare the *plats du jour.* U **Fossu** serves the least expensive *menu* at 58F. House wines tend to be top-notch. Look for *rapo,* a wonderful dessert wine that is now unfortunately seldom produced.

Mirroring Bastia on the other side of the Cap (20km from Bastia on the inland road), **St-Florent** is a modern beach resort built around an old port. There's nothing to see here, and you won't even be able to find a crêpe at a decent price. Stop at **Patrimonio,** a tiny village 5km from St-Florent, for local wine at very good prices (5F per liter in your own bottle or sack, 10-15F per bottle). The region is one of Corsica's first and finest wine producers.

Traveling along the *corniche* around the Cap is not particularly easy. Check with the *syndicat* in Bastia for excursions and up-to-date bus information. **Cars Micheli** (tel. 95-35-61-08) organizes a one-day circuit of the Cap from Bastia, passing through, but not stopping in, 18 small villages (leaves daily at 9am from 1, rue du Nouveau Port; returns at 5pm; 80F). The same company runs afternoon buses Monday, Tuesday, Thursday, and Saturday (June 15-Oct. 4) from Bastia to Morsiglia via Macinaggio, Rogliano, and Centuri. (Buses leave 4:30pm, return Wednesday only from Morsiglia at 7am.) On Monday, Wednesday, and Friday at 4pm, **Cars Saladini** (tel. 95-35-43-88) sends buses to Rogliano along the same circuit. Hitchhiking is next to impossible here since the drivers are mostly tourists.

Côte Orientale

The island's only relatively flat road stretches from Bastia to Porto-Vecchio, closely following the Côte Orientale (Corsica's east coast). Seemingly one long suburb of Bastia, the area is mobbed by families cluttering the unattractive, granular beaches. Inland, along the **Plaine Orientale,** the land is heavily cultivated with grapevines and fruit trees, or thick with *maquis* (underbrush). East of Corte lies the **Castagniccia,** a low, hilly region filled with chestnut trees (chestnut flour was once a staple of the Corsican diet). A car will make it easier to explore the virtually untoured back roads of this area. The road southeast from Corte (N200) will take you to the **Etang de Diana** on the coast; the water here is calm and abnormally salty. **Porto-Vecchio** has little to see except tourists. Still surrounded by its sixteenth-century Genoese walls, the city streets are narrow and winding, and the 10-meter-thick walls have been hollowed out for use as homes, stores, and restaurants. From **Porte Genoise** (formerly the city's main gateway), there is a panoramic view of the port and the inlet of the Tyrrhenian Sea on which Porto-Vecchio lies. The **Plage de Palombaggia,** 9km to the south, is a picture-postcard beach with a crescent of fine sand shaded by parasol-like pine trees. **Trinitours** (tel. 95-70-13-83) operates buses to the beaches (July-Aug. only, Mon.-Sat. 10am, return from the beach 6pm). The **Syndicat d'Initiative,** place de l'Hôtel de Ville (tel. 95-70-09-58), can provide information on campgrounds and transportation. (Open July-Aug. Mon.-Fri. 9am-noon and 4:30-8:30pm, Sat.-Sun. 10am-noon and 5-8pm; June and

Sept. Mon.-Fri. 9am-noon and 4-8pm, Sat. 9am-noon.) **Rapides Bleus,** 7, rue Jean Jaurès (tel. 95-70-10-36), runs two buses per day (1 Sun.) between Bastia and Porto-Vecchio (June 15-Sept. 15, 3 hr., 80F). **Autocars Balesi** (tel. 95-70-14-50; 95-21-28-01 in Ajaccio) sends one bus per day (at 6am) to Ajaccio (July-Aug. only, none Sun., 77F). **Ollandini** sends buses to Bonifacio (2 per day, 15 min.), as does **Trinitours** (1 per day at noon, return from Bonifacio at 7:30pm). If you absolutely must stay in Porto-Vecchio, **Hôtel Panorama,** 12, rue Jean-Nicoli (tel. 95-70-07-96), offers clean rooms (105-120F, with shower 130-180F. Breakfast 19F). **Hôtel le Mistral,** rue Jean-Nicoli (tel. 95-70-08-53), has reasonably decent rooms. (Singles 110F. Doubles 155F, with shower 165F. Triples 175-195F. Extra bed 65F. Breakfast 20F.) You may prefer the campground down the hill, **La Matonara** (tel. 95-70-35-05).

Bonifacio

Clinging limpet-like to the rocks above the sea, Bonifacio was once designed to keep intruders out. Now it welcomes them by the score. The town's long harbor is a haven for tourists—shops lining the quay hawk T-shirts, key chains, underwear, and earrings, all emblazoned with the bandana-wrapped Moor's head, symbol of Corsica. The town's *citadelle* commands a majestic view of Sardinia, 13km away across the straits, and of the towering Corsican cliffs. The Sardinian dialect has found its way into the local language, making it difficult even for other Corsicans to understand the town's residents. Bonifacio was founded as a fortress (the French Foreign Legion still sets up camp here), and despite the ravages of the climate, you will notice that virtually every house on the old streets of the citadel still has a steep staircase whose lowest flight can be raised like a mini-drawbridge in case of invasion. Below the town, you can swim and sun among the rocks at the foot of the cliffs.

Bonifacio is difficult to reach since it doesn't lie on the train line. However, buses run between Bonifacio and Porto-Vecchio twice per day, with a connecting bus to Bastia in the morning only (Mon.-Sat. 7am and 1:45pm, ½ hr.). Two buses per day (Mon.-Sat., 1 Sun.) connect Bonifacio to Ajaccio (6:30am and 1:45pm., 3½ hr., 92F). Contact the **Ollandini** office, 26, quai Comparetti (tel. 95-73-01-28), on the port. (Open June-Sept. Mon.-Sat. 8:30am-noon and 2-6pm; Oct.-May Mon.-Fri. 8:30am-noon and 1:30-6pm, Sat. 8:30am-noon.)

You can also leave town by sea—on a ferry to Sardinia. **Saremar** (tel. 95-73-00-96) sails for **Santa Teresa** (May-Sept. 3 per day, Oct.-April 2 per day; 1 hr.; 44F) and for **La Maddalena** (daily, 2½ hr., 57F). Their office is open daily from 8:30 to 10:30am, 11:30am to 2:30pm, and 3 to 5pm. **NAV.AR.MA. Lines** (tel. 95-73-00-29) also goes to Santa Teresa (mid-June to mid-Sept. 5 per day, 45F; office open daily 7:30am-8:30pm). All boats leave from the **Gare Maritime** at the very end of quai Comparetti, beneath the walls of the upper city. You can buy your tickets shortly before departure time.

If you want to go out to sea without crossing international borders, consider the one-hour excursion to the now-deserted islands of **Lavezzi** and **Cavello** (every 20 min., round-trip 100F), which leaves from the *port de plaisance* in front of all the restaurants. The islands offer a magnificent view of Bonifacio. You can also visit the **grottes** of Bonifacio by boat (20 min., 45F).

The **Syndicat d'Initiative,** place d'Armes (tel. 95-73-03-48), in the *citadelle,* has a very friendly staff and a free pamphlet with all the information you need. Inquire about rooms in private homes. (Open Mon.-Sat. 9am-noon and 3-6pm.) A **branch office** operates out of a kiosk on quai Comparetti (open June-Sept. Mon.-Sat. 9am-noon and 4-7pm). Next to the *syndicat* are kiosks with **currency exchange.** The **post office** is off Montée Rastello, the long staircase which leads to the *citadelle* (open Mon.-Fri. 9:30am-12:30pm and 3-6pm, Sat. 9am-noon). The **postal code** for Bonifacio is 20169.

Accommodations and Camping

Bonifacio is another Corsican town where you won't find a room much later than noon in the summer. Hotels are few and expensive, clustering with most of the restaurants along the port below the city. The *syndicat* and its branch office can give you a list of hotels and campgrounds and tell you about rooms available in private homes. Travelers who have been sleeping on beaches can take advantage of the hot showers (10F) at **Artisanat Tounet,** quai Comparetti (tel. 95-73-11-17). (Open July-Aug. 9am-2am; June and Sept. 9am-8pm.)

Hôtel des Etrangers, av. Sylvère Bohn (tel. 95-73-01-09), at the entrance to the lower town, 300m from the port. The only 1-star hotel without obligatory *pension.* Rooms expensive nevertheless. Doubles with shower and private toilet 150-270F. Breakfast included.

Hôtel les Voyageurs, quai Camparetti (tel. 95-73-00-46). A fun place to take a *demi-pension.* 200F per person, obligatory in summer. Otherwise, doubles 100F, with shower 120F. While rooms are straightforward, the very good and creative **restaurant** has a wild tropical decor, with stenciled green walls. *Menus* from 55F.

Hôtel la Pergola, 13, quai Comparetti (tel. 95-73-13-56 in summer, 95-73-06-16 in winter). Spacious rooms, all with showers. Obligatory *demi-pension* in summer 200F per person. Otherwise rooms 100F, with shower 120F.

Camping: There are several campgrounds in the area. **Relais de a'Araguina** is the closest, the most expensive, and the least desirable. 1-2 people 43F. **Cavallo Monto,** route de Porto-Vecchio (tel. 95-73-04-66), 2km away. In the direction of the Phare de Pertusato (5km) is 4-star **Camping des Iles.**

Food

Every *boulangerie* in Bonifacio sells its own version of *pain des morts* ("bread of the dead"—a non-lethal raisin-and-walnut concoction), the town's self-declared contribution to Corsican cuisine.

La Loggia, 2, rue de la Loggia (tel. 95-73-08-56), in the *citadelle* next to the Eglise Ste-Marie Majeure. Graceful rose-colored, neo-classical interior; outdoor seating in primary-colored chairs. Salads, including *tabouli* 20F; crêpes 9-18F. Open July-Aug. daily 10am-1am, in off-season 10am-7:30pm.

L'Agora, av. Carotolla (tel. 95-73-00-44) in the citadel. A sophisticated terrace above the port with bar, restaurant, and disco downstairs. You can get away with an affordable bill—order pizza, pasta, or salad (35-50F). Opens at 9am for coffee. Disco open until 6am.

Near Bonifacio

The road from Bonifacio northwest to Ajaccio crawls through mountains and offers intermittent glimpses of the sea in the distance. Try to leave the main route and explore some of the isolated villages. Along the coast, you will find unusual natural formations, such as the **Rocher du Lion** at **Roccapina,** a rock bearing the exact likeness of a lion. An elephant sits beside it.

Considered in 1839 "*la ville la plus corse des villes Corses*" by Corsican writer Prosper Merimée, the town of **Sartène** is built on granite, surrounded by megalithic stones and fantastically shaped rock faces. Like Bonifacio, Sartène sponsors **La Catenacciu,** a Good Friday procession imported from Seville. A red-hooded Christ bearing a wooden cross and dragging a long chain walks through the candlelit streets of the old town in a re-enactment of the Calvary drama. Sartène wine has a reputation for being both good and strong. Although most of the local vineyards are now only terraces on the mountainsides, **La Cave Sartenèse** in place Porta continues to pour the potent nectar (3.50F per glass, bottles from 14F). You can rent a tent at **Camping Olva** (tel. 95-77-11-58), 5km from Sartène on the mountain road D69. (20F per tent, 18F per person.) The **Syndicat d'Initiative** in Sartène is on cours Saraneli (tel. 95-77-05-37). Sartène is a stop on the Ajaccio-Bonifacio bus line (2 per day, 2 hr., 54F from Ajaccio).

Propriano, a popular summer resort set on the sandy beaches of the Gulf of Valinco, is also a busy fishing village. **Hôtel Le Bellevue,** 9, av. Napoléon (tel. 95-76-01-86), on the port, has a view of the port and the ocean. Rooms are big, clean, and well-furnished. (July-Aug. doubles 140-150F, with shower 200-220F. Breakfast 20F.) You can compose your own *menu* at the **Restaurant Mal Assis,** rue Général de Gaulle (tel. 95-76-01-49), across from the tourist office. Individual dishes are reasonably priced, so 50F should fill you up. (Omelettes 20F, lasagna 40F. Open daily noon-2:30pm and 7pm-1am.) The **Syndicat d'Initiative,** 17, rue Général-de-Gaulle (tel. 95-76-01-49), has a very competent staff and can help you with transportation and hotels, although they do not make reservations. You can change money here as well. (Open Mon.-Sat. 9am-noon and 3-7pm; in off-season Mon.-Fri. 9am-noon and 2-6pm.) Across the street at #4 is the **Ollandini** bus line (tel. 95-76-00-76), which makes excursions to various sights including the archeological site of **Filitosa,** where recently uncovered faces carved into stone monoliths observe the tides ebb and flow (Mon., Wed., and Fri.; 3½ hr.; 50F). Buses to Ajaccio leave twice per day (2 hr., 46F). Buses also run twice per day to Bonifacio (2 hr., 42F), Sartène (½ hr., 12F), and Porto-Vecchio (2 hr. 20 min., 47F). The office is open Monday through Saturday from 8:30am to noon and 2 to 6pm.

Two kilometers from Propriano are a few campgrounds near the ocean and an **auberge de jeunesse** at the **Centre Equestre de Barachi** (tel. 95-76-19-48) with slightly cramped co-ed dorm rooms, kitchen facilities, a restaurant, and a washing machine (40F per night, meals 30F). Next to the youth hostel, **Camping Colomba** (tel. 95-76-06-42) is clean and cheery and has a restaurant. (18F per person, 6F per tent.) At **Camping Corsica** (tel. 95-76-00-57), you can rent a 4-person tent with electricity.

Alps (Savoie-Dauphiné)

After museum corridors and enervating urban centers, this imposing, startling, and most spectacular of European landscapes will refresh and exhilarate. Indeed, the strong, silent mountains will bore no one with the details of recorded history. The Alps include towering peaks, green pastures, commercialized tourist centers, and villages next to cascading waterfalls. Gentle curves grow to tame mountains in such pre-Alpine regions as the Chartreuse Valley, or to more rugged crags in the Vercors range; they reach a crescendo with towering Mont Blanc.

The Alps themselves are divided into two regions, Savoie and Dauphiné. Dauphiné, the lower region, comprises the Chartreuse Valley and the Vercors mountains, the sporting and university center of Grenoble, and some magnificent, unspoiled mountain ranges. Grenoble has been the capital of the region since the fourteenth century, when Louis XI designated the town as the permanent parliamentary seat. To the northeast of La Tour du Pin, Berlioz's birthplace, you will find numerous late medieval châteaux.

Savoie bears the name of one of the oldest European royal houses. After 1000 C.E. this region of the Alps became the possession of Humbert aux Blanches Mains, founder of the House of Savoie and a vassal of the German emperor. Savoie's union with France in 1860 came about by choice and compatiblity of language and culture.

The Olympic Games that will take place here in 1992 have already stimulated an Alpine renaissance. However, the enchanting old town of Chambéry has not as yet been discovered by swarms of tourists, while throngs of worldly fun-seekers descend on Annecy for the hectic summer season. Finally, soaring, majestic mountains dominate the horizon in the international resort of Chamonix.

Train lines efficiently link the Alps's main cities to other cities in France, Italy, and Switzerland, while a thorough bus system serves even the most remote villages. This is fortunate, since distances can be considerable, the roads are arduous, and hitching on back roads can leave travelers stranded between destinations.

Once you're off the train, down from the bus, or out of the car, the most logical direction in which to proceed is up. Flowery meadows, icy lakes, and magnificent panoramic views await experienced and amateur hikers alike. Most towns have sports shops that rent appropriate footwear for about 30F per day, even on Sunday, and local *syndicats* will often provide free trail guides. Trails are clearly marked, but serious climbers should invest in a *Topo-Guide* (hiking map). Talk to the experts at the **Club Alpin Français** or the **Compagnie des Guides;** they provide updated information on trail and weather conditions, and will suggest hikes suited to your ability.

Skiing in the Alps can be expensive, but if you plan properly, your trip can be an exercise in frugality, not a farewell to your life's savings. Begin making arrangements in September or at least six to eight weeks in advance. The least crowded and cheapest months to go are January, March, and April. Remember that most resorts close in October and November.

The area is well endowed with campgrounds and youth hostels. Ski resorts, such as Chamonix, often have chalet-dormitories, and the Club Alpin maintains mountain refuges. Unofficial camping, although often illegal, is quite common. Always ask permission before setting up camp on private property.

Food here has a Swiss twist. Regional specialties include *fondue savoyarde* (a blend of 3 Alpine cheeses) and *raclette* (a strong Swiss cheese melted on an electric heater and served with boiled potatoes). *Gratin dauphinois,* a delicious local vegetable dish, involves potatoes baked in a cream and cheese sauce. The area also cures excellent ham, and nets superb trout from the cold mountain streams. The famous *montagne* cheeses are mild and creamy: *Tomme de Savoie, St-Marcellin* (half goat's milk), and *Reblochon.* Try the excellent white wines of Apremont, Ayse, and Chignin and the rich reds produced at Montmélian and St-Jean-de-la-Porte. For dessert, try the *roseaux d'Annecy* (chocolate-covered liqueurs), *St-Genux* (a kind of *brioche* with pink praline on top), and the *gâteau de Savoie* (a light sponge cake). *Eaux de vie,* strong liqueurs distilled from fruits, are popular here, especially *framboise,* made from local raspberries.

Grenoble

Most of ancient Grenoble lies hidden by the clean lines of contemporary buildings. The 390,000 people in the greater Grenoble area take great pride in their city's role as the industrial, cultural, and sporting capital of the Alps. Founded in the fourteenth century by Humbert II, Grenoble's university is one of France's largest and also one of the most cosmopolitan, hosting many American exchange programs. Its presence accounts for the city's numerous cafes, shaggy radicals, fascinating bookshops, and serious politics. Still, Grenoble has its share of the problems that accompany urban sprawl, such as smokestacks and pickpockets. In short, Grenoble is a lively town and, if it weren't for tourists standing in lines everywhere, it might even be pleasant. The city is well situated for trips into the mountains, but don't make it your only Alpine stop.

Orientation and Practical Information

Grenoble sits at the confluence of the Isère and Drac Rivers. The rivers border the town on the west and the north.

Public transportation in Grenoble is efficient. The tramway and buses cost 5.50F a ride, 33F for a book of 10 tickets. The tramway runs every 10 minutes from 5am to 10pm or so. Buses run from about 6am to 9pm. Transit maps are posted at every stop, and you can get your own at the **TAG** desk in the tourist office or the office to the right of the train station. From the station, take the tramway (*direction:* "Grand Place") to the Maison du Tourisme stop, take your first left and then your first right. On foot, just walk along the tramway tracks (10 min.).

You may want to invest in the **Guide DAHU,** a guide to restaurants and entertainment written by Grenoble students with razor-sharp wits (available in *tabacs*). As always, watch your purses and wallets in the city.

Maison du Tourisme: 14, rue de la République (tel. 76-54-34-36), in the center of town. Information on public transportation, trains, mountain excursions, and guided tours. Free map with an incomplete street index. (Better maps are dispensed for 2F from rotating billboards around town). Will reserve hotel rooms free in Grenoble, 25F anywhere in France. Open in summer Mon.-Sat. 9am-7pm; in off-season Mon.-Sat. 9am-6pm. **SNCF** and **TAG** (local public transportation) offices on the premises. Open Mon.-Fri. 9am-6pm, Sat. 9am-12:30pm and 1:30-6pm.

Club Alpin Français: 32, av. Felix Viallet (tel. 76-87-03-73). Advice on all mountain activities. Organizes group hiking, mountaineering, ice-climbing, and parachuting trips. Map library. Supervises mountain refuges (54F per night, club members 27F). Club membership (mainly an insurance policy) 266F, ages 18-25 150F. Open Mon. 2-4pm, Tues.-Fri. 2-7pm, Sat. 9am-noon and 2-5pm.

CIMES (Centre Informations Montagnes et Sentiers): Maison de la Randonnée, 7, rue Voltaire (tel. 76-51-76-00). Organizes hiking trips. Detailed guides of hiking, mountaineering and cross-country skiing routes for alpine areas (59F). Detailed maps (58F). Have some idea of what you want to do before you go. Open Mon.-Fri. 9am-noon and 2-6pm, Sat. 10am-noon and 2-6pm.

Travel Agency: Jeunes sans Frontière-Wastells, 50, av. Alsace-Lorraine (tel. 76-47-34-54), near the train station, and 20, av. Félix-Viallet (tel. 76-46-36-39). BIJ tickets and cheap excursion packages. Both offices open Mon.-Fri. 9am-noon and 2-6:30pm, Sat. 9am-noon and 2-6pm.

Centre Régional d'Information Jeunesse, 8, rue Voltaire (tel. 76-54-70-38), near the tourist office. Free ride board service. Information on housing, sports, and cultural events. Carte Jeune 60F. Open Mon.-Fri. 1-7pm.

Currency Exchange: Banque Nationale de Paris, rue de la République, across from the tourist office. Open Tues.-Fri. 8:05-11:55am and 1:15-5:05pm, Sat. 8:05-11:55am and 1:10-4pm. No currency exchange after 4pm. **Banque Populaire,** place Notre Dame. Open Tues.-Fri. 8:30am-noon and 1:30-6pm, Sat. 8:30am-noon and 1:30-5pm.

Post Office: Bd. Maréchal-Lyautey (tel. 76-76-14-14). **Currency exchange** and **telephones. Postal code:** 38000. Open Mon.-Fri. 8am-6:45pm, Sat. 8am-noon.

Airport: Aéroport de Grenoble St-Geoirs, St-Etienne de St-Geoirs (tel. 76-65-48-48). 8 buses per day leave from the *gare routière*.

Train Station: Place de la Gare (tel. 76-47-50-50; for reservations 76-47-54-27). Almost hourly trains to Valence (80 min., 58F), Chambéry (1 hr., 41.50F), Annecy (2 hr., 67F), Chamonix (5½ hr., 127F), Voiron (20 min., 20F), Avignon (3 hr., 122F), Lyon (2 hr., 73F). To Strasbourg (5-7 per day, 9 hr.) and Paris (5-7 per day, 5-8 hr.) via Lyon. Information office open Mon.-Fri. 8:30am-7:30pm, Sat. 9am-6pm.

Bus Station: Gare Routière, to the left of the train station. 4 companies offer summer excursions, service to ski resorts, and surrounding towns. **VFD** (tel. 76-47-77-77) is the biggest. Office open daily 7:40-11:30am and 2:30-6pm. For other companies, call 76-87-90-31. To Chambery (10 per day, 1 hr., 39F), Voiron (2 per day, 3 hr., 22F), Les Deux Alpes (2 per day, 1 hr., 72F), Alpe d'Huez (2 per day, 45 min., 68F), Chamrousse (2 per day, 1½ hr., 48F), and Briançon (7 per day, 1 hr., 110F).

Taxi: Tel. 76-54-42-54.

Car Rental: Avis, 22, cours Jean-Jaurès (tel. 76-47-52-72). Only one of many possibilities (see tourist office for others).

Bike Rental and Climbing Equipment: Borel Sport, 42, rue Alsace-Lorraine (tel. 76-46-47-46). Bicycles 47F per day, deposit 800F. Rents mountain climbing equipment. Shoes 20-35F per day. Open Tues.-Sat. 9am-noon and 2:30-7pm. **Objectif Montagne,** 18, rue Marceau Leyssieux (tel. 76-51-58-76), way out in St-Martin d'Heres. Specializes in renting mountaineering equipment. Open daily 9am-7pm.

Hitching: Allostop, at the Centre Régional Jeunesse. You pay 40F and share gas expenses with the driver. Open Mon.-Fri. 1-6pm. The area is well served by freeways, so the smaller roads see almost no through traffic. Hitching can be difficult. If hitching long-distance, you'll be best off taking a bus to Valence, where you'll have access to the major highways.

Bookstores: Just Books, 1, rue de la Paix (tel. 76-44-78-81). Sizable, entirely English collection of paperbacks, including the full line of everybody's favorite travel series: *Let's Go.*

Laundromats: 65, place St-Bruno (tel. 76-96-28-03). 12F per load. Open daily 7am-7pm. 4, rue Bayard. Wash 13F, dry 4F, soap 2F. Open daily 7am-9pm. 18, rue Chenoise. Wash 13F, dry 2F. Open daily 7am-9pm. 90, cours Berriat. Wash 12F, dry 3F. Open daily 7am-9pm. Rue Alphand, behind the tourist office. Wash 15F, dry 4F. Open daily 7am-10pm.

Women's Center: Centre d'Information Féminin, 9, rue Raoul Blanchard (tel. 76-54-08-19). Open Mon.-Tues. and Thurs.-Fri. 1-6pm.

Pharmacy: 5, rue Philis de la Charce, at rue Raoul Blanchard in *centre ville.* Open Tues.-Sat. 9am-noon and 2-7pm.

Mountain Rescue: Secours en Montagne, Tel. 76-21-44-44.

Hospital: Centre Hospitalier Régional de Grenoble, La Tronche (tel. 76-42-81-21).

Medical Emergency: SAMU, Tel. 76-42-42-42.

Police: Bd. Marèchal Leclerc (tel. 76-60-40-40). **Police Emergency:** Tel. 17.

Accommodations and Camping

Aside from the small but sufficient number of budget hotels, Grenoble is well endowed with *foyers*. These are especially suitable for longer stays; see the tourist office for a complete list.

Auberge de Jeunesse (IYHF), av. du Grésivaudan, Echirolles (tel. 76-09-33-52), about 4km out of town. Take bus #8 from cours Jean Jaurès (1 block straight ahead from the train station) or from the tourist office to La Quinzaine. It's on the right a block behind the Casino market. You can also walk down cours Jean Jaurès and turn right just before the Casino market. A modern building with a garden, bar, game room, cooking facilities, and TV. As always, watch your valuables. Rooms with 4-6 people 45F. Doubles 56F per person. Breakfast included. Open daily 7-10am and 5:30-11pm. Ask for the door combination if out late.

La Maison de L'Etudiante, 4 rue Ste-Ursule (tel. 76-42-00-84), near place Notre Dame. From the tourist office, follow place Ste-Claire to place Notre Dame and take rue du Vieux Temple. Ordinary rooms in a friendly atmosphere. Quiet street close to the center. Kitchen facilities, TV, and a piano. Singles 50F. Doubles with 2 beds 70F. Sheets included. Make reservations a week in advance. Accepts men and women travelers June 15-Sept. 15. Open daily 9am-noon and 2-5pm.

Foyer les Ecrins, 36, rue Christophe-Turc (tel. 76-09-40-74). Take bus #13 from place Victor Hugo. Looks like a run-down college dorm from the outside, but the rooms are pleasant enough. Restaurant, TV rooms, and cafeteria. Kitchenettes on each hall. 3-night minimum stay. Singles 3 nights 210F, 4 nights 260F, 5 nights 300F, and so forth. Office open 8:30am-noon and 2-7pm.

Hôtel de la Poste, 25, rue de la Poste (tel. 76-46-67-25), in the center of the pedestrian zone. A class operation. Fine rooms in an ancient building. Singles 65F. Doubles 80F. Triples and quads 120F. Showers included. Breakfast 15F.

Hôtel Colbert, 1, rue Colbert (tel. 76-46-46-65), a 5-min. walk from the train station. Take a right on rue Joseph Rey, hug the tracks, and turn left on rue Colbert. Large, tidy rooms with brass beds. Singles 70F. Doubles with 1 bed 85F, doubles and triples with 2 beds 130F. Triples with 3 beds 180F. Showers 15F. Breakfast 17F.

Camping: Camping Municipal, 15, av. Beaumarchais (tel. 76-96-19-87), on the way to the hostel. Take bus #8 towards the hostel (or walk along cours Jean Jaurès), and get off at Albert Reynier. Not particularly pleasant but passable. No reservations or long stays. 4.45F per person, 3.20F per student, 2.40F per site.

Food

The immigrant quarter around **rue Chenoise** bristles with cheap restaurants with a North African flair (*menus* 40F), as does rue St-Laurent in the old town across the river. For supplies, try **Prisunic,** across from the tourist office (open Mon.-Sat. 8:30am-7pm) or **Supermarket Casino,** at the youth hostel (open Mon.-Sat. 8:30am-9pm). Hit the *boulangeries* and *confiseries* for tarts and chocolates made with the local *noix de Grenoble* (walnuts). The big **markets** are at place St-Bruno, near the station on the other side of the tracks, and rue Joseph Rey, where cours Jean Jaurès meets the railroad tracks. (Both open Mon.-Sat. 8am-1pm.) The friendly covered market, Monday through Saturday mornings in place Ste-Claire (near the tourist office), has all you could want.

Le Cantilène, 11, rue Beyle-Stendhal (tel. 76-43-05-19), near the post office. Small and boisterous. 45F *menu.* Evening specials such as *moules-frites* (mussels with fries) 35F. Open Mon.-Sat. 11:30am-2pm and 7-10:30pm.

La Baleine, 20, rue Chenoise (tel. 76-54-65-54). A colorful, upbeat *crêperie-restaurant* serving French and North African specialties. *Coquelet aux champignons* 40F, *couscous* 40F. Open Tues.-Sat. noon-2pm and 7-11pm.

Restaurant Indochinois, 13, rue Raoul Blanchard (tel 76-51-33-57), behind the tourist office. Good, filling Vietnamese cuisine. Full meal (in and out in ½ hr.) 35F. Egg rolls at the counter 3F each. Open daily 10:30am-10:30pm.

Restaurant de la Plage, 2, rue St-Hughes (tel. 76-51-38-85), just off place Notre Dame. Follow place Ste-Claire from the tourist office. A beach, in the Alps? The restaurant that dares to be laid-back. *Plat du jour* 38F, *menu* 50F. Open Mon.-Fri. noon-2pm and 7-11pm.

La Panse, 2, rue de la Paix (tel. 76-54-09-54). Always crowded with loyal locals. Reasonably priced, ambrosial French cuisine. Simple 70F *menu,* and a gourmet 150F *menu,* including *pâté de hareng aux whiskey et truffes* (herring *pâté* with whiskey and truffles). Open Mon.-Fri. 8am-2pm and 5-10:30pm.

University Restaurants: Scattered around town. One at 5, rue Arsonval, usually closed in summer. Call CROUS (tel. 76-87-07-62) to find out what's open. Buy a ticket from a student waiting in line (10F).

Sights and Entertainment

A futuristic bubble of a cablecar (the *téléphérique de la Bastille*) pops out of the city every two minutes from quai Stéphane-Jay and whisks you up to the imposing **Bastille** (475m) in three minutes flat. (Open July-Aug. Mon. 10am-midnight, Tues.-Sun. 9am-midnight; April-June and Sept.-Oct. Mon. 10am-7:30pm, Tues.-Sat. 9am-midnight, Sun. 9am-7:30pm; Nov.-March daily 10am-7:30pm. One way 16F, round-trip 25F; students one way 8.50F, round-trip 13F.) At the top you'll enjoy a sweeping panorama of Grenoble's orange roofs encircled by mountains. From here, the ambitious can climb the mountain walls on well-marked trails of varying difficulty. Climb down through the delightful **Jardin des Dauphins** and **Parc Guy Pape.** (Open, weather permitting, daily June-Aug. 9am-7:30pm; April-May and Sept.-Oct. 9am-7pm; Nov.-Feb. 9am-4pm; March 9am-5:30pm. For general information on the *téléphérique,* call 76-44-33-65 or 76-51-00-00.)

The **Musée Dauphinois,** rue Maurice-Gignoux (tel. 76-87-66-77), halfway down the hill from the Bastille, is one of the most stylish and well-organized collections of regional folk art. (Open Wed.-Mon. 9am-noon and 2-6pm. Admission 8F, students and seniors 4F, Wed. free.)

Students and immigrants now occupy the eighteenth-century houses on the riverbank, Grenoble's most attractive and most urbane neighborhood. Victorian **Pont St-Laurent,** an early suspension bridge, occupies the former site of a Gallo-Roman bridge. Next to the manicured **Jardin de Ville,** the elaborate Renaissance **Palais de Justice** deliberates. There are no organized visits, but you can usually peek in at the intricately carved ceilings. The **Musée de Peinture et de Sculpture,** place Verdun (tel. 76-54-09-82), houses an adequate collection of Egyptian art, Renaissance and baroque paintings, and a notable modern collection. There are works by Matisse and Delaunay, and a flashy room with geometrical designs and works by Calder, from which you can exit to the street through a tunnel. (Open Wed.-Mon. 10am-noon and 2-6pm. Admission 8F, students 4F, Wed. free.) The Alps were a stronghold of the Resistance, and history buffs should make a point of visiting the **Musée de la Résistance,** 14, rue J.J. Rousseau (tel. 76-44-51-81; open Wed.-Sat. 3-6pm; free). A renovated warehouse at 155, cours Berriat (take tramway A to Berriat) houses **MAGASIN** (Center National d'Art Contemporain), an exhibition area for temporary displays of modern art (tel. 76-21-95-84; open Tues.-Sun. 12:30-7pm; admission 8F, ages under 25 4F). Guided tours of the town leave from place St-André around 10am Monday through Saturday during the summer. For information, contact **Service Animation du Centre d'Archéologie** (tel. 76-44-78-68).

Nightclubs, bars, and cafes entertain Grenoble by night. Consult the *Guide DAHU* for the "in" places. The **King Charly Pub,** 2, rue de Sault (tel. 76-47-29-72), attracts an international student crowd. (Open Mon.-Sat. 11:30am-1am.) **L'Etalon,** 1, rue Alphonse-Terray (tel. 76-49-20-95), has a reputation for being a meat market. (Open Mon.-Sat. 3pm-1am.) The upscale nightclub, **Palazzo,** 7, av. de Vizille (tel. 76-96-07-97), is packed six nights a week. (Cover 80F, cocktails around 60F. Open Mon.-Sat.) One favorite student disco is **Le Club des Etudiants,** 50-52, rue St-Laurent (tel. 76-42-00-68). You must show student ID to get in. (Cover about 35F. Open Thurs.-Sat. 10pm-3am. Often closed in summer.) **Le Crocodile,** 1, Grande Rue (tel. 76-42-74-45), is a chic cafe with live bands. (Open Mon.-Sat. 2pm-1am.) **Le George V,** 124, cours Berriat (tel. 76-73-64-47), is a popular gay disco. (Open Fri.-Tues.) **L'Entrepot,** rue Auguste Gerin (tel. 76-48-21-48), spotlights local jazz and rock. (Open Mon.-Sat. from 8pm on.)

Grenoble hosts no end of festivals, none of which is free. Pick up the bimonthly journal, *Grenoble Spectacles,* for a complete listing of events (available at the tourist office). The **Festival du Court Métrage** (short films) takes place July 5-9. Contact the Cinémathèque Française, 21, rue Génissieu (tel. 76-24-13-83), for details. The world-famous **Festival International du Roman et du Film Noir** occurs during the second week of October. For more information, contact Association Grenoble-Polar, 21, rue Génissieu (tel. 76-24-13-83).

Near Grenoble

The monks of the **Monastère de la Grande Chartreuse** sought to produce the elixir of long life but came up instead with the celebrated Chartreuse liqueur. The monastery's architecture was the prototype for the "charterhouse style" that has influenced communal institutions and hermitages around the world. Built in 1084 by St-Bruno, it was destroyed twice—once during the Revolution and again by the Germans in 1940. You cannot visit the monastery, but there is an excellent view of it from **Correrie**, about 1km from the main road. The **museum** in Correrie (tel. 76-88-60-45) faithfully depicts the monks' daily routine. (Open April-Sept. Mon.-Sat. 9am-noon and 2-6:30pm. Admission 10F.) You can reach Correrie by taking a bus to nearby **Voiron** from Grenoble's *gare routière* (5 per day, 45 min., 22F). While in Voiron, sample the liqueurs in the **Caves de la Grande Chartreuse**, 10, bd. Edgar Kofler (tel. 76-05-81-77; open daily Easter-Oct. 8-11:30am and 2-6:30pm, Nov.-April 8-11:30am and 2-5:30pm). Ten kilometers north of Voiron are the deep blue waters of **Lac de Paladru,** where you can swim, sail, and camp. Free beaches and **camping** await at Charavines (tel. 76-06-60-09), Paladru (tel. 76-32-30-53), Bilieu (tel. 76-06-62-41), Le Pin (tel. 76-06-63-14), and Montferrat (tel. 76-32-30-02); ask at the Grenoble *syndicat* for the *Lac de Paladru* brochure. Four buses per day run to the lake (45 min., 28F). At the **Prieuré de Chirens,** halfway between Voiron and the lake, is an annual **Festival de musique de chambre et d'arts plastiques** (Chamber Music and Sculpture Festival), held from late June to mid-August. For more information, contact the Voiron *syndicat,* place de la Republique, 38500 Voiron (tel. 76-05-00-38).

The charming resort town of **St-Pierre de Chartreuse** is 2km away in the Chartreuse Valley, surrounded by wooded pathways. The 15-km route near **St-Laurent du Pont** passes through some of the most picturesque countryside in the Alps; this road is now considered a national monument. The resort offers swimming, tennis, and golf in summer.

The *Syndicat d'Initiative* is located in St-Laurent du Pont (tel. 76-88-62-08; **postal code:** 38380). **Camping La Martinière** (tel. 76-88-60-36) is in nearby **Martinière** (40F per 2 people). The smaller and cheaper **Camping Charmant Som** (tel. 76-88-62-39) is in St-Hughes (15.20F per 2 people).

Site of the 1968 Winter Olympics, in which native son Jean-Claude Killy won all three downhill events, Grenoble is the gateway to some of the Alps's most renowned ski resorts. The two biggest are **Alpe d'Huez** (*syndicat* tel. 76-80-35-41; **postal code:** 38750), 63km from Grenoble, and **Les Deux Alpes** (*syndicat* tel. 76-79-22-00; **postal code:** 38860), 75km from Grenoble. Buses to Alpe d'Huez (4 per day, 2 hr., 68F) and Les Deux Alpes (3 per day, 2½ hr., 72F) leave from the *gare routière* in Grenoble. A ski-lift ticket will cost about 135F. These two resorts also offer limited summer skiing. The **Auberge de Jeunesse** in Alpe d'Huez is on chemin de la Goutte (tel. 76-80-37-37). You can exchange currency at the *syndicat* in Alpe d'Huez. For snow conditions call 76-80-34-32 in Alpe d'Huez or 78-58-33-33 for general information. Closer to Grenoble (30km), **Chamrousse** (*syndicat* tel. 76-89-92-65; **postal code:** 38410) is also a major resort. The two **Auberges de Jeunesse (IYHF)** (tel. 76-89-91-14 and 76-89-91-31) are both 1½km away in St-Martin d'Uriage and both open June 15 to Aug. 15 and Oct. 14 to March 5). Less glittery but somewhat more affordable are **Villard-de-Lans** (*syndicat* tel. 76-95-70-38; open Dec.), **St-Nigier** (*syndicat* tel. 76-53-40-60), **Lans-en-Vencours** (*syndicat* tel. 76-95-42-62; open mid-Dec. to April), and **St-Pierre** (*syndicat* tel. 76-88-62-08; open mid-Dec. to April). These smaller areas sell lift tickets for about 60-75F. You can rent ski equipment at the resorts for 110-160F per day. In summer, the resorts welcome hikers, bikers, and sun-seekers.

To the east lie the Hautes-Alps, with **Briançon** at their center. You can reach them through Val d'Isère, over the *iseran* pass from the north, or by the scenic **route**

des Grandes Alpes. Scenic buses from Grenoble's *gare routière* make the trip twice per day (3 hr., 110F). In July, the renowned **Tour de France** bicycle race passes through on nearby N6, a spectacular but steep and grueling road for cyclists.

Chambéry

Sitting at the foot of the Chartreuse and Bauges mountains, in a valley bordered by Lac du Bourget and Val d'Isère, Chambéry was for centuries the capital of Savoie. An elegant, lovingly preserved *vieille ville* graces the city, and the château from which the Dukes of Savoie ruled the region for centuries dominates the skyline. Colorful feudal banners and whimsical *trompe-l'oeil* murals decorate medieval walls and welcome tourists, of which thankfully few think to stop in this small, charming town.

Orientation and Practical Information

Chambéry lies on the Lyon-Chamonix line, about one hour from Grenoble, three to four hours from Chamonix, 1½ hours from Lyon, and five to six hours from Paris. From the station, walk left a few blocks, then cross place du Centenaire to bd. de la Colonne, the tourist office, and the center of town.

Office de Tourisme: 24, bd. de la Colonne (tel. 79-33-42-47). Disabled access from the other side at 19, av. des Ducs de Savoie. Ask for a free copy of *15 jours à Chambéry,* a bimonthly list of activities, events, and practical information. Also pick up their hiking book, *Sentiers autour de Chambéry.* In summer, the office sponsors a nightly tour of the old quarter and 2 daily tours of the château (15F, students 8F). Information on accommodations and sights also available. Open Mon.-Sat. 9am-noon and 2-6pm.

Association Départementale de Tourisme de la Savoie: 24, bd. de la Colonne (tel. 79-85-12-45), in the same building as the tourist office. Information on the surrounding area. Information about ski resorts. Open Mon.-Sat. 9am-noon and 2-6pm.

Club Alpin Français, 70, rue Croix d'Or (tel. 79-33-05-52). Information and advice on hiking and mountaineering in the area. Open Tues.-Fri. 5:30-7:30pm, Sat. 10am-noon.

Travel Agency: Wasteels, 17, Faubourg Reclus (tel. 79-33-04-63), off rue Ducs de Savoie across place Centenaire from the tourist office. Open Mon.-Fri. 9-11:45am and 2-6:30pm, Sat. 9-11:45am.

Centre d'Information et de Documentation Jeunesse (CIDJ): 4, place de la Gare, across from the train station. Information on sports, hostels, and *foyers.* Bulletin board posts rides, jobs, baby-sitting, and housing information. BIJ/Transalpino tickets. Open Mon.-Fri. 9am-noon and 2-6pm.

Post Office: Place Paul Vidal (tel. 79-69-10-69). **Telephones** and **currency exchange. Postal code:** 73000. Open Mon.-Fri. 8am-7pm, Sat. 8am-noon.

Train Station: Place de la R. Sommeiller (tel. 79-85-50-50; for reservations 79-62-35-26). Trains at least every hour to Lyon (1½-2 hr., 63F), Grenoble (1-2 hr., 41F), Aix-les Bains (12 per day, 15 min., 12F), Annecy (12 per day, 45 min., 37F), and Geneva (8 per day, 1½ hr., 60F). Many to Paris via Lyon (5½ hr.). Information office open Mon.-Fri. 8am-12:20pm and 1:30-6:50pm, Sat. 8am-12:20pm and 1:30-5:50pm.

Bus Station: Gare Routière, place de la R. Sommeiller, across from the train station. Many companies share this central depot. Try **VFD** first (tel. 79-69-28-78). For all other companies, call 79-69-11-88. To Le Chateland (3 per day, 1½ hr., 36F). Regional buses to Annecy (8 per day, 1 hr., 31F), Aix-les-Bains (8 per day, 20 min., 10.50F), and Grenoble (6 per day, 1 hr., 36.50F). Excursions to the Grande Chartreuse (95F), Chamonix (130F), Venice (397F), Geneva and Yvoire (86F), Turin (135F), and Zermatt (190F). Call VFD for information on other trips. **STAC,** 18, av. des Chevaliers Tireurs (tel. 79-69-61-12). Local buses. Get a schedule at the tourist office.

Taxi: Tel. 79-62-33-72.

Bike Rental: D. Brouard, 28, av. de Turin (tel. 79-70-13-54). In the Motobecane store on the way out of town, next to the fire station. 45F per day plus deposit.

Laundromat: 37, place Monge. Wash 12F, dry 1F, soap 4F. Open daily 7am-10pm.

Centre d'Information sur les Droits des Femmes, 22, rue Jawerie (tel. 79-85-49-13). Open on a walk-in basis Mon.-Fri. 2-5pm.

Hospital: Centre Hospitalier, place François-Chion (tel. 79-62-93-70).

Medical Emergency: SAMU, Tel. 79-69-25-25.

Police: 585, av. de la Boisse (tel. 79-96-17-17).

Police Emergency: Tel. 17.

Accommodations and Camping

Chambéry has few hotels, but what it lacks in quantity it makes up for in quality—many are pleasant, inexpensive, and rarely full. The *foyer* is even nicer than most hotels.

Maison des Jeunes et de la Culture (MJC), 311, Faubourg-Montmélian (tel. 79-75-13-23). From the station, take a left at place de la R. Sommelier and bear left onto rue des Ducs de Savoie. Follow the canal to the first bridge and turn right. The *maison* is on your left (15 min.). From the train station, take bus B or E (5F). Welcomes all ages year-round. Comfortable dorm singles 50F, doubles 70F. Sheets 20F. No lockout. No guests after 9:30pm. Office open July-Aug. Tues.-Fri. 1-9pm, Sat.-Mon. 8am-8pm; Sept.-June daily 8am-8pm.

Hôtel le Maurennais, 2, rue Ste-Barbe (tel. 79-69-42-78). The cheapest hotel in town. Sits in the shadow of the château. Singles 50F. Doubles 62F.

Hôtel de la Banche, 10, place de l'Hôtel de Ville (tel. 79-33-15-62). Small, with a bar downstairs. Excellent location in an old, wood-beamed house. Singles and doubles 95F, with shower 130F. Breakfast 16F. Often booked.

Hôtel du Porche, 126-128, rue Dessaix (tel. 79-85-31-82), hidden between rue de la République and rue de la Croix d'Or. A fantastic location with an ancient street on one side and a lovely square on the other. Singles from 75F. Doubles from 78F. Breakfast 17F.

Hôtel Savoyard, 35, place Monge (tel. 79-35-36-55), not far from the center of town. A small, cozy hotel, attached to a good restaurant. Singles and doubles 85F, with shower 130F. Restaurant serves 51-89F *menus,* as well as fondue and *raclette* for 52-62F per person (minimum 2 people).

Camping: The nearest is **Camping le Nivolet** (tel. 79-33-19-48) north of town in Bessens. Open April-Sept.

Food

Several cheap pizzerias; *crêperies,* and a few regional restaurants spice up the pedestrian zone in the center of town, especially rue du Croix d'Or. *Charcuteries* and *épiceries* on place de Genève and at the foot of place St-Léger make gourmet meals cheap and easy. Les Halles on place de Genève house a covered **market** on Tuesday, Thursday, and Saturday from 6am to noon. Also try the **Laiterie des Halles,** 4, rue de l'Herberie, which offers a mouth-watering selection of local cheeses such as *Chevrolin* and *Beaufort.* **Prisunic,** place de l'Hôtel de Ville, is the cheapest place to buy groceries. (Open Mon.-Sat. 8:15am-12:10pm and 2:15-7pm.)

Cafétéria Olympie, 2, av. de Bassens (tel. 79-75-25-12), in the same building as the Maison des Jeunes. Best quantity-to-price ratio. Full meals 25F. Open Mon.-Fri. 11:30am-3pm and 6:30-9pm, Sat. 11:30am-3pm.

La Frite Dorée, 13, place Monge (tel. 79-33-30-65). A filling 4-course, 38F *menu* in an elegant setting. Open Thurs.-Mon. noon-2pm and 7:30-10pm, Tues. noon-2pm.

Paprika, 188, Faubourg-Montmélian (tel. 79-75-13-45). Hearty Hungarian cooking. 50F *menu.* Open June-Aug. Wed.-Sat. for lunch and dinner, Tues. for dinner; Sept.-May Wed.-Sun. for lunch and dinner, Tues. for dinner.

Le Clap, 4, rue Ste-Barbe (tel. 76-96-27-08), next to the Hôtel le Maurennais. Share your dinner with portraits of your favorite film stars. Open Tues.-Sat. noon-2pm and 7-10pm, Mon. 7-10pm.

Sights

For six centuries, independent Savoie's power emanated from the imposing **Château des Ducs de Savoie.** (Obligatory tours July-Aug. daily at 10:30am, 2:30pm, 3:30pm, 4:30pm, and 5:30pm; June and Sept. daily at 10:30am and 2:30pm; March-May and Oct.-Nov. Sat. at 2:15pm, Sun. at 3:30pm. Admission 12F, students 8F.) The energetic tour guides brim with history, art, and anecdote. The château's last prominent master was King Vittorio Emmanuel, who presided over Italy's unification. **Ste-Chapelle,** painted in *trompe-l'oeil* in the nineteenth century, proudly housed the *sainte sueur,* Christ's alleged burial cloth, from 1502 to 1578, when, by an Italian ruse, the shroud found its way across the Alps to Turin, where it has stayed ever since. There are half-hour carillon concerts in the Ste-Chapelle Saturday at 11:30am and 6:30pm. From the château, take rue Boigne to the remarkable **Fontaine des Eléphants,** the most photographed monument in Chambéry. The statue was erected in 1838 to honor Count de Boigne, a general who gained fame and fortune in India.

Take the time to stroll through **Vieux Chambéry** and admire the beautiful *hôtels particuliers* on rue Croix-d'Or. The tourist office will provide a list of the most interesting mansions in the city. (Tours of the old city leave from place Château July-Aug. at 4pm and 9pm; June and Sept. at 4pm; March-May and Oct.-Nov., Sat. at 4pm. Admission 15F, students 10F.) The **Musée des Beaux Arts,** place du Palais de Justice, contains a medium-sized collection of Italian paintings including Uccello's *Portrait d'un jeune homme.* (Open Wed.-Mon. 10am-noon and 2-6pm. Free.) The surprisingly uncrowded **Musée Savoisien,** on bd. du Théâtre in an old Franciscan convent, displays some delightful primitives from Savoie in one of the cloister galleries. (Open Wed.-Mon. 10am-noon and 2-6pm. Free.) Two kilometers out of town on the chemin des Charmettes stands the **Musée des Charmettes,** the house where Jean-Jacques Rousseau lived with Mme. de Warrens. The interior has been reconstructed and now displays Rousseau memorabilia. It is accessible only by foot: From place Monge, take av. de la République to chemin des Charmettes. (Open April-Sept. Wed.-Mon. 10am-noon and 2-6pm; Oct.-March Wed.-Mon. 10am-noon and 2-4:30pm. Admission 5F.)

Gardens abound in Chambéry—the **Jardins du Verney;** the **Clos Savoiroux,** with its statue of Rousseau; and the **Parc des Loisirs de Buisson Rond,** with its fine rose garden, are just a few of the spots available for secluded picnics. On Bastille Day dancing breaks out in the streets in front of the Hôtel de Ville, and a folklore pageant is held in the stadium. Every year for 10 days in September, the **Foire de Savoie** raises local spirits, and in early October, a series of small festivals enlivens the town.

Aix-les-Bains

On the sedate **Lac du Bourget,** France's largest lake, lies the equally sedate town of Aix-les-Bains. Renowned for its thermal baths, the area has become an elegant *ville d'eau* (water town), attracting primarily an older, well-off crowd who come to cure their ailments—from rheumatism to *ennui.* Endless games of *boules,* manicured parks, and elegant nineteenth-century *hôtels* set the tone for this fountain of faded youth, though things pick up a little on the busy lakeside, where a more dynamic crowd mills about the restaurants, campsites, and beaches.

Orientation and Practical Information

Aix-les-Bains lies just 10 minutes by train north of Chambéry on the main train line. The center of town is up the hill from the train station, while the lake and beach are a 20-minute walk in the opposite direction. From the station, take bus #2 to the beach (6F). For the *syndicat* and the center of town, follow av. Général de Gaulle and turn left just before the Thermes Nationaux. The **Syndicat d'Initiative,** place Maurice Mollard (tel. 79-35-05-92), distributes decent free maps (a more complete map costs 12F) and a glossy tourist guide. (Open April-Sept.

Mon.-Sat. 9am-noon and 2-7pm, Sun. 10am-noon and 4:30-6:30pm; Oct.-March Mon.-Fri. 9am-noon and 2-6pm, Sat. 9am-noon.) The **post office** is on av. Victoria at av. Maris de Solms (tel. 79-33-15-15). The **postal code** is 73100. (Open Mon.-Fri. 8am-7pm, Sat. 8am-noon.) **Banque Populaire,** rue de Genève, offers **currency exchange.** (Open Mon.-Thurs. 8:15am-12:15pm and 1:30-5:10pm, Fri. 8:15am-12:15pm and 1:30-4:10pm.) **Trains** leave almost hourly for Chambéry (10 min., 12F), Annecy (45 min., 29.50F), and Grenoble (1¼ hr., 48F). Rent **bikes** at 45, bd. de Lattre de Tassigny (tel. 79-88-81-10) for 45F per day. This store also sells used hiking boots for 150-250F. (Open Mon.-Sat. 9am-7:30pm.)

Accommodations, Camping, and Food

As is typical in thermal spots, the town is loaded with hotels, many of which are reasonably priced. One-star hotels may attach a 1.50F nightly tax to your bill. A few hotels require reservations in summer.

Auberge de Jeunesse, promenade de Sierroz (tel. 79-88-32-88). From the train station, take a left to the carrefour des Hôpitaux (the second roundabout), bear left onto tree-lined av. du Grand Port, and continue to the lake. Turn left and then left again just after the creek (30 min.). Or take bus #2 to the left of the station and get off at the Camping stop. A beautiful, modern hostel with a cornfield out back. 4 min. from the lake. Members only, 33F. Sheets 11F. Breakfast 10F, meals 33F. Open Dec. 15-Oct. 31.

Hôtel les Deux Savoies, 12, av. du Grand Port (tel. 79-35-14-86). Decent rooms with hardwood floors not too far from *centre ville.* New management took over July 1988. Singles 65F. Doubles 85F. Breakfast 16F.

Avenue Hôtel, 16, av. du Grand Port (tel. 79-35-24-63). A little fancier than its neighbor. Singles 70F. Doubles 75F. Shower on the floor below. Breakfast 16F.

Hôtel Brasserie de Savoie, 43, bd. Wilson (tel. 79-35-20-69), 1 block to the right of the train station. Tasteful doubles 78F, with shower 125F. Showers 9.50F. Breakfast 16F.

Camping Municipal Sierroz, large and conveniently located across from the lake (tel. 79-61-21-43), about 2km from the station just before you reach the youth hostel. Showers, grocery store. 11F per person, 22F per tent. 44F for 4 or more people. Reservations required 1 month in advance July-Aug. Office open Feb. 15-Nov. 15 daily 8am-noon and 3-7pm.

Cheap, lively restaurants are rare. Many restaurants line rue de Genève and rue Albert 1er, behind the *syndicat.* For the more economically minded, a large **market** fills place Clemenceau on Wednesdays and Saturdays, and there is a **Prisunic** supermarket at 15, rue de Genève. **La Quimperoise,** 4, rue Albert 1er (tel. 79-88-99-48), serves excellent crêpes for 9-40F. (Open Tues.-Sat. noon-11pm, Sun. 7-11pm.) **Cafétéria Casino,** 8, rue du Casino, has the air of an ice-cream parlor and a gazebo at once. Try their delicious fruit melba for 14F. (*Plat du jour* 32F. Open daily 11am-10pm.) **La Petite Auberge,** 76, rue de Genève, serves a 55F fondue and a 32F *menu.* Near the *syndicat,* **Campanus,** place du Revard, a lively cafe with outdoor seating, serves crêpes for 18-22F, omelettes for 22-25F. (Open Thurs.-Tues.)

Sights and Entertainment

The **Thermes Nationaux** themselves, Aix-les-Bains's *raison d'être,* give tours of the new baths, followed by a descent underground to view the remains of the ancient Roman ones. Outside, one can visit the grottos and sulphur springs. Tours leave from opposite the tourist office on place Maurice-Mollard. (May-Sept. Mon.-Sat. at 3pm; Oct.-April Wed. and Sat. at 3pm or call 79-35-38-50 for an appointment. Admission 5F.) Treatments in the baths involve mud, mineral water, massage, and money. An underwater massage costs 60-90F. The **Musée du Docteur Fauré,** bd. des Côtes (tel. 76-61-06-57), diverts spirits sodden by bath water with works by Sisley, Pissarro, Renoir, Cézanne, and Rodin. (Open April 15-Oct. 16 Wed.-Mon. 10am-noon and 2-6pm; Oct. 17-March 30 Wed.-Sun. 10am-noon and 2-6pm. Admission 10F.)

The best reason to stay overnight in Aix-les-Bains is to take the morning excursion to the **Abbaye d'Hautecombe.** This Benedictine abbey, completely restored in the nineteenth century, houses the tombs of the princes of Savoie and seems to float on the still lake. You can hear masses sung in Gregorian chant. Visiting the abbey is free, but donations are appreciated. The only means of transportation is a boat that departs from Aix's Grand Port (July-Aug. Tues., Fri., and Sun. at 2:15pm, 2:45pm, 3:15pm, 3:45pm, and 4:30pm; June and Sept. 9:50am, 2:45pm, and 3:45pm; May and Oct. 2:45pm). The excursion takes 3¼ hour and costs 30F. A special Sunday trip to attend the mass at the abbey leaves at 8:30am. Call 79-35-05-19 or 79-61-45-75 for more information.

Aix hosts a variety of concerts (mostly free) in the **Théâtre de Verdure** in late July. Larger concerts take place at the Palais du Congress. For two or three days in the last week of August, Aix puts on a lakeside **Fête des Fleurs** (Flower Festival), with fireworks, singing, and general cheer. The little town of **Le Revard,** a 20-minute bus ride from Aix, is surrounded by an extensive network of trails for cross-country skiing in winter (Dec. 15-April 15), and overlooks a stupendous vista of Lac du Bourget to one side and Mont Blanc to the other. Buses leave from the kiosk in the Parc de Verdure (Sept.-June daily at 10:50am and 1:15pm). For information call **Gonnet Excursions** (tel. 79-61-01-78). You can also take a two-hour hike up to Le Revard. The well-marked trail starts at the base of the Les Mentens *téléphérique* in **Mouxy,** 4km east of Aix-les-Bains.

Annecy

No other French city combines so many forms of Alpine beauty as Annecy. In town, narrow cobblestone streets wind past flower-lined canals and stately castles. Grassy spaces, shady groves, and beach grace the lake. Windsurfers, pedalboats, and swans share the brilliantly green water, while mountain peaks preside over the entire scene. In high season droves of tourists come to soak up all this goodness, making for crowded streets and the most frenetically social summer season the French Alps know.

Orientation and Practical Information

Touching a lake, Annecy is easily reached by rail from Lyon, Grenoble, and Chambéry. The channeled river slices east to west through the heart of the old town, the château on one side and place Notre Dame and the main shopping district on the other. From the train and bus stations, walk straight ahead on rue de la Gare about 3 blocks, then turn left down rue Royale for 5 blocks to the tourist office, the center of town, and the lake.

Maison du Tourisme: 1, rue Jean Jaurès (tel. 50-45-00-33), at place de la Libération on the ground floor of a modern, glass complex by the lake. Free maps. Information on hiking, hotels, campgrounds, rural lodgings, excursions to nearby towns, and mountain climbing. Guided tours (25F) every afternoon (in English on Wed.). **Currency exchange** available June and Sept. Sat.-Sun. 9am-noon and 2-6:30pm; July-Aug. daily 5-6:30pm. Office open June-Sept. daily 9am-noon and 1:45-6:30pm; Oct.-May Tues.-Sat. 9am-noon and 1:45-6:30pm, Sun. 3-6pm.

Post Office: 4, rue des Glières (tel. 50-45-10-19), around the corner from rue de la Poste and down the street from the train station. **Currency exchange** on the ground floor, **telephones** in the basement. **Postal code:** 74000. Open Mon.-Fri. 8am-7pm, Sat. 8am-noon.

Club Alpin Français: 38, av. du Parmelan (tel. 50-45-52-76), at rue de Mortillet. Information on mountain activities and organized group trips. Open Wed. 3-7pm, Fri. 5:30-7pm, and Sat. 10am-noon.

Train Station: Place de la Gare (tel. 50-51-66-66). To Grenoble (9 per day, 2 hr., 72F), Aix-les-Bains (1 per hr., 15 min., 26F), Chambéry (10 per day, 45 min., 38F), Chamonix (8 per day, 2-2½ hr., 68F), Lyon (8 per day, 2 hr., 82F), Paris (by TGV 8 per day, 4½ hr., 285F with required 13F reservation; by night train, 1 per day, 6-8 hr.), and Nice (4 per day, 6 hr.,

305F). Information office open Mon.-Sat. 8am-7:15pm, Sun. 9am-7:15pm. Station open daily 5am-11:30pm.

Bus Station: Gare Routière, adjacent to the train station. **Voyages Crolard** (tel. 50-45-08-12) provides regular service to Talloires (9 per day, 1 Sun.; 25 min.; 9.70F), La Clusaz (4-7 per day, 1¼ hr., 26F), and Chamonix (1 per day, none Sun.; 2½ hr.; 63F) and 1-day excursions to Geneva (July-Aug. daily, 75F), Turin (Sat., 125F), and l'Abbaye d'Hautecombe (Wed., 66F). **Frossard** (tel. 50-45-73-90) offers slightly cheaper day- and ½-day trips in summer to La Grande Chartreuse (Mon., 88F), l'Abbaye d'Hautecombe (Fri., 63F), and Zermatt (Sat., 175F). Also offers regular service to Genève (6 per day, none Sun.; 1¼ hr.; 33.50F), Grenoble (4 per day, 2 hr., 50F), and Lyon (2 per day, 4 hr., 77F). **Francony** (tel. 50-45-02-43) runs one bus per day to Chamonix (3 hr., 52F). Call **SAT** (tel. 50-37-22-13) for schedules and rates to Morzine and Avioraz.

Urban Buses: SIBRA Tel. 50-51-70-53. Tickets 5F. *Carnet* of 8 24F. Get a bus map and schedule from the tourist office or the kiosk on rue de la Préfecture (open Mon.-Sat. 8:30am-7pm).

Bike Rental: Loca Sports, 37, av. de Loverchy (tel. 50-45-44-33), 10 min. from *centre ville.* 50F per day, with lower rates for longer rentals. Also at the **train station.** 37F per ½-day, 47F per day, deposit 100F.

Bookstore: Persan Bleu, 9bis, rue Prés Fauré. A small English-language selection.

Laundromats: Pressing, in the Nouvelles Galeries complex on bd. du Lycée. From the station, turn left onto av. de Brogny and bear right onto bd. du Lycée (10 min.). Wash 14F, dry 5.50F per 15 min., soap 3F. **Les Lavandières,** rue de Chausseurs. **Self-Laverie,** 9, rue Louis-Armand.

Public Swimming Pool: Rue des Marquisats, on the lake. Admission 10.50F, ages under 18 6.80F. Open Mon.-Sat. 10am-7pm, Sun. 9am-7pm.

Hospital: Av. des Trésums (tel. 50-88-33-33).

Medical Emergency: SAMU, Tel. 50-51-21-21.

Police: 15, rue des Marquisats (tel. 50-45-21-61).

Accommodations and Camping

A popular resort, Annecy has high prices to match its high temperatures. Try the Maison des Jeunes, the hostel, or one of the many small campgrounds. Do not arrive in the afternoon during July and August expecting to find a cheap room. If you arrive in the morning, you can usually find a room for a night or two. For a stay of a week or longer in peak season, you must reserve two months in advance (earlier for festival weeks). September is a better time to come—the weather is pleasant and the town less crowded. The hotels in neighboring towns are no cheaper.

Auberge de Jeunesse "La Grande Jeanne" (IYHF), 16, route de Semnoz (tel. 50-45-33-19). Take the bus marked "Semnoz" from the Hôtel de Ville (6F), or follow the directions to the Maison des Jeunes below but bear left on chemin de Belvedere at the *stade nautique* and continue straight for 4km, the last 2km up a hill where hitching is usually successful. Your arduous trek will be rewarded by a comfortable chalet (4 per room). 45F. Breakfast included. Meals 34F. No curfew. Office open 5-10pm.

Maison des Jeunes et de la Culture (MJC), 52, rue des Marquisats (tel. 50-45-08-80), on the lake, a 10-min. walk from *centre ville.* Take bus #1 from the station or the tourist office to the Marquisats stop (every 15 min., last bus 8pm, 5F; Sun. and holidays take bus A instead). Or, from the tourist office, follow quai E. Chappus onto rue des Marquisats for about 500m. A modern building, set amid pines with a gorgeous view of the lake and mountains. Comfortable rooms. TV and recreation areas. More expensive than the hostel, but worth it. Singles 60F. Doubles 90F. Triples 120F. Sheets included. Breakfast 13F. Cafeteria meals 31F. Snackbar offers sandwiches, drinks, and ice cream. Call Mon.-Fri. 9am-3pm for reservations. No curfew. Office open 24 hours.

Maison de la Jeune Fille, 1, av. du Rhône (tel. 50-45-34-81), at av. d'Aléry. Accepts men and women July-Aug.; women only Sept.-June. One-week minimum stay. Clean, ordinary singles 85F including obligatory breakfast and 1 meal, 106F with all 3 meals. Separate cafeteria meals 28F. Office open Mon.-Fri. 8-11am and 5:45-7:30pm. No curfew.

Hôtel des Alpes, 12, rue de la Poste (tel. 50-45-04-56), centrally located near the post office and train station. Small and comfortable, though some rooms are noisy. Singles 71-77F. Doubles from 90F, with shower 138F. Breakfast 19F. Showers 16F.

Hôtel du Château, 16, rampe du Château (tel. 50-45-27-66), up a winding ramp, near the castle in a secluded part of the old town. Lovely old walls and climbing flowers. Singles and doubles with shower 110F. 2 beds 140F. Triples 200F. Showers 10F. Breakfast 16F. Open Dec. 15-Oct. 15. Book early.

Hôtel Savoyard, 41, av. de Cran (tel. 50-57-08-08), in a quiet residential area behind the train station. Turn left and walk over the tracks onto av. Berthollet, then left onto av. de Cran. Distant, quiet, and clean enough. Singles or doubles 80F. Triples 110F. Showers 8F. Breakfast 15F. Open March-Oct.

Dozens of small **campgrounds** border the lake in the town of **Albigny,** which can be reached by Voyages Crolard buses leaving from the *gare routière* or by following av. d'Albigny from the tourist office. The larger **Belvedere,** route de Semnoz (tel. 50-45-48-30), on the same road as the hostel, is closer and usually packed. The food store sells staples at reasonable prices. (Open Dec. 15-Oct. 15.)

Food

Annecy restaurants tempt the belly but not the thrifty pocket; lovely lakeside picnics are probably your best choice. Taste cheese, sample cherries, or just join the merriment at the **markets** on Tuesday, Friday, and Sunday mornings around place Ste-Claire or Saturday mornings on bd. Taine. Less exciting but more convenient is the well-stocked **Prisunic** on rue du Lac at place Notre Dame. (Open Mon.-Sat. 8:45am-12:15pm and 2:15-7pm.) The cafeterias at the MJC and the Maison de la Jeune Fille serve heaps of food to anyone who will pay. Avoid the overpriced, pseudo-Italian tourist traps called restaurants that line the canal. Smaller, cheaper, ethnic restaurants cluster around Faubourt Ste-Claire.

Chez Petros, 15, Faubourg Ste-Claire (tel. 50-45-50-26), near the end of rue Ste-Claire. The only Greek restaurant, brags the owner/manager/cook, in the Haute-Savoie. Try the *guiros* (27F), with the *feuilles de vins* (rolled grape leaves) as an appetizer. Open daily 11am-3pm and 6:30pm-1am; in off-season Mon.-Sat. only.

Tarte Julie, place Ste-Claire (tel. 50-45-38-62). Julie's decorator had a checkered career. Sumptuous tarts for dinner or dessert (20-30F). Pizza from 23F. Open Tues.-Sun. 10am-10pm.

Au Bord du Thiou, 4, place St-François-de-Sales, on the canal near the Palais de l'Ile. Good for salads (10-30F), crêpes (from 17F), and ice cream. Specialties include the *fermière,* made with eggs and cheese, and liqueur dessert crêpes. Open daily noon-2pm and 5pm-midnight; in off-season 5pm-midnight.

Le Cellier, 7, rue Perrière (tel. 50-45-79-90), in the heart of the old town. Less pretentious than its neighbors. Pizza 32-49F, *plat du jour* 39F. Open daily noon-2pm and 6:30-11pm.

Cafétéria Le Petit Pierre, 8, rue de l'Annexion (tel. 50-51-22-47). From the tourist office, take rue Vaugelas and turn left on rue de l'Annexion. The best quantity-to-price ratio in town. Main dishes 20-34F. Open daily 11am-2:30pm and 6:30-11pm.

Au Lilas Rose, passage de l'Evéché (tel. 50-45-37-08). Prize location. A variety of dishes from *fondue savoyarde* (51F per person) to trout (53F) or pizza (30F). Open daily 11:45am-2:30pm and 6:45-11pm.

Sights

In Annecy's old town, venerable, pastel-colored houses, canals with baroque locks, old churches, and tourists collide. The **Palais de l'Ile,** a twelfth-century prison, juts out incongruously on a tiny island in the middle of the river. The brilliant green canals brighten the neighborhood and showcase the swans. Climb up to the **Château d'Annecy,** overlooking the town and the lake. The well-preserved castle displays a fairly interesting folklore and natural history collection. Majestic parlors resound with the squeak of your footsteps. The château also houses an ongoing series of expositions, ranging from classical portraits to modern sculpture in unexplored media. (Open Tues.-Sun. 10am-noon and 2-6pm. Admission 7F, students 3.50F.)

You haven't experienced the beauty of the Lac d'Annecy until you've taken the boat tour. **La Compagnie des Bateaux à Vapeur,** 6, place aux Bois (tel. 50-51-08-40), conducts cruises around the lake that dock for frequent photo breaks (2-3 per day, 1½ hr., 52F). The main beach charges 10F (ages under 12 5F), but you can find free places to swim all along the shore. The **plage de Sevrier,** a few kilometers past the MJC on rue des Marquisats, allows some breathing space. The **Champs de Mars** is one of the world's premier sunning and frisbee sites. Around the Jardin Public you can rent windsurfers, pedal boats, motor-launches, and small outboard boats.

The lakeside towns of **St-Jorioz; Doussard; Menthon-St-Bernard**—birthplace of St-Bernard, founder of the famed Hospices; **Duingt**—beloved of Cézanne; and **Talloires** are all within 20km of Annecy and accessible by bus. The tourist office in Annecy provides a brochure describing their main attractions. All offer a smorgasbord of swimming, boating, hiking, tennis, and evening entertainment. The **Fête du Lac** enlivens the first Saturday in August with fireworks and water shows (admission 35-180F). Each year the floats on the lake take on different themes; "Monsters and Legends," "Adventures in the Far West," and "Beyond the Planet Earth" have been themes in the past. The **Festival de la Vieille Ville** (1st 2 weeks in July) features free concerts and performances in the streets and churches and a few, big-time performances (UB40 came in 1988). There is dancing nightly at **Le Pop,** near the *pop plage* on av. d'Albigny.

Near Annecy

The **Gorges du Fier,** a canyon carved by melting prehistoric glaciers, about 10km from Annecy, is one of the more spectacular sights in the Alps. Waterfalls roar over scarred cliffs to crash on the rocks below. (Open Easter-Oct. 16 daily 9am-6:15pm. Admission a stiff 18F for the 40-min. walk. Call 50-46-23-07 for more information.) The medieval **Château de Montrottier** lies five minutes up the hill from the entrance to the *gorges*. The castle's tower provides a superb view of Mont Blanc. The castle itself contains centuries-old Asian costumes, armor, and pottery. (Open June-Aug. daily 10am-noon and 2-6pm; Easter-May and Sept.-Oct. 15 Wed.-Mon. only. Obligatory, informative tour 18F, students 15F. Call 50-46-23-02 for more information.) To get to the *gorges* and the château, take the Voyages Crolard excursion bus (2-3 per week; tel. 50-45-09-12 for information), plan your schedules ahead, and take the train to **Lovagny** then walk the 800m to the *gorges* (3 per day stop at Lovagny at odd hours, 10 min., 7F). Or, take bus A to the end of the line at Poisy and walk or hitch the 4km to Lovagny and the château.

Ask at the Annecy tourist office for a guide suggesting hikes around the lake. **La Forêt du Cret du Maure,** next to the Parc Regional du Semnoz (near the youth hostel), is peaceful, flowery, and fragrant (tourist office sells a guidebook for 8F). **Talloires,** 13km from Annecy, makes a good starting point for hikes to **La Cascade d'Angon** (1 hr.) and the **Ermitage de St-Germain** (45 min.), with a beautiful Alpine garden. (See Practical Information for buses to Taillores.)

In winter, hotel prices drop, and Annecy becomes a quiet base for skiing in Savoie. The nearest ski resort is **La Clusaz** (buses leave from the *gare routière* in Annecy). Contact the **Office de Tourisme** in La Clusaz (tel. 50-02-60-92; **postal code:** 74220) for information. La Clusaz's small **Auberge de Jeunesse Chalet "Marcoret" (IYHF),** sits in an idyllic setting.

In the Facigny area north of Annecy, **Samoëns** has a lovely **Jardin Alpin** whose waterfalls, small ponds, and terraces decorate eight acres of exotic and native Alpine plants. (Open daily 8am-noon and 1:30-7pm; in off-season 8am-noon and 1:30-5pm.) The **Auberge de Jeunesse "Beau Site" (IYHF),** in La Coutettaz (tel. 50-79-14-86), is located 1km out of the town of Morzine. A tough mountain leg of the Tour de France finishes in **Morzine** in the middle of July. **Lac de Montriond,** a sparkling mountain lake at an altitude of 1164m, splashes against its banks near **Avoriaz,** a chic resort without automobiles, accessible only by cablecar. **Flaine,** dubbed the "intellectual's ski resort," is a relatively new establishment with avant-garde films, galleries, and remarkably good skiing in winter. For more information, contact the *syndicat* in Morzine (tel. 50-79-03-45; **postal code:** 74110). The nearest train station is Les Cluses, 30km away. Call **SAT** (tel. 50-37-22-13) for bus schedules.

Chamonix

Mountains—menacing, wrathful mountains—strain mightily to pierce the clean blue sky. Chamonix is the profaned altar from which to worship these Alpine gods ranged above in an imposing pantheon. Mont Blanc (at 4807m, Europe's highest peak) and lesser cousins loom over awestruck mortals scurrying about in the valley below.

Each year, a close-knit fraternity of mountain climbers and guides climb a mountain in memory of their fallen colleagues. Chamonix's main streets are named after such mountaineers, who dedicated their lives to the pursuit of conquering yet more precarious peaks.

Directions and locations are often expressed in altitude—Chamonix is at 1035m and everything else is up. Chamonix embraces both the central town and the complex of nearby villages, scattered between forests and mountains. Les Bossons, Les Pèlerins, Les Praz, Les Bois, Les Tines, Lavancher, Les Chosalets, Argentière, Montroc, and Le Tour all spread along the narrow valley, bounded on one side by the Mont Blanc range and by the Aiguilles Rouges chain on the other. Buses and trains serve the valley well. The Himalayas or the Andes may have more mountain per square meter, but only in Chamoix do so many mechanical conveniences carry you up with so little effort.

Orientation and Practical Information

The center of town lies at the intersection of the three main commercial streets: avenue Michel Croz, rue du Docteur Paccard, and rue Joseph Vallot. From the train station, walk straight ahead to the town center; zigzag a little to the left and continue uphill to the tourist office, the bus station, and the Maison de la Montagne.

Office de Tourisme: Place du Triangle (tel. 50-53-00-24). Efficient, modern center with a list of hotels and dormitories and a helpful map of campsites. Everything in English. Efficient, free hotel-finding service. Hotel reservations (tel. 50-53-23-33) require a 30% deposit. Sells the *Carte des Sentiers d'Eté* (hiking map, 20F) and *Chamonix Magazine,* a useful bi-weekly bulletin (3F in summer, free in winter). Open daily July-Aug. 8:30am-7:30pm; Sept.-June 8:30am-12:30pm and 2-7pm.

Maison de la Montagne: Place de l'Eglise next to the church. The **Office de Haute Montagne** (tel. 50-53-22-08) stocks detailed maps (37F), a weather monitor, a library of hiking and mountaineering guides, and a knowledgeable staff. Open June 13-Sept. 30 daily 8:30am-noon and 2:30-6:30pm; June 1-June 12 and Oct. daily 8:30am-noon; Nov.-May Mon.-Tues. and Thurs. 8:30am-noon. **Compagnie des Guides** (tel. 50-53-00-88) organizes skiing and climbing lessons and leads guided hikes in summer, guided ski trips in winter. Ski from the *Aiguille du Midi* or take a weeklong skiing trip to Zermatt, Switzerland. Open daily 8:30am-noon and 2-7:30pm. The **meteorological station** (tel. 50-53-03-40) is open daily 9-11am and 4:30-6pm.

Club Alpin Français: 136, av. Michel-Croz (tel. 50-53-16-03). Information on mountain refuges and road conditions. Their bulletin board matches drivers, riders, and hiking partners. If you're considering an extensive stay, a one-year membership gets you 50% off all Alpine refuges, insurance, and participation in their semi-professional skiing and hiking expeditions. Open July-Aug. daily 9am-noon and 3:30-7pm; Sept.-June Mon.-Tues. and Thurs.-Fri. 3:30-7pm, Sat. 9am-noon.

Post Office: Place Jacques-Balmat (tel. 50-53-15-90). **Telephones,** telex, and Poste Restante. **Postal code:** 74400. Open July-Aug. Mon.-Fri. 8am-7pm, Sat. 8am-noon; Sept.-June Mon.-Fri. 8am-noon and 2-6pm, Sat. 8am-noon.

Train Station: Av. de la Gare (tel. 50-53-00-44). Trains almost hourly to St.-Gervais (35 min., 20F), change for Annecy (5 per day, 2 hr., 67F), Aix-les-Bains (6 per day, 2½ hr., 85F), Chambéry (6 per day, 3 hr., 90F), Lyon (6 per day, 4-5 hr., 132F), and Martigny, Switzerland (6 per day, 1½ hr., 64F) with transfers to Montreux. Information office open daily 8am-noon and 2-6:30pm.

Bus Station: Place de l'Eglise (tel. 50-53-05-55). Every ½ hr. in summer, every 15 min. in winter, and every hr. in off-season, buses go up and down the entire valley to Les Pèlerins, Les Praz, Les Houches, Argentière. Tickets 5.50-22F. *Carnets* of 6 (30F) and 10 (45F) tickets. Summer excursion buses go to Interlaken and Grindelwald (Tues., 180F), Venice (Fri., 330F), Zermatt (Sat., 180F), and Turin (Sat., 170F). Tour of Lac Leman (Thurs., 143F) and Mont Blanc (Tues., 143F). **Société Alpes Transports,** at the train station (tel. 50-78-05-33), provides regular service to Annecy (2 per day, 2¾ hr.), Grenoble (1 per day, 3½ hr.), Genève (1 per day, 2 hr.), and Courmayeur, Italy (6 per day, 40 min.).

Bike Rental: Le Grand Bi, 240, av. du Bois du Bouchet (tel. 50-53-14-16). 3-speeds 30F per ½-day, 40F per day. 10-speeds 33F per ½-day, 45F per day. Mountain bikes 55F per ½-day, 60F per day. Bicycle-built-for-two 80F per ½-day, 100F per day. Deposit 500F or passport. Open Mon.-Sat. 8:30am-6pm. **Mountain Bike,** 138, rue des Moulins (tel. 50-53-48-56). Run by an Australian and an Englishman. High quality mountain bikes 60F per ½-day, 100F per day, 500F per week. Open May-Nov. 9am-7pm.

Hiking Equipment and Ski Rental: Sanglard Sports, 31, rue Michel Croz (tel. 50-53-24-70), in the very center of town. Staff speaks English. Hiking boots 25F per day, mountain climbing boots 35F per day. Average pair of skis and boots 80F per day. Open daily 9am-noon and 2:30-7:30pm.

Laundromat: Lav'matic, 40, impasse Primevère, to the left of rue Vallot a few blocks up from the supermarket. Wash 20F, dry 10F per 20 min., soap 2F. Open daily 7:30am-9pm.

Weather Forecast: Issued 3 times per day by the meteorological office in the Maison de la Montagne. Bulletins in the window of the Pharmacie Mont Blanc and the Club Alpin Français.

Hospital: Hôpital de Chamonix, rue Vallot (tel. 50-53-04-74).

Mountain Rescue: PGHM Secours en Montagne, route de la Mollard (tel. 50-53-16-89). Accident victims or "their heirs" are responsible for all expenses. Cheap accident insurance available here, at the Club Alpin Français, and at the Office de Haute Montagne. A good idea to register any serious hiking itinerary here. Open 24 hours.

Medical Emergency: Tel. 50-53-02-10.

Police: Tel. 50-53-10-97.

Accommodations and Camping

Mountain chalets with dormitory accommodations (5-6 per room, bare mattresses, hall showers) combine affordability with splendid settings: 35-40F per night buys you a bed far from the urban bustle. Many places close in the off-season (Oct.-Nov. and May). All hotels and many dormitories require reservations (preferably 6 weeks in advance) for the hectic school vacations (Dec. and Feb.) but usually have some space during January, March, and April. If you choose to camp, be prepared for chilly nights.

Auberge de Jeunesse (IYHF), 103, montée Jacques Balmat (tel. 50-53-14-52), in Les Pèlerins. Take the bus from place de l'Eglise toward Les Houches, get off at Pèlerins Ecole, and follow the signs uphill to the hostel. If you're coming by train, get off at Les Pèlerins, and follow the signs up the hill (15 min.). Total renovation will be completed by summer 1989. Simple and clean. A bit inconvenient for visiting Chamonix. 25% discount on all *téléphériques*. Kitchen facilities available. 49F. Sheets 13F. Some doubles available. 10F extra per person to reserve a double. Nonmembers 15F more per night (up to 6 nights). Breakfast included. Meals 34F. Office open Dec.-Sept. daily 8-10am and 5-10pm, but you can drop your bags off anytime. No curfew.

Gîtes d'Etape: Chalet Ski Station, 6, route des Moussoux (tel. 50-53-20-25). Walk up the steep hill past the tourist office and church to the *téléphérique* of Brévent, and turn left (10-15 min.). A splendid view of the entire Mont Blanc range. Friendly atmosphere. No kitchen but a space for cooking if you have a camp stove. Many long-term residents during ski season. 33F. Sheets 8F. Shower 4F. Reception open 8am-11pm. No curfew.

La Montagne, 789, promenade des Crêmeries (tel. 50-53-11-60). From the train station, walk to the right on av. du Bois du Bouchet, then left into the *bois* at the signs (15 min.). Splendid home and garden in the woods. Mostly French residents. Kitchen facilities. Bunk beds in a cramped dormitory 31F. Tepid showers included. Lights out at 10:30pm, curfew 11pm, and nightly inspection for vagabonds. Office open daily 5-10pm.

Chamoniard Volant (Chalet le Chamoniard), 45, route de la Frasse (tel. 50-53-14-09), 10 min. from the town center across from the *bois.* Walk on av. du Bois du Bouchet, and turn right at the signs. Run by a young French couple, who speak English. Many young American and British travelers here. Chummy co-ed dorms (4-6 per room) with kitchen facilities and an optional 18F continental breakfast. Dinner 53F (warn manager the morning before). 40F. Sheets 10F the 1st night, free thereafter. No curfew. Office open daily 10am-10pm.

Le Corzolet, 186, av. du Bouchet (tel. 50-53-16-58), 10 min. from the train station. Walk straight ahead and take your 1st right. In an old house with balconies, surrounded by a sunny yard. No kitchen. Singles 75-90F. Doubles 138F. Showers included. Breakfast 18F.

Les Grands Charmoz, 468, chemin de Cristalliers (tel. 50-53-45-57). Walking right on av. du Bois de Boucher, go right under the train tracks after the bike rental, take a sharp right, and it's the 2nd house on the left. Run by a hospitable American couple—homesick Yankees should phone ahead to reserve one of the comfortable rooms. Beautiful kitchen and occasional garden barbecue. Dorm accommodations 41F. Doubles 122F. Triples 143F. Sheets and showers included. They'll do your wash for 15F.

Camping: Many people pitch tents in the Bois du Bouchet, but the police are cracking down on this illegal practice. Other squatters have found more creative plots, near the top of the *téléphérique* of La Flegère, for example. The tourist office dispenses a map and bill of particulars on the 20 campgrounds in the area. Most have good views, hot showers, and refreshingly few trailers. Several campsites lie near the foot of the Aiguille du Midi *téléphérique.* **L'Ile des Barrats,** route des Pèlerins (tel. 50-53-11-75), is the nicest. From the *téléphérique,* turn left and look to your right (16F per person, 14F per tent; office open June 15-Sept. 15 8am-9pm). **Les Rosiers,** 121, clos des Rosières (tel. 50-53-10-42), off route de Praz, the closest on the other side of Chamonix, always has space for a tent. Follow rue Vallot for 1-2km or take a bus to Les Nants (14F per person, 7F per tent; office open 8am-9pm).

Smaller, neighboring villages maintain more secluded chalets away from the crowds. The tourist office has a list of over 10. **La Boerne,** in Tré-le-Champ (tel. 50-54-05-14), just out of Montroc and accessible by bus from Chamonix, stands out. Thirty-two francs earns you a bed in a cleverly renovated barn.

Food

Don't stray from the basics in Chamonix. Anything but the *fondue savoyarde* or *raclette* will likely break the bank. Luckily, most chalets have kitchens, relief for the restaurant-weary traveler. The well-stocked **Supermarché Payot Pertin,** 117, rue Joseph Vallot, is by far the cheapest place to buy groceries (open Mon.-Sat. 8:15am-7:30pm, Sun. 8:30am-12:15pm). **Markets** occur Saturday mornings at place du Mont Blanc and Tuesday mornings in Chamonix Sud, near the foot of the Aiguille du Midi *téléphérique.* A *croix de Savoie,* a heavenly *brioche* and cream pastry, will satisfy any sugar addiction.

Le Fer à Cheval, 118, rue Whymper (tel. 50-53-13-22), at place du Mont Blanc. This cozy roadside spot has a reputation for serving the best fondue in the valley. Make reservations. *Fondue savoyarde* 35F, *fondue bourguinonne* 50F. Crêpes 12-20F. Open Tues.-Sun. noon-midnight.

Brasserie des Sports, rue Joseph Vallot (tel. 50-53-00-46). Simple food at affordable prices. *Fondue savoyarde* 35F; *menus* 35F and 45F. Open Wed.-Mon. noon-2pm and 6:30-9pm; in off-season Wed.-Sat. and Mon. only.

Restaurant Robinson, 307, chemin des Crêmeries (tel. 50-53-45-87), in the Bois du Bouchet. Follow the signs from av. du Bois du Bouchet. A beautiful wooded setting. Outdoor seating available. Swiss fondue 38F, omelettes from 15F, *menu* 68F. Open June-Sept. daily noon-2pm and 7-9pm.

Le Boule de Neige, rue Joseph Vallot (tel. 50-53-04-08). A skier's restaurant run by a boisterous family. Steak and fries 34F, *fondue savoyard* 35F, *menu* 46F. Open daily noon-2:15pm and 7-9pm.

Le Ferme de la Côte, 250, route Henriette d'Angeville (tel. 50-53-13-24). Charming ambience, glorious view, and delicious food. *Raclette* 65F, *fondue savoyarde* 46F. Open daily noon-2pm and 7-10pm.

Sights and Entertainment

An intricate web of trails wraps around Chamonix, each clearly marked by lines painted on trees to indicate varying degrees of difficulty. Wander along almost any road for views of the mountains, Alpine flowers, or stretches of woodland. The 20F hiking map of the area available at the tourist office color-codes all the trails according to difficulty and is well worth the investment. Serious climbers should buy the IGN topographic map (37F), available at the Office de Haute Montagne and local bookstores. The best trail guide is the *Guide Vallot* available at the **Presse du Mont Blanc,** rue de Docteur Paccard. Whatever your skill, a few precautions are in order: Bring warm, waterproof clothing and wear sturdy shoes—hiking boots are wise. Do not underestimate the length of your hike. The tourist office hiking map gives an accurate estimate of hiking times for most trails. You might want to discuss any serious plans with someone in the Office de Haute Montagne. *Téléphériques* **give you access to the higher, more aesthetically rewarding trails quickly but can wreak havoc on your budget.**

One of the more spectacular hiking trails leads up to **Lac Blanc,** a gemlike, turquoise mountain lake dominated by snow-covered peaks. The south-facing slope commands marvelous views of Mont Blanc. Take a bus (5.50F), hitch, or walk (25 min.) along rue Vallot/route de Praz to the town of Les Praz and the La Flegère *téléphérique* (one-way 24F, round-trip 37F; last descent 5:20pm). From the top of the *téléphérique,* turn right and climb the strenuous, well-marked trail for about 90 minutes. Pack a lunch. The more energetic can take the *téléphérique* of Le Brévent up the hill from the tourist office (one way 28F, round-trip 38F), follow the **Grand Balcon Sud** trail for two hours to the La Flegère *téléphérique* and continue up from there. The **Petit Balcon Nord** or the berry-lined **Petit Balcon Sud** are less demanding but still worthwhile.

For a longer excursion, try the **Tour du Mont Blanc.** The 6-day trail passes through France, Italy, and Switzerland and refuges are conveniently located about six-hour hikes apart.

The prices of the **Aiguille du Midi** *téléphérique,* the highest, most spectacular cablecar in the world, are as steep as the trajectory but it's worth it. The crowds may be suffocating and the waits interminable but no one is disappointed. Cars leave regularly from the station in South Chamonix, but go as early as you can since crowds and clouds usually gather by mid-afternoon. The simplest trip takes you to Plan de l'Aiguille (one way 25F, round-trip 35F), but most people continue right through the clouds to the next *étape,* the Aiguille du Midi (one way 80F, round-trip 110F from Chamonix; elevator to the summit for a slightly better view 8F). The round-trip to the summit takes at least 1½ hour From the Midi, you can continue to a third stage, Gare Helbrouner in Italy (one way 110F, round-trip 160F from Chamonix; take your passport), and if you've got money to burn, you can continue on to the Italian town of Courmayeur. No matter how far up the mountain you go, take very warm clothes and expect a wait for the car back down. The Helbrouner station is also an approach to rather limited summer skiing. Inquire at the tourist office before you go; ski rentals are available at most sports stores in Chamonix.

A much cheaper but less dazzling alternative is the two-part *téléphérique* Brévent. The *télécabine* to Planpraz costs 28F one way, 38F round-trip, and the *téléphérique* to Brévent costs 38F one way, 60F round-trip. From the top, the view stretches over the entire Mont Blanc range across the valley. The walk down from Planpraz is not too strenuous.

One of the strangest attractions in Chamonix is the **Mer de Glace,** a glacier that moves 30m each year. Special trains run from a small station next to the main *gare* (May-Sept. 8am-6pm; one way 30F, round-trip 43F), but you might prefer the one-hour hike. Nearby via *téléphérique* (7F) or a short hike is **La Grotte de Glace,** a kitschy cave in which the ice has been carved into imaginative shapes, including a grand piano and sofa set. (Admission 7.50F.) Go only if you enjoy being surrounded by tourists.

Chamonix is not exclusively a hiker's club in summer. Biking in the relatively flat Chamonix valley is a pleasant way to get around (see Practical Information). The Olympic indoor ice-skating rink costs 15F. (Skate rental 11F. Open Thurs.-Tues 3-6pm, Wed. 3-6pm and 9-11pm.) The Musée Alpin, off av. Michel Croz (tel. 50-53-25-93), is more interesting than most folklore museums and displays paintings and photographs of Mont Blanc from every conceivable angle. (Open daily June-Sept. 2-7pm; Christmas-Easter 3-7pm.)

Skiing in Chamonix challenges even the best skiers, but there is plenty of mountain here for everybody. You can buy a day pass on one *téléphérique* (in La Flegère 90F per day) or a *skipass,* which allows you access to *téléphériques* up and down the valley (2-day skipass 265F, 3-day 385F, 1 week 795F). Unfortunately, you often have to take the shuttle bus from one *téléphérique* to another. Over 16 stores in Chamonix rent skis.

After a day in the mountains, kick back at **La Choucas,** 206, rue Docteur Paccard (tel. 50-53-03-23), a popular change of scene with a bistro-cafe club atmosphere and a large video screen usually showing mountaineering and ski movies.

Val d'Isère

The yellow and violet flowers that color the banks of the Isère River cast an alluring and soporific spell. They lull the hamlet of Val d'Isère back into its once-peaceful Alpine slumber and seem to struggle against the commercialization of this cherished valley. Nevertheless, supermarkets, hotels, and sports shops sprout like the meadow dandelions. Particularly in winter, the town attracts a jet-set clientele; prices and pretensions here are as formidable as the skiing. Ever-increasing numbers of peak-lovers are discovering the splendid **Parc National de la Vanoise.** The mountains here inspire less awe than the Mont Blanc range in Chamonix to the north, and the town itself offers little of interest, but the skiing borders on unearthly. It provides by far the best reason for taking the long trip to Val d'Isère.

Orientation and Practical Information

Val d'Isère nestles in the Isère River Valley, due east of Chambéry and a few kilometers from the Italian border.

No trains run to Val d'Isère. The nearest train station is in **Bourg St-Maurice,** 30km north. Two to five trains per day arrive in Bourg St-Maurice, one a night train from Paris (9 hr.) and the others from Chambéry (2 hr., 63F). Board the bus for Val d'Isère (42F), or **Les Boisses** (37F) if you are going to the hostel.

There are no street names in Val d'Isère; fortunately there is only one nameless main street. The bus follows some disconcertingly narrow and precipitous mountain roads. Main street slopes gently upward from the exit to town. From the bus stop, walk up for about 100m and the tourist office will be on your left.

Office de Tourisme, Boîte Postale 28 (tel. 79-06-10-83). Free maps, glossy brochures, and hotel reservations. Everything in English. Friendly staff. Open daily Dec.-May 8 8:30am-7:30pm; June 25-Aug. 30 8:30am-12:30pm and 2:30-7:30pm; Sept.-Nov. and May-June 9am-noon and 2:30-7pm.

Currency Exchange: Banque Populaire, 75m down from tourist office (tel. 79-06-05-57). Open Mon.-Thurs. 9am-noon and 2-5:30pm, Fri. 9am-noon and 2:30-4:30pm.

Post Office, across from tourist office (tel. 79-06-06-99). **Postal Code:** 73150. Open Mon.-Fri. 9am-noon and 2-5pm, Sat. 9am-noon.

Buses: Autocars Martin, 100m down the main street from tourist office (tel. 79-06-00-42). Main office at place de la Gare (tel. 79-07-04-49), in Bourg St-Maurice. Buses coordinated with train schedules. In winter, buses to **Genève** airport (3 per day, 5 per day on weekends; 4 hr.; 205F). Buses to and from Les Boisses and the youth hostel (5 per day in winter, 2-3 per day in summer; 10 min.; 11F). Daily excursions (55-160F) usually leaving around 10:45am. Office open Wed.-Mon. 9:30am-noon and 2:30-7pm.

Bike rental: Jean Sports, 100m up from tourist office (tel. 79-06-04-44). 10-speeds 30F per ½-day, 50F per day. Mountain bikes 50F per ½-day, 80F per day. Open daily 8am-noon and 2:30-7pm.

Ski Information: Tel. 79-06-25-55.

Ski Patrol: Tel. 79-06-02-10.

Accommodations, Camping, and Food

Hotel rooms in Val d'Isère cost a bundle—reserve early at the hostel or the refuge. To rent an apartment for a week or more, contact the tourist office or **Val d'Isère Agence** (tel. 79-06-15-22) for a list of those available.

Auberge de Jeunesse "Les Clarines" (IYHF), 10km out of town (tel. 79-07-10-61), in Tignes. Take the bus marked "Tignes/Val Claret" from Bourg St-Maurice or Val d'Isère and get off at Les Boisses. Spotless rooms and a friendly atmosphere. Ski from door to *téléphérique.* Reserve in Sept. for Dec. and Feb.; 6 weeks ahead for Jan., March, and April. 4-person rooms have their own showers. 38F. Shower included. Sheets 11F. Nonmembers 15F more per night up to 6 nights. Hearty meals 34F. Good breakfast 15F. Office open 5-10pm but you can drop off bags all day (the bus from Bourg St-Maurice gives you about 10 min. before heading to Val d'Isère). Ask for a key if out past 10pm. Open mid-Nov. to mid-May and mid-June to mid-Sept., depending on ski season dates.

Gîte d'Etape: Refuge le Prarion, a 1-hr. walk and then a 45-min. hike from town (tel. 79-06-06-02). Head up from town for about 1 hr. to the National Park parking lot. (The shuttle to le Fornet takes you about half-way.) From there it's an exhilarating (exhausting?), well-marked hike up to a stream-carved mountain valley. Cozy. Ski to and from ski lifts during the spring. Popular base for ski-touring. Call ahead to reserve. 45F. Meals 75F. Breakfast 30F. Kitchen facilities available. Open March 15-May 20 and June 15-Sept. 15, depending on snow levels.

Hôtel le Floçon, 200m up from the tourist office off the main street (tel. 79-06-04-19). Best hotel deal in Val d'Isère and not cheap. All rooms with private bathroom and breakfast included. In summer, singles 110F, doubles 185F, triples 250F, quads 1800F per week. In winter, singles 136F, doubles 226F, triples 300F, quads 3500F per week. Open Dec.-April and July-Aug., depending on snow levels. Reserve early.

Camping: Camping les Richardes, 500m up from tourist office (tel. 79-06-00-50). Plain campsite in a beautiful setting, refreshingly unencumbered by trailers. 6F per person, 4F per tent. Crowded during Aug. Office open June 15-Sept. 15 daily 7:50am-12:50pm and 2-8pm. Although camping off campgrounds is officially illegal, many travelers pitch a tent off the road above the campground. Camping in the National Park carries a 450F fine.

Cheap restaurants don't exist in Val d'Isère. The well-stocked supermarkets, **Supermarché Banco** and **Supermarché Unico,** allow you to eat economically. The town's most popular pizzeria, **La Pedrix Blanche** (tel. 79-06-12-09), serves a 55F *plat du jour* and pizza from 35F.

Sights

If Val d'Isère isn't the best ski resort in the world, it's close to the top. Over 100 chairs and *téléphériques* afford access to 400km of trails. Val d'Isère doesn't present the trickiest slopes, but no skier will ever be bored. Lift tickets cost 100F per ½-day, 148F per day, and get progressively cheaper per day over longer periods. A new *téléphérique* and seven ski lifts serve a few mediocre ski runs on the **Glacier Pissalis** during July and August. A summer ski lift ticket (good 7:30am-1pm) costs 100F.

Hikers should procure the profusely detailed *Guide des Promenades de Val d'Isère* (10F) and a hiking map (15F) from the tourist office. Among the 40 walks described are the trips to **Rocher de Bellevarde** and **Tête du Solaise,** the most popular destinations from Val d'Isère. A *téléphérique* can whisk you part way to Rocher or to the **Tête,** and unrelentingly spectacular mountain vistas reward the next hour or so of legwork. The hike alongside a steep gorge up to the refuge raises spirits as well.

Central France

Central France designates a group of historically linked cities. Together they supported and upheld the French monarchy when it was threatened by the English, though when the French cleared their country of the enemy, the capital moved to Paris. Some say the real France begins and ends in Paris, but here people willingly stop on the street to answer your questions and lavish compliments on your broken French. Not only is the region friendlier, but its pace is slower, and the historical and architectural offerings of the small towns equally remarkable. Unfortunately, this largely industrial area is economically depressed—few tourists pass through throwing their francs into the rugged soil.

France's second largest city and capital of Lyonnais, Lyon is historically renowned for its silk exchange and medieval fairs. Northwest of Lyon, Moulins, ancient capital of Bourbonnais and of the French dynasty of the Bourbons, is a thriving agricultural center that figured as an important crossing point from Occupied into Vichy France. Montluçon, in western Auvergne, is an industrial city that still preserves a charming medieval core. On the northern outskirts of the Massif Central, west of Nevers, is the architecturally notable town of Bourges. George Sand's *pays,* Limoges, a porcelain-manufacturing town set among the terraced pastures and waterways of Limousin, lies at the southwestern apex of Central France, directly west of Lyon.

Transportation in the countryside is largely by private bus companies with limited networks. Fortunately, railroads crisscross the countryside, making many tiny villages accessible. The cities are on major SNCF lines and convenient to each other. The train and bus schedules, however, are designed with the local, not the tourist, in mind. Plan trips ahead so you aren't left stranded. Hitching is feasible as long as you stay on the *routes nationales* and the main roads.

Lyon

Lyon is known for three things: wealth, food, and a resolute *froideur* (coldness) towards outsiders. Neither do the residents of France's commercial and gastronomic center deny in the slightest their notorious aloofness. Old *lyonnais* wisdom has it that prosperous Lyon, always preeminent in trade at the confluence of the Rhône and Saône, was plagued throughout the Middle Ages by pillagers. As a result, Lyon's citizens became suspicious of innocent interlopers and learned to hide their prosperity by eschewing extravagant dress and building a city with an austere facade. Lyon's mascot, the marionette Guignol, who has been mercilessly disparaging kings, ministers, presidents, and police officers for over 150 years, epitomizes this distrustful attitude. Despite this preface, Lyon is undeniably a good place to visit: Excellent museums, varied nightlife, a friendly student population, and reasonably-priced accommodations await travelers.

Orientation and Practical Information

The Saône and the Rhône cleave Lyon into three parts. Vieux Lyon (the old city) unfolds on the west bank of the Saône. East of the Rhône is an area long considered uninspiring and colorless. Finished in 1975, the mammoth Part-Dieu commercial center, train station and painstakingly modernistic shopping mall, hasn't added much brio to this sprawling expanse of warehouses, private homes, and university buildings. Between the Saône and the Rhône lies the main north-south artery of this spit of land, the pedestrian zone, which starts at the Perrache train station in the south and runs across place Carnot up rue Victor Hugo to place Bellecour, continuing along rue de la République to place des Terreaux. Like Paris, Lyon is divided into *arrondissements.* There is no easy way to decipher this system.

The simplest way to sort out the buses and metro is with the expensive orange *Plan Guide Blay* (25F), available at any *tabac,* but it's possible to make do with the free maps of the city, buses, and metro available from the *syndicat.* The metro runs from 5am to midnight, with connections every three to 10 minutes. Tickets cost 6.40F or 31.50F for a *carnet* of six. As you enter the metro, you must validate your ticket; it will then be good for one hour in one direction—bus and *funiculaire* (trolley) connections can be made within this hour. *Funiculaires* go from place St-Jean to the Théâtre Romain and the Musée Gallo-Romain (both in the Fourvière quarter), but run only until 8pm.

On Saturdays, you can buy on the buses *Samedi Bleu* tickets, which allow unlimited travel on the **TCL** network (tel. 78-71-70-00). Lyon is considered a safe town. Solitary travelers can walk at any hour in the area between the Perrache train station and place des Terreaux. Drug-pushers haunt the area around Croix-Pâquet, but if you ignore them, they'll let you alone.

Office de Tourisme: Place Bellecour (tel. 78-42-25-75), 10-min. walk along rue Victor Hugo. You can also take the metro (2 stops from the Perrache station). Excellent introduction to Lyon, *Lyon Vous Aimerez..., available here. Prices for the accommodation service based on the number of stars (1-star 5F, 2-star 10F, anywhere in France 30F). Open June 15-Sept. 15 daily 9am-7pm; Sept. 16-June 14 Mon.-Sat. 9am-5pm.* **Annex,** at the **Perrache** train station, in the connecting building called Centre d'Echange (tel. 78-89-62-42). Not as informed or well-stocked with brochures as the Bellecour office, but will still make reservations. Changes cash but not travelers' checks. Open June 15-Sept. 15 Mon.-Sat. 9am-12:30pm and 2-6:30pm; Sept. 16-June 14 Mon.-Sat. 9am-12:30pm and 2-4pm. Another annex in **Villeurbanne,** 3, rue Aristiole Briand (tel. 78-68-13-20), east of the Rhône. Open Mon.-Fri. 9am-6:15pm, Sat. 9am-5pm.

CROUS: 59, rue de la Madeleine (tel. 78-72-55-47). Information on university housing and cafeterias. Open July 15-Aug. Mon.-Fri. 1:30-4:30pm; Sept.-July 14 Mon.-Fri. 8:30am-12:15pm and 1:30-4:30pm.

Budget Travel: Wasteels, at the Centre d'Echange connected to Perrache (tel. 78-37-80-17). Open Mon.-Fri. 9am-noon and 1-7pm, Sat. 9am-noon and 1-6pm. **Magic Bus,** 78, rue Ney (tel. 78-65-06-65). A trans-Europe budget bus company. Open Mon. 2-7pm, Tues.-Fri. 10am-12:30pm, Sat. 10am-1pm.

IYHF: 5, place Bellecour (tel. 78-42-21-88). A main office that sells membership cards and offers information on all France's hostels and IYHF-sponsored summer trips. A week of horseback riding, meals included, 1710F. Open Mon.-Fri. 2-6pm.

Centre Régional d'Information pour Jeunes (CRIJ): 9, quai des Célestins (tel. 78-37-15-28). Lists of jobs, *au pair* opportunities, and sports. Open Mon. 1-6:30pm, Tues.-Thurs. 10:30am-6:30pm, Fri. 10:30am-5pm, Sat. 10:30am-12:30pm.

Consulates: U.S., 7, quai Général Sarrail, 6ème (tel. 78-24-68-49). Open Mon.-Fri. 9am-noon and 4:30-5pm. **U.K.,** 24, rue Childebert (tel. 78-37-59-57). Open Mon.-Fri. 9am-12:30pm and 2-5:30pm.

American Express: 6, rue Childebert (tel. 78-37-40-69), just up rue de la République from place Bellecour. Open for exchange (with 5F commission) May-Sept. Mon.-Fri. 9am-noon and 2-5:30pm, Sat. 9am-noon; Oct.-April Mon.-Fri. 9am-noon and 2-5:30pm.

Post Office: Place Antonin Poncet (tel. 78-71-70-00), next to place Bellecour. Regular service and Poste Restante open Mon.-Fri. 8am-7pm, Sat. 8am-noon. **Telephone** and telegraph services open Mon.-Sat. 8am-midnight, Sun. 8am-2pm. **Postal Code:** 69002.

Airport: Aéroport Lyon-Satolas, 30km east of Lyon (tel. 72-22-72-21). Direct flights to Paris, London, Berlin, Casablanca. **Satobuses** leave from Perrache via Part-Dieu (Mon.-Fri. 5am-9pm every 20 min., Sat. 1-9pm and Sun. every 30 min.; 45 min.; 35F).

Train Stations: There are two, the most central being **Perrache,** on the southern part of the strip of land between the Saône and Rhône rivers (tel. 78-92-50-50). Sprawling mall with shops, bars, and currency exchange (open daily 5am-midnight). SOS Voyageurs here offers a place to leave bags, get oriented, and, if you're stuck, find lodgings. Open 8am-7pm, but there is a 24-hour bell you can ring if necessary. The SNCF information and reservation desk is open Mon.-Sat. 8am-7:30pm, Sun. 9am-noon and 2-6:30pm. **Part-Dieu,** in the middle of the business district of the same name, and southeast of Perrache. Thomas Cook Exchange office. Open daily 7am-9pm. Also has a blissfully understanding SOS Voyageurs staff. TGV

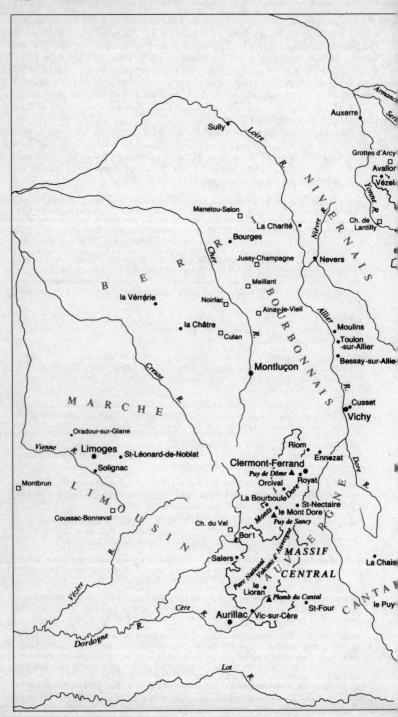

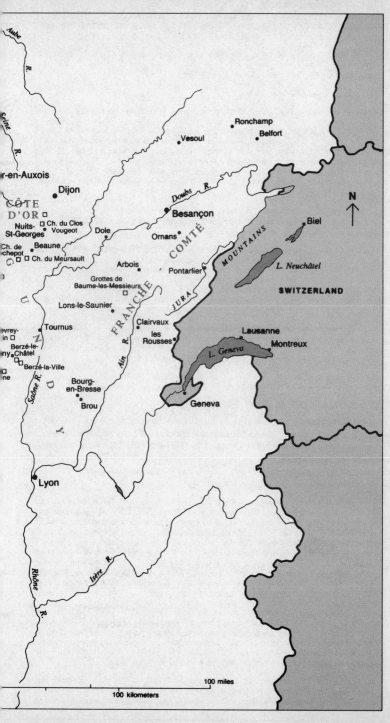

trains to Paris (7 per day, 2 hr., 250F). Trains to Dijon (12 per day, 2-2½ hr., 110F), Grenoble (12 per day, 2 hr., 130F), Strasbourg (8 per day, 7 hr., 130F), Geneva (7 per day, 2 hr., 90F), Marseille (every 2 hr., 3-4 hr., 180F), Nice (every 2 hr., 6 hr., 250F).

Bus Station: On the bottom floor of the Perrache train station (tel. 78-42-27-39). Open daily 6:30am-7pm. To Annecy (2 per day, 4 hr., 60F), Vienne (3-4 per day, 35 min., 28.50F), Annonay (3-4 per day, 2 hr., 60F), Grenoble (67F).

Taxis: Taxis Lyonnaise, Tel. 78-26-81-81.

Police: Place Antonin Poncet (tel. 78-42-49-91), next to place Bellecour and the post office.

Hitching: For Paris, the *autoroute* approaches are difficult to hitch on; take bus #2, 5, 19, 21, 22, or 31, and stand past pont Monton at the intersection with the N6. For Grenoble, take bus #39 as far as the rotary at bd. Pinel. Sad to say, there have been tales of 3-day waits for rides out of Lyon. **Allostop,** 8, rue de la Bombarde (tel. 78-42-38-29), will match you with a driver for a 40F fee plus 0.16F per km. Open Mon.-Fri. 3:30-6:30pm, Sat. 10am-noon. **Lyon Stop,** 29, rue Pasteur (tel. 78-58-65-29). Open Mon.-Thurs. 9am-noon and 1-6pm, Fri. 9am-noon and 1-5pm.

Laundromat: 10, rue Mourget. Take pont Bonaparte across the Saône to the old city, and follow the street; the laundromat is on your left just before place St-Jean. Wash 15F per 7kg, dry 2F per 10 min. Open daily 7am-9pm.

Disabled People: L'Association des Paralysés de France, 23, rue Sala (tel. 78-38-01-18). Has information and publishes a guide listing disabled-access for all of Lyon, *Guide d'Accessibilité pour Personnes Handicapées,* available also at the place Bellecour tourist office.

All-night pharmacy: Pharmacie Blanchet, 5, place des Cordeliers (tel. 78-42-12-42), in the *centre ville* between pont Lafayette and rue de la République. For each neighborhood's *pharmacie de garde,* consult newspapers or any pharmacy's door.

Medical Emergency: Hôpital Edouard Herriot, 5, place Arsonval (tel. 78-53-81-11). Best-equipped to handle serious emergencies, but far from center of town. For little boo-boos, go to **Hôpital Hôtel-Dieu,** 1, place de l'Hôpital (tel. 78-42-70-80), near quai du Rhône. **SOS Médecin,** Tel. 78-83-51-51. For home visits. **SAMU** ambulances, Tel. 15.

Police Emergency: Tel. 17.

Accommodations and Camping

A financial center, Lyon fills with business people during the week. The centrally located hotels are often packed Monday to Thursday nights and then empty over the weekend. However, even if the hotels near Perrache are full, cheap accommodations abound in *centre ville.* Also try the hotels near place des Terreaux, which are less popular with the financial types. CROUS (see Practical Information) has information on lodgings in dorms for longer stays.

Auberge de Jeunesse (IYHF), 51, rue Roger Salengro, Vénissieux (tel. 78-76-39-23), in a suburb of Lyon. Take the metro to Bellecour and bus #35 to George Lévy (30 min.); after 9pm, take bus #53 from Perrache to Etats-Unis-Viviani, and walk ½km along the train tracks. From Part-Dieu, take bus #36 to Vivani Joliot-Curie (last bus at 11:15pm, but call ahead if you'll be late). Big (130 beds), friendly cinderblock hostel. Almost always room; but it is a good idea during summer to check-in early. They'll set up a cot if all beds are full. Bar upstairs serves drinks and food for 10-20F until about 10pm. Especially in Sept. there are grape-picking jobs listed at the hostel. 34F per night. Breakfast 11F. No lockout, but office closed noon-5pm. You cannot use the bedrooms then, but other facilities are open. Curfew 11:30pm. Hostel card required (50F for ages 18-26).

Centre International de Séjour, 46, rue du Commandant Pegoud (tel. 78-01-23-45), far from the center of town. From Perrache, take bus #53 to Etats-Unis-Beauvisage (last bus at 11:30pm, 15 min.). From Part-Dieu, take bus #36. A hopping place with 24-hour check-in. You can hear any language from Italian to Hindi. Modern but crowded rooms, almost as expensive as a hotel in town. Singles 95F, doubles 75F, triples 65F, quads 60F (all prices per person). Self-service meals from 30F. Showers and breakfast included.

Residence Benjamin Delessert, 145, av. Jean Jaurès (tel. 78-72-86-77). From Perrache, take any bus that goes to J. Macé, walk under the train tracks for about 5-10 min., and look to your left. From Part-Dieu, take the subway to Macé. Large, plain dorm rooms with comfortable beds. Singles 58F. Doubles 53F per person. Breakfast 8F. Full meals 23F. Open July-Aug.

Hôtel Croix-Pâquet, 11, place Croix-Pâquet (tel. 78-28-51-49), in Terreaux. Walk up rue Romarin from place des Terreaux to place Croix-Pâquet. Enter from the 4th floor off the courtyard. Soothingly snug rooms. Singles 80F. Doubles 100F, with shower 130F. Showers 10F. Breakfast 15F.

Hôtel Select Home, 22, rue des Capucins (tel. 78-28-26-92), in Terreaux. On the 3rd floor of what must have been a warehouse in the wholesale clothing district. The friendly proprietor speaks English and 10 other languages. Call ahead; the 12 rooms fill fast. Singles 57F, doubles 70F.

Liberty Hotel, 3, rue Jean Larrivée (tel. 78-60-02-65). Cross the Rhône to the east; on Pont de la Guillotière, take your 2nd left—the hotel will be on your right. From the scarlet-painted lobby to the more subtle ornamentation in the large rooms, it is clear that the warm owners take pleasure in improving their hotel. All rooms with showers come with TV. Sometimes full during the week. Singles or doubles 108F, with shower 160F. Triples 170, with shower 190F. Shower 15F. Breakfast 18.50F.

Hôtel Alexandra, 49, rue Victor Hugo, 2ème (tel. 78-37-75-79). This big, old hotel would be perfect, with enormous, renovated rooms and exceptionally pleasant management, if there were hall showers, and if rooms with showers were not so expensive because they come with TV. Often close to filled during the week. Singles 94F, with shower 160F. Doubles 104F, with shower 172F. Triples with shower 199F.

Camping: Dardilly, Tel. 78-35-64-55. An easy bus ride from Lyon: From the Hôtel de Ville take bus #19 (*direction* "Ecully-Dardilly") to the Parc d'Affaires stop. One of the most beautiful camping sites in the Rhône Valley. Bar and restaurant. Open March-Oct.

Food

Some of France's best restaurants and cooking schools are located in Lyon, where the ideal is to allow each ingredient to retain and contribute its particular taste to the finished dish. Although renowned for *haute cuisine* and great chefs, Lyon treasures most the unassuming *mâchon* (snack) offered at her beloved *bouchons*. Only 20 authentic *bouchons* remain. *Bouchon* means cork, and the association is obvious, but it also may refer to the clientele in the old days; they had to rub down (*bouchonner*) their horses before their meal. The essential component of a *bouchon* is a charismatic *patron* (boss) who lets the red wine flow freely, who allows you to come in at any hour, and who produces a tasty, solid *mâchon*. Extremely rich and filling, the fare includes *cochonailles* (hot pork dishes), *tripes à la lyonnaise* (heavy on the onions and vinegar), and *andouillette* (sausage made of chitterlings). The original *bouchons* can be found in Terreaux, although the most pleasant (and tourist-ridden) in Vieux Lyon offer outdoor seating on narrow, cobblestoned streets.

Rue Mercière, near place Bellecour, is not nearly so scenic, but has many restaurants with 50F *menus*. The **university restaurants** in Villeurbanne serve cheap but unappetizing food. Ask at the tourist office for names and locations. Three large open **markets** are held Tuesday through Sunday mornings at quai St-Antoine on bd. de la Croix Rousse (on the Rhône), and on quai Victor Augagneur.

Elie et Henry, 21, rue Jean Larrivée (tel. 78-60-57-32). Cross pont de la Guillotière to the east bank of the Rhône, and continue going straight; rue Jean Larrivée is on your left. Classy atmosphere and good prices for seafood and traditional fare. 41F and 55F *menus*. Open Mon.-Fri. noon-2pm and 7-10pm, Sat. 7-10pm.

La Montaleau, 24, montée St-Sebastien (tel. 78-27-00-28), near the Croix-Pâquet metro stop. Unique meals served in a whimsical room crawling with vines. Delicious vegetarian *pâté* (16F) and hummus platter (20F). Open Sept.-June Mon.-Fri. noon-2pm, Thurs.-Sat. 7:30-11pm.

Titi Lyonnais, 2, rue Chaponnay 3ème (tel. 78-60-83-02), on the east bank of the Rhône by pont Wilson. Popular with locals. *Cuisine lyonnaise.* 62F *menu* with a wide choice and a serving of wine. Open Sept.-June Tues.-Sat. noon-1:30pm and 7:30-9:30pm, Sun. noon-1:30pm.

Café de Jura, 25, rue Tupin (tel. 78-42-20-57), the 6th block north on your left from Hôtel-Dieu. A true *bouchon* run by a charmer with a handle-bar mustache named Henri. New selection of entrées every day (32-55F). Open at 7:30am; lunch noon-2pm, dinner 7:30-10:30pm.

Le 21, 21, quai Romain Rolland (tel. 78-37-34-19). Boasts that it is a genuine *bouchon lyonnais,* but looks more like a fancy nightclub. Delicious food, but plan on spending 75F for a full meal, about average for the area. Open Mon.-Sat. for dinner only.

Garioud, 14, rue du Palais-Grillet (tel. 78-37-04-71), off rue de la République. A restaurant serving great *cuisine lyonnaise;* your least expensive way to sample food of the masters. *Menus* 80F, 155F, and 182F. Open Mon.-Fri. noon-2pm and 7:30-10pm, Sat. 7:30-10pm.

Le Petit Garioud, 26, rue Ferrandière (tel. 78-37-76-27), down the block from "big" Garioud. Elegant. Delicately prepared, if not overabundant, 62F *menu* served in a museum-like atmosphere. Open Mon.-Sat. noon-2pm and 7-11pm.

Sights

Whoever thinks there is nothing to do in Lyon has not yet cultivated a taste for *la flânerie* (strolling). Start at **place Bellecour,** fringed by shops and flower stalls and dominated by an equestrian statue of Louis XIV in the center. If you've been traveling through small towns in Burgundy and desire a big-city atmosphere, head out of the square along rue de la République or its parallel, rue du Président Edouard Herriot, to **Terreaux,** a pleasant *quartier.* At place des Terreaux, the ornate Renaissance **Hôtel de Ville** stands guard opposite the **Musée des Beaux Arts.** Farther north around rue des Capucins and place Croix-Pâquet is a somewhat dilapidated but very vibrant warehouse district, next to a small park.

A brief walk across the Saône leads to the most intriguing part of town, **Vieux Lyon,** a showcase of restored Renaissance architecture along ancient, dark, cobblestoned streets. The old city consists of the St-Paul, St-Georges, and St-Jean quarters. Note the mullioned windows and the many curious details, such as the smirking gargoyle at 11, place Neuve St-Jean, and the spiral staircase at 32, rue Doyenne. During the Renaissance, the intriguing *traboules* (from the Latin *trans ambulare,* to walk across) were built to compensate for the lack of crosswalks. Connecting the neighborhood widthwise, these passages helped protect silk as it was transported through the city in stormy weather. The passages were also used by the Resistance (of which Lyon was the center) to thwart the Nazis, who couldn't find the entrances to the *traboules.* You will have equal trouble visiting the passages unless you have the *Liste des Traboules* from the tourist office. They are closed after dark, which is the best time to see the ancient buildings in Vieux Lyon highlighted by spotlights. These renovated buildings are now the most costly residences in Lyon, forming a lively neighborhood full of people and cafes. Also useful for exploring this area is the booklet *Lyon, Rendez-vous avec la Renaissance.* A particularly interesting church in the St-Jean quarter is **Cathédrale St-Jean,** in the *bourguignon* style. Its northern transept has an astronomical clock that shows the feast days from 600 years ago all the way to the year 2000. (Open Mon.-Fri. 7:30am-noon and 2-7:30pm, Sat.-Sun. 2-5pm.)

Documents and photos of the Lyon Resistance are displayed in the **Musée de la Résistance,** 5, rue Boileau, on the east bank of the Rhône. (Open Wed.-Sun. 10:30am-noon and 1-6pm. Free.) Dedicated to the culture of West Africa, an integral part of France's colonial history and current economy, the fine **Musée Africain** is located at 150, cours Gambetta. Cross pont de la Guillotière to the east bank of the Rhône and continue a few blocks straight along cours Gambetta. (Open Wed.-Sun. 2-6pm. Admission 10F.)

From the **Fourvière Esplanade** above Vieux Lyon, you can gaze down on the urban sprawl. On the summit of the hill, built at the insistence of Lyon women, rises the extravagant nineteenth-century **Basilique de Fourvière,** as over-stuffed as the confections in the *pâtisseries* below. (Open daily 8am-noon and 2-6pm.) On the descent, you will pass the still-used (from opera to rock) **Théâtre Romain.** (Open daily 9am-nightfall. Free.) This hillside marks the site where Lugdunum was founded in 43 B.C.E. Julius Caesar made the colony the commercial and military center of Gaul. Also on the Fourvière hill, the **Musée Gallo-Romain,** 17, rue Cléberg, displays a collection of mosaics, swords, rings, statues, and money from Lyon's Roman past. (Open Wed.-Sun. 9:30am-noon and 2-6pm. Free.)

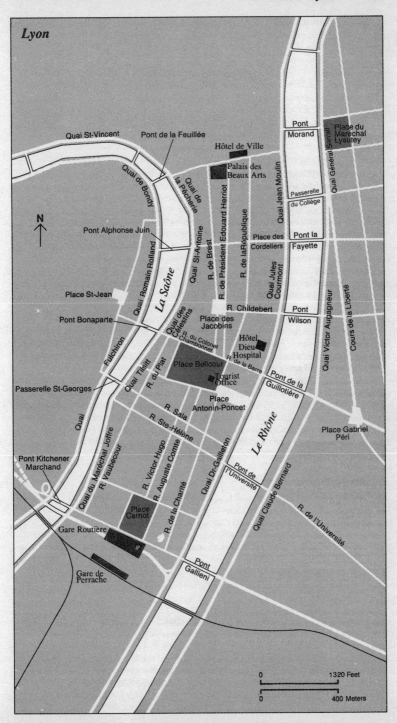

Lyon

Quai St-Vincent
Pont de la Feuillée
Hôtel de Ville
Palais des Beaux Arts
Quai de Bondy
Quai de la Pêcherie
Quai de la Pêcherie
Pont Morand
Place du Maréchal Lyautey
Quai Général Sarrail
Quai Jean Moulin
Passerelle du Collège
Pont Alphonse Juin
Quai Romain Rolland
Quai St-Antoine
R. de Brest
R. de Président Edouard Herriot
R. de la République
Place des Cordeliers
Pont la Fayette
N
La Saône
Quai Jules Courmont
Quai Victor Augagneur
Cours de la Liberté
Place St-Jean
R. Childebert
Pont Wilson
Pont Bonaparte
Quai des Célestins
R. du Colonel Chambonnet
Place des Jacobins
Hôtel Dieu Hospital
R. de la Barre
Fulchiron
Quai Tilsitt
R. du Plat
Place Bellecour
Tourist Office
Pont de la Guillotière
Passerelle St-Georges
Quai
Le Rhône
R. Sala
Place Antonin-Poncet
Place Gabriel Péri
R. Ste-Hélène
Quai Dr-Gailleton
Pont Kitchener Marchand
Quai du Maréchal Joffre
R. Vaubecour
R. Victor Hugo
R. Auguste Comte
R. de la Charité
Pont de l'Université
Quai Claude Bernard
R. de l'Université
Place Carnot
Gare Routière
Pont Gallieni
Gare de Perrache

0   1320 Feet
0   400 Meters

In jarring contrast to Vieux Lyon, modern Lyon is made up of sleek buildings and space-age conveniences. Worth a visit for its ultra-modern train station is the **District Part-Dieu.** Those with shopping to do will surely find what they want in the immense shopping complex opposite the station. The **Tour Crédit Lyonnais,** on the other side of the mall, symbolizes commercial Lyon. Next to it, the **Auditorium Maurice Ravel** beautifully exemplifies functional modern architecture.

There are 26 museums in Lyon—pick up a list at the *syndicat.* The **Musée des Beaux Arts** in the Palais St-Pierre houses a large and exciting collection of paintings and sculpture that includes works by Spanish and Dutch masters (El Greco, Zurbarán, Rembrandt, and Ruisdael), two rooms of impressionism (Manet, Monet, Morisot, Sisley, Renoir, Dégas, Van Gogh), and several rooms of excellent early twentieth-century canvases (Picasso, Matisse, Dufy, and more). (Open Wed.-Sun. 10:30am-6pm. Free.) After rushing through the exhibits, you can take a breather in the beautiful sculpture garden in the museum's courtyard.

Lyon seems to revel in its former position as center of the European silk industry. At the turn of the eighteenth century, 28,000 looms operated in Lyon. Working in a sweat-shop atmosphere, the silk workers were driven to riot against the profiteers that controlled the business. Although silk manufacturing is based elsewhere today, you can see an extraordinary collection of silk and embroidery ranging from the Coptic to the oriental at the **Musée Historique des Tissues,** 34, rue de la Charité. (Open Tues.-Sun. 10am-noon and 2-5:30pm. Admission 12F.) The **Musée Lyonnais des Arts Decoratifs,** down the street, displays porcelain, silver, and tapestry from various periods in the history of French furniture. (Open Tues.-Sun. 10am-noon and 2-5:30pm. Free with ticket from Musée des Tissues.) **La Maison des Canuts,** 10-12, rue d'Ivry, demonstrates the actual weaving techniques of the *canuts lyonnais* (silk workers), best known for their velvet and silk artisanship. (Open Mon.-Sat. 9am-noon and 2-6pm. Admission 4F.) **The Musée des Marionettes** in Hôtel Gadagne exhibits the famous Lyon puppets, including Guignol, as well as an international collection. (Open Wed.-Mon. 10:45am-6pm. Free.)

When urban fatigue sets in, leave the city noise behind for the roses of the **Parc de la Tête d'Or,** Lyon's botanical garden. Here you can bounce about on a pony or in a go-cart and tour the park in a mini-train. (Open in summer daily 6am-10pm; in off-season 8am-8pm.) And for something completely different, take a boat trip along the Saône and Rhône. Boats leave from quai des Célestins (April-Nov. daily 2pm, 3pm, 5pm, and 6pm for an hour-long trip). Contact **Navig'Inter,** 3, rue de l'Arbre-Sec (tel. 78-27-78-02), for more information.

Entertainment

Lyon supports a variety of resident theaters as well as an opera company, but the highlight of its cultural activities comes during the month of June with one of two annually alternating music and dance festivals. (Obtain schedules from the tourist office.) The first weekend of September, you can see big puppet parades and little puppet theaters at the **Festival International de la Marionette,** in the Centre Commercial Part-Dieu (tel. 78-62-90-13). **Le Nouveau Guignol de Lyon** also stages puppet shows for adults in winter. (Sept. 15-June 15. Admission 42F.) For information, call 78-37-31-79. On summer afternoons, free children's puppet shows take place in the Parc de la Tête-d'Or.

Starting on July 1, a host of international jazz celebrities invades Vienne, a town right outside Lyon and accessible by bus or train. The **Festival du Jazz à Vienne** lasts almost two weeks and features many free outdoor concerts by jazz stars of every stylistic persuasion. (Tickets 105F, students 95F.) For information, call 74-85-00-05 or the Vienne *office de tourisme* (tel. 74-85-12-62). There is a youth hostel in Vienne (tel. 74-53-21-97). The **Festival Hector Berlioz** is just that—a week of his music, performed and discussed. The festival takes place during the third week of September in odd-numbered years in La Côte St-André, not far from Lyon. (Call 78-60-85-40 for more information.) December 8, windows light up with candles and streets fill with parades for the **Fête de la Vierge,** to honor the Virgin Mary for having protected Lyon from the plague. This has been a tradition since 1852.

The tourist office keeps on top of nightlife and can give you an updated list. The disco **Cercle des Arts,** 17, rue Désiré, juggles everything: dancing, comedy, magic shows (tel. 78-30-82-59). (Open Wed.-Sun. 10pm-dawn.) At **J.M. Pub,** 15, rue Ste-Catherine (tel. 78-29-45-47), Saturday night is drag queen night in a comfortable bar with arm chairs and videos. (Open daily 5pm-1am.) Lesbians will enjoy the bar **Damier,** 8, rue St-Georges (tel. 78-38-07-09), which turns into a disco on Friday and Saturday. (Open Sun.-Tues. and Thurs. 5pm-1am; Wed., Fri., and Sat. 5pm-3am.) A particularly welcoming **Club Caraïbes,** 5, rue Terme (tel. 78-28-50-55), has drinking and dancing to Caribbean and African beats. (Open Fri.-Sat. 10pm-5am.) To find out what is going on in Lyon every week, pick up a copy of the *Lyon-Poche,* available at newsstands for 7.50F.

Near Lyon: Bourg-en-Bresse

Once the center of a druidic cult, Bourg-en-Bresse, 60km northeast of Lyon, now puts everything into its poultry industry and large **animal fairs,** held on the first and third Wednesday of each month. Animal husbandry aside, you would do well to focus your attention on marvelous **Eglise de Brou.** Constructed between 1505 and 1536 at the behest of Margaret of Austria as a tomb for her husband, the church is built in the Flamboyant Gothic style; its western facade is a marvel of Gothic decoration. The tomb of Philibert le Beau lies in the middle of the building, flanked by the tombs of his wife and his mother. (Open daily June-Sept. 9am-7pm; Oct.-March 10am-noon and 2-6:30pm.) Take bus #2 from the train station to the center of Bourg-en-Bresse (place Carriat), and change to #1 to Brou. Also worth a visit are the sixteenth-century Gothic **Eglise Notre-Dame** and **rue Bourgmayer,** where most of the remaining old houses of the city stand. The town puts on a *son et lumière* every Thursday, Saturday, and Sunday at 9:30pm from June to September.

The **Syndicat d'Initiative,** 6, av. Alsace-Lorraine (tel. 74-22-49-40), makes free room reservations and outlines a walking tour by pamphlet. (Open June 15-Sept. 15 Mon.-Sat. 8:30am-7:30pm; Sept. 16-June 14 Mon.-Sat. 8:30am-noon and 2-6:30pm.) The **train station,** av. P. Sémard, has hourly departures to Lyon, and frequent service to Dijon and Mâcon. Bourg is also a TGV stop on the Paris-Geneva line. Should you decide to stay, you'll easily find accommodations on av. A. Baudin, opposite the station. Try **La Genève,** 24, av. A. Baudin (tel. 74-21-02-59), which has singles for 90F, with bath 120F. Breakfast is 15F. There is also a **campground** on *terrain municipal* (tel. 74-22-27-79; open March-Oct.). **Chez Mémé,** 24, bd. de Brou (tel. 74-22-36-82), serves good *menus* from 40F.

Moulins

The town came into being in the tenth century when Archambault, a member of the French royal family, built his mistress a château on the river Allier. Moulins was named for the water wheels mounted on boats that positioned themselves in the strongest river currents. These characteristic barges had the unfortunate habit of running into other boats, and this inconvenient energy system was soon shelved. Today, only a part of Archambault's humble gift, the **Château des Ducs,** still stands, and the former capital of the *Bourbonnais* relaxes with quiet courtyards and a *vieille ville* of half-timbered houses. On place de l'Hôtel de Ville in the center of town, the sixteenth-century **Jacquemart** clock tower chimes every 15 minutes. The mechanical figures Jacques, Jacquette (his wife), Jacquelin and Jacqueline (their son and daughter) cheerfully parcel out the flow of time.

Stop by the tourist office and pick up their pamphlet (in English) that outlines a walking tour of the *vieille ville.* The tour stops at the house where Joan of Arc stayed, at the ruins of the **Château d'Anne de Beaujeu,** and at the **Cathédrale Notre Dame.** Stained-glass windows of Anne de Beaujeu and Pierre II de Bourbon in prayer, a Flamboyant Gothic choir and ambulatory, and the famous **Triptyque du Maître de Moulins** all recommend the beautiful cathedral. (*Tryptique* open daily 9am-noon and 2-6pm. Admission 9F, students 5F.) The tour concludes at the peak of the cathedral's tower, whence you can enjoy the best view of Moulins. The **Musée de Folklore et des Moulins**, 6, place de l'Ancien Palais (tel. 70-44-39-03), exhibits a substantial collection of old farm tools, household irons, hats, dolls, and religious statues. (Open Fri.-Wed. 10am-noon and 3-6:30pm. Admission 10F.) The **Musée d'Art et d'Archéologie**, place du Colonel Laussedat (tel. 70-44-22-98), features artifacts from the Egyptians to the nineteenth century. (Open Wed.-Mon. 10am-noon and 2-6pm. Admission 10F.)

Moulins sits on the east bank of the river Allier. From the train station, take av. du Général Leclerc straight ahead until you hit a building. Pick yourself up, dust yourself off, take a left, and take a right on rue de l'Horloge for the tourist office. The **Office de Tourisme**, place de l'Hôtel de Ville (tel. 70-44-14-14), across from the Jacquemart, has free maps, a list of all hotels and restaurants in Moulins, and a self-guided walking tour of the old town. (Open June 15-Sept. 15 Mon.-Sat. 9am-noon and 2-7pm, Sun. 9am-noon; Sept. 15-June 15 Tues.-Sat. 9am-noon and 2-6:30pm.) The **post office**, 6, rue Théodore de Banville (tel. 70-20-13-86), at rue Berthelot, has **currency exchange.** Moulins's **postal code** is 03000. (Post office open Mon.-Fri. 8am-7pm, Sat. 8am-noon.) About 6 trains per day run to Lyon (2¼ hr., 55F) and Bourges (1 hr., 62F). More than 10 per day run to Clermont-Ferrand (1½ hr., 64F). (Information office open Mon.-Sat. 9am-7pm, Sun. 9am-noon and 2-6:45pm. Call 70-46-50-50.) **Société Lyonnaise**, 23, av. Théodore Banville, is about the only bank open during lunch. (Open Mon.-Thurs. 8am-4:50pm, Fri. 8am-3:50pm.)

The **Foyer des Jeunes Travailleurs**, 60, rue de Bourgogne, functions as the local auberge de jeunesse. This friendly hostel occupies an old townhouse with a spacious garden, a TV room, a ping-pong table, a volleyball court and washing machines (4F). There is almost always space. (Singles and doubles 40F, without hostel card 50F. Breakfast 11F, sheets 15F. Lunch or dinner (Mon.-Fri. only) 28F. Reception open Mon.-Fri. 6:30am-midnight, Sat. 7am-midnight, Sun. 9am-midnight.) The **Hôtel de l'Agriculture**, 15, cours Vincent d'Indy (tel. 70-44-08-58), has an old-fashioned porch entrance and a bar, replete with birdcages. (Singles 70F. Doubles 80F, with shower 110F. Breakfast 18F.) **La Taverne de France**, 8, rue des Bouchers (tel. 70-44-04-82), much closer to the center of town, features doubles with stained carpets for 65F and a jolly bunch of locals in the bar downstairs. The **Camping Municipal** (tel. 70-44-19-29) is on the river, just south of Moulins's one-automobile bridge about 2km from the station. (4.20F per person, 2.10F per site, 2.10F per car. Open June-Sept. but some people pitch tents earlier and later.)

Nevers

At the confluence of the Loire and the Allier rivers, the landscape of Nevers, made famous by Marguerite Duras's novel and screenplay, *Hiroshima, mon amour,* more closely resembles the gentle farmland and forests of neighboring Berry than the Morvan or the vineyards of Burgundy. Carefully tended parks and squares separate dainty streets lined with shops. Life here proceeds at a peaceful, relaxed pace. The city revolves around place Carnot. From the train station, head straight on av. Général de Gaulle for 4 blocks. The **Office de Tourisme**, 31, rue du Rempart (tel. 86-54-07-03), will be on your right, across the square. Ask for the brochure *Bienvenue à Nevers,* which describes architectural landmarks in the area. They also operate an accommodation service (5F) and distribute information on visiting the local châteaux by car. (Open Mon.-Sat. 9am-12:30pm and 2-6:30pm.) The **post office,** square J.B. Thevenard, has **currency exchange.** (Open Mon.-Fri. 8am-6:30pm, Sat. 8am-noon, and holidays that fall on Mon. or Sat. 8am-noon.) Nevers's **postal code** is 58000. The **Centre d'Accueil Universitaire**, 57, Faubourg du Grand Mouësse (tel. 86-30-00-02), can help travelers find cheap housing. **Trains** from the Loire Valley and the Massif Central pass through Nevers to Dijon (4-5 per day, 3 hr., 114F), Lyon (6 per day, 3 hr., 133F), and Paris (8 per day, 2½ hr., 133F). **Bike rental** is available at the station (35F per ½-day, 45F per day, deposit 300F). The **Hôtel de la Paix,** 50, av. Général de Gaulle (tel. 86-57-23-93), approaches elegance. (Singles and doubles 68F, with shower 120F. Breakfast 17F. Lunch and dinner *menus* 50F.) The **Hôtel Villa du Parc,** 16-18, rue de Lourdes (tel. 86-61-09-48), has bright, flowery rooms and a luxurious TV lounge; Nevers's big park is right across the street. (Singles and doubles 70-75F, with bathroom 125F. Extra bed 35F. Breakfast 16.50F.) The **Hôtel de l'Avenue,** 38, av. Colbert (tel. 86-01-01-97), is a bit distant but a good bargain. (Doubles 60-65F. Ask for a key if out past 11pm.) The **Camping Municipal** (tel. 86-37-56-52), with a nearby swimming pool, is on the other side of the river. From the cathedral, follow rue de la Cathédrale to the river, cross the bridge, and turn left. (4.20F per person, 2.10F per tent. Open March-Oct.) An indoor **market** takes place every morning but Sunday on av. Général de Gaulle just before place Carnot. The cafeteria **Le Paris,** 7, place Guy Coquille offers large servings for little money in a tolerable atmosphere. (Open Mon.-Sat. 11am-2:30pm and 6-9:30pm.)

Sights

To the right of place Carnot, coming from the train station, stands the **Cathédrale St-Cyr et Ste-Juliette,** a melange of architectural styles developed between the tenth and sixteenth centuries. The rare blend is exemplified by the two chapels at the front of the nave: One, to the west, is in a somber Roman style; the other, to the east, is Flamboyant Gothic. Opposite the cathedral, the **Palais Ducal,** a beautiful example of Renaissance architecture, offers a majestic view of the Loire. Less visited than other comparable churches, the beautiful eleventh-century **Eglise St-Etienne** is built of several circular chapels radiating from the circular nave. As you walk up av. Général de Gaulle from the train station to place Carnot, look for the remains of the town fortifications on your right. The **Porte du Croux,** the strong tower housing the guards' rooms, now harbors a Romanesque sculpture museum (open Wed. and Sat. 2-4pm). From Porte du Croux, explore the stretch of gardens that hedges in the old ramparts down to the river.

Nevers is also known for its fine ceramics, some of which perch delicately in the **Musée de Faïences,** rue St-Genest. (Open Wed.-Mon. 10am-12:30pm and 2-6:30pm. Admission 5F.) Four *faïence* factories still exist in the city, the oldest dating from the seventeenth century.

Near Nevers: La Charité-sur-Loire

Twenty-three kilometers north of Nevers (an easy 25-min. train ride), the red roofs, church spire, and ramparts of La Charité emerge from the greenery on the banks of the Loire. Founded in the eleventh century by Cluniac monks, La Charité grew in power and wealth until it was known as "the older sister" of Cluny, with 400 dependent monasteries throughout Europe. Pilgrims often stopped here on the way to Santiago de Compostela. However, a fire in 1559 and then the Wars of Religion wrought almost total destruction. Given to the Protestants as part of the peace settlement, La Charité slowly declined; only 12 monks remained by the time of the Revolution.

Important because of its church and monastery, tiny La Charité makes a pleasant daytrip. The monastery is slowly being restored, although a three-day fire in the nineteenth century destroyed most of the buildings. The impressive twelfth-century **Eglise Notre-Dame** dominates the town with its Romanesque tower and monastery. Finely crafted stained-glass windows illuminate the simple and elegant interior. The short climb from the church to the ramparts will reward you with a splendid view of the town's medieval houses and the river.

Those wishing to spend the night should try the **Hôtel La Terminus,** 23, av. Gambetta. (Open Tues.-Sat.) Across the bridge, **Camping de la Saulaie** (tel. 86-70-00-

83) enjoys its own view of the Loire and is near a swimming pool and beach. (Open June 15-Sept. 15.) A picnic lunch on the ramparts with food from a *boulangerie* is the best way to cope with the dearth of high-quality, inexpensive restaurants in La Charité. The **Bar de la Plage,** located just across the river, to the right at the end of the bridge, has a pleasant view of the Loire and the city. From the station, take a left on av. de la Gare and then a right on av. Gambetta to reach the center of town. The **Syndicat d'Initiative,** 49, Grande-Rue (tel. 86-70-16-12), opposite the Hôtel de Ville, will give you information on the monastery and La Charité's other sights. (Open Mon.-Sat. 10:30am-noon and 3-6:30pm.) The **train station** (tel. 86-70-03-02) is located at the top of the hill to the east of town. The station also rents **bicycles.**

Bourges

Bourges wallowed in glory between 1422 and 1437 as the capital of France and the stronghold of Charles VII's power. Now Bourges plays a more modest role as the capital of Berry; it still has not lost all its pomp, however. The magnificent cathedral and imposing château transport the imagination back to the time of Charles VII's wars against the English Angevins and Burgundians. Modern Bourges has developed into quite a cultural center; the spring festival attracts visitors from all over France.

Orientation and Practical Information

Bourges is 221km from Paris and sits on the major train route between Orléans (105km) and the Loire Valley to the north, and Montluçon (93km) and the Massif Central to the south. The medium-sized city is a maze of small streets within a roughly pentagonal traffic ring. Avenue H. Laudrier, along with its continuation, avenue Jean Jaurès, leads directly south from the train station to this ring, in which rue Moyenne is the principal north-south artery.

Office de Tourisme: 21, rue Victor Hugo (tel. 48-24-75-33), by the cathedral. 15 min. from the train station. Head straight from the station on av. H. Laudier, which becomes av. Jean Jaurès. Bear left onto rue du Commerce, which becomes rue Moyenne and leads to the office. Efficient, friendly, English-speaking staff. Request the larger, more detailed map. Accommodations service (5F). 2-hr. walking tours (French only) leave July-Sept. daily (14F, students 11F); night tours July-Sept. Fri.-Sat. at 8:15pm (20F, students 16F). Open July-Sept. 15 Mon.-Sat. 9am-12:30pm and 1:30-7pm; Sept. 16-June Mon.-Sat. 9am-noon and 2-6pm.

Currency Exchange: Banks closed Mon. except **Crédit Agricole,** 69, rue d'Auron. Open Mon.-Fri. 8:30am-noon and 1:45-5pm. More convenient to the center is **Banque Nationale de Paris,** 43, rue Moyenne. Open Tues.-Sat. 8:30am-noon and 1:40-5:15pm.

Post Office: 29, rue Moyenne (tel. 48-24-21-01). **Currency exchange** and **telephones. Postal Code:** 18000. Open Mon.-Fri. 8am-7pm, Sat. 8am-noon.

Train Station: Place Général Leclerc (tel. 48-65-50-50). Bourges is just off the main north-south train line. Many destinations require a transfer at nearby Vierzon. About 6 trains per day to Paris (2½ hr., 123F), Orléans (1¼ hr., 65F), Tours (1½ hr., 82F), and Lyon (3¼ hr., 162F). 10 per day to Clermont-Ferrand (2½ hr., 114F). Information office open daily 9am-7pm.

Bus Station: Gare Routière, rue du Champs de Foire (tel. 48-24-36-42). Easy connections to La Charité (1 hr. 20 min.), and Jussy-Champagne and Châteauneuf (40 min. each). Unfortunately, buses leaving for the châteaux along route Jacques-Coeur depart in the evening and return the following morning. Reduced service during school vacations.

Car Rental: Locomat, 29, av. Jean Jaurès (tel. 48-24-02-94). 260F per day includes unlimited mileage and all taxes. Discounts on longer rentals. Minimum age 23. Deposit 1500F. You must return car to Bourges.

Bike Rental: At the **youth hostel.** Members: 15F per ½-day, 25F per day, and 150F per week. Nonmembers: 20F per ½-day, 30F per day. Student ID and 250F deposit. Also at the **train station** (tel. 48-24-58-09). 35F per ½-day, 45F per day, deposit 300F.

Hitching: For Lyon, the Alps, and the Midi, take rue Jean Baffier (bus #3 for N153). For Tours and Orléans, av. d'Orléans at av. des Près de Roi (N76). For Paris, av. de Général de Gaulle (N140).

Laundromat: 117, rue Edouard Valliant. Wash 20F, dry 5F per 12 min. Open daily 7am-8pm. Also at 79, av. Marcel Haegelan. Open daily 7am-8pm.

Showers: Centre Nautique Municipal de Bourges, 11, av. du 11 Novembre (tel. 48-24-42-90). Open Thurs.-Sat. 9:30am-12:30pm and 1:30-7pm, Fri. 9am-12:30pm and 1:30-7:30pm, Sun. 8am-12:30pm. Showers 5.40F, bath 7.10F.

Battered Women: Tel. 48-24-87-65.

Pharmacy: Pharmacie Centrale, 11, rue Moyenne. Open Tues.-Fri. 9am-noon and 2-7pm, Sat. 9am-noon and 2-6pm.

Hospital: Centre Hospitalier, 34, rue Gambon (tel. 48-68-40-00).

Police: 6, av. d'Orléans (tel. 48-24-42-46).

Police Emergency: Tel. 17.

Accommodations and Camping

Hotels in Bourges are rather scarce, rather expensive, and often closed in August. You might want to let the tourist office find you a room.

Auberge de Jeunesse (IYHF), 22, rue Henri Sellier (tel. 48-24-58-09), in a wooded site overlooking a stream. A 10-min. walk from the center of town, but a good 25 min. from the train station. Walk straight from the station down av. H. Laudrier, and turn right onto bd. Gambetta to bd. Juranville and bd. d'Auron; turn left onto Lamarck, right onto Messire Jacques, and left onto rue Henri Sellier. Or take bus #1 from the station, get off at Château-d'Eau, turn right on rue Charles Cochet, and right again onto rue Henri Sellier (5 min.). Basic, above-average hostel with a well-equipped kitchen, TV room, and washing machines (10F, dry 2F per 5 min.). 34F, nonmembers 49F. Sheets 12F, sleeping bag 8F. Breakfast 11F, dinner 34F. Popular with school groups, but there is almost always space during the summer. Office open 7-10am and 5-10pm. Curfew 11pm (negotiable).

Hôtel L'Etape, 4, rue Raphael Cassanova (tel. 48-70-59-47), just off rue Juranville. Tucked into a quiet street close to downtown area. Kind managers. Clean singles and doubles 80F. Breakfast 14F. Closed in Aug. for 15 days.

Au Rendez-vous des Amis, 6, av. Marc Dormoy (tel. 48-70-81-80). A hike from the center, but a 5-min. walk from the train station. Turn left onto av. Pierre Semard from the station and then right after the overpass. The cheapest place in town. Often filled with workers. Singles 65F. Doubles 70F. Breakfast 14F. Open Jan. 2-Dec. 24.

Hôtel de la Nation, 24, place de la Nation (tel. 48-24-11-96). Slightly cramped but in a good location. Singles 80F. Doubles 95F. Showers 13F. Breakfast 18F. Open Mon.-Sat., closed last 2 weeks in Aug. and at the end of the year.

Camping: Camping Municipal, 26, bd. de l'Industrie (tel. 48-20-16-85). Follow directions to the hostel, but continue on rue Henri Sellier away from *centre ville,* and turn right on bd. de l'Industrie. Open March 15-Nov. 15.

Food

Restaurants can be expensive; you might have to spend 50F to sample the local cuisine. The area around place Gordaine is filled with reputable, slightly expensive restaurants. A winter specialty is *poulet en barbouille,* chicken roasted in the regional red wine. Ask at any *boulangerie* for the local *galette de pommes de terre,* a flat potato cake usually served hot. The best-known local cheese is *chavignot,* which you can buy at the huge **farmer's market** held Saturday mornings at place de la Nation. The other big market takes place on Thursday until 1pm at place des Marronniers. Smaller markets occur Wednesday at la Chancellerie, Friday at place Gordaine, and Sunday at place St-Bonnet.

Chez Charles, 19, rue des Ecoles (tel. 24-80-18-02), just off rue Juranville. Receive a robust "bon appétit" from the cook. 4-course *menu* 33F.

Au Rendez-vous des Amis, 6, av. Marx Dornoy (tel. 48-70-81-80), beneath the hotel of the same name. Friendly, family-style restaurant. 5-course *menus* 38F and 42F. Open daily.

La Main à la Pat, 108, rue Bourbonnoux, behind the cathedral. Warm atmosphere, with loud chattering and a wood fire for pizzas (21F and up). Pesto 30F. Seafood pizza 43F. Take-out pizza also. Open Tues.-Sun. noon-2pm and 7pm-midnight.

Au Sénat, 8, rue de la Poissonnerie (tel. 48-24-02-56), off place Gordaine. One of the most affordable places for local food such as *poulet en barbouille* (similar to *coq au vin,* 42F) and *crotin* cheese (warmed and served on toast, 32F); but expensive nonetheless—the "tourist" *menu* is 67.50F. The wood-paneled, fire-warmed dining room creates an authentic atmosphere that's worth the price.

Comptoir Mirebeau, 59, rue Mirebeau (tel. 48-65-77-86). Unpretentious, decent, and cheap. Serves a 28F *plat du jour* on an otherwise overpriced street. Open 11am-11pm.

Sights and Entertainment

Cathédrale St-Etienne, one of France's most beautiful monuments, is a spectacular Gothic accomplishment visible for miles around. Five elaborately sculpted portals embellish the thirteenth-century facade. The center portal, with a chilling representation of the Last Judgment in the tympanum, is considered a Gothic masterpiece. In the center of the facade gleams a rose window, 10m in diameter. The interior of the cathedral gives the impression of fragility with its exceptionally tall nave that's supported by narrow piers with slender pillars surrounding the central column. The beautiful stained-glass windows of 1215-1225 remain remarkably well preserved. Come on a sunny day and watch them glow from gold to blue. The first medallioned window on the north side (on the left as you face the altar) shows the story of Lazarus and the Last Judgment. The two bright tapestries just to the left of the south door represent St-Etienne and his miracles. (Open daily 7am-noon and 2-6pm.)

If you have time, visit the cathedral's **tower** and **crypt** (also known as the Eglise Souterraine or Underground Church). Not much remains in the crypt except for a white marble figure of the Duke of Berry. The grotesque figures in the opening corridor are wonderfully repulsive—there's even a medieval mooner to greet you. Twelve large windows grace the crypt, so you won't be left completely in the dark. The obligatory half-hour tour leaves at times marked next to the north entrance. (Open Mon.-Sat. 9-11:30am and 2-5:30pm, Sun. 2-5:30pm. Admission 15F, ages 18-24 and over 60 9F.) A splendid half-hour audio-visual presentation with period music traces the artistic heritage of Bourges and Berry. (June-Sept. Tues.-Sat. at 10:30am, 2:30pm, 3:30pm, and 4:30pm, Sun. no morning shows; July-Aug. additional shows at 10am and 11am. Free.)

The **Palais Jacques-Coeur,** built by Charles VII's powerful and talented minister of finance, remains one of the most sumptuous urban buildings from the late Middle Ages, every bit as extravagant as the châteaux of the Loire, yet eminently more accessible. The fortified west face, with its towers and plain walls, makes an interesting contrast to the much more delicate decoration of the east face. On the base of the octagonal staircase tower, you can still see the inscription of Jacques Coeur's motto—"*A vaillants coeurs, riens impossible*" ("To bold hearts, nothing is impossible"). Throughout the palace you'll find Coeur's stamp, hearts for Jacques "Coeur" and *coquilles St-Jacques.* The obligatory 45-minute tour winds past storerooms, reception halls, and bedrooms, of which no two are alike. The tours are in French, but a printed English translation is available from the front desk. (Tours at 10:15am, 11:10am, 2:15pm, 3:15pm, and 4:10pm. Admission 15F, ages 18-24 and over 60 9F. A 25F ticket admits you to the crypt and tours at the cathedral as well.)

After scaling the heights, come down to earth for a stroll in the fine **Jardins de l'Hôtel de Ville** behind the cathedral. Summer concerts often take place amid the profusion of flowers and cool reed ponds. **Musée du Berry** includes a collection of prehistoric and Gallo-Roman remains in an elegant sixteenth-century *hôtel* on rue des Arènes; the **Hôtel Lallemant,** a luxurious Renaissance house on rue Bourbonnoux, was built by a rich fifteenth-century merchant and furnished from different periods. (Both open Wed.-Mon. 10am-noon and 2-6pm. Admission 7F, students 4F, Wed. free.) The **Musée Estève** 13, rue Edouard-Branly, houses the work of the talented modern artist Maurice Estève, a native of the region. (Open Wed.-Sat. 10am-noon and 2-6pm, Sun. 2-6pm, Mon. 10am-noon and 2-6pm. Admission 12F, students 6F.)

For two weeks at the beginning of April, this well-to-do town engages in an ebullient spring celebration. The **Festival Printemps de Bourges** fills the air with the sounds of folk, jazz, and rock 'n' roll. Well over one hundred thousand fun-seekers descend on Bourges every year to enjoy the music, performed by amateurs as well as established talent. The atmosphere is informal, and some of the concerts free (although most tickets cost 35-40F). For information contact l'Association Printemps de Bourges, 5, rue Sampson (tel. 48-24-30-50). From mid-July through August the tourist office sponsors **Ballades à Bourges,** concerts ranging from classical to rock, and theater and folklore groups. Tickets go on sale one hour before showtime at the concert spot (often a church or park), or one week in advance at the tourist office.

Châteaux on Route Jacques-Coeur

The châteaux along route Jacques-Coeur hardly compare with the grandest châteaux of the Loire, but are nonetheless impressive. A visit here is likely to be much more personal, as many of these old residences are still inhabited and all are situated in quiet little towns. None of the châteaux lies more than 90km from Bourges, and the tourist office provides helpful pamphlets on each of them, complete with explicit maps, photographs, and English descriptions. When contemplating a daytrip from Bourges, keep in mind that buses run only once per day to the châteaux, returning the following morning.

Sixty-nine kilometers south of Bourges on the Châteauroux-Montluçon train line, **Culan** perches gracefully atop a steep crag. Built in the eleventh century, it is furnished with fifteenth-century chests, Renaissance furniture, and fifteenth- and sixteenth-century tapestries and paintings. (Open Thurs.-Tues. May 16-Oct. 1 9-11:30am and 2-6:30pm; Jan.-Feb. 9-11:30am and 2-5pm; Feb. 3-May 15 9-11:30am and 2-6pm. Admission 15F, students 8F.) A few miles north of Culan is **Ainay-le-Vieil** (tel. 48-63-50-67), also known as Little Carcassonne because of its octagonal Romanesque towers. Most impressive is the beautifully carved facade of the Italian Renaissance manor. A fantastically carved fireplace and lovely polychromed ceilings grace the interior. (Open April-Oct. daily 10am-noon and 2-7pm; Feb.-March and Nov. Wed.-Mon. only. Admission 16F, students 8F.) Ainay is a stop on the train line between Bourges and Montluçon (tel. 48-63-30-58). Set in a lovely park with a pond, 35km south of Bourges, is **Château Meillant** (tel. 48-63-30-58). This early Renaissance château was built by Charles I d'Amboise and incorporates both medieval and Flamboyant Gothic elements influenced by the Renaissance. (Open March-Nov. 15 daily 9-11:45am and 2-6:45pm; Nov. 16-Feb. 28 9am-noon and 2-5pm. Admission 16F, students 8F.) The abbey of **Noirlac** (tel. 48-96-23-64), not far from Meillant, is a beautifully regular twelfth-century structure surrounded by gardens. This cistercian abbey was founded in 1150 by Bernard of Clairvaux. (Open April-Sept. daily 10am-noon and 2-6pm; Oct.-March Wed.-Mon. 10am-noon and 2-5pm. Admission 12F, students 6F.) Other interesting châteaux in the area include **Menetou-Salon,** an overly ornate mansion from the end of the Renaissance (open July-Nov. Wed.-Mon. 10am-noon and 2-6pm, March 19-June Wed.-Mon. 2-6pm; admission 16F, students 8F), and **Jussy-Champagne** (tel. 48-25-00-61), a small seventeenth-century brick and stone château with a large garden (open March 25-Nov. 15 daily 9-11:45am and 2-6:30pm; admission 5F). Forty kilometers north of Bourges stands **La Verrerie,** a lovely fifteenth-century Renaissance château situated on a small lake in the middle of a forest (open 10am-noon and 2-7pm).

Montluçon

A wall around Montluçon's medieval *cité* has kept it pristine, while a new tire industry has whipped the surrounding town into a commercial center. Now, careful development is seeping through the stone walls, although residents have always considered the *cité* a working part of Montluçon. Wood-beamed buildings with thick walls and short doorways fill the old town. Monluçon does have plenty of small-town charm, but alas, there just isn't that much to see.

At the core of the *cité* stands the commanding **Château des Ducs de Bourbon.** Constructed during the Hundred Years' War to defend the town against the English, it is the only remaining château of the Bourbon dukes. Its large parade ground commands an impressive view of the city and river. Housed in the château, the **Musée du Château des Ducs de Bourbon** exhibits archeological finds from the region and rusting farm implements. Up the winding castle steps, you'll find an interesting collection devoted entirely to the traditional stringed instrument of Auvergnat folk music, *la vielle.* The instrument's carved, violin-like neck depicts eighteenth-century political caricatures. (Open March 15-Oct. 15 Wed.-Mon. 10am-noon and 2-6pm; Oct. 15-Mar. 15 Wed.-Mon. 2-6pm. Admission 6F, students 4F. Oct.-June free on Wed.) **Eglise Notre Dame** was begun in the twelfth century as a Romanesque church. The choir, in Flamboyant Gothic, was not finished until the fifteenth century. A sensitively sculpted rendition of a popular conception of the *pietà* sits in a chapel to your left as you face the altar.

Take some time to wander aimlessly past the seventeenth-century houses in the well-preserved old town. Stop in to greet the bookseller at 3, rue des Cinq Piliers, or the iron artisan just across the street. Saturdays until 2:30pm, the whole inner town is closed off and vegetable stalls take over the narrow, winding streets. To escape the bustle, venture into the **Jardin Publique Wilson,** a pleasant park off bd. Carnot, and a peaceful place for a picnic. Amateur musicians play just about every night at the friendly co-op bar, **Le Guingois,** rue de la Réunion (tel. 70-05-88-18). For the first half of July, the old city comes alive for **Montluçon en Fête.** The **Festival de l'Instrument de Musique** organizes concerts during the third week in May.

Orientation and Practical Information

Montluçon lies roughly in the center of the triangle formed by Limoges, Bourges, and Clermont-Ferrand. Montluçon's walled city is circled by **boulevard de Courtais,** the main commercial street. Avenue Marx Dormoy leads from the train station past the *syndicat* and the post office to the base of the château.

Syndicat d'Initiative: 1ter, av. Marx Dormoy (tel. 70-05-05-92). From the train station, follow Marx Dormoy for 2 blocks; the *syndicat* is on the right near the foot of the castle. Don't expect much more than a free map and a meager booklet describing walking tours. Open Tues. 10am-noon and 3-6:30pm, Wed.-Sat. 9:30am-noon and 3-6:30pm.

Currency Exchange: Banque Nationale de Paris, 47, bd. de Courtais. Open Tues.-Fri. 8:20am-noon and 1:40-5:30pm, Sat. 8:20am-noon and 1:40-5pm.

Post Office: Place Piquand (tel. 70-28-22-97), at the base of the château. **Telephones** and **currency exchange. Postal code:** 03100. Open Mon.-Fri. 8am-7pm, Sat. 8am-noon.

Train Station: Rue de Bruxelles (tel. 70-05-50-50). Frequent service to Clermont-Ferrand (6 per day, 1 hr., 62F) and Bourges (4 per day, 2 hr., 57F). Also to Paris (4 per day, 3¾ hr., 167F), Tours (6 per day, 3 hr., 127F), and Limoges (5 per day, 2 hr., 83F). Bus service has replaced train lines to Moulins and Châteauroux. Information office open Mon.-Sat. 9am-noon and 2-7pm, Sun. 9:15am-noon and 2:15-6:45pm. Station open daily 5:10am-8:50pm.

Bus Station: Gare Routière, quai Rouget de l'Isle (tel. 70-05-39-97), near the river Cher. From the château, take bd. de Courtais to rue du Faubourg St-Pierre, and turn left along the river. 4 buses per day to Culan (around 35F) and Moulins (around 65F). Office open Mon. 10:45am-noon and 2-6pm, Tues.-Fri. 8:15am-noon and 2-6pm, Sat. 8:45am-noon. **City buses: Transports Urbains Montluçonnais (TUM),** rue Canaris (tel. 70-29-08-22). Tickets 3.70F for travel in 1 zone, 7.40F for 2 zones. Book of 10 tickets: 27F for 1 zone, 54F for 2. Get a schedule from the *syndicat.*

Taxi: Tel. 70-05-40-40.

Laundromat: Lavomatique, 3, rue Barathon; 10, rue Raquin; and 61, rue Charles Péguy. Wash 12F, dry 1F per 5 min. Open daily 7am-7pm.

Pharmacy: Pharmacie Centrale, 39, bd. de Courtais. Open Mon.-Sat. 8:45am-noon and 1:45-7pm. **Emergency Pharmacy,** tel. 70-02-15-15.

Hospital: Centre Hospitalier, 18, av. du 8 Mai (tel. 70-05-77-77).

Medical Emergency: Tel. 18

Ambulance: SAMU, tel. 70-28-11-11.

Police: Tel. 70-05-15-40.

Police Emergency: Tel. 17

Accommodations, Camping, and Food

It's a shame that there is so little to see in Montluçon because there are so many inexpensive places to stay. The exemplary **Auberge de Jeunesse Montluçon (IYHF),** 34, rue Notre-Dame (tel. 70-05-20-84), surrounds a garden courtyard in the old city. From the station, take av. Marx Dormoy to bd. Courtais, turn right and follow bd. Courtais to the Hôtel de Ville, turn left, climb up to rue Notre Dame, and turn right. During the year, the hostel functions as **Foyer des Jeunes Travailleurs** and accepts travelers only if there is space (there usually is). Officially a hostel from June 15 through September 15, it provides spotless facilities, including a library, TV lounge, ping-pong table, and washing machines, all in a family atmosphere. (Singles 50F including sheets and breakfast. Tasty meals 27F. Ask for a key if out past 11pm.) The **Hôtel le Celtic,** 5, rue Barathon (tel. 70-05-28-79), 1 block south of bd. Courtais (entrance at 1, rue Corneille), has cozy rooms with decent country furnishings and a friendly, English-speaking manager. (Singles and doubles 75-80F, with shower 90F. Breakfast 20F.) The **Hôtel des Deux Gares,** 7, rue de Bruxelles (tel. 70-05-06-58), two minutes to the right of the station, has spacious singles and doubles for 65F and a restaurant downstairs that offers a satisfying 40F *menu.* The **Hôtel de la Charrure d'Or,** 4, rue Racine (tel. 70-05-05-05), near the Hôtel le Celtic, has a loud bar complete with a barking dog downstairs but passable singles for 55F and doubles for 60F. The **Camping Municipal,** route de Néris-Clermont (tel. 70-05-39-53), is a two-star site 5km out of town on RN144. Take bus #1 from rue des Forges and bd. de Courtais.

Monluçon's culinary specialty is *pâté de pommes de terre.* Eaten hot or cold, this pastry is filled with a mixture of mashed potatoes and cream and can be found in *boulangeries* as well as restaurants. The main **market** is held Saturday morning in the old city, and a market also takes place Wednesday and Sunday mornings at Ville Gozet, across the river from *centre ville.* Monoprix, a **supermarket** at rue Marx Dormoy and bd. de Courtais, sells just about everything you'll need. (Open Mon.-Thurs. 8:45am-12:15pm and 2-7:15pm, Fri. 8:45am-12:15pm and 2-8pm.) **Chez Renée,** 33, rue des Forges (tel. 70-28-30-91), 2 blocks from bd. de Courtais, offers a substantial five-course *menu* for 42F. The elegant and intimate **Hostellerie du Thé-âtre,** 1, rue Croix Verte (tel. 70-05-07-27), in the old city near the hostel, serves omelettes (18F), *plats du jour* such as *escalope pavée* (a veal dish, 35F), and a 50F *menu.* **La Vie en Rose,** 7, rue de la Fontaine (tel. 70-03-88-79), in the heart of old Montluçon, serves traditional specialities such as *pâté de pommes de terre* (15F) in a pink, fern-bar setting with youth appeal (*plat du jour* 32F). **La Pizza Tutti,** 2, rue Grande (tel. 70-28-21-13), serves pizza from 20F and a 35F lunch *menu.*

Near Montluçon

Thirty-five kilometers north of Montluçon, east of the main road between Montluçon and Bourges (N144), lies the untamed **Forêt de Tronçais.** Deep in the heart of this forest, grand oak trees shelter burgeoning mushrooms; only wildlife, birds, and rustling leaves can be heard. The **Syndicat Mixte pour l'Aménagement Touristique du Pays de Tronçais** (tel. 70-67-55-89) will provide you with details. *Syndicats* in Montluçon, Bourges, and Vichy will also give you a map of the region and a list of hotels and campgrounds. The nearest **train station** (tel. 70-07-92-08) is in the town of **Urçay,** on the main train line between Montluçon (4 per day, ¾ hr.) and Bourges (3 per day, 1¼ hr.). The campground in Urçay, **Camping de la Plage du Cher** (tel. 70-06-93-30) is within walking distance of the forest (2km east on D978). If you have a car or bike, take a short trip to the village of **St-Bonnet-Tronçais** (east on D978 for about 10km and left on D39 for 2km). In St-Bonnet-Tronçais there is a 3-star campground, **Camping de Champfossé** (tel. 70-06-11-30). For information on other accommodations, call the *syndicat* at 70-67-55-89. The **Office National des Forêts** organizes tours of the forest that leave from the Rond du Vieux Morat in St-Bonnet (July-Aug. Thurs.-Mon. at 3pm, 2 hr., 10F).

Limoges

Limoges is celebrated for its fine porcelain, but the city is much less attractive than its product. The old quarter and porcelain museums merit only a day's visit at most. Patches of interesting streets are sewn in amidst bland, dead-end areas, and the city's personality seems to waver between that of a small town and an industrial city. Although Limoges harbors quite a few students, they don't seem to generate much energy. Perhaps the peaceful surrounding countryside and the nearby village of Oradour-sur-Glane (see Near Limoges) are the best reasons to come to the area. Limoges lies about four hours south of Paris-Austerlitz (10-12 trains per day, 191F). Other connections include Brive (10 per day, 1-1½ hr., 57F), Aurillac (6 per day, 3 hr., 107F), Lyon (4 per day, 6 hr., 200F), and Bordeaux (4 per day, 2 hr., 118F).

The city stretches roughly northwest from the Vienne river. The most interesting part of town, called La Boucherie, lies south and west of the tourist office. From the train station, take av. du Général de Gaulle and head straight across place Jourdan for the **tourist office,** bd. des Fleurus (tel. 55-34-46-87), which gives out good free maps and no end of brochures. (Open Mon.-Sat. 9am-noon and 2-6:30pm.) The office also gives two-hour guided tours of the city every Monday and Thursday in July and August. (Mon. at 4pm, Thurs. 10am. 16F.) The **Maison du Tourisme Haut-Vienne,** 4, place Denis Dussoubs (tel. 55-79-04-04), will provide you with a map of the entire region and all the information you need on the outlying area. (Open June 15-Sept. 15 Mon.-Fri. 9am-noon and 1:30-5:30pm, Sat. 10am-12:30pm and 1:30-5pm; Sept. 16-June 14 Mon.-Fri. 9am-noon and 1:30-5:30pm.) The **Centre d'Information Jeunesse,** 23, bd. Carnot (tel. 55-32-72-72), distributes information on student and cultural activities. (Open Mon.-Fri. 9am-6:30pm, Sat. 9am-noon and 2-5:30pm.) **CROUS,** rue Alexis-Carrel (tel. 55-01-46-12), has information for students on housing and university restaurants. The **gare routière** is at place des Charentes. Regional buses are unreliable and inconvenient (2-3 buses per day to Oradour-sur-Glane, 40 min., about 15F). Hitching on the rural roads around Limoges is difficult but possible. **Urban buses** cost 5F per ride. Ask at the tourist office for a bus map. You can wash your socks at the **laundromat** at 28, rue Delescluzes. (Open daily 7am-9pm. Wash 10F, dry 2F per 7 min.)

You will have no trouble finding a room in Limoges. The **Foyer des Jeunes Travailleuses/Auberge de Jeunesse,** 20, rue Encombe Vineuse (tel. 55-77-63-97), 15 minutes from the station, has sparkling clean singles for 38F (nonmbers 53F); take rue Théodore Bac to place Carnot, make a left onto av. Adrien Tarrade, and take the first left to the hostel. The *foyer* becomes a youth hostel only from June to August, but during the rest of the year they accept travelers for 53F per night if there is space. (Open 7am-2am. Breakfast 11F, sheets 11F.) The **Hôtel de France,** 23, cours Bugeaud (tel. 55-77-78-92), two minutes from the station (follow the left side of the park) offers large, clean singles and doubles for 65-70F; the manager speaks English. The **Hôtel de Lyon,** 3, rue Georges Dumas (tel. 55-34-43-79), just below the Jardin de l'Evêché, 10-15 minutes from the station, has small, tasteful singles for 65-72F, doubles for 75F. The closest **campground** is **Camping de la Vallée de l'Aurence** (tel. 55-38-49-43), 5km east of Limoges.

There are many good restaurants in Limoges, but none is particularly inexpensive. You can find the best restaurants around **place des Bancs.** An indoor **market** occurs at place de la Motte every morning and a larger market Saturday mornings at place Marceau. Several **university restaurants** dot Limoges. Call **CROUS** (tel. 55-01-46-12) for information. **Café Leopold,** in old Limoges, 27, rue Haute-Vienne (tel. 55-32-28-49), offers a *plat du jour* plus three vegetables for 37F. (Open Mon. for lunch, Tues.-Sat. for lunch and dinner.) **Le Paris,** 7, place Denis Dussoubs (tel. 55-77-48-31), caters to a raucous student crowd. Their "menu of the moment" (about 40F) may include *moules gambrinus* (mussels with onions and brown beer) and a selection from their list of 140 beers.

For a long look at Limoges's traditional artistry, the **Musée National Adrien-Dubouché,** av. St-Surin, houses the largest collection of porcelain in Europe. Exhibits range from Delft *faïence* to English Wedgewood and include displays of the dinner services of Napoleon I, Ulysses S. Grant, Elizabeth II, and the late Shah of Iran. (Open Wed.-Mon. 10am-noon and 1:30-5pm. Admission 15F, ages 18-25 and over 60 8F.) From July through September a free exhibit of porcelain and enamel is held at the Palais du Verdurier. (Open daily 9am-12:30pm and 2-6:30pm.) In the **Centre de Démonstration des Porcelaines** (tel. 55-30-21-86), you can see it all in nonstop video and live demonstrations. (Open daily 8am-7:30pm.) The factory is in an industrial zone on av. John Kennedy. Take bus #15 from the Hôtel de Ville (*direction* "Magret"). The **Musée Municipal de Limoges,** next to the cathedral, displays an excellent exhibit of the town's enamel products, which date from the twelfth to the twentieth century. (Open June-Sept. Wed.-Mon. 10-11:45am and 2-5:45pm; Oct.-May Wed.-Mon. 10-11:45am and 2-4:45pm. Free.)

You'll enjoy a good view of **Cathédrale St-Etienne** and its bell tower from the elegant and well-kept **Jardin de l'Evêché.** Of particular note is the facade of the north end of the transept, characteristic of the Flamboyant style, with the characteristic flame-like motif in the tympanum, and a fine rose window. Limoges's old quarter, **La Boucherie,** a district of narrow streets and medieval houses, has been home to the town's butchers since the tenth century.

Near Limoges

On June 10, 1944, Nazi soldiers massacred the entire village of **Oradour-sur-Glane.** Only a handful of the 600 inhabitants survived. Since that day, this martyred village has been left untouched. Obsolete electrical wires dangle from slanting poles, and 1944 automobiles rust on the road. The women and children were slaughtered in the town church; stare hard enough at the walls and you will see fingernail imprints. Two to three buses a day run from place des Charentes in Limoges (40 min., about 15F). To hitch, follow N141 to D9 (about 25km).

The wooded valley, ancient châteaux, and numerous lakes of the Limousin countryside make enticing attractions for cyclists and motorists. Unfortunately, trains and buses run infrequently. If you have the time, hitching might be your best way to travel. The village of **Solignac,** 13km south of Limoges on D704, is dignified by a huge, domed, twelfth-century church in the Périgord style. Inside the choir, the bas-reliefs decorate the curiously carved portal and the wooden misericords. A half-hour climb brings you to the ruins of the **Château de Chalusset,** an excellent example of medieval military architecture. From Limoges, two to three trains per day run to Solignac (10 min., 10F).

Thirty kilometers east of Limoges lies **St-Léonard de Noblet,** an ancient town that looks out over the Vienne river. The town's twelfth-century Romanesque church is an amalgam of styles and techniques. From Limoges, trains make the trip three to four times per day (25 min., 9F). **Aubusson,** 50km east of Limoges, advertises itself as *la capitale de la tapisserie;* tapestry-weaving has been an art there since the eighth century. The town is full of private galleries displaying local handiwork;

from June 15 through September 30, you can also visit the collections at the **Hôtel de Ville.** (Open daily 9:30am-noon and 2-6:30pm.) Obtain details from the **Syndicat d'Initiative** on rue Vielle (tel. 55-66-32-12), in the pedestrian zone. (Open Mon.-Fri. 9am-noon and 2-6:30pm.) Hiking trails with wonderful panoramas skirt the cliffs surrounding the town; 20km south is **Lac de Vassivière,** surrounded by campgrounds and offering abundant swimming, canoeing, sailing, and windsurfing. During the summer, free shuttle buses circle the lake and transport passengers 10km to and from the nearest train station in Eymontier. **Camping Châteaucourt** (tel. 55-69-22-40) is in nearby Beaumont-du-Lac. The entire region around Limoges is littered with châteaux, inaccessible by public transport: **Coussac-Bonneval, Montbrun,** and **Brie** are just three of the feudal castles in the beautiful countryside.

Auvergne

Tourism has only recently invaded this rugged farming region in the center of France. Parts of Auvergne, long inaccessible except by difficult overland routes, still resist creeping modernization. Large, isolated tracts and tiny villages checker the hills, watched over by sturdy cathedrals and churches built of local volcanic stone. The numerous feudal châteaux retain their original character, virtually untouched by Renaissance embellishments. Auvergne's characteristic mountains (extinct volcanoes) reinforce its denial of time.

Nucleus of the Massif Central, Auvergne embraces some of the most attractive and unspoiled countryside in France. Sadly, the region's strongly independent farmers struggle at a level of poverty unknown in most of France. The population has declined steadily since the beginning of the century, as inhabitants move to more prosperous industrial cities. Those who do remain show a fierce pride in their region and culture. A traditional saying runs, translated loosely, "Among other peoples, I boast of being French. Among the French, I boast of being *Auvergnat.*" The locals will share their love for the land with an appreciative visitor.

In late summer, small villages hold traditional *fêtes patronales,* which culminate in the exuberant *bourrée,* a dance to the strains of the *cabrette,* a type of bagpipe. Among the region's special dishes are *la potée,* a stew simmered for hours containing everything but the kitchen sink, and *tripaux d'Aurillac,* mutton wrapped in tripe. Massif dairy farms produce a great variety of cheeses, the most renowned being Cantal, St-Nectaire, and Bleu d'Auvergne.

Transportation in Auvergne can be slow. Trains stop frequently as they wind through the scenic countryside, and it may take several connections to get to the more remote villages. Either stick to the main lines that branch out from Clermont, or resign yourself to beautiful views at a leisurely pace. Hitching can also be complicated since major towns are not always connected by major roads; with a good map and a little perseverance, however, you can usually get short rides from locals. The steep, winding roads of central Auvergne help only those bikers training for the Tour de France, but hiking is a viable and popular way to see this area. The small roads twisting through the farms and villages make for pleasant walks.

Le Puy

Le Puy (Luh-PWEE) occupies one of the most extraordinary sites in France. In a bowl of gentle mountains, three jutting needles of volcanic rock tower over the red-tile roofs of the city: one balancing eleventh-century Chapelle St-Michel d'Aiguilhe, another the enormous crimson statue of *la Vierge* (the Virgin Mary), the third serving as a launching point for hand gliders. The narrow cobblestoned streets trimmed with reddish volcanic stone ascend steeply to the magnificent Romanesque Cathédrale Notre-Dame, still an important pilgrimage site. Le Puy has an interesting history similar to that of Clermont-Ferrand, but has been spared the heavy development. Indeed, the town is so quiet that it is fitting that lace-making is Le Puy's special calling. A few days here are a good antidote to overcrowded cities. The town also makes a fine base for excursions to the surrounding villages and farms.

Orientation and Practical Information

Le Puy is not always easily accessible by rail. Trains run regularly from St-Etienne (Châteaucreux) and Lyon, but if you're heading south from Clermont-Ferrand or north from Nîmes, you'll have to change at tiny St-Georges d'Aurac, where a small train will take you on the beautiful one-hour ride to Le Puy. From the train station, walk left, along av. Charles Dupuy, and then left onto bd. Maréchal Fayolle. After a five-minute walk you will reach two adjacent squares, place Michelet and place de Breuil. The tourist office and most of the hotels are here and on adjacent bd. St-Louis; the cathedral and *vieille ville* are just to the north up the hill.

Office de Tourisme: Place du Breuil (tel. 71-09-38-41). Amiable staff with basic English will make hotel reservations for free. Hiking suggestions, a shower of brochures, and guided tours of the city in French (in July 1 per day, in Aug. 2 per day; 2 hr.; 20F). If you're tired of long-winded walking tours, try the *petit train touristique,* a 45-min. ride through the city (9am-noon and 2-7pm, every hr., 22F). Summer excursions to Chaise-Dieu, St-Flour, Lac Bouchet, and nearby châteaux (50-125F). Pick up a copy of *La Haute Loire,* which describes the location, population, and services of nearby villages. Open July-Aug. daily 9am-6:30pm; Sept.-June Mon.-Sat. 9am-noon and 2-6:30pm.

Post Office: 8, av. de la Dentelle (tel. 71-09-00-03), a 5-min. walk east of the tourist office. **Telephones** and **currency exchange. Postal code:** 43000. Open Mon.-Fri. 8am-7pm, Sat. 8am-noon.

Train Station: Place Maréchal-Leclerc (tel. 71-02-50-50). To Lyon direct in summer (3 per day, 2½ hr., 82F). To St-Etienne (Châteaucreux), where you can take a train to Lyon (5 per day, 2½ hr., 54F). To Clermont-Ferrand via St-Georges d'Aurac (6 per day, 2-3 hr., 82F). Open daily 4:30am-midnight, until 10pm for ticket sales or reservations.

Bus Station: Place Maréchal Leclerc (tel. 71-09-25-60), next to the train station. Useful booklet *Horaire Rail-Air-Route en Haute-Loire,* with times for all transportation around the area, is available free. To St-Etienne (2 per day, 2½ hr., 30F), Yssingeaux (2 per day, 45 min., 14F), La Chaise-Dieu (1 per day, 1 hr., 24.70F), Polignac (1 per day, 5 min., 5F). To Lyon via St-Etienne (2 per day, 4 hr., 60F). Open Mon.-Sat. 8:30am-12:30pm and 2:30-7pm.

Taxis: Radio-cars (tel. 71-05-42-43).

Laundromat: 12, rue Chèvrerie, at rue Boucherie Basse. Wash 12F, dry 6F per 5 min. Dry cleaning 42F. Open Mon.-Sat. 7:30am-8pm.

Public Showers: Av. de la Cathédrale. Open Fri. 1:30-8pm, Sat. 8am-noon and 1:30-8pm, Sun. 8-11:30am. Free.

All-night Pharmacy: Call the police or look on the door of any pharmacy for that night's *pharmacie de garde.*

Medical Emergency: Centre Hospitalier, bd. Dr. Chantemesse (tel. 71-05-66-77), 10 min. from the center of town. Follow bd. St-Louis towards the highway to Clermont-Ferrand. SAMU ambulances, Tel. 71-02-02-02.

Police: Place Michelet (tel. 71-02-34-55).

Police Emergency: Tel. 17.

Accommodations and Camping

Numerous cheap hotels cluster around place du Breuil, especially on busy bd. Maréchal Fayolle. Phone reservation will usually be enough here, and even in July and August, rooms are usually available in the morning. The youth hostel is pleasant and centrally located. The tourist office has lists of *foyers,* most of which are for women.

Centre Pierre Cardinal (IYHF), Jules Vallés (tel. 71-05-52-40). From place Michelet, take rue Porteil d'Avignon north to the dead end, and turn right on rue Général Lafayette—the hostel is up the hill to your left, in a beautiful building overlooking Le Puy (a 10-min. walk). Friendly atmosphere and excellent kitchen facilities. 24F per night. Sheets 13F. Generous breakfast 6F. Lunch and dinner (served if there are enough people in the hostel) 25F—order 1 day in advance. Usually open 7am-11pm; if closed during the day, check after 8pm. Curfew 11pm.

Grand Hôtel Lafayette, 17, bd. St-Louis (tel. 71-09-32-85), in a quiet courtyard. Intriguing remains of a once-grand hotel: huge rooms filled with antiquated furniture, cavernous halls, a now-defunct iron-grill elevator, dusty silk flowers in the lobby. Singles and doubles 70F, with shower 100F. Feeble hall showers 10F. Breakfast 15F. Open Jan. 1-Dec. 22.

Hôtel des Cordeliers, 17, rue des Cordelières (tel. 71-09-01-12), off rue Crozatier, which is off bd. Maréchal Fayolle. Big rooms cleverly decorated by the somewhat whacky owner of this hotel and restaurant. Singles and doubles 85F. Triples with showers 140F. Hall showers included. Breakfast 15F.

Hôtel le Progrès, 51, bd. Maréchal Fayolle (tel. 71-09-34-35). Small but clean rooms. Singles 70F, with shower 90F. Doubles 80F, with shower 100F. Triples with shower 125F. Hall showers included. Breakfast 15F.

Hôtel le Régional, 36, bd. Maréchal Fayolle (tel. 71-09-37-74), a short walk from place Michelet, on your right. Adequate rooms over a lively bar, on the noisy corner of av. Dupuy. Singles or doubles 68F, with shower 94F. Triples with shower 140-160F. Hall showers included. Breakfast 9F.

Camping: Camping Municipal Bouthezard, chemin Rodéric (tel. 71-09-55-09), in the northwest corner of town. Walk up bd. St-Louis, continue on bd. Carnot, turn right at the dead end on av. d'Aiguille, and the site will be on your left (2km). Bus #7 goes there 7 times per day (10 min., 4.50F).

Food

Most restaurant food is expensive but unusually good. The cheapest, most satisfyingly authentic fare can be bought at the Saturday farmer's **market** on place du Plot (open 6am-12:30pm). Try homemade apricot jam (15F per jar) or the milky *chèvre* (goat) cheese from Yssingeaux (2F) on bread. Every bar and many stores (which often give free samples) serve the slimy green after-dinner potion *verveine*. Made from a collection of indigenous herbs, just a nip of *verveine* will go straight to the gray matter.

Restaurant des Cordeliers, 17, rue des Cordeliers (tel. 71-09-01-12), at the end of a small alley. Chummy neighborhood joint with a variety of tasty victuals at reasonable prices. Plain 45F *menu* and a whopping 58F *menu.* Open daily noon-2pm and 7:30-10pm.

Au Relais de Notre-Dame, 29, rue Cardinal de Polignac (tel. 71-02-35-63), near the cathedral on a peaceful street. Simple 3-course lunch *menu* 30F, *à la carte* 20-35F. Open noon-1:30pm.

Le Regina, 34, bd. Maréchal Fayolle (tel. 71-09-14-71). Pizza and *crudités* 38F, served in comfortable booths. Open daily noon-2pm and 7pm-midnight.

Cafétéria Casino, av. de la Dentelle (tel. 71-09-65-65), at rue Pierre Farigoule, a 2-min. walk southeast from place Michelet. On the 2nd floor of the supermarket bearing the same name. Surprisingly good cafeteria food for 19-45F. Wine 5.50F per 1/3 carafe. Open daily 8:30am-8pm. **Self du Breuil,** place du Breuil et Michelet (tel. 71-02-30-66), right next to the tourist office, also serves cafeteria-style food.

Sights

A long procession of streets and steps climbs dramatically to the facade of **Cathédrale Notre-Dame,** one of the most striking and unusual Romanesque churches in Auvergne. Built of alternating light and dark volcanic stones, and seasoned with a strong Byzantine influence, this cathedral soars with oriental arches. The Virgin Mary's black-skinned likeness, draped in the town's chief product, lace, rests on the main altar. These Black Virgins are common throughout central France. Some dismiss the phenomenon as discoloration by countless incense-ridden church masses. More reasonable explanations are that its original creator (possibly St-Luke) modeled his statue after the dark Judean women or that it was later painted that way to acknowledge the victims of the black plague. Most plausible of all, crusaders brought the statue home from the Middle East, where Mary was seen as endowed, as were all the local women, with a tawny complexion. The original Black Virgin went up in the French Revolution's flames—but its replacement is still revered, and on August 15 (Assumption Day), the town celebrates its faith as the statue is paraded through the streets. The cathedral is open daily from 8am until about 6pm. (Free tours leave from the nave July-Sept. at about 11am and 3:30pm.) Visitors to the cathedral may write messages to Mary in a small notebook. Peruse the moving and amusing requests (several are supplications for success on the *baccalauréat*).

Adjoining the cathedral, the curiously appealing **cloître** sports bright red tiles on Byzantine arches. The intricate frieze of hilarious faces and mythical beasts is barely visible under the edge of the roof. The 15F admission (students 9F) also gives entry to the **Trésor d'Art Religieux** and the **Chapelle des Reliques,** decorated with the celebrated mural of *Les Arts Libéraux.* (Open in summer daily 9am-noon and 2-6pm; in off-season shorter hours.)

From the sacred city, you can climb up the **Rocher Corneille** for a tremendous view of the surrounding area. If high isn't high enough, a staircase takes you up the cramped statue of the Virgin and Child for a view from Mary's halo. (Open May-Sept. daily 9am-7pm; Oct.-Nov. and Feb-March 15 Wed.-Mon. 10am-5pm; March 16-April 9am-6pm. Admission 6F.) On the edge of town, you'll find the eleventh-century **Chapelle St-Michel d'Aiguilhe,** which crowns a narrow, 80-m spike of volcanic rock. (Open daily Feb. 2-4pm; March-Nov. 10am-noon and 2-6pm. Admission 5F.)

Saturday is *marché* day in Le Puy, and practically every square in town puts on its own extravaganza. From 6am to 12:30pm, farmers bring what they've grown (fruits, vegetables) and made (cheeses, breads, jams, honey), plus live chickens, rabbits, and puppies to **Place du Plot.** The adjacent Place du Clauzel hosts an all-day **antiques market.** Bargaining for the items on sale, which include World War II medals, pipe paraphernalia, and old silverware, is *de rigueur* (Saturday until 6pm). **Place du Breuil** has the biggest spread of them all. At this flea market you can find new and used clothing, hardware, toiletries, and footwear galore (Saturday until 6pm). From September 11 to September 18, all Le Puy goes Renaissance for the **Roi de l'Oiseau.** For a week, people dress in period costume, jugglers and minstrels wander the streets, food and drink in the *vieille ville* can be purchased only with the currency minted for the festival, and there is a different theatrical presentation each day. The celebration culminates with the crowning of the town's best archer. (Admission to nightly shows at 9pm 70F, but 35F if you go Renaissance too.)

A 5-km walk from Le Puy (or 1 of 4 daily buses from the *gare routière*), the **Forteresse de Polignac** once housed the most powerful family in the area. The ruins and site still make an interesting visit (follow bd. St-Louis past the bridge to the N102). (Open daily Easter-Nov. 1 9:30am-noon and 2:30-7pm.) Fifty kilometers north is the ancient mountain town of **La Chaise-Dieu,** best known for its Gothic Abbaye St-Robert, which houses the chilling fresco *Danse macabre.* (Open June-Sept. daily 9am-noon and 2-7pm; Sept.-June Wed.-Mon. 10am-noon and 2-5pm.) A festival of French music is also held at the abbey (late Aug.-early Sept).

Clermont-Ferrand

Home of the Michelin tire empire, Clermont-Ferrand testifies to the recent industrialization of central France. The city hardly looks like the Auvergne you would expect: Factory chimneys puff merrily, and the city climbs onto the mountainsides. Stop here to spend some time with the thriving student population or to look over the old streets and monuments, but there's no need to prolong your visit. A lovely countryside awaits you nearby.

Orientation and Practical Information

Clermont-Ferrand lies about midway between Paris and Marseille. Major train lines from Paris and Lyon pass through and continue on to Nîmes, Béziers, and Toulouse. Stop at the tourist office in the train station for a good, free map and a pamphlet describing walking tours.

The center of Clermont, place de Jaude, is a 20-minute walk west of the train station. City buses will take you just about anywhere for 5.60F, or you can buy a *carnet* of 10 tickets for 40F at the TZC kiosk in place de Jaude. Buses #2 and 4 go from the train station to place de Jaude; bus #2 continues to the main tourist office. To reach the center on foot, go left from the train station on av. de l'Union

Soviétique and then right on av. Carnot; follow av. Carnot and av. Joffre west and down the hill to place de Jaude. From here take rue Gonod, which becomes bd. Charles de Gaulle; turn left on bd. Gergovia for the main tourist office.

Office de Tourisme: Main office, 69, bd. Gergovia (tel. 73-93-30-20). Plenty of glossy brochures and a free map; look for the monthly publication of information and events, *Le Mois à Clermont-Ferrand.* The tourist guide *Loisirs Eté* (15F) provides a comprehensive listing of leisure activities. **SNCF** operates a train information and reservation booth here as well. Open June-Sept. Mon.-Sat. 8:30am-7pm, Sun. 9am-noon and 2-6pm; Oct.-May Mon.-Fri. 8:45am-6:30pm, Sat. 9am-noon and 2-6pm. **Train station annex** (tel. 73-91-87-89) has all the regional information the main office does. English spoken. Open Mon.-Sat. 9:15-11:30am and 12:15-5pm. **Place de Jaude annex** and **Montferrand annex,** 22, rue de la Rodade (tel. 73-25-15-14), are open June-Sept. Mon.-Sat. 9am-noon and 2-6pm. **Musée de Ranquet annex,** 34, rue des Gras (tel. 73-36-80-30). Guided tours leave 2-3 times per week at 3pm from this office. Open June-Sept. Tues-Sat. 9am-noon and 2-6pm.

Comité Départemental du Tourisme: 17, place Delille (tel. 73-91-14-40). Best offfice to contact for information on the greater Clermont area.

Chamina: 5, rue Pierre-le-Vénérable (tel. 73-90-94-82). Exceedingly helpful organization that distributes maps and plans hiking and climbing trips in the Massif. Distributes *Le Colporteur,* a free, comprehensive guide on hiking, camping, and biking in the region. Open Mon.-Fri. 9am-6pm.

Travel Agency: Havas Voyages, 25, av. des Etats-Unis (tel. 73-37-48-36). Open Mon.-Fri. 9am-noon and 2-6pm, Sat. 9am-noon and 2-5pm.

Centre d'Information Jeunesse Auvergne: 8, place de Regensburg (tel. 73-35-55-00), behind the Home-Dôme *foyer.* From the tourist office, go left along bd. Gergovia, take your 6th left onto rue du 8 Mai 1945, and follow it to the end; the center will be on your right. Information on youth activities and lodging in student dorms in summer. Also information on hiking and canoeing. Open July-Aug. Mon.-Fri. 8:30am-5:30pm; Sept.-June Mon.-Fri. 8:30am-5:30pm, Sat. 9am-noon.

Currency Exchange: Crédit Agricole, 2, av. des Etats-Unis (tel. 73-37-19-71), on place Gaillard. Open Mon.-Fri. 8:45am-noon and 1:30-6:15pm, Sat. 8:45am-noon and 1:30-4:30pm.

Post Office: 1, rue Louis Renon (tel. 73-30-61-57). From place de Jaude, go west on av. Colonel Gaspard, turn right down rue M. de Lattre, and the post office will be on your left. **Telephone** and **telegram** services. **Postal code:** 63000. Open Mon.-Fri. 8am-7pm, Sat. 8am-noon.

Train Station: Av. de l'Union Soviétique (tel. 73-92-50-50). Most Auvergne connections, such as those to Le Puy and Aurillac, require changes. Main lines link you to Lyon (7 per day, 3 hr., 113F), Toulouse (5 per day, 6½ hr., 185F), Marseille (at least 4 per day, 2½ hr., 200F), and Paris-Gare-de-Lyon (at least 4 per day, 4 hr., 192F).

Bus Station: Bd. Gergovia (tel. 73-93-13-61), next to the tourist office. Inner-city and to nearby villages. To Montluçon (2 per day, 3 hr.) and Riou (4 per day, 30 min.), Moulins (2 per day, 2 hr.). Information office open Mon.-Sat. 8:30am-6:30pm. **Autobus Urbans,** Tel. 73-26-44-90. Information office at place de Jaude open Mon.-Fri. 8:30am-6:30pm, Sat. 8:30am-12:15pm.

Bike Rental: At the **train station.** 37F per ½-day, 47F per day, deposit 300F.

Laundromats: Place Renoux. Wash 16F, dry 2F per 5 min. Open daily 7am-8pm. Also at 62, av. Charras. Wash 16F, dry 2F per 5 min. Open daily 7am-8pm.

Pharmacy, 28, av. des Etats-Unis (tel. 73-37-50-39), off place de Jaude. Handy condom dispenser outside (10F). Open Tues.-Sat. 9am-7pm, Mon. 2-7pm.

Hospital: Hôpital St-Jacques, 30, place Henri-Dunant (tel. 73-26-57-00).

Ambulance: SAMU, Tel. 73-27-33-33.

Police: Tel. 73-92-10-70.

Police Emergency: Tel. 17.

Accommodations

Clermont has more than its share of hostel-like lodgings. The Centre d'Information Jeunesse will help you find summer student housing or a place in one of several *foyers*. Hotels are most crowded from April to June, but there is usually space.

Auberge de Jeunesse (IYHF), 55, av. de l'Union Soviétique (tel. 73-92-26-39), near the train station. Convenient for those just getting off the train, but not ideal for visiting the city. Basic dormitory accommodations, small kitchen, and pit toilets. 34F per person. Sheets 11F. Open Dec.-Oct. 7-9:30am and 5-10:30pm.

Foyer St-Jean, Auberge de Jeunesse, 17, rue Gaultier de Biauzat (tel. 73-92-49-70), less than 10 min. north of place de Jaude. Singles 50F. Sheets 10F. Breakfast included. Lunch or dinner 31F. Open all day.

Foyer International de Jeunes "Home-Dôme," 12, place de Regensburg (tel. 73-93-07-82). Take bus #18 from place de Jaude (last bus at 8:30pm), or walk southwest on av. Julien, turn left on rue Bonnabaud, right on bd. Pasteur, and then follow rue du 8 Mai 1945 (10 min. from *centre ville*, ½ hr. from station). Tired dorm singles 58F. Breakfast included. Lunch or dinner 33F. Call ahead if you'll be arriving late.

Hôtel le Savoy, 22, rue de la Préfecture (tel. 73-36-27-22), east of place de Jaude. Strangely shaped, small rooms, but central location and great antique elevator. Singles 70F. Doubles 80F, with shower 90F. Breakfast 15F.

Hôtel Foch, 22, rue Maréchal Foch (tel. 73-93-48-40), 2 blocks from place de Jaude. Convenient, friendly, and comfortable. Singles and doubles with good mattresses 75F, with shower 90F. Showers 12F. Breakfast with homemade jam 15F.

Hotel Bellevue, 1, av. Union Soviétique (tel. 73-92-43-12). Turn left out of the station (2 min.). Best bargain in the immediate area. Singles 69F. Doubles 75F.

Food

Stalk rue St-Dominique behind the cathedral for ethnic and student-type restaurants. The area's specialty, *la potée,* is a heavy soup of meat and vegetables, and meals always end with the local cheeses. Purchase fruit and cheese at the large **market** held Tuesday through Saturday mornings in place St-Pierre, below the cathedral. The two *foyers* (see above) serve good, inexpensive cafeteria-style food to non-guests as well as guests.

Le Stromboli, 18, rue du Cheval Blanc (tel. 73-37-22-47). Attractive and popular. Pasta 18-32F, pizza 26-35F, salad with hearts of palm and other exotica 25F. Open Tues.-Sat. noon-2pm and 7:15-11pm, Mon. 7:15-11pm.

Le Bougnat, 29, rue des Chaussetiers (tel. 73-36-36-98). Contrived *auvergnat* atmosphere. Local cuisine. 50F lunch *menu*. 80F *menu* is a gourmet delight. Try *tripes à l'auvergnate* or *la potée.* Open Mon. 8-10pm, Tues.-Sat. noon-2pm and 7:30pm-midnight.

Auberge Auvergnate, 37, rue des Vieillards (tel. 73-37-82-68). Reasonably-priced regional cuisine. *Menus* at 48F and 70F. *Plat du jour* 32F. Open Mon.-Sat.

Djerba, 18, rue Jeanne d'Arc (tel. 73-92-91-91), close to the youth hostel. Tunisian fare with *couscous* from 30F. Lunch *menu* 45F, dinner 75F. Open daily noon-2pm and 6pm-midnight.

Chez Ben, 10, rue des Chaussetiers. Main dishes 30F. *Plat du Jour* 20F. Specialty: *couscous.* Open daily noon-11pm.

Sights and Entertainment

The center of the city is lively **place de Jaude,** built around a dramatic statue of the *auvergnat* chieftain Vercingétorix, leader of Gaul's resistance to the occupying Romans. The stone in Clermont's *ville noire* is not dirty; it's volcanic. Walk on to the Renaissance **Fontaine d'Amboise;** from here follow rue du Port to **Basilique de Notre-Dame-du-Port,** a heavy twelfth-century church built in pure *auvergnat* Romanesque style. Stroll around the back to see the harmonious geometric layers of arches around the gallery. The spacious crypt, easily reached by steps on either side of the altar, echoes the outline of the chancel. (Open daily 9am-noon and 2-6pm.)

Gothic **Cathédrale Notre-Dame** was built only a quarter of a century later than the basilica, but after a revolution in architectural technique. Its slender spires (constructed of volcanic stone brought from nearby Volvic) form graceful silhouettes against the sky. Climb the steep, winding steps of the tower over the northern transept (3F) for a splendid view of the city and the Puy de Dôme to the west.

Clermont-Ferrand was once two distinct cities: the episcopal city of Clermont, and Montferrand, founded in the twelfth century by the dukes of Auvergne to rival their neighbor's power. The two merged in the eighteenth century. **Vieux Montferrand** is quiet and sparsely populated compared to its industrial neighbor. Buses #1, 9, 10, and 16 take you from the northeast corner of place de Jaude to place de la Fontaine, at the foot of **rue Guesde.** Intriguing courtyards and facades line this street. Continue up the hill to the thirteenth-century **Notre Dame-de-Prosperité.** Built out of volcanic stone, it stands on the site of the long-demolished château of the *auvergnat* dukes.

Back in the center of town, several museums offer shelter on a rainy day: The **Musée du Ranquet,** 1, petite rue St-Pierre, off rue des Gras, contains exhibits of regional art and history; the **Musée Bargoin,** 45, rue Baillainvilliers, houses archaeological exhibits and painting galleries; and the **Musée Lecoq,** 15, rue Bardou, is a natural history museum. This last stands next to the **Jardin Public,** a fine place for a picnic with its lakes, lawns, and small zoo. (All museums open Tues.-Sat. 10am-noon and 2-5pm. Sun. 2-5pm. Free.)

A large student population animates Clermont throughout the year. **Thoren's,** 16, place de Jaude, is a plush bar with a powerful sound system (open Sept.-July Mon.-Sat.). **Le Clown,** 65bis, av. Anatole France, behind the train station, is run by a jazz enthusiast who stages late-night improvisations (Mon. and Thurs.-Sat.).

Every year in early February, filmmakers from all over Europe flock to Clermont-Ferrand's **Festival International du Court Métrage** (Festival of Short Films). For information, contact Sauve Qui Peut le Court Métrage, 26, rue des Jacobins (tel. 73-91-65-73).

Near Clermont-Ferrand

The **Parc Naturel Régional des Volcans d'Auvergne** was founded in 1967 to save the unspoiled natural scenery of the area from industrial development and to promote the tradition of cottage industry and agriculture. Historical monuments in the park, including medieval castles built from volcanic stone and churches in the local Romanesque style, have been restored. Hiking paths through the most picturesque parts of the region are marked and are catalogued in a booklet available at the tourist office. The protected area includes three main sections—the **Monts Dore,** the **Monts du Cantal,** and the **Monts Dômes**—the last of which most clearly exhibits the profiles of extinct volcanoes. Swim in a chilly, clear crater lake to touch the cold heart of a now extinguished volcano.

The highest point of the volcanic domes is **Puy de Dôme** (1465m), a massive flat-topped peak. A toll road winds its way to the top, and tour buses leave Monday mornings in summer from the train station and place de Jaude (inquire at the tourist office for details). If you're up for a long walk, take city bus #14 from Clermont to Royat, then follow the Col de Ceyssat for about 6km until you reach the *sentier de muletiers,* a Roman footpath which will lead you to the top in about an hour. The panoramic view from this summit is magnificent, extending over an eighth of France when the weather is clear. Two small towns set among the most beautiful of the Monts Dore are **Orcival** and **St-Nectaire,** both with magnificent Romanesque churches. Each is served by occasional buses from Clermont and excursion buses from nearby Mont Dore.

Le Mont Dore

Le Mont Dore suffers from a split personality: in summer, thousands of *curistes* hobble into the Etablissement Thermale to heal their rheumatism and respiratory ailments; in winter skiers take over the resort town. Le Mont Dore's jagged, volcanic peaks provide good skiing in the Massif Central. The spring thaw reveals emerald green slopes, criss-crossed by splendid hiking trails. The awesome natural beauty of these mountains inspires both love and fear. Unfortunately, if you don't hike, ski, ache, or wheeze, this town has very little allure. You might be amused by the tour offered by the **Etablissement Thermal** on place du Pantheon (3F). Five of the springs used today were first channeled by the Romans, and the center (built 1817-1823) has grand arcades and granite Roman columns. The facetious guide does a stand-up comedy routine as he leads visitors through the main halls and concludes the tour by giving them a pungent whiff of a *douche nasale gazeuse*.

From the train station, climb straight up av. Michel Bertrand and follow the signs to the **Office de Tourisme,** av. de la Libération (tel. 73-65-20-21), which distributes free maps, organizes hikes and tours in the region (½-day tours 40F, at 1:45pm; full-day 80F, at 8am), and runs a hotel reservation service (tel. 73-65-09-00) for 25% of the first night's stay (reservation must be made 10 days in advance). (Open Mon.-Sat. 9am-12:30pm and 2-6:30pm, Sun. and holidays 10am-noon and 4-6pm.) The **Post Office,** place Charles de Gaulle (tel. 73-65-09-86), has **telephones.** Le Mont Dore's **postal code** is 63240. (Open Mon.-Fri. 8am-7pm, Sat. 8am-noon.) The **train station**is at place de la Gare (tel. 73-92-50-50). Six trains per day run to Laqueille (20 min., 9.50F) with changes to Clermont-Ferrand (1½ hr., 46F). One train per day runs direct to Paris (8 hrs., 222F).

Hotels are crowded during the winter and summer seasons, but you can usually find a room. The **Auberge de Jeunesse (IYHF),** route du Sancy (tel. 73-65-03-53), is 5km from the station (all uphill). Buses run in the afternoon in summer and all day in winter. Ask to be dropped off at the *auberge de jeunesse,* which is a chalet on a ski slope. If all else fails, the owner will pick you up. Filled with families during the winter (reserve 2 weeks ahead), the hostel usually has space during summer, but always call before you arrive. (34F per night. Breakfast 11F. Meals 34F. No lockout.) **Hôtel la Grande Vitesse,** av. Guyot Dessaigne (tel. 73-65-00-52), is a mere two minutes from the station and offers perfectly satisfactory singles (48F) and doubles (75F). **Hôtel Helvetia,** 5, rue de la Saigne (tel. 73-65-01-67), is cozy and clean with a good restaurant downstairs. (Singles and doubles 60-80F.) There are four **campgrounds** in and around Le Mont Dore: **Les Crouzets,** av. des Crouzets (tel. 73-65-21-60), across from the train station (8.50 per person, 4.25 per site, 3.20 per car; open Nov.-Sept.); **La Plage Verte,** route de la Tour d'Auvergne (tel. 73-65-09-85; open May 20-Sept. 20); **Domaine de la Grande Cascade,** route de Besse (tel. 73-65-06-23); and **L'Esquiladou,** chemin des Gentianes (tel. 73-65-20-00), 1km behind the train station.

Just about every restaurant in Le Mont Dore posts a 45-55F dinner *menu.* Follow your nose, or try **L'Etape Fleuris,** 1, rue Montloisier (tel. 73-65-02-20). A covered **market** occurs every morning in place de la République, and an open-air market in the same place Friday until 4pm. Try the local cheeses, and sample the pastries made with *myrtille* berries from the mountains. Before you hit the trail, stock up on groceries at the **Supermarché Suma,** behind the train station. (Open Mon.-Sat. 9am-12:30pm and 2:30-7:30pm, Sun. 9am-noon.)

Near Le Mont Dore

Le Mont Dore is a medium-sized ski area; most hot-dog skiers go elsewhere. The base of the slopes is **Le Sancy,** 5km out of town on route de Sancy (and right next to the hostel). Le Mont Dore and the area surrounding it have recently been connected to the Super Besse area. You can buy lift tickets for just Le Mont Dore (60F per ½-day, 80F per day, 145F per 2 days) or for both powdery masses (90F per day, 210F per 3 days, 400F per 7 days). For acrophobic skiers, Le Mont Dore offers over 400km of cross-country trails.

During summer, don't miss the opportunity to get to the mountains—minimal effort will net you generous rewards. The Grande Randonnée and other trails criss-cross this area, and the tourist office can help you find a route suited to your endurance. Before you set off on a serious hike (4 hrs. or more), you should get a detailed map, 37-57F, available at the tourist office). Contact the *gendarmerie* at the base of Puy de Sancy (tel. 73-65-05-03) and have them approve your route. **Vallée de Sancy** will give you an overview of the region. Start at the **Salon de Capucin** (1249m), which you can reach by foot or by a funicular classified as a historical monument because it dates back to 1898 (one way 7.50F). From there you can continue through the **Puy de Ciergue** (1691m) to the **Puy du Sancy** (1885m); the two-hour hike will take you along the *chemin de crètes* with all its old volcanoes, and past the source of the Dordogne; all the way you'll have a lovely panorama of the Massif Central. You can also reach Puy de Sancy by *téléphérique* (9am-noon and 1:30-5:30pm every 15-20 min., one way 18F, round-trip 23F); the summit is only a 20-minute climb away. For beautiful wildflowers, visit the protected **Vallée de Chaude-four,** east of Puy de Sancy, with its many endangered species including **Daphne** and anemonies. Volcanic lakes along the trail, including **Lac Serviere**, 20km northeast of Le Mont Dore, and **Lac de Guery,** 7km north, are suitable for windsurfing, sailing, and fishing, and are sometimes warm enough for swimming. An alternate 25-minute walk on the route to Besse leads to the **Grande Cascade,** where you can stand under the projecting rocks behind falling water. If you'd rather not roam around on your own, **Tourisme en Auvergne,** place des Moulins (tel. 73-65-22-55), organizes excursions from Le Mont Dore for 40-120F. The *syndicat* has more details.

Five kilometers away lies the mountain resort of **La Bourboule,** another *station thermale* and cross-country ski center. The town's natural setting rivals that of Le Mont Dore. The **Syndicat d'Initiative,** av. Agis Ledru (tel. 73-81-07-99), can help you organize your stay. For accommodations, try **Hôtel les Thermes,** bd. Georges Clemenceau (tel. 73-81-09-24), or **Hôtel Banne d'Ordanche,** av. Général Leclerc (tel. 73-81-09-57), above the train station. There is a **camping municipal** on av. de Lattre de Tassigny (tel. 73-81-10-20).

Riom

In the seventeenth century, Riom and Clermont were great commercial and cultural rivals. Riom soon yielded its status as a powerful metropolis, but maintained sophisticated tastes. Many ornate *hôtels particuliers* (bourgeois mansions) and half-timbered houses remain from its days of glory, though now a wide circular boulevard has replaced the old city ramparts. The modern *Riomois* are exuberantly proud of their sleepy little town; ask a simple history question and you may get a lecture in return; ask for directions to the clock-tower and you may get a guided tour.

The most impressive townhouses are the **Maison des Consuls,** rue de l'Hôtel de Ville, and the **Hôtel Guimoneau,** 12, rue de l'Horloge, with its beautiful courtyard and sculptured stairway (walk through the arch next to the tower to reach the latter). More moving still is the celebrated fourteenth-century statue of the Madonna and Child, called the *Vierge à l'Oiseau,* housed in the relatively simple **Eglise Notre-Dame-du-Marthuret.** The tender, playful exchange between mother and child is unexpectedly realistic—a sharp contrast to Auvergne's more somber, Romanesque renditions of the subject. The **Ste-Chapelle,** the only remaining vestige of the **Palais de Justice,** built in the fourteenth century by Jean de Berry, frames exquisite stained-glass windows. (Obligatory tour given July-Aug. Mon.-Fri. 3-5:30pm. Admission 10F.) Also worth a visit is the **Musée Régionale Folklorique d'Auvergne,** 10bis, rue Delile, near the Palais de Justice. It shelters a varied collection of local arts and crafts, costumes, and musical instruments peculiar to Auvergne. (Open April-Sept. Wed.-Mon. 10am-noon and 2-5:30pm; Oct.-March Wed.-Sun. 10am-noon and 2-4:30pm. Admission 10F, students 5F.) The beautifully renovated **Musée de Mandet,** 4, rue de l'Hôtel de Ville, in a seventeenth-century *hôtel particulier,* preserves a delightful collection of Gallo-Roman bronzes and pottery, early French and Flemish paintings and sculpture, and an extensive if unexciting collection of paintings from the seventeenth to the nineteenth centuries. More intriguing is the portrait gallery on the second floor. (Same hours and admission as the Musée Régional; 15F admits you to both museums.) All that is worth seeing in Riom is in the old town. From the station, head straight on rue Jeanne d'Arc and turn right on rue du Commerce for the *centre ville* and the *syndicat.* The friendly **Syndicat d'Initiative,** 16, rue du Commerce (tel. 73-88-59-45), will provide you with an annotated walking tour of Riom's sixteenth-century *hôtels particuliers* and a free but undetailed map. (Open May 15-Oct. 15 Mon.-Sat. 9am-12:30pm and 2-6:30pm; Oct. 15-March 15 Mon.-Fri. 9am-12:30pm; March 15-May 15 Mon.-Fri. 9am-12:30pm and 2-6pm.)

Accommodations don't pose any problems. A few affordable places lie near bd. Dessaix, including **Hôtel du Square,** 26, bd. Dessaix (tel. 73-38-46-52), with comfortable and appealing rooms from 70F, breakfast 15F. **Hôtel des Sports,** 44, rue de Commerce (tel. 73-38-00-59), next to the post office, tenders clean, basic accommodations for 60-85F, breakfast 15F; the traffic on rue de Commerce makes the front rooms noisy. There is a fine three-star campground, **Clos de Balenède,** route de la Piscine (tel. 73-86-02-47), at the entrance to **Châtel-Guyon,** a pleasant resort town 5km from Riom. (Full facilities, including washing machines.) Buses (tel. 73-86-03-22) leave for Châtel-Guyon every 2-3 hours from place J.B. Laurent. The locals' favorite restaurant, **L'Ane Gris,** 13, rue Gomot (tel. 73-38-25-10), a block off rue du Commerce, serves dishes like *le gros steak pour le gars qui a faim* (the big steak for the guy who is hungry) for 40-60F. (Open Tues.-Sat. 11:50am-2pm and 7:30-10pm.) **Chez Dédé,** 56, rue du Commerce (tel. 73-38-28-63), a family-style restaurant, serves a 38F *menu.* (Open Mon.-Fri. 11:30am-2pm and 7-9:30pm.) The **market,** Saturday mornings on rue du Commerce, provides the best food bargains in town. Every year, Riom hosts **Piano à Riom,** an international piano festival. (Tickets 80F, ages under 25 40F. For information call the *syndicat.*)

Vichy

Vichy's chief preoccupation is restoring the health— especially the wine-sodden livers—of the silver-haired from *le tout Paris* who descend on the town in great numbers every summer to "take the water" and stroll around parks and gardens. Everyone seems to come to Vichy to go on a health kick. Sports facilities cover almost as many acres as the entire *centre ville,* and multi-colored sweatsuits dominate the fashion scene. There is no denying that Vichy's lush parks are beautiful, or that the atmosphere becomes a bit festive during summer, but Vichy still lacks vigor.

Orientation and Practical Information

Vichy occupies a bend in the Allier river, about 100km northeast of Clermont-Ferrand. The river borders the *centre ville* to the south and west (regardless of how it may appear on the tourist office map). The center of activity is the **Parc des Sources** across from the tourist office. From the station, walk straight on rue de Paris; at the fork, take a left on rue Georges Clemenceau, then a quick right on rue Sornin. The **Office de Tourisme,** 19, rue du Parc (tel. 70-98-71-94), will be straight ahead of you across the park. The office has rather bad free maps and a good map for 4F. They help find rooms for free, and operate a **currency exchange** on weekends for a 20F commission. They also provide a comprehensive booklet of suggested walking and car tours in Vichy and the region. (Open July-Aug. Mon.-Sat. 9am-12:30pm and 2-8pm, Sun. 9:30am-12:30pm and 3-7pm; May-June and Sept. Mon.-Sat. 9am-12:15pm and 2-7pm, Sun. 9:30am-12:30pm and 3-7pm; Oct.-April Mon.-Fri. 9am-noon and 2-6:15pm, Sat. 9am-noon.) The **post office,** place

Charles de Gaulle (tel. 70-59-90-90), also has a **currency exchange** at competitive rates. (Open Mon.-Fri. 8am-7pm, Sat. 8am-noon.) The **train station,** place de la Gare (tel. 70-46-50-50), rents **bikes** (37F per ½-day, 47F per day, deposit 300F). Trains run to Clermont-Ferrand 12 times per day (1½ hr., 37F) and to Paris six times per day (4 hr., 174F). (Information office open Mon.-Sat. 9am-6:30pm, Sun. 9am-12:15pm and 2-6:30pm.) For information on **urban buses,** call 70-97-75-75 or 70-98-77-04. Buses for the surrounding region and Montluçon (3 per day, 2¾ hr.) leave from **gare routière,** place Charles de Gaulle. (Office open Mon.-Fri. 8-11:45am and 2-5:45pm.)

Accommodations, Camping, and Food

The quality of hotels in Vichy is high, although the price need not be. In summer you should book ahead. The **Auberge de Jeunesse (IYHF),** 19, rue du Stade, Belle-rive (tel. 70-32-25-14), across the river by pont de Bellerive, scrapes the bottom of the hostel barrel. There are no showers, the pit toilets are in a shack outside, but there is always a bed in the fairly clean dormitories. Kitchen facilities are available, and camping is permitted on the premises (15F per person). For the hostel or for other campgrounds (see below), take bus #4 from the train station and get out right after the bridge; cross the street and head towards the Le Bellerive sign atop the high-rise hotel. Follow the lamp-lined path onto rue du Stade and the hostel. (30F per person. Open April-Oct. daily 8am-10pm.) The **Hôtel Antilles,** 16, rue Desbrest (tel. 70-98-27-01), very close to the center, has pleasant singles for 45F and doubles off a courtyard for 66F. (Open April-Oct.) The **Hôtel Iéna,** 56, bd. Kennedy, has small but cheery rooms that are a great deal if you don't mind climbing four flights. (Singles 52F, doubles 75F. Breakfast 16F.) The **Hôtel de Surville,** 25, rue de Tou-raine (tel. 70-32-26-33), in a dainty old building, provides tastefully decorated, sunny rooms at low prices. (Singles 55F, doubles 70F. Breakfast 10F.) The four-star campsite **Les Acacias,** by the river at Bellerive (tel. 70-32-36-22), is the nearest of several campgrounds along the river bank. (2 people 42F, 3 people 54.50F; 10F cheaper in Sept. Swimming pool and showers included. Open March-Oct. 8:30am-10pm.) From the hostel, head down rue de la Grange to the river.

Restaurants abound in Vichy. **Le Fochotel,** 7, rue Foch (tel. 70-32-37-12), offers the best quality for the price. A popular self- or waiter-service spot, it serves 15-30F entrees in an elegant setting. **Le Cyrano Bar-Brasserie,** rue Foch, serves a no-nonsense *plat du jour* for 32F. The restaurant beneath the *Hôtel de la Nièvre,* 17-19, av. de Gramont (tel. 70-31-82-77), bills a 44F *menu* that includes *pâté de campagne.* Buy your own food at the large covered **market** in place du Grand Marché (Tues.-Sun. until 12:30pm).

Sights and Entertainment

In the glass and white cast-iron **Halle des Sources,** you can sit among the palm trees and watch the *curistes* file into the surrounding establishments every morning to get their daily dose of the lukewarm carbonate-laden water (8F per glass). This stuff is horrid, but if you drink what they give you, you can refill your bottle with a weaker version from the **Source des Célestins** on bd. Kennedy.

Up av. Thermale is the **Maison du Missionaire,** where religious orders stay while taking the cure. It houses a strange collection of mementoes from missions in former French colonies. Check out the paintings of missionaries on camel- and lion-back, and the photographs of missionaries subsequently killed by disgruntled natives. They also display model ships, stuffed animals, and crafts and artifacts of the Asian and African cultures.

Across the river the **Maison des Jeunes** shows films and sponsors activities throughout the year, and the nearby **Centre Omnisport** coordinates tennis courts, gymnasia, and kayaking on the river (tel. 70-32-04-68). You can rent windsurfers along the river, or buy a seven-day *passeport sportif* from the **base municipale,** by quai d'Allier on the beach. The pass allows you one week's use of the city's windsurfing equipment, sailboats, tennis courts, swimming pools, and canoes/kayaks. An outdoor swimming pool and a beach (no swimming allowed at the beach) lie across the river by the campground and youth hostel.

Three kilometers east of Vichy is the town of **Cusset,** displaying a grand collection of fifteenth- and sixteenth-century houses on rue St-Arloing. The *syndicat* in either Vichy or Cusset (rue St-Arloing; tel. 70-31-39-41) can provide you with a clear map of this area that carefully documents the important houses and courtyards.

The area around Vichy has many remarkable Romanesque churches. To the north are **Bessay-sur-Allier** and **Toulon-sur-Allier;** to the south, the church at **Ennezat** has a pure *auvergnat* Romanesque nave and a Gothic choir. All these towns make an easy daytrip from Vichy, and are served by the bus line **CFIT,** which departs from the *gare routière,* place Charles de Gaulle, in Vichy. All except Ennezat are also on train lines. **SNCF excursions** leave for various natural and architectural sights in the area (about 50F). **Châtel-Montagne** and **Château Lopalisse** are both about 25km from town, but inaccessible by public transportation.

Aurillac

Aurillac lies among steep green hills in a basin encircled by high volcanic ranges. In centuries past, Aurillac was fairly isolated, though it managed to maintain faint ties with Languedoc and Aquitaine. The town produced an abbey that returned the favor by producing the first French Pope, Sylvester II, in the tenth century. Unfortunately, the abbey along with most of the town was razed by Protestants in 1552, during the Wars of Religion. Still rather isolated, but with a lively and well-preserved *vieille ville,* Aurillac serves as a good base for excursions into southwestern Auvergne.

Be aware, however, that something strange happens between Clermont-Ferrand and Aurillac—phonemes shift: The *Cantaliens* tack on a nasal twang to words ending in "n," which end up rhyming with *meringue* (as in pie). If you can ordinarily understand a few words of French but haven't a clue about what these people are saying, don't fret.

All that remains of the original thirteenth century fortress, **Château St-Etienne,** is a dingy tower that overlooks the city. In the renovated château next door, the **Maison des Volcans** houses an extensive exhibit on the volcanoes and the geology of Auvergne. (Open July-Aug. Mon.-Sat. 10am-6:30pm; Sept.-June Mon. 2-5:30pm, Tues.-Fri. 8:30am-noon and 2-5:30pm, Sat. 8:30am-noon. Admission 10F, students 5F.) The château's gardens afford a panorama of Aurillac and the Jordanne river valley. The **Musée Cantalien,** 8, place de la Paix (tel. 71-48-42-56), displays an interesting collection of rocks, minerals, regional flora and fauna, and archeological finds, while the **Musée H. de Pariev,** also at 8, place de la Paix, exhibits paintings from the seventeenth through twentieth centures. (Both museums open Mon. and Wed.-Sat. 10am-noon and 2-6pm, Sun. 2-6pm.) **La Sellerie,** place de la Paix, a recently converted stable, is devoted to contemporary photography. (Open June-Sept. Mon.-Sat 1-7pm. Free.)

In recent years the town has developed a reputation as a center for avant-garde visual and performing arts. **Eclat d'Aurillac,** an international street-theatre festival in the last week of August, is unique in Europe. Last year's schedule included plays in outdoor tents, store windows, and moving trains (most shows free, some 60F). For information contact Information Bureau d'Eclat, Jardin des Carmes, 37, rue des Carmes (tel. 71-48-77-22). The **Festival de Création Choréographique d'Aurillac** features the most modern dance for three days in mid-July. (Tickets 35-200F.) Contact the Office Culturel d'Animations et Fêtes, 37, rue des Carmes (tel. 71-48-86-00), for information on **Café Musique,** a series of free concerts in local cafes, and other festivals.

From the station turn right, bear left onto rue de la Gare, and continue straight to place du Square, the center of town and location of the **Office de Tourisme** (tel. 71-48-46-58). The friendly but busy staff will give you a good, free map, information on the area, and help you find a room. They also organize walking tours (1½ hr., 15F) and bus excursions (70-160F); they hand out annotated walking tours and operate a **currency exchange** in July and August when the banks are closed. (Open July-Aug. daily 9am-12:30pm and 2-7:30pm; Sept.-June Mon.-Sat. 9am-noon and 2-6:30pm.) The **Comité Départemental du Tourisme,** 22, rue Guy-de-Veyre (tel. 71-48-53-54), distributes information on cheap lodging, camping, hiking, and food. Visit this office before venturing off into the Cantal. **Trains** run to Toulouse (5 per day, 3 hr., 113F), Brive (6 per day, 57F), and Clermont-Ferrand (6 per day, 3 hr., 88F). The **train station** is on place Pierre Semard (tel. 71-48-50-50; information office open Mon.-Sat. 7:15am-noon and 12:30-8pm, Sun. 7:15am-noon and 12:30-7pm). **Bike rental** is available here (37F per ½-day, 47F per day, deposit 300F). **Urban buses,** 8, rue Denis Papin (tel. 71-64-54-55), cost 5F a ride. **Regional buses** all stop at the *gare routière* in the parking lot to the left of the station. A schedule is posted in the train station. The main **post office** is on rue Salvador Allende (tel. 71-64-33-33; open Mon.-Sat. 8am-7pm, Sat. 8am-noon). The **postal code** is 15000. The more convenient **branch office** is at 3, rue Rieu (tel. 71-48-14-04; open Mon.-Fri. 8:30am-noon and 1:30-5pm, Sat. 8am-noon). Poste Restante letters must be marked "Préfecture" to arrive at the branch office. **Banque Nationàle de Paris** is at 6, place du Square. (Open Tues.-Sat. 8:20-11:55am and 1:35-5:25pm.)

Generally, Aurillac hotels do not fill. The city contains what might well be the accommodations opportunity of a lifetime. The **Château St-Etienne** (tel. 71-48-49-09) offers beds in simple rooms at extraordinarily low prices. (Singles 50F. Doubles 80F. Sheets and shower included. Single for 2 weeks 560F, for 1 month 750F. Kitchen facilities available. Call ahead.) From place du Square, head up rue Delzons, bear right onto bd. d'Auriques and left onto rue du Château St-Etienne, following the signs to the château. The **Foyer des Jeunes Travailleurs,** 25, av. de Tivoli (tel. (71-63-56-94), offers ordinary singles for 50F, 32F if you're female and there's more than one person in your room. (Showers included. Office open daily 8:30am-9pm.) Take bus #1 from the station or place du Square (*direction:* "Arpajon"), and ask to be dropped off at the *foyer.* The **Hôtel Bosc-Lapier,** 19, av. du 4 Septembre (tel. 71-48-26-85), five minutes from the station, has recently refurbished rooms with hardwood floors. (Singles and doubles 70F. 45F *menu* in restaurant.) More central is the **Hôtel Le Pont Rouge,** 1, bd. du Pont-Rouge (tel. 71-48-05-33). (Rooms 80F. Showers 10F. Breakfast 15F.)

The best meal bargain in Aurillac is probably the cafeteria at the *foyer.* For 34F you get five courses that approach a gourmet meal. Ask for a lot and they heap food on your plate. (Open daily noon-1pm and 7-8pm. Call the *foyer* to make sure the hours have not been changed.) You'll probably find yourself eating at **Le Bistro,** av. Gambetta (tel. 71-48-01-04), as it's central, almost always open, economical (*plats du jour* 30F), and friendly. **Aux Délices Gravier,** 22, cours Monthyon (tel. 71-64-38-90), serves sit-down cafeteria food cheaply. (Omelette 10F, salad 8F, *steak-frites* 30F.) There is a covered **market** at place de l'Hôtel de Ville on Wednesday and Saturday mornings. Just across the street from the *foyer* is a **Supermarket Topco** (open Mon.-Fri. 8:30am-12:30pm and 3-6:30pm, Sat. 8:30am-12:30pm and 2:30-7:30pm).

Cantal Countryside

The volcanic mountains of the Cantal are older and greener than the Monts Dôme to the northeast. Slow trains wind past feudal *châteaux* and ancient farmhouses (called *burons*); bell-bearing bovines seem genuinely surprised to see people walking down the country roads. Remember, however, not to count on getting anywhere in the Cantal fast. Touring the area without a car can be inconvenient. It may be preferable to use Aurillac as a base for your excursions.

Before you wander too far out into the countryside, you should probably stop by the Comité Départemental du Tourisme in Aurillac (see Aurillac Practical Information). They distribute a detailed, free map (a necessity); a complete list of hotels, *gîtes d'etape,* and campgrounds; the *Cantal Green Guide* (in English), with information on accommodations, camping, and sights; *Le Colporteur,* with complete information on touring the area; and booklets on cheeses and châteaux. The tourist office in Aurillac offers less comprehensive information but will give you printed descriptions of towns and lists of campgrounds and hotels, and will even book a room in neighboring towns for free. *La Montagne,* a local newspaper, usually lists events and festivals in the region (3.60F).

The region is not well served by trains. There are 3 main lines: Clermont-Ferrand to Aurillac to Toulouse (6 per day), Aurillac to Bort-les-Orgues (3 per day), and Bort-les-Orgues to Neussargues (3 per day). Three SNCF buses per day run from Bort-les-Orgues to Ussel. Schedules are designed to suit locals, but if you plan your trains ahead, you can see a good section of the countryside without too many delays. SNCF organizes train tours of the region (11 hr., 170F). Call SNCF Service Voyagers (tel. 71-48-89-46) for information.

Sixteen private bus companies serve the region. No office organizes them all, so trying to coordinate bus schedules can be frustrating. Check the schedules posted at the train station, or ask each driver individually for a schedule of his line. Most buses leave from the *gare routière,* to the left of the Aurillac train station.

The hilly terrain that challenges Tour de France veterans can torture the amateur cyclist. If steep hills don't faze you, rent a bike at the Aurillac train station.

By sticking to the train line between Aurillac and Neussargues (on the way to Clermont-Ferrand), you can cover a lovely stretch of countryside. Five minutes by train from Aurillac, the feudal **Château de Pesteils** glowers over the tiny village of **Polminhac.** From fourteenth-century towers to the imposing dungeon, the fortress exudes the strength that rebuffed several invasions. The seventeenth-century wing sports finely-painted ceilings and furniture and Aubusson tapestries. (Tel. 71-47-40-03. Open May 15-June and Sept. 2:30-5:30pm; July-Aug. 10am-noon and 2:30-6pm.) The **Camping Val de Cère** (tel. 71-47-40-07) is open June 15 to September 15. If you camp, prepare for chilly evenings.

The next train stop is **Vic-sur-Cère,** a popular summer resort in a beautiful valley by the Cère River, with an interesting Romanesque church and old city and several walking paths in the surrounding mountains. Walk in the direction of Thiézac to the **Pas de Cère, Rocher de Muret,** or the **Grotte des Huguenots.** The valley is a good place for cycling. **Camping les Tilleuls** (tel. 71-47-51-75) is open from April through September. For further information, contact the **Office de Tourisme,** Pavillion du Parc (tel. 71-47-50-68), 15800 Vic-sur-Cère.

Le Lioran is the major ski resort in the Cantal, and in summer ski runs become hiking trails. A *téléphérique* whisks you to a short distance from the **Plomb du Cantal** (1855m). From the train station, turn left, take the first right (following the signs to the *téléphérique*), and climb the 1km up to the ski area and hiking trails. The **Office de Tourisme** (tel. 71-49-50-08), at the foot of the *téléphérique,* distributes information on skiing and hiking. There are no cheap hotels in Le Lioran but the **Laveissiere Campground** lies 6km outside town (tel. 71-20-04-42). Stop off for a half-hour or so to see the old town of **Murat.**

St-Flour, on the eastern edge of the Cantal, sits high on a plateau. The mere sight of an entire town so sharply elevated merits the trip. The ancient houses of the old city are built around the severe Gothic **Cathédrale St-Pierre.** The graceful interior of the cathedral has a cavernous nave and a remarkably beautiful fifteenth-century wooden crucifix called *le Bon Dieu Noir.* (Open daily 10am-noon and 2-6pm.) The **Musée de la Haute Auvergne,** in the Hôtel de Ville, contains several rooms representing *auvergnat* folklore and a few rooms devoted entirely to the traditional *auvergnat* instrument, the *cabrette* (similar to a bagpipe). (Open June-Sept. Obligatory tour Mon.-Fri. at 10am, 11am, 2pm, 3pm, 4pm, and 5pm. Admission 12F, students 5F.) The **Musée Douet,** next to the cathedral in the **Ancienne Maison Consulaire,** contains several richly furnished rooms, ancient arms, and various paintings and sculptures. (Open May-Oct. 15. Obligatory tour at 10am, 11am, noon, 2:45pm, 3:45pm, 4:45pm, 5:45pm, and 6:45pm. Admission 7F, students 4F.) The **Office de Tourisme** is at 2, place des Armes (tel. 71-60-22-50), in the center of the *haute ville.*

(Open July-Aug. Mon.-Sat. 9am-noon and 2-7pm, Sun. 10am-noon and 3-6pm; Sept.-June Mon.-Sat. 9am-noon and 2-6pm, Sun. 10am-noon and 2-6pm.) The **Hôtel Au Bon Coin,** 2, av. des Lacs (tel. 71-60-14-31), serves excellent, simple meals and offers singles for 70F, doubles for 80F. (Restaurant open June-Sept. daily noon-2pm and 7-9pm. Hotel open Sept.-June.) **Camping des Orgues,** off av. du Dr. Mallet (tel. 71-60-14-41), is a two-star site with tennis courts and a good view.

Ten kilometers southeast of St-Flour is the **Viaduc de Garabit,** a huge metallic bridge designed by none other than Gustave Eiffel, and yes, it does resemble the Eiffel Tower. There is no public transportation. Hitch along N9. Thirty kilometers south of St-Flour lies **Chaudes-Aigues** (showed-ZEG), a medieval city and thermal center with the hottest waters in Europe (82°C). Two buses connect the towns daily. For details, call the **Office de Tourisme** in St-Flour, or in Chaudes-Aigues (tel. 71-23-52-75). Two hours north by train from Aurillac is **Bort-les-Orgues** (3 per day, 56F). The town itself is unattractive but is a good place to start hikes in the beautiful valley of the Dordogne River and the nearby **Lac du Barrage de Bort.** Bort-les-Orgues is actually closer to Le Mont Dore (40km south on N89) than Aurillac but there is no train line; **trains** connect Bort-les-Orgues to Neussargues (44F), and SNCF **buses** run between Bort-les-Orgues and Ussel (33F). For accommodations, try **Hôtel du Barrage,** 851, av. de la Gare (tel. 55-96-73-22), which offers clean, ordinary singles and doubles for 64F (breakfast 13.50F). Get a list of the many campgrounds in the area from the *Syndicat d'Initiative,* place Marmontel (tel. 55-96-02-49). A small **Auberge de Jeunesse** is 30km away in Ussel (tel. 55-96-13-17). Take av. Carnot from the train station to rue Pasteur on the left. (30F per night. Office open 8am-10pm.)

Six kilometers from Bort, the **Château du Val** once overlooked the sleepy Dordogne, but after the construction of the dam at Bort, it was magically transformed into a Gothic castle dramatically surrounded by a lake. The castle tends to look more impressive on postcards. Nevertheless, the solid, rustic interior makes an interesting visit. (Open Jan.-Nov. Wed.-Mon. 9am-noon and 2-6pm. To see the courtyard 2F. To see the castle on an obligatory tour 8F. To get there, follow N122 north for 5km out of Bort, then turn left on the well-marked road for 2km down to the lake. The busy roads are unpleasant to walk along, so try to hitch a ride.

About midway between Bort and Aurillac, **Salers** is a tourist-thronged but nonetheless beautiful old town set on a plateau overlooking the Maronne Valley. The town's medieval flavor has been preserved without making the town seem artificial. The somber **Eglise St. Mathieu** contains renowned **mise au tombeau** (entombment) sculpture and five Aubusson tapestries. The elegantly simple **Chapelle Notre-Dame de Lorette** (2 min. out of town off D680) shelters souls and an occasional chirping sparrow. From the **esplanade de Barouze** (a great place for a picnic), you have a panoramic view of the peaceful valley. Salers is inaccessible by public transportation. Hitch a ride from Mauriac (on the Bort-Aurillac train line). More locals travel on the road from Salers to Mauriac, so even if you're coming from or going to Aurillac, you should probably take this road (D22). The **Syndicat d'Initiative,** place Tissandier d'Escous (tel. 71-40-70-68), in the center of town, will direct you to hotels and campgrounds. (Open July-Aug. 10am-7pm; June 10am-noon and 2:30-6pm; April-May and Sept.-Oct. 11am-noon and 2:30-5:30pm.)

The main road from Mauriac to Aurillac (D922) passes through many timeless villages. The towns of **St-Martin Valmeroux, St-Chamant,** and **St-Cernin** all contain enchanting fifteenth- and sixteenth-century churches. The majestic **Chateau d'Anjony** is 5km off D922 in the village of Tournemire (tel. 71-47-61-67; open Easter-Oct. 2-6:30pm).

Burgundy
(Bourgogne)

Encompassing the upper valley of the Saône and its surrounding hills—the Côte d'Or, the Plateau de Langres, and the wild, forested Morvan, Burgundy is best known for its Romanesque architecture and the 40 million bottles of wine it produces each year. Today, the hills that provided feudal lords control over important passes leading toward Paris and the northern provinces are covered with vineyards that, despite their small size, produce great wines: Beaujolais comes from the area south of Mâcon, fine white wines—notably the dry Pouilly-Fuissé—from the Mâconnais, white Chablis from Auxerre, and full-bodied reds—Vougeot, Chambertin, Nuits—from the Côte d'Or, which stretches from Santenay north to Dijon. Roads throughout the wine-producing areas are dotted with signs advertising *dégustations*—free samplings of wine at local *caves*. Ask at any *syndicat* for a list of *viticulteurs* who offer tastings.

Opportunities to help in the annual grape *vendange* (harvest) are plentiful during September and October, but the work is physically taxing. For information, contact the Centre Régional de Jeunes Agriculteurs, 41, rue de Mulhouse, Dijon (tel. 80-30-84-96); or the Agence Nationale pour les Emplois, 6, bd. St-Jacques, Beaune (tel. 80-22-16-72). You can also go directly to the local vineyards, where they are less picky about requiring a work permit of foreign workers. Youth centers (see Dijon Practical Information) also have information on grape and cherry (in summer) harvest jobs; if your French is shaky, the staff can sometimes be persuaded to call around for you.

While the wine certainly is, as the locals say, Burgundy's best ambassador, the locals themselves and their beautiful surroundings make Burgundy a fine places to visit. Most vacationers will find even driving through the verdant landscape a moving experience—in more ways than one. Spend a few days in one of the countless tiny villages. The people's amiability, hospitality, and playfulness differ pleasantly from most French people's disposition. As jobs and education take young adults elsewhere, many villages seem to be top-heavy on the age scale. Often dressed in the blue cotton French work outfit and woolen beret, the older men cane themselves around town. They think nothing of ordering their *vin rouge* early on a Sunday morning, and the bartenders say that they come back to the bar so frequently that you might as well not remove their drained glasses. Don't offer that gray, bent man a hand as he hobbles about at an impossibly slow pace, for he has found great strength in tradition and in wine.

Burgundy is also rich in art and architecture: The Roman conquest of Gaul began in the area around Autun, and the impressive Gallo-Roman ruins of that city, combined with the thousands of Roman objects displayed in regional museums, constitute a fascinating historical legacy. The pamphlet *Bourgogne Archéologique,* free at most tourist offices, lists excavation sites and noteworthy museums throughout the region. Romanesque and Gothic architecture flourished in Burgundy, and each village church claims that its tympanum or altar *retable* is the most original in the province. Later, an eleventh- and twelfth-century building craze produced churches and abbeys decorated by an inexplicable and bewitching mix of biblical and fantastic, perhaps Celtic, stone carvings.

Centered on its wine-based sauces, Burgundy's renowned cuisine includes such specialties as *boeuf bourguignon, coq au vin,* Dijon *moutardes* (made with white wine instead of vinegar), and *kir* (a beverage concocted with white wine and *crème de Cassis*—blackcurrant brandy). Other culinary delights include *gougère* (a soft bread made with *pâté à choux* and cheese), *escargots* (cooked in lots of butter and garlic), and *quenelles* (little dumplings made with anything from fish to veal).

Hotels, particularly in the big cities, are relatively expensive, but hostels and *foyers* are common in the region. In the Yonne campsites are located amidst rolling pastures by rivers, and in the Morvan by lakes and forests; often sites are also found at the foot of spectacular mountains. For a list of campgrounds, ask at the tourist office for *Camping en Bourgogne, 1989.* Since the region's winding, hilly roads will strain the knees of all but the veteran cyclist, check altitude points on a map (try *Michelin's*). Burgundy is fairly well-serviced by trains, and daily or twice-daily buses fill in the gaps. The TGV runs directly between Paris, Dijon, and Beaure. Keep in mind that towns' banking days vary (some are open Mon.-Fri., others Tues.-Sat.); you could be left without a place to get cash on either the weekend or Monday.

Cultural festivals abound, especially during summer, in Burgundy. From mid-July to mid-August, Burgundy hosts **Musique en Bourgogne;** classical and early music concerts are performed in the cathedrals and churches of Sens, Beaune, Vézelay, Tournus, and other towns. Ask for the *Petit guide des manifestations musicales en Bourgogne,* available at any *syndicat.*

If Burgundy has won you over, a few useful organizations help those planning an extended stay. Volunteers are always needed on archeological sites throughout the region. If interested, contact Direction des Antiquités de Bourgogne, 39, rue Vannerie, 21000 Dijon (tel. 80-67-17-67). The Centre de Rencontres Internationales (CRISD), at 1, bd. Champillion, 21000 Dijon (tel. 80-71-32-12), arranges trips for younger people, including a three-day exploration of Dijon, a wine festival, and language holidays. Also a good place to study language is the Centre International d'Etudes Françaises (CIEF), 36, rue Chabot-Charmy, 21000 Dijon (80-66-20-49).

Cluny

Cluny became an immensely influential intellectual and artistic center in the twelfth century as headquarters of the Benedictine order, with 2000 dependent abbeys. Today it remains one of the most important names in Romanesque art. Though the abbey itself is now a gaping hole, the style and technical perfection of the surviving carved capitals retain their medieval character. This charming village with narrow, winding streets is a refreshing change from the larger Burgundian cities. A short walk from any part of town leads to cow-fields. Tiny hamlets, constructed of rough-hewn stone, dot the rolling hills around Cluny and transport the imagination to another era.

Orientation and Practical Information

Cluny sits in the Grosne River valley, about 20km west of the main Dijon-Lyon train line. To reach Cluny, take the train to Chalon-sur-Saône or to Mâcon, then the SNCF bus (free with railpass) through the beautiful Beaujolais countryside; the road wanders past farms, forests, and gentle valleys. The bus drops you off on rue Porte de Paris. From there, turn left down to rue des Tanneries and bear right onto rue Filaterie, which first becomes rue Lamartine then rue Mercière; this main road leads to the tourist office.

Syndicat d'Initiative: 6, rue Mercière (tel. 85-59-05-34). Helpful staff in a well-stocked office. Free maps. **Currency exchange** when banks are closed. Will call hotels or map out bicycle trips and other excursions. Walking tours of the town (mid-June to mid-Sept. daily or depending on demand at 3:30pm, 12F). Open June 15-Sept. 15 daily 9:30am-6:30pm; March-June 15 and Sept. 15-Oct. Mon.-Sat. 9:30am-12:15pm and 2:15-6pm; Nov.-Feb. Tues.-Sat. 2:30-5:30pm.

Post Office: Rue de la Poste. **Postal code:** 71250. Open Mon.-Fri. 8am-noon and 2-7pm, Sat. 8am-noon.

Buses: SNCF, Tel. 85-38-50-50 in Mâcon; 85-93-50-50 in Chalon-sur-Saône. All schedules are posted at the *syndicat* or at the more central stop outside Cluny Séjour, on rue Porte de Paris. To Taizé (8 per day, 10 min., 10F), Cormatin (6 per day, 20 min., 13F), Mâcon (8 per day, ½ hr., 17F), and Chalon-sur-Saône (6 per day, 1½ hr., 35F).

Bike Rental: Hôtel Moderne, Pont de l'Etang (tel. 85-59-05-65). 10F per hr., 30F per ½-day, 50F per day. Picnic basket 60F. Open 24 hours.

Medical Emergency: SMUR, Tel. 85-34-33-00.

Police: Route de Mâcon (tel. 85-59-06-32). **Police Emergency:** Tel. 17.

Accommodations and Camping

Cluny has only a few hotels and even fewer budget hotels. Reservations a few days in advance are usually necessary in summer. The large hostellike installation is better than most hostels. Another alternative is to make the town a daytrip from Mâcon, Chalon-sur-Saône, or a long daytrip from Lyon.

Cluny Séjour, rue Porte de Paris (tel. 85-59-08-83), behind the bus stop and a 3-min. walk from the abbey. Sparkling clean modern hostel in a renovated 18th-century building that usually has space. Beautiful wooden bunk beds in a co-ed dormitory 39F (sleeping bag or sheet sack required). Singles 90F. Doubles 100F. Triples 150F. Breakfast and hot showers included. Strict curfew 10pm in the dorm; no curfew in individual rooms. Reception open 7-11am and 5:30-10pm.

Hôtel de l'Abbaye, av. de la Gare (tel. 85-59-11-14), 10 min. from the center of town. Follow rue Lamartine/rue Filaterie down to the place du Commerce, and bear right onto av. de la Gare. Elegant and popular—be sure to reserve. Singles and doubles 79-108F, with shower 140F. The restaurant downstairs has *menus* for 68F and 94F. Open March-Nov. Closed Sun. evenings except June-Aug.

Hôtel du Commerce, 8, place du Commerce (tel. 85-59-03-09). Well-located, clean, and comfortable. Spotless, recently renovated singles and doubles 100-145F, with shower 135F. Hall showers 15F. Breakfast 22F. Make reservations. Closed Sun. Nov.-April.

Camping: Camping Municipal St-Vital, rue des Griottins (tel. 85-59-08-34). Follow rue Filaterie to rue de la Levée across the river, and turn right to this 3-star site next to a swimming pool. Often full July-Aug.; usually space if you arrive in early afternoon. Office sells ice-cream. Adults 8F, children 4F, 4.50F per tent or car. Office open June-Sept. 8am-10pm.

Food

Cafes and *salons du thé* outnumber restaurants in Cluny, which may be just as well for budget eaters. **Supermarché Lion** is a large supermarket on av. de la Gare past the Auberge du Cheval Blanc. (Open Tues.-Sat. 8:45am-12:15pm and 2:30-7:15pm, Sun. 9am-noon.) For coffee and dessert, try either of the two *salons du thé* on rue Lamartine, **Pâtisserie au Succès** and **Le Péché Mignon,** or the **Café de la Nation,** off rue Lamartine.

Restaurant de la Renaissance, 47, rue Mercière (tel. 85-59-01-59), on the continuation of rue Lamartine. Serves large portions of food to hungry working people of the town. The back room is elegant but a bit stuffy. *Plats du jour* from 35F. 50F *menu.* Open Oct.-Aug. daily 7:30am-8:30pm.

Les Marronniers, 20, av. de la Gare (tel. 85-59-07-95). A simple restaurant. Popular with locals. Large 47F *menu.* Open Tues.-Sat. noon-2pm and 7-8:30pm, Sun. noon-2pm.

La Petite Auberge, 18, place du Commerce (tel. 85-59-02-96). Salads 10-19F, good pizza 26-34F. *Côte de veau grillé* 41F. The staff hustles around to jazz tapes. Open Thurs.-Tues. noon-1:15pm and 7:15-9:30pm.

Auberge du Cheval Blanc, 1, rue Porte de Mâcon (tel. 85-59-01-13). Family-style meals in a pretty stone building. 65-150F *menus.* Open Sun.-Fri. noon-1:30pm and 6-9pm.

Sights

The **Abbaye** at Cluny was founded in 910 as part of an effort to purify monasticism. The Cluniacs reacted to increasing secular leadership in monastic centers by demanding that the abbot have supreme control over the abbey and be responsible only to the pope. For hundreds of years afterward, Cluny was the pillar of Christian piety, and the center of a network of satellite abbeys that spanned the continent. With power and opulence, however, came a relaxation of discipline. When the Cluniac abbey was brought under the dominion of the king of France in the fifteenth century, the ensuing decadence and religious wars eroded its power. It was greatly damaged during the Revolution, when its stones were sold off with the approval of the authorities.

Today, the only thing left to see is the southern part of the transept, but this alone gives you an idea of the majestic dimensions of the original building. The largest in all of Christendom until the construction of St-Peter's in Rome, the church at its peak could house 1000 pilgrims in its adjoining buildings. It contained 1200 capitals, many of which survived a fall of 30m when the columns on which they rested were mined, and are exhibited today in the vaulted thirteenth-century refectory. (Obligatory tours 22F, ages 18-24 12F, children 5F. Open daily July-Sept. 9am-6pm, tours every ½ hr.; April-June and Oct. 9:30am-noon and 2-6pm, tours every ½ hr.; Nov.-March 10am-noon and 2-4pm, tours every hr.)

To grasp the extent of the abbey's former grandeur and influence, go to the fifteenth-century Palais Jean de Bourbon to see the well-documented artifacts at the **Musée Ochier.** (Open daily June 15-Sept. 15 9:30am-noon and 2-6:30pm; Jan. 15-June 15 and Sept. 15-Dec. 20 10am-noon and 2-6pm. Admission 4F.) You can get a magnificent overview of the abbey and the valley by climbing the **Tour des Fromages;** enter through the *syndicat.* (Same hours as *syndicat.* Admission 5F, students 3F.) The humble twelfth-century **Eglise St-Marcel** (its steeple was added in the 16th century) houses an interesting exhibit on the life of a Benedictine monk (free). The **Eglise Notre-Dame** was built in pure thirteenth-century Burgundian style.

Near Cluny

South of Cluny the magnificently situated castle **Berzé-le-Châtel** overlooks the abrupt slopes and crags of the Bois Clair Pass. (Open April-Oct. daily 9am-noon and 2-6pm, but you can visit only the terrace. Free.) A few kilometers down N79 is **Berzé-le-Ville** with its **Chapelle Monacale** and notable twelfth-century frescoes. (Tel. 85-36-66-52. Open Easter-Nov. Mon. and Wed.-Sat. 9:30am-noon and 2-6pm, Sun. 2-6pm. Admission 10F, students 5F.) Twelve kilometers south of Cluny on D22 is **Château St-Point,** home of the poet Lamartine, with a small museum. Nearby **Lac St-Point-Lamartine** has sailboat rentals and year-round camping. There is no public transport to any of the above, so you'll have to improvise.

Four buses per day embark on the one-and-a-half-hour trip to **Basilique de Paray-le-Monial,** a well-proportioned smaller replica of the former abbey at Cluny. Here, in the nineteenth century, St-Margaret Mary Alacoque, then a humble nun, supposedly had her vision of the Sacred Heart of Jesus. Today the site draws pilgrims from all over the world. (Open May-Sept. 9am-noon and 1-7pm; April and Oct. 1-7pm. Free.) The **Musée d'Art Sacré du Hiéron** is devoted to religious sculpture and paintings; most notable is the tympanum from Anzy-le-Duc, considered a masterpiece of Burgundian Romanesque sculpture. (Tel. 85-88-85-80. Open May-Sept. daily 9am-noon and 1:30-6:30pm. Admission 10F.)

The road between Cluny and Tournus passes village after enchanted village, each with its own beautiful Romanesque church. A bus can take you as far as Cormatin; halfway you will find the religious community of **Taizé.** Brother Roger, its founder, settled here in the 1940s and sheltered political refugees in his home. Today, this small village with its modest twelfth-century church has become a bustling religious center. Every summer several thousand young Christians congregate here for singing, serious religious discussion, and good-natured revelry. Phone ahead (tel. 85-50-14-14) if you intend to stay. Bring a sleeping bag for the tents or bunks. They charge about 25F or whatever you can pay. For more information write Taizé communauté, 71250 Cluny.

Ten minutes (12km) farther by bus is **Château Cormatin.** This seventeenth-century castle possesses the best-preserved and most complete Louis XIII interior in France. The richly painted walls, complemented by period furniture, are shown off by knowledgeable guides; an English translation of the one-hour tour is available. (Open April 1-18 daily; May and June weekends and holidays; July-Oct. daily 10am-noon and 2:30-6:30pm. Admission 22F, students 15F.)

Halfway between Cormatin and Tournus and accessible only by car or bicycle on ill-traveled roads is the quiet town of **Brancion.** Its small Romanesque church retains some original frescoes; a map and description in English (9F) takes you on a treasure hunt through the ruins of its castle. But most magnificent is the view overlooking the lush valleys and hills of the countryside, where you can see villages as far as Cormatin.

Tournus

Situated midway between Chalon-sur-Saône and Mâcon on the Saône River, Tournus straddles the border of two distinct Burgundian regions—to the east lie the flat plains of Bresse, criss-crossed by gently undulating rivers and lakes; to the west, the more hilly, vine-covered Tournugeois are dotted with hundreds of Romanesque churches. Tournus has made its own contribution to Romanesque architecture—a magnificent church and monastery. The town also possesses two museums and an array of characteristic, ramshackle houses lining the peaceful, green banks of the Saône. In modern Tournus, working-class bars sidle alongside churches. The town awkwardly combines its agricultural brawn and crowds of tourists with the bygone grace of its religious buildings.

Orientation and Practical Information

Tournus is long and narrow, running along the west bank of the Saône. The main avenue, rue Docteur Pivey, which becomes rue de la République, then rue Desiré Mathivet, runs through place Lacretelle, place Carnot, and place de l'Hôtel de Ville, where the action, such as it is, can be found.

Office de Tourisme: Place Carnot (tel. 85-51-13-10). From the station, walk right on av. Gambetta then left on rue Docteur Privey. In a half-timbered building with a knowledgeable but reticent staff. Excellent free city maps. Accommodations service. Brochures on châteaux and Romanesque churches (in English). Map of the small roads connecting the above (1F), especially useful for biking or hitching. **Currency exchange** Mon. in July-Aug. when banks are closed. Open July-Aug. daily 9am-noon and 3-7pm; March-June and Sept.-Oct. daily 9am-noon and 2-6pm; Nov.-Feb. Sat. 10am-noon.

Post Office: Rue du Puits des Sept Fontaines (tel. 85-51-15-16). Take the bridge under the train tracks at place de l'Arc and bear right, following the PTT signs. **Postal code:** 71700. Open Mon.-Fri. 8am-noon and 2-6pm, Sat. 8am-noon.

Train Station: Av. Gambetta (tel. 85-51-07-30). Tournus is on the Paris-Lyon route. To Paris (5 per day, 3½ hr.). 10 trains per day to Dijon (1½ hr., 56F), Chalon-sur-Saône (15 min., 18.50F), Mâcon (25 min., 26F), and Lyon (1½ hr., 63F). 8 per day to Beaune (1 hr.), some requiring a transfer at Dijon.

Bus Station: Call the *gare routière* in Chalon-sur-Sâone (tel. 85-48-79-04) or Mâcon (tel. 85-38-13-85) for information. Schedules at Café du Centre, 6, quai de Verdun (tel. 85-51-01-69). To Chalon-sur-Saône (6 per day, 40 min., 18F), Mâcon (3 per day, 1½ hr., 21.60F), and Lyon (1 per day, 3 hr.). Buses leave from quai de Verdun and from the train station.

Hitching: Hitch north or south on the RN6, which runs right through Tournus. Avoid lightly traveled D56 toward Cluny.

Hospital: Hôpital de Belnay, route de St-Gengoux (tel. 85-51-02-22).

Ambulance: SARL, 5, av. du Clos Mouron (tel. 85-51-11-03).

Police: Gendarmerie, 9, av. de la Résistance (tel. 85-51-12-34; in emergencies 17).

Accommodations, Camping, and Food

Tournus's hotels charge more than they are worth, leaving a conspicuous gap in the under-70F range.

Hôtel de la Madeleine, 15, rue Désiré-Mathivet (tel. 85-51-05-83). Clean rooms in the back have a narrow passageway view onto the Saône. Singles and doubles 80F, with 2 beds 100F. No showers. Breakfast 18F.

Hôtel Aux Terrasses, 18, av. du 23 Janvier (tel. 85-51-01-74), on the continuation of the main street. Classy 2-star establishment. Singles 80F. Doubles 92F, with shower 115F. Triples and quads 138F, with shower 155F. Breakfast 17F. Often booked; call a day ahead if you plan to arrive on Sun.

Hôtel de l'Hôtel de Ville, place de l'Hôtel de Ville (tel. 85-51-07-33). Ordinary, clean rooms in a central location. Singles and doubles 100F, with bath 130F. Extra bed 40F. Breakfast 18F.

Hôtel Terminus, 21, av. Gambetta (tel. 85-51-05-54), next to the train station and 4 min. from the church. Singles and doubles from 75F. Breakfast 18F. Open Feb.-Dec.

Camping: Le Pas Fleury, Tel. 85-51-16-58. Follow av. Général-Leclerc or av. du 23 Janvier out of town to N6 (*direction* "Lyon"), and turn left. The 1-star site is at the river's edge, behind the track field, near a pool and tennis courts. English spoken. Crowded July-Aug. but always has room for a tent. No reservations. 4F per person, 3F per tent, 2F per car, hot showers included. Open April-Sept.

Tournus is probably the best place to try *quenelles au brochet,* dumplings made with *pâté à choux* and fish and served with a creamy sauce. Many hotels double as restaurants and serve homecooked meals for around 55F. The outdoor **market** (Sat. mornings on rue de la République) goes from one end of town to the other and sells about anything you could want. **Confiserie Fagot,** 42, rue de la Rpública, confects *pain d'épices,* a spicy cake unique to the region. (Open Tues.-Sat. 9am-noon and 2:15-7pm.) **Au Bon Accueil,** 31, rue Chanay (tel. 85-51-12-18), a local favorite, offers excellent *menus* from 52F, but is a 15-minute walk from *centre ville.* To get there, walk under the tracks on the continuation of rue Dorey. (Open Sun.-Fri. noon-2pm and 7-9pm.) **Le Voleur de Temps,** 32, rue Docteur Privey (tel. 85-40-71-93), features an uncontrived country atmosphere and an ambitious young chef. (Vegetarian *menu* 48F, carnivore *menu* 54F. Open Thurs.-Mon.) Get your *quenelles au brochet* in the 58F *menu* at the elegant **Restaurant l'Abbaye,** 12, rue Lion-Godin (tel. 85-51-11-63). (Open daily noon-2pm and 7-10pm.) Down the block, **Restaurant R. Gras,** 2, rue Fénelon (tel. 85-57-07-25), has a light 55F *menu* featuring *poulet rôti* (roast chicken). (Open Mon.-Sat. noon-2pm and 7:30-9:30pm.) Staples wait to jump into your arms from the shelves of **Supermarché Champion,** av. de la Resistance, off av. Gambetta. (Open Mon.-Thurs. 8:30am-12:30pm and 2:30-7pm, Fri. 8:30am-12:30pm and 2:30-7:30pm, Sat. 8:30am-7pm, Sun. 8:30am-noon.)

Sights

Abbatiale St-Philibert reminds you emphatically of the power of old stone. The austere monumental facade and the massive unadorned columns inside demonstrate powerful simplicity. **Chapelle Supérieure St-Michel,** upstairs above the narthex, accommodated, at one time or another, both prisoners and pilgrims. The narthex is the oldest surviving part of the early tenth-century structure. The transverse-ribbing of the nave's barrel vaults is unique among Romanesque patterns. Returning to the street, you will find the refectory next door and **Eglise St-Valérien** farther on (both now used as exhibition spaces). On the other side of the cloister, behind the abbey on rue A. Thibaudet, is the excellent **Musée Bourguignon,** rue Perrin de Puycousin. You'll be guided rather quickly through rooms furnished in eighteenth-century Burgundian style and containing period costumes, utensils, textiles, and ironwork. (Open April-Oct. Wed.-Mon. 9am-noon and 2-6pm. Admission 6F, students 4F.) **Musée Greuze,** rue de Collège by place de Lacretelle, maintains a large collection of works by Greuze, a popular, sentimental eighteenth-century artist. (Open April-

Nov. Tues.-Sat. 9:30am-noon and 2-6:30pm, Sun. 2-6:30pm. Admission 6F, students 4F.) In the old town, somber facades conceal some ornate Renaissance courtyards, the most interesting of which are at #13, 21 and 63, rue de la République. Cross the Saône and you'll be in the countryside.

Charlieu

In the ninth century, Benedictine monks fleeing invading Normans established a new monastery at Charlieu. They called their settlement *Carus locus* in Latin, *cher lieu* (dear place) in French; it soon came under the mantle of the prosperous abbey at nearby Cluny. In the late thirteenth century, the bourgeoisie, hostile to its tight-fisted Benedictine overlords, helped establish a Franciscan monastery, a more benevolent order. At this time, Charlieu was at its most prosperous with a colossal 5000 inhabitants, outnumbered only by Lyon. The city fell into decline after the fifteenth century, when major byways were re-routed through Beaune, but was revived somewhat at the beginning of the nineteenth century, with the introduction of the silk industry from Lyon. Nestled in the country, Charlieu is now a sleepy town with two lovely, historically important churches.

Orientation and Practical Information

Charlieu is located about 20km north of the town of Roanne and about 100km northwest of Lyon.

The nearest train station is in Roanne, on the main rail line west of Lyon. Trains run hourly to Lyon (1¼ hr., 58F) and St-Germain-de-Fossé (40 min., 43F) with transfers to all points west. (Call 77-37-50-50 for SNCF information.) **Buses** to Charlieu leave from the *gare routière* next to the Roanne train station (4 per day, 40 min., 9.30F). You can also take a bus to Pouilly-sur-Charlieu (8 per day, 20 min., 7.40F) and walk or hitch the last 4km along D487 to Charlieu. (Call 77-71-24-03 for bus information.) You can usually get a ride from Roanne at least to Pouilly-sur-Charlieu. Take bus #2 to the Roanne stop.

Charlieu's *centre ville* forms a square and is bordered by a busy street that changes names seven times. The buses stop at place St-Philbert. The **Syndicat d'Initiative** (tel. 77-60-12-42), located in the *place,* distributes a free map, a pamphlet describing the circuit of churches in the region, and little advice. (Open March-Dec. Tues.-Sat. 10am-noon and 3-6pm.) The **post office,** 6, bd. Jacquard (tel. 77-69-06-53), is at the other end of rue Charles de Gaulle from the *syndicat.* (Open Mon.-Fri. 8am-noon and 2-6pm, Sat. 8am-noon.) The **postal code** is 42190. Rent **bikes** at B. Auroy, 6, rue André Farinet (tel. 77-60-25-20), off rue Charles de Gaulle. (25F per ½-day, 50F per day. Open Tues.-Sat. 8am-12:30pm and 2-8pm.)

Accommodations, Camping, and Food

There are few hotels in Charlieu; fortunately, few tourists fill them. The **Hôtel Lion d'Or,** place de la Porcherie (tel. 77-60-29-36), down the street from the post office, offers beautiful, large rooms with elegant wood and brass beds. (Singles and doubles 85F, hall shower included. Extra bed 18F.) The **Hôtel du Champ de Foire,** place de la Bouverie (tel. 77-60-04-46), has large singles and doubles for 80F (showers 8F). The cozy restaurant downstairs serves a 55F *menu.* **Pizzeria l'Etna,** 31, rue Jean Morec (tel. 77-60-00-54), 1 block up from place St-Philbert, serves pizza from 22F. (Open Tues.-Sat. noon-2pm and 7-10pm, Sun. 7-10pm.) **Le Sornin** at 6, place de la Bouverie (tel. 77-60-03-74), will feast you handsomely for 50-70F. (Open Tues.-Sun.) Fill your picnic basket at the **market** on Wednesday and Saturday mornings in place St-Philbert, and enjoy it on the banks of the Sornin. Rue Riottier takes you from the post office to the riverside **Camping Municipal** (tel. 77-69-01-70), with tennis courts and a swimming pool next door. (8.75F per person, 5.15F per tent. Hot showers included. English spoken. Office open April-Sept. daily 8am-10pm. Swimming pool charges 9.30F per person.)

Sights

Three successive churches were built on the site of **Abbaye Benedictine,** the last of which was destroyed during the Revolution and subsequently auctioned off piece by piece. An informative 45-minute tour (text in English) takes you to a room above the Chapelle du Prieur, from where you can see traces of the foundations superimposed on one another. The southern portal is adorned with an image of Christ wreathed in a mandorla (almond-shaped aureole), gracefully balanced by two angels and fantastic animals symbolizing the four evangelists. The heads of all the figures were guillotined by over-zealous revolutionaries.

To the left as you leave the abbey lies the Franciscan **Couvent des Cordeliers** (called *cordeliers* for the cords used to tie the monks' robes). Happily, the **cloître** was saved from being moved to California to decorate a millionaire's tennis court when outraged locals had the French government declare it a national monument. The animal and human iconography of the sculpted capitals on its pillars is unique in Europe. Guides take small groups around pillar by pillar explaining the symbolic meaning of each. Once you understand, stroll back around the cloister to see the sculptures as they were intended to be seen, circling meditatively. (Convent tours every half-hour, abbey tours every 45 min. Admission 10F, students 7F; to both 15F, students 12F, including a temporary exhibition near the abbey. Abbey and convent open June 15-Sept. 15 daily 9am-noon and 2-7pm; April-June 15 and Sept. 15-Sept. 30 Wed.-Mon. 9am-noon and 2-7pm; Oct.-Nov. and Feb.-March Thurs.-Mon. 9am-noon and 2-7pm.)

The **Circuit des Eglises Romanes** makes a good bike or car daytrip and is a great way to see the countryside. Ask at the *syndicat* for a map and description of the churches, the most important of which are Châteauneuf, Bois Ste-Marie, Paray-le-Monial, Anzy-le-Duc, Semur-en-Bois, and Iguerande. It's a long way to go on a bike, but you can easily shorten your route.

Autun

Roman ruins, an outstanding cathedral, and the beautiful surrounding valley brighten this otherwise gray town, founded by Augustus in 10 B.C.E. as *Augustodonum.* By the Middle Ages, Autun had been invaded and pillaged several times, and divided into two cities: a religious center, and an economic and industrial settlement. In 1120, the ground-breaking for the cathedral and the arrival of the relics of St-Lazare drew pilgrims who ultimately brought in enough wealth to build up the city and reunite the two halves. Prosperity in the seventeenth and eighteenth centuries contributed several beautiful *hôtels particuliers* to Autun, many of which (especially around place du Champ de Mars) are now being restored.

Orientation and Practical Information

The main street, **avenue Charles de Gaulle,** leads from the train station to place du Champ de Mars. Rue St-Saulge and rue aux Cordiers both run from place du Champ de Mars into rue Chauchien, which changes name two times and ends up at the cathedral in the heart of the old city.

Office de Tourisme: 3, av. Charles de Gaulle (tel. 85-52-20-34 or 85-86-30-00), off place du Champ de Mars. Helpful English-speaking staff. Map, a booklet on Autun, and a list of hotels and restaurants. **Currency exchange** when banks are closed. Accommodations service 1F. In summer, guided tours of the city start here daily at 10am and 3pm (14F, students 10F). Open Easter-Sept. Mon.-Sat. 9am-noon and 2-7pm, Sun. 10am-noon and 3-6pm; in off-season Mon.-Fri. 9am-noon and 2-6pm, Sat. 2-6pm.

Post Office: Rue Pernette (tel. 85-52-05-85), up rue de la Grille from the train station. **Telephones. Postal code:** 71400. Open Mon.-Fri. 8:30am-7pm, Sat. 8:30am-noon.

Train Station: Place de la Gare (tel. 85-52-28-01), on av. de la République. TGV trains from Paris and Lyon stop at Le Creusot, from where Autun-bound buses depart daily (Mon.-Fri.

6 per day, 3 Sat., 1 Sun.; 50 min.; 29F). Train service from Chalon-sur-Saône, along the Dijon-Paris line, is continued by a special SNCF bus (3 per day, 1 hr. 20 min.). If you really, *really* want to make the entire trip by train, you'll have to change 2-4 times in tiny towns with huge names. The train station in Mâcon has a schedule of how to get to Autun; it looks like a final exam in Advanced Logic.

Bus Station: 13, av. de la République (tel. 85-52-30-02). The office is up the street to the left of the station, but buses leave from the station. To Dijon daily at 5:10pm (2 hr. 20 min., 55F).

Medical Emergency: Clinique du Parc, Tel. 85-52-18-34.

Police: Rue de la Jambe-de-Bois (tel. 85-52-18-01).

Police Emergency: Tel. 17.

Accommodations and Camping

The least expensive lodgings are located near the train station. Make reservations in summer, or ask at the tourist office.

Hôtel de France, place de la Gare (tel. 85-52-14-00). Magnificent stairways decorated with interesting photographs. Fine rooms. Singles from 66F. Doubles from 70F, with shower 100F. Breakfast 17F. Open Mon.-Sat. and Sun. after 5:30pm.

Hôtel le Grand Café, 19, rue de Lattre de Tassigny (tel. 85-52-27-66), on place du Champ de Mars. Central location. Quite luxurious—rooms with showers. Singles and doubles from 97F. Breakfast 15F.

Camping Municipal de la Porte d'Arroux, 1½km from town (tel. 85-52-10-82), past the bridge. A 3-star campground with swimming, fishing, and other water sports. Restaurant and grocery store nearby. 7F per person, 5.20F per tent. Open Easter-Nov.

Food

Autun supports a wide selection of fairly-priced restaurants serving regional cuisine. The **market** is held on Wednesday and Friday mornings in place du Champ de Mars.

Restaurant Lardreau, 58, av. Charles de Gaulle (tel. 85-52-16-74). A small, cozy place with 48F and 65F *menus,* the latter featuring *fondue de volaille au porto* (chicken fondue with port). Open Jan.-Nov. daily noon-2pm and 7-9pm.

Chalet Bleu, 3, rue Jeannin (tel. 85-86-27-30), near place du Champ de Mars. A super-spiffy place run by one of France's award-winning chefs. *Menus* 65F, 90F, and 150F. Open July-May Wed.-Mon.

Auberge de la Bourgogne, 39, place du Champ de Mars (tel. 85-52-20-96). A family restaurant serving regional specialties. 68F *menu.* Open Tues.-Sat. noon-2pm and 7-9pm, Sun. noon-2pm.

Tête Noire, 1-3, rue de l'Arquebuse (tel. 85-52-25-39), in a hotel 1 block from place de Champ de Mars. 54F "tourist" *menu* offers a horsemeat hamburger. Those who have just decided they don't eat red meat will enjoy the excellent *menu pêcheur* (72F). Open April-Feb. Sun.-Fri.

Sights and Entertainment

In its heyday, Autun was the largest city in Roman Gaul—with a population of about 70,000, it was more than twice its present size. Furthermore, it was the only city to boast a circus, theater, and amphitheater. Today most of this splendor has evaporated. The circus, for example, is now an expanse of field, although aerial surveys done in the 1970s detected the remains of the foundations deep beneath the surface of the ground. Standing 200m away is a huge, heavy brick structure called the **Temple de Janus.** Evidence suggests that it was actually dedicated to Demeter, built away from the city so that the decadence and sexual frivolity of the goddess's followers wouldn't shock the townspeople. Others believe it was a temple to the Gaulish god Esus (the equivalent of the Roman Mars). In either case, the ruin is a rare example of a temple built in Gaulish form using Roman construction techniques. Two of the city's four Roman gates are also still standing: **Porte d'Arroux** on rue de Paris and **Porte de St-André** on rue Faubourg St-André. The **Théâtre Antique**, once capable of seating 30,000 enthralled spectators, is now a nice spot for a picnic. From here you can see the weird, conical **Pierre de Couhard**, 1km away on the hillside. No one knew what it was until excavations unearthed a plaque cursing anyone who dared disturb the eternal slumber of the man buried inside.

The intricately carved capitals in the outstanding **Cathédrale St-Lazare** recall those at the basilica in Vézelay, also constructed between 1120 and 1140. The magnificent tympanum of the Last Judgment over the central portal, a phantasmagoric vision in fresco, along with many of the capitals, is the work of Autun native Gislebertus. The original, lead-covered **beffroi** was destroyed by lightning in 1469; the current stone one was built at the end of the fifteenth century. To combine aural and visual experience, make your ascent (3F) as the bells ring the hour. At 10pm on summer nights, the cathedral wall plays host to a majestic sound and light show in French, "Autun aux Cent Visages" ("The Hundred Faces of Autun"; 25F).

Down the street, the **Musée Rolin** occupies a fifteenth-century hotel belonging to Chancellor Nicholas Rolin. Even if you don't have time to inspect the well-orchestrated Gallo-Roman exhibit, examine the three delicate statues from the tomb of St-Lazare, and Gislebertus's *Eve*, which captures the moment of the Fall with remarkable poignancy. (Open March 16-Sept. 9:30am-noon and 2-6:30pm; Oct.-Nov. 15 10am-noon and 2-5pm; Nov. 16-March 15 10am-noon and 2-4pm. Admission 7F, students 3.50F.) Larger, less interesting Gallo-Roman architectural fragments are displayed in the **Musée Lapidaire,** 10, rue St-Nicolas. (Open April 16-Sept. 10am-noon and 2-6pm; Oct.-April 15 10am-noon and 2-4pm. Free.)

Around the corner from the cathedral is the **Tour des Ursulines** and the ruins of the city fortifications, with a splendid view of the cathedral. Three kilometers up Mont Jou from St-Lazare is the **Croix de la Libération,** towering handsomely over the city and the surrounding area. You'll have to walk or hitchhike, as there are no buses. On the edge of town, on av. du 2*ème* Dragon, you will find a small lake surrounded by swimming, tennis, and riding facilities.

Every year in July, the festival **Musique en Morvan** brings an international sampling of young people's choirs to Autun. Concerts throughout the summer take place at the Château of Arnay-le-Duc and at the Eglise Saulieu, both nearby.

Near Autun

Autun is planted at the southeastern corner of the **Parc Naturel du Morvan.** Twenty-four kilometers away, **Mont Beuvray** and **St-Léger-sous-Beuvray** are graced with magnificent scenery and the remains of a Roman military outpost. Twenty-five kilometers southeast of Autun on D978 lies **Château de Couches,** surrounded by trees and enclosing a pleasant courtyard. (50-min. tour July-Aug. daily 3-6pm. Admission 12F, students 6F.) **Château de Sully,** 15km northwest of Autun on D326 and 4km from D973, was called the "Fontainebleu of Burgundy" by Madame de Sévigné. Birthplace of Marshall MacMahon, nineteenth-century president of France, this sixteenth-century palace today provides ample shelter to the Duke of Magenta. (No entry to interior. Gardens open Easter-Sept. 8am-6pm. Admission 5F.) Huge **Lac des Setton,** about 40km northwest, offers extensive camping, sailing, and skiing in a superb setting. You can rent **bikes** for excursions into the countryside at the train station (45F per day, deposit 250F and ID). The tourist office sells a leaflet that details six bicycle tours through the Morvan (5F).

Sens

The relatively large town of Sens makes a pleasant stopover (or even a daytrip from Paris or Dijon) because of its agreeable inhabitants and its famous prototypical Gothic cathedral, St-Etienne.

Named for an ancient Celtic tribe, the Senoni, Sens was one of the first great Gallic towns to wield power. When the city was the ecclesiastical center of France, even the bishops of Paris answered to the archbishop of Sens. The Wars of Religion saw a decline in the town's fortunes, however, and Sens was tossed around among counties and provinces before finally landing in Bourgogne.

Cathédrale St-Etienne is celebrated as France's first authentically Gothic cathedral and was reputedly the model for Canterbury Cathedral in England. Construction began in 1140, but changes and additions continued into the sixteenth century. Note particularly the four blue-toned stained-glass windows in the north ambulatory (aisle by the chancel); the window farthest to the left depicts the life and martyrdom of St-Thomas à Becket, who visited Sens. The cathedral's treasury holds a rich array of relics and liturgical vestments that belonged to two of Canterbury's renowned archbishops, St-Thomas and Edward of Abingdon. (The cathedral has been under repair since 1983; parts of the building may be shut as the project continues.) In July, tours of the cathedral are given in French or English (1 hr., 10F). Next door, **Palais Synodal** contained at one time the ecclesiastical court. Downstairs is the courtroom where heretics were condemned. The system of cells off the vaulted passageway has remained untouched since its construction and is the most complete thirteenth-century prison complex in France. It is fascinating to see what kind of wall etchings the condemned chose to decorate their cells. You may have to ask the custodians to show you these rooms—they're happy to do so. The cathedral treasury and the collections of the **Musée Municipal** are exhibited in the Henry II wing of the former residence of the archbishops. The museum's collection is mostly Gallo-Roman. (Open June-Sept. Wed.-Mon. 10am-noon and 2-6pm; Oct.-May Wed. and Sat.-Sun. 10am-noon and 2-6pm, Mon. and Thurs.-Fri. 2-6pm. Admission 8F.)

Before you leave Sens wander around the back streets in search of the half-timbered houses, Renaissance and neoclassical *hôtels particuliers* whose beams and posts are sometimes adorned with decorative or religious figures. The *syndicat*'s guide mentions almost all of them, including the notable **Maison d'Abraham,** on rue de la République at rue Jean Cousin. Its carved wood beams depict the tree of Jesse.

Practical Information, Accommodations, and Food

Sens is on the Paris-Dijon train line, with frequent service both to Paris (1½ hr., 62F) and Dijon (2 hr., 104F). If you're headed for Champagne, **Trec** (tel. 25-82-23-43) sends two to four **buses** per day during the week from outside the train station and near the tourist office to Troyes for a train connection (2 hr., about 49F). The **Syndicat d'Initiative,** place Jean Jaurès (tel. 86-65-19-49), will supply you with maps, historical commentaries, and accommodations listings. (Hotel reservations 5F. Currency exchange in summer. Open daily July-Aug. 9am-noon and 1:30-7:30pm; Sept.-June Mon.-Tues. and Thurs.-Sat. 9am-noon and 1:30-6:15pm.) From the station, walk down av. Vauban, cross the river, and follow the signs left on the curving road (20 min.). The cathedral is just 2 blocks away.

Sens has many reasonably priced hotels, but the restaurants are on the expensive side. A sincere welcome awaits you at the **Hôtel des Deux Ponts,** 22, av. Lucien-Cornet (tel. 86-65-26-81), on the main road into town from the train station, just over the first bridge. (Decent singles 60F. Doubles 75-130F. Good 45F *menu.* Reception open Mon.-Sat.) The newly renovated **Hôtel Esplanade,** 2, bd. du Mail (tel. 86-65-20-95), off place Jean Jaurès, offers well-decorated rooms, all with TV. (Singles and doubles 75-145F. Hall shower included. Reception open Mon.-Sat.) **Camping Municipal Entre-deux-Vannes** (tel. 86-65-64-71) is right outside town on route de Lyon. (8F per night. Open June-Nov.) The cheapest meals in town are the enormous *couscous* platters (30F and up) at **Chez Said,** 89, rue du Général-de-Gaulle (tel. 86-65-40-46). Adequate rooms are also available (singles or doubles 80F, with shower 120F), but you'll have to go by an initially sweet-looking St-Bernard the size of a cow to get to them.

Auxerre

Auxerre has achieved what all Burgundian towns desire: a balance between past and present. Accommodating the departure *en masse* from the countryside (a trend since the 2nd half of the last century), Auxerre more than tripled its population, became an industrial center, and has been connected by railroad to the rest of France. Where for centuries wine production was the chief livelihood, only one Auxerre vineyard remains today, and tourism contributes significantly to the local economy. Miraculously, Auxerre evolved gracefully; the town offers many amenities (train and bus transport, reasonably priced hotels and restaurants), making it an excellent base for exploring the Yonne region of Burgundy. The residents, who decorate their city with flowers and this year established a new museum, seem to care about continuing improvement. What is best, Auxerre has not fully moved into the 1980s: With the utter calm of dusk, it becomes centuries younger. Gallo-Roman antiques invoke its childhood, and the yet unadulterated farmland, still visible from town limits, reminds visitors of its birth.

Orientation and Practical Information

Auxerre lies 52km north of Vézalay and Avallon. The *vieille ville* is on the west bank of the Yonne, forming a maze of crooked streets within a traffic ring.

Syndicat d'Initiative: 1-2, quai de la République (tel. 86-52-06-19), below the cathedral on the bank of the Yonne. Good city map, information on sights, and a 7F accommodations service. Open June 15-Sept. 15 daily 9:30am-12:30pm and 2-7pm; in off-season Mon.-Sat. 9am-12:30pm and 2-6:30pm. **Branch office,** 16, place des Cordeliers (tel. 86-51-10-27), adjacent to the pedestrian streets. Open June 15-Sept. 15 Mon. 2:30-6:45pm, Tues.-Sat. 10am-12:30pm and 2:30-6:45pm.

Bureau d'Information Jeunesse de l'Yonne (BIJY): 70, rue du Pont (tel. 86-51-68-75), on the street off point Paul Bert. Tons of information on travel, work (including archeological digs), and sports. Open Mon.-Fri. 9am-noon and 1:30-6pm.

Currency Exchange: Banque Populaire de L'Yonne (BPY), 18-22, place des Cordeliers (tel. 86-52-53-81). Accepts most types of traveler's checks. Commission 1%. Open Mon.-Fri. 8:30-11:55am and 1:35-5:30pm.

Post Office: Place Charles-Surugue (tel. 86-51-37-46), in the town center. **Telephones. Postal code:** 89000. Open Mon.-Fri. 8am-7pm, Sat. 8am-noon.

Train Station: Rue Paul Doumer (tel. 86-46-50-50), on the east side of the Yonne. To Paris (7 per day, 2½ hr., 97F), Lyon (7 per day, 4½ hr., 167F), Avallon (7 per day, 1 hr. 15 min., 37F), Autun (7 per day, 3 hr. 20 min., 76F), and Sermizelles (7 per day, 1 hr. 15 min., 30.50F).

Bus Station: Place Migraines (tel. 86-46-90-66), just outside the northwest corner of the inner city. Frequent connections to Avallon and the surrounding area.

Bike Rental: SNCF, at the train station (tel. 86-46-95-06). 47F per day, deposit 300F. You must show, but not leave, a piece of ID.

All-night Pharmacy: *Pharmacie de garde* changes nightly; call the police, see the listing in any local newspaper, or check the door of any pharmacy for the location.

Hospital: Hôpital Général, bd. de Verdun (tel. 86-46-07-09).

Medical Emergency: SMUR, Tel. 86-46-45-67.

Police: Bd. Vaulabelle (tel. 86-51-42-44).

Police Emergency: Tel. 17.

Accommodations, Camping, and Food

Auxerre has two IYHF-affiliated *foyers*. Both accept men and women. **Jeunes Travailleurs** is closer to the train station, and **Jeunes Travailleuses** closer to *centre ville*. The BIJY (see Practical Information) has a list of local farmers who welcome campers and help them discover the joys of fresh farm products.

Foyer des Jeunes Travailleurs (IYHF), 16, av. de la Résistance (tel. 86-46-95-11). From the train station, walk south along the tracks to the end of the platform, then cross the tracks on the little footbridge. Continue straight and you'll see the signs and a modest high-rise on the right (10 min.). Singles 54F. Breakfast included. Meals 30F.

Foyer des Jeunes Travailleuses (IYHF), 16, bd. Vaulabelle (tel. 86-52-45-38). From the train station, follow the signs to *centre ville,* cross the bridge, and turn left; the 1st right is rue Vaulabelle. The *foyer* is in an inconspicuous apartment building to the left, set back from the street and past a gas station, only 5 min. from the *vieille ville.* Singles 60F. Breakfast included. Meals 30F.

Hôtel de la Renomée, 27, rue d'Egleny (tel. 86-52-03-53), in the *vieille ville.* Stately and quiet rooms 80F, with shower 100F. Hall showers included. Open Mon.-Sat.; closed 3 weeks in Aug. Restaurant downstairs has *menus* from 39F.

Hôtel de la Porte de Paris, 5, rue St-Germain (tel. 86-46-90-09), on the edge of *vieille ville.* The owner, Jacques, runs a pleasant, clean hotel-bar. Almost always full by evening, but a very high turnover rate. Singles or doubles with shower 98F. Triple with shower 130F. Quad with shower 180F. Breakfast 15F.

Camping: 3-star site, route de Vaux (tel. 86-52-11-15), south of town on D163. A shady spot along the Yonne, with TV, laundry facilities, and a pool nearby. Open April-Oct.

Auxerre has many restaurants that offer filling 40-45F *menus.* Try **Restaurant L'Ancien Chai,** 12, rue de la Fraternité (tel. 86-52-39-62), which offers a good 38F *menu* at lunch and a grand 52F *menu* at both lunch and dinner. (Open Mon.-Fri. noon-1:30pm and 7-9:30pm, Sat. noon-1:30pm.) The **Pony Express,** 113, rue de Paris (tel. 86-52-83-44), a few blocks off the pedestrian area, also serves a 38F *menu,* but you can eat about the same quantity for less *a la carte* in this super-cheap restaurant. (Open daily noon-2pm and 7-9:30pm.) Tuesday, Friday, and Saturday are **market** days from 9am to 1pm in place de l'Arquelouse; Sunday, the market is held at the same time in place Degas.

Sights

Thirteenth-century **Cathédrale St-Etienne** is an elegant Gothic structure with a flamboyant facade. Bas-reliefs on the portals depict biblical accounts of the Creation, the Garden of Eden, and Noah's Ark. The interior is especially remarkable for its magnificent thirteenth- and sixteenth-century stained-glass windows: Closer to eye level than in many other churches, they narrate the stories of David and Saul and of St-Joseph. For 8F you can see the small **treasury** with its enamel work, illuminated manuscripts, and fifth-century tunic of St-Germain, and then be let in to see the eleventh-century **crypt,** where you'll find the ochre fresco *Christ on Horseback,* the only representation of its sort in the entire history of art. (Open Mon.-Sat. 9am-noon and 2-6pm, Sun. 2-6pm.)

Abbaye St-Germain was the site of several pilgrimages in honor of St-Germain, and was an educational center for pupils from all of Europe. The fame of the Gothic abbey rests on its Carolingian **crypts,** dating from the ninth century, a veritable underground church containing the oldest frescoes in France. (Open Wed.-Mon. Obligatory tours every ½ hr. 9-11:30am and 2-5:30pm. Admission 7.50F.) Included in the admission price is the adjacent **Musée d'Art et d'Histoire,** a new museum with a collection concentrating on the artifacts of four centuries of Roman occupation.

The crooked streets of the old town, departing from central place des Cordeliers, along with the lovely skyline from the Yonne, form an intriguing cityscape. Stroll around the pedestrian zone to see the old houses and **Tour de l'Horloge,** a fifteenth-century clocktower with two faces. **Musée Leblanc-Duvernoy,** 9bis, rue d'Egleny, in the west part of town, contains five Beauvais tapestries from the eighteenth century, as well as a collection of porcelain. (Open May-Oct. Wed.-Mon. 10:30am-noon and 2-6pm; Nov. 15-April Wed.-Mon. 10:30am-noon and 2-5:30pm. Admission 6F, ages under 16 free.)

A good dance place, open nightly from 10pm except Sundays, is **Le Magaly's,** 32, rue du Pont (tel. 86-51-73-45), down the street from the youth center.

Vézelay

Before his first election, Mitterand came here to reflect amidst the inspiring medieval architecture. Perched high on a hill overlooking fecund Burgundy farmland, this small town has enchanted visitors for centuries. Vézelay remains an ideal stopover for overstimulated travelers who wish to find a more traditional, tranquil side of France.

Before you actually enter the **Basilique de la Madeleine,** your climb to reach it will be rewarded by an exhilarating perspective on the valley below. Carved in about 1125, the **tympanum** expounds the Apostles' duty after Jesus' ascension. The bizarre array of characters in the carvings immediately adjacent symbolize the strange peoples in distant lands that the apostles must enlighten. The capitals of the columns are more difficult to see but are an even more intriguing mix of the prosaic, the biblical, and the supernatural.

However, the greatest of treasures, or so thought the throngs of pilgrims in the Middle Ages, are the remains of a woman supposed to be Mary Magdalene contained in the tomb in the crypt, which is accessible by the right transept. Each year on July 22, pilgrims still come to pay homage to *la Madeleine.* A helpful 15F booklet (available in English) sold near the entrance describes, with photos, the capitals and tympanum. One or two free tours (usually in French) are given daily according to a schedule posted on the south door. (Church open July-Aug. daily 7am-7pm, basilica illuminated Tues. and Fri. 9:30-10:30pm; Sept.-June sunrise-sunset.) A **museum** above the chapter room contains sculpture removed from the church and gives you a good idea of what Viollet-le-Duc's nineteenth-century restoration of the building must have involved. From Monday to Saturday in July and August, you can climb the tortuous, narrow staircase of the tower (5F) for a wonderful view of the entire town and surrounding hills. It was here that St. Francis of Assisi decided to establish his first French brotherhood. The first Franciscan abbey in France, destroyed during the Revolution, has been rebuilt in its original place alongside the church.

Vézelay lies in the northwest corner of the national **Parc du Morvan.** The tourist office sells a booklet, *Itineraire Pédestre* (5F), which offers maps for short walks around the sights. Most rewarding is the view of the basilica, high upon a hill. The office also sells maps and guides to the Morvan: the Grand Randonné (GR) goes along the perimeter of the Morvan, and GR13 cuts through the center. If you're planning to explore the area, the 60F or so you pay for either book is well worth it for the listings of emergency telephone numbers and *gîtes ruraux,* which appear every 25km or so.

Practical Information, Accommodations, and Food

Vézelay's **Syndicat d'Initiative,** rue St-Pierre (tel. 86-33-23-69), is just below the church and will **exchange currency.** (Open April-Oct. Mon.-Tues. and Thurs.-Sat. 10am-1pm and 2-6pm, Sun. 10am-noon; Nov.-March shorter hours.) The **post office** is halfway up the hill on rue St-Etienne (open Mon.-Fri. 9am-noon and 2-5pm, Sat. 9am-noon). **Trains** run from Auxerre to Sermizelles (5 per day, ¾ hr.), from where a bus shuttles passengers to Vézelay once in the morning and once in the afternoon. **Buses** from Avallon keep roughly the same schedule; the bus for Avallon leaves around 6:30pm. The Auxerre, Avallon, and Vézelay *syndicats* have the schedule. You may also call the transport company, **Cars de la Madeleine** (tel. 86-33-25-67). Hitching from the station and in the area is easy.

Run by Pax Christi, a Catholic peace movement, the **Centre de Rencontres Internationales,** rue des Ecoles (tel. 86-33-26-73), offers central and inexpensive accommodations. The facilities are simple, but the staff is attentive and friendly. The upper floors offer fantastic views. (42F per person. IYHF card required. Breakfast included. Lunch and dinner 33F. Open July-Sept. 5. For reservations earlier in the year call 43-36-36-68 in Paris.) Located on a peaceful, rural site, the **Auberge de Jeunesse (IYHF),** route de l'Etang (tel. 86-33-24-18), less than 1km from town, has slightly more luxurious accommodations with only four per room. Follow the signs towards the *gendarmerie* from the base of the hill to the left. (34F per person. IYHF card required. Kitchen facilities. Lockout noon-6pm. Open June-Sept.) **Camping** is available behind the hostel.

Vézelay's restaurants are expensive, so you may want to stick to a take-out sandwich or crêpe from the nameless *crêperie* at 3, rue St-Etienne (tel. 86-33-23-64; open daily July-Aug. 11am-9pm; April-June and Sept.-Oct. 11am-7pm). A decent 54F *menu* is available at **Hôtel du Cheval Blanc,** place du Champ de Foire (tel. 86-33-22-12). (Open Sat.-Wed. noon-2pm and 7-9:30pm, Thurs. noon-2pm.) **Peyarot,** 39, rue St-Etienne (tel. 86-33-62-51), offers elaborate salads and *assiettes bourguignonnes* at equally elaborate prices. (*Menus* 68F and 90F. Open daily noon-5pm and 7:30pm-late.) **Express Marché,** near the bottom of the street, is Vézelay's only supermarket.

Avallon and the Morvan

Fortunately for travelers in Bourgogne, recent industrialization in Avallon has spawned numerous cheap hotels and restaurants. In the past 50 years, Avallon has more than tripled in size. Nevertheless, in the *vieille ville* or while climbing around the ramparts, it is possible to find the Avallon of old, originally named *Aballo* by the Druids (nothing mysterious—just means little apple).

High on a granite mountain, the old city of Avallon sits proudly on medieval ramparts. Enter by the **Tour de l'Horloge** and visit **Eglise Collégiale St-Lazare,** whose eleventh-century origins are most evident in its two Romanesque portals. The large one to the left is covered with zodiac signs, angels, vine leaves, and the old men of the Apocalypse; the smaller one to the right is decorated with carved flowers and plants. (Open Easter-Nov. daily 7:30am-6:30pm.) The **Musée de l'Avallonais,** housed in the 1653 **Ancien Collège,** contains a lovely Gallo-Roman mosaic, the *Mercure de Ste-Vertut,* and the well-known statuette of a god from Charancy. (Open June 15-Sept. 15 Wed.-Mon. 10am-noon and 3-7pm; in off-season only during school vacations. Admission 2F, students 1F.) **Promenade de la Petite Porte,** along the ramparts, offers an excellent view of the Vallée du Cousin. For a vista including both the valley and the city, cross the ravine to Parc des Chaumes, about 2km away (follow rue de Lyon to rue de la Goulotte to av. du Parc des Chaumes). Before climbing to the peak, pack a lunch with *specialités bourguignonnes* such as *gougère* (a cabbage *pâté* with gruyère cheese), available at the *boulangeries* and *charcuteries.* A huge **Maximarché** awaits customers on rue des Ecoles, by the train station (open Mon.-Sat.), and a covered **market** is held on Saturday mornings by place Général de Gaulle and in place des Odeberts in the center of town. The tourist office distributes lists of hikes through the area's valleys, medieval sanctuaries, and fortresses. These take anywhere from a few hours to a few days; the longer tours include information on places to stay (*gîtes d'étape*). You can also buy a complete map of the Morvan with plans for hikes (36F).

Situated at the north edge of the huge **Parc Naturel du Morvan,** Avallon is a good starting point for excursions into the region. For information on horseback riding, canoeing, sailing, and sightseeing in the park, contact the **Maison du Parc Naturel Régional du Morvan,** St.-Brisson, 58230 Montesauche (tel. 86-78-70-16).

Practical Information, Accommodations, and Food

The **Office de Tourisme** in Avallon, 4, rue Bocquillot (tel. 86-34-14-19), right next to St-Lazare, has information on the park and the city and will help you find a hotel room (5F). (Open June-Sept. daily 9:30am-7:30pm; Oct.-May Mon. 2-6:30pm, Tues.-Sat. 9:30am-12:30pm and 2-6:30pm.) When the tourist office is closed, call the **mairie,** 37-39, Grande Rue (tel. 86-34-13-50). **Bikes** can be rented only at the station (47F per day, ID and 300F deposit required). The region is very hilly so remember to check altitude points on a map before setting out. (For general hiking, the *Carte IGN* is recommended.) Vézelay is only 15km away and, except for a steep climb at the end, the route is relatively flat if you go via Vallée du Cousin. You can also take **Cars de la Madeleine** (tel. 86-33-25-67), an inefficient fleet of buses that run once per day on weekdays to Vézelay. Departing around 8am, the buses return around 6:30pm; the trip takes a half-hour each way. There is no return bus on Saturday. Pick up a timetable at the tourist office. Six **trains** per day go to Laroche, with connections to Paris (43F), and Auxerre (1 hr., 37F); three trains per day run to Autun (2 hr., 51F). One train on Wednesday goes to Paris directly (3 hr., 118F). **Buses**, operated by Transco (tel. 80-43-58-97), run to Dijon (2 per day, 2½ hr., 67.50F), with a stop in Semur-en-Auxois (about 20F). These buses depart from the train station.

On the edge of town toward Vézelay is the **Foyer des Jeunes Travailleurs**, 10, av. de Victor Hugo (tel. 86-34-01-88), which offers singles in a modern high-rise. (Members 56F. Breakfast 11F. Lunch or dinner 33F.) **Au Bon Accueil**, 4, rue de l'Hôpital (tel. 86-34-09-33), is the most economical hotel in town. (Singles 75F. Doubles 85F, with shower 90F. Reception open Mon.-Sat.) The restaurant below serves *menus* for 40F and 69F. **Hôtel St-Vincent**, 3, rue de Paris (tel. 86-34-04-53), off place d'Odeberts, has friendly management, clean rooms with sagging beds covered with fake fur blankets, and a lively bar and restaurant. (Singles and doubles 90F, with shower 105F. Open mid-Oct. to Sept.) **Camping Municipal de Sous-Roche** (tel. 86-34-10-39) lies 2km away; walk along route de Lourmes and then climb back to the picturesque, clean, and quiet three-star campsite. It's next to a river, with fishing and a restaurant. (Open March 15-Oct. 15.)

The restaurant at **Hôtel du Parc**, 3, place de la Gare (tel. 86-34-17-00), serves fantastic *menus* for 47F, 66F, and 105F. In the center of town, **Restaurant de l'Horloge**, right outside Porte de l'Horloge, offers 42F *menus*, but you're probably better off at any of the three well-stocked *charcuteries* on Grande Rue Aristide Briand.

Semur-en-Auxois

In 606 the monks of the Abbaye de Flavigny signed their charter in a village they called *Sene muros*, the "old walls." This is the earliest written record of Semur-en-Auxois, although legend attributes its founding to Hercules. The exact age of the city is unknown; at any rate, its age has lent Semur-en-Auxois charm. Today this tiny, provincial town of cobblestones and archways, perches above a bend in the Armançon River. It and its graceful church and impressive fortifications are often ignored by tourists, but shouldn't be. Try to visit on a Saturday, Sunday, or holiday night in July and August, when the *vieille ville* is illuminated (about 10pm-midnight). Especially beautiful views can be had from the pont Joly, pont Pinard, and quai d'Armançon.

Graceful **Eglise de Notre Dame** contrasts sharply with Semur's four hardy defense towers. This hilltop fortress is best approached by walking down to pont Pinard and following the Armançon River around the village to **pont Joly.** From here you can see above the huge granite **Tour de l'Orle d'Or**, the dungeon of the dismantled château, which, in spite of walls 5m thick, is cracked in one long split almost from base to summit. For the opposite view of the valley, climb the tower to the top of Semur. (Open July-Aug. daily 10am-noon and 2-6pm. Guided tour in French, 30 min., 8F.) Along rue Buffon lie the oldest houses and the largest number of shops. Semur also has an eclectic **Musée Municipal,** rue J. J. Colenot, containing important manuscripts and rooms devoted to painting, archeology, and natural history. (Open daily. Free.) Every May 31 and the preceding Sunday, Semur hosts thrilling horse races.

Practical Information, Accommodations, and Food

Semur is not far from a train stop between Paris and Dijon; get off at Les Laumes and step onto the Semur-bound bus (3 per day, 30 min., 13F). The same bus company, **Transco** (tel. 80-43-58-97), runs buses throughout the entire Côte d'Or, connecting Semur directly, with Dijon (Mon.-Sat. 2 per day, 1 Sun.; 1½ hr.; 40.80F), Avallon (same frequency, 1 hr., about 20F), and Saulieu (same frequency, 50 min., 12F). If you're waiting to make that train-bus change in Les Laumes, the **Hôtel de la Gare,** across the street, is run by a wonderful family that really knows how to do *coq au vin* right. Semur's **Syndicat d'Initiative,** place Gustave Gaveau (tel. 80-97-05-96), at the head of rue de la Liberté, posts bus schedules and dispenses maps and a list of hotels. (Open July-Aug. Mon.-Sat. 8:45am-noon and 2-6:30pm, Sun. 10am-noon and 3-6pm; Sept.-June Mon. 2-6:30pm, Tues.-Fri. 8:45am-noon and 2-6:30pm, Sat. 8:45am-noon, Sun. 3-6pm.)

Your best bet for accommodations is the **Foyer des Jeunes Travailleurs,** which doubles as an **Auberge de Jeunesse (IYHF),** 1, rue du Champ de Foire (tel. 80-97-10-22). Walk down rue de la Liberté away from the center of town, and turn left on rue du Champ de Foire. The hostel is a modern structure located in a shady park. There is almost always space and, if not, they'll send you to their annex. You must ring the doorbell to enter after 10pm; reception is open all day. (Singles 32F. Sheets 10.20F. Breakfast 7F. Self-service lunch 32F and dinner 30F. Meals are served Sept.-July Mon.-Sat.) There are a few budget hotels in town, but by far the best, because of the plush rooms and the wholesome woman who runs it, is **Hotel-Bar du Commerce,** 19, rue de la Liberté (tel. 80-97-00-18), in the center of town across from the tourist office. (Singles with shower 120F. Doubles with shower 160F. Huge breakfast 20F.) A **campground** lies 3km south of Semur on scenic Lac du Pont. (Open May-Sept. 7F per night.)

The cheapest decent meal in town may be found at **Sagittaire,** 15, rue de la Liberté (tel. 80-97-23-91), with a lunch *menu* and pizzas from 13F. (Open May to mid-Sept. Tues.-Sun. noon-2pm and 7:15-10pm; mid-Sept. to April Tues.-Sat. only.) The tiny Semur **market,** also on rue de la Liberté, sells local farm products. (Thurs. and Sat. mornings.)

Near Semur

Twenty-three kilometers from Semur, north of Les Launes and accessible only by car, stands lovely twelfth-century **Abbaye de Fontenay,** built completely in the Romanesque style as a Cistercian abbey. Visiting the abbey's dorm, bakery, and infirmary will show you what life as a monk was like 800 years ago. (Open daily 9am-noon and 2:30-6:30pm. Admission 24F.) Six kilometers from Semur is eighteenth-century **Château de Lantilly.** (Open Wed.-Mon. 10am-noon and 2:30-6pm. Admission 15F.) Semur is in the center of the **Route des Ducs de Bourgogne;** the tourist office can give you information on nearby châteaux, most of which are accessible only by car.

Perched on a hill at the edge of the Morvan, **Saulieu** is known for its twelfth-century **Basilique St-Andoche,** which lies off place Docteur Rochore. A free brochure (in French only) describes the delicately carved capitals. (Open daily 8:30am-6pm.) Next door, **Musée François Pompon** features the works of the popular turn-of-the-century sculptor from Saulieu, Pompon, in a reconstruction of a traditional Morvan home. (Open daily 10am-noon and 2-7pm. Admission 6F, students 4F.) The **Office de Tourisme** occupies a kiosk on rue Argentine (tel. 80-64-09-22), and distributes information on trails and *gîtes ruraux.* It's wise to buy the GR (*Grand Route du Pays*) book (50F); it supplies maps and recommends lodgings. Or buy map #306, put out by the *Institute Geographique National* (36F), the best map of the area.

Several inexpensive hotel-restaurants are scattered along the main drag in town, rue Grillot and rue Argentine (1 road, 2 names). **Au Petit Marguery** at 4, rue Argentine (tel. 80-64-13-58), offers singles for 80F, doubles or more from 130F. Breakfast is 17F. (Closed Jan. and Sun. nights.) Across the street at 1, rue Grillot is a larger establishment, **Hôtel de la Poste** (tel. 80-64-05-67), with singles from 100F and doubles from 150F. **Camping le Perron,** 500m north of town (tel. 80-64-16-19), is a three-star site. (Open March-Nov.) Several stores along rue de la Foire and place des Terreaux stock picnic provisions.

Buses will take you to and from Dijon (1-2 per day, 2½ hr., 61.20F) and Semur (1-2 per day, 35 min., 20.40F). **Trains** run from Autun (3 per day, 1 hr., 36F) and Auxerre (13 per day, 2 hr., 52F). From Paris, change trains at Auxerre (4 hr., 132.50F).

Beaune

Proud and prosperous, Beaune has existed for centuries with one purpose: wine. The entire town urges tourists to imbibe the precious yet freely-flowing nectar. Surrounding vineyards make incursions into the city itself, and the almost sacred wine is stored in the crypts of former churches. Only 20 minutes by train from Dijon, Beaune makes an excellent daytrip.

Orientation and Practical Information

The center of town is laid out roughly like a grid inside a large circle, with rue Carnot leading directly south from Dijon to the Hôtel Dieu on place Carnot. From the train station, walk straight ahead on av. du 8 Septembre. Continue as the pavement turns to cobblestones until you reach place Monge. Perpendicular to this is **rue Carnot,** which becomes **rue de Lorraine.** Turn left to place Carnot, then take a right to the tourist office.

Office de Tourisme: Rue Hôtel Dieu (tel. 80-22-24-51), across from Hôtel Dieu. Well-equipped. Free maps. English well spoken. **Currency exchange** when banks are closed. Accommodations service. Lists of tour-offering *caves* in the region. Free guided tours of the town (in French) July-Aug. daily at 3pm. Open daily June-Sept. 9am-midnight; March-May and Oct.-Nov. 9am-10pm; Dec.-Feb. 9am-7:15pm.

Travel Agency: Havas Voyages, 8, rue Lorraine (tel. 80-22-25-39), or **Wagon-Lit Tourisme,** 25, rue de Lorraine. Open Mon. 2-7pm, Tues.-Fri. 9am-7pm, Sat. 9am-noon.

Post Office: Rue de la Poste (tel. 80-22-22-32). **Telephones** and **currency exchange. Postal code:** 21200. Open Mon.-Fri. 8am-7pm, Sat. 8am-noon.

Train Station: Av. du 8 Septembre (tel. 80-44-50-50). Beaune is on the Dijon-Lyon train line. To Lyon (6 per day, 2½ hr., 85F), Dijon (12 per day, ½ hr., 27F), and Nevers (4 per day, 2½ hr., 91F). The TGV to Paris stops in Beaune twice per day (2 hr., 171F plus 13F reservation fee).

Bus Station: Transco, Tel. 80-71-40-34. Buses depart from rue Maufoux at bd. Bretonnière. To Chalon-sur-Saône (2 per day, 45 min.), Autun (1 per day, 1½ hr.), and Dijon (8 per day, 1 hr., 27.20F), making local stops at all the important wine centers along the Côte d'Or.

Bike Rentals: At the station (tel. 80-22-80-56). 37F per ½-day, 47F per day, deposit 300F.

Laundromat: Next to the supermarket, off place Madeleine. Wash 15F, dry 15F, soap 5F. Open daily 7am-8pm. Also at 24, rue du Faubourg St-Nicolas, but with slower machines. Open daily 7am-8:30pm.

Hospital: Centre Hospitalier, av. Guigone de Salins (tel. 80-24-75-75).

Medical Emegency: Tel. 80-26-60-46 or 80-22-23-09 for ambulance.

Police: Av. Général de Gaulle (tel. 80-24-64-00).

Police Emergency: Tel. 17.

Accommodations, Camping, and Food

Finding a room is difficult if you don't have reservations as the place is jammed with tourists. Most hotels have space in the morning but fill by afternoon. You can always base yourself in Dijon or at the youth hostel in Chalon-sur-Saône (see Near Beaune), both only 20-minute train rides away.

Hôtel Rousseau, 11, place Madeleine (tel. 80-22-13-59). Turn left from the train station for 3 blocks and then right on rue du Faubourg Madeleine. Beautiful wooden beds in clean rooms off a garden courtyard, and a salty old manager who lays down the law. No baths or showers. Breakfast included. Singles from 80F. Doubles from 110F. Strict curfew 1am.

Auberge de la Gare, 11, av. des Lyonnais (tel. 80-22-11-13), 3 blocks left of the train station. No-nonsense, decent hotel with a cheap restaurant. Singles and doubles 80F.

Hôtel le Foch, 24, bd. Foch (tel. 80-22-04-29). Take av. de la République from the tourist office. Musty and none too clean, but cheap. Singles and doubles 75F.

Hôtel de France, 35, av. du 8 Septembre (tel. 80-22-19-99), facing the train station and all its noise. May have a room when others don't. Recently renovated. Tasteful and comfortable. Singles and doubles 120F.

Camping Municipal: Les Cent-Vignes, 10, rue Dubois (tel. 80-22-03-91), 500m from the town center off rue du Faubourg St-Nicolas. Head north on rue Lorraine from place Monge. Often infested with trailers. Always has some space in the morning and always full by mid-afternoon in summer. Reservations accepted by mail before May 30. 10F per person, 8F per tent, 5F per car. Hot showers included. Open March 15-Oct. **Camping Municipal de la Grappe d'Or,** 10km south in Meursault (tel. 80-21-22-48). A 3-star site with swimming pool. Open April-Oct. 15.

Most restaurants in Beaune are expensive. The **Supermarché Casino,** 28, rue du Faubourg Madeleine (open Mon.-Sat. 9am-7:30pm), is the cheapest place to buy food, and a large **market** takes place Saturday mornings at place Carnot. Not just a hotel, the **Auberge de la Gare** serves an honest five-course meal for 42F. (Open daily noon-2pm and 7:30-8:30pm.) Hospitable **Brelinette,** 6, rue du Faubourg Madeleine, a continuation of rue d'Alsace (tel. 80-22-63-94), serves delicious regional dishes and *menus* for 50F, 60F, and 85F. (Open July-Aug. daily noon-2pm and 7-10pm; Sept.-June Thurs.-Tues. noon-2pm and 7-10pm.) Next door at #2, **L'Eschelier** (tel. 80-22-22-40) serves similar food in a more austere environment. (53F *menu. Plat du jour* such as *poulet rôti* 36F. Open Mon.-Sat. 12:15-2pm and 7:30-9:30pm.)

Sights and Entertainment

A trip to Beaune would be incomplete without a visit underground to one of the numerous *caves.* The tourist office has information on all those open to public *dégustation,* with hours and fees.

Patriarche, the largest company, owns many of these operations; some connoisseurs argue that mass production debases this company's product. The **Marché aux Vins,** near the Hôtel Dieu, is the most prestigious of the Beaune *caves.* For 30F, you are given a glass and free rein to sample 37 of Burgundy's finest wines. You can easily drink three or four times your entrance fee. (Open April-Nov. daily 9:30am-noon and 2:30-6:30pm; Dec.-March Sun. 9:30am-noon and 2:30-4:30pm.) Don't drink your limit too quickly—the best wines always come near the end. Save your most discerning palate for *les grands crus* (the great labels), or bring along some bread to slow alcohol absorption.

The oldest *caves* are the **Halle aux Vins** in the ninth-century crypt of the former Eglise St-Martin. (Free *dégustation.* Open April-Sept. daily 10am-noon and 2-7pm; Oct.-March Mon.-Sat. 10am-noon and 2-6pm.) **Maison Calvet,** 6, bd. Perpreuil, whose cobwebbed *caves* are 3km-long, gives tours, tastings, and a slide show to explain the production and storage processes. (Open Tues.-Sun. 9-11:30am and 2-5pm.) The **Caves des Cordeliers,** next to the Hôtel Dieu, features an inferior tour but satisfactory sampling *du tonneau* (from the keg). (Open daily 9am-noon and 2:30-7pm.) The schmaltzy tour offered by **Maison Patriarche Père et Fils,** rue du Collège, leads past astonishing numbers of dusty, aging bottles lying thousands deep along 9km of tunnels. Fortunately, the tour omits most of the tunnels and culminates in an energetic, if short, tasting session. (Open March 5-Dec. 18 9-11:30am and 2-5:30pm. Admission 30F, but drink up—proceeds go to charity.) When you emerge from subterranean Beaune, go to beautiful **Parc de la Bouzaise** beyond the city ramparts or **Square des Lions** just within the ramparts and take a breather.

The **Hôtel Dieu** helps support itself with an annual sale from the produce of its extensive vineyards. This landmark of Burgundian architecture was constructed as a refuge for the poor by Nicholas Rolin, Chancellor of Burgundy and a most effective tax collector. Rolin commissioned the colorful courtyard roof tiles and Roger Van der Weyden's *The Last Judgment;* both illustrate the political and cultural ties this region once maintained with Flanders. The informative tour explains the daily operation of the infirmary, chapel, kitchen, and pharmacy. (Open June 28-Sept. 7 daily 9am-6:45pm; Sept. 8-June 27 9-11:40am and 2-6pm. Admission 17F, students 12F, ages 6-14 6F. 45-min. tours every 15 min. in French only. Free pamphlet in English.)

The **Musée du Vin** is bottled in the **Hôtel des Ducs de Bourgogne,** and shelved in the picturesque pedestrian zone. Its exhibits on winemaking and tapestry-weaving are incomprehensible; bring your dictionary. (Open April-Sept. daily 9am-noon and 1:30-7pm; Oct.-March Wed.-Mon. 10am-noon and 2-5:30pm. Admission 9F, students 6F. Free tours July and Aug. hourly.) The ticket also admits you to the **Musée des Beaux Arts** and the **Musée Etienne-Jules Marey,** both on rue de l'Hôtel de Ville next to the police station. The former has a mediocre collection of Gallo-Roman funerary monuments and paintings by Félix Ziem, a local nineteenth-century artist. The latter, though, is exceptional, especially if you're interested in the history of photography. Marey, also a *Beaunois,* is considered the inventor of motion photography (chronophotography), the precursor of cinematography. Marey even invented a camera that supposedly took 2000 pictures per second. (Open Easter-April and Sept. 16-Nov. Wed.-Mon. 10am-noon and 2-5:30pm; May-June 15 Wed.-Mon. 9am-noon and 2-6:30pm; June 16-Sept. 15 daily 9am-noon and 2-6:30pm.)

In the center of town, the **Basilique Collégiale Notre-Dame** merits a visit for its fifteenth-century Flemish tapestries depicting the life of the Virgin Mary, and a venerated twelfth-century carved wooden Virgin. This is yet another church modeled after the abbey at Cluny.

The third weekend in November brings the festivities and wines of the **Vente des Vins des Hospices de Beaune,** when the wines produced by the Hôtel Dieu are sold off. Ritzy dinners with famous guests of honor are held in nearby châteaux the nights preceding the *vente.* These are open to the public but you must make reservations one or two years in advance.

Near Beaune: Chalon-sur-Saône

South of Beaune on the banks of the Saône sprawls the bustling city of **Chalon-sur-Saône,** with 80,000 inhabitants, a youth hostel, and two noteworthy museums. The **Musée Nicéphore-Nièpce,** 28, quai des Messageries, is the city's pride and joy. Nièpce, born in Chalon in 1765, was a prolific inventor credited with the invention of photography in 1822. The fascinating large museum, housed in an eighteenth-century *hôtel* overlooking the river, contains an exceptional collection of cameras, from the very first ever made to the one used on the moon by the Apollo mission. (Open Wed.-Mon. 9:30am-noon and 2-5:30pm. Admission 10F, students 5F.) **Musée Denon,** on place de l'Hôtel de Ville, showcases a distinctive archeological collection featuring Bronze Age implements and the outstanding 18,000-year-old *Silex de Volgu.* French, Italian, Flemish and Dutch canvases from the seventeenth-and eighteenth- centuries are also displayed. The nineteenth-century exhibition halls showcase Géricault's *Tête de Nègre.* (Open Wed.-Mon. 9:30am-noon and 2-5:30pm. Admission 10F, students 5F.) Chalon's **Cathédrale St-Vincent** is a handsome twelfth-century structure with interesting capitals and a fifteenth-century cloister. For a lovely view, cross pont St-Laurent to the small island in the middle of the Saône and climb the **Tour du Doyenné,** near the ancient hospital. (Open April-Sept. Mon.-Fri. 2-4:30pm.) Every year, Chalon hosts one of the most exuberant pre-Lenten festivals in France, which may explain why so many of the town's babies are born eight months after Easter.

Finding a room in Chalon is not difficult. The **Auberge de Jeunesse,** rue d'Amsterdam (tel. 85-46-62-77), overlooks the river, has a kitchen, and is next to a swimming pool and sailing club. (34F. Sheets 13F. Office open Jan. 15-Dec. 15 daily 7-10am and 5:30-10:30pm.) From the train station, walk straight down av. Jean Jaurès, and continue under the highway and past the tourist office as it changes to bd. de la République. Turn left on rue du Général Leclerc at the tall cement monument (place de l'Obélisque), go to the river, turn left, and continue along the river to the hostel (25 min.). Or take bus #15. **Hôtel Gloriette,** 27, rue Gloriette (tel. 85-48-23-35), is the town's cheapest, but is no slouch. (Singles from 58F. Doubles from 75-80F. Breakfast 17F. Showers 12F. Closed Sun. noon-8pm.) **Camping Municipal de la Butte** (tel. 85-48-26-86) is a three-star, riverside site in nearby St-Marcel. (8F per person, 12F per site.) Follow the directons to the hostel but cross the bridge when you come to it, continue straight across two islands, and turn left along the river on rue Julien Lenevu.

Fleurs d'Asie, 20, av. Jean Jaurès (tel. 85-48-68-34), offers simple, Vietnamese *menus* for 36F and up. (Open Thurs.-Tues.) There is a **Supermarché Casino** on av. Nicéphore-Nièpce, just off av. Jean Jaurès, 2 blocks from the train station. (Open Mon.-Sat. 8:30am-8pm.)

The **Office de Tourisme** (tel. 85-48-37-97) is in place Chabas on bd. de la République. (Open Mon.-Sat. 9am-12:30pm and 1:30-7pm.) The **post office** is on place de l'Obélisque at bd. de la République. (Open Mon.-Fri. 8:30am-7pm, Sat. 8:30am-noon.) The **postal code** is 71100.

Côte d'Or: The Wine Route

Ever since the Roman invasion brought wine-making to Burgundy, the Côte d'Or has produced some of the world's most notable wines, the *grands crus.* Charlemagne kept his personal vineyard at Aloxe-Cortone, and Louis XIV happily quaffed his Nuits-St-Georges on doctor's orders.

One of the four *départements* that make up Burgundy (the others are Nièvre, Saône et Loire, and Yonne), this thin 60km strip that runs from Dijon to Beaune is more correctly called the **Côte de Nuits,** the region where Musigny, Clos de Vougeot, and Chambertin wines are produced. The **Côte de Beaune,** in the south, is the place of origin for Montrachet whites and Corton and Pommard reds.

While many *caves* offer free *dégustations,* however, a few gulps of wine are hardly worth the long, costly bus rides in between *caves.* And while the bigger growers expect many tasters and few buyers, the smaller growers hope that tasters are at least seriously considering buying. Buy something you like, and have it at lunch when the *caves* (and buses) are taking a break. Between your tastings, take the time to appreciate the undeniably beautiful countryside and to experience the wonderfully dilatory pace of life in the farming villages. Bourgogne has issued an outstanding series of brochures to help you do that, and all tourist offices should be well stocked. Ask for *Châteaux en Côte d'Or* (detailed information on all sites, not just castles), *Circuits en Côte d'Or* (suggested routes for drivers), and *Route des Forges et des Mines* (discussion of Burgundy's historical steel industry), as well as booklets on hotels and camping. Many of these brochures are available in English. For those still intent on wine tasting, the Dijon tourist office sells a colorful map *Le Vignoble de Bourgogne* (10F); the Beaune office has the even more useful (and free) *Liste des Viticulteurs et Négotiants-Eleveurs de la Côte d'Or et de l'Yonne,* in which *viticulteurs* with a glass next to their name welcome visits to their *caves* and offer *dégustations.*

By car, take D122, the **Route des Grands Crus,** through the rolling hills covered with vines and punctuated by wine châteaux. A more scenic and convenient method of transport than the train is the bus along the *route de vin* (see Dijon Practical Information). The bus schedule reads more like a wine list, with stops at all the major vineyards. One of the best wineries to visit is at the tenth-century **Château de Gevre-Chambertin,** just south of Dijon (tel. 80-34-36-13), which combines a smattering of history with a visit to its extensive *caves.* (Open Fri.-Wed. 10am-noon and 2-6pm, Sun. 11:30am-noon and 2-6pm. Tour lasts 30 min., 15F.)

Nearby **Reulle-Vergy** offers a municipal **Musée des Arts et Traditions des Hautes Côtes** with semi-interesting displays on the region's geology, geography, flora, fauna, archeology, viticulture, agriculture, and history. (Open July-Sept. daily 2-6:30pm. Admission 6F.) The town also harbors the ruins of ninth-century **Monastère de St-Vivant** and the twelfth-century **Eglise St-Saturnin** with its fifteenth-century polychromed wood reliquaries. Well worth a visit, though accessible only by car, is the **Château de Rochepot,** remarkable for its seductive hilltop setting and its interiors, as well as the nearby twelfth-century Roman church. Both lie about 10km southwest of Beaune. The paper *Eté 1989,* free at the tourist office, has up-to-date listings of events, museums, monuments, and other points of interest on the Côte d'Or.

Dijon

There was no way, in 1513, that the resolutely independent *Dijonnais* would surrender to the 30,000 Swiss holding their small city in seige. Negotiations faltered until, in a stroke of Burgundian brilliance, they sent a multitude of wine casks across enemy lines. The Swiss, with the generosity of utter inebriation, acquiesced and retreated, saving Dijon.

Episodes such as this fill the pages of Dijon's particularly colorful history. The city encompasses a well-restored *vieille ville,* a myriad of churches, museums and festivals, plus the students of the prominent university who keep the ancient city young: A perfect metropolitan compliment to, and base from which to explore, the boondocks of Bourgogne.

Orientation and Practical Information

Convenient by train to most of France, Dijon is two-and-a-half hours south of Paris, one-and-a-half north of Lyon, and about eight hours north of the Côte d'Azur. The city is relatively small and compact, convenient for pedestrians. The main east-west axis, the pedestrian zone of **rue de la Liberté,** runs roughly from **place Darcy,** where the *syndicat* is located, to **place St-Michel.** From the train station, follow av. Maréchal Foch straight to place Darcy, a few minutes away. The *vieille ville,* as well as most sites, rests on the small streets radiating from rue de la Liberté to the north and south.

Office de Tourisme: Place Darcy (tel. 80-43-42-12). Accommodations service 6F plus 1.50F per star. **Currency exchange** without commission. Maps in English. Not as well-informed on the *route de vin* here as in Beaune. The pamphlet, *Circuits en Côte d'Or,* lists things to see and do in the region. Ask for the extremely useful introduction to Dijon called *Divio 1989.* It's free and, if they won't give you a copy, explain that you're staying in town a long time. Open Sept.-July Mon.-Sat. 9am-noon and 2-8:30pm, Sun. 10am-noon and 2-7:30pm; Aug. Mon.-Sat. 9am-8:30pm, Sun 10am-7:30pm. July-Sept. guided walking tours leave daily at 3pm and 4:30pm (1½ hr.; 18F, students 10F).

Student Travel: Wasteels, 16, av. Maréchal Foch (tel. 80-43-65-34). BIJ tickets. Open Mon.-Sat. 9am-noon and 2-6pm. If you're under 26, you can get BIJ tickets for 25% less at **Autostop Bourgogne** (see Hitchhiking).

Centre d'Information Jeunesse de Bourgogne (CIJB): 22, rue Audra (tel. 80-30-35-56). Friendly. Information on accommodations, French classes for foreigners, festivals, cheap restaurants, wine harvesting, sports, and travel throughout France. Willing to call around for work if you can't speak French. Open Sept.-June Mon. noon-6pm, Tues.-Fri. 10am-6pm, Sat. 9am-noon; July-Aug. Mon.-Fri. only.

CROUS: 3, rue du Docteur Marat (tel. 80-30-76-33). Offers information on the plentiful university housing and cafeterias. Open Mon.-Fri. 9-11:30am and 2-4:30pm.

Post Office: Place Grangier (tel. 80-43-81-00), close to place Darcy. **Postal code:** 21000. Open Mon.-Fri. 8am-7pm, Sat. 8am-noon. Poste Restante, **telephones,** and stamps available only until 11am on Sat.

Train Station: SNCF, at the end of av. Maréchal Foch (tel. 80-41-50-50; for reservations 80-43-52-56). Station and ticket booth open 24 hours. Reservation and information desk open Mon.-Sat. 8:30am-7pm, Sun. 9am-noon and 2-7pm. *SOS Voyageurs* (tel. 80-43-16-34) is open Mon.-Fri. 8am-7pm, Sat. until 6pm. To Paris by TGV (5 per day, 1½ hr., 164F not including 13F reservation). To Lyon (every hr., 2 hr., 104F), Beaune (3 per day, ½ hr., 29F), Les Laumes (3 per day, 30 min., 25F), Besançon (10 per day, 1 hr., 56F), Gevrey-Chambertin (6 per day, 10 min., 12F), Strasbourg (1 per day, 4 hr., 174F), Nice (6 per day, 7½ hr., 338F)

Bus Station: Av. Maréchal Foch (tel. 80-43-58-97), connecting with the train station. Information and ticket booth open Mon.-Fri. 8:30am-12:30pm and 2:30-6:30pm, Sat. 8:30am-12:30pm, Sun. (in a small booth outside) 11am-12:30pm and 5-7:45pm. You can also by tickets aboard. To Avallon (2 per day, 2½-3 hr., 67.50F) via Semur-en-Auxois (1½ hr., 40.80F). To Gevrey-Chambertin (Mon.-Sat. 5 per day, 3 on Sun.; ½ hr.; 10.20F). The most convenient, scenic way to travel the *route de vin,* 8 buses per day including Beaune (1 hr., 27.20F) and Nuits St. George (40 min., 17F). The 12:15pm continues all the way to Antun (2½ hr., 59F).

Municipal Buses: STRD, booth in place Grangier (tel. 80-30-60-90). Covers greater Dijon Mon.-Sat. 6am-8:30pm, Sun. 1-8:30pm. Tickets 4.90F, 12-trip pass 36F.

Car Rental: Budget, 4, rue Millotet (tel. 80-45-05-55), near place Darcy. Ford Fiesta 181F per day, 2.56F per km; 1959F per week with unlimited mileage. Deposit, in cash or on credit card, 1500F. Must be 21 or over, and have had license for at least 1 yr. Open Mon.-Sat. 8am-noon and 2-6pm; call at other times.

Bike Rental: Cycles Pouilly, 3, rue de Tivoli (tel. 80-66-61-75).

Hitchhiking: For Paris via Sens, take av. Albert 1er. For the south, take av. Jean Jaurès (N74 for Chalon). **Autostop Bourgogne,** 22, rue Audra (tel. 80-30-71-55), in the same office as the youth center CIJB. They'll do their best to match you with a driver. Pay 30F per voyage or 80F per year. Pay the driver 16 centimes per km. Open Mon. noon-6pm, Tues.-Fri. 10am-6pm, Sat. 9am-noon; July-Aug. Mon.-Fri. only.

Markets: Halle Centrale: Follow rue François Rude from rue de la Liberté. Everything under the sun, prices reasonable but not remarkable. Open Tues. and Fri. until 1pm, Sat. all-day.

Laundromats: 36, rue Guillaume Tell, just above the train station. Wash 22F, dry 2F per 6 min. Open daily 7am-9pm. Also rue J. J. Rousseau at rue d'Assas, place de la République. Wash 20F, dry 2F per 5 min. Open daily 6am-8:30pm.

SOS Amitié: Tel. 80-67-15-15. When you need a pal.

SOS Femmes Battues: Tel. 80-46-21-66. For women in need.

All-Night Pharmacy: The *pharmacie de garde* changes nightly; consult the local newspaper or the door of any pharmacy.

Medical Emergency: Hôpital Général, 3, rue Faubourg Raines (tel. 80-41-81-41).

Police: 2, place Suquet (tel. 80-41-81-05).

Police Emergency: Tel. 17.

Accommodations and Camping

Dijon offers many cheap accommodations options, including a youth hostel, *foyers,* and university dorm rooms. From mid-July to mid-August and the first week of September reasonably priced hotels fill quickly, so reserve a place early or use the accommodations service at the tourist office.

Auberge de Jeunesse (IYHF), Centre de Rencontres Internationales, 1, bd. Champollion (tel. 80-71-32-12), a 4-km ride from the station. Take bus #5 from the "Bar Bleu" in place Grangier toward Epirey at the end of the line, or bus #6 from place Darcy. A classic, concrete "mega-hostel," complete with electronic surveillance, a bar and disco, and screaming school groups. Hosts language programs in summer for foreigners. Fills quickly in July and Aug., so call ahead and pick up keys early in the day. Singles 75F. Doubles 65F per person. 5- to 8-bed dorms 45F. Breakfast included. Self-service dinner 34F.

Foyer International d'Etudiants, av. Maréchal Leclerc (tel. 80-71-51-01). Take bus #4 (*direction* "Grezille"), and get off at Parc des Sports. Really the best deal in town—sleek and shiny. Rooms 47F. Breakfast 8F. Cafeteria lunch 19F. Travelers admitted year-round if there's room.

University Dorm Rooms: Residence Universitaire (R.U.) Mansard, bd. Mansard (tel. 80-66-18-22), and **Residence Universitaire Montmuzard,** bd. Gabriel (tel. 80-39-68-01). 2 stops away from each other on bus #9. Take the bus from the train station or place Darcy to Mansard for R.U. Mansard or to Faculté des Sciences for R.U. Montmuzard. Clean, comfortable singles available July-Sept. Students 45F, non-students 65F. Often full in Aug., so call ahead. Cafeterias at Mansard (tel. 80-66-39-85) open in Aug. only, at Montmuzard (tel. 80-39-69-01) in July only. Breakfast 8F. Lunch or dinner 22F, with a student card (sometimes *any* student card) 9.30F.

Hôtel de la Gare, 16, rue Mariotte (tel. 80-30-46-61). From the train or bus station, go down rue A. Remy; rue Mariotte is on your left. Cramped and dilapidated but not unclean. Convenient and usually has space if you arrive before 7pm. Best prices in Dijon. Pleasant management and amusing door keys fashioned from tennis balls. Singles 70-90F, with shower 110F. Doubles 105F, with shower 125F. Triples 140F, with shower 155F. Breakfast included.

Hôtel du Miroir, 7, rue Bossuet (tel. 80-30-54-81), just off rue de la Liberté. Central but quiet, located down an alley and upstairs. Spacious, clean rooms and friendly management. Singles 80F, with shower 100F. Doubles 80F, with shower 130F. Triples 140F, with shower 150F. Room for 5 220F. Showers 16F. Breakfast in cafe below about 18F.

Hôtel du Sauvage, 64, rue Monge (tel. 80-41-31-21), near Eglise St-Jean and not far from place Darcy. Lavish rooms around a tranquil courtyard with a well and canopy of vines. Singles and doubles 95F, with shower 130F. Triples and quads with shower 220F. Shower 15F. Breakfast 17F. Open Jan.-Dec. 24.

Hôtel Confort, 12, rue Jules Mercier (tel. 80-30-37-47), on an alley off rue de la Liberté. Delightful rooms but the highlight is the breakfast room mural that'll make you feel you're at sea. Singles and doubles 85-100F, with shower 120F, and TV 145F. Triples with shower 150F. Baths 20F. Breakfast 18F.

Hôtel du Théâtre, 3, rue des Bons Enfants (tel. 80-67-15-41), on a quiet side street off place de la Libération. Average rooms, run by a sweetheart of a lady. But no hall showers. Especially full weeknights. Singles and doubles 73F, with shower 128F. Breakfast 15F.

Hôtel Monge, 20, rue Monge (tel. 80-30-55-41), up the street from Hôtel du Sauvage. Set away from the street over a courtyard. Clean rooms with mattresses to die for. Singles 90F, with shower 130F. Doubles 95F, with shower 135F. Triples and quads about 150F. Showers 15F. Breakfast 17F.

Camping: Camping Municipal du Lac, bd. Kir and av. Albert 1*er* (tel. 80-43-54-72). On a beautiful lake about 2km from town, behind the train station and past the Natural History Museum. Spacious, with good facilities. 8F per night. Open April-Nov. 15. **Camping l'Orée du Bois,** route d'Etaules, Darois (tel. 80-35-60-22), 9km out of town. A 2-star campground with a pool nearby. 8.50F per night. Open May-Sept.

Food

Dijon's reputation as a gastronomic paradise has existed since Gallo-Roman and which seems to have elevated restaurant prices. There is a large **supermarket** in the basement of the Nouvelles Galleries on rue de la Liberté. (See also Practical Information for open-air markets.) *Charcuteries* are a particularly good place to try different *dijonnais* specialties. Buy 100g of *jambon persillé* (a ham *pâté* with parsley), *tarte bourguignon* (a pie with meat and mushrooms in a creamy sauce) or *quiche aux champignons* (mushroom quiche) and picnic in the **Jardin de l'Arquebuse** behind the train station. *Dijonnais* chefs take every possible opportunity to garnish their delicacies with heavy portions of their vinegars, wines, and mayonnaise. University cafeterias stay open all summer (see university housing under Accommodations).

Le Grilladou, 29, rue J.J. Rousseau (tel. 80-74-42-23), off place de la République. Cooking like yesteryear: over a wood fire, smack in the middle of the dining room. Lunch *menu* 45F. Assorted *brochettes* 28F. Smoked salmon salad 32F. Generous lunch/dinner *menu* 59F. Open Mon.-Sat. noon-2pm and 7pm-midnight, Sun. 7pm-midnight.

Au Bec Fin, 47, rue Jeannin (tel. 80-66-17-77). Rue Jeannin starts behind Notre Dame, about 1 block north of rue de la Liberté. *Menus* 42F (noon only), 60F, and 75F. 54F buys 4 courses: Try the *galantine de volaille* followed by a spicy *colombo de porc*, a choice of regional cheeses, and a delicious lemon mousse in raspberry sauce. Open Mon.-Fri. noon-1:30pm and 7:30-10:30pm, Sat. 7:30-10:30pm.

Moulin à Vent, 8, place Françoise Rudé (tel. 80-30-81-43), near the ducal palace and open market. In a half-timbered house with window boxes loaded with geraniums and white iron tables and chairs outside. Generous 65F and 85F *menus*. Excellent *boeuf bourguignon*. Open Tues.-Sat. noon-2pm and 7-9:30pm.

Mélodine, 6, av. Maréchal Foch (tel. 80-45-51-00), straight down from the train station. A large but pleasant self-service restaurant. Huge selection of salad, cheese, and pastry buffet. A variety of hot meals. Full meals cost 30-45F. If it's your birthday, they'll give you a surprise. Open daily 11am-11pm. 10% less for students 11am-noon and 1:30-11pm.

Le Vinarium, 23, place Bossuet (tel. 80-30-36-23), by Eglise St-Jean in a thirteenth-century crypt. Four 115-160F *menus* from different parts of Burgundy. *Boeuf bourguignon, jambon persillé,* and *charlotte* (a cake made with ladyfingers) worth the investment. A tad touristy. Open Mon. 7:30pm-late, Tues.-Sat noon-2pm and 7:30-10pm.

Sights

The pride of Dijon, located in the center of town on place de la Libération, is the imposing **Palais des Ducs de Bourgogne,** with the enormous kitchen that once produced Burgundy's finest cuisine. Climb **Tour Philippe Le Bon** for an outstanding view of Dijon and her hinterland. (Open Wed.-Mon. 9:30-11:30am and 2:30-5:30pm. Admission 5F, students free.) The **Musée des Beaux Arts** occupies a modern part of the palace and houses a wonderful collection of paintings from many periods. The medieval ties between Flanders and Burgundy are represented by an exceptional group of Flemish primitives. The museum's collection also includes paintings by Caracci, Veronese, and Titian, and by French artists from Mignard to Manet. The most famous gallery in the museum is the **Salle des Gardes,** dominated by two huge mausoleums of Philippe le Hardi and Jean sans Peur. Note the 41-statuette funeral procession at the base of Philippe's tomb, sculpted by the fourteenth-century master Claus Sluter. (Open Mon. and Wed.-Sat. 10am-6pm, Sun. 10am-12:30pm and 2-6pm. Admission 8F, students free.)

From the palace, walk along rue des Forges and the neighboring streets for a look at the nobles' grand residences (the tourist office has a list of the flashiest homes). Be sure to look at the courtyard of #34, the **Hôtel Chambellan,** which is now the *siège du syndicat d'initiative* (the location of its administrative offices). The demure exterior gives no indication of the extravagant Gothic courtyard within. If you enjoy strolling down medieval streets, don't miss **rue de la Chouette** and **rue Verrerie** (the grooved center of the pavement was the sewage conduit in the seventeenth-century). Note the different *eschaugettes* (watch towers) protruding from the corners of the Renaissance houses.

Nearby, seventeenth-century **Eglise de Notre Dame** was built in Burgundian Gothic style; its facade is a gargoyle extravaganza, each creature assuming a different pose or expression. A surprisingly haggard statue of Mary, to whom the church is dedicated, rests to the right of the main altar. Above the right tower sits the **Horloge à Jacquemart.** The clock and bell were commissioned by Philippe le Hardi in 1382 after his victory over the Flemish. Originally, a single figure hammered the bell each hour, but in 1610 the lonely male statue was given a spouse, then a son to strike the half hour, and finally, in 1881, a daughter to announce the quarter hour. This continual carillon is audible everywhere in Dijon.

A few blocks away on place St-Michel, the **Eglise Saint-Michel** incorporates both Gothic and Renaissance styles. In a fit of fancy, one stoneworker mixed mythological and biblical themes together—behold the result over the central portal. To the left of the altar rest the remains of a nun whose faith and writings inspired the people of Dijon. Her life is described in French near the entrance. Just off place Darcy, at 4, rue Docteur Maret, reigns the **Cathédrale St-Bénigne,** which houses a former monk's dorm room and a circular crypt. Right next door is the **Musée Ar-**

chéologique, 5, rue Docteur Maret. Artifacts document life and art in the Côte d'Azur from prehistoric times to the present. (Open Wed.-Mon. 9am-noon and 2-6pm. Admission 7F, students free.)

Across place de la Libération is the **Musée Magnin,** 4, rue des Bons Enfants, a sumptuous documentary of seventeenth-century living. Though paintings by Poussin, David, and many others hang on the walls, the museum is most interesting for the elegance of its period furnishings. Look for the wood-paneled passageway on the second floor. (Open Wed.-Mon. 9am-noon and 2-6pm. Admission 10F.)

Philippe le Hardi commissioned Claus Sluter to build the **Chartreuse de Champmol** on the western edge of town to house his family's tombs, which now all lie in the Musée des Beaux Arts. The entrance is on bd. Chanoine Kir. From place Darcy, follow bd. de Sevigne, go under the train overpass, and continue on av. Albert 1er. Partly destroyed in 1793, the **Puits de Moïse** (literally, the Well of Moses, but actually the base of a chapel on which Moses figures prominently) and the **portal** depict the six prophets.The sculpture group is on the grounds of a *hôpital psychiatrique.* (Open to the public 9am-6pm.)

Entertainment

Be sure to stop in at the **Grey Poupon** store, 32, rue de la Liberté, which has been making mustard since 1777, and has an exhibit of antique jars. You can also buy decorated mustard jars. (Open Mon.-Sat. 8:30am-noon and 2-7pm.) In nearby place François Rudé, on one side of rue de la Liberté, you can hire a *calèche* (horse and carriage) for a tour of Dijon (only July-Aug.). Throughout June, Dijon plays host to many of the world's best symphony orchestras and chamber groups during its **Eté Musical** (musical summer). From mid-June to mid-August, **Estivade** presents dance, music, and theater in the streets. **Grenier de Bourgogne** organizes free jazz and entertainment in the park by place Darcy throughout the summer. Dijon devotes a week in the first half of September to the **Fête de la Vigne.** Begun in 1946 just after the devastation of the second world war, this festival celebrates the fruit of the vine: Parades and parties take over the streets as people flock to the city for this now-famous international event.

The best source for information on films, festivals, and Dijon's numerous amateur and professional theater productions is *Dijon Nuit et Jour,* available free from the tourist office and *tabacs.* Opera, classical music concerts, and operettas are performed in season (mid-Oct. to late April) at the **Théâtre de Dijon,** place du Théâtre (tel. 80-32-78-00), a beautiful eighteenth-century opera house. (Tickets 150F, students 75F.) Investigate the shows at **Nouveau Théâtre de Bourgogne,** located at Théâtre du Parvis St-Jean, place Bossuet. (The theater was once a church.) The box office opens at 5pm, and there are productions throughout the year.

Dijon is as rich in bars and nightclubs as it is in art and history. **Le Carillon,** 2, rue Musette (tel. 80-30-63-71), and **La Cathédrale,** 4, place St-Bénigne (tel. 80-30-42-10), are two bars especially popular with students. **Le Messire Bar,** 3, rue Jules Mercier (tel. 80-30-16-40), is a friendly, dark nightclub with flashing lights and a warm clientele (open until 2am). For a complete list of bars, nightclubs, and restaurants, as well as shops and services of interest to young people, get a copy of *Divio '89.*

Franche-Comté

Franche-Comté ascends like an enormous stairway from the plains of central France to the mountains of Switzerland, with flat-topped wooded mountains rising from shallow rivers. Long a contested border region, the area is scattered with fortifications. A Celtic tribe in the second century C.E. settled along the banks of the Doubs River and named their town, later to become Besançon, Vesontio. The region first came under German rule but was ceded to Philippe le Bel of France. The Hapsburgs annexed the area into their empire. A short time later, in 1556, the Spanish took over the war-tossed region. Even the Archdukes of Austria ruled over the region before it finally became part of France.

Franche-Comté, now undeniably French at its core, has been garnished by layers of distinctly foreign flavors. Heavy-set churches with bell-shaped roofs on their towers, and names such as Lopez and Mendez remain from the period of Spanish rule, while the remote agricultural areas seem a little Swiss.

The region's beauty and history go underground as well: The sheer dimensions and strange, contorted beauty of the dozens of grottos and caves in the countryside are awe-inspiring. Don't, however, ignore their functional aspect—many served throughout history as shelter for primitive dwellers or as refuge in times of war. The Jura and Vosges mountain ranges provide abundant inspiration for nature lovers. With over 5000km of rushing torrents, meandering streams, and placid lakes, Franche-Comté is a paradise for canoe and kayak enthusiasts.

Spreading along the banks of the Doubs River, the capital city of Besançon serves as a university town as well as a watch-making center. The *route horlogère,* a tourist circuit, begins here and extends east to the Swiss city of Neuchâtel. Belfort, on the border of Alsace, is a bustling commercial city dominated by a solemn fortress and distinguished by the huge sandstone lion carved at the base of its château. Dole's once formidable power as capital of the *Comté de Bourgogne* has long since faded, leaving a quiet, friendly town. To the south, Arbois, a medieval town ensconced in vineyards, tempts with tours and wine samples from its *caves.* The quiet towns of Poligny and Pontarlier make convenient bases for exploring the vast expanses of unspoiled forest.

The regional cuisine is hearty, worthy of the mountain country that supplies it, but you'll find the flavors extremely delicate. Arbois wines go well with mild *Comté,* the cheese of the region. The *eaux-de-vie* of Fougerolles, in contrast, are sharp and very strong. Be sure to try the smoked hams, sausages, and cured meats, and in season (July-Sept.) the fresh trout from local rivers, along with mushrooms from the hills.

Trams run frequently between all cities in the region and the Monts Jura bus company operates fairly complete service to smaller towns and excursions into the mountains (see Dole or Besonçon Practical Information). Hitchhiking works about as well as elsewhere in France—not always easy.

Besançon

Hidden in the most mountainous terrain in the region, this horseshoe bend in the river Doubs has been a cultural center for centuries. Besançon, however, is now gaining prominence as the administrative capital of the Franche-Comté and as home to a dynamic university. Thousands of students, French and foreign, who attend either the university or the renowned language school, add excitement to this already attractive town. Besançon's verdant valley contains a treasure chest of Roman legacies, works of art, and historical idiosyncrasies.

Orientation and Practical Information

The center of Besançon is bordered on one side by the fortress and on all other sides by the river Doubs. The old town is an easy 10-minute walk downhill from the station, across the river. Look for signs that read *centre ville*. Walk straight ahead down the stairs, turn left on the main road, and take the first right onto av. Foch. Follow av. Foch down to the river and bear left along the bank to the tourist office.

Office de Tourisme: 2, place de l'Armée Française (tel. 81-80-92-55). This friendly facility has information on regional excursions and festivals, and will supply a list of hotels and restaurants or book a room for free. **Currency exchange** when the banks are closed. Open July-Aug. Mon. 10am-noon and 1:30-7pm, Tues.-Fri. 9am-noon and 1:30-7pm, Sat. 9am-noon and 1:30-6pm, Sun. 10am-1pm; Sept.-June Mon.-Fri. 9am-noon and 1:30-6pm, Sat. 9am-noon and 1:45-5pm.

Centre d'Information et d'Acceuil Municipal: 2, rue Megevand (tel. 81-83-08-24). Come here for further information and for the free practical guide *Besançon Mode d'Emploi.* Open Mon.-Fri. 8am-noon and 1:30-6pm, Sat. 9am-noon.

Centre Information Jeunesse (CIJ): 27, rue de la République (tel. 81-83-20-40). A friendly center and the best place to go for information on local sports and skiing or hiking excursions in the countryside. BIJ/Transalpino tickets. Ride board and Cartes Jeunes (60F). Open Mon. 2-7pm, Tues.-Fri. 10am-noon and 2-7pm, Sat. 2-6pm.

Post Office: 19, rue Proudhon (tel. 81-82-23-12), off rue de la République. **Telephones** and **currency exchange. Postal code:** 25000. Open Mon.-Fri. 8am-7pm, Sat. 8am-noon. To have mail delivered here, address it "Poste Restante, rue Proudhon, 25000 Besançon." The **main office** 4, rue Demangel (tel. 81-53-81-12), is way out in the new town. Take bus #8 to the 2nd stop, then walk 1 block to rue Démangel.

Train Station: Av. de la Paix (tel. 81-53-50-50). By way of Dole and Dijon, Besançon is about 4 hr. from Paris's Gare de Lyon (6 direct per day, 6 via Dijon; 189F). Local connections run to Lyon (8 per day, 2½ hr., 109F), Belfort (12 per day, 1 hr., 55F), Strasbourg (8 per day, 2¼ hr., 127F), and Dijon (12 per day, 1 hr., 55F). Office open Mon.-Sat. 8:30am-6:30pm, Sun. 9:30am-12:30pm and 2-6:30pm.

Bus Station: Monts-Jura, 9, rue Proudhon (tel. 81-88-11-33), on the left off rue de la République coming from the tourist office. To Pontarlier via Ornans (4 per day, 1½-2 hr., 31F) and Villers-le-Lac (leaves in the evening and returns the following afternoon, 38.50F). 3 buses per week to Salins-les-Bains in the foothills of the Jura (Mon., Wed., and Fri. at 6pm; 1 hr.; 28.50F), returning the following afternoon. Office open Mon.-Sat. 9am-noon and 2-6:30pm. **CTB,** 46, rue de Trey (tel. 81-50-28-55). Efficient city bus system. 4.90F per hr., *carnet* of 10 tickets 36.80F.

Car Rental: Europcar, 7, av. Foch (tel. 81-80-33-39), 1 min. from train station. Small car with unlimited mileage 2500F per week. **Avis,** 7, place Flore (tel. 81-80-91-08).

Bike Rental: Cycles Robert, 6, rue de la Préfecture (tel. 81-82-19-12). 35F per ½-day, 60F per day, 120F per weekend (3 days), 220F per week, deposit 1000F. Open Tues.-Sun. 9am-noon and 2-7pm. Also at the **train station.** 37F per ½-day, 47F per day, deposit 300F. Open Mon.-Sat. 5:30am-11pm.

Laundromat: 54, rue Bersot, near the bus station. Wash 12F, dry 5F per 20 min. Open 7am-8pm.

Hospital: Centre Hospitalier Régional, 2, place St-Jacques (tel. 81-52-33-22). From the tourist office, continue down rue de la République, which becomes rue de l'Ormée de Chambres.

Medical Emergency: SAMU, Tel. 81-52-15-15.

Police: Av. de la Gare d'Eau (tel. 81-82-03-67).

Police Emergency: Tel. 17.

Accommodations

Hotels in Besançon are generally pleasant—but you pay dearly. Fortunately, finding a room in one of the inexpensive *foyers* isn't tough, and the CROUS service can find you space in university buildings.

University Housing: CROUS, Service d'Accueil d'Etudiants Etrangers, 38, av. Observatoire, bldg. B (tel. 81-50-26-88), is the administrative office. To get yourself a room July-Sept. go to the **Cité Universitaire.** From the tourist office, cross the bridge and take bus #7 (*direction:* "Campus") to the Université stop. Head to bldg. A-B, to the right of the Resto U. Mon.-Fri. 10-11:45am and 1-4:15pm go to the *secrétariat,* where you pay and get a room. Other times go directly to the *concierge* in the lobby of the same building. Ordinary dorm singles 50F, with student ID 30F, with Carte Jeune 40F. CROUS offices can also arrange longer stays in university housing.

Centre International de Séjour, 19, rue Martin-du-Gard (tel. 81-50-07-54), near the university. Take bus #8 from the station to the Epitaphe stop. Approximates a youth hostel. Singles 70F. Doubles with two beds 48F per person. Triples or quads 42F per person. Breakfast 13F. Meals 40F. Picnic lunch 25F. Office sells *télécartes.* Rarely full. Reservations for up to 1-week stays accepted up to 1 week in advance. Office open 7am-1am.

Foyer des Jeunes Filles, 18, rue de la Cassotte (tel. 81-80-90-01). From the train station, walk straight downhill for 10 min., bearing left; or take any bus that goes to place Flore—rue de la Cassotte runs off the *place.* Women only. Maintained by nuns and long-term boarders. Friendly. Prices depend on 1001 factors (length of stay, age, pension, etc.). Singles 30F. Sheets 20F. Breakfast included. Office open daily 8am-10pm.

Hôtel le Levant, 9, rue des Boucheries (tel. 81-81-07-88), on place de la Révolution. From the tourist office, cross the bridge and turn right on av. E. Cusenier. Good location. Respectable, clean singles and doubles without windows 70-82F. Breakfast 18F. Lively restaurant and street downstairs.

Hôtel Regina, 91, Grande Rue (tel. 81-81-50-22), smack in the middle of town. Amazingly quiet spot on an alley. Singles and doubles 89.50F. No hall showers but the manager may let you use one of the room showers. Breakfast 17.50F.

Hôtel Granvelle, 13, rue du Général Lecourbe (tel. 81-81-33-92), in the old town on the way to the *citadelle.* Friendly management. Rooms are clean and comfortable. 2-stars, but a few cheap rooms. Singles and doubles from 88F.

Hôtel Florel, 6, rue de la Viotte (tel. 81-80-41-08), 2 min. to the left of the train station. Nice, but not quite worth the price. Singles 80-140F. Doubles 115-150F. Triples. Breakfast 18F.

Camping: Camping de la Plage, route de Belfort (tel. 81-88-04-26), in Chalezeule northeast of the city. Take bus #1 towards Palente and ask for the *camping.* A 4-star municipal campground. Access to nearby pool. Adults 8F, children 4F, tents 6-18F.

Food

Plenty of atmospheric, hole-in-the-wall restaurants cater to Besançon's cosmopolitan student population. Rue des Boucheries amasses a good selection of restaurants. **Pub de l'Etoile,** place de la Révolution, is often full of young *Bisontins.* Tuesday through Saturday afternoons, visit the outdoor **market** in place de la Révolution. *Comté* cheese is abundant here; among the famous *Arbois* wines is unique *vin jaune* (rather expensive), which tastes like sherry and goes well with *Comté.* Along rue des Granges many excellent *charcuteries* purvey *jambon de Haut Doubs,* a regional smoked ham. Inexpensive pizzerias line rue Bersot.

University Restaurants: The best food deals in Besançon. Mediocre but weighty cafeteria meals 20F. Buy a ticket from a student in line (10F). *À la carte* options are slightly more expensive. **Restaurant Canot,** 73, quai Veil-Picard, entrance on rue A. Janvier, across the river from the old town. Open Sept.-June Mon.-Sat. 11:30am-1:15pm and 6:30-7:50pm; July-Aug. Mon.-Sat. 11:30am-1:15pm. **Restaurant La Bouluie** at the *cité universitaire* (follow directions in Accommodations). Open Mon.-Sat. 11:30am-1:15pm and 6:30-7:50pm.

Le Levant, 9, rue des Boucheries (tel. 81-81-07-88). Always crowded. Try the regional specialties or the 39.50F *menu.* Open Sun.-Fri. noon-2pm and 7-9:30pm.

La Boîte à Sandwiches, 21, rue du Lycée (tel. 81-83-47-46), the next street to your right after Grande Rue, from rue de la République. Snacks and light meals—the French answer to fast food. Sandwiches of every stripe 10-37F, tasty salads such as *le fermier* (with artichokes and chicken) 14-24F. Open Mon.-Fri. 11am-2pm and 5:30-10pm, Sat. 11am-2pm.

Le P'tit Loup, 9, rue du Lycée (tel. 81-83-19-19), down the street from La Boîte. Stone walls with designer salads and elegant main dishes. Try the *filet mignon au poivre vert* (42F). Open Mon.-Sat. for lunch and dinner.

Le Fairouz, 9, rue Claude-Pouillet (tel. 81-82-06-80). A cute place with Syrian and Lebanese specialties. Full meals about 80F. Syrian background music, 3 vivid watercolors of nudes hanging lopsidedly on the wall, and a friendly, overworked waiter. Open Mon.-Fri. noon-2pm and 7-11pm, Sat. 7-11pm.

Sights and Entertainment

The **Citadelle,** built in 1674 by Vauban on the site of an ancient Gallo-Roman acropolis, rises from sheer rock over the green mountains and the winding Doubs. Climb to the top of the walls for a magnificent view of the old town. Vauban's works, built to thwart the Swiss, are described in the brochure *A la recherche de Vauban et de ses successeurs en Franche-Comté,* available from tourist offices. The buildings within the *citadelle* house a variety of museums: The **Musée Populaire Comtois** (folklore museum) has exhibits on native arts and crafts, agricultural techniques, cheesemaking, milking, and so forth. The **Musée de la Résistance et de la Déportation** presents a painfully detailed documentation of the French Resistance movement and the Vichy government, as well as a collection of artwork by prisoners in concentration camps. The walls of the Citadelle also encircle the **Musée d'Histoire Naturelle** (natural history museum), a small **aquarium,** and a **zoo.** (Museums open Wed.-Mon. 9:15am-6:15pm. Aquarium and zoo open daily 9:15am-6:15pm. Admission Wed.-Mon. to everything a worthwhile 20F, ages 10-18 10F, ages under 10 free. Admission Tues. to aquarium and zoo 10F.) To reach the citadel, take Grande Rue to rue des Fusilles, a steep and winding road, or take the tourist train that departs from the parking Rivotte on the southeast corner of the old town (40 min. tour on the way up, 20F).

At the foot of the citadel stands **Porte Noire,** a weighty second-century Roman triumphal arch, and the marvelously ornate eighteenth-century **Cathédrale St-Jean,** a double-apsed church with no main facade. (Tour of the church's treasures July-Aug. Sat. at 5pm, 15F.) Behind the church ticks the locally-crafted **Horloge Astronomique,** the sum of 30,000 parts. Daily at noon a puppet Christ leaps from his tomb as Hope blesses Faith and Charity, and two soldiers doze at their posts despite the ringing bells; another thrilling presentation occurs at 3pm, and less flamboyant mechanical theatrics occur every hour. (Admission 15F, students 9F.)

Past Porte Noire and along Grande Rue, the elegant **Renaissance Palais Granvelle** now houses the **Musée Historique de Besançon Doubs,** with a seventeenth-century Bruges tapestry depicting cameo scenes from the life of Charles V. (Open Wed.-Mon. 9:30am-noon and 2-6pm. Admission 10F, students 5F, Sun. free.) In summer free folk dance and classical music concerts are given in the courtyard; check the schedule in the tourist office, and show up early. The **Musée des Beaux Arts** displays major works by Matisse, Courbet, Renoir, Picasso, and Renaissance Italian masters, as well as exhibits on regional archeology, rosaries, Egyptian mummies, and crystal *horlogerie* (clock-making). (Same hours and admission fees as the history museum.)

Les Vedettes Bisontines (tel. 81-68-13-25) offers *bateau-mouche* cruises on the Doubs that depart daily from Pont de la République, near the tourist office. (July-Sept. 14 Mon.-Fri. at 10:30am, 2:30pm, and 4:30pm, Sat.-Sun. at 10:30am, 2pm, 4pm, and 6pm; April-June and Sept. 15-Oct. 5 fewer runs; 1¼ hr.; 37F.) **Piscine du Sport Nautique Bisontine,** av. de Chardonnet (tel. 81-80-56-01), on the same side of the river as the tourist office near pont de Bregille (tel. 81-82-50-01), offers instruction in sculling, canoeing, and kayaking (introductory course 50F; open 9:30am-noon and 2-6pm). They also have a pleasant outdoor swimming pool (same hours; admission 14F).

The **Festival de Musique de Besançon,** the first two weeks of September, features world-famous classical musicians and is the only remaining competition for young orchestra conductors in the world. (Tickets 70-170F, students 25-50F.) **Jazz en Franche-Comté** brings a plethora of free jazz concerts during June and July. The tourist office publishes a comprehensive list of all cultural events. Besançon maintains several *boîtes de nuit* (nightclubs), most with 50F covers. **Pimm's Club** features

French Top 40 in one room, and anything else (from the tango to Jacques Brel) in the other. **Excaliber** caters to a younger, new-wave crowd.

Near Besançon

Besançon is a good base for excursions into the **Jura.** You can explore the dozens of grottoes and underground rivers in the region on your own, or take advantage of organized activities such as guided walks in the national forests of Poligny and Pontarlier. Call the central Jura tourist office at 84-24-19-64, or pick up a copy of *Welcome to Jura,* which contains information on kayaking and hiking through the Jura massif.

A charming small town of graceful stone buildings and windowboxes overflowing with begonias and geraniums, **Poligny** is accessible by train directly from Besançon (about 5 per day, 1 hr.). To get to the main street, Grande Rue, take a right at the end of the road from the train station. It's a 12-minute walk, but you can stop in the small, shady park halfway and watch the old men playing *boules.* Poligny has a beautiful church, **Eglise Collégiale Saint-Hippolyte,** with a vivid portrayal of the saint's martyrdom above the door and a lovely polychrome statue of the Virgin and Child beneath it. Nearby, is fifteenth-century **Couvent des Clarisses.** If you want to spend the night, **Hôtel-Restaurant Les Charmilles,** route de Dole (tel. 84-37-24-51), is two minutes from the train station on your left. (Doubles 110F, triples 132F. Breakfast 18F. Closed Dec. 20-Jan. 20 and first week in Sept.) A nice place for a drink or a light meal is **Snack Bar Hôtel de Ville,** opposite its namesake on Grande Rue, with an ample 52F *menu.* The **Syndicat d'Initiative** is down the street at #85 (tel. 84-37-24-21).

Pontarlier, near the border of Switzerland, a good-sized town and a gastronomic paradise, produces a variety of liqueurs, chocolates, honey, and smoked hams, and boasts of being the capital of mountain *gruyère.* Eight footpaths take you through the lovely forest or to nearby attractions, and city-lovers will enjoy the clean town center with its seventeenth- and eighteenth-century buildings and extensive sports facilities (including a large, open-air pool complex). Nearby **Super-Pontarlier** is a ski resort on Montagne du Larmont. In town, stay at the **Auberge de Jeunesse** on rue Marpaud (tel. 81-39-06-57), or try **Les Gentianes** (tel. 81-39-19-73), a three-star campsite near the Paul Robbe municipal stadium. The **Syndicat d'Initiative** is in the Hôtel de Ville (tel. 81-46-48-33). To get to Pontarlier, take a train from Mouchard. **Ornans,** accessible by bus, is home to the **Musée Gustave Courbet,** Courbet's house, complete with many of his works.

Belfort

Belfort is pretty much a one-horse town, that one horse being the seventeenth-century military château with its expansive additions. Strategically overlooking the east-west road in the gap between the Vosges and the Jura, the rock of Belfort was first fortified in 1226. Vauban gave both the château and the old city a massive and sophisticated set of walls beginning in 1687. The three sieges for which Belfort is most famous occurred in the nineteenth century—the last and most bloody mounted during the Franco-Prussian War.

Neither quaint nor graceful, though half-ruined, the red-walled citadel still betrays its grim military function. The heavy-set towers of the **Cathédrale St-Christophe** link Belfort to the Spanish legacy of Franche-Comté; the bleak post-war pedestrian streets such as the **Faubourg de France,** lined with shops selling *choucroute,* beer, and pretzels, recall Alsace-Lorraine.

Most streets in the pentagonal old city turn into trails that wind up the rock to the **Château de Belfort.** (Open May-Oct. Wed.-Mon. 8am-noon and 2-7pm; Nov.-April Wed.-Mon. 10am-noon and 2-5pm.) The 10F charge admits you to ramparts and tunnels and to several small museums, one of which contains savage military artifacts—firearms, bayonets, and fortifications. The view of the Jura and the

Vosges, however, can be breathtaking on a clear day. On your way down, be sure to visit the 24-meter-wide **Lion,** sculpted from rock by Bartholdi (also responsible for the Statue of Liberty) to honor the defenders of Belfort in 1870-71. (Lion open daily 8am-6:45pm. Admission 3F.) If you liked the first climb, you might scale the hill west across the valley to **La Tour de la Miotte,** a turret built on the ruins of **Château de Montfort.**

The old town, a roughly pentagonal area at the base of the château, contains most sights. From the train station, walk several meters to your left and down rue Faubourg de France; turn left at the grouping of modern marble columns, and the tourist office is 20m farther on your right. The **Office de Tourisme,** place de la Commune (tel. 84-28-12-23), in a sleek new office in the pedestrian zone, will give you a rather confusing map that is, fortunately, indexed. Also pick up the publication *Le mois à Belfort,* which lists current events and expositions. (Open June-Aug. Mon.-Sat. 9am-12:15pm and 1:45-7pm, Sun. 10am-noon; Sept.-May Mon.-Sat. 9am-12:15pm and 1:45-6pm, Sun. 10am-noon.) A tourist office brochure, *Randonnées pèdestres autour de Belfort,* takes you through the forests on **la colline de Salbert,** a hill just outside of town, or on a two-hour walking tour around the fort and ramparts. The tourist office conducts guided tours to the old town and the magnificent organ in the cathedral (June-Aug. Thurs. at 3pm; 15F, students 8F).

Accommodations, Camping, and Food

You should have no trouble finding a cheap, clean room in Belfort. Some university housing is available for travelers from June to September; you must contact the CROUS office in Besançon to get a room (see Besançon accommodations). The **Hotel Vauban,** 4, rue du Magasin (tel. 84-21-59-37) offers some comfortable singles for 70 to 80F and doubles from 85F. (Breakfast 18F. Extra bed 35F.) The **Hôtel du Centre,** 11, rue du Magasin (tel. 84-28-67-80), across the street, offers some amazingly cheap rooms. (Singles and doubles from 50F, with shower 75F. Open Sept.-July Mon.-Sat.) The **Nouvel Hôtel,** 56, rue Faubourg de France (tel. 84-28-28-78), has clean rooms. (Singles 70F. Doubles 75F. Showers 10F.) To indulge yourself with a view of the cathedral, stay at the **Hôtel St-Christophe,** place d'Armes (tel. 84-28-02-14), with singles and doubles from 90F. (Showers included. Breakfast 17F.) *Menus* in the restaurant downstairs start at 41F. The **Camping Municipal,** promenade d'Essert (tel. 84-21-03-30), a 10-minute walk to the left and behind the train station, occupies a pleasant grassy mound in a shady park. (5F per person, 3F per tent. Open April 27-Sept. 27.) In the old city, **Dame Charlotte,** 2, place de la Grande Fontaine (tel. 84-28-18-62), a graceful place, concocts two surprisingly affordable *menus* for 39F and 59F. (Open Mon. 7-9:30pm, Tues.-Sat. noon-2:30pm and 7-9:30pm.) Wednesday, Friday and Saturday mornings a **market** is held on rue Docteur Fréry on the old-town bank of the river; Tuesday, Thursday, and Sunday mornings at the Marché des Vosges, on av. Jean Juarès, 20 minutes from *centre ville.*

Near Belfort

Twenty minutes from Belfort by train on the way to Vesoul lies the picturesque town of **Ronchamp,** surrounded by wooded hills. On one of these hills, lightning struck down an eighteenth-century church in 1913. The church was reconstructed only to be destroyed by Allied bombardments in 1944. The celebrated architect Le Corbusier built the third version of **Notre-Dame-du-Haut,** an asymmetrical church with a roof like a billowing sail, in 1955. This extraordinary example of Le Corbusier's architectural genius has become one of the most visited churches in France. (Open daily 9am-7pm. Admission 5F, ages 6-12 3F. For information, call 84-20-65-13.) Also in town is the **Musée de la Mine,** featuring exhibits relating to regional mines. (Open May-Sept. 15 daily 3-6pm.) A train for Ronchamp leaves the Belfort station at 6:30am (½ hr., 15F) and returns around 6pm. A train to Ronchamp also leaves from Vesoul around 6:30am (40 min., 29F) and returns around 5:30pm. One bus per day leaving about noon runs from Vesoul to Ronchamp (½ hr., 32F).

A brand new **Auberge de Jeunesse (IYHF)**will be constructed by the summer of 1989 in the unattractive town of **Vesoul.** The hostel will be in the Zone du Loisir du Lac, next to a campground (30F per night). Call the campground (tel. 84-76-22-86) for information. From the train station, turn left for about 500m, bear right onto rue Magnot, turn right at the next intersection, and take a left at the big round-about (2.8km, about 30 min.) The office will probably be open daily 8-10am and 5-10pm.

The cheapest hotel in town is **Au Point Central,** 9, rue des Casernes (tel.84-75-19-95), near the Hôtel de Ville, with singles from 64F, doubles from 81F. **Ty Per,** 7, rue Baron Bouvier (tel. 84-76-59-83), is a Breton *creêperie* with poor lighting but decent crêpes. (Open Tues.-Sun. 11am-11pm.) **Chez Corinne,** 5, rue du Breuil, as-sembles a hearty *menu* for 55F and a *plat du jour* for 30.50F. There is a **Prisunic** supermarket on rue Commandant Girardot. (Open Mon.-Sat. 8:30am-12:30pm and 2-7pm.) To get to the tourist office from the station, turn right, take the first left onto rue Commandant Girardot, and follow the signs. The **post office,** rue Com-mandant Girardot (tel. 84-75-28-34), has **currency exchange.** (Open Mon.-Fri. 8am-7pm, Sat. 8am-noon.) Vesoul's **postal code** is 70000.

Arbois

Situated in the valley of the Cuissance River, at the foot of the Jura Mountains, this serene village is the center of the millinarian *jurassien* vineyards and a lovely alternative to the more touristed wine *caves* and fields of Burgundy. Arbois was the childhood home of Louis Pasteur. It's easy to see why the chemist returned here year after year.

Orientation and Practical Information

Less than 50km from Besançon, Arbois is served frequently by trains and buses. The central square of the town, **place de la Liberté,** is 1 block up the bus terminus, and a good 15-minute walk from the train station. Turn left at the end of av. de la Gare, following the signs for *centre ville;* stay on av. Pasteur, the main street, across the river (it becomes rue de Courcelles and then Grande Rue) until you hit the main square. Everything in this compact town is near this square or on the nar-row multi-named main street.

Office de Tourisme: 10, rue de l'Hôtel de Ville (tel. 84-66-07-45), in the Hôtel de Ville, off place de la Liberté. Dispenses train and bus schedules, a map, and a list of hotels and restau-rants. The friendly staff will tell you which hotels probably have vacancies, and which *caves* are open to the public. Ask for the leaflet on countryside tours. Open July-Aug. Mon. 2:30-6:30pm, Tues.-Sat. 9:30am-noon and 2:30-6:30pm, Sun. 10am-noon; Sept.-June Mon. 2-6:30pm, Tues.-Sat. 9:30am-noon and 2:30-6pm.

Currency Exchange: Banque Populaire, 13, rue de l'Hôtel de Ville (tel. 84-66-09-66). Open Mon.-Fri. 8:30am-noon and 1:45-6pm. **Crédit Agricole,** 58, Grande Rue (tel. 84-66-16-99). Open Tues.-Fri. 8:30am-noon and 1:30-6pm, Sat. 8:30am-noon and 1:30-4:30pm.

Post Office: Av. Général-Delort (tel. 84-66-01-21), off place de la Liberté. **Telephones. Postal code:** 39600. Open Mon.-Fri. 8am-noon and 2:30-5:30pm, Sat. 8am-noon.

Train Station: Route de Dole (tel. 84-47-50-50). To Dijon (6 per day, with transfers, 1 hr.), Lons-le-Saunier (7 per day, ½ hr., 33F), Besançon (6 per day, ½ hr., 34F), and Lyon (6 per day, 2 hr., 87F).

Bus Station: SNCF buses (free with railpasses) stop at place Notre-Dame across from the Hôtel des Messageries. To Lons-le-Saunier (2 per day, 1 hr.) and Monchaud (7 per day, 5 min.). Schedules posted at the stops; ask at the train station or tourist office. For other destina-tions, call **Cars Monts-Jura** (tel. 84-82-00-03).

Bike Rental: Patrick Aviet, 1, rue de Bourgogne (tel. 84-66-03-13). Decent 10-speeds 30F per ½-day, 50F per day, 210F per week. Open Mon.-Sat. 8:30am-noon and 2-5pm.

Police: 17, av. Général-Delort (tel. 84-66-14-25).

Police Emergency: Tel. 17.

Accommodations, Camping, and Food

Arbois is mainly a seasonal town, with only 4000 permanent residents. There aren't many hotels, but you shouldn't have trouble finding a room.

Hôtel des Messageries, 2, rue de Courcelles or promenade Pasteur (tel. 84-66-15-45), 2 blocks from place de la Liberté. An exquisite old hotel with a bar downstairs and a *salon* upstairs. Management is attentive, pleasant, and helpful. Singles and doubles from 100F. The hall shower is wonderful. Breakfast 20F. Open March-Nov.

Hôtel le Memphisto, 33, place de Faramand (tel. 84-66-06-49), near the church. Comfortable, spacious rooms. Singles 80F. Doubles 100F. Pizzeria below has a 45F *menu.*

La Poste, 71, Grande Rue (tel. 84-66-13-22), above a bar. Basic and clean with easy-going management. Singles 70F. Doubles 102F. Showers 10F. Breakfast 19F. The restaurant downstairs serves *steak-frites* for 31F.

Camping: Camping des Vignes, av. Général-Leclerc (tel. 84-66-14-12), about 1km outside town next to an Olympic-sized swimming pool. Follow the signs from place de la Liberté. A 3-star site. Open April-Sept.

Around place de Faramand a number of cafes serve basic 40F *menus* (appetizer, *steak-frites,* and dessert). The best restaurant, **La Finette, Taverne d'Arbois,** 22, av. Pasteur (tel. 84-66-06-78), uses wooden barrels for tables and offers a hearty 63F menu. Their *mâchons* (snacks) can be a meal in themselves—try the *fondue des trois cantons* (30F). (Open daily 9am-midnight.) The **Restaurant des Arcades,** 22, Grande Rue (tel. 84-66-06-81), near place de la Liberté, serves substantial meals including an artichoke *vinaigrette* for 46F. (Open Tues.-Sat. noon-2pm.) Breakfast in Arbois features *pain au lait* (a soft sweet bun found only in this region). A **market** is held Tuesday and Friday until 1pm in place de Champs de Mars. A huge **market** for the entire region takes place on the first Tuesday of the month at the same place.

Sights and Entertainment

Come to Arbois to savor *jurassien* wines and learn about different winemaking techniques. **Henri Maire,** the biggest wine-producer in the region, shows a free 20-minute film in English and French, a sumptuous portrayal of wine cultivation. Daily guided tours of the vineyards are followed by a traditional *dégustation.* The visit takes you to *caves* where red, white, and even yellow wines are produced. This *vin jaune* (yellow wine) is expensive and takes six years to make; 20% of it turns to vinegar. The guides are generous with the wine. You will also get an *apéritif* (try *Montagnard,* a sweet rose-colored wine). Henri Maire also makes *vin de paille* (straw wine), a sweet white made by pressing grapes dried on straw. *Vin fou* is another local product, and resembles champagne. (Hours vary; ask at Henri Maire's shop in the main square. Free.) Frequent tours of *caves,* including free tastings, are also given by **Fruitière Vinicole D'Arbois,** 2, rue des Fosses (July-Sept. 15). Go only if you can't make a tour at Maire—these *caves* usually cater to bus tours. Visit the **Musée de la Vigne et du Vin** only if you want to spend 15 minutes in a cellar with dust-covered implements and run-down displays. (Open mid-June to Nov. Wed.-Mon. 10am-noon and 3-7pm. Admission 6.60F, students 3.30F, ages under 16 free. For 10F you'll get a pass good here and at the municipal museum in the center of town.) The tourist office distributes a list of smaller wine-making operations, but only the large businesses will give tastings. At smaller houses, you should at least offer to pay for the tasting (*payer la dégustation*) if you don't buy a bottle.

Arbois was Louis Pasteur's childhood home and later his vacation retreat from the university where he taught. The ivy-covered **Maison Pasteur** still contains his original furniture. (Open for guided visits Wed.-Mon. 9am-noon and 2-6pm, Sun. 9am-noon and 2-5pm. Ring the bell to summon the guide. Admission 10F, students 5F.) The house preserves the laboratory where Pasteur did his experiments on fermentation. The small vineyard that he owned is now privately cultivated by Henri Maire; a film on Pasteur's life is shown several times per day in Henri Maire's shop.

For a view of Arbois sheltered amidst fields of grapes, climb to the top of the bell tower of **Eglise St-Just** (visits 3 times per day at 11am, 4pm, and 5:30 or 6pm). You will be rewarded with a demonstration of the church bells and a spectacular view of the valley and town. (It is customary to tip the guide.) Be sure you do your wine-tasting afterwards. The church is a melange: early Romanesque nave, late Gothic chapels and vaulted ceiling, and a sixteenth- to eighteenth-century bell tower. A restful, 15-minute *circuit pédestre* begins outside the church and passes an old waterwheel, a bubbling brook, vegetable gardens, and grazing sheep.

Arbois is the site of several festivals each year. The largest is the **Grande Fête des Vins** (last Sun. in July), when dancers and others in local garb proceed down the main street and wine flows freely. There's a raffle whose first prize is the winner's weight in wine, so stop dieting. In September and October smaller wine festivals correspond to the harvests of various wines.

About 5km from Arbois on CD107 are the haunting **Grottes des Planches**, hollowed out 250m underground by a subterranean river. (45-min. tours June-Sept. daily 9am-noon and 2-6:30pm; April and Oct. 10am-noon and 2-6pm.) You can't get to the caves by public transportation—walk, hitch, or try to get a ride on one of the many tour buses passing through Arbois (they often have extra seats). Your efforts will be rewarded by eroded galleries and misshapen protuberances of golden rock. You'll also be able to cool off in the caves, perennially 12°C.

Lons-le-Saunier

The ancient town of Lons-le-Saunier took its name from prehistoric salted wells, flavored by deep subterranean deposits, which no longer exist. Nevertheless, this bustling but boring commercial city doesn't seem very old. Lons-le Saunier is a thermal resort and a base for excursions into the Jura, but otherwise doesn't merit a trip. The main square, **place de la Liberté,** is surrounded by cafes and elegant tea parlors. Walking south from place de la Liberté along rue St-Désiré, you will come to **Eglise St-Désiré**, whose interior is pure eleventh-century Romanesque, despite recent alterations. Note the intricate stained-glass windows behind the altar.

The **Maison de Tourisme,** 1, rue Pasteur (tel. 84-24-65-01), will supply you with maps, descriptions, walking tours, lists of cultural events, *L'Eté Lédonien* (Summer at Lons), and information on sights in the area. (Open Mon.-Sat. 8:30am-noon and 2-6pm.) For information on hiking and other sports in the Jura, contact the **Centre Information de Jeunesse,** nearby at 15, av. Thurel (tel. 84-24-39-05). The friendly staff doesn't speak English, but knows about hitching, cheap lodging, and cultural events and sells BIJ/Transalpino tickets. (Open Mon.-Fri. 2-6pm.) The **post office,** 2bis, av. Aristide Briand (tel 84-24-01-60), has **telephones** and **currency exchange.** (Open Mon.-Fri. 8am-7pm, Sat. 8am-noon.)

The **Hôtel le Glacier,** 1, place Philippe de Chalon (tel. 84-47-26-89), offers singles and doubles that are slightly cramped but clean enough for 58F. (Showers 6F. Obligatory breakfast 16F.) The **Excelsior Hotel,** 3, rue Pasteur (tel. 84-24-02-82), next to the tourist office, offers acceptable, small singles from 74F. (Showers 10F. Breakfast 15F.) **Hôtel du Cheval Rouge,** 47, rue Lecourbe (tel. 84-47-20-44), a fine two-star establishment, is fronted by a tiny, flower-filled patio. (Singles and doubles from 85F.) **Café des Amis,** 36, rue Lecourbe (tel. 84-47-20-56), serves filling *menus* for 40F or 44F, *plat du jour* with dessert 36F. (Open Tues.-Sun. noon-2pm and 7-around 9pm.) **Ile d'Asie,** 9, rue de Vallière (tel. 84-47-19-66), serves Vietnamese specialties for 30-40F. (Open Tues.-Sat. noon-2pm and 7:30-10:30pm, Mon. 7:30-10:30pm.) But you may want to save your appetite for a slab of delicious *Comté* cheese in one of the *crémeries;* many of the *Comtés* are refined in Lons, and the best are those aged the longest. Not as renowned as a gourmet speciality, the backpackers' staple *La Vache qui Rit* is also produced here.

The natural wonder of Franche-Comté deserves exploration. For bus schedules to **Les Grottes de Baume,** where strangely-formed caves resemble mushroom fields, and **Lac du Chalain,** a crystal clear mountain lake that has become a popular resort, call **Cars Credoz** (tel. 84-24-51-47) or ask at the tourist office. The **Cascades du Hérisson** are not far from Lons and are served by the **RDIJ** bus service (tel. 84-24-31-25). Hitching is possible, but light traffic might slow you down. There are eight *cascades* in all. Surrounded by thick woods, these watercourses plunge off tables of broken layered rock. **Le Saut Girard** forces its way down a ravine and is one of the most dramatic of the falls; **L'Eventail** (The Fan) is the most graceful, with intricate veils of water hissing down tall stairs of stone.

Dole

Dole was established as a monastic village: Monks walked the narrow streets as bells rang out from Eglise Notre-Dame, the largest church in Franche-Comté. The town then thrived as a university town. Later, Dole reached its cultural and political peak as the capital of the Comté de Bourgogne. However, Louis XI threw a tantrum and razed the town to its foundations, and Dole has never recovered. A working-class town, Dole now enjoys small squares, a beautiful, deep-green canal, and friendly people, overshadowed by its more dynamic and flamboyant neighbor Besançon.

Orientation and Practical Information

Dole is located midway between Dijon and Besançon. The town stretches along the Doubs. **Place Grévy,** just a few blocks north of the river, marks the center of town. From the train station, turn left and follow av. Aristide Briand to the second left, just past the post office, and take rue du Gouvernement to the *syndicat.*

Syndicat d'Initiative: 6, place Grévy (tel. 84-72-11-22). List of hotels and a free map of the city. Ask for a copy of *Jura été,* which has a listing of cultural events. Open July-Aug. Tues.-Sat. 8:30am-noon and 2-7pm; Sept.-June Tues.-Fri. 8:30am-noon and 2-6pm, Sat. 8:30am-noon and 2-5pm.

Post Office: 3, av. Aristide Briand (tel. 84-82-15-71). **Telephones,** cash advances on Visa or Mastercard, and **currency exchange,** plus a wheelchair ramp. **Postal code:** 39100. Open Mon.-Fri. 8am-6:30pm, Sat. 8am-noon.

Train Station: Place de la Gare (tel. 84-47-50-50), 5 min. from the center of town. To Dijon (10 per day, 30 min., 32F), Besançon (10 per day, 30 min., 31F), and Strasbourg (10 per day, 3½ hr., 145F). SNCF bus to Lons-le-Saunier (4 per day, 1¼ hr., 48F.)

Buses: Monts Jura, 98, bd. du Président Wilson (tel. 84-82-00-03). Excursions to the Jura mountains.

Hospital: Centre Hospitalier, av. L. Jouhaux (tel. 84-72-81-21).

Police: Commissariat de Police, 1, rue du 21 Janvier (tel. 84-72-01-68).

Accommodations and Camping

Comfortable student *foyers* open their doors to budget travelers throughout the year. Barring quirks of fate, Dole's several cheap hotels generally have space.

Foyer des Jeunes Travailleurs: Foyer St-Jean (IYHF), place Jean XXIII (tel. 84-82-36-74), a 15-min. walk from the station. Walk straight ahead, turn right on bd. du Président Wilson (the main street), turn left at the 3rd light (rue des Paters), and head toward the hideous modern church. Clean singles 42F. Sheets included. Croissants (2.50F) and coffee (3F) for breakfast. Lunch (noon-12:45pm) or dinner (7-7:45pm) 30F. You should have no problem getting a room here even July-Aug. **Washing machines** 20F, dry 10F. **Bike Rental** 15F per ½-day, 30F per day, 50F per weekend. Office open Mon.-Fri. 8:30am-10pm, Sat.-Sun. noon-1pm and 7-11pm. No curfew.

Foyer Féminin Dolois, 8, rue Charles Sauria (tel. 84-82-15-21). From the train station, take av. Aristide Briand, turn right on rue du Collège de l'Arc, and then take the 1st left onto rue Charles Sauria. Men and women accepted. In an old convent with long corridors and spacious rooms. Singles 60F, ages over 25 65F. Sheets, showers, and breakfast included. Office open daily 8am-7pm. Curfew midnight.

Hôtel Moderne, 40, av. Aristide Briand (tel. 84-72-27-04), across from the station. Singles and doubles 65F, with bath 110-150F. Breakfast 17F. Smoke-filled bar below.

Auberge du Grand Cerf, 6, rue Arney (tel. 84-72-11-68), off place Grévy. Many regulars stay here. Clean and comfortable. Singles 60F. Doubles 80F. Breakfast 14F. Open Sept.-July.

Hôtel de Voyageur, 34, av. Aristide Briand (tel. 84-72-18-73). A little run-down. Tiny, spartan singles 60-70F. Doubles 90F, with shower 100F. Breakfast 16F.

Hôtel le Lion d'Or, 9, rue Arney (tel. 84-72-11-68), near place Grévy. Cramped and oppressive. Singles 60F. Doubles 90F. No showers. Restaurant downstairs is more pleasant and vaguely resembles a hunting lodge. 58F *menu*.

Camping du Pasquier, a 10-min. walk from place Grévy (tel. 84-72-02-61), on the river. One of the best views of the town and Eglise Notre-Dame. Hot showers. Open March-Oct.

Food

Cafes and *salons de thé* abound in the area around place Grévy and rue de Besançon, but, beacons for tourists, they charge high prices. Fortunately, there are food shops in the same area, so put together your own meal and eat by the river. Tuesday, Thursday, and Saturday mornings, the **market,** place du Marché, opposite the church, will supply you with generous portions of local specialties. There is an **Intermarché** supermarket on bd. du Président Wilson on the way to the Foyer des Jeunes Travailleurs.

Restaurant Associative, 8, rue Charles Sauria. Enter through the *foyer* and pay 33F at the desk. Down the stairs and through a door marked "Sortie" for the best bargain in town. 5-course, sit-down meals including wine. Popular with locals. Open daily noon-2pm and 7-7:30pm.

La Demi-Lune, 39, rue Pasteur (tel. 84-72-65-17). Particularly pleasant with a vaulted cellar next to the Maison Pasteur. Great tables on the canal. Salads and crêpes 9-37F. Open March-Sept. and Nov.-Jan. Thurs.-Tues. noon-2pm and 7pm-midnight.

Restaurant Le Grand Cerf, 6, rue Arney. Hearty 35F and 45F *menus.* Open Sept.-July daily 7am-8pm.

Buffet de la Gare, place de la Gare (tel. 84-72-13-78). A fancy station restaurant that is actually recommended by the townspeople. 54F *menu,* but *à la carte* entrees come in larger portions and are garnished with fries. Open Fri.-Wed. 11:15am-2pm and 7-9pm, Thurs. 11:15am-2pm.

Sights

The sixteenth-century **Eglise Notre-Dame** with its 74-meter steeple dominates the downtown district. It contains some beautifully vivid stained-glass windows. Interesting **Hôtel Terrier de Santans,** 44, rue de Besançon, preserves three staircases from the sixteenth, seventeenth, and eighteenth centuries. From rue de Besançon, take a right on rue de la Bière as you approach place Grévy. This narrow street leads down the hill to rue Pasteur: At #27 stands the **Collège des Orphelins Nobles de Broissia,** and at #43, the **Maison Natale de Louis Pasteur.** The town has made this a veritable shrine, collecting anything remotely associated with Pasteur, from old clothing to flasks of liquid used in his experiments on fermentation. You can buy small guides in English for 1F, or else just look at the old photos and papers on your own. (Open April-Oct. Mon. and Wed.-Sat. 10am-noon and 2-7pm, Sun. 2-5pm. Admission 10F, students 5F.)

A small arch to the right of the house leads to the **Canal des Tanneurs,** where Pasteur's father cured hides. Down the street at #20 is the **Hôtel de Champagney,** with its pretty balcony. Dole has scores of similar sixteenth- through eighteenth-century residences; the **Musée Municipal,** 85, rue des Arènes, contains paintings and sculptures from foreign schools—works by Vouet, Lebrun, Courbet, and others—as well as an archeological section with Gaelic, Gallo-Roman, and Merovingian displays. (Open Wed.-Mon. 10am-noon and 2-6pm. Admission 5.50F, students 2.75F.) The tourist office conducts guided tours (10-15F) of Dole (Wed. at 10am), the basilica (Mon. and Wed.-Fri. at 3:30pm), and the Hôtel Dieu (Thurs. at 10am, Tues. and Fri. at 3pm).

Alsace-Lorraine

Alsace and Lorraine have served France and Germany as political pawns since the third and fourth centuries, when barbarian tribes first swept westward into these regions. They have been invaded repeatedly ever since, more recently during the Franco-Prussian War of 1870-71 and during both world wars. The result has been less hybridization than alchemy. The product strangely supercedes the sum of its parts. Listen closely: Is that German you hear? No, and it certainly isn't French—the people speak a dialect understood only by themselves.

Although Alsace and Lorraine have together endured over a millennium of shifting political fortunes, they also remain separate in fundamental ways. While well preserved, Alsace caters to an international tourist crowd; Lorraine, alternately wooded and industrial, offers a quiet and undisturbed view of French life at its everyday best.

Alsace displays a wide range of architectural styles, from the Carolingian polygonal-style church at Ottmarsheim and the octagonal Alsatian-Romanesque towers in Sélestat to the Gothic splendor of Erwin de Steinbach's masterpiece—the facades of the cathedral of Strasbourg. The fields and vineyards that carpet Alsace's Rhine Valley give way abruptly to the long, forest-covered ridge of the Vosges mountains. At the foot of these hills stretches the *route du vin,* a string of vineyards and picturesque villages that runs about 140km from Marlenheim to Thann—the wine cellars here fortify hikers starting out on the long trails that wind up into the hills. Hundreds of miles of trails dotted with overnight refuges (*fermes auberges*) have been marked. Maps and guides are available from Club Vosgien, 4, rue de la Douane, Strasbourg (tel. 88-32-57-96, open Mon.-Fri. 9am-noon and 2-5pm), and tourist offices.

Nowhere does Alsace's German heritage manifest itself so strongly as in its cuisine. Among the traditional dishes are *tarte à l'oignon, pâté de foie gras, choucroute garnie* (sauerkraut cooked in white wine sauce and heaped with sausages and ham), *coq au Riesling* (chicken in a white wine sauce), and *baeckaoffe* (a casserole of marinated beef, pork, lamb, and potatoes that must sometimes be ordered a day in advance). *Tarte flambée,* another popular specialty, is made with bacon and traditionally cooked in a wood stove. Vegetarians, unfortunately, will find slim pickings here; beware the *tarte à l'oignon,* which generally contains hidden ham. Cheeses include the Germanic *Münster* and *Emmenthal.* The Alsatian vineyards produce six white wines and one dry rosé called *Pinot Noir. Reisling,* dry but fruity, is the "king" of the local wines, while *Gewurtztraminer* is extraordinarily fragrant.

Lorraine, to the west of Alsace, derives its name from the Frankish Emperor Lothair. In 843, the Treaty of Verdun divided Charlemagne's empire among three of his grandsons, and the boundaries of these kingdoms still have some political validity. Charles the Bald received an area roughly corresponding to modern France, Louis the German got Germany, and Lothair was granted a "middle kingdom," including Lotharingia, or Lorraine. Annexed by France in 1766 on the death of Stanislas, its last duke, the duchy became a pawn once again a century later during the Franco-Prussian War, when it invariably served as a bargaining point for other, more desirable, areas.

Devastated by two world wars, Lorraine retains relatively little of its past. The cities, rebuilt, can seem solemn and graceless—still in mourning, it seems, for the millions of dead who virtually covered its fields. Only a few towns were spared destruction: Bar-le-Duc, former capital of the splendid and powerful duchy of Bar, preserves its watchful *tour de l'horloge* and ancient *ville haute,* both of which overlook a newer center. Metz, a former fortress town and cultural center, boasts the luminous Cathédrale St-Etienne and Basilique St-Pierre-aux-Nonnais, one of the oldest churches in France. In chilling contrast, however, is Verdun. Reduced to rubble in WWI, the city and its surroundings are haunted by dozens of military cemeteries and echoing crypts.

What Lorraine's culinary specialties may lack in delicacy, they make up in heartiness: The bread is heavier than most, and potatoes or white cabbage are the usual accompaniment to meals. Bacon, butter, and cream are key ingredients in many dishes, as in *quiche Lorraine*, the region's claim to gastronomic fame. It was originally a peasant dish in which a hollowed-out loaf of stale bread was filled with egg custard and a few bits of meat. *Pâtés* are hearty and often made with marinated veal and beef. The *ramequin* is a tasty cake, and other sweets include *madeleines* from Commercy, *macaroons* from Nancy, and *dragées* from Verdun. If you complete your visit to Alsace-Lorraine without sampling the *gâteau Fôret-Noire* (Black-Forest cake), don't get on the train.

A word of caution: The French attribute it to German influence, but whatever its origin, a tendency to enforce regulations to an extent unthinkable elsewhere in France pervades the region. Expect regular and brusque examinations by *contrôleurs* (conductors) aboard buses and trains; losing your bus ticket before the end of the ride or forgetting to validate your train ticket on the platform could cost you 100F—no exceptions or excuses.

Strasbourg

Strasbourg impressed both Goethe and Rousseau—a feat probably not duplicated by any other city. Straddling the German border, Strasbourg has inherited customs from both countries. The covered bridges and overhanging half-timbered houses look German; the Gothic churches, wide boulevards, and spacious squares recall France. Part of the German Holy Roman Empire in the Middle Ages, Strasbourg nonetheless leaned toward Paris and was first attached to France in 1681. Nor did the more recent German presence in the city (1870-1918 and 1940-1944) sway the natives' allegiance to France. Strasbourg is now the seat of the 21-nation Council of Europe, an economic regulatory board. Serving as a Rhine port, large university town, the home of a considerable Chasidic Jewish community, and a cultural center, the city handles its duties with grace. Border crossings are fairly hassle-free, making a daytrip to Germany convenient.

Orientation and Practical Information

The old city is virtually an island at the center of Strasbourg, bounded on all sides by a large canal. From the station, go straight on rue du Maire-Kuss and over the bridge to Grand'-rue, which leads directly to the cathedral via rue Gutenberg and rue Hallebardes. If you make a right after crossing the *quai* from the train station, you will arrive at **La Petite France,** an attractive neighborhood of old Alsatian houses, narrow canals, and restaurants.

Office de Tourisme: The most convenient of the 3 offices is in a kiosk opposite the train station at place de la Gare (tel. 88-32-51-49). It's almost as comprehensive as the one centrally located at 10, place Gutenberg (tel. 88-32-57-07), although the latter is more likely to have up-to-the-minute information on local events. Helpful 2F brochure, available in English, with an adequate map, descriptions of sights, and a street index. Bus maps, brochures on festivals, a monthly brochure called *Strasbourg actualités* (which covers various events, including the sessions of the European Parliament), and *Saison d'été à Strasbourg* (which lists summer events). Offices open June-Sept. 8am-7pm; Oct.-May Mon.-Fri. 9am-12:30pm and 1:45-6pm; the Bureau Gutenberg keeps these hours Sat. as well.

Student Travel: CROUS: 1, quai du Maire-Dietrich (tel. 88-36-16-91). Will try to set you up in a dorm for 50F per night. Meal vouchers 19F. BIJ/Transalpino tickets, Britrail passes, French rail passes, and ISICs. Lists hours and locations of student dining halls after Feb. Open Mon.-Fri. 9-11:45am and 2-4pm. **Centre d'Information Jeunesse d'Alsace,** 7, rue des Ecrivains (tel. 88-37-33-33). Mainly for locals but provides information on occasional, organized junkets to the surrounding area.

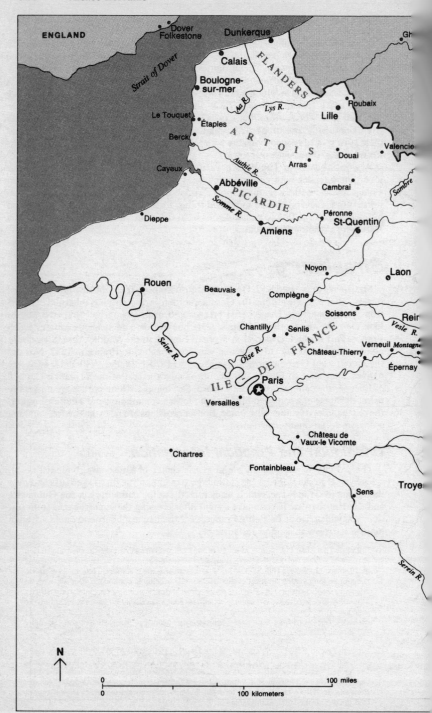

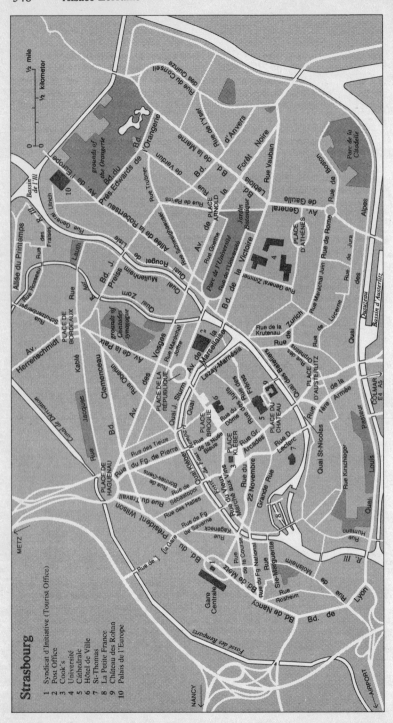

Strasbourg

1 Syndicat d'Initiative (Tourist Office)
2 Post Office
3 Cook's
4 Université
5 Cathédrale
6 Hôtel de Ville
7 St-Thomas
8 La Petite France
9 Château des Rohan
10 Palais de l'Europe

Consulates: U.S., 15, av. d'Alsace (tel. 88-35-31-04), next to pont John F. Kennedy. Open daily 9:30am-noon and 2-5pm. **Canada,** 10, place du Temple Neuf (tel. 88-32-65-96).

Currency Exchange: CIAL Bank (Crédit Industriel d'Alsace-Lorraine), 14, rue de la Nuée Bleue. Open Mon.-Fri. 8:15am-noon and 1:15-5pm. Also a window at the train station. Open daily 9am-8pm.

Post Office: Main branch, 5, av. de la Marseillaise. Poste Restante. **Telephones. Postal code:** 67000. Open Mon.-Fri. 8am-6:30pm, Sat. 8am-noon. **Branches** at the train station and place de la Cathédrale.

Train Station: Place de la Gare (tel. 88-22-50-50). Strasbourg is a major European rail junction. To Paris (4½ hr., 240F), Luxembourg (2½ hr.), Frankfurt (2½ hr.), Zurich (3 hr.), Vienna (11 hr.), Rome (15 hr.), and London (12 hr.). Frequent connections to Colmar (42F), Mulhouse (61F), Molsheim (14F), and Obernai (22F).

Bus Stations: Place de la Gare (tel. 88-28-20-30), and place des Halles (tel. 88-28-90-80). Office open Mon.-Fri. 6:15am-7pm. Maps from tourist offices. Local buses are convenient. Tickets 5.50F, *carnet* of 5 20F. Available from banks, vending machines, and *tabacs* within sight of a bus stop. Only a few buses go to the larger towns (Obernai and Saverne) along the *route du vin.*

Bike Rental: At the train station. 3-speed 45F per day, 10-speed 55F per day. Check at *bagages consigne.*

Hitching: For Paris, take bus #2, 12, or 22 to route des Romains. For Colmar, try bus #3, 13, or 23 to bd. de Lyon, and then follow the signs for Colmar to the highway ramp. **Allostop,** 5, rue du Général Zimmer (tel. 88-37-13-13), near the university off bd. de la Victoire. Arranges rides to a variety of cities: 40F per ride, annual membership 140F. **IYHF cards** here. Open Mon.-Fri. 2-6:30pm, Sat. 10am-noon.

Laundromat: 18, rue Edel; 3, rue des Tripiers; or 17, rue Jacques Peirotes (tel. 88-36-12-68). Wash 17F, dry 3F.

Public Baths: 10, bd. de la Victoire (tel. 88-35-51-56). Heated swimming pool open Mon.-Sat. noon-7:30pm. Admission 10F, students 6F. Laneless and lawless pool. Admission to the sauna or *bain-romain* 50F. Massage (8:15am-noon and 2-6:30pm) 80F, but these are single-sex at alternate times, so call before you go.

Rape Crisis: SOS Femmes, 16, quai Kleber (tel. 88-75-10-79 or 88-35-25-69). Open 2-7pm.

Medical Emergency: Tel. 17 for ambulances. **SAMU,** Tel. 88-33-33-33.

Police: 11, rue de la Nuée-Bleue (tel. 88-32-99-08).

Police Emergency: Tel. 17.

Accommodations and Camping

Strasbourg is extremely popular. The city has quite a few unpleasant budget hotels, and the good places fill quickly in summer. There are several budget hotels near the main train station, but the area is not particularly safe at night. Student dormitories open their doors to travelers from June to September (singles 49F), but availability may be limited. Despite the presence of two hostels, and a third one that should be completed by 1989, phone reservations a day or two in advance are often necessary. **CROUS** may provide a creative alternative (see Practical Information).

Auberge de Jeunesse René Cassin (IYHF), 9, rue de l'Auberge de Jeunesse (tel. 88-30-26-46), 2km from station. Take bus #3, 13, or 23 from rue du Vieux-Marché-aux-Vins. To get to the bus stop from the train station, go up rue du Maire-Kuss, cross the canal, and take the 2nd left. Wait in the covered booth for the bus (5.50F). An international meeting point. Game room. Bar open until 1am. Dorm beds 42F. Singles 85F. Doubles and triples 65F per person. Breakfast included, hearty lunch or dinner 30F. Camping 22F per person including breakfast. Reception open 7am-midnight.

CIARUS (Centre International d'Accueil de Strasbourg), 7, rue Finkmatt (tel. 88-32-12-12). From the train station, take rue de Maire-Kuss to the canal, and take a left to rue Finkmatt (10 min.). A sparkling new hostel affiliated with the YMCA. Excellent facilities, concerned management, and central location. 8- or 12-bed rooms 40F. Singles 97F. Breakfast 13F. Lunch and dinner 36F.

Auberge de Jeunesse, Centre International de Rencontres du Parc du Rhin, rue des Cavaliers (tel. 88-60-10-20), on the Rhine across from Germany. Take bus #11 from the train station to Pont-du-Rhin. Projected 1989 opening, but call ahead. Singles 130F. Doubles 70F per person. Triples 60F per person. Sheets and breakfast included. Lunch and dinner 40F. Open daily 7am-midnight.

Hôtel au Cycliste, 8, rue des Bateliers (tel. 88-36-20-01), near Eglise Ste-Madeleine. A pleasant hotel next to the river. Singles from 68F. Doubles 75-80F. Bath or shower 10F. Breakfast 14F. Usually closed at some point in June and July. Make reservations.

Hôtel Patricia, 1a, rue de Puits (tel. 88-32-14-60), behind Eglise St-Thomas, in the old town between rue de l'Ail and rue de Serruriers. A bit hard to find but in a nice location. Tranquility and comfort at a reasonable price. Singles 68F. Doubles 77-80F. Breakfast 15F.

Hôtel du Jura, 5, rue du Marché (tel. 88-32-12-72), near the station inside the old city off rue du Vieux-Marché-aux-Vins. Clean and comfortable. Singles and doubles 85F. Breakfast 17F. Curfew midnight. Closed noon-2pm.

Hôtel Victoria, 7-9, rue du Maire-Kuss (tel. 88-32-13-06), 5 min. from the train station on the street leading to the town center. Clean and cheap. Singles 65-80F. Doubles 75-115F. Reception open 4am-1am.

Hôtel Elisa, 3, rue Goethe (tel. 88-61-17-84), near the botanical gardens and old university. Pleasant and quiet, but full in summer; reserve as far ahead as possible. Singles and doubles 100-165F. Showers included. Breakfast 18F.

Hôtel Michelet, 48, rue du Vieux-Marché-aux-Poissons (tel. 88-32-47-38). Enthusiastic proprietors and decent facilities. Singles and doubles 65-135F. Showers 10F. Breakfast 15F.

Camping: La Montagne Verte, Terrain Municipal, rue du Schnokeloch (tel. 88-30-25-46), next to youth hostel. Take bus #3, 13, or 23 to Nid de Cigogne. Excellent facilities include showers, tennis courts, a bar, and restaurant (*menus* 35F and 50F). Open March-Oct. 7am-10pm. Adults 6.75F, ages under 10 3.60F, 6.75F per tent, electricity 5.70F. **Baggersee,** route de Colmar (tel. 88-39-03-40), on Lac du Baggersee. Take bus #13 or 23 (*direction* "Graffenstaden-Fegersheim") as far as Baggersee. Also excellent. Adults 8.50F, ages under 7 3.50F, 9F per tent, electricity 8F. Open 24 hours.

Food

Restaurants around the cathedral and La Petite France tend to be expensive. Think twice about ordering the *choucroute garnie,* which often turns out to be multicolored hot dogs in bland sauerkraut. Slightly dubious sausage stands abound; you may choose to take a turn for the *wurst.* Try the area around **Les Halles**for cheap if unremarkable French, Moroccan, or Chinese fare.

Au Pont St-Martin, 13-15, rue des Moulins (tel. 88-32-45-13). You can't miss this enormous, 3-tiered, riverside restaurant in picturesque La Petite France, catering to tourists and locals alike. The volume keeps their prices a little lower than their neighbors'. Portions are generous, at least. Dinner *menu* and 3-course lunch *menu* 50F.

La Plouzinette, 9, place St-Etienne (tel. 88-35-47-06), east of the cathedral. A small, pleasant *traiteur* with dozens of crepes for under 22F and picnic tables facing the square. Kirsch and Grand-Marnier *flambées* 26F. A great place for lunch. Open Mon.-Sat. 11:30am-10:30pm.

Restaurant de la Place, 16, rue des Tonneliers (tel. 88-32-53-54), off rue de la Douane. Small and homey. *Plat du jour* 26F, with entree 30F, with entree and coffee or tea 34F, but only for lunch Mon.-Fri. *A la carte* is not so cheap, but offers a good *gigot d'agneau* (leg of lamb) for 44F. Fri. is *paella* night. Open Mon.-Sat. 11:45am-2pm and 7pm-late.

Royal Saigon, 8, rue de l'Ecurie, off rue de la Douane. Full of locals, Asian and otherwise. Unusual Chinese and Vietnamese dishes 25-38F. The specials tend to be extremely spicy, but excellent. If you call a day in advance, the chef will prepare exotic dishes such as Chinese mushrooms stuffed with shark's fin. Open Tues.-Sun. 7:30-10:30pm. Right next door, **Les Quatre Saisons** (tel. 88-22-36-82) serves a *plat du jour* for 30F and pizza for 22-28F. Open Thurs.-Mon. 11:30am-2:30pm and 6:30-11:30pm, Tues. 11:30am-2:30pm.

Restaurant d'Quetsch, 6, rue du Faisan (tel. 88-36-31-01), on a side street between the cathedral and place St-Etienne. Not cheap, but serves excellent regional food to a young and sophisticated crowd. *Plat du jour* (noon-1:30pm) 45F, evening *menu* 80F. Open Sept.-July Mon.-Sat.

Chez Faisan and **Chez Aldo,** 8, rue du Faison, (tel. 88-36-00-49). Design your own pizzas and salads (30F) or order the *plat du jour* (36F).

FEC, place St-Etienne. The best of the student restaurants. Tickets 19F, local students 9F. Other student restaurants are **Paul Appel,** 10, rue de Palerme (tel. 88-35-66-00); **Esplanade,** 32, bd. de la Victoire (tel. 88-61-32-57); **Gallia,** 1, place de l'Université; and **Le Minotaure,** next door. Only the 1st 2 are open in summer. Inquire at CROUS (see Practical Information) to find out which are open and when.

Health Food Store: Ginseng Diététique, 5, place de l'Homme-de-Fer (tel. 88-32-20-20). Enthusiastic management. Open Mon. 3-7pm, Tues.-Fri. 9:30am-12:15pm and 2-6pm, Sat. 10am-noon and 2-6pm.

Sights

The ornate Gothic **Cathédrale de Strasbourg** was constructed from rose-colored Vosges sandstone between the eleventh and fifteenth centuries. Its famous single-towered profile has become a city trademark. Inside, the **Horloge Astronomique** (astronomical clock) shows the technical wizardry of Swiss clock makers in the sixteenth century: The apostles parade out of the face, and a cock crows to greet St. Peter. (Guided visits daily at 12:30pm. Admission 2F, tickets sold at the tourist office.) While waiting to see the clock's display, you can examine the cathedral's central **Pilier des Anges** (Doomsday Pillar), rising in the middle of the interior and decorated by an anonymous thirteenth-century master from Chartres. The same artist also produced the statues flanking the south portal, which portray the church and the synagogue as two women. The cathedral's 142-m tower made it the tallest monument in Christendom until the last century. If you climb the tower for a view, you'll be following in the footsteps of the young Goethe, who suffered from acute acrophobia and would climb up regularly as a measure of self-discipline. (Tower open in summer 9am-6pm. Admission 5.70F, students 2.60F.) The cathedral is being renovated because of recently discovered structural problems, but you can still enter at the south portal. (Open daily 9am-6pm.) The informative *son et lumière* presentation within presents a dramatic history of the city and cathedral, in German at 8pm and in French at 9pm. (April 22-Sept. daily. Admission 21F, students 12F.)

The museums are all near the cathedral. **Musée Alsacien,** 23, quai St-Nicolas, houses an interesting display of handicrafts, costumes, furniture, and regional art. The **Maison de l'Oeuvre Notre-Dame,** opposite the cathedral, occupies a fourteenth- to sixteenth-century mansion with sculpture, stained glass, and other artifacts from the Romanesque, Gothic, and Renaissance periods. The palatial **Château des Rohan,** a magnificent eighteenth-century building commissioned by the first Cardinal de Rohan-Soubise, houses a trinity of small, noteworthy museums: They focus on archeology, fine arts, and decorative arts. By the river, the **Ancienne Douane** (old customs house) shelters the pleasant **Musée d'Art Moderne,** with works by Klimt, Chagall, Klee, and Arp (a *Strasbourgeois*), as well as many impressionists. (All museums open April-Sept. Wed.-Mon. 10am-noon and 2-6pm; Oct.-March Mon. and Wed.-Sat. 2-6pm, Sun. 10am-noon and 2-6pm. Admission to the private chambers, fine and decorative arts collections in the Château des Rohan 6F, students 3F. All other museums 4F, students 2F.)

Forgettable boat tours of the old city's canals are given every half-hour from 10:30am to 9pm (1¼ hr., 40F; tickets and boarding in front of the Château des Rohan on place du Vieux-Marché-aux-Poissons). Equally dull tours on miniature, open-air trolleys leave every half-hour from in front of the cathedral (45 min., 17F).

The **Palais de l'Europe,** composed of Vosges sandstone and oxidized aluminum, was opened by former French president Giscard in 1977 to house the Council of Europe, as well as the European Parliament. When either organization is in session, you may register at the desk (bring your passport) for a look from the visitor's gallery, where headsets translating the debates into several languages are available. (Guided visits Mon.-Fri. 9-11am and 3-5pm every hr.) Across the street lies peaceful

Parc de l'Orangerie, designed by Le Nôtre, architect of Versailles, in 1692. Sadly, the animals in the small zoo aren't as well cared for as the flowers.

La Petite France, the old tanner's district, remains one of Strasbourg's prettiest and most visited neighborhoods. Tall Alsatian houses with steep roofs and carved wooden facades overlook narrow canals and locks that raise and lower boats on their way through the area. The streets here are full of budget-breaking cafes and tea-rooms.

Goethe, Napoleon, and Metternich were all alumni of the **Université de Strasbourg,** established in the seventeenth century. Follow bd. de la Victoire or rue de Zurich out to the new university quarters at the esplanade. The seven faculties are located in the area known as Palais de l'Université, which extends across bd. de la Victoire to rue Goethe and rue de l'Université, where there are beautiful botanical gardens and parks.

Entertainment

For information on all kinds of free entertainment, summer visitors should pick up the brochure *Saison d'été à Strasbourg* (Summer Season in Strasbourg) or the more complete *Strasbourg actualités* (Strasbourg Events) at the tourist office. In the courtyard of **Château des Rohan** a series of folk dancing demonstrations take place in June, July, and August. From June through mid-September, free concerts are given on Thursday at 8:30pm in **Parc des Contades** and once per week in the **Pavilion Joséphine** in the **Parc de l'Orangerie.** June brings the celebrated **Festival International de Musique;** for information, contact the Société des Amis de la Musique, 24, rue de la Mésange (tel. 88-32-43-10). Some concerts are free. A contemporary music festival, **Musica,** occurs in September or October. In the past it has featured such novelties as music played underwater in the public swimming pool. October through June, the **Orchestre Philharmonique de Strasbourg** performs at the Palais de la Musique et des Congrès, behind place de Bordeaux.

Productions of the **Théâtre National de Strasbourg** are staged at their resident theater, 7, place de la République (tei. 88-35-44-52). Tickets cost 45-68F, students 30-47F. Opera, operetta, and ballet are performed by **Opéra du Rhin** in the opera house, 19, place Broglie (tel. 88-36-43-41). Tickets cost 30-170F. November and December brings the annual **Festival Mimes et Clowns,** 1, rue du Pont St-Martin (tel. 88-32-74-01), along with the **Festival Européen de Cinéma d'Art et d'Essai,** 32, rue du Vieux-Marché-aux-Vins (tel. 88-32-12-30).

For less formal (and cheaper) entertainment, spend an evening in place de la Cathédrale. In summer, musicians play classical or folk music, and mimes, comedians, and acrobats perform for huge crowds in the evenings.

Among the area nightclubs and discos, you might try **Cintra,** 11, place des Etudiants (tel. 88-32-42-16), or **Don Juan,** 9, rue de la Course (tel. 88-32-44-62). Both are open Sunday to Friday.

Near Strasbourg: The Route du Vin

The back roads connecting the many small towns and extensive vineyards, known as the *route du vin,* offer a rich sampling Alsace's varied bouquets. The vineyards are interspersed with medieval ruins and small villages, whose charms are hardly diminished by their popularity. The route is easily covered by car; many hills make bicycling difficult. Hitching is also slow. You'll want plenty of time to stop for *dégustations* in various wine *caves;* the tourist offices at Strasbourg and Colmar provide information on specific routes and *caves,* and sponsor expensive weekly tours (around 80F) in summer.

Several of the larger towns are accessible by local trains. **Molsheim,** the largest, is popular and located breathtakingly at the foot of the Vosges. The town hall, the **Metzig,** has a tower, clock, and moondial from the sixteenth century, and near the center the small **Musée Regional** displays wine equipment and local curiosities. Pick up information here. (Open Mon.-Fri. 2-6pm. Free.)

Riquewihr, 60km south of Strasbourg, is widely considered the most beautiful town on the route. Enclosed by a wall, the sixteenth-century village lures thousands of tourists in summer, and prices for food and lodging are high. Built in 1291, the **Musée du Dolder,** in the Tour du Dolder, houses a collection of fifteenth-century firearms (open May-Oct. 5 daily 9am-noon and 1:30-6pm; admission 3F), while the beautiful **Tour des Voleurs** (Thieves' Tower) contains a bloodcurling torture chamber with a collection of evil-looking devices (open Easter-Oct. daily 9am-noon and 1:30-6pm; admission 3F). The **Syndicat d'Initiative,** 22, rue du Général de Gaulle (tel. 89-47-80-80), distributes a list of rooms in private houses. Prices vary; the cheapest run from 85F. (Open daily June and Sept. 10am-noon and 2-7pm; July-Aug. 10am-7pm.) Otherwise, the four-star **Camping International** (tel. 89-47-90-08) 1km from the town center (open April-Oct.).

A few kilometers south of Riquewihr lies the ancient, flower-filled village of Kaysersberg. Sitting at the entrance of the Weiss Valley and dominated by the ruined fortress that guarded it in the thirteenth century, Kaysersberg is just as attractive as Riquewihr, but not as tourist-oriented. A cluster of 500-year-old houses surrounds the village's fifteenth-century fortified bridge. **Eglise Ste-Croix,** dating from the thirteenth century, is home to Jean Bogartz's outstanding *retable,* completed in 1518. Located off a medieval courtyard at 62, rue du Général de Gaulle, the town's **musée** displays some excellent polychrome statues and an extremely prized fourteenth-century statue of the Virgin. (Open July-Aug. daily 10am-noon and 2-6pm; June and Sept.-Oct. Sat.-Sun. only.) Kaysersberg was also the birthplace of Nobel Prize-winning physician and musician Albert Schweitzer; you can now visit the **Centre Culturel Albert Schweitzer,** 126, rue du Général de Gaulle. (Open May-Oct. daily 9am-noon and 2-6pm. Admission 5F.) Farther along the street near the entrance to town is the **Syndicat d'Initiative** (tel. 89-78-22-78), on the ground floor of the town hall. (Open in summer Sat.-Thurs. 8am-noon and 2-6pm, Fri. 8am-noon and 2-5pm; in off-season Mon.-Thurs. 8am-noon and 1-5pm, Fri. 8am-noon and 1-4pm.) The **municipal campground** outside of town on rue des Acacias (tel. 89-47-14-47) is open from April through September. (7.60F per person, 6.15F per tent.)

Kintzheim, closer to Strasbourg and near Sélestat on the edge of the *route du vin,* possesses a remarkable library of priceless Merovingian documents. The **Syndicat d'Initiative,** place de la Fontaine (tel. 88-82-09-90 in summer; 88-82-09-88 in winter), can supply you with brochures of the area's sights. (Open in summer daily 10am-12:30pm and 2:30-6:30pm.) The ruined **Château de Kintzheim** now holds Europe's best-known aviary of predatory birds: Eagles, vultures, and falcons fly only a few meters above your head. (Open April-Sept. daily from 2pm; Oct.-Nov. 11 Wed. and Sat.-Sun. only.) As you climb into the mountains fringing the town, you'll come to **La Montagne des Singes.** Don't miss this opportunity to watch 300 Moroccan macaques (otherwise known as Barbary Apes) cavort freely in 20 hectares of enclosed Vosgian forest. (Open April-Sept. Mon.-Sat. 10am-noon and 1:30-7pm, longer hours Sun. Admission, including a handful of popcorn to feed the macaques, 20F.) Ascend to the 755-m peak of the mountain, where you'll join hundreds of other tourists at the **Château du Haut Koenigsbourg.** Commanding a splendid panorama of the Rhine valley, this large fortress complex was first constructed in the twelfth century. Burned by the Swedish in 1618 during the Thirty Years' War, it was occupied and rebuilt by Emperor William II of Germany in the late nineteenth century. (Open March 16-Sept. daily 9am-noon and 1-6pm; Oct.-Jan. 5 and Feb. 5-March 15 daily 9am-noon and 1-4pm. Admission 21F.) No accommodations exist at the top of the mountain, and those in the valley are expensive. A good alternative is the **Camping Rural,** 1, route de Sélestat (tel. 88-92-21-35), 3km from Kintzheim in tiny Orschwiller. The closest you can get by bus to Kintzheim and its surrounding sights is St-Hippolyte, a charming village itself; from there you'll have to walk or hitch the remaining distance.

If you're heading back to Strasbourg, try to go through **Obernai, Dambach-la-Ville,** and nearby **Scherwiller,** quaint villages couched amid vineyards. Several of the local *caves* offer *dégustations.* During the autumn grape harvests, the towns along the *route du vin* come alive with colorful bacchanalian festivals. Watch for vine wreaths hung outside establishments where *vin nouveau* is available.

Colmar

Colmar promises you a glimpse of the real Alsace. Only 30 minutes south of Strasbourg by train, it is surrounded by vineyards and overshadowed by the craggy Vosges mountains. However, prices are high, industrial smoke often obscures the mountains, and the mostly modern town has neither the sophisticated allure of Strasbourg nor the rustic charm of the wine villages. Still, proximity to the countryside, the *vieille ville* of magnificently preserved fifteenth- and sixteenth-century half-timbered houses, Grünewald's Issenheim Altarpiece, and Schongauer's *Virgin of the Rosebush* may lure you here and leave you with few regrets. Take a hike—in the peaceful countryside, that is—or settle into a small *brasserie* for some local philosophy.

Practical Information

Office de Tourisme: 4, rue des Unterlinden (tel. 89-41-02-29), across from the Unterlinden Museum. List of hotels, restaurants, and campgrounds, and a helpful city map. Also reserves hotel rooms; if all are full, they can probably locate a room in a private home. Organized tours to the villages of the region. Open mid-June to mid-Sept. Mon.-Fri. 8am-12:30pm and 1:30-7pm, Sat. 9am-noon and 2-6pm, Sun. 9:30am-12:30pm.

Post Office: 36-38, av. de la République, across from a lovely park. **Postal code:** 68000. Open Mon.-Fri. 8am-7pm, Sat. 8am-noon and 2-4pm. Open Sun. 8am-noon for telegrams, telephones, and Poste Restante only.

Train Station: Place de la Gare (tel. 89-41-66-80). To Paris (6 per day, 5 hr., 242F), Basel (Bâle), Switzerland (15 per day, 1 hr., 50F), and Nancy (3 per day, 2 hr., 115F). Countless runs to Strasbourg (½ hr., 40F) and Mulhorse (½ hr., 20F).

Bus Tours: Several private companies serve Riquewihr, St-Hippolyte, Kaysersberg, Ribeauville, and Eguisheim on the *route du vin.* The tourist office distributes *Actualités de Colmar,* listing schedules and destinations. **Voyages Pauli,** 6, rue Berthe Molly (tel. 89-41-66-80), offers organized tours of the region and beyond. To Fribourg, Germany, and the Black Forest, the Oberland Bernois (Switzerland) including Interlaken and Lucerne, and Lake Constance. Combined Rhine cruise and steam-train trip. Unfortunately, you can seldom choose your destination, but must resign yourself to the trip of the day. Office open Mon. 2-6pm, Tues.-Fri. 8:30am-noon and 2-6pm, Sat. 8:30am-noon.

Bike Rental: At the train station (tel. 89-23-17-17). 3-speeds 35F per ½-day (5am-1pm or 1-9pm), 45F per day. 10-speeds 45F per ½-day, 55F per day.

Markets: Place du Marché-aux-Fruits Thurs. 6am-6pm; place de la Cathédrale Thurs. 6am-6pm and Sat. noon-6pm; place des Dominicains Sat. noon-6pm (mostly clothes). Flea market 1st and 3rd Fri. of each month.

Laundromat: 8, rue Turenne, through La Petite Venise off the main canal. Wash 10F, dry 2F per 5 min. Open daily 8am-9pm.

Medical Emergency: SMUR, Tel. 18.

Police: 6, rue du Chasseur (tel. 89-41-08-00).

Police Emergency: Tel. 17.

Accommodations and Camping

You shouldn't have any trouble finding accommodations in Colmar.

Auberge de Jeunesse (IYHF), 6, rue St-Niklaas (tel. 89-41-33-08), about 20 min. from the station down av. de la Liberté, away from the center of town. Turn left from the station, cross the tracks, and double back on the other side until you reach av. de la Liberté. Or take bus #1 or 2 from the station to av. de Paris, and walk back along av. de la Liberté. A new building with basic facilities, but dark. Curfew in summer midnight; in off-season 11pm. Reception open March-Oct.

Maison des Jeunes (Centre International de Séjour), 17, Camille-Schlumberger (tel. 89-41-26-87), 3 blocks from the station in a pleasant residential neighborhood, 10 min. from the center of town. Probably the best deal in Colmar. TV room, beer, and soda in the evening. 38F per person. Breakfast 14F. Curfew 11pm. Registration 2-11pm.

La Chaumière, 74, av. de la République (tel. 89-41-08-99), near the station. Clean, simple rooms; most face a courtyard. Bar downstairs is a local hangout. Singles 75-160F. Doubles 90-170F. Showers 15F. Breakfast 15F.

Camping: A 3-star site (tel. 89-41-15-94), about ½km out of town. Take route de Neuf Brisach (RN415) out of town and across the Ill River. Or take bus #1 (*direction* "Wihr") to plage d'Ill.

Food

Inexpensive restaurants are hard to come by in Colmar, so you may have to choose between breaking the bank and another night of cheese sandwiches. Several concessions on rue des Clefs serve piping hot *tartes flambées* and pizza.

La Taverne, 2, impasse de la Maison Rouge (tel. 89-41-70-33). An elegant restaurant. Specialties include *salades composées* (27F), a fixed lunch *menu,* and a dinner *menu.* Try the pear sherbet for dessert. Open Tues.-Fri. for lunch and dinner, Mon. and Sat. for dinner.

A la Fleur, 3, rue du Consul Souverain (tel. 89-41-28-33), near La Taverne. Its outdoor tables encourage people-watching. Basic *menu du jour* 40F, omelettes 20F, quiche 16F. Open Thurs.-Mon. 9am-11pm, Tues. breakfast and lunch only.

Le Stéréo, 12, rue des Marchands (tel. 89-41-24-79). Slightly faded decor. Pizza and *steak frites* from 27F. Open Wed.-Mon. 11:45am-1:30pm and 6:40-11pm.

Auberge de l'Ill, 8, rue de l'Ill (tel. 89-71-83-23), near the campground. 2km northeast of town on route de Neuf Brisach (RN415) just 2 blocks beyond the canal. Take bus #1 towards Horbourg, stopping at Dornig. A real trek from the center, but definitely worth the trip. Where locals go for a special night out. The restaurant serves some of the largest portions you'll see in France. Main courses 40-80F. Salads and spaghetti from 32F. Open Wed.-Mon. afternoon. Call ahead or be prepared to wait.

Cafétéria Flunch, 8, av. de la République (tel. 89-23-56-56), at place Rapp. An orgy of plastic self-service. Cheap, filling meals 30-50F. You will be charged for everything—bread, sauce, and air. Open Mon.-Fri. 11am-2:30pm and 5:30-9:30pm, Sat.-Sun. 11am-9pm. **L'Ami Frit,** across the street in a parking lot, is a busy take-out with hamburgers for under 10F. You can eat in the lovely park beyond the parking lot. Open daily 8am-midnight.

Sights and Entertainment

Colmar's restored half-timbered houses are excellent examples of the regional architecture and of the local habit of painting plaster in various pastel shades. For the finest examples, visit the **Quartier des Tanneurs,** then follow rue des Tanneurs over a small canal to the delightful area called **La Petite Venise.** The multi-colored roof and amber-colored stone of **Collégiale St-Martin** stand out in the old section. Set among the ancient homes around rue des Marchands, a beautiful fourteenth-century house with Gothic windows faces the church. Two blocks to the west on place des Dominicains, **Eglise des Dominicains** displays Martin Schongauer's intricate *Virgin of the Rosebush* in its choir, as well as lovely fourteenth-century stained-glass windows. (Altar open for viewing April-Oct. daily 10am-6pm. Admission 5F, students 3F.)

The extraordinary **Musée Unterlinden,** place Unterlinden, contains a large collection of medieval religious art in a former Dominican convent that retains its cloister and chapel. The collection is famous for its primitive Alsatian masters and Mathias Grünewald's *Issenheim Altarpiece,* which blends the naturalistic and the fantastic. Two rooms in the basement display modern art, including a tapestry rendition of Picasso's *Guernica.* (Open April-Oct. daily 9am-6pm; Nov.-March 9am-noon and 2-6pm. Admission 17F, students 8F.) If you have time, visit the **Musée Bartholdi,**

30, rue des Marchands, across from the Maison Pfister (a famous sixteenth-century house). The former home of Frédéric Auguste Bartholdi, designer of the Statue of Liberty, this museum displays Colmar memorabilia from the eleventh through the nineteenth centuries. (Open May-Oct. daily 10am-noon and 2-6pm; Nov.-April Sat.-Sun. only. Admission 6F, students 3F.)

Every Tuesday evening at 9pm from June to September, Colmar hosts a folk-arts exhibition at place de l'Ancienne-Douane. Many free **concerts** occur during the summer (ask at the *syndicat* for information). During the **Fêtes Musicales d'Ete,** held Thursdays June through August, Eglise des Dominicains hosts evening concerts. (Tickets 40F, ages under 21 25F; the *syndicat* has a schedule.) The annual **Alsatian Wine Festival** is held in early August, with wine, beer, and agricultural equipment for all. The end of August and beginning of September bring **Jours Choucroute** (Sauerkraut Days), two weeks filled with feasting, dancing, wine and beer, and—guess again—*choucroute.*

Mulhouse

Annexed by the Germans in 1871, treated as occupied territory in both world wars, and bombed by the Allies prior to its liberation in 1945, the modern city of Mulhouse (pronounced Moo-LOOZ in French, Mool-HOW-zen in German) cannot count beauty among its virtues. Mulhouse welcomes you instead with an odd collection of museums.

Practical Information

Office de Tourisme: 9, av. Foch (tel. 89-45-68-31). From the train station, go to the far right corner of place du Général-de-Gaulle, across from a garden on rue Foch. Friendly staff and tons of useful brochures. The map looks like a poor photocopy of an eleventh-century manuscript written during a plague by a dying monk with a runny pen. If you need a room, the staff will find you one for free. Open June-Sept. Mon.-Sat. 9am-8pm, Sun. 10am-1pm; Oct.-May Mon.-Sat. 9am-noon and 2-7pm. **Annex,** at Musée de l'Automobile, 192, av. de Colmar. Open June-Sept. daily 10am-noon and 2-6pm.

Post Office: 3, place du Général-de-Gaulle. **Telephones.** Poste Restante. **Postal code:** 68055 or 68200. Open Mon.-Fri. 8am-7pm, Sat. 8am-noon.

Airport: Mulhouse-Bâle International Airport, on the Swiss border. Take the special Aéroport Bus from the train station (18F). Buses also run to and from Freiburg, Germany and Basel, Switzerland.

Train Station: Place du Général-de-Gaulle (tel. 89-46-50-50; for reservations 89-45-62-83). Mulhouse is on a direct rail line between Strasbourg (1½ hr., 60F), Colmar (45 min., 20F), and Basel, Switzerland (every ½ hr., 25 min., 30F). Services continues south to Milan (6 per day, 6 hr.) and Venice (6 per day, 11 hr.). To Metz (9 per day, 2½ hr., 128F). **Lockers** 3F per day, **baggage check** 10F per day.

Bus Station: Gare Routière, to the right as you face the train station (tel. 89-45-36-56). Both local and intercity. To Colmar (8 per day, 1½ hr., 20.50F). Local bus tickets 4F, a *carnet* of 6 15F. Maps and reliable timetables at every stop.

Public Baths and Swimming Pool: Etablissement de Bains, rue Pierre Curie (tel. 89-42-19-91), north off av. du Président and close to the center of town. Both open Tues. 2-7:15pm, Wed.-Thurs. and Sat. 8-11:45am and 2-7:15pm, Fri. 8am-7:15pm. Pool also open Mon. 2-7:15pm and Tues. 8-11:45am.

Medical Emergency: SAMU, Tel. 89-42-22-44.

Police Emergency: Tel. 17.

Accommodations and Camping

If you really must stay the night, the hostel may prove to be your best bet, as inexpensive hotels are hard to find.

Auberge de Jeunesse (IYHF), 37, rue de l'Illberg (tel. 89-42-63-28), 2km from downtown. Take bus #3 or 8 to Porte Jeune, then take bus #1 or 2 to Salle des Sports. Aging but pleasant, with a kitchen and TV. 35F per person. Sheets 11F. Breakfast 10F. Reception open 7-10am and 5-10pm. Curfew 11pm.

La Taverne, 26, rue de la Justice (tel. 89-45-14-92). From the train station, take av. de Maréchal Foch through place de la République to rue de Sauvage, then turn right on rue de la Justice. One of the more centrally-located budget hotels. Plain, well-lit rooms above a restaurant. Singles and doubles from 80F. Breakfast 15F.

Hôtel St-Hubert, 2, rue du Château zu Rhein (tel. 89-42-74-39), at the same bus stop as the youth hostel. The prices are right. Singles 68F. Doubles 80F. Showers 10F. Breakfast 16F. Reception open Sept. 2-Feb. 16 and March 2-Aug. 17 Tues.-Sun.

Hôtel Schoenberg, 14, rue Schoenberg (tel. 89-44-19-41). 11 rooms in a townhouse with a friendly, if eccentric, proprietor. A 15-min. walk from the station and the center of town: Take a left over the pont d'Altkirch and a right on av. d'Altkirch. A 3-min. bus ride to the zoo: take #8 to Maison de Convalescence St-Damien. Singles from 72F. Doubles 105F. Open Sept.-July Mon.-Sat.

Le Pavilion, 29, rue des Boulangers (tel. 89-45-85-90), on a pedestrian street in the middle of the old part of town. Small hotel with adequate rooms. Often fills up. Singles 75-91F. Doubles 91-150F. Open Sept. 16-Aug. 24.

Camping: Camping de l'Ill, 1, rue Pierre de Coubertin (tel. 89-42-63-28 or 89-06-20-66), near the youth hostel. A 3-star spot with sports facilities, a grocery store, and restaurant. Popular family spot, though there's generally room for tents. 11.30F per person. Open April-Sept.

Food

Mulhouse will satisfy your craving for Alsatian cuisine. Many restaurants serve inexpensive selections of authentic staples such as *baeckaoffe* (a bracing meal of stewed beef, lamb, pork, and potatoes), *choucroute,* and *andouillettes* (chitterling sausages). Other specialties include *tarte à l'oignon, flammeküche (tarte flambée),* and *kougelhopf* and *birewecke* (sweet bread with raisins or other dried fruit).

Auberge du Vieux Mulhouse, 8, rue des Archives (tel. 89-45-84-18), next to the Hôtel de Ville. A steaming interior and outdoor tables. Heaping platters of succulent Alsatian dishes. Various types of *choucroute* around 40F. 65F *menu.* Ordering *à la carte* is only a little more expensive. Open Mon.-Sat. noon-2pm and 7pm-midnight.

Brasserie Degermann, 46, rue des Franciscans (tel. 89-45-32-77). Only one of several traditional restaurants south of av. du Président Kennedy along rue du Couvent and its extension, rue des Bons Enfants. Low-key. Drinks, snacks, omelettes (32F). Alsatian dishes with fascinating names (*surlawerla* with *rösti,* and *haxala* on *choucroute*). 60F *menu.* Open Sept. 3-Aug. 16.

La Grillothèque, 41, av. Kennedy (tel. 89-80-24-44). Looks like a run-down fast-food joint from the outside, but the silk-covered ceiling and classical columns inside add sophistication. Vaguely international fare such as steak and spaghetti; they also serve a *tarte flambée* for 32F and a *menu* with *viande garnie* for 40F.

La Tête du Chou, 14, rue des Trois Rois (tel. 89-46-22-17). Vegetarian food in a room lit by candles and large paper orbs. Militantly *nouveau.* Most main dishes less than 45F. Try the *petits choux au fromage blanc* (little cabbages with white cheese, 42F) or the vegetable *pâté tarte* (42F). Open Mon.-Sat. noon-2pm and 7-11pm.

Sights

In Mulhouse, even the most compatible of travel relationships fall apart. Mulhouse equals museums—many varied and obscure museums that will enthrall some and bore others to tears. All close on Tuesdays, so plan accordingly. The tourist office distributes sheets with museum hours, addresses, and locations, with relevant bus information.

Place de la Réunion is the kernel of the old town. There you'll find **Temple St-Etienne,** in Gothic Revival style, with fourteenth-century stained-glass windows from an earlier church. (Open Mon. and Wed.-Sat. 10am-noon and 2-6pm, Sun. 2-6pm.) The **Hôtel de Ville,** the former town hall, also occupies the *place.* The Renaissance building's exterior revels in *trompe l'oeil* and shades of pink and gold. Today it retains only its painted ceilings and *salle de conseil* from that period, and is the beautifully maintained location of the **Musée Historique,** which displays local archeological finds and cultural artifacts. (Open June 15-Sept. 10am-noon and 2-6pm; ask at the tourist office for off-season hours. Admission 6F, students 3F.) Taking rue Guillaume Tell to the right as you face the Hôtel de Ville will bring you to the **Musée des Beaux Arts,** 4, place Guillaume Tell. Recently revamped, its collections include some impressive Gothic sculpture and paintings by masters such as Van Dyck, Ruysdael, and the school of Cranach. (Same hours and prices as above.)

Groups of Americans have been known to charter planes in order to visit the **Musée National de l'Automobile,** 192, av. de Colmar (tel. 89-42-29-17). Bus #2 or 7 from place de l'Europe can take you there somewhat less expensively. (Open Wed.-Mon. 10am-6pm. Admission a hefty 29F, students 18F.) This collection of cars, over 70 different makes, includes more than 100 Bugattis; two of these are Royal Bugattis, the special passion of the Swiss Schlumpf brothers, former owners of the collection. Their cache was discovered in the '70s, when unemployed textile workers came upon it in a warehouse, just days after the brothers had left the country. The **Musée Française du Chemin de Fer,** 2, rue Alfred de Glehn (tel. 89-42-25-67), allegedly has the largest collection of railway material on the continent. Take bus #1 from place de l'Europe. The stately old carriages are exhibited in a converted train station also housing the **Musée du Sapeur Pompier,** which illustrates the history of fire-fighting techniques. (Open daily April-Sept. 9am-6pm; Oct.-March 10am-5pm. Admission to both museums 25F.)

The **Musée de l'Impression sur Etoffes,** 3, rue des Bonnes Gens (tel. 89-45-51-20), is the only museum of its kind. Walk to the right as you leave the train station on rue Henner. Its collection is of both artistic and technical merit, showing the process of printing on cotton that *Mulhousiens* helped develop. Original examples of the intricate fabrics printed in the late eighteenth and early nineteenth centuries are on display, as well as some Asian textiles. (Open Wed.-Mon. 10am-noon and 2-6pm. Admission 18F, students 12F.) The **Musée du Papier Peint,** 28, rue Zuber (tel. 89-64-24-56), in nearby Rixheim, has the world's largest collection of wallpaper—over 130,000 varieties compiled by the manufacturer Zuber et Compagnie from 1791 to the present. (Same hours and prices as the Musée de l'Impression sur Etoffes. Admission to both 27F, students 18F.) Take bus #10 ("Porte de Bâle").

Epinal

Sitting on the banks of the Moselle River, modern Epinal is a city of 40,000 with little charm. Known since 1796 for the production of artistic renditions of village folk by the Imagerie Pellerin factory, the town is now home to the fascinating **Musée International de l'Imagerie,** on Ile de la Moselle. The museum's magnificent prints, sketches, and watercolors by Boucher, Gaurdi, Tiepolo, and others are augmented by a major collection of popular *images* from the earliest wood-cuts to present examples. (Open July-Aug. Wed.-Mon. 10am-noon and 2-7pm; May-June and Sept. 10am-noon and 2-6pm; Oct.-April 10am-noon and 2-5pm. Admission 18F, students 12F.) **Basilique St-Maurice,** in the center of town, is a wonderful church with a square tower and the fourteenth-century Portail des Bourgeois, which, though severely mutilated during the Revolution, still retains its grandeur. The only natural beauty to be found in town is the **Parc du Château,** off rue d'Ambrail; it surrounds the ruins of a medieval castle, and, at 20 hectares, is one of the largest wooded parks in France. (Open in summer 7:30am-8pm; in off-season shorter hours.)

The **Office de Tourisme,** 13, rue de la Comédie (tel. 29-82-53-32), is not the most helpful. (Open July-Aug. Mon.-Sat. 9am-7pm, Sun. 10am-noon and 4-7pm; Sept.-June Mon.-Sat. 9am-12:30pm and 1:30-7pm.) **Hôtel du Commerce,** 13-15, place des Vosges (tel. 29-34-21-65), is in one of Epinal's historic squares and has rooms from 65F. The **Terrain de Camping du Parc du Château,** chemin du Chaperon Rouge off Faubourg d'Ambrail (tel. 29-34-43-65), is a three-star site. **Au Grand Cerf,** 1, place Edmond Henry (tel. 29-34-38-67), has tables on the square behind the basilica, and *menus* for 57F and 67F. (Open Sept.-July Tues.-Sun.) Epinal is 70km from Nancy and 140km from Strasbourg. The **train station** (tel. 29-35-13-69) and **bus station** (tel. 29-82-54-82) are both in place du Général de Gaulle.

Nancy

Nancy has preserved fine examples of Baroque architecture. The gilded gates surrounding place Stanislas and the intricate facades of the old buildings evoke the finesse of another era. The city goes back to the eleventh century, when Gérard d'Alsace, founder of the hereditary duchy of Lorraine, built a fortified castle on a piece of land between two marshes of the Meurthe River. Today, Nancy is a city of monuments, museums, overpriced shops, and modern, steel-and-glass structures against an older background. Its numerous academic and technical institutions as well as its physical beauty make it the cultural hub of Lorraine.

Orientation and Practical Information

The center of town lies only a short distance from the train station. Leaving the *gare* to your left, take a right on rue Raymond-Poincaré, which turns into rue Stanislas, opening directly onto the main square, place Stanislas.

Learn the bus system or wear sturdy shoes. Nancy sprawls across a huge valley, and sights are far between.

Syndicat d'Initiative, 14, place Stanislas (tel. 83-35-22-41), to the right of the triumphal arch. The friendly, eager staff will find you a room free. They'll also load you up with dozens of brochures and maps. Tours of the city in French at 3pm (17F) and 9pm (20F), including the Hôtel de Ville (1 hr.). Open Mon.-Sat. 9am-7pm, Sun. 10am-1pm.

Post Office: Rue Pierre-Fourier, behind the Hôtel de Ville, 1 block from place Stanislas. Open Mon.-Fri. 8am-7pm, Sat. 8am-noon.

Train Station: Place Thiers (tel. 83-56-50-50). Frequent connections to Lunéville (23.50F), Strasbourg (80F), Metz (36F), and Paris (175F) via Verdun.

Buses: Rapides de Lorraine, place de la Cathédrale (tel. 83-32-34-20). **Transcar: Les Courriers Mosellans,** place Colonel-Driant (tel. 83-32-23-58).

Swimming Pool: Grande Piscine, rue Sergent Blandau. It's wound-or-be-wounded in this 4-pool complex. Open Mon.-Sat. 9am-noon and 2-7:40pm, Sun. 9am-noon. Admission 18F.

Medical Emergency: Tel. 15.

Police: Commissariat Central, 38, bd. Lobau (tel. 83-32-34-20).

Police Emergency: Tel. 17.

Accommodations, Camping, and Food

Hôtel Pasteur, 47, rue Pasteur (tel. 83-40-29-85), on the other side of town from the train station. Turn left on either rue Patton or rue Kennedy behind the station, right on rue de Mon-Désert, and left on rue Graffigny to rue Pasteur. Singles and doubles 70F. Breakfast 14F. Sometimes closed on Sun.; call ahead.

Centre d'Accueil de Remicourt, rue de Vandoeuvre, Villiers-lès-Nancy (tel. 83-27-73-67), 4km southwest of town in Château de Remicourt. Buy a bus ticket at the *consigne-baggages* desk in the train station. Take bus #4 from the station to Basch and walk left past 3 lights along bd. des Aiguillettes uphill (25 min.). Bus #26 stops uphill from the hostel but runs only Mon.-Sat. 7am-7:45pm. To your left you will see the castle across a park. Spectacularly inconvenient location. Extremely solicitous management. Bar and kitchen. Singles with sheets 33F. Breakfast 9F. Lockout 10:30pm.

Hôtel Le Jean Jaurès, 14, bd. Jean-Jaurès (tel. 83-27-74-14), on a continuation of rues Patton and Kennedy. A 2-star establishment with some cheaper rooms. Telephones in rooms. Singles from 75F. Doubles from 85F.

Camping de Brabrois, on RN74 towards Dijon (tel. 83-27-74-14). A 2-star site with telephones and showers. 3.75F per person, 4.10F per tent.

Most of Nancy's budget restaurants are undistinguished. The art-nouveau **l'Excelsior,** 50, rue Henry Poincaré (tel. 83-35-24-57), across from the station, is a *café-brasserie* popular with students. (Open 7am-1am. *Menus* 55F and 70F.) **Le Vaudemont,** 4, place Vaudemont (tel. 83-37-05-70), caters to a slightly older crowd. It serves an elegant 60F *menu* that includes a local dish and quiche. (Open 11am-midnight.) For full meals with German flair, try **Taverne Mutzig,** 45, rue des Dominicains (tel. 83-32-10-65), which serves *menus* from 56F and presents a band Sunday nights. **Caf' Conc' du Téméraire,** 17, Grande Rue (tel. 83-37-46-91), in the old city, is a smoke-filled cave with live blues and '30s jazz Wednesday nights for 100F, dinner included. Call to reserve. (55F *menu;* open noon-2pm and 6pm-2am.) **La Jouverte,** just down the street at #31, serves nutritious vegetarian meals from 55F. You can also buy food at the indoor/outdoor **market** held in the *place* in front of Eglise St-Sébastien (open Mon.-Sat. 9am-noon and 2-5pm).

Sights and Entertainment

Designed by eighteenth-century architect Hêré, magnificent **place Stanislas** marks Nancy's center. The seventeenth-century **Hôtel de Ville** is decorated with handsome eighteenth-century facades, balustrades, gilt-tipped wrought-iron railings, and the Neptune and Amphitrite fountains. The square is most spectacular at night during the *son et lumière* presentation around 10pm. The Bastille Day celebration here is fabulous, said to be rivaled only by the festivities in Paris.

The **Musée des Beaux-Arts,** 3, place Stanislas, has an impressive collection of seventeenth-century paintings, notably by Claude Lorraine, and a good selection of modern works by Matisse, Modigliani, and Dufy. (Open Wed.-Sun. 10am-noon and 2-6pm, Mon. 10am-noon. Admission 12F, students 8F.) Pass under Porte Roy-the finest of Nancy's seven triumphal arches, and descend to **Parc Pépinière,** a blend of English and French garden styles and the site of frequent summer concerts, with a **zoo** where peacocks strut about freely, and an outdoor cafe. Treat your senses to the **rose garden,** blooming spring through summer with an astounding collection of varieties and colors. Around to the left, the **Palais Ducal** houses the **Musée Lorraine,** an eclectic collection from 2000 years of the province's history. It includes paintings, sculpture, Roman artifacts, costumes, tapestries from the ducal palace, and the standard of Henry II, reputedly the oldest French flag in existence. (Open in summer Wed.-Sun. 10am-noon and 2-6pm. Admission 16F, students 11F.)

A walk through the **Arc de Triomphe** from place Stanislas takes you to the eighteenth-century **place de la Carrière.** At the end of this courtyard, twisting streets lead to **Porte de la Craffe.** These impressive guard towers are all that remain of the fourteenth-century fortifications. On the periphery of the city, opposite the station, is the **Musée de l'Ecole de Nancy,** 36, rue du Sergent-Blandan (tel. 83-40-14-86), France's contribution to art nouveau. It contains rooms with carved wood paneling, furniture, and glasswork, notably that of Emile Gallé. (Open in summer 10am-noon and 2-6pm; in off-season Wed.-Mon. 10am-noon and 2-5pm. Admission 12F.) Also of interest is the **Musée des Arts et Traditions Populaires** in the Couvent des Cordeliers, 66, Grande Rue, with displays evoking Lorraine lifestyles before the industrial era. (Open Thurs.-Sun. 10am-noon and 2-6pm. Admission 12F, students 8F.) Other museums include the museums of zoology and geology, and the **Musée du Fer,** which traces the history of iron production through three millennia.

In mid-October, the **Festival de Jazz** showcases an international covey of musicians, swinging from dusk to dawn in a tent in Parc de la Pepinière. In winter, **La Comédie de Lorraine** produces excellent contemporary plays. Every two months, the tourist office puts out a free pamphlet, *Spectacles à Nancy,* which has complete listings of expositions in progress and free concerts, theater productions, and movies. For the latest in video-dance excitement, try **Le Studio,** 23, rue des Maréchaux (tel. 83-37-00-09; open Mon.-Sat. 6pm-2am).

Lunéville

> This town was not reached by our researcher in 1988.

Duke Leopold fled to this negligible, calamity-ridden town from a Nancy occupied by French troops. Here, he and Duchess Elizabeth-Charlotte fashioned a vital, elegant court; his château became known as "the Versailles of the last dukes of Lorraine and Bar." Leopold laid out wide boulevards and squares based on the formal conceptions of eighteenth-century urban planning, and began building Eglise St-Jacques. When his son, François III, abandoned Lunéville for the grand duchy of Tuscany and the hand of Maria-Teresa of Austria, Lorraine passed to Louis XV. He in turn entrusted it to his father-in-law Stanislas Leczynski, the dethroned adventurer-king of Poland, to smooth Lorraine's passage into French hands. Stanislas built the flamboyant place Stanislas in Nancy, completed Eglise St-Jacques in effusive eastern-European baroque style, and made his court into an important intellectual center, drawing literati such as Voltaire. Upon Stanislas's death, Lorraine became French.

Lunéville's marvelous château, set amongst verdant gardens and lakes, makes the city an attractive daytrip from either Nancy or Metz.

Orientation and Practical Information

Lunéville lies between Nancy and Strasbourg and is an easy daytrip from Nancy via the Paris-Strasbourg train line. To reach the center of town from the station, walk straight ahead and bear left. Everything of interest is within a small radius of the old town.

Syndicat d'Initiative: Place de la 2ème D.C. (tel. 83-74-06-55), in the château's left wing, to your right as you face the building. Chock-full of pamphlets, but a bit confusing—it's best if you have a question in mind. Maps and a charming homespun walking-tour guide, *Un jour à Lunéville.* Also *Lunéville programme,* a monthly listing of local events. Open daily 9am-noon and 2-6pm.

Post Office: Rue Sarrebourg (tel. 83-73-19-32).

Train Station: 2, place Pierre Sémard (tel. 83-73-13-14; for reservations 83-73-01-28). Lunéville is on the main line between Paris (4 hr., 177F) and Strasbourg (1½ hr., 63F). Connections from Nancy (at least every 2 hr., 25 min., 23.50F).

Bus Station: Gare Routière, place Monseigneur Ruch (tel. 83-32-34-20), in Nancy. Call for information about buses from Nancy, which take triple the train time but cost just as much.

Hitching: For Nancy and Paris along Faubourg de Nancy off place des Carmes, north of the center (RN4). For Baccarat and St-Dié along rue de la Libération, to the right of and behind the station (RN59).

Medical Emergency: Centre Hospitalier St-Jacques, rue Level (tel. 83-73-17-49).

Police: 2, rue Caumont la Force (tel. 83-73-02-07).

Accommodations and Camping

Reservations are often necessary when conventions invade this popular destination. Plan ahead. Avoid the overpriced hotels on rue d'Alsace.

Hôtel Saint-Nicolas, 1, rue Chanzy (tel. 83-73-20-12), across from the château in a beautiful location. A 15-min. walk from the train station, down rue de la République and across the canal. Pleasant owners. Some rooms with views. Singles and doubles 67-100F. Showers 20F. Breakfast 16F.

Hôtel l'Evêché, 6, rue Carnot (tel. 83-73-00-50), straight down from the train station. Singles and doubles 70-90F. Restaurant downstairs with 45-67F *menus.*

Hôtel de l'Agriculture, 14, place du Rempart (tel. 83-73-00-61), off rue de la République, a few blocks from the château. Cheap. Singles 58F. The vinyl-and-plastic bar below serves a 43F *menu.* Open Mon.-Sat.

Camping: Camping Municipal de Lunéville, 69, quai des Petits Bosquets (tel. 83-73-37-58), at the foot of the château's extensive parc des Bosquets. Reception open daily 8am-9pm. Open April-Oct.

Food

Most of Lunéville's restaurants cluster near the château; rue de Lorraine is lined with *salons de thé, brasseries,* and a few ethnic restaurants.

Au Point Chaud, place du 2ème D.C. (tel. 83-73-20-86), opposite the tourist office. A good place for a quick snack or a light meal. From *frites* to crêpes to quiche, and local pastries such as *baba Stanislas,* a cream puff soaked in brandy (reputedly a creation of the Duke himself); the well-known *St-Jacques;* and the *Lunévillois.* Menus 31-45F. Open daily 11:15am-9pm.

Les Bosquets, 78, rue de Lorraine (tel. 83-74-00-14). Evokes rural manorial living and serves a luncheon *menu* Mon.-Fri. for 50F. Otherwise, make a careful *à la carte* selection for 55F. Try their *truite meunière* (trout with a butter sauce). Open Sun.-Thurs. noon-2pm and 7-9:15pm, Fri. noon-2pm.

Le Lunéville, 43, rue de la République (tel. 83-73-16-39). Appetizing 52F *menu* features a *tournedos de porc. A la carte* here is expensive (40-74F). Open Tues. and Thurs.-Sun. noon-3:30pm and 7pm-late, Wed. noon-3:30pm.

Sights

Château de Lunéville was designed by Boffrand, a disciple of Mansart, and its gardens were laid out by Le Nôtre's nephew. The majestic space enclosed by the palace's two wings, the artificial lakes, and the receding perspective of les Bosquets are direct quotations from Versailles. (*Son et lumière* by the south gate July-Aug. Fri.-Sat. at 9:30pm, Sept. 8:30pm; in off-season by appointment only. In bad weather and off-season held in the chapel.) The château houses the Musée Municipal (open Wed.-Mon. 10am-noon and 2-6pm; students 4F), with a military museum, historical museum, and collection of enameled ceramics from Lunéville and nearby St-Clément. Lunéville *faïences* have been renowned since the eighteenth century for their decoration, especially the floral patterns, rustic scenes, and chinoiseries, whose motifs are eighteenth-century interpretations of Asian design. Eglise St-Jacques was built on the plans of Boffrand and Héré, designer of Nancy's place Stanislas. The church is surmounted by two cupolas a la Borromini.

In the courtyard at 45, rue de la République, you'll find a twisting seventeenth-century stairway and stone medallions. The Maison du Marchand, 15, rue de Lorraine, is a baroque building in pink sandstone built during Stanislas's reign. Less fanciful architecture lines rue du Château.

Baccarat, only 15km away, has a Musée de la Crystalline, tracing the history of the famous glassworks founded in 1764 and revived around 1816. (Open June 15-July 15 daily 2-6:30pm; July 15-Sept. 15 10am-noon and 2-6:30pm; Sept. 15-June 15 Sat.-Sun. 2-6:30pm.) Contact the Syndicat d'Initiative, Résidence Centre, rue Division-LeClerc (tel. 83-75-13-37), for details. The *syndicat* in Lunéville also has information.

Metz

Less congested than Nancy and more cosmopolitan than Bar-le-Duc, Metz (MaYSS) extends an easygoing yet lively welcome to the traveler passing through. Metz was already an old fortified town in Caesar's time. Later it flourished, with Toul and Verdun, as one of three premier bishoprics. The twelfth-century Gothic

Cathédrale St-Etienne dates from this period. French by the Treaty of Westphalia, then German by the Treaty of Frankfurt, Metz was one of the principal strongholds of the Germans' western front in World War II. It's now a pleasant balance of old and modern architectural forms. Its **Musée Municipal** testifies to the city's efforts to infuse its artistic life with new energy.

Orientation and Practical Information

Metz is 150km northwest of Strasbourg, 350km east of Paris, and north of Nancy along the Moselle River, where it meets the Seille River. The train station is located in a fashionable neighborhood originally built by the Germans. From the train station, turn right and follow the contour of the gardens, making a left at rue Haute-Seille. Take another left at en Fourinirue until you reach the cathedral and the tourist office (20 min.).

Office de Tourisme: By far the most convenient is the branch in the **train station.** More information than you could ever want. Maps, calendars, and descriptions of monuments. Will find you a room for a deposit of half the night's fee. Open Mon.-Fri. 11am-1pm and 1:45-7:30pm. **Main office,** place d'Armes (tel. 87-75-65-21), in the center of town. 2-hr. tours of the city leave from here Mon.-Sat. at 9:30am and 2:30pm. Call a day ahead to request an English-speaking guide. Open Mon.-Fri. 9am-7pm, Sat. 9am-6:30pm, Sun. 10am-1pm and 3-5pm.

Post Office: 1, place Général-de-Gaulle (tel. 87-63-13-55), across from the train station. **Telephones. Postal Code:** 57007.

Train Station: Place Général-de-Gaulle (tel. 87-36-50-50; for reservations 87-66-82-22). To Nancy (every hr., 1 hr., 36F), Strasbourg (every 2 hr., 1½ hr., 80F), Luxembourg (every 2 hr., 1½ hr., 43F), Mulhouse (7 per day, 2½ hr., 128F), Lyon (6 per day, 5 hr., 206F), and Verdun (1 per day, 1 hr., 43F).

Bus Station: Place Coislin (tel. 87-75-26-62). Mostly local routes. To Verdun (6 per day, 2 hr.). Municipal buses and minibuses frequent and thorough. Route information at tourist office.

Market: Tues. and Thurs. mornings on place St-Jacques; Sat. morning on place du Marché.

Swimming Pools: Metz Plage, place du Luxembourg (tel. 87-32-42-49). Open Mon. 3-6pm, Wed. 9-11:40am and 2:30-5pm, Sat. 2-5pm, Sun. 9-11:40am. **Piscine Olympique,** rue Lothaire (tel. 87-63-77-29).

Hospital: Hôpital Notre Dame-de-Bon-Secours, 1, place Phillipe-de-Vignuelles (tel. 87-55-31-31).

Medical Emergency: SAMU, Tel. 87-62-27-11.

Police: Tel. 87-75-09-83.

Police Emergency: Tel. 17.

Accommodations, Camping, and Food

Hotels are usually expensive, and the few reasonable ones are far from the center of town. But Metz provides decent, cheap lodging with its hostel and foyer.

Auberge de Jeunesse, allée de Metz Plage (tel. 87-30-44-02), on the far side of town from the train station. Take bus #11 from the station to Pontifroy. Located right next to the Moselle River. An airy and simple hostel with obliging management. A good deal at 28F per person. Sheets 12F. Breakfast 12F. Reception open until 9am and 5-10pm. Call early in the day; fills fast.

Foyer Carrefour (IYHF), 6, rue Marchant (tel. 87-75-07-26). Continue to the right from the tourist office, turn right on rue St-Georges, then left on rue Marchant. A newer but dismal hostel that doubles as a *foyer* for young French workers. A definite 2nd choice. Singles with cold shower 56F. Lunch and dinner 30F.

Métropole, 5, place Général-de-Gaulle (tel. 87-66-26-22), across from the train station. Singles and doubles 70-85F. Breakfast 17F.

Camping: Metz-Plage, in a beautiful tree-shaded spot next to the Moselle and the youth hostel (tel. 87-32-42-49). Telephones, showers, indoor swimming pool, and skating rink nearby. 9F per person with tent, 5F per extra person. Open May 13-Dec. 10.

Several unabashedly touristic restaurants line av. Robert Schumann off place de la République. Join the animated crowd at **Hacienda,** 4, rue Ste-Barbe (tel. 87-31-29-03), across the river from the youth hostel. They dish out huge servings of the Spanish or French *plat du jour* on their 56F *menu.* Make it clear if you want something smaller—and less expensive. (Open daily 7:30am-1am.) **L'Etna,** 19, rue Dupont des Loges, parallel to rue Schumann, has local specialties but unattractive decor (*menu* 60F, *andouillettes* 30F). **Cafétéria Flunch,** 17, rue des Clercs (tel. 87-74-44-88), serves decent food at reasonable prices (main dishes from 30F) and is open daily 9am-10pm.

Sights and Entertainment

The tourist office distributes an exhaustive guide, *Rambles through Metz.* The cathedral and museum are off **place d'Armes,** an eighteenth-century square designed by Blondel, where a cloister and four churches once stood. **Cathédrale St-Etienne** possesses arresting stained-glass windows. On the west side of the nave, opposite Chappelle du Sacré-Coeur, is Hermann de Münster's monstrous rose window. Chagall's windows, in yellow, blue, red, and purple, are on the left as you face the north transept, and farther along the left where the ambulatory girdles the choir.

If you abandon place d'Armes to the right of the Hôtel de Ville, rue du Chanoine Collin, you will find the **Musée d'Art et d'Histoire,** 2, rue du Haut-Poirier. A wealth of Gallo-Roman sculpture testifies to Metz's importance as a Roman frontier town. The section on domestic architecture exhibits wooden interiors of entire medieval and Renaissance homes. The art museum houses works by the school of Metz, the Italian school, Corot, Zurbarán, and others. Dramatically lit or mounted in order to re-create their original settings, the paintings are arranged in rooms dedicated to themes such as "daily life" and "religious architecture." Rue des Clercs leads from place d'Armes to place de la République and the **esplanade,** a French garden with a balustrade overlooking the Moselle valley. To the left along the esplanade is **Basilique St-Pierre-aux-Nonnais,** one of the oldest churches in France and currently under reconstruction. Built on fourth- and seventh-century foundations, it underwent alterations until the fifteenth century.

The tourist office puts out a monthly *Calendrier des manifestations* (Calendar of Events, free). Its slicker magazine, *Vivre à Metz* (free), lists sports and cultural events. From July 14 through August, there is a *son et lumière* show at 10pm on the esplanade. For three weeks in late June and early July, the **Festival Etonnante Musique** (tel. 87-36-16-70) schedules performances of different kinds of music and dance. The **Fête de la Mirabelle** on the last weekend in August and the first weekend in September features fireworks, bands, and a parade led by the cherry-plum queen. November brings a contemporary music festival, **Rencontres Internationales de Musique Contemporaine,** with many free events. Check with the tourist office for performance dates and locations.

Verdun

The large, bomb-shaped chocolate candy sold at the tourist office, the forbidding Musée de la Bataille de Verdun at Fleury, and the military trophies scattered about town honor the million lives lost during the inconclusive battles centered on Verdun and Metz in World War I. Devastated by the war, Verdun has miraculously avoided the atrocious reconstruction that was the fate of so many other French cities. Much of Verdun is modern and commercial, built to blend pleasantly with the remnants of the original town. The flowing Meuse River, with its tree-lined banks, graces the center of the city, and the twin towers of the restored cathedral, outlined against the sky, recall a more peaceful past.

Verdun probably isn't worth visiting unless you have a special interest to research here. It is difficult to get to Verdun. Trains run infrequently from Nancy and **Châlons-sur-Marne,** and buses from Metz and Bar-le-Duc run in the morning. It is almost impossible to get out.

Practical Information

The bus and train stations face each other on either end of av. Garibaldi. The *centre ville* is to the west, enclosed within a loop of the Meuse.

Office de Tourisme: Place de la Nation (tel. 29-84-18-85), opposite Porte Chaussée. Maps of Verdun and the battlefields nearby. 4-hr. bus tour to all the principal sights (May-Sept. 15 daily at 2pm from the tourist office). Open June-Sept. 15 Mon.-Sat. 9am-12:15pm and 1:45-6:30pm, Sun. 9am-12:15pm and 1:45-5pm; Oct.-May 9am-noon and 2-5:30pm.

Post Office: Bd. de la Victoire. **Postal Code:** 55100.

Train Station: Place Maurice Genevoix (tel. 29-86-25-65). To Paris (7 per day, 3 hr., 124F), Châlons-sur-Marne (7 per day, 1½ hr., 55F), Nancy (2 per day, 2 hr.), and Metz (2 per day, 1¾ hr., 41F).

Bus Station: Place Vauban (tel. 29-86-02-71). To Metz (6 per day, 1¾ hr., 52F) and Bar-le-Duc (6 per day, 1 hr.).

Bike Rental: At the train station. 38F, deposit 250F. Battlefields are not more than 8km away.

Market: Fri. 9am-noon on rue de Rû.

Swimming Pool: Piscine de la Galavaude, at the edge of the city center (tel. 29-86-15-62), next to the stadium.

Medical Emergency: Tel. 15.

Police: Tel. 29-86-00-17.

Accommodations and Food

Hôtel de la Porte Chaussée, to the right of Porte Chaussée (tel. 29-86-00-78), overlooking the river. Clean and sunny. Singles 55F. Doubles 60-120F. Showers 10F. Breakfast 15F.

Hôtel Verdunois, 13, av. Garibaldi (tel. 29-86-17-45). Spacious rooms, sagging beds. Singles from 53.50F. Doubles 72F. Breakfast 10.30F.

Hôtel de Metz, 12, rue Edmond Robin (tel. 29-86-00-15), off the river. Cheap, airless singles from 40F. Clean, comfortable singles 52F. Breakfast 11F.

Des Deux Gares, 23, av. Garibaldi (tel. 29-86-64-03), is a *brasserie* serving a tasty *menu* for 40F. (Closed Sun. in winter.) Although its name is somewhat misleading, **Bowling de Verdun,** rue de 8 Mai (tel. 29-84-30-39), is an elegant restaurant and bowling alley, with a filling 45F *menu. A la carte* dishes are 40F. Bowling costs 15F, Saturday and Sunday 18F, plus 5F for shoe rental. (Open noon-3pm and 7pm-midnight.) Cross the river at pont Chausée and follow rue de la Liberté; signs to your right will point you there.

Sights

Two gateways remain from earlier forts, **Porte Châtel** on place St-Paul, a drawbridge with a war statue by Rodin, and **Porte Chaussée,** on the quai des Londres, in the Bastille style, through which troops and supplies were brought during the Great War. Past the gateway stretches the **Monument à la Victoire,** a flight of 72 granite steps surmounted by a resolute warrior figure and cannons aimed at the German front. Its crypt encloses gravestones with war decorations. (Open 9am-noon and 2-6pm.) Nearby is the **Musée de la Princerie,** a sixteenth-century mansion housing vestiges of Verdun's past. The arms, armor, sculpture, and archeology sections are notable.

Cathédrale Notre Dame, on the highest point in the city, was begun in 1048 with two choirs and two transepts. On the south side of the edifice, the cloister is divided into three galleries, one from the fourteenth century and the others from the sixteenth century. The cathedral's organ was the most powerful in Lorraine until the drought of 1976 warped its wooden parts. The **Citadelle Souterraine,** constructed on the site of the ancient Abbaye de St-Vanne, served as shelter for soldiers during the World War I. The 7km of underground galleries were equipped with everything necessary to support an army, including nine large ovens that could cook almost 29,000 rations of bread in 24 hours. (Open July-Aug. daily 9am-12:30pm and 2-6:30pm; Sept.-June hours vary slightly.)

Battlefields encircle the city 8km deep, a swath encompassing entire villages annihilated in the war. Two of the most frequently visited forts are **Fort de Vaux** and **Fort de Douaumont.** (Both open Feb.-March and Oct.-Dec. 10am-4:30pm; April-June 15 and Sept. 9am-6pm; June 15-Aug. 9am-7pm. Admission 10F.) Damp subterranean tunnels and gun casements are shrouded in ominous silence. The advantage of visiting Douaumont is that other sights lie along the same road: The **Mémorial-Musée de Fleury,** before Douaumont, displays models, uniforms, artillery, and reconstructed battlefields. (Open April-Sept. daily 9am-6pm; Oct.-March 9am-noon and 2-5pm. Admission 12F.) Near the fort is the **Ossuaire de Douaumont,** a rocket-shaped mausoleum containing the bones of 100,000 soldiers. (Open May-Sept. daily 9am-6pm; Oct.-April 9am-noon and 2-5:30pm. Admission 10F.) The **Tranchée des Baïonnettes** nearby honors an entire platoon of infantry buried alive in a trench.

Bar-le-Duc

You may want to come to Bar-le-Duc, a tiny, red-roofed village in a quiet, green valley, just to breathe the air. Capital of the ancient duchy of Bar, Bar-le-Duc's name derives from the barriers built by the Celts to repel invading Huns in the fifth century. The unscrupulous House of Bar inaugurated the region's golden age in the late thirteenth century. Its northern border extended to Luxembourg, its southern border to Burgundy. Court life flourished throughout the late Middle Ages and the Renaissance, but the golden age ended abruptly: The city was ravaged by plague and the Thirty Years' War, and only a fragment of the fortress-castle was standing when Bar passed into French hands after Duke Stanislas died in 1766. Bar-le-Duc's most famous product, its widely-exported *confiture de groseilles épinées* (seedless currant jam), has been locally produced since the beginning of the fifteenth century. The enterprise so expanded that by the eve of the Revolution, Bar-le-Duc was churning out 50,000 jars per year. Production has since settled down to a small cottage industry.

During World War I, Bar was an important transport and relief base to the Verdun battlefields, but escaped the heavy bombardments suffered by other cities. The steep cobblestone streets, the esplanade of the citadel, and the Renaissance facades on rue du Bourg all recall the former prominence of the town. Largely undisturbed since the eighteenth century, Bar has led to a life of tranquil obscurity. There is not much for the traveler to do in Bar-le-Duc—therein may lie its secret. Hike up into the woods, stroll along the canal, spend a day by the pool. Eat, sleep, make a friend—and drink in all that green.

Orientation and Practical Information

The town is roughly divided between the *ville haute,* on the hill, and the *ville basse,* in the valley. The *ville haute* is the older part of the city, with what remains of the castle. The train station and commercial center are in the *ville basse.* To reach either, walk straight out of the station. Once the street twists and slopes up, you have passed through the *ville basse.* Beyond is the center of the *ville haute.* To reach the neighborhood behind the train station, where the pool, Hôtel Bertrand, and the

Parc Varin Bernier are located, make a left from the station onto rue de Sebastopol, and make the next left onto rue St-Mihiel. You will have to climb the steep trestle to cross over the tracks.

Syndicat d'Initiative: 12, rue Lapique (tel. 29-79-11-13). Walk straight ahead from the train station, across the square, and down rue de la Gare, which becomes rue Lapique. The office is on the corner, in the left wing of the Hôtel de Ville. Although a new office with a friendly staff, you may be left to fend for yourself with a map and a list of hotels. Guided tours of the town leave July 5-Aug. Sat. at 3pm (1½ hr.). Open Tues.-Sat. 10am-noon and 2-6pm.

Post Office: 32, bd. de la Rochelle (tel. 29-45-17-33). **Telephones. Postal code:** 55000. Poste Restante at this office: 55013 Bar-le-Duc CEDEX. Open Mon.-Fri. 8am-7pm, Sat. 8am-noon.

Train Station: Place de la République (tel. 29-45-50-50). To Paris and Strasbourg (7-8 per day, 2¼ hr., 130F).

Bus Station: Gare Routière, place Reggio (tel. 29-79-34-35). To Verdun (6 per day, every 2 hr.).

Markets: To the left of rue André Theuriet coming from place Exelmans. Tues. and Sat., with a smaller one Thurs.

Laundromat: 10, rue du Bourg. Wash 7F, soap 3F, dry 1F. Open 7am-8pm.

Swimming Pool: 34, rue de la Piscine (tel. 29-79-09-06). In summer, full-to-bursting with screaming, splashing children. But worth the 10.50F for the sunbathing and gorgeous view. Open May-Sept. daily 9am-7:45pm.

Medical Emergency: SMUR, Tel. 29-79-11-13.

Police: Gendarmerie, 19, rue Louis Joblot (tel. 29-79-02-80).

Police Emergency: Tel. 17.

Accommodations, Camping, and Food

Intimate Bar-le-Duc is not equipped to accommodate many guests. Phone ahead or be prepared to move on to less idyllic towns such as Nancy. Most of the hotels and restaurants are in the *basse ville,* and a small grocery store is in the upper part of town.

Hôtel Bertrand, 19, rue de l'Etoile (tel. 29-79-02-97). Turn right from rue de St-Mihiel to place de l'Etoile. One of the finest hotels of its class in France. Well-maintained. Kind, concerned management. Down comforters and spotless bathrooms. Singles and doubles 65F. Rooms with 2 beds 100F, with bathroom 135F.

Hôtel Exelmans, 5, rue du Gué (tel. 29-76-21-06). On a small street in the center of town, on the far side of the Ornain if you're coming from the station. A clean, tight business. Closest to the city center. Singles and doubles from 55-82F. Showers 11F. Breakfast 15F. Open mid-Jan. to Dec.

Camping: Camping Municipal, behind the station (tel. 29-79-17-33), in the Parc Varin Bernier. 4F per person, 1.70F per tent, 8F per car. Open April-Oct. 1.

In the *ville haute,* **Grill de la Tour,** 15, rue du Baile (tel. 29-76-14-08), occupies an old guard tower with a crackling fire, low heavy beams, and a 50F *menu.* (Open Mon.-Sat. noon-1:30pm and 7-8:30pm.) **Restaurant la Chaumière,** 44, rue St-Jean (tel. 29-76-11-82), sports an Alpine look with dark wood and a cuckoo clock. The four-course *menu* is 55F. (Open Mon. noon-1:15pm, Tues.-Sun. noon-1:15pm and 7:30-9pm.) **Student Cafeteria,** at the Accueil des Jeunes, 2, place Exelmans (tel. 29-79-17-26), will fill you up with cheap if somewhat greasy food. Meal tickets cost 20F for students under 25, 25F for students over 25. (Open Mon.-Fri. 11:30am-12:45pm and 7-7:45pm, Sat. 11:30am-12:45pm.) Opposite the train station, **Restaurant de la Gare,** 2, place de la République (tel. 29-79-01-45), posts a standard 45F *menu.*

Sights

To reach the *ville haute,* take rue de l'Horloge off av. du Château to the left, and zigzag uphill along the steep, winding streets. Alsatian timber houses stand alongside sophisticated buildings such as the sixteenth-century *hôtel* of the Florainville family, which bears French and *barrois* coats of arms. **Eglise St-Pierre,** Gothic in structure and Renaissance in proportion, dominates the square. The **Tombe de René de Chalon** in the transept (called the *squelette,* or skeleton) is Ligier Richier's gruesome portrait of Chalon three years after his death. The triumphant pose of the figure against time and decay symbolizes the Christian hope of resurrection.

Between place St-Pierre and rue des Ducs lies **La Halle,** once a marketplace. In the other direction lies the entrance to what remains of the **château.** A map there, where rue François de Guise forks off to the right, shows its much larger original plan. The **esplanade** (with a magnificent view of the city), **Porte Romaine** (a relic of the original Roman settlement dating from the first century C.E.), and **Neufchâtel** (sixteenth-century, built but never occupied by Duc Charles III) are the only remaining structures. Neufchâtel now houses the **Musée Barrois,** which displays exhibits on *barrois* archeology, popular traditions, military history, and arts. (Open June-Sept. 15 Mon.-Fri. 2-6pm, Sat.-Sun. 3-6pm; Oct.-May Wed. and Sat.-Sun. 3-6pm. Admission Thurs.-Tues. 4F, Wed. free.) Avenue du Château roughly traces the outline of the ancient fort. The fourteenth-century **Pont Notre Dame,** once lined with shops and rebuilt entirely in the '50s, leads to the thirteenth-century **Eglise de Notre Dame,** with an eighteenth-century facade. Notre Dame eclipsed St-Pierre when the nobility shifted the town's center from the *ville haute* to the *ville basse;* this displacement has allowed the preservation of the *ville haute.* The **Parc Varin Bernier,** off rue St-Mihiel behind the train station, beckons with sublime shade. Feed the ducks or watch the water shimmer along the canal path.

Champagne

Brothers, brothers, come quickly!
I am drinking stars!

—*Dom Perignon*

Grapevines have existed in the Champagne region since the Tertiary period, but it was under the Romans that a systematic program of wine production for commerce was undertaken. The natural effervescence of champagne enchanted everyone who tasted it, but it was difficult to control. Not until the seventeenth century did a few individuals, among them the cellarer of the Abbey of Hautvillers—Dom Perignon—succeed in producing champagne of consistent quality. From that moment on, the wine's popularity expanded incredibly; it became known as the "king of wines and the wine of kings," and even Voltaire wrote of its noble properties.

You may be shocked to learn that you have seldom if ever drunk "real" champagne. According to French law, the name champagne can be used only for wines vinted from grapes of the region and produced according to the rigorous and time-honored *méthode champenoise,* which involves the blending of three different varieties of grape, two stages of fermentation, and the frequent realignment of bottles by *remueurs* (highly paid bottle turners) for an even distribution of the *ferment* or deposit. And even if you have taken the plunge, a little extra experience can't hurt—economist John Maynard Keynes once confessed that his one regret in life was not having drunk enough champagne. Make up for lost time by visiting the region's numerous wine cellars (*caves*). As each manufacturer will remind you, it's the area's unique combination of altitude, climate, chalky soil, and cellars carved from limestone that makes champagne production possible. The fascinating *caves* are redolent with penicillin mold, which thrives in the damp, cool air. Some *caves* have operated since Roman times; a few stretch along a 20-mile underground network, and others are decorated with impressive bas-reliefs.

Connoisseurs ask for a *coupe de champagne,* never the more vulgar *verre* (glass), in any bar, while gourmands enjoy the effervescent wine in the sauces of regional specialities such as *volaille au champagne* (poultry) or *civet d'oie* (goose stew). Buying by the bottle can be expensive; stick to Monoprix supermarkets for the best deals.

Once you have exhausted your money supply on the bubbly, take time to explore the region's less expensive attractions. To the French, this quiet and fruitful region, so often torn by war, means much more than a single liquid product. French civilization is deeply ingrained in the chalky soil, in some places going back 2000 years to important Roman administrative centers. The Middle Ages saw a flourishing high culture that carved its dreams in stone and wove them on the great looms of Troyes and Provins. Roman legionnaires fought barbarian tribes here; the region was again a battlefield in the Hundred Years' War, and the towers of Reims inspired Joan of Arc. Thousands died in the wars of Reformation and in the slaughter of WWI and WWII. Yet, throughout all turmoil, the grape harvest continued. And when WWII ended and France regained control over Champagne, the bubbles flowed freely in the national celebration.

Reims, the region's capital, is a vibrant cultural center with one of France's best-known cathedrals and an impressive basilica. Epernay exudes an air of wealth that emanates from its numerous, world-famous *caves,* which stretch literally for miles underground. Châlons-sur-Marne, outside the cultural area, is a quiet town of ancient churches, and Troyes, in the south, is a lively city of monuments and museums devoted to such diverse subjects as bonnetry and modern art.

Champagne is a great place for excursions into the countryside by car, bike, or foot. If you are driving or hitchhiking, follow any of the *routes de champagne* through the Montagne de Reims, the Marne Valley, or the *côtes des blancs.* Tourist offices distribute route maps; ask for the pamphlet *The Champagne Road.* You can wander off alone to visit the small villages and lakes dotting the region south and west of Epernay. Champagne's two national parks are ideal for hiking. The tourist office in Troyes has information on the Forêt d'Orient, while the tourist office in Reims sells a booklet of trails through the Parc Naturel de la Montagne de Reims (12F). The Forêt de Verzy, a curious forest of twisted, umbrella-shaped dwarf beeches (*tortillards*), and the vast Forêt de Germaine are also notable. Camping is easy and undisturbed. Trains connect the major towns and buses can bring you to smaller villages well off the tourist route.

Reims

Reims is, above all, a survivor. Regularly invaded, first in 3 C.E. by Vandals, more recently by German troups in 1870, 1914 and 1944, and, finally, by tourists year after year, the city has displayed tremendous resilience by making the best of rebuilding opportunities. Reims has also had its share of wealth and prestige. Twenty-five kings from Clovis to Charles X were crowned here; later, textile industries flourished and now champagne production thrives.

Though various sights testify to the glory of the city's past, veering from the main tourist routes uncovers a less attractive metropolis, where six out of seven houses have been rebuilt since the Great War with little attention to aesthetics.

Orientation and Practical Information

Unlike many French cities of its size, Reims was built not on a river, but on ancient trade routes. The city lies on a plain 30km north of the Marne River and 154km east of Paris. The scenic train ride from Paris's Gare de l'Est takes an hour and a half. Because the city is on a secondary rail line, connections to other cities often involve changing trains. The tourist office and most of the sights lie within easy walking distance east of the train station.

Office de Tourisme: 2, rue de Machault, next to the cathedral in the ruins of the old chapter-house. Ask the efficient, trilingual staff for the well-indexed town map *Plan de l'office de tourisme.* They also sell the *Plan Blay,* which shows all bus-routes. Lists of *caves* (wine cellars) and day hikes around Reims (*Promenades autour de Reims*). Pamphlet (*Reims en Champagne*) with museum hours and local festival dates. Open in summer Mon.-Sat. 9am-7:30pm, Sun. and holidays 10:30am-noon and 2-5pm; in winter Mon.-Sat. 10am-12:30pm and 1:30-5:30pm.

Post Office: Main office, rue Olivier-Métra and place de Boulingrin (tel. 26-88-44-22), near the Porte Mars. Poste Restante **postal code:** 51084; residential and commercial postal code: 51100. **Branch office,** 1, rue Cérès (place Royale), closer to the tourist office. Both open Mon.-Fri. 8:30am-6:30pm, Sat. 8:30am-noon.

Train Station: Bd. Joffre (tel. 26-88-50-50), across the park from the town center and place Drouet d'Erlon. To Laon (4 per day, 1 hr., 36F), Epernay (18 per day, ½ hr., 23F), Paris (12 per day around 6-7am, noon, and 5-9pm; 1½ hr.; 84F), and Luxembourg (2 per day, 3 hr., 115F). Lockers, **baggage service** (open daily 5:45am-8:30pm), an information desk next to the ticket counter, and a SNCF travel agency (open Mon.-Fri. 9am-12:30pm and 2-6:30pm, Sat. 9:30am-12:30pm and 2:30-5:30pm). The booth marked *Accueil* provides information only about the station itself; if you're in a pinch, the *Accueil* or the train information counter will give you a map of the city.

Bus Station: Transport Urbains de Reims (TUR). Buses stop in front of the train station. Although tickets can be bought at the station, the main information and ticket office is at 6, rue Chanzy (tel. 26-88-25-38), at the theater. Local buses leave from here. 10F *carnet* available at bars or tabacs. Ask at the tourist office about buses to Epernay, Laon, and Châlons-sur-Marne. No *gare routière* here.

Taxi: Tel. 26-88-05-05.

Hitching: For Paris, it's best to follow N31 via Soissons; take bus B or #2, *direction* Tinquieux. For Luxembourg, try N380; take bus B, *direction* Point de Witry, and get off at the terminus. To hitch a ride on a canal barge in the direction of Burgundy, go to the old port on bd. Paul-Doumer.

Lost and Found: Objets Trouvés, Tel. 26-09-21-04.

Markets: Every morning at different locations; ask at the tourist office.

Laundromat: 24, rue de Cernay; 32, rue Dr. Thomas.

Women's Center: SOS Femmes, Tel. 26-40-13-45.

Gay and Lesbian Services: Francine à Reims, Tel. 26-88-40-01. **Oméga,** tel. 29-86-23-72. Anonymity guaranteed.

Pharmacy: Grande Pharmacie Régional, 14, rue Cadrant St-Pierre (tel. 26-88-20-23).

Medical Emergency: Service Médicale d'Urgence (SAMU), 45, rue Cognacq Jay (tel. 26-06-07-08).

Police: 3, rue Rockefeller (tel. 26-88-21-12).

Accommodations and Camping

You must make reservations in this popular city, even at the youth hostel. There is a cluster of inexpensive hotels on **rue de Thillois** and **place Drouet d'Erlon.** Ask at the tourist office about options in *foyers* (workers' dormitories).

Auberge de Jeunesse (IYHF)/Centre International de Séjour, 1, chausée Bocquaine (tel. 26-40-52-60), across from Parc Leo Lagrange, beside Espace André Malraux. A 15-min. walk from the station. Continue straight from the train station, turn right at the far side of the gardens, follow bd. Général Leclerc, and cross the bridge. Take your first left on chausée Bocquaine; the hostel is on the left. Expensive for a hostel, but excellent facilities: kitchen, book exchange, TV. Singles 63F. Doubles 60F per person. Breakfast included. Curfew 11pm.

Auberge de Jeunesse, rue du Bassin (tel. 26-97-90-10), at Verzy 20km south of Reims. No public transportation. Open 7-10am and 5-10pm.

University Housing: CROUS, 34, bd. Henry Vasnier (tel. 26-85-50-16). Take bus D at the train station to Yser (2-3km). Accepts travelers in July and Aug. 40F per person.

Hôtel d'Alsace, 6, rue Général Sarrail (tel. 26-47-44-08), near the station and not far from the sights. Delightful proprietor has helpful advice and brochures. Bright, cheery hallways and large, simply furnished rooms. Bar downstairs. Singles and doubles 69F, with bathroom 116F. Showers 10F. Breakfast 17F.

Hôtel Linguet, 14, rue Linguet (tel. 26-47-31-89), on a quiet residential street. Clean rooms; some have fireplaces and stained-glass windows. Friendly management. Courtyard decorated with bonsai trees and dining room with fish tanks. Recently renovated bathrooms. Singles 65F. Doubles 70F. Showers 10F. Breakfast 16F.

Hôtel Thillois, rue Thillois (tel. 26-40-65-65). Nervous management. Simple rooms. Singles from 55F. Doubles from 70F. Showers 10F. Breakfast 15F.

Au Bon Accueil, 31, rue Thillois (tel. 26-88-55-74). Only 10 min. from the station. Reasonable prices. Singles from 65F. Doubles from 75F. Showers 10F. Breakfast 15F.

Camping: Camping-Airotel de Champagne, av. Hoche, route de Châlons (tel. 26-85-41-22), 8-9km from downtown. Take bus #2 from the theater. 3-star site with 3-day limit. Open Easter-Sept. 30.

Food and Drink

Reims may be the best place to sample local specialties since convenient restaurants often offer reasonably-priced *menus*. Place Drouet-Erlon is lined with fast food places, fancy cafes, and bars where *Rémois* exercise their *joie de vivre*. Students gather at pizza restaurants along rue Gambetta.

Avoid buying expensive bottles of champagne which are bulky and heavy. Take the tour at Mumm for a free taste of the local brew or order a *coupe de champagne* in any bar.

Le Colibri, 12, rue de Chanzy (tel. 26-47-50-67), facing the cathedral. A popular restaurant and bar. At night you can reserve a table with a view of the illuminated cathedral. *Menus* 40-110F. *Plat du jour* 25F. Open daily 11am-10:30pm.

Ancien Pavillon, 2, bd. Jules César (tel. 26-47-63-95), on the corner of the 2nd spoke off place de la République. Take a left from the station. Small, with wood ceiling beams and carved furniture. English-speaking host. *Menus* from 45F feature traditional *campagnard* dishes. Specialties include kidney flambée. Open Sept.-July Mon.-Fri. noon-2pm and 7-9:30pm, Sat. 7-10pm. Call for reservations.

Le Flamm' Steak, 17, rue Libergier (tel. 26-47-04-06), 2 blocks from the cathedral. A variety of delicious regional dishes and tasty crêpes cooked before your eyes. The candle-lit setting upstairs is cozy, even at noon. Dinner crêpes 14-21F, dessert 9-21F, main dishes 17-60F, *menus* 40-65F. Try the *mousseline de truite.* Open Oct.-Aug. Mon.-Sat. 10:30am-1:30pm and 6:30-10:30pm, Sun. 10:30am-1:30pm.

Le Nôtre Dame, rue de Chanzy, next to le Colibri. A little more elegant than its neighbor with *menus* at 45F, 65F, and 130F.

Les Brisants, 13, rue de Chativesle (tel. 26-40-60-41), off place Drouet d'Erlon. Sit inside the refreshing pastel green room or in the courtyard during summer. *Galettes* (dinner crêpes) 22-43F, main dishes 32-61F, *menu* 56F. Open daily noon-2:30pm and 7-10:30pm. Reservations recommended on weekends.

La Boule d'Or, 39, rue Thiers. Excellent value, homey atmosphere, fresh food. *Menus* 44F, 56F, and 66F. Try the *pâté champenois* (10F) and *plat du jour* (30F). Open Tues.-Sun. 9am-10pm.

Cafétéria, in the Espace André Malraux beside the youth hostel, the 2nd building on your left after crossing the Pont de Vesle. Don't let the name deceive you; there is waiter service and creative, tasty cuisine. *Menu* only 38F. Open Sept.-July Tues.-Sat. noon-2pm and 5-9pm.

Sights and Entertainment

Since the year 496, when the Frankish king Clovis was baptized here, bringing the Faith of Rome to the people of France, coronation at Reims has been the *sine qua non* of legitimacy for French monarchs. Joan of Arc's mission was to deliver the indecisive Charles VII to Reims so the French could unite behind a strong monarch and drive "Les Goddams"—as the English were called because of their penchant for the expression—back across the channel.

A half-hour tour of Reims in a minitrain leaves from the tourist office (daily every ½ hr. 9am-8pm, 20F). Despite visible damage from the Great War, the restored Gothic **Cathédrale de Notre Dame** stands fully equal to the coronations that have been held inside it. The present cathedral, the third to occupy this site, is built of blocks of golden limestone quarried in the Champagne *caves* beginning in 1211. The west facade contains a spectacular rose window, with deep blue glass made from lapis lazuli. The simple interior epitomizes medieval harmony and unity. Be sure to examine the tapestries that portray scenes from the *Song of Songs* and Jesus' infancy (usually on display in summer). Note Chagall's windows in the apse depicting the same events in modern style. You must enter the cathedral from place de Cardinal de Luçon. (Open July-Aug. daily 9am-8pm.) For guided tours in English, ask at the tourist office or buy the *Guide de Visite* (30F) in the cathedral.

Next to the cathedral stands the **Palais du Tau,** the former archiepiscopal palace, so named because the original floor plan resembled a "T." A museum here houses exquisite tapestries, statuary from the cathedral (including a Goliath-sized Goliath), and the extravagant gold and velvet coronation vestments of Charles X. The cathedral's dazzling treasure, housed in two exhibition halls, includes Charlemagne's talisman from the ninth century and the twelfth-century chalice from which 20 kings received communion. (Open in summer daily 10am-noon and 2-6pm; off-season daily 10am-noon and 2-5pm. Admission 16F, students 9F.)

To the east lies the less-visited, but equally worthwhile **Basilique St-Remi,** a Gothic renovation of a Carolingian Romanesque church reputed to contain the tombs of many of France's earliest kings. St-Remi, through his baptism of Clovis, is credited with cementing the French people's bond with Catholicism. His tomb, behind the altar, was rebuilt in 1847 and features statues from an earlier monument. The interior of the basilica is 122m long but only 28m wide, giving it the air of a huge, dark vault. Adjacent to the church is the **Abbaye St-Remi,** 53, rue St-Simon, the city's archeological museum. (Open Mon.-Fri. 2-6pm, Sat.-Sun. 2-7pm.) Admission to this and most city museums is 7F, though an 11F *billet commun* (valid for 1 month) allows you to visit six museums except the Palais du Tau.

When walking around the cathedral near rues Colbert and Carnot, notice **Place Royale,** restored to look as it did during the reign of Louis XV. A statue of Louis XV by Cartellier stands in the center. (The original *place* by Pigalle was destroyed during the Revolution.)

The **Salle de Reddition,** 12, rue Franklin Roosevelt, is the simple schoolroom where the Germans surrendered to the Allies on May 7, 1945. It has recently been jazzed up and is chock-full of war history. (Open March-Nov. Wed.-Mon. 10am-noon and 2-6pm. Admission 7F.)

Formerly an abbey, the **Musée St-Denis,** 8, rue Chanzy, displays an eclectic collection of paintings and tapestries. The ground floor contains ceramics and enamel works. Upstairs, you'll find a set of portrait sketches by the Cranachs, elder and younger, and a fine collection of French art, including an extensive Corot cache and two rooms of impressionist works by Pissarro, Sisley, Monet, Dufy, and others. (Open Wed.-Mon. 10:30am-noon and 2-6pm. Admission 7F.)

For a glimpse of Reims' august past, walk around the **Porte Mars,** by place de la République, a Corinthian-style triumphal arch erected in honor of Augustus sometime in the fourth century. The enormous three-arched monument still bears some bas-reliefs depicting Jupiter and Leda, and Romulus and Remus.

Exploring Reims' *caves* will convince you that wine is a tenet of the quotidian French creed. Some *caves* were built from chapels; others house illuminated shrines to St-Jean, patron saint of *cavistes.* Indeed, Dom Perignon, the individual who invented the *méthode champenoise,* was a monk. The *syndicat* stocks a map with a list of the *caves* open to the public; most organize free tours, but only **Mumm,** 34, rue Champ-de-Mars (tel. 26-40-22-73), still offers free samples. The *caves* are usually open Monday through Saturday from 9 to 11am and 2 to 5pm, and sometimes on Sunday afternoons; each schedule is listed on the map. Tours in French last 15-40 minutes; English tours are given on request.

The palatial **Pommery** *caves* at 5, place du Général Gouraud, probably give the most elegant tour. **Taittinger,** 9, place St-Nicaise (tel. 26-85-45-35), formerly the crypt of an abbey, has some of the eeriest and most ancient *caves;* if not a bar-hop, their tour is at least a solid history lesson, beginning with a slide show. **Piper-Heidsieck,** 51, bd. Henry Vasnier (tel. 26-85-01-94), takes you around their cellars on a little electric train, but you must call first. **Veuve Clicquot-Ponsardin,** 1, place des Droits-de-l'Homme (tel. 26-85-24-08), leads mediocre tours, but screens a fine film (shown only on advance request) about Madame Clicquot, La Grande Dame in the history of champagne production. (Open April-July Mon.-Sat. 9-11am and 2-5pm.)

For a change of pace, take a bus from the theater, 6, rue de Chanzy, to the **Musée d'Automobiles Françaises,** which displays French cars dating from 1891 to the present. (Open April-Nov. 10am-noon and 2-7pm. Admission 25F, students 18F, children under 10 free.)

Entertainment

A university town, Reims is full of effervescent nightlife. The hot discos are **L'Echiquier,** 110, av. Jean-Jaurès (tel. 26-89-12-38; open Fri.-Sun.), and **Club St-Pierre,** 43, bd. Général Leclerc. **Le Sunshine,** 114, rue du Barbatre, is one of many clubs offering jazz. Reims is justifiably proud of its **Théâtre de la Comédie,** 1, rue Eugene-Wiet (tel. 26-85-60-00), which regularly bills exceptional plays.

Epernay

Although both Reims and Troyes have laid historical claims to being the capital of Champagne, Epernay, surrounded by plush vineyards, is without a doubt the center of champagne production, an art form in this city. Miles of subterranean cellars contain 700 million bottles of "the king of wines." Epernay is strategically located at the crossroads of grape growing, with the light *Chardonnay* to the south and the dark *Pinot meunier* and *Pinot noir* to the northwest and northeast, respectively. These fruits yield sparkling wines via Moët & Chandon, Perrier-Jouet, Mercier, de Castellane, and other companies. The palatial nineteenth- and twentieth-century mansions above ground are nourished by the liquid gold below.

Orientation and Practical Information

Epernay straddles the Marne in the heart of the Champagne vineyard country. By train it is a half-hour south of Reims and only 90 minutes east of Paris (Gare de l'Est).

Office de Tourisme d'Epernay et sa Region: 7, av. de Champagne (tel. 26-55-33-00). From the train station, walk straight ahead and through the square to rue Gambetta. Follow this to place de la République, and take av. de Champagne. The office is 3 doors in on your left. Information on Epernay's wine houses and plans for 3 different *routes de Champagne* to towns within 30km. Ask for the pamphet *Epernay et sa Région.* Open Easter and in summer Mon.-Sat. 9:30am-6:30pm; off-season Mon.-Sat. 10am-5:30pm.

Post Office: Place Hughes Plomb (tel. 26-53-12-31). **Telephones** here. **Postal code:** 51200. Open Mon.-Fri. 8am-7pm, Sat. 8am-noon.

Train Station: Tel. 26-88-50-50. Epernay is on the main rail line between Paris and the east. Frequent service to Paris (every 1-2 hr., 74F) and Reims (22F). Also to Strasbourg (3 per day, 170F), Metz, Laon, and Luxembourg.

Bus Station: Gare Routière, place Notre-Dame (tel. 26-51-92-10). Buses to surrounding towns (2-3 per day to each town) and to Châlons-sur-Marne (5 per day).

Taxis: 35-55F for a ½ day. Price negotiable. Haggle.

Car Rental: Dewitte Frères, 70, rue de Champrot (tel. 26-54-11-92). Taxis as well.

Bike Rental: Buffet, 20, rempart Perrier (tel. 26-53-09-42).

Harvest Work (Vendanges): L'Agence National pour l'Emploi (ANPE), 11, rue Jean Moët, 51200 Epernay (tel. 26-51-01-33). Harvesting begins in late Sept., and employment confirmation is usually available after June. Foreign workers usually have no problems. Send for information as early as possible. Open Mon.-Fri. 9am-noon and 2-5pm.

Medical Emergency: Hôpital Auban-Moët, 137, rue de l'Hôpital (tel. 26-54-11-11).

Police: Tel. 26-54-11-17.

Accommodations and Food

MJC Centre International de Séjour, 8, rue de Reims (tel. 26-55-40-82), a 3-min. walk from the station. Bear left along the square and turn left onto rue de Reims. A pleasant, if pricey hostel and *foyer.* Call ahead, as rooms fill quickly in summer. Singles 62F. Breakfast, sheets, lockers, and showers included. Cafeteria meals 32F.

Hôtel St-Pierre, 1, rue Jeanne d'Arc (tel. 26-54-40-80), on a quiet street about 10 min. from the station and worth the walk. Elegant rooms and kind management. Singles and doubles from 65F, with shower 115F. Breakfast 19F. Open Sept. 7-Aug. 10.

Hôtel le Progrès, 6, rue des Berceaux (tel. 26-55-24-75). Comfortable, renovated singles and doubles 90-140F. Breakfast 18F, served in a pretty, skylit room. Check in at **Bar le Progrès,** a lively hangout on place de la République.

Hôtel du Nord, 50, rue Edouard Vaillant (tel. 26-51-52-65), a 10-min. walk from the station away from downtown. Clean, simple rooms. Singles and doubles 64-78F. Breakfast 13F. The restaurant downstairs serves affordable family-style meals.

Generally, cuisine fit for a royal banquet accompanies the luxurious liquid of Epernay. Your cheapest option is **MJC Cafeteria,** 8, rue de Reims, which serves standard cafeteria fare at 32F. (Open daily 11:30am-1:30pm and 6:45-8pm.) Across the square from the station, **Restaurant l'Hermite,** 3, place Thiers (tel. 26-55-24-05), offers a 52F *menu* on starched pink tablecloths. To celebrate, order their 120F *menu.* (Open Mon.-Sat., closed Wed. evening.) **Restaurant Mekong,** 30, rue du Dr. Verron (tel. 26-51-94-67), to the left of Notre Dame, serves a 48F Chinese *menu* and main dishes from 35F. (Open Tues.-Sun. noon-2pm and 7:30-10:30pm.) Across the river from the train station, **La Terrasse,** 7, quai de Marne (tel. 26-55-26-05), is one of Epernay's more pleasant affordable restaurants, serving a simple 52F *menu* and jazzier menus for 98F and 120F. (Open Tues.-Sun. noon-2pm and 7-9:30pm; closed last 2 weeks in July.) Also across the river, **Les Routiers,** 13, rue J.J. Rousseau, offers a 50F *menu* that includes drinks.

Sights and Entertainment

Epernay compensates for its lack of conventional historical monuments with the tastes and smells that emanate from sweeping **avenue de Champagne,** distinguished by its mansions, gardens, and monumental champagne firms. The best known is **Moët et Chandon,** 20, av. de Champagne (tel. 26-54-71-11). The 45-minute tours (some in English) are informative and end with a free tasting. The firm's lobby exhibits menus from state banquets, royal bills of sale, and a hat that belonged to Napoleon, souvenir of the emperor's friendship with Jean-Rémy Moët and of his frequent visits to the *caves.* (Open in summer Mon.-Sat. 9:30am-12:30pm and 2-5:30pm, Sun. and holidays 9:30am-noon and 2-4pm; off-season Mon.-Fri 9:30am-12:30pm and 2-5:30pm. Free.) Moët also owns the beautiful gardens across the street; they are private property, but many visitors step into the courtyard off the street to admire the intricately-interwoven flower beds, the shallow reflecting pool, and the graceful pavilion beyond. A 10-minute walk down the avenue at #75 is **Mercier** (tel. 26-54-75-26 or 26-51-71-11). Eugène Mercier's firm has long been known for its flamboyant gestures (the President of France once visited the *caves* in a carriage driven by 4 white horses); the tour features transport by electric train and a free sample. (Open April 1-Oct. 31 Mon.-Sat. 9:30am-noon and 2-5pm, Sun. and holidays 9am-6pm.) The most informative champagne museum is at **de Castellane,** 57, rue de Verdun (tel. 26-55-15-33), across the street from Mercier; de Castellane offers tours in English and tastings. Stop first at the **Jardin de Papillons,** where 200 butterflies emerge from cocoons every week. (Open May-Oct. 10am-noon and 2-6pm.) The most concise overview of champagne and Epernay is a 20-minute slide show at 19, av. de Champagne (tel. 26-54-49-51). (Open 10:30am-6:30pm; shown in English, French, and German.) At the **Musée du Champagne et de Préhistoire,** 13, av. de Champagne, ascend to the top floor to view an exceptional collection of archeological finds. (Open Wed.-Mon. 10am-noon and 2-5pm.)

Despite the preoccupation with fermentation, nightlife is not forgotten here. Side by side at 12 and 14, rue Pierre Sémard, near the train station, are **Club St-Jean** (tel. 26-55-26-42) and **Le Chinatown** (tel. 26-51-89-07), a new wave club. Both charge a cover of 50F. **Le Pénélope,** 25, rue de l'Hôpital (tel. 26-54-58-74), is another lively disco.

Châlons-sur-Marne

For centuries big names have used Châlons-sur-Marne as a sort of hotel—Marie Antoinette spent the night and left a triumphal arch behind her—but nobody has stayed here for long. Lacking the monumental majesty of Reims and Epernay's effervescence, Châlons remains a *petit village.* Although much less visited than its Champagne cousins, the town is trimmed with serene parks and canals, dignified old houses, and fine churches.

Orientation and Practical Information

Châlons-sur-Marne, as its full name implies, lies on the Marne River, on the main railway line between Paris's Gare de l'Est (2 hr.) and Strasbourg (3 hr.). The center is a 15-min. walk east of the station; turn left on rue Jaurès and continue down rue de la Marne, or catch buses A,D, or K, which follow the same route past the tourist office to the Hôtel de Ville.

Office de Tourisme: 3, quai des Arts (tel. 26-65-17-89). Just before you reach the Hôtel de Ville, a sign will indicate a pedestrian zone on your left. Their pamphlet, *le petit guide de Châlons,* has a map, lists hotels and restaurants, and describes monuments (French only). Open July-Aug. Mon. 9am-noon and 1:30-6:30pm, Tues.-Fri. 9am-12:30pm and 1:30-6:30pm, Sat. 9am-12:30pm and 2-6:30pm; Sept.-June Mon.-Sat. only.

Post Office: 36, rue Jaurès, around the corner from the station. **Postal code: 51000. Telephones** here. Open Mon.-Fri. 9am-noon and 2-6:30pm, Sat. 9am-noon.

Train Station: Place de la Gare (tel. 26-88-50-50). Trains leave for Reims every 2 hr. and pass through Epernay.

Bus Station: There is no *gare routière,* but **STDM** (tel. 26-65-17-07) runs buses that leave from the train station and place Tissier. Local buses leave from rue de Vaux (tel. 26-64-07-82).

Medical Emergency: Tel. 26-64-91-91.

Police: Rue de Jessaint (tel. 26-68-17-17).

Accommodations, Camping, and Food

The possibilities won't dazzle you. The **Auberge de Jeunesse (IYHF),** rue Kellerman (tel. 26-68-13-56), is located on rue Chevalier as it runs through the park, through a gate on your right. Open to all individual hostelers in July and August only. (34F per person. Breakfast 12F. Reception open 7-10am and 5-11pm.) The most pleasant establishment is **Hôtel Jolly,** 12, rue de la Charrière (tel. 26-68-09-47), near the hostel. (Singles and doubles 63F, with shower 75-95F. Breakfast 12F.) A friendly English speaker manages the convenient **Hôtel de Chemin de Fer,** rue de la Gare (tel. 26-68-21-25), across from the train station. (Singles and doubles from 70F, with WC 112F. Breakfast 15F.) The fine *menu* is prepared by an excellent restaurant's cook. **Hôtel de la Comédie,** 12, quai Notre Dame (tel. 26-68-10-45), by Notre-Dame-en-Vaux, has a decaying facade and small, simple rooms. (Singles and doubles 63-71F. Showers included. Breakfast 14F.) There's **camping** just south of town on av. des Alliés (tel. 26-68-38-00). Railpass holders and even others might find it worthwhile to stay in Reims or Epernay and make Châlons a daytrip.

Traiteurs (like *charcuteries*) serve the cheapest lunches in town. **Machet,** 59, rue de la Marne, serves quiche for 6F, *allumette au jambon* (a ham pastry) for only 3.30F. Ask the chef to warm the cold specialties. At 32, rue de Jaurès, near the station, **A Marion** has a tempting selection of salads. Young *Châlonnais* favor delicious if smallish pizzas (23-28F) at **Il Fluvio,** 18, rue Pasteur, a lively place decorated with plastic grapes and wagon-wheels (open 7:30-11pm). There is a fruit and meat **market** on Wednesday and Saturday mornings in place d'Art. For fun at night, sample a few of the 100 whiskeys at **La Cocktailerie,** 26, place de la République (tel. 26-65-10-27); their ice cream *coupes* are also good, though less potent. (Open Mon.-Sat. 5pm-3am.) Gay men and lesbians willing to pay for an elegant atmosphere, food, and drink may enjoy **La Table du Goûteur,** 14, rue André Hubert (tel. 26-21-09-49).

Sights

If you speak French, the *syndicat*'s tour is a magnificent introduction to the city. It lasts two to three hours; covers churches, parks, museums, and *hôtels particuliers* (mansions); and varies every time it is given. The experience is well worth the 11F charge, since you are admitted to corners otherwise locked or obscure. (Tours from the tourist office July 1-Sept. 15 Tues.-Sat. at 2:30pm.) If you don't speak French or are here in the off-season, the office will give you a map and a description in English of the museums and churches.

Châlons has several churches that exemplify different periods of the town's 2000-year history. In the center, facing one of the many ancient canals of Châlons, stands **Eglise de Notre-Dame en Vaux,** a church begun in 1180 whose thirteenth- and sixteenth-century stained-glass rose windows are set in the same pattern as those at Chartres, but on a smaller scale. Wednesdays and Saturdays the church's 56 bells supply the market just outside with resounding background music. (Open Mon.-Sat. 9am-noon and 2-6pm.) From the side street to the north, enter the **Musée du Cloître,** where medieval cathedral relics decapitated during the Revolution have been reunited with their heads. (Open Tues.-Sun. 10am-noon and 2-5pm. Admission 15F, students 9F, children 5F.) Eglise St-Alpin, off place Foch, features striking Renaissance windows in *grisaille,* white tinted delicately with yellows. They depict the life of the saint in the age of Attila. To visit, call the tourist office.

Notable windows might also beckon you to **Cathédrale St-Etienne** (12th through 16th centuries), where St-Stephen's painful death by stoning is commemorated in lush windows and stone carvings. Note the dark green in much of the glass—a hallmark of Châlons, just as blue is of Chartres. Because renovations continue, you must enter at the southern side of the church. Stroll through **Le petit Jard,** with its pleasant canal-side walks, rare trees, and a turreted Henri IV fortification built on a bridge over the river. Enter the garden at the corner of bd. Victor Hugo and av. du Leclerc. (Open May 1-Sept. 31 6:45am-11pm; Oct. 1-April 30 7:30am-6:30pm.) Châlons's municipal library, housed in the seventeenth-century **Hôtel des Dubois de Crancé,** jealously guards what is supposedly Marie Antoinette's prayerbook, in which she wrote, at 4:30am on the day of her execution, "My god, have pity on me! My eyes no longer have tears to cry on you, my poor children, adieu, adieu! Marie-Antoinette." You can't see the actual autograph, but attendants at the circulation counter can give you a booklet with photographs, which argue for and against the document's authenticity. The **Musée Municipal,** on place Godart, by the library displays a collection of statues representing Hindu deities, a reconstruction of a traditional *champenois* interior, local sculptures from the Middle Ages, and a small section of painting, including a winter scene by Josse de Momper. (Open Mon. and Wed.-Sat. 2-6pm, Sun. 2:30-6:30pm.) The **Musée Garinet-Goethe-Schiller,** 13, rue Pasteur, preserves the atmosphere of a wealthy *châlonnais* townhouse of the nineteenth century, with period furniture and an eclectic assortment of objects from all ages and all civilizations. (Open Wed.-Mon. 2-6pm.) On Midsummer's Eve (June 21) Châlons holds an all-night **music festival** in place de la République. If a boat ride through the local canals or a sound and light show, **Basilique de Lumière,** held in nearby Epine appeal to you, inquire at the Châlons tourist office.

Troyes

Troyes (pronounced like the French "3," *trois*) belongs to the province of Champagne not because of its *caves*—it has none—but only because of a strategic move by the counts of Champagne, who acquired it in the tenth century. These vigorous and liberal princes built a city that fostered a large Jewish community and then, in the Renaissance, created its own school of sculpture. When in 1524 the town was destroyed by fire for a third time, its artists redesigned it with the churches, gabled houses, tiny streets, and secret passages that you see today; the downtown area, *Bouchon de Champagne* (Champagne cork), is named for its shape. Troyes provides a relaxing introduction to the region; the grandeur of its tree-lined boulevards and of the **Cathédrale St-Pierre et St-Paul** complements the charming pedestrian zone that surrounds **Eglise Ste-Madeleine.** Note the half-timbered buildings reminiscent of Alsace, sometimes obscured by neon-lit shops, galleries, and cafes.

Orientation and Practical Information

Troyes is only about 130km south of Reims, about two and a half hours by bus or car. If you're traveling by train, you'll have to go through Paris—and spend about four hours doing it. Fortunately, train-connections between Paris-Est and Troyes are frequent.

The station at Troyes is only a block from the tourist office and 2 blocks from the rectangular old city, where almost all of the shops, restaurants, and hotels are located. To get to the cathedral, follow rue Charbonnet to place St-Remy; turn at rue Pithou and continue south for 5 blocks.

Office de Tourisme: 16, bd. Carnot (tel. 25-73-00-36), across from the train station, on the right. Guided walking tours of the city daily at 3pm and 8pm (2½ hr., 25F). Open July-Sept. 15 daily 9am-8:30pm, Sun. 10am-noon and 3-6pm; Sept. 16-June Mon.-Sat. 9am-12:30pm and 2-6:30pm. There is an **annex** at 24, quai Dampierre (tel. 25-73-36-88), in an old house opposite the Musée de la Pharmacie. Open July-Sept. 15 Tues.-Sat. 9am-12:30pm and 2-6:30pm.

Post Office: Rue Louis Ulbach (tel. 25-73-49-22), a street running south of the pedestrian zone in the Bouchon de Champagne. **Postal code:** 10000. **Telephones** here. Open Mon.-Fri. 8am-7pm, Sat. 8am-noon.

Train Station: Tel. 25-73-50-50. Surprisingly few destinations are directly linked to Troyes. Most involve a trip to Paris-Est (1½ hr., 84F). The main east line, however, serves Chaumont, Belfort, Mulhouse, and Basel (Switzerland), with trains running every 1-2 hr. during the day.

Bus Station: Buses depart next to the train station, which posts a bus schedule. Regional schedules at the tourist office for 5F. Information at 15, rue Gustave Michel (tel. 25-82-23-43). To Sens (7 per day, 1½ hr., 46F). To Châlons-sur-Marne (3 per day, 2 hr., 55F).

Taxis: Taxis Troyens, Tel. 25-78-30-30, in the circle outside the station. **Taxi Mestre,** 168, rue Général de Gaulle (tel. 25-73-07-40).

Car Rental: Interent, Tel. 25-80-50-07 or 25-73-53-22.

Markets: Les Halles, in the Hôtel de Ville. Traditional farmers from the Aube region, modern shops, and a bar.

Laundromat: Lavomatique, 13a, rue de Preize.

Pharmacy: Pharmacie de la République, rue de la République, near the Hôtel de Ville. Open Mon.-Sat.

Medical Emergency: Tel. 25-49-55-33.

Police: Tel. 25-73-44-88.

Accommodations and Camping

Troyes has many inexpensive hotels. Private homes open their doors for bed and breakfast, although some are on the periphery of town and are not convenient. Places for short stays are available mostly in summer. Make reservations if your visit coincides with the annual Foire de Champagne, a champagne producers' convention (June 3-12).

Auberge de Jeunesse (IYHF), 2, rue Jules Ferry (tel. 25-82-00-65), 5km from Troyes in Rosières. Take bus #6B (*direction* Chartreux) from the tourist office to the last stop. From there, take bus #11 to the hostel, or walk 2.2km down a country road. Set in an old farmhouse complete with fireplace, garden, and gardener, the hostel is well worth the trek. 34F with hostel card. No breakfast. Check-in from 6pm. Open year-round.

Hôtel du Théâtre, 35, rue Lebocey (tel. 25-73-18-47), on the northern limit of the Bouchon de Champagne. Warm and engaging proprietor. Better than average rooms. *Menus* starting at 39F downstairs. Singles 69F, with shower 103F. Doubles 88F, with shower 113F. Breakfast 15F. Open Sept.-July Tues.-Sun. evening.

Hôtel Le Marigny, 3, rue Charbonnet (tel. 25-73-10-67). A rickety, half-timbered hotel at the edge of the old town. Singles 65-130F. Doubles 85-170F, with a third bed 190F. Breakfast 18F. Beware, renovations and newly installed TVs may raise prices.

Hôtel de Paris, 54, rue Roger Salengro (tel. 25-73-11-70). A stylish 2-star hotel with a lovely garden terrace. Proprietor calls the decor *"style vieille France."* Singles 74-130F, doubles 85-168F. Breakfast 18F. Open Jan. 10-Dec. 22. Reservations recommended.

Hôtel Thiers, 59, rue Général de Gaulle (tel. 25-73-40-66). 2-star singles 85-105F, doubles 110-130F.

Hôtel Butat, 50, rue Turennes (tel. 25-73-77-39). Centrally located. Telephones in rooms. Singles 80-160F, doubles 100-180F. Reservations recommended.

Camping: Camping Municipal, on RN60, 10150 Pont-Sainte-Marie (tel. 25-87-02-64). A 2-star site with showers, shopping facilities, and a restaurant. 15F per person. Open April 15-Oct. 15.

Food

The Quartier St-Jean is full of *crêperies* and inviting little restaurants (especially on rue Paillot de Montabert and rue Champeaux). For lunch, make yourself a picnic and take it to **place de la Libération,** a lovely park with fountains, flowers, and ice cream vendors. You may want to try *andouillette à la mode de Troyes,* a small chitterling sausage served throughout France.

L'Accroche Coeur, 24, rue de la Trinité (tel. 25-73-27-36). Serves traditional dishes (including *andouillettes*) in a non-traditional setting. 42F and 47F *menus,* entrees 36-56F.

Crêperie la Tourelle, 9, rue Champeaux (tel. 25-73-22-40), just east of the Church St-Jean. Pocket-sized *crêperie* right in the middle of things. Tables trail out onto the sidewalk, and plates are passed through the windows. Homemade crêpes 10-30F. Open Tues.-Fri. until 9:30pm, Sat.-Sun. until 11pm.

Le Café du Musée, 59, rue de la Cité (tel. 25-80-58-64), near the cathedral. Famous for its selection of beer—12 brands on tap, 60 in bottles. Open Mon.-Sat. 10am-3am. The rustic restaurant upstairs offers local fare of good quality. 48F *menu.*

Le Tricasse, rue Charbonnier. Local musicians entertain the *Troyens* who frequent this popular bar.

Le Grand Café, 4, rue Champeaux (tel. 25-73-25-60), right in the *secteur piétonnier. Menu* 52F. Try the *flan froid d'aubergines à la tomate fraiche* (cold eggplant souffle with tomato sauce). You pay for the central location here. Open Sun.-Fri. 2:40-10:30pm, Sat. 2:40pm-midnight.

Sights and Entertainment

Troyes's **Cathédrale St-Pierre et St-Paul** was begun in the thirteenth century, expanded in the sixteenth, and like many others, never finished. Inside, 112 stained-glass windows light the airy nave and choir, one of the longest in France. (Open July 1-Sept. 15 daily 9am-noon and 2-7pm; in off-season daily 9am-noon and 2-5pm.) The adjacent **trésorerie** (treasury) contains the jewels of the counts of Champagne. (Open in summer 9:30am-noon and 2:30-6pm; in off-season 2:30-6:30pm.) Built in 1150, **Ste-Madeleine,** the city's oldest church, is distinguished by its delicate stone lacework. Because of recent vandalism, Ste-Madeleine and **St-Urbain** are closed to the public. However, visits may be arranged through the tourist office and are well worth the effort; Sunday masses are also open to the public. By the same arrangement you can see **Eglise St-Jean,** restored after the fire of 1524. Its altar-screens were carved by Girandon, a local master. Henry IV married the heiress of France in an earlier version of this church, kicking off the turmoil that Joan of Arc confronted many years later. Troyes combines history and theater in **Cathédral de Lumière,** a sound and light show exploring the magical qualities of the stained-glass windows. (Shows June 24-Sept. 23. Admission 15-30F from the tourist office.)

In the ancient Episcopal Palace next to the cathedral on place St-Pierre, the **Musée d'Art Moderne—Collection Pierre et Denise Levy** contains one of France's best collections of modern art, with 350 paintings and over 1300 drawings and sketches from 1850 to 1950. Among them are works by Braque, Cézanne, Degas, Dufy, Matisse, Modigliani, Picasso, and Rouault. (Open Wed.-Mon. 11am-6pm;

guided tours Sat.-Sun. at 11am, 2:30pm, and 4pm.) On the other side of the cathedral at 31, rue Chrétien-de-Troyes, the eclectic **Musée St-Loup,** housed in the old
Abbaye St-Loup, presents a fascinating if somewhat disorganized mixture of Merovingian weaponry, Gallo-Roman statuettes, medieval sculpture, and fifteenth-
through twentieth-century painting. A glass door (locked) on the second floor allows you to admire the largest library hall in France, once the dormitory of the
abbey's monks in the seventeenth and eighteenth centuries. The room contains
90,000 volumes, with over 4000 precious manuscripts from the seventh through
eighteenth centuries and 46,000 volumes from the sixteenth century alone. (Open
Wed.-Mon. 10am-noon and 2-6pm.) The **Musée Historique de Troyes,** housed in
the sixteenth-century Hôtel de Vauluisant on rue de Vauluisant, exhibits religious
articles, documents, and pieces of Renaissance *troyen* sculpture. In the same complex is France's only **Musée de la Bonneterie,** a collection of gloves, hats, and ho-
siery, for which Troyes is famous. The **Pharmacie de l'Hôtel-Dieu,** quai des Comtes
de Champagne, houses a rare sixteenth-century apothecary with 320 painted wood
boxes and 2140 *faïence* receptacles; the adjoining **Musée des Hôpitaux** contains old
documents and a collection of ancient bust reliquaries. (Museums open Wed.-Mon.
10am-noon and 2-6pm.) Ten francs will admit you to all of Troyes's museums except the Maison de l'Outil et de la Pensée Ouvrière and the Musée Marguerite Bourgeoys. A ticket to just one of the museums costs 5F.

Be sure to visit the **Maison de l'Outil et de la Pensée Ouvrière,** 7, rue de la Trinité,
a museum devoted to tools of the region. The building that houses the museum is
a marvelously restored sixteenth-century *hôtel.* Although the collection is poorly
documented, the beautiful implements speak for themselves. (Open daily 9am-noon
and 2-6pm. Admission 5F.) **Musée Marguerite Bourgeoys,** 8, rue de l'Isle, is not
really worth a visit unless you're interested in hagiography. The museum has displays on the life and works of Marguerite Bourgeoys, a native *Troyenne* of the seventeenth century who founded the Congrégation Notre Dame in Montréal and was
canonized by John Paul II in 1982. (Open in summer daily; in off-season Mon.-Sat.
only. Free.)

Perhaps the best way to explore Troyes is to wander through the streets around
the handicraft museum. In contrast to the commercial Quartier St-Jean, the area
is residential and its sixteenth-century buildings show the extent of Troyes's restoration and preservation efforts.

Shopping opportunities and movie theaters are abundant on rue Emile-Zola,
where only occasionally do the houses remind you of Troyes's long history. The
best dancing is at **K.V.O.,** cour de la Gare (tel. 25-78-22-35), in the Grand Hôtel
across from the station, where a mature crowd gathers nightly.

Near Troyes

Twenty-five kilometers from Troyes (45 min. by bus) is the **Forêt d'Orient,** a
peaceful wooded area set above a large, clear lake with fine swimming. For train
and bus connections call SNCF (tel. 25-72-50-50). This national park is a popular
stop for vacationing families migrating from the north to the south of France. For
a boat ride on the lake, call **L'Ondine de l'Orient** (tel. 25-41-21-64), or ask at the
Troyes tourist office. If you can get to **Lusigny-sur-Barse,** you'll find a **campground**
(tel. 25-41-20-01) and a **gîte rurale,** 5, rue du 8 Mai (tel. 25-21-31-99). There are
cheap **gîtes d'étape** at La Loge aux Chèvres (tel. 25-41-35-57), Amance (same tel.),
and Rouilly-Sacey (tel. 25-75-77-94). Maps of pedestrian circuits and rental bicycles
are available at the **Maison du Parc,** on the edge of the lake about 5km northeast
of **Mesnil St-Père.** A bus connects Troyes with Mesnil St-Père (¾ hr., tel. 25-82-
25-43), where there is an **Auberge de Jeunesse (IYHF)** with 24 beds and meals.
(Singles 30F; open May-Oct.) On the lake, **Camping de la Voie Colette** (tel. 25-45-
27-15) is a two-star site with showers, a restaurant, swimming, and sailing. (Open
March-Oct.) For details on excursions, camping facilities, and a list of *gîtes ruraux*
(rural bed and breakfasts), contact the tourist office in Troyes.

An hour by train from Troyes lies **Chaumont,** a town of 30,000 inhabitants which lost most of its charm during World War II bombings. Encroached on by ugly residential complexes and modern commercial blocks, the remaining streets of the old city harbor two monuments of interest. **Basilique St-Jean** is a thirteenth-century structure with an overly ornate, somewhat tacky interior. In the back, however, a small chapel contains the impressive *Sépulcre de Chaumont,* a group of 10 polychrome statues grieving over the body of Christ. This fifteenth-century ensemble is unique because the central position is occupied not by the Virgin Mary, but by Mary Magdalene. Note the remarkable facial expressions. A few blocks away, at the end of rue du Palais, the tenth-century square **donjon** looms over the **Palais de Justice.** The tree-lined promenade in front offers wonderful views of the Suize Valley and of the **Faubourg des Tanneries,** an area of town where tanners cured skins for centuries. Next door, the **Musée de Chaumont** devotes a section to the daily lives of women in the nineteenth century. (Open Wed.-Mon. 2:30-5:30pm.)

Accommodations in Chaumont are, without exception, expensive. An **Auberge de Jeunesse,** 11, rue Decrés (no tel.), offers beds for 32F a night. (Open only July 1-Aug. 31.) **Camping Municipal Parc Ste-Marie,** on rue des Tanneries (tel. 25-32-11-98), is another option. (Open April-Sept.) **Hôtel de France,** 25, rue Toupot (tel. 25-03-01-11), is pretty and slightly expensive, with a restaurant downstairs. (Singles and doubles from 105F, breakfast 25F. Open year-round.) Restaurants are also expensive: Make your own meal with produce from the **market** on place des Halles (Wed. and Sat. mornings).

Chaumont's **Syndicat d'Initiative** is in a stone pavilion on bd. Thiers (tel. 25-03-04-74). From the train station, turn right as you exit, climb the stairs at the end of the parking lot, turn right, and cross the tracks, and then take a left on bd. Thiers. (Open July-Sept. 15 Mon.-Fri. 9-11:30am and 2-5pm; Sept. 16-June Mon.-Fri. 2-5pm.) The **Post Office** and the **police** (tel. 25-32-65-00) are on rue Victoire de la Marne.

The North

The memory of war is never far from the towns and villages of northern France. The world's battlefronts have moved back and forth across the region four times in this century alone. Nearly every town bears scars from the wanton bombing of World War II, German-built concrete observation towers still watch over the land, and cemeteries stand as reminders of the massacres at Arras in the historical region of Flandre (Flanders), at the Somme in Picardie, and at Cambrai in Artois. In addition, the north has always been the industrial center of France. In recent years, labor-oriented political parties have made substantial gains and assumed control of several city governments.

Despite the twin ravages of war and industry, the area sees considerable numbers of tourists, many of them en route to England via the coastal ports of Boulogne, Calais, and Dunkerque, and others making their way to Belgium. Boulogne and Calais lie in the region known as the Pas de Calais, traditionally a battlefield for Western Europe and a strategic center for the control of the English Channel during World War II.

The best course for a tourist in this region of smog and battle scars is to bypass the overpriced major ports and to make a pilgrimage to the great cathedrals built here during the twelfth and thirteenth centuries. As testimony to both a devout spirit and a new prosperity, Laon and Noyon were the first towns to erect great churches with arching vaults; their construction led to heroic efforts in a mature Gothic style at Amiens and at Reims, in Champagne. No longer a major industrial center and now the cultural and commercial focus of northern France, Lille's manageable urban environment harbors a respected fine arts museum. If you're coming from Paris, you'll appreciate the countryside here—a pleasant change from urban congestion. In Picardie, undulating fields of wheat extend in all directions, dotted occasionally with clumps of trees or a rare wooden windmill. Along the coast, the terrain is more rugged. Chalk cliffs line the beaches, and agriculture gives way to livestock; cows and sheep graze within a few feet of collapsed concrete bunkers and rolls of rusty barbed wire.

Although trains run frequently, many of the smaller towns, such as Laon and Noyon, are difficult to reach even by bus. *Autoroutes* make for easy driving but somewhat tedious hitching. Bicycling is a good option, especially between cathedral towns; the terrain is flat, but there are a few tough hills, and trucks and frequent rains can be a nuisance.

Unfortunately, the north has become one of the more expensive areas of France: Both food and accommodations here will cost you dearly. Nor is the region renowned for its cuisine, although it does prepare some intriguing Flemish specialties. Try *pâté de canard* (duck *pâté*), *galette* (a salty crêpe), *ficelle picarde* (a cheese, ham, and mushroom crêpe), and *ouillette* (a particularly slimy type of sausage).

Boulogne

In 636 C.E., a boat carrying only a statue of the Virgin Mary washed up on the beach of Boulogne, which subsequently became the site of a famous pilgrimage. Today, the devout have been replaced by tourists, who pile off the dozens of ferries and hovercrafts that make the crossing between France and England each day. A no-nonsense industrial atmosphere presides over Boulogne, one of the largest fishing ports in continental Europe. Dismal rain clouds also hover over the city with remarkable frequency.

On the last Sunday in June, the **Fête du Cygne** (Festival of the Swan) in the *vieille ville* features exhibitions of local artwork. Call the *syndicat* for more information.

Orientation and Practical Information

Boulogne is 240km north-northwest of Paris, 120km west of Lille, and 120km
southwest of Ostende. The city has two main train stations, Gare Maritime, by the
ferries, and Gare Boulogne-Ville, from which most trains leave. To reach place
Frédéric Sauvage from Gare Boulogne-Ville, cross bd. Voltaire, go to the right of
the tall buildings, and follow rue Ferdinand Buissᴑn. Turn left on bd. Daunou. The
place lies just before the second bridge. A covered pedestrian walkway connects the
ferry terminal to Pont Marquet. Cross the bridge to place Frédéric Sauvage and
the tourist office. A free shuttlebus runs to the Hoverspeed terminal from the Hoverport.

Syndicat d'Initiative: Place Frédéric Sauvage (tel. 21-31-68-38). Friendly and helpful. English
spoken. Crowded with ferry travelers. Accommodations service and map, plus brochures on
all ferry lines. Open July-Aug. daily 10am-7pm; Sept.-June Tues.-Fri. 9am-6pm.

Currency Exchange: Banks open Mon.-Fri. 9am-noon and 2-5pm. Bank at Hoverport and
Ferry Terminal open daily.

Post Office: Place Frédéric Sauvage (tel. 21-31-65-40), near the *syndicat.* **Telephones. Postal
code:** 62200. Open Mon.-Fri. 8:30am-6:30pm, Sat. 8:30am-noon.

Port Information: Sealink, Car Ferry Terminal. The booking office is across from the Hoverspeed terminal near the *syndicat* (tel. 21-30-25-11). To Folkestone (6 per day, 1 hr. 50 min.;
one way 162F, round-trip within 5 days 256F; same-day return to Folkestone 114F, Canterbury 140F, London 222F). 15% student discount with ISIC. **P. & O. European Ferries,** Gare
Maritime. The Booking office is next to Sealink's booking office across from the Hoverspeed
terminal (tel. 21-31-78-00). To Dover (in summer every 3 hr; one way 156F, round-trip within
8 days 252F). Booking office open Mon.-Wed. 9am-6pm, Thurs.-Fri. 9am-5:30pm, Sat. 9am-
noon. **Hoverspeed** terminal on bd. Chanzy (tel. 21-30-27-26), next to the canal. To Dover
(in summer every 1-2 hr., winter service varies with the day of the week; one way 174F, same-
day return with early morning departure 108F, round-trip within 5 days 300F). On all three
lines bicycles sail for free.

Train Stations: Gare Boulogne-Ville, bd. Voltaire (tel. 21-80-50-50). To Paris (5 per day, 3
hr., 125F) and Calais (every ½-2 hr., ½-2 hr., 29F). Information office open Mon.-Sat. 9am-
7pm, Sun. 9:30am-noon and 2:15-7pm. **Gare Maritime,** Car Ferry Terminal. Less frequent
service to Paris, connecting with ferry arrivals.

City Buses: Autobus Urbains, 6, rue Alexandre Guilmant (tel. 21-91-06-03). Regular city
bus lines in all directions have central stop at place de France. A minibus (#10) circulates
in the *centre ville.*

Laundromats: Laverie Automatique, rue Nationale, right by the railway bridge. Wash 12F,
dry 2F. Open 5:30am-9:30pm. Another on rue de Lille, across from the cathedral.

Medical Emergency: Tel. 15.

Police: Rue Perrochel (tel. 21-83-12-34).

Police Emergency: Tel. 17.

Accommodations and Food

Hotels in Boulogne fill quickly, so reserve in advance or show up early.

Auberge de Jeunesse (IYHF), 36, rue de la Port Gayole (tel. 21-31-48-22), a 10-min. walk
from Gare Centrale. Take a right on bd. Voltaire, walk 1 block, turn right on bd. Beaucers
to rue de Brequerecque, turn left, and go up the hill. In summer they put beds in a tent out
back to make more room, but these also fill quickly. Rents bikes and organizes day- and weekend trips. If you ask ahead of time, you can leave your bags during closed hours. 45F per
night. Sheets 11F. Camping out back 13F in your own tent, 33.50F in hostel's tent. Breakfast
included. Office open 7:30am-noon and 5-11pm.

Hôtel Hamiot, 1, rue Faidherbe (tel. 21-31-44-20). A 1-star place facing the beach. Singles
80F, doubles 90F. Bath 16F. Breakfast 16F. **Hôtel le Sleeping,** 18, bd. Daunou (tel. 21-80-
62-79). Reasonably close to Gare Boulogne-Ville. Singles and doubles 70-140F. Breakfast
17F.

Hôtel le Mirador, 2, rue de la Lampe (tel. 21-31-38-08), off bd. Daunou. Singles and doubles 103-150F.

Hôtel des Arts, 102, bd. Gambetta (tel. 21-31-53-31). Singles 78-112F, doubles 94-139F.

Camping: Moulin Wibert, bd. Ste-Beuve (tel. 21-31-40-29), 2km west of the tourist office (quai Gambetta turns into bd. Ste-Beuve). Open April-Oct. 15.

The restaurant situation doesn't improve on the hotel scene. Gaudy tourist traps and *friteries* abound in the area near the port and around place Dalton, but you'll find lots of *crêperies* and *brasseries* around the cathedral in the *vieille ville*. On Wednesdays and Saturdays from 7:30am to 1:30pm, place Dalton comes to life with an excellent open-air **market.** Omnivores will enjoy the fish and grilled meat specialties at **Le Nabucco,** 78, bd. Gambetta (tel. 21-30-27-45), overlooking the port. *Menus* are 52F and 90F; the *plat du jour* is 38F. (Open Mon.-Tues. and Thurs.-Sat. noon-2:30pm and 7-11:30pm, Sun. noon-2:30pm.) **Vie Claire,** 22, place des Victoires (tel. 21-31-61-66), a health-food store, offers a vegetarian lunch *menu* for 49F. (Open Tues.-Sat. 8:45am-12:45pm and 2:30-7:30pm.) You can find fish and chips at **Union de la Marine,** 18, quai Gambetta (tel. 21-31-38-83). They serve *menus* for 50F and 90F, and meat dishes as well. (Open Mon.-Tues. and Thurs.-Fri. noon-7pm, Sat.-Sun. noon-11pm.) **Presto,** Centre Commercial de la Lane (tel. 21-31-31-48), is a decent cafeteria overlooking the sea.

Sights

Built on the site of the ancient Roman *castrum* and completely enclosed by sturdy thirteenth-century ramparts, Boulogne's old city is watched over by the immense cupola of **Basilique Notre-Dame.** This structure, ornate and imposing, dates only from the nineteenth century, but sits atop the fascinating, labyrinthine **crypts** of an earlier eleventh-century edifice. One of the 14 chambers of the crypt shelters the vestiges of a third-century Roman temple; another exhibits the statues and chalices that constitute the cathedral's treasure. (Crypt open Mon. and Wed.-Sat. 9-11:45am and 2-6pm, Tues. 2-6pm, Sun. 2:30-6pm. Admission 6F.) Next to the cathedral, the **beffroi** (belfry), a thirteenth-century store tower that once served as the *donjon* for the counts of Boulogne, oversees the port and all its activity. (Open Mon.-Fri. 8am-noon and 2-6pm, Sat. 8am-noon.) The **Centre National de la Mer** will open at the old casino in 1989, providing an opportunity to study sea life and the fishing industry.

Around 10km north of Boulogne near **Landrethun** lies the **Forteresse de Mimoyecques** (tel. 21-87-10-34 or 21-92-92-47), a gigantic underground construction excavated by hand from October, 1943 to July, 1944 by 5000 political prisoners from 18 countries occupied by Nazi Germany. Another 10 days of excavation and the Germans would have been able to launch 6000 V3s on London daily. A memorial in the 600m-long main tunnel commemorates Joseph Kennedy, who was killed while flying in the Allied air attack that destroyed the fortress. (July-Aug. guided tours daily on the hr. 10am-6pm; Easter-June and Sept. to mid-Nov. daily 2-6pm. Tours last 1 hr.) To get to Landrethun from Boulogne, take the N1 to Marquise, then take a right on the D231 in the direction of Guines. From Calais, take the N1 to Leubringhen and follow the signs eastward on the D231. Public transportation does not exist here, and hitching is difficult because most cars carry so much luggage they have no room for passengers.

Calais

Ever since Richard Coeur de Lion and his crusaders arrived here in 1189 on their way to Jerusalem, travelers have chosen Calais as the main crossing point between England and the Continent. Today, Calais sees over 15,000 visitors and as many as 160 channel crossings daily, and in 1993, when Eurotunnel is slated for completion, all those leaving Folkestone, England, will also arrive in Calais. Completely rebuilt after World War II, the town has become a heap of flashing neon and chintzy shops, but it does have a few redeeming features. Its most interesting building, the flamboyant **Hôtel de Ville,** is a twentieth-century construction in the Flemish Renaissance style.

The Hôtel is the backdrop for Rodin's evocative sculpture, the *Burghers of Calais,* which recalls a near-tragic moment in the final year of the Hundred Years' War: England's King Edward III had agreed to hang the mayor and several prominent citizens rather than slaughter all the city's inhabitants; the burghers decided to sacrifice their lives for their townsfolk, and their heroism prompted the impassioned and successful eleventh-hour intervention of Edward's French wife, Philippine. Calais remained British until François de Guise reclaimed it for the French in 1558. Calais's history is much more interesting than the town proper, and apart from the Hôtel de Ville, there is little to see here.

Parc St-Pierre relieves the urban landscape with spreading trees and orderly flower beds. A German-built blockhouse in the middle of the park contains the well-camouflaged **Musée de Guerre.** (Open June-Sept. 15 daily 10am-4:30pm. Admission 8F, students 5F, children 4F.) For Calais's forte—the beach, turn left from the station and walk straight down rue Royale.

Orientation and Practical Information

Calais is two and a half hours from Paris's Gare du Nord, and has two train stations: Gare Calais-Ville and Gare Calais-Maritime (near the ferry and hovercraft ports). Sealink runs a free shuttle bus between the ferry terminal and the Calais-Ville station. Otherwise, walk down the quay away from the terminal, turn left after the overpass, cross the bridge, cross place de Suède, and go down rue de Londres. Cross place de l'Angleterre by the church, and follow rue de Strasbourg. A right on rue de Rome will bring you to Calais's main road. The *syndicat* is immediately to your left. The Calais-Ville station lies beyond that, across the canal. From the Hoverport, follow rue du Nord along the canal, and turn left at the bridge onto rue Mollien. After many blocks, you'll pass the Hôtel de Ville on your left and come to Calais's main road, **bd. Jacquard,** which becomes **rue Royale** as you head toward the port. The Calais-Ville station and the *syndicat* are to your right.

Syndicat d'Initiative: 12, bd. Clemenceau (tel. 21-96-62-40), about 1 block away and across the street to the left of the Calais-Ville station. City map with no street names, ferry information, an accommodations list (free), and accommodations service (10F). Open July-Aug. Mon.-Sat. 9am-7:30pm, Sun. 10am-1pm and 4:30-7:30pm; Sept.-June Mon.-Sat. 9am-12:30pm and 2:30-6:30pm (closes at 6pm in winter).

Currency Exchange: Banque Populaire du Nord, 2, bd. Lafayette, just off bd. Jacquard. Open Mon.-Fri. 8:30am-5:45pm. Also at the **car ferry station** (tel. 21-96-67-75). Open 24 hours.

Post Office: 174, rue Mollien (tel. 21-96-55-30), on place d'Alsace. **Telephones. Postal code:** 62100. Open Mon.-Fri. 8:30am-6:30pm, Sat. 8:30am-noon.

Port Information: Sealink, Car Ferry Terminal (tel. 21-96-70-70). To Dover/Folkestone (every ½-2 hr.; 90 min.; one way 156F, round-trip within 5 days 246F, same-day return to Dover 110F). To Canterbury (140F) and London (210F). 15% student reduction with ISIC. **Booking office** at 2, place d'Armes (tel. 21-34-55-00). **Townsend Thoresen,** Car Ferry Terminal (tel. 21-97-21-21). To Dover (in summer every 1½ hr., in off-season every 2-3 hr.; 75 min.; one way 156F, round-trip within 5 days 252F, same-day return to Canterbury 146-158F). To London (191-253F). **Booking office** at 44, place d'Armes (tel. 21-34-41-90). **Hoverspeed,** Hoverport (tel. 21-96-67-10). To Dover (April-Sept. every ½-1 hr., Oct.-March service varies with the day of the week; 35 min.; one way 174F, same-day return 108F, round-trip within 5 days 300F). On all three lines bicycles sail for free.

Airport: Aérodrome de Calais-Marck, Tel. 21-82-71-02.

Train Station: Gare Calais-Ville, bd. Jacquard (tel. 21-34-40-17). Frequent service to Paris (2½ hr., 142F), Lille (1½-3 hr., 58F), and Boulogne (30-40 min., 29F). Information office open Mon.-Sat. 9am-7pm, Sun. 9:30am-12:35pm and 2:35-7pm. **Gare Calais Maritime,** Car Ferry Terminal Service. To Paris only in the afternoon. Open daily 8am-9pm. Helpful information office, with free city maps, open daily 9:15-11:15am and 2:15-7:50pm.

Hitching: For Paris, try bd. Gambetta or bd. Victor Hugo, which leads to the A26. Good luck.

Laundromat: Rue des Thermes at rue des Prêtres. Open 6am-10pm.

Ambulance and Medical Emergency: SMUR, Tel. 21-96-72-19. 24-hour emergency service.

Police: Place de Lorraine (tel. 21-34-37-00).

Police Emergency: Tel. 17.

Accommodations, Camping, and Food

If you're looking for a place to stay on this teeming shore, you won't have too much trouble, but don't expect anything special.

Point Accueil Jeunes/Maison Pour Tous, 81, bd. Jacquard (tel. 21-34-69-53), a huge modern building near the Hôtel de Ville. Not affiliated with IYHF. 35F per night. Reception open 5-10pm. Curfew midnight. Open July-Aug.

Hôtel du Cygne, 32, rue Jean Jaurès (tel. 21-34-55-18), off bd. Jacquard next to the Hôtel de Ville and 3 min. from the Calais-Ville station. Dim but clean. English spoken. Singles 82F, doubles 120F. Showers 5F. Breakfast 15F.

Au Mouton Blanc, 44, rue de Vauxhall (tel. 21-34-71-52), off bd. Jacquard about 5 blocks south of the Calais-Ville station. Small, fills up fast. Older guests, but lively. Simplest singles and doubles 70F. Doubles with shower and toilet 140F. Similar quads 160F. Triples with bath 170F. Breakfast 14F. Open July 15-June Mon. noon-Sun. evening. No reservations accepted. Restaurant downstairs has a pleasing 45F *menu. Demi-pension* includes room, breakfast, and dinner (130F).

Hôtel Le Littoral, 71, rue Aristide Briand (tel. 21-34-47-28), across from Parc St-Pierre. A white building with peeling paint. Singles 95F. Doubles 101-131F, with shower 150F. Breakfast included. Closed last 2 weeks in Sept., but not every year. The ground-floor restaurant serves a 48F *menu.* Open daily noon-2pm and 7-9pm.

Le Pot d'Etain, 7, rue Darnel (tel. 21-36-62-08), behind the municipal theater. 7 rooms above a *brasserie.* Singles 60F. Doubles 75F, with shower 90F. Quads with shower 120F. Breakfast 15-18F. Open daily 7am-11pm. Next door at #9, **La Douce France** (tel. 21-36-55-00) has more or less clean but unattractive singles and doubles with showers for 90F. Open daily.

Camping: Municipal Campgrounds, 26, av. Raymond Poincaré (tel. 21-97-99-00; in high season 21-34-73-25), right on the coast. Follow rue Royale. Drive in even if the office is closed. Tents packed together in high season, but sites well maintained. The weather is often windy and rainy here. 4.60F per person, children 2.60F. 7.20F per site. Electricity 5.50F. Tax 2F. Showers 3.50F. Reception open July-Aug. Mon.-Tues. and Fri.-Sun. 6:30am-9:30pm, Wed.-Thurs. 7am-9pm; Sept.-June Mon.-Fri. 8am-noon and 2-5pm, Sat. 8-11am.

Dining in Calais is not a gastronomic delight, but a few good places do exist among the ubiquitous sidewalk *friteries.* Try **Aux Trois Suisses,** 14, bd. Jacquard (tel. 21-34-33-30), where the service is excruciatingly slow but the food invigorating and well prepared. They offer no *menu,* but *à la carte* selections run 18-56F for a main course. Omelettes are 13-15.50F. The restaurant is upstairs. (Open Wed.-Mon. noon-8:30pm, Tues. noon-5pm.) A charming place decorated in lavender with candelabras on all tables, **Le Guéridon Gourmand,** 22, rue Jean Jaurès (tel. 21-34-29-95), next to the Hôtel de Ville, serves excellent *menus* (60F and 93F) that feature delectable dishes such as stuffed crab *thermidor.* Main courses are 17-72F. (Open daily 11am-3pm and 6-11pm.) **Le Terminal,** at the car-ferry terminal (tel. 21-96-46-20), and **Le Templier,** at the beach, (tel. 21-97-57-09) are decent self-service cafeterias.

Dunkerque

A fishing village and small port in the tenth century, Dunkerque survived Flemish, Burgundian, Spanish, and English rule until it became French in 1662, when Charles II of England sold it to Louis XIV. France's third largest sea port, the city specializes more in industrial efficiency than in aesthetic appeal. Nonetheless, Dunkerque takes pride in its delicate Gothic **Eglise St-Eloi,** constructed in the fifteenth century with the bell tower that has since been relocated across the street. Several old Flemish-style paintings line its walls, including a *Last Supper* in which the Apostles wear characteristic Flemish garb.

Before you leave, visit Dunkerque's prize, the **Musée d'Art Contemporain,** rue des Bains (tel. 28-59-21-65), across the bridge from the youth hostel. The building itself, shaped like a folded paper sailor's hat, merits a look as much as the collection of French art (1960-80) inside. The garden around it is uniquely landscaped with piles of twisted metal and chaotic arrangements of massive stones that together suggest nature's revenge on the classical French tradition of geometrically designed gardens. (Open Wed.-Mon. 10am-7pm. Admission 6F, students 3F. Guided tours on request.) The **Musée des Beaux-Arts** on place du Général de Gaulle (tel. 28-66-21-57), near the theater, houses an important collection of seventeenth- and eighteenth-century paintings. In the basement, an exhibition entitled *Dunkerque en guerre* presents documents from 1939-1945. (Open Wed.-Mon. 10am-noon and 2-6pm. Admission 6F, students 3F.) **Musée Aquariophile** (aquarium), 35, av. du Casino, displays large tanks of exotic fish. (Open Wed.-Mon. 10am-noon and 2-6pm. Admission 6F, students 3F.)

To reach Dunkerque's **Auberge de Jeunesse,** place Paul Asseman (tel. 28-63-36-34), follow rue des Fusiliers Marins to the left of the train station, along the quay, take rue de Leughenaer to place de la Victoire; turn left at the statue on rue des Bains, cross the canal, turn left, and walk along the canal. Or, take bus #3 or 3a to the Piscine stop, walk to your left in place Paul Asseman, and the hostel will be on your right. (Buses every 10 minutes from the train station.) The children who attend school here make fascinating company and are enthralled by foreign visitors. (Open 7:30-10:30am and 5:30-10:30pm. 34F per night. Breakfast 9.50F. Dinner 36F.) Get the tourist office's detailed list of Dunkerque's many affordable hotels and restaurants and choose your own. Among the possibilities are **Hôtel Modern,** 2-4, rue Nationale (tel. 28-66-80-24), in the center of town above a bar that caters to a student crowd. (Singles from 62F, doubles from 81F.) **Hôtel Terminus Nord,** 2, place de la Gare (tel. 28-66-54-26), also has a bar downstairs and features simple rooms. (Singles 68F, with shower 88F. Doubles 110F, with shower 125F.) If you like spacious rooms, try **Hôtel Tigre,** 8, rue Clemenceau (tel. 28-66-75-17). (Singles 90-150F, doubles 110-180F.) Dunkerque has a three-star campsite, **Dunkerque-Malo-les-bains,** bd. de l'Europe (tel. 28-69-26-68), complete with pool. Take bus #3 to the Au Collège Gaspard Malo stop. (Open March-Nov.)

If you can afford to spend a bit more than usual for dinner, **Craquelon,** 7, place Jeanne d'Arc (tel. 28-63-49-78), will place you in an art gallery setting where the *menu,* here called a *palette* and designed to complement the exhibit on the wall, will please your palate (90F); entrées cost 50F. (Open noon-late.) **Huchette,** 19, rue Marengo (tel. 28-66-15-34), offers 28-55F *galettes* and dessert crêpes with background jazz. The **Tête d'Ail,** 24, rue Terquem, is decorated with strings of garlic; fear no vampires. (Salads 28-35F; lunch *menu* 45F; dinner *menu* 65F; entrees 38-66F.)

Dunkerque lies on the RN1 between Calais (40km away) and the Belgian border (20km away), about 274km from Paris. **Sallyline** (tel. 28-21-43-44) runs **ferries** between Dunkerque Port-Ouest and Ramsgate (5 per day; 2½ hr.; 88F, same-day return 100F, round-trip within 5 days 200F; bicycles sail for free). They also organize various "escapades" in England using a combination of ferry and bus. Their one-day round-trip tour to London departs at 8:30am and returns at 2:30am. (Adults 245F, children 205F.) For information and tickets, contact Sallyline, place Emile Bollaert (tel. 28-63-23-80; open Tues.-Sat. 2-7pm). **Transalpino,** 3, rue Alfred Dumont (open Tues.-Fri. 9:15am-noon and 2-6:30pm), also has ferry and other travel information.

Trains leave from the Dunkerque station (tel. 28-66-50-50) for Lille (8 per day, 1 hr.), Paris (4 per day, 3 hr.), Calais (4 per day), and Arras (5 per day, 2 Sun.). To reach the tourist office from the station, head down rue du Chemin de Fer for

about 2 blocks. Cross the complicated intersection and turn left onto rue des Fusiliers Marins. Follow this street and then turn right onto rue de l'Amiral Ronarch.
The **Syndicat d'Initiative** (tel. 28-66-79-21) lies straight ahead in the belfry on place
du Beffroi. You can **exchange money** here when banks are closed. (Open July-Aug.
Mon.-Fri. 9am-6:30pm, Sat. 9-11:30am; Sept.-June Mon.-Fri. 9am-noon and 2-
6pm, Sat. 9-11:30am; also May-Sept. Sun. 9-11:30am.) Train travelers might address themselves to **Dunkerque Informations** (tel. 28-66-46-90), right in front of the
train station. (Open daily 8am-noon and 2-6pm.) If you arrive late, inquire at the
helpful **Cotaxi** next door (tel. 28-66-73-00). The **post office** is on rue Pres. Poincaré
at place du Général de Gaulle. (Open Mon.-Fri. 8:30am-6pm, Sat. 8:30am-noon.)

Lille

The largest city in the north, Lille vibrates with the activity of 50,000 students
as it transforms itself into a university town. Once the center of French steel production, after World War II the city developed a thriving service industry manifest in
countless shops and restaurants crammed into endless streets. Commerce continues
to flourish, as Lille lies right on the Pas-de-Calais (steps of Calais, which connect
Paris and the port). In addition, much of France's beer is brewed here. Originally,
the city belonged to the Duchy of Flanders and retains much of its bustling Flemish
character, evident in the Flemish townhouses lining rue Esquermoise off place de
Gaulle.

Orientation and Practical Information

By train, Lille is two hours from Paris's Gare du Nord and one hour from Calais.
Fortunately, the train station is centrally located. Place de Gaulle is straight down
rue Faidherbe, place Rihour just off there. Lille has a fully automatic metro, but
the maps are hard to decipher and most places are within walking distance. (Metro
tickets 6.30F per ride, *carnet* of 10 46.50F.) Both the area around the train station
and around the Wazemmes Market may be dangerous at night.

Office de Tourisme: Place Rihour (tel. 20-30-81-00), in the remaining fragment of a fifteenth-
century castle. Group tours. Also, women's information and referral service. Open Mon. 1-
6pm, Tues.-Sat. 10am-6pm. The **information center** at the train station can give you a list
of accommodations and a map.

Centre Régional d'Information de la Jeunesse, 2, rue Nicolas Leblanc (tel. 20-57-86-04), at
place de la République next to the post office. Open Mon.-Tues. and Thurs.-Fri. 1-6:30pm,
Wed. 9:30am-6:30pm.

Post Office: Main office, 7, place de la République (tel. 20-54-70-13). Poste Restante address:
Bureau PTT, Lille R.P., 59000. **Currency exchange** and **telephones.** Open Mon.-Fri. 8am-
7pm, Sat. 8am-noon. **Branch office,** behind the Vieille Bourse and place de Gaulle, on bd.
Carnotard at place du Théâtre. Poste Restante address: Lille Bourse, 59001. **Postal code:**
59000. Open Mon.-Fri. 8am-6:30pm, Sat. 8am-noon.

Airport: Aéroport de Lille-Lesquin, Tel. 20-87-92-00.

Train Station: Place de Gare (tel. 20-74-50-50). To Paris (every 1-2 hr., 2-2½ hr., 129F),
Calais (regular service every 2 hr., 2½ hr., 61F; express service 2 per day, 1½ hr., 66F),
and Boulogne (77F). Information office open Mon.-Sat. 6:45am-8pm, Sun. and holidays 8am-
8pm.

Bus Station: Rue le Corbusier (tel. 20-06-01-33), next to the train station.

Metro Information Office: Place des Buisses (tel. 20-91-92-01), next to the train station.

Hitching: Allostop, on the Palais Rihour with the tourist office (tel. 20-57-96-69). Matches
riders with drivers for 30F per ride, plus 16 centimes per km. Open Mon.-Fri. 2-6pm, Sat.
10am-noon.

Bookstores: Book 'n Broc, 17, rue Henri Kolb (tel. 20-40-10-02), off rue Léon Gambetta near
place de la République. Friendly used bookstore. Gladly buys and sells English books. **Librai-**

rie des Femmes, 19, rue du Cirque (tel. 20-51-54-88). Women's bookstore also serving as a center for lesbian and feminist activities, which have, unfortunately, diminished in recent years. Location may change so check with the tourist office.

Laundromats: On rue d'Arras at rue de Fontenoy. Open daily 6am-9pm. Another on rue Colbert. Open Mon.-Sat. 7:30am-8pm.

Centre d'Information des Droits de la Femme, 17, quai du Wault (tel. 20-54-27-66). Open Mon.-Fri. 9am-12:30pm. **Union Féminine Civique et Sociale,** 131, rue Jacquemare Giélée (tel. 20-54-91-97). Open 1st and 3rd Mon. of month 10am-1pm, Tues. 2-5pm, and Thurs. 9am-noon.

Hospital: Cité Hospitalière, place de Verdun (tel. 20-51-92-80).

Police: 6bis, rue du Maréchal Vaillant (tel. 20-86-17-17).

Police Emergency: Tel. 17.

Accommodations

Decent hotels are expensive in Lille. Hotels cluster around the train station, but the area can be dangerous at night. Check with the tourist office or with **CROUS,** 74, rue de Cambrai (tel. 20-56-93-40 or 20-52-84-00), about university housing during the summer, or about *foyers* year-round. (Open July-Aug. Mon.-Fri. 9am-noon and 2-4pm; Sept.-June Mon.-Fri. 9am-noon and 1-4pm.)

Auberge de Jeunesse (IYHF), 1, av. Julien Destrée (tel. 20-52-76-02), next to the Foire Internationale. Turn left down rue de Tournai from the train station. Take the pedestrian underpass beneath the highway, then cross the parking lot, and go under the overpass. A pleasant place. 50F, nonmembers 70F. Sheets and breakfast included. Camping in back 26F, nonmembers 46F. Breakfast included. Technically open daily 7-9am and 5-11pm, but hours are flexible. Open mid-Jan. to Nov.

Relais Européen de la Jeunesse (UCRIF), 40, rue de Thumesnil (tel. 20-52-69-75). Cheap, decent student housing in dormlike rooms. A hike from the center of town. 65F per night. Breakfast included.

Hôtel le Floréal, 21, rue Ste-Anne (tel. 20-06-36-21). Attractive rooms with lumpy mattresses. Decent proprietor, but the hotel is in a bad part of town. Singles 65-80F. Singles and doubles with shower 120F. Doubles with W.C. 140F. Breakfast 13F. Open Aug.-June 24 hours.

Hôtel Faidherbe, 42, place de la Gare (tel. 20-06-27-93). Immaculate but dimly lit. Sagging mattresses. Singles 75F, with shower 82-95F. Doubles 90F, with shower 120F. Breakfast 13F. Open daily.

Hôtel des Voyageurs, 10, place de la Gare, or 28, rue du Priez (tel. 20-06-43-14). Elevator. Spacious singles with sink 56F. Doubles with sink 70F. Singles or doubles with shower 95F. Breakfast 12F. Reception open 24 hours. Open Aug. 3-Dec. 24 and Jan. 2-June 30.

Hôtel St-Maurice, 8, parvis St-Maurice (tel. 20-06-27-40), about 100m from the station. Pleasant rooms and pleasant service. Singles 100F. Doubles 125F, with shower 160F. Triples with shower 180F. Breakfast 18.50F.

Hôtel Constantin, 5, rue des Fossés (tel. 20-54-32-26), near place Rihour. For a few more francs, you can escape from the station area into the agreeable pedestrian district. Singles and doubles 80F, with shower 130F. Breakfast 17F. Open daily.

Camping: The nearest campsite is **Les Ramiers,** rue César Loriden (tel. 20-23-13-42) in Bondues. Take the bus from Lille to Bondues Centre. Open May-Oct. For more information about camping in the area, call **Camping Club de Lille,** 13, rue Baggio (tel. 20-53-77-40).

Food

If you're looking for quick refueling, head to the pedestrian area around rue de Béthune, where you'll find satisfying take-out food such as *baguette* sandwiches, fruit from stands, pastries, pizza, ice cream, and salads. Lille is known for its poultry, fish, cheese, and *genièvre* (a liqueur based on juniper berries). **Supermarkets** are located on rue Léon Gambetta and on rue de Paris at av. Pres. Kennedy. (Open Tues.-Sat. 8:30am-12:30pm and 3-7pm, Mon. 3-7pm.)

Au Cordon Bleu, 24, place des Reignaux (tel. 20-06-48-66), near the station. Hearty authentic food and atmosphere. *Plat du jour* 25-28F, *menus* 44F, 53F, and 68F. Open Mon.-Fri. 11:30am-2pm and 6:45-9:30pm.

La Pierrade, 15, rue Ste-Anne. Filling and tasty dishes you cook yourself on a hot stone plate. Lunch *menu* 42F, entrees 25-40F.

Le Pekin, 18, rue du Priez (tel. 20-06-10-16), ½ block from place de la Gare. 3-course Chinese lunch *menus* 38F, service not included. Extensive *à la carte* selections. Open daily noon-3pm and 7pm-late.

La Crêperie de Beaurepaire, 1, rue St-Etienne (tel. 20-54-60-54), in an alley-like street parallel to rue Nationale, 2 blocks from place de Gaulle. You can sit outside in the cobblestoned courtyard. Lots of students indoors. *Galettes* 9-28F, dessert crêpes 9-26F, and delicious cider. Open Mon.-Sat. 11:45am-2pm and 7-10:45pm.

Aux Bretons, rue Colbert, across from the market. 38F *menu* features traditional veal, rabbit, and horse-meat dishes.

Sights and Entertainment

How much would you pay to see Thierry Bouts's triptych panels, sculptures by Rodin, and a collection of eighteenth-century pieces of *faïence* manufactured in Lille? What about if the offer was beefed up with Gothic statues, impressionist paintings, and works by Picasso, Sonia Delaunay, Grommaire, and Poliakoff? If you say 5F, congratulations—you're a winner. For this small fee you can spend many merry hours in one of the finest museums in France, Lille's outstanding **Musée des Beaux Arts,** on place de la République. (Open Wed.-Mon. 9:30am-12:30pm and 2-6pm; free Wed. and Sat. afternoon.) Your ticket also admits you to the **Musée de l'Hôspice Comtesse,** 32, rue de la Monnaie, founded in 1237 by Jeanne Constantinople, Comtesse de Flandre, and used as a hospital in the fifteenth century. The museum displays some old furniture and art works, but is most notable for the beautiful Flemish tilework on its walls. (Open Wed.-Mon. 10am-12:30pm and 2-6pm; free Wed. and Sat. afternoon.) Just off rue de la Monnaie (entrance off rue du Cirque) is **Cathédrale de Notre Dame de la Treille,** a neo-Gothic church begun in the last century and left unfinished. Despite the unappealing brick of the west facade, the church contains some lovely chapels and interesting choir masonry. In the crypt is the **Musée Diocésain d'Art Religieux,** exhibiting sacred art from the seventeenth through the twentieth centuries. (Open Sat. 4-5pm, 1st Sun. of each month 11am-noon. Free.)

The *Vieille Bourse* (Old Stock Exchange), on place de Gaulle between rue des Sept Acaches and rue Manneliers, is a masterpiece of the Flemish Renaissance style. Charles de Gaulle was born in Lille—you can visit the museum and birthplace: 9, rue Princesse (open Wed.-Sun. 10am-noon and 2-5pm). Place de Gaulle is nicknamed the "Grand Place" by all Lille residents. Second-hand book sellers and a few traffickers in bric-a-brac hold a daily market in its courtyard.

The ancient and imposing star-shaped **citadelle** on the north side of Lille was restored in the seventeenth century by the Marquis de Vauban, as were many of the fortresses in this area. To get over the moat and inside (it is still used as an army base), you must either sign up for a group tour at the tourist office (Sun. 3-5pm only, 30F), or convince the guard that you're enlisted in the French army. The exquisitely maintained **Jardin Vauban** across the street is also worth exploring. Other sights include the triumphal **Paris Gate** on bd. Louis XIV, and, near the station, **Eglise St-Maurice,** an ancient, blackened Gothic church built in the Flemish *hallerkirk* style—that is, with five naves of equal height.

Although the modern university lies several kilometers outside the city, most of its students live in Lille, supporting an active nightlife. For information on student activities, check at the tourist office or the **Centre Régional d'Information pour la Jeunesse** (see Practical Information). **Rive Gauche,** 3, rue St-Etienne, is reputedly the best disco in Lille proper. (Open 11pm-late.) **Le Molière,** rue Léon Trulin, near the theater, caters to gay men, while **Le Tropicana,** rue de la Clé, hosts mixed gay crowds.

Near Lille: St-Omer

A little more than 60km from Lille on the road to Calais and Dunkerque, the town of St-Omer offers some of northern France's best-kept secrets. Begun in the thirteenth century, **Basilique Notre-Dame** rises in the center of the old city, a huge, majestic structure. The vast interior contains numerous works of art, including an astronomic clock constructed in 1558, a venerated statue of Our Lady of Miracles from the thirteenth century, and the eighth-century tombs of St-Erkembode and St-Omer. Two blocks away on rue Carnot, the eighteenth-century **Hôtel Sandelin** now houses an excellent museum. On the ground floor, several rooms looking out onto a well-kept garden are arranged in the Louis XV style; the *salle du Trésor* showcases the celebrated *Pied de Croix de St. Bertin,* the gilt and enameled base of a cross attributed to Godefroy de Huy. The two upper stories exhibit ceramics, including a series of 750 Delft pieces. (Open Thurs.-Fri. 10am-noon and 2-5pm, Wed. and Sat.-Sun. 10am-noon and 2-6pm. Admission 7.50F.) In the lower part of town, the **ruines de St-Bertin,** the vestiges of the fifteenth-century abbey of St-Bertin, lend a romantic note to a grim neighborhood of gray row houses.

If you intend to stay overnight, head for the **Hôtel St-Louis,** 25, rue d'Arras (tel. 21-38-35-21), a few blocks below the basilica. Among the hotel's amenities are a lively bar, restaurant, TV room, and comfortable bedrooms. (Singles and doubles with shower 79-108F. Rooms with toilet and shower 102-192F. Extra bed 35F. Breakfast 19F.) The town's **Office de Tourisme,** bd. Pierre Guillain (tel. 21-98-70-00), is in place Painlevé. From the train station, cross the bridge and walk straight ahead until place Victor Hugo; bear right on rue des Cantons, and turn right on rue Henri Dupuis; bear left to enter place Painlevé, where you'll see the modern, glass office. (Open Mon.-Fri. 8am-noon and 2-6pm, Sat. 2:30-5:30pm, Sun. and holidays 9am-noon.) The **train station,** a vast, lugubrious structure that is downright spooky at night, lies light-years away from the center of town (20-25 min. on foot for earthlings), across the canal on place du 8 Mai, 1945. Trains run to Basel (2 per day), Hazebrouck (3-4 per day), Lille (Mon.-Sat. 5 per day, 3 Sun.), Calais (Mon.-Sat. 6 per day, 2 Sun.), Boulogne (Mon.-Fri. 6 per day, 3 Sat, 2 Sun.), and Arras (Mon.-Fri. 2 per day, Sat.-Sun. 1 per day).

Arras

Although historians argue that the name Arras is derived from "*arras*" (tapestry hangings) produced here during the sixteenth century, legend maintains that the name plays on the words "*à rats*" (to rats); in the Middle Ages, rats overran the hapless bourg, thus enabling the king of France to conquer the territory. The annual **Fête des Rats** celebrates the beloved animals every Whit Sunday, but the festival, which may include parades and expositions, fails to do justice to the city's long history. Although usually associated with twentieth-century trench warfare, Arras dates from the twelfth century and the era of Spanish domination. Though badly damaged during the Revolution and again in 1914-1915, Arras still retains many of its medieval buildings. Its chief architectural treasures, Grande Place and Petite Place, display reconstructed Flemish facades undisturbed by automobiles.

Orientation and Practical Information

Arras is on the main route from Paris to Lille. To get to Grande Place, take the road to the right of the deceptively mislabeled tourist office across from the train station. Beyond the gas station, the road becomes rue Pasteur; take the third right.

Tourist Office: Petite Place or place des Héros (tel. 21-51-26-95), in the Hôtel de Ville. Open May-Sept. Mon.-Sat. 9am-noon and 2-6pm; Oct.-April Mon.-Fri. 9am-noon and 2-5:30pm, Sat. 9-11:30am and 2-5pm.

Post Office: Rue Gambetta, 1 block down from the train station. **Postal code:** 62000. Open Mon.-Fri. 8am-6:30pm, Sat. 8am-noon.

Train Station: Place Maréchal Foch (tel. 21-71-00-42). Open 24 hours. Ticket office open 7am-7pm. Information hotline open daily 7am-9pm (tel. 21-73-50-50). To Paris (15 per day, 102F), Lille via Douai (20 per day, 38F), Dunkerque (10 per day, 63F), and Amiens (5 per day, 42F).

Bus Station: STCRA, in front of the train station (tel. 21-58-08-58). Inter-city buses only. You can pick up a map of the stops at the tourist office.

Laundromat: Superlave, place Vivani, near the tourist office. **Lavomatique,** rue Frédéric de Georges (tel. 21-61-88-44).

Swimming Pool: Piscine Desbin, rue Bocquet Flochel (tel. 21-58-00-33). **Piscine Georges Daullé,** rue Rouault (tel. 21-07-16-67).

Hospital: 57, av. Winston Churchill (tel. 21-21-48-01). Take bus B, C, D, H, M, or Z.

Medical Emergency: SAMU, Tel. 21-21-51-51.

Police Emergency: Tel. 17.

Accommodations, Camping, and Food

Few cheap hotels set up shop in Arras; those in the two-digit range are rare. Pick up a complete list at the tourist office. The best accommodations are the renovated rooms at the centrally located youth hostel.

Auberge de Jeunesse, 59, Grande Place (tel. 21-25-54-53). Kitchen facilities. 34F per night. Sheets 11F. Breakfast 11F. Curfew 11pm. Open 7:30-10:30am and 5-11pm.

Hôtel des Grandes Arcades, 12, Grande Place (tel. 21-23-30-89). Fairly clean rooms. Singles 82F and 95F. Doubles 84.50-108F. Triples 114F. The restaurant downstairs is popular with local business people at lunch (*menus* 50F, 68F, and 94F). Open Mon.-Sat. 12:15-2:30pm and 7:30-9:30pm.

Hôtel Le Réfuge, 10, place de l'Ancien Rivage (tel. 21-55-16-54), far northwest of the Grande Place. Cleanliness is not a priority. *Demi-pension* (110F) includes room, breakfast, and unappetizing dinner. Singles and doubles 75F, with shower 120F.

Camping. Closed for renovation. Call the tourist office for information.

La Cicciolina, 38, Grande Place (tel. 21-55-78-64), at the end of an alley, serves Italian food in an Italian-villa setting. The *menu* is 55F, spaghetti 26F, and pizza 20-30F. (Open Mon.-Sat. noon-2pm and 5pm-late.) **La Cave,** 50, Grande Place (tel. 21-58-53-84), is a popular place in—you guessed it—an old cellar. The 55F *menu* allows a wide selection of dishes; more expensive house specialties include *choucroutes* (60F and 65F) and *magret de canard* (duck, 90F). (Open Tues.-Sat. noon-3am, Mon. midday only.) Place des Héros and adjoining squares erupt in boisterous color every Wednesday, Thursday, and Saturday morning during Arras's open **market.**

Sights

The **Hôtel de Ville** near the marketplace dates from the fifteenth century, but the façade was rebuilt in the early sixteenth century after a fire destroyed the exterior. The style is pure French concentrate, with no mix of Flemish influence. By special arrangement with the concierge or with the guide at the tourist office, you can climb its blackened Gothic tower or ride the elevator to the top. For information, call Service des Boves (tel. 21-51-48-30). Serene **Grande Place** is an empty space bordered by 155 homogeneous, fifteenth-century Flemish townhouses, whose first floors are collectively supported by 345 columns. This inspired Gothic composition was sliced down the middle by barbed wire during World War I when the

French and Germans occupied opposite sides, yet it shows few war scars. Boutiques, bars, and cafes line **place des Héros,** a block away, smaller and more animated.

Near the town hall stretch miles of interconnected subterranean **tunnels** (called "Les Boves"), originally built to house medieval chalk miners. They've served as refuges during different wars and most recently, as a shelter and hospital for British soldiers during World War I. (Tours of the tunnels leave from the Hôtel de Ville May-Sept. Tues.-Sat. 10am-noon and 2-6pm, Sun. 10am-noon and 3-6:30pm; Oct.-April Tues.-Sat. 2-6pm, Sun. 10:30am-12:30pm and 3-6:30pm. ½-hr. tours 7F, 50-min. tours 14F, students and ages under 16 half-price. Call 21-51-48-30 for information.)

Eighteenth-century **Abbaye de St-Vaast,** almost totally destroyed during the bombardment and fire of 1915 but now reconstructed, shelters the fine **Musée des Beaux Arts** (tel. 21-71-26-43). The museum exhibits paintings by local artists, one Delacroix, and one Corot. (Open Wed.-Mon. 10am-noon and 2-5pm. Admission 4F, students 2F.) The adjacent **Musée de la Résistance** maintains a single unexciting room of Vichy France memorabilia. (Open April-Oct. Wed.-Mon. 10am-noon and 2-5:30pm, Sun. 3-5:30pm; Nov.-May Wed.-Mon. 10am-noon and 2-5pm, Sun. 3-5pm.) Work on the domed **cathédrale** began in 1783 but, interrupted by the Revolution, was not completed until 1833 under the Restoration monarchy. The facade features an *escalier monumental* leading down to sunken rue des Teinturies. (Open 9am-noon and 2-7pm.) Arrageois's preferred discos include **La Guillo** in Grande Place and **Le Pago** in Petite Place.

Near Arras

Eight kilometers northeast of Arras along the RN25 is the **Vimy Memorial** to the 75,000 Canadians killed in World War I. During the summer, tours of the trenches are given by lively young Canadian guides brimming with information about Arras and the war. (Open daily 10am-6pm; tours May-Sept. only. Admission 3F. For more information, call 21-48-72-29.)

Fifteen minutes away, **Douai** bustles with all the energy that is lacking in Arras. Fountains splash merrily in the place d'Armes, sidewalk cafes overflow with people, and masses of shoppers rush frantically from store to store. (The tourist office leads **tours** of the town May-Oct. on the 1st Sat. and 3rd Wed. of each month 2:30-4:30pm or by appointment. 15F.) Originally the Roman settlement of Duacum, Douai has experienced several metamorphoses through the centuries, including reconstruction by the celebrated seventeenth-century military architect, the Marquis de Vauban. Its central attraction is the splendid **campanile** (bell tower) rising out of the Hôtel de Ville and topped by a sculpted lion. The carillon, rung in concert (every Sat. 10:45-11:45am and holidays 11am-noon), contain some of the largest bells in Europe. If your knees have recovered from the Arras ascent, you can climb Douai's bell tower as part of a guided tour that includes the town hall. (Open July-Aug. Mon.-Fri. and Sun. 10am-noon and 2:30-5:30pm; Sept.-March Sun. 2:30-5:30pm; April-June Mon.-Fri. 10am-noon and 2:30-5:30pm, Sun. 2:30-5:30pm. Admission 7F, students 3.50F.) Of the old city walls, only the gates have been preserved; the **Porte d'Arras** and the **Porte de Valenciennes** date from the fifteenth century.

The sixteenth-century **Chartreuse,** rue des Chartreux, now functions as the **Musée de Douai** and displays some interesting sixteenth-century Dutch and nineteenth-century French art, as well as fine leaded windows in the Gothic cloisters. (Open Mon. and Wed.-Sat. 10am-noon and 2-5pm, Sun. and holidays 10am-noon and 3-6pm. Admission 7F.) During the last week of June and the first few weeks of July, Douai hosts the **Fêtes de Géant** (Festivals of the Giant), during which an enormous family of mannequins is paraded through the streets, and concerts, exhibitions, and sporting competitions are held each night.

Douai is not interesting enough to hold you overnight. If, however, you decide to stay, be warned that even one-star hotels charge incredibly high prices for the sparest of rooms. **Hôtel de Paris,** 53, place d'Armes (tel. 27-88-95-63), a decent two-star hotel, is in the center of town. (Singles 110F, with shower 170F. Doubles 145F,

with shower 200F. Breakfast 20F.) Slightly cheaper, **Hôtel St-Jacques,** 99, place
Carnot (tel. 27-88-67-05), offers singles and doubles with bathroom for 105F. The
restaurant below serves eight kinds of *couscous* for 46-71.50F. (Open noon-3pm and
7-11pm.) No youth hostel nor campground graces Douai, but there are three campgrounds in Aubigny-au-bac between Douai and Cambrai.

Trains from Paris-Nord and Arras run to Douai at least every hour. Trains run
to Paris (every 2 hr., 2 hr., 115F), Arras (hourly, 20 min., 18.40F), and Lille (hourly,
½ hr., 26F). The **Office de Tourisme** (tel. 27-88-26-79) is in the Hôtel du Dauphin,
70, place d'Armes. (Open Mon. 10am-noon and 2-6pm, Tues.-Fri. 9am-noon and
2-6pm, Sat. 2-6pm, Sun. 2:30-5:30pm.) To reach the tourist office from the train
station, cross place de la Gare and turn left on av. du Maréchal Leclerc; follow this
for several blocks. When you pass the post office on your right, take a right onto
place d'Armes.

Amiens

" . . . Of Gothic, mind you!" exulted John Ruskin about the Amiens Cathedral,
"Gothic clear of Roman tradition, and of Arabian taint; Gothic pure, authoritative,
unsurpassable, and inaccessible." Amiens's cathedral is undoubtedly one of the finest Gothic specimens in Europe. Unfortunately, Amiens hides many assets behind
ramshackle buildings, treeless avenues, and disappointing concrete plazas. World
Wars I and II left distinct scars on the city. Fortunately, the **Quartier St. Lev** on
the Somme still preserves a rich antiquity, while the abundant *Hortillonages* (market
gardens) flourish to compensate for the defects of the *centre ville.*

Orientation and Practical Information

Direct rail links connect Amiens to Rouen, Boulogne, Arras, and Paris. To reach
the center of town from the train station at the east end of town, head straight down
rue de Noyon. The street changes names several times, eventually becoming rue
des Trois Cailloux when it runs into place Gambetta. The cathedral and one of the
syndicats are off to your right down rue des Sergents; rue de la République is to
your left. Head straight down rue Delambre, which turns into rue Gressert, and
the main *syndicat* is in front of you on the left, in the Maison de la Culture. At
night lone travelers should beware of the Cirque area.

Syndicat d'Initiative: Rue Jean Catelas (tel. 22-91-79-28), in the Maison de la Culture. Provides helpful information on the town and a map of northern France. English spoken. Open
Mon.-Sat. 10am-12:15pm and 2-7pm. **Branch office** outside the cathedral, 20, place de Notre
Dame. Open daily 10am-12:15pm and 2-6pm. **Office** in the train station. Open Mon.-Sat.
9am-6pm, Sun. and holidays 9am-noon and 2-6pm, if renovating schedule does not temporarily close the office. All 3 are friendly and can book hotel rooms.

Centre Régionale d'Information Jeunesse (CRIJ): 56, rue du Vivier (tel. 22-91-21-31). Helpful clearinghouse of information for youth about Amiens and the Picardie region. Lists cheap
foyers, and books cheap excursions. Open Mon. 2-5:30pm, Tues.-Fri. 9:30am-12:30pm and
2-5:30pm.

CROUS: 25, rue St-Leu (tel. 22-91-84-33). Be sure to call or visit if you're staying a while.
Books cheap university housing, sells student meal tickets and BIJ/Transalpino tickets. Baby-
sitting and job placement services too. Open Mon.-Fri. 9am-5pm.

Post Office: 7, rue des Vergeaux, 2 long blocks from the cathedral. Poste Restante 2.20F
per letter. **Telephones. Postal code:** 80000. Open Mon.-Fri. 8am-7pm, Sat. 8am-noon.

Train Station: Gare du Nord, rue Jules Barni (tel. 22-92-50-50). To and from Paris (frequent,
1½ hr., 72F), Calais via Boulogne (7 per day, 2¼ hr., 89F), Rouen (every 3 hr., 68F). The
station may be undergoing renovation.

Bus Station: SEMTA, Rue Vallée St-Ladre (tel. 22-43-84-00), 1 block to the right of the train
station.

Markets: All day Thurs. and Sat. in **place du Marché** near the *syndicat;* every Sat. 9am-1pm at the **marché sur l'eau** on place Parmentier by the Somme. Call 22-91-79-28 for information.

Laundromat: 1, rue St-Maurice and 197, rue Jules Barni.

Hospital: Place Victor Pauchet (tel. 22-44-25-25).

Police: Rue des Jacobins (tel. 22-92-06-43).

Police Emergency: Tel. 17.

Accommodations and Camping

Hotels surround the train station, but most are expensive. Amiens's cheaper hotels tend to be tiny and filled with regulars. University singles are available from July through September (37F). Check with CROUS (see Practical Information).

Auberge de Jeunesse (IYHF), on an unnamed street off bd. Beauvillé (tel. 22-44-54-21), 1km from the station. Turn right from the station onto bd. d'Alsace Lorraine and follow the signs for the campground. Turn left before the Elf station, at the sign reading Accès Piétons. From place Gambetta, head down rue des Sergents past the cathedral and turn right on rue des Francs Muriers. Follow the river and turn left on bd. d'Alsace Lorraine. The hostel is by a lake, in the middle of the campground (same office for hostel and campground). Kitchen facilities but no breakfast. Spectacular views of the cathedral. All rules strictly enforced. Hot water in morning only. 32F per night, sleep sacks included. Office open daily 7am-noon and 2-8pm. No morning lockout. Curfew 10:30pm. Open mid-March to mid-Dec.

Hôtel L'Alsace-Lorraine, 18, rue de la Morlière (tel. 22-91-35-71), by the train station. If you can afford them, rooms are lovely and bright. In the pleasant courtyard the city seems like a distant memory. Singles from 100F. Doubles from 130F, with shower 160F. Breakfast 21F.

Hôtel de Normandie, 1bis, rue Lamartine (tel. 22-91-74-99), near the train station on a quiet side street, close to the cathedral. Sparkling, clean rooms and a charming breakfast room, plus parking in a garage (14F), but ask for a window or you may not get one. Rooms from 125F. Breakfast 20F. Closed Sun. noon-5pm.

Camping: Municipal de l'Etang St-Pierre, by the youth hostel (tel. 22-44-54-21). 2-star site with a splendid view of the cathedral. 4F per person plus 2.20F per site, 2.20F per car. Electricity 4.50-15F. Open April-Sept. For more camping information, call 22-92-44-44.

Food

Local dishes include duck pie, mushrooms, *"Amiens Tiles"* (chocolate and almonds), and *ficelle picarde* (a stuffed crêpe). See Practical Information for markets in town. CROUS has information about university restaurants and sells meal tickets (13F); you can get those tickets for 6.50F if you buy from a student. Provisions of all kinds can be bought in place de Beauvais near the tourist office.

La Soupe à Cailloux, 16, rue des Bondes (tel. 22-91-92-70), on the banks of the Somme in the Quartier St. Leu. Vegetarian and non-vegetarian dishes served both indoors and on the new terrace. Try the sensational salads (small 22F, large 33F). All-natural ingredients. Some English spoken. Lunch *menus* 51F and 74F. Open Tues.-Sat. noon-2pm and 7-10:30pm.

Miami, 44/50 rue des Trois Cailloux (tel. 22-91-48-27). So it's a cafeteria, it has pizzazz. Cheapest meal in town 22-40F. Salad bar for the health-conscious, massive plates of fries for the homesick. Open daily 7am-10:30pm.

La Corne du Boeuf, 30-36, rue des Beauvais (tel. 22-91-77-65). The *crudités* (raw vegetables) for 13.80F and *menu* at 41.50F can't be beat. Open Mon.-Sat. noon-2pm and 7-11pm.

La Mangeoire, 3, rue des Sergents (tel. 22-91-11-28). Slightly rowdy atmosphere. Country crêpes and *galettes* 6-29F, a 32.50F *menu*, and bowls of *cidre* (slightly alcoholic carbonated cider). Open Sept.-July Tues.-Sat. 11:30am-2:30pm and 5-11pm.

Sights

When the leaders of Amiens decided to rebuild their **Cathédrale de Notre Dame** in 1220, they sought to outdo the achievements at Laon and Chartres by making theirs even higher and more ornate. The west facade, with its surprisingly short towers, incorporates an astounding complexity of statuary and sculptural detail. Seen as a whole, the interior seems too tall and too vast to be visually inviting; nonetheless, it sings magnificence. Amiens's cathedral incarnates a vision of unity whose intricacy is rivaled by few other buildings. (Open daily 7:30am-noon and 2-7pm.)

The **Musée de Picardie**, 48, rue de la République (tel. 22-91-36-44), harbors a fine collection of classical paintings and an archeology exhibit. The galerie de Nieuwerkerke contains masterpieces by the brotherhood of Puy Notre Dame d'Amiens, a literary society that became a religious one devoted to glorifying the Virgin. (Open Tues.-Fri. 10am-12:30pm and 2-6pm, Sat. 10am-noon and 2-6pm. Free.) Next door stands the **Bibliothèque** (tel. 22-91-58-58), an elegant building dating from 1860, with gardens in front. A wonderful place to spend a few hours, the library also shows free video documentaries and films. (Open Tues.-Sun. 10am-7pm.) The graceful, seventeenth-century **Hôtel de Berny**, 7, rue du Musée (tel. 22-77-06-85), presents various displays and documents on local history. The building houses beautifully carved wood furniture and is itself a fine example of Louis XIII architecture.

Perfect for a sunny afternoon, the **Hortillonages** (market gardens) still supply Amiens's produce but also display decorative flora. (Open spring and summer daily 10am-noon and 2-6pm.) Call the *syndicat* about barge tours (19F).

Science fiction fans might want to venture to the tomb of **Jules Verne,** who spent most of his life in Amiens and wrote his imaginative novels here. The house where he lived and wrote, at the corner of bd. Jules Verne and rue Charles Dubois (tel. 22-45-37-84), is open to the public (Tues.-Sat. 2-6pm). He lies buried among nineteenth-century mausoleums in the **cimitière de la Madeleine.** Because the city lacks discos, Amiens nightlife revolves around clubs with live music. **La Lune de Pirates,** 17, rue Bélu (tel. 22-97-88-47); **Le Lucullus,** 58, rue de la République (tel. 22-91-77-33); and **Au Jockey,** rue Ernest-Cauvin, attract local crowds.

Compiègne

Unlike most cities in the north, Compiègne keeps its factories discreetly in the background, displaying instead its stone and half-timbered houses, tranquil river, and well-manicured parks. Founded in 877 by Charles the Bald's grandson, Compiègne has served as a royal country residence since the time of Louis XV. Napoleon I and Napoleon III also made it their home. The town specializes in ending wars: Joan of Arc was taken prisoner in Compiègne by the English in 1429, and on November 11, 1918, the armistice ending World War I was signed here. Compiègne was heavily damaged in World War II, but it has maintained its historic flair.

Orientation and Practical Information

Compiègne is an hour from Paris's Gare du Nord, and easily accessible from Amiens or Laon. The train station is across the river from the center of town. To get to the center of town, cross place de la Gare in front of the station, turn right, and then left onto the bridge. Follow this road to the center and to the tourist office in the Hôtel de Ville. Free bus service runs throughout town from the train station, most buses stopping at the Hôtel de Ville, but the town's sights and accommodations are easily reached on foot.

Office de Tourisme: Place de l'Hôtel de Ville (tel. 44-40-01-00), in the Hôtel de Ville. Free pamphlet of hotels and restaurants with all places marked on the map at the end. List of sights with hours and prices. Ask for the booklet *Du Roman au Gothique par les Forêts Royales de l'Oise*, with maps, practical information, and descriptions of monuments in and around the forests of Oise. Open Mon.-Tues. and Thurs.-Fri. 9am-noon and 1:45-6pm, Wed. and Sat. 9am-noon and 1:30-6pm, Sun. 8:30am-noon and 2:30-5:30pm; in off-season Sun. hours are 9:30am-noon.

CROUS: 6bis, rue Winston Churchill (tel. 44-20-36-28). Housing and meal tickets. Open Mon.-Fri. 8:30am-noon and 1:30-7pm.

Post Office: Rue des Domeliers (tel. 44-40-13-88). Poste Restante. **Postal code:** 60200. Open Mon.-Fri. 8am-7pm, Sat. 8am-noon.

Train Station: Place de la Gare (tel. 44-21-50-50). To Paris (several trains in the early morning, otherwise infrequent; 1 hr.; 49F), Amiens (mornings and early evenings only, 1-1½ hr., 47F), Laon (frequent service, 1½ hr., 41F), Lille (via Creil or Aulnoye, frequent service, 3 hr., 97F), and Noyon (frequent service, ½ hr., 16F). Information office open Mon.-Sat. 8:45am-7:30pm, Sun. 8:30am-noon and 2:45-5pm.

Bus Station: Cars Acary, 10, rue d'Amiens (tel. 44-83-36-26). City and local buses leave from place de la Gare. The tourist office has a complete schedule of intra-city stops, as well as those in surrounding areas. There are also two private bus companies in Compiègne: **Cars Charlot,** rue du Pont des Rets (tel. 44-40-21-09), in Choisy-au-Bac, with buses to and from Pierrefonds. Also **Cars STEPA,** 1, rue d'Amiens (tel. 44-83-38-75).

Bicycle Rental: At the **train station.** 45F per day, deposit 250F.

Laundromat: Le Lavoir, 29, rue du Port à Bateaux (tel. 44-23-10-16). Your laundry will be washed (20F), dried (5F), and ready in 1 hr. Open 7:30am-9pm.

Swimming Pools: Piscine Municipale d'Hiver, 15, av. de Huy (tel. 44-20-46-06). Admission 9.40F. Open in winter only. **Bassin d'Eté,** 2, cours Guynemer (tel. 44-40-05-41). Admission 9.40F. Open June-Aug. daily 9:30am-7:30pm except Mon. morning. This pool also has **public baths.** Showers 4.20F, baths 5.20F (open Sat. only).

Medical Emergency: Hôpital Général, 42, rue de Paris (tel. 44-20-99-20).

Police: 41, rue St-Germain (tel. 44-20-16-36).

Police Emergency: Tel. 17.

Accommodations, Camping, and Food

Although Compiègne merits an overnight stay, the few reasonably priced hotels fill quickly; start looking early in the day.

Auberge de Jeunesse (IYHF), 6, rue Pasteur (tel. 44-40-26-00), near the St-Antoine church. Members 22F. Sheets 9F. Use of kitchen 7F. No meals. Lockout 10am-6pm. Curfew 10pm.

Maison de l'Europe, 61, rue St-Lazare (tel. 44-40-26-00). Caters to travelers, but a walk from the town center. Kitchen facilities. 21.50F per night. Sheets included.

Hôtel St-Antoine, 17, rue de Paris (tel. 44-23-22-27). Most likely to have space. Bar downstairs. Singles 70-90F, doubles 80-110F. Breakfast 15F. Office open Tues.-Sun. Hotel open Sept. 2-Feb. 2 and Feb. 14-Aug. 8.

Le But Hôtel, 35, cours Guynemer (tel. 44-23-31-06), on the river. Decent rooms above a slightly raucous *brasserie*. Singles and doubles 60F, with shower 75F. Breakfast 15F. Hotel and restaurant open Aug.-June Sat.-Thurs. Reservations recommended.

Camping Municipal, av. du Baron R. de Soultrait (tel. 44-20-28-58). From Palais National, follow av. Royale southeast out of town for 2km. Beautifully situated on a 3-mile ave. of "Beaux Monts," the old Palais Grounds, designed by Napoleon in 1810 as a gift for his wife, Marie-Louisa, in the Forêt de Compiègne. Clean. 6.30F per person, ages under 7 2.10F. 5.20F per site, 2.30F per car. Electricity 4.90F. Showers 5.50F. Open March 15-Nov. 14.

Most of the better hotels have 45-52F *menus*. If you're in the mood to pack a picnic lunch, check out the formidable variety of fresh vegetables, fruit, and cheese at **Les Halles du Grenier à Sel,** on rue de Lombard at rue de l'Etoile. (Open Mon.-Fri. 8:30am-12:30pm and 3-7pm, Sat. 7am-6pm.)

Le Phnom Penh, 13, rue des Lombards (tel. 44-40-09-45), in the pedestrian zone. 3-course *menu* 51F. Delicious but not quite filling. Cambodian dishes 38-55F. Open Sun. and Tues.-Fri. noon-2:30pm and 7-9:30pm, Sat. noon-2:30pm.

Crêperie Melissa, 4, rue des Cordeliers (tel. 44-40-19-37), next to Le Phnom Penh. Excellent crêpes and *galettes* in a *salon de thé*. Crêpes 26.50F. Open Wed.-Mon. 11am-midnight.

La Sangria, 87, rue de Paris (tel. 44-86-19-84), 10 min. from the town center. Delicious Spanish cuisine. *Menus* 30F (lunch only), 56F, and 88F. Spanish *à la carte* specialties 30-50F. Open Thurs.-Tues. noon-1:45pm and 7pm-midnight.

L'Igloo, 31, rue de Paris (tel. 44-23-13-93). Crêpes (7-25F) and ice cream dishes (13-25F) in a small, candlelit den. Open Mon.-Fri. noon-2pm and 7-10:15pm, Sat. 7pm-1am, Sun. 7-9pm.

Sol Pouce, 29, rue de Paris (tel. 44-25-13-93). For a quick lunch, try the 30F *menu*. Entrees 12-20F. Open Mon.-Fri. 11:30am-2:30pm.

Sights

Restored to evoke the grandeur of its days as a "country cottage" for France's monarchs, Louis XV's château, the **Palais National,** down rue des Minimes behind the tourist office, flaunts huge ballrooms with chandeliers decorated in First and Second Empire styles under Napoleon as well as the first pinball machine. The palace also includes a **Musée du Second Empire** (tel. 44-40-02-02; ask the head guard), and a **Musée de la Voiture** (tel. 44-40-04-37), full of ancient bicycles, tricycles for two, and carriages, including the ostentatious vehicles wallpapered with artistic paintings in which Napoleon and Marie Antoinette used to go for spins. (Global ticket for all 3 museums 21F; students, seniors, and Sun. and holidays 11F.) The only way you can visit the palace is to take a tour with a guide who delivers an exhausting supply of anecdotes. (Tours Wed.-Mon. 9:30am-noon and 1:30-5pm. Last admission ½ hr. before closing.) The **Musée de la Figurine Historique,** in the annex of the beautiful Hôtel de Ville (tel. 44-40-26-00), houses an absolutely fascinating collection of small figurines representing all aspects of military and civilian life from the Merovingian era onwards. (Open March-Oct. Tues.-Sun. 9am-noon and 2-6pm; Nov.-Feb. 9am-noon and 2-5pm. Admission 8.40F, students 4.20F.)

The château's sculpted **parc** is beautifully maintained and makes an excellent picnic spot. Wander to the edge of the gardens, through the gilded gate, and you'll find yourself in the **Forêt de Compiègne,** miles of untamed greenery, long the hunting ground of kings, and now ideal for strolling, hiking, biking, or horseback riding (inquire at the *syndicat*). Six kilometers into the forest sits the **Clairière de l'Armistice** (Armistice Clearing), where the treaty that ended World War I was signed in a railway carriage, now berthed in a small museum with a simple monument. (Open April-Oct. daily 8am-noon and 1:30-6:30pm; Nov.-March Wed.-Mon. 9am-noon and 2-5:30pm. Admission 3F.)

Another tranquil spot in Compiègne is **Parc de Songeons,** off rue d'Austerlitz, by the river. All that remains of a former **abbaye** stands there silently: Several ivy-covered arches support nothing but air, framing a beautiful view of the river. Next to the park, **Musée Vivenel** displays Greek vases and various artifacts. (Admission 9F, students 5F). **Eglise St-Jacques,** place St-Jacques, exhibits the opulence of the Catholic Church with its wood carvings, paintings, chandeliers, and gilded decor—all gifts of Louis XV.

Near Compiègne

Twenty kilometers from Compiègne along D973 sits the medieval **Château de Pierrefonds,** an imposing, turreted fortress entirely restored by Viollet le Duc under Napoleon III. (Open April-Sept. Wed.-Mon. 10am-noon and 2-6pm; Oct.-March Thurs.-Mon. 10am-noon and 2-4pm; last entry ½ hr. before closing. Admission 11F, ages 18-25 and seniors 5.50F, ages under 18 2F.) The **forêt** around the town of **Pierrefonds** is crossed by several walking paths. Three buses per day (Mon.-Sat.) leave from quai #2 at the train station in Compiègne for Pierrefonds. (Contact **Cars Charlot,** tel. 44-40-21-09.) The *syndicat* has timetables. It's pleasant to cycle through the forest as well. In Pierrefonds, the **Office de Tourisme** is on place de l'Hôtel de Ville (tel. 44-42-81-44; open April 15-Oct. 15 Wed.-Mon. 10am-noon and 2-6pm).

Noyon, the smallest of the great cathedral towns of the north, lies 24km northeast of Compiègne along the N32. The town has suffered bad luck, invaded first by the Normans, then by the Spaniards in the sixteenth century, and occupied during both World Wars. But the *Noyonnais* are proud of their city's past. Charlemagne was crowned King of Neustrie here in 768, and Hugh Capet's coronation as King of France took place in 987. The town is also known as the birthplace of **John Calvin;**

the house where he was born has been restored as a fine museum, and contains pictures, engravings, and original works by Calvin on the Reformation. (Open April-Oct. Wed.-Mon. 10am-noon and 2:30-5pm.) Noyon's twelfth-century **cathédrale,** whose exterior rivals that of Amiens, is a fine example of transitional architecture, boldly integrating Romanesque and Gothic traditions. (Open daily mid-April to mid-Oct. 9am-noon and 2-6pm; mid-Oct. to mid-April 9am-noon and 2-4pm.) Flanking the cathedral is the fifteenth-century **bibliothèque,** with a collection of 4000 precious volumes, including a ninth-century illuminated gospel. (Guided visits July-Oct. Thurs. and Sat. at 2:30pm and 5pm.) Every second weekend in June, Noyon gathers a wide assortment of antique cars to cruise its narrow streets during the **Festival de l'Automobile.**

M. Colotte presides at the **Syndicat d'Initiative,** place de l'Hôtel de Ville (tel. 44-44-21-88; open June-Sept. Mon. 2-6pm, Tues.-Sat. 9:30am-noon and 2-6pm, Sun. 9:30am-noon; Oct.-May Tues.-Sat. only). He can suggest daytrips, particularly to the majestic **Abbaye Notre-Dame d'Ourscamp** (tel. 44-76-98-08 or 44-76-77-81), 15km toward Compiègne in tiny **Chiry-Ourscamp.** If you want to stay in Noyon, head for the two-star hotel **Le Grillon,** 37, rue St-Eloi (tel. 44-09-14-18), with clean singles and doubles with shower for 105-130F. Its restaurant concocts a 55F *menu.* (Open Mon.-Sat. noon-2pm and 7-9pm.) A pleasant **Camping Municipal,** 24, rue Hoche (tel. 44-44-02-97), off bd. Carnot, is a 15-minute walk from the station. (2.20F per person, 1.30F per site, 1.15 per car. Electricity 5F.) If that camping ground is still undergoing renovations, **Camping "La Montagne,"** rue de Mauconseil (tel. 44-76-98-29), is 3km away near Ourscamp. (7F per person, 2.50F per car. Electricity 7-12F.) A small group of restaurants assembles off bd. Mony with 45-55F *menus.* **La Galimafree Crêperie,** 27, rue J. Abel LeFranc, off place St-Martin entices with tasty crêpes (7.50-37F), a 36F *menu,* and a 20F children's *menu.* (Open Tues.-Fri. and Sun. noon-2:30pm and 6-10pm, Sat. 5:30-10pm.)

You can get to Noyon by train from Compiègne (frequent service, 15 min., 17.60F), from Paris's Gare du Nord (11 per day, 1-1½ hr., 58F), or from Laon (3 per day, change at Tergnier, 1 hr., 34F). **Trains** leave Noyon for Compiègne (frequent service), Paris (9 per day), and Laon (7 per day). Bus #8 (Cars Acary) runs twice per day from Compiègne and stops at the train station in Noyon. The ticket office (tel. 44-44-00-61) at the *gare* is open from 5am to 9:40pm.

Laon

Laon is one of the little-known attractions of northern France. Like the perched villages in the southern Bouches du Rhône or Assisi and Urbino on the plains of Tuscany, Laon rests on a hill in the midst of flat land, an unexpected butte crowned by a magnificent cathedral. The whitewashed stone of the *haute ville* on the hilltop presents a welcome change from the gray, industrial cities that pervade this region.

Orientation and Practical Information

Laon is not blessed with frequent train service. Trains to Laon run from Amiens, St-Quentin, and Paris-Nord. Once outside the station, you'll see why the city has rarely been attacked; the way to the *haute ville* is straight up. (The hill proved too much for even Napoleon, who failed to take Laon in 1814.) If climbing the 280 steps doesn't take your breath away, the view from the top will. From there, take the footpath across the street, then the ramp up onto the rampart, and turn left for the cathedral. The new **Chemin des Dames,** scheduled to open in September, 1988, is the first tramway in France. It transports passengers from the station to the *haute ville* every six minutes. The main road through the *haute ville* lies on the other side of the cathedral and changes names several times: rue du Cloître by the cathedral, then rue St-Jean, and rue St-Martin at the other end.

Syndicat d'Initiative: Place du Parvis (tel. 23-20-28-62), in a trailer next to the cathedral gates. Pamphlet in English and a map. Guided tours in French Mon.-Fri. by appointment;

Sat., Sun., and holidays at 4pm (15F per 2 hr.). Open Easter-Sept. daily 9am-noon and 2-7pm; Oct.-Easter 9am-noon and 2-6pm.

Comité Départemental du Tourisme de l'Aisne: 1, rue St-Martin (tel. 23-20-45-54). Loads of information about daytrips to the Picardie countryside, as well as swimming, hiking, biking, camping, and antique-hunting. Ask for the excellent *Cyclotourisme: guide pratique*, rent a bike from the office for 12F per ½ day (not always available), and bike into the **Forêts de St-Gobain.** Open Mon.-Thurs. 8:30am-noon and 1:30-6pm, Fri. 8:30am-noon and 1:30-5pm.

Post Office: Place des Frères le Nain at the corner of rue des Cordeliers and rue Pourier, in the *haute ville.* Open Mon.-Fri. 8am-6:30pm, Sat. 8am-noon. **Main office** (for Poste Restante) in the *ville basse* at place de la Gare. **Postal code:** 02000. Open Mon.-Fri. 8am-7pm, Sat. 8am-noon.

Train Station: Place de la Gare (tel. 23-79-10-79), in the *ville basse* down the road from the 280 steps. To Paris (every 1-3 hr., 1¾ hr., 74F), Amiens (6 per day, 2 hr., 58F), and Calais (change at Amiens, 133F).

Hospital: Center Hospitalier de Laon, rue Dévisme (tel. 23-24-33-33 or 23-20-20-20), by Eglise St-Martin in a beautiful seventeenth-century building.

Police: Bd. de Lyon (tel. 23-23-23-82), 1 block left of the train station.

Police Emergency: Tel. 17.

Accommodations, Camping, and Food

The *haute ville* is a lovely place to spend the night, but the few hotels tend to fill by late afternoon in high season, and 280 steps becomes quite a climb with a heavy pack.

Maison des Jeunes, 20, rue du Cloître (tel. 23-20-27-64). The nearest thing to a youth hostel. Primarily a *foyer* for young workers, so you'll have interesting company. Rooms are dimly lit and clinical. 30 singles and doubles for 60F. Sheets and breakfast included. Cafeteria serves 3 meals per day; dinner with beer or wine 27.20F. You must sleep here to eat here. Hostel card required; age limit 25. Reception usually closed weekends.

Les Chevaliers, 3, rue Serrurier (tel. 23-23-43-78), just off place du Général Leclerc. Respectable and quiet 2-star hotel with agreeable, rather expensive rooms. Singles from 110F, doubles from 165F, triples with bathroom 240F. Showers 18F. Breakfast 21F. Reception open daily 6:30am-midnight. Midnight curfew. Closed around Feb. 15-March 10.

Hôtel Welcome, 2, av. Carnot (tel. 23-23-06-11), between the station and the hill. Only 3 steps to climb instead of 280. Large, clean, carpeted rooms; soft mattresses. Singles and doubles 68-120F, doubles and triples 110-120F. Showers 15F. Breakfast 16F. Closed Sun. in winter. Two other hotels on av. Carnot offer cheap, decent rooms. **Le Vauclair,** at #16 (tel. 23-23-02-08) offers simple rooms (60-130F, breakfast 16F, showers 15F). **Le Nord-Est** at #11 (tel. 23-23-25-55) is slightly more expensive (singles 70F, doubles and triples 115F, bath 22F; breakfast 18F) and is closed weekends.

Camping: Camping Municipal, near the *stade municipal* (tel. 23-23-29-07), on the southern side of the *ville basse.* Clean sites and washing facilities. 7.50F per person, ages 4-7 4F, ages under 4 free. 4.50F per tent, 4.50F per car. There is a bar and you can also get cooked meals. Open April-Oct.

The few restaurants in the *ville basse* generally have unexceptional *menus,* but **Au Traineau,** 12 av. Carnot, across from the movie theater, offers a special *tarte au maroille* (cheese tart, 12F) and a daily special (28F), while jazz music flows in the background and a giant, static sleigh (*traineau*) dominates the foreground. Live piano music Fri. and Sat. nights. Open weekdays 11:30am-2pm and 7pm-1am, Fri.-Sat. 7pm-3am. Restaurants in the *ville haute* tend to be expensive. Supermarkets and the Maison des Jeunes's excellent **cafeteria** are better options, and the park by the Panoramic Pool makes a gorgeous picnic spot. For fresh croissants and oven-warm *pain gris,* stop in before noon at the friendly **Boulangerie Berthelin,** place St-Julien, next to the Crédit Immobilier (tel. 23-23-12-88; open Mon.-Sat. 7am-7:30pm). **Les Chevaliers,** on the ground floor of the hotel at 3, rue Serrurier (tel. 23-23-43-78), is a cozy restaurant. There is no *menu,* but the price of the main course

(38-45F) includes wine and coffee. Everything is excellent: Try the *pommes de terre Grand'mère* (potatoes and garlic sausage with bits of bacon cooked in a fresh cream and tarragon sauce) or one of the tasty omelettes. (Open Mon. and Wed.-Thurs. noon-2pm and 7-8:30pm, Tues. and Fri.-Sat. noon-2pm. Bar and cafe open Mon.-Fri. 11am-midnight, Sat. 11am-8pm, Sun. 11am-4pm.) The elegant **Restaurant des Chenizelles,** rue du Bourg (tel. 23-23-02-34), across from the town hall and next to historic porte de Chenizelles, serves a 59F *menu* and entrees starting at 40F. The owner recommends reservations. (Open Tues.-Sun. noon-around 3:30pm and 7pm-late; Mon. lunch only.)

Sights

Laon's history goes back to Roman times and includes a spell as capital of France under the Carolingian kings. Its fertile ground yielded Charlemagne's legendary companion Roland and, in modern times, the artistic le Nain brothers and Father Marquette (a priest from New France who, together with a trader named Joliette, was the first European to explore the Mississippi). Napoleon lost the Battle of Laon to the Prussians in 1814, and abdicated shortly afterward.

Easily defended and fortified, the *haute ville* is completely surrounded by medieval ramparts, pierced only by the city gates, and commands a spectacular view of the countryside for 50km around. Note especially **Porte d'Ardon,** at the end of rue Porte d'Ardon off rue des Cordeliers.

Laon's centerpiece is **Cathédrale de Notre Dame,** built in the 1100s and thus the first of France's great cathedrals in the Gothic style. Sturdy Romanesque pillars support the buoyant Gothic vaulting above, a visual metaphor for the triumph of the Gothic over the Romanesque style. Stand in the center and look up at the tower, where the ribbing reaches down like octopus tentacles. The exterior ornamentation of the four lavish towers is based on the number eight. The carved cows' heads peep through the columns to commemorate the oxen that helped haul the stone to the plateau. Visitors are sometimes allowed to climb the towers, but only during guided tours. Consult the *syndicat* for more information.

Eglise St-Martin, at the other end of the *haute ville,* is a less fanciful example of primitive Gothic architecture from the twelfth and thirteenth centuries. To visit the interior, ask at 4, av. de la République. Two blocks from the main cathedral on rue Georges Hermant sit the **Musée Municipale,** with a distinguished collection of Greek vases, and the thirteenth-century **Chapelle des Templiers,** a charming octagonal building with several additions. Inside are two statue-columns of prophets from the cathedral facade and the carved fourteenth-century "skeleton" of Guillaume de Harcigny, physician to Charles VI. (Both open April-Sept. Wed.-Mon. 10am-noon and 2-6pm; Oct.-March 10am-noon and 2-5pm. Admission 6F, students 3F.)

To get to the unbeatable, heated, indoor **Piscine Municipale,** go down rue St-Martin and follow the signs around the top of the ramparts by the hospital. The walk along the ramparts is breathtaking, as is the view through the pool's glass doors. (Open Mon. 2-8pm, Tues.-Fri. 10am-8pm, Sat. 10am-7pm, Sun. 9am-1pm. Adults 7.30F.) The **Maison des Arts et des Loisirs,** place Aubry, regularly sponsors exhibitions, concerts, and plays. (Open Tues.-Sat. 12:30-7pm, Sun. 3-7pm.) Every year it organizes the festive **Heures Médiévales** with colorful drama, music, and dancing in the streets for three weeks (early Sept.). Actors dress in medieval costumes, local bars keep the liquor flowing, and everyone has a good time. Ask at the *Maison* about the annual international film festival held in March and April.

LANGUAGE

Glossary

The following glossary of words is a supplement to the section on Language in the General Introduction. Here you will find an compilation of all the French terms *Let's Go* has used in its Sights sections. The gender of the noun is either indicated in parentheses or by the article (*la,* feminine; *le,* masculine). The glossary is followed by an addendum listing phrases you may find helpful during your stay in France.

French	English
l'abbatiale (f.)	abbey
l'abbaye (f.)	abbey
l'aile (f.)	wing
l'allée (f.)	lane, avenue
l'arc (m.)	arch
les arènes (f.)	arena
l'atelier (m.)	studio, workshop
l'auberge (f.)	inn; tavern
la banlieue	suburb
le baptistère	baptistery
la basilique	basilica
la basse ville	lower town
la bastide	walled town
le bateau	boat
le beffroi	bell tower
la bibliothèque	library
le bois	forest
la bourse	stock exchange
la calanque	creek; cove
le campanile	bell tower
le cap	cape, foreland
le carnet	booklet, notebook
la cave	(wine) cellar
le centre ville	downtown, town center
la chambre	room
la chambre d'hôte	rural B&B
le champ	field
la chapelle	chapel
la chartreuse	charterhouse
le château	castle
le cimetière	cemetery

le cirque	mountain basin; amphitheater; circus
la cité	city; housing development
le cloître	cloister
le col	pass
la corniche	cliff road, coastal road; cornice
la côte	coast
le couvent	convent
la croix	cross
le cru	wineyard; vintage
la dégustation	wine tasting
le donjon	castle keep; dungeon
la douane	customs
l'école (f.)	school
l'église (f.)	church
l'escalier (m.)	stairway
l'evêché (m.)	bishop's palace; bishopric
la faïence	crockery, earthenware
la falaise	cliff
le faubourg	quarter
la fête	holiday; festival
la fête votive	patron saint festival
les feux d'artifices (m.)	fireworks
la foire	fair
la fontaine	fountain
la forêt	forest
le gîte d'étape	simple rural lodging for horseback riders, cyclists, or hikers, not drivers
le gîte rural	rural B&B
la gorge	gorge; pass
le gouffre	gulf, pit
la halle	market hall, covered market
la haute ville	upper town
l'horloge (f.)	clock
l'hôtel (particulier) (m.)	mansion (town house)
l'hôtel de ville (m.)	town hall
l'île(f)	island
le lac (m.)	lake
le logis	lodging, dwelling
la mairie	town hall
le marché	market
le mas	farm- or country-house
le mont	mountain
la mosquée	mosque
le mur	wall

le musée	museum
l'ossuaire (m.)	charnel house
le pic	peak
le pilier	pillar
la place	square
la plage	beach
la pointe	headland, promontory
le pont	bridge
la porte	gate; mountain pass
le puy	peak
le quartier	quarter, neighborhood
la randonnée	run, hike
la rencontre	meeting
la roche	boulder
le rocher	rock; crag
la rue	street
la salle (capitulaire)	hall (capitular)
le salon	drawing or living room
le sentier	path, lane
le tabac	store selling cigarettes, stamps, and other small items, often located inside a cafe
la tapisserie	tapestry
le téléphérique	suspended cable car
les thermes (m.)	hot springs
la tour	tower
le trésor	treasure
la trésorerie	treasury
la vendange	grape harvest; vintage season
la verrerie	glassworks
la vieille ville	old town

Helpful Phrases

please	s'il vous plaît
thank you	thank you
hello	bonjour
good evening	bonsoir
How are you?	Çomment allez-vous?
I am well.	Je vais bien.
goodbye	au revoir
Excuse me.	Excusez-moi.
Do you speak English?	Parlez-vous anglais?
I need . . .	J'ai besoin de . . .

I would like . . .	Je voudrais . . .
I want . . .	Je veux . . .
I don't want . . .	Je ne veux pas . . .
The bill, please.	L'addition, s'il vous plaît.
Where is/are . . .	Où est/sont . . . ?
. . . the bathroom?	. . . le w.c.? (vay say)
. . . the police?	. . . la police?
to the right	à droite
to the left	à gauche
straight ahead	tout droit
a room	une chambre
double room	pour deux
single room	pour une personne
a shower	une douche
breakfast	le petit déjeuner
lunch	le déjeuner
dinner	le dîner
with	avec
without	sans
shower included	douch comprise
breakfast included	petit déjeuner compris

INDEX